For Reference

Not to be taken from this room

GREAT
AMERICAN
COURT CASES

GREAT AMERICAN COURT CASES

Volume I:
Individual Liberties

FIRST EDITION

Mark Mikula and
L. Mpho Mabunda,
Editors

Allison McClintic Marion,
Associate Editor

The Gale Group

DETROIT • SAN FRANCISCO • LONDON • BOSTON • WOODBRIDGE, CT

Staff

Mark F. Mikula, L. Mpho Mabunda, Editors

Allison McClintic Marion, Dawn R. Barry, Rebecca Parks, Dave Oblender, Associate Editors
Elizabeth Shaw, Brian J. Koski, Gloria Lam, Catherine Donaldson, Assistant Editors
Linda S. Hubbard, Managing Editor, Multicultural Team

Susan Trosky, Permissions Manager
Margaret A. Chamberlain, Permissions Specialist

Victoria B. Cariappa, Research Manager
Barbara McNeil, Research Specialist

Evi Seoud, Assistant Production Manager

Cynthia Baldwin, Product Design Manager
Eric Johnson, Art Director

Barbara Yarrow, Graphic Services Manager
Randy A. Bassett, Image Database Supervisor
Robert Duncan, Imaging Specialist

Theresa Rocklin, Manager, Technical Support Services
Jeffrey Muhr, Technical Support

Library of Congress Cataloging-in-Publication Data

Great American court cases / Mark F. Mikula and L. Mpho Mabunda, editors;
Allison McClintic Marion, associate editor. -- 1st ed.
      p. cm.
    Includes bibliographical references and index.
      Contents: v. 1. Individual liberties -- v. 2. Criminal justice -- v. 3. Equal protection and family law
-- v. 4. Business and government.
      ISBN 078762947-0 (set).
      1. Law--United States.--Cases. 2. Civil rights--United States-Cases. I. Mikula, Mark F. II. Mabunda,
L. Mpho., 1967-. III. Marion, Allison McClintic.
KF385.A4g68 1999
349.73--dc2
                                99-11419
                                CIP

Copyright © 1999
The Gale Group
27500 Drake Road
Farmington Hills, MI 48331-3535
http://www.galegroup.com
800-877-4253
248-699-4253

ISBN 0-7876-2947-2 (set) Vol 1 ISBN 0-7876-2948-0; Vol 2 ISBN 0-7876-2949-9;
Vol 3 ISBN 0-7876-2950-2; Vol 4 ISBN 0-7876-2951-0

10 9 8 7 6 5 4 3 2 1

CONTENTS

Volume I

Individual Liberties

(Consult this index for all the cases, people, events, and subjects covered in Vols. I–IV)

CONTENTS

Volume II, III, IV

This abbreviated view shows just the issues covered in the other volumes. Consult the Cumulative Index that appears in each volume for all the cases, people, events, and subjects in all four volumes.

PREFACE

U.S. citizens take comfort and pride in living under the rule of law. Our elected representatives write and enforce the laws that govern everything from familial relationships to the dealings of multi-billion-dollar corporations, from the quality of the air to the content of the programs broadcast through it. But it is the judicial system that interprets the meaning of the law and makes it tangible to the average citizen through the drama of trials and the force of court orders and judicial opinions.

The four volumes of *Great American Court Cases* profile nearly 800 judicial proceedings. The editors consulted textbooks, curriculum guides, and authoritative Internet sites to identify cases studied for their influence on the development of key aspects of law in the United States. Although the majority of the cases resulted in decisions by the U.S. Supreme Court, nearly 60 cases from state courts or lower-level federal jurisdictions are included because of their impact or their role in an emerging point of law. Comprehensiveness requires that fundamental cases from the nineteenth century and earlier, such as *Marbury v. Madison* (1803) and *Swift v. Tyson* (1842), are included. This is especially true in Volume IV, which covers how laws have shaped the government. Nevertheless, to serve the information needs of today's users, most of the cases are from the twentieth century, with emphasis on the last three decades.

Scope and Arrangement

The case profiles are grouped according to the legal principle on which they reflect, with each volume covering one or two broad areas of the law as follows:

c *Volume I: Individual Liberties* includes cases that have influenced such First and Second Amendment issues as freedom of the press, privacy, the right to bear arms, and the legal concerns emerging from the growth of the Internet. Libel, the Establishment Clause, and other important facets of freedom of speech and freedom of religion are treated in separate essays with their own cases.

c *Volume II: Criminal Justice* covers cases that establish the rights of the accused before, during, and after trial, or address criminal law and procedure, search and seizure, drug laws, the jury, damages, and capital punishment.

c *Volume III: Equal Protection and Family Law* includes cases related to two broad areas of law. Equal protection issues covered in this volume include the broad range of civil rights related issues, from affirmative action, segregation, and voting rights to the special concerns of immigrants, juveniles, the disabled, and gay and lesbian citizens. Family issues covered include child support and custody and reproductive rights. Sexual harassment and the right to die are also represented in this volume.

c *Volume IV: Business and Government* also encompasses two major spheres of the law. Consumer protection, antitrust, and labor-related cases supplement the business fundamentals of contracts and corporate law. The government cases document the legal evolution of the branches of the federal government as well as the federal government's relation to state power. Separate topics address environmental law, military issues, national security, taxation, and the legal history of Native American issues. Appendixes in this volume also present the full text of the U.S. Constitution and its amendments and a chronological table of Supreme Court justices.

Coverage

Issue overviews, averaging 2,000 words in length, provide the context for the case profiles that follow. Case discussions range from 750 to 2,000 words according to their complexity and importance. Each provides the background of the case and issues involved, the main arguments presented by each side, and an explanation of the court's decision, as well as the legal, political, and social impact of the decision. Excerpts from the majority, concurring, and dissenting opinions are often included. Cross-references lead the user to related cases, while suggestions for further reading launch in-depth

Deciphering Legal Citations

Great American Court Cases includes citations for the cases covered in the profiles. Three sources, *United States Reports* (U.S.), the *Supreme Court Reporter* (S.Ct.), and the *Lawyers' Edition* (L.Ed.), all cite Supreme Court cases in separate series, resulting in three distinct citation numbers for each case. The citations for *Great American Court Cases*, in most cases, are drawn from *United States Reports*. On rare occasions, because there is a lag between the time that a case is heard and the time that its companion volume is published, the citation has been drawn from another reporter, usually the *Supreme Court Reporter*. In all cases, the structure of the citation is as follows: the volume number precedes the abbreviation for the reporter and is followed by the page number. For instance, *Davis v. Bandemer*, 478 U.S. 109, is included in volume 478 of *United States Reports*, beginning on page 109. Citations for cases tried below the level of the Supreme Court follow a similar structure with an abbreviation for the reporter associated with the lower court falling between the volume and page number. The case *In re Quinlan*, 355 A.2d 647, is covered in volume 355 of the *Atlantic Reporter*, second series (cases for states in the East), beginning on page 355.

research. Within each issue section, the cases are arranged from earliest to most recent to indicate the evolution of precedent.

The editors have had to make hard choices when a single case has bearing on more than one issue, as often occurs. The landmark reproductive rights decision in *Roe v. Wade*, for example, is based upon an assertion of privacy rights, so the case could have been placed with either issue. Also, the case of *Marbury v. Madison*, while establishing the concept of judicial review, dealt foremost with a separation of powers issue at the time that it was decided, meriting its inclusion in the separation of powers section of Volume IV. Users should consult the cumulative index that appears in each volume to find cases throughout the set that apply to a particular topic.

A small percentage (under 10 percent) of cases were previously covered in *Women's Rights on Trial* or *Great American Trials*, both Gale products. Selection criteria for each publication were different, but the *Great American Court Cases* editors preferred this slight overlap to omission of landmark cases. Entry elements particular to *Great American Court Cases*, such as the Supreme Court justices' votes, have been added to the material, along with updating as appropriate.

The editors determined that with the focus on constitutional law, sensationalistic cases, such as the O. J. Simpson trial and the trial of Ted Kaczynski, were more appropriately covered in the sidebars that complement the main text rather than receiving full treatment in the main body of the text. Also, at the time of publication, the impeachment trial of Bill Clinton had not reached its conclusion. It, therefore, does not receive coverage in this series.

Additional Features

Great American Court Cases has several features to enhance its usefulness to students and non-professional researchers:

The **legal citation** appears at the head of each case profile, enabling researchers to access the authoritative records of the court action. The "Deciphering Legal Citations" sidebar that is part of this preface explains the elements that make up the citations and remarks on the abbreviations for the various series, called "reporters," where records are published.

Each case opens with a **factbox** so the user can quickly scan (when available): the names of litigants; the initiating litigant's claim; the names of chief lawyers on each side; the name of the judge or justice who wrote the majority opinion or decision, as well as names of those who concurred or dissented; the date and location of the decision; the summary of the decision and comments on the decision's significance.

Sidebars in the case profiles highlight interesting aspects of the legal process or arguments, key participants, or related facts and incidents. Some outline the arguments for and against a particular issue or line of reasoning, which will promote critical thinking as well as fuel debates or mock-trials. Some also discuss related cases that did not warrant their inclusion as a main case in the text.

Approximately **300 photographs and graphics** depict individuals and events related to the cases.

A broad overview of the court system and the disciplines of law is presented in a general essay regarding the structure of the legal system.

Contributors have tried to present the issues and proceedings in language accessible to high school, college, and public library users. Legal terms must sometimes be used for precision, however, so a **glossary** of more than 600 words and phrases appears in each volume.

Users interested in a particular case can locate it by name (e.g., *Brown v. Board of Education*) in the **Alphabetical Listing of Cases** in the back of each volume. Those who wish to trace the changing focus of legal interest and opinion over time will find the **Chronological Listing of Cases** in the back of each volume helpful.

A **Cumulative Index** to cases, people, events, and subjects appears in each volume. The Cumulative Index is repeated in each volume to ensure that multiple users of the set have simultaneous access to its complete contents.

Audience for Great American Court Cases

The four volumes of *Great American Court Cases* cover more U.S. Supreme Court and state or lower federal court cases in greater depth than other works for a nonprofessional user. The selection of issues and cases, the consistent treatment, and the minimal use of legal jargon were designed with the student user in mind. Court cases bring important issues into focus in a dramatic way. They are increasingly used in curricula for studies of U.S. government, civics, history, and journalism. Law magnet school and pre-law courses can use *Great American Court Cases* to introduce important content in an accessible manner, while mock court programs will find a wide range of source material here. Students with interdisciplinary writing assignments and exercises in critical thinking will also find inspiration. Beyond the classroom, a broad range of people from activists to history buffs and Court TV watchers, will find the set compelling and useful.

Acknowledgments

Leah Knight, Meggin Condino, and Linda Irvin conceptualized *Great American Court Cases* and solicited feedback from potential users. A number of public and school librarians as well as teachers contributed to the development of the set. While several provided early input, Hilda Weisburg of Morristown High School in New Jersey continued to answer questions to help shape the product through its development. Kathy Nemeh and Diane Carter reviewed selected material for legal accuracy.

Two websites, which are freely available to the public, proved indispensible as resources for fact gathering and checking. These websites are the Findlaw site located at http://www.findlaw.com and the Oyez Oyez Oyez site located at http://court.it-services.nwu.edu.oyez.

Suggestions Are Welcome

The editors welcome suggestions on any aspect of this work. Please send comments to: Editors, *Great American Court Cases*, Gale Group, 27500 Drake Rd., Farmington Hills, MI 48331.

THE AMERICAN LEGAL SYSTEM

The most basic function of the American legal system is to maintain peace by resolving disputes. Federal and state courts, tribunals, and administrative bodies do this by applying laws to cases between specific individuals or organizations.

The primary sources of applicable law are federal and state constitutions, statutes, and administrative regulations. Constitutions establish the structure of government, define and limit its power, and seek to protect individuals from unreasonable or unlawful exercises of that power. Legislatures enact statutes—criminal laws, for example—that govern a wide variety of conduct. Administrative bodies promulgate regulations to govern specific areas of business, such as telecommunications and securities.

In theory, courts apply these existing laws rather than creating new law. The legislatures and administrative bodies, however, cannot always anticipate every possible set of circumstances, and the laws do not clearly dictate a result in every case. Frequently, too, the law is intentionally vague to give the courts flexibility to interpret it in ways which serve general public policies rather than to accomplish specific results. There are, however, constitutional limits on how vague a law may be. In general, it must fairly apprise individuals of behavior that it prohibits or compels.

In practice, then, American courts often make law when they decide cases. Under the doctrine of *stare decisis*, courts at the same or lower level in the judicial hierarchy must follow the first court's interpretation of the law in subsequent cases with similar facts. Higher courts in the judicial hierarchy may either accept the lower court's interpretation or reverse it by interpreting the law differently. Courts in other states may rely on the first court's interpretation as persuasive authority concerning the application of similar laws in their states. This tradition of binding and persuasive authority is a by-product of the American judicial system's origins in the common law system of England.

Origins of the American Judicial System: State Judicial Systems

When America declared its independence in 1776, the 13 original colonies had largely informal judicial systems based loosely on the English system of common law. Common law is the body of law that developed in English courts on a case-by-case basis. Under the common law, judges placed great reliance on decisions in prior cases with similar facts. Although state courts today apply laws enacted by legislatures and administrative bodies, they continue the common law tradition of case-by-case interpretation of these laws and reliance on prior judicial decisions.

As the United States expanded southward and westward, it acquired Mexican, Spanish, and French territories, which had legal systems based on the European civil law tradition. Under that tradition, courts in Europe applied detailed civil codes that the legislatures had designed to resolve all potential disputes. Civil codes reflected the natural law concept that there are unchanging, God-made laws that govern human behavior. Unlike in common law systems, civil law courts were not supposed to interpret the law beyond what was provided in the civil codes—they simply resolved disputes by applying the appropriate portion of the code. While the English common law tradition dominated the formation of American state legal systems, remnants of the civil law tradition exist even today, most notably in Louisiana, which based its legal system on the civil law of France.

Origins of the American Judicial System: Federal Judiciary

The federal judiciary was born in 1789 upon adoption of the U.S. Constitution, which vested the judicial power of the United States in "one supreme Court, and in such inferior Courts as the Congress may from time to time ordain and establish." The Constitution created a judicial system that contains elements of both the common and civil law traditions. The latter is evident in one of the purposes expressed in the Constitution's preamble—to "secure the Blessings of Liberty." The

Constitution, however, is subject to case-by-case interpretation by the U.S. Supreme Court, which usually limits itself by the principle of *stare decisis.*

Origins of the American Judicial System: Federalism

The existence of separate federal and state judicial systems in the United States is a hallmark of federalism, which means these systems share authority to resolve legal disputes in their geographic boundaries. Federal and state courts sometimes have concurrent jurisdiction to resolve disputes arising from the same set of circumstances. For instance, federal and state authorities both took judicial action following the bombing of the Alfred P. Murrah Federal Building in Oklahoma City in 1995. Federal and state courts occasionally have exclusive jurisdiction over certain areas of the law. State courts, for instance, typically have exclusive jurisdiction to handle child custody disputes, while federal courts exclusively handle bankruptcy cases. The U.S. Constitution determines whether state and federal courts have concurrent or exclusive jurisdiction over a particular issue.

Structure and Operation of the Courts: Judicial Hierarchy

American state court systems are hierarchical. Most states have trial courts of general jurisdiction where the judges preside over all types of cases, both civil and criminal. Most states also have special courts of limited jurisdiction that hear only certain kinds of cases— domestic relations and family court, juvenile court, and courts for the administration of wills are typical examples. There also are state courts of inferior jurisdiction, such as justices of the peace, small claims court, and traffic court, that handle petty matters. Appeals from all lower courts usually go first to an intermediate appellate court, often called the court of appeals, and then to the state's highest court, often called the supreme court. When a case involves application of the U.S. Constitution or federal law, the parties sometimes may appeal from the state's highest court to the U.S. Supreme Court.

The federal judiciary is similarly hierarchical. Federal district courts handle trials in civil and criminal cases, and appeals from some federal administrative agencies. The federal judiciary also has special courts of limited jurisdiction, such as the Court of Federal Claims, the Court of International Trade, and the Tax Court. Appeals from federal district courts go to one of 11 numbered circuit courts of appeals covering different geographical regions, or to the District of Columbia Court of Appeals. Appeals from the Court of Federal Claims and the Court of International Trade go to the Federal Court of Appeals. Parties may appeal a case from the appellate courts to the U.S. Supreme Court.

Structure and Operation of the Courts: Criminal and Civil Procedure

The progress of a case through the court system is governed by rules of procedure. There are separate rules of civil and criminal procedure because criminal cases require special constitutional safeguards for the accused. The following illustration explains the procedure in a civil case, which generally is a dispute between private individuals. Some of the notable differences between civil and criminal procedures are noted in this discussion.

Rules of civil procedure define and limit the roles of the various persons in a case. The party who brings a case is called the plaintiff, and the person being sued is the defendant. (In criminal cases there is a prosecutor instead of a plaintiff.) As the American legal system is adversarial, the parties are represented by lawyers who must zealously protect their clients' interests. A jury typically hears the evidence and determines the outcome under the substantive law as instructed by the judge. The judge acts as a referee to enforce the rules and explain the applicable law.

While the federal and state courts each have their own rules of civil procedure, the federal process is fairly representative. A federal case begins when a plaintiff files a complaint and summons in a federal district court. The complaint explains the nature of the plaintiff's claim against the defendant. The summons notifies the defendant to appear and to answer the complaint by either admitting or denying the plaintiff's allegations. If the defendant fails to appear and answer, the court may enter a default judgment against the defendant and order the relief sought by the plaintiff. If the defendant appears, he typically files an answer that denies the plaintiff's allegations. The plaintiff's complaint, the defendant's answer, and any reply by the plaintiff are called the pleadings.

The defendant next may file a motion to dismiss, which argues that even if the plaintiff proves everything in his pleadings, the law does not provide any relief. If the judge grants this motion, she dismisses the case. If not, the parties proceed to the discovery phase.

The purpose of discovery is to help the parties identify and narrow the issues for trial, and to require the parties to disclose all of their evidence. The parties begin discovery by making mandatory disclosures containing basic information, such as the identity of persons and documents with evidence related to the pleadings. The parties then answer interrogatories and take depositions. Interrogatories are written questions that a party must answer in writing under an oath that acknowledges a penalty for perjury. Depositions are oral, transcribed proceedings by which a prospective witness, who also is under oath, answers verbal questions posed by the lawyers. Interrogatory answers and deposition transcripts may be used at trial as evidence or to impeach a witness's testimony if she contradicts what she said during discovery.

After discovery, the defendant may make a motion for summary judgment, which argues that even with everything that discovery has revealed, the plaintiff is unable to prove a violation of law warranting relief. If the judge grants this motion, she dismisses the case. Otherwise the case proceeds to trial.

The trial begins when the judge and parties pick a jury. (In civil cases for which there was no right to a jury trial upon adoption of the U.S. Constitution, or when the parties do not want a jury trial, the parties have a bench trial before a judge without a jury.) In some cases a grand jury, consisting usually of 23 members, is called to determine whether grounds exist for a criminal proceeding to be initiated by the state. To pick the jury, the judge or lawyers pose questions to prospective jurors. After hearing the answers, the parties may dismiss a set number of prospective jurors for any reason, although they may not discriminate unlawfully. The parties further may dismiss an unlimited number of jurors for good cause, such as bias in the prospective juror's responses.

Once they have selected 12 jurors, the lawyers present opening statements, which give the jury a roadmap of what the evidence will prove. The plaintiff then presents his case by the testimony of witnesses and the admission of documents into the record of evidence. The presentation is governed by rules of evidence, which the judge enforces to determine what the jury can and cannot hear. The rules of evidence are supposed to give the jury only the most reliable evidence. The defendant is allowed to cross-examine the plaintiff's witnesses to challenge their accuracy, truthfulness, and bias. The defendant presents his evidence after the plaintiff, who then may cross-examine the defendant's witnesses.

At the close of the evidence, each party may ask the judge to enter judgment in his favor on the ground that a reasonable jury could only reach one verdict under the evidence presented. If the judge denies this motion, she instructs the jury about the applicable substantive law, the lawyers make closing arguments to explain the result their clients seek, and the jury retires to deliberate and reach a verdict. After the jury (or the judge in a bench trial) delivers its verdict, each party may ask the judge to reverse the verdict or order a new trial based upon errors the judge made applying the rules of procedure, rules of evidence, or substantive law. If these motions are denied, the parties may file a notice of appeal to the proper circuit court of appeals. Notably, if a person is found not guilty in a criminal proceeding that is not declared a mistrial, that person cannot be tried again for the same crime. This concept of dou-

ble jeopardy has its origin in the Fifth Amendment, which prevents people from being placed at risk of conviction more than once for a single offense.

Cases in the courts of appeals are heard by a panel of three judges. The parties file briefs that explain the errors they think the trial judge made under the rules of procedure, rules of evidence, or substantive law. The court of appeals does not hear the evidence anew, but relies on the record—the trial testimony and documents entered into evidence before the district court. The court also might hear oral argument, during which the parties' lawyers may respond to questions posed by the judges on the panel. The judges then study the record, briefs, and oral argument, discuss the case among themselves, vote on the result, and issue a decision based on the majority vote.

Dissatisfied parties may appeal to the U.S. Supreme Court, which is composed of nine justices. The procedure is similar to that in the courts of appeal, with one major exception: a party first must file a petition for a writ of *certiorari* to convince the Supreme Court that the case is important enough to warrant consideration. The Supreme Court grants the writ—by a vote of four or more justices—for only approximately five percent of the thousands of petitions it receives each year. These lucky few file briefs and engage in oral argument as they did before the court of appeals. After the justices vote, one of the justices voting in the majority writes an opinion explaining the Court's decision. Dissatisfied parties have no further avenue of appeal from this court of last resort.

Structure and Operation of the Courts: Alternative Dispute Resolution

The procedure for pursuing a case, especially a civil case, from trial through appeal is time-consuming. It can take one or more years to get a verdict in the trial court, and five or more years for an appeal to the court of appeals and the Supreme Court. The legal fees and other costs can amount to hundreds of thousands or millions of dollars. The vast majority of civil cases thus settle before going to trial, which means the parties resolve their dispute by agreement. Most criminal cases also settle, a process called plea-bargaining.

Efforts to reduce costs in civil cases have popularized an area of legal procedure called alternative dispute resolution, or ADR. Arbitration, the best known form of ADR, is an informal, abbreviated trial where one or more neutral arbitrators hears and decides the case like a judge and jury. Conciliation, a less common form of ADR, involves submission of the dispute to a neutral third party for her investigation and recommendation. With mediation the parties try to negotiate a resolution with the assistance and guidance of a neutral mediator.

Today many contracts include a clause that requires parties to use ADR to resolve their disagreements. Whether or not they have a contract, many parties voluntarily pursue ADR before going to court. State courts increasingly require parties in certain types of cases to try arbitration or mediation before proceeding to trial. The American Arbitration Association and other organizations support these efforts by designing ADR systems and procedures.

Types of Law

In the United States, where most courts hear cases concerning all areas of law, categorizing the laws is largely arbitrary. In *An Introduction to the Legal System of the United States*, Professor E. Allan Farnsworth suggested a useful distinction between public and private law. Public law generally concerns disputes between the government and individuals. Private law concerns disputes between private individuals.

Types of Law: Public Law

Public law, as described by Professor Farnsworth, includes constitutional, criminal, trade regulation, labor, and tax law. Constitutional law is embodied in the decisions of the U.S. Supreme Court that interpret the federal Constitution. Many of these cases concern whether conduct by the legislative or executive branches of the federal government violate constitutional definitions or limitations on their powers. Under the "political question" doctrine, however, the Supreme Court will decline to decide such a case if the Constitution reserves the issue for the legislative or executive branch without judicial interference.

A large majority of constitutional law cases concern the protection of individual rights from unlawful federal conduct. The Bill of Rights, which comprises the first ten amendments to the Constitution, is the primary source of these rights. For example, the First Amendment protects the freedom of speech, while the Fourth Amendment protects the right to be free from unreasonable search and seizure. The Constitution also protects individual rights from unlawful state conduct. The most important source of this protection is the Fourteenth Amendment, which contains the Due Process and Equal Protection Clauses. By interpretation of these clauses, the U.S. Supreme Court has applied the rights and protections found in the Bill of Rights to state conduct.

Criminal law mostly appears in state penal codes. These codes, while largely based on the common law of England, reflect an effort to arrive at uniform, reliable definitions of crimes. The codes define everything from felonies, such as murder and rape, to misdemeanors and petty offenses. There also are federal sources of criminal law, most notably relating to interstate conduct, such as drug trafficking and fraudulent use of the mails. Another important source of federal criminal law is the statute that protects civil rights, such as the right to be free from discrimination on the basis of race, color, or creed. Criminal law cases also can involve issues of constitutional law, such as the rights of the accused to remain silent and to be represented by an attorney.

Trade regulation includes antitrust law, which seeks to prevent monopolies and other restraints of trade under America's system of free enterprise. It also includes laws designed to prevent unfair competition among businesses. Labor law protects the well-being of employees and the rights and duties of labor unions. Tax law primarily concerns the federal income tax.

Types of Law: Private Law

Private law, often referred to as civil law, includes tort, contract, family, commercial, and property law. States are the primary source of private law. Tort law is a system of providing compensation between individuals for private wrongs, such as battery and defamation. The enforcement of promises or obligations between individuals is the subject of contract law. Family law deals with the relationships between husband and wife or parent and child: marriage and divorce; spousal abuse and support; and child custody, abuse, support, and adoption. Commercial law, derived primarily from the Uniform Commercial Code, governs the sale and lease of goods. Property law governs transactions in real estate.

The Appointment of Judges

The process for appointing state judges varies from state to state. Most state trial judges are elected by popular vote or by the state legislature. The supreme court judges in most states are appointed for a fixed term by the governor, and then periodically stand unopposed for reelection based on their records. In some states the judges of the highest court are elected by popular vote. State judges usually serve for a fixed term of years or for life, and can be removed only for gross misconduct by formal proceedings.

Federal judges are appointed by the president with the advice and consent of the Senate. This process typically results in the appointment of judges who are members of the president's political party. If the Senate judiciary committee is controlled by the president's opposition party, the confirmation process can be hotly contested. Federal judges are appointed for life, and can be removed only by impeachment and conviction by Congress.

The Role of Judges

State and federal judges perform various important roles in the American legal system. Trial judges referee cases under the rules of procedure and evidence. The trial judge also instructs the jury concerning the substantive law that is applicable to the case. In bench trials, the judge determines the facts, law, and result without a jury. The role of appellate judges is to review the record of evidence before the trial court, decide the applicable substantive law, and either affirm or reverse the result below. In doing so, the appellate judge may announce principles of law for application by trial judges in future cases.

Limitations on Judicial Power

In *Marbury v. Madison* (1803), the Supreme Court said "[i]t is emphatically the province and duty of the judicial department to say what the law is." Judicial power, however, is not unlimited. The U.S. Constitution is the primary source for limitations on federal judicial power. The Constitution constrains federal courts to hear only "cases and controversies," which means actual cases rather than hypothetical situations or stale disputes. Under the political question doctrine, federal courts will not address issues reserved to the legislative or executive branches of the federal government. Congressional authority under the Constitution also limits judicial power. Congress may impeach and convict federal judges for "Treason, Bribery, or other high Crimes and Misdemeanors." If Congress is dissatisfied with a court's interpretation of a statute, it may pass legislation to correct the interpretation, as long as it acts within the constitutional limitations on its own power.

Similarly, state judicial power is restricted by state constitutions, the process for selection and removal of state judges, and the ultimate supremacy of the U.S. Constitution over both state and federal statutes and case law.

Bibliography and Further Reading

Calvi, James V., and Susan Coleman. *American Law and Legal Systems,* 3d ed. Upper Saddle River: Prentice Hall, 1997.

Farnsworth, E. Allan. *An Introduction to the Legal System of the United States,* 3d ed. New York: Oceana Publications, Inc., 1996.

Fowler, Michael Ross. *With Justice for All? The Nature of the American Legal System.* Upper Saddle River: Prentice Hall, 1998.

Van Dervort, Thomas R. *Equal Justice Under the Law.* Minneapolis/Saint Paul: West Publishing Company, 1994.

CONTRIBUTORS

Shannon Armitage

Beth Babini

Holly Barton

Daniel Brannen

Carol Brennan

Michael Broyles

ByLine Communications

Holly Caldwell

Jo-Ann Canning

Diane Carter

Richard Chapman

Chapterhouse

Linda Clemmons

Amy Cooper

Richard Cretan

Julie Davis

Michael Eggert

Grant Eldridge

Robert Gluck

Joel Golden

Carrie Golus

Nancy Gordon

Connor Gorry

Bridget Hall

Richard Clay Hanes

Lauri Harding

James Heiberg

Karl Heil

Robert Jacobson

Constance Johnson

Lois Kallunki

John Kane

Christine Kelley

Edward Knappman

Judson Knight

Paul Kobel

Jacqueline Maurice

Olivia Miller

Nancy Moore

Melynda Neal

New England Publishing Associates

Helene Northway

Carol Page

Akomea Poku-Kankam

Debra Reilly

Mary Scarbrough

Robert Schnakenberg

Bryan Schneider

Maria Sheler-Edwards

Elizabeth Shostak

Ginger Strand

Karen Troshynski-Thomas

Katherine Wagner

Linda Walton

Michael Watkins

Daniel Wisher

Susan Wood

Lisa Wroble

FREEDOM OF ASSEMBLY

Fundamental Rights

Every day, Americans exercise the freedoms of association and assembly. Both freedoms protect expressive choices. They let individuals decide what to think and say, with whom to agree or disagree, and when and how to do so. The freedom of association safeguards membership in organizations, regardless of whether individuals, groups, or even the government approve. The freedom of assembly allows people to gather in public to express their beliefs, happily or in the angriest protest. Fundamental to a free society, these rights are not always easily enjoyed. Majorities can find their ideologies threatened, and government officials can see some kinds of association and assembly as dangerous. The exercise of these freedoms has repeatedly provoked controversies that test the nation's commitment to constitutional liberties.

The right of assembly is as old as the Bill of Rights of the United States Constitution. Article I of the Bill of Rights guarantees "the right of the people peaceably to assemble, and to petition the Government for a redress of grievances." The framers of the Constitution protected these civil liberties because British authorities had repressed them during the colonial period. Particularly infuriating had been the refusal of the British king to answer the colonists' petitions, despite this right having been guaranteed in the English Bill of Rights of 1689. Thus, in the drafting of the First Amendment, the protections against government interference in speech and religion were joined to that of assembly and petition. In every era since, these rights have played a major role in shaping important historical events, from the gathering of two million anti-slavery petitions by abolitionists in the late 1830s, to the nineteenth and twentieth century marches of suffragettes on behalf of women's voting rights, to the demonstrations of the Civil Rights movement in the 1950s and 1960s, and the anti-war protests of the same period.

Like speech rights, the right of assembly is not absolute. It is even somewhat weaker. The Supreme Court has ruled that the First Amendment does not give as much protection to assembly as it does to "pure speech," a distinction observed in cases such as *Cox v. Louisiana* (1965). Lawmakers thus have regulated assembly in numerous ways, from requiring the issuance of permits to declaring when, where and for how long public demonstrations may occur. The Court has often recognized the importance of these reasonable regulations. In *Cox v. New Hampshire* (1941), it upheld a state law whose permit requirement for parades was intended to keep sidewalks and streets open for traffic. Government limits on assembling in particular public sites have been upheld, too, as witnessed in the decision *Adderley v. Florida* (1966), which allowed a state to ban demonstrations on jail premises. By the 1980s, courts required that such regulations must be narrowly tailored to serve a significant government interest, not control the content of the proposed assembly, and leave open alternative means for public expression.

Political Expression

Government abridgments draw close scrutiny from the courts. While the First Amendment's definition of "peaceable" assembly is open to wide interpretation, twentieth century courts have refused to allow it to be used as a blanket excuse for any government control. The modern trend has its roots in *De Jonge v. Oregon* (1937), one of the earliest cases to emphasize the importance of assembly rights. Dirk De Jonge, a Communist party member, had organized a meeting in Portland, Oregon, to protest police violence against striking workers. Though the meeting was peaceful, the state convicted him for selling Communist pamphlets in violation of a statute prohibiting "any unlawful acts or methods as a means of accomplishing or effecting industrial or political change or revolution." In overturning the conviction, the Supreme Court declared that "peaceable assembly for lawful discussion cannot be made a crime." Moreover, the right of assembly was "equally fundamental" to that of freedom of speech and the press. Three years later, in another milestone, *Thornhill v. Alabama* (1940), the Court gave protection to union picketing. Overturning a state law that prohibited picketing, the 8–1 decision observed that labor demonstrations were "indispensable to the effective and intelligent use of the process of popular government to shape the destiny of modern industrial society."

In recent decades, political expression has received the greatest protection, although this change came slowly. The many public demonstrations of the Civil Rights movement, for example, produced violent reactions from citizens opposed to voting rights and integration for African Americans, and courts in southern states often convicted demonstrators for breaching the peace. In *Edwards v. South Carolina* (1963), the Supreme Court reversed the convictions of almost 200 black students who protested discrimination by marching in orderly fashion on the state capitol grounds. The *Edwards* decision made it clear that states could not punish "the peaceful expression of unpopular views." Controversial decisions would follow, occasionally outraging society while reminding it that even the least popular groups could assemble legally. Such a decision was *Smith v. Collin* (1978), which ordered the Chicago suburb of Skokie, Illinois, to permit the American Nazi Party to march in neighborhoods inhabited by 70,000 Jewish residents, many of whom were Holocaust survivors. Skokie's local ordinances, which controlled the content of speech and the clothing of marchers, were held unconstitutional. "[I]f these civil rights are to remain vital for all," the federal court held, "they must protect not only those society deems acceptable, but also those whose ideas it quite justifiably rejects and despises."

Freedom of Association

Unlike the right of assembly, the Constitution makes no mention of the freedom of association. Through the late 1950s, decisions that broached the question of association considered it to be an aspect of other First Amendment liberties. This early view emerged in cases challenging the extent of Congress' power to question witnesses. They concerned the hearings of the House Committee on Un-American Activities (HUAC), during which lawmakers compelled reluctant witnesses to testify about the political associations of themselves, their friends, relatives, and colleagues, in an all-out attempt to identify Communists and so-called sympathizers. Refusal to testify could lead to charges of contempt. The Supreme Court curbed this power in *Watkins v. United States* (1957), holding that the use of such inquisitorial powers violated rights of association and privacy, endangered witnesses, and might even make other citizens avoid unpopular political ideas and assembling in groups.

In 1958, the Supreme Court took a defining step in *NAACP v. Alabama ex rel. Patterson.* The case grew out of the tumultuous struggle for civil rights. Alabama officials had resisted school desegregation and boycott efforts by the National Association for the Advancement of Colored People (NAACP), but when the organization persisted, prosecutors tried to prevent it from doing any further business in the state. Eventually, the state won a lower court order forcing the NAACP to dis-

close its membership records, which the organization refused to do in order to protect its members' safety. After the trial court fined it $100,000 for contempt, the Supreme Court reversed this decision and allowed the list to be kept private. Justice John Marshall Harlan II was persuaded by the NAACP's argument that forced disclosure of its membership would lead to economic reprisals, physical threats, and other kinds of public hostility. The state had failed to show a compelling interest that could outweigh these dangers. The contempt finding thus deprived the NAACP's members of their due process rights under the Fourth Amendment, and crucially, their constitutional right to free association. This right existed in the close relationship between the First Amendment rights of speech and assembly. Though enunciating the right for the first time, Justice Harlan noted that it "has been considered an essential element of the American political process since the early days of the nation's existence."

Following *Patterson*, the Supreme Court quickly issued similar decisions protecting individuals from divulging their association with groups. Again, in *Bates v. Little Rock* (1959), it allowed the NAACP to resist disclosing its membership lists. *Shelton v. Tucker* (1960) considered an Arkansas teacher competency statute which mandated that, as part of their review, teachers disclose every organization to which they had belonged. Evaluating a teacher's competency on this standard, the Court ruled, was too sweeping an invasion of her associational rights.

The Cold War era, characterized by extreme government suspicion of subversive activity, provided the Court with considerable opportunities to balance the rights of government and individuals. Here its decisions were inconsistent. Unlike the NAACP, the American Communist Party could be forced to disclose the names of its members because, as the Court held in *Communist Party v. Subversive Activities Control Board* (1961), the organization's activities posed dangers which the government had a substantial interest in controlling. Several cases challenged the constitutionality of the Smith Act of 1940, which prohibited conspiring to overthrow the government or merely promoting beliefs that advocated doing so. In particular, two cases challenged the law's restrictions on membership in groups committed to these ends. The Court determined that membership alone was insufficient grounds for conviction, but that convictions were constitutional when an individual was an active member who not only knew about the group's illegal activities but also intended to further them. Thus it upheld a conviction in *Scales v. United States* (1961) but overturned another in *Noto v. United States* (1961).

In cases decided in the 1970s and later, the Court looked negatively on attempts to make individuals espouse ideas or beliefs. Just as there was a right to associate, so, too, was there a right not to associate. Compelling association was unconstitutional, as was made clear in *Abood v. Detroit Board of Education* (1977). In *Abood*, Detroit school board employees were free not to join a union, but still had to pay a service fee that was equal to union dues. By compelling them to pay for political causes to which they were opposed, held the Court, board officials had violated the employees' right to choose not to associate. A similar decision was reached in *Keller v. State Bar of California* (1990), limiting the use of attorneys' mandatory state bar membership dues. Only if the bar showed that the dues were used for regulating and improving the legal profession could the dues be used to further political causes with which the members disagreed.

However, the right against compelled association proved to be far from absolute. When organizations claimed it in defense of discriminatory practices, the Supreme Court intervened to break down exclusive barriers to membership. This trend began in 1984 with *Roberts v. U.S. Jaycees*. After several women sued the national Jaycees, whose bylaws limited membership to men age 18 to 35, the organization defended its policy as an exercise of its free association rights. The Minnesota Supreme Court found the Jaycees had illegally discriminated on the basis of gender, and the Supreme Court agreed. It ruled that infringements on the right to association were sometimes constitutional, if they served important state interests and as long as the restrictions were unrelated to "the suppression of ideas". More state anti-discrimination laws were seen to promote the same valid interests in cases such as *Rotary International v. Rotary Club of Duarte* (1987) and *New York State Club Association v. City of New York* (1988), where clubs were forced to open their doors to all races and sexes.

In modern rulings, the importance of ideas and beliefs in the right to association stands paramount in Supreme Court doctrine. Time and again, it has emphasized that the right to association derives from the First Amendment and, as such, is protected only when it is asserted along with a First Amendment right. Thus it is not merely enough to claim that associational rights are violated simply because any kind of restriction

exists, as did the plaintiffs who unsuccessfully challenged an ordinance in *City of Dallas v. Stanglin* (1989) that barred adults from entering dance halls for teenagers. An expressive purpose must be present to trigger constitutional protection. This purpose can be expressed in any number of ways, including through economic means. A boycott against white-owned businesses was held to be legal in *National Association for the Advancement of Colored People v. Claiborne Hardware Co.* (1982) because it was designed to further the goals of civil rights, but a boycott by trial lawyers who wanted higher fees to represent poor clients was held to have no First Amendment protection in *FTC v. Superior Court Trial Lawyers Association* (1990), because the lawyers' goal expressed no political ideas.

See also: **Freedom of Speech, Freedom of Religion**

Bibliography and Further Reading

Burns, Gwinda L. "Case Comment: Roberts v. United States Jaycees." *Thurgood Marshall Law Review*, Spring 1985

Demac, Donna. *State of the First Amendment*. Multimedia book in PDF file form obtained from www.freedomforum.org. Arlington: Freedom Forum, 1997

Hall, Kermit L., ed. *The Oxford Companion to the Supreme Court of the United States*. New York: Oxford University Press, 1992

Jameson, Ann H. "Roberts v. United States Jaycees: Discriminatory Membership Policy of a National Organization Held Not Protected by First Amendment Freedom of Association." *Catholic University Law Review*, Summer 1985

Schwartz, Bernard. *A History of the Supreme Court*. New York: Oxford University Press, 1993

Spangler, Shannon L. "Freedom of Association—Explanation of the Underlying Concepts—Republican Party of Connecticut v. Tashjian." *University of Kansas Law Review*, Summer 1986

West's Encyclopedia of American Law. St. Paul: West Group, 1998

EX PARTE GARLAND

Legal Citation: 71 U.S 333 (1867)

Petitioner
Augustus H. Garland

Respondent
United States

Petitioner's Claim
That the act of Congress of 24 January 1865, which required all lawyers who practiced before a federal court to swear that they had no sympathy toward the Confederacy, was unconstitutional.

Chief Lawyers for Petitioner
Matthew H. Carpenter, Reverdy Johnson

Chief Lawyers for Respondent
Henry Stanbery, U.S. Attorney General; James Speed

Justices for the Court
Nathan Clifford, Stephen Johnson Field (writing for the Court), Robert Cooper Grier, Samuel Nelson, James Moore Wayne

Justices Dissenting
Salmon Portland Chase, David Davis, Samuel Freeman Miller, Noah Haynes Swayne

Place
Washington, D.C.

Date of Decision
14 January 1867

Decision
Federal and state governments may not require loyalty oaths.

Significance
Two important precedents were re-established. First, the president has full power to pardon anyone of all crimes, either before, during or after persecution and that the pardon clears the individuals of any consequences that may have arisen from the action from which they were to be punished. Second, laws may not be established that would punish someone, in the broadest sense of the word, *ex post facto*.

During the December term of 1860, the petitioner, Garland, was admitted as an attorney and counselor of the Supreme Court, and took and subscribed the oath then required. In March of 1865, this rule was changed by the addition of a clause requiring administration of the oath, in conformity with the acts of Congress of 2 July 1862, and 24 January 1865. The act of 2 July 1862, required that every person hereafter "elected or appointed to any office of honor or profit under the government of the United States . . . shall subscribe the following oath: I do solemnly swear that I have never voluntarily borne arms against the United States since I have been a citizen thereof, etc . . . " This act was extended to attorneys in the United States after 24 January 1865, and stated that no person should be permitted to practice in the Supreme Court or other courts unless they took the oath set forth in the act of 2 July 1862.

On 15 July 1865, Garland was pardoned by President Andrew Johnson for taking part in the Civil War. He then produced this pardon for the Supreme Court and asked permission to continue to practice as an attorney and counselor of the Court, without taking the above oath. He rested his application upon two grounds: first, the act of 24 January 1865, so far as it affects its status in the Court, is unconstitutional and void; second, that if the act was constitutional, he is released from compliance with its provisions by the pardon of the president.

Justice Field delivered the opinion of the Court, for the petitioner, with Justices Wayne, Nelson, Grier and Clifford concurring. The judgment was declared on the following three grounds:

1) A pardon reached the punishment prescribed for an offense and the guilt of the offender. If granted before conviction it prevents any of the penalties and disabilities consequent upon conviction from attaching; if granted after conviction it removes the penalties and disabilities and restores him to all his civil rights. The petitioner in this case having received a full pardon for all offenses committed by his participation, direct or implied, in the Rebellion, is relieved from all penalties and disabilities attached to the offense of treason, committed by such participation. For that offense

The U.S. Supreme Court, 1868. © Photograph by Brady and Company. The Library of Congress/Corbis.

he is beyond the reach of punishment of any kind. He cannot, therefore, be excluded by reason of that offense from continuing in the enjoyment of a previously acquired right to appear as an attorney and counselor in the Federal courts.

2) The act of Congress of 24 January 1865 operates as a legislative decree excluding from the practice of law in the courts of the United States all parties who have offended in any of the particulars enumerated. Exclusion from the practice of law in the federal courts, or from any other avocations of life for past conduct is punishment for such conduct. In the exclusion which the act adjudges it imposes a punishment for some of the acts specified which were not punishable at the time they were committed, and for other of the acts it adds new punishment to that before prescribed, and it is thus within the inhibition of the Constitution against the passage of an *ex post facto* law.

3) Attorneys and counselors hold their offices during good behavior, and can only be deprived of it for misconduct ascertained and declared by the judgment of the court after opportunity to be heard has been afforded. Their admission and their exclusion are the exercise of judicial power only. The admitted power of Congress to prescribe qualifications for the office of attorney and counselor in the federal courts cannot be exercised as a means for infliction of punishment for the past conduct of such officers, against the inhibition of the Constitution.

It was thus ordered that the prayer of the petitioner be granted and the amendment of the second rule of the court, which requires the oath prescribed in the act of 24 January 1865, to be taken by attorneys and counselors, having been unadvisedly adopted, be rescinded.

Justice Miller dissented with Justices Chase, Swayne, and Davis. Miller stated that it is at all times the exercise of delicate power of the Supreme Court to declare that the Congress of the nation has assumed an authority not belonging to it and, by violating the Constitution, has rendered void its attempt at legislation. Unable to see this incompatibility in the act of Congress, but entertaining a strong conviction that the act is within the competency of the Congress, he dissented.

Related Cases
Cummings v. Missouri, 4 Wall. 277 (1867).
In re North, 62 F.3d 1434 (1994).
In re Abrams, 689 A.2d 6 (1997).

Bibliography and Further Reading
Biskupic, Joan, and Elder Witt, eds. *Congressional Quarterly's Guide to the U.S. Supreme Court,* 3rd ed. Washington, DC: Congressional Quarterly, Inc., 1996.

Johnson, John W. *Historic U.S. Court Cases, 1690–1990: An Encyclopedia*. New York: Garland Publishing, 1992.

WHITNEY V. CALIFORNIA

Legal Citation: 274 U.S. 357 (1927)

Appellant
Charlotte Anita Whitney

Appellee
People of the State of California

Appellant's Claim
That a 1919 California criminal syndicalism law violated the First Amendment guarantees of freedom of speech and association.

Chief Lawyers for Appellant
Walter H. Pollak, Walter Nelles

Chief Lawyers for Appellee
John H. Riordan, U. S. Webb

Justices for the Court
Louis D. Brandeis, Pierce Butler, Oliver Wendell Holmes, James Clark McReynolds, Edward Terry Sanford (writing for the Court), Harlan Fiske Stone, George Sutherland, William Howard Taft, Willis Van Devanter

Justices Dissenting
None

Place
Washington, D.C.

Date of Decision
26 May 1927

Decision
The Supreme Court upheld the California law.

Significance
The concurrence was actually more important than the opinion of the Court in *Whitney*.

In 1919, California passed a law criminalizing syndicalism, a philosophy which advocated bringing government and industry under the control of labor through "direct action," such as strikes. The law was aimed chiefly at the International Workers of the World (IWW), or "Wobblies," a radical labor group then active in the West.

The first important prosecution under the law was of Charlotte Anita Whitney, a social activist and prominent member of the Socialist Party. In 1919 she was arrested while participating in a convention organized by the Communist Labor Party (CLP), a radical California-based offshoot of the Socialist Party. At trial, Whitney did not deny her brief association with the CLP, and the prosecution seized the opportunity to associate her with the IWW, whose goals had been endorsed by the CLP. Whitney was convicted of violating the anti-syndicalism law, and after the California Court of Appeals upheld her conviction, she appealed to the U.S. Supreme Court.

Supreme Court Upholds California Criminal Syndicalism Law

The conservative Court headed by Taft voted 9-0 to uphold the California statute, as well as Whitney's conviction. As Justice Sanford wrote in his opinion for the Court, the state has the right—even the duty—to protect itself and its citizens from violent political action. However, although the vote was unanimous, there was more than one opinion in the case, and it is Justice Brandeis's concurrence that has lent *Whitney* lasting significance.

Whitney's attorneys seemed not to have done well by her. (California governor C. C. Young pardoned Whitney a few months after the case.) Brandeis reasoned that if they had argued for a "clear and present danger" standard by which to judge her behavior, the Court might have reversed her conviction. Brandeis was joined in this opinion by Justice Holmes, the originator of the test. Holmes first used the phrase "clear and present danger" in *Schenck v. United States* (1919) to describe a situation where it is permissible for government to restrict speech otherwise protected by the First Amendment. In *Schenck*, the Court unanimously upheld the convictions of socialists who had distrib-

The California Criminal Syndicalism Act

As with the era of McCarthyism in the 1950s, the Red Scare of the late 1910s and early 1920s followed a world war. In both cases, the winding down of international hostilities had been attended by the spread of Communism: thus after World War II, Communists took over numerous countries in Europe, and to many Americans, a Soviet takeover of the United States seemed possible if not imminent.

Responding to fears inspired by the "Wobblies" (the Industrial Workers of the World), as well as by Communists and other agitators, Idaho in 1917 passed a criminal syndicalism law which became the model for California's and that of most other states. Much like its predecessor in Idaho, the 1919 California act defined "criminal syndicalism" as "any doctrine or precept advocating, teaching, or aiding and abetting the commission of crime, sabotage . . . or unlawful acts of force

. . . as a means of accomplishing a change in industrial ownership . . . or effecting any political change." Likewise the California act, in accordance with the Idaho model, defined participation in "criminal syndicalism" as "a felony . . . punishable by imprisonment."

In the heyday of the Red Scare, from 1917 to 1920, no fewer than 22 states and territories adopted criminal syndicalism laws, and eight others considered adopting them. But by the 1930s—a period when American sympathy for Communism was its highest point, due to the Great Depression—most criminal syndicalism laws had fallen into disuse. The Supreme Court overturned its *Whitney* ruling once and for all with *Brandenburg v. Ohio* in 1969.

Source(s): Levy, Leonard W., ed. *Encyclopedia of the American Constitution.* New York: Macmillan, 1986.

uted antiwar literature to men going through the conscription process during World War I. Holmes, like his fellow justices, found that the government had a right to intercept these communications which might interfere with army recruitment in time of war.

As it had after World War II, a Red Scare period followed in the wake of World War I. Whitney was a victim of that period, found guilty not so much of acts but of associations. Brandeis's opinion in *Whitney* made it clear that when it came to dissident speech, there

should be a distinction made between mere association and dangerous acts:

> Fear of serious injury alone cannot justify suppression of free speech and assembly . . . To justify suppression of free speech there must be reasonable ground to fear that serious evil will result if free speech is practiced. There must be reasonable ground to believe that the danger apprehended is imminent. There must be reasonable ground to believe that the evil

Andrew Ona (left) and Anita Whitney.
© UPI/Corbis-Bettmann.

to be prevented is a serious one . . . But even advocacy of violations, however reprehensible morally, is not a justification for denying free speech where the advocacy falls short of incitement and there is nothing to indicate that the advocacy would be immediately acted on . . . In order to support a finding of clear and present danger it must be shown either that immediate serious violence was to be expected or was advocated, or that the past conduct furnished reason to believe that such advocacy was then contemplated.

This was the test that Brandeis believed should be applied to a statute which, like the California anti-syndicalism law, defined speech itself as a criminal offense. The Supreme Court never fully developed the clear and present danger standard, and in *Dennis v. United States* (1951), the Court did away with the immediacy requirement to uphold the convictions of 11 Communist Party leaders during the height of the post-World War II Red Scare. Then, in *Brandenburg v. Ohio* (1969), the clear and present danger test resurfaced as a rationale for overturning the conviction of a Ku Klux Klan leader convicted of advocating criminal syndicalism. *Brandenburg* overturned *Whitney,* but a modified version of the California criminal syndicalism law remained on the books.

Related Cases
Schenck v. United States, 249 U.S. 47 (1919).
Dennis v. United States, 341 U.S. 494 (1951).
Brandenburg v. Ohio, 395 U.S. 444 (1969).

Bibliography and Further Reading
Abernathy, Mabra Glenn. *The Right of Assembly and Association,* 2nd ed., rev. Columbia: University of South Carolina Press, 1981.

Johnson, John W., ed. *Historic U.S. Court Cases, 1690–1990: An Encyclopedia.* New York: Garland Publishing, 1992.

Preston, William. *Aliens and Dissenters: Federal Suppression of Radicals, 1903-1933.* Urbana: University of Illinois Press, 1994.

Renshaw, Patrick. *The Wobblies: The Story of Syndicalism in the United States.* Garden City, NY: Doubleday, 1967.

DE JONGE V. OREGON

Legal Citation: 299 U.S. 353 (1937)

Appellant
Dirk De Jonge

Appellee
State of Oregon

Appellant's Claim
That an Oregon statute outlawing criminal syndicalism, the advocacy of change of government or business ownership by violence or other unlawful means, violates the right to freedom of assembly, which is protected by the First Amendment.

Chief Lawyer for Appellant
Osmond K. Fraenkel

Chief Lawyer for Appellee
Maurice E. Tarshis

Justices for the Court
Louis D. Brandeis, Pierce Butler, Benjamin N. Cardozo, Charles Evans Hughes (writing for the Court), James Clark McReynolds, Owen Josephus Roberts, George Sutherland, Willis Van Devanter

Justices Dissenting
None (Harlan Fiske Stone did not participate)

Place
Washington, D.C.

Date of Decision
4 January 1937

Decision
Declaring that peaceable assembly is as fully protected as freedom of speech, the Supreme Court reversed Dirk De Jonge's conviction and overturned the Oregon statute.

Significance
De Jonge marked the first time the right of free assembly was made applicable to the states by means of the Due Process Clause of the Fourteenth Amendment.

On 27 July 1934, Dirk De Jonge, a member of the Communist Party, participated in a party meeting in Portland, Oregon. The meeting had been called by the Communist Party to protest illegal raids on workers' halls and homes, as well as the shooting of striking longshoremen by Portland police. De Jonge spoke to a group, estimated to have been between 150 and 300 people, on these topics, afterward urging those present to recruit more members for the party and attempting to sell some Communist literature. While the meeting was still in progress, it was raided by the police, who seized some of the literature and took De Jonge and others who were conducting the meeting into custody. They were charged under the Oregon criminal syndicalism law, which outlawed participation in a meeting held under the auspices of the Communist Party.

At his trial De Jonge made a motion for acquittal, claiming that there was insufficient evidence to convict him under the statute. He then appealed the trial court's denial of his motion to the state supreme court, which upheld his conviction. He turned finally to the U.S. Supreme Court.

Oregon's criminal syndicalism statute was just one of 20 such state laws passed between the years of 1917 and 1929 as part of an effort to outlaw the radical labor organization, the Industrial Workers of the World (IWW) or "Wobblies." A large number of convictions under the syndicalism laws took place in the West, where the Wobblies were most active. During the Red Scare that followed World War I and the Bolshevik Revolution in Russia, the U.S. Supreme Court upheld the constitutionality of several of the criminal syndicalism laws. But as public alarm about Communist infiltration diminished and the power of the Wobblies faded, the attitude of the Court towards syndicalism also relaxed.

Court Finds Freedom of Assembly Protected from State Infringement

Writing for a unanimous Court, Chief Justice Hughes found that De Jonge, who had done no more than participate in a meeting called to air grievances, not to advocate government overthrow, had been wrongfully convicted. His rights to freedom of assembly, guaranteed at the federal level by the First Amendment, could not, because of the Fourteenth Amendment, be abridged by the state. Freedom of assembly, Chief Justice Hughes pointedly said, was as fundamentally important to our republic as freedom of speech.

> The greater the importance of safeguarding the community from incitements to overthrow of our institutions by force and violence, the more imperative is the need to preserve inviolate the constitutional rights if free speech, free press and free assembly in order to maintain the opportunity for free political discussion, to the end that government may be responsive to the will of the people and that changes, if desired, may be obtained by peaceful means. Therein lies the security of the Republic, the very foundation of constitutional government . . . It follows from these considerations that, consistent with the Federal Constitution, peaceable assembly cannot be made a crime.

De Jonge was the first case to make freedom of assembly applicable at the state level, thus contributing to the movement to incorporate the Bill of Rights into the Fourteenth Amendment, which assures that no state shall "deprive any person of life, liberty, or due process of law." The decision was in fact a harbinger; it was not until later in 1937, with *Palko v. Connecticut* that the Court formally announced its belief that some of the privileges and immunities of the Bill of Rights were so fundamental that states were obliged to respect them under the Due Process Clause of the Fourteenth Amendment.

Related Cases
Stromberg v. California, 283 U.S. 359 (1931).
Palko v. Connecticut, 302 U.S. 319 (1937).
Yates v. United States, 355 U.S. 66 (1957).

Bibliography and Further Reading
Abernathy, M. Glenn. *The Right of Assembly and Association,* 2nd ed. Columbia: University of South Carolina Press, 1981.

Salerno, Salvatore. *Red November, Black November: Culture and Community in the Industrial Workers of the World.* Albany: State University of New York Press, 1989.

Worton, Stanley N. *Freedom of Assembly and Petition.* Rochelle Park, NJ: Hayden Book Co., 1975.

COX V. NEW HAMPSHIRE

Legal Citation: 312 U.S. 569 (1941)

Appellant
Cox, et al.

Appellee
State of New Hampshire

Appellant's Claim
That a state statute prohibiting a parade or procession upon a public street without a special license violated the Fourteenth Amendment by interfering with appellant's First Amendment rights of free speech, press, worship and assembly and by vesting unreasonable and arbitrary power in the licensing authority.

Chief Lawyers for Appellant
Hayden Covington, Joseph F. Rutherford

Chief Lawyer for Appellee
Frank R. Kenison

Justices for the Court
Charles Evans Hughes (writing for the Court), Harlan Fiske Stone, Owen Josephus Roberts, Hugo Lafayette Black, Stanley Forman Reed, Felix Frankfurter, William O. Douglas, Frank Murphy

Justices Dissenting
None

Place
Washington, D.C.

Date of Decision
31 March 1941

Decision
Requiring a permit for a parade or procession upon a public street was a proper exercise of the state's authority and did not violate the appellants' constitutional rights.

Significance
The decision established the right of local governments to require a permit to conduct a parade or procession upon a public street. However, permit decisions had to be made according to uniform, nondiscriminatory standards based upon public convenience and safety to satisfy the Fourteenth Amendment. Validating permit requirements for parades meant that local governments received advance notice of parades allowing them the opportunity to plan policing activities to minimize disorder and inconvenience to passersby.

The First Amendment to the U.S. Constitution guarantees freedom of speech and peaceable assembly. Together these protect the right of U.S. citizens to peacefully gather and parade or demonstrate. In the early 1900s, as U.S. cities grew and increasing numbers of persons exercised these First Amendment rights in streets and parks, cities attempted to control the use of public areas through ordinances requiring permits or licenses. Many of these ordinances were vaguely written and failed to specify criteria for obtaining a permit.

In 1941, 68 Jehovah's Witnesses were convicted in a New Hampshire municipal court for violating a state statute which prohibited parades and processions on public streets without a license. The facts were undisputed that the Witnesses had engaged in an "information march" on the sidewalks in the city's business district while carrying placards and handing out leaflets to passersby. During the march, groups of 15 to 20 people marched in single file down sidewalks in the district, interfering with normal foot travel. Upon appeal to a New Hampshire Superior Court, a trial *de novo* was held, in which the appellate court heard the case as if the lower court trial never occurred. In the trial *de novo,* a jury again found the Witnesses guilty. Five of the Witnesses appealed to the New Hampshire Supreme Court.

In the state supreme court, appellants claimed that the statute was invalid under the Fourteenth Amendment of the U.S. Constitution because it deprived them of their First Amendment rights of freedom of worship, freedom of speech and press, and freedom of assembly, vested unreasonable and unlimited arbitrary and discriminatory powers in the licensing authority, and was vague and indefinite. The state supreme court overruled these contentions and affirmed that the appellants were in fact taking part in a parade or procession on the public streets, despite their claim that they were disseminating religious literature as a form of worship. According to the state Supreme Court, "It was a march in formation, and its advertising and informatory purpose did not make it otherwise . . . It is immaterial that its tactics were few and simple. It is enough that it proceeded in ordered and close file as a collective body of persons on the city streets." The state Supreme Court also concluded that because the statute prohibited only use of the streets by organized formations of persons, and not distribution of information, speech, or use of the streets by unorganized groups of people, any interference with liberty of speech and writing was slight.

As to the claim that the licensing authority's power was unreasonable and unlimited, the state Supreme Court replied that the statute mandated that the authority's discretion be exercised with "uniformity of method of treatment upon the facts of each application, free from improper or inappropriate considerations and from unfair discrimination, with reference to the convenience of public use of the highways." The state Supreme Court construed the statute to include this mandate, even though the language itself arguably set no specific limits. The state Supreme Court affirmed the convictions, and appellants took their case to the U.S. Supreme Court.

Parade Permit Constitutional

In a unanimous decision, the U.S. Supreme Court held that the statute as construed by the state Supreme Court did not infringe on any constitutional right of the appellants. First, the U.S. Supreme Court stated that the sole issue to be decided was the question of the statute's validity as applied to the appellants' conduct in taking part in a parade or procession on the public streets without a permit. The Court would not address issues of the statute's validity as applied to distribution of literature, carrying of placards, holding public meetings, or expressing religious beliefs. The Court also concluded that there was no ground for challenging the state court's ruling that the appellants had in fact engaged in a parade or procession.

Turning to the sole issue before it, the Court began by stating that a municipality's authority "to impose regulations in order to assure the safety and convenience of the people in the use of public highways has never been regarded as inconsistent with civil liberties but rather as one of the means of safeguarding the good order upon which they ultimately depend." The Court said further, ". . . Where a restriction of the use of highways in that relation is designed to promote the public convenience in the interest of all, it cannot be disregarded by the attempted exercise of some civil right which in other circumstances would be entitled to protection." The Court then concluded by restating the question to be decided,

> [since] regulation of the use of the streets for parades and processions is a traditional exercise of control by local government, the question in a particular case is whether that control is exerted so as not to deny or unwarrantedly abridge the right of assembly and the opportunities for the communication of thought and the discussion of public questions immemorially associated with resort to public places.

Looking to the opinion of the New Hampshire Supreme Court and relying on that court's limiting construction of the state statute, the U.S. Supreme Court found it impossible to say that the limited authority conferred by the licensing provisions of the statute in question, as thus construed by the state court, contravened any constitutional right. The Court concluded that, since a municipality undoubtedly has authority to control the use of its public streets for parades or processions, it cannot be denied authority to give consideration, without unfair discrimination, to time, place and manner in relation to the other proper uses of the streets.

As to fact that under the statute the license fee ranged from $300 to a nominal amount, the Supreme Court rejected the appellants' contention that a flat fee should be charged. The Court perceived no constitutional ground for denying to local governments flexibility in the adjustment of fees based upon the stated purpose of the parade or procession. In the Court's opinion, this flexibility would tend to conserve rather than impair the liberty sought.

The Court also concluded that there was no evidence in this case that the statute had been administered otherwise than in the fair and non-discriminatory manner that the state court had construed it to require. The Court distinguished previous decisions of the U.S. Supreme Court invalidating municipal ordinances regulating expressive activities. Those previous rulings did not apply because in each case the invalidated ordinance included either an element of censorship or prohibition of the dissemination of information that interfered with First Amendment activity. In this case, the only issue was the right to take part in a parade without a permit.

Impact

Prior to the decision in *Cox,* the U.S. Supreme Court had struck down, under the First and Fourteenth Amendments, numerous ordinances imposing permit requirements on expressive activity in public places, such as streets and parks, because the ordinances gave government officials uncontrolled discretion whether to issue the permits. After *Cox,* local governments were allowed to regulate competing uses of public forums by using a permit scheme to impose reasonable time, place, and manner restrictions on those wishing to hold a march, parade, or rally. In addition, *Cox* allowed local governments to give a different degree of protection under the First and Fourteenth Amendments to those who communicated ideas by patrolling, marching, and picketing on streets and highways and those who communicated ideas by pure speech. Permit systems were deemed constitutionally valid so long as the discretion of the issuing official was limited to questions of times, places, and manners, and was not based on the content of the message. The reasonable time, place and manner restriction of *Cox* was subsequently applied to governments' attempts to regulate a wide range of religious, social, economic, and political activity.

Related Cases

Davis v. Massachusetts, 167 U.S. 43 (1897).
Hague v. Committiee for Industrial Organization, 307 U.S. 496 (1939).
Poulos v. New Hampshire, 345 U.S. 395 (1953).
Cox v. Louisiana, 379 U.S. 536 (1965).
Walker v. City of Birmingham, 388 U.S. 307 (1967).
Lehman v. City of Shaker Heights, 418 U.S. 298 (1974).

Heffron v. Int'l Soc. for Krishna Consc., 452 U.S. 640 (1981).
Forsyth County v. The Nationalist Movement, 505 U.S. 123 (1992).

Bibliography and Further Reading

McCoy, Ralph E. *Freedom of the Press, An Annotated Bibliography.* Electronic Ed. CNI / AAUP Project, Library Affairs, SIUC. January 10, 1995.

Owen, Ralph D., "Jehovah's Witnesses and Their Four Freedoms." *University of Detroit Law Journal,* 14:111-34, March 1951.

AMERICAN COMMUNICATIONS ASSOCIATION V. DOUDS

Legal Citation: 339 U.S. 382 (1950)

Petitioner
American Communications Association, C.I.O.

Respondent
Charles T. Douds, Regional Director of the National Labor Relations Board

Petitioner's Claim
That the requirement of the 1947 Taft-Hartley Labor Management Relations Act that union officials affirm in writing that they are not members of the Communist Party violates their First Amendment Rights.

Chief Lawyer for Petitioner
Victor Rabinowitz

Chief Lawyer for Respondent
Philip B. Perlman, U.S. Solicitor General

Justices for the Court
Harold Burton, Felix Frankfurter, Robert H. Jackson, Stanley Forman Reed, Fred Moore Vinson (writing for the Court)

Justices Dissenting
Hugo Lafayette Black (William O. Douglas, Tom C. Clark, and Sherman Minton did not participate)

Place
Washington, D.C.

Date of Decision
8 May 1950

Decision
Declaring that the threat of political strikes outweighed the First Amendment rights of labor leaders, the Court upheld the provision at issue.

Significance
Douds, which has never been overturned but is of doubtful value as legal precedent, reflected the Cold War era, when paranoia about Communist infiltration was uppermost in the public consciousness.

The Taft-Hartley Labor-Management Relations Act, which Congress passed in 1947, was intended to reduce the power labor unions gained under President Franklin Roosevelt's New Deal programs of the 1930s. Prior to 1937, when Roosevelt threatened to "pack" the Court—increasing the number of justices on the Court so that it would reflect his own views, the justices had consistently endorsed a *laissez-faire* approach to economic issues that favored employers over workers. After 1937, however, the Court switched course, supporting New Deal innovations that provided workers and their unions with more and more statutory rights.

With the Taft-Hartley Act, Congress proposed to shift the balance of power away from unions, while at the same time curbing what many legislators regarded as the increasing influence of the Communist Party on union leadership. The act contained a number of proscriptions, including restrictions on the right of members to select their own representatives, and the requirement that union leaders swear they were not members of the Communist Party. If these requirements were not met, the noncomplying unions ran the risk of losing National Labor Relations Board (NLRB) protections against unfair labor practices. Some labor unions regarded such provisions to be violations of their members' First Amendment rights of political freedom and declined to observe them. When the NLRB threatened to hold a representative election in a bargaining unit that was already represented by the American Communications Association of the Congress of Industrial Organizations (CIO), the CIO went to court to obtain an injunction to prevent the election from occurring. After the Federal District Court of the Southern District of New York dismissed its suit, the CIO applied to the U.S. Supreme Court for review of this decision.

Although the Supreme Court was ostensibly unaffected by the political passions of the day, *Douds* is evidence that the Court was influenced by the Cold War. The perceived threat to national security posed by alleged Communist infiltration of labor unions prompted the Court to disregard the First Amendment's guarantees of the fundamental political freedoms, the rights of free speech, and free association.

The Taft-Hartley Labor-Management Relations Act

Usually referred to simply as the Taft-Hartley Act, the full name for the omnibus 1947 law was the "Taft-Hartley Labor-Management Relations Act." Its sponsors were Robert A. Taft, a senator from Ohio, and Fred A. Hartley, a representative from New Jersey.

The Taft-Hartley Act supplemented and amended the Wagner-Connery National Labor Relations Act of 1935, commonly called either the Wagner Act or the NLRA, the implementation of which was overseen by the National Labor Relations Board (NLRB). In the 1930s, the power of labor unions was on the rise, and sympathy with business was at a low point; but by 1947, business was once again on the offensive in its relations with unions—and the nation as a whole was gripped by fear of Communism, which in some minds was closely tied with unionism.

Among its numerous provisions was a ban on closed shops—that is, work environments in which union control was so strong that no non-union workers were allowed—and the administration of an oath whereby union leaders would certify that none among their ranks belonged to the Communist party.

Source(s): Bacon, Donald C., et al., eds. *The Encyclopedia of the United States Congress.* New York: Simon & Schuster, 1995.

The Court got around the First Amendment by reasoning that the Taft-Hartley provision was intended to protect society against harmful acts—politically motivated strikes—rather than harmful ideas. Writing for the Court, Chief Justice Vinson argued:

> Government's interest here is not in preventing the dissemination of Communist doctrine or the holding of particular beliefs because it is feared that unlawful action will result therefrom if free speech is practiced. Its interest is in protecting the free flow of commerce from what Congress considers to be substantial evils of conduct that are not the products of speech at all. Section 9(h) [of the Taft-Hartley Act], in other words, does not interfere with speech because Congress fears the consequences of speech; it regulates harmful conduct which Congress has determined is carried on by persons who may be identified by their political affiliations and beliefs.

If nothing else, *Douds* demonstrates the adaptability of the Constitution's Commerce Clause as a rationale for addressing seemingly unrelated issues. On its face, political affiliation would appear to have no direct bearing on interstate commerce. Retrospectively, many commentators view the Court's argument as disingen-

uous. But the highly publicized Communist witch hunt that was then being conducted by Senator Joseph McCarthy had a powerful impact—apparently affecting even the Supreme Court. As McCarthy's hold on the public consciousness relaxed, however, the need for loyalty pledges dissipated. Although *Douds* itself was not overruled, the statute that took the place of section 9(h) of Taft-Hartley was specifically struck down in *United States v. Brown* (1965).

Related Cases
United States v. Brown, 381 U.S. 437 (1965).
Levine v. Supreme Court of Wisconsin, 679 F.Supp. 1478 (1988)

Bibliography and Further Reading
Atleson, James B. *Values and Assumptions in American Labor Law*. Amherst: University of Massachusetts Press, 1983.

Forbath, William E. *Law and the Shaping of the American Labor Movement*. Cambridge, MA: Harvard University Press, 1991.

Tomlins, Christopher L. *The State and the Unions: Labor Relations, Law, and the Organized Labor Movement in America, 1880-1960*. New York: Cambridge University Press, 1985.

ADLER ET AL. V. BOARD OF EDUCATION OF THE CITY OF NEW YORK

Legal Citation: 342 U.S. 485 (1952)

Appellants
Two parents of school children, and four teachers

Appellees
New York City Board of Education

Appellants' Claim
The Supreme Court should invalidate the Feinberg Law, which declared it illegal for school teachers to "advocate, advise, teach, or embrace" the overthrow of the government by force and violence.

Chief Lawyer for Appellants
Osmond K. Fraenkel

Chief Lawyer for Appellees
Michael A Castaldi

Justices for the Court
Harold Burton, Tom C. Clark, Robert H. Jackson, Sherman Minton (writing for the Court), Stanley Forman Reed, Fred Moore Vinson

Justices Dissenting
Hugo Lafayette Black, William O. Douglas, Felix Frankfurter

Place
Washington, D.C.

Date of Decision
3 March 1952

Decision
The Court affirmed lower court rulings that the Feinberg Law was constitutional.

Significance
The decision upheld New York's right not to hire teachers belonging to subversive organizations. In fact, no one ever was denied a job or fired on these grounds. Nevertheless, a later court found the same New York law in violation of the First Amendment (*Keyishian v. Board of Regents,* 1967).

In the early 1950s, during the Cold War with the Soviet Union, the Supreme Court decided a number of cases concerning the constitutional rights of Communists and others seeking to overthrow the government by force and violence. *Adler* was the first case to consider programs that monitored or screened the loyalty of public school teachers.

For a number of years, New York's Civil Service Law had barred public employment to anyone "advocating the overthrow of the Government by force, violence, or any unlawful means." Another section of the law disqualified any member of a "society or group" that taught or advocated such action. In 1949, the Feinberg Law authorized the state board of regents to implement the rules by drawing up a list of subversive organizations. Feinberg required public hearings, subject to judicial review, both to list an organization and also to deny employment to an individual.

When the case was brought, no one had been fired or threatened with discharge under the Feinberg Law. A group of taxpayers, parents, and teachers had sued, asking that the law be declared unconstitutional before it was implemented (a so-called "declaratory judgement"). They argued that the Feinberg Law would intimidate public school employees. Hence it would limit their exercise of the First Amendment right to free speech. (The Court in earlier cases had incorporated the First Amendment into the Fourteenth Amendment, which forbids states from depriving anyone of "liberty" without "due process.") When New York courts had ruled against the Adler group, it appealed to the Supreme Court.

By a vote of 6-3, the Court affirmed the state court rulings. It thus upheld both the standards and the procedures imposed by the Feinberg Act. Justices Black and Douglas dissented on the case's merits. Justice Frankfurter dissented on a procedural matter.

Justice Minton wrote for the majority. Minton referred back to *Gitlow v. New York* (1925) in upholding disqualification of persons advocating violent overthrow. He cited *Garner v. Board of the Public Works of the City of Los Angeles* (1951) in upholding ineligibility because of membership in a subversive organization.

The Feinberg Law

New York state's Feinberg Law, passed in 1949, was a product of post-World War II fears concerning the spread of Communism and "subversion." It was designed to aid in the enforcement of two earlier laws, one passed in 1917—during an earlier "Red Scare," brought on by the victory of Communism in Russia and the spread of Communist sympathies among workers in the United States—and the other in 1939.

The 1917 statute designated "the utterance of any treasonable or seditious word or words or the doing of any treasonable or seditious act" an offense for which an employee of the state's public school systems could be dismissed. As for the 1939 law, it made any person who called for the overthrow of the government by force, or who published material advocating such overthrow, or who organized or joined any society advocating such overthrow, ineligible for employment in the state's civil service or educational systems.

Under the Feinberg Law, the State Board of Regents was charged with implementing rules to govern the dismissal and ineligibility requirements of the two ear-

lier statutes. Likewise the Board was required to identify all subversive organizations operating in the state, and to establish rules whereby membership in any such organization was grounds for disqualification or dismissal from any job in the state's public school system.

Though it applied to the state as a whole, the Feinberg Law was in fact directed toward that part of the state most likely to draw radicals: New York City. During the next several years, hundreds of teachers in the city resigned; then in 1956, the state's education commissioner issued a new order which made it possible for persons who had formerly—but not currently—been members of subversive organizations to retain their jobs. With its decision in *Keyishian v. Board of Regents of the University of the State of New York* (1967), the U.S. Supreme Court invalidated the 1917 and 1939 laws, and in effect overruled *Adler*.

Source(s): Folts, James D. *History of the University of the State of New York and the State Education Department, 1784-1996* (1996). http://unix2.nysed.gov.

These cases had affirmed the legitimacy of investigating past conduct and past loyalty as qualifications for public employment.

Good conduct and loyalty, Minton continued, are especially desirable in public school teachers:

> A teacher works in a sensitive area in a school room. There he shapes the attitude of young minds towards the society in which they live. In this, the state has a vital concern.

> New York has a legitimate police power "to protect the schools from pollution."

Just because someone is disqualified from employment as a teacher, "he is not thereby denied the right of free speech and assembly." No one has a right to public employment. A person remained free under this law to say and do whatever he wants—so long as he did not seek to be a public school teacher.

Minton also found nothing wrong with the rule that a person was disqualified simply for belonging to a listed organization. The New York courts had held that a person would be ineligible only if he knew about the organization's purpose. It is reasonable to assume, Minton wrote, that "the member by his membership supports the thing the organization stands for, namely, the overthrow of government by unlawful means."

Justice Frankfurter dissented on procedural grounds. The New York system would be governed by administrative regulations that had not yet been written. In effect, the Court was being asked to "adjudicate claims against its constitutionality before the scheme has been put into operation."

Justices Black and Douglas dissented on First Amendment grounds. Justice Black declared that, under the First Amendment,

> public officials cannot be constitutionally vested with powers to select the ideas people can think about, censor the public views they can express, or choose the persons or groups people can associate with. Public officials with such power are not public servants; they are public masters.

Justice Douglas asserted the Feinberg Law was based on guilt by association. A teacher could be disqualified for employment because of membership in an organization found to be "subversive." But this determination was made at a proceeding "to which the teacher is not a party" and at which she might not even be present. Douglas also dissented on the broader grounds that the First Amendment requires absolute freedom of speech.

> The Constitution guarantees freedom of thought and expression to everyone in our

society. All are entitled to it; and none needs it more than the teacher.

Related Cases

Gitlow v. New York, 268 U.S. 652 (1925).
United Public Workers v. Mitchell, 330 U.S. 75 (1947).
Garner v. Board of Public Works of the City of Los Angeles, 341 U.S. 716 (1951).
Keyishian v. Board of Regents of the University of the State of New York, 385 U.S. 589 (1967).

Bibliography and Further Reading

Emerson, Thomas I. *The System of Freedom of Expression.* New York: Random House, 1970.

Kalvern, Harry. *A Worthy Tradition: Freedom of Speech in America.* New York: Harper & Row, 1988.

Wiecek, William. *Liberty under Law: The Supreme Court in American Life.* Baltimore: Johns Hopkins University Press, 1988.

PENNSYLVANIA V. NELSON

Legal Citation: 350 U.S. 497 (1956)

Petitioner
Commonwealth of Pennsylvania

Respondent
Steve Nelson

Petitioner's Claim
That the Pennsylvania Supreme Court erred in overturning the conviction of Nelson, a Communist Party leader, under the state's antisedition law.

Chief Lawyer for Petitioner
Frank F. Truscott, Special Deputy Attorney General of Pennsylvania

Chief Lawyer for Respondent
Herbert S. Thatcher

Justices for the Court
Hugo Lafayette Black, Tom C. Clark, William O. Douglas, Felix Frankfurter, John Marshall Harlan II, Earl Warren (writing for the Court)

Justices Dissenting
Harold Burton, Sherman Minton, Stanley Forman Reed

Place
Washington, D.C.

Date of Decision
2 April 1956

Decision
The U.S. Supreme Court found the Pennsylvania antisedition law unconstitutional and upheld the reversal of Nelson's conviction.

Significance
The outcome in *Nelson* epitomized, for some, the ultraliberalism of the Court headed by Chief Justice Warren. Continual efforts of conservatives to pass legislation to overturn the decision were blocked.

Steve Nelson was an acknowledged member of the Communist Party. He was convicted in state court of violating the Pennsylvania Sedition Act, which outlawed subversive organizations. He was sentenced to 20 years in jail and a fine of $10,000, plus court costs. The superior court affirmed this decision, but on appeal, it was overturned by the Pennsylvania Supreme Court. This outcome was based on a determination that there was no evidence presented at trial that triggered the state antisedition law. Neither Nelson nor the Communist Party advocated overthrow of the government of Pennsylvania. Instead, said the state supreme court, Nelson had only threatened the federal government, thus violating the federal antisedition statute known as the Smith Act of 1940.

Pennsylvania petitioned the U.S. Supreme Court for review of this decision, which was based on the notion of pre-emption, the rule stating that when a federal law occupies a given field, it prevails over conflicting state legislation. The Supreme Court agreed. Writing for the six-member majority, Chief Justice Warren stated that:

> Since we find that Congress has occupied the field to the exclusion of parallel state legislation, that the dominant interest of the Federal Government precludes state intervention, and that administration of state Acts would conflict with the operation of the federal plan, we are convinced that the decision of the Supreme Court of Pennsylvania is unassailable.

Cold Warriors Outraged by Court's Decision in Favor of Communist Party Leader

In the mid-1950s, the liberal Court led by Chief Justice Warren came head-to-head with the conservative paranoia that helped fuel the communist witch hunt led by Senator Joseph McCarthy. Those who believed that there was an international communist conspiracy to overthrown the U.S. government, and who agreed with McCarthy that communists had infiltrated all sectors of American society, were often the same people who bitterly denounced the Warren Court. Feelings ran so high that the chief justice's public appearances were sometimes boycotted, and movements to impeach him cropped up from time to time. For the most ardent anti-communist warriors in the Cold War, Warren's opinion in *Nelson*—which seemed the equivalent of letting an admitted communist off on a technicality—was the last straw.

A powerful movement sprang up in Congress to pass legislation that would overturn *Nelson* and prevent anything like it from happening again. However, cooler heads eventually prevailed. The attempt to overturn *Nelson* was tied to a broader legislative proposal to block all implied federal pre-emption of state laws. Congress soon realized that the "technicality" which had freed Steven Nelson was in fact an important principle: the effectiveness of federal legislation is undermined when comparable but conflicting state statutes are permitted to dominate. Even some of those in Congress who were advocates of states' rights (the principle that individual state sovereignty should usually prevail over a strong federal government) found the prospect of doing away with federal preemption undesirable.

Although *Nelson* spelled the end for the Pennsylvania antisedition statute, other state antisedition laws remained on the books. Later, they were revived by various state legislators to justify arrests of demonstrators during the civil rights movement of the 1950s and 1960s and the anti-Vietnam War protests of the 1960s and 1970s.

Related Cases

Gitlow v. New York, 268 U.S. 652 (1925).
Whitney v. California, 274 U.S. 357 (1927).
Dennis v. United States, 341 U.S. 494 (1951).

Bibliography and Further Reading

Belknap, Michal R. *Cold War Political Justice: The Smith Act, the Communist Party, and American Civil Liberties.* Westport, CT: Greenwood Press, 1977.

Kutler, Stanley I. *The American Inquisition: Justice and Injustice in the Cold War.* New York, NY: Hill and Wang, 1982.

Zimmerman, Joseph F. *Federal Preemption: The Silent Revolution.* Ames: Iowa State University Press, 1991.

SLOCHOWER V. BOARD OF EDUCATION OF NEW YORK

Legal Citation: 350 U.S. 551 (1956)

Appellant
Harry Slochower

Appellee
Board of Higher Education of the city of New York

Appellant's Claim
That a provision of the city's charter prohibiting the use by employees of the Fifth Amendment privilege against self-incrimination violated his due process rights.

Chief Lawyer for Appellant
Ephraim S. London

Chief Lawyer for Appellee
Daniel T. Scannell

Justices for the Court
Tom C. Clark (writing for the Court), John Marshall Harlan II, Stanley Forman Reed, Sherman Minton, Earl Warren

Justices Dissenting
Hugo Lafayette Black, Harold Burton, William O. Douglas, Felix Frankfurter

Place
Washington, D.C.

Date of Decision
9 April 1956

Decision
The Supreme Court found the provision unconstitutional.

Significance
The closeness of the vote shows how the justices have been influenced by politics and current affairs. The provision in question clearly was unconstitutional, making employment conditional upon surrender of a constitutional right.

Harry Slochower was a tenured professor at Brooklyn College, an institution administered by New York City, when he was called before the Senate Subcommittee on Internal Security. It was 1952, the height of the Red Scare and anti-communist paranoia that later settled into a Cold War. Slochower told the committee that he was not himself a communist. The committee was interested in finding out if he knew others who were. Slochower was willing to answer questions about those he had associated with since 1941. About the period prior to 1941, however, he declined to testify, invoking his Fifth Amendment privilege against self-incrimination.

Shortly after his appearance before the committee, Slochower received word that he had been dismissed from his job "pursuant to the provisions of Section 903 of the New York City charter." Slochower's tenure meant that he could only be fired for cause, and only after a hearing and an appeal. Section 903 of the city charter, however, made refusal to testify about matters related to official conduct equivalent to a resignation. In effect, Slochower had been forced to resign for asserting his constitutional rights.

Slochower pursued his case through the New York courts, to no avail. He then appealed to the U.S. Supreme Court.

Court Upholds Privilege Against Self-Incrimination and Reinstates Professor

The Court found the charter provision used to dismiss Slochower unconstitutional and the manner in which he had been let go an arbitrary violation of due process. Writing for the Court, Justice Clark observed that the charter provision had converted the privilege against self-incrimination into a presumption of guilt:

> [W]e must condemn the practice of imputing a sinister meaning to the exercise of a person's right under the Fifth Amendment. The right of an accused person to refuse to testify . . . was so important to our forefathers that they raised it to the dignity of a constitutional enactment . . . The privilege against self-incrimination would be reduced to a hollow mockery if its exercise could be taken as equivalent either to

The Fifth Amendment

In the popular culture, particularly on television, the Fifth Amendment is best-known for its association with persons on trial "taking the Fifth," or refusing to testify against themselves. This right against self-incrimination—"No person . . . shall be compelled in any criminal case to be a witness against himself"—is just one of the many rights contained in the amendment, which was added to the Constitution along with nine others in the Bill of Rights in 1791.

Among the other significant rights contained in the Fifth Amendment are the prohibition of "double jeop-

ardy," meaning that no one can be tried twice for the same crime. The Fifth Amendment also provides that a civilian accused of a "capital or otherwise infamous crime" has a right to indictment by a grand jury; and it protects citizens from seizure of property "for public use, without just compensation."

Source(s): Hurwitz, Howard L. *An Encyclopedic Dictionary of American History.* New York: Washington Square Press, 1974.

a confession of guilt or a conclusive presumption of perjury.

It seemed a simple enough case. And yet Slochower won his victory by the narrowest of margins: one vote. The dissenters focused on Slochower's duty of loyalty to his employer and on the employer's right to protect itself. This right of self-protection seemed to loom especially large in the dissenters' minds because the

employer was a local government institution and Slochower was a public employee responsible for molding young minds. Clearly there was an underlying assumption of guilt in these justices' minds, just as there had been in those of the members of the board who fired Harry Slochower.

By the time Slochower was called before the Senate committee, the board had known for at least a dozen years about his pre-1941 Communist Party affiliation. In retrospect, his fate appears to be much like that of suspected "Fifth Amendment Communists" called before the House Un-American Activities Committee (HUAC) who lost their positions after they failed to answer questions about themselves or to "name names" of others with possible communist connections. HUAC and the communist witch hunt reached their zenith just as Slochower was called to testify. In 1954, the witch hunt lost much of its momentum when Senator Joseph McCarthy, who had made a name for himself by employing HUAC methods, was publicly discredited. Plainly, however, feelings about communist infiltration of American society still ran high for some time afterward—even among members of the nation's highest judicial tribunal.

Related Cases
Adler v. Board of Education, 342 U.S. 485 (1952).
Ullmann v. United States, 350 U.S. 422 (1956).

Bibliography and Further Reading
Diamond, Sigmund. *Compromised Campus: The Collaboration of Universities with the Intelligence Community, 1945-1955.* New York, NY: Oxford University Press, 1992.

Ladd, Everett Carll, and Seymour Martin Lipsett. *The Divided Academy: Professors and Politics.* NY: McGraw-Hill, 1975.

Schrecker, Ellen. *No Ivory Tower: McCarthyism and the Universities New York.* New York, NY: Oxford University Press, 1986.

Ephraim S. London. © AP/Wide World Photos.

KENT V. DULLES

Legal Citation: 357 U.S. 116 (1958)

Appellant
Rockwell Kent

Appellee
John Foster Dulles, U.S. Secretary of State

Appellant's Claim
That the State Department's denial of a passport to an acknowledged communist violates the right to travel and the First Amendment right of free association.

Chief Lawyer for Appellant
Leonard B. Boudin

Chief Lawyer for Appellee
J. Lee Rankin, U.S. Solicitor General

Justices for the Court
Hugo Lafayette Black, William J. Brennan, Jr., William O. Douglas (writing for the Court), Felix Frankfurter, Earl Warren

Justices Dissenting
Harold Burton, Tom C. Clark, John Marshall Harlan II, Charles Evans Whittaker

Place
Washington, D.C.

Date of Decision
16 June 1958

Decision
The Supreme Court ruled that it was unconstitutional for the State Department to withhold a passport based on the beliefs or associations of an applicant.

Significance
Kent v. Dulles arose from the general fear of communism that characterized the 1950s, the period known as the McCarthy era. Its long-lasting impact was the recognition of a constitutionally-protected right to travel abroad.

During the 1950s, the nation was engaged in a Cold War with the U.S.S.R. and its communist allies. American fears about a world-wide communist plot were fueled by Senator Joseph McCarthy of Wisconsin, who conducted a witch hunt for communists that touched most aspects of society and stopped only when it challenged the loyalty of high ranking members of the military.

Amidst this climate of fear, Rockwell Kent, well-known painter and acknowledged member of the Communist Party, applied for a passport in order to travel to England and to attend a conference of the World Council of Peace in Helsinki, Finland. The passport office denied his application on grounds that he was a communist. The only way he could be issued a passport was to file an affidavit indicating that he was not a communist. Kent declined to do so, instead applying to the U.S. District Court for the District of Columbia for a declaration that the passport office rules were unconstitutional. When the district court decided instead that he had no case, Kent applied to the U.S. Supreme Court for review of this decision.

Supreme Court Recognizes a New Fundamental Right: Foreign Travel

Four of the members of the Court joined in the opinion of Justice Douglas that although Congress had granted the secretary of state the power to issue passports, the statute granting this authority did not also confer the prerogative to withhold passports because of the beliefs or associations of passport applicants. This seemed a highly legalistic rationale for overruling the secretary of state, but the vote was a close one, and Justice Frankfurter agreed to sign on to Douglas's opinion only if it were based on a narrow statutory reading.

Douglas's actual reasons for overruling the passport office grew out of the First Amendment. He agreed with Kent that the passport office's policy of not issuing passports to communists violated the First Amendment's guarantee of freedom of association. More importantly, Douglas saw in the Fifth Amendment's guarantee that "No person shall be . . . deprived of life, liberty, or property, without due process of law," a right to travel:

The Right to Travel

The right to travel does not appear in any explicit provision of the Constitution. Nonetheless, this right is clearly implied, simply by virtue of the freedoms suggested elsewhere in the document.

Nor is it a right to be taken lightly, as is clear when one considers the situation under the Communist system that dominated Russia for most of the twentieth century. International travel, unless one were a member of the Communist Party or an otherwise privileged individual such as an athlete or author, was usually out of the question; but even travel within the nation—what Americans would call interstate travel—was rigidly controlled by means of internal passports. If one lived in Kiev and wanted to visit a relative in Leningrad (now St. Petersburg), one could not simply jump in an air-

plane: forms had to be filled out, and the machinery of bureaucracy had to undergo its slow, grinding process.

It is ironic, then, that the most significant challenges to freedom of international travel have occurred in reaction to Communism in such cases as *Aptheker v. Secretary of State* (1964), in which the Supreme Court invalidated the State Department's denial of passports for members of the Communist party; and *Zemel v. Rusk* (1966), when the Court upheld the denial of a passport to travel to Cuba.

Source(s): Levy, Leonard W., ed. *Encyclopedia of the American Constitution*. New York: Macmillan, 1986.

The right to travel is a part of the "liberty" of which the citizen cannot be deprived without due process of law under the Fifth Amendment . . . Freedom of movement across frontiers in either direction, and inside frontiers as well, was a part of our heritage. Travel abroad, like travel within the country, may be necessary for a livelihood. It may be as close to the heart of the individual as the choice of what he eats, or wears, or reads. Freedom of movement is basic in our scheme of values.

The immediate impact of *Kent v. Dulles* was that questions about Communist Party affiliations were removed from the passport application. Kent was issued a passport. Cold War era laws ordering members of communist organizations to register with the Subversive Activities Control Board were overruled in *Aptheker v. Secretary of State* (1964). Fear of what American communists might do if they were permitted to travel abroad abated along with fear of the Red Menace.

The right to foreign travel remained on the books, however. It seemed to at least four members of the *Kent* Court to be a natural extension of the right to travel within the United States—even of the fundamental concept of liberty itself. While the Court has upheld the constitutionality of some passport restrictions—for example, the ban on tourist travel to Cuba at issue in *Regan v. Wald* (1984)—it has not overruled *Kent v. Dulles*.

Rockwell Kent, an American artist, was denied a passport for his Communist affiliations. © Archive Photos.

Related Cases

Browder v. United States, 312 U.S. 335 (1941).

Edwards v. California, 314 U.S. 160 (1941).

Aptheker v. Secretary of State, 378 U.S. 500 (1964).

Regan v. Wald, 468 U.S. 222 (1984).

Bibliography and Further Reading

Gillon, Steven M., and Diane B. Kunz. *America During the Cold War*. Fort Worth, TX: Harcourt Brace Jovanovich, 1993.

Houseman, Gerald L. *The Right of Mobility*. Port Washington, NY: Kennikat Press, 1979.

Hull, Elizabeth. *Taking Liberties: National Barriers to the Free Flow of Ideas*. New York, NY: Praeger, 1990.

NATIONAL ASSOCIATION FOR THE ADVANCEMENT OF COLORED PEOPLE V. ALABAMA

Legal Citation: 357 U.S. 449 (1958)

Petitioner
National Association for the Advancement of Colored People

Respondent
State of Alabama

Petitioner's Claim
That the state of Alabama could not force the association to produce a list including the names and addresses of its members and agents, and that a temporary restraining order barring the association from operation in Alabama was unconstitutional.

Chief Lawyer for Petitioner
Robert L. Carter

Chief Lawyer for Respondent
Edmond L. Rinehart, Assistant Attorney General of Alabama

Justices for the Court
Hugo Lafayette Black, William J. Brennan, Jr., Harold Burton, Tom C. Clark, William O. Douglas, John Marshall Harlan II (writing for the Court), Potter Stewart, Earl Warren, Charles Evans Whittaker

Justices Dissenting
None

Place
Washington, D.C.

Date of Decision
30 June 1958

Decision
That the state's demand for a complete membership list was unconstitutional given Fourteenth Amendment protection of the right of free association and the right of pursuit of one's lawful interests; the Court did allow the restraining order barring the association from operating in Alabama to stand by refusing to consider the association's challenge.

Significance
By ensuring the privacy of members of associations pursuing legal ends, the Court protected supporters of the Civil Rights Movement who might have faced persecution had their names been known, and thereby aided the movement in attracting new members. The refusal to consider the association's challenge to the state restraining order effectively prevented the NAACP from operating in Alabama until 1964.

The 1950s were a period of great social change in the southern United States. In the aftermath of World War II, during which many African Americans rose to positions of responsibility in the military and industry, new challenges emerged to those southern social structures which included racial segregation. Organizations representing the interests of African Americans, such as the National Association for the Advancement of Colored People (NAACP), began wielding increased influence and receiving some assistance from federal authorities in areas including school desegregation. This newfound power brought a reaction from state and local authorities and from citizen groups willing to use threats and physical intimidation to protect the social status quo.

In December of 1955, Rosa Parks, an African American, refused to relinquish her seat to a white person on a Montgomery, Alabama bus in violation of city law. Parks was subsequently arrested and convicted, touching off a boycott by African Americans of the Montgomery public transportation system. As the boycott continued, tensions heightened and, in June 1956, Alabama attorney general John Patterson took action to curtail the NAACP's influence in the state, enjoining the NAACP to produce lists of its members and contributors. His actions were based on the grounds that the NAACP had failed to adhere to state requirements that organizations which were headquartered out-of-state had to file charters with the secretary of state, designate a place of business in the state, and name an agent to receive service of process. The NAACP quickly complied with these requirements, but refused to provide the membership and contributor lists. The Alabama State Circuit Court cited the NAACP for contempt for failure to provide the lists, and also issued an order restraining the association from operating in Alabama until it produced the lists required. Two appeals to the Alabama Supreme Court to review the contempt judgement by the NAACP were rejected, but the U.S. Supreme Court agreed on *certiorari* to hear the case.

Lawyers for the state of Alabama argued that the Supreme Court did not have jurisdiction in this case since the Alabama Supreme Court had denied *certiorari* on the (nonfederal) grounds that the NAACP was pursuing an incorrect appellate remedy under state law. NAACP attorneys countered that Alabama's order for the association to produce a list of its members and benefactors violated the Due Process Clause of the Fourteenth Amendment, guaranteeing individuals the right to form associations in support of their common and lawful beliefs. They further asserted that Alabama's temporary restraining order barring the NAACP from operations in the state was unconstitutional on Fourteenth Amendment Grounds.

Justice Harlan delivered the opinion of the Court. Alabama's contention that the Court lacked jurisdiction in the case was rejected, the Court believing that *certiorari* rather than appeal was the most proper way to review action in the case to date. The Court also held that the NAACP was not obliged to disclose its membership and donor lists, stating that:

> . . . advocacy of both public and private points of view, particularly controversial ones, is undeniably enhanced by group association . . . [it is] beyond debate that freedom to engage in association for the advancement of beliefs and ideas is an inseparable aspect of the "liberty" assured by the Due Process Clause of the Fourteenth Amendment, which embraces freedom of speech . . . [Furthermore], inviolability of privacy in group association may be in many circumstances indispensable to preservation of freedom of association, particularly where a group espouses dissident beliefs.

Finally, the Court ruled against the NAACP in the matter of the state of Alabama's restraining order against the association. The Court essentially agreed with the state of Alabama's argument regarding the disclosure of membership and donor lists, holding that since the NAACP had never received a hearing in a state court regarding the merits of the restraining order, the Supreme Court did not have jurisdiction over the matter.

Although the Court's refusal to remove the state restraining order greatly restricted NAACP activities in Alabama for more than a decade, its decision not to compel the association to disclose its membership and donor lists proved of great benefit to the Civil Rights Movement and to other causes of a socially or politically controversial nature. The ability of dissident groups to keep their membership a secret makes their individual members far less easy to target for intimidation or discrimination, which in turn allows such groups far greater scope for broad-based recruitment.

Related Cases

Pierce v. Society of Sisters, 268 U.S. 510 (1925).
Gitlow v. New York, 268 U.S. 652 (1925).
Near v. Minnesota, 283 U.S. 697 (1931).
Ashwander v. Tennessee Valley Authority, 297 U.S. 288 (1936).
DeJonge v. Oregon, 299 U.S. 353 (1937).
Palko v. Connecticut, 302 U.S. 319 (1937).
Cantwell v. Connecticut, 310 U.S. 296 (1940).
American Communications Association v. Douds, 339 U.S. 382 (1950).

Bibliography and Further Reading

Biskupic, Joan and Elder Witt. *Congressional Quarterly's Guide to the U.S. Supreme Court,* 3rd ed. Washington, DC: Congressional Quarterly, Inc., 1996.

Branch, Taylor. *Parting the Waters.* New York: Simon and Schuster, 1988.

Cushman, Robert F. *Leading Constitutional Decisions.* Englewood Cliffs, NJ: Prentice-Hall, Inc., 1982.

Greenberg, Jack. *Crusaders in the Courts.* New York: Basic Books, 1994.

Hall, Kermit L., ed. *The Oxford Companion to the Supreme Court of the United States.* New York: Oxford University Press, 1992.

SHELTON V. TUCKER

Legal Citation: 364 U.S. 479 (1960)

Appellants
B. T. Shelton, et al.

Appellees
Everett Tucker, et al.

Appellants' Claim
That the state of Arkansas violated the constitutional rights of personal, associational, and academic liberty by requiring teachers to disclose all their organizational affiliations as a condition for employment.

Chief Lawyers for Appellants
Robert L. Carter, Edwin E. Dunaway

Chief Lawyers for Appellees
Herschel H. Friday Jr, Louis L. Ramsay Jr., Robert V. Light

Justices for the Court
Hugo Lafayette Black, William J. Brennan, Jr., William O. Douglas, Potter Stewart (writing for the Court), Earl Warren

Justices Dissenting
Tom C. Clark, Felix Frankfurter, John Marshall Harlan II, Charles Evans Whittaker

Place
Washington, D.C.

Date of Decision
12 December 1960

Decision
Upheld appellants' claim.

Significance
For the second time in two years, the Court asserted an individual's implicit constitutional right to freedom of association, a right that came under attack in the South as a backlash to the Civil Rights Movement.

Since its beginnings in 1909, the National Association for the Advancement of Colored People (NAACP) has fought for equal rights for African Americans. Founded by both blacks and whites, the NAACP helped end segregation and lobbied for a federal anti-lynching law. In the 1950s, its major victory came with the historic Supreme Court decision in *Brown v. Board of Education* (1954), which outlawed so-called "separate but equal" schooling. The NAACP's legal successes and its prominence in the Civil Rights Movement made it a target for Southerners who opposed racial equality.

In 1958, the state of Alabama took the NAACP to court after the organization refused to turn over its membership list. Making the list public, the NAACP said, would endanger its members' jobs or physical safety. The Supreme Court, in *National Association for the Advancement of Colored People v. Alabama* (1958) unanimously agreed with the NAACP, ruling that its members had a constitutional right of association. This right was implied in the First Amendment's right to freedom of assembly, and was protected from state attack by the Fourteenth Amendment's Due Process Clause. This decision marked the first time the Court acknowledged this right.

The *NAACP* ruling, however, did not stop the attempts to single out members of that civil rights group. In 1958, Arkansas passed Article 10, a law affecting state teachers. The act said that every teacher who worked at a state-supported school or college had to list every group they had belonged or contributed money to during the previous five years. They would have to fill out a similar affidavit every year as a condition of their employment—Arkansas did not have tenure for its teachers, so a teacher's contract was reviewed every year. In the past, laws asking about organizational ties were designed to ferret out Communists or their sympathizers, but Act 10 was specifically designed to identify teachers affiliated with the NAACP.

Three Teachers Refuse to Comply

B. T. Shelton, an African American, had taught in Arkansas schools for 25 years. He was also a member of the NAACP. Before the 1959 school year, he was asked to comply with Act 10; he refused and was fired.

Two other Arkansas teachers, Max Carr and Ernest Gephardt, refused to fill out the affidavits required by Act 10, though they listed some of their memberships and agreed to answer any questions regarding their qualifications to teach. They, too, were fired. All three men contested their firings in court, saying their right to personal, associational, and academic freedom had been denied. The Arkansas courts, however, upheld Act 10 and the men appealed to the federal district court, which affirmed the state courts. The issue then went to the U.S. Supreme Court.

The U.S. Supreme Court did not address the civil rights implications of *Shelton* and the targeting of the NAACP. Instead, the Court focused on the general issue of asking all teachers for their membership affiliations, and whether it related to the state's right to hire quality teachers. In a 5-4 decision, the Court said Act 10 was too broad and therefore violated the petitioners' right of association.

Writing for the Court, Justice Stewart said ". . . there can be no question of the relevance of a State's inquiry into the fitness and competence of its teachers." But Act 10, he continued, went too far:

> . . . [T]o compel a teacher to disclose his every associational tie is to impair that teacher's right of free association, a right closely allied to freedom of speech and a right which, like freedom of speech, lies at the foundation of a free society. Such interference with personal freedom is conspicuously accented when the teacher serves at the absolute will of those to whom the disclosure must be made . . . the pressure upon a teacher to avoid any ties which might displease those who control his professional destiny would be constant and heavy . . . Many such relationships could have no possible bearing upon the teacher's occupational competence or fitness.

In his dissent, Justice Harlan said the right of free association is not absolute. Unlike *National Association for the Advancement of Colored People v. Alabama,* where the state did not have a legitimate interest in the membership information, in this instance Arkansas did: ". . . [I]nformation about a teacher's associations may be useful to school authorities in determining the moral, professional, and social qualifications of the teacher . . ." On its face, the statute was constitutional; if at a later date Arkansas used Act 10 in some discriminatory way, the Court may have reason to act.

Other NAACP Cases

A third case dealing with the NAACP and the freedom of association came three years after *Shelton.* In *National Association for the Advancement of Colored People v. Button* (1963), the Court struck down a Virginia law preventing the NAACP from providing legal support in cases it was not a party to or in which it had no financial interest. The same year, in *Gibson v. Florida Legislative Investigation Committee,* the Court overturned the contempt conviction of an NAACP official who refused to testify about members' past or current relationship with the Communist Party.

In the 1980s, freedom of association cases moved away from racial equality and turned toward sexual equality. In a series of cases, the Court ruled that some previously all-male clubs and organizations had to let women join. The Court said that in those cases, society's interest in ensuring equal treatment of women outweighed the freedom of "expressive association"— association of people who share common values and seek to pursue a particular goal. The rulings affected the U.S. Jaycees, the Rotary Club International, and a private New York club.

Related Cases

Brown v. Board of Education, 347 U.S. 483 (1954).

National Association for the Advancement of Colored People v. Alabama, 360 U.S. 240 (1958).

National Association for the Advancement of Colored People v. Button, 371 U.S. 415 (1963).

Gibson v. Florida Legislative Investigation Committee, 372 U.S. 539 (1963).

Bibliography and Further Reading

Biskupic, Joan, and Elder Witt. *Guide to the U.S. Supreme Court,* 3rd edition. Washington, DC: Congressional Quarterly, Inc., 1997.

Foner, Eric, and John Garraty eds. *The Reader's Companion to American History.* Boston: Houghton Mifflin, 1991.

Hall, Kermit L., ed. *The Oxford Companion to the Supreme Court of the United States.* New York: Oxford Press, 1992.

New York Times, 13 December 1960.

Witt, Elder, ed. *The Supreme Court A to Z. CQ's Encyclopedia of American Government.* Washington, DC: Congressional Quarterly, Inc., 1993.

COMMUNIST PARTY OF THE UNITED STATES V. SUBVERSIVE ACTIVITIES CONTROL BOARD

Legal Citation: 367 U.S. 1 (1961)

Petitioner
Communist Party of the United States of America

Respondent
Subversive Activities Control Board

Petitioner's Claim
That provisions of the 1950 Internal Security Act (the McCarran Act) requiring Communist organizations to register with the attorney general are unconstitutional either as bills of attainder, imposing punishment without benefit of trial, or as violations of the First Amendment.

Chief Lawyers for Petitioner
John J. Abt and Joseph Forer

Chief Lawyer for Respondent
J. Lee Rankin, U.S. Solicitor General

Justices for the Court
Tom C. Clark, Felix Frankfurter (writing for the Court), John Marshall Harlan II, Potter Stewart, Charles Evans Whittaker

Justices Dissenting
Hugo Lafayette Black, William J. Brennan, Jr., William O. Douglas, Earl Warren

Place
Washington, D.C.

Date of Decision
5 June 1961

Decision
The U.S. Supreme Court upheld the registration requirement.

Significance
Although the Court did not rule against the McCarran Act in this first test of its constitutionality, as more cases challenging various penalties associated with noncompliance with the act came before the Court, the Court struck them down one after another until the act was gutted.

In 1950, over a veto cast by President Harry Truman, Congress passed the Internal Security Act, popularly known as the McCarran Act. Passed at the height of the Cold War, when national paranoia about Communist infiltration and subversion was at fever pitch, the act was intended to root out the Communist Party in the United States. Convinced that secrecy was one of the party's greatest weapons, Congress required in the McCarran Act that all Communist organizations register with the attorney general. The Subversive Activities Control Board (SACB) was created to oversee the registration procedure, which also required that registered organizations disclose the names of their officers and the sources of their funds. The SACB promptly ordered the Communist Party of America to register, which it declined to do.

The party, arguing that the registration requirement was unconstitutional, fought the SACB for nearly 11 years, ultimately appealing the registration order to the U.S. District Court of the District of Columbia, where the appeal was rejected. The party finally turned to the Supreme Court.

The party's primary arguments were that the registration requirement was either unconstitutional as a bill of attainder or a violation of the First Amendment rights of freedom of speech and association. Article I of the Constitution outlaws bills of attainder at both the state and federal levels. This prohibition against government-imposed penalties without benefit of trial was of clear importance to the drafters of the nation's foundation document, who wanted there to be both a clear distinction between legislative and judicial functions in government and a government of laws, not men. The party's other argument against the registration requirement was that it violated guarantees established in the First Amendment, arguably the most fundamental guarantee embodied in the Bill of Rights.

Nonetheless, the Supreme Court upheld the registration requirement. The opinion of the Court, written by Justice Frankfurter, stated that since the only issue properly before the Court was the constitutionality of the registration requirement, which in itself included no provisions as to regulation or penalties, the SACB had behaved appropriately in ordering the Communist

Party to register. Indeed, the opinion went to considerable lengths to validate the SACB's mission:

> . . . Congress has found that there exists a world Communist movement, foreign-controlled, whose purpose it is by whatever means necessary to establish Communist totalitarian dictatorship in the countries throughout the world . . . Congress has found that in furthering this purpose, the foreign government controlling the world Communist movement establishes in various countries action organizations which, dominated from abroad, endeavor to bring about the overthrow of existing governments . . . And Congress has found . . . that a Communist network exists in the United States . . . The purpose of the Subversive Activities Control Act is said to be to prevent the worldwide Communist conspiracy from accomplishing its purpose in this country . . . It is not for the courts to re-examine the validity of these legislative findings and reject them.

In cases such as *Yates v. United States* (1957), which reversed the convictions of California Communist leaders under the anti-Communist Smith Act, the Court had already rejected such legislative findings. The passage quoted above gives some hint of why, in this case and several others decided around the same time, the Court retreated from its earlier opposition to the antisubversive legislation of the 1950s.

In the wake of decisions like *Yates,* conservative legislators grew alarmed and threatened to adopt legislation curtailing the Court's right to hear appeals in subversion cases. Before this threat could be realized, however, Justice Frankfurter, an advocate of judicial restraint towards legislation, and Justice Harlan changed their voting postures, shifting from support of civil liberties to concern for national defense. But after Frankfurter's retirement in 1962, the balance shifted back again, and by the time the penalties associated with failing to register with the SACB came before the Court in cases such as *Aptheker v. Secretary of State* (1964), the Court had reverted to its earlier liberalism.

Related Cases

Yates v. United States, 354 U.S. 298 (1957).

Aptheker v. Secretary of State, 378 U.S. 500 (1964).

Albertson v. SACB, 382 U.S. 70 (1965).

United States v. Robel, 389 U.S. 258 (1967).

Bibliography and Further Reading

Abernathy, M. Glenn. *The Right of Assembly and Association, 2nd ed.* Columbia: University of South Carolina Press, 1981.

Caute, David. *The Great Fear: The Anti-Communist Purge Under Truman and Eisenhower.* New York: Simon and Schuster, 1977.

Haynes, John Earl. *Red Scare or Red Menace?: American Communism and Anticommunism in the Cold War Era.* Chicago: Ivan R. Dee, 1966.

SCALES V. UNITED STATES

Legal Citation: 367 U.S. 203 (1961)

Petitioner
Junius Irving Scales

Respondent
United States

Petitioner's Claim
That the membership clause of the Smith Act, which makes it a crime to belong "knowingly" to an organization advocating overthrow of the government, violates the rights of free speech and association, as well as due process.

Chief Lawyer for Petitioner
Telford Taylor

Chief Lawyer for Respondent
John F. Davis

Justices for the Court
Tom C. Clark, Felix Frankfurter, John Marshall Harlan II (writing for the Court), Potter Stewart, Charles Evans Whittaker

Justices Dissenting
Hugo Lafayette Black, William J. Brennan, Jr., William O. Douglas, Earl Warren

Place
Washington, D.C.

Date of Decision
5 June 1961

Decision
The Supreme Court upheld the constitutionality of the membership clause of the Smith Act and Scales's conviction under its terms.

Significance
In the 1960s, the federal courts were still prosecuting members of the Communist Party. In *Scales*, the Supreme Court distinguished between Scales's "active" membership in the party and merely belonging.

In the wake of World War II, the United States became concerned about Soviet domination of Central and Eastern Europe. Policy makers in Washington, D.C. were determined to contain the growth of Soviet imperialism, both abroad and at home. The American Communist party in fact posed little threat to the federal government, but Congress passed many laws aimed at removing party members not just from government, but from American society at large. The anti-communist movement reached fever pitch when the political opportunist, Senator Joseph McCarthy, and the notorious House Committee on Un-American Activities began holding public hearings in an effort to root out domestic subversivism.

The Smith Act, a product of pre-war anxiety, became part of the Cold War on communism. Adopted in 1940 before the U.S. had actually entered World War II, the legislation—properly called Title I of the Alien Registration Act—was decidedly xenophobic, requiring the fingerprinting of all aliens in the country. Its true aim, however, was to check subversive activity. It imposed penalties on anyone attempting to disrupt the morale of the armed forces or advocating violent overthrow of the government. It also outlawed membership in any organization dedicated to this goal.

The Smith Act was rarely invoked during the war. After World War II ended, though, it saw active use as a tool for prosecuting domestic communists. After the Supreme Court upheld the convictions of 12 Communist Party Central Committee members under the act in *Dennis v. United States* (1951), the act helped to secure indictments of state party leaders all over the country. After the Korean War ended in 1953 and Senator McCarthy was publicly discredited in 1954, the communist witch hunt abated somewhat. The Supreme Court led by Chief Justice Warren began to back away from the government prosecution of communists. On what became known as "Red Monday," 17 June 1957, the Court ruled against the government in several cases involving alleged subversiveness, including a number of California communist leaders who had been convicted under the Smith Act.

A backlash followed. Conservative members of Congress mounted a campaign to take jurisdiction in sub-

The Smith Act

The Smith Act, properly known as the Alien Registration Act, became famous for its use during the anti-Communist campaigns of the late 1940s and 1950s. Yet like the House Un-American Activities Committee (HUAC), another fixture of the era, the Smith Act began life at a time when fascism and Nazism were viable systems, and it was designed to counteract these threats as much as Communism.

The Smith Act forbade the printing or display of materials that called for the overthrow of the federal government, and outlawed teaching or organizing of activities aimed toward overthrow. Likewise it made it illegal to belong to an organization which supported such overthrow. The first major prosecution of Communists under the Smith Act occurred in 1943, when a group that supported Leon Trotsky (a leader of the Russian Revolution murdered by Stalin in 1940) was convicted in Minneapolis; but the full-scale use of the act against Communists began in the late 1940s. A number of Supreme Court rulings during the 1950s and early 1960s, including *Scales*, greatly restricted the scope of the Smith Act.

Source(s): Levy, Leonard W., ed. *Encyclopedia of the American Constitution.* New York: Macmillan, 1986.

version cases away from the Supreme Court. The effort failed, but it did move the Court back towards the right politically—if only temporarily. One of the cases resulting from this switch in orientation was *Scales v. United States*.

Supreme Court Reverses Course on Communism

Junius Scales was a Communist Party activist who was convicted in the U.S. District Court for the Middle District of North Carolina of having violated the Smith Act's membership clause. His appeal of this felony conviction failed, and Scales took his case to the U.S. Supreme Court. Writing for the 5-4 majority that upheld Scales's conviction, Justice Harlan explained that it was the "active" nature of Scales's involvement that violated the law:

> [None] of the criminal provisions [of the Smith Act] shall be *construed* so as to make "membership" in a Communist organization "per se a violation." . . . Although we think that the membership clause on its face goes beyond making mere Party membership a violation, in that it requires a showing both of illegal Party purposes and of a member's knowledge of such purposes, we regard the first sentence . . . as a clear warrant for construing the clause as requiring not only knowing membership, but active and purposive membership, purposive that is as to the organization's criminal ends.

By interpreting the membership clause this way, the Court was able to get around Scales's First and Fifth Amendment objections. If membership in a subversive organization was not by itself a crime, then the Smith Act could not rob Scales of his right to speak his mind and associate with whomever he pleased. "Active" membership in an organization that plotted the violent overthrow of the government, however, crossed the line into criminality—and pursuing criminals cannot be construed as a violation of due process.

Scales involved some very fancy footwork. The same day that the Court decided this case, in *Noto v. United States* (1961) it also overturned the Smith Act conviction of a Communist Party member who was apparently less active than Junius Scales had been. The coalition of conservative opinion that produced *Scales* was an unstable one. After the retirement of Justice Frankfurter in 1962, Justice Harlan—and the other members of the Court—turned once again to their civil rights orientation, invalidating many legal leftovers from the Cold War.

Related Cases
Schenck v. United States, 249 U.S. 47 (1919).
Dennis v. United States, 341 U.S. 494 (1951).
Yates v. United States, 354 U.S. 298 (1957).
Noto v. United States, 367 U.S. 290 (1961).

Bibliography and Further Reading
Belknap, Michael R., ed. *American Political Trials*, rev. ed. Westport, CT: Greenwood Press, 1994.

———. *Cold War Political Justice: The Smith Act, the Communist Party, and American Civil Liberties*. Westport, CT: Greenwood Press, 1977.

Kutler, Stanley I. *The American Inquisition: Justice and Injustice in the Cold War*. New York: Hill and Wang, 1982.

NATIONAL ASSOCIATION FOR THE ADVANCEMENT OF COLORED PEOPLE V. BUTTON

Legal Citation: 371 U.S. 415 (1963)

Petitioner
NAACP

Respondent
Robert Y. Button, Attorney General of Virginia

Petitioner's Claim
That Chapter 33 of the Virginia Acts of Assembly, Extra Session 1956, violated its Fourteenth Amendment rights.

Chief Lawyer for Petitioner
Robert L. Carter

Chief Lawyer for Respondent
Henry T. Wickham

Justices for the Court
Hugo Lafayette Black, William J. Brennan, Jr. (writing for the Court), William O. Douglas, Arthur Goldberg, Earl Warren

Justices Dissenting
Tom C. Clark, John Marshall Harlan II, Potter Stewart, Byron R. White

Place
Washington, D.C.

Date of Decision
14 January 1963

Decision
The Court, reversing the decision of the Virginia Supreme Court of Appeals, held that Chapter 33 of the Virginia Acts of Assembly, Extra Session 1956, was unconstitutional because it violated the First and Fourteenth Amendments.

Significance
The decision affirmed the NAACP's freedoms of speech and association in the face of attacks from the state. The Virginia statute would have sharply curtailed the legal activities of the NAACP, which was working to desegregate schools by means of litigation.

The Battle for Desegregation

When *Brown v. Board of Education* ordered an end to school segregation in 1954, Virginia reacted violently. In spring of 1956, Senator Byrd coined the phrase "massive resistance" to characterize Virginia's response. The state adopted a resolution to "take all appropriate measures honorably, legally and constitutionally available . . . [in order] to resist [the Court's] illegal encroachment upon [Virginia's] sovereign powers." (S.J.Res. 3, 1956 Va. Acts 1213.)

Meanwhile, the NAACP's Legal Defense Fund was concentrating its efforts on claiming the *Brown* victory. Their chief strategy was litigation: staff attorneys represented those who were denied desegregated schooling. Ordinarily, the NAACP funded only suits in which NAACP attorneys were retained, though there were exceptions to this. Although the NAACP did not direct the attorney's actions in a suit, staff attorneys were expected to follow NAACP policies. States in the South—Virginia and others—responded with legislation designed to hinder or evict the organization. A string of Supreme Court cases answered these efforts.

The NAACP Sues

In 1957, the NAACP and the NAACP Legal Defense Fund sued to restrain the enforcement of Chapters 31, 32, 33, 35, and 36 of the Virginia Acts of Assembly, 1956 Extra Session. The organization claimed that the statutes violated its right to freedom of association under the Fourteenth Amendment. Each of the statutes was clearly aimed at the NAACP's legal campaign.

Chapter 31 stated that in order for a group or person to solicit funds to finance a suit, they must be one of the litigants. However, this could be avoided if the person filed organizational information (such as membership lists and financial records) with the state. Chapter 32, purportedly to preserve "interracial harmony and tranquility," required organizations that dealt with racial issues (including those funding litigation "in behalf of any race or color") to register with the state. Chapter 33 expanded the definition of "solicitation," making it illegal for an attorney to work for someone who was not a party in a suit, and who had no financial interest in the suit. It also outlawed solicitation for an attorney by such a third party. Chapter 35 defined "barratry" as "stirring up litigation." Chapter 36 made it illegal for anyone not directly involved in a lawsuit to offer or accept assistance to help another institute or continue a suit.

The U.S. District Court for the Eastern District of Virginia struck down Chapters 31, 32, and 35. The court abstained from judgment on Chapters 33 and 36, and instead waited for interpretation from a state court. The NAACP then took the case to the circuit court, which ruled against it. The Virginia Supreme Court of Appeals upheld that ruling for Chapter 33, but reversed it for Chapter 36. With only Chapter 33 remaining law, then, the NAACP petitioned the U.S. Supreme Court for a writ of *certiorari,* which was granted.

Petitioner's Claims

The NAACP had argued that the statute deprived it of property without due process and violated its right to equal protection. These two claims were dismissed by the Court. In regard to due process, the Court found that the statute was within the range of permissible regulations. Equal protection was not an issue because technically the statute applied to many groups, not just to the NAACP or to African Americans (as the Court wrote, "that the petitioner happens to be engaged in activities of expression and association on behalf of the rights of Negro children to equal opportunity is constitutionally irrelevant to the grounds of our decision"). The NAACP also claimed that the statute violated its First Amendment freedoms of speech and association, as extended under the Fourteenth Amendment. It was on these grounds that the Court struck down the statute.

State's Interests Do Not Justify Suppression of Speech

The Court rejected Virginia's first claim that "solicitation" was not protected by the First Amendment. "[T]he First Amendment," Justice Brennan wrote, delivering the majority decision, ". . . protects vigorous advocacy, certainly of lawful ends, against government intrusion." Arguing against a narrow interpretation of speech and assembly, he pointed to the decision in *National Association for the Advancement of Colored People v. Alabama* (1958), which protected the right "to engage in association for the advancement of beliefs and ideas." He pointed out that some minorities cannot reach their goals by voting, and these groups often rightly turn to litigation, which may then become their most meaningful form of political association.

The Court also found the statute so vague that "solicitation" could be interpreted as a simple referral to an attorney. The danger presented here was that it would be illegal to tell people that their rights were being violated and then direct them to a particular lawyer. "There thus inheres in the statute the gravest danger of

smothering all discussion looking to the eventual institution of litigation on behalf of the rights of members of an unpopular minority." Furthermore, a vague law may easily be used to oppress unpopular groups. Given the racially polarized political climate in Virginia at the time, the statute could have struck a great blow to the civil rights movement. (Justice Douglas, in his concurrence, noted that in fact the act was "not applied across the board to all groups that use this method of obtaining and managing litigation, but instead reflects a legislative purpose to penalize the NAACP because it promotes desegregation of the races.")

Virginia's second claim was that states traditionally had a legitimate interest in regulating professional conduct. Barratry, persistent incitement of litigation; maintenance, unlawful interference in a suit by providing money to either part; and champerty, assistance by someone outside the suit in exchange for a share of the matter in suit; had never been protected behavior. The Court agreed that the state had a valid interest, but an interest in maintaining proper professional behavior did not outweigh constitutional rights.

The NAACP's behavior did not meet traditional criteria for unprofessional legal conduct—it was neither malicious, avaricious, nor harmful to the public. As the Court pointed out, "Lawsuits attacking racial discrimination, at least in Virginia, are neither very profitable nor very popular." The NAACP, rather than seeking personal gain for its attorneys, aimed to vindicate the constitutional rights of its clients. Therefore, the state's regulation was not important enough to justify overruling freedom of speech. The Court ruled for the petitioner.

Justice White concurred in part and dissented in part. He agreed with the Court that the Virginia statute was unconstitutional. However, he agreed with the dissent that the actual legal practices of the NAACP were subject to regulation.

Professional Conduct Not Protected

Justice Harlan, joined by Justices Clark and Stewart, dissented. The dissent began with an acknowledgment:

> No member of this Court would disagree that the validity of state action claimed to infringe rights assured by the Fourteenth Amendment is to be judged by the same basic constitutional standards whether or not racial problems are involved. No worse setback could befall the great principles established by *Brown v. Board of Education* . . . than to give fair-minded persons reason to think other-wise.

Having said that, Harlan went on to say that state regulation of the NAACP's practice was probably constitutional (though not wise).

He critically reviewed the organization's activities: The NAACP did aggressively seek out cases, a practice that often resulted in abnormal attorney-client relationships. The organization identified potential litigants, and NAACP attorneys attended meetings bearing blank forms for these target litigants to sign. In some cases clients did not personally interact with the attorneys representing them.

NAACP attorneys were also likely to maintain an agenda not necessarily set by their clients' own goals. For example, staff attorneys were directed by the NAACP to always fight for desegregated education, even if their clients preferred equal facilities. The result, White charged, was a distorted relationship to which the state could reasonably object.

In response to the majority's arguments, the dissent pointed out that even if litigation is a form of political expression, it may still be regulated. Furthermore, the state has a legitimate interest in regulation, and plentiful legal precedent to support its regulations. Finally, the dissent argued, the statute was not as vague as the Court had claimed. Even if it were, the proper course would be to resolve the ambiguity, rather than reject the entire statute.

Impact

NAACP v. Button was of obvious importance in the Civil Rights movement, and the school desegregation movement in particular. But as Brennan noted, the case was not decided on the grounds of equal protection. Rather, it dealt with the freedoms of speech and association. Its impact would thus be felt equally by labor unions and other groups. In *Brotherhood of Railroad Trainmen*

v. Virginia State Bar (1964), the Court extended *National Association for the Advancement of Colored People v. Button* to protect unions' referral of members to attorneys. This and subsequent cases involving group legal service would reshape the previously more personal attorney-client relationship, affecting not only the rights of various groups but also the professional conduct of the law.

Related Cases

Brown v. Board of Education, 347 U.S. 483 (1954).
National Association for the Advancement of Colored People v. Alabama, 357 U.S. 449 (1958).
Brotherhood of Railroad Trainmen v. Virginia State Bar, 377 U.S. 1 (1964).
United Mine Workers v. Illinois State Bar Association, 389 U.S. 217 (1967).

Bibliography and Further Reading

Cushman, Robert F., and Susan P. Koniak. *Leading Constitutional Decisions.* Englewood Cliffs, NJ: Prentice-Hall, 1987.

Hall, Kermit L., ed. *The Oxford Companion to the Supreme Court.* New York: Oxford University Press, 1992.

Spong, William B., Jr. "From Button to Bates—Road to the Marketplace?" *Virginia Bar Association Journal* 12, no. 4, Fall 1986, pp. 5-8.

Tobias, Carl. "Public School Desegregation in Virginia during the Post-*Brown* Decade." *William and Mary Law Review* 37, Summer 1996, pp. 1261-1306.

APTHEKER V. SECRETARY OF STATE

Legal Citation: 378 U.S. 500 (1964)

Appellant
Herbert Aptheker

Appellee
Dean Rusk, U.S. Secretary of State

Appellant's Claim
That the provision of the Internal Security Act of 1950 denying passports to members of the American Communist Party interferes with the constitutional right to travel.

Chief Lawyers for Appellant
John J. Abt, Joseph Forer

Chief Lawyer for Appellee
Abram Chayes

Justices for the Court
Hugo Lafayette Black, William J. Brennan, Jr., William O. Douglas, Arthur Goldberg (writing for the Court), Potter Stewart, Earl Warren

Justices Dissenting
Tom C. Clark, John Marshall Harlan II, Byron R. White

Place
Washington, D.C.

Date of Decision
22 June 1964

Decision
The provision denying passports was struck down as unconstitutional.

Significance
The decision effectively established a constitutional right to travel. Although this particular decision barred government from denying passports to members of allegedly subversive organizations, the principle was soon applied to uphold the government's right to prohibit discrimination in public accommodations, such as motels, against African Americans.

The Passport Act of 1926 gave the secretary of state the power to issue passports to American citizens. During the Cold War, however, when paranoia about Communist infiltration was high, the U.S. State Department adopted a policy of denying passports needed for foreign travel to American Communists. In *Kent v. Dulles* (1958), the Supreme Court, arguing that the right to travel was a fundamental right guaranteed by the Fifth Amendment, declared this policy unconstitutional.

In 1950, however, Congress had passed the Internal Security Act, also known as the McCarran Act, requiring registration of members of the Communist Party of America with the attorney general. Once registered, individuals were, among other things, denied passports. The registration provisions of the McCarran Act had been upheld by the Court in *Communist Party of the United States v. Subversive Activities Control Board* (1961), but now the chairman of the American Communist Party filed suit challenging the constitutionality of the provision denying passports to registered persons. The U.S. District Court for the District of Columbia upheld the constitutionality of the provision, and Aptheker petitioned the U.S. Supreme Court for review of this decision.

In a 6-3 vote, the Court overturned the decision of the district court, basing its opinion on the view that the provision was too broad on its face, indiscriminately restricting the right to travel both of actual subversives and passive, "unknowing" members of the Communist Party. Congress had, said Justice Goldberg for the majority, "less drastic" means of achieving the goal of safeguarding national security. The right to travel, although not absolute, is a constitutional liberty closely related to freedom of speech and of association:

> Since freedom of association is itself guaranteed in the First Amendment, restrictions imposed upon the right to travel cannot be dismissed by asserting that the right to travel could be fully exercised if the individual would first yield up his membership in a given organization.

This emphasis on the right to travel was to remain very much on the justices' minds. In the fall of the

The Subversive Activities Control Act

The Subversive Activities Control Act was part of a larger piece of legislation, the McCarran Internal Security Act of 1950. It was named for Senator Patrick A. McCarran, a Democrat from Nevada who supported Wisconsin's anti-Communist senator, Joseph McCarthy. Contained within the McCarran Act were the Subversive Activities Control Act, and the Emergency Detention Act of 1950.

The Subversive Activities Control Act amended espionage, sabotage, alien exclusion, deportation, immigration, and nationality laws already on the books, and set up a five-member Subversive Activities Control Board (SACB) to oversee the registration of suspected "Communist-action" and "Communist-front" groups. During the 1950s, the SACB reviewed a number of organizations, and it won a Supreme Court victory with *Communist Party of the United States v. Subversive Activities Control Board* (1961). But *Albertson v. Subversive Activities Control Board* (1965) struck a blow against the board, and it began to lose power. In 1974 President Nixon in effect ended the SACB by cutting off its funding.

Source(s): Bacon, Donald C., et al., eds. *The Encyclopedia of the United States Congress.* New York: Simon & Schuster, 1995.

---

same year in which they handed down their decision in *Aptheker,* they delivered their opinion in an important civil rights case, *Heart of Atlanta Motel v. United States,* in which Congress's power under the Commerce Clause to regulate business affecting interstate commerce was cited as the rationale for outlawing racial discrimination in a privately-owned place of accommodation. In essence, by not providing African Americans with a place to stay, the Heart of Atlanta Motel was unconstitutionally restricting their right to travel. The prevailing mood of the Court during the activist era overseen by Chief Justice Warren restored civil liberties—including the right to travel—both to political dissidents and to racial minorities.

Related Cases

Kent v. Dulles, 357 U.S. 116 (1958).
Communist Party of the United States v. Subversive Acivities Control Board, 367 U.S. 1 (1961).
Heart of Atlanta Motel v. United States, 349 U.S. 241 (1964).

Bibliography and Further Reading

Aptheker, Herbert. *The Era of McCarthyism,* 2nd ed. New York: Marzani & Munsell, 1962.

Belknap, Michal R. *Cold War Political Justice: The Smith Act, the Communist Party, and American Civil Liberties.* Westport, CT: Greenwood Press, 1977.

Johnson, John W. *Historic U.S. Court Cases, 1690–1990: An Encyclopedia,* Vol 2. New York: Garland Publishing, 1992.

Library of Congress, Legislative Reference Service. *Passports and the Right to Travel: A Study of Administrative Control of the Citizen.* Washington, DC: U.S. Government Printing Office, 1966.

Elizabeth Flynn founded the American Civil Liberties Union and was a member of the Communist Party, c. 1913. © Hulton-Deutsch Collection/Corbis.

LAMONT V. POSTMASTER GENERAL OF THE UNITED STATES

Legal Citation: 381 U.S. 301 (1965)

Appellant
Corliss Lamont

Appellee
John F. Fixa, U.S. Postmaster General

Appellant's Claim
That a federal statute requiring the postmaster to destroy any mail from foreign countries determined to be communist propaganda unless the addressee returns a reply card indicating his desire to receive the mail violated his free speech rights under the First Amendment.

Chief Lawyer for Appellant
Leonard B. Boudin

Chief Lawyer for Appellee
Archibald Cox, U.S. Solicitor General

Justices for the Court
Hugo Lafayette Black, William J. Brennan, Jr., Tom C. Clark, William O. Douglas (writing for the Court), Arthur Goldberg, John Marshall Harlan II, Potter Stewart, Earl Warren

Justices Dissenting
None (Byron R. White did not participate)

Place
Washington, D.C.

Date of Decision
24 May 1965

Decision
That the statute requiring the addressee to return a reply card in order to receive mail designated as communist propaganda infringed on the addressee's unfettered right to free speech under the First Amendment.

Significance
The Court's decision reiterated the Court's previous decisions that the government has no power to place even minor restrictions on the right of free speech under the First Amendment to the Constitution. It also reiterated the central idea behind the First Amendment, that the freedom to speak one's mind protects the right to speak on topics which are politically unpopular.

Following the end of World War II, and fueled in large part by the Cold War between the United States and the Soviet Union, a great fear arose in the United States of people associated with the Communist party or generally holding communist beliefs. This era was marked by blacklisting of members of the media and entertainment industries with ties to communists, Congressional investigation of communists and non-communists alike, and a general distrust of anyone sympathizing with communists or communist beliefs. This period was also marked by government attempts in the 1950s and 1960s to monitor U.S. citizens suspected of being communists.

Part of this paranoia was reflected in the Postal Service Act of 1962. Section 305 of this act required the postal service to detain any unsealed mail, such as magazines and pamphlets but not including sealed letters, designated as "communist political propaganda" which was sent into the United States from a foreign country. The post office was then required to notify the addressee that the mail had been received and would be delivered only at the addressee's request.

In 1963, a copy of a pamphlet called "Peking Review #12" was sent to Dr. Corliss Lamont, who published and distributed pamphlets in the United States. Pursuant to the Postal Service Act, the post office detained the pamphlet and sent Lamont a card notifying him that the material had been detained. Instead of sending to the post office a reply card indicating that he wished to receive the material, Lamont filed a lawsuit in the U.S. District Court for the Southern District of New York, claiming that the statute infringed on his right to free speech under the First Amendment to the U.S. Constitution. A three-judge panel of the district court dismissed the complaint, concluding that Lamont's claim was moot because the post office construed his filing of the lawsuit as an indication that he wished to receive the pamphlet and delivered it to him. Meanwhile, Leif Helberg instituted a similar challenge to the law in the U.S. District Court for the Northern District of California. That court, however, found that the statute was unconstitutional.

Court Sets Broad Free Speech Protections

The government appealed the decision in the California case, and Lamont appealed the district court's decision in the New York case, to the U.S. Supreme Court, which decided the cases together. The Supreme Court found that the statute was an unconstitutional restriction on the right to free speech.

The Court first rejected the government's argument that, because the government has no duty to provide for a postal service, the law did not involve any official action restricting the free speech rights of citizens wishing to receive material designated as communist propaganda. Quoting from Justice Oliver Wendell Holmes's dissenting opinion in the 1921 case of *United States ex rel. Milwaukee Social Democratic Publishing Co. v. Burleson,* the Court stated that "[t]he United States may give up the post-office when it sees fit, but while it carries it on the use of mails is almost as much a part of free speech as the right to use our tongues." Thus, the Court concluded, Congress by passing a statute was attempting to abridge the free speech rights of citizens to receive this material.

The Court also rejected the government's argument that the statute did not infringe on the right to free speech. The government argued that people could still receive material designated as communist propaganda by sending back the reply card directing the post office to deliver the material. Thus, the government argued, the statute involved only inconvenience, and not an abridgment of the right to free speech. The Court rejected this argument, reasoning that the statute requires an affirmative act on the part of the addressee in order to receive the prohibited materials. The Court also reasoned that people would be deterred from sending back the reply card, for fear that the government or others would label them communists. In his concurring opinion, Justice Brennan expressed the Court's view thusly: "[I]nhibition as well as prohibition against the exercise of precious First Amendment rights is a power denied to government . . . [W]e cannot sustain an intrusion on First Amendment rights on the ground that the intrusion is only a minor one." Thus, the Court found that the statute was unconstitutional.

Impact

The Court's decision, coming at the height of the country's fear of communism during the Cold War, reaffirmed the central tenet of the First Amendment's guarantee of freedom of speech: That freedom of speech protects speech on unpopular topics and advocacy of unpopular political ideas. Thus, the Court signaled that government may not impose any burdens on the right of the people to speak their minds concerning political and social issues. Since the Court's decision in *Lamont,* the Court has consistently held to this interpretation of the First Amendment's protection of the freedom of speech.

Related Cases

United States ex rel. Milwaukee Social Democratic Publishing Co. v. Burleson, 255 U.S. 407 (1921).

National Association for the Advancement of Colored Persons v. Alabama ex rel. Patterson, 357 U.S. 449 (1958).

United States Postal Service v. Council of Greenburgh Civic Associations, 453 U.S. 114 (1981).

Meese v. Keene, 481 U.S. 465 (1987).

Denver Area Educational Telecommunications Consortium, Inc. v. Federal Communications Commission, 116 S. Ct. 2374 (1996).

Bibliography and Further Reading

Haynes, John Earl. *Red Scare or Red Menace?: American Communism and Anticommunism in the Cold War Era.* Chicago: Ivan R. Dee, 1996.

Hunt, John G., ed. *The Dissenters: America's Voice of Opposition.* New York: Gramercy Press, 1993.

Schrecker, Ellen. *The Age of McCarthyism: A Brief History with Documents.* Boston: Bedford Books, 1994.

Smolla, Rodney A. *Free Speech in an Open Society.* New York: Knopf, 1992.

ADDERLEY V. FLORIDA

Legal Citation: 385 U.S. 39 (1966)

Petitioner
Harriett Louise Adderley, et al.

Respondent
State of Florida

Petitioner's Claim
That the arrest of 107 demonstrators petitioning on the property of the Leon County jail was a breach of their rights to free speech, assembly, petition, equal protection of the laws, and due process of law.

Chief Lawyer for Petitioner
Richard Yale Feder

Chief Lawyer for Respondent
William D. Roth, Assistant Attorney General of Florida

Justices for the Court
Hugo Lafayette Black (writing for the Court), William O. Douglas, John Marshall Harlan II, Potter Stewart, Byron R. White

Justices Dissenting
William J. Brennan, Jr., William O. Douglas, Abe Fortas, Earl Warren

Place
Washington, D.C.

Date of Decision
14 November 1966

Decision
Upheld the decision affirmed by the Florida Circuit Court and the district court of appeals allowing the protection of public property through the use of private property trespass law. Also ruled that the plaintiffs' First and Fourteenth Amendment rights were not violated.

Significance
Because the state was considered the private owner of the county jail, and because of the large number of petitioners, the Supreme Court deemed it relevant to agree with the charge of trespassing with malicious and mischievous intent that was bestowed by the lower courts. This ruling raised the question of how much power the "custodian" of a public property can wield without suppressing the First and Fourteenth Amendment rights held by a group or an individual.

One of the defining features of the 1960s was civil unrest. The United States was a country torn apart by opposing sentiments of the war in Vietnam and by the laws and mores of racial segregation. During this time of protest rallies, demonstrations, and marches, the privileges set forth by the First Amendment were stretched to the limit, not only by demonstrators, but by the officers assigned to protect and enforce these rights.

In 1966 a group of Florida A&M University (FAMU) students demonstrated against the racial segregation of a local movie theater. These protesters were arrested, and what followed established the foundation of what became known as the *Adderley v. Florida* case.

On the day following this incident, approximately 200 FAMU students, Harriett Louise Adderley among them, marched from the university to the Leon County jail to protest the arrest of their fellow students as well as state and local policies of racial segregation. This protest was in the form hand clapping and singing songs concerned with freedom; no placards were used.

Initially the group took position within feet of the first step to the entrance of the jail. A deputy sheriff, fearing that they might enter, asked the group to move back from the door. The entire gathering did as requested, subsequently blocking the jail driveway and congregating partially on a grassy area of the jail's property. It is important to note that this particular entrance and driveway were primarily used by the sheriff's department for the transportation of prisoners and by commercial vehicles—not by the public.

At this point someone called the sheriff, who was away from the jail on business. Upon his return, the sheriff immediately determined the safety status of the jail, then opened conversation with the leaders of the protest (known only as Mr. White and Mr. Blue). He informed them they were trespassing and that he would give the group ten minutes to leave or he would begin arresting them. Neither leader attempted to disperse the crowd; however, one of them told the sheriff that they had every intention of being arrested.

After the allotted ten minutes had passed, the sheriff informed the protesters that he was the legal custodian of the jail property and that they were trespassing. He continued by stating that if they did not leave immediately he would arrest them. Some members of the group left, while others remained; some even sat down. At no time did the sheriff ever take exception to the songs and speech of the group. After waiting for up to four minutes (all participants were unclear concerning the time period), the sheriff ordered the arrest of the remaining 107 demonstrators. The petitioners (32 of the 107 demonstrators) were found guilty of trespassing under a Florida trespass statute that prohibited trespassing with "malicious or mischievous intent."

The petitioners contended that the conviction deprived them of their rights to free speech, petition, assembly, due process of law, and protection of the laws as stated in the Fourteenth Amendment. They backed their argument with references to *Edwards v. South Carolina* (1963) and *Cox v. Louisiana* (1965). The *Edwards* case contained many similarities to *Adderley v. Florida* in that it also dealt with a large number of people on public property demonstrating against segregation and singing. The similarities end there, however; in *Edwards,* the demonstrators were on the grounds of the South Carolina State Capitol with permission of state officials—not in an area that is infrequently used by the public, such as a jail. The demonstrators in the *Edwards* case were charged with breach of peace, a law that was subsequently proven to be so indefinite and broad that it was invalidated. The *Cox* case benefited from the same outcome.

The petitioners also insisted that the trespass law was void due to vagueness and that there were few solid pieces of evidence to back up the account as presented by the sheriff and his officers. After being processed by the Florida Circuit Court and then by the Florida District Court of Appeal, the Supreme Court would decide if the rights of the plaintiffs had been violated.

The Supreme Court considered the case and determined that there was ample evidence supplied for the arrest and that the rights of the petitioners had not been violated. However, the means in which this was determined made this quite a unique case: it all hinged on the use of the Florida trespass statute.

This statute dealt with a particular type of conduct—trespassing with malicious and/or mischievous intent. Indeed, the petitioners did not argue with the definitions set forth by the trial court to the jury: The word

> malicious means that the wrongful act shall be done voluntarily, unlawfully and without excuse or justification . . . Mischievous . . . means that the alleged trespass shall be inclined to cause petty and trivial trouble, annoyance and vexation to others . . .

In this case it was quite simple to prove that, according to the definition, a mischievous act was taking

place. The fact that one of the protestors informed the sheriff of a desire to be arrested was all the evidence that the Court needed to prove mischievous intent. With this, the Court was able to find the petitioners guilty of trespassing.

Because the acts of the sheriff were based upon the situation of trespass rather than the speech and songs of the demonstrators, the Supreme Court deemed that the petitioners' rights to freedom of speech, assembly, press, and petition were not violated. Because of this, the invocations of *Edwards v. South Carolina* and *Cox v. Louisiana* were considered irrelevant.

A controversy arose concerning the unique use of the Florida trespass statute to protect the jail. In effect, people were being convicted of trespassing on public property. The Supreme Court determined that a state has the right to control the use of its own property and that the state, Florida in this case, is no less than the private owner of the jail and its property. According to the Supreme Court, nothing in the U.S. Constitution prevents a state's fair enforcement of its own criminal trespass statute against anyone refusing to obey the sheriff's order. The jail differed from a park or state capitol grounds in that it was an edifice built for security purposes, not for public use.

Impact

This reasoning did not sit well with some. Chief Justice Warren and Justices Brennan, Fortas, and Douglas expressed a decidedly negative opinion concerning the power the majority opinion afforded to a "custodian" of public property. They felt that such discretion placed at the whim of any public official, regardless of his status, would place those who assert their First Amendment rights in jeopardy. Despite this reservation, *Adderley v. Florida* proved to be useful in later Supreme Court cases—not as an example of a violation of the First Amendment—but as a dividing line for which types of public property can be used for public speaking.

Related Cases

Edwards v. South Carolina, 372 U.S. 229 (1963).
Cox v. Louisiana, 379 U.S. 559 (1965).

Bibliography and Further Reading

Biskupic, Joan and Elder Witt, eds. *Congressional Quarterly's Guide to the U.S. Supreme Court,* 3rd ed. Washington, DC: Congressional Quarterly, Inc., 1996.

Cushman, Robert F. *Cases in Constitutional Law,* 7th ed. Englewood Cliffs, NJ: Prentice-Hall, Inc., 1989.

Cushman, Robert F. *Leading Constitutional Decisions.* Englewood Cliffs, NJ: Prentice-Hall, Inc., 1982.

Konvitz, Milton R., ed. *Bill of Rights Reader,* 5th ed. Ithaca, NY: Cornell University Press, 1973.

KEYISHIAN V. BOARD OF REGENTS OF THE UNIVERSITY OF THE STATE OF NEW YORK

Legal Citation: 385 U.S. 589 (1967)

Appellant
Harry Keyishian

Appellee
Board of Regents of the University of the State of New York

Appellant's Claim
That various New York state statutes and administrative regulations disqualifying teachers who are deemed subversive or who have belonged to subversive organizations are unconstitutional.

Chief Lawyer for Appellant
Richard Lipsitz

Chief Lawyers for Appellee
Ruth V. Iles, Assistant Attorney General of New York, and John C. Crary, Jr.

Justices for the Court
Hugo Lafayette Black, William J. Brennan, Jr. (writing for the Court), William O. Douglas, Abe Fortas, Earl Warren

Justices Dissenting
Tom C. Clark, John Marshall Harlan II, Potter Stewart, Byron R. White

Place
Washington, D.C.

Date of Decision
23 January 1967

Decision
The Supreme Court struck the New York rules down, citing their vagueness.

Significance
In *Keyishian*, the Court upheld the principle of educational freedom and at the same time did away with the state's ability to force an individual to surrender constitutional rights as a condition of employment.

New York State first passed a law prohibiting those charged with treasonous words or acts from teaching in the public school system in 1917. In 1939, the state passed another law that disqualified anyone who advocated violent overthrow of the government or who belonged to an organization that advocated such a doctrine from employment in the educational system or the civil service. The 1939 law charged the State Board of Regents with drawing up procedures for disqualification, as well as a list of "subversive" organizations, such as the Communist Party. The board was also directed to state in its regulations that membership in any of the listed organizations constituted evidence for disqualification. A 1953 amendment to the 1939 law—passed during the height of the McCarthy era communist witch hunts that poisoned the atmosphere of the early 1950s—extended its application to include personnel at any institution of higher education operated by the state.

Harry Keyishian was an instructor in English at the privately owned and operated University of Buffalo in 1962 when it was merged with the publicly supported State University of New York. When he refused to comply with the state requirement that he sign a certificate stating that he was not a communist, his one-year teaching contract was not renewed. Together with other instructors who refused to sign, he brought an action in federal court claiming that the state laws and regulations at issue were unconstitutional. After the U.S. District Court for the Western District of New York ruled against Keyishian, he appealed to the U.S. Supreme Court.

Supreme Court Upholds Principle of Academic Freedom

By the time Keyishian's case went to trial, much of the paranoid hysteria about communist infiltration associated with the Cold War and Senator Joseph McCarthy's campaign to purge leftists from public life had abated. Still, the rules of the State University of New York remained on the books, and the State Board of Regents was determined to enforce them. Keyishian and others saw the rules as an abridgement of his First Amendment rights to freedom of speech and freedom of association. More ominously, he argued, they threatened academic freedom.

Five of the nine justices of the Supreme Court agreed with him. Writing for the majority, Justice Brennan stressed:

> Our Nation is deeply committed to safeguarding academic freedom, which is of transcendent value to all of us and not merely to the teachers concerned. That freedom is therefore a special concern of the First Amendment, which does not tolerate laws that cast a pall of orthodoxy over the classroom . . . The classroom is peculiarly the "marketplace of ideas."

But the Court chose reasons other than strictly First Amendment concerns for overturning the New York laws. As Justice Brennan noted, regulations which affect the First Amendment must be drafted with great care and specificity. In the case of the New York laws at issue, the wording was vague and ambiguous and had resulted in a maze of regulation and administrative machinery that made it difficult for those affected to know when or how—or even if—they were in compliance. The rules therefore could result in a distinct "chilling effect" on those who had to guess which conduct or utterance might cost them their jobs. An instructor might be violating the law simply by carrying a copy of the Communist Manifesto on the street, or by discussing in class the principles of certain abstract political doctrines. The laws carried no requirement that the teacher have a specific intent to overthrow the government or to further the goals of the prohibited organizations; mere membership was enough to cost him or her a job.

The statutes at issue were "void for vagueness," a judicial doctrine which holds that laws are unconstitutional when they are vague as to what persons fall within their scope or what conduct is forbidden. The New York rules, said Justice Brennan, violate not only First Amendment freedoms, but the guarantee of procedural due process. After *Keyishian,* New York State employees were no longer required to surrender their constitutional rights in order to obtain or hang on to their jobs.

Related Cases

DeJonge v. Oregon, 299 U.S. 353 (1937).
Herndon v. Lowry, 301 U.S. 242 (1937).
Adler v. Board of Education, 342 U.S. 485 (1952).
Yates v. United States, 354 U.S. 298 (1957).
Scales v. United States, 367 U.S. 203 (1961).

Bibliography and Further Reading

Bosmajian, Haig, ed. *Academic Freedom.* New York, NY: Neal-Schuman, 1989.

Diamond, Sigmund. *Compromised Campus: The Collaboration of Universities With the Intelligence Community, 1945-1955.* New York, NY: Oxford University Press, 1992.

Dickman, Howard, ed. *The Imperiled Academy.* New Brunswick, NJ: Transaction Publishers, 1993.

BROADRICK V. OKLAHOMA

Legal Citation: 413 U.S. 601 (1973)

Appellant
William M. Broadrick and two other state employees

Appellee
Oklahoma State Personnel Board

Appellant's Claim
That Section 818 of the Oklahoma State Merit System Act, which forbids state employees from taking part in political fund-raising or campaigning except as private citizens, was overbroad and vague, thus forbidding activities which are constitutionally protected under the First Amendment.

Chief Lawyer for Appellant
John C. Buckingham

Chief Lawyer for Appellee
Mike D. Martin, Assistant Attorney General of Oklahoma

Justices for the Court
Harry A. Blackmun, Warren E. Burger, Thurgood Marshall, Lewis F. Powell, Jr., William H. Rehnquist, Potter Stewart, Byron R. White (writing for the Court)

Justices Dissenting
William J. Brennan, Jr., William O. Douglas

Place
Washington, D.C.

Date of Decision
25 June 1973

Decision
That Section 818 was constitutional as applied to the actions for which appellants were charged, and that it was not sufficiently overbroad to justify their challenge that it might be applied unconstitutionally to others.

Significance
Broadrick v. Oklahoma raised difficult First Amendment questions in its focus on the right of public employees to participate in politics. While the Constitution can hardly be construed to justify the use of public office to promote political ends, higher officials in the federal and lower governments belong to political parties, and daily function in the capacity of promoting their parties' ends. The case also marked the high point of the reaction to the concept of First Amendment "overbreadth" associated with the Court of former Chief Justice Earl Warren.

The appellants in *Broadrick v. Oklahoma,* all three of them Oklahoma state employees, were charged by the Oklahoma State Personnel Board for violation of Section 818 of the Oklahoma Merit System of Personnel Administration Act. The latter forbids employees of the state from soliciting funds or campaigning for, or belonging to, any political party except as a private citizen. The three appellants were charged for their active participation in the 1970 reelection campaign of Ray C. Jones, a state corporation commissioner—and their superior. On several occasions at the commission's Oil and Gas Conservation Division, they allegedly asked other corporation commission employees to take part in campaign work or to recommend others who might participate in the campaign. Two of the three were charged with soliciting campaign funds from commission employees, and one was charged with receiving and distributing campaign posters.

When the three appellants took their case to the Federal District Court of the Western District of Oklahoma, at issue were two clauses in Section 818. The first of these, in paragraph six, stated that "[n]o employee in the classified service . . . shall, directly or indirectly, solicit, receive, or in any manner be concerned in soliciting or receiving any assessment . . . or contribution for any political organization, candidacy or other political purpose." The second was in paragraph seven, which provided that no such employee "shall be a member of any national, state or local committee of a political party, or any officer or member of a committee of a partisan political club, or a candidate for nomination or election to any paid public office."

The law, the appellants charged, was overly broad in its application, and could be used to forbid constitutionally protected forms of free speech, such as the use of campaign buttons or bumper stickers. However, they did not dispute the constitutionality of the law as applied to their own circumstances, but only called into question its possible future application. The three-judge panel of the district court upheld the law, and the appellants took the case to the Supreme Court.

"Overbreadth" Called into Question

Earlier on the same day that the Court reviewed the case of *Broadrick v. Oklahoma,* it heard a similar case involving federal, rather than state, employees. In *Civil Service Commission v. Letter Carriers,* the law in question was Section 9(a) of the Hatch Act, which provides that no federal employee shall "use his official authority or influence for the purpose of interfering with or affecting the result of an election" or "take part in political management or in political campaigns." Evidently the Court did not consider this law "overbroad," because it upheld the Hatch Act by 6-3 vote.

In delivering the opinion of the Court in *Broadrick,* Justice White cited not only the Hatch Act, but laws similar to Section 818 which prevailed in all 49 of the other states. Thus he established that such provisions are relatively uniform, and that they are not ambiguous: "Without question," he said, "a broad range of political activities and conduct is proscribed by the section." He cited another proscription in Section 818, one which the appellants did not dispute, which prohibited discrimination against any state employee for his or her political beliefs—thus perhaps establishing a link between the prohibition of political discrimination on the one hand, and that of active campaigning and solicitation on the other.

In clarifying the case at hand, Justice White noted that the appellants did not consider the legitimacy of Section 818 as it applied to them, but were challenging it on the basis of its possible overbreadth and vagueness. White discounted this claim: "Whatever other problems there are with Section 818, it is all but frivolous to suggest that the section fails to give adequate warning of what activities it proscribes, or fails to set out 'explicit standards' for those who must apply it." Though he conceded that "[w]ords inevitably contain germs of uncertainty," and that the prohibitions in Section 818 might not satisfy "those intent on finding fault at any cost," he affirmed that Section 818 was spelled out in terms clear enough for any person using ordinary common sense to understand.

White had little use for the appellants' claim that, even if the law was correct when applied to them, it could be misapplied to others. Implied in the traditions of constitutional interpretation, he said, is the idea that a person clearly guilty under a given statute cannot challenge that statute simply on the grounds that it might be misapplied to somebody else. "These principles," he said, "rest on more than the fussiness of judges. They reflect the conviction that, under our constitutional system, courts are not roving commissions assigned to pass judgment on the validity of the Nation's laws." There were limited exceptions, he said, especially instances in which those who are not parties to a suit stand to lose due to its outcome, as in the case of *National Association for the Advancement of Colored People v. Alabama* (1958). But *Broadrick* was not one of those instances, according to White, so he, along with Chief Justice Burger and Justices Blackmun, Powell, and Rehnquist, voted to affirm the decision of the district court.

The Dissent on First Amendment Grounds

Two dissenting opinions were filed in *Broadrick v. Oklahoma.* The first of these came from Justice Douglas, who contrasted the case with *Connally v. General Construction,* which involved a state law forbidding a contractor to pay workers "less than the current rate of *per diem* wages in the locality where the work is performed." The Court, Douglas noted, had held that the law in question was too vague, and by that standard, Section 818 would be similarly judged too vague. The First Amendment, he said, does not just protect "private" speech, but public speech as well, and therefore "I do not see how government can deprive its employees of the right to speak, write, assemble, or petition once the office is closed and the employee is home on his own." Therefore Douglas voted to reverse the judgment of the lower court.

Justice Brennan also dissented, in an opinion in which Justices Stewart and Marshall joined. In Brennan's view, the decision in *Broadrick* was "a wholly unjustified retreat from fundamental and previously well established First and Fourteenth Amendment principles." He called into question White's reference to "substantial overbreadth" in the Court's opinion, when White had said, "where conduct and not merely speech is involved . . . the overbreadth of a statute must not only be real, but substantial as well, judged in relation to the statute's plainly legitimate sweep." This idea, Brennan said, was at odds with previous Court decisions, such as that in *Coates v. Cincinnati* (1971).

And even with regard to the *Letter Carriers* case decided earlier that day, Brennan said, there were differences between Section 818 and the Hatch Act. The latter, he said, was much more well-defined than Section 818. By providing that employees have the right to express their political views in private, he said, Section 818 implies that they have no right to do so publicly. On these and other bases, he held that Oklahoma had failed "to provide the necessary 'sensitive tools' to carry out the 'separation of legitimate from illegitimate speech'."

Related Cases

Connally v. General Construction Co., 269 U.S. 385 (1926).
National Association for the Advancement of Colored People v. Alabama, 377 U.S. 288 (1958).
Coates v. Cincinnati, 402 U.S. 611 (1971).
Civil Service Commission v. Letter Carriers, 413 U.S. 548 (1973).

Bibliography and Further Reading

Biskupic, Joan and Elder Witt, eds. *Congressional Quarterly's Guide to the U.S. Supreme Court,* 3rd ed. Washington, DC: Congressional Quarterly, Inc., 1996.

Levy, Leonard W., ed. *Encyclopedia of the American Constitution,* New York: Macmillan, 1986.

Witt, Elder, ed. *The Supreme Court A to Z,* Washington, DC: Congressional Quarterly, 1993.

COMMUNIST PARTY OF INDIANA V. WHITCOMB

Legal Citation: 414 U.S. 441 (1974)

Appellant
The Communist Party of Indiana, certain of its officers and potential voters, and its candidates for president and vice-president in the 1972 general election

Appellee
The Indiana state election board and its members

Appellant's Claim
That the state's rule requiring political parties to submit a written oath stating that they will not advocate the overthrow of the federal, state or local government by violence or force in order to be placed on an election ballot was a violation of the First and Fourteenth Amendments.

Chief Lawyer for Appellant
Sanford Jay Rosen

Chief Lawyer for Appellee
Theodore L. Sendak, Attorney General of Indiana

Justices for the Court
Harry A. Blackmun, William J. Brennan, Jr. (writing for the Court), Warren E. Burger, William O. Douglas, Thurgood Marshall, Lewis F. Powell, Jr., William H. Rehnquist, Potter Stewart, Byron R. White

Justices Dissenting
None

Place
Washington, D.C.

Date of Decision
9 January 1974

Decision
That the law which forced the party to declare its non-intention to overthrow the government was unconstitutional.

Significance
Reaffirmed the Court's established position declaring loyalty oaths unconstitutional.

In the 1972 presidential election the Communist Party in the United States fielded a slate of candidates for president and vice-president. The Communist Party of Indiana fielded a slate for the first time and attempted to get those candidates on the state ballot. Indiana had a law, however, that stated no political party could get on the ballot unless it first submitted a written pledge stating that it had no intention of ever advocating the overthrow of the government, whether local, state or national, by any means involving violence or force. The Communist Party declined to file such a pledge, and was therefore denied a place on the ballot. The party filed a motion with the district court in that state asking that the law be ruled unconstitutional and that the party be ordered placed on the ballot. A three-judge court ruled that the party must be placed on the ballot if it filed the oath.

The party responded by filing the pledge in writing, but with a disclaimer of sorts. A note on the pledge pointed out that "The term advocate as used herein has the meaning given it by the Supreme Court of the United States in *Yates v. United States* . . . 'the advocacy and teaching of concrete action for the forcible overthrow of the government, and not of principles divorced from action.'" The election board found the pledge in that form to not meet its satisfaction, and again denied the party a place on the ballot, and the party again sought help from the district court, but was denied. The party briefly sought emergency help from the U.S. Supreme Court, but agreed to withdraw that request as the district court agreed to reconsider its earlier ruling and decide if a pledge that was consistent with the *Yates* decision should be sufficient to meet the law's requirements. The court eventually decided not to reverse its earlier decision, however, and the party was forced to take its case to the Supreme Court at the end of November, too late to be placed on the ballot but not too late to prove its point and win its case.

The state sent Attorney General Theodore L. Sendak to argue its case. Sendak pleaded:

> It is fraudulent for a group seeking by violent revolution to overthrow our democratic form of government to disguise itself as a political party and use the very forms of the democracy

it seeks to subvert in order to gain support and carry on its nefarious ends.

Court Strikes Law Down

The Supreme Court was unanimous in deciding that the district courts ruled incorrectly, striking down Indiana's law. Justice Brennan, writing the majority opinion, said:

This principle that 'the constitutional guarantees of free speech and free press do not permit a state to forbid or proscribe advocacy of the use of force or of law violation except where such advocacy is directed to inciting or producing imminent lawless action and is likely to incite or produce such action' has been applied not only to statutes that directly forbid or proscribe advocacy, . . . but also to regulatory schemes that determine eligibility for public employment, . . . tax exemptions, . . . and moral fitness justifying disbarment. Appellees argue that the principle should nevertheless not obtain in cases of state regulation of access to the ballot. We perceive no reason to make an exception, and appellees suggest none. Indeed, all of the reasons for application of the principle in the other contexts are equally applicable here.

The Court also emphasized the importance of the case to the integrity of the political process, quoting previous decisions:

Thus, burdening access to the ballot, rights of association in the political party of one's choice, interests in casting an effective vote and in running for office, not because the party urges others "to do something, now or in the future . . . [but] . . . merely to believe in something" (Yates) is to infringe interests certainly as substantial as those in public employment, tax exemption, or the practice of law. For "the right to exercise the franchise in a free and unimpaired manner is preservative of other basic civil and political rights . . ." (Reynolds v. Sims) "Other rights, even the most basic, are illusory if the right to vote is undermined." (Wesberry v. Sanders)

Justice Powell was joined in a concurring opinion by three other justices, in which he agreed with the result but felt the decision should have been reached for a much more basic issue, that the Democratic and Republican Parties had also not filed affidavits promising they would not advocate the violent overthrow of the government. He wrote:

In my view it was quite unnecessary to reach the issue addressed by the Court. It was established at trial that the appellees had certified the Democratic and Republican Parties despite the failure of party officials to submit the prescribed affidavits . . . In Williams v. Rhodes, . . . this Court held that a discriminatory preference for established parties under a state's electoral system can be justified only by a "compelling state interest." In the present case, no colorable justification has been offered for placing on appellants burdens not imposed on the two established parties. It follows that the appellees' discriminatory application of the Indiana statute denied appellants equal protection under the Fourteenth Amendment.

The lasting import of the case, however, came in the confirmation of a principle the Court had earlier stated in the National Association for the Advancement of Colored People v. Button case:

Precision of a regulation must be the touchstone in an area so closely touching our most precious freedoms.

Related Cases

National Association for the Advancement of Colored People v. Button, 371 U.S. 145 (1963).
Wesberry v. Sanders, 376 U.S. 1 (1964).
Reynolds v. Sims, 377 U.S. 533 (1964).
Williams v. Rhodes, 393 U.S. 523 (1968).

Bibliography and Further Reading

American Bar Association Journal, March 1974, p. 322.

Biskupic, Joan, and Elder Witt, eds. Congressional Quarterly's Guide to the U.S. Supreme Court, 3rd ed. Washington, DC: Congressional Quarterly, Inc., 1996.

Indiana Law Review, Vol. 8, no. 1, p. 102.

In re Primus

Legal Citation: 436 U.S. 412 (1978)

Appellant
Edna Smith Primus

Appellee
Supreme Court of South Carolina

Appellant's Claim
That the Disciplinary Board of the South Carolina Supreme Court, by issuing Primus a public reprimand, violated her First Amendment rights to freely engage in association as a political activity, as a cooperating lawyer with the ACLU.

Chief Lawyer for Appellant
Ray P. McClain

Chief Lawyer for Appellee
Richard B. Kale, Jr., Assistant Attorney General of South Carolina

Justices for the Court
Harry A. Blackmun, Warren E. Burger, Thurgood Marshall, Lewis F. Powell, Jr. (writing for the Court), John Paul Stevens, Potter Stewart, Byron R. White

Justices Dissenting
William H. Rehnquist (William J. Brennan, Jr., did not participate)

Place
Washington, D.C.

Date of Decision
30 May 1978

Decision
The Court overturned the decision of the South Carolina Supreme Court and determined that Primus acted within her rights to free association as a representative of the ACLU, and should not have been reprimanded for improper solicitation.

Significance
This decision upheld the First Amendment protections for nonprofit organizations with political aims, allowing such groups to approach potential litigants to offer legal advice, explain the rights of individuals, and to encourage the use of litigation as a political action.

In 1973, Edna Smith Primus was working as a paid legal consultant for the South Carolina Council on Human Relations, and was a cooperating lawyer for the American Civil Liberties Union (ACLU), for which she received no pay. During that summer, newspapers began reporting that pregnant mothers receiving Medicaid in Aiken County, South Carolina were being sterilized or threatened with sterilization, in order to continue receiving care under the Medicaid program. Primus was sent as a representative of the council to speak to a group of the women who had been sterilized, to advise them concerning their legal rights. In August of 1973, the ACLU told Primus that free legal representation could be offered to the women who had been sterilized. Primus then wrote a letter to Mary Etta Williams, a woman who had been sterilized, and who had expressed interest in bringing a suit against the doctor who had sterilized her. Williams gave a copy of this letter to her doctor after she had decided not to sue. The letter became the basis of a formal complaint against Edna Smith Primus, filed with the Board of Commissioners on Grievances and Discipline of the South Carolina Supreme Court.

Primus was accused of improper solicitation on the behalf of the ACLU, which the board claimed would have benefited financially if the potential client had sued and won money damages. Codes of ethics for lawyers and various state regulations prohibit direct solicitation which would result in gain by lawyers, with the aim of protecting the public from pressure. Primus claimed that her actions did not represent improper solicitation, but were protected by both the First and Fourteenth Amendments as she would not gain from representing Williams, but would be advancing a civil liberties political agenda. The South Carolina Supreme Court rejected these arguments and issued a public reprimand.

The primary question in this case was over the nature of the activities of the appellant and the ACLU. While the state supreme court claimed that Primus was soliciting for the ACLU with the intention of financial gain, the ACLU and the appellant claimed that her solicitation was protected, based on the decision in *National Association for the Advancement of Colored Peo-*

ple v. Button (1963). In that case, the U.S. Supreme Court decided that the NAACP, "for the purpose of furthering the civil-rights objectives of the organization and its members was held to come within the right 'to engage in association for the advancement of beliefs and ideas.'" While the Court did not deny the rights of states to create legislation which protects the public from "undue influence, overreaching, misrepresentation, invasion of privacy, conflict of interest, and lay interference that potentially are present in solicitation of prospective clients by lawyers," it clearly protected the freedom of nonprofit groups, such as labor unions, to freely associate. This was upheld in cases such as *United Transportation Union v. Michigan Bar* (1971) and *Mine Workers v. Illinois Bar Association* (1994). If the ACLU's intention was primarily to provide legal counsel, and to profit accordingly, Primus's action would probably be worthy of a reprimand. But the Court found that the ACLU was an organization with political interests, as are the NAACP and labor unions. The ACLU only becomes involved in litigation concerning civil liberties, and the Court acknowledged that "it has engaged in the defense of unpopular causes and unpopular defendants and has represented individuals in litigation that has defined the scope of constitutional protection in areas such as political dissent, juvenile rights, prisoners' rights, military law, amnesty, and

privacy." The ACLU is a "bona fide, nonprofit organization that pursues litigation as a vehicle for effective political expression and association, as well as a means of communicating useful information to the public."

The Court, by rejecting the South Carolina Supreme Court's decision to reprimand Primus, took a strong stand against limiting freedom of speech and association. By protecting these rights, not just for individuals but also for active nonprofit organizations, the Court was protecting the free discussion of politics, and open public debate. The case also indicated that potentially troubling or unpopular opinions, such as those expressed by the ACLU, the NAACP, or labor groups, could not be suppressed by the states.

Related Cases
National Association for the Advancement of Colored People v. Button, 371 U.S. 415 (1963).
United Transportation Union v. Michigan Bar, 401 U.S. 576 (1971).
Mine Workers v. Illinois Bar Association, 389 U.S. 217 (1994).

Bibliography and Further Reading
Biskupic, Joan and Elder Witt. *Congressional Quarterly's Guide to the U.S. Supreme Court,* 3rd ed. Washington, DC: Congressional Quarterly, Inc., 1996.

ROBERTS V. U.S. JAYCEES

Legal Citation: 468 U.S. 609 (1984)

Appellants
Kathryn R. Roberts, Acting Commissioner, Minnesota Department of Human Rights, et al.

Appellee
U.S. Jaycees

Appellants' Claim
That Minnesota's Human Rights Act was constitutional and required the Jaycees to admit women as regular members.

Chief Lawyer for Appellants
Richard L. Varco, Jr.

Chief Lawyer for Appellee
Carl D. Hall, Jr.

Justices for the Court
William J. Brennan, Jr. (writing for the Court), Thurgood Marshall, Sandra Day O'Connor, Lewis F. Powell, Jr., William H. Rehnquist, John Paul Stevens, Byron R. White

Justices Dissenting
Harry A. Blackmun (Warren E. Burger did not participate)

Place
Washington, D.C.

Date of Decision
3 July 1984

Decision
Minnesota's Human Rights Act was constitutional. Requiring the Jaycees to admit women as regular members in accordance with the act's provisions did not violate that organization's right to freedom of association.

Significance
This was the first in a series of Supreme Court decisions that opened many previously all-male organizations to women.

The U.S. Jaycees, originally known as the Junior Chamber of Commerce, is a nonprofit membership corporation founded in 1920. Its national headquarters are in Tulsa, Oklahoma. Its purpose is to "promote and foster the growth and development of young men's civic organizations in the United States . . ." It also meant to encourage "genuine Americanism" and "to develop true friendship and understanding among young men of all nations."

At that time, regular membership was open only to males between the ages of 18 and 35. Men over the age limit and women were permitted to become associate members. As such, they still paid dues—although somewhat less than regular members—but they could not vote, hold office, or take part in its awards or training programs.

Rebellion in the Ranks

Despite the rule against women, two chapters—one in Minneapolis (1974) and the other in St. Paul (1975)—admitted women to full membership. Women became a significant presence in both local chapters, even serving on their boards of directors. As a consequence, the national organization declared all members of those chapters ineligible to run for the organization's state or national offices, to receive its awards, or to have their votes counted at the Jaycees' national conventions. The chapters then learned that the national board would meet to consider a motion to revoke their charters.

Minneapolis' and St. Paul's Jaycees immediately filed discrimination complaints with the Minnesota Department of Human Rights, claiming that if they excluded women—as the national board was demanding—they would be in violation of the state's Human Rights Act. The commissioner agreed and ordered a Human Rights Department hearing examiner to conduct an evidentiary hearing.

The Jaycees' national board fired back with a lawsuit against the commissioner and other state representatives in the U.S. District Court for the District of Minnesota. If the act were enforced, they claimed, male members would be deprived of their constitutional rights of free speech and association. The court dismissed the suit but

Exclusive Clubs and Discrimination

Inasmuch as a club truly is private, the Constitution offers little to impede its members from restricting membership. Not only is there an idea of freedom of association derived from the First Amendment, but the Constitution itself is designed to place restraints on government, not on individuals. Yet where discrimination on the basis of gender, ethnicity, or other such factors can be clearly demonstrated, and where a club is clearly public, then the Supreme Court has tended to support a "compelling state interest" that overrides the desires of the club's members to keep out others.

If an individual can compel a club to open its doors, as occurred in *Roberts*, could such an exercise of civil rights jeopardize civil liberties in some other sector? The Constitution is a document with almost nothing to say about the private lives of citizens. To accommodate the government's intrusion into personal associations in the Constitution might be equally as dangerous as permitting acts of blatant discrimination.

Source(s): Leonard W. Levy, ed. *Encyclopedia of the American Constitution.* New York: Macmillan, 1986.

---

left the national Jaycees room to sue again if the Human Rights Department examiner ruled against them.

Never Say Die

The department examiner did rule against the national board, classifying the Jaycees organization as a "place of public accommodation" within the meaning of Minnesota's Human Rights Act. Therefore, excluding women was an unfair discriminatory practice. The Jaycees renewed its suit before the district court, which then referred the question to the Minnesota Supreme Court.

Having already ruled in 1981 that the state human rights act could be applied to any "public business facility," the state supreme court also determined that the Jaycees "(a) is a 'business' in that it sells goods and extends privileges in exchange for annual membership dues; (b) is a 'public' business based on its unselective criteria; and (c) is a public business 'facility' in that it conducts its activities in fixed and mobile sites within the state of Minnesota."

The national Jaycees then amended its district court complaint to add the charge that the act, as interpreted by the Minnesota Supreme Court, was unconstitutional and overly broad. The district court upheld the act and that ruling was appealed to the Court of Appeals for the Eighth Circuit.

That court reversed the lower court decision in 1983. The Jaycees' right to determine its membership was protected by the First Amendment freedom of association, since "political and public causes, selected by the membership," is a large part of the Jaycees' reason for being. The court of appeals also held that the Minnesota act was "vague as construed and applied" and therefore in violation of the due process clause of the Fourteenth Amendment.

The Supreme Court Decides

Kathryn R. Roberts, the acting commissioner of the Minnesota Department of Human Rights, appealed to

the U.S. Supreme Court. On 18 April 1984, Richard L. Varco, Jr., argued that the act was not unconstitutionally broad or vague and that Minnesota could require the Jaycees to admit women. Carl D. Hall, Jr. argued for the Jaycees that the Fourteenth Amendment requires that laws be clearly written and that rights of free speech and association would be violated by a requirement to admit women.

Justice Brennan delivered the Court's opinion. He began by pointing out the differences between two aspects of the First Amendment's right of association: "freedom of intimate association" and "freedom of expressive association."

Associations protected by the right of intimate association, Brennan explained, would include family relationships and other associations "distinguished by such attributes as relative smallness, a high degree of selectivity in decisions to begin and maintain the affiliation, and seclusion from others in critical aspects of the relationship." Associations formed in the context of "a large business enterprise" did not involve such concerns. The Jaycees—as an organization with no other membership criteria than age and sex, and as an organization with a history of permitting the partial but routine association of women and others deemed ineligible for membership—was "clearly . . . outside of the category of relationships worthy of this kind of constitutional protection."

Turning to constitutional protection of the "freedom of expressive association," Brennan noted that "an individual's freedom to speak, worship, and to petition the government for the redress of grievances" included the "freedom to engage in group effort toward those ends . . ." So, while the right to engage in such "protected activities" was "plainly implicated" in the case under consideration, Brennan pointed out that the "right to associate for expressive purposes is not . . . absolute. Infringements on that right may be justified by regulations adopted to serve compelling state interests . . ."

Richard L. Varco, Jr., represents Kathryn R. Roberts before the U.S. Supreme Court. © Reproduced by permission of Richard L. Varco.

Minnesota had a compelling state interest in ending sex discrimination, Brennan concluded, and that interest justified the impact of its Human Rights Amendment on the Jaycees.

To further illustrate the compelling nature of the state's interest, Brennan discussed the nineteenth-century passage of public accommodation laws intended to end racial discrimination, and their expansion over time, "both with respect to the number and type of covered facilities and the groups against whom discrimination is forbidden." He referred to the Court's 1964 decision in *Heart of Atlanta Motel v. United States,* which upheld the Civil Rights Act of 1964's prohibitions on racial discrimination in places of public accommodation. In that case, Brennan quoted, the Court recognized that the law's "fundamental object . . . was to vindicate the deprivation of personal dignity that surely accompanies denials of equal access to public establishments." The Court now recognized that such a "stigmatizing injury, and the denial of equal opportunities that accompanies it, is surely felt as strongly by persons suffering discrimination on the basis of their sex as by those treated differently because of their race." *Roberts v. U.S. Jaycees* was followed by two other Supreme Court decisions granting women access to previously all-male organizations or establishments: *Rotary International v. Rotary Club of Duarte* (1987) and *New York State Club Association, Inc. v. New York City* (1988).

Related Cases

Heart of Atlanta Motel v. United States, 379 U.S. 241 (1964).

Beynon v. St. George-Dixie Lodge No. 1743, Benev. and Protective Order of Elks, 854 P.2d 513 (1993).

South Boston Allied War Veterans Council v. City of Boston, 875 F.Supp 891 (1995).

Mauro v. Arpaio, 147 F.3d 1137 (1998).

Bibliography and Further Reading

Goldstein, Leslie Friedman. *The Constitutional Rights of Women: Cases in Law and Social Change,* rev. ed. Madison: University of Wisconsin Press, 1989.

Hoff, Joan. *Law, Gender & Injustice: A Legal History of U.S. Women.* New York: New York University Press, 1991.

Mezey, Susan Gluck. *In Pursuit of Equality: Women, Public Policy, and the Federal Courts.* New York: St. Martin's Press, 1992.

O'Connor, Sandra Day. "Women and the Constitution: A Bicentennial Perspective," in *Women, Politics and the Constitution,* Naomi B. Lynn, ed. New York: Harrington Park Press, 1990.

Ross, Susan Deller, Isabelle Katz Pinzler, Deborah A. Ellis, and Kary L. Moss. *The Rights of Women: The Basic ACLU Guide to Women's Rights.* Carbondale: Southern Illinois University Press, 1993.

BOOS V. BARRY

Legal Citation: 485 U.S. 312 (1988)

Petitioners
Michael Boos, Bridget M. Brooker, J. Michael Waller, Father R. David Finzer

Respondents
Marian Barry, Mayor of Washington, D.C., and other officials of the District of Columbia

Petitioners' Claim
That Section 22-1115 of the District of Columbia Code, which forbade the display of any sign within 500 feet of a foreign embassy if that sign brings the foreign government into "public odium" or "public disrepute," and also prohibited congregation of three or more persons within 500 feet of a foreign embassy, was in violation of the First Amendment's protection of free speech.

Chief Lawyer for Petitioners
Raymond D. Battocchi

Chief Lawyer for Respondents
Edward E. Schwab

Justices for the Court
William J. Brennan, Jr., Thurgood Marshall, Sandra Day O'Connor (writing for the Court), Antonin Scalia, John Paul Stevens

Justices Dissenting
Harry A. Blackmun, William H. Rehnquist, Byron R. White (Anthony M. Kennedy did not participate)

Place
Washington, D.C.

Date of Decision
22 March 1988

Decision
The decision of the lower court was affirmed in part and reversed in part, the finding being that the display clause of Section 22-1115 was in violation of the First Amendment, but the congregation clause was not.

Significance
Boos v. Barry opened the way for more direct picketing of foreign embassies and other installations representative of a foreign government on U.S. soil. More significantly, it expanded the realm of protected speech under the First Amendment. On the other hand, it allowed certain aspects of public congregation for the purposes of protest to remain questionable. Thus it could be used, for instance, in decisions relating to protests outside abortion clinics.

In 1988, both Russia and Nicaragua were under the control of Communist governments; the regime in the latter nation being financially sponsored in large part by the leadership of the former. Examples of human rights offenses by the two governments included the imprisonment of physicist Anatoly Sakharov by the Soviet Union; the suppression of the Solidarity movement in Poland, a Soviet satellite nation at that time; and the brutal prosecution of the war with anti-government *Contra* forces by the Sandinista regime in Nicaragua. Bridget M. Brooker and Michael Boos both wished to display signs reading "RELEASE SAKHAROV" and "SOLIDARITY" in front of the Soviet embassy, and J. Michael Waller wanted to put up a sign that said "STOP THE KILLING" in front of the Nicaraguan embassy. All three wished to hold assemblies of more than two persons within 500 feet of these official buildings, and they were aware that D.C. Code Section 22-1115 prevented them from doing so. Therefore they joined with Father R. David Finzer in bringing a facial First Amendment challenge to the District of Columbia statute, naming as respondents the mayor and other law enforcement officials of the district.

Enacted by Congress in 1938, Section 22-1115 was created under the authority of Article I, Section 8, Clause 10 of the U.S. Constitution to "define and punish . . . Offenses against the Law of Nations." The law made it unlawful, within 500 feet of a foreign embassy of the District of Columbia, to display a flag, banner, placard, or other device with the purpose of intimidating, coercing, or "bring[ing] into public odium" any foreign government, or individual or organization representing that foreign government. It also prohibited persons from congregation within 500 feet of such a building or premises. (Congregation, under D.C. common law, was defined as an assemblage of three or more people.) The first part of this law, the basis for the petition by Boos and others, was called the "display clause," the second part the "congregation clause."

The respondents submitted a motion for summary judgment to the district court, which granted it, using as precedent the case of *Frend v. United States* (1938), which had upheld Section 22-1115 against First Amend-

Foreign Embassies

Along with its many federal buildings and headquarters of national organizations, the city of Washington, D.C. is dotted with foreign embassies. There are the vast facilities representing large nations which enjoy significant interaction with the United States, embassies which in many cases employ hundreds of staff members. But there are also embassies for countries such as Luxembourg, a nation smaller than many U.S. counties; or Mongolia, which has fewer people than Chicago.

Large or small, however, a certain feature applies to all embassies and consulates (commercial delegations located in cities other than the capital). That is the concept of *extraterritoriality*, an agreement of international law which exempts diplomatic personnel from the legal jurisdiction of the host country. For Americans overseas, extraterritoriality has often been a saving grace, as for instance when a U.S. citizen wrongfully accused of a crime by authorities under a dictatorial regime obtains asylum in a U.S. facility. On the other hand, the concept of extraterritoriality raises considerable ire at home, often for relatively petty reasons: for instance, Washingtonians are routinely annoyed to find cars bearing embassy license plates parked in "no parking" slots.

More serious was the abuse of extraterritoriality committed by officials at the Libyan People's Bureau (i.e. embassy) in London on 22 April 1984. After persons inside opened fire on bystanders and killed a British policewoman, British authorities demanded that the Libyans turn over the perpetrators. The Libyans refused to do so, and the incident led to the severing of diplomatic ties between Britain and Libya.

Source(s): Jentleson, Bruce W. and Thomas G. Paterson, eds. *Encyclopedia of U.S. Foreign Relations*. New York: Oxford University Press, 1997.

---

ment questions. The case went on to the U.S. Court of Appeals, District of Columbia Circuit, on which sat Robert Bork, who had recently been nominated for the Supreme Court by President Ronald Reagan and rejected by the Senate. A divided panel affirmed the motion of the lower court, but though it considered the *Frend* case "persuasive precedent," the court of appeals decided that the *Frend* decision was not binding because the Supreme Court, in the 50 years that had passed since 1938, had "developed constitutional law in ways that must be taken into account."

In reviewing *Boos v. Barry,* the court of appeals considered the display and congregation clauses separately, and found both constitutional. Though the display clause restricted speech on the basis of content, which taken by itself would be unconstitutional, in this case the court found sufficient justification in view of the "compelling governmental interest" represented, as well as the fact that the law was narrowly drawn for the specific purpose of serving that interest. With regard to the congregation clause, the court of appeals held that, properly construed, the clause simply allows police to disperse crowds when those crowds present a threat to peace or security, and therefore is permissible under the First Amendment.

A Five-Part Decision

Justice O'Connor delivered the opinion for the Court, a complex five-part decision over the second part of which the Court was split. In Part I, she stated that the Court reversed the court of appeals with regard to the display clause, but affirmed it in the area of the con-

gregation clause. In this she was joined by Justices Brennan, Marshall, Stevens, and Scalia.

The Split Over Part II

In Part II-A, Justice O'Connor, joined by Justices Stevens and Scalia, found that the display clause was indeed content-based, since its prohibition of picketing was based on whether or not the picket signs were critical of the government in question. Even if it were construed as content-neutral because it does not choose between different viewpoints, she said, it still violated the First Amendment by prohibiting an entire category of speech—signs critical of a foreign government. She also rejected the argument that the clause was content-neutral on the basis of the claim that its purpose was not to suppress free speech, but rather "the secondary effect" of upholding the obligation to protect foreign diplomats from speech offensive to them. She used as her basis *Renton v. Playtime Theatres* (1986), which established that the phrase "secondary effects" applies to secondary features associated with a type of speech, but not with its content.

Justices Brennan and Marshall, while agreeing with O'Connor that even under the *Renton* analysis, the display clause was content-based, disagreed with her use of it as a basis. Since the *Renton* case related to sexually explicit materials and not political speech, they said, it presented "dangers" in that it could be used to deny free speech on the basis of the possible offense such speech could cause. Therefore they were opposed to content-based denial of free speech regardless of the reasoning behind it.

Part II-B also turned on the issue of content-based political speech, and in this O'Connor was joined by the same majority as in Part I. Citing an earlier case involving pornographer Larry Flynt, publisher of *Hustler* magazine, and the Rev. Jerry Falwell, O'Connor noted that the Court had made it clear that American citizens must tolerate offensive speech in order to preserve freedom. In the present situation, she said, the Court was not persuaded that there was a compelling difference between American citizens and foreign officials which would entitle the latter to be protected from offensive speech. After review of possible arguments, the Court held that even if the interest of protecting the dignity of foreign officials could be shown as "compelling," the display clause was in violation of the First Amendment.

Parts III, IV, and V

The Court was unanimous on Part III, which addressed the petitioners' facial overbreadth challenge to the congregation clause, holding that it gave the police unrestricted authority to suppress demonstrations. While the clause could be considered to violate free speech if taken alone, the Court stated, in line with the display clause and the Court of Appeals' interpretation of the law as applying only to the dispersal of demonstrations directed at an embassy, it was sufficiently narrow not to constitute a violation of free speech. Therefore the Court upheld the lower court's ruling.

In Part IV, the Court addressed the petitioners' claims that their right to equal protection was in question because Section 22-1116 excludes labor picketing from the forms of protest prohibited under Section 22-1115. This, however, was not a valid argument,

O'Connor stated, because 22-1116 could not be construed to protect violent labor picketing. Since the display clause had already been found unconstitutional, 22-1116 could only apply to the congregation clause. So, if labor picketers were not violent, their protests were in effect no different from any other kind of protests—all of which would be permitted so long as they constituted no threat to the peace. (Thus the Court's ruling on 22-1115 would make 22-1116 superfluous.) The Court was unanimous on Part IV.

In Part V, O'Connor spoke for the same majority as in Parts I and II-B when she concluded that the display clause was unconstitutional on its face because it was content-based and not sufficiently narrow to be construed as serving a compelling state interest. The Court also concluded in Part V that the congregation clause was not unconstitutional on its face. Thus the Court reversed the judgment of the Court of Appeals in part, and affirmed it in part.

In a dissent joined by Justices Blackmun and White, Chief Justice Rehnquist agreed with Judge Bork's decision in the lower court, upholding the display clause. The three dissenters agreed with the rest of the Court that the congregation clause was not unconstitutional.

Related Cases

Frend v. United States, 69 App. D.C. 281,100 (1938).
Renton v. Playtime Theaters, 475 U.S. 41 (1986).
Hustler Magazine v. Falwell, 485 U.S. 46 (1988).

Bibliography and Further Reading

Hall, Kermit L., ed. *The Oxford Companion to the Supreme Court of the United States.* New York: Oxford University Press, 1992.

RUTAN V. REPUBLICAN PARTY OF ILLINOIS

Legal Citation: 497 U.S. 62 (1990)

Petitioner
Cynthia Rutan, et al.

Respondent
Republican Party of Illinois, et al.

Petitioner's Claim
That the Republican governor of Illinois violated their First Amendment freedom of association by requiring they support the Republican Party to receive state jobs, transfers, recalls, or promotions.

Chief Lawyer for Petitioner
Mary Lee Leahy

Chief Lawyer for Respondent
Thomas P. Sullivan

Justices for the Court
Harry A. Blackmun, William J. Brennan, Jr. (writing for the Court), Thurgood Marshall, John Paul Stevens, Byron R. White

Justices Dissenting
Anthony M. Kennedy, Sandra Day O'Connor, William H. Rehnquist, Antonin Scalia

Place
Washington, D.C.

Date of Decision
21 June 1990

Decision
The Court found for the petitioner, expanding the First Amendment protection against dismissal from low-level government positions based on party affiliation, which had been established in two earlier cases.

Significance
Rutan was a further blow to the patronage system at all levels of government.

During most of the nineteenth century, American politicians followed the maxim, "To the victor belong the spoils." When a political party took control of a government, it appointed its loyal supporters throughout the bureaucracy. This "spoils system," also called patronage, helped parties earn money, as people who wanted government jobs contributed campaign funds, and sometimes even kicked back part of their pay to the party. Patronage, however, also led to illiterate clerks filling low-level jobs, and other incompetence at all levels of government.

Criticism of patronage grew, and in 1883 the first Civil Service Act was passed. To obtain most federal jobs, prospective employees now had to take an exam to show they were qualified. Test scores, not political affiliation, assured a job. Only high-level officials were appointed by government leaders, based on party loyalty. Over the years, civil service reform spread to state and local governments, and Congress passed a major Civil Service Act as recently as 1978.

Despite these reforms, issues about government hiring practices and party affiliation still stirred controversy. In 1980, Illinois governor Jim Thompson, a Republican, ordered a hiring freeze for government workers. When an existing job had to be filled, because of death, resignation, or the like, Thompson's office approved every new hire. This system might not have caused a problem, except that support of the Republican party seemed to be the major criterion for getting a state job.

State Workers Challenge the System
Cynthia Rutan, a rehabilitation counselor, had worked for the state of Illinois since 1974. Starting in 1981, she was denied promotions to supervisory positions because, she claimed, she was not a Republican faithful. A road equipment operator for the state, Franklin Taylor, said he was denied a promotion because local Republican officials did not support him. Three other people had similar experiences. James W. Moore had not been hired because Republican officials did not back him; two others were not recalled after layoffs because they were Democrats. The five brought suit against the Republican Party of Illinois, claiming Gov-

ernor Thompson's hiring policy was unconstitutional under the First Amendment.

As well as protecting freedom of speech and religion, the First Amendment guarantees the freedom of assembly. The Supreme Court has interpreted that to mean people have the freedom to associate with any group they want to associate with. Low-level government workers, for example, should be able to join any political party and not have that membership impact their employment. The Court had taken that position in *Elrod v. Burns* (1976) and *Branti v. Finkel* (1980). In those cases, the Court said a person's political association was not grounds for dismissal from a government position. Now, Rutan and the other Illinois workers wanted the same protection in their circumstances.

In district court, Rutan and the other plaintiffs' claims were dismissed. When the case went to the court of appeals, the court affirmed part of the lower court's decision and reversed another. The appeals court said that basing hiring decisions on political affiliation did not contradict the First Amendment, so it dismissed Moore's claim. But the court ordered a rehearing for Rutan and the other three plaintiffs. The court also noted that the precedents set in *Elrod* and *Branti* only applied to employment practices that were the "substantial equivalent of a dismissal." Rutan, Taylor, and Moore then asked the Supreme Court to review this constitutional standard, as well as the dismissal of Moore's claim.

Another Blow to Patronage

In a 5-4 vote, the Court said the state of Illinois, or any government, could not refuse to transfer, promote, recall, or hire workers because of their political affiliation. "To the victor," began Justice Brennan's opinion, "belong only those spoils that may be constitutionally obtained." Brennan relied heavily on the arguments in *Elrod* and *Branti,* and said that although no one has a right to a government job, the government may not deny a job on grounds that deny constitutional freedom—such as freedom of association.

The Court was clear that its ruling applied, as in the past, only to low-level employees. It recognized the need for an administration to choose higher-ranking officials based on political loyalty. However, people like Rutan, Taylor, and Moore should not have to compromise their political beliefs to ensure favorable treatment in the government workplace.

Justice Scalia wrote a lengthy dissent, arguing that the issue of political patronage ". . . is a policy question to be decided by the people's representatives." Scalia believed that patronage had helped strengthen the two-party system in America, and its longevity argued for its effectiveness. Justice Stevens, in a concurring opinion, responded directly to Scalia's dissent. Regarding the point on the longevity of patronage, Stevens said the

James Thompson, Governor of Illinois. © AP/Wide World Photos.

same argument could have been made for slavery, but that was hardly grounds for promoting it.

Scalia not only argued against the decision in *Rutan,* but also wanted to overturn the earlier rulings in *Elrod* and *Branti.* Those decisions, he said, "by contributing to the decline of party strength, have also contributed to the growth of interest-group politics in the last decade."

Coincidentally, the *Rutan* decisions came down on the same day the Senate refused to override a veto by President George Bush. Bush had rejected a bill that would have let federal employees become more involved in political activities. Legal reporter Linda Greenhouse, of the *New York Times,* saw the two events as complementary: "One says, in effect, that government has to keep those whom it hires out of politics, while the other says it has to keep politics out of the decision of whom to hire."

Related Cases

West Virginia Board of Education v. Barnette, 319 U.S. 624 (1943).
Keyishian v. Board of Regents of University of New York, 385 U.S. 589 (1967).
Buckley v. Valeo, 424 U.S. 1 (1976).
Elrod v. Burns, 427 U.S. 347 (1976).
Branti v. Finkel, 445 U.S. 507 (1980).
Wygant v. Jackson Board of Education, 476 U.S. 267 (1986).

Bibliography and Further Reading

Desai, Uday, and John A. Hamman. "Images and Reality in Local Government Personnel Practices." *Public Administration Review,* July-August 1994, pp. 391.

Roback, Thomas H., and Janet C. Vinzant. "The Consitution and the Patronage-merit Debate." *Public Personnel Management,* fall 1994, pp. 501.

Vinazant, Janet C., and Thomas H. Roback, "Dilemmas of Legitimacy." *Administration & Society,* February 1994, pp. 443.

TIMMONS V. TWIN CITIES AREA NEW PARTY

Legal Citation: 520 U.S. 351 (1997)

Petitioner
Michele L. Timmons, Acting Director, Ramsey County Department of Property Records and Revenue

Respondent
Twin Cities Area New Party

Petitioner's Claim
A candidate running for office could not participate in elections as a nominee representing more then one political party. Minnesota's statute imposing prohibition of "fusion appearance" on a ballot, therefore, did not jeopardize associational rights.

Chief Lawyer for Petitioner
Richard S. Slowes

Chief Lawyer for Respondent
Laurence H. Tribe

Justices for the Court
Stephen Breyer, Anthony M. Kennedy, Sandra Day O'Connor, William H. Rehnquist (writing for the Court), Antonin Scalia, Clarence Thomas

Justices Dissenting
Ruth Bader Ginsburg, John Paul Stevens, David H. Souter

Place
Washington D.C.

Date of Decision
28 April 1997

Decision
Respondent's (New Party's) constitutional rights under First and Fourteenth Amendment were not violated by provisions of Minnesota's statute prohibiting "fusion" candidates. Statutory restrictions were held permissible.

Significance
The fusion ban imposed under Minnesota statute was challenged by respondents (New Party), because it imposed severe burdens that restrained associational rights of minor political parties. The U.S. Supreme Court decided that the "anti-fusion law" was not a burden that infringed on the respondent's rights (i.e., prohibiting New Party's nomination of a candidate already running for office as a candidate of another political party). Conversely, respondent believed that the right to associate and create their electoral strategy should be protected by the Constitution's First and Fourteenth Amendment.

Electoral procedures evolved through American history in order to reduce possibilities of electoral abuse. After 1888, balloting protocols changed to the "Australian ballot system" (ballots contained either names of candidates and the parties by which they were nominated). It was considered an important departure from the then, widely-accepted balloting custom when voters did not know which party a candidate belonged to (ballots contained only the names of candidates).

Since 1888, when balloting adapted to the new system, states have dealt with many reforms, bans, multiple party nominations, and other changes and exceptions to the electoral process but the basic format of American balloting is still the Australian ballot system. One of the outcomes of such procedural change meant that fusion candidacies were not supported by many states. In fact, many states responded to multiple nominations by barring and prohibiting them.

In April of 1994, a minor political party, Twin Cities Area New Party, chose Andy Dawkins as their candidate running for state office as a nominee of the Minnesota Democratic Farmer Labor Party. He did not oppose the dual nomination and, in effect, thus established double candidacy for the 1994 general elections. Dawkins did not actually become a New Party member, he just signed the "required affidavit of candidacy" needed for nomination by New Party. Under Minnesota statute, the state banned his candidacy as nominee of two parties. Because that statute prohibited a second "appearance" on the ballot of a candidate already nominated by one party, New Party's nominating petition was denied under Minnesota law.

Believing that their associational rights under the First and Fourteenth Amendments were violated, New Party challenged Minnesota's statute and its "anti-fusion laws." Fusion is defined as nomination of one candidate by more than one political party. The U.S. District Court ruled in favor of the petitioner finding that "Minnesota's fusion ban was valid and [a] nondiscriminatory regulation of the election process." However, the U.S. Court of Appeals reversed the decision because of "restrictive and burdening" provisions under Minnesota's law that jeopardized the constitutional rights of New Party. They found no merit in the reasons which the state felt justified excluding "fusion candidacies for elected office."

The U.S. Court of Appeals decided in favor of the respondent, New Party. They held that provisions under Minnesota's law burdened New Party's freedom to participate in elections with nominees which the respondent believed to be the best representatives of their "ideologies and preferences." The court found no compelling state concern which justified anti-fusion laws banning multiple party nominations. The decision posited that because minor parties usually broaden their chances to win elections by using the benefits of fusion and political association, the preclusive regulations of Minnesota law lessened New Party's chances of winning and, therefore, intruded on constitutionally-guaranteed associational rights.

Arguing Fusion

The First Amendment enables political parties to associate and freely express their political platform. Parties are absolutely free to determine who will represent party ideas and send the party message to voters. As pointed out in *FindLaw Annotated Constitution,* the political association between parties is considered an "integral part of basic constitutional freedom." However, in order to achieve party in political competition, minor parties usually use candidate "fusion," (multiple nominations) as a convenient way to increase their chances to win an election. New Party believed that Minnesota's "fusion ban" was therefore a wholly inappropriate prohibition that violated their rights under the First and Fourteenth Amendment. They claimed that nomination of another party's candidate was a proper and legal way to deliver their political platform to potential voters. The attorney for New Party reasoned that parties have an unquestionable right to choose who will be the bearer of their political ideas. Thus, in presenting its case before the court, counsel for New Party contended that a "fusion ban burdens its right to communicate its choice of nominees on the ballot on terms equal to those offered other parties, and the right of the party's supporters and other voters to receive information." Further, the respondent's attorney argued that New Party did not believe there existed any valid state interest to preclude nomination of a candidate who was already nominated for elections by another party.

Representing the petitioner before the U.S. Supreme Court, counsel for the state of Minnesota argued that minor parties must use their own political platforms and avoid exploitation of other candidates' popularity to make a significant "step forward" in the "political struggle" for voters. He maintained that, as enacted, the Minnesota's statute was justified in order to provide electoral stability, prevent voter confusion and ballot manipulation, and promote candidate competition. The state felt attaining voters could be misled if New

Party was allowed to take advantage of the popularity of another party's candidate. Counsel for the petitioner argued that access to a ballot should be determined by a party's own merit, rather than a "fusion strategy," which could confuse potential voters into voting for a particular, popular candidate even if they were not acquainted with the (fusion) party's own views.

The U.S. Supreme Court agreed with the plaintiff's claim and overturned the appellate court. The majority decision held that Minnesota's statute did not contain restrictive regulations which intruded on the rights of political parties that employ fusion candidacy. They considered Minnesota's law a reasonable act which did not seriously infringe on freedoms of association under the First and Fourteenth Amendment. Although the Court recognized that the Constitution guarantees substantial rights regarding political association, they believed that a ban on double candidacies prevented electoral abuse and maintained electoral fairness.

In rendering their decision, the Court cited as precedent the same cases which New Party's attorney used to support his arguments in court: *Eu v. San Francisco County Democratic Central Committee* (1989) and *Tashijan v. Republican Party of Connecticut* (1992). Unlike counsel for the respondent, Justice Rehnquist found no similarity—the cases cited, he pointed out, violated a core of associational rights and interfered in the internal structure of political parties. Conversely, Minnesota statute did not ban New Party from endorsing or choosing members; they were only forbidden to nominate persons who were already candidates endorsed by another party. The Court reasoned that if New Party wanted to have Andy Dawkins as their representative on the ballot, they had to convince him to be their candidate and forego nomination by another party. Rehnquist further reasoned that Minnesota's statute did not prevent New Party from independently choosing to endorse any candidate they wished. The statute did not deny political participation in elections nor intrude on how the New Party organized politically.

In writing the majority decision, Rehnquist emphasized that although the provisions of First Amendment provide minor parties with the possibility of creating fusion strategies which may enable them to enlarge the popular base of their nominees, that possibility should not be considered a privilege that states may not restrain. He reasoned that because Minnesota's fusion ban did not prohibit New Party's access to the ballot that the restrictive requirements of the statute were not "severe burdens" that jeopardized New Party's First and Fourteenth Amendment associational rights. Burdens imposed by Minnesota's statute were not so high as to be considered irregular, rather, they recognized the state's interest in protecting correctness of competition. Moreover, not permitting fusion candidacies supported the state's interest in maintaining the integrity of their political system because, Rehnquist wrote, "the State need not narrowly tailor the means it chooses to promote ballot integrity."

The majority opinion further cited a previous ban upheld by the Supreme Court which contained restrictive provisions much more prohibitive than the Minnesota statute. (A disaffiliation rule in California, *Storer v. Brown* [1974], precluded any appearance on a ballot if a candidate was previously affiliated with another party during the electoral year.) Conversely, the only restraint under Minnesota's law was to forbid the possibility of a candidate appearing twice on the same ballot due to her/his nomination by more than one party. While the Court explained that they did not depreciate the "wisdom of fusion," they asserted that Minnesota's fusion ban was "sufficiently weighty to justify the limitation on Party's rights," which, in turn, served to preserve the traditional, American two-party system.

Impact

The Court's decision was opposed bitterly by third parties who felt robbed of a strategy that, once viable, served to enlarge their influence in the political process. Among dissenters, the American Civil Liberties Union was the loudest in criticizing the ruling of the Court, calling its decision a "strike down of anti-fusion law." The crux of their objection reasoned that if the two party system was permanently privileged in the courts, minor political parties would never get an opportunity to achieve political parity.

Regardless of opposition by minority parties and independent organizations, the U.S. Supreme Court jus-

tified the existence of the state of Minnesota's anti-fusion statute and found it only restrictive on a party's right to choose and select candidates already nominated by another party—burdens imposed were, therefore, justifiable and minor. The Court held that Minnesota's law served to avoid ballot manipulation and factionalism and justifiably maintained a two-party system as well. In essence, the decision of the Court did not recognize multiple nominations as a significant, legitimate means by which minor parties might achieve their political interests. The decision of the U.S. Supreme Court supported an American tendency to preserve and privilege a two-party system by limiting association rights of minority parties.

Related Cases

Storer v. Brown, 415 U.S. 724 (1974).

Anderson v. Celebrezze, 460 U.S. 780 (1983).

Munro v. Socialist Workers Party, 479 U.S. 189 (1986).

Tashijan v. Republican Party of Conn., 479 U.S. 208 (1986).

Eu v. San Francisco County Democratic Central Comm., 489 U.S. 214 (1989).

Norman v. Reed, 502 U.S. 279 (1992).

Burdick v. Takushi, 504 U.S. 428 (1992).

Bibliography and Further Reading

American Civil Liberties Union *ACLU in the Courts: ACLU Summary of the 1996 Supreme Court Term Major Civil Liberties* http://www.aclu.org

Hansen, Richard L. "Entrenching the Duopoly." *Supreme Court Review*, Annual 1997, pp. 331.

FREEDOM OF RELIGION

Religious Belief

Among the unique characteristics of being human is the ability to create and communicate abstract thoughts such as religious beliefs. For much of human history religion has served as a means to socially unify individuals into groups. Early in the human experience, religion likely served to explain natural events and create order out of the world. The doctrine of salvation evolved based on the belief that individuals are in danger, either physically or spiritually, from which they must be saved. Religion thus served to order and regulate peoples' lives in addition to defining their place in the natural world. Religion has also served as an expression of a community's moral values and collective beliefs. Religious doctrines explain how the world is and how it should be.

Through the Constitution the country's founders created a world in which religion could flourish, but not dominate social order. But, at the time the Constitution was drafted, this country had a relatively homogeneous, mostly Protestant Christian population. Religion was primarily a set of beliefs and practices associated with a divine being, and was thereby theistic in nature. In the increasingly secular (non-religious) world of twentieth century Western Society, freedom of religion gained a different meaning than in eighteenth century America. The eight major religions practiced to various degrees in the United States by the late twentieth century were Christianity, Judaism, Islam, Buddhism, Confucianism, Hinduism, and Taoism. Though state and federal laws cannot interfere with such diverse religious beliefs and opinions, laws can restrict actual practice. Deciding what specific circumstances allow governmental interference with religious conduct has formed the basis for much confusion and debate.

Growth of Religious Tolerance

Religious intolerance of seventeenth century England, in which religious strife precipitated political turmoil, greatly influenced the colonists. However, the various colonies treated religious toleration differently. The Puritans, greatly persecuted in England, imposed their own religious values in Massachusetts and became the persecutors. Maryland, in an effort to attract settlers, passed the Religion Toleration Act in 1649 marking an early recognition of the freedom of belief. However, the act primarily addressed the freedom of Christians. John Locke, famed English philosopher and early proponent of freedom of thought, wrote the Carolina constitution in 1669. Possibly the most influential action in the colonies regarding religious toleration was the adoption of the 1663 Charter of Rhode Island. The charter, actually created in reaction to persecution by the Puritans, marked the first inclusion of religious liberty in a colony charter.

Across the ocean in the mother country, the adoption of the English Bill of Rights of 1689, though addressing social classes rather than individuals, planted more seeds for the recognition of human rights. The document built on the much earlier 1215 Magna Carta of feudal England which initiated the idea certain fundamental rights existed upon which states could not infringe.

By the 1740s a religious revival movement known as the Great Awakening swept through the colonies spurred by evangelical ministers. The Anglican Church of England became a chief target of dissatisfaction while broader support for various minority sects found in the colonies grew. Consequently, ties with England eroded and the expansion of the free exercise to worship spurred an increasing mood of independence.

By the late 1700s colonial leaders were well under the influence of the Enlightenment, a philosophical movement primarily in Europe promoting freedom of the mind and a more individual approach to religious, social, political, and economic issues through reason and science. Previously unquestioned authority was no longer blindly followed by many. More specifically to religion, the Enlightenment brought skepticism about many Christian beliefs. The right of people to revolt against oppressive authority rose from the movement.

Framers of the Constitution captured this mood in the First Amendment which states, "Congress shall make no law respecting an establishment of religion, or prohibiting the free exercise thereof." Thus was born two key constitutional clauses on religious freedom to guide the new nation: the Establishment Clause and the Free Exercise Clause. However, the idea of religious freedom in early U.S. history consisted of government support and approval of Judeo-Christian faiths and toleration of others. But as James Madison pointed out, toleration is not the same as full liberty.

Religion and the Courts

The earliest court cases addressing free exercise of religion focused on the issue of polygamy practiced among the Mormons (members of the Church of Jesus Christ of Latter-Day Saints). Federal territorial laws in Utah and Idaho prohibited plural marriages and denied the right to vote to those who advocated such lifestyles, respectively. Perhaps largely influenced by the overwhelming Protestant majority in the nation at the time, the Court in *Reynolds v. United States* (1879) and *Davis v. Beason* (1890) upheld the restrictive laws against polygamist marriages and ruled the free exercise of religion "must be subordinate to the criminal laws of the country." Similarly, in *Jacobson v. Massachusetts* (1905) the Court upheld state law requiring mandatory vaccination opposed by Seventh-Day Adventists based on religious convictions. Like criminal laws, public safety took precedence over religious belief.

Major changes in the American population occurred around the beginning of the twentieth century. Protestant domination further dwindled as immigration from eastern and southern Europe increased the numbers of Catholics and Jews. The United States was becoming more pluralistic (multiple religious traditions) just as it was becoming more secular driven by new Darwinian scientific ideas and increasing interest in socialism. The Court overturned an Oregon state law enacted during a wave of anti-Catholic sentiment requiring all children to attend public schools in *Pierce v. Society of Sisters* (1925).

In the twentieth century, freedom of religion became integrally related to the other protected freedoms in the First Amendment—speech, press, and association. What good are one's views, if they cannot be freely expressed and practiced jointly with others? Such relationships were highlighted in the 1938 *Lovell v. City of Griffin* case involving Jehovah's Witnesses. A local ordinance prohibited distribution of leaflets on public property, but the Court ruled the ordinance was too broad a restraint on the press, and hence was unconstitutional.

The 1940s brought a series of important free exercise rulings. In *Cantwell v. Connecticut* (1940) the Court extended the Free Exercise Clause to the states by overturning a Connecticut state law that prohibited solicitation for religious causes without a license certifying the religion as *bona fide*. The Court held that the entire First Amendment had been incorporated into the Fourteenth Amendment, and thus were included in one's right to due process of law. Freedom of religion became

an assumed fundamental right, free of any level of governmental intervention. In 1943 the Court in *Murdock v. Pennsylvania* held that a peddler's license fee applied to door-to-door sales of religious literature constituted a tax on the free exercise of religion, and thus was unconstitutional. Also in 1943 in *West Virginia State Board of Education v. Barnette,* the Court broke from a standard weighing the secular purpose of a rule by holding that a requirement that school children must salute the flag on a daily basis was unconstitutional when conflicting with their Jehovah Witness religious beliefs. Justice Robert H. Jackson wrote, "we apply the . . . Constitution with no fear that freedom to be intellectually and spiritually diverse . . . will disintegrate the social organization. To believe that patriotism will not flourish if patriotic ceremonies are voluntary and spontaneous instead of a compulsory routine is to make an unflattering estimate of the appeal of our institutions to free minds." In the 1944 *United States v. Ballard* case, the Court also held that the government cannot question the truth of religious beliefs, even if fraud may be involved.

The secular purpose test commonly applied by the Court in the 1940s and 1950s was exemplified in a 1961 case. In *Braunfeld v. Brown* the Court upheld a state Sunday-closing law challenged by an Orthodox Jewish store-owner. The owner argued he needed to be open for business on Sundays due to his closure on Saturdays for religious observances. The Court found no violation of the Free Exercise Clause because the closing law only made his religious practice more expensive, but did not restrict it. The Court found the goals sufficiently secular with no other practical means to avoid the indirect burden on religious practice.

The 1960s and 1970s brought tougher restrictions on government involvement in religious matters. In 1963 in *Sherbert v. Verner* the Court established the stricter "compelling interest" test. Only a compelling state interest could justify restrictions on religious liberty. The Court reinstated unemployment compensation benefits to a Seventh-Day Adventist fired for refusing to work Saturdays, her Sabbath. The *Sherbert* test was later applied when Amish parents refused to send their children to high school because the values taught were contrary to Amish beliefs (*Wisconsin v. Yoder* [1972]). The Court in *Yoder* found no compelling reason for enforcement of the state law against Amish citizens.

The Changing Concept of Religion

After World War II and the inception of the Cold War, a revival of religion grew again but this time more integrally, including Catholics and Jews into a new Judeo-Christian tradition reflecting the ever increasing pluralism. Although Congress amended the Pledge of Allegiance by adding "under God" after "One nation," belief systems not based on the belief in a divine being gained prominence in the United States, including Buddhism, Taoism, and "Secular Humanism." In *Torcaso v. Watkins* (1961), the Court wrote that "those religions based on a belief in the existence of God as against those religions founded on different beliefs" may not be favored. Military draft cases of the 1960s broadened the view of religion to include non-traditional belief systems. The Court held in 1965 that a person did not have to believe in a Supreme Being, a theistic belief, to claim conscientious objector status to military service. In 1970 the Court held this status applied to persons objecting to war simply on moral grounds. Theistic religions could not be favored over non-theistic beliefs.

With the continually changing perception of what religion was, in 1981 a circuit court in *Africa v. Pennsylvania* attempted to define religion in a new expanded form. For a belief to be religious it must address fundamental questions about deep and imponderable matters, and be comprehensive rather than narrow in scope. It may commonly involve tangible symbols such as clergy or texts. These traits would tend to distinguish religions from personal philosophical views.

Debates over what religion is in constitutional law persisted as religious values and beliefs became increasingly important in U.S. politics. The concept must be broad and inclusive enough to recognize a variety of faiths, yet not so broad as to hinder government in supporting moral goals. Some suggested using different definitions for the two religious clauses with a narrower perception of traditional religions under the Free Exercise Clause, and more broadly belief systems of all types under the Establishment Clause. Proponents of narrower definitions fell back to what the framers considered religion, which was theistic and not just moral views on subjects. To them belief in a superior power distinguished religion from moral beliefs. Such would not necessarily be the case with the narrower interpretation.

Toward a More Neutral Government

In the late 1970s, social backlash to a series of Court cases, primarily concerning the Establishment Clause, led to fundamental changes in American politics and, eventually, the makeup of the Court. Some saw the backlash as a response to free exercise concepts posing a threat to the declining white Judeo-Christian dominance as the character of the U.S. population changed. Importantly, in 1990 the Court backed away from the strict *Sherbert* compelling interest test in *Employment Division v. Smith*. The Court held that Oregon state law could prohibit sacramental use of peyote without violating free exercise. The Court created a neutrality test in which a law could be upheld if it were determined "a valid and neutral law of general applicability" that happens to infringe on religious practices.

By the late 1990s the role of free exercise still meant government could not: (1) interfere with religious belief; (2) restrict religious expression without passing the strict standards of free speech; and, (3) treat religious activities in a discriminatory manner. In regard to the third element, *Smith* more clearly established that government could restrict religious activity no matter how minimal government interest may be if the law is neutral. Neutral meant restrictions apply to all citizens equally regardless of their religious beliefs. By significantly increasing the ability of states to interfere with religious practice, the *Smith* case held that protection of religious practices often falls more into the political realm of legal accommodation rather than being constitutionally required.

Dropping the compelling interest test in *Smith* spurred proponents of broad free exercise rights to seek other avenues for legal protection, including federal and state laws and state constitutions. In the 1993 book *The Culture of Disbelief*, author Stephen Carter argued that for religious exercise to be truly free, people must be free to engage in practices the larger society condemns. Also in 1993 Congress passed the Religious Freedom Restoration Act which reinstated the compelling interest standard. However, in 1997 the Court ruled against the constitutionality of the act in *City of Boerne v. Flores* as it applied to state and local governments. The decision was based on Congress overstepping its constitutional separation of powers authority and impinging on Supreme Court responsibilities.

After four centuries in a progression toward greater freedom of religion, the public debate over the role of religion in society highlighted a major feature of American life. Balancing between protection of individuals' religious beliefs, their social duties, and the protection of the rights of others continued to be at the core of discourse.

See also: **Establishment of Religion**

Bibliography and Further Reading
Carter, Stephen. *The Culture of Disbelief: How American Law and Politics Trivialize Religious Devotion*. New York: Basic Books, 1993.

Choper, Jesse H. *Securing Religious Liberty: Principles for Judicial Interpretation of Religion Clauses*. Chicago: The University of Chicago Press, 1995.

Evans, Bette Novit. *Interpreting the free exercise of religion: The Constitution and American Pluralism*. Chapel Hill, NC: University of North Carolina Press, 1997.

Frankel, Marvin E. *Faith and Freedom: Religious Liberty in America*. New York: Hill and Wang, 1994.

Kramnick, Isaac, and R. Laurence Moore. *The Godless Constitution: The Case Against Religious Correctness*. New York: W. W. Norton & Company, 1996.

Lynn, Barry W., Marc D. Stern, and Oliver S. Thomas. *The Right to Religious Liberty: The Basic ACLU Guide to Religious Rights.* Carbondale: Southern Illinois University Press, 1995.

Noonan, John T., Jr. *The Lustre of Our Country: The American Experience of Religious Freedom.* Berkeley: University of California Press, 1998.

Smith, Steven D. *Foreordained Failure: The Quest for a Constitutional Principle of Religious Freedom.* New York: Oxford University Press, 1995.

TENNESSEE V. SCOPES

Legal Citation: 278 S.W. 57 (1925)

Plaintiff
State of Tennessee

Defendant
John Thomas Scopes

Chief Prosecutors
William Jennings Bryan; A.T. Stewart, Attorney General of Tennessee

Chief Defense Lawyers
Clarence Darrow, Arthur Garfield Hays, Dudley Field Malone

Judge
John T. Raulston

Place
Dayton, Tennessee

Date of Decision
21 July 1925

Decision
Guilty; however, neither side won the case because the decision was reversed on a technicality involving the judge's error in imposing a fine that legally could only be set by the jury.

Significance
The trial checked the influence of Fundamentalism in public education and stripped William Jennings Bryan of his dignity as a key figure in American political history. It also marked the displacement of religious faith and rural values by scientific skepticism and cosmopolitanism as the dominant strains in American thought.

Rarely has the American psyche been so at odds with itself as in the early 1920s. In the cities, Americans were dancing to the opening bars of the Jazz Age, debating Sigmund Freud's theories and swigging bootleg liquor in defiance of Prohibition. In the rural heartland, particularly in the South, believers in old-fashioned values were caught up in a wave of religious revivalism. Preachers damned modern scientific rationalism in all its guises and upheld a strict and literal interpretation of the Bible as the only source of truth. A showdown between modernists and traditionalists to decide which would dominate American culture seemed inevitable. Both sides itched for a decisive battle.

Fundamentalists were particularly galled by the gains modernism had made in public schools, where the teaching of Charles Darwin's theory of evolution by natural selection had supplanted the Biblical story of creation. To them, it seemed their tax dollars were being spent to turn their own children against—even to scoff at—the religion of their parents. Led by William Jennings Bryan, the thrice-defeated presidential candidate of populism, the Fundamentalists tried to drive the Darwinian "heresy" out of the schools by legislative fiat.

In Tennessee a bill sponsored by John Washington Butler was enacted in February of 1925, declaring it unlawful for a teacher in any school supported by state funds "to teach any theory that denies the story of the divine creation of man as taught in the Bible, and to teach instead that man has descended from a lower order of animals." Fearful that if the Tennessee law went unchallenged other states would soon pass similar bills, the American Civil Liberties Union (ACLU) immediately announced it would defend any teacher charged with violating the Butler Act.

A few weeks later, in the little town of Dayton, a transplanted New Yorker with Darwinian views got into a debate at the local drugstore soda fountain with two Fundamentalist lawyers. However much they fought over evolution and whether mankind and monkeys were close relatives, they quickly agreed that a trial to test the law would do wonders for Dayton's commerce. The 24-year-old science teacher of the local high school, John Thomas Scopes, was recruited that very afternoon

Teaching Evolutionism

In most science classrooms in public schools across the country, students learn that the origin of life on this planet evolved over millions of years. For many Americans, however, the theory of evolution is just one possible start of life on earth and not necessarily the correct one. These opponents of evolution-based teaching look to the biblical account in Genesis for the beginnings of organic life. They say that evolution does not offer an explanation between the vast differences between humans and other living forms. They contend that there is no scientific validity to the theory of evolution.

But evolution advocates cite the fact that the scientific community accepts the theory of evolution as the only acceptable scientific view. They state that there is substantial evidence to support Charles Darwin's theory of evolution through natural selection. Natural selection, as described by Darwin in 1858, is the process that allows a species to evolve and adapt to its environment over a period of time. This happens when a species has a certain feature that enables it to survive and then passes that feature onto its offspring.

Source(s): Spaid, Elizabeth Levitan. "Scopes Revisited: South Puts Creationism Into Classroom." *The Christian Science Monitor*, 8 March 1996.

to be the legal guinea pig. Just as quickly, the ACLU confirmed it was prepared to defend Scopes.

Using a state-approved textbook, Scopes taught a lesson on evolutionary theory on 24 April to his Rhea County High School science class. Arrested on 7 May, Scopes was quickly indicted by the grand jury, setting the stage for what newspaper headline writers were already calling the "Monkey Trial."

The Circus Comes to Dayton

The legal teams fielded by both sides guaranteed the press attention they and Dayton's business leaders craved. The ACLU dispatched its chief attorney, Arthur Garfield Hays, and his partner, Dudley Field Malone, along with Clarence Darrow. Darrow, who had made his reputation by defending controversial clients, became the chief lawyer for the defense. A militant agnostic, he had long been on a personal crusade against resurgent Fundamentalism, and he saw the *Scopes* trial as the perfect opportunity to kick the wobbly intellectual props out from under that ideology.

Personifying the Fundamentalist world view, the star of the prosecution team was none other than William Jennings Bryan. No one was more holier-than-thou or more effective on the stump in defending old-fashioned rural America's Fundamentalist values than "The Great Commoner," as he liked to be called.

Pro- and anti-evolutionists alike billed the trial as a winner-take-all debate between incompatible ideologies, a forensic Armageddon between religion and science, faith and reason, traditional and modern values, the forces of light and the forces of darkness. Scientists and intellectuals were horrified at the prospect of a state barring scientific knowledge from the classroom. Civil libertarians saw the case as a crucial test of academic

freedom, which had to be defended regardless of the prevailing religious beliefs of the local population. Fundamentalists proclaimed the case a last-ditch battle to save the souls of their children from atheism.

Big-city editors recognized it as a circus and sent their most waspish reporters and columnists to poke fun at the locals. Dozens of new telegraph lines had to be strung into Dayton to handle their cable traffic. In addition to the lawyers and reporters, the town was overrun with itinerant preachers, commercial hucksters, eccentrics of every stripe, and numerous chimpanzees accompanied by their trainers. Monkey dolls, umbrellas with monkey handles, and dozens of other souvenirs with a monkey motif were put on sale.

Despite the circus-like atmosphere, the trial was no laughing matter for Bryan. Arriving a few days early, he preached to a large audience, "The contest between evolution and Christianity is a duel to the death . . . If evolution wins in Dayton, Christianity goes."

Evolution on Trial

The trial began Friday, 10 July 1925, with Judge John T. Raulston presiding. More than 900 spectators packed the sweltering courtroom. Because of an error in the original indictment, most of the first morning was spent selecting another grand jury and drawing up a new indictment. With that task done, a trial jury of 10 farmers, a schoolteacher and a clerk was quickly impaneled, and the court adjourned for the weekend.

On the first business day of the trial, the defense tried and failed to quash the indictment on grounds that the law violated both the Fourteenth Amendment to the U.S. Constitution, which states that no one may be deprived of rights without due process of law, and the freedom of religion clause of the First Amendment.

Clarence Darrow (left) and William Jennings Bryan at the Scopes trial, 1925. © AP/Wide World Photos.

Describing the Butler Act to be "as brazen and as bold an attempt to destroy learning as was ever made in the Middle Ages," Darrow predicted there would be a natural progression from the forbidding of the teaching of evolution in public schools to the banning of books and censoring of newspapers.

The opening statement for the prosecution was made the next day by A.T. Stewart, the attorney general of Tennessee, who charged Scopes with contradicting the Biblical story of Creation, thus violating the Butler Act. Responding for the defense, Dudley Malone insisted that for Scopes to be convicted the state had to prove two things: that he had denied the Biblical story of creation and that he had taught instead that man descended from a lower order of animals. Proving both would considerably complicate the prosecution's task. (While Scopes had admitted teaching evolution, there was no evidence he had denied the Bible's version of man's origins.) Malone conceded there was there were some apparent contradictions between the Darwinian and Biblical accounts of creation, but he noted that many people managed to reconcile the two theories. Only the Fundamentalists maintained that science and religion were totally incompatible on the subject.

The prosecution's case was presented briskly. The superintendent of the Rhea County school system testified that Scopes had admitted teaching evolution in a biology class. Stewart then offered a King James Version of the Bible as evidence of what the Butler Act described as the Biblical account of Creation. The judge accepted this as evidence over the objection of Arthur Garfield Hays, who pointed out that there were several different versions of the Bible.

Scopes' students testified that he had taught that mammals had evolved from one-cell organisms and that humans share the classification "mammal" with monkeys, cats, etc. The owner of the local drugstore where Scopes had purchased the textbook he used to teach evolution acknowledged that the state had authorized sale of the textbook. Darrow and the druggist read aloud portions on Darwin. To counter, Steward read the first two chapters of the Old Testament's Genesis into the record. With that, the prosecution rested.

The next day, Thursday, 16 July, the defense started calling its witnesses, beginning with a zoologist from Johns Hopkins University. The prosecution objected, arguing the evidence was inadmissible and irrelevant since the jury did not need to understand evolutionary theory to decide whether Scopes had violated the law in teaching it.

Bryan seized this opportunity to give his major speech of the trial. Clutching the offending textbook in one hand and a palm fan in the other, he belittled the theory of evolution and ridiculed a diagram in the textbook. Bryan charged that Darwinism produced agnostics and atheists, thus weakening moral standards. As evidence of this, he claimed it had inspired the German philosopher Friedrich Nietzsche, whose writings, in turn, had motivated the Chicago "thrill-killers," Nathan Leopold and Richard Loeb. Darrow, who had been the defense attorney in that case, angrily objected, stating that Bryan was misrepresenting Nietzsche's views to prejudice the jury; Judge Raulston overruled him. Bryan closed on a defiant note, assuring his audience that the Bible would survive attacks by scientists trying to reconcile it with evolution. Although some of his quips provoked appreciative laughter from spectators, observers noted that the speech lacked the eloquence and punch of Bryan's best stump performances.

Dudley Malone, presenting the defense's last argument for the admissibility of scientific evidence, charged the Fundamentalists with suppressing new ideas out of fear and claiming they had a monopoly on the truth. Malone proclaimed: "The truth always wins . . . The truth does not need the forces of Government. The truth does not need Mr. Bryan. The truth is imperishable," Malone declared. "We feel we stand with progress . . . We feel we stand with fundamental freedom in America. We are not afraid. Where is the fear? We defy it!" Although Malone's speech received more applause than Bryan's, it failed to persuade the judge.

The phrase "descended from a lower order of animals" was clear enough to define evolution under the law, Judge Raulston decided, ruling out the admissibility of scientific testimony.

Enraged by this decision, Arthur Hays requested the judge at least permit the expert statements to be entered into the court record, not to be heard by the jury, but to be available to an appeals court. Avoiding cross-examination of its expert witnesses, the defense lawyers submitted their written statements, summaries of which went into the record.

Darrow Deflates Bryan

The trial, which had been moved to the courthouse lawn to accommodate the crowds, seemed to be winding down when defense attorney Hays dropped a bombshell: He called William Jennings Bryan to the stand as an expert on the Bible. This was an unheard-of legal tactic, but, with jaunty overconfidence, Bryan sprang up to accept the dare and the doubtful judge agreed. Darrow, whose skill at trapping witnesses with their own words was legendary, dropped his previously gentle manner when Bryan took the stand. First, he got Bryan to state every word in the Bible was literally true. He then asked how the Old Testament figure Cain got a wife if he, Adam, Eve, and Abel were the only four people on earth at the time, as the Bible said. Next, Clarence Darrow pointed out that the Book of Genesis states that the serpent who tempted Eve in the Garden of Eden was condemned by God to slither on its belly, Darrow then asked Bryan if before that, had the snake walked on its tail? The more Darrow attacked, the more entangled Bryan became in contradictions, and the more foolish he and his cause appeared.

Sweating and shaking, Bryan shocked his own supporters by admitting he did not think the earth was made in six 24-hour days, as a literal reading of the Bible suggested. This was significant, since literalism was the cornerstone of Fundamentalist doctrine. The

personal antagonism between Darrow and Bryan charged the courtroom with electricity. Bryan accused Darrow of insulting the Bible. Darrow responded, "I am examining you on your fool ideas that no Christian on earth believes."

Finally, after an hour and a half, Judge Raulston adjourned the proceedings in a transparent attempt to save Bryan further embarrassment. The next morning Bryan's testimony was described as irrelevant and removed from the record by the judge. The defense immediately rested, denying Bryan any opportunity to erase the previous day's humiliation.

Closing for the defense, Clarence Darrow stole the prosecution's lines by asking the jury to find Scopes guilty so that the case could be appealed. After nine minutes, the jury came back with a guilty verdict. In violation of Tennessee law, which required that the fine be set by the jury, Raulston advised the jury to let him fix the fine, an error that led the court of appeals to reject the original verdict. While the appeals court upheld the constitutionality of the Butler Act, it did not order a retrial for John Thomas Scopes, who by that time had given up teaching.

In a narrow sense, Scopes and the evolutionists lost the battle. But it was soon apparent that they had won the war. No attempt was made to enforce the Butler Act again, although it was not repealed until 1967. Within a few years, efforts to enforce similar laws in other states were also abandoned. The Supreme Court put the issue to rest in 1968, when it held a similar statute in Arkansas unconstitutional because it violated the separation of church and state required by the First Amendment of the Constitution.

But the *Scopes* trial is remembered not so much for its legal as its social and cultural significance. It marked a watershed in intellectual history; before *Scopes*, religious faith was the common, if not universal, premise of American thought; after *Scopes*, scientific skepticism prevailed. Friends and enemies alike viewed William Jennings Bryan's death just a few weeks after the trial ended as tolling the end of an era. A 1955 play and subsequent film based on the events in Dayton, Tennessee, *Inherit the Wind* by Jerome Lawrence and Robert Lee, ensured that the trial would remain among the most remembered courtroom battles in U.S. history.

Bibliography and Further Reading

Allen, Leslie H., ed. *Bryan And Darrow At Dayton: The Record And Documents Of The "Bible Evolution Trial."* New York: Arthur Lee, 1925.

Darrow, Clarence. *The Story Of My Life.* New York: Charles Scribner's Sons, 1932.

De Camp, L. Sprague. *The Great Monkey Trial.* Garden City, NY: Doubleday & Co., 1968.

Ginger, Raymond. *Six Days Or Forever: Tennessee v. John Thomas Scopes.* Boston: Beacon Press, 1958.

Hays, Arthur Garfield. *Let Freedom Ring.* New York: Boni & Liveright, 1928.

Johnson, John W., ed. *Historic U.S. Court Cases, 1690-1990: An Encyclopedia.* New York: Garland Publishing, 1992.

Koenig, Louis W. *Bryan: A Political Biography of William Jennings Bryan.* New York: G.P. Putnam's Sons, 1971.

Scopes, John. *Center of The Storm.* New York: Holt, Rinehart & Winston, 1967.

Tierney, Kevin. *Darrow: A Biography.* New York: T.Y. Crowell, 1979.

Tompkins, Jerry. *D-days at Dayton.* Baton Rouge: Louisiana State University Press, 1965.

CANTWELL V. CONNECTICUT

Legal Citation: 310 U.S. 296 (1940)

Appellant
Newton Cantwell

Appellee
State of Connecticut

Appellant's Claim
That a state law requiring prior official approval before soliciting door-to-door violates the First Amendment guarantee of freedom of religion.

Chief Lawyer for Appellant
Hayden C. Covington

Chief Lawyers for Appellee
Edwin S. Pickett and Francis A. Pallotti

Justices for the Court
Hugo Lafayette Black, William O. Douglas, Felix Frankfurter, Charles Evans Hughes, James Clark McReynolds, Frank Murphy, Stanley Forman Reed, Owen Josephus Roberts (writing for the Court), Harlan Fiske Stone

Justices Dissenting
None

Place
Washington, D.C.

Date of Decision
20 May 1940

Decision
While asserting that a state has the right to issue appropriate time, place, or manner restrictions on solicitation, the Court unanimously struck down the Connecticut statute as violative of the First Amendment.

Significance
Cantwell v. Connecticut was the first case to state that the First Amendment's Free Exercise of Religion Clause applies at the state level, and also the first to state what later became a standard canon of constitutional law: the "time, place, and manner" rule.

Newton Cantwell, together with his sons, Jesse and Russell, was arrested while individually going house to house in a heavily Catholic neighborhood of New Haven, Connecticut. As they went from one door to the next, the Cantwells, all of them members of the Jehovah's Witnesses, asked residents if they would like to accept a pamphlet or hear a record. Both of these items attacked Roman Catholicism. If the residents refused requests to buy a book, the Cantwells then solicited a donation that would go toward publication of more pamphlets.

Police arrested the Cantwells, charging them under a Connecticut statute requiring individuals to obtain permission from the secretary of public welfare prior to engaging in solicitation. After the Cantwells were convicted in trial court, they appealed to the state supreme court, which affirmed their convictions. They then turned to the U.S. Supreme Court.

The opinion of the Court, written by Justice Roberts, first dispensed with the argument that the First Amendment did not apply to the state of Connecticut. Clearly, said the Court, the Due Process Clause of the Fourteenth Amendment—which says that no state shall "deprive any person of life, liberty, or property without due process of law"—makes the First Amendment applicable at the state level. Here, for the first time, the Court specifically stated that the Free Exercise of Religion Clause of the First Amendment applies to states as well as to the federal government. "The First Amendment declares that Congress shall make no law respecting an establishment of religion or prohibiting the free exercise thereof. The Fourteenth Amendment has rendered the legislatures of the states as incompetent as Congress to enact such laws."

Court Develops the "Time, Place, and Manner" Rule

The Court went on to point out that there are two aspects to freedom of religion, and that although freedom of conscience cannot be restricted by law, some restraints can be placed on some acts of religious adherence.

[T]he Amendment embraces two concepts—freedom to believe and freedom to act. The first

"Time, Place, and Manner" Rule

The "time, place and manner" rule arose from a decision by the Supreme Court that the federal government, as well as states, were bound by the First Amendment's guarantees for religious freedom. The Court held that one of these guarantees, namely the rights of citizens to follow whatever religious beliefs they wish, is protected and absolute. However, the Court also stated that the amendment's Free-Exercise Clause, the right of citizens for free exercise of their religion, is not absolute. A citizen's free-exercise right must be weighed against the public interest and a state can regulate to ensure that it is practiced in a reasonable time, place, and manner.

Thus, a state cannot deny, totally, a child's right to pray in school, for instance, providing the prayer is done in a reasonable time, place, and manner and does not disturb other students. In the Court's view, the "time, place, and manner" rule is a general and nondiscriminatory restraint of religious practice and therefore does not violate the guarantees of the First Amendment.

Source(s): Eastland, Terry. *Religious Liberty in the Supreme Court*. Washington, DC: Ethics and Public Policy Center, 1993.

---

is absolute but, in the nature of things, the second cannot be . . . No one would contest the proposition that a state may not, by statute, wholly deny the right to preach or to disseminate religious views. Plainly such a previous and absolute restraint would violate the terms of the guarantee. It is equally clear that a state may by general and non-discriminatory legislation regulate the times, the places, and the manner of soliciting upon the streets, and or holding meetings thereon . . .

Federal courts would go on to hear many more cases concerning time, place, and manner restrictions—not all centering on freedom of religion. In each, the preliminary inquiry was whether or not the regulation at issue was truly neutral, or "non-discriminatory," in the words of Justice Roberts' *Cantwell* opinion. If so, the courts must then balance the interests of those who wish to practice their religion publicly against the interests of the larger society. Recently, as the "time, place, and manner" rule has become more and more refined, the Supreme Court has been granting government more lat-

itude in regulating the incidental effects of free expression and narrowing its definition of what constitutes a public forum, which must remain available to those wishing to exercise all of their First Amendment rights.

Related Cases
Reynolds v. United States, 98 U.S. 145 (1879).
Davis v. Beason, 133 U.S. 333 (1890).
Schneider v. New Jersey, 308 U.S. 147 (1939).
Cox v. New Hampshire, 312 U.S. 569 (1941).
Murdock v. Pennsylvania, 319 U.S. 105 (1943).

Bibliography and Further Reading
Church and State: The Supreme Court and the First Amendment. Chicago: University of Chicago Press, 1975.

McConnell, Michael W. "The Origins and Historical Understanding of Free Exercise of Religion." *Harvard Law Review* 103 (1990): 1410-1517.

Religious Liberty in the Supreme Court: The Cases that Define the Debate Over Church and State. Washington, DC: Ethics and Public Policy Center, 1993.

MINERSVILLE SCHOOL DISTRICT V. GOBITIS

Legal Citation: 310 U.S. 586 (1940)

Appellant
Minersville School District

Appellee
Walter Gobitis

Appellant's Claim
That forcing a schoolchild to salute the American flag in violation of her religious principles abridges her First Amendment right to exercise her faith freely.

Chief Lawyer for Appellant
Joseph W. Henderson

Chief Lawyers for Appellee
George K. Gardner and Joseph F. Rutherford

Justices for the Court
Hugo Lafayette Black, William O. Douglas, Felix Frankfurter (writing for the Court), Charles Evans Hughes, James Clark McReynolds, Frank Murphy, Stanley Forman Reed, Owen Josephus Roberts

Justices Dissenting
Harlan Fiske Stone

Place
Washington, D.C.

Date of Decision
3 June 1940

Decision
Arguing that the "felt necessities" of society outweigh the dictates of an individual's religious conscience, the Supreme Court upheld the state law mandating the flag salute.

Significance
World War II clearly influenced the outcome of this case, which was overturned three years later in *West Virginia State Board of Education v. Barnette* (1943).

The school board that controlled the public school in Minersville, Pennsylvania, required that both teachers and students salute the American flag as part of a daily school exercise. Lillian Gobitis, aged 12, and her brother William, aged 11, both attended the school. Both were from a family that belonged to the Jehovah's Witnesses, which taught that saluting the flag was forbidden by holy scripture. When the children refused to comply with the flag salute requirement, both were expelled from school.

Their parents were then obliged to put the Gobitis children in private schools, an expense the family could not afford. To be relieved of this burden, Walter Gobitis brought this suit in his own behalf and on behalf of his children. From the district court he obtained an injunction to prevent the school board from prohibiting his children from returning to public school. The injunction was upheld in the circuit court of appeals, a ruling the school board requested the U.S. Supreme Court to review.

Nationalism in Time of War Trumps the First Amendment

The basis for Gobitis's suit was the Free Exercise Clause of the First Amendment, which reads: "Congress shall make no law . . . prohibiting the free exercise [of religion]." Writing for the Court, Justice Frankfurter found that even this prohibition had its limits:

> Certainly the affirmative pursuit of one's convictions about the ultimate mystery of the universe and man's relation to it is placed beyond the reach of law. Government may not interfere with organized or individual expression of belief or disbelief . . . But the manifold character of man's religion may bring his conception of religious duty into conflict with the secular interests of his fellow-man . . . [T]o affirm that the freedom to follow conscience has itself no limits in the life of a society would deny that very plurality of principles which, as a matter of history, underlies protection of religious toleration.

As a matter of history, the individual beliefs of the Gobitis family were particularly at odds with the inter-

Jehovah's Witnesses and Public Schools

Jehovah's Witnesses are a Christian sect that gives sole allegiance to the kingdom of Jesus Christ. As a result, they refuse to salute any flag, vote, perform military service, or otherwise signify allegiance to any government. At times, these beliefs have brought members into conflict with the U.S. government. For instance, children who belong to the Jehovah's Witnesses have been expelled from public schools because they have refused to salute the U.S. flag in violation of their religion's teachings. The religion prohibits the worship of "graven images" and considers the American flag to be a graven image.

Source(s): Eastland, Terry. *Religious Liberty in the Supreme Court*. Washington, DC: Ethics and Public Policy Center, 1993.

ests of most members of society in 1940, when America was on the brink of entering World War II. Also as a matter of history, the Court had legal precedent for enforcing the flag salute requirement. As far back as *Reynolds v. United States* (1879), the Supreme Court had found that there could be a rational basis for punishing individuals for religiously motivated actions, so long as the state did not inquire into their beliefs. The issue in *Reynolds,* Mormon polygamy, was perhaps of a different order than refusing to pay homage to a symbol. For the Supreme Court in time of war, however, much more was at stake than a symbol: "We are dealing with an interest inferior to none in the hierarchy of legal values," wrote Frankfurter. "National unity is the basis of national security."

Only one of the justices, Stone, disagreed with this opinion. Just three years later, in *West Virginia State Board of Education v. Barnette* (1943), a majority of the Court voted in favor of the Jehovah's Witnesses in another flag salute case. *Gobitis* proved to be a highly criticized decision. It seemed to license abuse of religious nonconformists. The incidence of attacks on Jehovah's Witnesses in particular escalated dramatically. State authorities threatened to send children who refused to pledge allegiance to the flag to reformatories for juvenile delinquents. West Virginia passed a compulsory flag salute law modeled on the Court's opinion in *Gobitis. Barnette,* which used the First Amendment right of free speech as the grounds for overturning this law, was a marked retreat from everything *Gobitis* acknowledged.

Related Cases

Reynolds v. United States, 98 U.S. 145 (1879).
West Virginia State Board of Education v. Barnette, 319 U.S. 624 (1943).

Bibliography and Further Reading

Bosmajian, Haig A., ed. *Freedom of Religion*. New York, NY: Neal-Schuman, 1987.

Curtis, Michael Kent, ed. *The Constitution and the Flag*. New York, NY: Garland, 1993.

Johnson, John W., ed. *Historic U.S. Court Cases, 1690–1990: An Encyclopedia*. New York: Garland Publishing, 1992.

Stevens, Leonard A. *Salute! The Case of the Bible vs. the Flag*. New York, NY: Coward McCann & Geoghegan, 1973.

WEST VIRGINIA STATE BOARD OF EDUCATION V. BARNETTE

Legal Citation: 319 U.S. 624 (1943)

Appellant
West Virginia State Board of Education

Appellee
Walter Barnette

Appellant's Claim
That a state law mandating a daily salute of the American flag by public school children does not violate the First Amendment's guarantee of religious freedom.

Chief Lawyer for Appellant
W. Holt Wooddell

Chief Lawyer for Appellee
Hayden C. Covington

Justices for the Court
Hugo Lafayette Black, William O. Douglas, Robert H. Jackson (writing for the Court), Frank Murphy, Stanley Forman Reed, Owen Josephus Roberts

Justices Dissenting
Felix Frankfurter, Wiley Blount Rutledge, Harlan Fiske Stone

Place
Washington, D.C.

Date of Decision
14 June 1943

Decision
The Supreme Court struck down the West Virginia flag salute law.

Significance
The majority opinion in *Barnette* is one of the Court's greatest and most sweeping statements about the fundamental freedoms memorialized in the Bill of Rights.

The Jehovah's Witnesses have a long history of evoking the First Amendment to challenge state laws. In 1940, they lost a major court battle in *Minersville School District v. Gobitis,* in which the Supreme Court voted 8-1 that a Jehovah's Witness child could be expelled from a public school in Minersville, Pennsylvania, for refusing to salute the American flag on religious grounds. This outcome had been thought to be a product of prewar concerns about national loyalty—especially in view of Justice Frankfurter's discussion in the majority opinion of how only the "felt necessities" of society can override the First Amendment's guarantee of freedom of religion.

Somewhat unexpectedly, *Gobitis* produced a backlash. Some members of society interpreted the decision to mean that the Jehovah's Witnesses were un-American, and attacks on them increased, particularly after the United States entered World War II in 1941. These actions in turn sparked a reaction, and critics of the *Gobitis* decision proliferated. Even the American Legion supported a proposed law that would make saluting the flag a voluntary activity. Walter Barnette, a Jehovah's Witness, chose this moment to bring a suit challenging the West Virginia flag salute law, which had been modeled on the Court's opinion in *Gobitis*.

The U.S. District Court for the Southern District of West Virginia granted Barnette's request that the state school board be enjoined from enforcing the flag salute requirement. The school board then appealed this decision to the U.S. Supreme Court.

Supreme Court Holds That Compulsory Flag Ceremonies Violate Constitutional Guarantees of Free Speech

This time, by a vote of 6-3, the Supreme Court struck down a state flag salute law, overruling *Gobitis* in the process. But whereas the earlier decision had relied primarily on the First Amendment's Free Exercise of Religion Clause, the *Barnette* Court couched its decision in language evoking freedom of speech. The choice to salute the flag was speech, the Court said, and the First Amendment protected individuals from compelled speech. It almost did not matter that the Jehovah's Witnesses had religious objections to pledging allegiance

The Flag Salute

Can schoolchildren be compelled to state the Pledge of Allegiance or salute the U.S. flag? Those who say yes believe that children do not have a constitutional right to refuse to do so. Advocates say that loyalty to the nation and the government is important and that saluting the flag is one way to teach children to have loyalty for the country.

But those opposed to enforced flag salutes say that children should not have to make a statement of loy- alty if they do not wish. To make them do so, in turn, makes the action worthless. They also believe that children who are compelled to say the Pledge of Allegiance or salute the flag may one day resent the country that forced them to make these false statements or gestures.

Source(s): Eastland, Terry. *Religious Liberty in the Supreme Court.* Washington, DC: Ethics and Public Policy Center, 1993.

to the American flag; neither they, nor anyone, could be forced to verbally espouse beliefs they did not hold.

To underscore the interrelatedness of the fundamental freedoms memorialized in the first ten amendments to the Constitution, Justice Jackson, writing for the Court, delivered an oratory to the Bill of Rights:

> The very purpose of a Bill of Rights was to withdraw certain subjects from the vicissitudes of political controversy, to place them beyond the reach of majorities and officials and to establish them as legal principles to be applied by the courts. One's right to life, liberty, and property, to free speech, a free press, freedom of worship and assembly, and other fundamental rights may not be submitted to vote; they depend on the outcome of no elections.

After *Barnette,* the Court began to turn away from the belief-action doctrine altogether, creating religious exemption for believers of different stripes. In *Sherbert v. Verner* (1963), for example, the Court upheld a Seventh-Day Adventist's claim to unemployment benefits even though she declined to make herself available to work on Saturday (her Sabbath) as the law required. In *Wisconsin v. Yoder* (1972), the Court upheld the right

of Amish parents not to send their children to public schools past the eighth grade. But when the Amish asked the government for an exemption from paying Social Security taxes, the Court ruled against them in *United States v. Lee* (1982). Thereafter, Supreme Court decisions concerning the Free Exercise Clause steered away from constitutional exemptions for particular religious groups.

Related Cases

Reynolds v. United States, 98 U.S. 145 (1879).
Minersville School District v. Gobitis, 310 U.S. 586 (1940).
Wisconsin v. Yoder, 406 U.S. 205 (1972).

Bibliography and Further Reading

Curtis, Michael Kent, ed. *The Constitution and the Flag.* New York, NY: Garland, 1993.

Newton, Merlin Owen. *Armed with the Constitution: Jehovah's Witnesses in Alabama and the U.S. Supreme Court, 1939-1946.* Tuscaloosa: University of Alabama Press, 1995.

Stevens, Leonard A. *Salute! The Case of the Bible vs. the Flag.* New York, NY: Coward, McCann & Geoghegan, 1973.

EVERSON V. BOARD OF EDUCATION

Legal Citation: 330 U.S. 1 (1947)

Appellant
Arch R. Everson

Appellee
Board of Education of Ewing Township

Appellant's Claim
That a New Jersey law authorizing school boards to reimburse parents for the costs of transporting their children to schools, both public and parochial, violates the principle of separation of church and state.

Chief Lawyers for Appellant
Edward R. Burke and E. Hilton Jackson

Chief Lawyer for Appellee
William H. Speer

Justices for the Court
Hugo Lafayette Black (writing for the Court), William O. Douglas, Frank Murphy, Stanley Forman Reed, Fred Moore Vinson

Justices Dissenting
Harold Burton, Felix Frankfurter, Robert H. Jackson, Wiley Blount Rutledge

Place
Washington, D.C.

Date of Decision
10 February 1947

Decision
The Supreme Court upheld the statute, reasoning that it benefited parents, not church-affiliated schools.

Significance
Everson marked the first time the Court used the Fourteenth Amendment to apply the religion clauses of the First Amendment at the state level.

New Jersey passed a statute authorizing local school districts to make rules and contracts for the transportation of children to and from school. The Board of Education of Ewing Township, following this law, authorized reimbursement to parents of money spent by their children on public buses. When Arch Everson, a resident and taxpayer in the Ewing Township school district, learned that some of these monies were going to parents who sent their children to Catholic schools, he filed suit. While a New Jersey trial court agreed that the statute permitting state money to go to parents of parochial school students was unconstitutional, the New Jersey Supreme Court upheld the law. Everson then appealed this ruling to the U.S. Supreme Court.

In a lengthy opinion written for the Court majority, Justice Black recounted the history of religion in America. The earliest settlers, many of whom had come to this land seeking religious freedom, had determined that the best way to achieve that freedom was to give government no power to tax in order to aid religion, or the authority to support religion or any particular faith in any way. During the early years of the republic, 1785-1786, Thomas Jefferson and James Madison had led a successful revolt against a proposed state tax earmarked for support of the established church of Virginia. As part of his campaign, Madison wrote his famous "Memorial and Remonstrance" essay, in which he argued that no person, either believer or nonbeliever, should be taxed to support a religious institution of any kind. Black went on to discuss Jefferson's equally famous "Virginia Bill for Religious Liberty," which was enacted in place of the proposed tax. The philosophy of Madison and Jefferson regarding freedom of religion is clearly reflected in the First Amendment, which they helped to draft.

Court Rules the State Must Be Neutral, Not Antagonistic Toward Religion

Justice Black was a First Amendment absolutist, fond of quoting the opening words of this first element of the Bill of Rights: "Congress shall make no law respecting an establishment of religion, or prohibiting the free exercise thereof." It was, therefore, not surprising to find that he was the author of an opinion that seemed

Public and Private School Busing

Should parents be reimbursed for expenses incurred for busing their children to church schools? Opponents say that public funds used in this way is a clear violation of the separation of church and state because it forces the government to favor one religion over another. They contend that to allow this type of reimbursement opens the door for future entanglement between public funds and religious activities.

On the other hand, advocates say that reimbursement to families for private schools only indirectly supports church-run facilities and therefore falls outside the Establishment Clause of the First Amendment. They argue that the costs actually promote the public welfare and contend that transportation costs are no different than those incurred by the state when it provides crossing guards to assist children going to church schools. Additionally, since the reimbusement would be for all types of religious education facilities, it would not be a matter of the government treating any one religious entity preferentially to another.

Source(s): Eastland, Terry. *Religious Liberty in the Supreme Court.* Washington, DC: Ethics and Public Policy Center, 1993.

to be endorsing Everson's point of view. But in fact, for Black and four other justices, a literal reading of the First Amendment had the opposite result.

The meaning of the Free Exercise Clause of the First Amendment was not, for a majority of the *Everson* Court, just that government could not promote religion, but that it could not act as religion's adversary. The state, Black wrote, must remain neutral:

The "establishment of religion" clause of the First Amendment means at least this: Neither a state nor the Federal Government can set up a church. Neither can pass laws which aid one religion, aid all religions, or prefer one religion over another . . . No tax in any amount, large or small, can be levied to support any religious activities or institutions . . . In the words of Jefferson, the clause against establishment of religion by law was intended to erect "a wall of separation between Church and State."

This was the first time that the Supreme Court had, by means of the Fourteenth Amendment, made the Establishment Clause of the First Amendment applicable to individual states. On its face, the prohibition against state establishment of religion might seem to make the New Jersey school reimbursement statute unconstitutional. However, the Court reasoned, New Jersey cannot hamper its citizens from freely exercising their own religions. If the state extends tax benefits to parents of public school students, in order to remain truly neutral towards religion, it must also extend these benefits to parents of parochial school students.

Everson remains a valid legal precedent, primarily for its application of the religion clauses of the First Amendment to the states. It is most often cited, however, for its proposition that the founders' primary intention in drafting the First Amendment was to prevent government from setting up an official religion.

Related Cases
Watson v. Jones, 13 Wall. 679 (1872).
McGowan v. Maryland, 366 U.S. 429 (1961).
Engel v. Vitale, 370 U.S. 421 (1962).
Lemon v. Kurtzman, 403 U.S. 602 (1971).
Abington School District v. Schempp, 374 U.S. 203 (1973).
The Committee for Public Education and Religious Liberty v. Nyquist, 413 U.S. 561 (1973).

Bibliography and Further Reading
Eastland, Terry, ed. *Religious Liberty in the Supreme Court: The Cases that Define the Debate Over Church and State.* Washington, DC: Ethics and Public Policy Institute, 1993.

Everson, David H. *The Supreme Court as Policy-Maker: Three Studies on the Impact of Judicial Decisions,* 2nd ed. Carbondale: Southern Illinois University, 1972.

Howe, Mark De Wolfe. *The Garden and the Wilderness: Religion and Government in American Constitutional History.* Chicago, IL: University of Chicago Press, 1965.

ILLINOIS EX REL. McCOLLUM V. BOARD OF EDUCATION

Legal Citation: 333 U.S. 203 (1948)

Appellant
Vashti McCollum

Appellee
Board of Education of School District No. 71, Champaign County, Illinois

Appellant's Claim
That a policy of permitting limited religious instruction in public schools violated the Establishment Clause of the First Amendment.

Chief Lawyer for Appellant
Walter F. Dodd

Chief Lawyers for Appellee
Owen Rall and John L. Franklin

Justices for the Court
Hugo Lafayette Black (writing for the Court), Harold Burton, William O. Douglas, Felix Frankfurter, Robert H. Jackson, Frank Murphy, Wiley Blount Rutledge, Fred Moore Vinson

Justices Dissenting
Stanley Forman Reed

Place
Washington, D.C.

Date of Decision
8 March 1948

Decision
The Supreme Court held that the state could not permit religious instruction to take place in public school classrooms.

Significance
McCollum was one of the first Supreme Court decisions to address issues raised by the Establishment Clause of the First Amendment. In it, the Court affirmed that the wall separating church and state is both high and impregnable.

The Illinois school board provided space in its buildings for religious instruction to be given by teachers who were paid by various private religious groups, but subject to school board approval. Students could choose not to participate in the program, which offered Protestant, Catholic, or Jewish instruction for 30 to 45 minutes every week during regular school hours. Non participating students went elsewhere in the school buildings; participating students were required to attend.

Vashti McCollum, a resident and taxpayer in Champaign, Illinois, and a parent whose child was registered in the Champaign public schools, brought an action against the school board in state court. McCollum's action was in fact brought on her behalf by the state of Illinois, which is the import of the case title, *Illinois ex. rel McCollum*. Citing both the First and the Fourteenth Amendments, McCollum requested that the board be ordered to adopt and enforce regulations prohibiting religious instruction in her public school district. The district court found that the school board's program violated neither of the constitutional provisions McCollum invoked and denied her petition for *mandamus*—a request that a governmental entity be ordered to perform some necessary duty. When the state supreme court upheld this decision, McCollum appealed to the U.S. Supreme Court.

Wall Between Church and State Remains Intact

Justice Black, writing for the eight-member Court majority, cited an opinion he had written in another Establishment Clause case, *Everson v. Board of Education*, just the year before:

> [T]he First Amendment rests upon the premise that both religion and government can best work to achieve their lofty aims if each is left free from the other within its respective sphere. Or, as we said in the *Everson* case, the First Amendment has erected a wall between Church and State which must be kept high and impregnable.

The four justices who had dissented in *Everson*—Frankfurter, Jackson, Rutledge, and Burton—concurred here. Whereas in the earlier case a one-vote majority had upheld a state statute authorizing reimbursement of transportation costs to and from schools, including parochial schools, here the Court stood solidly behind a rejection of state support for religion. In *Everson* Black had emphasized state neutrality towards religion, but in *McCollum* the two clearly were too close for comfort:

> Here not only are the state's tax-supported public school buildings used for the dissemination of religious doctrines. The State also affords sectarian groups an invaluable aid in that it helps to provide pupils for their religious classes through use of the state's compulsory public school machinery. This is not separation of Church and State.

The *Everson* dissenters signed on to a concurring opinion, written by Justice Frankfurter, which emphasized an historical trend away from mixing religious and sectarian instruction in public schools.

However, Justice Frankfurter's concurrence also noted that in 1948 nearly two million students took part in "released time" activities such as the program for religious studies in Champaign, Illinois. In *Zorach v. Clauson* (1952), the Supreme Court would uphold a New York City practice of releasing students from public school so that they could receive instruction at religious centers of their own choosing. The Court was moving away from an absolute prohibition of any state support for religion and towards the "excessive entanglement" test for impermissible government involvement with religion that would be articulated in *Lemon v. Kurtzman* (1971).

Related Cases

Minersville School District v. Gobitis, 310 U.S. 586 (1940).
West Virginia State Board of Education v. Barnette, 319 U.S. 624 (1943).
Everson v. Board of Education, 330 U.S. 1 (1947).
Zorach v. Clausen, 343 U.S. 306 (1952).
School District of Abington Township v. Schempp, 274 U.S. 203 (1963).
Lemon v. Kurtzman, 403 U.S. 602 (1971).
Wallace v. Jaffree, 472 U.S. 38 (1985).

Vashti and Terry McCollum. © AP/Wide World Photos.

Bibliography and Further Reading

Eastland, Terry, ed. *Religious Liberty in the Supreme Court: The Cases That Define the Debate Over Church and State.* Washington, DC: Ethics and Public Policy Institute, 1993.

Johnson, John W., ed. *Historic U.S. Court Cases, 1690–1990: An Encyclopedia.* New York: Garland Publishing, 1992.

Levy, Leonard Williams. *The Establishment Clause: Religion and the First Amendment,* second edition. Chapel Hill: University of North Carolina Press, 1994.

Sikorski, Robert, ed. *Prayer in Public Schools and the Constitution, 1961-1992.* New York: Garland, 1993.

ZORACH V. CLAUSON

Legal Citation: 343 U.S. 306 (1952)

Appellant
Tessim Zorach

Appellee
Andrew G. Clauson, Jr.

Appellant's Claim
That New York City's program of "released time" for students to attend religious instruction away from school premises violated the First Amendment mandate of church-state separation.

Chief Lawyer for Appellant
Kenneth W. Greenawalt

Chief Lawyer for Appellee
Michael A. Castaldi

Justices for the Court
Harold Burton, Tom C. Clark, William O. Douglas (writing for the Court); Sherman Minton, Stanley Forman Reed, Fred Moore Vinson

Justices Dissenting
Hugo Lafayette Black, Felix Frankfurter, Robert H. Jackson

Place
Washington, D.C.

Date of Decision
28 April 1952

Decision
The Supreme Court upheld the program.

Significance
Although *Zorach* is at odds with other Supreme Court precedents, it has evolved into the Lemon test for acceptable state accommodation of religion.

In the 1940s, New York City adopted a program of "released time" that permitted public school students to take time off during the normal school day to attend religious instruction away from the actual school premises. Tessim Zorach, together with other taxpayers and parents in New York, brought suit against Andrew Clauson and other members of the city school board, challenging the program. After a series of New York state courts rejected his challenge, Zorach took his case to the U.S. Supreme Court.

Supreme Court Upholds "Released Time" Program

Zorach based his suit on the Establishment Clause of the First Amendment, which holds that: "Congress shall make no law respecting an establishment of religion . . . " Since the days of Thomas Jefferson, this clause of the Constitution has been interpreted to mean that "a wall of separation" exists between church and state. And since the Court decided *Everson v. Board of Education* in 1947, government has had to maintain an attitude of strict neutrality towards religion in order to keep that wall up.

The effort with regard to public schools has been especially fraught. In 1948, the Court considered the first of its "released time" cases, *Illinois ex rel. McCollum v. Board of Education*, in which religious instruction provided to public school students by independent teachers on school grounds was struck down. Just four years later, in *Zorach*, however, the Court upheld a similar "released time" program. The only obvious difference between the two programs was that in *Zorach* the religious instruction took place away from school property.

It is not easy to square *Zorach* with *McCollum*. Indeed, in later years, Justice Douglas, the author of the majority opinion in *Zorach* disavowed what he had to say there. But Douglas's opinion itself contains indications of why the Court has not only not reversed *Zorach*, but subsequently expanded upon it:

> We would have to press the concept of separation of Church and state to . . . extremes to condemn the present law on constitutional grounds . . . In each case the teacher requires

Public School Release Time

Public school release time is an arrangement that permits public school children to be dismissed from regularly scheduled classes for the purpose of attending religious instruction. According to the 30 April 1952, *New York Times* article, "Time Off for Religion," in 1952 there were 550,000 elementary school students in New York City eligible to take advantage of release time programs. Of that number, 105,467 actually participated.

The article stated that in 1952, there were 2,000,000 students nationwide that took sanctioned time off from school in order to receive religious training.

Source(s): Eastland, Terry. *Religious Liberty in the Supreme Court.* Washington, DC: Ethics and Public Policy Center, 1993.

parental consent in writing. In each case the teacher, in order to make sure the student is not a truant, goes further and requires a report from the priest, the rabbi, or the minister. The teacher in other words cooperates in a religious program to the extent of making it possible for her students to participate in it. Whether she does it occasionally for a few students, regularly for one, or pursuant to a systematized program designed to further the religious needs of all the students does not alter the character of the act.

The difference between the situations in *McCollum* and *Zorach* was the manner in which students confirmed participation. In *McCollum* the students had to opt out, and in the latter students had to make an affirmative effort to participate. The decision to engage in religious activities during school hours, in other words, was theirs and their parents'. This line of thought eventually led, in *Lemon v. Kurtzman* (1971), to the Lemon test for acceptable state accommodation of religion. In order for a statute or program not to violate the Establishment Clause, it must meet three requirements: 1) it must have a secular legislative purpose; 2) its primary purpose must neither advance nor inhibit religion; and 3) it must not foster excessive government entanglement with religion.

It is this third prong of the Lemon test that evolved from *Zorach*. If students—or better yet, their more independent parents—make the decision to participate in

religious activities only tangentially connected with the public schools, then the government itself avoids "excessive entanglement." Such thinking has led to decisions like *Board of Education v. Mergens* (1990), in which the Court upheld prayer meetings organized and held at a public high school during an "activity period" when students were free to attend a wide variety of other, secular events.

Related Cases
Everson v. Board of Education, 330 U.S. 1 (1947).
Illinois ex rel. McCollum v. Board of Education, 333 U.S. 203 (1948).
Lemon v. Kurtzman, 403 U.S. 602 (1971).
Board of Education v. Mergens, (1990).

Bibliography and Further Reading
Drakeman, Donald L. *Church-State Constitutional Issues: Making Sense of the Establishment Clause.* New York, NY: Greenwood Press, 1991.

Eastland, Terry, ed. *Religious Liberty in the Supreme Court: The Cases That Define the Debate Over Church and State.* Washington, DC: Ethics and Public Policy Center, 1993.

Johnson, John W., ed. *Historic U.S. Court Cases, 1690–1990: An Encyclopedia.* New York: Garland Publishing, 1992.

Nord, Warren A. *Religion & American Education: Rethinking a National Dilemma.* Chapel Hill: University of North Carolina Press, 1995.

BRAUNFELD V. BROWN

Legal Citation: 366 U.S. 599 (1961)

Appellant
Abraham Braunfeld, et al.

Appellee
Albert N. Brown, Commissioner of Police of Philadelphia, et al.

Appellant's Claim
That Philadelphia's blue laws, which force the closing of stores on Sundays, interfere with the free exercise of religion.

Chief Lawyer for Appellant
Theodore R. Mann

Chief Lawyer for the Appellee
David Berger

Justices for the Court
Hugo Lafayette Black, Tom C. Clark, Felix Frankfurter, John Marshall Harlan II, Charles Evans Whittaker, Earl Warren (writing for the Court)

Justices Dissenting
William J. Brennan, Jr., William O. Douglas, Potter Stewart

Place
Washington, D.C.

Date of Decision
29 May 1961

Decision
Upheld Pennsylvania's blue laws, deciding that they did not violate individual freedom of religion.

Significance
The Court considered whether a law which establishes a valid secular goal, but which results in indirect burdens for people of a particular religion, violates First Amendment rights to the freedom of religion. The Court decided that laws which do not prohibit the practice of a religion, even if they present related difficulties, cannot be considered unconstitutional.

"Blue laws" are state laws which prohibit non-essential or certain forms of commerce on Sundays, in order to create an uniform day of rest for the community. They have their origins in the colonial period, and were named for the color of the paper on which they were originally printed. In 1959, Pennsylvania passed just such a blue law, requiring shops and other businesses to remain closed on Sundays.

The appellant, Abraham Braunfeld, owned and operated a clothing and home furnishing store in Philadelphia. He was also an Orthodox Jew; his religion required him to observe the Sabbath, from sundown Friday to sundown Saturday, by engaging in no work and closing his shop. Because of the revenue lost on Friday evening and all day Saturday, Braunfeld relied on being open on Sundays. Braunfeld asserted that if he was required to also close his shop on Sundays, in accordance with the Pennsylvania blue law, he would necessarily suffer economic hardship, and would not be able to continue in his business. The appellant asserted that this interfered with his First Amendment right to the free exercise of religion. The case was dismissed at the state level and appealed to the U.S. Supreme Court.

The appellant in this case, as well as the appellants in *Two Guys from Harrison-Allentown, Inc., v. McGinley* argued that the Pennsylvania statute was an attempt to establish a religion, since the blue laws emerged from the Christian practice of refraining from work on Sunday. They also asserted that the statutes violated the Fourteenth Amendment, by not providing equal protection to people of different religious faiths. The Court had considered both of these arguments in *Two Guys from Harrison-Allentown, Inc. v. McGinley,* and had dismissed them as invalid. The Court had also found in *McGowan v. Maryland,* a related case, that the states had the right

> to set one day of the week apart from the others as a day of rest, repose, recreation and tranquility, a day when the hectic tempo of everyday existence ceases and a more pleasant atmosphere is created, a day which all members of the family and community have the opportunity to spend and enjoy together.

Blue Laws/Morality Laws

Blue laws seek to strictly legislate personal behavior in puritanical fashion, particularly on Sundays and holidays. The origin of the expression, "blue laws," goes back to 1781, and is attributed to Reverend Samuel A. Peters in his book, *A General History of Connecticut*. Peters coined the phrase, "blue laws," and makes reference to these laws supposedly in force in Connecticut. Some of the laws he named however, either didn't exist, or were less severe.

Blue laws became connected with New England's Puritans. In colonial America, similar restrictions on work, sports, and travel, and requirements to attend church on Sunday were common in the South as well as New England. Other blue laws have restricted the sale of alcohol and tobacco products on Sunday and holidays, or prohibit specific personal activities like dancing or playing cards.

Although some of these outdated laws are still on the books, many are not enforced today. In 1919 the federal government attempted to legislate the prohibition of alcohol altogether with the National Prohibition Act, the Eighteenth Amendment to the U.S. Constitution. It was repealed in 1933.

Source(s): *New Standard Encyclopedia*, Vol. 3, Chicago, IL: Standard Educational Corp., 1990.

This right, according to the Court, was a valid secular pursuit for states, and did not constitute the establishment of religion.

The question remaining before the Court, then, was whether or not the Pennsylvania blue law interfered with the appellant's free exercise of religion. The appellee did not dispute the appellant would suffer financially by being forced to close on Sunday. A significant amount of business was done on that day. On this question, the Court reaffirmed that

> Certain aspects of religious exercise cannot, in any way, be restricted or burdened by either federal or state legislation.

While holding this true, the Court also stated,

> the freedom to act, even when the action is in accord with one's religious convictions, is not totally free from legislative restrictions.

As long as the legislation was not directly interfering with religious practices, and was designed to promote some valid secular goal, it would not be considered unconstitutional. The Court asserted,

> To strike down, without the most critical scrutiny, legislation which imposes only an indirect burden on the exercise of religion, i.e., legislation which does not make unlawful the religious practice itself, would radically restrict the operating latitude of the legislature.

Another example of an indirect burden on the practice of religion is tax laws which limit the deductions available for donations to religion. Although the blue law in question would make practicing Orthodox Judaism more expensive, it did not prevent Orthodox Jews from abiding by the tenets of that religion, including refraining from work on Saturdays.

Impact

Justice Brennan wrote a dissenting opinion, in which he argued that the blue laws actually did infringe on the free exercise of religion. The burden which the laws created for the appellant, while indirect, was great; if Braunfeld had to close his shop on Sundays, he would not be able to continue in his business. Justice Brennan phrased the question as

> whether a state may put an individual to a choice between his business and his religion,

and argued that it was in fact unconstitutional to do so.

In the end, however, the case had limited impact on religious freedom. Shopping malls and chain stores changed the way business was done, and the blue laws which the case called into question were largely repealed as commerce in towns, cities, and suburbs grew.

Related Cases

Reynolds v. United States, 98 U.S. 145 (1879).
Prince v. Massachusetts, 321 U.S. 296 (1940).
McGowan v. Maryland, 366 U.S. 420 (1961).
Two Guys from Harrison-Allentown, Inc. v. McGinley, 366 U.S. 582 (1961).

Bibliography and Further Reading

Biskupic, Joan and Elder Witt, eds. *Congressional Quarterly's Guide to the U.S. Supreme Court*, 3rd ed. Washington, DC: Congressional Quarterly, Inc., 1996.

Hall, Kermit L., ed. *The Oxford Companion to the Supreme Court of the United States*. Oxford: Oxford University Press, 1992.

Witt, Elder, ed. *Congressional Quarterly's Guide to the U.S. Supreme Court*. Washington, DC: Congressional Quarterly, Inc., 1990.

ENGEL V. VITALE

Legal Citation: 370 U.S. 421 (1962)

Petitioner
Steven L. Engel, et al.

Respondent
William J. Vitale, et al.

Petitioner's Claim
That an official state prayer, even though it is nondenominational and voluntary, violates the First Amendment prohibition against state establishment of religion.

Chief Lawyer for Petitioner
William J. Butler

Chief Lawyer for Respondent
Bertram B. Daiker

Justices for the Court
Hugo Lafayette Black (writing for the Court), William J. Brennan, Jr., Tom C. Clark, William O. Douglas, John Marshall Harlan II, Earl Warren

Justices Dissenting
Potter Stewart (Felix Frankfurter and Byron R. White did not participate)

Place
Washington, D.C.

Date of Decision
25 June 1962

Decision
The Supreme Court declared that the creation of an official state prayer was unconstitutional.

Significance
The Court stated for the first time that the Constitution forbids public schools from sponsoring religious activities.

The First Amendment clearly forbids government from enacting any law "respecting an establishment of religion." Prior to hearing *Engel v. Vitale* in 1962, the Supreme Court had honored the formulation first put on this proscription by Thomas Jefferson that a "wall" separates church and state. But in earlier decisions such as *Zorach v. Clauson* (1952)—upholding a program permitting public school students to receive religious training during school hours, but off school premises—the Court had permitted there to be some accommodation between public schools and religious activities. In *Engel,* the Court would make the barrier between the two almost unbreachably high.

In 1962, the school board of New Hyde Park, New York required that the following prayer be spoken aloud by each class every morning in front of a teacher: "Almighty God, we acknowledge our dependence upon Thee, and we beg Thy blessings upon us, our parents, our teachers and our country." The nondenominational prayer had been composed and recommended by state officials. Parents of ten pupils in the school district responded by bringing suit in state court to stop the practice of mandated prayer in school. After the New York Court of Appeals upheld the decision of the trial court permitting public schools to use the prayer—so long as it was voluntary—the parents applied to the U.S. Supreme Court for review of this decision.

The parents were joined in their appeal by the American Civil Liberties Union and a variety of other groups, many of them associated with the Jewish religion. For its part, the school board was joined by Porter R. Chandler, a lawyer associated with the Roman Catholic Archdiocese of New York. While the parents and their supporters claimed that the state-sponsored prayer clearly violated the First Amendment, the school board argued, to the contrary, that because no one was obliged to say the prayer, and because it was not geared towards any particular religion, it conformed to the policy of free exercise of religion promoted by the U.S. Constitution.

Official State Prayer

Even though schoolchildren now have the right, under the First Amendment's free-exercise clause, to pray silently while at school, there are some who would like a state-sponsored school prayer. The proponents of school prayer believe that bringing religion into the classroom will make our society less violent. They also believe that not allowing prayer in school takes away the rights of those who wish to do so. They also argue that adopting a formal prayer does not force anyone to pray who does not want to.

Opponents to formal prayer argue that it is not a necessary activity and that it would force atheists and children in minority religions to conform with the majority. They also counter that allowing prayer into schools would be a clear violation of the First Amendment religious guarantees.

Source(s): Seelye, Katharine Q. "House Rejects Drive to Allow Formal Prayer in the Schools." *New York Times,* 5 June 1998.

Justice Black For the Majority Declares Public School Prayer Wholly Unconstitutional

Writing for the Court, Justice Black stated unequivocally that any religious activity sponsored by public schools was inherently unconstitutional:

> We think that in using its public school system to encourage recitation of the Regent's prayer, the State of New York has adopted a practice wholly inconsistent with the Establishment Clause . . . we think that the constitutional prohibition against laws respecting an establishment of religion must at least mean that in this country it is no part of the business of government to compose official prayers for any group of the American people to recite as a part of a religious program carried on by government.

Always a First Amendment fundamentalist who took the words of the amendment at face value, Black cited no other cases to support this contention, instead concentrating on British and American history to illustrate the strength of the founding fathers' prohibition against any intermingling of church and state affairs. In contrast, the lone dissenter, Justice Stewart, maintained that the Establishment Clause merely forbids government establishment of a state religion. At the time, Stewart's opinion was disregarded. More recently, however, the Court's attitude towards prayer in the schools has softened, and in 1985, in his dissenting opinion in *Wallace v. Jaffree* William Rehnquist—who became chief justice the following year—adopted Stewart's line of argument.

Related Cases
Zorach v. Clauson, 343 U.S. 306 (1952).
Wallace v. Jaffree, 472 U.S. 38 (1985).

First graders pause for a moment of silent prayer in South Carolina.
© Corbis-Bettmann.

Bibliography and Further Reading

Eastland, Terry, ed. *Religious Liberty in the Supreme Court: The Cases that Define the Debate Over Church and State.* Washington, DC: Ethics and Public Policy Institute, 1993.

Howe, Mark De Wolfe. *The Garden and the Wilderness: Religion and Government in American Constitutional History.* Chicago, IL: Chicago University Press, 1965.

Johnson, John W. *Historic U.S. Court Cases, 1690–1990: An Encyclopedia.* New York: Garland Publishing, 1992.

Miller, Robert T. and Ronald B. Flowers. *Toward Benevolent Neutrality: Church, State, and the Supreme Court.* Waco, TX: Markham Press Fund, 1992.

ABINGTON SCHOOL DISTRICT V. SCHEMPP

Legal Citation: 374 U.S. 203 (1963)

Appellant
School District of Abington Township, Pennsylvania

Appellee
Edward Lewis Schempp

Appellant's Claim
That a Pennsylvania law requiring daily Bible readings in public schools violates the First Amendment requirement of church-state separation.

Chief Lawyers for Appellant
John D. Killian III and Philip H. Ward III

Chief Lawyer for Appellee
Henry W. Sawyer III

Justices for the Court
Hugo Lafayette Black, William J. Brennan, Jr., Tom C. Clark (writing for the Court), William O. Douglas, Arthur Goldberg, John Marshall Harlan II, Earl Warren, Byron R. White

Justices Dissenting
Potter Stewart

Place
Washington, D.C.

Date of Decision
17 June 1963

Decision
The Supreme Court struck down the Pennsylvania statute by a vote of 8-1.

Significance
For the second time in two years, the Court headed by Chief Justice Warren handed down a decision prohibiting religion in the public schools. This time, because of the hostile response to the first decision, the Court outlined a clear standard for evaluating legislation that might offend the First Amendment's Establishment Clause.

In 1962, the Supreme Court decided the case of *Engel v. Vitale,* striking down the recitation of a state-authorized prayer in public schools. *Engel* was greeted with public outrage and was denounced by congressmen and cardinals alike. When Representative Frank Becker sponsored a constitutional amendment to overturn the decision, a Gallup Poll revealed that 76 percent of Americans supported this proposal. Becker's was in fact just one of 150 such amendments, all of which ultimately failed.

Schempp was, in a sense, a case meant to test the resolve of the justices and the public. The American Civil Liberties Union (ACLU) sought out the Schempps and argued their case for them. They were a Unitarian family with school age children living in Pennsylvania. They objected to a state law requiring that a Bible passage be read each morning in the public schools. Their case was joined with that of Madalyn Murray and her son William, professed atheists and residents of Baltimore, Maryland. The Murrays likewise objected to a state-sponsored program of daily Bible readings in the public schools. In the first case, the parents won their trial; in the second, the school board was victorious. The Supreme Court agreed to review both decisions as a means of clarifying any doubt that may have lingered in the wake of *Engel.*

Court Articulates a Test for Establishment Clause Questions

As in *Engel v. Vitale,* the vote was 8-1 against a state law authorizing public school sponsorship of activities resembling prayer. All but one of the justices clearly endorsed the First Amendment's opening passage: "Congress shall make no law respecting an establishment of religion . . ." All agreed that the Fourteenth Amendment's Due Process Clause made this prohibition binding on the states. This time, however, the opinion of the Court was written not by the First Amendment absolutist Black, who had written for the Court in *Engel,* but by the more moderate Clark. The Bible readings at issue here were just as unconstitutional as the state-sponsored prayer being questioned in the earlier case; the fact that the state had actually composed the nondenominational prayer in *Engel* made no difference. Lest there be any confusion about

Reading the Bible in Public School

Even though the Supreme Court has struck down state-sponsored Bible readings and clubs in public schools, these rulings have not ended the debate as to whether or not the Bible has a place in public schools. At issue is whether the Bible should be used as a history textbook in schools. Opponents say that while the Bible may be an historical document, it is not an accurate portrayal of history. They argue that to use the Bible as a textbook gives a religious view of history and thus an infringement of First Amendment religious liberties.

Source(s): "Dispute Settled over School Bible Courses." *Christian Century,* 1 April 1998.

what constituted acceptable legislation that touched on religion, Clark spelled out a test for constitutionality:

> The test may be stated as follows: what are the purpose and the primary effect of the enactment? If either is the advancement or inhibition of religion then the enactment exceeds the scope of legislative power as circumscribed by the Constitution. That is to say that to withstand the strictures of the Establishment Clause there must be a secular legislative purpose and a primary effect that neither advances nor inhibits religion.

Clark could hardly have been clearer. If added reinforcement were needed to reassure the public that the Court was not opposed to religion, the Catholic Justice Brennan wrote a 74-page concurring opinion reviewing the history of the First Amendment and the means by which the founding fathers had arrived at the Establishment Clause. And the Jewish Justice Goldberg wrote a second concurring endorsement of the opinion of the Court.

The lone dissenter, as in *Engel,* was Justice Stewart, who once again indicated that he found the Court's holding to be anti-religious. He felt the proper empha-

Edward L. Schempp stands with his family on the steps of the U.S. Supreme Court, 1963.
© UPI/Corbis-Bettmann.

sis in deciding such cases should be on the First Amendment's Free Exercise Clause, which adds that "Congress shall make no law . . . prohibiting the free exercise [of religion]." Although the *Schempp* Court plainly thought they had put the issue of school prayer to rest, it raged on. The American public and politicians remained keenly interested in religion and the public school system. Proposals for a constitutional amendment permitting school prayer continued to surface. Toward the end of the twentieth century, the Supreme Court grew more conservative in orientation, and more justices began to share Stewart's view of religion in the public schools.

Related Cases

Engel v. Vitale, 370 U.S. 421 (1962).

Bibliography and Further Reading

Alley, Robert S. *School Prayer: The Court, the Congress, and the First Amendment.* Buffalo, NY: Prometheus Books, 1994.

Drakeman, Donald L. *Church-State Constitutional Issues: Making Sense of the Establishment Clause.* New York, NY: Greenwood Press, 1991.

Levy, Leonard Williams. *The Establishment Clause: Religion and the First Amendment.* Chapel Hill: University of North Carolina Press, 1994.

SHERBERT V. VERNER

Legal Citation: 374 U.S. 398 (1963)

Appellant
Adeil Sherbert

Appellees
Verner, et al.

Appellant's Claim
That South Carolina's denial of unemployment benefits to a Seventh Day Adventist who refused to work on Saturdays constituted a violation of her constitutional right to freely exercise her religion.

Chief Lawyer for Appellant
Daniel R. McLeod

Chief Lawyer for Appellees
William D. Donnelly

Justices for the Court
Hugo Lafayette Black, William J. Brennan, Jr. (writing for the Court), Tom C. Clark, William O. Douglas, Arthur Goldberg, Potter Stewart, Earl Warren

Justices Dissenting
John Marshall Harlan II, Byron R. White

Place
Washington, D.C.

Date of Decision
17 June 1963

Decision
South Carolina's denial of unemployment benefits to Adeil Sherbert, a Seventh Day Adventist, was held to be a violation of her constitutional free exercise rights under the First Amendment.

Significance
The Supreme Court's decision in *Sherbert v. Verner* substantially broadened its protection of the Free Exercise Clause of the First Amendment.

Legal Context

Sherbert v. Verner was one in a long line of cases revolving around the issue of state restrictions on the free exercise of religion. The trend at the time this case was decided was toward narrower protection of free exercise. In the 1961 case of *Braunfeld v. Brown*, the Court held that a Pennsylvania "blue law" that banned certain stores from remaining open on Sunday did not violate the free exercise rights of an Orthodox Jewish shopkeeper who could not, for religious reasons, operate his shop on Saturday. This decision was essentially reaffirmed in *Gallagher v. Crown Kosher Market* (1961). In these cases, the Court concluded that restrictions on religious freedom are not unconstitutional if they impose only an indirect burden, such as loss of economic opportunities, on individuals.

Sherbert v. Verner presented a somewhat different set of circumstances. In this case, the appellant claimed to have suffered a direct and substantial economic burden. Adeil Sherbert, a member of the Seventh Day Adventist Church, was fired from her job because she refused to work on Saturdays, the Sabbath day of her faith. Sherbert attempted to find work elsewhere, but was turned down for a number of jobs because of her unwillingness to work Saturdays. She then applied for unemployment compensation from the state of South Carolina. The South Carolina Unemployment Compensation Act provided compensation for any individual who has made a good faith effort to accept available suitable work when offered. The state denied Sherbert's claim on the grounds that she had failed to accept jobs when offered. Sherbert appealed this denial of benefits, claiming her freedom to practice religion had been unfairly restricted. But the South Carolina Supreme Court upheld the unemployment commission's decision. Sherbert then appealed her case to the U.S. Supreme Court.

High Court Reverses

On 17 June 1963, the Supreme Court reversed the ruling of the South Carolina Supreme Court and ruled in Sherbert's favor. In contrast to the Sunday closing cases of the preceding sessions, the Court concluded that an unfairly heavy and direct burden had been

Sherbert Test

Named for the 1963 Supreme Court case *Sherbert v. Verner*, the Sherbert test greatly expanded the religious free-exercise clause in the First Amendment. The test weighs the free-exercise rights of a citizen against the rights of a state to regulate religious actions. Prior to the Sherbert test, a state could regulate the religious actions of citizens by proving it had a rational basis for doing so. As long as a state could satisfy the rational-basis burden—and it was not difficult to do so—the state's actions were considered constitutional.

However, the Sherbert test changed that by placing a greater burden onto the state. The test required a state government to demonstrate a "compelling interest," such as public health and safety, to justify restricting or infringing on a citizen's religious free-exercise rights. A state could only justify those types of action when it provided a "compelling interest" to do so.

Source(s): Eastland, Terry. *Religious Liberty in the Supreme Court.* Washington, DC: Ethics and Public Policy Center, 1993.

placed on Sherbert without a compelling state interest for doing so.

The Court did not expend much time in determining that Sherbert's right to the free exercise of her religion had indeed been impinged upon. Writing for the majority, Justice Brennan reasoned:

> [N]ot only is it apparent that appellant's declared ineligibility for benefits derives solely from the practice of her religion, but the pressure upon her to forego that practice is unmistakable. The ruling forces her to choose between following the precepts of her religion and forfeiting benefits, on the one hand, and abandoning one of the precepts of her religion in order to accept work, on the other hand. Governmental imposition of such a choice puts the same kind of burden upon the free exercise of religion as would a fine imposed against appellant for her Saturday worship.

Next, the Court turned to the question of whether the state of South Carolina had a compelling enough interest to curtail Sherbert's religious liberties and deny her unemployment benefits. It dismissed the state's claim that it had an interest in weeding out individuals who used bogus religious beliefs as a way of unscrupulously claiming compensation. "[E]ven if the possibility of spurious claims did threaten to dilute the fund and disrupt the scheduling of work," Brennan wrote, "it would plainly be incumbent upon the appellees to demonstrate that no alternative forms of regulation would combat such abuses without infringing First Amendment rights."

Finally, Brennan and his fellow justices explicitly denied that their ruling in this case amounted to an unconstitutional establishment of religion. He wrote:

> Our holding today is only that South Carolina may not constitutionally apply the eligibility provisions so as to constrain a worker to aban-

don his religious convictions respecting the day of rest. This holding but reaffirms a principle that we announced a decade and a half ago, namely that no State may "exclude individual Catholics, Lutherans, Mohammedans, Baptists, Jews, Methodists, Non-believers, Presbyterians, or the members of any other faith, because of their faith, or lack of it, from receiving the benefits of public welfare legislation."

Dissenting Opinion

Refusing to join in this "amen chorus" were Justices Harlan and White, who issued a dissent. They decried the precedent set by the Court in carving out a special religious exemption from the normal rules of state benefit eligibility. Writing for himself and White, Harlan opined: "To require South Carolina to so administer its laws as to pay public money to the appellant under the circumstances of this case is thus clearly to require the State to violate the Establishment Clause as construed by this Court." The majority's ruling would, in Harlan's opinion, force states to "single out for financial assistance those whose behavior is religiously motivated, even though it denies such assistance to others whose identical behavior (in this case, inability to work on Saturdays) is not religiously motivated."

Impact

The Supreme Court's decision in *Sherbert v. Verner* signaled a shift in the Court's attitude toward expanded protection for the free exercise of religion. In subsequent cases like *Thomas v. Review Board of the Indiana Employment Security Division* (1981), the Court further restricted a state's ability to deny benefits to religious observers.

Related Cases

Solomon v. South Carolina, 382 U.S. 204 (1965).
Russell v. Catherwood, 399 U.S. 936 (1970).
Roach v. United States, 406 U.S. 935 (1972).

Thomas v. Review Board of the Indiana Employment Security Division, 450 U.S. 707 (1981).

Bibliography and Further Reading

Biskupic, Joan, and Elder Witt, eds. *Congressional Quarterly's Guide to the U.S. Supreme Court,* 3rd ed. Washington, DC: Congressional Quarterly, Inc., 1996.

Chandler, Ralph C. *The Constitutional Law Dictionary.* Santa Barbara, CA: ABC-Clio, Inc., 1987.

GEORGETOWN COLLEGE v. JONES

Legal Citation: 118 U.S. App. D.C. 80 (1964)

Appellants
President and Directors of Georgetown College

Appellee
Jessie E. Jones

Appellants' Claim
That the school's hospital should be able to administer a blood transfusion to Mrs. Jones despite the Jones' refusal to permit the transfusion based on religious principle.

Chief Lawyers for Appellants
Peter R. Taft, Harold Ungar, Edward Bennett Williams

Chief Lawyers for Appellee
Ralph H. Decker, Bernard Margolius

Judge
J. Skelly Wright

Place
Washington, D.C.

Date of Decision
3 February 1964

Decision
Ruled in favor of Georgetown that all necessary blood transfusions to sustain life should be administered.

Significance
The decision supported the hospital's ethical concern in saving lives of patients admitted under their care despite the patient's and family's immediate wishes. Despite the expansion of civil liberties by the courts in the 1960s, the judicial system refused to recognize any right to refuse medical treatment for purely religious reasons.

One of the many Christian religious sects is a group called the Jehovah's Witnesses. The modern group by that name was founded in Pittsburgh, Pennsylvania in the 1870s by Charles Russell. By the late 1990s membership numbered 4.5 million people worldwide. Followers of the sect believe in the imminent end of the world, and in strictly following the literal words and commands of the Bible. One of these biblical commands is contained in Genesis chapter nine, which states that the consumption of blood is forbidden:

> And God went on to bless Noah and his sons and to say to them: "Be fruitful and become many and fill the earth. And a fear of you and a terror of you will continue upon every living creature of the earth and upon every flying creature of the heavens, upon everything that goes moving on the ground, and upon all the fishes of the sea. Into your hand they are now given. Every moving animal that is alive may serve as food for you. As in the case of the green vegetation, I do give it all to you. Only flesh with its soul—its blood—you must not eat."

In keeping with their literalist approach, the Jehovah's Witnesses traditionally would not eat blood sausages or blood puddings. They had few serious conflicts with the medical profession until the 1940s, when blood transfusions and the technology of blood storage in blood banks became standardized and commonplace. In 1945, a Jehovah's Witness publication called *The Watchtower* issued the ruling that blood transfusions were akin to consuming blood. Consequences to the individual who violates the prohibition are significant including excommunication from the church and forfeiting the prospect of eternal life.

Crisis Develops at Georgetown Hospital

In September of 1963, a young man named Jessie E. Jones brought his wife into the hospital operated by Georgetown College in Washington, D.C. Georgetown College, later known as Georgetown University, and the Georgetown University Hospital are world-famous institutions. Mrs. Jones, age 25 and mother of a 7 month old child, had suffered a ruptured ulcer and lost

Refusal of Treatment

When it comes time to choose a cure for a medical problem, members of faith-healing religions will turn to prayer rather than conventional medicine. These religions believe that faith in the healing power of God, not medical procedures, will heal them.

Over the years, court cases have been brought against those who believe in faith healing to force them to accept medical treatment and procedures, especially if the health of a third party, such as a fetus, is at stake. In the situation where a woman refuses medical treatment that could save the health of her child, the court must weigh the rights of the mother against the unborn child. Court-appointed advocates for the third party

contend that the rights of an unborn child must be ensured, even if this means forcing a pregnant woman to undergo unwanted medical treatment.

But those in favor of a patient's right to refuse treatment counter that the Constitution provides a right to privacy and the free exercise of religious beliefs. It would be a breach of the Constitution, proponents say, to make someone undergo conventional medical treatment when that is against the tenets of his religion.

Source(s): Crawford, Jan. "Caesarean Case Appeal is Rejected." *Chicago Tribune,* 17 December 1993.

---

two-thirds of her blood. The Joneses were both Jehovah's Witnesses. When Dr. Edwin Westura, the chief medical resident, said that Mrs. Jones would die unless given a blood transfusion, Jones refused to permit it.

Georgetown went to court for permission to give the necessary blood transfusions without Jones's consent. On 17 September 1963 the attorneys went to Judge Edward A. Tamm's chambers at the U.S. District Court for the District of Columbia and asked for an emergency order allowing the hospital to save Mrs. Jones's life. Judge Tamm refused. At 4:00 p.m. on the same day, the attorneys next went to the chambers of Judge J. Skelly Wright of the U.S. Court of Appeals for the District of Columbia Circuit, asking for an immediate review of Tamm's decision.

Judge Wright telephoned the hospital, and Dr. Westura confirmed that Mrs. Jones would die without a blood transfusion. Wright then went to the hospital with the attorneys, where he met Mr. Jones. Jones remained firm in his refusal to grant consent. Father Bunn, Georgetown's president, even came to plead with Jones to no avail. Westura and other doctors assigned to the case tried without success to explain that a transfusion is very different from drinking blood. At 5:20 p.m., Wright signed the legal orders prepared by Georgetown, and Mrs. Jones received blood transfusions that saved her life.

On 14 October 1963, Jones's attorneys, Ralph H. Decker and Bernard Margolius, filed a petition for rehearing before the full court of appeals to quash Wright's order. On 3 February 1964, the court of appeals denied Jones's petition because Mrs. Jones had long since recovered and left the hospital. There was a spirited dissent, however, by Circuit Judge Warren Burger, who subsequently became chief justice of the U.S. Supreme Court. Burger felt that the fact that Jones

had signed a release upon bringing his wife to the hospital took the case out of the court's jurisdiction. In effect, the college had the release for legal protection without court help.

Also on 3 February 1964 Wright issued his written opinion concerning his actions, which recited various legal precedents permitting courts to act in preservation of human life, and ended by stating:

> The final, and compelling, reason for granting the emergency writ was that a life hung in the balance. There was no time for research and reflection. Death could have mooted the cause in a matter of minutes, if action were not taken to preserve the status quo. To refuse to act, only to find later that the law required action, was a risk I was unwilling to accept. I determined to act on the side of life.

Jones appealed to the U.S. Supreme Court, but his petition was denied without comment on 15 June 1964.

Impact

Even though the 1960s was an era of increasing civil liberties, the Supreme Court under Chief Justice Earl Warren refused to overturn the court of appeals' *de facto* approval of Judge Wright's actions to save Mrs. Jones's life. Although the Supreme Court and the judicial system were increasingly sensitive to the rights of religious minorities, they drew the line when religious sensibilities meant that modern medical technology would be denied to a person in need. Later in 1986, the New York Supreme Court awarded damages to a Jehovah's Witness patient given blood products against his wishes. The Court in *Randolph v. City of New York* ruled a Jehovah's Witness could legally refuse treatment even if detrimental to his health.

Conflict between physicians and patients' religious beliefs led to several forms of response by health care teams. Two alternatives included coercion often in treating young patients and deception by not revealing the treatment administered when possible. The more increasingly common option was cooperation between the patient and staff in reaching a mutual understanding of the situation and the medical options available. Since the *Georgetown* decision, use of coercion and deception became accepted as ethically wrong in denying the autonomy of the patient, long respected in medical ethics. In fact, some feared such medical tactics would actually deter Jehovah's Witnesses from coming to hospitals at all, thus endangering lives where blood transfusions would not be a factor. The right of a patient to refuse blood transfusions based on religious reasons became well accepted ethically and legally, though still introducing additional stress on hospital staff in such situations. Some hospitals began asking Jehovah's Witnesses to sign waivers relieving hospitals of the threat of lawsuits. Most Jehovah's Witnesses began carrying medical directive cards expressing their refusal of blood transfusions under all circumstances.

Medical professionals had to accept and respect the patient's rights to refuse treatment and the patient's values and beliefs, even if death could result. A cooperative relationship between the medical profession and the sect evolved by the end of the 1990s. Jehovah's Witnesses divide blood products into two main categories. They will not accept transfusions of whole blood, red blood cells, plasma, white blood cells and platelets. Acceptable are immune globulins, vaccines, serum, hemophiliac preparations, and organ transplants. As a result, treatment of Jehovah's Witnesses often presented difficult situations for health care specialists, but new approaches in treating diseases such as leukemia were explored and shared in the medical profession.

The case also raised issues concerning ethical and legal responsibilities of hospitals and physicians who accept patients under their care. A physician's relationship with a patient is a voluntary one with no requirement to accept a particular person. But once a relationship is established, the doctor is legally responsible to provide medical treatment and can be held liable for not providing treatment. The case of *Cruzan v. Director, Missouri Department of Health* (1990) highlighted hospital employees' apprehensiveness to passively allow death without clear legal footing. In *Cruzan* the Court essentially ruled that the hospital was compelled to sustain life with whatever means available regardless of the desires of the immediate family when the wishes of the patient were not clear, either due to his current incapacitated state or lack of prior guidance.

Related Cases
Randolph v. City of New York, 117 A.2d. 44 (1986).
Cruzan v. Director, Missouri Department of Health, 497 U.S. 261 (1990).

Bibliography and Further Reading
Carroll, Patricia A. "When a Jehovah's Witness Refuses a Transfusion." *Nursing,* August, 1995.

Kelly, David F. *Critical Care Ethics: Treatment Decisions in American Hospitals.* Kansas City, MO: Sheed & Ward, 1991.

Malyon, David. "Transfusion-free Treatment of Jehovah's Witnesses: Respecting the Autonomous Patient's Rights." *Journal of Medical Ethics,* October 1998, 24(5): pp. 302.

Penton, M. James. *Apocalypse Delayed: the Story of Jehovah's Witnesses.* Buffalo, NY: University of Toronto Press, 1985.

Rosenthal, Elisabeth. "Blinded by the Light." *Discover.* August 1988, pp. 28-30.

LEMON V. KURTZMAN

Legal Citation: 403 U.S. 602 (1971)

Appellant
Alton J. Lemon

Appellee
David H. Kurtzman, Superintendent of Public Instruction of the Commonwealth of Pennsylvania

Appellant's Claim
That state payment of teachers of secular subjects in parochial schools violates the First Amendment mandate of separation of church and state.

Chief Lawyer for Appellant
Henry W. Sawyer III

Chief Lawyer for Appellee
J. Shane Creamer

Justices for the Court
Hugo Lafayette Black, Harry A. Blackmun, William J. Brennan, Jr., Warren E. Burger (writing for the Court), William O. Douglas, John Marshall Harlan II, Potter Stewart, Byron R. White

Justices Dissenting
None (Thurgood Marshall did not participate)

Place
Washington, D.C.

Date of Decision
28 June 1971

Decision
The Supreme Court struck down the state laws enabling such payments.

Significance
Lemon v. Kurtzman is important for establishing the "Lemon Test," a three-pronged test for determining whether a statute passes scrutiny under the First Amendment's prohibition of laws "respecting an establishment of religion."

Two separate state laws were at issue in *Lemon v. Kurtzman.* The first of these was the Rhode Island Salary Supplement Act of 1969; the second was the Pennsylvania Non-Public Elementary and Secondary Education Act of 1968. Both laws permitted state government to supplement the salaries of teachers of secular subjects in religious schools. Alton J. Lemon was one of the residents and taxpayers who challenged these laws in federal court, claiming they violated the First Amendment's prohibition against state establishment of religion. After his suit was dismissed by the federal district court, he appealed to the U.S. Supreme Court for review of this decision.

The first modern Supreme Court case concerning the First Amendment's Establishment of Religion Clause was *Everson v. Board of Education* (1947), in which the Court ruled that not only is government not allowed to favor one religion over another, it also cannot favor religion over secularism. *Abington School District v. Schempp* (1963) added the requirement that laws touching on freedom of religion must have a secular legislative function. And in 1968, in *Board of Education v. Allen,* the Court also concluded that the primary effect of such laws must neither advance nor restrict religion.

Supreme Court Establishes the Lemon Test

Before ruling on the constitutionality of the statutes before it, the Court set up a three-pronged test, which Chief Justice Warren, writing for the Court, called "cumulative criteria developed by the Court over many years." In order to pass the test, a law was obliged to meet the requirements of the First Amendment: 1) the law must have a secular (i.e., not religious) legislative purpose; 2) the law in its principle or primary effect must neither advance nor inhibit religion; and 3) the law must not foster excessive entanglement of church and state.

Both statutes failed the third requirement of no excessive entanglement. Burger's opinion admitted that the wall Thomas Jefferson said must be erected between church and state "far from being a 'wall,' is a blurred, indistinct, and variable barrier depending on all the circumstances of a particular relationship." To guarantee that church and state remained separated under such laws, government would have to involve itself in constant monitoring of religious schools, an involvement amounting to excessive entanglement. In the end, wrote Burger:

> The merit and benefits of these schools . . . are not the issue before us . . . The sole question is whether state aid to these schools can be squared with the dictates of the Religion Clauses. Under our system the choice has been made that government is to be entirely excluded from the area of religious instruction and churches excluded from the affairs of government. The Constitution decrees that religion must be a private matter . . . and that while some involvement and entanglement are inevitable, lines must be drawn.

Although the Court has not yet abandoned the Lemon test, it has found ways of modifying it significantly. Justice O'Connor, for example, has convinced most of her fellow justices to shift the emphasis of the second prong of the test to a consideration of whether or not the law conveys a message of government endorsement or disapproval of religion.

State governments, realizing that the Court itself often found the results of *Lemon* unsatisfactory, were quick to find ways around it. For instance, the Court has taken a lenient attitude towards state aid that goes directly to parochial school students and their parents, allowing the state to provide such things as free transportation and educational testing and counseling services—assistance also afforded public school students.

For the same reason, state tax deductions for educational expenses—regardless of whether they were incurred in public or religious institutions—have been allowed to stand. And in *Agostini v. Felton* (1997), the Court overturned a precedent set a decade earlier ruling out a New York City program that sent public school teachers to parochial schools to provide remedial education to disadvantaged students. In the intervening years, the Court said, the state had instituted safeguards to prevent excessive entanglement.

Related Cases
Everson v. Board of Education, 330 U.S. 1 (1947).
McCollum v. Board of Education for District 71, 333 U.S. 203 (1948).
Abington School District v. Schempp, 374 U.S. 203 (1963).
Board of Education v. Allen, 392 U.S. 236 (1968).
Aguilar v. Felton, 473 U.S. 402 (1985).
Agostini v. Felton, 117 S. Ct. 1997 (1997).

Bibliography and Further Reading
Healey, Robert M. "Thomas Jefferson's 'Wall': Absolute or Serpentine?" *Equal Separation: Understanding the Religion Clauses of the First Amendment.* ed. Paul J. Weber. New York, NY: Greenwood Press, 1990: pp. 123-148.

Levy, Leonard W. *The Establishment Clause: Religion and the First Amendment,* 2nd ed. Chapel Hill: University of North Carolina Press, 1994.

Pfeffer, Leo. *Religion, State, and the Burger Court.* Buffalo, NY: Prometheus Books, 1985.

WISCONSIN V. YODER

Legal Citation: 406 U.S. 205 (1972)

Petitioner
State of Wisconsin

Respondents
Jonas Yoder, Wallace Miller, Adin Yutzy

Petitioner's Claim
That three Amish parents violated state educational requirements by refusing to send their children to public school past the eighth grade.

Chief Lawyer for Petitioner
John W. Calhoun

Chief Lawyer for Respondents
William B. Ball

Justices for the Court
Harry A. Blackmun, William J. Brennan, Jr., Warren E. Burger (writing for the Court), Thurgood Marshall, Potter Stewart, Byron R. White

Justices Dissenting
William O. Douglas (Lewis F. Powell, Jr., and William H. Rehnquist did not participate)

Place
Washington, D.C.

Date of Decision
15 May 1972

Decision
That the Free Exercise Clause of the First Amendment exempted the Amish parents on religious grounds from obeying the state law.

Significance
Wisconsin v. Yoder interpreted the Free Exercise Clause by constructing a three-part test intended to balance state educational interests against the interests of religious freedom. This balancing test marked the height of the move away from the belief-action doctrine established in the nineteenth century. The decision also impacted debates regarding parental control of their children's education.

The Free Exercise Clause of the First Amendment has posed a challenge to those courts faced with conflicts between religion and the government. The clause, which protects the free exercise of religion, fails to define religion, leaves its protective parameters unclear, and invites a wide range of interpretations. Interpreting free exercise becomes especially tricky—and especially important—in a culturally diverse nation such as the United States, when members of a religious minority seek exemption from state or federal laws because of their religious beliefs.

In *Wisconsin v. Yoder,* the Supreme Court grappled with a clash between Amish religious convictions and state educational requirements. Three families belonging to two Amish sects—the Old Amish religion and the Conservative Amish Mennonite Church—refused to send their children to public school past the eighth grade. Though state law required all children to attend school until age 16, the parents of Frieda Yoder, Barbara Miller, and Vernon Yutzy insisted that their religion prohibited them from allowing their children to attend high school. The Amish felt that exposing their children to the mainstream, "worldly" values taught there, such as competition and materialism, would undermine the religious teachings central to their alternative lifestyle and world view. They preferred instead to prepare their children at home for the agricultural and domestic pursuits that awaited them as adults in the Amish community. Therefore they sought exemption from state law under the Free Exercise Clause.

The Court used a three-part test to decide the case. First, it asked whether the religious beliefs in question were sincerely held. Secondly, it asked whether state law did in fact seriously burden those beliefs. After answering in the affirmative to the first two parts, the Court went on to consider the balance of the state's interests against the free exercise interests of the Amish. It determined that in order to rule for the state, state interests had to override religious interests, and that there must be no other way for state interests to be met other than to impinge upon religious freedom. Here the Court found that the state's interest in educating children to be responsible, productive citizens did not override the Amish parents' right to protect their commu-

The Amish and Schooling

The Amish are a North American Protestant group, of Mennonite origin, that has maintained a conservative agricultural way of life. Because of their desire to retain a separate way of life, the Amish have had conflicts with the larger society, especially in the area of compulsory education. The Amish believe that the public educational system does not reflect their community's traditional values, such as humility, correctness, and efficient use of resources and time. Because of this, many Amish parents will not send their children to public high schools, believing that if their children continue with schooling, they will not be fit for the Amish way of life.

The difference between Amish cultural values and those of U.S. society at large is reflected in the instructional methods used in Amish-run elementary schools. The instruction in Amish schools is designed to sustain that community's cultural beliefs. Consequently, these teaching methods can be quite different from those used in public schools. For instance, Amish teachers do not encourage their students to stand out or be different from the other students so that children will learn humility and not become prideful.

Source(s): Fishman, Andrea R. "Worlds Together, Worlds Apart." *Phi Delta Kappan*, January 1996.

nity's religious beliefs by keeping their children out of high school.

The majority opinion emphasized the unique and pervasive nature of the Amish religion in rendering its decision. In an extensive inquiry into Amish religious beliefs and practices, the Court found that in an Amish community, religion, culture and daily life proved inseparable. Removing a child from his or her community for several hours a day thus would seriously undermine religious beliefs. The Court also discussed what it saw as the unbroken historical tradition of the Amish way of life, its isolation, and its rejection of modern conveniences and values. The majority opinion felt that the home-based education provided by the Amish beyond the eighth grade sufficiently prepared their children to function within and contribute to Amish society. The Court even went so far as to say that forcing these parents to send their children to high school threatened the very viability of the Amish religion and way of life.

The decision in *Wisconsin v. Yoder* brought together two areas of legal interpretation: parental control over education and the free exercise of religion. Between 1923 and 1927 a series of Supreme Court decisions— *Meyer v. Nebraska, Pierce v. Society of Sisters,* and *Farrington v. Tokushige*—established parents' constitutional right to exert control over their children's education, though strictly in a secular context. *Yoder* introduced a religious dimension to that debate.

Yoder also contributed to the Court's long-standing effort to interpret the Free Exercise Clause. In *Reynolds v. United States* (1879), the Court established the belief-action distinction, which held that though the First Amendment protected religious beliefs, citizens could still be held responsible for actions emanating from those beliefs that violated state or federal laws. In

Cantwell v. Connecticut (1940), the Court moved away from strict belief-action doctrine to rule that government could not place an undue burden on religious practice as well as belief. The Court extended free exercise protection to indirect, unintended restrictions on religious practice in *Sherbert v. Verner* (1963).

In 1972, *Wisconsin v. Yoder* elaborated on the *Sherbert* decision, developing the three-part balancing test and issuing what Samuel Brooks called, in a 1990 article for the *Valparaiso University Law Review,* the Court's "clearest statement of the factors used in analyzing free exercise claims" to date. Together, *Sherbert* and *Yoder* seemed thoroughly to renounce the belief-action doctrine of previous rulings. In the 1980s and 1990s, however, the Court rendered several decisions—including *United States v. Lee* (1982) and *Employment Division v. Smith* (1990)—that reestablished the belief-action distinction and limited religious exemptions from federal and state laws.

The Supreme Court's decision in *Wisconsin v. Yoder* elicited mixed reactions. To some, it seemed greatly to extend both constitutional protection of religious freedom and parental control over education. To others, the way in which the Court focused its ruling on the specific facts of the case and emphasized what it saw as the unique nature of the Amish situation, limited its precedential value and actually restricted religious exemptions in future cases. This restrictive aspect has received criticism from several factions, including advocates of parents' rights to protect their children from religiously objectionable portions of school curricula, advocates of complete home education, and those who support private religious schools' freedom from state regulation.

The *Yoder* decision caused other negative reactions as well. Some critics have faulted the Court for failing to consider the children's interests as distinct from their parents and their right to a lifestyle choice beyond the Amish community. Others have expressed concern with the Court's narrow definition of what kind of religion qualified for the exemption granted in *Yoder,* a definition that included the existence of an organized group holding common religious convictions and a belief in the literal interpretation of the Bible. Some Native American legal advocates have criticized subsequent courts for misapplying the principles established by *Yoder* to Native American religions, thus denying Indian people protection of their sacred sites against government use and development. Whether seen as a positive or negative move, it remains clear that far from settling debates over the meaning of the Free Exercise Clause, *Wisconsin v. Yoder* only added to its multiple interpretations.

Related Cases

Reynolds v. United States, 98 U.S. 145 (1879).
Meyer v. Nebraska, 262 U.S. 390 (1923).
Pierce v. Society of Sisters, 268 U.S. 510 (1925).
Cantwell v. Connecticut, 310 U.S. 296 (1940).

Bibliography and Further Reading

Bainton, Denise M. "State Regulation of Private Religious Schools and the State's Interest in Education." *Arizona Law Review,* Vol. 25, no. 1, winter 1983, pp. 123–149.

Brooks, Samuel D. "Native American Indians' Fruitless Search for First Amendment Protection of Their Sacred Religious Sites." *Valparaiso University Law Review,* Vol. 24, no. 3, spring 1990, pp. 521–551.

Gordon, James D. III. "*Wisconsin v. Yoder* and Religious Liberty." *Texas Law Review,* Vol. 74, no. 6, May 1996, pp. 1237–1240.

McVicker, Debra D. "The Interest of the Child in the Home Education Question: *Wisconsin v. Yoder* Re-examined." *Indiana Law Review,* Vol. 18, no. 3, summer 1985, pp. 711–729.

Tompkins, Dwight Edward. "An Argument For Privacy in Support of the Choice of Home Education by Parents." *Journal of Law and Education,* Vol. 20, no. 3, pp. 301–323.

STONE V. GRAHAM

Legal Citation: 449 U.S. 39 (1980)

Petitioner
William C. Stone, et al.

Respondent
James Graham, Superintendent of Public Instruction of Kentucky

Petitioner's Claim
That a Kentucky law requiring posting of the Ten Commandments in public schoolrooms violated the Establishment Clause of the First Amendment.

Chief Lawyer for Petitioner
William C. Stone

Chief Lawyer for Respondent
Edward L. Fossett

Justices for the Court
William J. Brennan, Jr., Thurgood Marshall, Lewis F. Powell, Jr., William H. Rehnquist, John Paul Stevens, Byron R. White (unsigned)

Justices Dissenting
Warren E. Burger, Harry A. Blackmun, Potter Stewart

Place
Washington, D.C.

Date of Decision
17 November 1980

Decision
Upheld Stone's claim and overturned a Kentucky Supreme Court decision allowing copies of the Ten Commandments to be posted in all public classrooms for secular (non-religious) purposes.

Significance
The ruling found that placement of a copy of the Ten Commandments in public classrooms constituted unlawful promotion of the Christian religious tradition. The Establishment Clause violation was largely based on the lack of integration of the Ten Commandments into a formal school curriculum. Various organizations and public school districts have since developed and adopted such curricula. The ruling also marked a growing trend by the Court to evaluate the purpose of state legislation in individual cases, not just the effects of laws.

In 1978 the state of Kentucky passed legislation requiring placement of a copy of the Ten Commandments, purchased with private donations, on the wall of each public school classroom. Also required was a notation in small print at the bottom of each display. The notice stated that the "secular application of the Ten Commandments is clearly seen in its adoption as the fundamental legal code of Western Civilization and the Common Law of the United States." Despite complaints, James Graham, Superintendent of Public Instruction in Kentucky, defended the stated secular purpose and emphasized the use of private funds. Stone filed suit with state court claiming the law violated the Establishment Clause of the First Amendment. The Establishment Clause states that, "Congress shall make no law respecting an establishment of religion." The clause guarantees separation of church (religion) and state (government). Government can neither favor one religion over another nor religion over non-religion.

The state court accepted the secular purpose as stated in the Kentucky law. The court found the action neither promoted or inhibited any religion or religious group nor involved the state excessively in religious matters. Appeal to the Kentucky Supreme Court led to affirmation of the lower court's finding through a tie vote. Stone then appealed to the U.S. Supreme Court.

Coercion in the Classroom?

Determining what degree of government action constitutes unlawful promotion of religious belief in the classroom has long been debated. In the 1963 *Abington School District v. Schempp* case, the Supreme Court established that government actions must have a "secular legislative purpose and a primary effect that neither advances nor inhibits religion" to not violate the Establishment Clause. This "purpose and effect" test was later merged with the concept of "entanglement" in the 1971 *Lemon v. Kurtzman* case to create the three-part Lemon test. The Lemon test asks three questions: (1) is the purpose of the legislation secular or religious; (2) does the primary effect of the legislation favor a particular religion, and (3) does the legislation result in excessive "entanglement" of the government. Entanglement refers to the degree of control and involvement the government finds itself having in a religious activity. The courts have defined three levels of government "favoritism" to determine the effect legislation poses: coercion, endorsement, and acknowledgment. The Supreme Court has consistently considered most religious-oriented activities in public school classrooms as coercion because school attendance is mandatory and children are particularly impressionistic, and hence are more susceptible to influence than adults. Rulings on the Establishment Clause are based on application of this test. Inclusion of *Abington* for legislative purpose, as a separate measure of constitutionality, substantially increased the range of government actions potentially violating the Establishment Clause.

The Supreme Court, in applying the Lemon test to determine if the Kentucky law was permissible under the Establishment Clause, came to a different conclusion than the two lower courts. In a majority opinion unsigned by the five justices, a 5-4 vote found the Kentucky law had no secular legislative purpose despite Kentucky's asserting the non-religious intent written in the law itself and in the disclaimer on each posting. The majority wrote that the "preeminent purpose [was] plainly religious" because the "Ten Commandments are undeniably a sacred text in Jewish and Christian faiths, and no legislative recital of a supposed secular purpose can blind us to that fact." The Court found the Ten Commandments had not been integrated into a school curriculum for purposes of study in history, civilization, ethics, or comparative religion. Hence, the posting served no valid public educational function. The majority also found that even though the copies of the Ten Commandments were purchased with private monies, public funds were still spent in administering the statute itself and that constituted excessive entanglement.

The Secular Impact of Religion

Joined in dissent by Justices Blackmun, Stewart and Chief Justice Burger, Justice Rehnquist asserted that the "Court's summary rejection of a secular purpose articulated by the legislature and confirmed by the state court is without precedent in Establishment Clause jurisprudence." He considered the questioning of Kentucky legislature intent highly inappropriate. The Court decision was thus assuming an implied unlawful religious purpose or desired effect by the state legislature and he believed this finding was unsupported by fact. Rehnquist wrote that the Court should accept Kentucky's statement in good faith and not rule the law void because the stated secular purpose might conflict with what others may see as religious. Rehnquist further wrote, "The Establishment Clause does not require that the public sector be insulated from all things which may have a religious significance or origin." In summary, he acknowledged the integral role of religion in U.S. history and government and that Kentucky was

appropriately instructing its students on the "secular impact of the Ten Commandments." Rehnquist finished by protesting the lack of oral arguments and legal briefs presented to the Court in this case.

Impact

The 1990s witnessed a nationwide spiritual revival and a rise in conservative Christian activism, including organizations such as the Promise Keepers and Christian Coalition. Groups such as these expressed an increasing desire for greater religious expression in public schools as well as government buildings. The number of student religious clubs in public schools also grew significantly, including Jewish and Muslim as well as Christian clubs.

Some believed that, owing to glaring inconsistencies in Supreme Court decisions involving the Establishment Clause, the resulting confusion in society inappropriately kept religion largely out of public schools. Minimally, this avoidance had resulted in generations of students who lack knowledge concerning the impact of religion on the United States and the world. Worse yet, many believed Court decisions banning prayer and other religious expressions, such as the posting of the Ten Commandments, contributed in the 1990s to a perceived significant moral decline in younger generations. For example, violent crime in public schools increasingly became a concern. Republican legislators came into power in the 1994 elections and promised to introduce a "school prayer" amendment. By 1998 Congress debated a proposed constitutional amendment, titled the Religious Freedom Amendment. The new amendment sought to recognize a new right to practice religion in public schools and on government property, including the display of religious symbols, such as the Ten Commandments, and allowing the use of public funds to support private religious schools.

Many hold the Ten Commandments as a cornerstone of Western civilization and the basis for the U.S. legal system. Similarly, the Court repeatedly recognized the substantial contributions religion made to historical events and social trends in the United States. Even the majority in *Abington,* which prohibited the daily reading of Bible verses in a public school, asserted that a student not exposed to religious ideas and texts would receive a less than full education by leaving them ignorant of the importance of religion in U.S. history. Consequently, critics believed the Court had been overzealous in the application of the Establishment Clause in a number of cases, including *Stone.*

Display of the Ten Commandments in public buildings continued to be an issue through the 1990s. A U.S. Circuit Court of Appeals prohibited a display in a Georgia courthouse in 1994. The American Civil Liberties Union of Alabama filed a lawsuit the following year to stop a state court judge from posting a wood carving of the Ten Commandments in his courtroom. By 1998 resolutions encouraging the display of the Ten Commandments in public buildings were introduced in both houses of Congress. Critics claimed that Christians and Jews were being accorded a privileged status in violation of the Establishment Clause.

In response to the growing public sentiment of the early 1990s, President Bill Clinton issued a Memorandum on Religious Expression in the Public Schools in July of 1995. The document recognized the role of religion and religious institutions in the history of the United States and asserted that "the First Amendment permits—and protects—a greater degree of religious expression in public schools than many Americans may now understand." The Clinton memorandum outlined several principles to guide public school districts in accommodating religious activity in schools. In support of curricula using religious material in the classroom, the 1995 Clinton memorandum stipulated that though "[p]ublic schools may not provide religious instruction, . . . they may teach *about* religion" (emphasis not added). Curriculum examples included history of religion, comparative religion, Bible-as-literature, and the role of religion in the history of the United States.

Curricula examining the Bible's influence in art and literature were taught in some public schools in the 1990s but were not free of contention. Organizations that actively pursued development and adoption of religious-oriented curricula in public schools included the Freedom Forum First Amendment Center of Vanderbilt University and the National Council on Bible Curriculum in Public Schools. Not all Christian organizations supported efforts to place religious materials in the classroom, choosing instead to emphasize respect and recognition of the increasing religious diversity in the nation.

Still, the 1990s witnessed a trend toward more leniency in introducing religious symbols in public places. The public supported efforts to bring moral values, as exemplified in the Ten Commandments, back into public activities as long as harmony and inclusiveness was promoted rather than division or exclusion. For instance, some Muslim groups did not oppose posting the Ten Commandments as long as it was not interpreted as excluding beliefs of other religions, but accepted as representative of the rich religious tradition in America. Toward the end of the 1990s, the place of religion in public schools continued to be the subject of substantial debate.

Aside from religion issues, the *Stone* decision also demonstrated an increased willingness of the Court to question the intent behind state legislation. The Court generally avoided passing judgement on the legitimacy of legislative actions in previous decisions. This new tendency led to more debate over the appropriateness of *Stone* and similar Supreme Court findings issued since.

Related Cases
Abington School District v. Schempp, 374 U.S. 203 (1963).
Lemon v. Kurtzman, 403 U.S. 602 (1971).
Lee v. Weisman, 505 U.S. 577 (1992).

Bibliography and Further Reading
Gedicks, Frederick M. *The Rhetoric of Church and State: A Critical Analysis of Religion Clause Jurisprudence.* Durham, NC: Duke University Press, 1995.

Hardy, Lawrence. "Bible Story: Walking a Fine Line Between Church and State, Schools Try to Teach the Bible." *The American School Board Journal.* April 1998.

Larue, Gerald A. "What Hasn't Been Said About the Ten Commandments Controversy." *The Humanist.* January-February 1998, vol. 58, no. 1.

"Posting Ten Commandments in Public Places Stirs Debate." *The Philadelphia Inquirer.* 8 March 1997.

Smith, Steven D. *Foreordained Failure: The Quest for a Constitutional Principle of Religious Freedom.* New York: Oxford University Press, 1995.

THOMAS V. REVIEW BOARD OF THE INDIANA EMPLOYMENT SECURITY DIVISION

Legal Citation: 450 U.S. 707 (1981)

Petitioner
Eddie C. Thomas

Respondent
Review Board of the Indiana Employment Security Division

Petitioner's Claim
That the Indiana Employment Security Division's refusal to grant unemployment benefits to Thomas, a Jehovah's Witness who quit his job for religious reasons, violated his right to free exercise of religion.

Chief Lawyer for Petitioner
Blanca Bianchi de la Torre

Chief Lawyer for Respondent
William E. Daily

Justices for the Court
Harry A. Blackmun, William J. Brennan, Jr., Warren E. Burger (writing for the Court), Thurgood Marshall, Lewis F. Powell, Jr., John Paul Stevens, Potter Stewart, Byron R. White

Justices Dissenting
William H. Rehnquist

Place
Washington, D.C.

Date of Decision
6 April 1981

Decision
The Indiana Employment Security Division did in fact violate Thomas' constitutional right to free exercise of religion under the First Amendment.

Significance
Thomas v. Review Board of the Indiana Employment Security Division reinforced earlier decisions that required the states to have a compelling interest when denying unemployment benefits to people who leave their jobs because of sincere religious convictions.

Eddie C. Thomas, a Jehovah's Witness, was employed by the Blaw-Knox Foundry and Machinery Company in Indiana as a sheet metal worker. After a year on the job, he found himself transferred to another department which produced turrets for military tanks. Since the manufacture of armaments violated his religious beliefs, Thomas asked for a second transfer. When he was told there were no other openings in departments unrelated to military production, he asked to be laid off. When this request was likewise refused, Thomas quit his job. Thomas then applied for unemployment compensation benefits and appeared at an administrative hearing to explain his beliefs. His request for benefits was denied, on the grounds that his decision to quit was not based on "good cause arising in connection with his work." The Indiana Employment Security Division affirmed this decision, which Thomas then appealed in the state court—on the grounds that the denial of benefits violated his right to the free exercise his religion.

The Lower Court Rulings

The Indiana Court of Appeals agreed with Thomas' argument and reversed the ruling of the Employment Security Division. The Employment Security Division then appealed to the Indiana Supreme Court, which vacated the court of appeals' decision. It asserted that Thomas' decision to quit was not an exercise of religious belief but "a personal-philosophical choice." It further ruled that whatever burden was being imposed on Thomas' First Amendment right to religious practice was greatly outweighed by the state of Indiana's need to keep the unemployment compensation fund financially sound. It could only do this by keeping strict eligibility rules to deter people from making fraudulent or frivolous unemployment claims. Finally, the Indiana Supreme Court determined that to give financial assistance to someone who left his job on religious grounds would violate the First Amendment clause prohibiting the establishment of a state religion. Not to be deterred, Thomas then appealed again—this time to the U.S. Supreme Court.

The Supreme Court Decides

On 6 April 1981, the Supreme Court issued its decision. By an 8-1 vote, it ruled in favor of Thomas and against the Indiana Employment Security Division. Chief Justice Burger wrote the majority opinion. The majority ruled that the denial of unemployment benefits in this case had in fact substantially infringed upon Thomas' free exercise of religion. Moreover, in the Court's opinion, the state of Indiana had failed to justify its decision to deny benefits to an extent that would outweigh the burden placed on Thomas. Regarding the Indiana Supreme Court's conclusion that Thomas' reasons for quitting were "philosophical" rather than religious, Burger wrote:

> In reaching this conclusion, the Indiana court seems to have placed considerable reliance on the facts that Thomas was "struggling" with his beliefs and that he was not able to "articulate" his belief precisely . . . Courts should not undertake to dissect religious beliefs because the believer admits that he is "struggling" with his position or because his beliefs are not articulated with the clarity and precision that a more sophisticated person might employ.

As to the review board's claim that forcing it to pay benefits to Thomas would violate the First Amendment's Establishment Clause, the Court rejected the notion that "to compel benefit payments to Thomas involves the state in fostering a religious faith." In addition, the Court dismissed the contention that the state had a "compelling interest" in deterring people from quitting jobs for "personal" reasons:

> There is no evidence in the record to indicate that the number of people who find themselves in the predicament of choosing between benefits and religious beliefs is large enough to create "widespread unemployment."

Justice Rehnquist dissented. He believed that to force Indiana to extend benefits to Thomas would violate the Establishment Clause as the Supreme Court had interpreted it in past cases:

I believe that although a State could choose to grant exemptions to religious persons from state unemployment regulations, a state is not constitutionally compelled to do so. If Indiana were to legislate what the Court today requires—an unemployment compensation law which permitted benefits to be granted to those persons who quit their jobs for religious reasons—the statute would "plainly" violate the Establishment Clause . . . [A]lthough the unemployment statute as a whole would be enacted to serve a secular legislative purpose, the proviso would clearly serve only a religious purpose. It would grant financial benefits for the sole purpose of accommodating religious beliefs.

Thomas v. Review Board of the Indiana Employment Security Division was an important case in the constitutional history of freedom of religion. It did not settle the matter once and for all, however. The Court would return again and again to the thorny question of where freedom of religion ends and the establishment of religion begins.

Related Cases
Stromberg v. California, 283 U.S. 359 (1931).
Cantwell v. Connecticut, 310 U.S. 296 (1940).
Everson v. Board of Education, 330 U.S. 1 (1947).
Walz v. Tax Commisioner, 397 U.S. 664 (1970).
Wisconsin v. Yoder, 406 U.S. 205 (1972).

Bibliography and Further Reading
Ducat, Craig R. and Harold W. Chase. *Constitutional Interpretation.* St. Paul, MN: West Publishing Company, 1988.

Greenslaw, Paul S., and John P. Kohl. "Religious Freedom and Unemployment Compensation Benefits." *Public Personnel Management,* Fall 1995.

Seeger, Steven C. "Restoring Rights to Rites." *Michigan Law Review,* March 1997, p. 1472.

VALLEY FORGE COLLEGE V. AMERICANS UNITED

Legal Citation: 454 U.S. 464 (1982)

Petitioner
Valley Forge Christian College

Respondent
Americans United for Separation of Church and State, Inc., et al.

Petitioner's Claim
That donation of a surplus federal facility to a private sectarian college did not violate the Establishment Clause of the First Amendment.

Chief Lawyer for Petitioner
C. Clark Hodgson, Jr.

Chief Lawyer for Respondent
Lee Boothby

Justices for the Court
Warren E. Burger, Lewis F. Powell, Jr., Sandra Day O'Connor, William H. Rehnquist (writing for the Court), Byron R. White

Justices Dissenting
Harry A. Blackmun, William J. Brennan, Jr., Thurgood Marshall, John Paul Stevens

Place
Washington, D.C.

Date of Decision
12 January 1982

Decision
Reversed a court of appeals finding that citizens can sue the government for spending public monies on religious institutions by claiming violation of the First Amendment's Establishment Clause.

Significance
The Supreme Court found that private taxpayers could not challenge federal spending programs in court without proving specific injuries. Without the show of injury, a requirement basic to the concept of "standing" before the courts, the complaint was considered a general grievance more appropriately directed towards the legislative or executive branches of government. Public pressure mounted for the Court to broaden its definition of standing. Using a narrow definition, government actions can potentially violate the Constitution with no one able to challenge in a timely manner.

In 1942, the Department of the Army acquired 181 acres of land northwest of Philadelphia, Pennsylvania. On a 77-acre part of the property, the government built Valley Forge General Hospital to provide medical care for members of the military. After 30 years of operation, the secretary of defense identified the hospital in April of 1973 for closure as part of a national plan to reduce the number of military installations in the United States. Declared surplus property, the facility was transferred to the Department of Health, Education, and Welfare (HEW) for disbursement.

Under authority of the Federal Property and Administrative Services Act of 1949, HEW was directed to award the property to a party showing "the greatest public benefit." In response to an application from Valley Forge Christian College, HEW transferred the property to the college in August of 1976. HEW did not charge the college for the $577,500 facility because of a 100 percent public benefit allowance calculated by the agency. The college, a nonprofit educational institution under supervision of the Assemblies of God religious order, was committed to use the facility solely for educational purposes for at least 30 years. The college expressed its intention to conduct "a program of education . . . meeting the accrediting standards of the State of Pennsylvania, the American Association of Bible Colleges, the Division of Education of the General Council of the Assemblies of God and the Veterans Administration."

Upon learning of the acquisition through a news release, four employees of the Americans United for Separation of Church and State, Inc., filed a lawsuit in U.S. district court in October of 1976. They sought to block the property transfer, charging violation of the First Amendment's Establishment Clause, which directs that the U.S. government can not provide support to religious organizations. Americans United, a nonprofit organization, claimed that due to the transfer their members "would be deprived of the fair and constitutional use of his (her) tax dollar . . . in violation of his (her) rights under the First Amendment." Americans United asserted the government should have been paid full value for the property since a religious-oriented organization could not legally benefit all Americans.

Taxpayer Standing

Prior to 1968, citizens claiming general injury as federal taxpayers in opposition to legislation authorizing government spending programs were routinely denied "standing" by the Court. Standing means that only persons considered directly affected by or involved in a dispute may sue in federal court. The persons initiating a suit must demonstrate clearly that they have "suffered some actual or threatened injury" as a result of supposedly unlawful activity, that the injury can be traced to the challenged action, and that it can be resolved by a court decision. Also, the injured party must be the one bringing legal action, not another party speaking on their behalf. These requirements also serve to protect those that may be the target of lawsuits by providing a factual forum for them to defend themselves and appeal unfavorable decisions. A taxpayer can challenge constitutionality of government spending under the various articles and amendments of the Constitution. Options include the Tax and Spend Clause of Article I, the Judicial Powers Clause of Article III, and the Establishment Clause of the First Amendment.

The restriction to federal taxpayer standing was established in 1923 by the *Frothingham v. Mellow* case. A taxpayer claimed financial injury by a federal law providing funds to states implementing programs to reduce maternal and infant mortality. Though the Court previously ruled taxpayers had standing to sue local governments over spending issues, the question of federal government spending had not been addressed. The Court ruled the taxpayer had no basis to bring suit by simply asserting that Congress was acting unconstitutionally. No specific injury to the individual could be identified. The Court asserted "the relation of a taxpayer to the United States is very different" than with local governments because their interest was "shared with millions of others." Any personal effects would be comparatively minor. The Court wrote, "The party who invokes the power [of judicial review] must be able to show not only that the (law) is invalid but that he has sustained or is immediately in danger of sustaining some direct injury as a result of its enforcement, and not merely that he suffers in some indefinite way in common with people generally."

The *Frothington* prohibition rigidly held until 1968 when the Court created a limited exception. In *Flast v. Cohen* (1968), the Court determined the Establishment Clause of the First Amendment provided sufficient connection between the taxpayer's constitutional claims and government spending to create standing.

In the *Valley Forge* case, the district court dismissed the lawsuit ruling that Americans United failed to demonstrate any actual injury other than disagreement with the government action. Americans United then appealed to the U.S. Court of Appeals which reversed

the lower court's decision. The court of appeals agreed with the district court's finding that American United lacked standing for suing as American taxpayers, but asserted that they "had standing merely as 'citizens,' claiming (injury) to their . . . right to a government that 'shall make no law respecting the establishment of religion.'" The college appealed to the Supreme Court.

In assessing Americans United's standing, Justice Rehnquist, writing on behalf of the 5-4 majority, found that Americans United were challenging the action by HEW under the Tax and Spending Clause of Article I, but HEW was actually operating under the Property Clause of Article IV. Taxpayer standing did not apply to land grant actions under that article. Rehnquist claimed that citizens as taxpayers could only challenge congressional spending, not spending by the executive branch of government. Rehnquist noted that the property in question was in Pennsylvania, the respondents lived in Maryland and Virginia with their office in Washington, D.C., and that they learned of the transfer through a news release. The Court concluded "that any connection between the challenged property transfer and respondents' tax burden is at best speculative and at worst nonexistent." In fact public funds spent in acquiring the property and building the facility were actually spent 30 years before Americans United claimed injury. In finding no specific injury, Rehnquist wrote that "standing is not measured by the intensity of the litigant's interest or fervor of this advocacy." In sum, Rehnquist wrote that the Establishment Clause does not provide citizens "a special license to roam the country in search of governmental wrongdoing and to reveal their discoveries in federal court. The federal courts were simply not [created] as [overseers] of the general welfare." Rehnquist sharply criticized the lower court by going out of their way in finding "an available plaintiff" to try the case. The Court reversed the court of appeals decision essentially overruling the Establishment Clause exemption of *Flast*.

Right to Sue

With Justices Marshall and Blackmun joining in dissent, Justice Brennan strongly protested the majority using "standing to slam the courthouse door against plaintiffs." He believed the Court had far more flexibility in determining standing under the Constitution. Brennan criticized the majority on several issues. First, he believed standing is not lost because many people may claim the same injury, contrary to the *Frothington* ruling. The Constitution does not draw distinction between large injuries and smaller ones. Secondly, under Article III, if a causal relationship can be identified, it does not matter how indirect. Thirdly, even though a taxpayer cannot sue for return of tax payments, they can file a complaint that public funds are being spent in violation of the Constitution. This question is not one of standing, but of legal rights.

Unlike any other clause in the Constitution, the Establishment Clause imposes a restriction on the power to tax based on manner of spending. This restriction was established in the 1947 *Everson v. Board of Education* case by stating, "No tax in any amount . . . can be levied to support any religious activities or institutions." Therefore, the Establishment Clause automatically gives citizens standing to challenge the spending of tax funds to advance religion. In addition, all taxpayers suffer the same injury under an Establishment Clause violation. Brennan added that taxpayers must be able to challenge Establishment Clause violations in court. Objections cannot be raised at the time of paying a tax since it is paid before the actual spending, and taxpayers cannot challenge the tax collectors, because there is no way of separating those monies that will be spent in support of religion from the general funds of the nation. Therefore, the taxpayer must be able to challenge at the time of the violation "in order to halt the . . . intolerable burden on his pocketbook, his conscience, and his constitutional rights."

Impact

The *Valley Forge* case centered on when taxpayers may challenge government spending in courts. As demonstrated by the sharply divided vote, the Court did not easily recognize collective public complaints. Individuals must establish personal standing to represent public interest. Court actions in the 1990s maintained these strict standards for standing. In April of 1998 the Supreme Court heard arguments in *NEA v. Finley* concerning standards imposed by Congress on fellowships and grants given by the National Endowment of the Arts. Identification of any precise injury to specific individuals were initial points the Court debated before considering whether to tackle First Amendment censorship questions. A taxpayer issue in the late 1990s was Congressional efforts to authorize spending public funds on private schools, many of which are parochial, through a special voucher, or coupon, system.

Congressional watchdog groups composed of taxpayers, such as People for the American Way, multiplied significantly in the 1990s. Such groups fear if important questions are left to elections rather than the courts, constitutional "relativism" would follow, resulting in fundamental rights changing with public mood swings. A broadening of standing by courts would possibly allow resolution of fundamental constitutional issues in the courts before national crises escalate, politically dividing the country.

Related Cases

Frothingham v. Mellow, 262 U.S. 447 (1923).
Everson v. Board of Education, 330 U.S. 1 (1947).
Flast v. Cohen, 392 U.S. 83 (1968).
National Endowment for the Arts v. Finley, U.S. 97-371 (1998).

Bibliography and Further Reading

"The Art of Avoidance: Supreme Court Puts on a Good Show, But It May Opt to Not Rule on Merits of a First Amendment Case Involving the NEA," *Casper Star-Tribune,* April 12, 1998.

Biskupic, Joan, and Elder Witt. *Guide to the U.S. Supreme Court.* Washington, DC: Congressional Quarterly, 1997.

MUELLER V. ALLEN

Legal Citation: 463 U.S. 388 (1983)

The First Amendment contains in its first clause that "Congress shall make no law respecting an establishment of religion." As interpreted by the Supreme Court, the Establishment Clause prohibits the government from promoting religious beliefs in any form. After passage of the Fourteenth Amendment, the clause was applied to state law as well.

In the twentieth century, the Supreme Court has considered a number of cases involving state support of parochial (also called sectarian) schooling. The Court has generally limited efforts to subsidize religious schooling, viewing those attempts as the establishment of religion. The Court, however, has found exceptions to those limits, and *Mueller v. Allen* is one of the most important of these.

Tax Breaks for All—in Theory

In 1955, the state of Minnesota allowed parents to deduct certain expenses on their state income tax relating to their children's education. The deductions were for tuition, books, and transportation, up to $500 for each student in grades K-6 and $700 for students in grades 7-12. Parents of students in either public or private schools could claim the deduction.

The deduction for tuition applied almost exclusively to parents who sent their children to private schools. Tuition was a far greater expense than books or transportation for those parents, most of whom enrolled their children in sectarian schools. A group of Minnesota taxpayers, including Van Mueller, believed the tax law in effect subsidized religious education, violating the Establishment Clause of the First Amendment.

The taxpayers sued the state of Minnesota in federal district court. They introduced statistics to back their claim. In 1978-79, of the 90,000 state students enrolled in private schools, almost all went to parochial institutions. Only 79 students in public schools paid any tuition, to attend schools outside of their local district. Despite these numbers, the court ruled that law was neutral: it did not advance or hinder the exercise of religious beliefs. Mueller appealed, and the court of appeals affirmed the lower court's decision. The U.S. Supreme Court then agreed to hear the case.

Petitioners
Van D. Mueller and June Noyes

Respondent
Clyde E. Allen, Minnesota Commissioner of Revenue

Petitioners' Claim
That a Minnesota statute allowing parents to deduct certain school expenses on their state income tax promoted religious schooling, violating the Establishment Clause of the First Amendment.

Chief Lawyer for Petitioners
William I. Kampf

Chief Lawyer for Respondent
Douglas C. Blomgren

Justices for the Court
Warren E. Burger, Sandra Day O'Connor, Lewis F. Powell, Jr., William H. Rehnquist (writing for the Court), Byron R. White

Justices Dissenting
Harry A. Blackmun, William J. Brennan, Jr., Thurgood Marshall, John Paul Stevens

Place
Washington, D.C.

Date of Decision
29 June 1983

Decision
Affirmed the decision of the lower courts that the tax statute did not violate the Establishment Clause.

Significance
For the first time, the Court let stand a law that in practice benefited parochial schooling, as a majority found the law was primarily secular.

Deducting Private School Expenses

Should taxpayers be allowed to deduct from their state income taxes expenses related to sending their children to religious schools? Proponents of the measure argue that these tax deductions are not religious in nature because they support a secular cause, namely the advancement of education. Further, they argue that these deductions give poorer students the opportunity to attend private schools.

Opponents argue that these deductions support religious activity and thus breach the Establishment Clause of First Amendment. In addition, they feel that if more students opt to leave public schools it could have the ill effect of eroding the public educational system. Finally, opponents argue that a great deal of state revenue would be lost with these deductions.

Source(s): Eastland, Terry. *Religious Liberty in the Supreme Court.* Washington, DC: Ethics and Public Policy Center, 1993.

Applying the "Lemon Test"

The Court affirmed the ruling of the lower court. In his opinion, Justice Rehnquist acknowledged that "Today's case is no exception to our oft-repeated statement that the Establishment Clause presents especially difficult questions of interpretation and application." But in 1971, in *Lemon v. Kurtzman* the Court created a test since adopted in other Establishment Clause cases. The so-called "Lemon test" subjects a law to three requirements: It must reflect a secular purpose; it must, in its primary effect, not advance nor inhibit religion; and it must avoid excessive government "entanglement" in religious practice. The Court used the Lemon test in *Mueller* and ruled in favor of the Minnesota tax law.

On the first point of the test, Rehnquist wrote that the law was clearly "secular and understandable," as its goal was to help parents pay for education costs. Helping parents with those costs served the greater good by ensuring well educated citizens. Rehnquist further reasoned the existence of private schools helped lower public schooling expenses for taxpayers.

For the second point, Rehnquist wrote, "The deduction is available for educational expenses incurred by all parties, including those whose children attend public schools and those whose children attend non-sectarian private schools or sectarian private schools." By helping so many groups, the law did not advance religion.

The ruling in *Mueller* differed from that of *Committee for Public Education and Religious Liberty v. Nyquist* (1973), in which the Court struck down New York tax laws that helped only parents who sent their children to private, mostly parochial, schools. Mueller and the other petitioners cited *Nyquist*, arguing that the Minnesota law had a similar effect as the laws that were prohibited in New York. As their statistics showed, the Minnesota law in practice helped subsidize religious education. The Court, however, was not swayed by the numbers and largely dismissed them in their decision.

Finally, on the third point, the Court held that the Minnesota tax did not "excessively entangle" the state with religion, even though the state might have to decide which text books were secular and which were sectarian. Previous rulings had found that making such evaluations did not violate the Establishment Clause.

A Strong Dissent

The *Mueller* decision spelled out the way states could help parents who sent their children to private schools, by allowing tax breaks apply to everyone. However, the dissenters in *Mueller* thought the decision ignored the true effect of Minnesota tax law: the subsidization of religious instruction. In his dissent, Justice Marshall opined that the Establishment Clause applied whether a subsidy for sectarian schooling was direct, as in *Nyquist*, or indirect, as in this case. Unlike Rehnquist, Marshall was influenced by the petitioners' statistics, and he concluded that they revealed the failure of the Minnesota tax law in the second part of the Lemon test. By almost exclusively helping parents who paid tuition for parochial schools, the tax did advance religion.

Marshall summed up his discomfort with the majority opinion:

> For the first time, the Court has upheld financial support for religious schools without any reason at all to assume that the support will be directed to the secular function of those schools and will not be used to support religious instruction. This result is flatly at odds with the fundamental principle that a State may provide no financial support whatsoever to promote religion.

Previously, the Court had allowed states to fund parochial schools for non-religious obligations and activities, but nothing that was specifically religious. The Court upheld that standard two years later in *Aguilar v. Felton*.

Related Cases

Lemon v. Kurtzman, 403 U.S. 602 (1971).
Committee for Public Education and Religious Liberty v. Nyquist, 413 U.S. 756 (1973).
Aguilar v. Felton, 473 U.S. 402 (1985).

Bibliography and Further Reading

Biskupic, Joan, and Elder Witt. *Guide to the U.S. Supreme Court.* Washington, DC: Congressional Quarterly, Inc., 1997.

Hall, Kermit L., ed. *The Oxford Companion to the Supreme Court of the United States.* New York: Oxford Press, 1992.

Kemerer, Frank R. and Kimi Lynn King. "Are School Vouchers Constitutional?" *Phi Delta Kappan,* December 1995, p. 307.

Nowak, John E., Ronald D. Rotunda, and J. Nelson Young. *Constitutional Law,* 2nd ed. St. Paul: West Publishing Company, 1984.

Padover, Saul, ed. *The World of the Founding Fathers.* New York: Thomas Yoseloff, 1960.

Peterson, Paul E. "A Report Card on School Choice." *Commentary,* October 1997, p. 29.

Shnayerson, Robert. *The Illustrated History of the Supreme Court of the United States.* New York: Harry A. Abrams, 1986.

Witt, Elder, ed. *The Supreme Court and Individual Rights.* Washington, DC: Congressional Quarterly, Inc., 1979.

Zelinsky, Edward A. "James Madison and Public Choice at Gucci Gulch: A Procedure Defense of Tax Expenditures and Tax Institutions." *Yale Law Journal,* March 1993, pp. 1165–1207.

MARSH V. CHAMBERS

Legal Citation: 463 U.S. 783 (1983)

Petitioner
Frank Marsh, Nebraska State Treasurer, et al.

Respondent
Ernest Chambers

Petitioner's Claim
That prayer led by a publicly paid chaplain to open Nebraska legislature sessions should not be found in violation of the First Amendment's Establishment Clause due to its historical and secular role.

Chief Lawyer for Petitioner
Shanler D. Cronk

Chief Lawyer for Respondent
Herbert J. Friedman

Justices for the Court
Harry A. Blackmun, Warren E. Burger (writing for the Court), Sandra Day O'Connor, Lewis F. Powell, Jr., William H. Rehnquist, Byron R. White

Justices Dissenting
William J. Brennan, Jr., Thurgood Marshall, John Paul Stevens

Place
Washington, D.C.

Date of Decision
5 July 1983

Decision
Upheld the state of Nebraska's claim and overturned two lower courts' decisions prohibiting legislative prayer and its public funded support.

Significance
The ruling found legislative prayer not in violation of the First Amendment based on an historical analysis rather than application of standard Court tests to determine applicability of the Establishment Clause. Legislative prayer plays an historic secular role in establishing a serious atmosphere for legislative work and does not promote a particular religion. Acceptance of ceremonial religious activities in governmental proceedings continues to foster debate as the Supreme Court wrestles with organized society's ability to recognize and accommodate religion.

For over a century the Nebraska legislature, similar to other state legislatures and even the U.S. Congress, opened each daily session with a prayer given by a chaplain paid with public funds. Presbyterian minister Robert E. Palmer had, in fact, been employed by the legislature for 16 years since 1965 to perform the duty. Issues concerning prayer had generally been resolved as they surfaced through the years. For instance, Palmer dropped reference to Christ from the prayer after receiving a complaint from a Jewish legislator. However, by 1980, disputes arose again within the legislature over the prayer. This time, no agreement was reached and legislator Ernest Chambers formally filed suit in Federal District Court seeking to end the practice.

Two clauses contained in the First Amendment concern freedom of religion: the Establishment Clause and the Free Exercise Clause. The complaint regarding Nebraska legislative prayer focused on the Establishment Clause, which states, "Congress shall make no law respecting an establishment of religion." The Establishment Clause guarantees the separation of church and government, more commonly known as the "separation of church and state" doctrine. Congress extended application of the Establishment Clause to state governments in the 1947 *Everson v. Board of Education* case. The Supreme Court subsequently established several tests to assess the constitutionality of laws and actions that came before it. The Lemon Test, formulated in the 1971 *Lemon v. Kurtzman* decision, has three parts, addressing purpose, effect, and involvement. To pass the test, government action must be: (1) only for secular purposes; (2) not to promote or prohibit a specific religion; and (3) not to "excessively entangle," meaning substantially involve, government in religious matters. Failure on any one of the three parts indicates a violation of the Establishment Clause.

Regarding Nebraska legislature prayer, the district court ruled in 1980 the prayer itself was not contrary to the Establishment Clause, but paying the chaplain from public funds was, and such use of funds must cease. Chambers appealed to the U.S. Court of Appeals. By applying the Lemon Test the court found the practice failed decisively. The 1982 decision held that

Ernest Chambers, 1968.
© Corbis-Bettmann.

repeated use of the same minister promoted a single religion and the use of state money led to entanglement. Consequently, the court ruled the Nebraska prayers fundamentally violated the Establishment Clause and ordered the entire practice to cease. The case then was petitioned by the state of Nebraska to the Supreme Court.

Is There an American Civil Religion?

On behalf of Nebraska, the state attorney general's office argued that the practice of legislative prayer was embedded in U.S. history, even performed in the U.S. Congress since the founding of the nation. The state contended that the prayers were not limited to any one religion and served a secular purpose by bringing order to the start of daily business and symbolizing the seriousness of that business before the legislature. The prayers were, in essence, "elements of the American civil religion." "Civil religion" refers to a general use of religious symbols and practices for ceremonial purposes, apart from actual worship in a particular religious tradition.

Chambers argued on the basis of the Lemon Test. He emphasized that: (1) the prayers' purpose was pro-

moting the Judeo-Christian tradition; (2) the use of the same clergyman established the effect of involving only a single denomination for over 16 years; and (3) the chaplain offered prayer at public expense thus constituting entanglement.

The Supreme Court, however, chose not to apply the Lemon Test in this case, instead focusing on the historic use of legislative prayer in the United States. Chief Justice Burger, in delivering the opinion of the Court for the 6-3 vote, recognized that the U.S. Congress had opened sessions with prayer for over 200 years following a practice begun by the Continental Congress in 1774. In fact, in September of 1789 Congress authorized the appointment of paid chaplains three days before reaching agreement on the wording of the First Amendment. On that same day, the House of Representatives passed a resolution requesting the President to set aside a Thanksgiving Day to acknowledge "the many signal favors of Almighty God." Burger noted that James Madison, an outspoken advocate of religious freedom and drafter of the Establishment Clause, was appointed the task of selecting a chaplain to open each session of the First Congress with prayer. Madison also personally voted for a bill authorizing public financial support. Burger thus wrote, "Clearly the men who wrote the First Amendment Religion Clauses did not view paid legislative chaplains and opening prayers as a violation of that Amendment." He emphasized "their actions reveal their intent." Burger concluded, "To invoke divine guidance on a public body entrusted with making the laws is not, in these circumstances, a violation of the Establishment Clause; it is simply a tolerable acknowledgment of beliefs widely held among the people of this country." That debate in the original Congress focused on this issue demonstrated the "subject was considered carefully" before adoption.

The Court recognized that "prayer is deeply embedded in the history and tradition of this country" and "the practice of legislative prayer has coexisted with the principles" of the First Amendment. In fact, court proceedings in the district court, court of appeals, and U.S. Supreme Court routinely opened with an announcement concluding, "God save the United States and this Honorable Court." The Court did not consider such prayers and statements as promoting a particular religious viewpoint. The Court, by reversing the opinion of the court of appeals, condoned the practice of legislative prayers.

A Nation in Change

Joined in dissent by Justice Marshall, Justice Brennan contended that "messages of history often tend to be ambiguous and not relevant to a society far more heterogeneous [diverse]" than 200 years earlier. Brennan believed application of the Lemon Test would have clearly demonstrated the practice of official invocational prayer in state legislatures is contrary to the Establishment Clause and unconstitutional. By not applying the test, Brennan stressed, the Court's finding was truly recognizing an exception "rather than reshaping Establishment Clause doctrine." Then in applying the Lemon Test elements, Brennan found legislative prayers placed at least "indirect coercive pressure upon religious minorities to conform," linked religious belief to the power and prestige of the state, and led to excessive entanglement by placing the state in a position of monitoring and overseeing the prayers, selecting a chaplain, and resolving complaints by legislators that arise. In sum, Brennan regarded the prayers as distinctly religious in nature, not secular, and stated that the quieting of legislators and the setting of a serious tone could be accomplished in some other manner.

Impact

The *Marsh* case and another that soon followed, *Lynch v. Donnelly* (1984), drew considerable criticism and debate due to apparent inconsistency with other Supreme Court decisions. The Court had not uniformly applied the Lemon Test designed to maintain government neutrality in religious matters, totally ignoring it in *Marsh*. Many advocates of a firm separation of church and state tried to limit the implications of this decision by asserting that the historical-based analysis used is unique to the legislative prayer question, as did Brennan in his dissent. Some became alarmed that, despite the Establishment Clause, the trend in the 1980s and 1990s was toward greater inclusion of religion in public programs. The *Marsh* decision served to further focus debate on the Establishment Clause and to what extent government action constitutes endorsing official religious belief.

Regarding the use of standard Establishment Clause tests by the Court, many justices believed the Lemon Test is too strict and difficult to apply consistently in all cases, specifically those in which tradition is a strong factor. Following *Marsh,* two other tests were offered by Supreme Court justices. Justice O'Connor created the Endorsement Test in 1984 to better evaluate the effect element in the Lemon Test. It seeks to determine if some plausible secular justification for a law exists and if the legislation actually endorses a religion. Unacceptable endorsement occurs when certain persons, such as religious minorities, are not treated as full members of a political community. In 1989 Justice Kennedy offered the Coercion Test. The test asserts that the Establishment Clause is violated only when a statute coerces an individual into accepting a particular religious doctrine. These two tests still require subjective determinations as demonstrated in *County of Allegheny v. ACLU.* In addition, law scholars consider the Coercion Test inconsistent with the intent of the First Amendment by ignoring unintended and more subtle restrictions on religious practice that regularly occur. Though the Lemon Test has been regularly criticized and even ignored, as in *Marsh,* no better test has been developed.

The Court stimulated further debate over the role of religion in government by accepting legislative prayer. The debate at times focused on the concept of "ceremonial deism." Deism is the belief in existence of a Supreme Being worthy of adoration. Ceremonial deism then means a more secular use of religious concepts in maintaining civil order in a society, as part of a civil religion. Other examples of ceremonial deism related to government action in the United States include invocations in courts, observance of Thanksgiving, the national motto "In God We Trust," the words "under God" in the Pledge of Allegiance, use of "in the year of our Lord" to date public documents, prayers in Presidential inaugurations, use of the Bible to administer oaths, and a National Day of Prayer. Protection of these uses from the Establishment Clause has been argued on the grounds that any particular religious meaning has been largely lost through their rote repetitious use in public. Thus they serve wholly secular purposes for inspiring commitment, celebrating patriotic values, and infusing a solemn context. They are not part of specific religious practice. Many believe ceremonial deism plays an integral role in preserving the integrity of civil society. Therefore, they believe such general public use of religious concepts should be exempt from Establishment Clause scrutiny. The Court still struggles over the issue of ceremonial deism and how to best accommodate it in the U.S. constitutional framework while prohibiting other religious practices.

Related Cases

Everson v. Board of Education of Ewing Township, 330 U.S. 1 (1947).
Lemon v. Kurtzman, 403 U.S. 602 (1971).
Lynch v. Donnelly, 465 U.S. 668 (1984).
County of Allegheny v. ACLU, 492 U.S. 573 (1989).

Bibliography and Further Reading

Bork, Robert H. "What to Do About the First Amendment." *Commentary,* February 1995.

Choper, Jesse H. *Securing Religious Liberty: Principles for Judicial Interpretation of Religion Clauses.* Chicago: The University of Chicago Press, 1995.

Levy, Leonard W. *The Establishment Clause: Religion and the First Amendment.* Chapel Hill, NC: The University of North Carolina Press, 1994.

Smith, Steven D. *Foreordained Failure: The Quest for a Constitutional Principle of Religious Freedom.* New York: Oxford University Press, 1995.

"Suit of the Week: City Needn't Offer an Anti-Prayer Prayer." *Liability Week,* 2 November 1998.

"The Supreme Court: Taking a Sledge Hammer to Jefferson's Wall." *Church & State,* September 1997, p. 16.

WALLACE V. JAFFREE

Legal Citation: 472 U.S. 38 (1985)

Appellant
George C. Wallace, Governor of Alabama

Appellee
Ishmael Jaffree

Appellant's Claim
That public schools can provide students with a minute of silence each day for purposes of meditation or prayer without violating the doctrine of church-state separation.

Chief Lawyer for Appellant
John S. Baker, Jr.

Chief Lawyer for Appellee
Ronnie L. Williams

Justices for the Court
Harry A. Blackmun, William J. Brennan, Jr., Thurgood Marshall, Sandra Day O'Connor, Lewis F. Powell, Jr., John Paul Stevens (writing for the Court)

Justices Dissenting
Warren E. Burger, William H. Rehnquist, Byron R. White

Place
Washington, D.C.

Date of Decision
4 December 1984

Decision
The Supreme Court struck down the Alabama "moment of silence" statute.

Significance
The Court remained firm in its opposition to statutes like Alabama's, which was clearly intended to reintroduce prayer into the schools. However, the Court did leave an opening for some other state to introduce a truly undefined, uncommitted "moment of silence" into its school system.

Ishmael Jaffree was a resident of Mobile County, Alabama. On 28 May 1982, he filed suit in federal district court on behalf of his three school-age children. They were, he claimed, being subjected to regular prayer services and other forms of religious indoctrination as a part of the regular school day. Jaffree named as defendants the governor of Alabama, George Wallace, and various other state officials. At a preliminary hearing in the case, state Senator Donald G. Holmes testified about the statute that permitted religious or quasi-religious activity in the Alabama public schools. He said that as the prime sponsor of the bill, his intention was to use the proposed legislation to return voluntary prayer to the public schools. When it was first passed in 1978, the statute had called for a minute of silence for "meditation." In 1981, the statute was amended so that the moment of silence could be spent in "meditation or voluntary prayer." Then in 1982, the law was changed again to permit teachers to lead "willing students" in a prayer to "Almighty God."

In the end, the district court concluded that there was no impediment to Alabama's establishment of a state religion. Jaffree then appealed this judgment to the federal appellate court, which overturned the district court's decision. Since the law in question clearly was meant to advance religion, it violated the Establishment Clause of the First Amendment, which reads: "Congress shall make no law respecting an establishment of religion . . ." Subsequent U.S. Supreme Court decisions had made the Establishment Clause applicable to the states, as well as the federal government. After this decision, the Supreme Court granted Governor Wallace's petition for review, but agreed only to address the constitutionality of the 1981 amendment to the Alabama "minute of silence" law.

There was some reason to believe that at this moment in history, the Court might be open to some quasi-religious observation in the public schools. Popular response to the Court's decisions upholding a wall between church and state in *Engel v. Vitale* (1962) and *Abington School District v. Schempp* (1963) had been negative, and ever since 1971, polls had consistently shown that more than 75 percent of respondents favored school prayer. When Ronald Reagan was

Moment of Silence

Is it constitutional to require a moment of silence at the beginning of the day in a public school? Opponents believe a "moment of silence" law is an unconstitutional attempt to bring prayer back into the public schools. They contend that in order for the law to be constitutional, it must state that the silent time be spent for meditation only and not suggest that it be for prayer. For instance, they argue that a law that allows students the opportunity for "meditation or voluntary prayer" has a religious purpose and therefore violates First Amendment rights.

Those in favor of the "moment of silence" feel that the law is constitutional epecially if it states that it is for "meditation or voluntary prayer." They argue that this makes it clearer that the child can use the time as they wish and are not being pressured to pray.

Source(s): Eastland, Terry. *Religious Liberty in the Supreme Court.* Washington, DC: Ethics and Public Policy Center, 1993.

elected president in 1980, he made no secret of his ambition to reintroduce prayer in the public schools. And the Court itself had shown some signs that it might be relenting. Recently it had ruled, in *Lynch v. Donnelly* (1984), that a city-sponsored Christmas display including a nativity creche did not violate the Establishment Clause.

Court Strikes Down "Minute of Silence" Law as Impermissible State Sponsorship of Religion

Writing for the Court, however, Justice Stevens made it immediately clear that the Alabama law, which was intended from its inception to reintroduce prayer into the schools, would not pass constitutional muster. The district court's conclusion that there was no constitutional barrier to state-sponsored religion was, he wrote, "remarkable." Stevens first rehearsed the history of the Establishment Clause. Then, applying the Court's latest test for deciding Establishment Clause questions, developed in *Lemon v. Kurtzman* (1971), he concluded that the Alabama statute lacked the necessary "secular purpose."

Stevens's opinion did, however, leave one small opening. If the Alabama legislature had simply left matters where they stood in 1978, he hinted, the outcome might have been different:

> The legislative intent to return prayer to the public schools is, of course, quite different from merely protecting every student's right to engage in voluntary prayer during an appropriate moment of silence during the school day. The 1978 statute already protected that right, containing nothing that prevented any student from engaging in voluntary prayer during a silent minute of meditation.

The separate concurring opinions of Justices Powell and O'Connor emphasized the point that some

"moment of silence" statutes might in fact be constitutional.

Related Cases

Engel v. Vitale, 370 U.S. 421 (1962).
Abington School District v. Schempp, 374 U.S. 203 (1963).
Lemon v. Kurtzman, 403 U.S. 602 (1971).
Lynch v. Donnelly, 465 U.S. 668 (1984).

George C. Wallace, Governor of Alabama, in 1972.
© *UPI/Corbis-Bettmann.*

Ishmael Jaffree (left) and his attorney, Ronnie Williams, outside the U.S. Supreme Court, 1984. © AP/Wide World Photos.

Bibliography and Further Reading

Alley, Robert S. *School Prayer: The Court, the Congress, and the First Amendment.* Buffalo, NY: Prometheus Books, 1994.

Johnson, John W., ed. *Historic U.S. Court Cases, 1690–1990: An Encyclopedia.* New York: Garland Publishing, 1992.

Keynes, Edward. *The Court vs. Congress: Prayer, Busing, and Abortion.* Durham, NC: Duke University Press, 1989.

Oaks, Dallin H., ed. *The Wall Between Church and State.* Chicago, IL: University of Chicago Press, 1963.

GRAND RAPIDS SCHOOL DISTRICT V. BALL

Legal Citation: 473 U.S. 373 (1985)

Petitioner
Grand Rapids School District, Michigan

Respondent
Six Grand Rapids, Michigan, taxpayers

Petitioner's Claim
That two local public-school programs, Shared Time and Community Education, violated the separation of church and state called for in the First Amendment by using public funds to support courses offered in religious schools.

Chief Lawyer for Petitioner
Kenneth F. Ripple, Special Assistant Attorney General of Michigan

Chief Lawyer for Respondent
A. E. Dick Howard

Justices for the Court
Harry A. Blackmun, William J. Brennan, Jr. (writing for the Court), Warren E. Burger, Thurgood Marshall, Sandra Day O'Connor, Lewis F. Powell, Jr., John Paul Stevens

Justices Dissenting
William H. Rehnquist, Byron R. White

Place
Washington, D.C.

Date of Decision
1 July 1985

Decision
That the Grand Rapids programs did indeed violate the First Amendment.

Significance
The Court's decision created a major barrier against using public funds for programs that take place within religious schools, making it more difficult to establish such programs and also damaging President Ronald Reagan's efforts to create a voucher system whereby parents could get tax credit or other public assistance for sending their children to private schools.

When the Bill of Rights was first added to the Constitution, Americans looked to European law to decide what they did and did not want their new country to be like. One of the aspects of European countries that most displeased the framers of the Constitution was the idea of an official church, one that was sanctioned, financially supported, or otherwise given special privileges by the government. In England, for example, the Church of England was the official church, and it was headed by the King of England. The colonists decided to insure that in America, church and state would be completely separate.

As a result, the First Amendment to the new Constitution held that "Congress shall make no law respecting an establishment of religion." In other words, Congress could not establish any religion as officially supported by the government. Nor could Congress interfere with the practice of any religion.

Separating Public and Religious Education

Over the years, the Supreme Court ruled on many different cases that involved the separation of church and state, particularly when it came to public education. For example, it allowed a public school system to loan secular (nonreligious) textbooks to religious school students. It also allowed public schools to provide medical diagnostic services to students in religious schools. On the other hand, it would not allow the public to fund salary supplements for religious school teachers, or to reimburse religious schools for tests they prepared.

Meanwhile, Congress was passing legislation that also affected the relationship between public and religious education. By 1985, the year of *Grand Rapids School District v. Ball,* Congress had mandated that public schools had to provide all students with certain forms of remedial services. This meant that somehow, public school districts had to reach out to private-school students, including parochial-school students, to insure that they got certain kinds of help and instruction. In Grand Rapids, the school district came up with two programs to fulfill this requirement: Shared Time and Community Education.

Shared Time funded courses during the regular school day that were supposed to supplement the "core curriculum" courses that every school, public or private, had to offer in order to be accredited by the state of Michigan. These supplementary courses were offered right in the private-school building during the regular school day. They included remedial and enrichment math, remedial and enrichment reading, art, music, and physical education. Typically, a nonpublic school student would attend these publicly funded classes for one or two periods a week, or about ten percent of his or her school time during the year. Although they taught in private schools, the Shared Time teachers were full-time public-school employees.

Community Education was a program offered throughout Grand Rapids, both in schools and at other sites—but only after the school day was done. Both children and adults could take Community Education classes, which included arts and crafts, home economics, Spanish, gymnastics, yearbook production, Christmas arts and crafts, drama, newspaper, humanities, chess, model building, and nature appreciation. Teachers of Community Education were part-time public school employees—that is, they were paid by the public school district only for teaching, say, one or two courses a week. If a Community Education course was taught within a private-school building, it was virtually certain that the teacher was also employed full-time during the day by that private school.

Although Shared Time and Community Education were not specifically directed to religious schools, the district court found that, in fact, most of the schools who used them were "religiously oriented" and their regular instruction was "pervasively sectarian." In other words, during these religious schools' regular school day, even when a class was about history, literature, or science, religious ideas would be brought into the discussion. However, there was no evidence that any religious instruction was offered as part of either of the publicly funded programs.

Taking the Lemon Test

Local taxpayers decided to challenge the constitutionality of spending public funds on programs that were offered within religious schools. Both the district court and the Sixth Circuit Court of Appeals agreed that the programs violated the First Amendment. Grand Rapids School District decided to take the case to the Supreme Court.

After what was apparently a bitter debate, the Court ruled 5-4 that the Community Education program violated the First Amendment, and 7-2 that the Shared Time program was in violation. Justice Brennan wrote the majority opinion, which laid out a sweeping prohibition against programs like the ones in Grand Rapids.

Brennan explained that he had been guided by a three-part test laid out in an earlier decision, *Lemon v. Kurtzman* (1971). The so-called "Lemon test" used three criterion to evaluate each case: 1) whether the law providing public funds to religious schools had a secular (nonreligious) purpose in mind; 2) whether the law either advanced or inhibited religion; and 3) whether the law lead to "an excessive government entanglement with religion."

Brennan believed that Grand Rapids had passed the first part of the Lemon test. Clearly, the purpose of the law funding Shared Time and Community Education had been to help some students supplement their education. No religious purpose was intended. The question was with the second part of the Lemon test, and whether a religious purpose had been achieved, even if the school district had not intended it.

Yes, answered Justice Brennan:

> We do not question that the religious school teachers employed by the Community Education program will attempt in good faith to perform their secular mission conscientiously. Nonetheless, there is a substantial risk that the religious message they are expected to convey during the regular school day will infuse the supposedly secular classes . . . Shared Time instructors are teaching academic subjects in religious schools in courses virtually indistinguishable from the other courses offered during the regular religious day. Teachers in such an atmosphere may well subtly (or overtly) conform their instruction to the environment in which they teach, while students will perceive the instruction in the context of the dominantly religious message of the institution.

The End of A Symbolic Union

Justice Brennan also believed that the Grand Rapids programs failed the third part of the Lemon test: "excessive government entanglement with religion." He wrote that even the "state-paid instructors" might be "influenced" by the religious atmosphere of the schools in which they worked, so that they might "subtly or overtly indoctrinate the students in particular religious tenets at public expense." Brennan said that for public schools to provide services in a religious school building was to create a "symbolic union of church and state."

Brennan had more concerns about where the process of private schools taking money from the public systems would stop. He worried that religious schools would stop teaching all their secular courses expecting the public schools to pick up their tabs. Then the public would truly be subsidizing religious education.

Of course, this arrangement was exactly what President Ronald Reagan, Secretary of Education William

Bennett, and others in the Reagan administration had been calling for. They had proposed a system whereby public schools would be replaced with vouchers or tax credits, so that all who paid taxes would be allowed to direct their share into any type of education they chose. That way, rather than sending a child to a free public school, a parent might use his or her tax credit or voucher to pay all or part of the tuition at a private or religious school.

By ruling as they did in *Grand Rapids School District v. Ball*, the Supreme Court would seem to be calling such a system unconstitutional. The day after the decision, Bennett assailed the decision, calling it a "ridiculous" expression of the Court's "fastidious disdain for religion that is hard to fathom." "Crazy," "terrible," and "badly reasoned," were just some of the words Bennett used to criticize the Court's ruling.

Related Cases

Lemon v. Kurtzman, 403 U.S. 602 (1971).

Aguilar v. Felton, 473 U.S. 402 (1985).

Agostini v. Felton, 117 S.Ct. 1997 (1997).

Bibliography and Further Reading

"Establishment of Religion." *Harvard Law Review,* November 1985, p. 173.

Fiske, Edward B. "Ruling Means Cities Must Work Out How to Get Help to Parochial Pupils." *New York Times,* 2 July 1985.

Gora, Joel M. "The Delicate Matter of Religion." *ABA Journal,* December 1985, p. 84.

Greenhouse, Linda. "High Court Bars Public Teachers in Church Schools." *New York Times,* 2 July 1985.

GOLDMAN V. WEINBERGER

Legal Citation: 475 U.S. 503 (1986)

Petitioner
S. Simcha Goldman

Respondent
Caspar W. Weinberger, U.S. Secretary of Defense, et al.

Petitioner's Claim
That the U.S. Air Force regulations on uniform dress preventing petitioner from wearing a yarmulke while on duty violate his First Amendment right to free exercise of religion, and that the Supreme Court reverse the U.S. Court of Appeals prior ruling that strict enforcement of Air Force regulations is permissible.

Chief Lawyer for Petitioner
Nathan Lewis

Chief Lawyer for Respondent
Kathryn A. Oberly

Justices for the Court
Warren E. Burger, Lewis F. Powell, Jr., William H. Rehnquist (writing for the Court), John Paul Stevens, Byron R. White

Justices Dissenting
Harry A. Blackmun, William J. Brennan, Jr., Thurgood Marshall, Sandra Day O'Connor

Place
Washington, D.C.

Date of Decision
25 March 1986

Decision
Upheld the lower court's ruling that the First Amendment does not require the U.S. Air Force to allow an Orthodox Jew to wear a yarmulke, which violates uniform regulations, while on duty.

Significance
The ruling affirmed that, because the military's interest in uniformity of dress is necessary for the strict obedience, unity, commitment, and morale required by the armed forces, the First Amendment's protection of free exercise of religion does not require the military to accommodate personnel whose religious beliefs require them to violate uniform regulations.

Although the First Amendment guarantees the free exercise of religion, religious beliefs sometimes conflict state interests, including a person's military duty. The Supreme Court has never held that a person has a constitutional right to be exempted from military service because of religious convictions, though it has upheld that statutory right. But even in rulings that have embraced a broad interpretation of religion, the Court has not said that the First Amendment protections outweigh the military's significant interest in maintaining a force ready and fit for the country's defense.

S. Simcha Goldman, an Orthodox Jew and ordained rabbi, joined the Armed Forces Health Professions Scholarship Program in 1973. This program provided him with financial support while he obtained his doctorate in psychology at Loyola University. After completing his degree, Goldman was required to serve one year of active duty for each year of his subsidized study. He became a commissioned officer in the U.S. Air Force, serving as a clinical psychologist at the mental health clinic at March Air Force Base in Riverside, California.

For some years Goldman wore his yarmulke, a skullcap required of Orthodox Jewish men, while on duty. Air Force uniform regulation (AFR) 35-10, however, states that "[h]eadgear will not be worn . . . [w]hile indoors except by armed security police in the performance of their duties." In 1981, when Goldman testified as a witness at a court-martial wearing his yarmulke, the opposing counsel complained to Hospital Commander Col. Joseph Gregory that the yarmulke was in violation of the uniform code. Col. Gregory then ordered Goldman not to wear his yarmulke outside the hospital. Goldman refused. Gregory then ordered Goldman not to wear his yarmulke even in the hospital, and warned him that failure to obey AFR 35-10 could result in a court-martial. Col. Gregory also withdrew a recommendation that Goldman's application to extend active service be approved.

Goldman then sued the secretary of defense on the grounds that AFR 35-10 violated his First Amendment right to free exercise of religion, since wearing a yarmulke is required by Orthodox belief. The U.S. District Court for the District of Columbia issued an injunction barring the Air Force from prohibiting

Goldman from wearing his yarmulke. The secretary of defense appealed, and the appellate court reversed the earlier decision. The Supreme Court agreed to review the matter because of its importance.

The Government's Interest In Defense

In its analysis, the Supreme Court considered two issues: whether AFR 35-10 interfered with Goldman's ability to practice his sincerely held religious beliefs, and whether the U.S. Air Force's interest in uniform regulations justified its imposing its strict dress code on those for whom religious belief requires exemption. The Court found that AFR 35-10 did clearly impose a burden on Goldman's ability to perform his religious duties. But the Court determined that the military's interest in discipline is important enough to outweigh this burden.

Justice Rehnquist, writing for the majority, noted that "the military is, by necessity, a specialized society separate from civilian society" and "need not encourage debate or tolerate protest to the extent that such tolerance is required of the civilian state by the First Amendment." The Court also noted that it must give great deference to the professional opinion of military authorities when judging a matter of military interest. U.S. Air Force authorities claimed that uniform regulations were necessary to create discipline, subordination, and a sense of unity essential to its military mission. The Court accepted this claim, and ruled that the Air Force was not required to allow Goldman to wear his yarmulke while on duty.

In a separate concurring opinion, Justice Stevens, joined by Justice White and Justice Powell, noted that the military's interest in uniform dress must be applied equally to members of all religions. Though a yarmulke is relatively unobtrusive, Justice Stevens pointed out other visible marks of religion such as dreadlocks for a Rastafarian or turbans for Sihks are obtrusive; if yarmulkes were excepted from military regulations, these would also have to be excepted. Yet dreadlocks and turbans can be considered "so extreme, so unusual, or so faddish an image that public confidence in his ability to perform his duties will be destroyed." Because the U.S. Air Force must not distinguish between religions in its enforcement of uniform regulations, Justice Stevens argued, yarmulkes should not be permitted.

A Passionate Dissent

Four justices, however, dissented. Justice Brennan, joined by Justice Marshall, wrote that, in finding against Goldman, the Court "abdicate[d] its role as principal expositor of the Constitution and protector of individual liberties in favor of credulous deference to unsupported assertions of military necessity." Justice Brennan chastised the Court for accepting the view of military authorities without question. The contention

Caspar Weinberger, U.S. Secretary of Defense. © The Library of Congress/Corbis.

that the wearing of a yarmulke undermined the Air Force's discipline "surpasse[d] belief," Brennan wrote. The Air Force, in his view, "failed utterly" to show that excepting yarmulkes from its dress code would interfere with its interest in discipline. Noting that it was particularly important for the military to be sensitive to the requirements of minority religions, Justice Brennan concluded that banning yarmulkes "is unworthy of our military because it is unnecessary."

Justice Blackmun also dissented for a different reason. He argued that there was no reason to believe that the interests of the U.S. Air Force would be harmed by allowing Orthodox Jews to wear yarmulkes while on duty, or by allowing other similar religious exceptions. Justices O'Connor and Marshall added that since the Air Force had not plausibly justified the need for its rigid enforcement of its dress code, the individual's assertion of the First Amendment right to free exercise of religion must prevail over the military's uniform policy.

Impact

The *Goldman* decision was consistent with the Supreme Court's history of balancing First Amendment rights against the government's interests. The Court has defended individual rights to the free exercise of religion and has accepted increasingly broad and tolerant views on religious diversity, but has stopped short of finding that religious beliefs are universally more important than legitimate government interests in matters such as defense, public safety, or public health. However, in *Church of Lukumi Babalu Aye v. City of Hialeah* (1993) the Court ruled that members of the Santeria religion were permitted under the First Amendment to violate public health laws by the ritual slaughter of animals in their religious ceremonies. The Court found that this was an instance in which the First Amendment right to free exercise of religion outweighed a compelling state interest.

Related Cases

Goldman v. Secretary of Defense, 530 F.Supp. 12 (1981).
Church of Lukumi Babalu Aye, Inc. v. City of Hialeah, 508 U.S. 520 (1993).

Bibliography and Further Reading

Evans, Bette Novit. *Interpreting the Free Exercise of Religion: The Constitution and American Pluralism.* Chapel Hill, NC: University of North Carolina Press, 1997.

Rotunda & Nowak, *Treatise on Constitutional Law: Substance and Procedure,* 2nd ed. Vol. 4-13, Chapter 21.

Silverglate, Harvey A. "Paying the Piper Who Protects Our Freedoms." *The National Law Journal,* April 29, 1996, p. A17.

EDWARDS V. AGUILLARD

Legal Citation: 482 U.S. 578 (1987)

Appellant
Edwin W. Edwards, Governor of Louisiana

Appellee
Don Aguillard

Appellant's Claim
The Creationism Act was legal.

Chief Lawyer for Appellant
Wendell R. Bird, Special Assistant Attorney General of Georgia

Chief Lawyer for Appellee
Jay Topkis

Justices for the Court
Harry A. Blackmun, William J. Brennan, Jr. (writing for the Court), Thurgood Marshall, Sandra Day O'Connor, Lewis F. Powell, Jr., John Paul Stevens, Byron R. White

Justices Dissenting
William H. Rehnquist, Antonin Scalia

Place
Washington, D.C.

Date of Decision
19 June 1987

Decision
The Creationism Act violated the Establishment Clause and was therefore unconstitutional.

Significance
The case is significant because it reaffirmed that the advancing of any religious doctrine violates the Establishment Clause of the First Amendment to the U.S. Constitution.

In June of 1987, the Supreme Court voted to reject a law passed by the state of Louisiana. The rejection of this Louisiana law was to set a precedent in religion and freedom of religion-related cases. The Louisiana law required teachers in the state to teach "creationism." Although some people believe creationism, also known as creation science, to be a fact, others believe it to be a theory—a proposed but unverified explanation. In dealing with the case of *Edwards v. Aguillard*, the High Court had to deal with many issues including creation science, evolution, religion, and education. In the end, the Supreme Court ruled that the Louisiana law violated the Establishment Clause of the First Amendment to the U.S. Constitution. Because of this violation, the law was found to be unconstitutional.

To understand this case one must first understand the Louisiana law. Then one must come to understand how the Supreme Court justices arrived at their decision. The state of Louisiana passed a law it called "The Creationism Act." Under the Creationism Act teachers were required to teach both the theory of evolution and the theory of creation science.

The theory of evolution states that human beings evolved, or came into being gradually, over time. The theory of creation science disagrees with the theory of evolution. Creation scientists believe the origin of life did not happen over time, and that humans did not evolve from lower life forms. Louisiana's Creationism Act said if one theory is taught to students, then both theories must be presented. Challenging the Creationism Act were Louisiana parents, religious leaders, and teachers. A Federal District Court declared that Louisiana's Creationism Act was unconstitutional and both the court of appeals and the U.S. Supreme Court upheld the Federal District Court's decision.

The U.S. Constitution's Establishment Clause prohibits the passage of any law that takes away an individual's freedom of religion, whether that person selects a religion or decides on no religion at all. The question the Supreme Court asked itself was did the passage by the state of Louisiana of its Creationism Act violate the Establishment Clause? Based on its long history dealing with the religion clauses of the First Amendment, the Supreme Court had developed what became known

---

Creationism Act

The Creationism Act was a 1981 Louisiana law that sought to bar the teaching of evolution in public school classes unless "creation science" was also taught as a possible origin of organic life. The theory of evolution proposes that animals and humans evolved from one or two primitive life forms over 3 million years ago in a process of natural selection. Creation science, how-ever, dates the start of human life on earth back 6,000 years ago as described in the book of Genesis in the Bible.

Source(s): Sanders, Alain I. "LAW: Memories of the Monkey Trial." *Time,* 29 June 1997.

---

as the Lemon test. The Lemon test allowed the Supreme Court to decide whether or not a certain piece of legislation violated the Establishment Clause.

The Lemon test itself evolved over time. Many cases, including *Everson v. Board of Education, Engel v. Vitale, McGowan v. Maryland, Committee for Public Education and Religious Liberty v. Nyquist,* and the case lending the test its name—*Lemon v. Kurtzman* in 1971—among others, provided precedents on which to build the Lemon test. The Lemon test the Supreme Court used to decide whether or not the act violated the clause included the justices' answers to three separate questions. The justices found that the answers to their questions were: 1) Yes, the legislature passed the law with a non-religious purpose. 2) Yes, the prmary effect of the law was to advance or inhibit religion. And, 3) Yes, the law created an excessive meshing of religion with government. So, by answering yes to its three part question concerning the violation of the Establishment Clause, the Supreme Court ruled against the passage of the act.

The Supreme Court, in making its decision, brought to light several points about the Creationism Act that were discriminatory. The act required that teachers develop curriculum guides for creationism but not for evolution. The Supreme Court said this was discrimination. The act forbade local school boards from discriminating against creation-scientists, but not teachers who taught the theory of evolution. The Supreme Court said this was discrimination. And, the High Court noted, the act endorses the creation-science-held religious belief that a supernatural being created human beings. This, the justices agreed, violates the First Amendment to the Constitution.

By challenging the constitutionality of the act in court, the Louisiana parents, teachers and religious leaders participated in what became a landmark case dealing with freedom of and from religion. After the Supreme Court ruled, Louisiana Governor Edwards along with others involved in the educational system in Louisiana agreed not to implement the Creationism Act. In summary, the case is significant because it reaffirmed that the advancing of any religious doctrine violates the Establishment Clause of the First Amendment to the U.S. Constitution.

Related Cases
Everson v. Board of Education, 330 U.S. 1 (1947).
McGowan v. Maryland, 366 U.S. 429 (1961).
Engel v. Vitale, 370 U.S. 421 (1962).
Lemon v. Kurtzman, 403 U.S. 602 (1971).
Committee for Public Education and Religious Liberty v. Nyquist, 413 U.S. 756 (1973).

Bibliography and Further Reading
Benen, Steve. "Evolving Debate." *Church & State,* October 1998, p. 13.

Biskupic, Joan, and Elder Witt, eds. *Congressional Quarterly's Guide to the U.S. Supreme Court,* 3rd ed. Washington, DC: Congressional Quarterly, Inc., 1996.

Lemonick, Michael D. "Dumping on Darwin." *Time,* March 18, 1996, p. 81.

Schmidt, Karen. "Creationists Evolve New Strategy." *Science,* July 26, 1996, p. 420.

COUNTY OF ALLEGHENY V. ACLU

Legal Citation: 492 U.S. 573 (1989)

Petitioner
County of Allegheny

Respondent
American Civil Liberties Union, et al.

Petitioner's Claim
That two separate holiday displays (involving a creche and a menorah, respectively) on public property do not violate the First Amendment's Establishment of Religion Clause.

Chief Lawyer for Petitioner
Roslyn Litman

Chief Lawyer for Respondent
Peter Buscemi

Justices for the Court
(Part one, against the creche display) Harry A. Blackmun (writing for the Court), William J. Brennan, Jr., Thurgood Marshall, Sandra Day O'Connor, John Paul Stevens; (part two, for the menorah display) Harry A. Blackman (writing for the Court), Anthony M. Kennedy, Sandra Day O'Connor, William H. Rehenquist, Antonin Scalia, Byron R. White

Justices Dissenting
(Part one, for the creche) Anthony M. Kennedy, William H. Rehnquist, Antonin Scalia, Byron R. White; (part two, against the menorah) William J. Brennan, Jr., Thurgood Marhsall, John P. Stevens

Place
Washington, D.C.

Date of Decision
3 July 1989

Decision
By different majorities, the Court banned the display of the creche but permitted the display of the menorah.

Significance
The Supreme Court found that Allegheny County violated the Establishment Clause by displaying a creche in the county courthouse because it had the unconstitutional effect of conveying government-endorsed Christianity. However, the menorah, which was displayed in the City-County Building along with a Christmas tree, was permissible because it was displayed in such a way as to be viewed as a secular symbol, given "its particular, physical setting." This decision established that the main factor in determining the constitutionality of public holiday decorations is the context in which they are displayed.

During every Christmas holiday season since 1981, a creche donated by the Holy Name Society, a Roman Catholic organization, had been on display in front of the grand staircase inside the Allegheny County Courthouse. The creche bore a plaque attributing its donation to the Holy Name Society. Along with figures of Jesus, Mary, Joseph, shepherds, animals, and wise men, the creche depicted an angel bearing a banner that said, "Gloria in Excelsis Deo!" which translates as "Glory to God in the highest." The creche stood alone in front of the staircase as the main element on display, surrounded by poinsettias and two evergreen trees, as placed there by the county. Santa Claus figures and other Christmas decorations were arranged around the courthouse, but no other secular decorations were displayed near the staircase.

The county used the creche as the setting for its Christmas carol program, which also included other songs. From 3 December to 23 December 1986, high school choirs and other musical groups performed a two-hour program each weekday at lunchtime. The county issued a press release identifying the program as a county-sponsored event and connected the program to the creche.

A block away from the courthouse, another holiday display involving a Christmas tree and menorah was placed in front of the City-County Building, a building owned jointly by the city of Pittsburgh and Allegheny County. The 45 foot tree was erected and decorated by city employees in keeping with a long-standing tradition. Next to the tree was an 18-foot menorah. The menorah was owned by Chabad, a Jewish organization, but since 1982, it had been stored, displayed, and removed by the city each year. At the tree's base was a sign that bore the mayor's name and the message: "During this holiday season, the city of Pittsburgh salutes liberty. Let these festive lights remind us that we are the keepers of the flame of liberty and our legacy of freedom." The tree was up from 17 December 1986 to 13 January 1987 and the menorah from 22 December 1986 to 13 January 1987.

On 10 December 1986 the Pittsburgh chapter of the American Civil Liberties Union (ACLU) and seven local residents filed suit in Federal District Court to enjoin

Allegheny County from displaying the creche and the city of Pittsburgh from displaying the menorah. The ACLU claimed that displays such as the creche and the menorah violate the Establishment of Religion Clause of the First Amendment.

On 8 May 1987 the district court denied the ACLU's claim. Citing *Lynch v. Donnelly* (1984), a landmark Supreme Court decision that established a constitutional mandate for religious accommodation, the court held that the creche and the menorah did not violate the Establishment Clause. The court concluded that the displays had a secular purpose and did not create an excessive entanglement of government with religion.

The ACLU filed an appeal with the U.S. Court of Appeals. A divided panel of the court of appeals reversed the district court's decision. The court stated that despite being located near secular decorations, "neither the creche nor the menorah can reasonably be deemed to have been subsumed by a larger display of non-religious items." The displays, the court found, had the impermissible effect of endorsing religion, and thus violated the Establishment of Religion Clause of the First Amendment.

The Supreme Court decided the case on 3 July 1989. By different majorities the Court found that the menorah did not advance religion in such a way as to violate the Establishment of Religion Clause, but the creche did violate the Establishment Clause because the county, in associating with the display, was not merely acknowledging Christmas as a cultural phenomenon, but celebrating and promoting a holiday with a blatant Christian message.

Justice Blackmun, writing for the majority, said that the menorah was displayed in such a way as not to endorse religion but was used to create a secular winter holiday setting, of which Christmas and Chanukah are both part. Chanukah—for which the menorah is the primary symbol—has both religious and secular connotations. Although the menorah is a symbol with religious meaning, Chanukah does not have a preeminently secular symbolic equivalent, as Christmas has with Santa Claus and reindeer. Blackmun said, "[I]t would be a form of discrimination against Jews to allow Pittsburgh to celebrate Christmas as a cultural tradition while simultaneously disallowing the city's acknowledgment of Chanukah as a contemporaneous cultural tradition."

In her opinion, Justice O'Connor expressed the view that the creche display was different than the one in

Lynch v. Donnelly. In *Lynch* the creche was on private property and included traditional secular holiday symbols, while the Allegheny creche had the unconstitutional effect of conveying government-endorsed Christianity. She further concluded that the menorah, in its "particular physical setting" did not have the effect of endorsing religion, regardless of whether the menorah is considered a religious or secular symbol. She argued that the display conveyed "a message of pluralism and freedom to choose one's own beliefs."

Justice Kennedy, along with Justices White and Scalia and Chief Justice Rehnquist, dissented on the creche decision. Kennedy wrote: "This view of the Establishment Clause reflects an unjustified hostility toward religion, a hostility inconsistent with our history and our precedents . . . The creche display is constitutional, and, for the same reasons, the display of a menorah by the city of Pittsburgh is permissible as well."

The Controversy Continues

The debate over religious displays in Pittsburgh, as well as in the rest of the United States, has not ended since the *Allegheny* decision. In 1996 The Ku Klux Klan petitioned to display a cross bearing the Klan's insignia in the county courthouse courtyard. The petition came just five days after a coalition of local black clergy asked the commissioners for permission to erect a creche in the courthouse courtyard. Allegheny County Commissioner Bob Cranmer withdrew his support of the creche display after receiving the Klan's request. Cranmer said, "I think it is necessary that we take a prudent position and not permit the use of the courtyard as a public forum."

Related Cases

Lemon v. Kurtzman, 403 U.S. 602 (1971).
Lynch v. Donnelly, 465 U.S. 668 (1984).
Scarsdale v. McCreary, 471 U.S. 83 (1985).
Capitol Square Review and Advisory Board et al. v. Pinette et al., 515 U.S. 753 (1995).

Bibliography and Further Reading

Ahn, Laura. "This is Not a Creche." *Yale Law Journal,* April 1998, pp. 1969–1974.

Hall, Kermit, ed. *The Oxford Companion to the Supreme Court of the United States.* New York: Oxford Press, 1992.

Witt, Elder, ed. *The Supreme Court A to Z.* CQ's Encyclopedia of American Government. Washington, DC: Congressional Quarterly, Inc., 1993.

LEE V. WEISMAN

Legal Citation: 505 U.S. 577 (1992)

Petitioners
Robert E. Lee, et al.

Respondent
Daniel Weisman

Petitioners' Claim
That nonsectarian prayers offered as invocations and benedictions at public school graduation ceremonies do not represent an infringement of the Establishment Clause suggesting separation of church and state.

Chief Lawyer for Petitioners
Charles J. Cooper

Chief Lawyer for Respondent
Sandra A. Blanding

Justices for the Court
Harry A. Blackmun, Anthony M. Kennedy (writing for the
Court), Sandra Day O'Connor, David H. Souter, John Paul
Stevens

Justices Dissenting
William H. Rehnquist, Antonin Scalia, Clarence Thomas,
Byron R. White

Place
Washington, D.C.

Date of Decision
24 June 1992

Decision
Affirmed rulings of the district court and court of appeals,
which held that, regardless of their content, the offering of
prayers at public school graduation ceremonies constituted
a violation of the Establishment Clause.

Significance
The ruling constituted a political, if not legal, surprise. With
the Supreme Court comprising a majority of justices
appointed by conservative presidents, a decision validating
the use of prayer in the public schools was anticipated by
many. With this decision, the Court affirmed earlier rulings
such as *Wallace v. Jaffree* (1985) and *Marsh v. Chambers*
(1983). Significantly, the Court also refused a direct request
from the administration of President George Bush to review
the test for violation of the Establishment Clause developed
in *Lemon v. Kurtzman* (1971).

Political Landscape

Amid what many people saw as increasing social disorder and lawlessness in the 1980s, a strong political
movement emerged favoring a more prominent role for
religion within the public schools of the United States.
This movement particularly emphasized the supposed
benefits of prayer in the public schools, believing that
a renewed emphasis on religious teachings in a school
setting would lessen the perceived waywardness of
youth. By the same token, many people feared that the
introduction of religion into the public schools would
constitute a dangerous abridgement of the Establishment Clause of the U.S. Constitution, which many interpret as calling for the complete separation of church and
state. Throughout the decade of the 1980s, conservative
presidents Ronald Reagan and George Bush appointed
new members to the Supreme Court, including O'Connor, Scalia, Souter, and Thomas, who many hoped
would vote to reverse earlier Court rulings barring the
introduction of religious teachings or practices into the
public schools. A challenge to legal precedent was
eagerly awaited by proponents of school prayer.

Graduation Traditions

For many years it was customary for the principals of
middle and high schools in Providence, Rhode Island
to invite religious leaders to give nonsectarian prayers
as invocations and benedictions at school-sponsored
graduation ceremonies. The school system had, in fact,
prepared guidelines for clergy delivering such prayers,
to insure that the prayers would not include any direct
references to specific deities or saints. Despite this effort
of the schools to make the prayers innocuous and all-
inclusive, a middle school student, Deborah Weisman,
and her father, Daniel, objected to the use of any prayer
at her 29 June 1989 graduation ceremony. Four days
prior to the ceremony, the Weismans sought a temporary restraining order from the U.S. District Court for
the District of Rhode Island to prohibit the use of prayer
at Deborah's graduation. This motion was denied due
to a lack of time to fully consider the case, and the graduation ceremony was conducted as planned. Daniel
Weisman then filed for a permanent injunction against
the use of prayers at future graduation ceremonies from
the district court.

Application of Lemon

The district court held that the use of prayer at public school graduation ceremonies did constitute a violation of the Establishment Clause. To reach its verdict, the district court applied the three-pronged test for establishing infringement of the Establishment Clause devised in *Lemon v. Kurtzman.* The so-called Lemon Test directed that any state-sponsored program, in order to adhere to the Establishment Clause, must: reflect a clearly secular purpose; have a primary effect that neither advances nor inhibits religion; and avoid excessive government entanglement with religion. The district court did not comment on the first or third stipulations of the Lemon Test, but noted that the use of prayer at official public school functions violated the second clause, in that by having prayer of any kind at a state function the idea of religion in general was advanced. Robert E. Lee, principal of the Nathan Bishop Middle School of Providence, Rhode Island, and representing the petitioners, appealed the case to the U.S. Court of Appeals for the First Circuit. The court of appeals upheld the ruling of the district court, and expanded its scope by stating that the practice of using prayer at official school functions in fact violated all three prongs of the Lemon Test. The petitioners then appealed the case to the Supreme Court, which heard arguments on 6 November 1991.

A Test for Lemon

In its argument before the Supreme Court, the petitioners maintained that prayer represents an appropriate and effective means to enable students and parents to seek spiritual guidance at important events such as school graduations. The Court was unmoved by either this logic or the prevailing conservative political climate, however, and upheld the ruling of the appeals court by a vote of 5-4. Justice Kennedy, writing for the majority, made a distinction between this case and *Marsh v. Chambers,* when the Court had ruled that the use of a prayer to open a state legislature's session did not constitute a violation of the Establishment Clause. Kennedy maintained that the opening of a legislature, comprising entirely adults who are there of their own free will cannot be realistically compared to a school graduation, where numerous peer, parental, and social pressures for attendance exist. The Court also noted that school children are particularly susceptible to coercion through the schools, and as such the behavior of schools with regard to the Establishment Clause must be able to withstand especially careful scrutiny. Justices Blackmun, O'Connor, and Stevens concurred, adding that the Lemon Test was applicable and represented a

straightforward means of assessing compliance with the Establishment Clause. Justices O'Connor, Souter, and Stevens also wrote separately to maintain that the Establishment Clause should not only be construed as prohibiting the government from favoring one religion over another, but also as barring government support for religion as opposed to nonreligion. Justices Rehnquist, Thomas, and White, in dissenting from the majority, noted the pervasive tradition of using prayers as invocations and benedictions at a number of non-religious events, viewing such prayers as being essentially nonreligious in intent when used in this manner.

Impact

Lee v. Weisman represented a major political blow for proponents of prayer in the public schools. The decision came as something of a surprise to many legal and political analysts, but was in keeping with precedents established by the Court in similar cases. In *Engel v. Vitale* (1962), the Court barred prayer in the public schools as an unhealthy union of church and state. This position was affirmed and expanded in *Abington School District v. Schempp* (1963), in which the Court ruled that school-sponsored devotional activities and Bible readings were unconstitutional under the Establishment Clause. The Court has continued to adhere to a rigorous interpretation of the Establishment Clause in cases including *Board of Education of Kiryas Joel v. Grumet* (1994), where the Court found that the creation of a special school district to accommodate the needs of a community comprising entirely of Hasidic Jews was unconstitutional under the Establishment Clause.

Related Cases

Engel v. Vitale, 370 U.S. 430 (1962).
Abington School District v. Schempp, 374 U.S. 203 (1963).
Lemon v. Kurtzman, 403 U.S. 602 (1971).
Marsh v. Chambers, 463 U.S. 783 (1983).
Wallace v. Jaffree, 472 U.S. 38 (1985).
Board of Education of Kiryas Joel v. Grumet, 93 U.S. 517 (1994).

Bibliography and Further Reading

Biskupic, Joan, and Elder Witt, eds. *Guide to the U.S. Supreme Court,* 3rd ed. Washington, DC: Congressional Quarterly Inc., 1990, 491.

Biskupic, Joan, ed. *Supreme Court Yearbook 1991–1992,* Washington, DC: Congressional Quarterly Inc.

Lawton, Kim A. "Do Students Have a Prayer?" *Christianity Today,* 21 June 1993, p. 45.

CHURCH OF LUKUMI BABALU AYE, INC. V. CITY OF HIALEAH

Legal Citation: 508 U.S. 520 (1993)

Petitioner
Church of Lukumi Babalu Aye, Inc.

Respondent
City of Hialeah

Petitioner's Claim
Animal sacrifices should be allowed in rituals of religion.

Chief Lawyers for Petitioner
Douglas Laycock, Jeanne Baker, Steven R. Shapiro, Jorge A. Duarte

Chief Lawyers for Respondent
Richard G. Garrett, Stuart H. Singer, Steven M. Goldsmith

Justices for the Court
Harry A. Blackmun, Anthony M. Kennedy (writing for the Court), Sandra Day O'Connor, William H. Rehnquist, Antonin Scalia, David H. Souter, John Paul Stevens, Clarence Thomas, Byron R. White

Justices Dissenting
None

Place
Washington, D.C.

Date of Decision
11 June 1993

Decision
Religious sacrifices are allowable.

Significance
The Supreme Court unanimously declared that religious rituals involving animal sacrifices are allowed under First Amendment rights.

Santeria, a Cuban form of voodoo, combines Roman Catholicism and African tribal religions. West African slaves brought the religion to Cuba in the 1500s. The Santeria religion came to the United States via the Caribbean where Yoruba slaves brought it from West Africa. There are an estimated 70,000 followers in South Florida, mainly in the Dade County area, with as many as 800,000 nationwide. Santeria believers worship "orishas," a deity or god identified with a figure from Christianity. When help is sought from these "orishas," a ritual sacrifice is made. Animals sacrificed in Santeria rituals include doves, ducks, chickens, guinea pigs, goats, sheep, and turtles. After Santeria worshipers cut the carotid artery in the animal's neck, they cook and eat the animal except during healing and death rituals.

After the Church of Lukumi Babalu Aye, Inc., leased land in Hialeah, Florida, and said it would build a house of worship there, the Hialeah City Council passed resolutions declaring the city's commitment to prohibiting animal sacrifices. The church filed suit. The suit stated that the rights of church members were being violated. These rights were due members, the church claimed, under the Free Exercise Clause of the First Amendment. Both the district court and the court of appeals ruled in favor of the city of Hialeah.

Although differing in their approaches to this case, the Supreme Court justices unanimously agreed to reverse the lower court rulings. Echoing the High Court's opinion, Supreme Court Justice Kennedy said the laws enacted by the city of Hialeah were null and void. The ordinances were deemed invalid because they suppressed Santeria religious worship. According to Linda Greenhouse of the *New York Times,* Kennedy said "killings that are no more necessary or humane in almost all other circumstances are unpunished."

The Supreme Court said the laws enacted by the city of Hialeah violated America's commitment to freedom of religion. Although it is a non-profit religious organization, the church was accused of engaging in practices inconsistent with public morals including cruelty to animals. Still, this prohibition of ritual animal sacrifice violated freedom of religion, a constitutional right granted to all U.S. citizens.

Related Cases

Swanson By and Through Swanson v. Guthrie Independent School Dist. No. I-L, 135 F.3d 694 (1998).

Bibliography and Further Reading

Boadle, Anthony. *Reuters,* 22 May 1997.

Greenhouse, Linda. "Court, Citing Religious Freedom, Voids a Ban on Animal Sacrifice." *New York Times,* 12 June 1993.

Rohter, Larry. "Santeria Faithful Hail Court Ruling." *New York Times,* 13 June 1993.

BOARD OF EDUCATION OF KIRYAS JOEL V. GRUMET

Legal Citation: 93 U.S. 517 (1994)

Petitioner
Board of Education of Kiryas Joel Village School District

Respondent
Louis Grumet, et al.

Petitioner's Claim
That Chapter 748 of New York State Law, enabling creation of a separate school district to provide special education to the children of Kiryas Joel village, did not violate the Establishment Clause of the U.S. Constitution mandating the separation of church and state.

Chief Lawyer for Petitioner
Nathan Lewin

Chief Lawyer for Respondent
Jay Worona

Justices for the Court
Harry A. Blackmun, Ruth Bader Ginsburg, Anthony M. Kennedy, Sandra Day O'Connor, David H. Souter (writing for the Court), John Paul Stevens

Justices Dissenting
Antonin Scalia, William H. Rehnquist, Clarence Thomas

Place
Washington, D.C.

Date of Decision
27 June 1994

Decision
Denied the petitioner's claim and upheld the decisions of the New York state trial court and New York court of appeals, which ruled that Chapter 748 of New York State Law impermissibly advanced religion.

Significance
The ruling provided further elaboration of the test for deciding violation of the Establishment Clause created in *Lemon v. Kurtzman* (1971). While neither affirming nor completely abandoning the Lemon test, the Court referred to *Lemon* throughout its decision. Despite this reference to *Lemon*, several justices deemed the Lemon test flawed, leaving the future method of decision in Establishment Clause issues in doubt.

Kiryas Joel

Circumstances peculiar to the village of Kiryas Joel led to this case. In the early twentieth century the Jews living in the vicinity of Satmar, a town near the border of Romania and Hungary, became a distinct religious community, the Satmar Hasidim, under the leadership of Grand Rebbe Joel Teitelbaum. Following the Holocaust the Satmar Hasidim emigrated to the Williamsburg section of Brooklyn, New York. In the early 1970s the Satmars purchased an undeveloped area within the town of Monroe, New York, with the intent of creating a village made up exclusively of their followers. The Satmars achieved incorporation of their village, named Kiryas Joel, in 1977. The village of Kiryas Joel, with its homogeneous population sharing a single religious belief, maintained a private school system offering an Orthodox Jewish curriculum, including segregation of the sexes and emphasis on Torah teachings and limited instruction in secular subjects. The village had no public school system prior to 1989, in that there were no non-Satmar students in the district. With no public school system, Kiryas Joel did not provide special education courses and services to children with disabilities. To meet this need the adjoining Monroe-Woodbury, New York public schools offered special education services to Kiryas Joel students in 1984.

Retrenchment and Renewed Controversy

Two U.S. Supreme Court decisions handed down on 1 July 1985, rendered the accommodation between the Monroe-Woodbury and Kiryas Joel schools unacceptable. In *Grand Rapids School District v. Ball* (1985), the Supreme Court ruled that the Grand Rapids public schools had violated the Constitution by providing remedial education and religious enrichment programs to nonpublic schools, whether during or after regular school hours. Then, in *Aguilar v. Felton,* (1985), the Supreme Court ruled, 5-4, that New York state statutes allowing provision of public school remedial education and counseling services to private school students were unconstitutional. In light of these rulings the arrangement reached by the Monroe-Woodbury schools and the Kiryas Joel schools was scrapped, and the search for a new arrangement began. Meanwhile, Satmar children

Orthodox Jews denounce the Kiryas Joel School District's arguments before the U.S. Supreme Court. © Photograph by Gary A. Cameron. Archive Photos.

with disabilities had to attend the Monroe-Woodbury schools, hire their own private tutors, or forego special education altogether. This situation was unacceptable to Satmar parents, who began to lobby for a political solution to their problem. Finally, in July of 1989, the New York State legislature adopted State Law Chapter 748, which constituted Kiryas Joel as a separate, public school district for the exclusive purpose of providing special education services to students with disabilities. Governor Mario Cuomo had some misgivings about Chapter 748, given that the law specifically benefited members of one religious sect, but signed the law in the belief that it represented a satisfactory compromise for the peculiar situation faced by Kiryas Joel. Before the new Kiryas Joel school board commenced operations, however, the New York State School Boards Association brought suit against the State Education Department, alleging that Chapter 748 violated both the state and federal Establishment Clauses barring formation of state-sponsored religious organizations.

Lower Court Rulings

The first ruling in *Grumet v. New York State Education Department* was delivered by the New York State trial court, which found that Chapter 748 failed all three tests for determining violation of the Establishment Clause as laid out in the Supreme Court's decision in *Lemon v. Kurtzman*: it lacked at least one legitimate secular purpose; its primary effect was to advance a particular religious belief; and it resulted in excessive government entanglement in religion. As such, it was unconstitutional at both the state and federal levels. Subsequent legal actions at the state level resulted in

rulings from the appellate division and the court of appeals upholding the trial court's findings. Following these rulings the Board of Education of Kiryas Joel appealed the case to the U.S. Supreme Court.

Challenging the Lemon Test

The Supreme Court heard arguments in the case on 30 March 1994, and many legal observers were eager to see if the Court would use the case as a platform for the confirmation, amendment, or overthrow of the three-pronged Lemon test for determining violations of the Establishment Clause. However, when the Court's decision was handed down on 27 June 1994, the use of *Lemon* as a test was neither confirmed nor abandoned. The Court upheld the rulings of the New York state trial and appeals courts by a 6-3 margin. Justice Souter, writing for the majority, maintained that this case more closely resembled *Larkin v. Grendel's Den* (1982) than *Lemon*. In *Larkin,* the Court struck down a Massachusetts state statute allowing religious bodies the ability to veto applications for liquor licenses by establishments planning to operate within 500 feet of any church, synagogue, or parochial school. Stating that although the state had a legitimate interest in protecting religious organizations, allowing such organizations veto power over a state regulatory function created an unconstitutional "fusion of governmental and religious functions." Souter further elaborated the similarity between *Board of Education of Kiryas Joel v. Grumet* and *Larkin,* pointing out that

> the Establishment Clause problem presented
> by Chapter 748 is more subtle, but it resem-

bles the issue raised in *Larkin* to the extent that the earlier case teaches that a State may not delegate its civic authority to a group chosen according to religious criterion.

Significantly, despite its reliance on *Larkin*, the Court also made reference to *Lemon*, in that by accommodating the needs of a particular religious sect, Chapter 748 had the effect of advancing religion. Justice O'Connor, while concurring with the majority, advanced the position that Chapter 748 was unconstitutional only in that it provided no assurance that the state would provide similar benefits "equally to other religious (and non-religious) groups."

Legal Impact

The Court's ruling in *Board of Education of Kiryas Joel v. Grumet* failed to confirm or abandon the Lemon test of constitutionality under the Establishment Clause. Although it relied most heavily on *Larkin* in reaching its decision, the Court also did mention that Chapter 748 had a primary effect of advancing religion, in violation of one prong of the Lemon test. Perhaps the most significant portion of the Court's decision was that contributed by Justice O'Connor, which was used as a basis for rewriting of New York State Law Chapter 748 by Governor Cuomo and legislative leaders so as to make the statute equally applicable to any municipality. As of 1999, the constitutionality of this new statute had yet to be determined.

Related Cases

Lemon v. Kurtzman, 403 U.S. 602 (1971).
Larkin v. Grendel's Den, 459 U.S. 116 (1982).
Grand Rapids School District v. Ball, 473 U.S. 373 (1985).
Aguilar v. Felton, 473 U.S. 402 (1985).

Bibliography and Further Reading

"Church-State Separation Case to be Heard." *The Christian Century,* January 5, 1994, p. 8–10.

Coyle, Marcia. "Drawing a New Line on Religion?" *National Law Journal,* April 4, 1994, p. A1.

Rabkin, Jeremy "The Curious Case of Kiryas Joel." *Commentary,* November 1994, p. 59.

Simon, Barbara A., Esq., "Kiryas Joel's Impact on Separation," http://www.ifas.org/fw/9410/kiryas.

ROSENBERGER V. UNIVERSITY OF VIRGINIA

Legal Citation: 515 U.S. 819 (1995)

Petitioner
Ronald W. Rosenberger, Wide Awake Productions, and others

Respondent
Rectors and Visitors of the University of Virginia and others

Petitioner's Claim
That denying commonly available school funds to a student religious organization by a public university violated the First Amendment's Speech Clause.

Chief Lawyer for Petitioner
Michael W. McConnell

Chief Lawyer for Respondent
John C. Jefferies, Jr.

Justices for the Court
Anthony M. Kennedy (writing for the Court), Sandra Day O'Connor, William H. Rehnquist, Antonin Scalia, Clarence Thomas

Justices Dissenting
Stephen Breyer, Ruth Bader Ginsburg, David H. Souter, John Paul Stevens

Place
Washington, D.C.

Date of Decision
29 June 1995

Decision
The Court ruled in favor of Rosenberger by finding that the University of Virginia violated the Free Speech Clause of the First Amendment and must provide financial support to a student religious publication as it does to other student publications.

Significance
The Court found the university's actions were essentially suppressing student speech in violation of the First Amendment's Speech Clause. The ruling, following on an earlier Court decision supporting the use of public school facilities for religious purposes, significantly expanded public support for religious activities. Critics of the decision lamented that the Court again avoided the Establishment Clause issue by relying on Speech Clause considerations as in other recent cases.

Two First Amendment clauses apply to religious practice. The Establishment Clause prohibits government from establishing or promoting religious beliefs. The Free Exercise Clause prohibits governments from restricting individuals from practicing religion. The two often clash in that protecting religious practice from disruption could be construed as promotion when carried too far. Government must maintain neutrality in dealing with religious matters, and is prohibited from passing laws, which aid or inhibit religion, or prefer one religion to another. Similarly, the Speech Clause of the First Amendment allows individuals to express personal beliefs without well-founded government restriction. What some may see as protection of expressing religious viewpoints, others may see as promotion of those viewpoints, depending on the nature of the particular circumstance.

The Supreme Court consistently upheld students' rights to express themselves on university and college campuses. The Fourteenth Amendment to the Constitution extended these protections to state governments and state funded universities. In *Westside Community Board of Education v. Mergens* (1990), the Court held that Bible clubs and prayer groups could meet on public secondary school campuses. The case provided a broadened interpretation of the Equal Access Act of 1984 in which Congress prohibited discrimination against students because of their religious beliefs.

Jefferson's University

Founded by Thomas Jefferson in 1819, the University of Virginia is one of the oldest and most highly respected institutions of higher education in the nation. Over 17,000 undergraduate and graduate students annually enroll at the school. As part of the Commonwealth of Virginia, the university is subject to the First and Fourteenth amendments.

The University routinely provided monetary support from its Student Activities Fund to commercial costs for printing a variety of publications produced by student organizations. The Student Activities Fund, itself funded from mandatory student fees, was designed to support a broad range of extracurricular student activities related to the university's educational purpose. The student organizations had to include in their contracts and in all written materials a disclaimer stating that they were independent of the university and that the university was not responsible for the content.

A University of Virginia student, Ronald W. Rosenberger, applied for $5,800 from the Student Activities Fund to help subsidize the publishing expenses of a Christian magazine, *Wide Awake,* initiated in 1990. Based on the religious nature of the publication, the university refused Rosenberger's request. Because of Establishment Clause concerns, the university had adopted funding guidelines prohibiting financial support for publications promoting a particular belief about a supreme being or "ultimate reality."

The existing university structure provided no recourse to the denied students for contesting the University policy. With few other options available, Wide Awake Productions and three of its editors and members including Rosenberger filed suit in U.S. District Court for the Western District of Virginia. Rosenberger claimed the Student Activities Fund's policy to selectively refuse payments for printing costs solely on the basis of religious viewpoints violated constitutional rights to freedom of speech and press. Rosenberger also alleged his rights to the free exercise of religion and to equal protection under the law were violated as well.

The suit sought monies for the magazine's printing costs, an injunction against further enforcement of the school policy, and reimbursement of attorney's fees. Upon request for a summary judgment, the district court ruled in favor of the university. The district court ruled that the university's Establishment Clause concern over supporting "religious activities" was sufficient justification for denying payment and that Wide Awake Production's speech rights were not violated.

Rosenberger appealed the decision to the U.S. Court of Appeals for the Fourth Circuit. The appeals court disagreed with the district court opinion concerning Speech Clause violations. The court held that the fund guidelines did discriminate on the basis of speech content. The appeals court ruled that, while the state need not support the speech, a violation of the Speech Clause resulted when the university selectively denied payments, normally available to student organizations. Nevertheless, the appeals court affirmed the district court judgment when considering the religion issues. The court concluded such discrimination by the university was justified by the "compelling interest in maintaining strict separation of church and state." Rosenberger next appealed to the Supreme Court. The Court issued a writ of *certiorari,* a written order commanding the U.S. Court of Appeals for the Fourth Circuit to forward the proceedings of a case for review.

An Issue of Speech

By a narrow majority of 5-4, the Court reversed the two lower court decisions. Justice Anthony M. Kennedy,

writing for the majority, wrote that the University had violated the Constitution through "viewpoint discrimination" and that funding the paper would not violate the Establishment Clause.

Kennedy relied heavily on the Court's earlier decision in *Lamb's Chapel v. Center Moriches Union Free School District* (1993) in deciding the case. In *Lamb's Chapel,* a public school denied a religious organization permission to show a religious film in a public school building even when the property was not in use for school purposes. The school district had an existing policy of allowing certain uses during "off hours," but specifically excluded building use for religious activities. The Court found that by favoring non-religious over religious viewpoints the school policy violated the Free Speech Clause. The Court went on to find that the showing of a religious film on school property did not violate the Establishment Clause because the film was not shown during school hours, did not receive school sponsorship, and was open to the public. The school board policy for making the facilities available to groups after normal school hours had in essence created an "open forum" for expression of all viewpoints.

Kennedy asserted that under the First and Fourteenth amendments the government could not restrict speech based on the content of its message. Kennedy wrote,

> In the realm of private speech or expression, government regulation may not favor one speaker over another. Discrimination against speech because of its message is presumed to be unconstitutional. These rules informed our determination that the government offends the First Amendment when it imposes financial burdens on certain speakers based on the content of their expression. When the government targets not subject matter but particular views taken by speakers on a subject, the violation of the First Amendment is all the more blatant.

Kennedy pointed out that such viewpoint discrimination was a form of content discrimination. He concluded that the government must refrain from restricting speech when the specific ideology or opinion of the speaker was the basis for the policy.

Kennedy, noting that fundamental First Amendment speech principles were at stake, identified two dangers present in this case. The first was granting a state entity the power to examine publications to determine if they were based on some "ultimate" idea. The second danger was the chilling of individual thought and expression. Kennedy wrote, "That danger is especially real in the University setting, where the State acts against a background and tradition of thought and experiment that is at the center of our intellectual and philosophic tradition."

The Uniqueness of Religion Cases

Justice Sandra Day O'Connor, in writing a concurring opinion, sought to limit the utility of the decision as a precedent for other forms of direct public financial aid to religious activities. She emphasized that in this case the student publications were actually independent of the university and included disclaimers in every issue to that effect. In addition, the Student Activity Fund payments were sent directly to the printer, not to the students themselves. She also underscored that *Wide Awake* was only one among a large number of school funded student publications. Lastly, O'Connor asserted the funds were not normal government revenue but derived from student payments, the distribution was administered by students, and the funds were available only to students who paid their fees.

Justice David H. Souter was joined by Justices John Paul Stevens, Ruth Bader Ginsburg, and Steven Breyer, in dissent. Souter wrote, "The Court today, for the first time, approves direct funding of core religious activities by an arm of the State." Souter contended that the university's use of mandatory student fees to pay printing costs for a religious publication constituted a direct subsidy forbidden under the Establishment Clause. Souter asserted the indirect funding cases heard by the majority as precedence were fundamentally different.

Souter concluded,

> Thus the Court's reasoning requires a university that funds private publications about any primarily non-religious topic also to fund publications primarily espousing adherence to or rejection of religion. . . . The Court's contrary holding amounts to a significant reformulation of our viewpoint discrimination precedents and will significantly expand access to limited-access forums.

Impact

Rosenberger was the fourth in a series of Supreme Court cases since 1981 in the post-Warren Court era that ruled public institutions could offer support to religious organizations or activities when the benefits were provided neutrally to all groups, religious and secular. A state law or policy providing funding support to individuals or organizations without regard to religion was no longer considered in violation of the Establishment Clause. However, O'Connor's concurring opinion in *Rosenberger* made it very clear that precedents in Establishment Clause cases have narrow implications. Each case, O'Connor wrote, must be examined in regard to its specific nature to determine their relation to constitutional protections.

Critics decried use of public money to support a Christian magazine. They noted the Court had ruled that the university founded by Thomas Jefferson, chief architect of the Establishment Clause, must spend public money to support religious comment. On the other hand, the decision was viewed as a victory by the Religious Right. As fallout from the decision, government institutions seeking to avoid the subsidy of religious activity were left with the option of not supporting any type of public forum. The series of decisions supporting use of public funds for religious activities further fueled the efforts by some to use public tax monies to support private religious schools through tuition vouchers given directly to families.

Related Cases

Widmar v. Vincent, 454 U.S. 263 (1981).
Westside Community Board of Education v. Mergens, 496 U.S. 226 (1990).
Lamb's Chapel v. Center Moriches School District, 508 U.S. 385 (1993).

Bibliography and Further Reading

Coyle, Marcia. "Court Face-off in School Fee Case." *The National Law Journal,* March 13, 1995.

Doerr, Edd. "Wobbly Wall." *The Humanist,* September-October 1995.

Gaffney, Edward, Jr. "At Jefferson's University: Freedom From, not of, Religion?" *Commonwealth,* April 21, 1995.

Gedicks, Frederick M. *The Rhetoric of Church and State: A Critical Analysis of Religious Clause Jurisprudence.* Durham, NC: Duke University Press, 1995.

CITY OF BOERNE V. FLORES

Legal Citation: 117 S. Ct. 2157 (1997)

Petitioner
City of Boerne, Texas

Respondent
Father P. F. Flores, Archbishop of San Antonio, and the United States

Petitioner's Claim
That the Religious Freedom Restoration Act exceeded Congress' constitutional powers under the Fourteenth Amendment.

Chief Lawyer for Petitioner
Marci A. Hamilton

Chief Lawyers for Respondent
Douglas Laycock and Walter Dellinger

Justices for the Court
Ruth Bader Ginsburg, Anthony M. Kennedy (writing for the Court), William H. Rehnquist, Antonin Scalia, John Paul Stevens, Clarence Thomas

Justices Dissenting
Stephen Breyer, Sandra Day O'Connor, David H. Souter

Place
Washington, D.C.

Date of Decision
25 June 1997

Decision
Ruled in favor of Boerne, overturning two lower court decisions, and held that Congress impermissibly intruded on the powers of the states to enact laws for the general health and welfare of their citizens by enacting the Religious Freedom Restoration Act.

Significance
The Court's decision placed distinct limits on the power of Congress to regulate areas traditionally subject to state, not federal, regulation. The decision also limited the power of Congress to pass statutes overturning Supreme Court interpretations of constitutional provisions.

The First Amendment to the Constitution provides, in part, that "Congress shall make no law . . . prohibiting the free exercise" of religion. Prior to 1990, any law which burdened a religious practice was invalid under the First Amendment unless it met the "compelling interest test." Under this test, which is the strictest test that can be applied to a law or governmental action, a law is invalid unless it serves a "compelling" interest of the government and is narrowly drawn to serve that interest. However, in 1990, the Supreme Court decided in *Employment Division v. Smith* that a law not directed specifically towards a religious practice, but generally applicable to all citizens equally need not satisfy the compelling interest test even if it burdens a religious practice. Thus, for example, a law prohibiting the use of drugs is valid even though certain Native American religions use the drug as part of their religious ceremony.

In 1993, Congress passed the Religious Freedom Restoration Act (RFRA) to restore the compelling interest test applied by the Supreme Court prior to *Smith*. The RFRA provided that if a federal, state, or local law of general applicability "substantially burdened" a person's exercise of religion, then the law was invalid unless it could pass the strict scrutiny test. Essentially, the RFRA overturned the Supreme Court's decision in *Smith*.

In the early 1990s, St. Peter Catholic Church in the city of Boerne, Texas, sought to expand its church building to accommodate its growing number of parishioners. Boerne is situated approximately 30 miles outside of San Antonio. The church structure, built in 1923, replicated the Spanish mission style of architecture important to the region's heritage. At about the same time, the Boerne City Council passed an ordinance authorizing its Historic Landmark Commission to prepare a plan for preservation of the city's historic landmarks. P. F. Flores, Archbishop of San Antonio applied for a permit to expand the church, which was denied because the city designated the area in which the church was located as a historic district. The archbishop filed a suit in the U.S. District Court for the Western District of Texas, arguing the ordinance violated the RFRA because it burdened the church members' exercise of religion and did not satisfy the compelling interest test. The district court found that the

Religious Freedom Restoration Act

Congress passed the Religious Freedom Restoration Act (RFRA) in 1993. The act was a response to a 1990 ruling by the Supreme Court that effectively ended the Court's established procedures for free-exercise protection. RFRA required federal courts to reinstate earlier and broader free-exercise standards.

RFRA was used to restore and defend a variety of religious freedoms, such as Muslims' wearing of head coverings. As part of RFRA, a state government had to provide a compelling justification for laws that substantially

interfered with an individual's religious practices. When the Supreme Court was ruling on the constitutionality of RFRA, a 90-member coalition of religious groups spoke out in support of the act. The Religious Freedom Restoration Act was deemed unconstitutional with the Supreme Court decision in *City of Boerne v. Flores* (1996).

Source(s): Marquand, Robert. "High Court Clips Protections for Religous Freedom in the U.S." *The Christian Science Monitor*, 26 June 1997.

RFRA was unconstitutional and upheld the ordinance. The archbishop then appealed to decision to the U.S. Court of Appeals for the Fifth Circuit, which concluded the RFRA was constitutional. This decision was appealed to the Supreme Court through a procedure known as a petition for writ of *certiorari*.

Court Limits Scope of Congressional Power

The Supreme Court reversed the decision of the court of appeals, finding the RFRA unconstitutional. Congress passed the RFRA pursuant to its powers under the Fourteenth Amendment. Section 1 of the Fourteenth Amendment prohibits a state from denying a person of due process of law and of the equal protection of the laws. Section 5 gives Congress the power to "enforce, by appropriate legislation, the provisions of "the Fourteenth Amendment. Justice Anthony Kennedy, writing for the 6-3 majority, concluded that the RFRA was not a proper exercise of power under Section 5 of the Fourteenth Amendment. Kennedy reasoned that by passing the RFRA, Congress was not "enforcing" any right guaranteed by the Fourteenth Amendment but was creating a new right. Kennedy wrote that,

> The design of the Amendment and the test of 5 are inconsistent with the suggestion that Congress has the power to decree the substance of the Fourteenth Amendment's restrictions on the States. Legislation which alters the meaning of the Free Exercise Clause cannot be said to be enforcing the Clause. Congress does not enforce a constitutional right by changing what the right is. It has been given the power "to enforce," not the power to determine what constitutes a constitutional violation.

In reaching his conclusion, Kennedy relied heavily on two principles governing the structure of the American government: separation of powers and federalism. Separation of powers describes the distribution of the powers of government among the executive, leg-

islative, and judicial branches of the government. According to Kennedy, the RFRA violated separation of powers principles because, ultimately, it is within the judiciary branch's scope of power to determine what the Constitution means. However, in enacting the RFRA, Congress substituted its own judgment for that of the Supreme Court. Kennedy also concluded that the RFRA violated principles of federalism. Federalism describes the relationship between the federal government and the state governments, in which the federal government has certain powers and the state governments have others. Kennedy wrote that the RFRA constituted "a considerable congressional intrusion into the States' traditional prerogatives and general authority to regulate for the health and welfare of their citizens."

Justice Sandra Day O'Connor, joined by Justices David H. Souter and Stephen Breyer, dissented. O'Connor did not disagree with the Court's opinion regarding interpretation of Congress' powers under Section 5 of the Fourteenth Amendment. However, she was very displeased with the earlier *Smith* ruling by the Court. O'Connor wrote, "In *Smith*, five Members of this Court without briefing or argument on the issue interpreted the Free Exercise Clause to permit the government to prohibit, without justification, conduct mandated by an individual's religious beliefs, so long as the prohibition is generally applicable." She asserted the decision "harmed religious liberty" and the Court should have overturned the decision in the *Boerne* case. O'Connor argued that "the Free Exercise Clause is not simply an antidiscrimination principle that protects only against those laws that single out religious practice for unfavorable treatment." The Clause is "an affirmative guarantee of the right to participate in religious practices . . . without . . . government interference." She concluded that government must have to justify any significant burdens on religious practice by a compelling state interest with restrictions narrowly designed to attain that interest.

Impact

The decision constituted the first significant restriction of congressional power to enforce the Fourteenth Amendment since the late 1800s. Indeed, the Court's decision was a marked contrast from the civil rights cases decided in the 1960s, which generally held that Congress' power under the Fourteenth Amendment was extremely broad. Even more significant, however, the Court's reliance on principles of federalism and separation of powers followed a trend of cases decided in the mid-1990s striking down federal laws on the grounds that those laws intruded into areas, particularly crime and safety, traditionally subject to regulation by the state governments. These rulings markedly retreated from the decisions of the 1960s which broadened Congress' powers under the Fourteenth Amendment.

In the wake of the *Boerne* decision, several efforts were mounted in Congress under public pressure to counter the Court's action. The Religious Liberty Protection Act was considered by Congress in 1998. The act would prohibit state and local governments from enacting land use legislation that would potentially burden religious exercise unless the laws promoted a compelling government interest. Critics, including the National League of Cities, feared the implications of the bill on cities' ability to regulate religious-based land uses through zoning ordinances.

What did pass Congress and was signed into law late in 1998 was the International Religious Freedom Act. The act sought to protect religious believers from persecution overseas. The law provides the president a range of options to penalize nations that allow such persecution. Some business and political leaders in the United States did not support the act fearing implications on foreign trade and possible implications to other foreign policy goals over such a globally sensitive issue. The act also formed a Commission on International Religious Liberty to monitor progress and advise Congress.

Congress also continued to pursue the proposed Religious Freedom Amendment to the Constitution, with little prospects for success. Many believed the proposed amendment would disrupt classrooms, allow religious displays on public property, and permit public tax support for sectarian schools. All of these efforts raised concerns over the United States imposing its notion of religious freedom on other cultures and domestically subjecting local religious minorities to various burdens by religious majorities.

Related Cases

Employment Division v. Smith, 494 U.S. 872 (1990).

Bibliography and Further Reading

Calabresi, Stephen G. "A Constitutional Revolution." *Wall Street Journal,* 10 July 1997.

Choper, Jesse H. *Securing Religious Liberty: Principles for Judicial Interpretation of the Religion Clauses.* Chicago: University of Chicago Press, 1995.

Currie, David P. "RFRA. (Religious Freedom Restoration Act of 1993)." *William and Mary Law Review,* Vol. 39 no. 3, 1998, pp. 637-644.

Linter, Jay. "The Right's Holy War." *The Nation,* 20 July 1998.

"Protecting Persecuted Christians." *The Christian Century,* 2 December 1998.

St. Peter Catholic Church in Boerne, Texas, 1996. © Photograph by Tommy Hultgren. AP/Wide World Photos.

FREEDOM OF RELIGION, ESTABLISHMENT CLAUSE

Church and State

In an 1802 letter President Thomas Jefferson wrote of a need to maintain a "wall of separation" between church and state so as to avoid unequal treatment of the young nation's citizens. The Establishment Clause of the Constitution has since become synonymous with the phrase "separation of church and state." The terms church and state have rather specific meanings in common usage. Church normally refers to a building used for public worship, particularly in the Christian religious tradition. The term church comes from the Greek word *kuriakon* meaning "of the Lord." The term state commonly refers to the 50 states composing the United States or similar political units in other countries. However, in constitutional law much broader meanings are involved for both. Church refers to any type or form of belief system, either organized religion or more personal beliefs. State refers to any collection of people politically organized under a single government.

Many cultures in the world do not clearly distinguish between the religious and non-religious aspects of their daily lives. However, peoples of Western Society, which primarily includes Europe and North America, commonly separate their religious life from everyday events. In addition to the distinction between religious and non-religious (secular), the United States has become an increasingly pluralistic society, characterized by the presence of multiple religious traditions. The use of Christian-associated materials and practices are often offensive to those who profess other religions, as well as to those who choose to practice no religion at all.

For many states, or governments, the church was envisioned as a principal means for maintaining social unity and suppressing unwanted ideas. However, the founders of the United States saw religion as a particularly divisive issue.

Development of Separation Concepts

Controversy over the relationship between church and state extends back at least to the Roman Empire following the adoption of Christianity as the state religion in the fourth century. At the height of church influence early in the thirteenth century, the Roman Catholic Pope issued a decree stating the church should have a voice in the civil governments of Europe. Such a proclamation led to significant conflicts with various European rulers. The strife that followed between the church and various governments lasted through much of the fifteenth century before peace was restored. The uneasy tranquility between the church and states quickly ended later in the sixteenth century when several Christian Protestant churches came into existence through the Reformation. The Reformation led to state churches being established in various nations often competing in violent conflict for power and control against the previously dominant Catholic Church. The authority of rulers to determine the religion of their subjects became generally accepted.

Consistent with the turmoil, England broke away from the Catholic Church in 1534 and established the English monarch as head of the sanctioned church of England, the Anglican Church. Through the next 150 years, religion was intensively intertwined with English politics. In 1688 King James II restored Catholicism as the state religion, but English politicians rebelled and the king fled. The following year England adopted a Bill of Rights prohibiting the king from maintaining an army, levying taxes, and being a member of the Roman Catholic Church. This English Bill of Rights, in addition to the previous Magna Carta of 1215 and Petition of Right of 1628 formed the basis for emerging English liberty.

During the period of English turmoil Jamestown and Plymouth were founded in America and the colonies began to be settled. Fresh in the minds of the Founders of the United States were the seventeenth century struggles in England and restrictions placed on those not conforming to the favored religion. In fact, many colonists left England for the colonies seeking religious freedom. Ironically, most of the original colonies soon adopted state-sanctioned religions. For that reason, the framers wrote in the First Amendment, "Congress shall make no law respecting an establishment of religion, or prohibiting the free exercise thereof." Thus were born two religious freedom clauses to the Constitution: the Establishment Clause and the Free Exercise Clause. The two clauses acting together ensure that government neither supports nor penalizes a religion.

The first case before the Supreme Court addressing the neutrality of government in religious disputes came in the 1872 *Watson v. Jones* case. The Court ruled that a dispute within the Presbyterian Church could not be resolved in the courts but only by the church officials. Thus the Constitution gave churches the freedom to manage their own affairs free from government intervention, even by the courts. Much later, a Russian Orthodox Church dispute led the Court to hold in *Kedroff v. St. Nicholas Cathedral* (1952) that the federal government could not intervene even if a church's authority is being exerted from a foreign country unfriendly toward the United States.

The full implication of the Establishment Clause on government actions, besides obviously forbidding the sanctioning of state churches, was not defined until 1947. In *Everson v. Board of Education,* a decision which denied state-funded transportation to children attending parochial schools, the Court wrote an extensive description of what the Establishment Clause means. The Court held that:

> Neither a state nor the Federal Government . . . can pass laws which aid one religion, aid all religions, or prefer one religion over another. Neither can government force nor influence a person to go to or to remain away from church against his will or force him to profess a belief or disbelief in any religion. No person can be punished for . . . religious beliefs or disbeliefs . . . No tax can be levied to support any religious activities or institutions.

The language was sufficiently broad to ensure government would not be able to use its power to support religion in any way.

Religion in the Public Classroom

Cases related to public schools soon dominated Establishment Clause court decisions. In the Warren and Burger Courts of the 1960s and 1970s the Court more fully defined the separation of church and state. Activities publicly accepted since public schools began operation in the United States in the mid-nineteenth century became prohibited. In 1962 the issue of officially sponsored prayer in public schools reached the Supreme Court. In *Engel v. Vitale* the Court held the encouragement by the public system of recitation of even a non-denominational prayer was "wholly inconsistent with the Establishment Clause." For a democratic society, the Court found it would be chaotic if a religion were sanctioned and then changed "each time a new administration is elected to office." On the heels of the school prayer issue was the question of Bible readings in public schools. As in *Engel,* the Court found that they were inappropriate activities in *Abington School District v. Schempp* (1963). Importantly, the *Abington* decision also

extended the establishment prohibition to state governments through the Fourteenth Amendment. The Court further adopted state legislative intent as an important factor in weighing the possible appearance of inappropriate religious endorsements.

The subject of school curricula came before the Supreme Court in 1968 in *Epperson v. Arkansas.* In a revisit of the famous 1925 *Scopes* trial and the subject of evolution, the Court unanimously ruled a state law prohibiting the teaching of evolution violated the First Amendment because the law expressly promoted religious beliefs. Later, in 1987 the Court also ruled against a Louisiana law requiring equal treatment of the creation theory where evolution is taught because the law sought to advance a religious viewpoint.

Aside from school prayer, Bible, and curricula issues, determining when government programs improperly benefitted religious activities was still not resolved. In the *Abington* case the Court began to tackle this confusion by creating a "purpose and effect" test. A government action must have a "secular legislative purpose and a primary effect that neither advances nor inhibits religion" for it to be valid. The rule for identifying Establishment Clause violations was further developed in *Lemon v. Kurtzman* (1971). The Court created a three prong test the stated: 1) the law must have a secular (i.e., not religious) legislative purpose; 2) the law in its principle or primary effect must neither advance nor inhibit religion; and 3) the law must not foster excessive entanglement of church and state. This test became known as the Lemon test.

The Lemon test was soon applied in another public school case, *Stone v. Graham* (1980), involving the posting of the Ten Commandments in classrooms. The Court strongly asserted that any religion-related activities in public schools may be viewed as coercion because of the mandatory nature of attendance and the susceptibility of youth to adult influences.

Many felt the Court decisions of the 1960s and 1970s were responsive to the increasingly diverse character of the American public. Yet, sharp reactions resulted primarily from conservative Protestant groups. In reaction to the *Stone* decision, religious organizations sought to more fully integrate religious materials into traditional school curricula, such as history classes, so as not to stand apart as religious instruction. Several unsuccessful efforts were made to pass school prayer constitutional amendments.

The Lemon Test Turns Sour

As religious activist groups became better organized, the Religious Right, led by a loose alliance of various organizations, rose in political prominence by 1980. The role of religion in America became a more visible issue. New Supreme Court appointments by presidents

Ronald Reagan and George Bush led to a distinct lowering of the "wall" between church and state. The Lemon test was found by the new justices to be too inflexible and even "hostile" toward religion. Accommodation of some religious activities was no longer considered equivalent to endorsement. The test became only selectively applied to particular cases much to the consternation of those wishing to maintain a more clear distinction between church and state.

The Court found in *Marsh v. Chambers* (1983) that prayer led by a publicly funded chaplain to open daily sessions of state legislatures did not violate the Establishment Clause. Unlike the classroom, the justices reasoned this activity involved adults not captive to the practice. In *Marsh,* the Court found the use of religion and religious symbols, such as the use of a Bible in oaths, had in many instances become so integrated in peoples' daily activities that their inclusion was more of a general ceremonial nature than actual worship in a particular religious tradition. The 1984 *Lynch v. Donnelly* decision drew additional attention in which the Court upheld the use of religious symbols on public property.

A perspective came to dominate: Just because government may not support religion through preferential treatment, as held in *Wallace v. Jaffree* (1985), such neutrality does not imply an absolute prohibition. Churches and practitioners of religion could not be denied commonly available public services, such as those related to public health and safety, normally available to all. In *Westside Community Board of Education v. Mergens* (1990) the Court upheld the 1984 federal Equal Access Act by allowing secondary school students to hold religious club meetings on public school property during non-instructional time as long as the facilities were also available to other secular student club activities. The key distinction was that school employees could not take a active role in religious club meetings except to ensure safety. In *Zobrest v. Catalina Foothills School District* (1993), the Court allowed state provision of a sign language interpreter to a deaf parochial school student under the Individuals with Disabilities Education Act (IDEA). The neutrality issue surfaced again in *Rosenberger v. University of Virginia* (1995) in which the Court held that school funding support of a campus religious-oriented newspaper did not violate the Establishment Clause since the funding program was otherwise neutrally applied to all school organizations . In fact, withholding such funds would actually violate the Constitution's Free Speech Clause. Providing public funds to parochial schools was determined to be inappropriate, but not when funds went directly to families whose children might attend parochial school.

A line of separation still existed though in the new era. In *Lee v. Weisman* (1992), the Court held that invocations and benedictions at secondary school gradua-

tions constituted an endorsement of religion and thus violated the Establishment Clause. Attendance was considered obligatory and school authorities selected the clergy and controlled the content of these gatherings.

A Public Moral Basis

A fundamental shift late in the twentieth century gave religious practice equal treatment under the law. Religious conduct became subject to the same laws as the rest of society rather than protected from general laws in the spirit of separation. This change opened the door to greater government aid to religious schools and organizations.

The debate over the meaning of the Establishment Clause often focused on interpreting the original intent of the framers. Some believed the framers only sought to keep the Federal government from meddling with religious policies of the states several of whom had established churches in 1791, and not restrict state activities as commonly inferred. Proponents of religious liberty claimed the First Amendment established principles of political morality. Any interpretation of the original intent or understanding could be misleading because of fundamental change in American society. With many more Americans being non-Protestant, Protestant prayers at public events can be even less tolerated than in 1791.

The issue of separation continued to be hotly debated as the twentieth century came to a close. Many, including organizations such as the Christian Coalition, believed religion continued to be inappropriately kept out of the classroom. Even the Clinton Administration outlined guidance for inclusion of religious topics in public school curricula. The Republican-lead Congress pushed for voluntary prayer in schools as states attempted to pass religious-based measures designed to protect Bible reading and mandate the teaching of "science creationism" in addition to evolution. Posting of the Ten Commandments in public buildings continued as an issue in Alabama state politics in 1998.

A broader public consensus seemed evident that government cannot be neutral to religion since religion is so important to morality and justice. A democracy requires a religious and moral basis. Many point to the role religious beliefs played in the civil rights movement of the 1960s. Though the "official" government position is to maintain a separation of church and state, a substantial majority of Americans wish to have governmental leaders reflect and be guided by religious faith and principles. In consequence, though the nation should be guided by religious values, it should be kept apart from religious matters. Recognizing the secular role of activities that include religious themes was yet to be clearly reconciled with the meaning and intent of the Establishment Clause. Though general agreement exists that some degree of separation between church and state is necessary, the tension of where to draw the line persists in the nation after two centuries.

See also: **Freedom of Religion**

Bibliography and Further Reading

Berg, Thomas C. *The State and Religion: In a Nutshell.* St. Paul, MN: West Group, 1998.

Eastland, Terry (ed.). *Religious Liberty in the Supreme Court: The Cases That Define the Debate Over Church and State.* Washington, DC: Ethics and Public Policy Center, 1993.

Flowers, Ronald B. *That Godless Court? Supreme Court Decisions on Church-State Relationships.* Louisville, KY: Westminster John Knox Press, 1994.

Gedicks, Frederick M. *The Rhetoric of Church and State: A Critical Analysis of Religious Clause Jurisprudence.* Durham, NC: Duke University Press, 1995.

Jelen, Ted G., and Clyde Wilcox. *Public Attitudes Toward Church and State.* Armonk, NY: M.E. Sharpe, 1995.

Levy, Leonard W. *The Establishment Clause: Religion and the First Amendment.* Chapel Hill, NC: The University of North Carolina Press, 1994.

Nord, Warren A. *Religion & American Education: Rethinking a National Dilemma.* Chapel Hill: University of North Carolina Press, 1995.

REYNOLDS V. UNITED STATES

Legal Citation: 98 U.S. 145 (1879)

Petitioner
George Reynolds

Respondent
United States

Petitioner's Claim
The Morrill Act, which made practice of polygamy a crime, violated his First Amendment right to freedom of religion.

Chief Lawyers for Petitioner
George W. Biddle and Ben Sheeks

Chief Lawyers for Respondent
Charles Devens, U.S. Attorney General, and Samuel F. Phillips, U.S. Solicitor General

Justices for the Court
Joseph P. Bradley, Nathan Clifford, Stephen Johnson Field, John Marshall Harlan I, Ward Hunt, Samuel Freeman Miller, William Strong, Noah Haynes Swayne, Morrison Remick Waite (writing for the Court)

Justices Dissenting
None

Place
Washington, D.C.

Date of Decision
5 May 1879

Decision
Polygamy was not protected by freedom of religion.

Significance
The Mormons, who settled Utah, permitted members of their religion to practice polygamy. In *Reynolds*, the Supreme Court held that federal legislation banning polygamy was constitutional and did not violate the Mormons' First Amendment right to free exercise of their religion. The *Reynolds* case still remains the leading Supreme Court decision that the First Amendment does not protect polygamy.

After a somewhat checkered history and a long trek westward, in the mid-nineteenth century the followers of a religious prophet named Joseph Smith settled the western lands that became the state of Utah. Their religion was called the Church of Jesus Christ of Latter-Day Saints, but most people called them the Mormons. They held a variety of novel beliefs, ranging from their conviction that Jesus Christ visited the American Indians to a prohibition against caffeine drinks such as coffee and tea. Their most controversial belief, however, was that a man could have more than one wife.

The rest of the United States knew about the Mormon practice of polygamy since 1852. Most Americans were traditional Christians and believed in monogamy, or having only one spouse. Until the Mormons arrived, however, there were no federal laws against bigamy or polygamy. The government left the Mormons alone for many years, but in 1862 President Abraham Lincoln signed the Morrill Anti-Bigamy Act into law. The Morrill Act outlawed polygamy throughout the United States in general and in Utah in particular. The government did not do much to enforce the law, however, because it was preoccupied by the Civil War.

Congress Strengthens the Anti-Bigamy Law

After the Civil War, Congress regained interest in the question of Mormon polygamy. Congress strengthened the Morill Act by passing the Poland Law in 1874. The Poland Law increased the powers of the federal judiciary within the territory of Utah. Because federal judges were federally appointed, they were more likely to be non-Mormons and thus more aggressive about enforcing the law.

Mormon leader Brigham Young and George Q. Cannon, territorial delegate to Congress and advisor to Young, decided to challenge the federal government in court. They were confident that if the government tried any Mormons for bigamy the U.S. Supreme Court would throw out the convictions, based on the First Amendment right to free exercise of their religion. Therefore, they planned to arrange for a "test case" to be brought to court. Young and Cannon chose Young's personal secretary, a devout Mormon and practicing polygamist, George Reynolds.

Young and Cannon were successful: the government indicted Reynolds for bigamy in October of 1874. Reynolds had to be re-tried, however, due to jury selection problems. The government indicted Reynolds again in October of 1875.

The government charged that Reynolds was currently married to both Mary Ann Tuddenham and Amelia Jane Schofield. The prosecution had little difficulty in proving that Reynolds lived with both women, despite some trouble in serving Amelia Jane Schofield with her subpoena. The following dialogue is an excerpt from the prosecution's questioning of Arthur Pratt, a deputy marshall sent to serve a subpoena on Amelia:

Question: State to the court what efforts you have made to serve it.

Answer: I went to the residence of Mr. Reynolds, and a lady was there, his first wife, and she told me that this woman was not there; that that was the only home that she had, but that she hadn't been there for two or three weeks. I went again this morning, and she was not there.

Question: Do you know anything about her home, where she resides?

Chief Justice Morrison Remick Waite, c. 1875. © Corbis-Bettmann.

Answer: I know where I found her before.

Question: Where?

Answer: At the same place.

Following more evidence of Reynolds's two marriages, which the defense had no chance of refuting, Judge White gave instructions to the jury. White's instructions smashed Reynolds's defense that by virtue of the First Amendment he was innocent because of his Mormon religious beliefs:

[if you find that Reynolds] deliberately married a second time, having a first wife living, the want of consciousness of evil intent, the want of understanding on his part that he was committing crime, did not excuse him, but the law inexorably, in such cases, implies criminal intent . . .

The jury found Reynolds guilty on 10 December 1875. On 6 July 1876, the territorial Supreme Court affirmed his sentence. Reynolds appealed to the U.S. Supreme Court. On 14 and 15 November 1878, Biddle and Sheeks argued to the Supreme Court that it must overturn Reynolds's conviction on the basis of the First Amendment.

The Supreme Court Destroys the Mormons' Hopes

On 6 January 1879, the Supreme Court upheld the trial court's decision. The Supreme Court said that the First Amendment did not protect polygamy, and based its decision upon historic American cultural values:

Polygamy has always been odious among the northern and western nations of Europe, and, until the establishment of the Mormon Church, was almost exclusively a feature of the life of Asiatic and of African people. At common law, the second marriage was always void, and from the earliest history of England polygamy has been treated as an offence against society . . . In the face of all this evidence, it is impossible to believe that the constitutional guaranty of religious freedom was intended to prohibit legislation in respect to this most important feature of social life. Marriage, while from its very nature a sacred obligation, is nevertheless, in most civilized nations, a civil contract, and usually regulated by law.

Therefore, the Supreme Court upheld Reynolds's sentence of two years imprisonment and a $500 fine. The Supreme Court's decision rocked the Mormons, who initially vowed to defy the Court but later seemed to accept the inevitable. In 1890, Mormon leader Wilford Woodruff issued a document called the Manifesto, which terminated "any marriages forbidden by the law of the land." After 1890, most Mormons abandoned polygamy.

George Reynolds and his twelve sons. © Utah State Historical Society.

The *Reynolds* case is still the leading Supreme Court decision that the First Amendment does not protect polygamy. In 1984, a U.S. District Court considered the case of Utah policeman Royston Potter, who was fired for bigamy. District Court Judge Sherman Christensen rejected Potter's First Amendment defense, and the United States Tenth Circuit Court of Appeals upheld Christensen's ruling. In October of 1985 the Supreme Court refused to hear Potter's appeal. By not listening to cases like Potter's, the Supreme Court has effectively decided to keep *Reynolds* as the law of the land.

Many legal scholars have criticized the Supreme Court for not modifying or overturning *Reynolds*. It has been over 100 years since the decision was handed down, and in many subsequent cases the Supreme Court has greatly expanded the First Amendment's legal protection for free exercise of religion. Further, in the 1960s and early 1970s the Supreme Court increased the Constitution's protection for the civil rights of women, minorities and other persons whose equality under the law had never been a part of the old "common law" cited in *Reynolds*. Logically, therefore, one could expect the Supreme Court to reconsider its position on the constitutionality of polygamy. To date, however, the Supreme Court has not reversed the ruling on polygamy it gave in *Reynolds*.

Related Cases

Potter v. Murray City, 760 F.2d 1065 (10th Cir. 1985).
Employment Division v. Smith, 485 U.S. 660 (1988).

Bibliography and Further Reading

Cannon, George Quayle. *A Review of the Decision of the Supreme Court of the United States, in the Case of Geo. Reynolds vs. the United States.* Salt Lake City: Deseret News Printing, 1879.

Casey, Kathryn. "An American Harem." *Ladies Home Journal,* February 1990, pp. 116–121.

Embry, Jessie L. *Mormon Polygamous Families: Life in the Principle.* Salt Lake City: University of Utah Press, 1987.

Firmage, Edwin Brown. *Zion in the Courts: a Legal History of the Church of Jesus Christ of Latter-Day Saints, 1830-1900.* Urbana: University of Illinois Press, 1988.

Foster, Lawrence. *Religion and Sexuality: the Shakers, the Mormons, and the Oneida Community.* Urbana: University of Illinois Press, 1984.

Johnson, John W., ed. *Historic U.S. Court Cases, 1690–1990: An Encyclopedia.* New York: Garland Publishing, 1992.

Wagoner, Richard S. *Mormon Polygamy: a History.* Salt Lake City: Signature Books, 1989.

EPPERSON V. ARKANSAS

Legal Citation: 393 U.S. 97 (1968)

Appellant
Susan Epperson

Appellee
State of Arkansas

Appellant's Claim
Arkansas law stating one can not teach evolution is unconstitutional.

Chief Lawyer for Appellant
Eugene R. Warren

Chief Lawyer for Appellee
Don Langston, Assistant Attorney General of Arkansas

Justices for the Court
Hugo Lafayette Black, William J. Brennan, Jr., William O. Douglas, Abe Fortas (writing for the Court), John Marshall Harlan II, Thurgood Marshall, Potter Stewart, Earl Warren

Justices Dissenting
None

Place
Washington, D.C.

Date of Decision
12 November 1968

Decision
The law against the teaching of evolution is unconstitutional.

Significance
The decision demanded that governments refuse to favor any particular religion or religious theory over another.

A young schoolteacher named Susan Epperson found herself caught in a dilemma at the beginning of the 1965 school year. Little did she know at that time that her dilemma would end up being solved by the justices of the U.S. Supreme Court in the landmark case *Epperson v. Arkansas*. Reminiscent of the famous Scopes monkey trial, *Tennessee v. Scopes,* of 1925, the significance of *Epperson v. Arkansas* is that our government cannot and should not favor any one religion over another.

At the beginning of the 1965 school year, Epperson, a woman with a master's degree in zoology from the University of Illinois, began to review the textbook she was told to use to teach her tenth grade biology class. A biology teacher at Central High School in Little Rock, Arkansas, Epperson realized, after reviewing the chapters in the textbook, that one of the chapters contained information about evolution. The theory of evolution is that humans developed over time from lower animal forms.

Epperson's dilemma was this: she was supposed to teach the class using the textbook. However, she knew if she taught the chapter on evolution contained in the textbook that she would be fired. She knew the school system would seek her dismissal because on the law books in the state of Arkansas at that time was a statute that made it against the law to teach evolution in any state supported school.

Filing suit in the local chancery court, Epperson sought to have the law deemed null and void and she wanted to prevent the school system from firing her. The chancery court said that the law violated the First and Fourteenth Amendments to the U.S. Constitution. The First Amendment grants all Americans freedom of speech and prevents the government from favoring one religion over another. The Fourteenth Amendment extends the First Amendment to the states. Epperson's dilemma continued as the case was appealed. The Arkansas Supreme Court reversed the decision of the chancery court. In a short statement, the Arkansas Supreme Court said the law was legal because the state has the power to decide what the curriculum is in its public schools. However, the Arkansas Supreme Court did not express any opinion as to whether or not the law allows a teacher to explain the theory of evolution.

Next came Epperson's appeal to the U.S. Supreme Court. The High Court reversed the Arkansas Supreme Court's decision and said that the Arkansas law could not stand. Justice Fortas explained the U.S. Supreme Court's view. He said that our democratic government must remain neutral when it comes to religious theory. In expressing the views of the Court, Justice Fortas quoted other precedent-setting cases including *Watson v. Jones.* In 1872, in *Watson v. Jones,* the U.S. Supreme Court said "the law knows no heresy, and is committed to the support of no dogma, the establishment of no sect."

In comparing *Epperson v. Arkansas* to other similar cases, the U.S. Supreme Court, it should be noted, took similar positions in two other cases. The High Court held closely to the separation between church and state in 1962 in *Engel v. Vitale* and in 1963 in *Abington School District v. Schempp.*

The U.S. Supreme Court in *Epperson v. Arkansas* told the American public, and especially its school systems that the protection of constitutional freedoms is vital in our schools. In addition to quoting from *Watson v. Jones,* Justice Fortas talked about other cases including *Everson v. Board of Education.* In *Everson v. Board of Education,* the U.S. Supreme Court upheld a state law that provided free bus service to school children, both public and private school children. During the *Everson* case the High Court said, "Neither a state nor the federal government can pass laws which aid one religion, aid all religions, or prefer one religion over another."

In *Epperson v. Arkansas* the U.S. Supreme Court went as far back as to quote Thomas Jefferson. Jefferson said the First Amendment to the Constitution was intended to erect a "wall of separation" between church and state. In making its decision in *Epperson,* the U.S. Supreme Court was aided by the precedents set in previous freedom of religion cases.

In summary, *Epperson v. Arkansas* is significant because it demanded governments refuse to favor any particular religion or religious theory over another. Governments must maintain a religious neutrality, the Supreme Court said in *Epperson.* If they do not, they are infringing on a person's constitutional rights set forth in the First and Fourteenth Amendments.

Related Cases
Watson v. Jones, 13 Wall. 679 (1872).
Everson v. Board of Education, 330 U.S. 1 (1947).
Engel v. Vitale, 370 U.S. 421 (1962).
Abington School District v. Schempp, 374 U.S. 203 (1963).

Bibliography and Further Reading
Biskupic, Joan, and Elder Witt, eds. *Congressional Quarterly's Guide to the U.S. Supreme Court,* 3rd ed. Washington, DC: Congressional Quarterly, Inc., 1996.

Chandler, Ralph C., Richard A. Enslen, and Peter G. Renstrom. *The Constitutional Law Dictionary, Volume 1, The First Amendment.* Santa Barbara: ABC-Clio, Inc., 1987.

Konvitz, Milton R., ed. *Bill of Rights Reader,* 5th ed. Ithaca, NY: Cornell University Press, 1973.

WALZ V. TAX COMMISSION

Legal Citation: 397 U.S. 664 (1970)

Appellant
Frederick Walz

Appellee
New York Tax Commission

Appellant's Claim
That a New York state property tax exemption granted to religious organizations constituted governmental establishment of religion, thus violating the First Amendment.

Chief Lawyer for Appellant
Edward J. Ennis

Chief Lawyer for Appellee
J. Lee Rankin

Justices for the Court
Hugo Lafayette Black, Harry A. Blackmun, William J. Brennan, Jr., Warren E. Burger (writing for the Court), John Marshall Harlan II, Thurgood Marshall, Potter Stewart, Byron R. White

Justices Dissenting
William O. Douglas

Place
Washington, D.C.

Date of Decision
4 May 1970

Decision
That the tax exemption did not constitute an establishment of religion and that it in fact avoided excessive entanglement between church and state, thus maintaining separation between the two.

Significance
In the *Walz* decision, the Supreme Court used the excessive entanglement test for the first time to regulate the relationship between church and state. For over a decade, this test remained the Court's most prominent method of interpreting cases involving the religion clauses.

The First Amendment to the U.S. Constitution contains the two religion clauses, which prohibit government from either establishing a state religion or restricting the free exercise of religion. Together, the Establishment Clause and the Free Exercise Clause work to ensure the separation of church and state and religious freedom. For the courts, however, steering between the two clauses has proved challenging. As Reka Potgieter Hoff explained in a 1991 article in the *Virginia Tax Review*, "an interpretation of the Free Exercise Clause to give religious groups space freely to exercise their different conceptions of religious belief and worship, exempt from otherwise legitimate governmental requirements, may in effect, amount to an establishment of religion." One area in which interpretation of the religion clauses has sparked controversy is that of taxation.

In 1968, a lawyer named Frederick Walz challenged Section 420(1) of the New York Real Property Tax Law in a New York court as a violation of the Establishment Clause of the First Amendment. The section in question provided a property tax exemption for religious organizations using property for religious purposes, as part of a wider exemption for public welfare organizations. Walz claimed that this exemption forced him, as a taxpayer and property owner, to make an indirect contribution to religious organizations. The New York courts ruled against Walz, as did the court of appeals in 1969. In 1970, the Supreme Court upheld the lower courts' decisions.

The Court emphasized several points in rendering its decision. First, it determined whether either the purpose of the exemption or its end result amounted to a state establishment of religion. In both cases, it found no violation of the Establishment Clause. It found instead that New York's tax exemption neither promoted nor inhibited religion; rather, it retained a healthy level of neutrality. In so ruling, the majority opinion insisted that a difference existed between a tax exemption—which gave indirect economic benefits to a religious organization—and the more direct support of a governmental subsidy.

The *Walz* decision also introduced the excessive entanglement test for the first time. This test deter-

Separation of Church and State

The First Amendment of the Constitution sets forth that Congress should not make any laws "respecting an establishment of religion, or prohibiting the free exercise thereof." The first part of the amendment is called the "Establishment Clause," and the second is called the "Free-Exercise Clause." In the broadest terms, these two clauses create a separation of church and state.

In order for the government to guarantee religious freedoms, many people believe that it must show neutrality and not favor one religion over another. This neutrality allows individuals the right to choose what religious views, if any, they wish to believe and the right to practice them however they see fit. To maintain this separation of church and state, the courts have generally ruled that all religious matter must be kept away from the public environment. By doing this, some liberties which might favor one faith over another, such as state-sponsored school prayer, must be abridged in order to ensure that the Constitution's basic religious liberties apply to all.

Source(s): Eastland, Terry. *Religious Liberty in the Supreme Court.* Washington, DC: Ethics and Public Policy Center, 1993.

mined whether a statute would bring the government into excessive involvement with religion through regular official surveillance. In applying the test, the justices had to consider not only the current state of affairs, but also whether entangling tensions might arise in the future. The Court decided that in this case, exempting religious organizations from the New York property tax actually created less entanglement than taxation would inevitably bring; therefore the tax exemption fostered a healthy separation of church and state.

The *Walz* Court took other factors into consideration as well. It argued that religious organizations provide services which contribute to the well-being of the community beyond a strictly religious context. These benefits, and the way in which the Court saw religious institutions as contributing to a pluralistic environment, encouraged it to support the tax exemption. The Court also felt that such exemptions helped to prevent discrimination against religion. Finally, the majority opinion found that New York and many other states had offered similar exemptions for many years without causing conflict between religion and the state; thus history sanctioned the practice.

Following the *Walz* decision, subsequent Supreme Court rulings used and expanded upon the ruling. First in *Lemon v. Kurtzman* (1971), and then in other cases throughout the 1970s and early 1980s, justices relied on the excessive entanglement test to monitor church-state relationships, particularly regarding the status of religious schools. Many of these decisions moved beyond the Establishment Clause issue raised by *Walz* to apply entanglement analysis to the Free Exercise Clause as well. Though the majority opinion in *Walz* did not explicitly discuss the Free Exercise Clause, it did imply a relationship to it. The Court justified the state accommodation of religious organizations embodied in a tax exemption—what Frederick Walz objected to as establishment of religion—by arguing that avoiding the oppressive entanglement of government tax regulation and surveillance allowed more room for the free operation of religion. In this way, the decision clearly marked an attempt by the Supreme Court to maneuver between the two religion clauses.

Walz v. Tax Commission sparked controversy among legal scholars interested in the balance between church and state. Several commentators objected to the Court's use of historical precedent to justify tax exemptions for religious organizations, insisting that the rapidly changing nature of the modern state-church relationship differed markedly from the context in which such exemptions first arose. In Kenneth Ripple's 1980 article in the *UCLA Law Review,* he decried the level of judicial subjectivity inherent in the excessive entanglement test's "prophylactic" function, which forced justices to predict possible future conflicts and move to prevent them.

One of the most comprehensive critiques of the *Walz* decision came from Douglas Rovens in a 1982 article for the *Southwestern University Law Review.* Rovens dismissed the Court's attempt to distinguish between a tax exemption and a direct subsidy, and condemned both as an unconstitutional establishment of religion. He also argued—in direct opposition to *Walz*— that tax exemptions for religious purposes actually created more excessive entanglement between church and state than taxation would, as they put the government in the dangerous position of defining what constituted religion and what did not. Finally, Rovens expressed concern with the possibility of growing numbers of "fraudulent" religious organizations and their leaders abusing tax exempt status to accumulate property wealth. As such responses show, at the controversial crossroads of church, state, religious freedom and taxation, no decision as influential as *Walz* could remain unchallenged.

Related Cases

Everson v. Board of Education, 330 U.S. 1 (1947).
Zorach v. Clausen, 343 U.S. 306 (1952).
Roth v. United States, 354 U.S. 476 (1957).
Engel v. Vitale, 370 U.S. 421 (1962).
School District of Abington Township v. Schempp, 374 U.S. 203 (1963).
Lemon v. Kurtzman, 403 U.S. 602 (1971).

Bibliography and Further Reading

Barham, Dean T. "The Parsonage Exclusion Under the Endorsement Test: Last Gasp or Second Wind?" *Virginia Tax Review,* Vol. 13, no. 2, fall 1993, pp. 397-422.

Hoff, Reka Potgieter. "The Financial Accountability of Churches for Federal Income Tax Purposes: Establishment or Free Exercise?" *Virginia Tax Review,* Vol. 11, no. 1, summer 1991, pp. 71-136.

Ripple, Kenneth F. "The Entanglement Test of the Religion Clauses – A Ten Year Assessment." *UCLA Law Review,* Vol. 27, no. 6, August 1980, pp. 1195-1239.

Rovens, Douglas J. "Religious Tax Exemptions: A Challenge to *Walz v. Tax Commission*." *Southwestern University Law Review,* Vol. 13, no. 1, winter 1982, pp. 129-167.

TILTON V. RICHARDSON

Legal Citation: 403 U.S. 672 (1971)

Appellant
Tilton, et al.

Appellee
Richardson, U.S. Secretary of Health, Education, and Welfare, et al.

Appellant's Claim
Institutions receiving federal monies were sectarian, therefore under Higher Education Facilities Act, they should not get monies.

Chief Lawyer for Appellant
Leo Pfeffer

Chief Lawyer for Appellee
Daniel M. Friedman

Justices for the Court
Harry A. Blackmun, Warren E. Burger (writing for the Court), John Marshall Harlan II, Potter Stewart, Byron R. White

Justices Dissenting
Hugo Lafayette Black, William J. Brennan, Jr., William O. Douglas, Thurgood Marshall

Place
Washington, D.C.

Date of Decision
28 June 1971

Decision
The Court ruled that money used for non-religious purposes did not violate the Establishment Clause. However, the Court did strike down the 20 year limitation.

Significance
The Court found that the constitutional rights of taxpayers were not violated simply by the government granting money to religious schools for secular facilities.

In 1971 a group of people from Connecticut protested in a court of law a statute called The Higher Education Facilities Act of 1963. The Higher Education Facilities Act of 1963 allowed the government to give money to church-related universities for buildings as long as these buildings were only used for non-religious educational purposes. The group of people who protested the act believed that four Connecticut-based church-related universities that received grant monies from the federal government were using the buildings for religious purposes. The universities said they did not violate the statute. When the case arrived at the U.S. Supreme Court, the justices, in a landmark 5-4 decision, voted to uphold the Higher Education Facilities Act of 1963. However, they made one change in the act. They changed the portion of the act that allowed a 20-year limit on the religious use of the buildings erected with the grant monies.

Chief Justice Burger voiced the majority opinion in *Tilton v. Richardson*. According to the *Constitutional Law Dictionary*, Burger said that the Higher Education Facilities Act of 1963 had a "legitimate secular objective entirely appropriate for government action without having the effect of advancing religion."

The reason the Court decided that the 20-year limit was unconstitutional, Burger said, was that "it cannot be assumed that a substantial structure has no value after that period and hence the unrestricted use of a valuable property is in effect a contribution of some value to a religious body."

The majority of justices in *Tilton v. Richardson* voiced the opinion that the act, when Congress passed it, was for providing opportunities for college educations. This, they said, had nothing to do with religion. The appellants, or people who protested the act in court, provided evidence they believed showed that the monies used did promote religious content. They believed that the act violated the Establishment or Free Exercise Clauses of the First Amendment to the U.S. Constitution.

Chief Justice Burger and Justices Stewart, Harlan, Blackmun and White agreed that the act did not violate the Establishment or Free Exercise Clauses of the First Amendment. These men arrived at their decision

Higher Education Act

The aim of the Higher Education Act is to define the purpose of programs used in higher education institutions, such as colleges and universities. The act is federally funded and and requires reauthorization every few years. Between its founding in 1965 through 1997, it was reauthorized seven times. In addition to establishing a program's purpose, the act defines who is eligible to participate in the program. It also provides procedures for distributing funds, which are made available to eligible students and institutions at the start of the academic year. The act sets annual federal spending limitations for each program.

Source(s): Wolanin, Thomas R. "A Primer on the Reauthorization of the Higher Education Act." *Change,* November/December 1997.

using a several criteria. First, the justices believed that Congress intended the act to include all colleges no matter what their affiliation. Secondly, the justices said legislative history backed up their opinions. Although other cases focused on the tension between the Establishment Clause and the Free Exercise Clause of the First Amendment, the justices noted, there existed no simple solution to such a problem.

> The Justices who voted to uphold the Act cited this constitutional passage to bolster their argument: "the security and welfare of the United States require that this and future generations of American youth be assured ample opportunity for the fullest development of their intellectual capacities, and that this opportunity will be jeopardized unless the Nation's colleges and universities are encouraged and assisted in their efforts to accommodate rapidly growing numbers of youth who aspire to a higher education."

The justices also concurred that religious teaching is not the main purpose of church-related colleges as it is in parochial secondary and elementary schools. Further, Justices Burger, Stewart, Harlan, Blackmun and White cited the *Bradfield v. Roberts* case of 1899. This case, they argued, showed that all financial aid to church-sponsored activities did not violate the religion clauses to the Constitution. Their conclusion was this: there was no evidence that the religion was involved in the use of the allotted monies to the universities.

However, the act did violate the religion clauses, Justices Burger, Stewart, Harlan, Blackmun and White

noted, in regard to the limitation for religious use of the buildings for 20 years. They said this restriction opens the buildings to use for other purposes at the end of the 20 years; therefore, it violates the religion clauses.

According to the *Constitutional Law Dictionary,* the opinion of the dissenters was "that even if the specific buildings funded under the grant were used only for secular (non-religious) purposes, religious institutions were aided by being able to use for religious purposes monies freed by the receipt of the federal grant." The dissenters believed that taxpayer's monies should not be used at a parochial school, be it elementary, secondary or collegiate. These justices said that the provision of monies, under the act, to these Connecticut colleges and universities, was indeed a violation of the Free Exercise Clause of the First Amendment.

Related Cases

Bradfield v. Roberts, 175 U.S. 291 (1899).
National Labor Relations Board v. Jones and Laughlin Steel Corp., 301 U.S. 1 (1937).
Everson v. Board of Education, 330 U.S. 1 (1947).
Abington School District v. Schempp, 374 U.S. 203 (1963).
Walz v. Tax Commission, 397 U.S. 664 (1970).

Bibliography and Further Reading

Biskupic, Joan, and Elder Witt, eds. *Congressional Quarterly's Guide to the U.S. Supreme Court,* 3rd ed. Washington, DC: Congressional Quarterly, Inc., 1996.

Chandler, Ralph C., Richard A. Enslen, and Peter G. Renstrom. *The Constitutional Law Dictionary: The First Amendment,* Volume 3, Santa Barbara: ABC-Clio, Inc., 1987.

LYNCH V. DONNELLY

Legal Citation: 465 U.S. 668 (1984)

Petitioner
Lynch, Mayor of Pawtucket, et al.

Respondent
Donnelly, et al.

Petitioner's Claim
A nativity scene should be allowed in public view.

Chief Lawyer for Petitioner
William F. McMahon

Chief Lawyer for Respondent
Amato A. DeLuca

Justices for the Court
Warren E. Burger (writing for the Court), Sandra Day O'Connor, Lewis F. Powell, Jr., William H. Rehnquist, Byron R. White

Justices Dissenting
Harry A. Blackmun, William J. Brennan, Jr., Thurgood Marshall, John Paul Stevens

Place
Washington, D.C.

Date of Decision
5 March 1984

Decision
The nativity scene was allowed to remain in view.

Significance
The case led many to believe that the Court was tempering its stand for the separation of church and state.

The case of *Lynch v. Donnelly*, decided by the U.S. Supreme Court 5 March 1984, became a landmark case regarding the separation of church and state. The case began as a dispute between a group of people who wanted a "creche" displayed in public and a group who did not. A "creche" is a nativity scene, a scene depicting the birth of Jesus Christ. The Supreme Court justices decided the "creche" displayed in Pawtucket, Rhode Island, did not violate the Establishment Clause of the U.S. Constitution. The Establishment Clause outlines the government's role in the separation between church and state. Part of the First Amendment to the U.S. Constitution, the Establishment Clause clearly prohibits any official establishment of a religion.

The case began when the city of Pawtucket put up its annual Christmas display. The display was put up in Pawtucket's downtown area as it had been for 40 years. The display contained other items besides the "creche." Among the other items were a Christmas tree, colored lights, Santa Claus's home, and animal figures.

After the display containing all these items was erected, a group of people filed a lawsuit claiming the display violated the Establishment Clause. The group filing the suit included residents of Pawtucket, members of the Rhode Island affiliate of the American Civil Liberties Union, and the union itself.

The decision in the case in district court commanded the city of Pawtucket not to include the "creche." The district court agreed that by including the "creche" the city had violated the Establishment Clause. The next stop in the appeals process was the First Circuit Court of Appeals. This court also commanded Pawtucket to remove the "creche," therefore upholding the decision of the district court.

However, the U.S. Supreme Court, in *Lynch v. Donnelly*, reversed the two lower court decisions, deciding to allow Pawtucket to display the "creche." The "creche" the High Court said, did not violate the Constitution's Establishment Clause.

When the 5-4 decision of the U.S. Supreme Court was announced, the *New York Times* described it as a considerable modification of the existing line between

Public Religious Displays

Seasonal religious displays on public property, such as a manger scene at Christmas, are often challenged in court on the grounds that they depict religious matter and therefore violate the concept of separation of church and state. Proponents say that the displays do not violate the First Amendment because they are not coercive in nature and do not pressure anyone to hold a specific religious belief. Those who oppose the displays counter that religious symbols do not have a place on public government property. When it comes to Supreme Court rulings on the issue, the Court has taken a middle ground. The Court has upheld religious symbols in a holiday display if the display includes symbols from other religions or nonreligious items.

Source(s): Hirsley, Michael. "Religious Display Needs Firm Court." *Chicago Tribune,* 20 December 1991.

church and state. Linda Greenburg of the *New York Times* wrote, "it significantly shifted the boundary in favor of religion."

In previous precedent setting cases regarding challenges to the Constitution's Establishment Clause, the U.S. Supreme Court had voted against religion. The Court's apparent accommodation of religion contrasted with its previous decisions. In 1971, in the case of *Lemon v. Kurtzman,* a practice was declared unconstitutional because it did not have a legitimate non-religious purpose.

The "Lemon Test"—a three part test used by Supreme Court justices to aid them in deciding if a practice had violated the Establishment Clause—came out of *Lemon v. Kurtzman.* However, in *Lynch v. Donnelly,* Chief Justice Burger stated that his court did not consider the "Lemon Test" as essential as other justices had in the past.

Instead of using the Lemon Test as a barometer in their decision making process, several justices in Burger's Court substituted a new test. Their test was simply the answer to the question of whether the Pawtucket practice of displaying the "creche" posed a real danger to the establishment of a state church. In other words, as Justice O'Connor stated at the time, whether the government in question intends to endorse or is perceived to be endorsing a particular religion.

Justices Burger, White, Powell, Rehnquist, and O'Connor opined that the U.S. Constitution commands that there should not only be tolerance of all religions, but accommodation of all religions. The Constitution, these five justices declared, forbids hostility toward any religion. In voting to reverse the two lower court decisions, these five Justices asserted that Pawtucket has not advanced any religion. The display, they affirmed, merely celebrates a holiday recognized by Congress as a national tradition.

Although five of the nine Supreme Court justices believed the "creche" did not pose any real danger, four justices dissented. Among the four was Justice Brennan. Brennan said that the "maintenance and display at pub-

lic expense of a symbol as distinctively sectarian as a creche simply cannot be squared with our prior cases."

Brennan and the other dissenters, Justices Marshall, Blackmun, and Stevens, said the "creche" was a recreation of an event that is at the center of Christianity. And, the dissenting justices concurred, Pawtucket's action in displaying the "creche" was a step toward establishing a religious preference. In summary, the dissenting justices agreed with the American Civil Liberties Union and the National Council of Churches that the display violated the Establishment Clause. Still, the Supreme Court's decision did not totally clarify the High Court's position on the Establishment Clause. Uncertainty was maintained because the justices reviewed *Lynch v. Donnelly* while taking into consideration that there were other items in the holiday display. Brennan and the other dissenters noted that it was not clear which way the Supreme Court would have voted had the display only contained the "creche."

Five years later, in a similar case the Supreme Court would rule differently. In 1989, in *County of Allegheny v. ACLU* the Supreme Court ruled that a "creche" displayed in a public building without anything else present in the display violated the Establishment Clause. Still, *Lynch v. Donnelly* is significant because it suggested an allowance for some religious adjustment in the concept of the separation of church and state.

Related Cases
Lemon v. Kurtzman, 403 U.S. 602 (1971).
County of Allegheny v. ACLU, 492 U.S. 573 (1989).

Bibliography and Further Reading
Balkin, J. M. "The Constitution of Status." *Yale Law Journal,* June 1997, pp. 2313–2374.

Clendinen, Dudley. "Ruling on Christmas Display Elates People in Pawtucket." *New York Times,* 6 March 1984.

Goodman, Jill Laurie. "Creches, Menorahs, and the Courts." *Tikkun,* January-Februrary 1995, p. 30.

Greenhouse, Linda. "High Court Rules Cities May Put Up Nativity Displays." *New York Times*, 6 March 1984.

Hall, Kermit L. *The Oxford Companion to the Supreme Court of the United States*, New York: Oxford University Press, 1992.

Kippenberg, Hans G. "Paying the Words Extra: Religious Discourse in the Supreme Court of the United States." *History of Religions*, November 1997, p. 184.

McGeevy, John T. "Religion and American Education: Rethinking a National Dilemma." *Commonweal*, 16 June 1995, p. 24.

Sachs, Benjamin I. "Whose Reasonableness Counts?" *Yale Law Journal*, March 1998, pp. 1523–1528.

ZOBREST V. CATALINA FOOTHILLS SCHOOL DISTRICT

Legal Citation: 509 U.S. 1 (1993)

Petitioner
Larry Zobrest, et al.

Respondent
Catalina Foothills School District

Petitioner's Claim
The government can pay to provide a sign language interpreter for a deaf student attending a parochial school without violating the constitutional separation of church and state.

Chief Lawyer for Petitioner
William B. Ball

Chief Lawyer for Respondent
John C. Richardson

Justices for the Court
Anthony M. Kennedy, William H. Rehnquist (writing for the Court), Antonin Scalia, Clarence Thomas, Byron R. White

Justices Dissenting
Harry A. Blackmun, Sandra Day O'Connor, John Paul Stevens, David H. Souter

Place
Washington, D.C.

Date of Decision
18 June 1993

Decision
Reversed lower court rulings and held that the provision of a sign language interpreter in a parochial school did not violate First Amendment prohibitions against the establishment of a state religion.

Significance
This narrow 5-4 decision was one in a long line of cases in which the Supreme Court struggled to strike the proper balance between permissible and impermissible state aid to parochial schools. The closeness of the decision indicated that the issue would continue to be debated in the future.

Historical Background

The U.S. Supreme Court has long affirmed the right of parents to send their children to parochial, or church-run, schools. However, the Court has acknowledged that there are limits to the type of assistance that states can provide to these schools and their students. Too much aid, or the wrong type of aid, can be challenged on the basis of the First Amendment's Establishment Clause prohibiting the establishment of a religion by the state. In numerous cases over the decades, the Court has struggled to define the limits of state aid to religious education. In some instances, it has issued bizarre or seemingly contradictory rulings. When the Court determined that a state could loan textbooks to religious schools, but not maps, an exasperated Sen. Daniel Patrick Moynihan was heard to remark, "What about atlases, or books of maps?" It was in this atmosphere of unclear boundaries that *Zobrest v. Catalina Foothills School District* was played out in 1993.

The Facts of the Case

Larry Zobrest, a deaf high school student in Arizona, requested that his school district provide him with a sign language interpreter as mandated under the federal Individuals with Disabilities Education Act. The school district declined, on the advice of the county attorney, claiming that such a provision would violate the establishment clause of the First Amendment to the Constitution. Arizona's attorney general concurred in this opinion, so Zobrest and his parents filed an action in U.S. District Court. Before the case was heard, both parties agreed that the provision for sign language instruction was in fact mandated by the Individuals with Disabilities Education Act, and that the school district would have supplied the interpreter if Zobrest had attended a non-religious school. But Zobrest and his parents disputed the claim that the aid they were seeking violated the separation of church and state and asked for reimbursement from the state for the cost of hiring their own sign language interpreter. The school district filed a motion for summary judgment on its claim that such aid violated the U.S. Constitution.

The Lower Courts Rule

The judge for the U.S. district court granted the Catalina Foothills School District's motion for summary judg-

---

The Lemon Test

The Lemon test, named for the Supreme Court case *Lemon v. Kurtzman,* uses a three-part test to determine if laws or government activities are considered unconstitutional. For instance, to determine if parochial school aid is constitutional, the test asks if the aid is for a religious purpose, promotes a religion, or requires excessive entanglement between government and religion. The importance of using the Lemon test to determine the constitutionality of parochial school aid can be seen in the impact that the result has on the large number of U.S. citizens who send their children to private schools.

At the time the Lemon test was adopted by the Court in 1971, there were 36 states considering measures to help parochial schools, according to a 10 July 1971, article in *The New Republic.* The article went on to state that 25 percent of Rhode Island's elementary-age children were enrolled in private schools and that 95 percent of those were parochial. In Pennsylvania, the article states, 20 percent of elementary pupils were in private school with 98 of those parochial institutions.

Source(s): "Parochial School Aid." *The New Republic,* 10 July 1971.

---

ment. It agreed with the district that such aid would promote a particular religious agenda at public expense and hence violate the establishment clause. The Zobrests then took their case to the U.S. Court of Appeals, which affirmed the district court's ruling. It held that the actions the Zobrests had requested would have represented an unconstitutional application of the Individuals with Disabilities Education Act. The Zobrests next appealed to the U.S. Supreme Court, which agreed to hear the case.

The Supreme Court Rules

On 18 June 1993, the Supreme Court issued its decision. Along narrow 5-4 lines, it reversed the rulings of the lower courts, holding that the First Amendment's establishment clause did not bar the Catalina Foothills School District from providing Zobrest with an interpreter. Chief Justice Rehnquist wrote the opinion for the five justice majority, with Justice Blackmun penning a dissent that was joined, in whole or in part, by three other justices.

The provision of a sign language interpreter, observed Chief Justice Rehnquist, was not an act of establishment of religion but "part of a general government program that distributes benefits neutrally to any child qualifying as handicapped." If an individual who is handicapped, in this case Larry Zobrest, chooses to attend a parochial school, Rehnquist went on to write, "we hold that the Establishment Clause does not prevent the school district from furnishing him with a sign-language interpreter there in order to facilitate his education."

The majority's opinion hinged in part on its contention that the sign language interpreter would in no way advance the school's religious agenda. "Nothing in this record suggests that a sign language interpreter would do more than accurately interpret whatever material is presented to the class as a whole," Rehnquist wrote.

Dissenting Opinions

Writing in dissent, Justice Blackmun contended that the Supreme Court should not have even weighed in on the constitutional questions in the case, since the issue of whether the Individuals with Disabilities Education Act requires the school district to provide an interpreter at a private school was still in doubt—and would have rendered the larger questions moot. On the issue of separation of church and state, Blackmun was unequivocal in asserting that the use of a public employee by a religious institution to promote a religious message was in violation of the Constitution. Blackmun wrote:

> Today, the Court unnecessarily addresses an important constitutional issue, disregarding longstanding principles of constitutional adjudication. In so doing, the Court holds that placement in a parochial school classroom of a public employee whose duty consists of relaying religious messages does not violate the Establishment Clause of the First Amendment. I disagree both with the Court's decision to reach this question and with its disposition on the merits.

In a separate dissent, Justice O'Connor agreed with Blackmun's assertion that the Court should have refused to even address the constitutional issue. She argued for vacating the lower court's decision on statutory grounds.

Disposition of the Case

James Zobrest had already completed high school by the time the Supreme Court ruled in his favor. However, the Catalina Foothills School District agreed to reimburse his parents for the cost of hiring their own sign language interpreter.

Impact

Zobrest v. Catalina Foothills School District was a loss for those who favor a strict interpretation of the Establishment Clause of the First Amendment. Future decisions will reveal whether this case laid down a clear marker for states in determining what type of aid they can provide to religious schools.

Related Cases

Helling v. McKinney, 509 U.S. 25 (1993).
Reno v. Catholic School Services, Inc., 509 U.S. 43 (1993).
Darby v. Cisneros, 509 U.S. 137 (1993).
Shalala v. Schaeffer, 509 U.S. 292 (1993).

Bibliography and Further Reading

Biskupic, Joan and Elder Witt, eds. *Congressional Quarterly's Guide to the U.S. Supreme Court,* 3rd ed. Washington, DC: Congressional Quarterly, Inc., 1996.

Coughlin, John J. "Religion, Education and the First Amendment." *America,* May 15, 1993, pp. 12.

"Court Rulings on Religion." *The Christian Century,* June 16, 1993, pp. 624.

Coyle, Marcia. "High Court Could Reshape Church-State." *The National Law Journal,* March 1, 1993, p. 1.

Drinan, Robert F. "A Glimmer of Hope for Aid to Catholic Schools." *America,* September 18, 1993, pp. 4.

Lawton, Kim A. "Trio of Rulings Clarifies Religious-Liberty Rights." *Christianity Today,* July 19, 1993, pp. 56.

FREEDOM OF SPEECH

Speech and Expression

The desire to exchange thoughts with others is considered a natural inclination of human nature. Common use of the term speech infers pure, or verbal, speech, a complex ability to communicate that distinguishes humans from other species. However, use of the term in U.S. law includes a much wider range of individual expression including speaking, writing, and even through behavior called symbolic speech. Therefore, free speech includes all forms of expression, including books, newspapers, magazines, radio, television, computer transmittals, motion pictures, and certain physical actions. Though the phrase freedom of expression is commonly used in courts, the term expression actually does not appear in the First Amendment. Its use, however, includes freedoms of speech, press, assembly, petition and association.

Throughout history many governments restricted speech for fear that the spread of ideas by the citizens could interfere with the government's conduct of business and create social disorder. Two kinds of interests are included in free speech, individual interests in expression and social interest in regard to protection from certain kinds of false or hurtful statements. Speech is a personal right that receives preferred treatment over property rights issues by the Supreme Court with speech cases receiving closer scrutiny. This preferred status is often called the "firstness" doctrine of the First Amendment.

The Origins of Free Speech Concerns

Struggles over attaining freedom of speech have a long history. Citizens of Athens in ancient Greece actually enjoyed considerable freedom of speech in the 400s B.C. Freedom of speech, though, was a central issue to the conflict between religion and politics throughout European history including the Reformation in the sixteenth century that gave rise to a new religious tradition of Protestantism. Speech restrictions issued by King James I led to a declaration of freedoms by Parliament in 1621. During the Enlightenment in the seventeenth and eighteenth centuries, speech was considered a natural right. Influential philosophers of England and France stressed the importance of the individual with

each person having a right to speak freely and participate in government. Freedom of expression thus became an important factor in the French Revolution leading to the 1789 Declaration of the Rights of Man.

The colonists were well aware of the English tradition of suppressing speech. In forming a democracy, the founders considered free speech absolutely necessary. Freedom of belief would have little meaning if thoughts could not be freely expressed and shared. In fact, a tradition of robust and rowdy expression was prevalent during the framing of the Constitution. The framers reasoned if government was to be governed by the people, then government can be only as effective as the citizens are informed. Influenced by the 1789 French declaration, the framers raised freedom of speech to yet another level involving constitutional law, more compelling than a declaration. In the end, the colonists struck a balance between absolute freedom and the English form of restricted freedom. The First Amendment read "Congress shall make no law . . . abridging the freedom of speech."

Speech and the Law

Debate in the Constitutional Congress over the First Amendment made it clear an unlimited right of expression was not intended despite the absolute wording of the clause. Ever since, the courts have sought to balance restrictions on individuals' speech rights and preservation of an orderly society. Government may restrain speech through suppression before the utterance is spoken (prior restraint) or through punishment after it is spoken. Also, protection of free speech must be compatible with protecting other rights such as privacy and right to a fair trial. Two very basic categories of expression were distinguished: pure expression and expression associated with conduct. Pure expression, consisting of spoken opinion to a voluntary audience, is almost fully protected from restrictions. Conduct is not. In *Cantwell v. Connecticut* (1940), a case focused on religious freedom, the Court held that the First Amendment "embraces two concepts—freedom to believe and freedom to act. The first is absolute, but . . . the second cannot be. Conduct remains subject to regulation for the protection of society." The

Court found in *Cox v. Louisiana* (1965) that "rights to free speech and assembly . . . do not mean that everyone with opinions . . . may address a group at any public place and at any time." Public order must be maintained or "liberty itself would be lost in the excesses of anarchy."

In *Cox*, the Court recognized several forms of speech restrictions including: (1) libel and slander that harm reputations; (2) speech that offends public decency by using obscenities or encouraging acts considered immoral; (3) laws against spying, treason, and urging violence that endangers life, property, or national security; and, (4) speech that invades peoples' right not to listen, such as city ordinances limiting the use of loudspeakers on public streets.

But where does the line fall between constitutionally protected conduct and unacceptable conduct that can be restrained by the government? That question has been tough for the courts to answer when tackling specific cases. In the 1950s, the Court introduced the "balancing doctrine" weighing speech rights against public interests which grew into the "compelling public interest" doctrine, which centered mainly on the rights of a community to voice their concerns and views about their locale. As dissatisfaction with the "compelling public interest" test grew, the Court focused more specifically on the laws in question looking for vagueness or overbreadth, or less restrictive alternatives.

Initially, some believed only political speech was meant to be protected. Others contended, even speech in error should receive protection so that the truth could eventually be discovered. Judicial interpretations of the First Amendment have steadily enlarged the definition of "speech" continually seeking to determine the kinds of speech protected by the First Amendment and those not protected. In 1977, the Court chose to add philosophical, economic, social, and other non-political fields to political discussion as protected speech in *Abood v. Detroit Board of Education*. In 1998, the Washington State Supreme Court overturned a state law prohibiting false political advertising by holding that the First Amendment even protects lies.

Speech and National Security

Many congressional limitations on free speech were imposed on the United States between the time of the Civil War and World War I. Such restrictions included the Sedition Act of 1798, which forbade any advocation of treason or the overthrow of the government; and martial law during and after Reconstruction. However, no important cases involving the free speech were decided by the Supreme Court until after World War I.

With the advent of World War I, fears stemming from war with Germany and the 1917 Russian Revolution compelled Congress to again pass restrictions on speech about treason, including the Espionage Act of 1917 and the Sedition Act of 1918. In the first case concerning free speech before the Supreme Court, *Schenck v. United States* (1919), the Court attempted to balance concerns over national security with free speech. The Court introduced the "clear and present danger" test which stated that speech raising a clear and present danger of causing results that Congress had authority to prevent was not protected under the First Amendment. In the decision, an enduring statement on the limitations of free speech was made by Justice Oliver Wendell Holmes in that one cannot be free to falsely shout fire in a theater and cause panic. The Clear and Present Danger test was the standard applied by courts to free speech cases for the next half century. Importantly in *Schenck*, the Court held that constitutional protections of speech extend beyond prior restraint concerns, including protection from punishment after speech is made under certain circumstances.

In another sedition trial, *Gitlow v. New York* (1925), the Court applied the free speech clause to state laws for the first time. National security restrictions on speech continued as the Cold War commenced with associated anti-subversive laws. The 1940 Smith Act (another act regarding treason) was upheld in *Dennis v. United States* when the Court held that advocating overthrow of the U.S. government by force was sufficient danger to warrant restriction. However, the Court later limited government restriction by holding that advocacy of specific action must be present to not be protected. The test of incitement toward imminent illegal action was further applied during the 1960s anti-war protest era in *Brandenburg v. Ohio* (1969), where the Court ruled that a person's words were protected by free speech if they did not incite unlawful actions.

The Many Sides of Speech

Public safety issues arose also, in which the Court sought to balance the rights of individuals making public speeches and an audience's right to hear the speech—with the government's responsibility to maintain public order and safety. In *Hague v. Committee for Industrial Organization* (1939) and *Cox v. New Hampshire* (1940) the Court affirmed the rights of individuals to deliver public speeches, but under "reasonable" limitations. Such limitations involved regulation of time, place, and manner.

The most perplexing cases before the Court involved questions of when individuals may incite others to act. Unpopular opinions, which needed constitutional protection most, were most likely to cause hostile reactions from listeners. When may government restrict such speech? The Court clarified that civil authorities must be acting to ensure safety, and not to suppress unfavorable speech. When are speech and expression not considered essential to communicate ideas and have little social value? One such area of speech is "fighting words" in which public insults are intended to raise violent responses. The first case addressing this issue, *Chaplinsky v. New Hampshire* (1942), established "fighting words" as a category of speech not protected by the Constitution.

In the 1990s the issue of hate crimes rose in prominence and states passed laws prohibiting expressions of racial, religious, or gender prejudice. The symbolic actions of cross burnings and swastika displays were included in prohibitions. The Court, in *R.A.V. v. City of St. Paul* (1992), overturned a hate crime ordinance because it prohibited expression based on content rather than invoking the "fighting words" doctrine. The case involved a questionable group that wished to hold a parade along a main street of the city of St. Paul.

Like libel, commercial speech, meaning speech proposing financial transactions such as advertising, was initially considered to be outside the realm of First Amendment protection. However, using the "marketplace of ideas" doctrine, the Court dropped the distinction between public information and advertising for strictly commercial purposes in the 1976 case *Virginia State Board of Pharmacy v. Virginia Citizens Consumer Council* holding that the free flow of information was necessary for a free enterprise system. Consequently, the First Amendment protected commercial advertising, but to a lesser degree than political and other noncommercial speech. In 1980 the Court held that corporations deserved much the same protections as individuals.

Another controversial form of speech addressed by Congress and the Courts involved political campaign spending and contribution limits. In reaction to Watergate revelations, Congress passed the Federal Election Campaign Act of 1974. The act revised limits on spending and contributions and established a system of public funding. A challenge against the law soon came to the Court in *Buckley v. Valeo* (1976). The Court ruled spending limits violated First Amendment protections citing the modern high costs of mass media communications. *Buckley* did uphold limits on contributions, citing the government's interest in preventing corruption. In a related case, the Court overturned a state law prohibiting corporations from spending to influence voters on local referendums in *First National Bank of Boston v. Bellotti* (1978).

As an employer, the government has greater flexibility to restrict its employees' speech. Such restrictions were elaborated in *Pickering v. Board of Education* (1968) and later in *Connick v. Myers* (1983) in which the Court sought to balance government interest in minimizing disruptive behavior and employee rights. Congress added statutory protections for employees who report work related wrong-doing to their employers or fellow employees (whistleblowers) by the Whistleblower Protection Act of 1989. Similarly, juveniles are accorded

approximately the same rights as adults when on trial, as established in the 1967 *In re Gault* decision. Government employees also face restrictions in their participation in political activities.

Speech and Modern Society

The late 1990s witnessed a number of key speech issues. In 1998 Mayor Rudolph Giuliani of New York City attempted to "civilize" the city by regulating certain activities including street vendors. A number of lawsuits claiming free speech violations resulted when higher fees were charged to operate newsstands and for street musicians. A case involving permit requirements for sidewalk artists went to a federal appeals court which held that selling art was a form of protected speech and could not be selectively regulated. The U.S. Supreme Court declined to hear the case. Highlighted was the tension between the city government attempting to manage its public spaces and people seeking to preach and sell their wares in public.

The courts continued to be asked what speech needed protection for the sake of democracy. Should it really include advertising, product labeling, or campaign contributions in cases with little clear connection to politics? Campaign spending and contributions were not pressing issues through most of the twentieth century. But with expansion of First Amendment protections to campaign contributions in 1976, the cash-driven electoral system of the 1990s evolved into what many believed to be counter to the democratic participatory ideals of the founders. Prohibiting regulation of campaign contributions appeared to place the political process under the influence of the wealthy. Fearing violation of free speech, Congress rejected a proposed constitutional amendment in 1998 that would have given Congress and the states authority to establish campaign spending limits.

In 1997 Congress passed the Communications Decency Act imposing criminal penalties for distributing "indecent" material. The Supreme Court in 1998 overturned the act based on free speech concerns. By the late 1990s it was becoming increasingly apparent that traditional means of censorship and conceptions of First Amendment rights did not readily apply to the new world of online media with technologically advanced forms of communication. Words were no longer associated with physically identifiable objects such as books and magazines, the cost of copying was greatly reduced, and even the concept of "publishing" changed. With the demise of decency laws and continued interest in regulating the range of Internet content, emphasis shifted from censorship by the sender of information and material to censorship by the receiver. New Internet access management software capabilities were created under direction of the World Wide Web Consortium to filter material being received on a content basis. The Consortium, an independent body supported by the internet industry, sought to formalize standards and protocols for the Web. Offensive or unwanted material could be blocked by the receiver. Congress also began considering legislation imposing self-rating requirements for internet information providers. Issues of free speech and personal privacy were central to deliberations.

A call came forward with the advent of technologically advanced systems to fundamentally refocus the application of the freedom of speech more to desired goals, rather than more narrowly focus on prohibitive forms of government regulation. Legislation was needed to protect free expression on its own merits, rather than allowing for such liberties to be protected only in a reactive mode. Concern grew over the increasing ability of private and corporate interests to restrict the free flow of information. The primary threat to censorship was no longer considered the government.

See also: **Freedom of Assembly, Internet, Libel, Obscenity, Freedom of the Press, Symbolic Speech**

Bibliography and Further Reading

Abel, Richard L. *Speaking Respect, Respecting Speech.* Chicago: University of Chicago Press, 1998.

Fish, Stanley E. *There's No Such Thing as Free Speech, and It's a Good Thing, Too.* New York: Oxford University Press, 1994.

Greenawalt, Kent. *Fighting Words: Individuals, Communities, and Liberties of Speech.* Princeton: Princeton University Press, 1995.

Hentoff, Nat. *The First Freedom: The Tumultuous History of Free Speech in America.* New York: Delacorte, 1980.

Smolla, Rodney A. *Free Speech in an Open Society.* New York: Knopf, 1992.

Sorenson, Karen. *Silencing the Net: The Threat to Freedom of Expression On-Line.* New York: Human Rights Watch, 1996.

Sunstein, Cass R. *Democracy and the Problem of Free Speech.* New York: The Free Press, 1993.

SCHENCK V. UNITED STATES

Legal Citation: 249 U.S. 47 (1919)

Appellant
Charles T. Schenck

Appellee
United States

Appellant's Claim
That his speech was protected by the First Amendment.

Chief Lawyers for Appellant
Henry J. Gibbons, Henry John Nelson

Chief Lawyer for Appellee
John Lord O'Brian

Justices for the Court
Louis D. Brandeis, John Hessin Clarke, William Rufus Day, Oliver Wendell Holmes (writing for the Court), Charles Evans Hughes, Joseph McKenna, James Clark McReynolds, Willis Van Devanter, Edward Douglass White

Justices Dissenting
None

Place
Washington, D.C.

Date of Decision
3 March 1919

Decision
Schenck's speech was not protected by the First Amendment and his conviction under the Espionage Act was upheld.

Significance
This case marked the first time the Supreme Court ruled directly on the extent to which the U.S. government may limit speech. It produced, in the affirmative opinion written by Justice Holmes, two of that fabled jurist's most memorable and oft-quoted statements on the law.

On 15 June 1917, just after the United States entered World War I, Congress passed the Espionage Act, which made it a federal crime to obstruct the country's war effort. The act closely followed the Conscription Act of 18 May, which enabled the government to draft men for military service.

At the Socialist party headquarters in Philadelphia, Pennsylvania, the executive committee quickly passed a resolution authorizing the printing of 15,000 leaflets, to be sent through the mails and otherwise distributed to men who had been drafted. The leaflets recited the first section of the Thirteenth Amendment to the U. S. Constitution, which states:

> Neither slavery nor involuntary servitude, except as a punishment for crime whereof the party shall have been duly convicted, shall exist within the United States or any place subject to their jurisdiction.

Advising the reader that a conscript is little better than a convict, the leaflets described conscription as despotism in its worst form and as a monstrous wrong against humanity in the interest of Wall Street's chosen few. "Do not submit to intimidation," said the leaflets, urging readers to petition for repeal of the Conscription Act.

"If you do not assert and support your rights," continued the leaflets, "you are helping to deny or disparage rights which it is the solemn duty of all citizens and residents of the United States to retain." Furthermore, the message implied that there was a conspiracy of cunning politicians and a mercenary capitalist press that would be aided even by silent consent to the conscription law, and it said the law lacked the power to send Americans to foreign shores to shoot the people of other countries.

"Largely Instrumental in Sending the Circulars About"

As general secretary of the Socialist party, Charles T. Schenck was in charge of the Philadelphia headquarters from which the leaflets were sent.

Schenck was soon arrested and indicted for sedition in conspiring to cause insubordination in the armed

Clear and Present Danger Test

The U.S. Supreme Court has never held that expressive freedoms of speech, press, and assembly are completely without limits. The difficulty lies in settling on a general standard or test to be applied in determining when a form of expression becomes so threatening to society that it deserves no constitutional protection and must be controlled by government.

Such judicial standards or tests, beginning with the "clear and present danger" test, emerged shortly after World War I. The "clear and present danger" test, formulated by Justice Oliver Wendell Holmes in 1919, provided that if actions create a danger to organized society so "clear and present . . . that they will bring about

. . . substantive evils" then government must attempt to prevent the activities. Holmes wrote the actions requiring intervention must be so imminently threatening they require "an immediate check . . . to save the country." In 1925 the "clear and present danger" test was weakened to the "bad tendency" test requiring only a threat of or tendency toward danger. Much later in 1969 the "clear and present danger" test returned with a "likely to incite" requirement added.

Source(s): Abraham, Henry J. and Barbara A. Perry. *Freedom & The Court: Civil Rights & Liberties in the United States.* New York: Oxford University Press, 1998.

forces and obstruction of recruitment and enlistment. No evidence was presented to prove that he had corrupted even one draftee. Rather, the publication of the pamphlets was itself considered proof enough of his guilt.

The defense presented a simple argument: Schenck had exercised the right guaranteed him by the First Amendment—-the right to speak freely on a public issue.

Found guilty, Schenck appealed through the district courts and to the Supreme Court, steadfastly insisting on his right to freedom of speech.

Schenck's defense argued that there was not enough evidence to prove that he himself was concerned with sending out the pamphlets. Reviewing the testimony, Holmes pointed out that Schenck was the general secretary of the Socialist party and was in charge of the headquarters from which the pamphlets were sent to men who had been called and accepted for military service. The general secretary's report of 20 August 1917, Holmes noted, said, "Obtained new leaflets from printer and started work addressing envelopes." Holmes also pointed out that "there was a resolve that Comrade Schenck be allowed $125 for sending leaflets through the mail."

"No reasonable man," concluded Holmes, "could doubt that the defendant Schenck was largely instrumental in sending the circulars about."

Justice Holmes wrote the opinion that was shared unanimously by the Court. Noting that no case had been made for the leaflets having actually caused any insurrection, he commented:

Of course the document would not have been sent unless it had been intended to have some effect, and we do not see what effect it could be expected to have upon persons subject to

the draft except to influence them to obstruct the carrying of it out.

Holmes agreed with the defense that the leaflets were entitled to First Amendment protection, but only in peacetime—not in wartime.

We admit that in many places and in ordinary times the defendants in saying all that was said in the circular would have been within their constitutional rights. But the character of every act depends upon the circumstances in which it is done. The most stringent protection of free speech would not protect a man in falsely shouting fire in a theater and causing a panic.

It may be noted in passing that Holmes never said the theater was crowded; posterity has consistently and mistakenly ascribed that adjective to the quotation. Next came the justice's second memorable phrase:

The question in every case is whether the words used are used in such circumstances and are of such a nature as to create a clear and present danger that they will bring about the substantive evils that Congress has a right to prevent.

The "clear and present danger," said Holmes, is a question of "proximity and degree." When a nation is at war many things that might be said in time of peace are such a hindrance to its effort that their utterance will not be endured so long as men fight and that no Court could regard them as protected by any constitutional right.

Finally, the justice observed, it made no difference that Schenck and his compatriots had failed to obstruct recruitment. "The statute," he said, "punishes conspiracies to obstruct as well as actual obstruction."

If the act [speaking or circulating a paper], its tendency and the intent with which it is done are the same, we perceive no ground for saying that success alone warrants making the act a crime.

With that, the judgments of the lower courts were affirmed. Charles T. Schenck, who had been sentenced to 10 years' imprisonment on each of the three counts of the indictment, but with the three terms to be served concurrently, was sent to federal prison.

The *Schenck* case, in establishing the "clear and present danger" criterion, marked a turning point in First Amendment thinking by the Court. Until then, Chief Justice White and other justices had permitted the government to suppress any speech that displayed a "dangerous tendency." Within months, moreover, Holmes refined his views on the First Amendment when seven of his colleagues found a "clear and present danger" in the *Abrams v. United States* case. A Russian-born American named Jacob Abrams had been found guilty of violating the Espionage Act when he scattered leaflets protesting the sending of American troops into Russia after the Revolution of 1917. Holmes' dissent objected that Abrams had been condemned not for what he did but for what he believed. The justice insisted that the First Amendment guaranteed one's right to freedom of opinion, if not (as in the *Schenck* case during wartime) of action. One may assume that Holmes would have continued to insist on the guarantee of this right during the dark days of McCarthyism and the House Un-American Activities Committee.

In 1927, Holmes again dissented when the Court upheld the conviction of Socialist Benjamin Gitlow under a New York state law for advocating criminal anarchy. Holmes found that Gitlow's publications, which advocated overthrowing the government, were protected by the Fourteenth Amendment's due process clause against interference by the state. The justice saw "no present danger of an attempt to overthrow the Government by force" in Gitlow's papers.

Related Cases
Abrams v. United States, 250 U.S. 616 (1919).
Gitlow v. United States, 268 U.S. 652 (1925).

Bibliography and Further Reading
Bowen, Catherine Drinker. *Yankee from Olympus: Justice Holmes and His Family.* Boston: Little, Brown and Co., 1943.

Burton, David H. *Oliver Wendell Holmes, Jr.* Boston: Twayne Publishers, Div. of G. K. Hall & Co., 1980.

Justice Oliver Wendell Holmes. © The Library of Congress/Corbis.

Commager, Henry Steele, and Milton Cantor. *Documents of American History.* Englewood Cliffs, NJ: Prentice Hall, 1988.

Friedman, Leon and Fred L. Israel, eds. *The Justices of the U.S. Supreme Court 1789-1969: Their Lives and Major Opinions.* New York: Chelsea House, 1969.

Johnson, John W., ed. *Historic U.S. Court Cases, 1690-1990: An Encyclopedia.* New York: Garland Publishing, 1992.

Novick, Sheldon M. *Honorable Justice: The Life of Oliver Wendell Holmes.* Boston: Little, Brown and Co., 1989.

Schnayerson, Robert. *The Illustrated History of the Supreme Court of the United States.* New York: Harry N. Abrams, 1986.

Witt, Elder, ed. *The Supreme Court and Individual Rights.* Washington, DC: Congressional Quarterly, 1980.

ABRAMS V. UNITED STATES

Legal Citation: 250 U.S. 616 (1919)

Appellants
Jacob Abrams, Mollie Steimer, Hyman Lachowsky, Samuel Lipman

Appellee
United States

Appellants' Claim
That they were not legally convicted of conspiracy to violate the Espionage Act of 1917.

Chief Lawyer for Appellants
Harry Weinberger

Chief Lawyer for Appellee
Robert T. Stewart

Justices for the Court
John Hessin Clarke (writing for the Court), William Rufus Day, Charles Evans Hughes, Joseph McKenna, James Clark McReynolds, Willis Van Devanter, Edward Douglass White

Justices Dissenting
Louis D. Brandeis, Oliver Wendell Holmes

Place
Washington, D.C.

Date of Decision
10 November 1919

Decision
Upheld the conviction and the Espionage Act as constitutional.

Significance
In his dissent, Holmes advanced a revised version of his own "clear and present danger" standard in *Schenck v. United States* The new standard gave greater protection to political speech, even during wartime. Holmes's reasoning was adopted by the Court during the 1930s and serves as the basis for legal doctrines upholding freedom of expression.

During World War I, the Supreme Court, for the first time, debated the meaning of the First Amendment's freedom of expression section, "Congress shall make no law . . . abridging the freedom of speech, or of the press . . ." President Abraham Lincoln's government had sternly subdued opposition during the Civil War. Rather than passing laws to suppress free speech, however, Lincoln had issued presidential decrees enforced through military power. After declaring martial law in an area, the army shut down or censored the newspapers. *Habeas corpus* was suspended, and persons accused of disloyal utterances were jailed without trial in military prisons.

In Uncharted Territory

Fewer than a dozen cases involving free expression had come before the Supreme Court prior to 1918. In these cases, the Court upheld federal and state laws limiting speech and other forms of expression that "tended" to have a bad effect. In *Patterson v. Colorado* (1907), for example, Justice Oliver Wendell Holmes had argued that freedom of the press meant merely freedom from censorship prior to publication. He thus had affirmed a state's power to punish even true statements tending to interfere with judicial proceedings. As a result, there were few precedents available when Congress passed the 1917 Espionage Act and the 1918 Sedition Act to curb dissent. These laws led to the first sustained Supreme Court interpretation of the extent to which political speech was to be protected in times of war.

Three cases were decided in March 1919: *Schenck v. United States, Frohwerk v. United States,* and *Debs v. United States.* In each of these cases, Justice Holmes wrote the decisions for the unanimous Court. Eight months later, in November 1919, the Court decided *Abrams v. United States* This time, Holmes was almost alone in dissenting from the majority decision.

Creating the Surveillance State

In June of 1917, two months after the U.S. entered the war, Congress passed the Espionage Act. The act established three basic wartime offenses: conveying false information intended to interfere with U.S. military operations, causing insubordination in the military,

Espionage Act of 1917

The Espionage Act of 1917 outlawed making false statements, in speech or writing, for the purpose of causing insubordination, or for suppressing or obstructing recruitment of men into the U.S. military at times of war. The act prohibited an individual or group from using the mail for transmitting materials containing statements outlawed under the act. Postmasters could refuse to distribute such materials.

Congress passed the Espionage Act at the beginning of World War I when national fervor and patriotism were at an unparalleled level. Fears, fueled by the success of the Bolshevick Revolution in Russia, precipitated intolerance for anarchists, foreigners, and pacifists. Any criticism of the government was viewed as criticism of the U.S. war effort and a threat to national security.

Historically, the act was linked with a much stronger law passed the following year, the Sedition Act of 1918. The Sedition Act imposed heavy fines and prison terms for persons speaking or writing anything critical of the government or its symbols such as the flag, the military uniform, or the Constitution. Although a vast majority of Americans supported both laws, some groups and individuals strenuously objected to them on grounds they blatantly disregarded the First Amendment's free speech guarantee.

Source(s): Biskupic, Joan and Elder Witt. *Guide to the U.S. Supreme Court.* Washington, DC: Congressional Quarterly, 1997.

---

and obstructing recruiting. In May of 1918, the Sedition Act added nine additional offenses. Taken together, these made it illegal to do, to say, or to write anything that might tend to hinder the war effort, support America's enemies, or bring contempt or disrespect upon the government, flag, uniform, or Constitution.

The constitutionality of the Espionage Act was upheld in *Schenck v. United States*. Charles Schenck was convicted of supervising the printing and distribution of a Socialist Party pamphlet that attacked the military draft. Writing for a unanimous Court, Justice Holmes affirmed Schenck's conviction.

Ignoring earlier free speech decisions, Holmes sketched out his own "clear and present danger" standard. Absolute freedom of speech, Holmes argued, would be absurd. "The most stringent protection of free speech would not protect a man in falsely shouting fire in a theatre and causing a panic."

Holmes then sketched two tests for protection of speech. The first tied protection to circumstances, ". . . whether the words used are used in such circumstances and are of such a nature as to create a clear and present danger that they will bring about the substantive evils that Congress had a right to prevent." The second test tied protection to intent. If the speaker intended to bring about those evils, "we perceive no ground for saying that success alone warrants making the act a crime."

A week after the *Schenck* decision, Holmes rendered two more unanimous opinions in Espionage Act cases. These opinions expressed an extremely limited view of First Amendment rights. They brought into question the meaning of Holmes's "clear and present danger" doctrine.

In *Frohwerk*, Holmes upheld the conviction of Jacob Frohwerk because his newspaper articles critical of the draft might "be enough to kindle a flame of resistance." In *Debs*, Holmes held that a speech by Eugene Debs, the Socialist leader, was intended to obstruct recruiting. In these decisions, Holmes did not mention his own "clear and present danger" test. Thus he did not analyze whether the words used might actually cause an "evil effect." It was enough that they might have a "tendency" to so do.

In formulating his "clear and present danger" doctrine, Holmes knew precisely where to draw the line between protected and unprotected speech. He was given a new opportunity to provide a clear demarcation when *Abrams* reached the court the following October.

Anarchists and War

Jacob Abrams and his codefendants—Hyman Lachowsky, Jacob Schwartz, Mollie Steimer, and Samuel Lipman—were Russian-born Jews living in the East Harlem section of New York. They became involved with the Yiddish-language paper *Der Shturm* (*The Storm*), which advocated anarchist doctrines and policies. With their fellow anarchists, they sought to destroy capitalism and government and create a collectivist but uncoerced society.

Although anarchists usually rejected Marxist socialism, many initially were dazzled by the Russian Revolution. During August 1918, the *Shturm* group reacted with passionate opposition when President Woodrow Wilson sent U.S. troops to Siberia. Samuel Lipman prepared an English pamphlet attacking U.S. intervention, while Jacob Schwartz wrote a much more militant version in Yiddish.

On 22 and 23 August, fellow anarchists distributed the leaflets by scattering them from rooftops in Manhattan. The New York police soon traced the leaflets to the *Shturm* group. Joined by army officers, the police interrogated the prisoners until each confessed. They later accused the officers of beatings and torture, and Jacob Schwartz died in prison the following October.

Trial and Appeal

The trial of Abrams and his associates began on 14 October 1918, before Henry DeLamar Clayton, an Alabama judge temporarily assigned to New York. A former congressman (author of the Clayton Anti-trust Act), Clayton hated Germany, especially after his beloved younger brother was killed in France by German soldiers.

Judge Clayton was overtly hostile throughout the trial. Despite a vigorous defense from attorney Harry Weinberger, a fellow anarchist, the jury convicted the defendants. On 25 October 1918, after delivering a two-hour tirade on the evils of Germany and Bolsheviks, Clayton sentenced Abrams, Lachowsky, and Lipman to 20 years and Steimer to 15 years in prison. Weinberger immediately appealed directly to the Supreme Court.

The Court heard oral arguments in *Abrams* on 21 October 1919. Assistant Attorney General Robert Stewart contended that the group had attempted to interfere with munitions production and had intended to overthrow the government by force. The First Amendment, he argued, did not apply because it merely protected the press from prior restraints.

Defense attorney Weinberger argued that the evidence did not support a guilty verdict. Moreover, the Espionage and Sedition Acts were unconstitutional because they violated the natural right of liberty of discussion. In any event, since the United States was not at war with the Soviet Union, the leaflets did not interfere with the war effort.

On 19 November 1919, the Court upheld the conviction of Abrams and his colleagues. Justice Clarke wrote the majority decision. The defendants' contention that the First Amendment protected their leaflets, Clarke wrote, "is definitely negated by *Schenck*."

Clarke quoted the leaflets selectively to show that there was enough evidence to convict the defendants. And Clarke tied their actions to the "clear and present danger test" in *Schenck*. The leaflets had been "circulated in the greatest port of our land," Clarke pointed out, at "the supreme crisis of the war." On the question of intent, Clarke brushed aside the argument that the anarchists wanted to protect the Soviet Union and not to help Germany. "Men must be held to have intended . . . the effects which their acts were likely to produce."

Clear and Present Danger—Phase Two

Holmes dissented, joined by Brandeis. Holmes centered his argument on the government's failure to prove intent. The word intent, he argued, often was vaguely used to mean only that a certain act had a tendency to cause a certain effect. But "when words are used exactly, a deed is not done with intent to produce a consequence unless that consequence is the aim of the deed." Intent means, in other words, that a person's goal is the proximate and immediate cause of a specific act.

Holmes asserted that he was following the *Schenck, Frohwerk,* and *Debs* decisions. In restating the "clear and present danger" standard, however, Holmes significantly revised it, by changing "present" to "imminent" and by adding "forthwith." Congress may punish only speech that "is intended to produce a clear and imminent danger that it will bring about forthwith certain substantive evils."

Holmes argued there was no danger that the defendants actually could damage the war effort.

> Now nobody can suppose that the surreptitious publishing of a silly leaflet by an unknown man, without more, would present any immediate danger that its opinions would hinder the success of the government arms or have any appreciable tendency to do so.

In any case, Abrams and his friends did not intend to harm the United States. Their only intent was to prevent interference with the revolution in Russia.

The Unending Search for Truth

In an eloquent final paragraph, for which the dissent is famous, Holmes discussed the connection between freedom of speech, the search for truth, and the value of experimentation. It is perfectly logical to persecute opposing views if one assumes one knows the truth.

> But when men have realized that time has upset many fighting faiths, they may come to believe even . . . that the ultimate good desired is better reached by free trade in ideas—that the best test of truth is the power of the thought to get itself accepted in the competition of the market . . . That is at any rate the theory of our Constitution . . . Only the emergency that makes it immediately dangerous to leave the correction of evil counsels to time warrants making any exception to the sweeping command, "Congress shall make no law abridging the freedom of speech."

The reasoning in Holmes' *Abrams* dissent significantly modifies his *Schenck* opinion eight months earlier. As Professor Richard Polenberg has shown in *Fighting Faiths,* Holmes spent considerable time during the summer of 1919 reconsidering his *Schenck* reasoning and reading about issues of free expression. Holmes discussed the case with Judge Learned Hand and Harvard Law School professor Zechariah Chafee, Jr., both libertarians on political discussion. He also met with English socialist Harold Laski, a visiting professor at Harvard. As a result, Holmes profoundly revised his *Schenck* reasoning and developed the more permissive doctrine he advanced in the *Abrams* dissent, nine months later.

Ultimately the revised "clear and imminent danger" standard in *Abrams* dissent became the position of the Court majority. But Holmes eloquent dissent did little for the *Abrams* defendants. After many months in prison, they were deported to the Soviet Union in 1921. But their homeland rejected them as well. Samuel Lipman was murdered during one of Stalin's purges, and Abrams and Mollie Steimer fled to lonely exile in Mexico City.

Related Cases
Patterson v. Colorado, 205 U.S. 454 (1907).
Schenk v. United States, 249 U.S. 47 (1919).

Frohwerk v. United States, 249 U.S. 204 (1919).
Debs v. United States, 249 U.S. 211 (1919).

Bibliography and Further Reading
Cohen, Jeremy. *Congress Shall Make No Law: Oliver Wendell Holmes, the First Amendment and Judicial Decision Making.* Ames: Iowa State University Press, 1989.

Johnson, John W. *Historic U.S. Court Cases, 1690–1990: An Encyclopedia,* Vol. 2. New York: Garland Publishing, 1992.

Kalven, Harry. *A Worthy Tradition: Freedom of Speech in America.* New York: Harper & Row, 1988.

Murphy, Paul. *World War I and the Origin of Civil Liberties in the United States.* New York: Norton, 1979.

Polenberg, Richard. *Fighting Faiths: The Abrams Case, the Supreme Court, and Free Speech.* New York, Viking, 1987.

Semonche, John E. *Charting the Future: The Supreme Court Responds to a Changing Society, 1890–1920.* Westport, CT: Greenwood, 1978.

Smith, Donald L. *Zechariah Chafee, Jr.: Defender of Liberty and Law.* Cambridge, MA: Harvard University Press, 1986.

GITLOW V. NEW YORK

Legal Citation: 268 U.S. 652 (1925)

Petitioner
Benjamin Gitlow, publisher of *The Revolutionary Age* newspaper

Respondent
State of New York

Petitioner's Claim
That a statute making a crime of anarchy violated the Due Process Clause of the Fourteenth Amendment.

Chief Lawyers for Petitioner
Walter Nelles and Walter H. Pollak

Chief Lawyers for Respondent
W.J. Weatherbee, Deputy Attorney General of New York, and John Caldwell Myers, Assistant District Attorney of New York County

Justices for the Court
Pierce Butler, James Clark McReynolds, Edward Terry Sanford (writing for the Court), Harlan Fiske Stone, George Sutherland, William Howard Taft, Willis Van Devanter

Justices Dissenting
Louis D. Brandeis, Oliver Wendell Holmes

Place
Washington, D.C.

Date of Decision
8 June 1925

Decision
Found Gitlow's conviction was constitutional.

Significance
Twofold: reinforced the then-common legal opinion that provocative political opinions which could be threatening enough to the public interest that freedom of speech could be abridged to silence it, but also was the first time the Supreme Court fully embraced the idea that the Fourteenth Amendment barred the states from denying their citizens freedom of speech without due process.

On 11 November 1919, New York City police officers raided the office of Benjamin Gitlow, a former city assemblyman from the Bronx, and Jim Larkin, a labor organizer, and filed against them charges of criminal anarchy. The two were members of the Communist Party, a radical offshoot of the Socialist Party, which they found to be too mainstream. The pair published a newspaper, *The Revolutionary Age,* and in it they had published the intellectual bible of their party, a treatise they called "The Left-Wing Manifesto." This manifesto called for the overthrow of the U.S. government and its capitalist system by violent revolution, and spelled out how this revolution was to take place, but did not specifically urge anyone to take action along these lines.

> It is not a problem of immediate revolution. It is a problem of the immediate revolutionary struggle. The revolutionary epoch of the final struggle against Capitalism may last for years and tens of years; but the Communist International offers a policy and program immediate and ultimate in scope, that provides for the immediate class struggle against Capitalism, in its revolutionary implications, and for the final act of the conquest of power. The old order is in decay. Civilization is in collapse. The proletarian revolution and the communist reconstruction of society—the struggle for these—is now indispensable.

Gitlow was convicted on the charges, and the conviction was upheld in the appellate court. In 1923 his case was heard by the U.S. Supreme Court. Defense attorney Walter Pollak issued one of his generation's most spirited and eloquent pleas for freedom of speech, saying:

> The citizen's liberty to take part in public affairs stands on another and broader footing. His exercise of his right is free not only in his own interest, but in the interest of the whole community. It is not for his benefit alone that he is permitted to express his views of law, government and politics, and propose his remedies. His views may be silly, his remedies preposterous. Their mere utterance creates some

Criminal Anarchy

Criminal anarchy is advocating, through either speech or writing, the overthrow of organized government by force, violence, or assassination. The term sedition is synonymous with criminal anarchy.

Sporadically in U.S. history, states became concerned about radical activities within their borders. They often felt the need to minimize threats by limiting free speech, free press, and free assembly through passage of criminal anarchy or sedition laws. New York's Criminal Anarchy Act appeared in 1902 after assassination of President William McKinley by a professed anarchist.

By 1919, following the Bolshevik Revolution in Russia, the end of World War I, and the emergence of labor unrest in the United States, Americans became fearful that revolution might erupt at home. Thirty-three states enacted sedition or criminal syndicalist (organized group) laws. These felony laws expanded criminal anarchy to include any individual or organization seeking political or industrial reform through crime, sabotage, or violence. Any person allowing the assembly of anarchists in a building could also be charged. Socialists, Communists, and members of labor unions were frequently singled out for prosecution. Doctrines of Fascism, Nazism, and Communism led to renewed fears of anarchism during the 1940s and 1950s. Civil rights unrest in the 1960s likewise produced these reactions.

Source(s): Murray, Robert K. *Red Scare: A Study of National Hysteria, 1919-1920.* New York: McGraw-Hill Book Company, 1964.

danger that unthinking members of the community may undertake to act upon them. But he is not to be punished either for their utterance—for the danger inherent in the doctrines themselves, as distinct from the danger arising from their utterance in particular circumstances. The citizen has a right to express, for the state may have an interest in hearing, any doctrine. Free government is premised upon the proposition that no human agency other than the ultimate good sense of the whole community can be trusted with power to gauge the dangerous tendency of mere expression of political doctrine. The utterance even of dangerous folly may be a valuable index of the need of wisdom. Folly may suggest wisdom. The liberty of opinion and expression which is essential to free government and which the Constitution protects, is thus an immunity from prosecution because of the intrinsic quality of the ideas expressed.

Victory for Free Speech

Ironically enough, when the Court finally ruled on the *Gitlow* case at the end of the following term in 1925, the ruling was that Gitlow's conviction was proper, but the significance of the case was a victory for freedom of speech. The reason was that two separate questions were involved in the *Gitlow* appeal. Both were questions which had been addressed numerous times by U.S. courts at all levels, up to and including the Supreme Court: One of the issues received the same judgment which had been fashionable in previous decisions, while the other for the first time was decided with a much different verdict.

The big change was that for the first time the Court decided that the Fourteenth Amendment, which forbade the states to deprive citizens of their liberty without due process of law, also forbade them to deny their citizens freedom of speech without due process.

> For present purposes we may and do assume that freedom of speech and of the press—which are protected by the First Amendment from abridgement by Congress—are among the fundamental personal rights and 'liberties' protected by the due process clause of the Fourteenth Amendment from impairment by the states.

This was the exact opposite of several rulings from the nineteenth century. In fact, the precedent, which had been cited many times and which seemed written in stone, held that the "liberty" referred to in the Fourteenth Amendment merely restricted the states from exacting physical restraints, such as imprisonment or confiscation of property, without due process. The other provisions of the Bill of Rights, i.e., freedom of speech, the press, religion, were all only binding to the federal government, and the individual states were free to agree with or ignore these freedoms as they saw fit. Over the first two decades of the twentieth century the Court had begun to waffle on the issue, sometimes hedging on the question, and sometimes declining to address it, but Justice Sanford's opinion on the *Gitlow* case was still an alarming step toward freedom of speech and away from states' rights.

That left, then, the second question of the trial, that of whether the state of New York had ample reason to deny Gitlow his freedom of speech to protect the public interest. The Court ruled, not unusually according to the sentiments of the times, that the manifesto was a threat to public stability and Gitlow's conviction was proper and just. Justice Sanford explained:

> When the legislative body has determined generally, in the constitutional exercise of its discretion, that utterances of a certain kind involve the danger of substantive evil that they may be punished, the question whether any specific utterance coming within the specified class is likely, in and of itself, to bring about the substantive evil, is not open to consideration.

The dissent, by Justices Holmes and Brandeis, would come to be the litmus test on freedom of speech issues in the coming decades:

> If what I think the correct test is applied, it is manifest that there was no present danger of an attempt to overthrow the government by force on the part of the admittedly small minority who shared the defendant's views. It is said that this manifesto was more than a theory, that it was an incitement. Every idea is an incitement. It offers itself for belief and if believed it is acted upon unless some other belief outweighs it or some failure of energy stifles the movement at birth. The only difference between the expression of an opinion and an incitement in the narrower sense is the speaker's enthusiasm for the result. Eloquence may set fire to reason. But whatever may be thought of the redundant discourse before us it had no chance of starting a present conflagration. If in the long run the benefits expressed in proletarian dictatorship are destined to be accepted by the dominant forces of the community, the only meaning of free speech is that they should be given their chance and have their way.

Related Cases

Stromberg v. California, 283 U.S. 359 (1931).
Chaplinsky v. New Hampshire, 315 U.S. 568 (1942).
Feiner v. New York, 340 U.S. 315 (1951).
Dennis v. United States, 341 U.S. 494 (1951).
Bigelow v. Virginia, 421 U.S. 809 (1975).
R.A.V. v. City of St. Paul, 505 U.S. 377 (1992).

Bibliography and Further Reading

Harvard Civil Rights—Civil Liberties Law Review, spring 1982, p. 1.

Harvard Law Review, Vol. 34, p. 431.

Johnson, John W., ed. *Historic U.S. Court Cases, 1690–1990: An Encyclopedia.* New York: Garland Publishing, 1992.

New York University Law Review, May 1994, p. 421.

Yale Law Journal, Vol. 35, p. 108.

CHAPLINSKY V. NEW HAMPSHIRE

Legal Citation: 315 U.S. 568 (1942).

Appellant
Walter Chaplinsky

Appellee
State of New Hampshire

Appellant's Claim
That a state statute prohibiting certain types of public speech violates the First Amendment guarantee of free speech.

Chief Lawyer for Appellant
Hayden C. Covington

Chief Lawyer for Appellee
Frank R. Kenison

Justices for the Court
Hugo Lafayette Black, James Francis Byrnes, William O. Douglas, Felix Frankfurter, Robert H. Jackson, Frank Murphy (writing for the Court), Stanley Forman Reed, Owen Josephus Roberts, Harlan Fiske Stone

Justices Dissenting
None

Place
Washington, D.C.

Date of Decision
9 March 1942

Decision
Reasoning that the Constitution does not protect some "well defined and narrowly limited" types of speech, the Supreme Court unanimously upheld both the statute and Chaplinsky's conviction under it.

Significance
Chaplinsky introduced a two-tiered approach to free speech, in which so-called "fighting words" and certain other categories of speech are placed outside the protection of the First Amendment.

Walter Chaplinsky, a Jehovah's Witness, had attracted a large and unruly crowd as he distributed religious tracts in the streets of Rochester, New Hampshire. Warned by a city marshall that the crowd was becoming riotous, Chaplinsky hurled insults at the officer, calling him a "racketeer" and a "Fascist." Chaplinsky was convicted in municipal court of having violated a state ordinance against the use of abusive language in public. His conviction was affirmed by the New Hampshire Supreme Court, and he appealed to the U.S. Supreme Court.

Court Develops Two-Tiered Theory of the First Amendment

Dismissing Chaplinsky's claim that his right to free exercise of his religion had been violated, Justice Murphy, writing for the unanimous Court, turned to the appellant's other First Amendment claim. The New Hampshire statute did not, the justices concluded, violate freedom of speech. The Court arrived at this conclusion by elaborating a two-tiered theory of the First Amendment.

> [I]t is well understood that the right of free speech is not absolute at all times and under all circumstances. There are certain well-defined and narrowly limited classes of speech, the prevention and punishment of which has never been thought to raise any constitutional problem. These include the lewd and obscene, the profane, the libelous, and the insulting or "fighting" words—those which by their very utterance inflict injury or tend to incite an immediate breach of the peace.

"Fighting words," like obscene ones, Murphy went on to say, contribute nothing in the way of ideas, and any value they might have is outweighed by an interest in social order and morality. This was an important distinction, for speech that is protected by the First Amendment is immune to government scrutiny of its content. Here, Murphy asserted, the words had essentially no content, but are only meant to provoke an immediate and violent reaction. In a sense, they were much like those that former Justice Oliver Wendell

---

Fighting Words

Although the U.S. Supreme Court has extended considerable constitutional protection to dissident speech, it recognized several areas of expression which fall outside First Amendment protection. These areas of expression include words which are lewd, obscene, profane, libelous, and "fighting." "Fighting words" are so offensive and inflammatory they will likely provoke a violent response from the individual being addressed. These words are calculated to inflict injury and incite an immediate breach of peace. Any benefit derived from them is clearly outweighed by repulsive repercussions to social order and morality.

Fighting words are words aimed intentionally at a specific individual rather than a group. The circumstances under which such speech is uttered is also important in identifying when speech is constitutionally unprotected.

If a municipality desires to forbid a particular kind of speech considered to be "fighting," the resulting law must be narrowly written. It must not include expressions which are merely offensive to someone, hurt their feelings, or cause resentment. Also, the law may not prohibit words based only on a particular bias, such as involving race or religion. The law could be judged unconstitutionally discriminatory. A prohibition must, therefore, outlaw all "fighting words."

Source(s): Biskupic, Joan and Elder Witt. *Guide to the U.S. Supreme Court.* (Washington, DC: Congressional Quarterly, 1997).

Holmes described in his famous dissent in *Schenck v. United States* (1919), one of the first Supreme Court opinions to attempt an interpretation of the First Amendment. Chaplinsky's epithets, like the words of a man shouting fire in a theater, presented "a clear and present danger" to public order.

Unlike Holmes' "clear and present danger" doctrine, which remains a part of First Amendment dogma, the "fighting words" analysis in *Chaplinsky* has been modified since the decision was handed down in 1942. *Chaplinsky* was the last case to uphold a conviction for the use of fighting words against a public official. *Edwards v. South Carolina* (1963) introduced the notion of a "heckler's veto," a doctrine which states that mere threats cannot trump free speech rights. In *Cohen v. California* (1971), the Court went further, stating that in order to override First Amendment protections, "fighting words" must provoke an immediate hostile reaction. What is more, the *Cohen* Court recognized that even threatening words have a communicative aspect that is worth protecting.

Cohen illustrates the erosion of *Chaplinsky*'s double standard on free speech. In the later case, a young man was convicted of disturbing the peace for wearing a jacket bearing the legend "F*** the Draft" while standing in a courthouse. The Supreme Court overturned his conviction, finding that neither the "vulgar" language on his jacket nor its provocative message were outside the ambit of First Amendment protection.

Related Cases
Schenck v. United States, 249 U.S. 47 (1919).
Edwards v. South Carolina, 372 U.S. 229 (1963).
Cohen v. California, 403 U.S. 15 (1971).
Bethel School District v. Fraser, 478 U.S. 675 (1986).

Bibliography and Further Reading
Greenawalt, Kent. *Fighting Words: Individuals, Communities, and Liberties of Speech.* Princeton, NJ: Princeton University Press, 1995.

Saunders, Kevin W. *Violence as Obscenity: Limiting the Media's First Amendment Protection.* Durham, NC: Duke University Press, 1996.

Speaking of Race, Speaking of Sex: Hate Speech, Civil Rights, and Civil Liberties. New York: New York University Press, 1994.

THOMAS V. COLLINS

Legal Citation: 323 U.S. 516 (1945)

Appellant
Roland J. Thomas

Appellee
Collins, Sheriff of Travis County, Texas

Appellant's Claim
That Texas law requiring union organizers to obtain a special license was an invalid restriction of the First Amendment right to free speech.

Chief Lawyers for Appellant
Lee Pressman, Ernest Goodman

Chief Lawyer for Appellee
Fagan Dickson

Justices for the Court
Hugo Lafayette Black, William O. Douglas, Frank Murphy, Robert H. Jackson, Wiley Blount Rutledge (writing for the Court)

Justices Dissenting
Owen Josephus Roberts, Harlan Fiske Stone, Stanley Forman Reed, Felix Frankfurter

Place
Washington, D.C.

Date of Decision
8 January 1945

Decision
Reversed Supreme Court of Texas decision upholding the contempt conviction of Thomas for ignoring a restraining order aimed at preventing him from making a union organizing speech without an organizer's license.

Significance
Thomas v. Collins arose during a period in which the relationship between unions and employers was undergoing a great deal of change. The case was part of a series of legal victories for labor, which included a ban on the intimidation by employers of workers attempting to organize. While the U.S. Supreme Court had expressed a willingness to restrict that kind of expression on the part of employers, it was less inclined to put limitations on the free speech rights of workers. *Thomas v. Collins* reinforced the doctrine that only in the presence of "clear and present danger" could that right be restricted.

Thomas v. Collins involved a Texas law that required labor union organizers to obtain a special license from the Texas secretary of state before engaging in membership recruitment. Roland Jay Thomas, president of the United Automobile, Aircraft and Agricultural Implements Workers (UAW) and a vice president of the Congress of Industrial Organizations (CIO), sought to challenge the constitutionality of the law. Thomas was involved in an effort to organize workers at the Humble Oil & Refining Company plant in Bay Town, Texas, into the Oil Workers Industrial Union, an affiliate of the CIO. Thomas traveled to Houston on 21 September 1943 in order to address a widely publicized mass meeting on the subject scheduled two days later.

About six hours before he was to speak, Thomas was served with a restraining order preventing him from doing so, on the grounds that he had not registered as an organizer. After consulting with his lawyers, Thomas decided that the Texas law requiring organizers to obtain an "organizer's card" was an illegal infringement of his right to free speech. Ignoring the restraining order, he went ahead with his planned speech. After the meeting, Thomas was arrested and subsequently convicted of contempt for violating the restraining order.

The Texas Supreme Court sustained the registration law, regarding it as a "valid exercise of the State's police power, taken 'for protection of the general welfare of the public, and particularly the laboring class.'" According to the Texas court the act, while "interfering to a certain extent with the right of the organizer to speak as the paid representative of the union," did not unduly impose "previous general restraint upon the right of free speech . . . It merely requires paid organizers to register with the Secretary of State before beginning to operate as such."

The case was appealed to the U.S. Supreme Court, where attorneys Lee Pressman and Ernest Goodman argued on Thomas's behalf that the Texas act did indeed impose such prior restraint on Thomas's right of free speech, in direct violation of the First and Fourteenth Amendments. The Supreme Court agreed, and the contempt conviction was reversed on a vote of 5-4. The majority opinion was written by Justice

Rutledge, with Justices Black, Douglas, and Murphy concurring. Rutledge's reasoning was that the only circumstances under which the First Amendment permitted restriction of free speech or free assembly were in the presence of clear and present danger. Alluding specifically to the *Thomas* case, he wrote that "Lawful public assemblies, involving no element of grave and immediate danger to an interest the State is entitled to protect, are not instruments of harm which require previous identification of the speakers." Since all Thomas had done was address a perfectly peaceful meeting, the requirement to register beforehand represented an invalid restriction of his rights.

While the decision was a victory for labor, there was reason for employers to take heart as well. In a separate concurring opinion, Justice Jackson pointed out the distinction between the regulation of speech and the regulation of a professional vocation. Jackson noted that it takes only a small step to push Thomas's actions into the realm of business activity, which does not enjoy the same constitutional protections as speech. He also indicated that employers should also be permitted unrestricted speech, a right which recent cases involving the National Labor Relations Board had denied them.

Justices Roberts, Stone, Reed, and Frankfurter dissented. To them, Thomas's speech fell into the category of mere business activity. As a professional union organizer, his work could be regulated as much as that of a doctor, lawyer, or stock broker. Roberts, in his dissenting opinion, wrote that "We may deem the statutory provision under review unnecessary or unwise, but it is not our function as judges to read our views of policy into a constitutional guarantee, in order to overthrow a state policy we do not personally approve . . ."

Impact

Although the balance of power between unions and employers has shifted repeatedly in the decades since *Thomas v. Collins,* the case ushered in a period of relative strength for organized labor during the postwar economic boom in the United States. In classifying union organizing as a protected form of expression rather than an economic activity, the Court played a part in creating what was one of the best periods for working-class America in the nation's history.

Related Cases
Martin v. Struthers, 319 U.S. 141 (1943).
Breard v. Alexandria, 341 U.S. 622 (1951).
Staub v. City of Baxley, 355 U.S. 313 (1958).

Bibliography and Further Reading
Business Week, January 13, 1945.

Emerson, Thomas I. *The System of Freedom of Expression.* New York: Random House, 1970.

Mason, Alpheus Thomas. *The Supreme Court from Taft to Burger,* Louisiana State University Press, 1979.

New Republic, January 22, 1945.

Time, January 22, 1945.

MARSH V. ALABAMA

Legal Citation: 326 U.S. 507 (1946)

Appellant
Grace Marsh

Appellee
State of Alabama

Appellant's Claim
That she had the freedom to distribute religious literature of the Jehovah's Witnesses on a "public" street in the company-owned town of Chickasaw, Alabama, despite the privately owned town's refusal to issue her a permit and the Alabama state law supporting property owners' right to ask individuals to leave their property.

Chief Lawyer for Appellant
Hayden C. Covington

Chief Lawyers for Appellee
William M. McQueen, Attorney General of Alabama, and John O. Harris, Assistant Attorney General of Alabama

Justices for the Court
Hugo Lafayette Black (writing for the Court), William O. Douglas, Felix Frankfurter, Robert H. Jackson, Frank Murphy, Owen Josephus Roberts, Wiley Blount Rutledge

Justices Dissenting
Harold Burton, Stanley Forman Reed, Harlan Fiske Stone (Robert H. Jackson did not participate)

Place
Washington, D.C.

Date of Decision
7 January 1946

Decision
The First and the Fourteenth Amendments prohibit states from imposing punishment on people who distribute religious literature, even in a company town; therefore, Marsh's conviction was overturned.

Significance
The *Marsh v. Alabama* decision was a landmark First Amendment case, further establishing the "preferred position" of freedom of religion, as opposed to the rights of property owners.

Grace Marsh was a Jehovah's Witness who wanted to distribute religious literature in downtown Chickasaw, Alabama. Chickasaw was a suburb of the city of Mobile—a suburb wholly owned by the Gulf Shipbuilding Corporation.

One day Marsh stood near the town post office, handing out leaflets. In the stores nearby, signs announced:

> This Is Private Property, and Without Written Permission, No Street House, or House Vendor, Agent or Solicitation of Any Kind Will Be Permitted.

Marsh was warned that she could not distribute literature without a permit, and officials made it clear that she would never be issued a permit. Marsh claimed that she had a right to hand out literature under the First Amendment of the Constitution, which protects freedom of religion and of the press. However, Marsh was arrested for violating an Alabama law that made it a crime for a person to stay on the property of someone who has asked that person to leave.

The Special Case of a Company Town

When Marsh's case finally made it to the Supreme Court, the Court faced an unusual situation. Certainly no government agency had the right to prohibit the distribution of religious literature in a public street. But Chickasaw was wholly owned by a private company. The Court needed to answer the question of what rights such a company had to regulate the activities that took place on its property.

The majority of the Court answered: When private property rights conflict with First Amendment freedoms, especially freedom of religion, the First Amendment freedoms should probably be preferred. The Court stressed that private property rights are especially likely to be limited when an owner has already more or less opened that property to the public. This was certainly the case in Chickasaw. In the words of Justice Black's majority opinion:

> . . . Chickasaw . . . has all the characteristics of any other American town. The property consists of residential buildings, streets, a system

of sewers, a sewage disposal plant and a "business block" on which business places are situated . . . [R]esidents . . . make use of a company-owned paved street and sidewalk located alongside the store fronts . . . Intersecting company-owned roads at each end of the business block lead into a four-lane public highway . . . In short the town and its shopping district are accessible to and freely used by the public in general . . .

Therefore, wrote Justice Black

Ownership does not always mean absolute dominion. The more an owner, for his [sic] advantage, opens up his property for use by the public in general, the more do his rights become circumscribed by the . . . rights of those who use it . . .

Moreover, Justice Black said, First Amendment rights were particularly precious—even more precious than property:

When we balance the constitutional rights of owners of property against those of people to enjoy freedom of the press and religion, as we must here, we remain mindful of the fact that the latter occupy a preferred position . . . Many people in the United States live in company-owned towns . . . Just as all other citizens they must make decisions which affect the welfare of community and nation. To act as good citizens they must be informed. In order to enable them to be properly informed their information must be uncensored.

The Rights of Property Owners

The Supreme Court therefore overturned Marsh's conviction, establishing the principle that privately owned places could also be public, and that freedom of religion was one of the most "preferred" freedoms in the nation. However, Justices Reed, Burton, and Chief Justice Stone dissented. As Justice Reed wrote:

It has never been held and is not now by this opinion of the Court that these [constitutional] rights [to freedom of religion, of speech, and of the press] are absolute either in respect to the manner or the place of their exercise . . . This is the first case to extend by law the privilege of religious exercises beyond public places or to private places without the assent of the owner . . .

Despite these objections, the majority decision in *Marsh* established an important principle. People who owned places that were treated as "public" had different obligations than the owners of individual homes.

The Consequences of *Marsh v. Alabama*

Despite the strong language of the majority decision in *Marsh*, its influence is rather difficult to determine. Certainly, in the 1946 case of *Tucker v. Texas*, the *Marsh* decision was directly applied. In *Tucker*, a town owned by the Federal Public Housing Authority tried to ban the distribution of religious literature. Because of *Marsh*, the Federal PHA was told that such a ban was unconstitutional.

However, in 1951, in *Breard v. Alexandria*, the Court ruled that a city ordinance can prohibit door-to-door selling. As commercial activity, selling does not have the same protected status as distributing religious literature.

Perhaps the two most dramatic results of *Marsh* took place in the 1960s and early 1970s. Starting in the 1960s, African American youths and their white supporters organized the first sit-ins—events in which people literally sat in at the lunch counters in local department and drugstores, waiting for African Americans to be served. Technically, these stores were privately owned. The Court might have agreed that private store or restaurant owners had the right to serve whomever they please. But thanks to *Marsh*, the Court found that by opening their stores to the public, the store owners had accrued certain obligations, such as to offer equal treatment to all customers.

A second key decision came in 1972, in the case of *Lloyd Corp. v. Tanner*. A privately owned shopping center wanted to prohibit the distribution of literature protesting the Vietnam War and the draft. In what appeared to be a sharp departure from *Marsh*, the Court ruled that private property owners had the right to forbid activities unrelated to the normal operations on that site. In other words, a lunch-counter operator could not refuse to serve lunch to customers based on race, but a shopping center owner could refuse to allow political literature to be given out. Whereas in *Marsh*, First Amendment rights had taken precedence, in *Lloyd*, the rights of property owners were considered more important.

Related Cases

Tucker v. Texas, 326 U.S. 517 (1946).
Breard v. City of Alexandria, 341 U.S. 622 (1951).
Lloyd Corp. v. Tanner, 407 U.S. 551 (1972).

Bibliography and Further Reading

Bartholomew, Paul C. *American Constitutional Law: Limitations on Government,* Vol. II. Totowa, NJ, Littlefield, Adams, 1970, 1978.

Pollak, Louis H., ed. *The Constitution and the Supreme Court: A Documentary History,* Vol. II. Cleveland: World Publishing Co., 1966.

Summaries of Leading Cases on the Constitution. Totowa, NJ: Littlefield, Adams & Co., 1976.

TERMINIELLO V. CHICAGO

Legal Citation: 337 U.S. 1 (1949)

Petitioner
Father Arthur Terminiello

Respondent
City of Chicago

Petitioner's Claim
That the Chicago ordinance against disturbing the peace violated Terminiello's right of free expression as guaranteed by the First Amendment.

Chief Lawyer for Petitioner
Albert W. Dilling

Chief Lawyer for Respondent
L. Louis Karton

Justices for the Court
Hugo Lafayette Black, William O. Douglas (writing for the Court), Frank Murphy, Stanley Forman Reed, Wiley Blount Rutledge

Justices Dissenting
Harold Burton, Felix Frankfurter, Robert H. Jackson, Fred Moore Vinson

Place
Washington, D.C.

Date of Decision
16 May 1949

Decision
Reversed Illinois decision affirming Terminiello's conviction for disturbing the peace on grounds that the trial judge's instructions to the jury defined "breach of peace" too narrowly.

Significance
The Court held that even speech that is designed to stir up anger and provoke disputes is protected by the First Amendment. While the right to free speech is not absolute, the Court chose to draw the line as to what types of speech created "a clear and present danger" far beyond the hate-mongering, mean-spirited kind in which Arthur Terminiello engaged.

Father Terminiello, sometimes called "the Father Coughlin of the South" because of his anti-Semitic rhetoric, was an Alabama priest who, at the time of this case, was under suspension by his church for distributing anti-Jewish literature. Well known for his controversial views on Jews, blacks, New Deal Democrats, and just about everybody else not white, Christian, and conservative, Terminiello came to Chicago from his home base of Birmingham. He was invited by a group called the Christian Veterans of America in 1946 in order to make a speech at the West End Women's Club.

Terminiello's appearance was attended by a capacity crowd of about 800. Meanwhile, a hostile mob of protesters, estimated at well over 1,000 people, gathered outside the auditorium. The tone of Terminiello's speech, which straightforwardly attacked "Communistic Zionistic Jews," African Americans, and Franklin D. Roosevelt, among others, incited the crowd outside to violence. Police were unable to contain the disturbance. Scores of rocks, bricks, bottles, and stink bombs were thrown, resulting in 28 broken windows, 17 arrests.

In the wake of the mayhem, an organization called the Chicago Civil Liberties Committee filed a complaint against Terminiello, claiming that he had violated a Chicago ordinance against disturbing the peace. The language of the ordinance declared it illegal to create a "diversion tending to a breach of the peace." Terminiello was convicted and fined $100 for his role in the disturbance. Two higher Illinois courts upheld the conviction. Terminiello eventually brought his case to the U.S. Supreme Court.

In a 5-4 decision, the Supreme Court reversed the ruling of the Illinois courts, and overturned Terminiello's conviction. Throughout the appeals process, Terminiello maintained that the Chicago ordinance under which he had been charged violated his constitutionally protected right of free speech. This argument found a degree of sympathy among the Supreme Court justices. Justice Douglas, in particular, had consistently voted to protect virtually all forms of expression throughout his career, and *Terminiello v. Chicago* was no exception. Writing for the majority, however, Douglas followed a much more subtle line of reasoning. The problem with Terminiello's conviction was not the

Chicago ordinance itself, but rather the instructions that had been given to the jury regarding how to interpret it. The trial court that first heard the case was advised that "breach of the peace" can be committed by speech that "stirs the public to anger, invites dispute, brings about a condition of unrest, or creates a disturbance."

To Douglas, this represented a view of public speech that was far too restrictive. In typical style, Douglas wrote:

> A function of free speech under our system of government is to invite dispute. It may indeed best serve its high purpose when it induces a condition of unrest, creates dissatisfaction with conditions as they are, or even stirs people to anger . . . That is why freedom of speech, though not absolute, . . . is nevertheless protected against censorship or punishment, unless shown likely to produce a clear and present danger of a serious substantive evil that rises far above public inconvenience, annoyance, or unrest . . . There is no room under our Constitution for a more restrictive view.

Annoying and inconvenient as it was, the evil incited by Terminiello's speech was not nearly substantive enough to qualify for restriction under Douglas's interpretation of the First Amendment.

So while the Court voted to void Terminiello's conviction, the justices were collectively unwilling to throw out the Chicago ordinance altogether. It was acceptable, they said in effect, to pass laws against disturbing the peace; but if the disturbance was in the form of speech, it had better be extraordinarily inflammatory if you expected a conviction to stick. The Court chose not to address the question of whether Terminiello's antics were likely to have caused a riot. Instead, it limited its decision to the validity of the Illinois court's procedures.

Several strong points were made by dissenting justices in *Terminiello*. In a long, emotional dissenting opinion, Justice Jackson was clearly influenced by his own recent experience as chief U.S. counsel at the Nuremberg trials of Nazi war criminals. To Jackson, Terminiello's language was too close to that of the fascists, whose defeat was considered important enough to justify going to war. Jackson wrote:

> An old proverb warns us to take heed lest we 'walk into a well from looking at the stars.' . . . This Court has gone far toward accepting the doctrine that civil liberty means the removal of all restraints from these crowds and that all local attempts to maintain order are impairments of the liberty of the citizen . . . There is danger that, if the Court does not temper its doctrinaire logic with a little practical wisdom, it will convert the constitutional Bill of Rights into a suicide pact.

Justices Vinson and Frankfurter dissented on other, more technical, grounds. They objected to Douglas's argument that Terminiello's conviction was flawed because of faulty jury instruction by the trial judge. Their reason: Terminiello and his attorneys never complained about it. The Supreme Court, as a rule, had no business tampering with a state court's procedures on issues that were raised by neither litigant.

Impact

The passage of Douglas's opinion quoted above became the key to opinions upholding First Amendment rights in public assembly cases for years to come. While *Terminiello* signaled a major victory for free speech, the victory was not complete. Douglas made clear that there was a point—namely, where it creates a clear and present danger—at which it was acceptable to restrict speech. Laws such as Chicago's could be reasonably applied. It was the way in which it was used against Terminiello that represented a violation of his rights. The Court held that the trial judge's definition of a "breach of peace" was too narrow, not that a valid definition was impossible.

Related Cases

Cantwell v. Connecticut, 310 U.S. 296 (1940).
Chaplinsky v. New Hampshire, 315 U.S. 568 (1942).
Kunz v. New York, 340 U.S. 290 (1951).
Feiner v. New York, 340 U.S. 315 (1951).

Bibliography and Further Reading

Emerson, Thomas I. *The System of Freedom of Expression,* New York: Random House, 1970.

Kalven, Harry, Jr. *A Worthy Tradition: Freedom of Speech in America.* New York: Harper and Row, 1988.

New Republic, May 30, 1949.

Newsweek, May 30, 1949.

Time, May 30, 1949.

Tresolini, Rocco J. *These Liberties.* New York: Lippincott, 1968.

FEINER V. NEW YORK

Legal Citation: 340 U.S. 315 (1951)

Petitioner
Irving Feiner

Respondent
State of New York

Petitioner's Claim
His First Amendment and free speech rights were violated.

Chief Lawyers for Petitioner
Sidney H. Greenberg and Emanuel Redfield

Chief Lawyer for Respondent
Dan J. Kelly

Justices for the Court
Harold Burton, Tom C. Clark, Felix Frankfurter, Robert H. Jackson, Stanley Forman Reed, Fred Moore Vinson (writing for the Court)

Justices Dissenting
Hugo Lafayette Black, William O. Douglas, Sherman Minton

Place
Washington, D.C.

Date of Decision
15 January 1951

Decision
The Court ruled that Feiner's arrest did not hamper his right to free speech.

Significance
With *Feiner v. New York*, the Supreme Court helped balance "clear and present danger" against free speech rights, in upholding Feiner's original misdemeanor conviction.

In our Constitution's First Amendment, a single phrase has caused more judicial hair-pulling and controversy than almost any other. The First Amendment reads in part that Congress can make no law, "abridging the freedom of speech." The U.S. Supreme Court has been involved with the Free Speech Clause more intently since the early 1920s. During this time, free speech issues and Court opinions have spread so far in different directions that it is impossible to define "free speech" exactly. No one phrase can sum up all of its meanings and ramifications.

It was about 6:30 on the evening of 8 March 1949 when Syracuse police officers received a call about an outside meeting on the corner of South McBride and Harrison. Two officers were sent to investigate. When the officers arrived, they found about 75 to 80 people listening to a college student, Irving Feiner.

The growing crowd filled the sidewalk and flowed into the street. Feiner was on the sidewalk, standing on a large wooden box. Using a loudspeaker system attached to his car, he was urging the audience to attend a meeting that evening in the Syracuse Hotel. His announcement was not limited to the time, place and whereabouts of this meeting. It included unsavory references to the American Legion, Syracuse's Mayor, and President Harry Truman, just to name a few.

When they arrived, the police officers did not interrupt Feiner. From across the street, they noticed that passing pedestrians had to walk in the street to maneuver past the crowd. In turn, this was causing traffic problems. When the police tried to get the crowd out of the street, some pushing, shoving and muttering emanated from the crowd. One of the officers went into a store and called the police station. Then both officers joined the crowd. They had no plan to arrest Feiner.

Several things happened. At this time Feiner was speaking in what has been described as a "loud, high-pitched voice." Witnesses got the impression that he was inciting the African Americans to rise up against the Caucasians and fight for their civil rights. Some of the people in the crowd became somewhat agitated about these remarks and passersby commented to the officers about their apparent lack of ability to handle

Sidewalk Speech

The "sidewalk speaker" or "soapbox orator" has long been part of America's urban landscape. Espousing various themes, generally political or religious in nature, his/her exuberant free expression at times raises questions about the limits of First Amendment protection. The Supreme Court's role has been to find a balance between the right of the individual to make a speech on public property, the right of listeners to assemble, and the government's responsibility to maintain public order and safety.

The First Amendment protects public free speech from states' and municipalities' regulations. Using public places, such as streets and parks for communication of ideas, is a privilege of the citizens which may not be limited or denied. One function of speech is to invite dispute and arouse, even anger, its listeners. Government is constitutionally justified in repressing expression only if a breach of peace or violence is threatened or actually occurs. Unless a clear and present danger exists, speech may not be restrained.

The courts consistently reject any prior restraints placed on speech. However, if enforced in a nondiscriminatory manner, government can regulate the time, place, and manner of speech, particularly speech that may interfere with other rightful uses of the space.

Source(s): Sunstein, Cass R. *Democracy and the Problem of Free Speech*. New York: The Free Press, 1993.

---

the crowd. At least one person threatened violence against Feiner if there was no police action.

The crowd was demonstrating feelings for and against Feiner to such a degree that the police judged a fight might erupt momentarily. One of the officers asked Feiner to step off the box, not to arrest him, but to get him to disperse his listeners. Feiner paid no attention. After a minute or so, the officer insisted that Feiner stop talking. Still, Feiner ignored him.

Now, the crowd was closing in on this activity. The police told Feiner they were arresting him and ordered him off of his box. One officer reached up to help him off of the box. As Feiner got off the box, he used the microphone one final time to say that "the law has arrived, and I suppose they will take over now." The police charged Feiner with violating section 722 of the Penal Law of New York. Essentially, he was charged with disorderly conduct.

During the ensuing trial, some testimony agreed with the police officers, but some testimony did not. The trial judge considered all of the evidence and concluded that the police actions to prevent a breach of the peace were proper and dictated by the events. Two review courts agreed. All of the courts agreed that it seemed as though the officers acted as they did, not because they disagreed with Feiner, but out of their duty to preserve the peace. Indeed, Feiner had not been arrested for his speech, but the aftermath.

The case then went to the U.S. Supreme Court where Chief Justice Vinson's opinion stated that considering all of the circumstances, Feiner's constitutional rights had not been violated. In a 6-3 decision, the Court confirmed the lower courts' decisions that the police officers were not attempting to suppress Feiner's opinions, but were attempting to prevent an impending civil disturbance.

Justice Black dissented, making three points. First, he said, that according to the facts, the crowd behavior seemed as though it was normal, all things considered and the idea of an impending riot was "far-fetched." Second, Black said that even if the circumstances were as the officers described, they ought not have interfered with the speaker. Their first duty was to protect the speaker. Black said that, according to the evidence, there had been no attempt at all to protect Feiner. Third, Feiner's resistance to the officer was justified in that he was not required by law to stop speaking just because a police officer requests this. According to Black, Feiner was entitled to know why he was being silenced and why he should cease engaging in a legal activity. The testimony was clear that at no time did the officer explain his reasoning to Feiner. The strength of Black's convictions were summed up when he wrote, "I understand that people in authoritarian countries must obey arbitrary orders. I had hoped there was no such duty in the United States."

Related Cases
Terminiello v. Chicago, 337 U.S. 1 (1949).
Kunz v. New York, 340 U.S. 290 (1951).
Edwards v. South Carolina, 372 U.S. 229 (1963).

Bibliography and Further Reading
Seidman, Louis M., Gerald R. Stone, Cass R. Sunstein, Mark V. Tushnet. *Constitutional Law*. Little, Brown and Company, 1986.

Lieberman, Jethro K. *The Evolving Constitution*. Random House, 1992.

DENNIS V. UNITED STATES

Legal Citation: 341 U.S. 494 (1951)

Petitioners
Eugene Dennis, Benjamin Davis, John Gates, Gil Green, Gus Hall, Irving Potash, Jack Stachel, Robert Thompson, John Williamson, Henry Winston, Carl Winter

Respondent
United States

Petitioners' Claim
That the Smith Act violates the First Amendment and other provisions of the Bill of Rights of the U.S. Constitution.

Chief Lawyers for Petitioners
George W. Crockett, Jr., Abraham J. Isserman, Harry Sacher

Chief Lawyers for Respondent
Philip B. Perlman, Irving S. Shapiro

Justices for the Court
Harold Burton, Felix Frankfurter, Robert H. Jackson, Sherman Minton, Stanley Forman Reed, Fred Moore Vinson (writing for the Court)

Justices Dissenting
Hugo Lafayette Black, William O. Douglas (Tom C. Clark did not participate)

Place
Washington, D.C.

Date of Decision
4 June 1951

Decision
Provisions of the Smith Act prohibiting willful advocacy of overthrow of government by force or violence, organization of any group for that purpose and conspiracy to violate such provisions were held not to violate the First Amendment or other provisions of the Bill of Rights.

Significance
The U.S. Supreme Court's review of this case provides a classic example of how the guarantees of the First Amendment must be balanced against the nation's need, as prescribed by Congress, to protect itself. The opinions written by the justices contain memorable expressions of this paradox.

The Alien Registration Act of 1940, known as the Smith Act, made it a crime "to knowingly or willfully advocate, abet, advise, or teach the duty, necessity, desirability, or propriety of overthrowing or destroying any government in the United States by force or violence." Publication or display of printed matter teaching or advocating overthrow of the government was forbidden, as was organizing any group that teaches, advocates, or encourages overthrow of government by force. Also against the law was "knowing" membership in any group dedicated to that end.

In July of 1948, Eugene Dennis, general secretary of the Communist Party in the United States, and ten other party leaders were indicted for violating the Smith Act by conspiring to organize groups that taught the overthrow of the government. In a sensational trial that lasted nine months and resulted in a record 16,000 pages of testimony, the defendants argued that First Amendment freedom of speech protected them. Finding that the leaders of the Communist Party were unwilling to work within the framework of democracy but, rather, intended to initiate a violent revolution, the jury convicted them all.

"Clear and Present Danger"

They appealed. The U.S. Court of Appeals applied the "clear and present danger test" of free speech that was originated by Supreme Court Justice Oliver Wendell Holmes in *Schenck v. United States* (1919), when Holmes, writing the opinion of the unanimous court, said:

> The question in every case is whether the words used are used in such circumstances and are of such a nature as to create a clear and present danger that they will bring about the substantive evils that Congress has a right to prevent.

Upholding the convictions, the court of appeals applied a "sliding scale" rule for the clear and present danger test, saying it "must ask whether the gravity of the 'evil,' discounted by its improbability, justifies such invasion of free speech as is necessary to avoid the danger."

Eugene Dennis, 1951. © AP/Wide World Photos.

The U.S. Supreme Court agreed to review the case from the standpoint of whether the Smith Act "inherently or as construed and applied in the instant case violates the First Amendment and other provisions of the Bill of Rights." Without Justice Clark participating, the eight other justices showed wide disagreement over how to measure the Smith Act's restraints on the freedom of speech and association guaranteed by the First Amendment. Chief Justice Vinson, with Justices Burton, Minton, and Reed, found that:

> Congress did not intend to eradicate the free discussion of political theories, to destroy the traditional rights of Americans to discuss and evaluate ideas without fear of governmental sanction [but] the formation of such a highly organized conspiracy, with rigidly disciplined members subject to call when the leaders felt that the time had come for action, coupled with the inflammable nature of world conditions, convince us that their convictions were justified . . . It is the existence of the conspiracy which creates the danger . . . If the ingredients of the reaction are present, we cannot bind the Government to wait until the catalyst is added.

Petitioners intended to overthrow the government of the United States as speedily as the circumstances would permit. Their conspiracy . . . created a "clear and present danger" . . . They were properly and constitutionally convicted for violation of the Smith Act.

"Beyond These Powers We Must Not Go"
Justice Frankfurter concurred, but wrote:

> It is a sobering fact that in sustaining the convictions before us we can hardly escape restriction on the interchange of ideas.

Congress, not the Supreme Court, he wrote, was responsible for reconciling such a conflict of values. The Court's job was to require substantial proof before conviction and to ensure fair procedures in enforcement of the law. "Beyond these powers," he wrote, "we must not go; we must scrupulously observe the narrow limits of judicial authority."

While also concurring, Justice Jackson wrote:

> The authors of the clear and present danger test never applied it to a case like this, nor would I. As proposed here, it means that the Communist plotting is protected during its period of incubation; its preliminary stages of organization and preparation are immune from the law; the Government can move only after imminent action is manifest, when it would, of course, be too late.

Jackson concluded: "There is no constitutional right to gang up on the Government."

Dissenters Cite Prior Censorship
Justices Douglas and Black wrote dissenting opinions. Black stated:

> The indictment is that they conspired to use speech or newspapers to teach and advocate the forcible overthrow of the Government. No matter how it is worded, this is a virulent form of prior censorship of speech and press, which I believe the First Amendment forbids.

Douglas wrote:

> We deal here with speech alone, not with speech *plus* acts of sabotage or unlawful conduct. Not a single seditious act is charged.

> Free speech—the glory of our system of government—should not be sacrificed on anything less than plain and objective proof of danger that the evil advocated is imminent. On the record no one can say that petitioners and their converts are in such a strategic position as to have even the slightest chance of achieving their aims.

The majority opinion concluded that the Smith Act "does not violate the First Amendment or other provisions of the Bill of Rights." As a result, not only did Dennis and his fellow appellants serve time in prison, but 121 second-rank U.S. Communist Party officials were prosecuted for conspiracy under the Smith Act. Other individual party members also were prosecuted. In every case tried between 1951 and 1956, convictions were obtained. All were affirmed by courts of appeal. All were denied review by the Supreme Court.

Related Cases

Abrams v. United States, 250 U.S. 616 (1919).
Gitlow v. New York, 268 U.S. 652 (1925).
Whitney v. California, 274 U.S. 357 (1927).
DeJonge v. Oregon, 299 U.S. 353 (1937).
Thornhill v. Alabama, 310 U.S. 88 (1940).
Cantwell v. Connecticut, 310 U.S. 296 (1940).
West Virginia Board of Education v. Barnette, 319 U.S. 624 (1943).

American Communications Association v. Douds, 339 U.S. 382 (1950).

Bibliography and Further Reading

Belfrage, Cedric. *The American Inquisition, 1945-1960.* Indianapolis: Bobbs Merrill Co. 1973.

Fast, Howard. *Being Red.* Boston: Houghton Mifflin, 1990.

Johnson, John W. *Historic U.S. Court Cases, 1690–1990: An Encyclopedia.* New York: Garland Publishing, 1992.

Hoover, J. Edgar. *Masters of Deceit.* New York: Henry Holt, 1958.

Klehr, Harvey. *The Heyday of American Communism: The Depression Decade.* New York: Basic Books, 1984.

Mitford, Jessica. *A Fine Old Conflict.* New York: Alfred A. Knopf, 1971.

Witt, Elder. *Guide to the U.S. Supreme Court.* Washington, DC: Congressional Quarterly Press, 1990.

JOSEPH BURSTYN, INC. V. WILSON, COMMISSIONER OF EDUCATION OF NEW YORK, ET AL.

Legal Citation: 343 U.S. 495 (1952)

Appellant
Joseph Burstyn, Inc.

Appellee
Lewis A. Wilson, New York Commissioner of Education

Appellant's Claim
The New York State should not have banned the showing of the film *The Miracle* on the grounds that the film was "sacrilegious."

Chief Lawyer for Appellant
Ephraim S. London

Chief Lawyers for Appellee
Charles A. Brind, Jr., and Wendell P. Brown, Solicitor General of New York

Justices for the Court
Hugo Lafayette Black, Harold Burton, Tom C. Clark (writing for the Court), William O. Douglas, Felix Frankfurter, Robert H. Jackson, Sherman Minton, Stanley Forman Reed, Fred Moore Vinson

Justices Dissenting
None

Place
Washington, D.C.

Date of Decision
26 May 1952

Decision
That New York should not permit a censor to restrict films on the grounds of "sacrilege."

Significance
This decision definitively established motion pictures as part of the "press" and therefore protected by the First Amendment. The decision condemned any use of religious notions as a means of making governmental decisions, and it also condemned vagueness in any language that concerned censorship.

In late 1950, an Italian film directed by world-famous director Roberto Rossellini and featuring the international star Anna Magnani opened at the Paris Theatre in New York. This was the unlikely beginning of one of the Supreme Court's key rulings on censorship, the film industry, and the separation of church and state.

A Controversial Film

In the words of film critic Bosley Crowther (quoted in one of the Supreme Court decisions), *The Miracle* was the story of a "poor, simple-minded girl" who tends goats on a mountain in rural Italy. One day she meets a bearded stranger, whom she decides is "St. Joseph, her favorite saint, and that he has come to take her to heaven, where she will be happy and free." The stranger gives the girl wine and "apparently ravishes her." When she wakes up, the stranger is gone, and she has no idea whether he was real or a dream. She meets an old priest who says that perhaps she did see a saint. Eventually, the village women discover that the girl is going to have a child, whom she believes to be the son of St. Joseph. Mocked by the villagers, the girl becomes an outcast. As her time approaches, she finds a small, deserted church, where she gives birth. Then, as Crowther described it:

> There is a dissolve, and when we next see her sad face, in close-up, it is full of a tender light. There is the cry of an unseen baby. The girl reaches towards it and murmurs, "My son! My love! My flesh!"

When the film was first shown at the Venice Film Festival, it was reviewed by *L'Osservatore Romano* the official newspaper of the Vatican. Although the critic, Piero Regnoli, found the film "pretentiously cerebral," he affirmed that "we continue to believe in Rosselini's art and we look forward to his next achievement."

When the 40-minute film was shown in New York—as part of a trilogy entitled *Ways of Love*—it was promptly attacked as "a sacrilegious and blasphemous mockery of Christian religious truth" by the national Legion of Decency, a private Catholic organization for film censorship whose rulings on films had considerable influence both in Hollywood and among the general public, Catholic and non-Catholic alike. On the

---

Sacrilege and the Arts

Religion has often found its way into contemporary artistic works. Occasionally, these depictions are an artist's interpretation of an event, and hold a great deal of religious meaning. Recently, there have been increasing instances when artistic license intermingles with religious art and leads to what some view as the ridiculing of religious belief, or even presenting the holy as perverse or provocative.

Sacrilege means irreverence of a religious place, person, concept, or viewpoint. The broad term encompasses expression ranging from profanity, mockery, and scorn, to desecration of anything holy using repulsive, shocking, hostile religious imagery. No faith is immune to harsh attacks but Christianity is a prime target.

Courts struggle with legislation outlawing sacrilege. The term is vague and indefinite. What to one individual is amusement may be blasphemous mockery to another. Laws against sacrilege are frequently considered constitutionally vague since the term is so imprecise. Exactly what is prohibited can often not be distinguished.

Source(s): "Why Is the Public When Confronted with Openly Anti-Catholic Imagery, Amused or Indifferent? What Are the Limits? Where Is the Outrage?" *The New York Times*, 16 May 1998.

---

other hand, New York film critics voted the trilogy "best foreign film" of 1950.

Sacrilege or Art?

In order to be shown in New York, a film had to be licensed by the state's Department of Education, under the supervision of the Board of Regents. A film could not get a license if:

> . . . such film or a part thereof is obscene, indecent, immoral, inhuman, sacrilegious, or is of such a character that its exhibition would tend to corrupt morals or incite to crime . . .

The Miracle had already been granted a license. But after it was shown, the New York State Board of Regents received "hundreds of letters, telegrams, post cards, affidavits and other communications" both protesting against and defending the movie. As a result, the regents took another look at the movie, and decided to rescind its license on the grounds that it was indeed "sacrilegious."

The regents had to consider that the notion of "sacrilege" is a tricky one, for it comes from within religion, not from any governmental or legal tradition. Joseph Burstyn, Inc., the film distributor, immediately brought suit against the regents' action, claiming that the licensing statute violated the Fourteenth Amendment by restraining freedom of speech and press, by breaking down the separation between church and state, and by making use of such a vague term making due process of law impossible.

When Burstyn's case made it to the New York Supreme Court, the judges upheld the state law, including its use of the term "sacrilegious." As that court held, there was "nothing mysterious" about the law or the term:

> It is simply this: that no religion, as that word is understood by the ordinary, reasonable person, shall be treated with contempt, mockery, scorn and ridicule . . .

Movies as Free Press

The Supreme Court, on the other hand, found that the New York law was unconstitutional, offending both the First and the Fourteenth Amendments. The High Court struck down the law and affirmed Joseph Burstyn, Inc.'s right to show *The Miracle* in New York State. However, in the course of handing down their decision, they did far more than that.

The majority decision, written by Justice Clark, established that motion pictures were now to be considered as an aspect of free speech and free press. The Court considered the argument that because movies are made for profit by large businesses, they do not constitute "free speech." It also considered the argument that motion pictures posses "a greater capacity for evil" than other types of expression, particularly in their ability to corrupt young people, and that therefore, they needed to be regulated more than other types of expression.

Yet the Court found both of these arguments unconvincing. Even if movies needed some regulation, Clark wrote, even if they needed more regulation than, say, books or newspapers, they still should not be subject to the kind of sweeping censorship inherent in the New York law.

Both Justice Clark and Justice Frankfurter, who wrote a concurring opinion, held that state government had no business prohibiting movies on the grounds that they were "sacrilegious." (The Court left open the possibility that movies could be prohibited for being "obscene.") As Frankfurter wrote:

A motion picture portraying Christ as divine—for example, a movie showing medieval Church art—would offend the religious opinions of the members of several Protestant denominations who do not believe in the Trinity, as well as those of a non-Christian faith. Conversely, one showing Christ as merely an ethical teacher could not but offend millions of Christians of many denominations. Which is "sacrilegious"? . . . To allow such vague, undefinable powers of censorship to be exercised is bound to have stultifying consequences on the creative process of literature and art . . . We not only do not know but cannot know what is condemnable by "sacrilegious." Frankfurter essentially questioned how anyone, save those to be governed by the statute could tell what was "sacrilegious."

Related Cases
Jacobellis v. Ohio, 378 U.S. 184 (1964).
Jenkins v. Georgia, 418 U.S. 153 (1974).

Bibliography and Further Reading
Bartholomew, Paul C. *American Constitutional Law, Limitations on Government.* Vol. II. Totowa, NJ: Littlefield, Adams, 1970, 1978.

Biskupic, Joan, and Elder Witt, eds. *Congressional Quarterly's Guide to the U.S. Supreme Court,* 3rd ed. Washington, DC: Congressional Quarterly, Inc., 1996.

YATES V. UNITED STATES

Legal Citation: 355 U.S. 66 (1957)

Petitioner
Oleta O'Connor Yates

Respondent
United States

Petitioner's Claim
That advocacy of future overthrow of the government is protected by the First Amendment guarantee of free speech.

Chief Lawyer for Petitioner
Ben Margolis

Chief Lawyer for Respondent
Philip R. Monahan

Justices for the Court
Harold Burton, Tom C. Clark, Felix Frankfurter, John Marshall Harlan II (writing for the Court), Earl Warren

Justices Dissenting
Hugo Lafayette Black, William O. Douglas, (William J. Brennan, Jr., and Charles Evans Whittaker did not participate)

Place
Washington, D.C.

Date of Decision
17 June 1957

Decision
The Supreme Court struck down the convictions of five of the appellants and referred the cases of the other nine (all were Communist Party leaders) back to the lower courts for retrial.

Significance
By declaring that advocacy of future action differed from plans for immediate government overthrow, *Yates* greatly curtailed the federal government's ability to prosecute subversives.

The Smith Act, also known as the Alien Registration Act, was adopted in 1940. America did not enter World War II until the following year, but the Smith Act was clearly a product of the nation's prewar anxiety. It contained provisions regarding admission, registration, and deportation of aliens living in the United States, but its most important sections concerned subversive activities. The act's conspiracy provisions imposed criminal penalties on anyone who "advocates, abets, advises, or teaches" the violent overthrow of the federal government, publishes subversive literature, organizes a subversive group, joins such a group, or conspires to commit any of these offenses.

The Smith Act was rarely used during the war, but afterward it became the government's primary tool for prosecuting domestic communists as fears of an international communist conspiracy spread. In 1951, the act was used to convict 12 members of the Communist Party's Central Committee. The Supreme Court upheld 11 of these convictions and the act itself in *Dennis v. United States* (1951). In *Dennis,* the Court found that leaders of the Communist Party posed a "grave and probable danger" to the government and that their words and deeds were therefore not protected by the First Amendment. The U.S. Department of Justice interpreted *Dennis* as license to prosecute Communists all around the country.

Supreme Court Distinguishes Advocacy of Doctrine from Advocacy of Action

But by the time 11 Communist Party leaders were convicted under the Smith Act in *Yates v. United States,* the mood of the country had shifted. The liberal Court led by Chief Justice Warren distinguished the situation of the communist leaders in *Dennis* from that of the current petitioners. While the former had established a seditious group which it maintained in readiness to overthrow the government, the latter were guilty only of advocating a doctrine which might lead to revolution at some undefined point in the future:

> In failing to distinguish between advocacy of forcible overthrow as an abstract doctrine and advocacy of action to that end, the District Court appears to have been led astray by the

Advocating Government Overthrow

Sporadically since its birth, the United States has struggled with subversive activity, both real and imagined. During the twentieth century concern about Communism and anarchists, those who advocated violent overthrow of the government, led to racial antagonism including racially-biased legislation and massive government probes into the affairs of aliens and citizens.

The period between 1917 and 1920 is known as the first Red Scare, the word "red" being synonymous with Communism. States enacted sedition laws making it unlawful to advocate violent political change or to be a member of a group that did. Aliens charged with anarchist beliefs were commonly deported. The Justice Department created the Radical Division headed by J. Edgar Hoover, later director of the Federal Bureau of Investigation.

A second Red Scare surfaced in 1938 with the beginning of World War II. Worries about fascism, Nazism, and Communism led to the formation of the House Un-American Activities Committee. Congress, focusing on preventing communist infiltration of the government, passed the Smith Act of 1940 and the Subversive Activities Control (McCarran) Act of 1950. U.S. citizens, unions, and even Hollywood became targets of investigations as Senator Joseph McCarthy led inquiries in the 1950s to identify Communists at the highest levels of U.S. government.

The Red scares largely ceased by the 1960s as Vietnam War controversies began.

Source(s): *West's Encyclopedia of American Law.* Minneapolis/St. Paul, MN: West Publishing, 1998.

holding in *Dennis* that advocacy of violent action to be taken at some future time was enough . . . This misconceives the situation confronting the Court in *Dennis* and what was held there . . . The essence of the *Dennis* holding was that indoctrination of a group in preparation for future violent action, as well as exhortation to immediate action . . . is not constitutionally protected when the group is of sufficient size and cohesiveness . . . to justify apprehension that action will occur. This is quite a different thing from the view of the District Court here that mere doctrinal justification of forcible overthrow . . . is punishable *per se* under the Smith Act.

Justices Black and Douglas dissented in part from the majority opinion written by Justice Harlan. Black and Douglas argued that the Smith Act should be declared unconstitutional as a violation of the First Amendment guarantees of free speech and freedom of association. In the end, however, although the Court threw out the convictions of all 11 petitioners in *Yates,* nine of the cases were sent back for retrial. The Court found that in two cases there was insufficient evidence to convict; in all the others, the Court indicated that clearer jury instructions the second time around would result in fairer trials.

Yates neither overruled *Dennis* nor held the Smith Act unconstitutional. In effect, however, the Warren Court's reinterpretation of *Dennis* rendered the conspiracy provisions of the act unenforceable. No further prosecutions were made under these provisions, despite the vitality of the Smith Act.

Related Cases
Dennis v. United States, 341 U.S. 494 (1951).
Barenblatt v. United States, 360 U.S. 109 (1959).
Scales v. United States, 367 U.S. 203 (1961).

Bibliography and Further Reading
Belknap, Michal R. *Cold War Political Justice: The Smith Act, the Communist Party, and American Civil Liberties.* Westport, CT: Greenwood Press, 1977.

Johnson, John W., ed. *Historic U.S. Court Cases, 1690-1990: An Encyclopedia.* New York: Garland Publishing, 1992.

Konvitz, Milton Ridvas. *Expanding Liberties: Freedom's Gains in Postwar America.* New York, NY: VIking Press, 1966.

Kutler, Stanley I. *The American Inquisition: Justice and Injustice in the Cold War.* New York, NY: Hill and Wang, 1982.

SPEISER V. RANDALL

Legal Citation: 357 U.S. 513 (1958)

Appellant
Lawrence Speiser

Appellee
Justin A. Randall, as Assessor of Contra Costa County, California

Appellant's Claim
That the California law denying property-tax exemption to veterans who refuse to sign a loyalty oath violates the Constitution.

Chief Lawyer for Appellant
Lawrence Speiser

Chief Lawyer for Appellee
George W. McClure

Justices for the Court
Hugo Lafayette Black, William J. Brennan, Jr. (writing for the Court), Harold Burton, William O. Douglas

Justices Dissenting
Tom C. Clark (Earl Warren did not participate)

Place
Washington, D.C.

Date of Decision
30 June 1958

Decision
Reversed the lower court's decision and upheld appellant's claim that the California law denying property-tax exemption to veterans who refuse to sign a loyalty oath violates the Constitution.

Significance
The ruling confirmed the types of speech protected under the First Amendment, and found that statutory provisions that force an individual to prove he is not engaged in criminal activities violate the Due Process Clause of the Fourteenth Amendment.

After World War II, the spread of Communism in Eastern Europe and Asia influenced both foreign and domestic policy in the United States. Measures to defend the country against the influence of communist agitators led to intense conflicts in the area of free speech and association. Communist Party members were prosecuted under the Smith Act (the Alien Registration Act of 1940), which made it illegal to advocate the overthrow of the government or to belong to any organization that held such beliefs. Loyalty oaths were required of many job applicants, and persons who belonged to the Communist Party or other groups considered subversive were often fired. Such activities, defendants argued, were unconstitutional because they violated the First Amendment's guarantee of freedom of speech. As Congress and the states passed anti-subversive legislation, the courts engaged in complex deliberations over the limits and protections of free speech.

Punishing Subversive Ideas

The state of California passed a law in 1954 requiring that a property-tax exemption for veterans be denied to anyone refusing to sign an oath of loyalty that stated "I do not advocate the overthrow of the Government of the United States or of the State of California by force or violence or other unlawful means, nor advocate the support of a foreign Government against the United States in event of hostilities." The appellant, an honorably discharged World War II veteran, struck the clause from the exemption form he filed for the 1954-55 tax year, arguing it violated the U.S. Constitution. The tax assessor denied the requested exemption only because the oath had not been signed. The appellant sought relief in the Superior Court of Contra Costa County, which found the relevant section of the California statute invalid under the Fourteenth Amendment. The California Supreme Court, however, reversed this decision. The U.S. Supreme Court considered the case along with that of Daniel Prince, another veteran denied exemption under similar circumstances.

In a decision reflecting the opinion of six members of the U.S. Supreme Court, Justice Brennan held that the California statute's requirement of a loyalty oath violated the Due Process Clause of the Fourteenth

Amendment because it placed the burden of proof on the individual. Justice Black concurred, stating that the First Amendment prohibited California from imposing a tax on belief and expression. Justice Douglas concurred with Justice Black, noting that the Constitution prohibits government from monitoring thought. Justice Clark dissented, and Chief Justice Warren did not participate in the decision.

Throughout its history, the Supreme Court has struggled with questions relating to free speech. In the period immediately following World War I, anti-sedition laws that criminalized anti-government speech were rigorously enforced and resulted in numerous convictions. Between 1919 and 1920, the Court heard six of these cases. In *Schenck v. United States* (1919) the Court relied on common law analysis to determine the boundaries between protected and proscribed speech. Justice Oliver Wendell Holmes, in his majority opinion, established that prohibited speech must present "a clear and present danger that [it] will bring about the substantive evils that Congress has a right to prevent." This became the standard judicial test for determining whether speech should be permitted or restricted.

In the next several years, the Court heard many cases involving aspects of national and state loyalty and security measures. In *Dennis v. United States,* the Court ruled that advocating the overthrow of the government in itself was not sufficient to warrant conviction unless it included not only "clear and present danger" but also incitement to action. The next year, the Court in *Wieman v. Updegraff* (1952), threw out a state loyalty law in Oklahoma that created "guilt by association." After the appointment of Earl Warren as Chief Justice in 1953, the Court began to move more quickly to identify the limits of criminal speech and to respond to what the majority on the Court considered excesses in prosecuting dissent. According to Paul L. Murphy in *The Constitution in Crisis Times,* the chief justice believed that the Court's role was "an active course in the pursuit of social justice" through "vigorous statutory interpretation, with an eye to bringing the operation of American legal institutions into harmony with professed American ideals." The Court did not want to deprive the legislative branch of the power to protect society from subversion, but it did act to moderate the extremes of such laws by focusing on procedural questions.

The Burden of Proof

In *Speiser v. Randall,* the state of California argued that its statute denied benefits only to those whose speech would be considered criminal by First Amendment standards and by the definitions arrived at by the Supreme Court. But the Court ruled that this was not the central issue. "[W]e assume without deciding," Justice Brennan wrote, "that California may deny tax exemptions to persons who engage in the proscribed

speech for which they might be fined or imprisoned." Instead, the Court focused on the matter of due process—the procedural safeguards guaranteed by the Constitution. Whether the veteran's speech was criminal or not, the Court reasoned, the California statute requiring the loyalty oath unjustly imposed the burden of proof on the appellant. "Due process commands that no man shall lose his liberty," the Court noted, "unless the Government has borne the burden of producing the evidence and convincing the factfinder of his guilt."

Shifting the burden of proof was particularly dangerous in this case, the Court ruled, because the speech in question fell close to the line distinguishing between protected and criminal speech. This created the danger that mistaken factfinding could end up inadvertently penalizing legitimate speech. A person burdened with the task of proving himself innocent, the Court reasoned, "must steer far wider of the unlawful zone than if the State must bear these burdens," and this could, in effect, create self-censorship that would deprive the individual of his or her right to speak freely.

Though the majority opinion emphasized the due process analysis, Justice Black, joined by Justice Douglas, issued a separate concurring opinion focusing on the importance of protecting free speech. He viewed the California statute as an example of "how dangerously far we have departed from the fundamental principles of freedom declared in the First Amendment" and called the case an example of the Communist witch-hunt mentality still gripping the country at the time.

Justice Clark's Dissent

Justice Clark dissented from the majority opinion. He did not agree that due process required the state of California to assume the burden of proof in this case. Furthermore, he noted that the law did not inhibit individuals' right to speak as they might wish, pointing out that the state would not take action against those who refused to sign the oath, but would simply not take any beneficial action for them. He concluded that "Refusal of the taxing sovereign's grace in order to avoid subsidizing or encouraging activity contrary to the sovereign's policy is an accepted practice."

Impact

The *Speiser* decision clarified that, though the Smith Act made it illegal to belong to any organization that advocated the violent overthrow of the government, individuals have the constitutional right to be considered innocent of a crime until proven guilty. It also established that the guarantee of due process under the law protects individuals from the burden of having to prove their innocence. In a subsequent case, *Elfbrandt v. Russell* (1966), which involved membership in a radical organization, the Court cited the *Speiser* decision when it declared "to presume that one who joins a subversive organization shares its illegal aims is forbidden—the state may not compel a citizen to prove that he has not engaged in criminal advocacy." And in *Baird v. State Bar of Arizona* (1971), the Court decided in favor of a bar applicant who claimed she had been denied admission based on her membership in the Communist Party. This case established that political beliefs or memberships cannot be used as the basis for refusing vocational licenses.

This does not mean, however, that the Court banned all loyalty oaths. In fact, loyalty statutes for public employees are still on the books in many states and, though challenges to such laws have sometimes succeeded, the Court in other cases has upheld these statutes. For example, in *Connell v. Higgenbotham* (1971), the Court invalidated a loyalty oath in Florida because it called for the summary dismissal of an employee who refused to sign it without giving the employee an opportunity to explain the refusal. But in *Cole v. Richardson* (1972), the Court upheld a loyalty oath.

Speiser also confirmed due process guarantees. For example, in *Smith v. California,* the Supreme Court ruled in favor of a bookstore owner who had been convicted of obscenity charges by having, on the store premises, a title deemed obscene. Using the analysis articulated in *Speiser,* the Court noted that the laws could not be applied "in a manner tending to cause even a self-imposed restriction of free expression." In its focus on due process, the *Speiser* case typified the general movement of the Warren Court toward more liberal interpretations of constitutional safeguards for individuals.

Confronted with a Congress that was hunting down alleged Communist Party members and passing harsh legislation against those it considered subversive (the Immunity Act of 1954, for example, allowed Congressional committees to obtain a federal judicial order compelling a witness to testify, despite the Fifth Amendment's guarantee of immunity, if the matter involved national security), the Supreme Court acted to counter the erosion of guaranteed individual rights. This strong role, in the opinion of some scholars, set the stage for civil rights activism in other areas, culminating in the passage of the Civil Rights Act of 1964.

Related Cases

Schenck v. United States, 249 U.S. 47 (1919).
Dennis v. United States, 341 U.S. 494 (1951).
Wieman v. Updegraff, 344 U.S. 183 (1952).
Elfbrandt v. Russell, 384 U.S. 11 (1966).
Baird v. State Bar of Arizona, 401 U.S. 1 (1971).
Connell v. Higgenbotham, 403 U.S. 207 (1971).
Cole v. Richardson, 405 U.S. 676 (1972).

Bibliography and Further Reading

Hentoff, Nat. *The First Freedom: The Tumultuous History of Free Speech in America.* New York: Delacorte, 1980.

Leiberman, Jethro K. *The Enduring Constitution: An Exploration of the First 200 Years.* New York: Harper and Row, 1987.

Leinwand, Gerald. *Freedom of Speech.* New York and Oxford: Facts on File, 1990.

McCloskey, Robert G. *The Modern Supreme Court.* Cambridge, MA: Harvard University Press, 1972.

Murphy, Paul L. *The Constitution in Crisis Times: 1918-1969.* New York: Harper and Row, 1972.

EDWARDS V. SOUTH CAROLINA

Legal Citation: 372 U.S. 229 (1963)

Appellant
James Edwards, Jr.

Appellee
State of South Carolina

Appellant's Claim
That the South Carolina common law crime of breach of the peace, as applied to a peaceful march to protest racial discrimination, infringes on the First Amendment guarantee of free speech.

Chief Lawyer for Appellant
Jack Greenberg

Chief Lawyer for Appellee
Lionel R. McLeod

Justices for the Court
Hugo Lafayette Black, William J. Brennan, Jr., William O. Douglas, Arthur Goldberg, John Marshall Harlan II, Potter Stewart, Earl Warren, Byron R. White

Justices Dissenting
Tom C. Clark

Place
Washington, D.C.

Date of Decision
25 February 1963

Decision
The Supreme Court struck down the convictions of the civil rights demonstrators for breach of peace.

Significance
Using the Due Process Clause of the Fourteenth Amendment, the Court made it illegal for states to criminalize peaceful expressions of unpopular views.

On the morning of 2 March 1961, roughly 200 African American high school and college students assembled at the Zion Baptist Church in Columbia, South Carolina. They proceeded to walk, in groups of 15, to the nearby state house grounds, an area open to the public. Their purpose in doing so was to protest segregation, a message they conveyed by peacefully carrying placards as they walked through the grounds. A small, quiet crowd gathered to watch them, and the police then informed them that they had 15 minutes to leave the premises. When the students responded by singing "The Star Spangled Banner" and other patriotic and religious songs, they were arrested and charged with breaching the peace, a crime under the common law of South Carolina.

Convicted and sentenced with small fines and jail sentences of up to 30 days, the students appealed their cases to the state supreme court, which upheld the convictions for an offense that even the appellate court admitted was only vaguely defined. The students then petitioned the U.S. Supreme Court for review of this decision.

The Supreme Court declared that the students' convictions violated their rights of free speech, free assembly, and the freedom to petition government for redress of grievances. All of these rights, the Court said, were assured by the Due Process Clause of the Fourteenth Amendment, which makes fundamental guarantees of the Bill of Rights binding upon the states. The arbitrariness and egregiousness of South Carolina's violation of the petitioners' rights was manifest in the fact that they were not convicted of having violated any proper statute, only an ill-defined rule:

> We do not review in this case criminal convictions resulting from the evenhanded application of a precise and narrowly drawn regulatory statute evincing a legislative judgment that certain specific conduct be limited or proscribed. If, for example, the petitioners had been convicted upon evidence that they had violated a law regulating traffic, or had disobeyed a law reasonably limiting the periods during which the State House grounds were open to the public, this would be a different case.

Uncodified Breach of Peace Crime Held Not a "Time, Place, and Manner" Restriction

Justice Stewart's opinion, expressing the views of the majority of the Court, was referring to the so-called "time, place, and manner" restrictions which are often upheld in First Amendment cases. The assumption implicit in the "time, place, and manner" doctrine is that where it is possible to distinguish between the message certain speech is intended to convey and the manner in which it is communicated, the latter may be reasonably regulated even though the former may not. Here, however, the evidence "showed no more than that the opinions which [the students] were peaceably expressing were sufficiently opposed to the views of the majority of the community to attract a crowd and necessitate police protection." Far from being precise and narrowly-drawn, the common law crime outlined by the South Carolina Supreme Court was so broad and ambiguous as to permit the state to impermissibly interfere with the message as well as the medium. In effect, with *Edwards*, the Supreme Court made it impossible for a southern state beset by peaceful demonstrations to fight back with vague, overly broad laws. This case is yet another example of how the Court headed by Earl Warren helped to create a legal climate in which the Civil Rights movement could flourish.

Bibliography and Further Reading

African Americans and the Living Constitution. Washington, DC: Smithsonian Institution Press, 1995.

Bell, Derrick A. *Race, Racism, and American Law,* 2nd ed. Boston: Little, Brown, 1980.

Worton, Stanley N. *Freedom of Assembly and Petition.* Rochelle Park, NJ: Hayden Book Co, 1975.

GIBSON V. FLORIDA LEGISLATIVE INVESTIGATION COMMITTEE

Legal Citation: 372 U.S. 539 (1963)

Petitioner
Theodore R. Gibson

Respondent
Florida Legislative Investigation Committee

Petitioner's Claim
That requiring the Miami branch of the National Association for the Advancement of Colored People to use its membership list during investigative hearings to determine if its membership included alleged Communists violated the members' constitutional right to freedom of association.

Chief Lawyer for Petitioner
Robert L. Carter

Chief Lawyer for Respondent
Mark R. Hawes

Justices for the Court
Hugo Lafayette Black, William J. Brennan, Jr., William O. Douglas, Arthur Goldberg (writing for the Court), Earl Warren

Justices Dissenting
Tom C. Clark, John Marshall Harlan II, Potter Stewart, Byron R. White

Place
Washington, D.C.

Date of Decision
25 March 1963

Decision
Upheld the petitioner's claim and reversed the Supreme Court of Florida's affirmance of the trial court's judgment of contempt.

Significance
Prior to *Gibson*, Supreme Court decisions in cases involving governmental investigation of subversive activities favored the production of membership lists when there was evidence that the people being investigated were associated with subversive organizations or activities. From a legal standpoint, *Gibson* protected associations from compelled disclosure of their membership lists absent a strong showing that the association itself was involved in subversive or illegal activities. From a social perspective, *Gibson* was a victory for civil rights organizations such as the NAACP who wanted the freedom to associate for their lawful activities without fear of governmental or societal reprisal.

Investigating Suspected Communists

In the wake of World War II, the alliance between the United States and the Union of Soviet Socialist Republics eroded as the Soviet Union engaged in military and political campaigns to extend its influence in Asia and Eastern Europe. This led to a resurrection of anti-Communist sentiment in the United States and the onset of the Cold War. Federal authorities waged this war in the United States during the 1940s and 1950s by investigating suspected Communists for prosecution under various laws including the Smith Act. The Smith Act had a section on sedition that penalized persons who advocated, or belonged to an organization that advocated, the destruction of the government by force.

At the same time, civil rights organizations such as the NAACP were engaged in efforts to ensure the political, educational, social, and economic quality of minorities in the United States. Such efforts resulted, for example, in the 1956 Supreme Court decision in *Brown v. Board of Education,* which outlawed segregation in public schools. Opponents of desegregation and other civil rights reforms, particularly in the South, engaged in efforts to eliminate the NAACP. Some opponents tried to capitalize on the anti-Communist fever by linking Communism with the civil rights movement. Anti-Communist and anti-NAACP sentiments converged in the *Gibson* case.

The *Gibson* case originated in Florida, where the state legislature authorized a series of committees to investigate Communists and other subversive persons and organizations. These committees developed a list of alleged Communists who had acted in the state of Florida. A 1956 committee began an investigation of the Miami branch of the NAACP purportedly to determine whether it had been infiltrated by some of the alleged Communists. A 1957 committee continued this investigation by issuing a subpoena for the entire membership list of the Miami NAACP. Its members refused to produce the list on the ground that it would interfere with their First Amendment right to freedom of association. The Supreme Court of Florida ultimately ruled that the committee could not require production of the entire list, but could require members to bring the list to committee hearings and to testify to whether certain alleged Communists appeared on the list as members of the Miami NAACP.

The Florida Legislative Investigation Committee continued the investigation in 1959. It relied on legislation that authorized it to investigate organizations whose principles or activities

> would constitute violence, or a violation of the laws of the state, or would be inimical to the well-being and orderly pursuit of their personal and business activities by the majority of citizens of this state.

Armed with this statute and the decision of the Supreme Court of Florida, the committee sought to compel petitioner Theodore R. Gibson, then president of the Miami branch, to appear before it and testify on the membership list. Gibson agreed to testify from memory to whether alleged Communists named by the committee were members of the Miami NAACP, but he refused to bring or use the membership list. A trial court found Gibson to be in contempt and sentenced him to six months in prison with a $1,200 fine.

On appeal to the Florida Supreme Court, Gibson argued that requiring him to testify by reference to the membership list impermissibly infringed on the members' First Amendment right to freedom of association because it might discourage membership for fear of public retaliation. Gibson relied on two prior decisions of the U.S. Supreme Court. In *National Association for the Advancement of Colored People v. Alabama* (1958) the state tried to require the association to file its entire membership list in order to determine the nature of its nonprofit business. In *Bates v. City of Little Rock* (1960) the municipality tried to require the association to file its entire membership list in order to determine the applicability of certain tax license requirements. In both cases the U.S. Supreme Court decided that without a compelling state interest, compulsory production of the membership lists of this legitimate organization violated its members' First Amendment right of association.

The committee argued before the Supreme Court of Florida that it had testimony from two witnesses that certain alleged Communists also were members of the Miami NAACP. The committee believed that such testimony gave Florida a compelling interest warranting investigation of the membership list. The committee relied in particular on *Uphaus v. Wyman* (1959), where the Supreme Court upheld a contempt conviction for refusal to produce the guest lists of the World Federation summer camp, an organization with known ties to Communism.

The Supreme Court of Florida ruled in favor of the committee. It recognized that when a government investigation intrudes on a private constitutional right, the government must show a compelling need that justifies subordinating the private right to the investiga-

Justice Arthur Goldberg. © Photograph by Harris and Ewing. Collection from the Supreme Court of the United States.

tion. The Court then relied on *Uphaus v. Wyman* to decide that the committee showed a compelling need with the evidence that alleged Communists were associated with the Miami NAACP.

The Supreme Court of Florida distinguished *National Association for the Advancement of Colored People v. Alabama* and *Bates v. City of Little Rock* on the ground that the Miami NAACP did not have evidence that use of its membership list would result in social or economic retribution against its members. Further, unlike in those cases, the committee did not seek production of the entire membership list. On balance, Florida's interest in investigating Communism outweighed the slight intrusion on the First Amendment rights of the members of the NAACP.

Strengthening the Individual Freedom of Association

The U.S. Supreme Court reversed with a 5-4 vote. Writing for the majority, Justice Goldberg began by noting that the freedom of speech and the related freedom of association guaranteed by the First and Fourteenth Amendments are "fundamental and highly prized, and need breathing space to survive." Compelled disclosure of membership in a legitimate organization may effectively restrain exercise of the freedom of association. On the other hand, the states have the power to conduct legislative investigations in order to protect their legitimate and vital interests. This includes the power to investigate Communist and subversive activities.

To strike a balance, Justice Goldberg articulated a slightly different test than the one applied by the Supreme Court of Florida. Relying on *National Association for the Advancement of Colored People v. Alabama,* the Supreme Court decided that when a legislative investigation infringes on the constitutional freedom of association, the government must show "a substantial relation between the information sought and a subject of overriding and compelling state interest." Applying this balancing test, the Supreme Court held that the committee failed to show a substantial relation between the NAACP and the alleged Communist activities.

The Court reached this conclusion by carefully scrutinizing the testimony concerning alleged Communist membership in the NAACP. The Court decided that the testimony was weak. It only proved that at some unspecified time in the years before the investigation, 14 alleged Communists may have been members of, or attended meetings of, the Miami NAACP. Absent any evidence that the 14 alleged Communists had substantial participation in or control of the Miami branch, which had 1000 members in total, the evidence of Communist infiltration was weak. Without evidence linking the NAACP itself to subversive activity, the committee did not have a compelling interest that outweighed the infringement on the right of association.

Justices Black and Douglas each wrote concurring opinions. While they agreed with the result of the majority opinion by Justice Goldberg, they believed that the First Amendment freedom of association was an absolute right not subject to a balancing test. Justice Douglas wrote:

> government is not only powerless to legislate with respect to membership in a lawful organization; it is also precluded from probing the intimacies of spiritual and intellectual relationships in the myriad of such societies and groups that exist in this country, regardless of the legislative purpose sought to be served.

Justifying the Legislative Power of Investigation

Justice Harlan wrote a dissenting opinion joined by Justices Clark, Stewart, and White. He noted that government evidence in Smith Act prosecutions showed that race relations were a prime target of Communist infiltration efforts. Despite this, the majority opinion

seemed to create a distinction between legislative power to investigate Communist infiltration of organizations and Communist activity by organizations. Justice Harlan did not think that the Supreme Court's prior decisions warranted such a distinction. Justice Harlan also believed that the majority's "substantial relation" test required an investigative committee to prove subversive activity before being allowed to investigate to find subversive activity. Justice Harlan thought such logic was faulty. He also believed that the committee's evidence of Communist membership in the Miami NAACP was a sufficient nexus to justify legislative investigation, particularly when the committee was not trying to require the Miami NAACP to produce its entire membership list.

Justice White also wrote a dissenting opinion in which he concluded that the effect of the majority's decision was to insulate from legislative inquiry the Communist Party's effective strategy of infiltrating and controlling legitimate organizations.

Subsequent Decisions

For a variety of political reasons, including the failure of the Communist Party to succeed in the United States, anti-Communist sentiments and activities calmed down after the mid-1950s. The Supreme Court did, however, have occasions to apply *Gibson* in later cases involving the First Amendment right to freedom of association. Most notably with respect to public disclosure, the Supreme Court in *Buckley v. Valeo* (1976) upheld the provisions of the Federal Election Campaign Act requiring disclosure of the names of persons making contributions to political campaigns. The Court relied on the government's substantial interest in allowing the public to make informed decisions on election day.

Related Cases

National Association for the Advancement of Colored People v. Alabama, 357 U.S. 449 (1958).
Gibson v. Florida Legislative Investigative Committee, 108 So.2d 729 (Fla. 1959).
Uphaus v. Wyman, 360 U.S. 72 (1959).
Bates v. City of Little Rock, 361 U.S. 516 (1960).
Buckley v. Valeo, 424 U.S. 1 (1976).

Bibliography and Further Reading

Biskupic, Joan and Elder Witt, eds. *Congressional Quarterly's Guide to the U.S. Supreme Court,* 3rd ed. Washington, DC: Congressional Quarterly, Inc., 1996.

Cushman, Robert F. *Leading Constitutional Decisions.* Englewood Cliffs, NJ: Prentice-Hall, Inc., 1982.

Haynes, John Earl. *Red Scare or Red Menace?: American Communism and Anticommunism in the Cold War Era.* Chicago: Ivan R. Dee, 1996.

COX V. LOUISIANA

Legal Citation: 855 S. Ct. 453 (I) and 476 (II) (1965)

Appellant
Reverend B. Elton Cox

Appellee
State of Louisiana

Appellant's Claim
That the convictions under a local breach-of-the-peace law of a minister leading a peaceful protest against segregation policies violated his First Amendment rights of free speech.

Chief Lawyers for Appellant
Nils Douglas (I) and Carl Rachlin (II)

Chief Lawyer for Appellee
Ralph L. Roy

Justices for the Court
Hugo L. Black, William J. Brennan, Jr., Tom C. Clark, William O. Douglas, Arthur Goldberg (writing for the Court), Potter Stewart, Earl Warren

Justices Dissenting
John Marshall Harlan II, Byron R. White

Place
Washington, D.C.

Date of Decision
18 January 1965

Decision
The two rulings were in favor of Cox and reversed two lower court decisions convicting him of illegal speech and assembly.

Significance
The decision effectively struck down as "unconstitutionally vague" state and local laws. The statutes were presumably intended to prevent breaches of the peace, but actually were designed to restrict and punish unpopular speech. The landmark ruling, however, reaffirmed the state and municipal governments' responsibility to regulate the time, place, and manner in which public places may be used by individuals exercising their constitutional freedom of expression rights. Such public places include parks, sidewalks, and streets.

When persons choose to exercise their rights of expression in public forums, questions of community peace and order arise. Activities conducted in open public forums have the potential to jeopardize public order, safety, and tranquility. An essential duty of government is to preserve order and protect citizens from violence, destruction of property, and restriction of free movement in public places. The government's commitment to free speech and assembly must be balanced with the obligation to maintain order. At what point is government constitutionally justified in restraining expression in order to prevent a breach of the peace?

To deal with expression in public places the justices developed legal guidelines distinct from those they use to deliberate pure speech cases. The Court established that the right to speak and assemble peacefully in public for lawful discussion is a privilege not to be diminished by states or cities, and that time, manner, and place of public speeches can be regulated only if done precisely and in a non-discriminatory fashion. In the 1940s the Court began to define standards to determine when public speech became menacing in a way causing a breach of peace. In *Cantwell v. Connecticut* (1940) the Court decided that the speech in question would have had to present a clear and present danger to be considered a menace to public peace. *Chaplinsky v. New Hampshire* (1942) established the doctrine of "fighting words," expressions so lewd, obscene, profane, libelous, or unsettling that they would likely incite immediate illegal behavior and should be prohibited.

The 1960s brought a sense of urgency to the issue of public order cases. The civil rights and Vietnam War protest movements produced varied forms of public expressions, such as mass demonstrations on college campuses and on public grounds, sit-ins, and protest rallies. In 1961 a group of black students marched peacefully onto the grounds of the South Carolina State Capital to protest discriminatory actions against "negroes." The resulting case, *Edwards v. South Carolina* (1963), built on the standards set in the 1940s by ruling that the threat of violence or actual violence is required before suppression of speech in a public forum is warranted.

Breach of Peace

The term "breach of peace" originated in England when kings reigned supreme. The king had a right to peace in his country and anyone disturbing the king's peace was arrested. Breach of peace law originated in common-law but in many states is governed by statute, a law passed by a legislative body. A similar term, "disorderly conduct," is strictly statutory law. Both terms refer to an intentional disruption of public peace, order, or safety of a community. Wide ranging examples include loud noises in a neighborhood, repugnant language in a public place, resisting arrest, destruction of property, and exhorting a crowd to gather. The behavior must clearly lead to disturbance or violence.

Statutes commonly specify which conduct is considered offensive so the public will know what exactly is pro-

hibited. On the other hand, some statutes are so all-encompassing that vagueness becomes a problem, such as those restricting boisterous conduct. Generally, the penalty for breach of peace is either a fine or imprisonment, or both.

In the twentieth century, arrests for breach of peace were frequently associated with the civil rights demonstrations of the 1960s. The Court found statutes in South Carolina and Louisiana unconstitutional on grounds of vagueness or lacking a disruption requirement.

Source(s): *West's Encyclopedia of American Law*. Minneapolis/St. Paul, MN: West Publishing, 1998.

Protests in Baton Rouge

On 14 December 1961, black students from Southern University picketed stores with racially segregated lunch counter service in Baton Rouge, Louisiana and urged a boycott of those stores as part of a general protest against segregation. The Congress of Racial Equality (CORE) organized the demonstration. The students were arrested and lodged in the parish jail located above the courthouse building. In reaction, a mass student meeting was held on campus and students resolved to demonstrate the next day in front of the courthouse.

The following day about 2,000 students began walking to downtown Baton Rouge. With student leaders of the local CORE chapter already in jail, the Reverend Mr. B. Elton Cox, a Field Secretary to CORE and ordained congregational minister, assumed leadership and cautioned the students to remain orderly and to walk to one side of the sidewalk as they marched toward the courthouse. Two high ranking officials of the city police department and sheriffs office approached and talked to Cox. Cox informed them that the students were marching to protest the student arrests "and also to protest discrimination." Cox told the officers that they would "march by the courthouse, say prayers, sing hymns, display signs, and conduct a peaceful program of protest." Cox declined a request by the officials to disband the group.

The students walked orderly to the courthouse where Police Chief Wingate White inquired about the purpose of the demonstration. Cox again outlined the purpose and activities and White instructed Cox that "he must confine" the demonstration "to the west side of the street," 101 feet from the courthouse steps. Approximately 80 police were stationed in the street between

the demonstrators and a group of 100 to 300 curious white people, mostly courthouse workers, gathered on the east side of the street. The program began and the 23 jailed students responded by singing.

Cox stated their purpose was to protest the illegal arrest and that they were not going to commit any violence. In his concluding remarks Cox urged the marchers to go downtown and seek service at the segregated lunch counters. "Muttering" and "grumbling" by the white onlookers began. Perceiving that Cox's speech would cause a disturbance in the city, the sheriff demanded that the demonstration break up immediately. When the demonstrations failed to disperse, police exploded tear gas and the students ran back toward downtown. Cox, trying to calm them, was one of the last to leave. No blacks participating in the demonstration were arrested.

The next day, Reverend Cox was arrested and charged with four offenses under Louisiana law, criminal conspiracy, disturbing the peace, obstructing public passages, and picketing before a courthouse. He was later acquitted of criminal conspiracy but convicted of the other three offenses and sentenced to a total of one year and nine months jail time and fined $5,700. In two separate judgements the Louisiana Supreme Court affirmed all three convictions. Both judgements were appealed.

The U.S. Supreme Court granted certiorari to both appeals. *Cox* I dealt with the convictions for disturbing the peace and obstructing public passages. *Cox* II concerned the conviction for picketing before a courthouse.

As in *Edwards,* the Court in *Cox* I reversed Reverend Cox's conviction, finding Louisiana's breach of the peace statute unconstitutionally broad. That is, it penalized persons who were legally exercising their rights of free speech and assembly. The Court found the practice of allowing local Baton Rouge officials total discretion in regulating the use of public streets in violation of the First and Fourteenth Amendments. Justice Arthur Goldberg delivered the Court's opinion.

No Breach of Peace

The Court unanimously ruled to set aside the convictions on the breach of the peace charge. Goldberg discussed five points in this reversal.

1. In considering the testimony of sheriff's officers, apparently the one objectionable part of the entire protest program came at the conclusion of Cox's speech when he urged students to go uptown and sit at lunch counters. The Court reasoned that this part of Cox's speech did not deprive the demonstration of its constitutional protection as free speech and assembly.

2. Although the students cheered, clapped, and sang loudly, they were well behaved throughout. The record does not support Louisiana's contention that the students' actions converted a peaceful assembly to a riotous one.

3. Louisiana argued that "violence was about to erupt." This threat of violence seemed to be based on the "mutterings" of the white group of citizens. However, Goldberg found no indication that any member of the white group threatened violence.

4. The Court found no evidence of the use of "fighting words."

5. In considering the Louisiana breach of peace statute, the Louisiana Supreme Court defined breach of peace as "to agitate, to arouse from a state of repose, to molest, to interrupt, to hinder, to disquiet." This definition allows persons to be prohibited from merely expressing unpopular views. Yet, the purpose of free speech in government is to be "provocative and challenging," inducing unrest, dissatisfaction, and even anger. Goldberg struck down the state law on the grounds that it was too broad within its scope of constitutionally protected speech and assembly.

Public Passages Not Obstructed

On this second charge, the Court voted 7-2 for reversal. Justices Byron R. White and John M. Harlan II dissented. Goldberg wrote that the Louisiana Obstructing Public Passages law as written "precludes all street assemblies and parades, (yet) it has not been so applied and enforced by the Baton Rouge authorities." City officials testified clearly that certain meetings and parades are permitted in Baton Rouge, even though they obstruct traffic, provided prior approval was obtained. Importantly, Goldberg pointed out that a state or municipality must so regulate city streets or other public facilities to assure the safe passage and convenience of the people and may, in a non-discriminatory application, regulate time, place, duration, or manner of the use of streets for public assemblies. However, Baton Rouge city authorities permitted or prohibited parades or street meetings at in a very *ad hoc* manner. This practice resulted in an unwarranted restriction of Cox's freedoms of speech and assembly protected under the First Amendment.

Picketing Before a Courthouse

The appeal on the third charge of picketing before a courthouse was reported separately as Cox II. The Court reversed the conviction by a vote of 5-4. Goldberg again wrote for the majority. The conviction was for violations of a Louisiana law which prohibited picketing or parading in or near a state court "with the intent of interfering with, obstructing or impeding the administration of justice, or with the intent of influencing any judge, juror, witness or court officer, in the discharge of his duty." Goldberg wrote that the law was appropriately narrowly written to protect the state's judicial system from pressures that demonstrations near a courthouse might create. The restriction did not infringe on free speech and assembly and was, therefore, valid. Goldberg also found that, in applying the statute, Louisiana could arrest and convict for the kind of demonstration which occurred near the Baton Rouge courthouse. However, the majority voted to reverse the conviction on the grounds that prior permission was granted by the police to conduct the demonstration on the far side of the street from the courthouse steps. Goldberg wrote, "to permit him to be convicted for exercising the privilege they told him was available would be to allow a type of entrapment violative of the Due Process Clause."

Impact

In public forums, *Cox* I affirmed the use of certain prerequisites, such as violence or the threat of violence or fighting words, to establish a true breach of peace. The Court reaffirmed that speech which merely produces discussion, arouses, disquiets, or angers is constitutionally protected. The Court also confirmed the duty of states or municipalities to assure the safety of its public places. Goldberg stated that authorities can "call a halt to a meeting which originally peaceful, becomes violent . . . set reasonable limits for assemblies . . . and then order them dispersed." *Cox* II reiterated that a state has a legitimate interest in protecting its judicial system from demonstrations near a courthouse which are designed to influence the administration of justice.

The above standards largely governed public order cases which followed. Near the end of the twentieth century, the Court continued to face questions of how far government may restrict the speech, manner, and place of protests. Civil rights, religion, and foreign policy dominated First Amendment litigation. Abortion became a public forum protest issue in the 1990s with free speech claimed by anti-abortion demonstrators. On the other hand, pro-choice proponents were concerned with guaranteeing individuals free access to abortion clinics without undue interference and pressure. In sum, the *Cox* standard still persisted holding that government can regulate speech in public places. But any restrictions cannot be based on the content of the speech, must be narrowly applied, must serve a significant government interest, and must leave other means available for the speech to occur. A clear message from *Cox* was that freedom of speech, though of utmost importance, was not absolute.

Related Cases

Cantwell v. Connecticut, 310 U.S. 296 (1940).
Chaplinsky v. New Hampshire, 315 U.S. 568 (1942).
Edwards v. South Carolina, 372 U.S. 229 (1963).
Adderley v. Florida, 385 U.S. 39 (1966).

Bibliography and Further Reading

Abernathy, M. Glenn, and Barbara A. Perry. *Civil Liberties Under the Constitution.* 6th Ed. Columbia, SC: University of South Carolina Press, 1993.

Epstein, Lee, and Thomas G. Walker. *Constitutional Law for a Changing America: Rights, Liberties, and Justice.* 2nd edition. Washington, DC: Congressional Quarterly Press, 1995.

Miller, Loren. *The Petitioners: The Story of the Supreme Court of the United States and the Negro.* New York: Random House, 1966.

FREEDMAN V. MARYLAND

Legal Citation: 380 U.S. 51 (1965)

Appellant
Ronald Freedman

Appellee
State of Maryland

Appellant's Claim
That Maryland's statute requiring that all films be submitted to a board of censors before being exhibited violated freedom of expression protected by the First Amendment.

Chief Lawyer for Appellant
Felix J. Bilgrey

Chief Lawyer for Appellee
Thomas B. Finan

Justices for the Court
Hugo Lafayette Black, William J. Brennan, Jr. (writing for the Court), Tom C. Clark, William O. Douglas, Arthur Goldberg, John Marshall Harlan II, Potter Stewart, Earl Warren, Byron R. White

Justices Dissenting
None

Place
Washington, D.C.

Date of Decision
1 March 1965

Decision
Deemed the procedures followed by Maryland's Motion Picture Censor Board unconstitutional.

Significance
The ruling outlined limitations on a state's right to require exhibitors to submit movies to a censoring authority prior to their being shown. Although the ruling did not go so far as to label all such "prior restraint"—i.e. banning something before the public sees it—unconstitutional, the Court's decision did establish guidelines aimed at protecting against the "undue inhibition of protected expression." The decision indicated that censorship procedures must: (1) place the burden of proving the film is not protected expression on the censors, (2) make provisions for a judicial procedure to impose a valid determination—i.e. the censor's decision cannot be final, and (3) require prompt determination "within a specified time period."

By the mid-1960s, official censorship of motion pictures was already clearly on the decline. As of 1964, the year *Freedman v. Maryland* was argued before the Supreme Court, only four states—Maryland, New York, Virginia, and Kansas—and a handful of municipalities had statutes requiring the submission of all films to a censorship board before they could be shown. Although the Court was still struggling with the seemingly impossible task of drawing the line between obscenity and protected expression, a series of Court decisions over the previous decade had brought into question the legitimacy of such "prior restraint" of various forms of expression. The *Freedman* case was the first to address the machinery of the censorship process, rather than the validity of all prior censorship or the boundaries of freedom of expression.

Under Maryland law, every movie had to be pre-screened and licensed by the board of censors before it could be shown at a public venue. The board could reject films it deemed were obscene, morally corrupt, or likely to incite crime. No limit was placed on how long the decision-making process could take. Ronald Freedman, a Baltimore theater manager, sought to challenge the legality of Maryland's film censorship statute. To test the law, Freedman informed the board in advance of his intention to screen a film without first putting it through the licensing process. The film he showed was *Revenge at Daybreak*, a story of the Irish Revolution. It was clearly not obscene, and, likely would have been approved had he submitted it to the board. He showed the movie in November of 1962, and was promptly arrested after the screening. In March of 1963, Freedman was convicted by the Baltimore Criminal Court of violating the censorship code and was fined $25.

Freedman's actions came on the heels of another Supreme Court ruling, *Times Film Corp. v. Chicago* (1961). That case involved a Chicago ordinance similar in most respects to the Maryland statute. In that case, Times Film Corp. argued that total constitutional protection should cover at least the initial showing of all films, regardless of their content. The Court ruled that a law requiring that all motion pictures be submitted for review prior to their showing was not auto-

Ronald L. Freedman (center) and William Hewitt with Richard C. Whiteford (left).
© AP/Wide World Photos.

matically unconstitutional. This left an important question regarding the circumstances which made such a requirement acceptable. In refusing to submit *Revenge at Daybreak,* Freedman hoped to demonstrate that laws such as Maryland's, which in effect made it a criminal act to show a perfectly benign movie without a license, represented an unreasonable threat to freedom of expression. Where the *Times Film* case had asked the Court to consider only the narrow question of whether prior restraint was ever constitutionally valid, *Freedman v. Maryland* broadened the issue to include other aspects of the statute.

The Supreme Court took up the *Freedman* case after Freedman's conviction was upheld by the Maryland Court of Appeals. Freedman's lawyer, Felix Bilgrey, had also represented Times Film Corp. in the earlier case. It was no secret that Bilgrey's ultimate goal was the same in both cases—namely, the elimination of routine film licensing. His main task here was to make clear the differences between the two cases. Since the *Times Film* decision removed the idea that a submission requirement was by its very nature unconstitutional, in the *Freedman* case Bilgrey turned his attention to the specifics of the Maryland statute. Rather than claiming

that prior submission should never be required, he asserted in the *Freedman* case that it must be considered in the context of the entire statute. The statute taken as a whole, Freedman claimed, represented an undue suppression of his right to free expression.

The state of Maryland, represented by Thomas Finan, argued essentially that the *Freedman* case was merely a rehashing of *Times Film.* Finan asserted that the importance of preventing the public from being exposed to pornography and other harmful material outweighed the film owner's or distributor's right to freedom of expression. But he also claimed that the existence of the *Freedman* case was a thinly disguised attempt to get the Supreme Court to overrule its previous decision in *Times Film,* in light of personnel changes that had taken place on the Court since 1961.

The Supreme Court ruled unanimously in Freedman's favor. Although the Court reversed the decision of the Maryland Court of Appeals, however, *Freedman v. Maryland* was not a clear-cut victory for the anti-censorship camp. Rather than taking an all or nothing view on the validity of prior censorship, the Court chose to travel the middle of the road. In siding with Freedman by accepting that this case was different from *Times Film,* the Court confirmed its view that prior restraint was sometimes acceptable, but it imposed guidelines under which such censorship procedures must operate.

Writing for the majority, Justice Brennan outlined the specific areas in which the Maryland statute failed to adequately protect film exhibitors' First and Fourteenth Amendment rights. Brennan wrote:

> The administration of a censorship system for motion pictures presents peculiar dangers to constitutionally protected speech. Unlike prosecution for obscenity, a censorship proceeding puts the initial burden on the exhibitor or distributor. Because the censor's business is to censor, there inheres the danger that he may well be less responsive than a court—part of an independent branch of government—to the constitutionally protected interests in free expression. And if it is made unduly onerous, by reason of delay or otherwise, to seek judicial review, the censor's determination may in practice be final.

In other words, the Court decided that the burden of proving that the film is not a form of expression protected by the Constitution must lie with the censor. Under the Maryland statute the burden of appealing the censor's decision had been carried by the film owner. Brennan also declared that an assurance of a prompt final judicial review must be given. The Maryland statute made no provisions for any judicial involvement of any kind, and the amount of time a determination could take was not limited. The ruling reduced the role of the censor. After deeming a film unacceptable, the censor now had to initiate judicial proceedings to have licensing withheld.

Although the vote to reverse was unanimous, Brennan's opinion represented the views of only seven justices. Douglas wrote a concurring opinion, joined by Black. Their view was that the Maryland statute was unconstitutional because any attempt to censor expression, be it a film, a book, or speech, was a violation of the First Amendment. Douglas wrote that "I do not

believe any form of censorship—no matter how speedy or prolonged it may be—is permissible . . . I would put an end to all forms and types of censorship and give full literal meaning to the command of the First Amendment."

In the long term, the requirements outlined in the *Freedman* case probably paved the way for the virtual death of state and local film censorship boards in the United States. It had several immediate effects as well. The ruling led directly to the elimination of prior censorship of movies in most of the places where it was in effect at the time. Those authorities that chose to retain such laws were forced to revamp them to incorporate the *Freedman* safeguards. *Freedman v. Maryland* also inspired a similar case dealing with the censorship of import films by the Federal Bureau of Customs. Since 1965, *Freedman* has come into play in countless cases involving instances of censorship and prior restraint, where the party being restrained claims that the rigorous standards created by the Court in *Freedman* were not met.

Related Cases
Mutual Film Corp. v. Industrial Commission, 236 U.S. 230 (1914).
Burstyn v. Wilson, 343 U.S. 495 (1952).
Kingsley International Pictures v. Regents, 360 U.S. 684 (1959).
Times Film Corp. v. Chicago, 365 U.S. 43 (1961).

Bibliography and Further Reading
DeGrazia, Edward. *Censorship Landmarks.* New York: Bowker, 1969.

Friedman, Leon. *Obscenity.* New York: Chelsea House, 1970.

Hixson, Richard F. *Pornography and the Justices.* Carbondale, IL: Southern Illinois University Press, 1996.

Randall, Richard S. *Censorship of the Movies.* Madison, WI: University of Wisconsin Press, 1968.

Weiler, A. H. "Censorship Seen in New Light." *New York Times,* March 3, 1965.

BROWN V. LOUISIANA

Legal Citation: 383 U.S. 131 (1966)

Petitioner
Henry Brown

Respondent
State of Louisiana

Petitioner's Claim
A breach of the peace statute that banned Louisiana residents from protesting in public facilities was unconstitutional because it violated the freedom of speech and assembly rights (First and Fourteenth Amendments) of five protesters.

Chief Lawyer for Petitioner
Carl Rachlin

Chief Lawyer for Respondent
Richard Kilbourne

Justices for the Court
William J. Brennan, Jr., William O. Douglas, Abe Fortas (writing for the Court), Earl Warren, Byron R. White

Justices Dissenting
Hugo Lafayette Black, Tom C. Clark, John Marshall Harlan II, Potter Stewart

Place
Washington, D.C.

Date of Decision
23 February 1966

Decision
Reversed the conviction of five men arrested after staging a protest in a public library over its policy of serving whites only.

Significance
This case, was the fourth in a four-year-period in which Louisiana's breach of peace statute was used to stop a peaceful demonstration over discriminatory practices. *Garner v. Louisiana* (1961) involved a sit-in at a lunch counter to protest service for whites only. In *Taylor v. Louisiana* (1962) blacks again protested the presence of bus depot that was for white customers only. In *Cox v. Louisiana* (1965) a man led a demonstration near the courthouse and jail to protest the arrest of other demonstrations. Each of the protests were orderly and peaceful and were over discriminatory practices that denied the protesters' rights that were guaranteed to them under the Constitution.

The Audubon Regional Library in Clinton, Louisiana, Parish of East Feliciana did not serve blacks. Instead blacks were expected to use one of two bookmobiles. The red bookmobile served whites and the blue bookmobile served blacks. On 7 March 1964, five young black males entered the adult reading room. One of the men, Brown, requested a book, "The Story of the Negro," by Arna Bontemps. The assistant librarian, after checking the card catalogue, discovered that the library did not have the book. She told Brown she would request it from the state library and he could pick it up from the bookmobile or it could be mailed to him. After the men failed to leave the library, the assistant librarian requested that they go. They did not. Brown sat down and the others stood nearby. The assistant librarian then went to the head librarian who also requested that the men leave. They did not. A short time later the sheriff arrived and asked the men to leave. Again, they refused. The sheriff arrested them. He had been notified that morning that members of the Congress of Racial Equality were planning a "sit-in" at the library. The sheriff witnessed the men enter the library and notified his deputies. The men were arrested and charged with intention to provoke a breach of peace and failure or refusal to leave a public building when ordered to do so.

The five men were tried and found guilty. Brown was sentenced to pay $150 for court costs or spend 90 days in jail. The four other men were sentenced to $35 for court costs or 15 days in jail. Under Louisiana law, the convictions were not appealable. The Louisiana Supreme Court denied their request for discretionary review because they could find no error. The Supreme Court granted *certiorari*.

In writing for the majority, Justice Fortas, first examined whether the protesters could be convicted simply for refusing to leave the library. He concluded that they could not since their protest was peaceful and blacks could not be denied access to the library, since whites were allowed inside. He then reviewed the conduct of the men while they were in the public room, and again, found that they had not violated the statute because "They sat and stood in the room, quietly, as monuments of protest against the segregation of the library." The state argued that the men were in fact served and by remaining proved their intention to disturb the peace and upset the librarian. However, Justice Fortas concluded that the arrest was a violation of the men's First and Fourteenth Amendment rights that guarantee freedom of speech and assembly and the right to ask the government for redress of grievances. He wrote:

> As this Court has repeatedly stated, these rights are not confined to verbal expression. They embrace appropriate types of action which certainly include the right to peaceable and orderly manner to protest by silent and reproachful presence, in a place where the protester has every right to be, the unconstitutional segregation of public facilities.

In a sharply worded dissenting opinion Justice Black took issue with the majority's reasoning. He disagreed that the Constitution prohibits any state from making "sit-ins" or "stand-ups" in public libraries illegal. Second, Black argued that the previous breach of the peace cases in Louisiana differed from *Brown v. Louisiana.* The decision in *Garner* was based on an older version of the breach of the peace statute. In *Taylor,* the Court decided that individuals could not be charged under the breach of the peace statute, if they were only protesting a white-only policy. Additionally, there was no evidence in that case that individuals who were only present to protest continued to do so after being asked to leave. In *Cox v. Louisiana* the issue involved was picketing and protesting on public streets. Black wrote:

> Public buildings such as libraries, schoolhouses, fire departments, courthouses, and executive mansions are maintained to perform certain specific and vital functions. Order and tranquillity of a sort entirely unknown to the public streets are essential to their normal operation. Contrary to the implications of the prevailing opinion it is incomprehensible to me that a State must measure disturbances in its libraries and on the streets with identical standards . . . In the public building, unlike the street, peace and quiet is a fast and necessary rule, and as a result there is much less room for police officers to abuse their authority in enforcing the public building part of the statute.

Justice Black also disagreed with the majority opinion that Louisiana was using the breach of peace statute to enforce a policy of denying use of the library based on race. There was no racial discrimination practiced in this case because the assistant librarian not only looked for the book that Brown requested, but also sent Brown the book two weeks later.

Impact

The Court's ruling in this case and in others proved vital to the Civil Rights struggles and to Vietnam war protests that would follow. Indeed, without these rulings the 1960s and early 1970s may have been a completely different period of time, especially for the Civil Rights movement. Yet, the Court's support was not to last. In the last line of Justice Black's opinion in *Brown v. Louisiana* he wrote: "The holding in this case today makes it more necessary than ever that we stop and look more closely at where we are going." That same year in *Adderley v. Florida* the Court appeared to follow Justice Black's advice. In that case, the Court upheld the convictions of 32 students at Florida A&M, a historically black college. The students went to a jail to protest the arrests of others demonstrating against racially discriminatory practices in that state.

Related Cases

Garner v. Louisiana, 368 U.S. 157 (1961).
Taylor v. Louisiana, 370 U.S. 154 (1962).
Cox v. Louisiana, 379 U.S. 536 (1965).
Adderley v. Florida, 385 U.S. 39 (1966).
Grayned v. Rockford, 408 U.S. 104 (1972).
Greer v. Spock, 424 U.S. 828 (1976).

Bibliography and Further Reading

Biskupic, Joan and Elder Witt. *Guide to the U.S. Supreme Court,* 3rd ed. Washington, DC: Congressional Quarterly Inc., 1997.

Gunther, Gerald and Kathleen Sullivan. *Constitutional Law* 13th ed. New York: The Foundation Press Inc., 1997.

Hall, Kermit L., ed. *The Oxford Companion to the Supreme Court of the United States.* New York: Oxford University Press. 1992.

WALKER V. BIRMINGHAM

Legal Citation: 388 U.S. 307 (1967)

Petitioners
Wyatt Tee Walker, et al.

Respondent
City of Birmingham, Alabama

Petitioners' Claim
That the conviction of Walker and seven other African American ministers, including Dr. Martin Luther King, Jr., on contempt charges stemming from their decision to disregard an injunction prohibiting them from participating in a Birmingham demonstration, should be reversed on grounds that the injunction violated their constitutionally protected rights to free speech and assembly, and was therefore invalid.

Chief Lawyer for Petitioners
Jack Greenberg

Chief Lawyers for Respondent
Earl McBee, J.M. Breckenridge

Justices for the Court
Potter Stewart (writing for the Court), Byron R. White, John Marshall Harlan II, Tom C. Clark, Hugo Lafayette Black

Justices Dissenting
Earl Warren, William J. Brennan, Jr., Abe Fortas, William O. Douglas

Place
Washington, D.C.

Date of Decision
12 June 1967

Decision
Affirmed Alabama Supreme Court decision upholding the contempt convictions of Reverends Walker, King, and six others.

Significance
In *Walker v. Birmingham,* the U.S. Supreme Court ruled that an individual may not deny an injunction, even if the injunction itself appears to be unconstitutional, without challenging the injunction's validity through the official mechanisms of judicial review. The Court, on a vote of 5-4, upheld the 1963 convictions of the Martin Luther King Jr. and seven other prominent black ministers, on charges that they inappropriately ignored an Alabama injunction aimed at stopping the group from demonstrating against discrimination in Birmingham. The demonstrations themselves were in violation of a Birmingham ordinance that required organizers to obtain a parade license. For a civil rights organizer in 1963, the very notion of obtaining such a license in Birmingham, Alabama, given its race relations climate, was absurd.

The demonstration that led to this case was part of a series of Birmingham protests organized by the Southern Christian Leadership Conference, led by Dr. King. After being refused a parade permit twice by Birmingham public safety commissioner Eugene Connor, the group decided to proceed with its planned demonstrations. Several African American protesters were arrested during marches on 6-7 April and 9-10 April for unlicensed parading. On the night of 10 April, an Alabama court issued an injunction enjoining King and his supporters from further unauthorized activity. The protesters chose to ignore the injunction, and proceeded with additional planned demonstrations on Good Friday, 12 April, and Easter Sunday, 14 April. Eight ministers, including King, were subsequently arrested, convicted of contempt, fined $50 each, and sentenced to five days in jail.

The trial court that heard the case declined to consider arguments regarding the constitutional status of either the Birmingham parade permit ordinance or the injunction. In convicting the eight clergymen, the court based its decision solely on the issues of whether the injunction was legally issued and whether the defendants had knowingly violated it. The Alabama Supreme Court likewise affirmed the decision. The justices of the U.S. Supreme Court had widely varying views of the case. A majority of justices acknowledged that the ordinance may very well have been unconstitutional, but that did not prevent them from voting to uphold the convictions.

The prevailing opinion, as written by Justice Stewart, was that King and his associates had no right to take the law into their own hands. Had the group fought the injunction through the channels of legal appeal, noted Stewart, it is quite possible that they would have won the right to demonstrate in Birmingham. "No man can be judge in his own case," wrote Stewart, "however exalted his station, however righteous his motives, and irrespective of his race, color, politics or religion." Quoting from *Howat v. Kansas* (1922) Stewart also wrote:

> An injunction duly issuing out of a court of general jurisdiction with equity powers, upon pleadings properly invoking its action, and

served upon pleadings properly invoking its action, and served upon persons made parties therein and within the jurisdiction, must be obeyed by them, however erroneous the action of the court may be.

In other words, if a court issues an injunction properly and in good faith, the individual must obey it until it is ruled invalid. Stewart then went on to describe circumstances under which this rule might not apply. Most important among these were instances "where the injunction was transparently invalid or had only a frivolous pretense to validity." It is exactly that sort of transparent invalidity and frivolity of pretense that some of Stewart's brethren believed were in play in *Walker v. Birmingham*. The four dissenting justices, to varying degrees, argued that the Birmingham parade permit ordinance and/or the injunction that ensued were "transparent" attempts to keep the ministers from asserting their protected right to free assembly. That being the case, the group was within their rights in ignoring both.

Chief Justice Warren, Justice Douglas, and Justice Brennan each wrote a dissenting opinion, and Justice Fortas concurred with all three. The dissenters based their arguments on the Court's longstanding approval of the right to disobey an invalid law. To these justices, *Walker* was a perfect example of individuals asserting that right. They also warned that allowing a state to use an injunction to impose prior restraint on speech without compelling cause would set a dangerous precedent. Warren wrote that "the *ex parte* temporary injunction has a long and odious history in this country, and its susceptibility to misuse is all too apparent from the facts of this case." His point was that such abuse of state power was likely to lead to weaker rather than greater respect for the law in the long run.

The fact that *Walker v. Birmingham* involved a contempt charge stemming from the injunction rather than a criminal charge involving the ordinance itself had an enormous impact on the case. By issuing an injunction, the Alabama court in effect guaranteed that the constitutionality of the Birmingham parade ordinance would not be the central issue of the case. Interestingly, that ordinance was held invalid by the U.S. Supreme Court two years later in *Shuttlesworth v. City of Birmingham* (1969), a case that involved circum-

Justice Potter Stewart. © Photograph by Chase LTD. Collection of the Supreme Court of the United States.

stances virtually identical to those of *Walker*. The strength of the dissenters' arguments in *Walker* played no small role in bringing about the eventual discarding of the Birmingham law.

Related Cases
Howat v. Kansas, 258 U.S. 181 (1922).
Thomas v. Collins, 323 U.S. 516 (1945).
Shuttlesworth v. Birmingham, 394 U.S. 147 (1969).

Bibliography and Further Reading
Emerson, Thomas I. *The System of Freedom of Expression.* New York: Random House, 1970.

New York Times, June 14, 1967.

Time, June 23, 1967.

ZWICKLER V. KOOTA

Legal Citation: 389 U.S. 241 (1967)

Appellant
Zwickler

Appellee
Koota, District Attorney of Kings County

Appellant's Claim
That section 781-b of the New York Penal Code violated the appellant's First Amendment rights.

Chief Lawyer for Appellant
Emanuel Redfield

Chief Lawyer for Appellee
Samuel A. Hirshowitz, First Assistant Attorney General of New York

Justices for the Court
Hugo Lafayette Black, William J. Brennan, Jr. (writing for the Court), Abe Fortas, Thurgood Marshall, William O. Douglas, Potter Stewart, Earl Warren, Byron R. White

Justices Dissenting
John Marshall Harlan II

Place
Washington, D.C.

Date of Decision
5 December 1967

Decision
Reversal of the district court's decision to abstain from hearing the case.

Significance
Zwickler presented an important question regarding the scope of the discretion of the district court to abstain from deciding the merits of a challenge that a state statute on its face violates the Constitution. The ruling established the facts for applying the "Doctrine of Abstention." Because there was no "special circumstance" warranting application of the abstention doctrine, a district court erred in refusing to hear a claim for a declaratory judgment. The decision established the principle that a federal court has to respect a suitor's choice of a federal forum for the hearing and decision of his federal constitutional claims. The principle that abstention cannot be used to give the state courts the first opportunity to vindicate a federal claim in First Amendment issues was established. The delay requiring recourse to the state courts might moot the constitutional right that a plaintiff seeks to protect.

Section 781-b of the New York Penal Law makes it a crime to distribute quantities of handbills which contain statements about a candidate in any election of public officers. The law requires that the name and post office address of the printer as well as that of the candidate must be on the handbill.

Zwickler was convicted of violating the statute by distributing anonymous handbills critical of the record of a U.S. Congressman seeking re-election at the 1964 elections. Zwickler appealed to the New York Court of Appeals. The court of appeals affirmed the conviction but offered no opinion. Zwickler then appealed to the New York Supreme Court. The court reversed the decision on the basis of state law.

Zwickler brought suit in district court under the Civil Rights Act of 1964 and the Declaratory Judgment Act. He sought declaratory and injunctive relief in the District Court for the Eastern District of New York. The basis of the suit was that the New York statute was repugnant to the guarantees of free expression secured by the U.S. Constitution. His contention was that the statute suffers from impermissible "overbreadth" that embraces anonymous handbills, both within, and outside the protection of the First Amendment.

A three-judge court, one judge dissenting, applied the doctrine of abstention and dismissed the complaint. The court remitted the case to the New York courts to assert a constitutional challenge. Zwickler appealed to the U.S. Supreme Court and the Court accepted the case. The basis of the appeal was that the discretion of the district courts to abstain from deciding the merits a state statute violates the Constitution.

An Important Reversal

By a majority vote of 8-1, the Supreme Court reversed the decision of the lower court, and remanded the case to the lower court for judgement. The district court applied the doctrine of abstention when "special circumstances" did not exist. The Supreme Court first considered whether abstention from the declaratory judgment sought by appellant was appropriate in the absence of his request for injunctive relief. They then considered whether abstention was justified because appellant also sought an injunction against future criminal prosecutions for violation of section 781-b of the New York Penal law.

Congress relied on the state courts to vindicate essential rights arising under the Constitution and federal laws during most of the nation's first century. The only exception was the twenty-fifth section of the Judiciary Act of 1789. This act provided for Supreme Court review when a state court denied a federal claim. After the Civil War, the policy was completely altered when nationalism dominated political thought. Congress gave the federal judiciary increased powers. The act of 3 March 1875 was the principal means of the broadening federal domain in the area of individual rights. This statute allowed Congress to give the federal courts a vast range of power, which had lain dormant in the Constitution since 1789. The federal courts ceased to be restricted tribunals of fair dealing between citizens of different states. They became the primary and powerful forum for vindicating every right given by the Constitution, the laws, and treaties of the United States.

Prior to the 1875 act, Congress passed the Civil Rights Act of 1871. This act allowed suit to be brought against "every person who, under color of any statute . . . subjects, or causes to be subjected, any citizen of the United States or other person . . . to the deprivation of any rights . . . secured by the Constitution and laws." It gave the district courts "original jurisdiction" of actions under state law of any right secured by the Constitution.

The Supreme Court held that in expanding federal judicial power, Congress imposed the duty upon all levels of the federal judiciary. It was a duty to give due respect to a suitor's choice of a federal forum for the hearing and decision of his federal constitutional claims. A federal court cannot escape from that duty because state courts also have the solemn responsibility to guard, enforce, and protect every right granted or secured by the Constitution of the United States.

The judge-developed doctrine of abstention was created in 1941 in *Railroad Commission of Texas v. Pullman Company*. This doctrine sanctions the use of the doctrine only in narrowly limited "special circumstances." One of the "special circumstances" is the susceptibility of a state statute to interpretation by the state courts that would avoid or modify a constitutional question. The Court argued that the district court applied this maxim.

The Supreme Court said that they were not reviewing the issue of construction of section 781-b of the New York Penal Law that would "avoid or modify the constitutional question." Zwickler's appeal was not based on the fact that the statute is void for "vagueness." Zwickler based his constitutional attack on the fact that the statute, although lacking neither clarity nor precision, was void for "overbreadth." This means that it violated the constitutional principle that "a gov-

ernmental purpose to control or prevent activities constitutionally subject to state regulation may not be achieved by means which sweep unnecessarily broadly and thereby invade the area of protected freedoms." Koota did not contest Zwickler's suggestion that 781-b is both clear and precise.

The Court used the principle established in *Livingston v. United States* (1960) as a guide to its decision. The principle is expressed as:

> Regard for the interest and sovereignty of the state and reluctance needlessly to adjudicate constitutional issues may require a federal District Court to abstain from adjudication if the parties may avail themselves of an appropriate procedure to obtain state interpretation of state laws requiring construction [*Harrison v. National Association for the Advancement of Colored People*]. The decision in *Harrison,* however, is not a broad encyclical commanding automatic remission to the state courts of all federal constitutional questions arising in the application of state statutes [*National Association for the Advancement of Colored People v. Bennett*]. Though never interpreted by a state court, if a state statute is not fairly subject to an interpretation, which will avoid or modify the federal constitutional question, it is the duty of a federal court to decide the federal question when presented to it. Any other course would impose expense and long delay upon the litigants without hope of its bearing fruit.

In *Turner v. City of Memphis* (1962), the Court vacated an abstention order. Its basis was that a declaratory judgment action ought to have been brought in the state court, before the federal court, in a Fourteenth Amendment issue. In *McNeese v. Board of Education* (1959), it was shown that abstention cannot be ordered simply to give state courts the first opportunity to vindicate the federal claim. In the *McNeese* case, the Court concluded that "we would defeat those purposes if we held that assertion of a federal claim in a federal court must await an attempt to vindicate the same claim in a state court." The Court ruled that the district court erred in refusing the Zwickler claim for declaratory judgement since there was no "special circumstance" to satisfy the doctrine of abstention.

Zwickler asked for an injunction against further prosecutions in violation of section 781-b of the New York penal code. He wanted to continue to distribute anonymous handbills in quantity in connection with election of party officials. The majority of the Supreme Court was of the opinion that abstention from deciding the declaratory judgment issue was justified because Zwickler had not shown "special circumstances" entitling him to an injunction against criminal prosecution. It would be the task of the district court on the remand to decide whether an injunction will be "necessary or appropriate" should Zwickler request for declaratory relief prevail.

Justice Harlan concurred but wrote a separate opinion. His opinion stressed a difference of view. He wrote "If, however, the opinion of the Court is intended to suggest that the central, or even a principal, issue in deciding the propriety of abstention is whether the complaint has alleged 'overbreadth,' or only 'vagueness,' with respect to the New York statute in question, I cannot agree." His main argument was based on the fact that neither principle has ever been definitively delimited by the Supreme Court, and a doctrine built upon their supposed differences would flounder because of lack of a foundation.

An Additional Reversal

The case reappeared in the Supreme Court as *Golden v. Zwickler* and was decided in March of 1969. The Court held that on the remand Zwickler would have to "establish the elements governing the issuance of a declaratory judgment," noting as relevant to that question that the congressman who had been the target of Zwickler's handbills had been elected to the Supreme Court of New York. On remand, the district court, without hearing evidence held that the essential elements for declaratory relief existed when this action was initiated. The Supreme Court ruled that the district court should have considered the facts at the time the case was heard on remand. The Court ruled that Zwickler did not establish the facts for declaratory judgement on remand. The district court decision was reversed and the case was remanded with direction to enter a new judgement to dismiss the complaint.

Impact

The ruling in this case established that the doctrine of abstention could only be applied in certain cases where special circumstances existed. It became a landmark case in establishing jurisdictional issues between the state and federal systems.

Related Cases

Railroad Commission of Texas v. Pullman Company, 312 U.S. 496 (1941).

Harrison v. National Association for the Advancement of Colored People, 360 U.S. 167 (1959).

National Association for the Advancement of Colored People v. Bennett, 360 U.S. 471 (1959).

McNeese v. Board of Education, 373 U.S. 668 (1959).

Livingston v. United States, 364 U.S. 281 (1960).

Turner v. City of Memphis, 369 U.S. 350 (1962).

Golden v. Zwickler, 394 U.S. 103 (1969).

Bibliography and Further Reading

Biskupic, Joan, and Elder Witt. *Congressional Quarterly's Guide to the U.S. Supreme Court,* 3rd ed. Washington, DC: Congressional Quarterly, Inc., 1996.

Freedom Forum Online. http://www.freedomforum.org/first/welcome.asp

RED LION BROADCASTING CO. V. FEDERAL COMMUNICATIONS COMMISSION

Legal Citation: 395 U.S. 367 (1969)

Petitioner
Red Lion Broadcasting Company, et al.

Respondent
Federal Communications Commission, et al.

Petitioner's Claim
That the Federal Communications Commission's Fairness Doctrine, which requires broadcasters to allow the subjects of personal attacks or political analyses equal time for rebuttal, violated their First Amendment right to freely determine the content of their programming.

Chief Lawyer for Petitioner
Roger Robb

Chief Lawyer for Respondent
Archibald Cox

Justices for the Court
Hugo Lafayette Black, William J. Brennan, Jr., John Marshall Harlan II, Thurgood Marshall, Potter Stewart, Earl Warren, Byron R. White (writing for the Court)

Justices Dissenting
None (William O. Douglas did not participate)

Place
Washington, D.C.

Date of Decision
9 June 1969

Decision
Denied the petitioner's claim, upholding a court of appeals ruling that the Fairness Doctrine did not violate the First Amendment right of broadcasters to determine the content of their programming.

Significance
The ruling upheld the Fairness Doctrine of the Federal Communications Commission, and insured the legal Right of Reply over broadcast media. Because there is a finite number of broadcast frequencies, the Court ruled that licensed broadcasters are obliged to present a variety of views on all subjects covered in their programming.

A Personal Attack on the Airwaves

On 27 November 1964, Pennsylvania radio station WGCB broadcast a 15-minute program by Reverend Billy James Hargis as part of its ongoing "Christian Crusade" series. In this program Rev. Hargis discussed author Fred J. Cook's work entitled *Goldwater: Extremist on the Right.* Rev. Hargis disagreed with the book's positions and found fault with Cook's political beliefs and personal and work history, stating that Cook had: been dismissed from a position with the *New York World Telegram* newspaper for fabricating a story; had subsequently worked for a Communist-affiliated publication; and had defended alleged Communist spy Alger Hiss and attacked the Federal Bureau of Investigation and its head, J. Edgar Hoover, in his writings. Cook subsequently heard the program, determined that it constituted a personal attack against him, and demanded free air time for a reply from WGCB. The station refused Cook's request and the matter was referred to the Federal Communications Commission (FCC). The FCC ruled that Rev. Hargis's program qualified as a personal attack on Cook, and that WGCB had failed to meet its obligation as a licensed broadcaster to provide a variety of viewpoints on all subjects covered in its programming. As such, the station was ordered to provide Cook with free air time.

The Fairness Doctrine

The advent of commercial radio in the 1920s constituted a revolution in popular communications. In the earliest days of commercial radio broadcasting, the allocation of broadcast frequencies was left to the private sector, resulting in a chaotic and virtually unusable broadcast spectrum. To sort out this chaos and protect the public interest in radio broadcasting, the federal government created the Federal Radio Commission (later the FCC) in 1927. This agency quickly reorganized the radio broadcasting industry, allocating fixed frequencies to licensed broadcasters and creating rules and regulations regarding radio station operations and, to some extent, programming. While pursuing its congressionally mandated responsibility to guard the public interest in radio broadcasting, the FCC determined in 1929 that the "public interest requires ample play for the free and fair competition of opposing views," a principle which the agency intended to apply "to all discussions of issues of importance to the public." By the end of the 1940s the FCC's efforts to ensure enlightened discussion of political issues from a variety of viewpoints had crystallized into the so-called Fairness Doctrine, which obligates broadcasters to offer free time for rebuttal and reply for commentators representing viewpoints differing from those presented in a station's programming.

Regulation of Content

WGCB objected to the FCC's ruling and in 1967 took the case to the U.S. Court of Appeals for the District of Columbia Circuit. The radio station maintained that, by forcing it to supply reply time to Clark, the FCC was regulating the content of its programming in violation of First Amendment protections of free speech. While the court of appeals considered the case, the FCC moved to clarify the Fairness Doctrine, particularly insofar as it applied to personal attacks and political editorials. As amended, the doctrine defined a personal attack as occurring "when, during the presentation of views on a controversial issue of public importance, an attack is made upon the honesty, character, integrity or like personal qualities of an identified person or group." The amended doctrine also prescribed a remedy for such attacks:

> the licensee shall, within a reasonable time . . . transmit to the person or group attacked (1) notification of the date, time and identification of the broadcast; (2) a script or tape (or an accurate summary if a script or tape is not available) of the attack; and (3) an offer of reasonable opportunity to respond over the licensee's facilities.

Although the court of appeals upheld the FCC in the *Red Lion* case, the amended Fairness Doctrine was almost simultaneously ruled unconstitutional by the U.S. District Court of Appeals for the Seventh Circuit in a parallel case, *United States v. Radio Television News Directors Association* (RTNDA). In light of these conflicting rulings the case moved to the U.S. Supreme Court, which heard arguments on 2 and 3 April 1969.

Freedom of Speech for Broadcasters and the People

In considering the case, the Supreme Court reviewed the history and purpose of the FCC. By a vote of 8-0, the Court upheld the decision of the Court of Appeals of the District of Columbia, and overruled the decision reached in *RTNDA*. Writing for the majority, Justice White noted that part of the function of the FCC is to maintain a diversity of views on the broadcast airwaves as a public trust. This function is made necessary by

the fact that the limited number of frequencies available makes it impossible for each individual to voice their opinions on the air. As such, FCC licensed broadcasting stations must function, as much as possible, as conduits for public dissemination of the views of those unable to obtain broadcasting licenses. "A license permits broadcasting, but the licensee has no constitutional right to be the one who holds the license or to monopolize a radio frequency to the exclusion of his fellow citizens." Furthermore, the Court interpreted the First Amendment as applying more to the duty of broadcasters to represent the views of those unable to broadcast than to the right of broadcasters to determine their own programming. "There is nothing in the First Amendment which prevents the Government from requiring a licensee to share his frequency with others and to conduct himself as a proxy or fiduciary with obligations to present those views and voices which are representative of his community and which would otherwise, by necessity, be barred from the airwaves."

Impact

The ruling upheld and solidified the use of the Fairness Doctrine in the regulation of political speech on the public airwaves. The Fairness Doctrine was, however, overtaken by events in due course. The Court seemed to back away from its position on the doctrine in *Miami Herald Publishing Company v. Tornillo* (1974), ruling that the right of reply did not apply to printed media. A final blow to the doctrine was delivered in 1987, when President Ronald Reagan vetoed legislation codifying the doctrine and the FCC abandoned it altogether shortly thereafter. Despite this retrenchment, the Court has continued to interpret the right of reply and personal attack rules as justifying the regulation of programming to ensure the airing of a variety of political viewpoints. In the 1981 case of *CBS v. FCC,* for instance, the Court ruled that broadcasters must allow "reasonable access" for all candidates for federal office.

Related Cases

CBS v. Democratic National Committee, 412 U.S. 97 (1973).
Miami Herald Publishing Company v. Tornillo, 418 U.S. 241 (1974).
CBS v. FCC, 453 U.S. 367 (1981).

Bibliography and Further Reading

Biskupic, Joan and Elder Witt, eds. *Guide to the Supreme Court of the United States.* Washington, DC: Congressional Quarterly Inc., 1997.

Cook, Don Lloyd. "Earthquakes and Aftershocks." *Journal of Public Policy & Marketing,* Spring 1998, p. 116.

Hall, Kermit L., ed. *Oxford Companion to the Supreme Court of the United States.* New York: Oxford University Press, 1992.

BRANDENBURG V. OHIO

Legal Citation: 395 U.S. 444 (1969)

Appellant
Clarence Brandenburg

Appellee
State of Ohio

Appellant's Claim
That conviction of Brandenburg under the Ohio Criminal Syndicalism Act violated the free speech clauses of the First and Fourteenth Amendments.

Chief Lawyer for Appellant
Allen Brown

Chief Lawyer for Appellee
Leonard Kirschner

Justices for the Court
Hugo L. Black, William J. Brennan, Jr., William O. Douglas, Abe Fortas, John M. Harlan II, Thurgood Marshall, Potter Stewart, Earl Warren, Byron R. White (unsigned)

Justices Dissenting
None

Place
Washington, D.C.

Date of Decision
9 June 1969

Decision
Ruled in favor of Brandenburg and overturned lower court decisions upholding Brandenburg's conviction under the Ohio Criminal Syndicalism Act.

Significance
The ruling reversed a previous Supreme Court decision setting a new precedent for the "clear and present danger" standard in First Amendment cases. The Court now held that a person's words were protected as free speech as long as they did not directly incite unlawful action. Concerns became raised later that the standard established in the decision was not appropriate in situations involving mass communications through the Internet and popular talkshows in the 1980s and 1990s.

Between 1917 and 1920 in the aftermath of World War I and the Russian Bolshevik Revolution, nationalism and patriotism swept the country at a fever pitch. At the same time, fear of communism and the people who supported it gripped America. Determined to suppress radicals and anarchists who would violently disrupt political and social order to bring about change, thirty-three states enacted sedition or criminal syndication laws. "Syndicates" are groups of people undertaking a project that they would not be able to attempt individually. To advocate, teach, or aid in an illegal act of violence to bring about political or industrial reform was now unlawful. These laws prohibited a person from organizing or meeting with any group that promoted "criminal syndicalism," meaning the attempted organized, violent takeover of the state.

The framework and standard by which future criminal syndicalism claims would be judged was formulated by Justice Oliver Wendell Holmes in *Schenck v. United States* (1919) which involved violations of the federal Espionage Act of 1917. The standard, known as the "clear and present danger" test, required deciding whether a person's words "create a clear and present danger that they will bring about substantive evils that Congress has a right to prevent. It is a question of proximity and degree."

Beginning with *Schenck* and for the following five decades, history echoed a valuable lesson: governments are more repressive in times of crisis and less restrictive in days of peace. The Supreme Court was continually pressed to decide where First Amendment protections end and the government's right or obligation to restrict threatening expression begins.

The year 1919 saw the Court affirm several more convictions using the clear and present danger test. Near the end of 1919, *Abrams v. United States* also involving Espionage Act violations pushed the test to a much more restrictive level. Moving away from the imminent danger language, *Abrams* emphasized that if the defendant's expressive words simply had a tendency to cause illegal actions, that was sufficient to convict. Justice Holmes dissented, reemphasizing his belief that expression could not be suppressed unless it constituted an immediate danger. Yet, with *Abrams* the clear and present danger standard evolved to the much more repressive constitutional interpretation, the "bad tendency" test. Continuing to combat the "Red Menace," two cases involving state criminal syndication statutes, *Gitlow v. New York* (1925) and *Whitney v. California* (1927), were judged using the bad tendency standard and the convictions upheld. In *Whitney,* Charlotte Whitney, a well known California heiress and member of the Oakland branch of the Socialist Party, was found guilty of organizing and associating with a party whose aim was to overthrow the United States government.

By the early 1930s Americans developed a strong self-consciousness of their civil liberty heritage. The fear of anarchists subsided and this trend was reflected in Court decisions reversing state criminal syndication convictions. The Court found these laws unnecessarily restrictive of the rights of free speech. The tide seemingly flowed back to the clear and present danger standard.

Following World War II, the emergence of the Cold War, a second Red Scare, and McCarthyism led many states in the late 1940s through the mid-1950s to pass or revitalize laws prohibiting organizations perceived as dangerous to the United States. The focus again was communist activity. The *Dennis v. United States* (1951) decision exhorted courts to consider if the "gravity of the evil, discounted by its improbability, justifies such invasion of free speech as is necessary to avoid the danger." Referred to as the clear and *probable* danger test, the ruling marked a return to the bad tendency views of the post-World War I period.

Once the second Red Scare passed, the Supreme Court, with a series of decisions handed down in the early 1960s, began defending expression and association against repressive legislation passed during the McCarthy era. Concurrently, the nation's focus shifted away from communism to civil rights and Vietnam War demonstrations. Some states began to look at their criminal syndication laws as a way to curb anti-government protests.

The Ohio Criminal Syndicalism Law

The Ohio Criminal Syndicalism statute, enacted in 1919, made a crime of advocating "the duty, necessity or propriety of crime sabotage, violence, or unlawful methods of terrorism as a means of accomplishing industrial or political reform" and "voluntary assembl[ing] with any society, group, or assemblage of persons formed to teach or advocate the doctrine of criminal syndicalism."

A Ku Klux Klan leader, Clarence Brandenburg, organized a rally in Hamilton County, Ohio. Before the rally, Brandenburg telephoned a Cincinnati television reporter, asking him to cover the event. The reporter and a cameraman attended the rally. About a dozen Klansmen participated. The Klansmen burned a cross

and Brandenburg dressed in full Klan regalia delivered a speech saying in part, "We're not a revengent [sic] organization, but if our President, our Congress, our Supreme Court, continue to suppress the white Caucasian race, it's possible that there might have to be some revengence [sic] taken." Klansmen shouted racist slogans against African Americans and demanded all Jews be sent to Israel.

The reporters taped the cross-burning and shouting of racist sentiments and broadcast them on the local news. Based on the films, Brandenburg was charged and later convicted of violating Ohio's Criminal Syndicalism Act. He appealed claiming the Ohio law violated his free speech rights under the First and Fourteenth amendments. The appeals court affirmed his conviction without offering an opinion. Brandenburg then appealed to the Ohio Supreme Court, which dismissed his appeal, claiming no substantial constitutional issues were involved. The U.S. Supreme Court agreed to hear the case.

Whitney Reversed

The unanimous decision of the court was delivered *per curiam,* which means the justice who authored the Court's decision was not identified. The Court reversed Brandenburg's conviction which was based on his racist speech suggesting the possibility of violence at some future time and found Ohio's Criminal Syndicalism Act invalid.

The Court's powerful but briefly written decision cited the numerous previous cases addressing the subject. According to the Court's decisions in the preceding cases, the courts

> . . . have fashioned the principle that the constitutional guarantees of free speech and free press do not permit a State to forbid or proscribe advocacy of the use of force or of law violation except where such advocacy is directed to inciting or producing imminent lawless action and is likely to incite or produce such action . . . A statute which fails to draw upon this distinction impermissibly intrudes upon the freedoms guaranteed by the First and Fourteenth Amendments. It sweeps within it condemnation speech which our Constitution has immunized from government control . . . measured by this test, Ohio's Criminal Syndicalism Act cannot be sustained . . . Such a statute falls within the condemnation of the First and Fourteenth Amendments.

Although the words never appear in the decision, the Court returned to Holmes' clear and present danger test and added the incitement test to it. No longer could a mere bad tendency suffice to support government suppression. Rather, suppression was allowed only if the expression directly incited action. Frequently referred to as the *Brandenburg* test, the justices affirmed the right to speak and organize even when the message and purpose is offensive to American values. Additionally, the *Whitney* decision was specifically overruled in this decision.

Justices William O. Douglas and Hugo L. Black, writing in a concurring opinion, would seemingly go a step further and remove all restrictions from speech by stating that they see no place in the spirit of the First Amendment for any clear and present danger test whatsoever.

Although having nothing to do with the Communist Party or groups dedicated to the violent overthrow of government, *Brandenburg,* the last major decision of the Warren Court, was highly regarded as the decision finally closing the door to the repressive McCarthy era.

Impact

Brandenburg, the Court's first review of a 1960s application of criminal syndication law, resulted in a landmark philosophy succinctly casting doubt on all such laws. To many, the decision reopened the door to the original clear and present danger restrictions. The *Brandenburg* decision provided First Amendment protection to public discourse important for self-governing societies to legitimately operate.

Some legal scholars acclaimed the *Brandenburg* test as the foundation for the modern interpretation of free speech. The test allowed for a greater degree of political discussion. People have the right to discuss the possibility of using violence to address social and political ills. Only when their words lead to direct action is the law broken. Later, some claimed the *Brandenburg* standard was outdated for the new high-speed, global communications era of the late 1980s and 1990s. They asserted speech clearly advocating illegal and murder-

ous violence that reaches mass audiences through the Internet or popular talk-show programs should be held to different standards. Examples used to illustrate which speech should not be constitutionally protected included the posting of bomb-making instructions over the Internet and radio talk-show hosts describing how to kill Federal law enforcement agents wearing protective gear. Critics argued the *Brandenburg* standard should only be applied to situations involving a limited number of immediate listeners. Odds of violence directly resulting from the speech advocating murderous actions over a mass communications medium was considered significantly greater than with smaller forums. It would take only a few people out of millions of "listeners" to lead to violent acts aimed at killing people. Such speech was considered quite different than calls for civil disobedience by Martin Luther King, Jr. in the 1960s.

Related Cases

Schenck v. United States, 249 U.S. 47 (1919).
Abrams v. United States, 250 U.S. 616 (1919).
Gitlow v. New York, 268 U.S. 652 (1925).
Whitney v. California, 274 U.S. 357 (1927).
Dennis v. United States, 341 U.S. 494 (1951).

Bibliography and Further Reading

Biskupic, Joan, and Elder Witt. *Guide to the U.S. Supreme Court.* 3rd edition. Washington, D.C: Congressional Quarterly, Inc., 1997.

Epstein, Lee, and Thomas G. Walker. *Constitutional Law for a Changing America: Rights, Liberties, and Justice.* 2nd edition. Washington, DC: Congressional Quarterly Press, 1995.

Sunstein, Cass R. "Is Violent Speech a Right?" *The American Prospect,* Summer 1995.

POLICE DEPARTMENT OF CHICAGO V. MOSLEY

Legal Citation: 408 U.S. 92 (1971)

Petitioners
Police Department of the City of Chicago, et al.

Respondent
Earl Mosley

Petitioners' Claim
That a Chicago city ordinance banning labor-related picketing next to a school was constitutional.

Chief Lawyer for Petitioners
Richard L. Curry

Chief Lawyer for Respondent
Harvey J. Barnett

Justices for the Court
Harry A. Blackmun, William J. Brennan, Jr., Warren E. Burger, William O. Douglas, Thurgood Marshall (writing for the Court), Lewis F. Powell, Jr., William H. Rehnquist, Potter Stewart, Byron R. White

Justices Dissenting
None

Place
Washington, D.C.

Date of Decision
26 June 1972

Decision
Denied the petitioners' claim and reversed the decision of the U.S. District Court for the Northern District of Illinois, affirming the decision of the Seventh Circuit Court of Appeals that the Chicago ordinance banning non-labor demonstrations next to schools violated the Equal Protection Clauses of the First and Fourteenth Amendments.

Significance
The ruling extended protection of an individual's right to freedom of speech and assembly which the Court had previously affirmed by striking down state ordinances banning demonstrations in the vicinity of state capitols: *Gregory v. City of Chicago* (1969) and parks: *Niemotko v. Maryland* (1951).

Public Forum Doctrine

Public demonstrations for social, political, or labor causes have been a part of American life since before the establishment of the United States. In fact, demonstrations played a major role in spurring the American Revolution, and the founding fathers were undoubtedly looking to protect public political expression in the writing of the First Amendment. Likewise, the Supreme Court has consistently ruled in favor of free public expression of political beliefs within certain parameters. In *Hague v. Committee for Industrial Organization* (1939) the Court established the public forum doctrine. This doctrine maintains that government may not prohibit free political speech or related activities, including demonstrations, distribution of printed materials, and public speaking in favor of or opposing various policies or organizations. During the 1960s the public forum doctrine was repeatedly challenged, as public demonstrations became commonplace.

In August of 1967 Earl Mosley, an employee of the U.S. Postal Department, began a solitary protest against the hiring and admissions policies of the Jones Commercial High School in Chicago, Illinois. By the standards of the 1960s, a decade replete with violent demonstrations, Mosley's protest was quite unobtrusive. His usual method of operations consisted of walking back and forth on the sidewalk in front of the school carry a placard bearing a slogan, such as "Jones High School Practices Black Discrimination. Jones High School Has A Black Quota." Mosley always conducted himself in an orderly manner, and his protest was entirely nonviolent. On 26 March 1968, with Mosley's protest still in progress, the city of Chicago passed Municipal Code Chapter 193-1 (i), which prohibited

> pickets or demonstrations on a public way within 150 feet of any primary or secondary school building while the school is in session and one-half hour before the school is in session and one-half hour after the school session has been concluded, provided that this subsection does not prohibit the peaceful picketing of any school involved in a labor dispute . . .

Upon hearing of the new ordinance, Mosley contacted the Chicago Police Department, which informed him that under the ordinance he would be arrested if he continued his protest. As such, Mosley resumed his protest at a distance of greater than 150 feet from the school, but found that the architecture and layout of the neighborhood rendered his picketing entirely ineffective at that distance. Finding his protest stymied, Mosley sought an injunction against Chapter 193-1 (i) in the district court.

Legal Proceedings

Mosley argued that Chapter 193-1 (i) punished activities protected by the First Amendment and that the ordinance also denied him equal protection in violation of the First and Fourteenth Amendments. The district court was unmoved by these arguments, however, and Mosley was forced to take his case to the Seventh Circuit Court of Appeals. The court of appeals reversed the district court's ruling, holding that since Chapter 193-1 (i) prohibited even peaceful protesting of many kinds it was too broad and "patently unconstitutional on its face." The Chicago Police Department then appealed the case to the Supreme Court, which heard arguments on 19 January 1972.

Time, Place, and Manner and Equal Protection

In addition to the public forum doctrine, the Supreme Court has developed the time, place, and manner rule for the adjudication of freedom of speech questions. This rule allows for regulation of certain types of speech by reason of its time, place, and manner, for instance, a zoning ordinance regulating the placement of adult theaters and bookstores, while not enabling governments to restrain speech in general. In considering cases under this rule, the Court has invariably held in favor of government regulation of speech only where there is a clear necessity for such regulation to maintain a public interest and such regulation is applied without distinction.

As such, the Court affirmed the decision of the court of appeals in this case, ruling by a vote of 9-0 that Chicago Municipal Code Chapter 193-1 (i) was unconstitutional in that it exempted peaceful labor picketing from its ban of demonstrations within 150 feet of school grounds. Justice Marshall, writing for the majority, noted that the Court struck down the Chicago ordinance only because, by exempting peaceful labor demonstrations, it did not seek to regulate speech based on that speech's time, place, and manner of conveyance, but rather its content.

Impact

Police Department of Chicago v. Mosley occupies an important place as an example of the application of the public forum doctrine and the time, place, and manner rule. The decision in this case was in keeping with those of *Edwards v. South Carolina* (1966) and *Niemotko v. Maryland* (1951) in that it denied states the right to ban protests occurring near specific buildings or locations. In subsequent rulings the primacy of the time, place, and manner rule and, in particular, the public forum doctrine have diminished to some extent, and the Court has often upheld ordinances and statutes regulating speech as long as such regulations apply equally with regard to the content of said speech.

Related Cases

Edwards v. South Carolina, 372 U.S. 229 (1966).
Gregory v. City of Chicago, 394 U.S. 111 (1969).
City Council of Los Angeles v. Taxpayers for Vincent, 466 U.S. 289 (1984).
Frisby v. Schultz, 487 U.S. 474 (1988).

Bibliography and Further Reading

Hall, Kermit L., ed. *Oxford Companion to the Supreme Court of the United States.* New York: Oxford University Press, 1992.

Whitehead, John. "Academic Freedom and the Rights of Religious Faculty." Rutherford Institute. http://campus.leaderu.com/real/ri-intro/freedom.

GRAYNED V. CITY OF ROCKFORD

Legal Citation: 408 U.S. 104 (1972)

Appellant
Richard Grayned

Appellee
City of Rockford

Appellant's Claim
That he should not have been convicted for his participation in a demonstration that allegedly violated the city of Rockford's anti-picketing and antinoise ordinances because the ordinances were overbroad and should be struck down.

Chief Lawyer for Appellant
Sophia H. Hall

Chief Lawyer for Appellee
William E. Collins

Justices for the Court
Harry A. Blackmun, William J. Brennan, Jr., Warren E. Burger, Thurgood Marshall (writing for the Court), Lewis F. Powell, Jr., William H. Rehnquist, Potter Stewart, Byron R. White

Justices Dissenting
William O. Douglas

Place
Washington, D.C.

Date of Decision
26 June 1972

Decision
That the anti-picketing ordinance was overbroad and was therefore invalid; that the antinoise ordinance, which prohibited only noise that took place near a public school and might disrupt school activity, was valid; and that therefore Grayned's conviction under the anti-picketing ordinance was reversed while his conviction under the antinoise ordinance was upheld.

Significance
Although the Court upheld the antinoise ordinance, it gave a ringing endorsement to the right of access to "a public forum," affirming that citizens have a broad right to freely express their political views in a variety of public places.

On 25 April 1969, some 200 people gathered outside of West Senior High School in Rockford, Illinois. This group had been trying to change things at West Senior High for some time. They had made formal proposals to the school board, but they had been turned down. Now they were staging a demonstration. The picket signs they carried told what their demands were: "Black cheerleaders to cheer too," "Black history with black teachers," "Equal rights, Negro counselors."

Most of the demonstrators were African American students who had been advised by a faculty member to choose this way of fighting for their rights. They were also joined by former students, family members, and other concerned citizens. Everyone had been told that they must walk quietly, hand in hand, no whispering, no talking. They gathered on a sidewalk about 100 feet from the school building, and began to march.

Who Made the Noise?

At this point, witnesses disagree about what happened. Demonstrators and their supporters claimed that the demonstrators remained quiet and orderly at all times. They admitted that there was noise, but they said that most of it came from the 25 police officers who were stationed nearby, using loudspeakers to explain that there was a law against this kind of picketing in Rockford and to tell demonstrators that they might be arrested.

Witnesses who supported the police told a different story. They said that the demonstrators cheered and chanted, insulting the police officers. They said that this noisy demonstration caused hundreds of students to jump up from their desks and line up at the windows to watch, that some demonstrators called to their friends to leave class and join the demonstration, that many students were late to class because they had been watching the demonstration, and that in general, the demonstration had seriously disrupted the school day.

Everyone agrees that the picketing lasted only 20 to 30 minutes, and that it was, in the words of one police officer, "very orderly." Everyone also agrees that Richard Grayned, whose brother and twin sisters were students at the school, made no noise whatsoever as

When is picketing constitutionally protected?

Picketing is normally a peaceful carrying of signs and banners clearly advertising a grievance or the purpose of a demonstration. It is a recognized means of communication.

Beginning in the 1930s, some states sought to hinder the development of labor unions by passing laws prohibiting pickets. The states argued picketing is conduct, not speech, and, therefore, not protected by the First Amendment. In 1941 the Supreme Court concluded, however, that peaceful picketing is a constitutionally protected means of transmitting ideas.

The guarantee of free expression has often been weighed against a state's desire to preserve public peace through picketing restrictions. Normally, picket-ing that becomes an instrument of force, vandalism, intimidation, or coercion is not protected by the First Amendment. Similarly, First Amendment protection does not apply to picketing that is part of other conduct violating state law. For example, if the purpose of picketing is to force an employer to replace his non-union workers with union workers, the activity would be contrary to a state's valid right-to-work law. The Court would uphold a state's action to stop the picketing. Therefore, the First Amendment protects from state restriction all non-violent picketing that is not part of other illegal conduct.

Source(s): Biskupic, Joan and Witt, Elder. *Guide to the U.S. Supreme Court.* Washington, DC: Congressional Quarterly, 1997.

he marched with the group. Nevertheless, he was one of some 40 demonstrators arrested.

Grayned—along with the other demonstrators—was arrested under two ordinances of the city of Rockford. One of them was an anti-picketing ordinance that prohibited picketing within a certain distance of a public school around the time that school was in session. Another was an antinoise ordinance that prohibited "the making of any noise or diversion which disturbs or tends to disturb the peace or good order of such school session or class thereof . . ."

Grayned was interested in more than just reversing his own conviction under the two ordinances. He wanted to strike down both laws, which made any kind of school-oriented demonstration impossible. Since the school board had not responded to their original demands, Grayned and others in his community wanted to be able to keep working to win their demands, through peaceful protests as well as through other means.

Broad Laws and Specific Restrictions

When Grayned's case finally made it to the Supreme Court, the Court had just recently ruled on another anti-picketing ordinance in the city of Chicago, very similar to the one in Rockford. The Court had invalidated the Chicago ordinance, and so they invalidated the Rockford one as well. That left only the antinoise ordinance.

The Court had to answer the two questions of whether the ordinance too was vague, and was it too broad. Those were the charges brought by Grayned. Clearly, a vague law is not a fair law, because its vagueness makes it too easy for police and juries to apply the law only against the people they don't like, rather than treating everyone equally. Likewise, a broad law, while outlawing some bad things, might at the same time outlaw some activities that are actually protected by the Constitution. To be fair, laws have to be precise and specific.

Justice Marshall, who wrote the decision for the Court, spent a great deal of time emphasizing that people have a right to protest, to express themselves freely, and to engage in protests that take place at or near a school, even while the school is in session. The right to free speech is protected by the First Amendment, and Marshall wanted to be sure that the Rockford law did not contradict the First Amendment in any way.

However, Marshall also pointed out that honoring the First Amendment does not mean that there are no restrictions on how ideas are expressed. He gave the example of people who want to hold two parades at once, on the same street. Clearly, a city has the right to give a permit to only one group, to prevent the disruption that having two parades would cause. Likewise, if people want to hold the parade on a busy street during rush hour, a city could forbid the parade on the grounds that it would cause too many traffic problems.

In other words, Marshall said, cities and other branches of government had the right to place "reasonable 'time, place and manner' regulations" to protect certain governmental interests. However, these regulations had to be so clear that no one could interpret them differently for different groups—they had to apply in the same way to everybody.

In addition, the regulations had to be so specific that they only prohibited the part of free expression that would actually interfere with those governmental interests. For example, a law might forbid someone from making a political speech in a library reading room, but the law should allow a silent protest in a library reading room, while allowing the noisier speech in a public park.

By those standards, Marshall said, the city of Rockford's ordinance was neither too vague nor too broad. The Court recognized that communities have a right to protect their schools. If noise or disturbances will disrupt the school day or incite students to leave the classroom, then certainly, the Court felt, a community has a right to take action. The city of Rockford's antinoise ordinance was precisely limited to just that type of noise that might disrupt the school day. Therefore, the Court upheld it—and Grayned's conviction under it.

The Lone Dissenter

Every one of the Court's nine justices agreed that the city of Rockford's antinoise ordinance was appropriately specific. However, Justice Douglas did dissent from one part of Marshall's opinion. He felt that the demonstration that Grayned had been a part of, which had always been intended as a silent demonstration,

was not actually in violation of the antinoise ordinance. "There was noise," Douglas wrote, "but most of it was made by the police . . ."

As a result, Douglas wrote, Grayned's conviction should certainly be overturned, even though Grayned's argument had not rested on his own behavior, but only the question of the ordinance being too broad. Douglas felt that if the ordinance really was not too broad, it should not be understood to apply to the demonstration that Grayned had been a part of—and it certainly should not have been applied to Grayned himself.

Related Cases

Thornhill v. Alabama, 310 U.S. 88 (1940).
Edwards v. South Carolina, 372 U.S. 229 (1963).
Adderley v. Florida, 385 U.S. 39 (1966).
Pruneyard Shopping Center v. Robins, 447 U.S. 74 (1980).
Schenck v. Pro-Choice Network of Western New York, 519 U.S. 357 (1997).

Bibliography and Further Reading

Werhan, Keither. "The Supreme Court's public forum doctrine and the return of formalism." *Cardozo Law Review,* Winter 1986, Vol. 7, No. 2, pp. 335-437.

GRAVEL V. UNITED STATES

Legal Citation: 408 U.S. 606 (1972)

Petitioner
Frank Gravel, U.S. Senator

Respondent
United States

Petitioner's Claim
That a senator's aide shares the protections guaranteeing the senator freedom of speech and debate.

Chief Lawyers for Petitioner
Robert J. Reinstein and Charles L. Fishman

Chief Lawyer for the Respondent
Erwin N. Griswold, U.S. Solicitor General

Justices for the Court
Harry A. Blackmun (announced the opinion), Warren E. Burger, Lewis F. Powell, Jr., William H. Rehnquist, Byron R. White (writing for the Court)

Justices Dissenting
William J. Brennan, Jr., William O. Douglas, Thurgood Marshall, Potter Stewart

Place
Washington, D.C.

Date of Decision
29 June 1972

Decision
That the privileges of the Speech or Debate Clause do extend to congressional aides, but not to activity outside the legislative process.

Significance
The Supreme Court ruled that congressional aides are in fact "alter egos" of the legislators for whom they work. As such, their speech receives special protection under the Constitution's Speech or Debate Clause.

The *Pentagon Papers* is the popular name given to a secret study done from 1967 to 1969 by a team of analysts for the U.S. Department of Defense. The 47-volume study (officially called "History of the U.S. Decision-Making Process on Vietnam Policy") sharply criticized the U.S. policies in Southeast Asia that led to the Vietnam War and stated that the government had misrepresented its role there to the American people. In 1971, Daniel Ellsberg, who had access to the study, released it to the *New York Times,* which began publishing excerpts in a series of articles.

On 29 June 1971, Senator Mike Gravel of Alaska called a meeting of the Senate Subcommittee on Public Buildings and Grounds. He began to read aloud from the *Pentagon Papers* and place their full text into the subcommittee's official record. Later, Gravel provided a copy of the documents to Beacon Press, a Boston publishing house, which did in fact publish them. A federal grand jury investigated to determine whether Gravel had broken the law in releasing the sensitive documents to the public. One of his aides, Leonard Rodberg, was called to testify before this grand jury. Gravel and Rodberg moved to block this action, on the grounds that Article I, Section 6 of the U.S. Constitution, known as the Speech or Debate Clause, extends immunity to the actions of congressional staff workers when they act on behalf of members of Congress.

The case came before the U.S. Court of Appeals, which issued a mixed decision. It held that the commercial publication of the *Papers* was not protected under the Speech or Debate Clause because it was not a legislative act. However, neither Gravel nor Rodberg could be questioned by a grand jury. The case was then appealed to the U.S. Supreme Court, which agreed to hear it and issued its ruling on 29 June 1972.

Private Publication Not Protected

The Supreme Court held against Senator Gravel on a 5-4 vote. The decision, written by Justice Blackmun, did support him on two counts, however. It upheld Gravel's contention that reading the *Papers* aloud in the subcommittee was protected by the Speech or Debate Clause:

Senator Mike Gravel, 1972. © AP/Wide World Photos.

The Speech or Debate Clause was designed to assure a coequal branch of the government wide freedom of speech, debate, and deliberation without intimidation or threats from the Executive Branch. It thus protects Members against prosecutions that directly impinge upon or threaten the legislative process. We have no doubt that Senator Gravel may not be made to answer . . . for the events that occurred at the subcommittee meeting.

The Court also agreed with Gravel that the Speech or Debate Clause extended to his aide, Rodberg:

We agree with the Court of Appeals that for the purpose of construing the privilege a Member and his aide are to be "treated as one" . . . [I]t is literally impossible, in view of the complexities of the modern legislative process, with Congress almost constantly in session and matters of legislative concern constantly proliferating, for Members of Congress to perform their legislative tasks without the help of aides and assistants; that the day-to-day work of such aides is so critical to the Members' performance that they must be treated as the latters' alter ego.

However, the Court held that Gravel's presentation of the *Papers* to a private publisher was not a legislative act, and thus was not protected by the Speech or Debate Clause:

[P]rivate publication by Senator Gravel . . . was in no way essential to the deliberations of the House; nor does questioning as to private publication threaten the integrity or independence of the House by impermissibly exposing its deliberations to executive influence . . . We cannot but conclude that the Senator's arrangements with Beacon Press were not part and parcel of the legislative process.

In short, the Court concluded that Rodberg could be questioned, but only under certain conditions:

The Speech or Debate Clause does not in our view extend immunity to Rodberg, as a Senator's aide, from testifying before the grand jury about the arrangement between Senator Gravel and Beacon Press or about his own participation, if any, in the alleged transaction, so long as legislative acts of the Senator are not impugned.

Gravel v. United States provided important clarification on the breadth of the Speech or Debate Clause of the Constitution.

Impact

The *Gravel* decision has been used to determine the scope of executive and judicial immunity under the Speech or Debate Clause. The important findings in *Gravel* were that a congressional aid enjoys the same immunity as a Member of Congress and that the immunity under the Speech or Debate Clause is limited to legislative activity. In *Stump v. Sparkman* (1978) the Court held that judges are also absolutely immune from liability for damages when performing judicial functions. However, consistent with *Gravel,* the Court found in *Dennis v. Sparks* (1980) that federal judges do not have immunity apart from performing their judicial function; in this case the Court found that federal judges are not immune from conspiracy charges and that co-conspirators cannot be considered "official aides" of a judge. Similarly, in *Nixon v. Fitzgerald* (1982) the Court defined the range of presidential immunity. Among their findings in this case, the Court determined that presidential aides are entitled to the same absolute immunity granted to congressional aides in *Gravel*

In many instances *Gravel* has been invoked to emphasize the limits of immunity under the Speech or Debate Clause. In *United States v. Gillok* (1980), for instance, the Court ruled that a state senator is not immune from prosecution in a federal court on the basis of the Speech or Debate Clause. Presidents Nixon and Clinton tested the boundaries of presidential immunity only to find that the same limitations found in *Gravel* applied to the executive branch as well.

Related Cases

United States v. Nixon, 418 U.S. 683 (1974).
Eastland v. United States Servicemen's Fund, 421 U.S. 491 (1975).
Nixon v. Fitzgerald, 457 U.S. 731 (1982).
Clinton v. Jones, 520 U.S. 681 (1997).

Bibliography and Further Reading

Chandler, Ralph C. *The Constitutional Law Dictionary.* Santa Barbara, CA: ABC-Clio, Inc., 1987.

Ducat, Craig R., and Harold W. Chase. *Constitutional Interpretation.* St. Paul, MN: West Publishing Company, 1988.

Encyclopedia of the American Constitution. New York, NY: Macmillan Publishing Company, 1986.

GERTZ V. ROBERT WELCH, INC.

Legal Citation: 418 U.S. 323 (1974)

Petitioner
Elmer Gertz

Respondent
Robert Welch, Inc.

Petitioner's Claim
That an article in the respondent's magazine had defamed him, and that the respondent was liable for damages.

Chief Lawyer for Petitioner
Wayne B. Giampietro

Chief Lawyer for Respondent
Clyde J. Watts

Justices for the Court
Harry A. Blackmun, Thurgood Marshall, Lewis F. Powell, Jr. (writing for the Court), William H. Rehnquist, Potter Stewart

Justices Dissenting
William J. Brennan, Jr., Warren E. Burger, William O. Douglas, Byron R. White

Place
Washington, D.C.

Date of Decision
25 June 1974

Decision
The Court overruled the court of appeals and district court rulings and held that the respondent was liable for damages.

Significance
The decision established a precedent for libel cases involving private individuals. Unlike public officials or public figures, private individuals did not need to establish actual malice in order to receive damages.

Defamation in Common Law

Laws governing defamation evolved from English common law and remained basically constant until the 1960s. Traditionally, plaintiffs in defamation suits needed only to prove that defendants had published defamatory statements about them. In most cases, unless defendants could establish that the statements were true, they were then subjected to strict liability. Strict liability, also known as liability without fault, applies to a defendant regardless of negligence. Thus a defendant who handles dangerous substances such as poisonous snakes—or words—is liable for any accidents that may occur, no matter how much care is exercised. The burden of proof was on defendants, as encouragement for them to check facts thoroughly before publication.

Damages were typically awarded without proof of actual loss. The loss in question was usually loss of reputation, and loss of reputation was difficult to establish in court. The actual (or compensatory) damages were often monetary sums arrived at with little reference to actual monetary loss. Punitive damages could then be awarded with proof of actual malice (knowingly or recklessly publishing falsehoods).

Precedent

In *New York Times v. Sullivan* (1964), the Court held that, except in a case of actual malice, the press enjoyed a constitutional protection against such liability if the defamed person was a public official. The Court reasoned that the common law burden of proof on the press would stifle free speech and discourage democratic debate. Decisions following *New York Times,* such as *Curtis Publishing Co. v. Butts* (1967), extended this protection to media statements about public figures, as well as public officials. One outstanding question was whether the media were still protected if the object of defamation was a private individual.

This was the question before the Court in *Rosenbloom v. Metromedia* (1971). The decision in *Rosenbloom* did little to clarify a confusing issue. The Court announced a variety of opinions, reflecting a range of approaches to the *New York Times* precedent. The plurality, composed of Brennan, Burger, and Blackmun, concluded that the *New York Times* standard applied to the private

Definition of a Public Figure

In 1974 the U.S. Supreme Court established the definition of a public figure. The case of *Gertz v. Robert Welch, Inc.* provided a useful characterization that could be applied by other courts deciding libel cases.

The Court allowed that while a person could become a "public figure" without specific action on his or her own, this happened rarely. Rather, they found it more likely that individuals had ". . . assumed roles of especial prominence in the affairs of society." For example, anyone running for political office becomes more vulnerable to public scrutiny and media attention. Other well known individuals like entertainers, writers, athletes, and other celebrities are considered public figures too.

In some instances, persons become viewed as public figures because of involvement in a controversial public issue. The general recognition accorded them as a result of the controversy may subsequently allow the person to influence the outcome of the issue. This may be referred to as the "public controversy" test.

Finally, the Court asserted that in many cases people are considered public figures because of the enormous power and influence they wield in general.

Elmer Gertz, 1958. © AP/Wide World Photos.

Source(s): Cornell. http://supct.law.cornell.edu/supct/. Findlaw, http://www.findlaw.com/casecode/supreme.html. http://law.vill.edu/Fed-Ct/Supreme/Flite/opinions. 418US323.htm.

individual, if the individual was involved in an event of public or general interest. Justice Black concurred, but on the grounds that the First Amendment granted the media absolute protection from liability. White also concurred, with yet another line of reasoning: Private individuals who were affected by or involved in official business of public servants were not protected.

Justice Harlan dissented. Private persons are less able to effectively, publicly rebut defamation. They have also not voluntarily exposed themselves to public scrutiny. Marshall wrote, in a dissent joined by Stewart, that the public or general interest test employed by the plurality would require that the Court decide "what information is relevant to self government." He also felt that the Court's decision did not sufficiently protect private persons from defamation. He concluded that that the states should be "essentially free to continue the evolution of the common law of defamation" using any standard other than strict liability.

The *Gertz* Case

It was in this confused legal context that Elmer Gertz brought his suit. Gertz, a lawyer, had represented the family of a murder victim in civil litigation against the murderer, a Chicago policeman named Richard Nuccio. The respondent's magazine, *American Opinion*, then

printed a story titled "FRAME-UP: Richard Nuccio and The War On Police." The story alleged that Gertz was part of a conspiracy to overthrow the police, in order to clear the way for a communist dictatorship. The article presented several falsehoods: that Gertz had a police file, that he was involved in Marxist organizations, that he was a Leninist. The managing editor of the magazine did not fact-check the article.

Gertz sued for libel in district court. Robert Welch, Inc., first moved to dismiss the complaint, as it did not make a specific claim for damages. The court ruled that Gertz need not claim special damages as the case involved libel *per se*. The respondent then filed a motion for summary judgment, claiming that Gertz was a public figure and that the article involved a matter of public concern. The district court dismissed the motion for summary judgment, but apparently agreed with the respondent that the *New York Times* standard applied for the reasons given. The burden was therefore on Gertz to show that the respondent had acted with actual malice.

In the trial, the court decided that because Gertz was not a public figure, the respondent was not protected, despite the fact that the article was on a matter of public interest. But after a jury awarded $50,000 to Gertz, the court reconsidered and ruled for the respondent, deciding that discussion of public speech was indeed protected.

The court of appeals, to which Gertz turned next, considered *Rosenbloom v. Metromedia, Inc.* (1971), a precedent for protecting any media presentation of a matter of public interest, not just those involving public figures. Because Gertz failed to present any evidence of actual malice, the court upheld the district court's ruling. The case then proceeded to the Supreme Court.

A Balance

The Court faced the same general problem here as in *Rosenbloom:* how to strike a balance between freedom of speech and of the press, on one hand, and the rights of the individual, on the other. Justice Powell, writing for the majority, laid out the dangers:

> Although the erroneous statement of fact is not worthy of constitutional protection, it is nevertheless inevitable in free debate . . . And the punishment of error runs the risk of inducing a cautious and restrictive exercise of the constitutionally guaranteed freedoms of speech and press . . . Allowing the media to avoid liability only by proving the truth of all injurious statements does not accord adequate protection to First Amendment liberties.

On the other hand, the state does have an interest in protecting the individual from wrongful injury by the press.

Rejecting the possibility that courts proceed on a case-by-case basis, the Court laid out some guidelines. Echoing Harlan in his *Rosenbloom* dissent, the Court noted that 1) private individuals cannot so easily rebut defamatory statements and 2) they have not voluntarily put themselves in the public eye, and thus do not willingly assume the risk of defamation. Therefore, "private individuals are not only more vulnerable to injury than public officials and public figures; they are also more deserving of recovery."

The Court repudiated *Rosenbloom*'s "public or general interest" test, claiming that it did not serve either side of the dispute. It did not adequately protect private individuals, but neither did it protect the media in cases in which the subject matter was not considered to be of public interest. And, again recalling a dissent in *Rosenbloom,* the Court noted Marshall's warning that the courts should not decide what information people need to govern themselves.

The Court left it to the states to define an appropriate standard of liability, as long as it was not strict liability. States might award damages in the absence of actual malice, but the Court set a limit: In cases using a standard less stringent than *New York Times,* plaintiffs could recover compensation only for actual injury. Juries would not be permitted to award punitive damages.

Gertz Not a Public Figure

Last, the Court addressed the respondent's argument that Gertz was in fact either a public figure or a public official. In the Court's view, he was neither. Unless all lawyers were regarded as "public officials," Gertz clearly did not belong in that category. As to the "public figure" designation, the Court identified two types: all-purpose and limited-purpose. The all-purpose public figure was famous (or notorious) in all contexts. The limited-purpose public figure was well-known, either voluntarily or not, in the context of one particular public controversy. Despite the fact that Gertz was active in professional organizations and civic groups, he was not well-known enough to qualify as a public figure.

The Court therefore reversed the lower court's ruling. The *New York Times* standard did not apply in this case. The original jury award of $50,000 had to be reconsidered, though, because the jury had imposed strict liability.

Impact

In *Gertz* the Court attempted to formulate a test to identify public figures. Lower courts have not been able to discern a clear precedent, though, particularly for the limited-purpose public figure. They have thus produced inconsistent and unpredictable judgments regarding who is a public figure. The effect is a press unsure of its protection when commenting on certain individuals, resulting perhaps in some self-censorship.

Related Cases

New York Times v. Sullivan, 376 U.S. 254 (1964).
Curtis Publishing Co. v. Butts, 388 U.S. 130 (1967).
Rosenbloom v. Metromedia, 403 U.S. 29 (1971).

Bibliography and Further Reading

Eaton, Joel D. "The American Law of Defamation Through *Gertz v. Robert Welch, Inc.* and Beyond: An Analytical Primer." *Virginia Law Review,* Vol. 61, no. 5, 1975, pp. 1350-1364.

Gifis, Steven H. *Law Dictionary,* 4th ed. Hauppauge, NY: Barron's, 1996.

Hall, Kermit L., ed. *The Oxford Companion to the Supreme Court.* New York: Oxford University Press, 1992.

Walton, Mark D. "The Public Figure Doctrine: A Reexamination of Gertz v. Robert Welch, Inc. in Light of Lower Federal Court Public Figure Formulations." *Northern Illinois Law Review,* Vol. 16, no. 1, 1995, pp. 141-173.

BIGELOW V. VIRGINIA

Legal Citation: 421 U.S. 809 (1975)

Appellant
Jeffrey C. Bigelow

Appellee
Commonwealth of Virginia

Appellant's Claim
That the Virginia statute banning abortion advertising under which he was convicted was an unconstitutional violation of his First Amendment rights.

Chief Lawyers for Appellant
Melvin L. Wulf and John C. Lowe

Chief Lawyer for Appellee
D. Patrick Lacy, Jr.

Justices for the Court
Harry A. Blackmun (writing for the Court), William J. Brennan, Jr., Warren E. Burger, William O. Douglas, Thurgood Marshall, Lewis F. Powell, Jr., Potter Stewart

Justices Dissenting
William H. Rehnquist, Byron R. White

Place
Washington, D.C.

Date of Decision
16 June 1975

Decision
Reversed Virginia Supreme Court decision upholding Bigelow's conviction for running an abortion advertisement in the newspaper he managed.

Significance
In *Bigelow v. Virginia*, the U.S. Supreme Court ruled that advertisements for abortion services and clinics were forms of expression protected by the First Amendment guarantee of freedom of speech and press. Prior to this ruling, which came two years after *Roe v. Wade*, (1973) it was not uncommon for states to restrict such advertising, even if it was for services in another state.

Jeffrey C. Bigelow was managing editor of the *Virginia Weekly*, a newspaper based in Charlottesville. In February of 1971 the paper ran an advertisement for the Women's Pavilion, a New York organization that helped women find abortion services. At the time, a Virginia statute was in effect making it a misdemeanor to "encourage or prompt the procuring of abortion." As the ad itself stated, abortions were legal in New York at the time, and there was no residency requirement for obtaining one in that state. Bigelow was tried and convicted for violating the state law.

Appealing the conviction, Bigelow's attorneys argued that the Virginia statute was a violation of his First Amendment right to freedom of the press. The law was also, according to Bigelow, overbroad, and therefore unconstitutional on those grounds as well. It is interesting to note that shortly after Bigelow's conviction, but long before it was overturned, the law was changed to apply only to abortions performed illegally in Virginia. Therefore the issue of the statute's overbroadness became moot.

The Virginia Supreme Court upheld Bigelow's conviction, ruling that because his activity "was of a purely commercial nature," it was not protected by the First Amendment. It also held that the statute was a proper consumer protection measure. In so ruling, the Virginia Supreme Court relied on a precedent it had set 25 years earlier that distinguished between protected speech and "commercial speech." First outlined in 1942 in the case *Valentine v. Chrestensen*, the Court's prevailing attitude was that commercial speech did not enjoy First Amendment protection because it had more to do with economic inducement than with the free and open exchange of ideas.

In considering *Bigelow*, the U.S. Supreme Court began to rethink its position on the distinction between protected and commercial speech in light of recent developments. A major factor was the general expansion of First Amendment freedoms that had taken place during the 1970s. More important, however, was the fact that the Court had recently decided *Roe v. Wade*, (1973) which made abortion a constitutionally protected right. With *Roe v. Wade* still fresh in the collective American mind, the Court ruled that since the advertisement in the *Virginia Weekly* conveyed truthful information about a matter of significant public interest, it merited First Amendment protection. In a 7-2 vote the Court overturned Bigelow's conviction and invalidated the Virginia law on which he was tried.

Writing for the majority, Justice Blackmun noted that:

> Advertising, like all public expression, may be subject to reasonable regulations that serve a legitimate public interest. To the extent that commercial activity is subject to regulation, the relationship of speech to that activity may be one factor, among others, to be considered in weighing the First Amendment interest against the governmental interest alleged. Advertising is not thereby stripped of all First Amendment protection. The relationship of speech to the marketplace of products or of services does not make it valueless in the marketplace of ideas . . .

In other words, an advertisement may have something of value to offer beyond its use as an attempt to get somebody to buy something. If it does, then it is entitled to First Amendment protection.

Dissenting, Justices Rehnquist and White did not subscribe to this reasoning. To them, commercial speech was commercial speech, regardless of whether it was about abortions or cattle feed. The state of Virginia therefore had every right to regulate the advertisement. In his dissenting opinion, Rehnquist wrote that the ad in the *Weekly* was "a classic commercial proposition directed towards the exchange of services rather than the exchange of ideas." Under earlier rulings, the ad was therefore entitled only to "the limited constitutional protection traditionally accorded commercial advertising."

Impact

Bigelow was an important link in the chain of decisions that broadened the constitutional protection afforded to commercial speech. The following year, the Court formalized that protection in *Virginia State Board of Pharmacy v. Virginia Citizens Consumer Council* (1976). The concepts addressed in *Bigelow* were extended further by *Carey v. Population Services International* (1997), in which the Court struck down a New York law prohibiting the advertising and sale of contraceptives to minors. As a result of these and other subsequent decisions, commercial speech now occupies a special niche as a "quasi-protected" form of expression.

Related Cases

Valentine v. Chrestensen, 316 U.S. 52 (1942).

Roe v. Wade, 413 U.S. 113 (1973).

Virginia State Board of Pharmacy v. Virginia Citizens Consumer Council, 425 U.S. 748 (1976).

Carey v. Population Services International, 431 U.S. 678 (1977).

Bibliography and Further Reading

Craig, Barbara H., and David M. O'Brien. *Abortion and American Politics*. New York: Chatham House, 1993.

Crawford, Alan Pell. "One Hand Clapping." *ADWEEK Eastern Edition,* July 12, 1993, p. 22.

Hall, Kermit L., ed., *Oxford Companion to the Supreme Court of the United States*. Oxford University Press, 1992.

New York Times. June 17, 1975.

GREER V. SPOCK

Legal Citation: 424 U.S. 828 (1976)

Petitioner
Commander Greer, Fort Dix Military Reservation

Respondents
Benjamin Spock, M.D., Julius Hobson, Linda Jenness, Andrew Pulley, et al.

Petitioner's Claim
That the Court should overturn two lower courts' rulings, which had forbidden him to interfere with candidates of the People's Party and the Socialist Workers Party as they distributed literature and held political meetings in areas of Fort Dix that were open to the public.

Chief Lawyer for Petitioner
Robert H. Bork, U.S. Solicitor General

Chief Lawyer for Respondents
David Kairys

Justices for the Court
Harry A. Blackmun, Warren E. Burger, Lewis F. Powell, Jr., William H. Rehnquist, Potter Stewart (writing for the Court), Byron R. White

Justices Dissenting
William J. Brennan, Jr., Thurgood Marshall, (John Paul Stevens did not participate)

Place
Washington, D.C.

Date of Decision
24 March 1976

Decision
The lower courts' injunctions were reversed, so that Commander Greer was free to ban pamphleteering and political meetings from the base if he so chose. He was not allowed to discriminate among candidates based on their political views, but he was permitted to ban some candidates if he thought they might threaten military discipline.

Significance
In this ruling, the Court promoted the notion that the First Amendment does not apply to areas that are not "public forums." The case greatly limited the political freedom of military personnel, while certifying the power of military officers to regulate the bases they command.

In 1972, U.S. involvement in the Vietnam War was still in full swing. Political protestors of all types attempted to mobilize public opinion against the war. One of the best-known opponents of the war was Benjamin Spock, M.D., whose book on baby and child care had helped to raise a generation.

Spock had become so deeply opposed to the war that he was running for president on a protest ticket sponsored by the People's Party, along with vice-presidential candidate Julius Hobson. The Socialist Workers Party, a small but very visible left-wing group, was also running a national ticket with an antiwar theme, offering Linda Jenness for president and Andrew Pulley for vice president.

Spock, Hobson, Jenness, and Pulley did not want to preach to just the converted, they wanted their message of peace to reach the very men who were being trained to fight in Vietnam. So on 9 September 1972, they wrote a joint letter to Major General Bert A. David, then commanding officer of Fort Dix, telling him that they were planning to come onto the base on 23 September to hand out campaign literature and hold a meeting to discuss election issues.

Fort Dix was a base devoted primarily to basic training for newly inducted army personnel. However, many areas of the base were open to the public, and civilians came onto the base at all hours. The base also housed the husbands and wives of soldiers and other army staff. The four antiwar activists wanted to reach this community.

A Military Mission

On 18 September, the candidates' request was denied. General David wrote a letter explaining his reasoning:

> The mission assigned to me . . . is to administer basic combat training to approximately 15,000 men at any given time. These men spend a period of eight weeks here during which they perform their training on very vigorous schedules occupying virtually all of their time . . . Political campaigning on Fort Dix cannot help but interfere with our training and other military missions.

Benjamin Spock speaks at a meeting, 1968. © AP/Wide World Photos.

Besides the possible disruptive effect, Dix had another reason for refusing to allow the People's Party or the Socialist Workers Party onto the base:

> To decide otherwise could also give the appearance that you or your campaign is supported by me in my official capacity. I feel that I am prohibited from doing this for any candidate for public office.

A Long Court Battle

Spock and his companions did not take this refusal lying down. On 29 September 1972, they went to court for the right to engage in political activity on the base. They asked the court to enjoin the commander from interfering with their campaign. The district court did not agree, but the court of appeals did. That court issued an injunction, which allowed Spock to conduct a campaign rally at a Fort Dix parking lot on 4 November 1972. Later court decisions seemed to further affirm the public's right to make political speeches or to distribute leaflets in areas of the base open to the public.

The various commanders of Fort Dix were also unwilling to give in. They too appealed, and the case eventually went to the Supreme Court. There, the Court

took the side of the commanders, affirming their right to decide what kind of political activity took place on their base.

To decide what kind of political activity can happen on a base, the Court had to define what kind of place a base was. If it was an ordinary public place, political activity there would be protected by the First Amendment, but as Justice Stewart wrote in the Court's majority opinion, the Court did not consider Fort Dix a public place:

> Since under the Constitution it is the basic function of a military installation like Fort Dix to train soldiers, not to provide a public forum, and since, as a necessary concomitant to this basic function, a commanding officer has the historically unquestioned power to exclude civilians from the area of his command, any notion that federal military installations, like municipal streets and parks, have traditionally served as a place for free public assembly and communication of thoughts by private citizens is false, and therefore respondents had no generalized constitutional right to make political speeches or distribute leaflets at Fort Dix.

Discrimination or Not?

The Court had approved the regulations that gave the commander the right to exclude civilians from the base. In the majority's view, the commander had acted fairly. He had said that no political candidate could speak or hold a meeting on the base. In the Court's view, that was fair and therefore, constitutional.

Justice Powell added that the Fort Dix regulations did allow "conventional political campaign literature." It might seem that to allow Democrats and Republicans to give out literature, while forbidding such freedom to the People's Party and the Socialist Workers Party, would be a kind of discrimination against certain types of speech, but Powell said that because of the special nature of the military, the Constitution did allow a base commander to exercise his judgment in that way. Although a commander could not "prevent distribution of a publication simply because he does not like its contents" or because it was "critical—even unfairly critical—of government policies or officials," he could prevent distribution of literature that he perceived "to be a clear danger to the loyalty, discipline, or morale of troops on the base under his command."

A Dissenting View

Justices Brennan and Marshall completely disagreed with the majority opinion. In their view, much of Fort Dix was a public place. Civilians came onto the base at all hours of the day and night, eating and talking freely with the recruits. Access to the base was so easy that there had been problems with muggings and prostitution. Moreover, said the dissenters, there was no basis for believing that distributing leaflets or having a meeting would impair the government's ability to train recruits or to maintain a national defense. Additonally, the fact that all types of political rallies had been excluded was no excuse. "An evenhanded exclusion of all public expression would no more pass muster than an evenhanded exclusion of all Roman Catholics," wrote Justice Brennan.

In the dissenters' view, the only thing that could justify the suppression of free speech on Fort Dix was the threat of a clear and present danger resulting from that speech. The dissenting justices did not see how such danger could result from peaceful leafleting or a campaign rally.

The case of *Spock v. Greer* has had severe consequences for the kinds of speech allowed or not allowed in military settings. The Court relied on this case to uphold Air Force, Navy, and Marine Corps regulations requiring service members to get permission from their commanders before they themselves could circulate petitions on their bases. *Greer* has also been used to define other arenas as "non-public" places where it is therefore permissible to restrict speech.

Related Cases
Rescue Army v. Municipal Court of City of Los Angeles, 331 U.S. 549 (1947).
United States ex rel. Toth v. Quarles, 350 U.S. 11 (1955).
Cafeteria Workers v. McElroy, 367 U.S. 886 (1961).
Adderley v. Florida, 385 U.S. 39 (1966).
Flower v. United States, 407 U.S. 197 (1972).
Houchins v. KQED, 438 U.S. 1 (1978).

Bibliography and Further Reading
"High Court Limits Military Rights." *New York Times,* 25 March 1976, p. 29.

Werhan, Keither. "The Supreme Court's public forum doctrine and the return of formalism." *Cardozo Law Review,* Vol. 7, no. 2, winter 1986, pp. 335-437.

VIRGINIA STATE BOARD OF PHARMACY V. VIRGINIA CITIZENS CONSUMER COUNCIL, INC.

Legal Citation: 425 U.S. 748 (1976)

Appellant
Virginia State Board of Pharmacy

Appellee
Virginia Citizens Consumer Council, Inc.

Chief Lawyer for Appellant
Anthony F. Troy

Chief Lawyer for Appellee
Alan B. Morrison

Justices for the Court
Harry A. Blackmun (writing for the Court), William J. Brennan, Jr., Warren E. Burger, Thurgood Marshall, Lewis F. Powell, Jr., Potter Stewart, Byron R. White

Justices Dissenting
William H. Rehnquist (John Paul Stevens did not participate)

Place
Washington, D.C.

Date of Decision
24 May 1976

Decision
The state of Virginia's statute making it "unprofessional conduct" for a pharmacist to dispense information on the price of prescription drugs was deemed unconstitutional, and the Virginia State Board of Pharmacy was enjoined from enforcing that portion of its professional code.

Significance
Certain types of commercial communication involving the conveyance of information about products or services are protected by the First Amendment to the U.S. Constitution.

The practice of pharmacy is regulated in Virginia by the State Board of Pharmacy (VSBP), which among its duties serves as a licensing body and promulgator of professional codes of conduct for pharmacists. Only licensed pharmacists may dispense prescription drugs in the state. In 1968, the board added to its code of conduct a clause stipulating that it would constitute unprofessional conduct for pharmacists to advertise information regarding the prices to be charged for prescription drugs.

The new clause was immediately challenged in Virginia state court by a retail drug manufacturer and one of its corporate pharmacists on the basis of a possible violation of the Due Process and Equal Protection Clauses of the Fourteenth Amendment, but the court upheld the statute and no appeal of the case was ever made.

In 1974 the Virginia Citizens Consumer Council, Inc. (VCCC), a nonprofit organization with many members who were regular purchasers of prescription drugs, joined another nonprofit organization and a private citizen resident in Virginia to bring suit in the U.S. District Court for the Eastern District of Virginia against the Virginia State Board of Pharmacy's prohibition against the advertising of prescription drug prices by pharmacists. This time the argument against the VSBP centered on its possible violation of the First Amendment right to free speech, and the district court held in favor of VCCC and enjoined the state from enforcing that portion of its pharmacy licensing statutes. The VCBP appealed the case to the U.S. Supreme Court, which heard arguments on 11 November 1975.

Attorneys for the VCCC argued that the organization's members were prevented from obtaining useful information that was not subject to interpretation of misrepresentation by the VSBP prohibition against advertisement of prescription drug prices by pharmacists. The state countered that so-called "commercial speech" is not protected by the First Amendment, since advertising and other corporate communications to the public must adhere to standards of truthfulness not applicable to other forms of speech. The State also maintained that excessive price competition could lead to the erosion of professionalism among pharmacists, who might be tempted to cut corners to reduce the amount of time spent in compounding and dispensing prescription medications.

On 24 May 1976, the U.S. Supreme Court decided in favor of the VCCC and upheld the injunction barring the state of Virginia from enforcing its prohibition of advertising prescription drug prices by pharmacists. Writing for the Court, Justice Blackmun stated that certain types of commercial communication were protected by the First Amendment, since "society may have a strong interest in the free flow of commercial communication," and "advertising, however tasteless and excessive it may seem, is nonetheless dissemination of information." Against this public need for consumer information, the state posed its need to ensure high standards of professional practice and conduct among pharmacists. While noting that the state's justifications could not be "entirely discounted," the Court replied that "the strength of these proffered justifications is greatly undermined by the fact that high professional standards, to a substantial extent, are guaranteed by the close regulation to which pharmacists in Virginia are subject." The Court also further stated that, while commercial speech is somewhat protected by the First Amendment, it must always remain subject to greater state scrutiny and regulation than other forms of speech. In the final analysis, the Court saw the issue as one of allowing the state to completely "suppress the dissemination of concededly truthful information about entirely lawful activity," which it could not allow on constitutional grounds. The lone dissenter, Justice Rehnquist, maintained that the First Amendment had been extended by the decision, since the state did not bar pharmacists from giving out price information to those who inquired, only from advertising. He also objected to the decision on the ground that there is a substantial social interest in decreasing dependency on drugs to cure "every ill, real or imaginary."

Justice Rehnquist's dissent underscores the importance of this decision, which did apply First Amendment protection to commercial speech more broadly than previously.

Related Cases

Williamson v. Lee Optical Co., 348 U.S. 483 (1955).
Bolger v. Youngs Drug Products Corp., 463 U.S. 60 (1983).
44 Liquormart Inc. v. Rhode Island, 116 S. Ct. 1495 (1996).

Bibliography and Further Reading

Cook, Don Lloyd. "Earthquakes and Aftershocks." *Journal of Public Policy & Marketing,* Spring 1998, pp. 116.

Garner, Donald W. "Banning Tobacco Billboards: The Case for Municipal Action." *The Journal of the American Medical Association,* April 24, 1996, pp. 1263.

Freedom of Speech and the U.S. Supreme Court. San Diego: Excellent Books, 1996.

Klinkner, Philip A. *The First Amendment.* Englewood Cliffs, NJ: Silver Burdett Press, 1991.

Langvardt, Arlen W., and Eric L. Richards. "The Death of Posadas and the Birth of Change in Commercial Speech Doctrine." *American Business Law Journal,* Summer 1997, pp. 483.

Reed, O. Lee. "Is Commerical Speech Really Less Valuable than Political Speech?" *American Business Law Journal,* Fall 1996, pp. 1.

Richards, Jef I. "Is 44 Liquormart a Turning Point?" *Journal of Public Policy & Marketing,* Spring 1997, pp. 156.

BATES V. STATE BAR OF ARIZONA

Legal Citation: 433 U.S. 350 (1977)

Appellants
John R. Bates, Van O'Steen

Appellee
State Bar of Arizona

Appellants' Claim
That state rules prohibiting lawyers from advertising violate the Sherman Antitrust Act by restraining trade, and violate the First Amendment by inhibiting free speech.

Chief Lawyer for Appellants
William C. Canby, Jr.

Chief Lawyer for Appellee
John P. Frank

Justices for the Court
Harry A. Blackmun (writing for the Court), William J. Brennan, Jr., Thurgood Marshall, Jr., John Paul Stevens, Byron R. White

Justices Dissenting
Warren E. Burger, Lewis F. Powell, William H. Rehnquist, Potter Stewart

Place
Washington, D.C.

Date of Decision
27 June 1977

Decision
Although the U.S. Supreme Court disregarded the petitioner's antitrust claim, citing their right of free speech, as well as the public's right to receive their message concerning competitive legal fees, the Court ruled in favor of lawyers John Bates and Van O'Steen.

Significance
By emphasizing the public's right to know about legal fees, the Court opened the profession up to greater competition and added to the development of the commercial speech doctrine, which extends some First Amendment protections to advertising.

John Bates and Van O'Steen were attorneys licensed to practice law in the state of Arizona. Together, they opened a legal clinic in Phoenix, and by accepting only a limited range of uncomplicated cases and making extensive use of such cost-saving measures as paralegal support and standardized legal forms, they were able to provide legal services for modest fees. After two years, they decided that their practice would only survive if they advertised their fees to the community. In doing so, however, they violated a state bar disciplinary rule—included in the rules of the Arizona Supreme Court—prohibiting lawyers from publicizing themselves commercially. The State Bar's Board of Governors responded by recommending that both Bates and O'Steen be suspended from the practice of law for a week. After the Arizona Supreme Court upheld their suspension, the two lawyers appealed this ruling directly to the U.S. Supreme Court.

Justice Blackmun, writing for the Court, had no trouble dispensing with Bates and O'Steen's argument that the Arizona disciplinary rule prohibiting lawyer advertising was an illegal restraint of trade. The Sherman Antitrust Act, which the appellants cited to support this proposition, did not apply to their case, as the disciplinary rule was an act of a sovereign state government which was not subject to federal regulation. The First Amendment argument, however, proved convincing.

Commercial Speech Doctrine Extended to Lawyer Advertising

A year earlier, in *Virginia State Board of Pharmacy v. Virginia Citizens Consumer Council* (1976), the Court had decided its first landmark commercial speech case. Justice Blackmun, who also wrote the opinion of the Court in the earlier case, had declared unconstitutional a statute barring advertising of prescription drug prices. The commercial speech doctrine provides that advertisements which convey valuable information to consumers merit some First Amendment protection. Such protection does not extend, however, to advertising that is false or misleading; unlike ordinary speech, commercial speech is subject to content regulation.

Bates extended the ruling in *Virginia State Board of Pharmacy* to attorney advertising. As in the earlier

Advertising Lawyers

Lawyer advertising provides customers with information about legal services, legal rights, and a direct means of finding an attorney. The advertising must be truthful, not misleading or deceptive in any way. Phone directories, newspapers, newsletters, radio, television, and Internet homepages are all considered appropriate media. Advertising standards are based on the American Bar Association's (ABA) Moral Code of Professional Responsibility. States can develop their own guidelines based on these standards.

A 1990 study by the ABA's Commission on Advertising concerning lawyer's perceptions about advertising acceptability showed variations by age groups. Of those younger than 35 years of age, 85 percent said

print and TV ads were acceptable *under certain conditions*. However, of those over 55, only 48 percent approved print and 65 percent television.

In a 1993 Gallup Poll commissioned by the ABA, 61 percent of respondents indicated their firms participated in at least one method of advertising. In 1993 lawyers spent $419 million on yellow page ads compared to $120 million on television.

Source(s): American Bar Association, *Lawyer Advertising at the Crossroads: Professional Policy Considerations.* Chicago: American Bar Association, Commission on Advertising, 1995.

case, the First Amendment protection afforded was limited.

> In holding that advertising by attorneys may not be subjected to blanket suppression, and that the advertisement at issue is protected, we, of course, do not hold that advertising by attorneys may not be regulated in any way . . . Advertising that is false, deceptive, or misleading of course is subject to restraint . . . In fact, because the public lacks sophistication concerning legal services, misstatements that might be overlooked or deemed unimportant in other advertising may be found quite inappropriate in legal advertising . . . As with other varieties of speech, it follows as well that there may be reasonable restrictions on the time, place, and manner of advertising.

The Court approved a "time, place, and manner" restriction the very next year in *Ohralik v. Ohio State Bar Association* (1978), in which a policy of barring all in-person solicitation by lawyers was upheld.

The concern expressed by the Arizona State Bar Association in *Bates* was that attorney advertising would have an adverse effect on professionalism. It was the same concern expressed by the Virginia Bar Association in *Goldfarb v. Virginia State Bar* (1975) two years earlier, when the Supreme Court prohibited the bar association from mandating a fee schedule. Just as Chief Justice Burger dismissed such concerns in *Goldfarb,* so Blackmun dismissed them in *Bates*. It was anachronistic to assert that lawyers are somehow above the "trade," he wrote, when the ban on advertising was apparently based on an antique British rule of etiquette and not on any ethical considerations. When bar associations object that price competition among lawyers will cut

into the quality of lawyering, they are advancing a disingenuous argument in an attempt to perpetuate the comprehensive self-regulation the profession had enjoyed for so long. With *Bates,* however, consumers were given access to important information that would

Justice Harry A. Blackmun. © Archive Photos.

help them to decide which lawyers were worth their money.

Related Cases

Goldfarb v. Virginia State Bar, 421 U.S. 773 (1975).
Virginia State Board of Pharmacy v. Virginia Citizens Consumer Council, 425 U.S. 748 (1976).
Ohralik v. Ohio Bar Association, 436 U.S. 447 (1978).

Bibliography and Further Reading

Advertising and Commercial Speech. Westport, CT: Meckler, 1990.

Andrews, Lori B. *Birth of a Salesman: Lawyer Advertising and Solicitation,* rev. ed. Chicago: ABA Press, 1981.

Fulkerson, Jennifer. "When Lawyers Advertise." *American Demographics,* June 1995, p. 54.

Hill, Louisa L. *Lawyer Advertising.* Westport, CT: Quorum, 1993.

Johnson, John W. *Historic U.S. Court Cases, 1690–1990: An Encyclopedia.* New York: Garland Publishing, 1992.

Resnick, Rosalind. "Florida Soliciting Rule Struck Down." *The National Law Journal,* January 18, 1993, p. 3.

FEDERAL COMMUNICATIONS COMMISSION V. PACIFICA FOUNDATION

Legal Citation: 438 U.S. 726 (1978)

Petitioner
Federal Communications Commission

Respondent
Pacifica Foundation, et al.

Petitioner's Claim
That "patently offensive," although not necessarily obscene, speech should be subject to federal regulation.

Chief Lawyer for Petitioner
Joseph A. Marino

Chief Lawyer for Respondent
Harry M. Plotkin

Justices for the Court
Harry A. Blackmun, Warren E. Burger, Lewis F. Powell, Jr., William H. Rehnquist, John Paul Stevens (writing for the Court)

Justices Dissenting
William J. Brennan, Jr., Thurgood Marshall, Potter Stewart, Byron R. White

Place
Washington, D.C.

Date of Decision
3 July 1978

Decision
Upheld the Federal Communications Commission (FCC), overturning a court of appeals ruling that speech can only be regulated when it is obscene or has "prurient appeal."

Significance
This ruling established the authority of the FCC to regulate the broadcast of "indecent" material, restricting such broadcasts to hours of the day when children would be unlikely to be in the audience. In its decision the Court also defined broadcast obscenity as "language that describes, in terms patently offensive as measured by contemporary community standards for the broadcast medium, sexual or excretory activities or organs."

Obscene or Offensive Speech

Throughout the history of the United States, tension has existed between the right of free expression and the tastes of individuals and groups. The difficulty of defining objectionable speech is readily apparent, for, as Justice John Marshall Harlan observed, "one man's vulgarity is another man's lyric." Despite its intractability, the question of exactly what comprises obscene or offensive speech lies at the heart of many court decisions surrounding First Amendment rights. Further complicating questions of objectionable speech is the proliferation of broadcast technology and the resulting pervasiveness of speech of all forms. Generally speaking, the Supreme Court has ruled that most types of speech are fully protected from censorship, although a few exceptions have been made. Libelous speech and false advertising, for instance, are not protected from censorship. Sounding of false alarms (such as yelling "fire!" in a crowded theater) or "fighting words" as defined in *Chaplinsky v. New Hampshire* (1942), are also forms of speech that are subject to government regulation. Short of these examples, however, lies a vast grey area of speech that is protected to some degree. Speech that could be construed as obscene falls into this latter category, with obscenity defined by the Court in *Miller v. California* (1973) as speech that

> (1) the average person, applying contemporary community standards, would find, taken as a whole, to appeal to a prurient interest; (2) depicts or describes in a patently offensive way sexual conduct specifically defined by state law; (3) lacks serious literary, artistic, political, or scientific value.

Filthy Words

Given the subjectiveness of the criteria for determining whether or not speech is patently offensive, it is not surprising that many performers and broadcasters have intentionally used speech that could be considered offensive in an effort to be entertaining. "Filthy Words," a monologue performed by comedian George Carlin in the early 1970s is a magnificent example of this type of entertainment. In this monologue Carlin listed seven words that he categorized as "the words

Freedom to Broadcast

The Supreme Court clearly extended First Amendment protections to the electronic media of radio and television. However, since these media can only operate over a limited number of public airways or frequencies, the government may regulate them to assure operational effectiveness and public benefit. Such limitations are considered prior restraint in the print media and not allowed.

Congress created the Federal Communications Commission (FCC) to implement its regulations over broadcasting. The FCC issues licenses to broadcast over specific airways, requires broadcasters to provide coverage of public interest issues, and prohibits certain language on the air. Licenses must be awarded neutrally so as not to favor one broadcaster's views over another's.

In the 1940s, the FCC developed a policy known as the "fairness doctrine." The doctrine required broadcasters to provide the opportunity for an individual whose views or records were attacked on air to respond. However, in 1987 the FCC voted to discard the doctrine. In two rulings in the 1970s the Court held that airing all views was not possible. Broadcasters retained the discretion of which views to air. Despite legal challenges, the FCC maintains authority to restrict hours during which offensive programming may be aired.

Source(s): Hindman, Elizabeth B. *Rights vs. Responsibilities: The Supreme Court and the Media.* Westport, CT: Greenwood Press, 1997.

you can't say, that you're not supposed to say all the time." He then proceeded to use these words repeatedly in a number of humorous contexts throughout the remainder of the performance. Given Carlin's prominence at the time, "Filthy Words" was recorded and distributed to radio stations across the United States.

Patently Offensive Language Hits the Fan

On 30 October 1973, at approximately 2:00 p.m., a New York City radio station owned by the Pacifica Foundation aired "Filthy Words" in its entirety. Among the listeners to the program were a motorist and his young son. The motorist strongly objected to the content of "Filthy Words," and sent a written complaint to the FCC within a few weeks of the broadcast. The FCC forwarded the complaint to the Pacifica Foundation, which responded that the monologue had been played as part of a serious examination of changing attitudes toward language, and that before the program listeners had been warned that it included "sensitive language which might be regarded as offensive to some." The Pacifica Foundation also advanced the view that George Carlin was a significant social satirist who used the potentially offensive language to "satirize as harmless and essentially silly our attitudes toward those words." The FCC ruled on the matter on 21 February 1975, finding in favor of the complainant and stating that the Pacifica Foundation could have been "the subject of administrative sanctions." The legal basis for the FCC's decision rested in 18 U.S.C. 1464 (1976) (hereinafter referred to as 1464), which forbids use of "any obscene, indecent, or profane language by means of radio communications," and 47 U.S.C. 303, which requires the FCC to "encourage the larger and more effective use of radio in the public interest." Finally, the FCC advanced

the position that it did not seek to prohibit the use of patently offensive speech but only to restrict its use to those times of day when it was unlikely that children would be in the audience.

Legal Proceedings

The Pacifica Foundation appealed the FCC ruling to the three judge panel of the U.S. Court of Appeals for the District of Columbia Circuit. By a 2-1 count the court of appeals reversed the FCC decision. The two judges favoring reversal were divided in their view of the case. Judge Tamm felt that the FCC had acted in violation of section 326 of the Communications Act, which forbids censorship. Chief Judge Bazelon observed that 326 does not cover language as described in 1464, but concurred in the decision due to his feeling that the provisions of 1464 should be interpreted more narrowly than was done in this case. The FCC appealed the case to the Supreme Court, which heard arguments on 18 and 19 April 1978.

The Court delivered its decision on 3 July 1978, reversing the decision of the court of appeals and upholding the FCC's right to regulate the broadcast of patently offensive language. Justice Stevens, writing for the majority, viewed the case as hinging on three questions: whether the form of censorship suggested by the FCC violated 326; whether the monologue was indecent within the definitions set forth in 1464; and whether the FCC order against the Pacifica Foundation constituted a violation of the First Amendment. On the first question the Court concluded that 326 did not preclude the subsequent review of programming that had already aired, and that it was "perfectly clear" that 326 "was not intended to limit the Commission's power to regulate the broadcast of obscene, indecent, or profane

Should Stand-Up Comics Be Censored?

In 1964, Lenny Bruce was brought to trial for using obscene words during a stand-up routine. Whereas mainstream comedians of his era remain in the popular imagination chiefly for their jokes, Bruce, who died in 1966, is viewed as an avant-garde figure who stood for free speech.

But some would ask if Bruce stood for free speech or filthy speech. Using the standards adopted by the Supreme Court in later obscenity cases, was there any "redeeming social value" to Bruce's humor?

Defenders of Bruce, on the other hand—a group which includes a number of civil libertarians—would say that

the free speech of a foul-mouthed comedian is all the more to be protected precisely because it does offend many people. If a society can decide which types of free speech to protect, and which to let fall prey to censorship, who can say where the lines will be drawn? Perhaps the very religious groups who would be least likely to feel sympathetic toward a Lenny Bruce might find themselves the next target for censorship.

Source(s): Daniel, Clifton, ed. *Chronicle of the Twentieth Century.* Mt. Kisko, NY: Chronicle, 1987.

language." Similarly, the Court ruled that the language contained in "Filthy Words" did qualify as indecent within the parameters of 1464. Finally, the Court ruled that the FCC's sanction of the Pacifica Foundation did not constitute a violation of the First Amendment, citing a precedent in the case of *Red Lion Broadcasting Co. v. Federal Communications Commission* (1969). In *Red Lion* the Court ruled that individuals do not have a constitutional right to communicate by broadcasting, since the electromagnetic spectrum can accommodate only a finite number of transmission frequencies. As such broadcasters are required to act in the public interest, since they, in effect, must represent the views of all those unable to obtain a broadcasting license. In fact, the Court decided that the pervasive nature of broadcasting technology, which can project words and images into anyone's home, justified unique forms of regulation of potentially objectionable material. Despite the apparent decisiveness of the ruling, Justice Stevens took pains to narrow the context of the case. The limited nature of the FCC's action in the case, that is, to merely issue what amounted to a warning and suggest that similar programming should air at hours of the day when children were unlikely to be in the audience, was a factor in the decision, as was the obviously intentional offensiveness of "Filthy Words." In the final analysis, however, the actual degree of offensiveness was relatively unimportant:

> It is appropriate, in conclusion, to emphasize the narrowness of our holding . . . As Mr. Justice Sutherland wrote, 'a nuisance may merely be a right thing in a wrong place,—like a pig in a parlor instead of the barnyard.' *Euclid v. Ambler Realty Co.,* 272 U.S. 365, 388. We simply hold that when the Commission finds that a pig has entered a parlor, the exercise of its regulatory power does not depend on proof that the pig is obscene.

Impact

Federal Communications Commission v. Pacifica Foundation established the principle that indecent, as opposed to obscene, speech that is broadcast on the public airwaves is subject to some degree of regulation. The Court's reliance on the definition of obscenity set forth in *Miller v. California* solidified the use of that definition in adjudicating First Amendment cases. The problem of determining the exact extent of an individual's freedom of speech remains intractable, as the Court was clear that its decision rested on narrow grounds peculiar to this case, thereby severely constraining the applicability of *Federal Communications Commission v. Pacifica Foundation* as a legal precedent.

Related Cases

Chaplinsky v. New Hampshire, 315 U.S. 568 (1942).
Red Lion Broadcasting Co. v. Federal Communications Commission, 395 U.S. 367 (1969).
Miller v. California, 413 U.S. 15 (1973).
New York v. Ferber, 458 U.S. 747 (1982).

Bibliography and Further Reading

Berman, Jerry, and Daniel J. Weitzner. "Abundance and User Control." *Yale Law Journal,* May 1995, pp. 1619.

Biskupic, Joan, and Elder Witt, eds. *Guide to the U.S. Supreme Court,* 3rd ed. Washington: Congressional Quarterly Inc., 1990.

Gewirtz, Paul. "Constitutional Law and New Technology." *Social Research,* Fall 1997, pp. 1191.

Petrillo, Matthew. "High Court Appears Divided on CDA." *Business Insurance,* April 7, 1997, pp. 7.

Volokh, Eugene. "Freedom of Speech, Shielding Children, and Transcending Balancing." *Supreme Court Review,* Annual 1997, pp. 141.

COLLIN V. SMITH

Legal Citation: 447 F.Supp. 676 (1978)

Plaintiff
Albert Smith, President of the Village of Skokie, Illinois

Defendant
Frank Collin, on behalf of the National Socialist Party of America

Plaintiff's Claim
That Skokie had illegally prevented the American Nazis from holding a political march.

Chief Lawyer for Plaintiff
Gilbert Gordon, Harvey Schwartz

Chief Defense Lawyer
David A. Goldberger

Judge
U.S. District Court Judge Bernard M. Decker

Place
Chicago, Illinois

Date of Decision
2 December 1977

Decision
That Skokie could not prevent the Nazis from marching.

Significance
Despite the fact that the Nazis had deliberately chosen a heavily Jewish community to march in, the courts stuck firm to the First Amendment principle that unpopular groups must be allowed to express their political opinions.

Prior to World War II, there was a small yet fairly significant Nazi movement in the United States, which grew out of the German-American Bund. After the war, the movement was discredited, and survived only due to the leadership of George Lincoln Rockwell, who was assassinated in 1967. As with other fringe groups, such as the Ku Klux Klan, hatred and prejudice kept the National Socialist Party of America alive with a small but vocal membership. In the mid-1970s, to generate publicity and attract new members, Nazi leader Frank Collin targeted the Chicago, Illinois suburb of Skokie as a site for a series of marches and demonstrations.

Over half of Skokie's 70,000 residents were Jewish, and many were survivors of German concentration camps. Seeing Nazi marchers and the swastika was bound to bring back tragic memories. Skokie was initially successful in getting an injunction against any Nazi marches from the Illinois state courts, but the Supreme Court summarily dismissed the injunction as unconstitutionally infringing the Nazis' First Amendment right to political expression. Determined to protect its Jewish residents, on 2 May 1977, Skokie decided to thwart the Nazis by passing a series of municipal ordinances. The ordinances required any group wishing to stage a public demonstration to obtain $350,000 in liability and property insurance, and forbade the dissemination of racist literature and the wearing of military-style uniforms by group members during such demonstrations. The Nazis promptly took Albert Smith, president of the Village of Skokie, and other municipal officials to court.

Nazis Must be Allowed to March

Ironically, both sides were represented by Jewish attorneys. David A. Goldberger from the American Civil Liberties Union represented the Nazis; Gilbert Gordon and Harvey Schwartz represented Smith and Skokie. The case was heard before U.S. District Court Judge Bernard M. Decker in Chicago on 2 December 1977.

Collin was brutally honest about his party's beliefs. He stated that the Nazis believed blacks were inferior, and that Jews were involved in an international financial and communist conspiracy. Further, Collin testified that the Nazis deliberately copied the military uniform style of the notorious "Brownshirts" of Hitler's Third Reich:

> We wear brown shirts with a dark brown tie, a swastika pin on the tie, a leather shoulder strap, a black belt with buckle, dark brown trousers, black engineer boots, and either a steel helmet or a cloth cap, depending on the situation, plus a swastika arm band on the left arm and an American flag patch on the right arm.

On 23 February 1978 Decker issued his decision. Stating that "it is better to allow those who preach racial hate to expend their venom in rhetoric rather than to be panicked into embarking on the dangerous course of permitting the government to decide what its citizens may say and hear," Decker held that the ordinances violated the First Amendment and were unenforceable.

Skokie appealed to the U.S. Court of Appeals for the Seventh Circuit, and the case was argued on 14 April 1978. On 22 May 1978, the Seventh Circuit refused to overturn Decker's decision:

> No authorities need be cited to establish the proposition, which the Village does not dispute, that First Amendment rights are truly precious and fundamental to our national life. Nor is this truth without relevance to the saddening historical images this case inevitably arouses. It is, after all, in part the fact that our constitutional system protects minorities unpopular at a particular time or place from government harassment and intimidation, that distinguishes life in this country from life under the Third Reich.

Finally, Skokie asked the Supreme Court to review the case, a procedure called "petition for a writ of *certiorari.*" On 16 October 1978 the justices of the Supreme Court voted to deny *certiorari,* and so Decker's original decision was upheld. Justices Harry Blackmun and Byron White, however, dissented. Blackmun and White felt that the Court should make an official pronouncement on the important First Amendment issues in the Skokie litigation, and not just let the lower court decision stand by default:

> [We] feel that the present case affords the Court an opportunity to consider whether, in the context of the facts that this record appears to present, there is no limit whatsoever to the exercise of free speech. There indeed may be no such limit, but when citizens assert, not casually but with deep conviction, that the proposed demonstration is scheduled at a place and in a manner that is taunting and overwhelmingly offensive to the citizens of that place, that assertion, uncomfortable though it may be for judges, deserves to be examined. It just might fall into the same category as one's "right" to cry "fire" in a crowded theater, for "the character of every act depends upon the circumstances in which it is done." [Quoting *Schenck v. United States.*]

There was now nothing to prevent Collin and the Nazis, victorious in the courts, from marching in Skokie. Collin, however, abruptly called the march off. Declaring that his aim had been to generate "pure agitation to restore our right to free speech," Collin proclaimed the whole affair a moral victory for the Nazis and never marched in Skokie. Whether the Skokie affair was a victory for the Nazis is debatable, but it was certainly a victory for the right of every minority group, no matter how unpopular, to express its political views without government interference.

Related Cases

Schenck v. United States, 249 U.S. 47 (1919).
Hurley v. Irish American GLIB Association, 515 U.S. 557 (1995).

Bibliography and Further Reading

Bartlett, Jonathan. *The First Amendment in a Free Society.* New York: H.W. Wilson, 1979.

Downs, Donald Alexander. *Nazis in Skokie: Freedom, Community, and the First Amendment.* Notre Dame, IN: University of Notre Dame Press, 1985.

Gross, Alan. "I Remember Skokie: a Cultural Defense." *Chicago.* February 1981, pp. 90-97.

Hamlin, David. *The Nazi/Skokie Conflict: a Civil Liberties Battle.* Boston: Beacon Press, 1980.

Neier, Aryeh. *Defending My Enemy: American Nazis, the Skokie Case, and the Risks of Freedom.* New York: E.P. Dutton, 1979.

HERBERT V. LANDO

Legal Citation: 441 U.S. 153 (1979)

Petitioner
Anthony Herbert

Respondents
Barry Lando, et al.

Petitioner's Claim
In a libel suit, a plaintiff should have the right to discover and inquire into the editorial process and states of mind of those responsible for the publication, in order to meet plaintiff's burden of proving "actual malice."

Chief Lawyer for Petitioner
Jonathan W. Lubbell

Chief Lawyer for Respondents
Floyd Abrams

Justices for the Court
Harry A. Blackmun, William J. Brennan, Jr., Warren E. Burger, Lewis F. Powell, Jr., William H. Rehnquist, John Paul Stevens, Byron R. White (writing for the Court)

Justices Dissenting
Thurgood Marshall, Potter Stewart

Place
Washington, D.C.

Date of Decision
18 April 1979

Decision
The Court reversed the court of appeals and reinstated the district court's ruling. The Court held that defendants have no privilege under the First Amendment which would bar a plaintiff from inquiring into the editorial process or states of mind of those involved in the alleged libel, if the inquiry was tailored to the production of evidence considered material to plaintiff's necessary burden of proof.

Significance
This decision was an important one in a chain of appellate cases delineating the boundaries of the press's right to publish information about private and public figures, and the burden of a plaintiff in a defamation case. The Supreme Court, contrary to defendants' arguments, did not believe that allowing the plaintiff to pursue the requested discovery would have a "chilling effect" on the press, nor cause the press undue or extra costs in producing the evidence requested.

Significant Facts

Anthony Herbert was a retired U.S. Army officer and a Vietnam veteran who had publicly accused his army superiors of war crimes and atrocities. Herbert and his accusations were the focus of a Columbia Broadcasting System, Inc. (CBS) television show, written and produced by Barry Lando, and narrated by Mike Wallace. Herbert filed a defamation lawsuit after the airing of the television program and the publication of a subsequent magazine article. He alleged that the program and article had falsely and maliciously portrayed him as a liar who created the war-crime charges just to cover up the real reason for his leaving the army.

During the course of discovery in the pending lawsuit, Herbert's attorney took depositions of several network employees, but responses to his questions were refused on grounds that the First Amendment protected against inquiry into the states of mind of those involved in the editing, producing or publishing process. A motion to compel answers was filed with the district court, which agreed with Herbert's attorney that the First Amendment afforded no such protections. The defendants appealed, and a divided court of appeals reversed, stating that there was an absolute privilege attached to the editorial process of a media defendant in a libel case. Herbert next petitioned the U.S. Supreme Court who agreed to hear the case on a writ of *certiorari*.

The State of the Law in 1979

Several years prior to this case, the Supreme Court had decided a landmark defamation case, *New York Times v. Sullivan* (1964), which distinguished "public officials" from private individuals in actions for defamation. In essence, the Court ruled that some First Amendment protections were to be afforded to speech and the press (media) in the reporting of news or information about public officials relating to their official conduct (the "honest error" defense). Accordingly, a public official who alleged defamation had the burden of proving that false statements were made with "actual malice," and were not "honest errors." This evidence burden was extended to "public figures" in two subsequent cases, *Curtis Publishing Co. v. Butts* (1967) and *Associated Press v. Walker* (1967). By the criteria outlined in these cases,

Herbert was clearly a "public figure," which he readily acknowledged.

According to these decisions, in order to prove "actual malice" in a defamation case, plaintiffs such as Herbert had to prove that the defendants published a false statement about them "with knowledge that it was false" or "with reckless disregard of whether it was false or not." Herbert readily conceded that this was his burden. However, it was Herbert's argument that, in order to prove the prerequisite "actual malice," he needed to gain access to information about the editorial process, particularly information about the thoughts, opinions, and conclusions of those who gathered information about Herbert and discussed it with their editorial colleagues. Conversely, defendants argued that the First Amendment precluded inquiry into these areas, that an absolute privilege should protect them from disclosure, and further, that submission to petitioner's inquiries would place substantial burden and cost upon defendants. They also argued that to not allow such a protective privilege would result in a "chilling effect" on the editorial process, would cause undue self-censorship, and would cause the suppression of truthful material.

The Court's Analysis

Writing for the majority, Justice White rearticulated from previous decisions, "the right of the public to receive suitable access to social, political, esthetic, moral, and other ideas and experiences," and to the "circulation of information to which the public is entitled in virtue of the constitutional guaranties." Noting that the media (including the present defendants) played an important role in providing the public with such information, White carefully assessed whether the creation of a protective privilege as requested by the defendants, "would significantly further these social values recognized by our prior decisions."

White concluded that neither the First Amendment nor the Court's prior decisions protected the media from inquiry into the thoughts, opinions, conclusions, or editorial processes used to gather or publish alleged defamatory information, if the inquiry would "produce evidence material to the proof of a critical element of the plaintiff's cause of action." Further, the Court saw no reason to modify established constitutional doctrines by affording the defendants the requested privilege, as the result would make plaintiff's burden of proving "knowing or reckless falsehood" almost insurmountable. Thus, the Court concluded, ". . . the present construction of the First Amendment should not be modified by creating the evidentiary privilege which the respondents now urge." Justice White also stated that "only knowing or reckless error will be discouraged," by the present construction, and that, "constitutional values will not be threatened."

Dissent on the Scope of Discovery

In two separate dissenting opinions, Justices Stewart and Marshall questioned the prudence of what they saw as overly-liberal discovery by plaintiffs in defamation cases. Justice Stewart concluded that information obtained (and opinions held) by editorial and media staff, which was not published, was simply not relevant to the case. Liability attached only to published defamatory information. Justice Marshall, in turn, was concerned with the unfettered ability of plaintiffs to harass defendants by excessive discovery requests, and saw a clear potential for abuse of the discovery process.

Justice Brennan, who concurred with the majority but dissented in part, believed that the Court should adopt a "qualified" rather than absolute privilege, as requested by defendants, so that plaintiffs in defamation cases could inquire into the previously-discussed areas, only after demonstrating to the trial court that the publication in question represented a *prima facie* defamatory falsehood.

Impact

The *Herbert v. Lando* decision became an important authority for plaintiffs in defamation cases to use in

Anthony Herbert makes a statement outside the U.S. District Court for New York, 1979. © AP/Wide World Photos.

support of compelled disclosure of certain information which, state by state, and court by court, previously had not enjoyed standardized judicial treatment. State and federal courts remained free to modify their respective rules of civil procedure, especially those concerning discovery, if it became apparent that abuse of discovery was a real, rather than perceived, concern. In a subsequent case, *Branzburg v. Hayes* (1972), a divided Supreme Court concluded, by a narrow margin, that the media must disclose the identities of confidential sources of information when testifying before grand juries in criminal matters or at criminal trials. Importantly, the Court noted that states were free to enact their own laws creating a privilege to newspersons, protecting them against being compelled to disclose confidential sources (so-called "shield laws," enacted in a majority of states). The Court also preserved the right of the media to obtain relief against harassment.

Related Cases

New York Times v. Sullivan, 376 U.S. 254 (1964).
Associated Press v. Walker, 379 U.S. 47 (1967).
Curtis Publishing Co. v. Butts 388 U.S. 130 (1967).
New York Times Company v. United States, 403 U.S. 713 (1971).
Branzburg v. Hayes, 408 U.S. 665 (1972).
Miami Herald Publishing Company v. Tornillo, 418 U.S. 241 (1974).
Gertz v. Robert Welch, Inc., 418 U.S. 323 (1974).
United States v. Nixon, 418 U.S. 683 (1974).
Time, Inc. v. Firestone, 424 U.S. 448 (1976).
Hustler Magazine v. Falwell, 485 U.S. 46 (1988).

Bibliography and Further Reading

Biskupic, Joan, and Elder Witt, eds. *Congressional Quarterly's Guide to the U.S. Supreme Court,* 3rd ed. Washington, DC: Congressional Quarterly, Inc., 1996.

HUTCHINSON V. PROXMIRE

Legal Citation: 443 U.S. 111 (1979)

Petitioner
Ronald Hutchinson

Respondent
Senator William Proxmire

Petitioner's Claim
That negative statements against Hutchinson issued by Senator Proxmire in a press release, a newsletter, and a television interview are not protected under the Speech or Debate Clause.

Chief Lawyer for Petitioner
Michael E. Cavanaugh

Chief Lawyer for Respondent
Alan Raywid

Justices for the Court
Harry A. Blackmun, Warren E. Burger (writing for the Court), William O. Douglas, Thurgood Marshall, Lewis F. Powell, Jr., William H. Rehnquist, Potter Stewart, Byron R. White

Justices Dissenting
William J. Brennan, Jr.

Place
Washington, D.C.

Date of Decision
26 June 1979

Decision
That the privileges of the Speech or Debate Clause do not extend to press releases, newsletters, and other communications not "essential to the deliberations of the Senate."

Significance
The Supreme Court ruled that a speech made on the floor of the Senate cannot be protected under the Speech or Debate Clause if it is reprinted in the form of a newsletter, an interview, or a release to the media. The decision reaffirmed the rule set down in *Gravel v. United States* regarding the nature of official communication.

In the mid-1970s, Senator William Proxmire became well-known for his "Golden Fleece of the Month Award." This dubious honor was given to persons and institutions whom the senator believed had wasted taxpayer money on ridiculous or unnecessary projects. In April of 1975, Proxmire gave one of these awards to Dr. Ronald Hutchinson of the National Science Foundation, for his research into the ways animals deal with stress. In a speech on the floor of the Senate, Proxmire ridiculed Hutchinson's work as the study of why monkeys "grind their teeth." This speech was protected under the Speech or Debate Clause of the U.S. Constitution, meaning Hutchinson could not sue Proxmire for libel.

However, Proxmire kept up his barrage against Hutchinson outside the Senate floor. He sent a newsletter to his constituents touting the Golden Fleece Award, issued a press release on the subject, and spoke about it in a television interview. In these communications, Proxmire referred to Hutchinson's work as "monkey business" and urged Congress to "put a stop to the bite Hutchinson and the bureaucrats who fund him have been taking out of the taxpayer." Hutchinson sued Proxmire for damages, claiming that Proxmire's remarks had damaged his professional reputation and hindered his ability to make a living as a scientist.

The District Court's Ruling
The federal district court ruled in favor of Proxmire. It held that the press release was part of the process by which a senator keeps constituents informed of his or her activities. As a result, it was protected by the Speech or Debate Clause. As for the interview and the newsletter, those too were held to be protected speech under the First Amendment. Later, an appeals court affirmed this ruling. It even added the newsletter to the category of "informing functions" protected by the Speech or Debate Clause. The courts threw out the damage claims made by Hutchinson against Proxmire.

The Supreme Court Steps In
Next, the U.S. Supreme Court chose to hear the case. It hoped to resolve several key issues, the first of which it stated very clearly:

Speech or Debate Clause

The Constitutional Convention of the late 1700s placed the Speech or Debate Clause into Article I, Section 6, Clause 1, of the U.S. Constitution. The clause protects members of Congress from prosecution for their activities related to the legislative process. Legislative activities within the Senate or House that may not be part of a prosecution against a member include speeches and debates, preparing committee reports, voting, conducting committee hearings, and any other task required by the nature and execution of the office.

Legislators are even protected from prosecution when accused of violating another individual's constitutional rights. The Supreme Court has held, "Legislators are immune from deterrents to the uninhibited discharge of the legislative duty . . . for the public good." The protection, although not absolute, extends to congressional aides if their duties involve legislative activities a member of Congress would perform.

Since protection is limited only to conduct which is part of the legislative process, legislators' remarks published in newsletters, made in press releases, or on television are not immune from prosecution. Taking a bribe to influence legislation also falls outside the immunity. In striking a balance, the clause can not be interpreted so broadly as to allow erosion of the legislature's integrity.

Source(s): Biskupic, Joan and Witt, Elder. *Guide to the U.S. Supreme Court.* Washington, DC: Congressional Quarterly, 1997.

Whether a Member of Congress is protected by the Speech or Debate Clause of the Constitution . . . against suits for allegedly defamatory statements made by a Member in press releases and newsletters.

Senator Willaim Proxmire. © The Library of Congress/Corbis.

The decision hinged on how the Court defined "legislative business":

> Whatever imprecision there may be in the term "legislative activities," it is clear that nothing in the explicit language of the [Speech or Debate] Clause suggests any intention to create an absolute privilege from liability or suit for defamatory statements made outside the Chamber.

After deliberating, eight of the nine justices—with only Justice Brennan dissenting—held against Proxmire. They chose to define "legislative activity" narrowly, excluding things like newsletters and press releases:

> Valuable and desirable as it may be in broad terms, the transmittal of such information by individual members in order to inform the public and other Members is not a part of the legislative function or the deliberations that make up the legislative process. As a result, transmittal of such information by press releases and newsletters is not protected by the Speech or Debate Clause.

The principle that press releases and newsletters are not a part of the legislative process had in fact been explicitly stated by the Court in an earlier case, *United States v. Brewster.* In that decision, the Court wrote:

> It is well known, of course, that Members of the Congress engage in many activities other than the purely legislative activities protected by the Speech or Debate Clause. These include . . . preparing so-called "news letters" to constituents, news releases, and speeches delivered outside the Congress.

Ronald Hutchinson sued Senator William Proxmire for libel.
© AP/Wide World Photos.

Finally, the Court addressed Senator Proxmire's contention that Ronald Hutchinson was a "public figure." If this were true, his libel claim would be invalid, because public figures can claim libel only when they are attacked by statements made with "actual malice" where the attacker knows that the claims are false. To be considered a public figure, Hutchinson would have to have regular and continuing access to the media or have thrust himself into the public spotlight. The Court found neither of these things to be true. Therefore, it held that Hutchinson was not a public figure and his claim of libel was valid.

Like *Gravel v. United States, Hutchinson v. Proxmire* provided important clarification on the breadth of the Speech or Debate Clause of the Constitution. It defined the nature of "legislative activities" more precisely than ever before and put clear limits on the speech protections afforded to members of Congress.

Related Cases

Long v. Ansell, 293 U.S. 76 (1934).
New York Times Co. v. Sullivan, 376 U.S. 254 (1964).
United States v. Brewster, 408 U.S. 501 (1972).
Gravel v. United States, 408 U.S. 606 (1972).
Doe v. McMillan, 412 U.S. 306 (1973).

Bibliography and Further Reading

Chandler, Ralph C. *The Constitutional Law Dictionary.* Santa Barbara, CA: ABC-Clio, Inc., 1987.

Ducat, Craig R. and Harold W. Chase. *Constitutional Interpretation.* St. Paul, MN: West Publishing Company, 1988.

Encyclopedia of the American Constitution. New York, NY: Macmillan Publishing Company, 1986.

SNEPP V. UNITED STATES

Legal Citation: 444 U.S. 507 (1980)

Appellant
Frank W. Snepp III

Appellee
U.S. Central Intelligence Agency (CIA)

Appellant's Claim
That CIA requirements for agency prepublication review of writings about the agency by employees and former employees constituted unconstitutional prior restraint on freedom of speech in violation of the First Amendment.

Chief Lawyers for Appellant
Alan M. Dershowitz, Bruce J. Ennis, Joel M. Gora, Mark H. Lynch, Jack D. Novik, John H. F. Shattuck, John Cary Sims, Geoffrey J. Vitt

Chief Lawyers for Appellee
David J. Anderson, Barbara Allen Babcock, William B. Cummings, Brook Hedge, Thomas S. Martin, Elizabeth Gere Whitaker, Glenn V. Whitaker, George P. Williams

Justices for the Court
Harry A. Blackmun, Warren E. Burger, Lewis F. Powell, Jr., William H. Rehnquist, Potter Stewart, Byron R. White (unsigned)

Justices Dissenting
William J. Brennan, Jr., Thurgood Marshall, John Paul Stevens

Place
Washington, D.C.

Date of Decision
19 February 1980

Decision
Upheld lower court decisions that a compelling government interest justifies publication safeguards in CIA employee contracts and waives their First Amendment rights to free speech.

Significance
The ruling recognized a situation where government compelling interest justified imposing a prior restraint on publications about the agency by employees and former employees. The United States successfully argued that uninhibited freedom to publish materials on CIA activities, even when classified information was not involved, still jeopardized international trust relationships with foreign nations. Critics feared the increasing use of such "contracts of silence" in government and private business waiving freedom of speech rights violated the First Amendment rights of the public to know potentially important information of public interest.

The CIA was established with the inception of the Cold War immediately following World War II in 1947. Created to protect national security in international affairs, the agency gathers intelligence for the U.S. government in an atmosphere of considerable secrecy and little media exposure. The CIA, whose director is a member of the President's cabinet, reports directly to the National Security Council. The agency, headquartered in McLean, Virginia, has "offices" in 130 foreign countries. Aspects of the CIA became more commonly known since the mid-1970s when a series of political controversies began. Still, the effectiveness of the CIA is governed by its ability to gather and distribute foreign intelligence in cooperation with numerous domestic and foreign information sources.

The authority of government to restrict speech prior to publication has been substantially limited by the Supreme Court since its landmark decision in *Near v. Minnesota* (1931). Freedom of expression from prior restraints was considered a fundamental right under the Constitution deriving from earlier English common law. The Court in *Near* did leave open that prior restraint might be justified for national security reasons in times of war.

On 16 September 1968 a young man named Frank W. Snepp III took the final step necessary to begin working for the Central Intelligence Agency. The job application process with the CIA is a long one, involving extensive background checks for issuing a security clearance and other procedures. That process for Snepp culminated in signing a secrecy agreement which obligated Snepp not to "publish or participate in the publication of" any material relating to the CIA's activities during Snepp's term of employment without "specific prior approval by the Agency."

Snepp worked for the CIA for more than seven years, serving two tours of duty with the CIA station in South Vietnam during the height of the Vietnam War. Snepp became disillusioned with the CIA's conduct in Vietnam, particularly with its role in the final stages of American withdrawal from Saigon in 1973. Snepp resigned from the CIA effective 23 January 1976 signing a termination secrecy agreement reiterating his obligation to obtain the "express written consent of the

Director of Central Intelligence" before publishing any materials about the CIA.

Snepp Writes *Decent Interval*

Despite the documents he had signed, Snepp went to the publishing company Random House with a book manuscript titled *Decent Interval*. The book described the American withdrawal from Vietnam and Saigon and offered unflattering details about the CIA's involvement. The book detailed CIA dishonesty and corruption during the U.S. pullout of Vietnam. Snepp received a $60,000 advance from Random House, and a contract calling for potentially lucrative royalties after publication. Though based on his experience in the CIA, Snepp never submitted the manuscript for agency approval.

Random House published the book in November of 1977. On 15 February 1978 the government filed suit against Snepp in the U.S. District Court for the Eastern District of Virginia. Because the book did not contain any information officially designated as classified, secret or top secret, the government took a conservative approach. Instead of criminal prosecution or seeking an injunction against publication of the book, the government asked the court for all of Snepp's profits as compensation for breach of contract. Snepp stood to lose everything under his contract with Random House.

The district court ruled in the government's favor on 7 July 1978, and the U.S. Court of Appeals for the Fourth Circuit largely affirmed the district court's actions on 20 March 1979 except for not allowing the government's right to the profits. Snepp appealed to the Supreme Court.

Both sides fielded extensive legal teams as the American Civil Liberties Union and the Authors League of America came to Snepp's assistance. CIA Director Admiral Stansfield Turner had been a key witness for the government before the district court testifying that Snepp's book had significantly damaged CIA operations. Turner claimed a "number of sources" had discontinued cooperation and others expressed concerns, including complaints from foreign intelligence services. In addition, the book most likely discouraged new potential sources from coming forward. Snepp argued the secrecy agreements violated his right under the Constitution's First Amendment to freely express himself, a right which cannot be contracted away. Snepp's lawyers were not allowed to cross-examine Turner concerning the harms to the agency he identified.

The Court, in an extraordinary move by not hearing oral arguments or accepting briefs on the issues, ruled on the case. A *per curiam* opinion was issued, meaning the author of the Court's decision was not identified. In rejecting Snepp's argument, the Court held the government could use employment agreements to bind its employees to vows of secrecy. The

Frank W. Snepp III. © AP/Wide World Photos.

majority wrote, "The Government has a compelling interest in protecting both the secrecy of information important to our national security and the appearance of confidentiality so essential to the effective operation of our foreign intelligence service. The agreement that Snepp signed is a reasonable means for protecting this vital interest." The Court reinstated the government's rights to the profits and required Snepp to obtain permission from the CIA in the future before speaking or writing about the agency for the rest of his life. The decision resulted in a substantial fine of $140,000 for Snepp. Ironically, Snepp must obtain permission from an organization he would seek to criticize.

Justice John Paul Stevens, joined by Justice William Brennan and Justice Thurgood Marshall, wrote in dissent. Stevens asserted no precedents existed for the government to seize the profits from Snepp's book when it revealed no confidential information. Stevens also questioned the conclusiveness of Turner's "truncated testimony" as to the actual harm Snepp's book posed. In addition, Stevens wrote that he saw no basis for the Court to dispense with the case so rapidly, particularly when the "prior restraint on a citizen's right to criticize his government" was at issue. Such a restraint should require the "censor" to more substantially justify its interest at stake.

Impact

Despite the Court's historic concern for First Amendment rights, the *Snepp* decision reaffirmed that the government is entitled to enforce contracts with its employees that prohibit publishing sensitive material without prior consent. However, the decision went beyond a relatively simple question of contract law. The ruling recognized national security concerns in a peace time era as sufficient compelling interest of government to impose a prior restraint on free speech. Such a ruling was contrary to previous Court decisions. Government reliance on national security concerns did not prevail in *New York Times Company v. United States* (1971) in trying to block publication of the Pentagon Papers. Also, in 1979 the government, though successfully gaining a temporary injunction, ultimately failed to successfully block publication of hydrogen bomb production information in *United States v. The Progressive, Inc.* (1979). Prior restraints were more commonly used to avoid inappropriate pretrial publicity in highly publicized criminal cases.

Critics of the ruling argued that only criminal penalties for after-the-fact publication was constitutional, though admittedly not very effective since the unwanted revelations would have already occurred. They also argued the prepublication constraints inevitably keep more information secret than necessary. The CIA was, through its broad oversight, suppressing criticism that did not involve confidential information by those most knowledgeable of the issue. Critics doubted the CIA actually had proven a compelling interest since the agency was not actually seeking to suppress confidential information, but merely to present the appearance of suppressing such information.

The *Snepp* decision in combination with two other decisions, *Haig v. Agee* (1981) and *United States v. The Progressive, Inc.* (1979), signaled to some the potential beginning of a new sedition era in which criticism of U.S. activities would not be protected by the First Amendment. The rise of enforcing seditious libel under the cloak of national security to many corresponded with an increase in political repression. In *Agee*, the Court actually questioned whether the CIA was truly only trying to suppress confidential information, or was actually unconstitutionally imposing content-based restrictions on speech through prior restraints. However, the end of the Cold War era appeared to diffuse the issue of apparent political suppression at least for a while.

A broader issue involved the growing use of "contracts of silence" which the government, as in the case of *Snepp,* and private companies were increasingly using to keep potentially important information from the public. The tension between freedom of contract and freedom of speech, particular the public's right to know drew increasing concern. Some contracts of silence, particularly involving matters of commerce, clearly have importance in protecting trade secrets, sensitive financial and personnel information, and even protecting personal privacy. However, out of court settlements involving confidentiality conditions could potentially withhold defective product information from the public. Physicians were discovered signing "gag" provisions with health care management organizations to withhold information from patients concerning financial incentives under which they practiced. Some critics believed courts should more carefully consider public interest in access to information under the First Amendment when hearing cases involving these contracts of silence. Contract law traditionally allowed courts to deny enforcement of contracts when they violated public policy. Some argued this authority should be extended to adverse effects on free speech when significant public interest is identified.

A fundamental question raised by *Snepp* continued to plague the courts. What extent of a constitutional right does the public have to know about government operations? The public right to know has been assumed to be an essential part of free speech necessary for a democracy to maintain an informed electorate. But how much access to information is necessary when the public is not actually involved in day-to-day decision-making of government affairs is yet to be resolved.

Related Cases

Near v. Minnesota, 283 U.S. 697 (1931).

New York Times Company v. United States, 403 U.S. 713 (1971).

United States v. The Progressive, 467 F.Supp. 990 (W.D. Wis. 1979).

Haig v. Agee, 453 U.S. 280 (1981).

Bibliography and Further Reading

Alter, Jonathan. "Slaying the Message." *Washington Monthly,* September 1981, pp. 43-50.

Garfield, Alan E. Promises of Silence: Contract Law and Freedom of Speech. *Cornell Law Review,* Vol. 83, pp. 261-364, 1998.

Mullin, Dennis, and Robert S. Dudney. "When CIA Spies Come in From the Cold." *U.S. News and World Report,* 28 September 1981, pp. 41-44.

Snepp, Frank. *Decent Interval: An Insider's Account of Saigon's Indecent End Told by the CIA's Chief Strategy Analyst in Vietnam.* New York: Vintage Books, 1978.

Snepp, Frank. "The CIA's Double Standard." *Newsweek,* 25 January 1982, p. 10.

PRUNEYARD SHOPPING CENTER V. ROBINS

Legal Citation: 447 U.S. 74 (1980)

Appellant
Pruneyard Shopping Center and Fred Sahadi, owner

Appellee
Michael Robins, et al.

Appellant's Claim
That a provision of the California Constitution guaranteeing an individual's right to free speech at privately owned shopping centers violates the owner's property and free speech rights under the First, Fifth and Fourteenth Amendments of the U.S. Constitution.

Chief Lawyer for Appellant
Max L. Gillam, Jr.

Chief Lawyer for Appellee
Philip L. Hammer

Justices for the Court
Harry A. Blackmun, William J. Brennan, Jr., Warren E. Burger, Thurgood Marshall, Lewis F. Powell, Jr., William H. Rehnquist (writing for the Court), John Paul Stevens, Potter Stewart, Byron R. White

Justices Dissenting
None

Place
Washington, D.C.

Date of Decision
9 June 1980

Decision
Denied the appellant's claim and affirmed the ruling of the California Supreme Court.

Significance
Although the Court had previously found that the Constitution did not guarantee freedom of speech at privately owned shopping centers, this ruling granted states a greater latitude of freedom under their own constitutions.

Starting in 1939, the U.S. Supreme Court began to develop the "public forum" doctrine in free speech issues. Controversial protests or leafleting were protected if they occurred in a public forum, though government could set limits on the "time, place and manner" of the speech. Most of the cases that further shaped this doctrine dealt with public spaces or government property. Eventually, the Court also considered if and when a privately owned area could serve as a public forum.

Shopping centers were often the subject of debate, as different political groups tried to picket or distribute information in these privately owned retail areas, and the owners tried to stop them. After some initial inconsistency in the Court's decisions regarding First Amendment protections in a shopping center, the Court clarified its stance in *Hudgens v. National Labor Relations Board* (1976). Shopping centers were not public forums, and they could restrict speech, as long as they did it independently, without any state involvement or encouragement.

In 1980, however, a California case tested whether states could compel a shopping center to allow some displays of expression, with certain time, place, and manner restrictions. On a Saturday afternoon, a group of high school students, including Michael Robins, set up a table in the central courtyard at the Pruneyard Shopping Center. The center included more than 65 stores, ten restaurants, and a movie theater. The students handed out pamphlets and collected signatures for a petition that criticized a United Nations resolution that condemned Zionism, a form of Jewish nationalism.

After a short while, a Pruneyard security guard told the students to leave, as their activities violated the shopping center's regulations against the circulation of petitions. Later, Robins and the other students sued the shopping center in California Superior Court.

The State's Constitutional Guarantee of Free Speech

Both the superior court and the California Court of Appeals ruled that the students did not have a federal or state constitutional right of expression at a privately

Are Malls Public Places?

Should privately owned malls or shopping centers be treated as public places? If the answer is yes, a mall owner cannot restrict the exercise of First Amendment freedoms on his property any more than governments can restrict expression in public places.

Proponents contend the general public has essentially unrestricted access to shopping malls. As such, malls serve the functional equivalent of a community's business district. Whether the mall is publicly or privately owned would not be apparent, and an individual would not normally be aware that he was on private property. Therefore, when a shopping mall owner invites the public onto his property to conduct business, he gives up a degree of privacy rights in the public interest.

Opponents point out that even though malls are generally accessible to the public, they do not have all the features of a public business district and still maintain their private character. The public has an invitation to come to the shopping center to do business with its tenants but has no open-ended invitation to use the center for any and all purposes. Privately-owned malls are not dedicated to public use and should not be required to permit activities unrelated to the mall's business.

Source(s): Joan Biskupic and Elder Witt, *Guide to the U.S. Supreme Court*. Washington, DC: Congressional Quarterly, 1997.

owned shopping center. The state supreme court, however, overruled this decision. In its interpretation of the state constitution, the supreme court said the students had a right of expression and petition on private property, as long as it was "reasonably exercised."

Fred Sahadi, the owner of Pruneyard, argued that giving people the right to distribute pamphlets at the center infringed on his property rights. The California Supreme Court disagreed, reasoning that Pruneyard attracted 25,000 people a day, and "a handful of additional orderly persons, soliciting signatures and distributing handbills . . . would not markedly dilute defendant's property rights."

Appealing the case to the U.S. Supreme Court, the Pruneyard owner again argued for the protection of his property rights. The Court had previously ruled that those rights included the right to exclude others from private property. Pruneyard also claimed that it had First Amendment rights not to be compelled by the state to let others use its land as a public forum. The Court, however, voted unanimously to affirm the decision of the California Supreme Court.

Justice Rehnquist wrote the decision, and he first examined the appellant's claims regarding property rights. He acknowledged that the Court earlier, in *Lloyd Corp. v. Tanner* (1972), stated that private property remains private, even when the public is invited to use the land for shopping or other purposes. But the *Lloyd* decision, Rehnquist continued, did not ". . . limit the authority of the State to exercise its police power or its sovereign right to adopt in its own Constitution individual liberties more expansive than those conferred by the Federal Constitution."

As far as the right to exclude, Pruneyard had argued that if it lost that right, the state was in effect unfairly "taking" its property, which was prohibited by the Fifth Amendment. But the Court said not every infringement on property rights constitutes a taking in the constitutional sense, and ensuring freedom of expression at the property owner's expense was not an unconstitutional taking. "There is nothing to suggest that preventing appellants from prohibiting this sort of activity will unreasonably impair the value or use of their property as a shopping center."

The First Amendment Concerns

On the First Amendment issue, the owner of the center cited a precedent that said states may not force an individual to display any kind of ideological message. The case cited, *Wooley v. Maynard* (1977) which involved a Jehovah's Witness who covered up the New Hampshire state motto, "Live Free or Die," on his car's license plate. Rehnquist, however, said that case was completely different from *Pruneyard*. The shopping center is open to the public, and the view expressed by a group distributing pamphlets would not necessarily be associated with the owner. Also, the state was not compelling Pruneyard to display one specific message. "Finally," Rehnquist concluded, ". . . appellants can expressly disavow any connection with the message simply by posting signs in the area where the speakers or handbillers stand."

Although all nine justices agreed with the judgment in *Pruneyard*, two of them took issue with the last section, regarding the First Amendment. Justice Powell, in an opinion joined by Justice White, asserted the appellants had not made a convincing argument. But Powell worried about other instances where property owners might be compelled to let others express opinions the owner did not share. "I do not interpret our decision today as a blanket approval for state efforts to transform privately owned commercial property into public forums. Any such state action would raise substantial federal constitutional questions not present in this case."

Related Cases

Village of Euclid v. Ambler Realty Co., 272 U.S. 365 (1926).

West Virginia State Board of Education v. Barnette, 319 U.S. 624 (1943).

Adamson v. California, 332 U.S. 46 (1947).

Lloyd Corp. v. Tanner, 407 U.S. 705 (1972).

Miami Herald Publishing Company v. Tornillo, 418 U.S. 241 (1974).

Hudgens v. National Labor Relations Board, 242 U.S. 507 (1976).

Young v. American Mini Theaters, 427 U.S. 50 (1976).

Wooley v. Maynard, 430 U.S. 705 (1977).

Bibliography and Further Reading

Brownstein, Alan E. "Constitutional Wish Granting and the Property Rights Genie." *Constitutional Commentary,* spring 1996, pp. 7–54.

Bullock, Scott G. "The Mall's in Their Court." *Reason,* August-September 1995, p. 46.

Elliott, Stephen P., ed. *A Reference Guide to the U.S. Supreme Court.* New York: Facts on File Publications, 1986.

Hall, Kermit L., ed. *The Oxford Companion to the Supreme Court of the United States.* New York: Oxford Press, 1992.

Nowak, John E., Ronald D. Rotunda, and J. Nelson Young. *Constitutional Law,* 2nd ed. St. Paul: West Publishing Company, 1984.

Yamada, David C. "Voices from the Cubicle: Protesting and Encouraging Private Employee Speech in the Post-Industrial Workplace." *Berkeley Journal of Employment and Labor Law,* summer 1998, pp. 1–59.

CENTRAL HUDSON GAS AND ELECTRIC CORP. V. PUBLIC SERVICE COMMISSION OF NEW YORK

Legal Citation: 447 U.S. 557 (1980)

Appellant
Central Hudson Gas and Electric Corp.

Appellee
Public Service Commission of New York

Appellant's Claim
That a regulation by the New York Public Service Commission, banning the use of promotional advertising by the electrical utility Central Hudson Gas and Electric Corp., was a restraint of commercial speech under the First and Fourteenth Amendments.

Chief Lawyer for the Appellant
Telford Taylor

Chief Lawyer for the Appellee
Peter H. Schiff

Justices for the Court
Harry A. Blackmun, William J. Brennan, Jr., Warren E. Burger, Thurgood Marshall, Lewis F. Powell, Jr. (writing for the Court), John Paul Stevens, Potter Stewart, Byron R. White

Justices Dissenting
William H. Rehnquist

Place
Washington, D.C.

Date of Decision
20 June 1980

Decision
The Court reversed the judgment of the New York Court of Appeals, and found that the restraint of commercial speech was a violation of the appellant's rights under the First and Fourteenth Amendments.

Significance
Central Hudson was the most significant case up to its time in establishing a framework for the practice of commercial speech. The case set in place a four-part test—which was not without controversy—for the constitutionality of state laws restraining commercial speech, which is somewhat more limited that ordinary free speech under the First Amendment.

In 1973, the oil-producing nations of the world raised the price of oil, which caused a severe "energy crisis" in the United States. As a response to the need to conserve fuel, the Public Service Commission of the State of New York ordered in December of 1973 that all electric utilities in the state desist from any form of advertising which "promot[es] the use of electricity."

Three years later, with the energy crisis over, the commission solicited public opinion as to the rule limiting promotional advertising. Central Hudson Gas and Electric Corporation, an electrical utility, opposed the rule on First Amendment grounds, claiming that it abridged free speech. In Central Hudson's advertising, the company encouraged customers to use energy at "off-peak" times such as late at night, when demand for electricity was low. This, the company reasoned, would ultimately encourage economy of energy.

However, the commission decided to continue with its ban, and on 25 February 1977, it clarified its position in a policy statement. The latter classified advertising as either "promotional," which was intended to increase consumption, or "institutional and informational," which in essence included all other advertising not obviously intended for the purpose of stimulating sales. Promotional advertising, the commission declared, ran counter to the continuing national policy of conserving energy.

The commission, which judged Central Hudson's advertising to be promotional in nature, acknowledged that its rule would not necessarily lead to greater energy conservation, since by restricting the advertising that would promote off-peak consumption, it would to some extent limit the "beneficial side-effects" that such advertising might have. Its rationale was that the use of additional power encouraged by such advertising would create higher rates for all users, since at that time electricity rates in New York state were not based on the more economically efficient system of marginal cost. As for informational advertising, the commission permitted that which would encourage "*shifts* of consumption" (emphasis in original) from high-demand to low-demand time periods. Despite the rather nebulous distinction between this and the so-called promotional advertising by Central Hudson, the commission reasoned that such informational advertising would not have the purpose of increasing overall consumption of energy. Promotional advertising, on the other hand, would give "misleading signals" to consumers because it would appear to encourage consumption of power.

Central Hudson took the commission to state court, charging that the order was a restraint of commercial speech, and violated the First and Fourteenth Amendments to the Constitution. The state and intermediate appellate courts upheld the commission's order, and the New York Court of Appeals affirmed. In so doing, the court cited the fact that, as an electrical utility, Central Hudson operated in a "noncompetitive market." As for the constitutional question of commercial speech, the Court reasoned, the state's interest in limiting consumption was more compelling that the utility's claim.

The Four-Part Test

The Supreme Court held 8-1 that the commission's order was unconstitutional. Justice Powell, who gave the Court's opinion, used a four-part test for the constitutionality of a law limiting commercial speech. First of all, a court must determine whether such speech is protected under the First Amendment. Assuming it passes that test, then it comes under a three-part formula for balancing interests. The components of this formula require the Court to question three aspects of the claim: whether or not the government's interest in the situation was "substantial"; whether or not the Court's regulation of the commercial speech in question "directly advanced" the government's interest; and whether that regulation would be "more extensive than necessary to serve that interest".

Powell addressed the question of the First Amendment's protection of free speech. Though such constitutional protection is "lesser" than that given to other guaranteed forms of expression, he said, it is indeed protected. Commercial speech must not be misleading, or encourage unlawful activity, whereas ordinary free speech need not meet those criteria in order to be protected. As for the question of whether or not Central Hudson's speech could be limited by virtue of the fact that it held a monopoly over the sale of electricity within its service area, Powell did not find this a compelling justification.

Given that Central Hudson's right to commercial speech was protected, Powell went on to ask if the commission's interest was "substantial." He did find that the commission had a substantial interest in limiting consumption; however, he did not find this "a constitutionally adequate reason for restricting protected speech[,] because the link between the advertising prohibition and appellant's rate structure is, at most, tenuous." In other words, whether or not the commission limited the advertising would have little bearing on the conservation of energy, and therefore it would not

"directly advance" the state's interest. And, he found, the regulation was more extensive than necessary, precisely because it would not directly lead to any decrease in consumption.

Questioning the Four-Part Test

Justices Brennan, Blackmun, and Stevens all concurred in the judgment, but they placed a finer point on questions of restricting free speech. Brennan, who joined in the opinions of his colleagues Blackmun and Stevens, cited the vagueness of the commission's distinction between promotional and informational or institutional advertising.

Blackmun, while agreeing that the four-part test was adequate in situations where the commercial speech was "misleading or coercive," did not think it sufficient in situations such as the one at hand, in which a government limited commercial speech for the purposes of creating a specific economic outcome. Comparing the case at hand to the Court's 1976 ruling in *Virginia State Board of Pharmacy v. Virginia Citizens Consumer Council*, Blackmun said that the four-part test would appear to make it permissible for a government to limit commercial speech if by so doing it served a compelling economic purpose. On the contrary, Blackmun reasoned, if the government has such an interest, it should make laws which deal directly with the issue—e.g., a law limiting electrical consumption—rather than abridging the freedom of commercial speech.

Justice Stevens likewise questioned the broad manner in which he believed the four-part test might be applied. Since, as the Court had stated, commercial speech was deserving of less protection that other forms of speech, he was concerned that the definition of commercial speech be as limited as possible in order that other forms would not accidentally be included under that heading as well. Therefore, he said, he could only concur in the result "because I do not consider this a 'commercial speech' case."

Nor did Justice Rehnquist, the Court's lone dissenter, though on an entirely different basis. Rehnquist disagreed with the Court's analysis for several reasons, the first of which was that he did not believe a state-created monopoly was entitled to free-speech protection under the First Amendment. Therefore, the commission's order was in his view an economic regulation rather than a regulation of speech. In line with his more sympathetic view toward the rights of states, he held that "the Court, in reaching its decision, improperly substitutes its own judgment for that of the state in deciding how a proper ban on promotional advertising should be drafted."

Related Cases

Virginia State Board of Pharmacy v. Virginia Citizens Consumer Council, 425 U.S. 748 (1976).
44 Liquormart, Inc. v. Rhode Island, 517 U.S. 484 (1996).

Bibliography and Further Reading

Biskupic, Joan and Elder Witt, eds. *Congressional Quarterly's Guide to the U.S. Supreme Court,* 3rd ed. Washington, DC: Congressional Quarterly, Inc., 1996.

Cook, Don Lloyd. "Earthquakes and Aftershocks." *Journal of Public Policy & Marketing,* Spring 1998, pp. 116.

Hamilton, Deborah L. "The First Amendment Status of Commercial Speech." *Michigan Law Review,* June 1996, pp. 2352.

Langvardt, Arlen, and Eric L. Richards. "The Death of Posadas and the Birth of Change in Commerical Speech Doctrine." *American Business Law Journal,* Summer 1997, pp. 483.

ISLAND TREES UNION FREE SCHOOL DISTRICT BOARD OF EDUCATION V. PICO

Legal Citation: 457 U.S. 853 (1982)

Plaintiff
Steven A. Pico, by his next friend, Frances Pico et al.

Defendant
Board of Education, Island Trees Union Free School District No. 26 et al.

Plaintiff's Claim
That the Island Trees School System Board of Education was violating the First Amendment by banning books from the school libraries.

Chief Lawyer for Plaintiff
Alan H. Levine

Chief Defense Lawyer
George W. Lipp, Jr.

Justices for the Court
Harry A. Blackmun, William J. Brennan, Jr. (writing for the Court), Thurgood Marshall, John Paul Stevens, Byron R. White

Justices Dissenting
Warren E. Burger, Sandra Day O'Connor, Lewis F. Powell, Jr., William H. Rehnquist

Place
Washington, D.C.

Date of Decision
25 June 1982.

Decision
The district court was in error in its summary judgment in its case that challenged a local school board's removal of library books.

Significance
With this case, school boards were constitutionally disabled from removing library books in order to deny access to ideas with which they disagreed for political reasons.

The *Board of Education v. Pico* was a case that raised many questions concerning the rights of students within the context of the First Amendment. The Constitution's First Amendment makes the United States different from all other countries by guaranteeing American citizens the right to feel, believe, and speak as they wish. One of the most controversial freedoms guaranteed to U.S. residents is the freedom of speech, detailed in the First Amendment's Free Speech Clause. This is not just the right for a person to say what he or she wants, but it has been extended, by the U.S. Supreme Court to mean that if the First Amendment guarantees a speaker's—or writer's—right to express individual ideas, then it follows that people are just as free to receive these ideas.

This concept clashes on occasion with a school board's responsibility to maintain and communicate community values. At the heart of the matter is the question of whether a school board has acted with the intention of communicating and protecting community values or its own beliefs. If the latter is the underlying motivation, there is a constitutional problem just as though a basically Democratic school board had banned any books voicing Republican doctrine, a Caucasian school board banned books about African Americans, or vice versa. In short, the U.S. Constitution forbids the official suppression of ideas, especially if the suppression is based on personal political views.

At the time of this controversy, Richard Ahrens was the president of the Board of Education of New York's Island Trees Union Free School District No. 26, Frank Martin was the vice president, and Patrick Hughes was among the board's members. They were some of the petitioners involved in this case, even though Pico, et al. originally brought the board to district court.

In September of 1975, Ahrens, Martin, and Hughes went to a conference sponsored by Parents of New York United (PONYU), a politically conservative group of parents who were having misgivings about New York State legislation regarding education. While at this conference, the three petitioners picked up lists of books that Ahrens called "objectionable," and Martin felt were "improper fare for school students." When it was determined that 11 of the listed books were in school libraries, the board "unofficially" directed the high school and junior high school principals to remove these books from the library shelves and take them to the board's offices so they could read them. Some of the books included were: *Slaughterhouse Five,* by Kurt Vonnegut, Jr.; *The Naked Ape,* by Desmond Morris; *Soul on Ice,* by Eldridge Cleaver; and *Best Short Stories of Negro Writers,* edited by Langston Hughes.

When the board officials had these books removed from the library shelves, the press reported their actions. To justify the removal, the board sent out a press release explaining that these books were, "anti-American, anti-Christian, anti-Semitic, and just plain filthy." The board felt that, "it is our duty, our moral obligation, to protect the children in our schools from this moral danger as surely as from physical and medical dangers."

Subsequently, the school board appointed a book review committee comprised of four school district parents and four Island Trees staff members, to read the books and recommend which should be kept in the library. Their criteria were "educational suitability," "good taste," "relevance," and "appropriateness to age and grade level."

The committee decided that the schools keep five of the books and remove two. As to the other four books, there were two that the committee could not agree on, one on which they took no position, and one that should be available with parental permission. The school board ignored the committee's decision and decided that the libraries would keep only one of the books, parental permission would be required for another, and the other nine would be removed. The board gave no reasons for its decisions.

Confronted with the school board's decision, several junior high and high school students brought suit against the school board to the U.S. District Court for the Eastern District of New York. They alleged that the board's actions resulted from personal opinion as to the moral, political, and social suitability of these books, and the students' First Amendment rights were being violated. They wanted the court to declare that the board was acting unconstitutionally, have the board return the books to the libraries, and not to interfere with the use of these books in the schools.

The district court granted the school board a summary judgment; that is, they construed the school board's interpretation of these books as fact. Based on this premise, the district court ruled that the school board acted on its conservative views that these books were immoral, in bad taste, vulgar, etc., rather than personally held religious or political beliefs. Therefore, the school board had not violated the students' First Amendment rights.

The U.S. Court of Appeals for the Second Circuit reversed the district court's judgment and sent the case back to be examined with a closer look at whether the students' First Amendment rights had been violated.

The Supreme Court agreed with the court of appeals. Justice Brennan offered an opinion joined by Justices Marshall and Stevens and partially by Justice Blackmun. Justice White concurred with the judgment, but did not join in the opinion. Chief Justice Burger and Justices Rehnquist, O'Connor, and Powell dissented.

In essence, the Supreme Court agreed that the students' First Amendment rights were violated by the removal of these books because the school board was trying to suppress ideas they simply did not like. They seemed not to be acting out of a genuine concern for the educational suitability of the content of these books.

Related Cases

Meyer v. Nebraska, 262 U.S. 390 (1923).

Pierce v. Society of Sisters, 268 U.S. 510 (1925).

West Virginia Board of Education v. Barnette, 319 U.S. 624 (1943).

Brown v. Louisiana, 383 U.S. 131 (1966).

Keyishian v. Board of Regents of the University of the State of New York, 385 U.S. 589 (1967).

Epperson v. Arkansas, 393 U.S. 97 (1968).

Tinker v. Des Moines Independent Community School District, 393 U.S. 503 (1969).

Ambach v. Norwick, 441 U.S. 68 (1979).

Bethel School District No. 403 v. Fraser, 478 U.S. 675 (1986).

Bibliography and Further Reading

Hentoff, Nat. "Censoring the Right to Live." *The Progressive,* Februrary 1995, p. 19.

Peck, Robert S. and Ann K. Symons. "Kids Have First Amendment Rights, Too." *American Libraries,* September 1997, p. 64.

Seidman, Louis M., Gerald R. Stone, Cass R. Sunstein, Mark V. Tushnet. *Constitutional Law.* Little, Brown and Company: 1986.

BOLGER V. YOUNGS DRUG PRODUCTS CORP.

Legal Citation: 463 U.S. 60 (1983)

Appellant
The United States Postal Service

Appellee
Youngs Drug Products Corporation

Appellant's Claim
The postal service should be allowed to ban the mailing of unsolicited advertisements about condoms.

Chief Lawyer for Appellant
David A. Strauss

Chief Lawyers for Appellee
Jerold S. Solovy, Robert L. Graham, Laura A. Kaster

Justices for the Court
Harry A. Blackmun, Warren E. Burger, Thurgood Marshall (writing for the Court), Sandra Day O'Connor, Lewis F. Powell, Jr., William H. Rehnquist, John Paul Stevens, Byron R. White

Justices Dissenting
None (William J. Brennan, Jr., did not participate)

Place
Washington, D.C.

Date of Decision
24 June 1983

Decision
The postal service could not ban unsolicited advertisements for contraceptives.

Significance
The Supreme Court provided a definition of "commercial speech." It identified criteria providing commercial speech with "qualified but substantial protection" under the First Amendment.

The Supreme Court has placed political speech at the heart of the First Amendment, which exists to promote informed self government. In part, the Court has protected artistic expression because it can serve as a vehicle for commentary on public issues. With this understanding of the amendment's purpose, the Court had held flatly in *Valentine v. Chrestensen* (1942) that the Constitution "imposes no . . . restraint on government." regarding the street distribution of "purely commercial advertising."

Bolger and other cases during the 1970s and 1980s modified earlier rulings, and the Court limited government interference with advertising. For the first time, the Court directly defined the difference between commercial and political speech. Although still not according it the absolute protection provided to political and artistic expression, the Court granted commercial speech substantial First Amendment protection.

Teaching Americans to Use Condoms
Youngs Drug Products Corporation manufactured, distributed, and sold condoms under various brand names. Youngs marketed its products primarily through sales to wholesalers. The latter in turn sold them to retailer pharmacists who then provided them to individual customers.

Youngs used different techniques to publicize and promote its products. In conjunction with its wholesalers and retailers, the company decided to undertake a campaign of unsolicited mass mailings to members of the public. It planned to send out fliers promoting condoms and other drugstore products. It also planned to mail purely informational pamphlets discussing the ways in which condoms can help prevent disease and facilitate family planning. These informational pamphlets would mention Youngs only at the end and solely as their sponsor.

Since 1873, federal law had prohibited the mailing of unsolicited advertisements for contraceptives. The postal service warned Youngs that its proposed mailings would violate this law. At Youngs request, the district court issued an injunction voiding the law, because it violated the company's First Amendment rights. The postal service appealed directly to the Supreme Court.

Political Speech and Commercial Speech

Eight justices affirmed the district court's decision, with Justice Marshall writing the Court's opinion. Marshall's opinion directly addressed the characteristics distinguishing commercial speech. If the pamphlets were a form of political speech, they were fully protected by the Constitution and not subject to governmental regulation. If they were commercial in nature, then they enjoyed only a lesser and "qualified" degree of protection.

Marshall agreed with the district court that Youngs' proposed mailings all involved commercial speech. The company conceded that the informational pamphlets were advertisements. They referred to a specific product, and Young was mailing them for commercial reasons.

In isolation, no one of these three factors necessarily turned Youngs' pamphlets into commercial speech. However, because all three factors simultaneously were present, the pamphlets clearly were commercial. They did not become political speech merely because they mentioned health issues. "Advertising which 'links a product to a current public debate' is not thereby entitled to the constitutional protection afforded noncommercial speech."

Youngs' proposed mailings "fall within the core notion of commercial speech—'speech which does no more than propose a commercial transaction.'" As such, Marshall stressed, the mailings were entitled to the "qualified but nonetheless substantial protection accorded to commercial speech."

When the Government May Regulate Commercial Speech

Marshall advanced two criteria for determining whether commercial speech enjoys First Amendment protection. One must ask if the statements were illegal or deceptive. They must also ask if banning the speech serves any substantial governmental interest.

In the case of commercial speech, the government can forbid advertising which promotes illegal and criminal acts. It also may outlaw "false, deceptive, or misleading sales techniques." Justice Marshall found no deception in the Youngs mailings. Thus they were entitled to First Amendment protection under criterion one.

Marshall then considered whether prohibiting the mailings served any "substantial governmental inter-

est." According to the government's attorneys, the ban on mailing would serve two interests. A ban would shield people from materials they would likely find offensive. It would also help parents control how their children learned about important subjects such as birth control.

Marshall rejected both of these government arguments. On the first issue of offensiveness, Marshall noted that an individual could still ask advertisers not to send mail that he found "erotically arousing or sexually provocative." But the government could not suppress speech just because it was offensive to some persons. In any event, those who were offended could avert their eyes or dispose of the mailings in a trash can.

Marshall found the second government interest more substantial. "Parents have an important 'guiding role' to play in the upbringing of their children . . . which presumptively includes counseling them on important decisions." However, a universal ban on mailings is not an effective way of achieving this limited objective.

By stopping Youngs' mailings, the government would assist only those parents who could not otherwise keep innocent children from confronting Young's pamphlets. To achieve this "marginal degree of protection," the government seeks to purge every mailbox of materials "entirely suitable for adults." But the government may not "reduce the adult population . . . to reading only what is fit for children." In addition, a ban on mailings would deny parents "truthful information bearing upon their ability to discuss birth control and to make informed decisions."

Related Cases

Valentine v. Chrestensen, 316 U.S. 52 (1942).
National Life Ins. Co. v. Phillips Publishing, Inc., 793 F.Supp. 627 (1992).
Gordon and Breach Science Publishers S.A. v. American Institute of Physics, 859 F.Supp. 1521 (1994).

Bibliography and Further Reading

Gartner, Michael. *Advertising and the First Amendment.* New York: Priority Press, 1989.

Hemmer, Joseph. *The Supreme Court and the First Amendment.* New York: Praeger, 1986.

Middleton, Kent. *The Law of Public Communication.* White Plains, New York: Longman, 1988.

FEDERAL ELECTION COMMISSION V. NATIONAL CONSERVATIVE POLITICAL ACTION COMMITTEE

Legal Citation: 470 U.S. 480 (1985)

Appellant
Federal Election Commission

Appellee
National Conservative Political Action Committee et al.

Appellant's Claim
That the National Conservative Political Action Committee violated the Presidential Election Campaign Fund Act by exceeding the $1,000 spending limit to support the election of a presidential candidate.

Chief Lawyer for Appellant
Charles N. Steele

Chief Lawyer for Appellee
Robert R. Sparks, Jr.

Justices for the Court
Harry A. Blackmun, William J. Brennan, Jr., Warren E. Burger, Sandra Day O'Connor, Lewis F. Powell, Jr., William H. Rehnquist (writing for the Court), John Paul Stevens

Justices Dissenting
Thurgood Marshall, Byron R. White

Place
Washington, D.C.

Date of Decision
18 March 1985

Decision
Upheld district court finding that expenditures prohibited by the Presidential Election Campaign Fund Act were protected by the First Amendment and could not be restricted by the government.

Significance
The U.S. Supreme Court found political spending restrictions in the Presidential Election Campaign Fund Act "substantially overbroad," inappropriately applying to small informal groups as well as highly organized national organizations. The Court did not consider a general fear of corruption sufficient to justify government restrictions. The Court found that political action committees are valuable tools for the common citizen to promote their political views in an era of mass media communications. Therefore, committee expenditures for presidential campaigns deserved First Amendment protection.

Political Contributions

In 1971 Congress passed two campaign finance reform laws, the Presidential Election Campaign Fund Act (FECA) and the Presidential Election Campaign Finance Act (PECFA), to address spiraling campaign costs. The acts set limits on campaign spending, required disclosure of contributors, and established a public funding system. Amendments in 1974 created the Federal Election Commission (FEC) to enforce provisions of both acts.

The Supreme Court ruled in *Buckley v. Valeo* (1976) that parts of FECA were unconstitutional. The Court upheld limitations on contributions by individuals to political organizations but ruled that spending restrictions by FECA on political committees were unconstitutional if the committees operated independently of candidates or the candidates' election committees. By finding that such limits infringed on freedom of speech, the Court wrote, "[V]irtually every means of communicating ideas in today's mass society requires the expenditure of money." The opinion equated free speech with the spending of money to promote political views. Chief Justice Rehnquist wrote,

> A restriction on the amount of money a person or group can spend on political communication during a campaign necessarily reduces the quantity of expression by restricting the number of issues discussed, the depth of their exploration, and the size of the audience reached.

In essence, this ruling legalized independent expenditures. Similarly the Court, in *First National Bank of Boston v. Bellotti* (1978), noted that spending to express political views "is the type of speech indispensable to decision making in a democracy."

Amendments to FECA in 1979 exempted from campaign spending limits certain monies given to parties rather than individual candidates. The money, called "soft money" in this case, could only be used for specific purposes, such as volunteer activities, voter registration efforts, and for campaign materials. This money can not go directly to specific candidates or to the candidates' election committees.

Political Action Committees

Politicians finance their election campaigns with their own money and donations. As of 1998, individuals are limited by law to donating $1,000 per candidate per election, and $25,000 to all candidates per year. Primary, general, and run-off elections count separately for application of the limit.

Political action committees, or PACs, collect and pool money from individuals for donations to candidates above the individual limits. Individuals may contribute $5,000 per year to a PAC. PACs are limited to donating $5,000 per candidate per election, and an unlimited total amount per year.

The Federal Election Commission, which oversees campaign contributions and enforces the legal limits, places PACs into four categories: corporate, labor, trade-health-membership, and nonconnected. Nonconnected PACs are unaffiliated with any other organization, and usually are formed to raise contributions for candidates supporting a particular issue or political ideology. The other PACs are affiliated with an existing organization, such as a manufacturer or labor union, which funds the operation of the PAC and decides how to contribute the money it collects.

Source(s): Clawson, Dan, Alan Neustadtl, and Mark Weller. *Dollars and Votes: How Business Campaign Contributions Subvert Democracy.* Philadelphia: Temple University Press, 1998.

Clawson, Dan, Alan Neustadtl, and Mark Weller. *Money Talks: Corporate PACs and Political Influence.* New York: BasicBooks, 1992.

As an unexpected outcome of these campaign finance reforms in the 1970s, political action committees, more commonly called PACs, burst on the national scene. PACs are formed by various corporations, labor groups, and other special interests to influence elections and lobby Congress and the administration for favors. PACs operate independently of political parties or candidate election committees. Given the Supreme Court rulings and "soft money" amendments, PACs quickly seized the opportunity to influence elections while legally avoiding spending limitations. Some special interest PACs are called "ideological" PACs because they primarily promote specific ideas or beliefs. With the rise of the New Right political movement, two ideological PACs, the National Conservative Political Action Committee (NCPAC) and Fund for a Conservative Majority (FCM), rapidly gained prominence promoting conservative political doctrine.

Extensive Spending

Anticipating PAC activity, the FEC and Common Cause, a long-time proponent of campaign finance reform, challenged the extensive spending by independent organizations with reference to provisions of PECFA. They filed suit in 1980 seeking to affirm the constitutionality of section 9012(f) of PECFA. The section stipulates that independent PACs could not spend more than $1,000 to support the election of a presidential candidate. The case quickly proceeded to the Supreme Court who reached a deadlock on the constitutional question. The deadlock left independent spending unaffected for the 1980 political campaign. As a result, NCPAC pioneered PAC independent spending strategies designed to defeat liberal Democrats in the 1980 elections. In 1980 NCPAC spent more than

$7 million and FCM more than $2 million on Ronald Reagan's election campaign in an effort to gain control of the White House for the conservative Republicans.

In May of 1983, the Democratic party and the Democratic National Committee became alarmed by NCPAC's and FCM's intent to spend even more monies to gain President Reagan's re-election in 1984. Consequently, they filed suit to determine the legality of the two PACs' activities. Shortly afterwards, FEC joined the Democrats in the suit.

The plaintiffs initially filed suit accusing NCPAC of violating PECFA with the Federal District Court of the Eastern District of Pennsylvania. The suit focused on the spending of the PACs. The three-judge panel found 9012(f) not constitutionally valid on grounds that any limitation on spending by the PACs would violate First Amendment rights of free speech and free association. The plaintiffs appealed to the Supreme Court.

Unconstitutional Political Spending Limitations

The issue before the Court was whether PECFA violated NCPAC's First Amendment rights of free speech and free association. In arguments before the Supreme Court, the PACs claimed their expenditures were independent of the political parties or candidates, hence beyond the intended prohibitions of 9012(f). They asserted that typical contributions to their organizations were quite modest in size, predominately representing the common citizen. The plaintiffs argued that actions by the PACs did not constitute free speech, but simply "speech by proxy" which should not receive full First Amendment protection. "Speech by proxy" means that one person receives from another authority to speak on their behalf. Hence, the leaders of PACs were speaking for all their contributors. They also argued the high expenditures of the two PACs could breed political corruption, or at least the appearance of corruption. As evidence they pointed to high level appointments in the Reagan administration of persons previously associated with PACs.

The Supreme Court affirmed the district court's ruling that 9012(f) was not constitutionally valid. First, writing for the majority, Chief Justice Rehnquist fell back on the earlier *Buckley* ruling by again noting the expense of promoting political views in a mass-media society. In this regard, the independent PACs constitute valuable tools expanding the individual's voice. To limit PACs' spending would inhibit free speech protected under the First Amendment. Secondly, freedom of association rights were also relevant in this case due to the PACs' reliance on public contributions. The Court argued that *Buckley* protected freedom of association of "large numbers of individuals of modest means" to join together and amplify their voices. Rehnquist stated,

> that the contributors obviously like the message they are hearing from these organizations and want to add their voices to that message; otherwise they would not part with their money.

Section 9012(f) violated their freedom of association guaranteed under the First Amendment. Thirdly, the majority found section 9012(f) to be "substantially overbroad" by applying to all groups, no matter of what size, thereby limiting smaller, less formal political groups. Lastly, using the Court-established principle that preventing corruption is the only constitutionally permissible government interest in regulating campaign spending, the Court held that the plaintiffs did not clearly explain the type of corruption feared. The possible appearance of corruption was not sufficient in this case to warrant concern. Rehnquist asserted that simple distrust does not constitute corruption. In conclusion, the Court held that the PACs' independent expenditures are entitled to First Amendment protection because they are designed to promote political views, not specific political campaigns.

No Right to Spend

In dissent joined by Justice Marshall, Justice White agreed with FEC that spending large sums of money breeds political corruption and threatens the integrity of political campaigns. White noted the informal but close relationship between ideological PACs and the political parties in a world of "tacit [unspoken] understandings and implied agreements." Also, White asserted political equality is undermined by the accumulations of wealth by the PACs. Therefore, government restrictions should enhance the voice of the individual citizen by limiting PAC expenditures. In direct opposition to Rehnquist, White criticized equating expenditures of money with actual free speech. White wrote, "the First Amendment protects the right to speak, not the right to spend." Individual citizens who contribute to PACs do not actually have the opportunity to voice their political views since the actual decisions on spending are made by only the few PAC leaders. Contributors to political committees were no more engaging in speech than those who contributed directly to political candidates for which there exist limitations. Hence, any limitations would pose only minor interference with First Amendment rights. White feared candidates would increasingly feel pressure to please the PAC spenders rather than the voters.

Impact

Federal Election Commission v. National Conservative Political Action Committee opened the door wider to extensive campaign spending and the continued political influence of PACs. Many believe the campaign finance system creates distrust and cynicism in the public and undermines concepts of integrity and fairness. To many, government seems increasingly remote from their influence and a tool of the rich and powerful special interest groups. However, reform is a strongly partisan issue as Republicans have demonstrated a greater ability than Democrats to raise large sums of funds, thus gaining a seemingly greater advantage in elections. President Clinton, recognizing this disadvantage of the Democrats, undertook extraordinary efforts to raise campaign funds for his 1996 re-election. The various tactics drew considerable debate.

Facts regarding the dangers of PACs are not clear, complicating reform efforts. Studies show that life spans of individual PACS are brief, particularly the conservative citizen PACs. *FEC v. NCPAC* came at the time of maximum influence exerted by NCPAC and FCM. As quickly as 1986, NCPAC came into debt and by the early 1990s exerted only a minor influence in campaigns. Corporate and labor PACs, proven more stable due to a more definite, cohesive supporter base, largely replaced "ideological" PACs. Extensive reform proposals include public financing for Congressional elections, and limitations on PAC "soft money" contributions and independent spending. Congressional efforts at reform died again in early 1998. Reforms passed in the 1990s tended to focus more on disclosure of activities to the public rather than actual regulation of activities. Despite strong disagreements over the role and influence of PACs, they persist in the American political scene and continue to enjoy protection under the First Amendment.

Related Cases

Buckley v. Valeo, 424 U.S. 1 (1976).
First National Bank of Boston v. Bellotti, 435 U.S. 765 (1978).

Federal Election Commission v. National Right to Work Committee, 459 U.S. 197 (1982).

Austin v. Michigan State Chamber of Commerce, 494 U.S. 652 (1990).

Federal Election Commission v. National Rifle Association Victory Fund, (1994).

Bibliography and Further Reading

Alexander, Herbert E. *Financing Politics: Money, Elections, & Political Reform,* Fourth Ed. Washington, D C: Congressional Quarterly Press, 1992.

Common Cause. http://www.commoncause.org

Dowd, Ann R. "Look Who's Cashing in on Congress." *Money Magazine,* December 1997.

Gais, Thomas. *Improper Influence: Campaign Finance Law, Political Interest Groups, and the Problem of Equality.* Ann Arbor: University of Michigan Press, 1996.

Hrebenar, Ronald J. *Interest Group Politics in America.* Third Edition. New York: M.E. Sharpe, Inc., 1997.

"'Issue-Advocacy' Groups to Play Bigger Role." *The Wall Street Journal,* 6 March 1998

Puchi, David C. "Federal Election Commission v. National Conservative Political Action Committee: A Judicial Cure for Congressional Overzealousness in Presidential Campaign Finance Regulation." *Denver University Law Review* Vol. 63, no. 4, 1986.

BELL V. U-32 BOARD OF EDUCATION

Legal Citation: 630 F.Supp. 939 (1986)

Plaintiff
Megara Bell et al.

Defendant
The U-32 Board of Education

Plaintiff's Claim
That the board of education had violated the First Amendment rights of the students.

Chief Lawyer for Plaintiff
Alan Rosenfield

Chief Defense Lawyer
Robert H. Opel

U.S. District Judge
Chief Judge Coffrin

Place
U.S. District Court, District of Vermont

Date of Decision
17 March 1986

Decision
The school board did not violate the First Amendment rights of the students.

Significance
School officials have the ability, when trying to keep a clean and productive learning environment, to stop certain sentiments, deemed inappropriate, from being spread throughout the student body.

The First Amendment guarantees U.S. residents freedom of speech, but it is one of the most difficult concepts to untangle. Freedom of speech covers so many different issues and has been the subject of so many different court cases that no one definition serves. No one phrase captures all of the meanings imbued to the guarantee of freedom of speech. Of course, there is one other issue: with so many people and so many freedoms, it is difficult to know where one person's freedom ends and another person's rights begins. An example of this is found in the case of *Bell v. U-32 Board of Education*.

Every spring, U-32 High School produced a musical. The audience, as it does in many school plays, consisted of other students, parents and other people from the community. The school acted as sponsor for these plays, providing funds, covering costs above ticket sales, providing rehearsal and performance locations, publicizing the plays, etc. Generally, the performers and stage crew were made up of students from seventh to twelfth grades. These students received grades as well as academic credits for participating in these productions because the play was considered part of the curriculum. Faculty staff members received extra compensation for directing the play and for general supervision of the production. Each January faculty members picked a play and the school board approved the production by appropriating funds.

Around 16 January 1984, the curriculum director spoke to the principal about the appropriateness of that year's choice. The chosen play for 1984 was called *Runaways*. The principal and superintendent of schools read the play, discussed it with various school administrators, faculty members who chose the play, the director and other involved faculty members. The final decision was that the school could not support this particular production. Their concerns revolved around the subject of the play and some of its content.

The play was about several runaway children who were reflecting about the home problems that drove them away from home and some of their problems out in the street. Much of the play contrasted nursery rhymes with relatively realistic portrayals of some issues faced by runaway children in rougher situations—

Performing Arts Censorship

The performing arts is a medium of communication of ideas protected by the First Amendment. Yet, no absolute freedom exists to exhibit every kind of film and theater. What is deemed obscene, indecent, or excessively violent is subject to censorship. Should this censorship exist?

Proponents of censorship emphasize the role of the performing arts as entertainment clearly affecting public attitudes, behaviors, and morals. Blatantly offensive performances encourage violence, sexual promiscuity, and drug abuse. Censorship is, therefore, vital to safeguard children and adults from pornography and excessive violence. Opponents of regulation counter that censorship threatens the free speech rights of playwrights, screenwriters, filmmakers, performers, and distributors. They contend that deciding what is obscene or excessive is highly subjective.

Proponents also support voluntary rating systems. Owners of theaters and video rental franchises maintain such systems keeps customer satisfaction high and their business healthy. Civil libertarians and professional entertainer organizations object, saying in reality the rating systems are not voluntary but imposed through intimidation. The systems are also arbitrary, showing signs of racism, gender bias, and favoring large studios with sufficient budgets to repeatedly edit. Lastly, opponents contend legislation passed in the 1990s to improve children's programming only served to impose the government's values on society.

Source(s): *West's Encyclopedia of American Law.* Minneapolis/St. Paul, MN: West Publishing, 1998.

things like drug abuse, alcohol, child prostitution, and rape. One especially graphic scene featured a murder and a rape. There was some profane language and some humor.

When the school's performing arts director appealed to the school board, they arranged for a special school board meeting three days later, on Monday, 23 January. This would allow time for a decision before auditions which were scheduled to begin on Tuesday, 24 January.

Notices for the meeting were posted in a store and the superintendent's office. Also, a local radio station broadcast public service announcements about the meeting. All of the school board members attended, except one. Several faculty members and students also attended so their views could be heard. However, without stating any reasons, the school board voted that the play not be produced. Soon after the meeting, the plaintiffs spoke with an attorney. The attorney asked the board to reconsider clarifying its reasons for its decision.

On 8 February 1984 the board sent a letter to the attorney that it would add a motion for reconsideration to the next regular meeting's agenda on 23 February. At the meeting, the board explained its decision. They said, essentially, that the play was inappropriate for students and the general community for various rea-

sons. The board said they disapproved of the play because it involved sexual activity, child abuse, sexual violence, drug abuse and other such matters. The board did note that the play did not advocate or glamorize any of these things. Furthermore, the board pointed out, the play was available in the school library and was used as a textbook in a humanities class. The board thought that with all the available plays, this particular production did not represent a proper allocation of school funds. The same day as the meeting, the students filed their court action.

The district court ruled that the school board's decision about the play would hold because this did not violate the First Amendment rights of the students. It did not violate the First Amendment rights of the students because a school board can establish curricula so as to uphold and communicate community values as long as this did not deny access to ideas and opinions of others just because they disagreed with those ideas.

Bibliography and Further Reading

Lieberman, Jethro K. *The Evolving Constitution.* Random House, 1992.

Seidman, Louis M., Gerald R. Stone, Cass R. Sunstein, Mark V. Tushnet. *Constitutional Law.* Little, Brown and Company, 1986.

POSADAS DE PUERTO RICO V. TOURISM COMPANY OF PUERTO RICO, ET AL.

Legal Citation: 478 U.S. 328 (1986)

Appellant
Posadas de Puerto Rico Associates

Appellees
Tourism Company of Puerto Rico, et al.

Appellant's Claim
That provisions and implementing regulations of Puerto Rico's Games of Chance Act of 1948 suppressed commercial speech in violation of the First Amendment and the equal protection and due process guarantees of the Constitution.

Chief Lawyer for Appellant
Maria Millagros Soto

Chief Lawyer for Appellees
Lino J. Saldana

Justices for the Court
Warren E. Burger, Sandra Day O'Connor, Lewis F. Powell, Jr., William H. Rehnquist (writing for the Court), Byron R. White

Justices Dissenting
Harry A. Blackmun, William J. Brennan, Jr., Thurgood Marshall, John Paul Stevens

Place
Washington, D.C.

Date of Decision
1 July 1986

Decision
Affirmed the decisions of the Puerto Rico Superior Court and the Puerto Rico Supreme Court that the act was constitutional.

Significance
The ruling continued a trend of the Court to allow the state greater latitude in the regulation of commercial speech related to activities deemed to be potentially harmful, such as smoking, consumption of alcohol, and gambling.

A Two-Edged Sword

The present effort of several U.S. cities to legalize casino gambling to spur economic growth has a number of predecessors. Many Caribbean islands, faced with limited traditional economic prospects, turned to gambling as a means of promoting tourism. Ironically, those who support the legalization of gambling view it primarily as an economic development strategy, all parties in the debates over the legalization of gambling agree that gambling produces some negative social effects. When Puerto Rico decided to legalize certain forms of casino gambling in the years immediately following World War II, its government clearly recognized the negative aspects of legal gambling, and constructed its legislation accordingly. The Puerto Rico Games of Chance Act of 1948 legalized roulette and dice and card games within licensed gambling rooms, but specified that such gambling rooms were to be for the exclusive use of tourists. The act also forbade the advertising of Puerto Rican gambling establishments within Puerto Rico. Although the act was expanded to allow the playing of bingo in 1972 and the operation of slot machines in 1974, its ban on the use of Puerto Rican casinos by residents of Puerto Rico remained intact.

What Constitutes Commercial Speech?

In 1975 a group of investors known as Posadas de Puerto Rico Associates began operation of the Condado Holiday Inn and Sands Casino in Puerto Rico. In 1978 Posadas was twice fined by the Tourism Company of Puerto Rico for violating the act's prohibition against advertising casino facilities within Puerto Rico. Posadas argued that the fines were unwarranted in that its casino had undertaken no mass market advertising, but was told by the company in 1979 that the prohibition against advertising contained in the act "includes the use of the 'casino' in matchbooks, lighters, envelopes, inter-office and/or external correspondence, invoices, napkins, brochures, menus, elevators, glasses, plates, lobbies, banners, flyers, paper holders, pencils, telephone books, directories, bulletin boards or in any hotel dependency or object which may be accessible to the public in Puerto Rico." Posadas then sought a declaration from the Superior Court of Puerto Rico that the act violated, both on its face and as interpreted by the company, constitutional protection of commercial speech.

Initial Ruling and a Constitutional Question?

The superior court ruled in favor of the company, with some reservations. It found that the act was not unconstitutional on its face, but that its interpretation by the company was overly stringent and did violate Posadas' First Amendment rights. The superior court ruled that the state did have a compelling interest in regulating speech regarding casinos since the sole intent of the act was "to contribute to the development of tourism," and the act specifically barred residents of Puerto Rico from gambling houses. Despite finding the act legally admissible and binding, the superior court did temper the strict interpretation of the act's prohibition of advertising applied by the company. Its ruling allowed suggestive words, such as "casino," to appear even in mass market advertising of gambling establishments within Puerto Rico, as long as these words were not emphasized within the advertisement, and such advertising was "addressed to tourists" and did not encourage residents of Puerto Rico to enter gambling houses. The superior court also allowed hotels and casinos to produce and distribute memorabilia and items of clothing bearing their name and logo on their premises. Posadas was not satisfied by this partial victory and appealed the case to the Puerto Rico Supreme Court, which agreed with the superior court that the act was not unconstitutional. Posadas then appealed the case to the U.S. Supreme Court, which heard arguments on 28 April 1986.

Regulation of Truthful Advertising

By a 5-4 margin the Supreme Court upheld the decision of the lower courts, ruling that the act was constitutional. The Court also agreed that discouraging participation in legal gambling by residents of Puerto Rico constituted a compelling state interest. In deciding on the constitutionality of the company's interpretation of the act, the Supreme Court applied the test for establishing violation of First Amendment protection of commercial speech developed in *Central Hudson Gas and Electric Corporation v. Public Service Commission of New York,* (1980).This test involves applying four questions to any commercial speech: does the speech promote a lawful activity and is it truthful?; is there a compelling state interest in regulating the speech?; do any regulations applied to the speech advance the state's compelling interest in such regulation?; are any regulations of the speech excessive to the state's compelling interest in such regulation? The Court ruled that the company's interpretation of the act met each of the four prongs of the *Central Hudson* test, and as such affirmed the decision of the superior court. The four dissenting justices advanced the position that commercial speech that promotes a lawful activity and is truthful in content should be afforded the same protection as other forms of speech.

Impact

Posadas de Puerto Rico v. Tourism Company of Puerto Rico, et al. confirmed the Court's willingness to allow greater state regulation of commercial speech in the name of a compelling state interest, as first seen in *Central Hudson.* Significantly, the Court split along its perceived political lines, with the more conservative justices constituting a majority. The decision also evidenced the Court's tendency to allow greater state regulation of speech-promoting activities perceived to be potentially harmful, such as the use of tobacco products, gambling, and consumption of alcohol.

Related Cases

Virginia Pharmacy Board v. Virginia Citizens Consumer Council, Inc., 425 U.S. 748 (1976).
Carey v. Population Services International, 431 U.S. 678 (1977).
Central Hudson Gas and Electric Corp. v. Public Service Commission of New York, 447 U.S. 557 (1980).
Zauderer v. Office of Disciplinary Counsel, 471 U.S. 626 (1985).
Renton v. Playtime Theaters, 475 U.S. 41 (1986).

Bibliography and Further Reading

Biskupic, Joan, and Elder Witt, eds. *Guide to the Supreme Court of the United States.* Washington, DC: Congressional Quarterly Inc., 1997.

Cook, Don Lloyd. "Earthquakes and Aftershocks: Implications for Marketers and Advertisers in Reno v. ACLU and the Litigation of the Communications Decency Act." *Journal of Public Policy & Marketing,* Spring 1998, p. 116.

Hall, Kermit L., ed. *Oxford Companion to the Supreme Court of the United States.* New York: Oxford University Press, 1992.

Langvardt, Arlen W. and Eric L. Richards. "The Death of Posadas and the Birth of Change in Commercial Speech Doctrine: Implications of 44 Liquormart." *American Business Law Journal,* Summer 1997, pp. 483-559.

Petty, Ross D. "Please Be Ad-Vised: The Legal Reference Guide for the Advertising Executive, 2nd Ed." *Journal of Public Policy & Marketing,* Spring 1997, p. 189.

Richards, Jef I. "Is 44 Liquormart a Turning Point?" *Journal of Public Policy & Marketing,* Spring 1997, p. 156.

BETHEL SCHOOL DISTRICT NO. 403 V. FRASER

Legal Citation: 478 U.S. 675 (1986)

Petitioner
Bethel School District in Pierce County, Washington State

Respondent
Matthew Fraser, a student at Bethel High School

Petitioner's Claim
School authorities should be permitted to discipline students that use language those authorities consider offensive.

Chief Lawyers for Petitioner
William A. Coats, Clifford D. Foster, Jr.

Chief Lawyers for Respondent
Jeffrey T. Haley and Charles S. Sims

Justices for the Court
Harry A. Blackmun, William J. Brennan, Jr., Warren E. Burger (writing for the Court), Sandra Day O'Connor, Lewis F. Powell, Jr., William H. Rehnquist, Byron R. White

Justices Dissenting
Thurgood Marshall, John Paul Stevens

Place
Washington, D.C.

Date of Decision
7 July 1986

Decision
The First Amendment did not prevent school authorities from disciplining Matthew Fraser for giving an "offensively lewd and indecent speech." School disciplinary codes only have to describe offenses in general terms; they need not be as detailed as a criminal code, which imposes harsh punishments.

Significance
Bethel was only the second case dealing with the legal rights of students. The Court ruled that students do not enjoy the full protection accorded to adults. Schools may limit student speech both to prevent disruption and also to instill fundamental values.

Jeff Held Firm Convictions

Matthew Fraser was a student with an outstanding academic record at Bethel High School. At a school assembly in April 1983, Fraser delivered a brief speech nominating a fellow student for office. The speech contained words which might have had a double meaning, with the second meaning referring to the act of sexual intercourse. In part, Fraser spoke as follows:

> I know a man who is firm—he's firm in his pants, he's firm in his shirt, his character is firm—but most . . . of all, his belief in you, the students of Bethel is firm.
>
> Jeff Kuhlman is a man who takes his point and pounds it in. If necessary, he'll take an issue and nail it to the wall. He doesn't attack things in spurts—he drives hard, pushing and pushing until finally—he succeeds.
>
> Jeff is a man who will go to the very end—even the climax, for each and every one of you.
>
> So vote for Jeff for A. S. B. vice-president—he'll never come between you and the best our high school can be.

Students were required to attend the assembly, and about 600 were present, some as young as 14. During Fraser's speech, some students hooted and yelled, and a few mimicked the sexual activities they thought Fraser was describing. Others were bewildered by the entire incident. No evidence was presented that anyone present was insulted or offended by Fraser's remarks.

Harsh Punishments for "Obscene" Language

The morning after the assembly, the assistant principal called Fraser into her office. School administrators, she told Fraser, had ruled that his speech violated a Bethel High rule prohibiting "obscene" language. The rule in question read: "Conduct which materially and substantially interferes with the educational process is prohibited, including the use of obscene, profane language or gestures."

Fraser admitted having given the speech described, and he said that he had intended to use a sexual

Student Free Speech

The U.S. Supreme Court generally recognizes more limitations to a student's First Amendment rights than it does to an adult's. However, a student's constitutional rights to freedom of speech and expression are not left at the schoolhouse door. They cannot be punished for expressing personal views in the cafeteria, playing fields, classrooms, or halls unless school staff has reason to believe the educational process has been disrupted or other students' rights infringed. Yet, the Court recognizes that when considering First Amendment rights, the special characteristics of a school's environment must be considered. Justice Byron R. White succinctly wrote, " A school need not tolerate student speech that is inconsistent with its basic educational mission." For example, speech advocating drug use or irresponsible sex would be inappropriate.

Determining if speech is contrary to basic school values rests with the schoolboard, not the federal courts. School-sponsored publications, performing arts productions, and other forms of expression produced by students must teach the lesson intended and be at an appropriate maturity level. To accomplish their educational goals, educators can require a higher standard of speech than might be demanded outside the school setting.

Source(s): Epstein, Lee, and Thomas G. Walker. *Constitutional Law for a Changing America: Rights, Liberties, and Justice.* Washington, DC: Congressional Quarterly Press, 1995.

metaphor. He was suspended from school for three days. Moreover, his name was removed from the list of candidates for speaker at the upcoming graduation exercises. The school district's grievance process affirmed Matthew's punishment, but he enjoyed more success when he sued in the district court.

Students are Persons Too

Prior to this case, the Supreme Court had granted students some rights enjoyed by adults. In *Tinker v. Des Moines Independent Community School District* (1969), the Court had ruled that three students could not be suspended for peacefully wearing black armbands (to protest U. S. involvement in the Vietnam War). Students are "persons" and thus are protected by the Fourteenth Amendment, which incorporates the First Amendment right to free speech.

Relying on the *Tinker* decision, the district court had held that Bethel High violated Matthew Fraser's First Amendment rights. The court also had concluded that the school's rules were vague and overbroad. In particular, removal from the graduation speaker list was not mentioned among possible punishments. Removing Fraser from the list thus violated the Fourteenth Amendment's due process clause.

The district court awarded Fraser damages and costs (amounting to $13,028). It also ordered that the school allow Fraser to speak at the graduation ceremonies. Elected graduation speaker by a write-in vote, Fraser did deliver the speech.

Again referring to the *Tinker* decision, the court of appeals affirmed the district court's judgement. The school district appealed to the Supreme Court.

Students Must Be Taught that Lewd Speech is Undemocratic

In reversing the lower courts, the justices ruled that the school district had the authority to punish Fraser. Joined by four others, Chief Justice Burger wrote the opinion of the Court. Justices Blackmun and Brennan concurred with the decision, but Brennan filed a separate opinion. Justices Marshall and Stevens filed dissenting opinions.

Burger declared that adults enjoy wide freedom in public discourse. However, "the constitutional rights of students in public school" are more limited than "the rights of adults in other settings." Burger argued that *Tinker* did not protect "offensive" speech. Nor did *Tinker* protect speech that is "materially disruptive."

Schools exist, Burger continued, to instill "the fundamental values necessary to the maintenance of a democratic political system." These democratic values "disfavor" the use of terms "highly offensive or threatening to others." In teaching these values, teachers and older students serve as role models just as parents do in the home.

> The schools, as instruments of the state, may determine that the essential lessons of civil, mature conduct cannot be conveyed in a school that tolerates, lewd, indecent, or offensive speech . . . A high school assembly or classroom is no place for a sexually explicit monologue . . . Accordingly, it was perfectly appropriate for the school to disassociate itself to make the point to the pupils that vulgar speech and lewd conduct is wholly inconsistent with the "fundamental values" of public school education.

Chief Justice Burger also ruled that school officials did not violate Fraser's due process rights. The school's regulations gave Fraser sufficient notice that "lewd" speech could subject him to sanctions. School rules need not be as rigidly precise as a criminal code.

What Some Considered Lewd Is Not Lewd to Others

Justice Brennan concurred with the majority's decision. However, he wrote a separate opinion that placed more limits on a school board's authority. Brennan stated that his colleagues grossly exaggerated in describing Fraser's remarks as "obscene," "vulgar," and "lewd." Having read the full text, Brennan found it "difficult to believe that it is the same speech the Court describes" The language Fraser used was very far indeed from the "very narrow class of 'obscene' speech" that is not protected by the First Amendment.

School officials do not, Brennan argued, have a "limitless authority" to regulate student speeches, such as Fraser's. If they acted to ensure that the assembly proceeded in any orderly manner, then they had the authority to suspend Fraser. But his speech might well have been protected "had he given it in school but under different circumstances."

In Justice Marshall's dissenting opinion, he argued that school officials never presented evidence that Fraser's speech had, in fact, disrupted education at Bethel High.

Justice Stevens also dissented. Stevens argued that Fraser had no reason to think he would be suspended for the speech given. As the lower courts had correctly ruled, his First and Fourteenth Amendment rights were violated because he did not receive "fair notice" of how the authorities would react.

The school rules forbade "disruptive" conduct. But there was no evidence that his speech was disruptive. And his language—although it involved a sexual metaphor—was not obviously "obscene" or "lewd." Before giving the speech, Fraser had questioned three teachers regarding its propriety. None of them suggested that he might be suspended for giving the speech. Fraser thus had no reason, Stevens concluded, to anticipate that he would be punished.

Related Cases

Tinker v. Des Moines Independent Community School District, 393 U.S. 503 (1969).

Chief Justice Warren E. Burger. © Photograph by Joseph Lavenburg, National Geographic. Collection of the Supreme Court of the United States.

Bibliography and Further Reading

Baldwin, Gordon B. "The Library Bill of Rights—A Critique." *Library Trends*, summer 1996, pp. 7.

Biskupic, Joan and Elder Witt, eds. *Congressional Quarterly's Guide to the U.S. Supreme Court*, 3rd ed. Washington, DC: Congressional Quarterly, Inc., 1996.

Lane, Robert. *Beyond the Schoolhouse Gate: Free Speech and the Inculcation of Values*. Philadelphia: Temple University Press, 1995.

Martinson, David L. "Vular, Indecent, and Offensive Student Speech." *The Clearing House*, July-August 1998, pp. 345.

Schuster, Joseph F. *The First Amendment in the Balance*. San Francisco: Austin & Winfield, 1993.

"The Supreme Court: A Principal's Best Friend." *Time*, July 10, 1995, p. 14.

AIRPORT COMMISSIONERS V. JEWS FOR JESUS, INC.

Legal Citation: 482 U.S. 569 (1987)

Petitioners
Board of Airport Commissioners of The City of Los Angeles, et al.

Respondents
Jews for Jesus, Inc., et al.

Petitioners' Claim
That a resolution adopted by airport commissioners, banning all First Amendment activities within the central terminal area at Los Angeles International Airport, does not violate the First Amendment.

Chief Lawyer for Petitioners
James R. Kapel

Chief Lawyer for Respondents
Jay Alan Sekulow

Justices for the Court
Harry A. Blackmun, William J. Brennan, Jr., Thurgood Marshall, Sandra Day O'Connor (writing for the Court), Lewis F. Powell, Jr., William H. Rehnquist, Antonin Scalia, John Paul Stevens, Byron R. White

Place
Washington, D.C.

Date of Decision
15 June 1987

Decision
The resolution violates the First Amendment.

Significance
The ruling invalidated a city airport's resolution banning all First Amendment activities in the central terminal. The Supreme Court decided that the resolution was substantially overbroad in violation of the First Amendment because its express language prohibited even talking and reading or the wearing of campaign buttons or symbolic clothing. The resolution was invalid, regardless of whether the airport was a public or nonpublic forum.

The First Amendment to the U.S. Constitution states:

> Congress shall make no law respecting an establishment of religion, or prohibiting the free exercise thereof; or abridging the freedom of speech, or of the press; or the right of the people peacefully to assemble, and to petition the government for a redress of grievances.

In the 1980s, religious organizations used commercial airports as a forum for the distribution of literature, the solicitation of funds, proselytizing new members, and other similar activities. Airport authorities, concerned with congestion and the disruption of airport business, enacted rules attempting to limit such activity. Religious groups challenged these rules under the First Amendment.

In 1983, the Board of Airport Commissioners of the city of Los Angeles adopted a resolution, which provided that "the Central Terminal Area at Los Angeles International Airport is not open for First Amendment activities by any individual and/or entity." The resolution also warned that

> if any individual or entity engages in First Amendment activities within the Central Terminal Area at Los Angeles International Airport, the City Attorney . . . is directed to institute appropriate litigation against such individual and/or entity to ensure compliance with this Policy.

In 1984, a minister with the religious group, Jews for Jesus, was stopped by an airport peace officer while distributing religious literature on a walkway in the central terminal. The minister was shown a copy of the resolution, told that his activities violated the resolution, and instructed to leave the facility. The minister was also warned that his refusal to leave would result in legal action by the city.

Jews for Jesus and its minister filed an action in the district court for the Central District of California claiming that the resolution was facially unconstitutional under both the California and U.S. Constitutions because it banned all speech in a public forum. They also claimed that the resolution was applied to Jews for

Jesus in a discriminatory manner and that it was unconstitutionally overbroad and vague. The district court ruled only on the first claim. The district court first found that the central terminal area was a traditional public forum under federal law, and then concluded that the resolution was facially unconstitutional under the U.S. Constitution. The Court of Appeals for the Ninth Circuit affirmed. The court of appeals concluded that "an airport complex is a traditional public forum," and held that the resolution was unconstitutional on its face under the U.S. Constitution. The Supreme Court granted the airport commissioners' petition for a writ of *certiorari* and ordered the court of appeals to forward the case to the Supreme Court for its review.

Resolution Unconstitutional

In a unanimous decision, the Supreme Court affirmed the ruling of the lower court. It found that the resolution was unconstitutional on its face under federal law because it banned all First Amendment activities in the airport. However, unlike the lower courts, the Supreme Court did not decide the issue of whether the airport was a public or nonpublic forum. Jews for Jesus claimed that the airport was a public forum, requiring the Supreme Court to strictly scrutinize the regulation of speech. The airport argued that the it was a nonpublic forum to which access may be reasonably restricted. In response, the Supreme Court acknowledged its ruling in *Perry Ed. Assn. v. Perry Local Educators' Assn.* (1993) that a less restrictive standard applies in First Amendment cases in which the expressive activity takes place in a nonpublic forum. However, because the resolution imposed an absolute ban on all First Amendment activities, the Court concluded that the resolution was unconstitutional, regardless of whether the airport was a public or nonpublic forum. Thus, the Court did not decide the forum issue because the decision was not necessary to the Court's ruling on the issue of constitutionality.

Writing for the unanimous Court, Justice O'Connor concluded that the resolution was facially unconstitutional because it violated the overbreadth doctrine of the First Amendment. Justice O'Connor explained that under the overbreadth doctrine, a person whose own speech or conduct is not protected by the Constitution may challenge a statute on its face if the statute also threatens to compromise the constitutionally protected activities of other persons not before the court. In addition, a party whose speech may not be constitutionally prohibited may also challenge a statute as overbroad if the speech of others would be chilled. According to West's *Words and Phrases,* the overbreadth doctrine is an exception to the general rule that a person to whom a statute may be constitutionally applied cannot challenge the statute on the ground that it may be unconstitutionally applied to others. The goal of the doctrine is to prevent the chilling effect of overbroad statutes. A chilling effect occurs when individuals restrict their

expressive activities rather than risk being prosecuted under such statutes.

An overbroad statute that encompasses both protected and unprotected speech and conduct will normally be struck down as facially invalid. However, as stated by the Supreme Court in *Broadrick v. Oklahoma* (1973), to invalidate a statute on its face, the overbreadth must be "substantial." A realistic danger that the statute itself will significantly compromise recognized First Amendment protections of parties not before the Court must be present for a statute to be facially challenged on overbreadth grounds. The Supreme Court determined that the airport's resolution was substantially overbroad because it banned all First Amendment activities in the central terminal area, rather than merely regulating expressive activity that might create problems such as congestion or the disruption of the activities of airport users. Justice O'Connor stated,

> On its face, the resolution at issue in this case reaches the universe of expressive activity, and, by prohibiting all protected expression, purports to create a virtual 'First Amendment Free Zone' at [the airport].

Justice O'Connor went on to say that by prohibiting all First Amendment activities, the resolution "prohibits even talking and reading, or the wearing of campaign buttons or symbolic clothing." Justice O'Connor concluded that "[u]nder such a sweeping ban, virtually every individual who enters [the airport] may be found to have violated the resolution by engaging in some First Amendment activity." She stated that it was "obvious that such a ban cannot be justified even if [the airport] were a nonpublic forum because no conceivable governmental interest would justify such an absolute prohibition of speech."

No Narrowing Interpretation Possible

The Supreme Court also chose not to give the California state courts an opportunity to limit the scope of the resolution before ruling on its constitutionality. The Court concluded that the express words of the resolution left no room to narrow its scope in a way that would avoid the federal constitutional questions.

In answer to the airport's claim that the statute was not substantially overbroad because it applied only to expressive activity unrelated to airport purposes, Justice O'Connor called the line between airport-related speech and nonairport-related speech "murky" and concluded that the vagueness of such a limiting construction would leave its enforcement open to abuse by airport officials.

Public Forum Issue Postponed

In a concurring opinion joined by Chief Justice Rehnquist, Justice White disagreed with the Court's decision to postpone a ruling on the issue of whether the airport was a public forum. Justice White also pointed out that the Court's failure to decide the issue did not mean that a majority of the Court agreed with the lower courts' conclusion that the airport was a traditional public forum.

Impact

The controversy over distribution of religious and political literature on government property continued into the 1990s. In 1992, the Supreme Court ruled in a 5-4 decision that an airport terminal operated by a public authority is a nonpublic forum, and that a ban on solicitation need only satisfy a reasonableness standard [*International Society for Krishna Consciousness v. Lee*]. The *Krishna Consciousness* case followed a 1990 Supreme Court decision by a plurality of the Court that a sidewalk on U.S. Post Office property was not a public forum [*United States v. Kokinda*]. In 1997, the city of Los Angeles enacted another ordinance banning all solicitations at city airports. The International Society of Krishna Consciousness of California and the Committee for Human Rights in Iran sued the city, alleging the ban violated the First Amendment and the California Constitution.

Attempts to further define the protections of the First Amendment also continued in Congress. In 1993, Congress passed the Religious Freedom Restoration Act, which required the government to show a compelling interest to justify any substantial restriction on religion, a traditional test that some members of Congress feared had been replaced by less restrictive standards. However, in 1997, The Supreme Court declared the act unconstitutional as applied to the states in *Boerne v. Flores*.

Related Cases

Tinker v. Des Moines Independent School District, 393 U.S. 503 (1969).

Broadrick v. Oklahoma, 413 U.S. 601 (1973).

Perry Ed. Assn. v. Perry Local Educators' Assn., 460 U.S. 37 (1983).

United States v. Kokinda, 497 U.S. 720 (1990).

International Society for Krishna Consciousness v. Lee, 505 U.S. 672 (1992).

Boerne v. Flores, 521 U.S. 507 (1997).

Bibliography and Further Reading

Laycock, D. "Equal Access and Moments of Silence: The Equal Status of Religious Speech by Private Speakers," 81 *Northwestern University Law Review* 1, 48 (1986).

New York Times, March 4, 1998.

Words and Phrases. St. Paul, MN: West Publishing Co., 1981.

RANKIN V. MCPHERSON

Legal Citation: 483 U.S. 378 (1987)

Petitioner
Constable Walter Rankin

Respondent
Ardith McPherson

Petitioner's Claim
That the respondent's dismissal was a reasonable exercise of the government's interest in maintaining an efficient workplace.

Chief Lawyer for Petitioner
Billy E. Lee

Chief Lawyer for Respondent
Lloyd N. Cutler

Justices for the Court
Harry A. Blackmun, William J. Brennan, Jr., Thurgood Marshall (writing for the Court), Lewis F. Powell, Jr., John Paul Stevens

Justices Dissenting
William H. Rehnquist, Sandra Day O'Connor, Antonin Scalia, Byron R. White

Place
Washington, D.C.

Date of Decision
24 June 1987

Decision
The Court held that the respondent's speech was on a matter of public concern, and was therefore protected by the First Amendment.

Significance
This case addressed the necessity of striking a balance between a public employer's right to maintain an efficient workplace and a public employee's right to free speech.

"I hope they get him"

Ardith McPherson was a probationary employee in the office of the constable of Harris County, Texas. Her job was to enter information into a computer. She worked in a room without a phone, and she had no contact with the public. Her job title was "deputy constable," but this signified little, as that was the job title of every employee in the constable's office.

On 30 March 1981, McPherson heard on the radio at work that someone had attempted to assassinate President Reagan. She speculated to her boyfriend, another deputy constable, that the would-be assassin was probably an African American, as Reagan's policies were particularly punitive to African Americans. She then commented, "If they go for him again, I hope they get him."

Another employee overheard this comment, and reported it to Constable Walter Rankin. The constable called McPherson into his office, and asked her if she had made the comment. She admitted doing so; Rankin fired her on the spot.

McPherson sued Rankin in district court for violating her First and Fourteenth Amendment rights of free speech. The district court used a three-question test developed in *Mt. Healthy City School District Board of Education v. Doyle* (1977): 1) Is the speech protected? 2) Did it play a substantial part in the decision to fire the employee? 3) If so, was it the deciding factor? In this case, only (1) was in question. The court answered "no," deciding that, on balance, Rankin's interest was more compelling.

McPherson then took her case to the circuit court of appeals. This court found "substantial issues of material fact." It therefore set aside the district court's judgment and sent the case back to be tried again.

The district court ruled for Rankin a second time, saying that McPherson's speech was not protected. McPherson appealed again to the circuit court. This time, the circuit court reversed the district court's judgment and sent the case back to district court for determination of an appropriate remedy. At this point, Rankin petitioned the Supreme Court for a writ of *certiorari*, which was granted.

Pickering and *Connick*

Two previous cases involving public employees' speech came to bear on this decision: *Pickering v. Board of Education* (1968) and *Connick v. Myers* (1983). *Pickering* involved a public school teacher dismissed for criticizing the board of education in a letter to the editor. The Court held that the teacher's dismissal violated his right to free speech. Justice Marshall, writing for the majority, explained that the Court's job was to "arrive at a balance between the interests of the teacher, as a citizen, in commenting upon matters of public concern and the interest of the State, as an employer, in promoting the efficiency of the public services it performs through its employees." The legacy of *Pickering* is a balancing test. The three-step Mt. Healthy test was a later elaboration on the Pickering balance.

The second case, *Connick v. Myers,* further refined the Pickering test by adding a threshold requirement. The case arose when an assistant district attorney circulated an inflammatory questionnaire in her office. After being dismissed for what was called her "mini-insurrection," she sued. The Supreme Court ruled against her, on the grounds that her speech did not address a matter of public concern. Thus *Connick* added the "public concern threshold" to the Pickering balance, resulting in the test that the *Rankin* Court would use.

Comment a Matter of Public Concern

Justice Marshall, writing for the majority, first addressed the threshold question of whether McPherson's comment was "speech on a matter of public concern." The Court found that it was, because an attempt on the president's life clearly concerned the public. The context of the comment, a conversation about the president's policies, also helped its public concern status.

The next question was whether McPherson's statement interfered with the office's ability to provide services efficiently. Marshall did not see any evidence that it had (though Scalia disputed this in his dissent). By Rankin's own testimony, he did not dismiss McPherson in order to maintain an efficient office. He did not ask himself whether or not the comment was disruptive. Rankin fired McPherson because he felt, on the basis of the comment, that she was unsuitable for employment in the constable's office.

Moreover, the specific job of the employee was worth considering. Marshall wrote that because McPherson's duties were so circumscribed, and because she served "no confidential, policymaking, or public contact role," she really had limited potential for disrupting the agency or diminishing public trust in the agency. The majority therefore found that, on balance, McPherson's discharge was unwarranted, and ruled for her.

In a concurrence, Justice Powell wondered "how this case has assumed constitutional dimensions and reached the Supreme Court of the United States."

To him, this was a relatively minor and clear-cut free speech case. Because McPherson's comment was made privately, the government's interest would have to be unusually great to override her rights in a Pickering balance.

"Simply Violent"

In contrast, Justice Scalia, dissenting, worried that in this case

> the Court significantly and irrationally expands the definition of "public concern"; it also carves out a new and very large class of employees—i.e., those in "nonpolicymaking" positions—who, if today's decision is to be believed, can never be disciplined for statements that fall within the Court's expanded definition.

Scalia departed from the majority on the nature of McPherson's speech. The subject matter alone did not qualify her comment as speech on a matter of public concern, he argued. The statement "I hope they get him" did not relate to self-government, did not constitute part of a public debate, and was not conducive to informed decision making (all criteria from earlier decisions). Her comment was simply violent. Scalia dismissed the conversation preceding the comment as nothing more than the motive for the offending comment.

Even if the speech were on a matter of public concern, though, Scalia still would not consider it protected. The issue was not whether she ought to have been fired. The issue was whether it was permissible to discipline her in some way for her comment. If the speech was protected, then no reprimand would be allowed.

Rankin did have a legitimate interest in disciplining McPherson, Scalia argued, explicitly contradicting the majority's finding that "there is no evidence that [McPherson's comment] interfered with the efficient functioning of the office." As proof, Scalia pointed to a statement from testimony, that the deputy reporting McPherson's comment to Rankin "was very upset because of [it]."

He also took issue with the Court's leniency toward the statements of "nonpolicymaking" employees. (The category of "nonpolicymaking employees" was not new to this case, contrary to Scalia's assertion. It arose first in reference to patronage cases, in *Elrod v. Burns* [1976], which recommended that patronage dismissals be limited to nonpolicymaking positions. In *Rankin,* however, the category was first used outside the context of a patronage case.) "Nonpolicymaking employees," Scalia objected, "can hurt working relationships and undermine public confidence in the organization every bit as much as policymaking employees."

Impact

This case expanded the category of "speech on a matter of public concern." At the time of the decision, some circuit courts of appeals were using the dissent's standard: speech on a matter of public concern informed citizens and helped them make democratic decisions. Some critics have noted that the Court did not provide a clear analysis of "public concern." If the expanded definition proves difficult to apply, courts may retreat from the *Connick* threshold requirement, back to the Pickering balancing.

Related Cases

Pickering v. Board of Education, 391 U.S. 563 (1968).
Elrod v. Burns, 427 U.S. 347 (1976).
Mt. Healthy City School District Board of Education v. Doyle, 429 U.S. 274 (1977).
Connick v. Myers, 461 U.S. 138 (1983).

Bibliography and Further Reading

Cox, Madeline E. "Constitutional Law—First Amendment—Public Employees' Right to Free Speech in the Workplace Expanded." *Seton Hall Law Review,* Vol. 19, no. 2, 1989, pp. 380–405.

Gerhold, Susan. "Constitutional Safeguard on Speech—Dismissal of Public Employee—Balancing Approach." *Duquesne Law Review,* Vol. 27, no. 1, fall, 1988, pp. 185–98.

Glovin, Richard M. "*Rankin v. McPherson:* The Court Handcuffs Public Employers." *Pacific Law Journal,* Vol. 19, no. 4 (1988): 1543–63.

Schiumo, Michael J. K. "A Proposal for Rethinking the 'Of Public Concern' Requirement of Pickering." *Communications and the Law,* June 1992.

WARD V. ROCK AGAINST RACISM

Legal Citation: 491 U.S. 781 (1989)

Petitioner
Benjamin R. Ward, New York City Police Commissioner

Respondent
Rock Against Racism

Petitioner's Claim
U.S. Circuit Court of Appeals ruling that a city guideline regulating sound volume as unconstitutional was in error.

Chief Lawyer for Petitioner
Leonard J. Koerner

Chief Lawyer for Respondent
William M. Kunstler

Justices for the Court
Harry A. Blackmun, Anthony M. Kennedy (writing for the Court), Sandra Day O'Connor, William H. Rehnquist, Antonin Scalia, Byron R. White

Justices Dissenting
William J. Brennan, Jr., Thurgood Marshall, John Paul Stevens

Place
Washington, D.C.

Date of Decision
22 June 1989

Decision
In favor of appellant Ward, reversing the appeal court decision.

Significance
Prompted by lawsuits over the volume of rock concerts, the Court found itself weighing the legality of local regulation versus the right to free speech.

Rock and A Loud Place

Amid a season of testimony about issues like civil rights and abortion, the 1989 Supreme Court got a lesson in how rock concerts are amplified. The result was a decision in which the Court divided over the intent of the First Amendment.

Starting in 1979, a New York anti-fascist organization called Rock Against Racism (RAR) began holding annual concerts at the Naumberg Acoustic Band Shell in Central Park. RAR's 1984 concert produced complaints from neighbors and park visitors in the nearby Sheep Meadow, a portion of Central Park reserved for "passive recreation." After repeated warnings to lower the volume, and two citations, city officials shut off the band shell's electricity, angering the crowd. When the city refused to issue a permit to RAR to use the band shell the following year and suggested alternate sites, the organization threatened legal action against the city. The two sides came to an agreement and a permit was issued, but the city began looking for a way to avoid repeating such disagreements.

The city decided to install a permanent sound system and contract an independent sound technician to run the equipment. Under new guidelines, all users of the Naumberg band shell would be required to use both the permanent amplification equipment and the sound engineer provided by the city. The system would thus be operated by someone familiar with the intricacies of the band shell's acoustics and would be less likely to simply turn up the volume in answer to any problems that might arise.

The 1986 summer season of concerts proceeded at the Naumberg band shell, but Rock Against Racism challenged the guidelines as an intrusion upon the First Amendment right to free expression. RARs initial legal challenge was unsuccessful. Noting that other users, ranging from reggae bands to opera companies, had been satisfied with the permanent system, the U.S. district court ruled that the guidelines were a valid constitutional regulation. Upon appeal, however, the U.S. Court of Appeals for the Second Circuit decided that the city had not protected the First Amendment by proving that its guidelines were the "least intrusive" means of regulating the sound volume. Instead, the court ruled, the city might have simply set a finite decibel level for all users with a warning that excessive volume would result in the system being turned off.

The court granted RAR an injunction against enforcement of the guidelines. While the injunction was in force, RARs annual concert took place, producing the usual complaints. After the concert was over, the issue of control over the Naumberg sound system remained undecided. RAR added a suit for damages and a request for a declaratory statement striking down the guidelines as invalid. Naming Police Commissioner Benjamin Ward as appellant, the city sought a reversal of the appeals court decision in the next highest judicial venue, the U.S. Supreme Court.

A Sound Lesson

The case was argued before the Court on 27 February 1989. RARs attorney, William M. Kunstler, explained to the justices how onstage microphones relay the sound of instruments and vocals through a central mixing board. From this console, a sound engineer balances the individual instruments into an overall "mix," controlling the volume and making necessary adjustments. Kunstler explained that using a sound engineer who was unfamiliar with a performer's music was similar to switching symphony conductors, each of whom was likely to have a different concept of how a piece of music was to be interpreted. By requiring that every performer use the city's sound engineer, the city was intruding upon the performers right to control the actual sound of their music. Consequently, Kunstler argued, the guidelines intruded upon the First Amendment right to free expression.

Kunstler also argued that the guidelines were excessively broad. While free expression is guaranteed by the First Amendment, laws governing the time, place, and manner of such expression are also legitimate. To avoid conflicts with the First Amendment, such laws are required to be "narrowly tailored to serve significant governmental interests"—for example, banning musical concerts is unconstitutional, but a "narrowly tailored" ordinance banning concerts between 11 p.m. and 6 a.m. can be valid in the interest of preserving public peace. To RAR and Kunstler, the city's assumption of utter control of all amplification at the Naumberg band shell overstepped the alleged goal of merely avoiding excessive noise beyond the band shell area.

When the Court returned with its decision on 22 June 1989, it agreed with the city that the guidelines were unobtrusive. In a decision written by Justice Anthony Kennedy, the majority agreed upon a number of things the controversial guidelines did not do. They did not authorize the suppression of free speech nor did they seek to ban rock concerts. The guidelines applied to all genres of music performed at the band shell and were therefore "content-neutral." The majority noted that

the guidelines required the hired sound engineer to defer to the wishes of the performers and their representatives in controlling the sound mix. Any interference with a performer's message by manipulating the sound quality was expressly forbidden by the guidelines.

The Court recognized the equal rights of citizens to avoid excessive noise or to enjoy the concerts in the park. Unlike the appeals court, however, the majority decided that the city was not required to prove that it had made an analysis of "less restrictive" alternatives to the guidelines. Since no proof had been offered that the city's regulation of the sound had been inadequate or substandard for the RAR concerts, the Court decided that the organization's claim that the guideline was unnecessarily broad had no merit.

Justices Kennedy, Rehnquist, White, O'Connor, and Scalia joined in the majority decision, with Justice Blackmun concurring in the result. The appeals court decision against Commissioner Ward and New York City was reversed. Yet the decision was not unanimous. Justices Brennan and Stevens joined in a dissenting opinion written by Justice Marshall.

If the city indeed deferred to each performer's wishes in mixing the sound, Marshall wondered why the city's

William Kunstler, 1995 © Photograph by Victor Irving Fisher.
AP/Wide World Photos.

engineer was necessary. Marshall and the dissenters felt that the majority opinion regarding "narrow tailoring" was inconsistent with the Court's own stand the previous year in its *Frisby v. Schultz* (1988) decision. In that case, the Court had defined a statute as being "narrowly tailored" only "if it targets and eliminates no more than the exact source of the 'evil' it seeks to remedy." Instead of adopting guidelines like those used by the National Park Service—monitoring the volume level at the perimeter of the event, conferring with the sponsors, and if necessary shutting off the power—New York City had interjected itself into the means by which performances were created. To adopt rules effecting a performance before a note was played amounted to an "impermissible prior restraint" of free speech. Giving government the freedom to legislate itself into the creative process, Justice Marshall felt, was to "eviscerate" the First Amendment right to free expression.

"Today's decision has significance far beyond the world of rock music," he warned, as if cautioning anyone who might have considered the issue before the Court to be frivolous. "Government no longer need bal-ance the effectiveness of regulation with the burdens on free speech. After today, government need only assert that it is most effective to control speech in advance of its expression."

Related Cases

United States v. O'Brien, 391 U.S. 367 (1968).
Grayned v. City of Rockford, 408 U.S. 104 (1972).
Wygant v. Jackson Board of Education, 476 U.S. 267 (1986).
Boos v. Barry, 485 U.S. 312 (1988).
Frisby v. Schultz, 487 U.S. 474 (1988).

Bibliography and Further Reading

Greenhouse, Linda. "Supreme Court Accord: Rock Music Is Loud." *New York Times,* 28 February 1989 p. A1.

Kunstler, William M. *My Life As A Radical Lawyer.* New York: Birch Lane, 1994.

Pareles, Jon. "Second-Guessing the First Amendment." *New York Times,* 12 March 1989, Section II 28.

UNIVERSITY OF PENNSYLVANIA v. EEOC

Legal Citation: 110 U.S. 577 (1990)

Petitioner
University of Pennsylvania

Respondent
Equal Employment Opportunity Commission

Petitioner's Claim
That the university has special privilege grounded in either common law or the First Amendment to prohibit disclosure of peer review materials relevant to racial, sexual, or national origin discrimination claims in tenure decisions.

Chief Lawyer for Petitioner
Rex E. Lee

Chief Lawyer for Respondent
Kenneth Winston Starr, U.S. Solicitor General

Justices for the Court
Harry A. Blackmun (writing for the Court), William J. Brennan, Jr., Anthony M. Kennedy, Sandra Day O'Connor, Thurgood Marshall, William H. Rehnquist, Antonin Scalia, John Paul Stevens, Byron R. White

Justices Dissenting
None

Place
Washington, D.C.

Date of Decision
9 January 1990

Decision
In a unanimous decision, upheld the court of appeals finding that neither common law nor a First Amendment academic freedom privilege protects peer review tenure materials.

Significance
The Supreme Court found universities had no special legal privilege for withholding court-requested materials. Academic freedoms indirectly protected by the First Amendment were individual freedoms, not institutional. The decision opened tenure-granting decisions to greater public scrutiny, protecting employees from discrimination based on sex, age, and national origin. The Court also maintained a reluctance to acknowledge new common law privileges.

Tenure at colleges or universities is a status granted to professors protecting them from abrupt dismissal. Tenure is an important achievement in a scholar's career and comes after years of research and teaching. During the tenure granting process, fellow professors critically evaluate the scholar's performance. Peer evaluations are commonly confidential to encourage candid evaluations of a candidate's qualifications.

Congress passed the Civil Rights Act in 1964. Title VII of the Act made it unlawful "to discriminate against any individual with respect to his compensation, terms, conditions, or privileges of employment because of such individual's race, color, religion, sex, or national origin." The act originally exempted institutions of higher learning. However, recognizing the widespread problem of discrimination in educational institutions, Congress expanded Title VII in 1972 to include universities.

Title VII also created the Equal Employment Opportunity Commission (EEOC) to investigate charges of discrimination. The EEOC was given a broad right of access to any "relevant" evidence for its enforcement duties. The confidential nature of peer review evaluations increasingly conflicted with the EEOC's needs for information. When universities refused information, the EEOC often responded with subpoenas through the courts.

The courts applied different methods to arrive at rulings, thus creating inconsistencies. The Third Circuit Court's *EEOC v. Franklin and Marshall College* (1986) decision denied the right to withhold confidential peer reviews. Some other circuit courts used a balancing test to decide between emphasis on academic freedom or discrimination. Another circuit court provided protection of tenure committee members' identities by omitting their names from files sent to the EEOC. The Supreme Court sought to resolve these conflicts by accepting the University of Pennsylvania (Penn) case.

Penn is a private institution of higher learning providing teaching and research in 12 different "schools" including the Wharton School of Business. In 1985, Wharton denied tenure to Rosalie Tung, an associate professor on the faculty. She filed a charge of discrimination with the EEOC alleging tenure was denied based on her race, sex, and national origin.

Tung claimed sexual harassment by the department chairman. When she insisted their relationship remain professional, he wrote a negative letter to Penn's Personnel Committee, which makes final decisions in tenure reviews. Tung claimed the majority of Wharton's faculty members gave her positive recommendations for tenure. Also, she named five male faculty members who received more favorable assessments than she, yet, according to Tung, her accomplishments and qualifications were equal to or better than their qualifications. Lastly, although not given any specific reason for tenure denial, Tung discovered the committee based its decision on the pretext that Wharton was not interested in China and related studies. She alleged the real reason was Wharton did not want a Chinese American woman on its faculty.

The EEOC agreed to investigate Tung's charge. To do so, they requested relevant information from Penn. When Penn refused to provide certain information, the EEOC issued a subpoena for, among other things, tenure review files of Tung and the five male faculty members Tung had named. Penn insisted the EEOC demonstrate a particular need in addition to showing relevance to obtain the peer review materials. The school insisted the peer documents were "privileged" information. For these purposes, privilege is defined as the legal ability to resist disclosure of certain document contents if a special need beyond relevance is not shown. The EEOC applied to the U.S. District Court for the Eastern District of Pennsylvania for enforcement of the subpoena and an enforcement order was issued. The Court of Appeals for the Third Circuit affirmed the enforcement decision and rejected Penn's claim of privilege.

Penn appealed to the Supreme Court and the Court issued a writ of *certiorari,* an order commanding the lower court to forward records of the case to the superior court so the case could be heard. The Court granted *certiorari* limited to the disclosure of the documents in question and did not seek to address discrimination allegations.

Two Claims Lead to One Question

Penn based its arguments on two claims: a common law privilege claim and a First Amendment academic freedom right. Because peer review is central to the functioning of universities, Penn asked the Court to recognize a "common law privilege against disclosure of confidential peer review materials." The common law claim was grounded in federal rules of evidence which provide that "the privilege of a witness . . . shall be governed by the principles of the common law as they may be interpreted by the courts of the United States in the light of reason and experience." Common law is generally based on reason and common sense rather than rigid laws. Although Penn conceded the information sought passed the relevance test, they con-

tended the EEOC did not have an absolute right to acquire such evidence and that it must show a special need. Penn stated such privilege claims have precedents in executive privilege for presidential communications and grand jury proceedings.

Penn also focused on First Amendment "academic freedom" concepts. Penn directed the Court to "language in prior cases acknowledging the crucial role universities play in dissemination of ideas in our society and recognizing academic freedom as a special concern of the First Amendment." One essential academic freedom a university possesses is deciding "on academic grounds who may teach" using the tenure process. Revealing peer review information could weaken education by interfering with tenure-granting decisions. With confidentiality lost, less candid evaluations would result in lower quality evaluations and appointment of less qualified tenured faculty. Penn alleged "that the quality of instruction and scholarship [will] decline as a result of the burden the EEOC subpoenas place on the peer review process." In previous cases before the Court, traditional academic freedom concerned an individual's right to speak or teach what they chose. Penn asked for a new institutional academic freedom for the university's procedures outside scrutiny, even when charges of discrimination are brought. Both claims resulted in the same question of whether a university can enjoy "a special privilege, grounded in either the common law or the First Amendment, to prevent disclosure of relevant peer review information."

No Academic Institutional Privilege

Unanimously, the Supreme Court upheld the court of appeals by finding neither a common law nor a First Amendment academic freedom privilege for peer tenure review materials. The Court directed Penn to comply with the subpoena and provide the EEOC all requested peer review information. In considering the common law privilege claim, the Court noted that Congress, in extending Title VII coverage to educational institutions, weighed academic autonomy against the high costs of discrimination. Congress decided preventing discrimination was more important than any risks opening peer review files would create. Therefore, it did not recognize a particular privilege for peer review documents. Blackmun reasoned that Penn "has not offered persuasive justification for its claim that this Court should go further than Congress thought necessary to safeguard confidentiality." In fact, the Court noted that for many universities confidentiality was not an issue, and open access to peer review files was the rule.

The Court endorsed court of appeals language that, "Clearly, an alleged perpetrator of discrimination can not be allowed to pick and choose the evidence which may be necessary for an agency investigation." Requiring the EEOC to give a specific reason for access to the information beyond a show of relevance would essentially give universities a weapon to frustrate investigations. Finally, no historical or constitutional basis existed granting privilege for peer review materials as there was for granting privileges for presidential and grand jury communication and documents.

In considering First Amendment academic freedom claims, the Court decided Penn was misguided. The Court found that the EEOC was not trying to tell universities to whom to grant tenure, who to teach, or what ideas will be taught. It was simply making sure such decisions were not based on race, sex, or national origin. Blackmun wrote, "The Commission is not providing criteria [guidelines] that (Penn) must use in selecting teachers. Nor is it preventing the university from using any criteria it may wish to use except those—including race, sex, and national origin—that are proscribed [banned] under Title VII." The Court, therefore, rejected Penn's request to expand the right of academic freedom to protect confidential peer review materials from disclosure. Penn was misguided at trying to expand academic freedom to university institutional procedures when freedom is individual.

Impact

The Court's ruling affected all university-level tenure and review committee decisions. It specified whose files could be looked at, by whom, and for what purpose. It placed a high degree of responsibility on university faculty to ensure an academic environment free of discrimination. The Penn case demonstrated the Court's reluctance in establishing new common law privileges.

Afterwards, the American Association of University Professors (AAUP) examined Penn's implications. They agreed on a statement favoring openness. The AAUP stressed faculty members should have full access to their files, access upon request to information in other faculty members' vitae, and ability for university grievance committees to obtain relevant information to decide cases.

A 1993 study revealed most universities did not believe peer review must be confidential to maintain its integrity. Another study indicated many institutions

changed aspects of their tenure and promotion process a year after Penn. Although tenure committee meetings remained closed at most universities, over half did not restrict access to peer review documents. This increased access to files at least increased the perception of truthfulness and fairness.

The rejection of a newly defined privilege based on constitutional academic freedom claims is perhaps the most significant part of the Penn decision. Blackmun wrote the Court, in fact, continued to show great respect for academic decision-making. The Court reiterated "free trade in ideas" and upheld traditional academic freedom. But it clarified the distinction between individual and institutional academic freedom by rejecting the extension of freedom to an institution's autonomy. Universities have no right to keep their procedures free from outside scrutiny. By the latter 1990s, debates over the appropriateness of affirmative action measures increased nationally. Just as with Penn, universities again considered prospects of claiming institutional academic freedom in protecting their affirmative action programs from judicial review by asserting such programs were essential for providing a high quality of "collective speech" on campus.

Related Cases

Sweezy v. New Hampshire, 354 U.S. 234 (1957).
Branzburg v. Hayes, 408 U.S. 665 (1972).
Regents of the University of California v. Bakke, 438 U.S. 265 (1978).
Jaffe v. Redmond, 116 S.Ct. 1923 (1996).

Bibliography and Further Reading

Flanigan, Jackson L., Michael D. Richardson, Kenneth E. Lane, and Dennis W. VanBerkum. "Pennsylvania v. EEOC: Tenure Decisions and Confidentiality." The NEA Higher Education Journal, Spring 1995.

Frost, Lynda E. "Shifting Meanings of Academic Freedom: An Analysis of Pennsylvania v. EEOC." Journal of College and University Law, Vol. 17, no. 3, 1991, pp. 329-350.

Galle, William P., Jr., and Clifford M. Koen. "Tenure and Promotion after Penn v. EEOC." Academe, September-October 1993.

AUSTIN V. MICHIGAN CHAMBER OF COMMERCE

Legal Citation: 494 U.S. 652 (1990)

Appellants
Richard H. Austin, Michigan Secretary of State, and Frank J. Kelley, Michigan Attorney General

Appellee
Michigan Chamber of Commerce

Appellants' Claim
That Section 54(1) of the Michigan Campaign Finance Act did not violate the First and Fourteenth Amendments to the Constitution.

Chief Lawyer for Appellants
Louis J. Caruso, Solicitor General of Michigan

Chief Lawyer for Appellee
Richard D. McLellan

Justices for the Court
Harry A. Blackmun, William J. Brennan, Jr., Thurgood Marshall (writing for the Court), William H. Rehnquist, John Paul Stevens, Byron R. White

Justices Dissenting
Anthony M. Kennedy, Sandra Day O'Connor, Antonin Scalia

Place
Washington, D.C.

Date of Decision
27 March 1990

Decision
The U.S. Supreme Court found Section 54(1) of the Michigan Campaign Finance Act not to be in violation of the First Amendment of the Constitution.

Significance
The case of *Austin v. Michigan Chamber of Commerce* dealt with many important issues regarding state laws to control and regulate political contributions and expenditures from corporations.

Case Background

The Michigan Chamber of Commerce opposed Section 54(1) of the Michigan Campaign Finance Act which did not allow the use of "corporate treasury funds for independent expenditures in support of or in opposition to any candidate in elections for state office." The chamber wanted to pay for a newspaper advertisement to support their choice for a candidate for Michigan's House of Representatives from the general treasury funds instead of from an independent fund that was "designated solely for political purposes." The Michigan Chamber of Commerce filed suit in federal district court against "state officials for declaratory and injunctive relief against enforcement of the statute," claiming that Section 54(1) was in violation of the First and Fourteenth Amendments to the Constitution. The federal district court found that the section was constitutional. However that decision was reversed by the court of appeals, holding that Section 54(1) was in violation of the First Amendment

> because (1) the chamber was a "nontraditional" corporation formed for essentially ideological purposes and to disseminate economic and political ideas, (2) the chamber's expenditures did not pose the threat or appearance of corruption, and (3) there was thus no compelling state interest that justified the infringement of the chamber's freedom of speech.

A First Amendment Violation or Protection Against Political Corruption?

The U.S. Supreme Court reversed the decision of the court of appeals. It held that Section 54(1) did not violate the First Amendment. Justice Marshall, who delivered the opinion of the Court, wrote that the statute was "supported by a compelling governmental interest in preventing political corruption" by limiting the corporation to the use of a special independent fund raised entirely for political purposes instead of using general treasury funds, which may have "little or no correlation to the public's support for a corporation's political ideas." The Supreme Court also felt that the statute was narrowly tailored to that end, and that the Michigan Chamber of Commerce did not merit exemption

Justice Thurgood Marshall.
© Photograph by Joseph Lavenburg, National Geographic. Collection of the Supreme Court of the United States.

"from the statute's restrictions as a voluntary political association." While the chamber of commerce claimed that the statute was "over inclusive for First Amendment purposes" because it included closely held corporations, the Supreme Court did not agree. The chamber also claimed the statute was "under inclusive" because it did not include unincorporated labor unions, but the Court found that "the state's decision to regulate only corporations was precisely tailored to serve the compelling state interest of eliminating from the political process the corrosive effects of political 'war chests' amassed with the aid of the legal advantages given to corporations."

The Supreme Court also considered the matter of whether the statute was a burden to the chamber's "freedom of expression," as was found by the Supreme Court in *Federal Election Commission v. Massachusetts Citizens for Life, Inc.* (1986). The Supreme Court did find that in this case, the statute was indeed a burden, and "must be justified by a compelling State interest," that interest being to regulate "political expenditures to avoid corruption or the appearance of corruption" (*Federal Election Commission v. National Conservative Political Action Committee* [1985]).

The Supreme Court then had to decide if the statute was in violation of the Equal Protection Clause of the Fourteenth Amendment. Because the Court found that the statute was "narrowly tailored to serve a compelling state interest," Section 54(1) did "pass muster under the Equal Protection Clause." Even though, as the Chamber argued, media corporations are exempt from the statute, it is justified due to the "unique role that the press plays" in providing information of "newsworthy events" to the public. The Supreme Court determined that the Michigan Campaign Finance Act did not violate the Equal Protection Clause, but rather "reduces the threat that huge corporate treasuries amassed with the aid of favorable state laws will be used to influence

unfairly the outcome of elections." Because the Supreme Court found that the Michigan Chamber of Commerce should not be made exempt from the Michigan Campaign Finance Act, the Court reversed the decision of the court of appeals.

Dissenting Opinions

Justices Scalia and Kennedy each filed dissenting opinions. Justice Scalia expressed his opinion that just because corporations are sometimes given "special advantages" by state laws and can have large treasuries, they should not be required "to forfeit their First Amendment rights," and that the statute was not sufficiently narrow in its construction. Justice Kennedy, who was joined by Justices O'Connor and Scalia, expressed a dissenting opinion because he felt that the statute was in violation of the First Amendment as it constituted a "censorship of speech." He felt that the act "prohibits corporations from speaking on a particular subject, the subject of candidate elections," and "discriminates on the basis of the speaker's identity," so that "the State censors what a particular segment of the political community might say with regard to candidates who stand for election." Thus, the Court's finding resulted in a decision "wholly at odds with the guar-

Richard Austin, Michigan Secretary of State. © Photograph by Dale Atkins. AP/Wide World Photos.

Frank Kelley, Michigan Attorney General. © AP/Wide World Photos.

antees of the First Amendment" (*Meyer v. Grant,* [1988] *Buckley v. Valeo,* [1976]). Kennedy agreed with Scalia that the act was not narrow enough and believed that "the Act does not meet our standards for laws that burden fundamental rights."

Impact

The case of *Austin v. Michigan Chamber of Commerce* has been cited in six U.S. Supreme Court cases and 11 Circuit Court cases, as of 1998. The role of the government in establishing limitations, policies, and restrictions on political campaign contributions, fundraising, and donations is constantly being evaluated. The many important issues involved here, such as freedom of speech and press, will surely continue to be contested in the courts of our country.

Related Cases

Police Department of Chicago v. Mosely, 408 U.S. 92 (1972).

Buckley v. Valeo, 424 U.S. 1 (1976).

FEC v. National Conservative Political Action Committee, 470 U.S. 480 (1985).

FEC v. Massachusetts Citizens for Life, Inc., 479 U.S. 238 (1986).

Meyer v. Grant, 486 U.S. 414 (1988).

Bibliography and Further Reading

Biskupic, Joan and Elder Witt, eds. *Congressional Quarterly's Guide to the U.S. Supreme Court,* 3rd ed. Washington, DC: Congressional Quarterly, Inc., 1996.

Burke, Thomas F., "The Concept of Corruption in Campaign Finance Law." *Constitutional Commentary,* spring 1997, pp. 127.

Levit, Kenneth J. "Campaign Finance Reform." *Yale Law Journal,* Nov. 1993, pp. 469.

SIMON & SCHUSTER V. MEMBERS OF THE NEW YORK STATE CRIME VICTIMS BOARD

Legal Citation: 502 U.S 105 (1991)

Petitioner
Simon & Schuster, Inc.

Respondent
New York Crime Victims Board

Petitioner's Claim
That New York's "Son of Sam" law restricts free speech and is therefore inconsistent with the First Amendment.

Chief Lawyer for Petitioner
Howard L. Zwickel

Chief Lawyer for Respondent
Ronald S. Rauchberg

Justices for the Court
Harry A. Blackmun, Anthony M. Kennedy, Sandra Day O'Connor (writing for the Court), William H. Rehnquist, Antonin Scalia, David H. Souter, John Paul Stevens, Byron R. White

Justices Dissenting
None (Clarence Thomas did not participate)

Place
Washington, D.C.

Date of Decision
10 December 1991

Decision
Overturned the two lower courts' decisions ruling that New York's Son of Sam law was inconsistent with the First Amendment.

Significance
The Supreme Court ruled that New York's particular Son of Sam law was overbroad. The law would penalize any book in which the author had admitted a crime. Also the Court ruled that the statute levied a financial penalty on a certain type of speech that it imposed on no other type of speech. The Supreme Court held that this particular law was unconstitutional, but since that time other constitutionally questionable Son of Sam laws have been passed in many states, including another in New York.

During the summer of 1977 the most sensational and widely reported story was a series of murders in New York City. When David Berkowitz was caught and identified as the killer, the New York State legislature wanted to make sure he did not profit from his killing spree. The state quickly passed a statute (New York Exec. Law 632-a) designed to prevent Berkowitz from selling his story and making money. More specifically, the law required any entity which entered into a contract with a person convicted or accused of a crime to give a copy of the contract as well as any income derived from the contract to the New York Crime Victims Board. The board would then deposit the payment into an escrow account to provide monetary judgements for crime victims who sued the accused or convicted person.

The case *Simon & Schuster v. New York State Crime Victims Board* began in 1986. Simon & Schuster, a large New York publishing house, entered into a contract with organized crime figure Henry Hill. In a 26-year career, Hill was involved in robberies, extortion, and selling drugs. Hill and author Nicholas Pileggi signed on with Simon & Schuster to write a book which would eventually become *Wiseguy: Life in a Mafia Family*. The Crime Victims Board learned of Hill and Pileggi's book in January of 1986. The board moved quickly to get all the financial records regarding the transactions between Simon & Schuster and Hill. After reviewing the contract the board ruled that the publishing house had broken the law and all the money paid to Hill should have been turned over to the board's escrow account for Hill's victims. The board also ordered Hill to turn over all monies he received from the project. In August of 1987, Simon & Schuster sued the board in U.S. District Court claiming the law violated the First Amendment. The district court found the statute consistent with the First Amendment and the Second Circuit Court of Appeals affirmed the lower court's ruling. Because the issue was likely to come up again, the U.S. Supreme Court granted *certiorari,* an order for the lower court to forward the case to the highest court.

The Supreme Court reversed the two lower court's rulings in an 8-0 vote (Justice Clarence Thomas took no part in the case). The Court's opinion, delivered by Justice O'Connor, held that New York chose to impose

---

Crime for Profit

Should crime pay? Do criminals, convicted or not, have the right to profit from selling their true crime stories to publishers or film makers?

Proponents maintain if criminals are not paid they will not write, and the public is extremely interested in crime, criminals, and criminal justice. Publicity surrounding crime arouses such curiosity. If criminals did not write, the public would be denied their right to read or view authentic versions of crime experience.

Publishing and film-making industries generate huge profits by commonly focusing on crime themes in a large number of works, including books, movies, and television programs. Bidding wars for criminals' stories occur. Perhaps marketing their story is the only asset the wrongdoer has left. The criminal or criminal's fam-

ily could use the money for legal debts and living expenses. Conversely, if the profits could be seized, crime victim restitution programs could be funded.

Lastly, proponents argue Henry David Thoreau's *Civil Disobedience* or the *Autobiography of Malcolm X* would never have been published, stifling the free exchange of ideas.

Opponents focus on the victim's loss being turned into profit for the wrongdoer. Payment for crime is unconscionable and offensive. Felons actually benefitting from vicious crimes could perhaps lead to more grisly crimes.

Source(s): Garbus, Martin. Let's Do Away with "Son of Sam" Laws. *Publisher's Weekly*, Vol. 242, no. 7, p. 19.

---

a financial penalty on one type of speech that it imposed on no other type of speech. The Court had previously ruled in *Leathers v. Medlock* that a statute which imposed a financial burden on speech because of its content was inconsistent with the First Amendment. Further, in *Arkansas Writers' Project, Inc. v. Ragland* the Court ruled that the content of speech could not be the basis for any special taxes. The Court wrote:

> We conclude simply that in the Son of Sam law, New York has singled out speech on a particular subject for a financial burden that it places on no other speech and no other income. The State's interest in compensating victims from the fruits of crime is a compelling one, but the Son of Sam law is not narrowly tailored to advance that objective. As a result, the statute is inconsistent with the First Amendment.

The Court ruled that the Son of Sam law was overbroad—that it was too general. This statute as it was written would include all types of literature and penalize any speech in which the author admitted a crime. Though Justice O'Connor acknowledged the exaggeration, this law would in theory punish the authors of such books as *The Autobiography of Malcolm X*, *Civil Disobedience* by Henry David Thoreau, and even *The Confessions of Saint Augustine*.

Another issue that the Court addressed was the rights of victims. The Court recognized that the state had a compelling interest in compensating crime victims and in preventing criminals from profiting from their mis-

deeds. Despite the Board's best attempts, it could not explain why the specific assets from a criminal telling his or her story should be isolated from all of their other earnings. In short, the Court did not see why the state should specifically limit the financial penalty to the money the lawbreaker earned from talking about his or her crime. In his agreement with the Court, Justice Kennedy concluded:

> I would recognize this opportunity to confirm our past holdings and to rule that the New York statute amounts to raw censorship based on content, censorship forbidden by the text of the First Amendment and well-settled principles protecting speech and the press. That ought to end the matter.

But the issue of victims' rights was a matter that was far from settled.

Almost immediately after the Supreme Court declared New York's law unconstitutional, the New York legislature passed a revised Son of Sam law on 24 July 1992. On 3 April 1997 the Crime Victims Board announced the first settlement under the new law. Warner Bros., Inc. payed the children of Bruce Kellog, who was murdered by teenagers hired by his wife, a $5,000 settlement after a production company owned by the entertainment giant made a TV movie about the crime. Earlier in 1997 New York Governor George E. Pataki and Attorney General Dennis C. Vacco sued organized crime figure Sammy "The Bull" Gravano as a result of his reported book deal. In addition to New York, Son of Sam laws have spread across the United States and Canada. The state of

Florida sued writer Sandra London under its *Civil Restitution Lien and Crime Victims' Remedy Act of 1994.* London sold the story of Danny Rolling, who murdered five college students in 1990. While this case and others like it have sprung up all over the country in the aftermath of *Simon & Schuster v. New York State Crime Victims Board,* the decision remained an important part of the body of law concerning commercial speech. The case is mentioned along with *Police Department of Chicago v. Mosley* in 1972 and *Arkansas Writers' Project, Inc. v. Ragland* in 1987 as an important safeguard of free speech—even that speech which may be unpopular or offensive.

Related Cases

Police Department of Chicago v. Mosley, 408 U.S. 92 (1972).
Arkansas Writers' Project v. Ragland, 481 U.S. 221 (1987).
Leathers v. Medlock, 499 U.S. 439 (1991).

Bibliography and Further Reading

Fabian, Ann. "Crime that Pays." *Yale Review,* October 1993, pp. 45.

The Gainesville Sun. http://www.sunone.com

Grogan, David. "Cashing in." *People Weekly,* August 8, 1994, pp. 26.

State of New York Press Releases. http://www.oag.state. ny.us

R.A.V. v. City of St. Paul

Legal Citation: 505 U.S. 377 (1992)

Petitioner
R.A.V.

Respondent
City of St. Paul, Minneapolis

Petitioner's Claim
That a St. Paul city ordinance banning all public displays of symbols that arouse anger on the basis of race, color, creed, religion, or gender was invalid under the First Amendment to the U.S. Constitution.

Chief Lawyer for Petitioner
Edward J. Cleary

Chief Lawyer for Respondent
Thomas J. Foley

Justices for the Court
Harry A. Blackmun, Anthony M. Kennedy, Sandra Day O'Connor, William H. Rehnquist (writing for the Court), Antonin Scalia, David H. Souter, John Paul Stevens, Clarence Thomas, Byron R. White

Justices Dissenting
None

Place
Washington, D.C.

Date of Decision
22 June 1992

Decision
Reversed the court of appeals ruling and held that the St. Paul ordinance did in fact violate First Amendment free speech protections.

Significance
The unanimous decision in this case clarified the concept of "fighting words" left unprotected under the First Amendment.

Fighting Words

In a 1941 decision, the U.S. Supreme Court defined "fighting words" as words that "by their very utterance inflict injury or tend to incite an immediate breach of the peace." It further held that such speech is not entitled to protection under the First Amendment to the U.S. Constitution. The decision in *R.A.V. v. City of St. Paul* hinged on how broadly and under what criteria a local government can define "fighting words."

In St. Paul, Minnesota, the local government enacted a law, the Bias-Motivated Crime Ordinance. It banned the display of symbols and objects which offend others on the basis of race, color, creed, religion, or gender. A white teenager challenged the law after he and two others were charged with burning a cross on the lawn of a black family. The teenager claimed that the law was too broadly drawn and violated his right to free speech. He first took his case to a state trial court.

The Lower Court's Rule

The trial court in Minnesota ruled in the teenager's favor. It held that the ordinance was overbroad and that it sought to regulate speech based on its content, not its impact (i.e. its potential to incite violence). The city of St. Paul then appealed to the Minnesota Supreme Court, which reversed the lower court's decision. The state supreme court construed the kind of speech banned in the ordinance to fall under the definition of "fighting words" left unprotected by the Constitution. It also expressed the view that the ordinance was a reasonable measure taken by the city to protect its citizens against bias-related crimes. Not satisfied with this decision, the teenager then appealed his case to the U.S. Supreme Court.

The Supreme Court Rules

On 22 June 1992, the Supreme Court issued its decision. In a unanimous vote, it reversed the Minnesota Supreme Court's ruling and decreed the St. Paul ordinance unconstitutional. Justice Scalia wrote a majority opinion signed by four other justices. The remaining four justices issued various opinions outlining their reasoning for coming to the same judgment.

"Let there be no mistake about our belief that burning a cross in someone's front yard is reprehensible," Scalia declared in his opinion. But he went on to decry the city of St. Paul's method for addressing the problem of bias crime. In his view, the ordinance was too selective in picking out certain topics and types or expression for official disfavor. "Selectivity of this sort creates the possibility that the city is seeking to handicap the expression of particular ideas," Scalia wrote—i.e. only ideas that incite on the basis of race, creed, religion, or gender. If a city wants to ban fighting words, Scalia declared, it must ban all fighting words, not those in a few selected categories. As he analogized, "[T]he government may proscribe libel; but it may not make the further content discrimination of proscribing only libel critical of the government." He went on to laud the city of St. Paul for taking steps to safeguard the human rights of all its citizens, but recommended other methods to pursue that end that did not infringe upon First Amendment rights.

In a separate opinion, Justice White joined in the judgment but expressed the decidedly different view that the government does in fact have a right to discriminate among different types of speech. He lampooned Scalia's "all-or-nothing" formulation for banning fighting words. As White wrote:

> It is inconsistent to hold that the government may proscribe an entire category of speech because the content of that speech is evil . . . but that the government may not treat a subset of that category differently without violating the First Amendment; the content of the subset is, by definition, worthless and undeserving of constitutional protection.

However, White agreed with Scalia that the St. Paul ordinance was too broadly drawn. "[T]he ordinance reaches conduct that is unprotected," White opined. "[I]t also makes criminal expressive conduct that causes only hurt feelings, offense, or resentment, and is protected by the First Amendment." Thus, in White's view,

if the ordinance had been tailored more narrowly to include only those expressions that truly incite violence, it would have passed constitutional muster.

Impact

The decision in *R.A.V. v. City of St. Paul* cast doubt on a number of state laws and university codes designed to prohibit prejudiced or offensive speech. Subsequent to this case, lawmakers became careful to craft laws that did not contain the content-based classifications struck down as unconstitutional here.

Related Cases

Wisconsin v. Mitchell, 508 U.S. 476 (1993).
Ladue v. Gilleo, 512 U.S. 43 (1994).
Kansas v. Hendricks, 521 U.S. 346 (1997).

Bibliography and Further Reading

Biskupic, Joan, and Elder Witt, eds. *Congressional Quarterly's Guide to the U.S. Supreme Court,* 3rd ed. Washington, DC: Congressional Quarterly, Inc., 1996.

Brooks, Thomas D. "First Amendment—Penalty Enhancement for Hate Crimes: Content Regulation, Questionable State Interests and Non-Traditional Sentencing." *Journal of Criminal Law and Criminology,* Winter-Spring 1994, pp. 703–742.

Dry, Murray. "Hate Speech and the Constitution." *Constitutional Commentary,* Winter 1994, pp. 501–513.

Lawrence, Frederick M. "The Punishment of Hate: Toward a Normative Theory of Bias-Motivated Crimes." *Michigan Law Review,* November 1994, pp. 320–381.

Post, Robert C. "Liberalism Divided: Freedom of Speech and the Many Uses of State Power." *Michigan Law Review,* May 1997, pp. 1517–1541.

Simon, Glenn E. "Cyberporn and Censorship: Constitutional Barriers to Preventing Access to Internet Pornography by Minors." *Journal of Criminal Law and Criminology,* Spring 1998, pp. 1015–1048.

INTERNATIONAL SOCIETY FOR KRISHNA CONSCIOUSNESS V. LEE

Legal Citation: 505 U.S. 672 (1992)

Petitioners
International Society for Krishna Consciousness, et al.

Respondent
Walter Lee, Police Superintendent of the Port Authority of New York and New Jersey

Petitioners' Claim
That the Port Authority of New York and New Jersey's regulations against soliciting funds and distributing literature inside airports under its control violated the First Amendment's protection of freedom of speech.

Chief Lawyer for Petitioners
Barry A. Fisher

Chief Lawyer for Respondent
Arthur P. Berg

Justices for the Court
Sandra Day O'Connor, William H. Rehnquist (writing for the Court), Antonin Scalia, Clarence Thomas, Byron R. White

Justices Dissenting
Harry A. Blackmun, Anthony M. Kennedy, David H. Souter, John Paul Stevens

Place
Washington, D.C.

Date of Decision
26 June 1992

Decision
Denied the petitioners' claim, upholding a court of appeals decision that airports did not constitute public fora, and as such are legally justified in regulating speech on their premises in a "reasonable" manner.

Significance
The ruling placed airports in the category of nonpublic fora for the purpose of evaluating government regulation of speech. Under the public forum doctrine, regulation of speech in nonpublic fora need only be "reasonable and content neutral."

Running the Gamut

Any air traveler in the United States during the 1970s and 1980s will well remember being accosted in airports by representatives of numerous political and religious organizations. Among the most ubiquitous of such groups was the International Society of Krishna Consciousness (ISKC), whose followers are obliged to perform an act known as "sankirtan." Sankirtan involves going into public places and distributing printed information and soliciting contributions for the ISKC. The members of the ISKC became so familiar a part of the landscape of airports in the United States that their presence became the focal point of humorous scenes in popular comedies such as the film *Airplane*. Although the followers of the ISKC were normally not aggressive in their solicitations, their presence caused anxiety among some travelers and caused already crowded air terminals to become even more congested.

The Port Authority of New York and New Jersey is responsible for the operation of the International Arrivals Building at Kennedy Airport and the Central Terminal Building at LaGuardia Airport in New York City and the North Terminal Building at the Newark Airport in Newark, New Jersey. In 1975, in order to relieve congestion at these facilities, and in response to customer complaints, the port authority adopted a regulation which prohibited the sales and distribution of literature and merchandise and solicitation of funds

> within the interior areas of buildings or structures at an air terminal if conducted by a person to or with passers-by in a continuous or repetitive manner.

The new regulation amounted to a ban on sankirtan within the air terminals operated by the port authority.

Hare Krishna and the Public Forum Doctrine

With their ability to perform sankirtan in airport terminals effectively eliminated, the ISKC sought legal recourse. They met with success initially, as the district court held that airport terminals are public fora, and that therefore any state regulation of speech within them must be narrowly drawn to support a "compelling

A Hare Krishna of Brooklyn solicits money and distributes literature at New York's John F. Kennedy International Airport, 1992. © AP/Wide World Photos.

state interest." As such, the ISKC was granted injunctive relief from the port authority's regulation against solicitation and distribution of literature. This ruling was in keeping with the so-called public forum doctrine, which has traditionally been used to evaluate state regulation of speech in government-owned places. Under the public forum doctrine, there are three categories of government (public) property: public fora such as streets, sidewalks, and parks, where communication among citizens has traditionally occurred; designated public fora, such as public university auditoriums, that have been opened for the express purpose of promoting certain types of communication; and nonpublic fora, comprising all government property that does not fall into the first two categories. The legal implications of a property's categorization are vast: the state can only regulate speech in public or designated fora in a narrowly defined manner designed to protect a compelling state interest. In a nonpublic forum, however, the state can only impose regulations on speech that are reasonable and neutral with regard to the speech's content. By ruling that airport terminals were public fora, the district court had to conclude that the port authority's regulation of speech within its terminals was overly broad. The port authority subsequently brought the case before the court of appeals, which reversed the district court's decision. The court of appeals held that airport terminals were not public fora and, as such, that the port authority's regulations met the standard of being reasonable and content neutral with regard to solicitation of funds. The appeals court found, however, that the port authority's ban on distribution of literature was in violation of the First Amendment. Following this partial victory with a partial setback, the ISKC

appealed the case to the U.S. Supreme Court, which heard arguments on 25 March 1992.

Defining a Public Forum

The ISKC advanced the position that "transportation nodes," such as railroad and bus stations, docks, and even Ellis Island are historically established public fora, and that airport terminals fall into the same category. The Court disagreed, and affirmed the decision of the court of appeals by a majority of 5-4. Chief Justice Rehnquist, writing for the majority, focused on the original definition of a public forum, developed by Justice Roberts in *Hague v. Committee for Industrial Organization,* (1939):

> (locations which) have immemorially been held in trust for the use of the public and, time out of mind, have been used for purposes of assembly, communicating thoughts between citizens, and discussing public questions.

In the Court's judgement the fact that air travel had only become common within the last 50 years ruled out classification of airports as being used from "time out of mind" for any purpose whatsoever. Furthermore, the use of airports for speech purposes was a recent development in the brief history of air travel. The argument of the ISKC, that airports should be classified in the same manner as traditional transportation nodes, was rejected on the basis that most transportation nodes have been privately owned, and the public forum doctrine can only be applied to publicly owned sites and facilities. The Court also pointed out that airports by their nature differ from other transportation nodes in many ways. For instance, everyone boarding an aircraft is forced to submit to a metal detection search to ensure passenger safety in flight. Finally, the Court observed that publicly owned airport facilities had been established for transportation and defense purposes, without regard for their use as fora for dissemination of information.

Having defined airport terminals as nonpublic fora, the Court had only to determine if the port authority's regulations were reasonable and content neutral. Given the pedestrian congestion at the port authority's air terminals and the rigid deadlines inherent to air travel, the Court ruled that the regulations in question were a reasonable measure to ensure freer flow of foot traffic within the terminals. It also determined that the regulation was content neutral, because it banned all solicitation and distribution of leaflets.

Impact

The ruling represented a more narrow interpretation of the public forum doctrine than had been made in the past. Such an interpretation was in keeping with the Court's more conservative leanings following the appointments of justices Kennedy, O'Connor, Souter, and Thomas by Presidents Ronald Reagan and George Bush during the 1980s. This case did not represent an unmitigated victory for the port authority, however. Despite its more narrow interpretation of the public forum doctrine the Court relied heavily on practical considerations, in this case relieving pedestrian congestion in airport terminals, in reaching its decision. As such, it was unwilling to allow the port authority to restrict speech under circumstances where exercise of such speech would not pose an undue inconvenience to air travelers. For this reason, the Court agreed with the court of appeals in a parallel case, *Lee v. International Society for Krishna Consciousness,* that the port authority could not ban distribution of literature within its terminals.

Related Cases

Hague v. Committee for Industrial Organization, 307 U.S. 486 (1939).

Perry Education Association v. Perry Local Educators' Association, 460 U.S. 37 (1983).

Board of Airport Commissioners of Los Angeles v. Jews for Jesus, 482 U.S. 569 (1983).

Cornelius v. NAACP Legal Defense and Education Fund, 473 U.S. 788 (1985).

United States v. Kokinda, 497 U.S. 720 (1990).

Bibliography and Further Reading

Biskupic, Joan and Elder Witt. *Congressional Quarterly's Guide to the U.S. Supreme Court,* 3rd ed. Washington, DC: Congressional Quarterly, Inc., 1996.

First Amendment Center Homepage. http://www.fac.org/legal/supcourt.

Kelling, George L. and Catherine M. Coles. "Disorder and the Court." *The Public Interest,* summer 1994, p. 57.

"Los Angeles City Council Approves Solicitation Ban at LAX." *Business Wire,* 21 March 1997.

LAMB'S CHAPEL V. CENTER MORICHES UNION FREE SCHOOL DISTRICT

Legal Citation: 508 U.S. 384 (1993)

Petitioner
Lamb's Chapel, et al.

Respondent
Center Moriches Union Free School District, et al.

Petitioner's Claim
That the Center Moriches Union Free School District violated the First Amendment rights of the Lamb's Chapel by not allowing them to use the school facilities for the showing of a religious-based film series on family values.

Chief Lawyer for Petitioner
Jay Alan Sekulow

Chief Lawyer for Respondent
John W. Hoefling

Justices for the Court
Harry A. Blackmun, Anthony M. Kennedy, Sandra Day O'Connor, William H. Rehnquist, Antonin Scalia, David H. Souter, John Paul Stevens, Clarence Thomas, Byron R. White (writing for the Court)

Justices Dissenting
None

Place
Washington, D.C.

Date of Decision
7 June 1993

Decision
Overturned the trial court and appeal's court decisions by stating that the claim by Lamb's Chapel alleging that they had been discriminated against on basis of religion was accurate.

Significance
By ruling in favor of the Lamb's Chapel, the Court sent a firm message regarding the role of "content" in First Amendment issues as well as taking what some viewed as a conservative stand on the freedom of religion.

In 1971 the Supreme Court, in *Lemon v. Kurtzman*, issued a standard on church and state relations that held government programs to three regulations. The programs: (1) had to have a secular (or nonreligious) purpose, (2) could not "advance or inhibit" religious practice, and (3) could not "lead to excessive governments entanglements in religion." This ruling has been used since to determine whether or not the right to free speech should come before the idea of the separation of church and state in the United States.

Over the years, this so-called Lemon Test has been called into service in many additional cases, but one that brought the controversy of the test to light dramatically was heard in 1993. The case revolved around the fact that New York State law allowed school districts to regulate the use of public school buildings after hours. The Center Moriches school district regularly allowed groups such as the Girl Scouts and the local Parent-Teacher Association to meet in its school buildings but decided to turn down any requests from religious organizations.

In 1988, John Steigerwald, the pastor of Lamb's Chapel, an evangelical Christian church in Long Island requested use of the school space. He wanted to host a six-part film series that would feature Dr. James Dobson, the president of the group Focus on Family. The school district asked for more information on the program and they were provided a pamphlet by Steigerwald, which included a description of Dobson as a licensed psychologist, author, and radio commentator. The brochure went on to say that Dr. Dobson's belief was that the media's influence on the American family could only be countered by a return to Christian values. The films, titled, "A Father Looks Back," "Power in Parenting: The Young Child," "Power in Parenting: The Adolescent," "The Family Under Fire," "Overcoming a Painful Childhood," and "The Heritage," focused on the "civil war of values" that Dr. Dobson felt was being waged in this country and Dr. Dobson's belief that a Christian perspective could strengthen the family.

The request by Lamb's Chapel to use the school facilities was turned down on the basis that the films were church-related. Their second application to use the space to show the films, which were described this time as "family-oriented movie[s]—from a Christian Perspective," was also turned down for the same reasons. During this time, the school district did allow, however, a New Age religious group called the "Mind Center" to sponsor a lecture series titled "Psychology and the Unknown," which was based on parapsychology and the unconscious mind. When asked by the district whether this was a religious series, its creator responded, "It was all science." This prompted the church to file suit in the district court. They asserted that by turning their request down, the school system was in violation of the Freedom of Speech and Assembly Clauses, the Free Exercise Clause, and the Establishment Clause of the First Amendment, as well as the Equal Protection Clause of the Fourteenth Amendment.

Was the School District Discriminatory?

When the church brought the case to the district court, it alleged that the school district had broken state law by discriminating against them on the basis of religion and restricting their right to free speech—two actions not allowed to be taken by a public institution. The court, however, ruled in favor of the district, affirming that the school facilities constituted a "limited public forum," that the laws that allowed usage of school facilities did not include "religious worship or instruction," and that the church had admitted that the films were to promote religious ideas, which, as a public institution, the district had no responsibility to do. It further ruled that if the school district had at any time granted space to other groups for religious purposes the church would have a case. Since the district had categorically disallowed all religious requests, the denial was within their rights.

The church appealed the decision to the court of appeals which upheld the ruling "in all respects." The court found that school property was not a traditional public forum when school was not in session and therefore it is subject to rules for public property only for "specified uses."

Federal Court

Following this ruling, Lamb's Church proceeded to take the case to the Supreme Court. In a unanimous decision, the rulings of the lower courts were overturned. In essence, the Court ruled that the district did violate the chapel's freedom of speech by refusing their request to show movies on their property solely because the movies had a religious theme. It also stated that granting permission to the chapel would not have constituted the district's endorsement of the films since the films would not be sponsored by the school during school hours or closed to the general public. The district acted in violation of the Chapel's First Amend-

ment rights. This was the Supreme Court's main reason for overturning the decisions of the lower courts.

Justice White wrote

> . . . although a speaker may be excluded from a nonpublic forum if he wishes to address a topic not encompassed within the purpose of the forum . . . or if he is not a member of the class of speakers for whose special benefit the forum was created . . ., the government violates the First Amendment when it denies access to a speaker solely to suppress the point of view he espouses on an otherwise includible subject

In making their determination, the Court invoked the somewhat controversial Lemon Test. Even justices who agreed that the district was in error, were not comfortable with the strictness of the Lemon Test. Justice Scalia wrote

> Like some ghoul in a late-night horror movie that repeatedly sits up in its grave and shuffles abroad, after being repeatedly killed and buried, Lemon stalks our Establishment Clause jurisprudence once again, frightening the little children and school attorneys of Center Moriches Union Free School District.

Right-wing Christian groups perceived the decision as a major victory. *The Christian Science Monitor* quoted Michael McConnell from the University of Chicago, whom they called "an expert on church-state relations," as saying "I don't think people realize how common it is for religious speakers to be suppressed in public schools. This decision says public spaces will not be treated as religion-free zones."

Still, the importance of the idea of separation of church and state was not overlooked in this ruling, as the Court drew fine lines between when and where the freedom of religious speech crosses the bounds of civic responsibility.

Related Cases
Lemon v. Kurtzman, 411 U.S. 192 (1973).
Bronx Household of Faith v. Community School District No. 10, 127 F.3d 207 (1997).
The Good News Club v. Milford Center School, 21 F.Supp.2d 147 (1998).

Bibliography and Further Reading

Boot, Max. "High Court Sends Signals On Church, State Issue." *Christian Science Monitor,* June 9, 1993.

Chemerinsky, Erwin. "Free Speech or Religious Freedom: Revisiting the Establishment Clause." *Trial,* December 1995, p. 16.

Coyle, Marcia. "Battles over Religion Still Rage at High Court." *The National Law Journal,* 21 June 1993, p. 5.

Lindsay, Ronald A. "School Prayer Thirty Years Later." *Free Inquiry,* Fall 1993, p. 6.

Stewart, David O. "Arguing Religion: Searching for Clear Commandments in This Term's Religion Cases." *ABA Journal,* August 1993, p. 48.

Wiggin, Carolyn. "A Funny Thing Happens When You Pay for a Forum: Mandatory Student Fees to Support Political Speech at Public Universities." *Yale Law Journal,* May 1994, pp. 2009–2038.

WISCONSIN V. MITCHELL

Legal Citation: 508 U.S. 476 (1993)

Petitioner
State of Wisconsin

Respondent
Todd Mitchell

Petitioner's Claim
That the Wisconsin statute allowing penalty enhancements for crimes motivated by the "race, religion, color, disability, sexual orientation, national origin or ancestry" of the victim was constitutional, and that respondent's enhanced sentence should stand.

Chief Lawyer for Petitioner
James E. Doyle, Attorney General of Wisconsin

Chief Lawyer for Respondent
Lynn S. Adelman

Justices for the Court
Harry A. Blackmun, Anthony M. Kennedy, Sandra Day O'Connor, William H. Rehnquist (writing for the Court), Antonin Scalia, David H. Souter, John Paul Stevens, Clarence Thomas, Byron R. White

Justices Dissenting
None

Place
Washington, D.C.

Date of Decision
11 June 1993

Decision
The Court decided that the Wisconsin statute did not violate the protections guaranteed by the First Amendment, and allowed the original sentence to stand.

Significance
With this decision, a line was drawn between First Amendment protected speech and criminal activity that had as its motive hate based on race, religion, or related biases. The Court did not broadly condone restrictions to expression, but did indicate that hate crimes can be considered more dangerous to society than crimes with other motives, and therefore could be punished more severely.

Todd Mitchell was one of a group of young black men who had been watching the movie *Mississippi Burning* in a Kenosha, Wisconsin apartment on 7 October 1989. The movie contains scenes of white men beating a black boy, and other racially-motivated violence against blacks. After viewing the movie, the men went outside onto the street. Mitchell made some remarks about wanting "to move on some white people," and when a white boy passed on the other side of the street, Mitchell said, "There goes a white boy; go get him." The group, including Mitchell, beat the boy severely, and stole his running shoes; the boy was in a coma for four days, but survived the attack.

In 1990, the Wisconsin legislature had passed a statute that allowed for enhanced penalties in cases in which the person being sentenced "[i]ntentionally selects the person against whom the crime . . . is committed or selects the property which is damaged or otherwise affected by the crime . . . because of the race, religion, color, disability, sexual orientation, national origin or ancestry of that person . . ." The circuit court which convicted Mitchell of aggravated battery cited this statute to enhance his sentence, from two to four years in prison. The statute was found to be unconstitutional by the Wisconsin Supreme Court, after the court of appeals rejected Mitchell's challenge; the case was then petitioned to the U.S. Supreme Court.

The arguments that Mitchell advanced, and which had been accepted by the state supreme court, were that the statute violated the First Amendment by punishing "offensive thought," and that the statute was unconstitutional because it was too broad and would have a "chilling effect" on individuals' speech. Mitchell asserted that the statute allowed the courts to punish the motive for selecting the victim, and "that the statute violates the First Amendment by punishing offenders' bigoted beliefs."

Mitchell's case was based on the tradition of the Court protecting speech, even speech which could be considered offensive or objectionable. In *R.A.V. v. City of St. Paul* (1992), for example, three young white men were charged with violating an ordinance which banned the use of symbols which "arouse anger, alarm, or resentment in others on the basis of race, color, creed, religion, or gender." The men had burned a cross on the property of a black family, recalling the activities of the Ku Klux Klan. The Court rejected the ordinance as unconstitutional, as it limited speech according to content, and because it allowed restrictions "based on hostility-or favoritism-toward the underlying message expressed." This precedent of protecting hate speech was the basis of Mitchell's arguments.

However, the U.S. Supreme Court rejected these arguments, citing *United States v. O'Brien* (1968): "Our cases reject the view that an apparently limitless variety of conduct can be labeled 'speech' whenever the person engaging in the conduct intends thereby to 'express an idea;'" and *National Association for the Advancement of Colored People v. Claiborne Hardware Co.* (1982): "The First Amendment does not protect violence." In accord with these cases, Justice Rehnquist wrote, "A physical assault is not, by any stretch of the imagination, expressive conduct protected by the First Amendment." The Court also found that the statute did not violate the Constitution, as it was suitably narrow; no credence was given to the idea that the statute would have a chilling effect on speech, as the legislation would only effect the sentencing phase of criminal proceedings.

The Court also had precedents which allowed the consideration of motive in criminal sentencing. In *Barclay v. Florida* (1983), for example, the Court had "allowed the sentencing judge to take into account the defendant's racial animus towards his victim"—the defendant was a member of the Black Liberation Army, and was attempting to provoke a "race war." And the Court recognized Wisconsin's reasoning for passing the statute: it "singles out for enhancement bias-inspired conduct because this conduct is thought to inflict greater individual and societal harm," and is "more likely to provoke retaliatory crimes, inflict distinct emotional harms on their victims, and incite community unrest." While the Court made no move to impede what could be considered "hate speech," it acknowledged that some crimes, when motivated by hatred, were subject to more severe punishments.

Related Cases

United States v. O'Brien, 391 U.S. 367 (1968).
National Association for the Advancement of Colored People v. Claiborne Hardware Co., 458 U.S. 886 (1982).
Barclay v. Florida, 463 U.S. 939 (1983).
R.A.V. v. City of St. Paul, 505 U.S. 377 (1992).

Bibliography and Further Reading

Biskupic, Joan, and Elder Witt, eds. *Congressional Quarterly's Guide to the U.S. Supreme Court.* Washington, DC: Congressional Quarterly, Inc., 1997.

Brooks, Thomas D. "First Amendment—Penalty Enhancement for Hate Crimes." *Journal of Criminal Law and Criminology*, winter-spring 1994, p. 703.

Dry, Murray. "Hate Speech and the Constitution." *Constitutional Commentary*, winter 1994, p. 501.

Greve, Michael. "Speech Impediments." *National Review*, October 10, 1994, p. 36.

Knoll, Erwin. "A Matter of Intent." *The Progressive*, August 1993, p. 4.

Lawrence, Frederick M. "The Punishment of Hate." *Michigan Law Review*, November 1994, pp. 320.

Rosen, Jeffrey. "Bad Thoughts." *The New Republic*, July 5, 1993, p. 15.

WATERS V. CHURCHILL

Legal Citation: 511 U.S. 661 (1994)

Petitioners
Cynthia Waters, Kathleen Davis

Respondent
Cheryl Churchill

Petitioners' Claim
That a public hospital employee's speech is not protected by the First Amendment when it disrupts the operational effectiveness and efficiency of the facility.

Chief Lawyer for Petitioners
Lawrence A. Marison

Chief Lawyer for Respondent
John J. Bisbee

Justices for the Court
Ruth Bader Ginsburg, Anthony M. Kennedy, Sandra Day O'Connor (writing for the Court), William H. Rehnquist, Antonin Scalia, David H. Souter, Clarence Thomas

Justices Dissenting
Harry A. Blackmun, John Paul Stevens

Place
Washington, D.C.

Date of Decision
31 May 1994

Decision
Upheld the hospital's claim and overturned a lower court's decision prohibiting the hospital from firing an employee based on what was thought to have been said.

Significance
The ruling established that the government as an employer can restrict its employees' speech under certain conditions, but the public employer must conduct a sufficient investigation before taking action. To avoid violating the First Amendment, the employer must establish a "reasonable belief" that the contested comments were either disruptive to the effectiveness and efficiency of the agency's operation or were not related to a topic of public interest. Left undefined were the investigative procedures an employer should follow in establishing that belief thus introducing greater uncertainty in an agency's accountability for personnel actions.

At dinner break in January of 1987 while on duty at McDonough District Hospital, a public hospital, nurses Cheryl Churchill and Melanie Perkins-Graham discussed work. Churchill worked in obstetrics and Perkins-Graham was considering a transfer to that department. A fellow worker, Mary Lou Ballew, overheard the discussion and, displeased with Churchill's remarks, relayed what she thought she heard to Cynthia Waters, Churchill's supervisor. Ballew claimed Churchill bitterly described an unfavorable work environment in obstetrics, blamed Waters and the hospital's vice president of nursing, Kathleen Davis, for the situation, and cited irreconcilable differences with Waters. The comments apparently led Perkins-Graham not to pursue the transfer.

When approached, Churchill provided a different version of her remarks. She claimed her comments focused primarily on certain training practices of the hospital that could possibly have lowered the quality of nursing care. Two other fellow workers who also overheard the discussion agreed with Churchill's account. Churchill claimed Ballew was biased against her due to a previous incident. Waters and Davis conducted several inquiries before firing Churchill for what they believed was said. Churchill filed a formal internal complaint with the hospital administration. The complaint was rejected following an interview and review of reports prepared by Waters and Davis. Churchill then filed suit claiming violation of her First Amendment rights to freedom of speech.

The Supreme Court previously provided guidance to lower courts for cases involving public employees' speech restrictions. The Court found in *Pickering v. Board of Education* (1968) that government can restrict its employees' speech to a greater extent than private citizens. The Court ruled disciplinary action against a public employee for speech "violates the First Amendment only if it is in retaliation for the employee's speech on a matter of public concern." Later in 1983, the Court developed a test in *Connick v. Myers* to better determine when a public employee may be appropriately disciplined or discharged for their speech. Essentially, the Court ruled that a public employee's speech is protected by the First Amendment if it is about

Whistleblower Protection Act of 1989

The Whistleblower Protection Act of 1989 protects the jobs of federal employees who report fraud, waste, abuse of authority, or mismanagement within the workplace. The act requires a worker to only prove his whistleblowing was "a contributing factor," not a "dominant" reason, in disciplinary actions brought against him. Employing agencies must prove with "clear and convincing evidence" that actions against an employee would have occurred even if the employee had not "blown the whistle." Office of Special Counsel (OSC) and the Merit System Protection Board (MSPB) are charged with investigating cases and protecting whistleblowers.

The OSC's primary role is to protect federal workers reporting incidents within their agencies. Responsibilities include forwarding worker complaints of employer harassment to the appropriate agency, investigating allegations of retribution, and filing complaints with the MSPB or recommending disciplinary action against employers. A worker can appeal directly to the MSPB only if the OSC drops the case or issues no reply to a complaint within 20 days. The OSC is required to respond to allegations of a "gross" nature.

The MSPB protects witnesses from harassment and encourages reluctant colleagues to testify. The MSPB also conducts hearings, appeals, special studies, and oversees the U.S. Office of Personnel Management's federal employment policies.

Source(s): *Congress and the Nation.* Vol. IX: 1993-1996: *A Review of Government and Politics.* Washington, DC: Congressional Quarterly, Inc., 1998.

---

a subject of public concern and not disruptive to the efficiency and effectiveness of an agency achieving its goals. The balancing test involved weighing interests in agency efficiency, employee performance, and workplace harmony against the employee's First Amendment rights.

In applying the *Connick* test, the U.S. District Court ruled in 1991 against Churchill claiming that neither version of the conversation was a matter of public concern, and, even if so, the disruption from her behavior erased any constitutional protection. The following year, the U.S. Court of Appeals reversed the district court's decision. By accepting Churchill's version of the conversation, the court found it a matter of public interest and not disruptive. Possible violations of state nursing regulations and the quality of nursing care at the hospital were matters of public interest. The court concluded that employee action should be based on what was actually said as determined by a jury trial, not what the employer thought was said. The U.S. Supreme Court accepted the case in 1993 to resolve the conflict between the two lower courts.

A Reasonable Belief

In *Waters,* the Court first had to determine whether to apply the *Connick* test to what the employer thought Churchill said, or what a jury might determine was said. Justice O'Connor, writing for the majority, found that the "*Connick* test should be applied to what the government employer reasonably thought was said," not what a jury might ultimately determine. O'Connor wrote that a government supervisor must be able to make personnel decisions based on common employment factors, such as past conduct, what others have

to say, people's believability, and other factors not normally a part of a court process. The court of appeals, in referring the case to a jury trial, did not adequately consider "the government's interest in efficient employment decision making." Therefore, the employer should not be required to follow common court procedure, but use more standard employment decision making processes without fear of lawsuit. O'Connor cautioned though that the decision-maker must reach their conclusion in good faith and not in some predetermined biased manner.

O'Connor then introduced a new requirement for making personnel decisions. She wrote the Court must have some means in assessing the "reasonableness of the employer's conclusions." The answer was that the employer must conduct an adequate investigation to establish a "reasonable belief" that the speech violated the First Amendment. So, if Waters and Davis truly believed Ballew's version and conducted an investigation to substantiate the facts, then they acted appropriately. Such an investigation need not be exhaustive. As stated by O'Connor, "Management can spend only so much of their time on any one employment decision." The Court found the investigation conducted by the hospital administration sufficient to establish a reasonable belief.

O'Connor further wrote that Churchill's speech, as reported by Ballew, was not of public interest, and, even if it were, the potential disruptiveness was sufficient to warrant personnel action. O'Connor considered discouraging an employee from seeking a transfer sufficiently disruptive to outweigh any First Amendment protection. In addition, Churchill's complaining threatened management's authority and her statements of irreconcilableness established doubt as to her future effectiveness as a nurse at the hospital. Even if part of Churchill's speech regarding training procedures was of public interest, the other speech regarding hospital administration decisions was not and that was sufficient for disciplinary action. The *Connick* test need only be applied to that part of the speech of public interest. O'Connor wrote, "An employee who makes an unprotected statement is not immunized from discipline by the fact that this statement is surrounded by protected statements." O'Connor directed the lower court to determine if Churchill was fired for the disruptive speech she made about hospital administration, or for some non-disruptive speech concerning training procedures.

Justice Scalia, joined by Kennedy and Thomas, concurred with the basic judgement of the majority but sharply differed on one key point. Scalia wrote that the employer should not be required to conduct an investigation before taking disciplinary action. This "right to an investigation" inappropriately creates for the employee "a broad new First Amendment right to an investigation before dismissal for speech." In effect, this decision changed the employer's responsibility from avoidance of retaliation motives, as directed in *Pickering,* to an ill-defined procedural responsibility. Scalia asserted no previous Court findings justified such a ruling.

She Said She Said

With Justice Blackmun joining in dissent, Justice Stevens wrote that the hospital should not be able to take disciplinary action based on what they thought was said. Blackmun wrote that public "agencies are often the site of sharp differences . . . When those who work together disagree, reports of speech are often skewed." Blackmun believed the majority opinion inappropriately favored "discipline, rather than further discussion, when such disputes arise." He believed the court of appeals requiring a trial to determine what was actually spoken should be pursued if the hospital could not resolve the issue without disciplinary action. Otherwise, public employees may not be able to "express their views on issues of public concern without fear of discipline or termination." Misconceptions by the employer should not be sufficient cause for violating an employee's First Amendment rights.

Impact

The basic concern of the Court in *Waters* was the relationship between the government and its employees in regard to regulation of their speech and how it differs from government regulation of private citizens' free speech. As the Court recognized, various laws require agencies to accomplish specific tasks. Employees are hired "to help with those tasks as effectively and effi-

ciently as possible." As a result, public employers have considerable flexibility to limit its employees' speech. When an employee deviates by speaking out disruptively, even on matters of public concern, the public employer must have some ability to correct the situation. The Court in *Waters* established a "reasonableness" test to protect employers who must take disciplinary actions.

Throughout history, the Court has held that a different relationship exists between the government and its employees than with private citizens. O'Connor wrote that in "many situations . . . the government must be able to restrict its employees' speech." Examples include offensive speech to the public or fellow employees, and participation in political campaigns. The finding in *New York Times v. Sullivan* (1964) that the First Amendment reflects the "profound national commitment to the principle that debate on public issues should be uninhibited, robust, and wide-open" does not necessarily apply to public employees. Providing a service to the public compels standards of conduct applied to public employees that would be considered too vague to apply to the common citizen. Therefore, the courts have provided greater flexibility to public employers in restricting activity of their employees than with the public at large regarding First Amendment protections.

As stated by Justice Souter, "First Amendment limitations on public employers . . . must reflect a balance of the public employer's interest in accomplishing its mission and the public employee's interest in speaking on matters of public concern." Some believed procedures for limiting the speech of employees in the public workplace as established in *Waters* served as a model for resolving harassment claims in private workplace settings as well. The Court ruling reinforced that speech disruptive to the mission of an organization may not be tolerated by the employer.

A year after the *Waters* case, the Supreme Court decided another public employee speech case in *United States v. National Treasury Employees Union* (1995). By amending the Ethics in Government Act of 1978, Congress sought to prohibit most executive branch federal employees from earning outside income by giving speeches or writing articles. The restriction applied even when the subject and second employer were totally unrelated to the employee's official public duties. In applying the balancing test, the Court found the law unconstitutional because the ban on the payment was essentially a ban on free speech. Payment served as an incentive toward free expression.

Added to the First Amendment constitutional protections of public employee's speech were statutory protections established by the Whistleblower Protection Act of 1989. The act further protected public employees from retaliation by employers for speaking out on matters of public interest about their employers and agency activities. The freedom of speech for public employees on matters of public interest in a non-disruptive manner was the focus of much activity through the 1990s.

Related Cases

New York Times v. Sullivan, 376 U.S. 254 (1964).
Pickering v. Board of Education, 391 U.S. 563 (1968).
Connick v. Myers, 461 U.S. 138 (1983).

United States v. National Treasury Employees Union, 513 U.S. 454 (1995).

Bibliography and Further Reading

Biskupic, Joan, and Elder Witt, eds. *Guide to the U.S. Supreme Court.* Washington, DC: Congressional Quarterly, 1997.

Shafroth, Frank. "Cities Gain Modest Protection from High Court Ruling on Speech."

LADUE V. GILLEO

Legal Citation: 513 U.S. 374 (1994)

Petitioner
City of Ladue, et al.

Respondent
Margaret P. Gilleo

Petitioner's Claim
That the city of Ladue's ban on residential signs except in ten exempted cases did not violate Margaret Gilleo's First Amendment right to free speech.

Chief Lawyer for Petitioner
Jordan B. Cherrick

Chief Lawyer for Respondent
Gerald P. Greiman

Justices for the Court
Harry A. Blackmun, Ruth Bader Ginsburg, Anthony M. Kennedy, Sandra Day O'Connor, William H. Rehnquist, Antonin Scalia, David H. Souter, John Paul Stevens (writing for the Court), Clarence Thomas

Justices Dissenting
None

Place
Washington, D.C.

Date of Decision
13 June 1994

Decision
Upheld the lower court's ruling that the city of Ladue's ban on residential signs did in fact violate Margaret Gilleo's First Amendment right to free speech.

Significance
The ruling affirmed the Supreme Court's belief that a city cannot infringe upon the free speech rights of its inhabitants without a compelling reason to do so. In this case the city's desire to reduce clutter in residential areas was found not to be compelling enough to justify a ban on signage.

The Facts of the Case

Margaret P. Gilleo, a citizen of Ladue, Missouri, placed a sign outside her home calling for an end to the Persian Gulf War. The city informed her that her sign was banned under a local law which prohibited signs in residential areas. Its justification for banning the sign was that widespread display of signs would make the city look cluttered and ugly. Gilleo fought to keep her sign where it was and won a case in district court stopping the city from enforcing its ordinance. She then placed another sign, reading "For Peace in the Gulf," in her front window. The Ladue City Council responded by passing a new law that banned all signs over a certain size that were not covered by ten specific exemptions (such as "For Sale" and "Beware of Dog" signs). The city hoped this new ban would pass constitutional muster. Margaret Gilleo believed it violated her right to free speech and filed a new action in district court challenging the revised law.

The Lower Courts Rule

The U.S. District Court for the Eastern District of Missouri found for Margaret Gilleo. It held the new law unconstitutional and ordered the city of Ladue to stop enforcing it. The case then went to the U.S. Court of Appeals, which affirmed the decision. It asserted the city was choosing to regulate Gilleo's free speech on the basis of what she was saying, rather than its stated reason of eliminating clutter. It also found that the city's reasons for banning signs, while valid, were not compelling enough to warrant such a content-based restriction. The city of Ladue then appealed this decision to the U.S. Supreme Court, which agreed to hear the case.

The Supreme Court Rules

On 13 June 1994, the Supreme Court issued its decision. It affirmed the rulings of the lower courts, holding that the new Ladue city ordinance violated Margaret Gilleo's right to free speech under the First Amendment to the U.S. Constitution. Justice Stevens wrote the opinion for the unanimous majority, with Justice O'Connor writing a concurring opinion The Supreme Court based its decision on four key points.

Margaret Gilleo holds the sign that she placed in her bedroom window, 1994. © AP/Wide World Photos.

The first point made by Stevens was that, although cities have a right to regulate the placement of signs, they cannot enforce the law selectively based on the messages contained in the signs. However, in this case, the Supreme Court accepted from the outset that the city of Ladue's law banning signs did not discriminate on the basis of content. It simply found that the city's interest in regulating clutter was outweighed by Gilleo's right to express her opinion.

In its second point, the Supreme Court asserted that the city of Ladue had "almost completely foreclosed" on a vital means of expression by its citizens. Even if not done on the basis of content, the banning of an entire media—in this case signs—poses too much of a threat to the free speech of citizens to be allowed to stand.

Third, the Court rejected the city's claim that Gilleo could have found other means of expressing her viewpoint, such as pamphlets or newspaper advertisements. The Court ruled that personal signs are a unique way of expressing one's opinion and cannot be equated with other methods of expression. As Justice Stevens wrote, "Residential signs are an unusually cheap and convenient form of communication. Especially for persons of modest means or limited mobility, a yard or window sign may have no practical substitute." Therefore the city could not choke off this avenue entirely without severe free speech repercussions.

Finally, the Court sought to put the issue at hand into a historical context. It affirmed Americans' special regard for individual liberty in the home and warned against government attempts to restrict a person's abil-

ity to speak there. The Court also suggested that Ladue residents' own interest in maintaining their property values would prompt them to police themselves on the issue of rampant proliferation of signs. Justice Stevens wrote, "We are confident that more temperate measures could in large part satisfy Ladue's stated regulatory needs without harm to the First Amendment rights of its citizens. As currently framed, however, the ordinance abridges those rights."

Impact

Ladue v. Gilleo reaffirmed the U.S. Supreme Court's commitment to strict scrutiny of all governmental attempts to restrict free speech. It established a precedent for future cases in which the balance between state regulation of signage and the rights of expression come into conflict.

Related Cases

First National Bank of Boston v. Bellotti, 435 U.S. 765 (1978).

Metromedia, Inc. v. San Diego, 453 U.S. 490 (1981).

Frisby v. Schultz, 487 U.S. 474 (1988).

Bibliography and Further Reading

Kennedy, David J. "Residential Associations as State Actors." *Yale Law Journal,* Vol. 105, no. 3, December 1995, pp. 761–793.

Newman, Judith, Mary M. Harrison, and Carolyn Kramer. "A Sign of the Times." *People Weekly,* March 21, 1994, pp. 115–117.

LEBRON V. NATIONAL RAILROAD PASSENGER CORPORATION

Legal Citation: 513 U.S. 374 (1995)

Petitioner
Michael A. Lebron

Respondent
National Railroad Passenger Corporation

Petitioner's Claim
That refusal to place an advertisement on Amtrak's Spectacular billboard had violated his First and Fifth Amendment rights.

Chief Lawyer for Petitioner
David D. Cole

Chief Lawyer for Respondent
Kevin T. Baine

Justices for the Court
Stephen Breyer, Ruth Bader Ginsburg, Anthony M. Kennedy, William H. Rehnquist, Antonin Scalia (writing for the Court), David H. Souter, John Paul Stevens, Clarence Thomas

Justices Dissenting
Sandra Day O'Connor

Place
Washington, D.C.

Date of Decision
21 February 1995

Decision
The Supreme Court reversed the decision of the U.S. Court of Appeals for the Second Circuit and held that Amtrak was a government agency. Therefore, Amtrak is part of the federal government subject to the free speech requirements of the First Amendment. As such, Amtrak could not prohibit political billboards from train stations.

Significance
The decision extended the First Amendment to corporations created by, and under the control of, the government in the case of an artist who argued successfully that Amtrak had been wrong to reject his billboard display because of its political message. The First Amendment bars only governments and instruments of government from infringing upon the freedom of speech. Private persons and corporations generally are free to regulate speech in whatever ways that they wish. The Court's holding that Amtrak is a part of government extends First Amendment protections to federally created corporations. The Supreme Court indicated that it might not extend these protections to other federally created corporations that are not as closely affiliated with and controlled by the government.

American concern about inefficiency in government dates back to the First Continental Congress. In over 200 years since the First Congress, reorganization has taken place, but the fundamental structure of government departments has changed little. However, their jurisdiction has grown. The Reinventing Government program of Vice President Al Gore is only the latest in a series of plans to reinvigorate the federal government.

Petitioner, Michael A. Lebron, created a billboard display that involved commentary on public issues. In August of 1991, he contacted Transportation Displays Incorporated (TDI), which managed the leasing of the billboards in Amtrak's Pennsylvania Station in New York City. He sought to display an advertisement on a large billboard known to New Yorkers as "the Spectacular." The Spectacular was a curved, illuminated billboard, approximately 103 feet long and 10 feet high. It dominated the main entrance to Penn Station's waiting room and ticket area.

On 30 November 1992, Lebron signed a contract with Transportation Displays Incorporated to display an advertisement on the Spectacular for two months beginning in January of 1993. The contract provided that all advertising was subject to approval of Transportation Displays Incorporated and Amtrak as to character, text, illustration, design and operation. Lebron declined to disclose the specific content of his advertisement throughout his negotiations with Transportation Displays Incorporated, but explained that it was political.

On 2 December 1992, he submitted to Transportation Displays Incorporated and Amtrak an advertisement. The advertisement was described by the district court:

> The work is a photomontage, accompanied by considerable text. Taking off on a widely circulated Coors beer advertisement which proclaims Coors to be the 'Right Beer,' Lebron's piece is captioned 'Is it the Right's Beer Now?' It includes photographic images of convivial drinkers of Coors beer, juxtaposed with a Nicaraguan village scene in which peasants are menaced by a can of Coors that hurtles towards them, leaving behind a trail of fire, as

if it were a missile. The accompanying text, appearing on either end of the montage, criticizes the Coors family for its support of right wing causes, particularly the contras in Nicaragua. Again taking off on Coors' advertising which uses the slogan of 'Silver Bullet' for its beer cans, the text proclaims that Coors is 'The Silver Bullet that aims The Far Right's political agenda at the heart of America.'

Amtrak did not approve the advertisement. Amtrak's policy was not to allow political advertising on the Spectacular Billboard. Lebron filed suit against Amtrak and Transportation Displays Incorporated. He claimed that refusal to place his advertisement on the Spectacular billboard had violated his First and Fifth Amendment rights. The district court ruled that Amtrak, because of its close ties to the federal government, was a government entity for First Amendment purposes. Rejection of Lebron's proposed advertisement violated the First Amendment. The district court granted Lebron an injunction and ordered Amtrak and Transportation Displays Incorporated to display Lebron's advertisement on the Spectacular.

The U.S. Court of Appeals for the Second Circuit reversed the decision. The court noted that Amtrak was, by the terms of the legislation that created it, not a government entity. It concluded that the federal government was not so involved with Amtrak that the latter's decisions could be considered federal action. The U.S. Supreme Court then issued a writ of *certiorari*, a written order commanding a lower court to forward the proceedings of a case for review, and took on the case.

An Important Reversal

By a majority ruling (8-1), the Supreme Court reversed the decision of the U.S. Court of Appeals for the Second Circuit. The Court relied on the confluence of a number of factors to conclude that Amtrak, a federally chartered for-profit corporation, is "part of the government" for "the purpose of individual rights guaranteed against the Government by the Constitution." Amtrak is wholly owned by the United States, and the government controls its board of directors. In incorporating Amtrak, Congress declared that it "will not be an agency or establishment of the United States Government," although it subjected Amtrak to the Government Corporation Control Act, and classified it as a mixed-ownership government corporation.

Amtrak was created by the Rail Passenger Service Act of 1970 (RPSA) to avert the threatened extinction of passenger trains in the interest of "the public convenience and necessity." The legislation established detailed goals for Amtrak, set forth its structure and powers, and assigned the appointment of a majority of its board of directors to the president.

In giving the majority opinion, Justice Scalia distinguished between two types of government corporations. The first type was that such as Conrail, in which the responsibilities of the federal directors are not different from those of the other directors. Each director had a role to operate the corporation at a profit for the benefit of its shareholders. In the second type of government corporations, such as Amtrak, the public directors had other duties besides profit.

The Court ruled that "where, as here, the government created a corporation by special law for the furtherance of governmental objectives, and retains for itself permanent authority to appoint a majority of that corporation's directors, the corporation is part of the Government for purposes of the First Amendment." There was a long history of corporations created and participated in by the United States for the achievement of governmental objectives. Amtrak's authorizing statute provided that it will not be an agency or establishment of the United States Government.

The Court relied on a number of factors to conclude that Amtrak is an agency of the United States for the purpose of individual rights guaranteed against the government by the Constitution. This conclusion accords with the public, judicial and congressional understanding over the years that government-created and government-controlled corporations are part of the government itself.

A Dissenting Opinion

In her dissent, Justice O'Connor said that the Court had avoided the issue that Amtrak was a private entity. Justice O'Connor wrote that she must continue to answer the question that is properly presented to the Court: whether Amtrak's decision to ban Lebron's speech, although made by a concededly private entity, is nevertheless attributable to the government and therefore considered state action for constitutional purposes. The conduct of a private entity is not subject to constitutional scrutiny if the challenged action resulted from the exercise of private choice, and not from state influence, or coercion.

Justice O'Connor saw no basis to credit to the government Amtrak's decision to disapprove Lebron's advertisement. Although there were a number of factors indicating government influence in Amtrak's management and operation, none suggested that the government had any effect on Amtrak's decision to turn down Lebron's proposal. The advertising policy that allegedly violated the First Amendment originated with a predecessor to Amtrak, the wholly private Pennsylvania Railroad Company. A prior lease by that company prohibited "any advertisement which in the judgement of Licensor is or might be deemed to be slanderous, libelous, unlawful, immoral, or offensive to good taste . . ." Amtrak continued this policy after it took over. The specific decision to disapprove Lebron's advertising was made by Amtrak's Vice President of Real Estate and Operations Development, who was not appointed by the president, nor by the president appointed board.

Lebron nevertheless contends that the board, through its approval of the advertising policy, controlled the adverse action against him. Justice O'Conner wrote, "it assumes that the board members sit as public officials and not as business directors, thus begging the question whether Amtrak is a Government agency or a private entity." The particular lease, which permitted Amtrak to disallow Lebron's billboard was neither reviewed, nor approved, directly by the board. The Amtrak Board approved only one contract between Amtrak and Transportation Displays Incorporated, the billboard leasing company that served as Amtrak's agent. In this case, no evidence suggested that the government controlled, coerced, or influenced Amtrak's decision, made according to corporate policy and private business judgment, to not approve of the advertisement proposed by Lebron.

Justice O'Conner wrote, "the Court of Appeals properly applied our precedents and did not impute Amtrak's decision to the Government. I would affirm on this basis and not reverse the Court of Appeals based on a theory that is foreign to this case. Respectfully, I dissent."

A Second Appeal

The nation's highest court reversed the ruling in 1995 and sent Lebron's case back to the appeals court. The justices had left undecided whether Amtrak had committed any free speech violation. Ordered to study Lebron's First Amendment arguments, the appeals court again ruled against him in October of 1995. "Amtrak's historical refusal to accept political advertisements such as Lebron's on the Spectacular is a rea-

sonable use of that forum that is neutral as to viewpoint," the appeals court ruled. The court of appeals denied a rehearing on 29 December 1995. Lebron again appealed to the Supreme Court, but it rejected his appeal on 27 May 1996.

Impact

The cases of *McCulloch v. Maryland* (1819) and *Osborn v. Bank of United States* (1819) set the foundation for the constitutional status of federal government corporations. These two decisions established three clear principles concerning a federal government corporation. First, the federal government may charter private corporations. Second, the presence of a minority of directors appointed by the president, or federal ownership of a minority of shares, did not make an otherwise private corporation into an agency. Third, the federal government may give special advantages and powers, such as state and federal tax exemptions or control of the money supply, to a private federal corporation. No subsequent court decision has seriously questioned any of these general principles. The Supreme Court's decision in this case added a fourth principle to the list: A corporation created for a public purpose over which the government retains permanent control is a federal government corporation.

Related Cases

McCulloch v. Maryland, 4 Wheat 316 (1819).
Osborn v. Bank of United States, 9 Wheat 738 (1819).
Burton v. Wilmington Park Authority, 365 U.S. 715 (1961).

Bibliography and Further Reading

Reinventing the Government Corporation. http://www.law.miami.edu/~froomkin/articles/reinvent.htm

USA Today. http://www.usatoday.com/news/court/nscot190.htm

McIntyre v. Ohio Elections Commission

Legal Citation: 514 U.S. 334 (1995)

Petitioner
Joseph McIntyre, Executor of the Estate of Margaret McIntyre

Respondent
Ohio Elections Commission

Petitioner's Claim
That 3599.09(A) of the Ohio Code violates the right to free speech under the First Amendment.

Chief Lawyer for Petitioner
David Goldberger

Chief Lawyer for Respondent
Andrew I. Sutter

Justices for the Court
Stephen Breyer, Ruth Bader Ginsburg, Anthony M. Kennedy, Sandra Day O'Connor, David H. Souter, John Paul Stevens (writing for the Court), Clarence Thomas

Justices Dissenting
William H. Rehnquist, Antonin Scalia

Place
Washington, D.C.

Date of Decision
19 April 1995

Decision
The Court, reversing a lower court's ruling, held that an Ohio statute prohibiting anonymous campaign literature was unconstitutional.

Significance
The ruling extended First Amendment protections to those who publish anonymously in a political context.

On 27 April 1988, outside a public meeting in Westerville, Ohio, a school official warned Margaret McIntyre that the pamphlets she was distributing were illegal. Her fliers opposed a proposed school levy; some were signed with her name, but others were only signed "Concerned Parents and Tax Payers." Despite the warning, McIntyre continued handing out her fliers the following evening.

In November, after the levy had passed, the same official filed a complaint against McIntyre with the Ohio Elections Commission. The commission fined McIntyre $100, as 3599.09(A) of the Ohio Code prohibited anonymous campaign literature. The Franklin County Court of Common Pleas reversed that decision, on the grounds that McIntyre had not misled the public or acted surreptitiously. The Ohio Court of Appeals reinstated the fine, based on the 1922 Ohio Supreme Court decision *State v. Babst* upholding the predecessor to the law in question. The dissent cited *Talley v. California* (1960) as a relevant, more recent case.

Talley v. California

The Supreme Court had decided in *Talley* that a Los Angeles city ordinance, barring handbills unless they are printed with the names and addresses of their authors or sponsors, violated the Fourteenth Amendment's protection of speech and press. As stated in the court transcripts, California argued that the ordinance was designed to "identify those responsible for fraud, false advertising and libel." However, there was nothing in the ordinance itself nor in its legislative history to support that claim; the ordinance uniformly banned all anonymous handbills.

Writing for the majority, Justice Black praised the historical role of anonymous publications: "Persecuted groups and sects from time to time throughout history have been able to criticize oppressive practices and laws either anonymously or not at all." He went on to note the importance of anonymous pamphlets in early American history, concluding "It is plain that anonymity has sometimes been assumed for the most constructive purposes."

In the *MacIntyre* case, though, the Ohio Supreme Court affirmed the court of appeals ruling, notwithstanding the Supreme Court decision in *Talley*. The Ohio law, the court claimed, differed from the ordinance in *Talley* because 3599.09(A) was meant to identify "those who distribute materials containing false statements." The dissent considered identification a significant burden, and feared that the requirement would silence some unpopular groups for fear of retaliation. The Supreme Court's ensuing decision echoed many of this dissent's arguments.

Regulation of the Electoral Process

Before the Supreme Court, Ohio argued that 3599.09(A) was a "reasonable regulation of the electoral process." As in *Talley,* though, the Court found that the statute was not limited to documents containing falsehoods. The Ohio statute differed from the Los Angeles ordinance, however, in its specific application to documents intended to sway voters. The Court's job in this case, then, was to "decided whether and to what extent the First Amendment's protection of anonymity encompasses documents intended to influence the electoral process."

"Exacting Scrutiny"

Rather than weigh the interests of the state against the rights of voters, as it had done in other cases regarding regulation of the electoral process, the Court here applied "exacting scrutiny." That is, it would "uphold the restriction only if it is narrowly tailored to serve an overriding state interest." The Court applied this strict standard because this case involved not just procedural issues, but free speech. In fact, 3599.09(A) applied to a central area of free speech: discussion of public issues.

Ohio argued that even by this standard, the statute was justified because of the importance of the state's interest in "preventing fraudulent and libelous statements and its interest in providing the electorate with relevant information." The question then was: Did this statute achieve those goals? The Court's answer was that it did not.

The identity of the author, according to the Court, was no different from any other information that might be contained in a document. In *Miami Herald Publishing Company v. Tornillo* (1960), the Court had decided that no one could be required to print all relevant information. In any case, the name and address of the author would add little information to a document.

Ohio already had other regulations prohibiting false statements during political campaigns. Thus, the statute in question acted primarily as an auxiliary to those regulations, and as a deterrent. Given its supporting role, and its obvious potential for use against authors of accurate and scrupulous documents, 3599.09(A) did more harm than good.

The Court rejected Ohio's argument that past decisions requiring disclosure —of the sources of corporate advertising (*First National Bank of Boston v. Bellotti* [1978]) and of campaign funds(*Buckley v. Valeo* [1976])—applied here. *Bellotti* was inapplicable, as corporations lack individuals' First Amendment protections. As for *Buckley,* the Court decided that, compared to identification of a leaflet's author, "Disclosure of an expenditure and its use, without more, reveals far less information . . . even though money may 'talk,' its speech is less specific, less personal and less provocative than a handbill—and as a result, when money supports an unpopular viewpoint it is less likely to precipitate retaliation."

Anonymity Part of Original Intent

Justice Thomas filed a concurring opinion agreeing with the Court's judgment, but not its reasoning. Thomas presented a history of anonymous publishing in the United States, to establish that the original intent of the First Amendment encompasses anonymous publishing. The Court's reasoning in the case, he argued, was largely irrelevant; it was the framers' understanding that was important.

. . . Or Perhaps Not

In his dissent Justice Scalia found it difficult to discern the original intent. Laws against anonymous pamphleteering were neither approved, nor clearly disapproved, at the time of adoption. Scalia acknowledged that "anonymous electioneering was not prohibited by law in 1791 or in 1868 [the year in which the Fourteenth Amendment was adopted]." This fact did not, however, establish anonymity as a constitutional right. Nor did any of Thomas's examples involve the electoral process, the context in *McIntyre*. In the absence of other evidence, Scalia turned to "the widespread and long-accepted practices of the American people." At the time of *McIntyre,* every state except California had a law similar to the Ohio statute. On this basis alone Scalia would decide for the respondent.

However, he went on to say that restriction of free speech was justified by protection of the electoral process. Furthermore, a general right to anonymity was not supported by precedent, and had been explicitly rejected in earlier cases. And finally, prohibiting anonymous political pamphlets does improve elections. A signing requirement deters those who would mislead the public or smear their opponents.

Justice Ginsburg, in a concurrence, called Scalia's dissent "stirring in its appreciation of democratic values." She pointed out, though, that previous cases supported the decision. She also qualified that decision to some degree: "We do not thereby hold that the State may not in other, larger circumstances, require the speaker to disclose its interest by disclosing its identity."

Impact

In 1998, most states required sponsors of political television advertisements to identify themselves in the advertisements. *McIntyre* may provide a way for political organizations to challenge that condition. Notably, the petitioner's lawyer in *McIntyre* did say that an identification requirement for television advertisements would be appropriate.

Another parallel is to Internet speech, which, like pamphleteering, falls into the category of "cheap speech." Internet "remailers" allow individuals to post messages anonymously; many object to the resulting lack of accountability. The arguments presented in *McIntyre* could equally well address that objection. On one hand, the author's identity may not always add relevant information. On the other hand, if the author's identity might create a bias against a message, anonymity could deliver a more open-minded audience.

However, this decision may prove conducive to dirty campaigning. Scalia noted in his dissent that "[t]he principal impediment against [mudslinging] is the reluctance of most individuals and organizations to be publicly associated with uncharitable and uncivil expression." With the *McIntyre* decision, the Court may have provided a way around that impediment.

Related Cases

State v. Babst, 135 N.E. 525 (1922).

Talley v. California, 362 U.S. 60 (1960).

Miami Herald Publishing Company v. Tornillo, 418 U.S. 241 (1974).

Buckley v. Valeo, 424 U.S. 1 (1976).

First National Bank of Boston v. Bellotti, 435 U.S. 765 (1978).

Bibliography and Further Reading

Biskupic, Joan. "Court Hears Case on Unsigned Leaflets." *Washington Post,* Thursday, 13 October 1994, p. A05.

Dupree, Thomas H., Jr. "Exposing the Stealth Candidate: Disclosure Statutes After *McIntyre v. Ohio Elections Commission.*" *University of Chicago Law Review,* Vol. 63, no. 3, summer 1996, pp. 1211-41.

Eyer, Sherri L. "From Whence It Comes—Is the Message More Revealing Than the Messenger? *McIntyre v. Ohio Elections Commission* 115 S.Ct. 1511 (1995)." *Dickinson Law Review,* Vol. 100, no. 4, summer 1996, pp. 1051-74.

Schwartz, John. "With E-Mail Privacy in Jeopardy, 'Remailer' Closes Up Shop." *Washington Post,* 16 September 1996, p. F19.

Tien, Lee. "Who's Afraid of Anonymous Speech? *McIntyre* and the Internet," *Oregon Law Review,* Vol. 75, no. 1, spring 1996, pp. 117-89.

HURLEY V. IRISH-AMERICAN GAY GROUP OF BOSTON

Legal Citation: 515 U.S. 557 (1995)

Petitioner
John J. Hurley and South Boston Allied War Veterans Council

Respondent
Irish-American Gay, Lesbian and Bisexual Group of Boston, et al.

Petitioner's Claim
That First Amendment Freedom of Speech protection extends to a private organizer's choice of which groups can participate in Boston's St. Patrick's Day Parade based on the content of their intended messages.

Chief Lawyers for Petitioner
Chester Darling and Dwight G. Duncan

Chief Lawyer for Respondent
John Ward

Justices for the Court
Stephen Breyer, Ruth Bader Ginsburg, Anthony M. Kennedy, Sandra Day O'Connor, William H. Rehnquist, Antonin Scalia, David H. Souter (writing for the Court), John Paul Stevens, Clarence Thomas

Justices Dissenting
None

Place
Washington, D.C.

Date of Decision
19 June 1995

Decision
Upheld the parade organizer's claim and overturned two lower courts' decisions that banned the organizer's practice of excluding groups from parades due to the messages they express.

Significance
The ruling recognized that privately organized parades are a form of private expression and are protected under the First Amendment. The private organizer can select which messages are expressed to onlookers and which messages left out. Denying participation of certain groups, in essence, exercises a right not to speak. However, many long established parades around the nation organized by private organizations are often considered civic in character thus blurring the distinction between private and public expression. The Supreme Court's decision broadened constitutionally protected symbolic speech by accepting a less focused message than in previous cases.

The Massachusetts public accommodations law has a long, colorful history. In common law, innkeepers, blacksmiths, and others serving the public could not refuse service without good reason. After the Civil War, the Commonwealth of Massachusetts was the first state to turn this principle into law expanding it to cover any "public place of amusement, public conveyance [transportation] or public meeting." The state legislature continued to broaden the scope to prohibit among other things, discrimination on the basis of "race, color, religious creed, national origin, sex, and sexual orientation." These provisions are well within the state's usual power to act when the legislature has reason to believe a given group could be a target of discrimination. The provisions were safe from First Amendment violation since the content of speech was not targeted.

As early as 1737 citizens of Boston observed the feast of the apostle to Ireland, St. Patrick. In 1776, the evacuation of British troops and Loyalists from Boston during the Revolutionary War created another cause for celebration. Both the feast of St. Patrick and the evacuation are commemorated every year on 17 March with a parade. Previously sponsored by the city of Boston, in 1947 the South Boston Allied War Veterans Council was granted authority to organize and conduct the St. Patrick's Day-Evacuation Day Parade. After 1947 the council, an unincorporated association of persons elected from various Boston veteran groups, annually applied for and received a parade permit. Organizations wishing to march in the parade applied to the council, who then selected the participants. The popular parade included up to 20,000 marchers and one million watchers in a single year.

In 1992, the council denied the Irish-American Gay, Lesbian and Bisexual Group of Boston (GLIB) a place in the parade. GLIB was formed specifically for the parade "in order to express its members' pride in their Irish heritage as openly gay, lesbian, and bisexual individuals in the community, and to support the like men and women who sought to march in the New York St. Patrick's Day parade." GLIB obtained a state court order and marched in the parade that year.

In 1993 GLIB applied to the council and was denied again. GLIB filed suit alleging the denial violated the

The Irish American Gay Lesbian and Bisexual Pride Group of Boston in a St. Patrick's Day Parade. © AP/Wide World Photos.

Massachusetts public accommodations law and the First Amendment of the U.S. Constitution, which protects freedom of speech and expression. GLIB argued the public accommodations law, as stated, prohibits "any distinction, discrimination or restriction on account of . . . sexual orientation . . . relative to the admission of any person to, or treatment in any place of public accommodation, resort, or amusement." A public accommodation is defined as "any place . . . which is open to and accepts the patronage [business] of the general public and . . . a boardwalk or other public highway [and] . . . a place of public amusement, recreation, sport, exercise or entertainment."

The trial court found in favor of GLIB. It ruled the parade, occurred in the public streets of South Boston for 47 years, provided "entertainment, amusement, and recreation to participants and spectators alike." The court identified a lack of selectivity in choosing participants since no particular procedures for admission existed, applications were voted on in batches, and at times groups simply joined on the day of parade. The court considered the parade a "public event" with the only common theme among the participants being their public involvement. The parade therefore was within the public accommodation definition. Exclusion of GLIB because of its message of proclaiming its members' sexual orientation clearly violated the public accommodations law. With respect to the alleged First Amendment violation, the trial court found the parade conveyed no specific theme therefore no specific expressive purpose was present. Consequently, no expression existed to violate.

The Supreme Judicial Court of Massachusetts affirmed the trial court's decision on all points. The U.S.

Supreme Court granted *certiorari*, agreed to hear the case, to "determine whether the requirement to admit a parade contingent [group] expressing a message not of the private organizer's own choosing violates the First Amendment."

Parades Are Expression Too

The Supreme Court unanimously held that First Amendment protection did apply to the council and that, being private organizers, they could exclude a group whose message was one which they did not wish to express. Justice Souter, delivering the opinion of the unanimous Court, wrote, "If there were no reason for a group of people to march from here to there except to reach a destination, they could make the trip without expressing any message beyond the fact of the march itself. Some might call such a procession a parade, but it would not be much of one." Real parades make "some sort of collective point, not just to each other but to bystanders along the way." If there is no media coverage, the parade might as well not happen. Souter continued, "Parades are thus a form of expression, not just motion" and integral to the marching is expression to make a point. In both *Gregory v. City of Chicago* (1969) and *Edwards v. South Carolina* (1963), the Court ruled that processions to express social points were protected by the First Amendment and "reflect an exercise of these basic constitutional rights in their most pristine and classic form." Protected expression in a parade was not limited to banners and songs, but extended to such symbolism as wearing arm bands or saluting a flag. Likewise, a parade need not have only one theme, but can have all sorts of messages, and a private organizer does not forfeit constitutional protection due to the inclusion of various messages.

Regarding the Massachusetts public accommodations law, the Supreme Court ruled that though the law was in keeping with the First Amendment the state court's application of the law violated the First Amendment. Souter wrote, "Although the state courts spoke of the parade as a place of public accommodation, it becomes apparent that the state court's application of the statute [law] had the effect of declaring the sponsor's [council's] speech or message itself to be the public accommodation." The Court disagreed.

The Court found the parade was expressive and the effect of the lower courts' rulings were to make the private organizer alter the message of its parade. In essence, the ruling forced the council to speak on a subject against their wishes. Also, if public accommodation is the message, as inappropriately considered by the lower court, any message produced by the council could then be changed and shaped by all those who wished to join and convey their own theme. Souter wrote that "this use of the State's power violates the fundamental rule of protection under the First Amendment, that a speaker has the autonomy [freedom] to choose the content of his own message." Furthermore, the speaker, in this case parade organizer, also had the right to decide "what not to say." The council could not only determine how to express values, opinions or endorsements, but also decide what to leave out altogether.

The council, by selecting specific units for the parade, expressed a sufficiently particular message in the eyes of the Court. The Court found the message the council disfavored was the suggestion that gay, lesbian, or bisexual people had as much claim to unqualified social acceptance as heterosexuals. The Court ruled that requiring this violated the council's First Amendment rights.

Impact

The *Hurley* decision held that privately organized parades were a form of symbolic private expression. The Supreme Court has found that symbolic speech was sufficient in some cases to deserve First Amendment protection. In 1941 the Court also determined that parades comprise such a form of protected symbolic speech, but they can also be subject to greater regulation than pure speech. For example, though laws must be nondiscriminatory in regulating parades, local governments can control when and where parades are held due to conflicts with other citizens' use of public places, such as city streets. In the 1974 *Spence v. Washington* case, the Court established a test to determine when actions constitute protected symbolic speech. Factors included whether a specific "particularized" message was intended, and whether an audience would be able to understand the message.

The Court in *Hurley* was accused of blurring distinctions regarding symbolic speech in two ways. In *Hurley*, the Court broadened the "particularized message" requirement by stating that "a narrow, succinctly articulable message is not a condition of constitutional speech." Though the St. Patrick's Day organizers had nothing in particular to express by its actions, still it was worthy of protected expression in the Court's eyes. Secondly, the blurring of private and public occurred in *Hurley*. Clearly, the Freedom of Speech Clause only applies to government actions. However, to many the St. Patrick's Day parade, held annually since the eighteenth century, was more a "civic" event than a private activity. In addition, local government action involved authorizing the private organizer, issuing a permit, and making available city streets. Yet the Court determined those factors irrelevant. The Court instead opposed the idea that government restrictions could be placed on essentially noncommercial speech and the "flow of ideas." The Court thus expanded what was considered protected speech and further confused the place of constitutional protections in what were considered by many civic parades. The *Hurley* decision again demonstrated the difficulty in both defining protected speech and establishing when a party has the right not to speak.

In the years following the Supreme Court ruling, Irish gay and lesbian groups in various cities continued to fight for inclusion in St. Patrick's Day parades. By the late 1990s gay and lesbian protests even began to be considered a traditional part of the events.

Related Cases

Edwards v. South Carolina, 372 U.S. 229 (1963).
Gregory v. City of Chicago, 394 U.S. 111 (1969).
Spence v. Washington, 418 U.S. 405 (1974).
Turner Broadcasting System, Inc. v. FCC., 520 U.S. 180 (1997).

Bibliography and Further Reading

Berkman, Harvey, Marcia Coyle and Claudia MacLachlan. "Toward Term's End, Court Rules on Aguilar, Taxes." *The National Law Journal,* July 3, 1995, p. A16.

Biskupic, Joan, and Elder Witt. *Guide to the U.S. Supreme Court.* Washington, DC: Congressional Quarterly, 1997.

Farrell, James C. "Should Irish Eyes Be Smiling: The Hidden Issue of State Action in Hurley v. Irish-American Gay, Lesbian and Bisexual Group of Boston." *St. John's Law Review,* Vol. 70, spring 1996, pp. 313.

Kozlowski, James C. "Gay Pride Message not Accommodated in City Parade Organized by Private Association." *Parks & Recreation,* September 1995, pp. 28.

Wackerman, Daniel T. "Mind's Eye." *America,* July 15, 1995, p. 5.

Waldman, Joshua. "Symbolic Speech and Social Meaning." *Columbia Law Review,* Vol. 97, October 1997, pp. 1844.

FLORIDA BAR V. WENT FOR IT, INC.

Legal Citation: 515 U.S. 618 (1995)

Petitioner
Florida State Bar

Respondent
Went For It, Inc., a lawyer referral service

Petitioner's Claim
A regulation of the Florida bar prohibiting direct-mail advertising targeting victims of accidents is an unconstitutional suppression of speech.

Chief Lawyer for Petitioner
Bruce S. Rogow

Chief Lawyer for Respondent
Barry Scott Richard

Justices for the Court
Stephen Breyer, Sandra Day O'Connor (writing for the Court), William H. Rehnquist, Antonin Scalia, Clarence Thomas

Justices Dissenting
Ruth Bader Ginsburg, Anthony M. Kennedy, David H. Souter, John Paul Stevens

Place
Washington, D.C.

Date of Decision
21 June 1995

Decision
Within certain limits, states may regulate advertising by lawyers.

Significance
Decision could signal a reversal of the trend during the 1980s and 1990s toward extension of First Amendment protection to commercial speech.

The Facts of the Case

In 1990 the Florida bar adopted a rule limiting the scope of direct-mail solicitation of business by attorneys. In cases of "personal injury," "wrongful death," "accident," or "disaster," lawyers were prohibited from sending targeted advertisements to victims or their relatives for a 30-day period following the occurrence of such events. The rule was created after the bar conducted a two-year study of the effect of lawyer advertising on public opinion, which concluded in 1989. According to the study, the public found such advertising highly offensive, and the rule was enacted in an attempt to improve the reputation of lawyers among the general public.

Went For It, Inc. was a lawyer referral service owned by G. Stewart McHenry. McHenry filed suit in U.S. District Court, claiming the 30-day prohibition on targeted direct-mail solicitation was an unconstitutional limit on speech. He claimed that he routinely sent such targeted solicitations in order to refer interested parties to lawyers who participated in his referral service and that he wanted to continue to do so.

Both Went for It and the Florida bar moved for summary judgment, and the district court referred the matter to a magistrate judge. The judge recommended the rule be upheld as constitutional, as a narrowly drawn rule that promoted a substantial government interest in protecting the privacy and tranquility of those who might receive and be offended by such advertisements. The district court, however, granted summary judgment to Went For It, in deference to the decision in *Bates v. State Bar of Arizona* (1977), which had struck down the prohibition of advertising the prices charged for certain legal services. The defendants appealed, and the higher court affirmed the judgment, again relying on *Bates* and *Shapero,* although it noted that it was "disturbed that *Bates* and its progeny require the decision." The Court granted *certiorari* in order to decide if the 30-day rule was a constitutionally permissible regulation of speech.

Commercial Speech and the First Amendment

The Court has traditionally construed the First Amendment as primarily protecting political speech, with "commercial" speech enjoying less protection. As late as 1942 the Court ruled in *Valentine v. Chrestensen,* a case involving prohibition of the distribution of handbills on a public street, that the First Amendment does not prohibit government regulation of "purely commercial advertising." This holding was followed until the Court struck down a ban on the advertising of prescription drug prices in *Virginia State Board of Pharmacy v. Virginia Citizens Consumer Council, Inc.* (1976). The following year the Court moved toward greater protection of commercial speech, striking down a ban on advertising the prices of certain legal services in *Bates v. Arizona.*

The scope of protection of commercial speech was clarified in *Central Hudson Gas and Electric Corp. v. Public Service Commission* (1980), in which the Court laid out a three-pronged test regarding the permissibility of government regulation of such speech: (1) the rule must be in support of a substantial government interest; (2) it must materially advance that interest; and (3) it must be no broader than necessary to accomplish its purpose. After *Central Hudson* the Court struck down bans on lawyer advertising in *Zauder v. Office of Disciplinary Counsel of Supreme Court of Ohio* (1985) and *Shapero v. Kentucky Bar Association* (1988). In *Shapero* a complete ban on direct-mail advertising by lawyers was found not to be an invasion of privacy and was struck down. The Court has also afforded protection to commercial speech in other cases not involving lawyers.

The Majority Decision

A bare 5-4 majority found that the rule was in fact permissible and reversed the ruling of the court of appeals, although both the majority and minority found the three-pronged test of *Central Hudson* applicable to the case at hand. The majority accepted the petitioner's claim of damage to the reputation of the bar by targeted direct-mail solicitations and found that the first requirement, a substantial state interest, was easily met by the petitioner, and several cases were quoted in which the Court found a substantial state interest in protecting the peace and privacy of citizens, indicating it did not find with the minority that the privacy implications of *Shapero* were valid as applied to this case.

In the opinion of the majority, the second prong of the test, that the rule must materially advance that interest, was met as well. The study results submitted by the petitioner well documented the adverse effects on public opinion of the solicitations, and the majority found them to be exhaustive and conclusive, rejecting the respondent's claim that the study had "no factual basis." It also rejected the minority's attack on the study's validity due to its lack of supporting documentation regarding methodology and other matters.

According to the majority, the petitioner's rule also met *Central Hudson*'s final requirement that the regulation be no broader than necessary to accomplish the desired goal. It rejected the respondent's claim that the rule was overbroad because it did not distinguish between major and minor traumas citizens might experience and that such a rule might prevent citizens from quickly learning what their legal options were in such situations. Justice O'Connor noted many other avenues by which citizens needing access to a lawyer could find one, including television and radio advertisements, billboards, non-targeted direct-mail advertisements, and yellow pages listings in telephone directories, and further noted that the prohibition was for a 30-day period only.

The Dissent

The minority opinion, written by Justice Kennedy, began by noting the inconsistency of barring lawyers from contacting a potential client in such a manner when lawyers representing other parties in cases or potential cases were not similarly barred from contacting that client. The minority also believed that the privacy interest rejected in *Shapero* also precluded regulation in this case, noting that "offensiveness" did not constitute grounds for the suppression of speech.

In the minority view, the petitioner's rule also failed all three parts of the *Central Hudson* test: The first part, a substantial state interest, was not present. The state's interest in protecting the privacy and tranquility of victims of trauma did not extend as far as prohibition of speech: "It is only where an audience is captive that we will assure its protection from some offensive speech." He quoted the finding in *Shapero* that "a letter, like a printed advertisement . . . can be put in a drawer . . . ignored, or discarded."

The petitioner's claim also did not meet the second requirement, that of materially advancing the interest at hand, according to the minority, who did not accept the study as proof, stating that it contained no "explanation of methodology":

> There is no description of the statistical universe or scientific framework that permits any productive use of the information the so-called Summary of Record contains . . . Our cases require something more than a few pages of self-serving and unsupported statements by the State to demonstrate that a regulation directly and materially advances the elimination of a real harm when the State seeks to suppress truthful and nondeceptive speech.

The petitioner's rule also failed the last requirement, that the regulation be no broader than necessary, in that it was a flat ban without regard to the severity of the trauma the victim experienced, while "criminal law routinely distinguishes degrees of bodily harm." Further, those most in need of services, those who "because of lack of education, linguistic ability, or familiarity with the legal system are unable to seek out legal services" are the ones most harmed by such a rule.

The dissent concluded by noting that the problem the Florida bar sought to address was largely "self-policing," since a person is unlikely to hire someone who offends them. And if such solicitations "reveal the social costs of the tort system as a whole," then energies should be put into reforming the system rather than suppressing that which exposes its weaknesses.

Impact

Florida Bar v. Went For It, Inc. was a reversal of the direction the Court had taken since the 1970s, that of extending further protection to commercial speech. The 5-4 decision of the Court left it unclear, however, how the Court will view future controversies regarding commercial speech, since only one justice viewing even a minor point differently in a different set of facts could conceivably result in a different outcome. In a *Villanova Law Review* article highly critical of the *Florida Bar* decision, Tara L. Lattomus claimed that "In the near future, attorneys can expect stricter regulation on advertising and their First Amendment rights relating to commercial speech."

Related Cases

Valentine v. Chrestensen, 316 U.S. 52 (1942).
Bigelow v. Virginia, 421 U.S. 809 (1975).
Virginia Board of Pharmacy v. Virginia Citizens Consumer Council, Inc., 425 U.S. 748 (1976).

Bates v. State Bar of Arizona, 433 U.S. 350 (1977).
In re Primus, 436 U.S. 412 (1978).
Central Hudson Gas and Electric Corp. v. Public Service Commission, 447 U.S. 557 (1980).
44 Liquormart, Inc. v. Rhode Island, 517 U.S. 484 (1996).

Bibliography and Further Reading

Elliot, Ralph Gregory. "Professional Image and Soliciting Counsel." *Connecticut Law Tribune,* 18 December, 1995.

Goolsby, Tonia S. "Florida Bar v. Went For It, Inc.: Does Ambulance-Chasing in Florida Justify Advertising Reform in Arkansas?" 49 *Arkansas Law Review* 795, 1997.

Lattomus, Tara L. "Offensiveness: The New Standard for First Amendment Legal Advertising Cases." 3 *Villanova Law Review* vol. 40 no. 4, 1995.

Moore, Susan Alice. "Florida Bar v. Went For It, Inc.: Refining the Constitutional Standard for Evaluating State Restrictions on Legal Advertising." 45 *Catholic University Law Review,* Summer 1996.

Richards, Jef I. "Is 44 Liquormart a turning point?" *Journal of Public Policy & Marketing,* Spring 1997.

Shoop, Julie Gannon. "Supreme Court upholds lawyer solicitation ban." *Trial,* August 1995.

CAPITOL SQUARE REVIEW AND ADVISORY BOARD V. PINETTE

Legal Citation: 515 U.S. 753 (1995)

Petitioner
Capitol Square Review and Advisory Board

Respondent
Vincent J. Pinette

Petitioner's Claim
Allowing the display of a large wooden cross in front of the state capitol violates the Establishment Clause because it could be interpreted as an endorsement of religion.

Chief Lawyer for Petitioner
Michael J. Renner

Chief Lawyer for Respondent
Benson A. Wolman

Justices for the Court
Stephen Breyer, Anthony M. Kennedy, Sandra Day O'Connor, William H. Rehnquist, Antonin Scalia (writing for the Court), David H. Souter, Clarence Thomas

Justices Dissenting
Ruth Bader Ginsburg, John Paul Stevens

Place
Washington, D.C.

Date of Decision
29 June 1995

Decision
Displaying a wooden cross in front of the Capital did not violate the Establishment Clause.

Significance
A religious symbol, even if displayed on or near a government building does not violate the Establishment Clause, which prohibits governments from sanctioning or endorsing a religion, if the facility is opened to any and all groups.

A Symbol of Hatred or Religious Display?

Capitol Square, is a ten-acre, state-owned plaza that surrounds the state capitol in Columbus, Ohio. The area was used frequently by various groups for displays such as nativity scenes. Use of the square was determined by a review board, which issued the permits. On November of 1993, after reversing a decision to ban holiday displays during December from Capitol Square, the board agreed to allow the state to put up its Christmas tree. Later, the board approved a rabbi's application to display a menorah. That same day, the board received a request from Donnie Carr, an officer of Ohio's Ku Klux Klan, to erect a cross on the square during the holidays. The board denied the request citing the Ohio and U.S. Constitutions ban on governments endorsing religion.

Two weeks later, the Ohio Klan's leader Vincent Pinette, filed suit in the U.S. District Court for the Southern District of Ohio, seeking to force the board to issue the permit. The board argued that it had denied the permit because of the Establishment Clause. The district court ruled that since the square was opened to all and that the Klan's cross was protected private expression, the board had to issue the permit. The district court issued the injunction and the board's request for emergency stay was denied. The board allowed the Klan to display its cross. It received and granted several permits to display crosses on Capitol Square during December of 1993 and January of 1994. The board appealed to the U.S. Court of Appeals for the Sixth Circuit, which affirmed the district court ruling. That decision agreed with a ruling by the Eleventh District Circuit, but conflicted with rulings in the Second and Fourth Circuits. The U.S. Supreme Court granted *certiorari*.

In writing for the majority Justice Scalia stated that the board relied on *County of Allegheny v. ACLU* (1989) and *Lynch v. Donnelly* (1984), but that both those cases were different from *Capitol Square Review*. In *Allegheny*, the Court ruled that the display of a privately-sponsored creche on the grand staircase of the Allegheny County Courthouse violated the Establishment Clause. That staircase, Scalia reasoned, was not open to all on an equal basis, so the county was in that case favoring sectarian religious expression. In *Lynch*, the Court ruled that the city's display of a creche did not violate the Establishment Clause because it did not endorse an established religion. Petitioners argued that because the cross was displayed so close to a symbol of government, that it could be mistaken as religious expression endorsed by the government, which they argued was a clear violation of the Establishment Clause. However, Scalia dismissed that argument. He wrote: "That proposition cannot be accepted, at least where, as here, the government has not fostered or encouraged the mistake." He further reasoned that it would have "radical implications for our public policy to suggest that neutral laws are invalid whenever hypothetical observers may—even reasonably—confuse an incidental benefit to religion with state endorsement." Scalia concluded that "Religious expression cannot violate the Establishment Clause where it is (1) purely private and (2) occurs in a traditional or designated public forum, publicly announced and open to all on equal terms."

Justice O'Connor in a separate opinion, joined by Justices Breyer and Souter, agreed with the majority conclusion, but offered a different analysis. Justice O'Connor reasoned that it is not unreasonable for a governmental body to protect itself against the mistaken assumption that privately expressed speech or symbols were endorsed by the government. O'Connor along with the other concurring justices concluded that the city of Columbus could have excluded the cross from the public square if they feared the message would have been attributed to the city. However, the justices did not view such a mistake possible in this case. Justice O'Connor explained that cross was on a public square and not on government property.

> In this case, I believe, the reasonable observer would view the Klan's cross display fully aware that Capitol Square is a public space in which a multiplicity of groups, both secular and religious, engage in expressive conduct . . . Moreover, this observer would certainly be able to read and understand an adequate disclaimer, which the Klan had informed the state it would include in the display at the time if applied for the permit. On the facts of this case, therefore, I conclude that the reasonable observer would not interpret the State's tolerance of the Klan's private religious display in Capitol Square as an endorsement of religion.

Justices Stevens and Ginsburg each filed separate dissenting opinions. Justice Stevens concluded that a vio-

lation of the Establishment Clause occurred when "some reasonable observers would attribute a religious message to the state." Justice Ginsburg reasoned that a disclaimer would not have removed the question of a government endorsing a religion. Ginsburg wrote: "Whether a court order allowing display of a cross, but demanding a sturdier disclaimer, could withstand Establishment Clause analysis is a question more difficult than the one this case poses."

Impact

This case considered the difficult question of freedom of speech versus freedom of religion. Under the U.S. Constitution both are of equal of importance. Yet, the problem for government officials in Columbus, Ohio and others faced with this dilemma is to refrain from restraining freedom of speech without seeming to endorse a particular religion. *Capitol Square Review* went a long way in establishing a test or standard for maintaining this important balance. As long as the area is opened to any and all, it cannot be constructed as endorsing an establish religion. However, maintaining that balance remains a delicate balancing act.

Related Cases

McGowan v. Maryland, 366 U.S. 420 (1961).
Lemon v. Kurtzman, 403 U.S. 602 (1970).
Widmar v. Vincent, 454 U.S. 263 (1981).
Marsh v. Chambers, 463 U.S. 783 (1983).
Lynch v. Donnelly, 465 U.S. 668 (1984).
County of Allegheny v. ACLU, 492 U.S. 573 (1989).
Lamb's Chapel v. Center Moriches Union Free School Dist., 508 U.S. 384 (1993).

Bibliography and Further Reading

Biskupic, Joan, and Elder Witt. *Guide to the U.S. Supreme Court,* 3rd ed. Washington, DC: Congressional Quarterly Inc., 1997.

Gunther, Gerald, and Kathleen Sullivan. *Constitutional Law,* 13th ed. New York: The Foundation Press Inc., 1997

Hall, Kermit L., ed. *The Oxford Companion to the Supreme Court of the United States.* New York: Oxford University Press, 1992.

Kozlowski, James. C. "KKK Cross on Capitol Square not Endorsement of Religion." *Parks & Recreation,* November 1995, pp. 20.

"The Sign of the Cross." *America,* July 15, 1995, p. 3.

44 LIQUORMART, INC. V. RHODE ISLAND

Legal Citation: 517 U.S. 484 (1996)

Petitioner
44 Liquormart, Inc., et al.

Respondent
State of Rhode Island, et al.

Petitioner's Claim
That a Rhode Island law prohibiting liquor retailers from advertising truthful information about liquor prices violated the liquor retailers' freedom of speech under the First Amendment.

Chief Lawyer for Petitioner
Evan T. Lawson

Chief Lawyer for Respondent
Rebecca T. Partington

Justices for the Court
Stephen Breyer, Ruth Bader Ginsburg, Anthony M. Kennedy, Sandra Day O'Connor, William H. Rehnquist, Antonin Scalia, David H. Souter, John Paul Stevens (writing for the Court), Clarence Thomas

Justices Dissenting
None

Place
Washington, D.C.

Date of Decision
13 May 1996

Decision
That Rhode Island's complete ban on advertising of liquor prices unconstitutionally restricted free speech in violation of the First Amendment.

Significance
Although disagreeing as to the exact method of applying the First Amendment's protection of free speech to statutes prohibiting truthful commercial speech, all the justices applied tests that make it extremely difficult, if not impossible, for such bans to withstand constitutional scrutiny. Thus, after the Court's decision, it is unlikely that complete bans on truthful advertising will ever be valid under the First Amendment.

The First Amendment to the U.S. Constitution provides, in part, that the government "shall make no law . . . abridging the freedom of speech[.]" Since the adoption of the First Amendment in 1792, it has been clear that the amendment protects speech by citizens on political issues and other matters of public concern. However, the Supreme Court has struggled to define the extent to which the amendment protects other areas of speech. One such area in which the Court has been inconsistent in defining the extent of the First Amendment's protection of speech involves so-called "commercial" speech, most notably advertising. In *44 Liquormart, Inc. v. Rhode Island*, the Court once again struggled on this subject.

In 1956, the state of Rhode Island passed a law prohibiting any liquor manufacturers, wholesalers, or retailers from advertising the price of alcoholic beverages. The theory behind the law was that it would discourage drinking because the advertising ban would force consumers to spend more time trying to locate the best deals for alcohol. In 1991, 44 Liquormart, an alcoholic beverage retailer, ran an advertisement in a Rhode Island newspaper. Although the ad did not explicitly state the price of any alcoholic beverages, it did show pictures of alcoholic beverages and low prices of other goods such as peanuts, potato chips, and soda pop. The Rhode Island Liquor Control Administrator concluded that the advertisement implied that 44 Liquormart was selling alcohol for bargain prices, and thus violated the state's ban an advertising of liquor prices. Accordingly, the administrator assessed a $400.00 fine against 44 Liquormart.

After paying the fine, 44 Liquormart, along with Peoples Super Liquor Stores, filed a lawsuit in the U.S. District Court for the District of Rhode Island. 44 Liquormart sought a declaration that the price advertising ban was an impermissible restriction on its right to free speech, and thus violated the First Amendment. The district court found that the statute was unconstitutional because it did not "directly advance" the state's interest in reducing alcohol consumption and restricted more speech than was necessary to promote the state's interest. Rhode Island appealed the decision to the U.S. Court of Appeals for the First Circuit, which reversed

Commercial Speech

Commercial speech is advertising or speech proposing a financial transaction and, with limitations, is protected by the First Amendment. Commercial speech serves significant interests of both the producers of goods and services and the consumers. Supreme Court Justice Harry A. Blackmun wrote, "The free flow of commercial information is indispensable to the proper allocation of resources in a free enterprise system."

Consumers rely on commercial speech for information about the quality and price of goods in order to make economic decisions. Examples of commercial speech are advertisements of products in a newspaper or magazine, television commercials, advertisements in the yellow pages, promotional advertisements by a public utility, and advertising by professionals such as lawyers.

The government can legally regulate commercial speech to prevent publication of false or misleading advertising. Therefore, commercial speech enjoys less freedom than noncommercial expression, such as political speech. The U.S. Supreme Court has suggested that citizens and their pocketbooks may be more vulnerable to false advertising than to false or overblown rhetoric by a politician. Therefore, the First Amendment protects commercial speech only as long as it is truthful and does not advertise illegal or harmful activity.

Source(s): Smolla, Rodney A. *Free Speech in an Open Society.* New York: Knopf, 1992.

---

the district court's decision. The court of appeals concluded that the price advertising ban was permissible because it advanced the state's interest in promoting temperance. The court of appeals reasoned that competitive price advertising would lower the prices for alcoholic beverages, and the lower prices in turn would result in increased consumption. Accordingly, the court of appeals concluded that the price advertising ban was permissible under the First Amendment.

44 Liquormart and Peoples Super Liquor Stores sought to appeal the decision to the U.S. Supreme Court by filing a petition for a writ of *certiorari*, which the Court granted. On appeal, the Court was unanimous in reversing the court of appeals and concluding that Rhode Island's ban on alcohol price advertising violated the First Amendment's guarantee of freedom of speech. However, the justices were unable to agree on the approach to follow in analyzing claims involving restrictions on truthful, non-misleading commercial speech, issuing four separate opinions.

Initially, all the justices agreed that the Twenty-first Amendment provided no support for the Rhode Island price advertising ban. In 1919, the Eighteenth Amendment was ratified, prohibiting the manufacture or sale of intoxicating liquors in the United States. The Era of Prohibition ushered in by the Eighteenth Amendment lasted until 1933, when the Twenty-first Amendment was ratified. The Twenty-first Amendment expressly repealed the Eighteenth Amendment. However, the amendment also provided that the states remained free to prohibit the sale and use of alcoholic beverages. Rhode Island argued that this portion of the Twenty-first Amendment altered the analysis for resolving claims involving commercial speech regulations related

to alcohol by giving such regulations a presumption of validity. All of the justices agreed with Justice Stevens's conclusion that "the Twenty-first Amendment does not qualify the constitutional prohibition against laws abridging the freedom of speech embodied in the First Amendment." However, beyond that, the justices disagreed over the appropriate test for analyzing challenges to laws prohibiting truthful commercial speech.

Justice O'Connor's Four Part Test

Justice O'Connor, writing an opinion which was joined by Chief Justice Rehnquist and Justices Souter and Breyer, thought that the Court should continue to apply the four part test established by the Court in the 1980 case of *Central Hudson Gas and Electric Corp. v. Public Service Commission of New York*. In *Central Hudson*, the Court found that a New York law prohibiting all promotional advertising by electric utilities violated the First Amendment. In doing so, the Court established a four part test for analyzing commercial speech claims under the First Amendment. Under this test, the Court first asks whether the speech is truthful and concerns lawful activity. If not, then the First Amendment provides no protection. If the speech is truthful and concerns lawful activity, then the Court asks whether the interest which the government seeks to advance is substantial. If it is not, then the regulation on speech is invalid. If the government interest is substantial, then the regulation will be upheld if it meets the third and fourth part of the test: the regulation must directly advance the government's interest, and may not restrict more speech than is necessary to advance that interest.

Justice O'Connor concluded that because *Central Hudson* involved a statute prohibiting truthful commercial advertising similar to the one involved in this case, there was no reason to depart from the *Central Hudson* four part test in analyzing the constitutionality of the Rhode Island price advertising ban. Applying the *Central Hudson* test, Justice O'Connor concluded that the Rhode Island price advertising ban was unconstitutional because it did not meet the fourth prong of the test. She reasoned that, assuming that the price advertising ban directly advanced Rhode Island's interest in reducing alcohol consumption, it nevertheless restricted more speech than was necessary to advance that interest. She reasoned that Rhode Island had other, more effective methods for reducing alcohol consumption, such as establishing minimum prices for alcohol, increasing sales taxes on alcoholic beverages, limiting purchase of alcohol, or conducting an educational campaign about the dangers of drinking. Thus, Justice O'Connor concluded that Rhode Island's price advertising ban failed to meet the *Central Hudson* standard and was an infringement on the First Amendment right to free speech.

Justice Stevens's Modified *Central Hudson* Test

In contrast to Justice O'Connor, Justice Stevens, who was joined in his opinion by Justices Kennedy and Ginsburg, proposed that the *Central Hudson* test be modified. While not abandoning that test entirely, Justice Stevens read the test more strictly than did Justice O'Connor. He reasoned that, in general, the Court has been more willing to uphold restrictions on commercial speech than on other forms of speech because the government has an interest in protecting consumers from commercial harms. However, he noted that such commercial harms are only present when the commercial speech is misleading, involves an illegal activity, or exerts "undue influence" over consumers. Because such concerns are not present when a company seeks to advertise using truthful information, under the *Central Hudson* test, laws which place a complete ban on truthful advertising should be examined by the Court with "special care" to ensure that they do not impermissibly restrict free speech. He noted that "speech prohibitions of this type will rarely survive constitutional review."

Applying his stricter version of the *Central Hudson* test, Justice Stevens concluded that the Rhode Island price advertising ban failed to meet both the third and fourth parts of the test. With respect to the third part, Justice Stevens found that there was no evidence that the advertising ban reduced consumption of alcoholic beverages. With respect to the fourth part of the test, Justice Stevens concluded, as did Justice O'Connor, that Rhode Island had a number of non-speech related means of reducing alcohol consumption, such as increased taxes, a limit on purchases of alcohol, or

an educational campaign. Thus, Justice Stevens likewise concluded that the Rhode Island law was unconstitutional.

Justice Thomas's *Per Se Approach*

Unlike the other justices, Justice Thomas thought that the *Central Hudson* test had no application to a complete ban on truthful advertising such as Rhode Island's ban on alcohol price advertising. In his view:

> In cases such as this, in which the government's asserted interest is to keep legal users of a product or service ignorant in order to manipulate their choices in the marketplace, the balancing test . . . should not be applied, in my view. Rather, such an 'interest' is *per se* illegitimate and can no more justify regulation of 'commercial' speech than it can justify regulation of 'noncommercial' speech.

He reasoned that, in a number of cases, the Court has recognized that consumers have a strong interest in the free flow of truthful commercial information and that the First Amendment does not permit the government to protect consumers from truthful information which may lead consumers to make choices which the government thinks are "bad." Justice Thomas reasoned that there is no reason to distinguish between truthful commercial speech and other forms of speech. He also noted that the *Central Hudson* test has proved difficult to apply in the courts and has lead to inconsistent results. Thus, Justice Thomas favored a categorical rule under which "all attempts to dissuade legal choices by citizens by keeping them ignorant are impermissible." Under this approach, Rhode Island's complete ban on advertising of liquor prices clearly violated the First Amendment.

Justice Scalia's Historical Approach

In a separate opinion, Justice Scalia "share[d] Justice Thomas's discomfort with the *Central Hudson* test," as well as Justice Stevens's "aversion towards paternalistic governmental policies that prevent men and women from hearing facts that might not be good for them." However, Justice Scalia thought that the First Amendment, outside of cases involving suppression of political ideas which the First Amendment was clearly designed to prohibit, should be interpreted according the historical practices of the American people. Nevertheless, Justice Scalia concluded that the Court did not have before it in this case sufficient information to determine what these practices were. Thus, he concluded that he "must resolve this case in accord with" the Court's existing law in this area, which he agreed with Justices Stevens and O'Connor compelled the conclusion that the Rhode Island statute was unconstitutional.

Impact

The Court's decision in *44 Liquormart* drastically altered the analysis for determining whether total bans on truthful advertising are permissible under the First Amendment. Seven of the justices applied the *Central Hudson* test, as Justice Thomas recognized both Justice Stevens's and Justice O'Connor's application of the fourth prong was much stricter than in previous cases. As Justice Thomas stated, their interpretations, "as a practical matter, go a long way toward the position" of Justice Thomas that complete bans of truthful advertising are always unconstitutional. Thus, after *44 Liquormart,* it is unlikely that the Court will uphold any blanket restrictions on truthful commercial speech.

Related Cases

Virginia Board of Pharmacy v. Virginia Citizens Consumer Council, Inc., 425 U.S. 748 (1976).
Linmark Associates, Inc. v. Willingboro, 431 U.S. 85 (1977).
Central Hudson Gas and Electric Corp. v. Public Service Commission of New York, 447 U.S. 557 (1980).
Posadas de Puerto Rico Associates v. Tourism Co. of Puerto Rico, 478 U.S. 328 (1986).
Rubin v. Coors Brewing Co., 514 U.S. 476 (1995).
Glickman v. Wileman Brothers and Elliott, 521 U.S. 457 (1997).

Bibliography and Further Reading

Haiman, Franklyn S. *Speech and Law in a Free Society.* Chicago: University of Chicago Press, 1981.

Richards, Jef I. "Is 44 Liquormart a Turning Point?" *Journal of Public Policy & Marketing,* Spring 1997, p. 156.

Rome, Edwin P., and William H. Roberts. *Commercial Free Speech: First Amendment Protection of Expression in Business.* Westport, CT: Quorum Books, 1985.

Wright, George R. *Selling Words: Free Speech in a Commercial Culture.* New York: New York University Press, 1997.

BOARD OF COUNTY COMMISSIONERS, WABAUNSEE COUNTY, KANSAS V. UMBEHR

Legal Citation: 518 U.S. 668 (1996)

Petitioner
Board of County Commissioners, Wabaunsee County, Kansas

Respondent
Keen A. Umbehr

Petitioner's Claim
Termination of his contract to perform services for the county after he criticized the conduct of county government officials violated his First Amendment free speech right.

Chief Lawyer for Petitioner
Donald Patterson

Chief Lawyer for Respondent
Robert A. Van Kirk

Justices for the Court
Stephen Breyer, Ruth Bader Ginsburg, Anthony M. Kennedy, Sandra Day O'Connor (writing for the Court), William H. Rehnquist, David H. Souter, John Paul Stevens

Justices Dissenting
Antonin Scalia, Clarence Thomas

Place
Washington, D.C.

Date of Decision
28 June 1996

Decision
The Court agreed that the petitioner's rights had been violated.

Significance
First Amendment protection against retaliation for political speech extended to independent contractors providing services to governments.

In 1981 Keen A. Umbehr entered into an agreement as an independent contractor with Wabaunsee County, Kansas, under which he would be the exclusive hauler of trash for all cities within the county, subject to acceptance of the agreement by each city. The terms of his contract stated that the arrangement would renew automatically each year, subject to termination by either party on 60 days' notice before the end of the year or renegotiation on 90 days' notice. One such renegotiation took place in 1985, and from 1985 to 1991 Keen A. Umbehr was the exclusive hauler of trash for six of the seven cities of Wabaunsee County, Kansas.

During that time Umbehr was actively critical of the conduct of the board of commissioners of the county. He wrote letters to and editorials in local newspapers and spoke out at meetings of the board of commissioners on various matters, including the violation of the Kansas Open Meetings Act by the board, which resulted in a consent order the board members signed. He even ran for election to the board but was defeated.

The board of commissioners terminated his trash-hauling contract with the county in 1991 by a 2-1 vote after an attempt to do so in 1990 was technically defective and thus unsuccessful. Umbehr filed suit against the members of the board both officially and individually, alleging that by losing his contract in retaliation for his criticism of the board he was in effect punished for exercising his First Amendment right to free speech.

His claim of suffering damages due to the retaliation of board members for his criticism was not challenged by the court. Nonetheless, the court granted summary judgment to the board, also holding that the members held qualified immunity as individuals. The court stated that because of his status as in independent contractor Umbehr did not enjoy the same level of protection afforded to government employees and therefore the First Amendment did not prevent the termination of his contract at the end of its annual term. Umbehr appealed to the U.S. Court of Appeals for the Tenth District.

The court of appeals held that Umbehr's status as an independent contractor rather than an employee did not render him less deserving of First Amendment protection: "an independent contractor is protected under the First Amendment from retaliatory government action, just as an employee would be." The court further stated that past analyses claiming that an independent contractor had "less at stake" and was less dependent on the government for employment than an employee were not backed up by empirical evidence. Thus the court declared that the "balancing test" devised in *Pickering v. Board of Education,* (1968) in which the firing of a teacher for his criticism of the local school board (his employer) was held to be a First Amendment violation, was applicable in this case. In *Pickering* the Court held that government

> has interests as an employer in regulating the speech of its employees . . . The problem in any case is to arrive at a balance between the interests of the teacher, as a citizen, in commenting upon matters of public concern and the interest of the State, as an employer . . . [Because] free and open debate is vital to informed decision-making by the electorate . . . [one's] exercise of his right to speak on issues of public importance may not furnish the basis for his dismissal from public employment.

The court of appeals reversed the holding of the lower court, remanding the case for further proceedings in which it would be determined whether the termination of the contract was in fact retaliatory. The board appealed to the U.S. Supreme Court, which granted *certiorari*.

The Court's Decision

The Court granted *certiorari* in order to resolve the conflict between the trial court and the appeals court "regarding whether and to what extent independent contractors are protected by the First Amendment," noting that in a number of cases federal courts had delivered conflicting opinions on this issue. The majority agreed with the opinion of the appeals court, however, both in holding that independent contractors are protected under the First Amendment and that the Pickering test was applicable in Umbehr's case. The case was again remanded for further proceedings in which Umbehr would have to prove that "the termination of his contract was motivated by his speech on a matter of public concern." Even if he did prove such motivation on the part of the board members, however, proof by the board members that they "would have terminated the contract regardless of his speech" would be a sufficient defense against his claim.

In analyzing the claims of the parties, the Court noted that both petitioner and respondent claimed that there was a distinction between independent contractors and employees. Both agreed that independent contractors work at a "greater remove from government

officials than do government employees," performing their work without direct day-to-day supervision, but they drew opposite conclusions from this fact. Umbehr argued that because he worked on his own, his speech could have no effect on the efficient operation of the government workplace. He further claimed that since he was an independent contractor, his speech would not be confused with that of a government official by the public. The board, on the other hand, claimed that such lack of direct supervision created the need for a government to contract with someone it trusted.

The majority, while stating that both claims were in fact reasonable and entitled to due consideration, nonetheless held that a "brightline rule" distinguishing independent contractors from employees "would leave First Amendment rights unduly dependent" on whether state law labels a government service provider's contract as a contract of employment or a contract for services. The majority also noted that "such formal distinctions . . . can be manipulated largely at the will of the government agencies concerned . . ." An approach more considerate of the vital First Amendment issue at stake was the application of the Pickering test to such situations, an approach which gave due deference to the interests of both parties. And by such application, Umbehr had the right to speak on matters of public concern without fear of retaliation, just as would a government employee. Thus the lower court reached the correct decision.

Justices Scalia and Thomas Dissent

Justice Scalia, joined by Thomas, delivered a dissent that by its very first sentence clearly revealed his frustration with the majority decision: ". . . this Court's Constitution-making process can be called 'reasoned adjudication' only in the most formalistic sense." Later in his opinion he was even more critical: "The Court must be living in another world. Day by day, case by case, it is busy designing a Constitution for a country I do not recognize."

To Scalia, there was no basis in affording Umbehr the protection the majority granted him; however undesirable, political patronage was "an American political tradition as old as the Republic," and "such traditions are the stuff out of which the Court's principles are to be formed." The public, through its representatives in government, has regulated the granting of government contracts in many and various ways, and should it see fit, it could further regulate. The Constitution, however, does not expressly proscribe such activity as occurred in the case at hand, and therefore it cannot be used to prevent it. Scalia also rejected the majority's refusal to distinguish between independent contractors and government employees, holding that independent contractors *were* less vulnerable than government employees, and lack of clear distinctions between the two would likely lead to excessive litigation.

Impact

The Court's decision in *Umbehr* extended the First Amendment protection enjoyed by government employees to independent contractors providing services to state and local governments. In addition to increased use of independent contractors by government, today's changed economic climate has caused many people to lose their jobs due to "downsizing" and become self-employed, at least in the strictly legal sense, by necessity rather than choice In a *Kansas Law Review* article, Brian Jacobs proposed extension of this protection to these contingent workers as well, who often perform the same jobs in the same environment as they did when employees. It is likely that *Umbehr* will be cited in cases involving dismissals of self-employed independent contractors of this type.

Related Cases

Pickering v. Board of Education, 391 U.S. 563 (1968).
Rutan v. Republican Party, 497 U.S. 62 (1990).
Waters v. Churchill, 511 U.S. 661 (1994).
O'Hare Truck Service, Inc. v. City of Northlake, 518 U.S. 712 (1996).

Bibliography and Further Reading

Berger, Mark. "Unjust Dismissal and the Contingent Worker: Restructuring Doctrine for the Restructured Worker." *Yale Policy and Law Review,* Vol. 16, January, 1997.

Cooper, Julie. "Board Of County Commissioners v. Umbehr: A Rejection of The Categorical Approach to First Amendment Analysis and an Affirmation Of the Core Values Underlying Free Speech Protection." *Widener Journal of Public Law,* Vol. 6, 1997.

Jacobs, Brian. "First Amendment Rights and Independent Contractors: The Law of Political Patronage in the Wake of *Umbehr* and *O'Hare Truck Service*." *Kansas Law Review,* Vol. 45., July 1997, p. 1299.

"Leading Cases." *Harvard Law Review,* Vol. 110, November 1996.

McCahan, Nancy S. "Justice Scalia's Constitutional Trinity: Originalism, Traditionalism, and The Rule of Law as Reflected in His Dissent in *O'Hare* and *Umbehr*." *St. Louis Law Journal,* Vol. 41, fall, 1997.

Post, Robert. "Justice for Scalia." *New York Review of Books,* Vol. XLV, no. 10, 11 June 1998.

Schwartz, Martin A. "Government Contractors and the First Amendment." *New York Law Journal,* 20 August 1996.

O'HARE TRUCK SERVICE, INC. V. CITY OF NORTHLAKE

Legal Citation: 518 U.S. 712 (1996)

Petitioner
O'Hare Truck Service, Inc.

Respondent
City of Northlake

Petitioner's Claim
That the removal of the truck service from the city's list of contractors was based on the owner's support for another political candidate, and therefore abridged his freedom of association.

Chief Lawyer for Petitioner
Harvey Grossman

Chief Lawyer for Respondent
Gary Feiersel

Justices for the Court
Stephen Breyer, Ruth Bader Ginsburg, Anthony M. Kennedy (writing for the Court), Sandra Day O'Connor, William H. Rehnquist, John Paul Stevens, David H. Souter

Justices Dissenting
Antonin Scalia, Clarence Thomas

Place
Washington, D.C.

Date of Decision
28 June 1996

Decision
The Court reversed the lower courts' rulings that free speech protections do not extend to government contractors, and remanded the case to the lower courts.

Significance
This case extended freedom of speech and association to government contractors as well as public employees.

O'Hare Truck Service, owned by John Gratzianna, had been on the city of Northlake's rotation list of towing services since 1965. Over almost 30 years, Gratzianna had donated money and services to various politicians to cultivate business. He had every indication that his company provided good service and that the city would continue to give him work. In 1993, the incumbent mayoral candidate, Reid Paxson, asked Gratzianna for a campaign contribution of "more than $1,000," according to a story by Joan Biskupic in the *Washington Post*. Not only did Gratzianna not contribute, he displayed posters for Paxson's opponent. Following Paxson's reelection, O'Hare Truck Service was removed from the city's rotation list. The ensuing court case was an important chapter in the history of U.S. patronage practices.

The Patronage System

Political patronage has been practiced throughout the history of the United States. George Washington, Thomas Jefferson, and John Adams all openly made patronage appointments; Washington's explicit policy was that high-level appointments would be based on patronage, low-level appointments on performance. Andrew Jackson entrenched the practice, giving personal attention to all patronage appointments. In 1883, the Pendleton Act, which created a Civil Service Commission and merit system, put a damper on patronage to some degree, but until the 1950s the courts basically held that no one had a right to public employment. In the latter half of the twentieth century, the courts turned their attention to the First Amendment rights of public employees.

Elrod, Branti, Rutan

Three Supreme Court cases defined these rights. In the first, *Elrod v. Burns* (1976), the Court held that public employees cannot be dismissed on the basis of their party affiliation. The Court found that patronage dismissals violate the First and Fourteenth Amendments. While employees' rights of political belief and affiliation are not absolute, the burden is on the government to show that it has a vital interest in making decisions based on patronage. The Court considered the argument that patronage ensured that an elected government's policies were not undercut by a rebellious staff, but thought this problem could be addressed by limiting patronage dismissals to policymaking or confidential positions.

The second case, *Branti v. Finkel* (1980), addressed the question of "policymaking positions." *Branti* was brought by two Republican assistant public defenders who were fired by a newly appointed Democratic public defender. This time, the Court held that the label "policymaking" was less important than the nature of the position. The question is whether "party affiliation is an appropriate requirement for the effective performance of the office." The Court argued that political allegiance was not a legitimate condition for employment as a public defender (and in fact, would undermine the effective performance of the office), and ruled for the assistant public defenders.

While *Elrod* and *Branti* dealt with dismissals, the third case, *Rutan v. Republican Party of Illinois* (1980), dealt with hirings and promotions. The case was brought by Illinois state employees after the newly elected governor turned all hiring and promotions decisions over to his office of personnel. The office based its decisions on employees' contributions to and support of the Republican Party. The Supreme Court found this practice unconstitutional.

After *Rutan,* it still was not clear whether these protections extended to independent contractors. The Fifth, Eighth, Ninth, and Tenth Circuit Courts extended the rule to include contractors, based on three arguments: a contractor's situation is analogous to an employee's; the government could easily contract out more jobs to evade existing patronage restrictions; and the suppression of speech was unconstitutional whatever the status of the individual. The Third and Seventh Circuit Courts, on the other hand, did not recognize protection for contractors, reasoning that contractors depend less on government business than did public employees. It was in this context that John Gratzianna brought suit.

The Case in the Lower Courts

Gratzianna sued in U.S. District Court for the Northern District of Illinois, for infringement of his First Amendment rights of political association. The district court dismissed the claim, because of the Seventh Circuit's position on protection for contractors. The Court of Appeals for the Seventh Circuit affirmed, saying that if *Elrod* were to be extended, it would have to be done by the Supreme Court. The Supreme Court then granted *certiorari,* citing the circuit split.

The Court's Judgment: Contractors Protected

The Court reversed the lower courts' ruling. Citing *Elrod* and *Branti,* Justice Kennedy wrote that "patron-

age does not justify the coercion of a person's political beliefs and associations." In such cases, in which affiliation is the sole basis of dismissal, there is no need to inquire whether the affiliation requirement was reasonable. However, he went on say that in cases that involve speech as well as affiliation, a balancing test from an earlier free speech case, *Pickering v. Board of Education,* would apply. (And he said that *O'Hare* might be such a case.) The *Pickering* test balances the employees' rights against the government's interests in the efficiency of its office. Kennedy then said that because the court of appeals had considered *O'Hare* to be an affiliation case, the Supreme Court would do likewise and try it as such.

The Court held that a contractor was protected to the same extent that public employees were. Kennedy responded to the city's arguments:

> Respondents insist the principles of Elrod and Branti have no force here, arguing that an independent contractor's First Amendment rights, unlike a public employees, must yield to the government's asserted countervailing interest in sustaining a patronage system. We cannot accept the proposition, however, that those who perform the government's work outside the formal employment relationship are subject to what we conclude is the direct and specific abridgement of First Amendment rights described in this complaint.

The Court rejected the Seventh Circuit's reasoning in distinguishing employees from contractors. An *amicus curiae* brief filed by the Towing and Recovery Association of America, Inc., indicated that government referrals account for 30 to 60 percent of contractors' business (for contractors that work with the government at all). The argument that contractors do not depend on government business, then, does not hold.

Kennedy briefly addressed the fear that this decision would spawn numerous suits. First, similar cases in the past had not resulted in excessive litigation. Second, government agencies were still allowed wide latitude in hiring and firing decisions. An agency might end a contract based on merit, or even on political affiliation, if that were relevant to the job. Thus, agencies would not be at the mercy of baseless lawsuits. What was unacceptable in this case was that the city offered no justification for its actions other than its interest in maintaining a patronage system. Having made the above judgments, the Court sent the case back to the lower courts, to decide whether the *Elrod-Branti* rule or the *Pickering* balancing test would apply.

Dissent: A Tradition of Patronage

Justice Scalia filed a dissent, joined by Justice Thomas. He began with a quotation from his dissent in *Rutan*:

When a practice not expressly prohibited by the text of the Bill of Rights bears the endorsement of a long tradition of open, widespread, and unchallenged use that dates back to the beginning of the Republic, we have no proper basis for striking it down.

The Supreme Court was not the proper forum for debating patronage, he claimed. The legislative branch had produced volumes of regulations for patronage practices; these "have brought to the field a degree of discrimination, discernment, and predictability that cannot be achieved by the blunt instrument of a constitutional prohibition."

Scalia further questioned the Court's failure to provide a clear precedent for deciding patronage cases. The distinction between pure affiliation cases and speech cases was confusing and pointless. He also argued that the court had hedged on whether the affiliation test was to be absolute when it allowed for some "case-by-case adjudication" in affiliation cases.

Impact

While this ruling may increase the risk of lawsuits against government employers, it also protects the freedoms of speech and association for independent contractors. These freedoms are particularly important in the late 1990s when government is contracting out more and more jobs.

Related Cases

Pickering v. Board of Education, 391 U.S. 563 (1968).
Elrod v. Burns, 427 U.S. 347 (1976).
Branti v. Finkel, 445 U.S. 507 (1980).
Connick v. Myers, 461 U.S. 138 (1983).
Rutan v. Republican Party of Illinois, 497 U.S. 62 (1990).

Bibliography and Further Reading

Biskupic, Joan. "It's Speech vs. Spoils In Patronage Dispute." *Washington Post,* March 19, 1996, p. A03.

Chemerinsky, Erwin. "Speech Rights of Government Contractors." *Trial,* Vol. 33, no. 1, January 1997, p. 64.

Eckersley, Brent C. "Constitutional Law: *Board of County Commissioners v. Umbehr* and *O'Hare Truck Service v. City of Northlake*—The Extension of First Amendment Protection to Independent Contractors—The Garbage Man Can Now Talk Trash!" *Oklahoma Law Review,* Vol. 50, no. 4, winter 1997, pp. 557–583.

Jackson, Brian. "First Amendment Rights and Independent Contractors: The Law of Political Patronage and Protected Speech in the Wake of *Umbehr* and *O'Hare Truck Service.*" *The University of Kansas Law Review,* Vol. 45, no. 4, July 1997, pp. 1299–326.

Koby, Michael H., and Paul Fischer. "The Supreme Court Cries 'Foul' to Patronage Contracting: Where Have You Gone Joe McDonough?" *New England Review,* Vol. 32, no. 1, fall 1997, pp. 1–45.

McCahan, Nancy S. "Justice Scalia's Constitutional Trinity: Originalism, Traditionalism and the Rule of Law as Reflected in His Dissent in *O'Hare* and *Umbehr.*" *St. Louis University Law Journal,* Vol. 41, no. 4, fall 1997, pp. 1435–76.

TURNER BROADCASTING SYSTEM V. FEDERAL COMMUNICATIONS COMMISSION

Legal Citation: 520 U.S. 180 (1997)

Appellant
Turner Broadcasting System, Inc., et al.

Appellee
Federal Communications Commission, et al.

Appellant's Claim
That the Federal Communications Commission was violating the First Amendment rights of cable operators by requiring them to broadcast local channels.

Chief Lawyer for Appellant
H. Bartow Farr III

Chief Lawyer for Appellee
Bruce Ennis

Justices for the Court
Stephen Breyer, Anthony M. Kennedy (writing for the Court), William H. Rehnquist, David H. Souter, John Paul Stevens

Justices Dissenting
Ruth Bader Ginsburg, Sandra Day O'Connor, Antonin Scalia, Clarence Thomas

Place
Washington, D.C.

Date of Decision
31 March 1997

Decision
Requiring cable systems to broadcast local stations was a "content neutral" decision and therefore did not violate the First Amendment rights of the systems.

Significance
The Court furthered the concept of content-neutrality in this case which has and will set the standard for future First Amendment cases involving newer forms of communication such as the Internet.

The History of Cable Television

In 1948, cable television was created as a way to access homes too remote for normal signals to reach. By setting antennas up on mountaintops and connecting homes to them, systems were able to provide television service for those who might not otherwise have it. In the late 1950s, these systems found that by offering their subscribers signals from other areas, rather than just local ones, they increased interest in their service. By 1962 850,000 subscribers were being served by about 800 systems.

Not surprisingly, local television stations viewed these services as competition. In response, the Federal Communications Commission (FCC) expanded its area of responsibility to include these systems and regulated their ability to access these distant signals. With the growth of satellite technology and increasing efforts by the cable industry, regulations throughout the 1970s lessened. The first pay network, Home Box Office (HBO) along with the emergence of a local television station that began using the new technology, WTBS, turned the home entertainment industry upside down. By the end of the 1970s nearly 15 million homes subscribed to cable television.

The 1984 Cable Act deregulated the cable industry, allowing business to begin to experiment with newer technologies and programming. According to the National Cable Television Association (NCTA), the industry spent an unprecedented $15 million "on program development," the "largest private construction project since World War II." In the following decade, cable networks began to market themselves to small focus group. For instance, networks would show programs that they thought would be interesting to women, or would only broadcast music-oriented shows or only sports. By 1998 seven in ten households who had televisions, subscribed to cable.

Regulation Begins

As systems began to carry more and more stations, they began to set up subscriber "tiers." The lowest and least expensive tier usually offers subscribers a compliment of local broadcast stations plus a selection of specialty networks chosen by the cable system. For a higher monthly fee, the subscriber gets a larger and more diverse selection of cable stations.

In 1992, overriding the veto of President George Bush, Congress passed the Cable Television Consumer Protection and Competition Act of 1992. The act allowed the FCC to regulate the cable industry and set minimum technical standards for broadcast, prohibited an area from allowing cable franchise monopolies, imposed restrictions of programmers who are affiliated with cable operations, and required operators to carry a minimum number of local broadcast stations. This so-called "must-carry" provision required, for example, that a cable system with more than 12 channels and more than 300 subscribers, set aside up to one-third of the channel space for any local broadcast station that requested it. Any station that did not make an official request did not have to be considered and if more than the required number asked for space, the cable system could choose those stations that it wanted to air. Any station that it did choose to carry, however, needed to be placed on the same numerical channel that they would be on if they were broadcasting. Similar rules were enacted regarding public television and educational broadcast channels.

This act was approved after three years of hearings during which Congress determined that the superior technical quality and financial strength of cable systems allowed the possibility that local stations were in danger of being economically ruined. Congress found that

> most subscribers to cable television systems do not or cannot maintain antennas to receive broadcast television services, do not have input selector switches to convert from a cable to antenna reception system, or cannot otherwise receive broadcast television services . . . The result is undue market power for the cable operator as compared to that of consumers and video programmers.

Also at issue was advertising revenue. The more subscribers a system has, the higher their advertising rates. If everyone has cable and they are not carrying local channels, then advertisers have no motivation to advertise on those local channels which will put them out of business.

Very quickly, many cable programmers and operators filed suit in the U.S. District Court of the District of Columbia against the United States and the FCC on the grounds that the must-carry rules were a violation of the systems' free speech as stated in the First Amendment. In a summary judgement the systems lost. The Court found that these regulations kept competition in the industry balanced and that local broadcasters were realistically in danger of being run out of business. The Court's dissenting opinion was on the grounds that in telling the systems that they had to carry local stations,

Ted Turner, 1995. © David P. Allen/Corbis.

the government was potentially forcing the systems to broadcast stations with content that they did not support and would otherwise not carry. There was also the argument made that this act might work to the detriment of the local stations.

> . . . because cable operators 'now carry the vast majority of local stations' and thus, to the extent that the rules have any effect at all, 'it will be only to replace the mix chosen by cable-casters—whose livelihoods depend largely on satisfying audience demand—with a mix derived from congressional dictate.

Cable operators felt the same way and lodged an appeal with the Federal Supreme Court. Justice Kennedy, writing for the majority who voted against the cable operators, agreed that cable systems were due some amount of First Amendment protection in light of their business of carrying speech. He admitted that

> . . . the must carry rules regulate cable speech in two respects: the rules reduce the number of channels over which cable operators exercise unfettered control, and they render it more difficult for cable programmers to compete for carriage on the limited channels remaining. He went on to explain, however,

that not every "interference" with free speech is contrary to the First Amendment.

The issue of content was at the heart of the Court's decision. The basic idea in the center of the First Amendment is that speech is free. One can choose to publish, broadcast or otherwise disseminate more or less whatever they choose as an individual. An entire government-regulated industry however can either print or not, broadcast or not. They can only discriminate due to content within very small parameters. "Laws that compel speakers to utter or distribute speech bearing a particular message are subject" to rigorous scrutiny whereas "regulations that are unrelated to the content of speech are subject to an intermediate level of scrutiny . . . because in most cases they pose a less substantial risk of excising certain ideas of viewpoints from the public dialogue."

The Court's first order of business then, became to determine whether the issues were based on content. As explained in the decision, laws can either be content-specific, such as those which ban individuals from handing out political statements too close to polling booths during elections although they would be free to hand out statements of other sorts, or content-neutral such as those prohibiting the posting of signs on public property regardless of what they say. Contrary to what cable operators thought, the court ruled that must-carry laws were content-neutral. "Nothing in the Act imposes a restriction, penalty, or burden by reason of the views, programs, or stations the cable operator has selected or will select. The number of channels a cable operator must set aside depends only on the operator's channel capacity." Likewise, the law says that every local channel has the opportunity to request to be carried, regardless of what the channel's message is or if it even has one.

The Court's findings went on to determine that "Congress' overriding objective in enacting must-carry was not to favor programming of a particular subject matter, viewpoint, or format, but rather to preserve access to free television programming for the 40 per-cent of Americans without cable." There was also the advertising revenue issue and in this too, the Court found that it would be too easy for cable operators to eliminate a major segment of their competition by simply not carrying local channels. The Court found that "the provisions are designed to guarantee the survival of a medium that has become a vital part of the Nation's communication system, and to ensure that every individual with a television set can obtain access to free television programming." It is important to note, that in his decision, Justice Kennedy noted that he did not feel that cable had been in the marketplace long enough to clearly judge the issue.

Back to District Court

Having found the legislation legal by a 5-4 vote, the Supreme Court sent the case back to the district court to see if they could determine whether the must-carry regulations "advanced an important governmental interest." The district court remained divided but ruled by a majority that Congress had enough information to come to the conclusion on 31 March 1997 that without the must-carry regulations that local broadcasters would be put in dire danger of losing their livelihoods.

Related Cases

United States v. O'Brien, 391 U.S. 367 (1968).
Red Lion Broadcasting, Co. v. FCC, 395 U.S. 367 (1969).
Miami Herald Publishing Company v. Tornillo, 418 U.S. 241 (1974).

Bibliography and Further Reading

Huber, Peter. "Must-carry and the Bill of Rights." *Forbes,* August 29, 1994, p. 94.

MacLachlan, Claudia. "Cable Operators Dismayed by 'Must Carry' Ruling." *The National Law Journal,* December 25, 1995, p. A14.

Trigoboff, Dan. "Cable Takes Another Shot at Supreme Court." *Broadcasting & Cable,* September 30, 1996, p. 18.

GLICKMAN V. WILEMAN BROTHERS & ELLIOTT, INC.

Legal Citation: 521 U.S. 457 (1997)

Petitioner
Dan Glickman, U.S. Secretary of Agriculture

Respondent
Wileman Brothers & Elliott, Inc., et al.

Petitioner's Claim
That the monetary assessments required by the Agricultural Marketing Agreement Act of 1937 for generic advertising did not violate the First Amendment and should be allowed to stand.

Chief Lawyer for Petitioner
Walter Dellinger

Chief Lawyer for Respondent
Thomas E. Campagne

Justices for the Court
Stephen Breyer, Ruth Bader Ginsburg, Anthony M. Kennedy, Sandra Day O'Connor, John Paul Stevens (writing for the Court)

Justices Dissenting
William H. Rehnquist, Antonin Scalia, David H. Souter, Clarence Thomas

Place
Washington, D.C.

Date of Decision
25 June 1997

Decision
The Court held that the requirement to contribute to generic advertising did not violate the freedoms of speech or belief protected by the First Amendment.

Significance
The decision limited the First Amendment protection of commercial speech, particularly in cases where legislation introduced by the states or Congress regulated matters of trade. Because the case did not involve compelled political or ideological speech, and was considered integral to the regulation of the market, the majority found that the advertising did not violate the First Amendment. The impact of the decision was limited, however, as several justices dissented, and the decision was limited to the producers of agricultural products.

In 1937, Congress passed the Agricultural Marketing Agreement Act (AMAA), which was designed to protect the public by regulating the agricultural market. Congress saw fit to exempt agriculture from the antitrust regulations which protect competition in other markets, in order to create a collective atmosphere. The market as a whole would settle on product standards, prices, and other factors. This collectivism would benefit the public, ensuring quality products at reasonable prices. The AMAA authorized, as part of the collective action of agricultural groups, generic advertising and promotion of products. Collective actions are mandated by marketing orders, which are drafted by committees and must be approved by a majority of producers. Wileman Brothers & Elliott, Inc., objected in 1988 to two such marketing orders, which required California tree fruit producers to contribute to generic advertising.

Wileman Brothers & Elliott, Inc. was a large producer and marketer of California tree fruit, a classification which included nectarines, plums, pears, and peaches. The company refused to pay the assessments for generic advertising, arguing that the assessments took funds away from more specific advertising relating to the brands it marketed, and that it disagreed with some of the advertising itself. The Court rejected the argument that the generic advertising took resources away from more specific advertising, because "[t]his is equally true . . . of assessments to cover employee benefits, inspection fees, or any other activity that is authorized by a marketing order." The financial requirements of the assessments could not, of themselves, be understood to restrict speech. The company also objected on First Amendment grounds, arguing that it should not be coerced into financing any kind of speech.

Following the company's refusal to pay the assessments, an administrative law judge ruled for Wileman Brothers & Elliott, Inc.; the secretary of agriculture, though, reversed this ruling, and the Ninth District Court agreed. Wileman Brothers then argued the case in the court of appeals, which ruled that enforced financing of the advertising was a violation of First Amendment guarantees to freedom of speech, because the advertising represented compelled speech. The

Dan Glickman, U.S. Secretary of Agriculture, 1997. © AP/Wide World Photos.

Department of Agriculture then appealed to the U.S. Supreme Court, which overturned the court of appeals' decision.

The Court's decision was primarily based on two related cases: *Abood v. Detroit Board of Education* (1977) and *Keller v. State Bar of California* (1990). In *Abood v. Detroit Board of Education,* the Court had addressed the concerns of state employees who were required to pay union dues, some of which were to be directed toward publications expressing political opinions. The Court in that case ruled that state employees could not be forced to pay for ideological speech; the ruling was interpreted in the case at hand as follows: "*Abood . . .* did not announce a broad First Amendment right not to be compelled to provide financial support for any organization that conducts expressive activities. Rather, *Abood* merely recognized a First Amendment interest in not being compelled to contribute to an organization whose expressive activities conflict with one's 'freedom of belief.'" *Keller v. State Bar of California* was a similar case, allowing California bar members' dues to finance information geared toward educating the public, but barred compelling members to endorse political views. The majority of the Court understood the generic advertising to be a similar kind of nonideological, non-

political speech, which Congress had authorized in order to regulate the market. Besides these precedents, the Court also considered the kinds of laws which do limit speech, and found that the advertising assessments had little similarity to them. As Justice Stevens wrote,

> Three characteristics of the regulatory scheme at issue distinguish it from laws that we have found to abridge the freedom of speech protected by the First Amendment. First, the marketing orders impose no restraint on the freedom of any producer to communicate any message to any audience. Second, they do not compel any person to engage in any actual or symbolic speech. Third, they do not compel the producers to endorse or finance any political or ideological views.

But four of the justices dissented with the majority opinion. There was a concern that commercial speech was receiving less protection than other forms of speech, and that this case represented a setback regarding that speech. The dissenting justices also expressed doubt as to whether the generic advertising in question helped in any tangible way to regulate the market. The basis of the dissent was that the case failed the test for acceptable limits on commercial speech set forth in *Central Hudson Gas and Electric Corp. v. Public Service Commission* (1980). In that case, it was determined that commercial speech could only be limited (or, in *Glickman,* compelled) if government regulation required it. The dissenting justices felt that the compelled generic advertising was excessive, and not pertinent to regulation of the market.

Because of the strong arguments of the dissenting writers and the very limited nature of the regulations in question, this case will probably not have a wide impact on matters of free speech. The majority opinion made it clear that the First Amendment would not allow any coercion to political or ideological speech, and that the ruling at hand dealt specifically with the Agricultural Marketing Agreement Act. But defenders of commercial speech cite the case as a blow to the protections of the First Amendment.

Related Cases
Abood v. Detroit Board of Education, 431 U.S. 209 (1977).
Central Hudson Gas and Electric Corp. v. Public Service Commission, 447 U.S. 557 (1980).
Keller v. State Bar of California, 496 U.S. 1 (1990).

Bibliography and Further Reading
First Amendment Center. http://www.fac.org.

"Government-Compelled Fruit Advertising not in Violation of First Amendment." *Business Wire,* 25 June 1997.

Greenhouse, Linda. "Agricultural Marketing Effort is Constitutional, Court Says." *New York Times,* 26 June 1997, p. C25.

"PFAW: The Supreme Court in Review." *M2 Presswire,* 30 June 1997.

MAINSTREAM LOUDOUN ET AL. V. BOARD OF TRUSTEES OF THE LOUDOUN COUNTY LIBRARY ET AL.

Legal Citation: 241 F.Supp. 252 (E.D. Va. 1998)

Plaintiff
Mainstream Loudoun Association and ten members

Defendant
Board of Trustees of the Loudoun County Library and Douglas Henderson

Plaintiff's Claim
That the Loudoun County Library violated the Speech Clause of the First Amendment by restricting patrons' access to certain Internet sites.

Chief Lawyer for Plaintiff
Robert Corn-Revere

Chief Defense Lawyer
Kenneth C. Bass III

Judge
Leonie M. Brinkema

Place
Alexandria, Virginia

Date of Decision
7 April 1998

Decision
Ruled in favor of Mainstream Loudoun by finding that the Loudoun County Library must revise its Internet access policy to not violate the First Amendment's Speech Clause.

Significance
The ruling upheld constitutional rights of library users by affirming that First Amendment freedoms fully apply to public library Internet access. The decision set a legal standard for assessing Internet use restrictions in future cases. With the clarification of First Amendment protections applied to public Internet use, libraries searched for legal means to control access, particularly for children who hold fewer First Amendment rights.

The rapid growth of the Internet in the 1990s and its use in public libraries raised new complex legal and policy questions. Clearly, the shear volume of information on the Internet meant that much unreliable, illegal, and clearly dangerous material was more accessible to individuals. By the late 1990s, the computer industry had developed software capable of screening Internet material considered "inappropriate." About 15 percent of public libraries in the United States installed the filters on at least some their computer terminals according to a survey by the American Library Association (ALA). Such filter programs were immediately criticized by civil libertarians charging the programs, while ineffective in blocking out all undesirable materials, did block out much material considered appropriate for viewing. The ALA argued that users of the Internet in public libraries were the only ones who should determine what is appropriate for them to view. On the other hand, a Ohio library's funding was threatened by community members unless the library installed filters. Few libraries fully supported the ALA position.

The U.S. Supreme Court, in the unanimous 1997 *Reno v. ACLU* ruling striking down key provisions of the Communications Decency Act, noted the potential use of such software as a legally preferable alternative to legislation limiting speech. In response, various states considered legislation promoting the use of such software, or other means of content restriction in public schools and libraries.

The Internet Filtering Dilemma

In the wake of the *Reno* ruling, Senator John McCain, R-Arizona, sponsored The Internet School Filtering Act that would require schools and libraries to use filtering or blocking systems for publicly accessible computers. The proposed law would restrict availability of certain telecommunications discounts and withhold funding support to public schools and libraries if filtering or blocking software were not used. Critics charged any legislation requiring all inappropriate material be blocked was not constitutionally feasible given software technology. All commonly available filtering technology would likely be over-inclusive in what it restricts. Additionally, constitutional tests used in courts to assess obscenity and indecency included a key "community standards" element. Consequently, any law requiring that access be blocked to "obscene," "indecent," or "illegal" material would require implementation based on local community standards of what was considered undesirable. With little legal guidance, including court decisions, libraries struggled to establish workable compromises.

Loudoun Chooses Restricted Access

The Loudoun County public library system in Virginia consisted of six branches and, like many public libraries, provided public access to the Internet and the World Wide Web. A library board of trustees controlled and managed the library. Board members, appointed by county officials, adopted bylaws, rules and regulations to guide operation and use of the library system.

In October of 1997, the library board voted to adopt an Internet sexual harassment policy requiring Internet site-blocking software be installed on all library computers. The primary purpose was to block children's access to sexually explicit material. The policy also required blocking other material judged "harmful to juveniles" under Virginia law. The library board selected a commercial software product, X-Stop, to limit access to such sites.

Shortly afterwards, a local citizens' association known as Mainstream Loudoun and ten adult members of Mainstream who were patrons of the Loudoun County public libraries filed suit against the Board of Trustees of the Loudoun County Public Library, including its five board members, and against Douglas Henderson, Loudoun County's director of library services. Mainstream sought a court-ordered injunction blocking further use of the blocking software and eliminating the policy.

Mainstream, represented by the American Civil Liberties Union, claimed the library blocked their access to such protected speech as the Quaker Home Page, the Zero Population Growth website, and a site for the American Association of University Women-Maryland. They also charged no clear criteria existed for the blocking decisions, thus Mainstream's receipt of constitutionally protected materials on the Internet was illegally restricted.

The library policy was essentially asking the software to conduct a legal test to determine what material was inappropriate. Mainstream further argued that library policy requiring all computer terminals be placed in full view of others actually increased, rather than decreased, a risk that library patrons might view material they may consider offensive. Such public placement of terminals might also pose a restrictive effect by discouraging patrons from viewing even unfiltered material. Mainstream charged that, ironically, the filtering software

could potentially block material on the Internet that was actually available to library patrons on the library's shelves.

The Board responded that the new policy was patterned after an existing policy restricting the library from obtaining certain objectionable materials when requested by patrons. The Board argued that accessing material by computer at an Internet site was the same as using library facilities to request an interlibrary loan of the material. The Board contended that as far as they knew "no court has ever held that libraries are required by the First Amendment to fulfill a patron's request to obtain a pornographic film through an interlibrary loan." Furthermore, they argued the Supreme Court in *Board of Education v. Pico* (1982) held that school boards should have the freedom to decide what materials to add to their library collections.

Protection by Subtraction

Judge Leonie M. Brinkema wrote that "the central question before this court is whether a public library may, without violating the First Amendment, enforce content-based restrictions on access to Internet speech." The Board had sought to portray the Internet as a vast interlibrary loan system. Restricting Internet access to selected materials was merely a decision not to acquire such materials, not a decision to remove them from a library's collection. On the other hand, Mainstream considered the Internet a set of electronic encyclopedias. The board's policy essentially "blacked out" selected articles they, or a computer software company, considered inappropriate for adult and juvenile patrons.

Brinkema found the Board's interlibrary loan argument unpersuasive since the Internet connection and its benefits were already present within the library. Library staff was not needed to arrange for the transfer of any material already available to an Internet-connected library computer. Brinkema wrote that, to the contrary, software restricting access to certain material actually removed access to material already available in the library.

Brinkema, coincidentally a former librarian, thus found in favor of Mainstream Loudoun. The judge's strongly worded opinion upheld First Amendment rights of library users by affirming that freedom of speech fully applied to library Internet access. Brinkema concluded the Board distorted the nature of the Internet. She held that the Internet more clearly resembled Mainstream's analogy to encyclopedias, and the library board's action was more of a removal decision. Brinkema wrote,

> all, or nearly all, Internet publications are jointly available for a single price. Indeed, it costs a library more to restrict the content of

its collection by means of blocking software than it does for the library to offer unrestricted access to all Internet publications . . . Accordingly, considerations of cost or physical resources cannot justify a public library's decision to restrict access to Internet materials.

Brinkema characterized public libraries as places encouraging freewheeling inquiry. Consequently, library boards did not enjoy the same discretion in removing or restricting materials as public school boards. In fact, Brinkema noted the Court in *Pico* "justified giving public schools broad discretion to remove books in part by noting that such materials remained available in public libraries."

Brinkema concluded the First Amendment clearly applied to and limited a public library's discretion to place content-based restrictions on the access to constitutionally protected materials in its collection. A public library could not determine what was acceptable in politics, nationalism, religion, or other matters of opinion. Brinkema wrote, "Adults are deemed to have acquired the maturity needed to participate fully in a democratic society, and their right to speak and receive speech is entitled to full First Amendment protection." The judge continued, "We are therefore left with the First Amendment's central tenet that content-based restrictions on speech must be justified by a compelling governmental interest and must be narrowly tailored to achieve that end." Therefore, "the Library Board may not thereafter selectively restrict certain categories of Internet speech because it disfavors their content."

Brinkema noted that "plaintiffs allege that the X-Stop filtering software chosen by defendants restricts many publications which are not obscene or pornographic." They also noted that X-Stop was not completely effective at blocking access to pornographic materials addressed in the policy. The relationship of a California corporation's criteria for blocking materials to legal definitions of obscenity or child pornography was unknown. Brinkema, noting the policy included prohibition of materials considered harmful to juveniles, ruled the Board could not, in the interest of protecting children, limit speech available to adults to only what is considered fit for children.

Impact

The *Loudoun* decision was the first major court case challenging public library use of Internet filters. The decision in issuing a permanent injunction against the filtering policy supported unrestricted access to the

Internet in public libraries. The Virginia library's policy was considered a form of prior restraint on the distribution of speech. Following the ruling, the Loudoun library board voted to allow adults unfiltered Internet access and parental permission slips for children to use unfiltered computers.

Though the Board was concerned that the *Loudoun* decision undercut the traditional role of librarians in deciding what materials a library should acquire, the court was clear that the decision only applied to the unique world of the Internet. In the realm of books, librarians continued to make acquisition choices. In the Internet world, all information is equally available at no additional cost with the click of a mouse.

Though the decision only applied to eastern Virginia, the effects were felt throughout the nation as libraries began to reassess their own policies toward Internet use. Left unanswered by the decision was whether it was constitutionally acceptable to use such filters on terminals set aside for children. The *Loudoun* decision reinforced the principle that minors hold fewer constitutionally protected rights than adults. Many public schools already required parental permission before allowing students access to the Internet on school computers.

Libraries also considered use of other measures, such as using privacy screens or optional filter by-pass codes. Another option was for public libraries to purchase some form of limited Internet access identifying only particular sites desired. The Internet served in the 1990s to test the constitutional notions of freedom of speech and press in ways that were previously unimaginable.

Related Cases

Board of Education v. Pico, 457 U.S. 853 (1982).
Reno v. American Civil Liberties Union, 512 U.S. 844 (1997).

Bibliography and Further Reading

Childs, Kelvin. "Federal Court: Library Can't Filter Internet Access." *Editor & Publisher,* 5 December 1998.

Fitzhugh, John H. "Public Library Internet Limits Spark Litigation," *The National Law Journal,* October 26, 1998.

Godwin, Mike. *Cyber Rights: Defending Free Speech in the Digital Age.* New York: Times Books, 1998.

Kahin, Brian, and Charles Nesson. *Borders in cyberspace: information policy and the global information infrastructure.* Cambridge, MA: MIT Press, 1997.

Mainstream Loudoun. http://Loudoun.net/mainstream

CRAWFORD-EL V. BRITTON

Legal Citation: 118 S.Ct. 1584 (1998)

Petitioner
Leonard Rollon Crawford-El

Respondent
Patricia Britton

Petitioner's Claim
That the district court's direct evidence rule and the appeals court's "clear and convincing evidence" standard for persons seeking to sue government officials should be rejected.

Chief Lawyer for Petitioner
Daniel M. Schember

Chief Lawyer for Respondent
John M. Ferren

Justices for the Court
Stephen Breyer, Ruth Bader Ginsburg, Anthony M. Kennedy, David H. Souter, John Paul Stevens (writing for the Court)

Justices Dissenting
Sandra Day O'Connor, William H. Rehnquist, Antonin Scalia, Clarence Thomas

Place
Washington, D.C.

Date of Decision
4 May 1998

Decision
The Court rejected the court of appeals' "unprecedented" introduction of a new standard that plaintiffs must meet in order to bring suit against government officials, on the grounds that the change undermines the law providing remedies for violations of federal rights.

Significance
The ruling in this case attempted to strike a balance between a plaintiff's right to seek redress for alleged violations of federal rights by government employees, and government employees' need for protection against frivolous law suits. The District of Columbia Court of Appeals held in this case that the petitioner's suit failed because he did not present "clear and convincing evidence" at the outset that the prison official's motives were as charged. The Supreme Court rejected the court of appeals' "clear and convincing evidence" test because it was new, without precedent, and, most important, would make it more difficult for all classes of plaintiffs with legitimate grievances to seek remedies for violations of their federal rights.

Crawford-El v. Britton presents an apparent paradox. Citizens are entitled to bring suit against government officials when they believe they have been wronged, but in order to do their jobs, government officials must be free from harassment by petty and frivolous claims. Accordingly, the first line of defense for a government official accused of a tort ("a wrong") by a citizen is to claim immunity from the lawsuit by asking for a summary judgment against his or her accuser. The claim of immunity kills the legal proceedings, in effect, before all the pretrial activities—"discovery," evidence-gathering, depositions, and the like—can begin. But the citizen bringing suit—the plaintiff—can overcome that first line of defense in a variety of ways, providing his or her complaint is judged by the courts to have merit. In other words, with the exception of the president of the United States (who has absolute immunity against being taken to court), government officials have the presumption of immunity from lawsuits while in office, but citizens can overcome those immunities—again, assuming their claims are substantial rather than frivolous.

In the United States, the idea that government officials are sometimes immune from suit dates at least from 1824, in a Supreme Court ruling. In 1871, Congress enacted a modest law protecting citizens against constitutional violations committed against them by government officials; this law produced 21 cases in its first 50 years of existence, according to Justice Scalia in his dissenting opinion in this case. Because of the way a 1961 Supreme Court ruling expanded this statute, "tens of thousands" of suits pour into the federal courts each year, and, as Justice Scalia put it, the Supreme Court is engaged "in a losing struggle to prevent the Constitution from degenerating into a general tort law." In fiscal 1997, for example, there were 41,215 civil rights suits filed in federal courts by prison inmates. It is therefore extremely important that federal courts have clear guidelines for distinguishing between the frivolous and the substantive, and, at the same time, for protecting the right of plaintiffs to bring suit.

At the time of this case, Crawford-El was serving a life sentence in the District of Columbia's correctional system; he was litigious (a "jail-house lawyer") and out-

Inmate Conditions

In the decade from 1985 to 1996, the total U.S. prison population grew from 744,208 to 1,630,940, a growth rate of 7.8 percent a year. Severe prison overcrowding had become a major problem throughout the nation by the mid-1990s.

Factors contributing to overcrowded conditions included get-tough-on-crime laws and the "war on drugs." These initiatives led to the elimination of parole for certain crimes, requirements for longer sentences, and an increase in the types of crimes requiring imprisonment. Only nine states operated below their bed capacity with the national average being 130 percent of capacity. The federal prison system and several states reported populations exceeding 150 percent capacity. Despite a huge prison-building program in the 1980s, California prisons remained overcrowded at 175 per-

cent of capacity in 1997. Accommodating inmate population means double bunking in single cells and transporting inmates from state to state where empty beds can be found.

The new rapidly constructed prisons generally have only minimal facilities required to house and maintain prisoners. Rehabilitation has given way to keeping order. Maximum security prisoners spend 22 to 23 hours a day in barren cells. Recreation occurs in exercise "cages" and access to education, self-help programs, and health care is minimal.

Source(s): Austin, James and John Irwin. *It's About Time: America's Imprisonment Binge*. Belmont, CA: Wadsworth Publishing Company, 1994.

---

spoken. On several occasions in the late 1980s, his outspokenness allegedly brought verbal disapproval from Patricia Britton, a corrections administrator. In 1988 Crawford-El and several other inmates were transferred to the county jail in Spokane, Washington, and after several more transfers, Crawford-El ended up in a federal prison in Florida. Three boxes of his personal belongings, including legal materials, were transferred separately; when they arrived back in Washington, the respondent in this case, Patricia Britton, asked Crawford-El's brother-in-law (also a corrections officer) to pick them up and forward them to Crawford-El. He received the boxes several months after his arrival in Florida. Crawford-El sued Britton, claiming she had diverted the boxes containing his legal materials in order to interfere with his constitutional right of access to the courts; later, he added the complaint that Britton diverted his boxes in retaliation for his exercising his First Amendment rights.

The case bounced back and forth between district court and the court of appeals for several years, the question at all times involving the adequacy or appropriateness of Crawford-El's legal efforts to overcome Britton's first line of defense—the qualified-immunity-from-suit defense. Finally, in 1996, a bare majority of the court of appeals sent the case back to district court once again, this time saying that the unless the petitioner could offer "clear and convincing evidence" about the respondent's "state-of-mind" and motives when she diverted the boxes, judgment should be entered in favor of the respondent. Of the five opinions written by the court of appeals, three agreed with the newly announced standard calling for "clear and convincing evidence," one stated a preference for the

"objective standard" announced in *Harlow v. Fitzgerald* (1982), and a dissenting opinion (signed by four judges) thought the newly announced standard was unauthorized. Thus, the question of what plaintiffs can do to overcome a defendant's first line of defense was unresolved and less clear than it had been. Thus the Supreme Court decided to hear the case—"despite the relative unimportance of the facts of this particular case."

Noting that the court of appeals thought its new standard was a corollary to the Supreme Court's ruling in *Harlow v. Fitzgerald*, Justice Stevens re-examined *Harlow*, the problem of which hinged on the idea that a government official's state of mind is "easy to allege and hard to disprove." Before *Harlow*, a plaintiff could get to trial with "bare allegations of malice," which involved a subjective judgment about the defendant's state of mind at the time of his or her action; after *Harlow*, that type of allegation was no longer allowed. Instead, the standard was now objective: in Justice Powell's words, ". . . government officials . . . are shielded from liability for civil damages, insofar as their conduct does not violate clearly established statutory or constitutional rights of which a reasonable person would have known." In other words, if Britton diverted Crawford-El's boxes because she hated him, that would not necessarily prove that she retaliated against him for exercising his First Amendment rights.

At the same time, Justice Stevens wrote, *Harlow*'s shift to an exclusively objective standard of evidence-evaluation "does not justify a rule that places a thumb on the defendant's side of the scales," as did the "clear and convincing evidence" standard invented by the court of appeals. Their "new rule" is "a blunt instrument that carries a high cost, for its rule also imposes a heightened standard of proof . . . upon plaintiffs with bond fide constitutional claims." Further, "it lacks any common law pedigree and alters the cause of action itself in a way that undermines remedies for the violation of federal rights." In short, *Harlow* had nothing to do with the present case. New rules are the business of the legislative branch and the judiciary. Justice Stevens then sent ("remanded") the case back to the court of appeals.

In conclusion, mindful of his ruling's potential for generating even more cases in an already crowded field, and mindful of the friend-of-the-court briefs filed by 34 states supporting the court of appeals' new rule, Justice Stevens reminded judges of the "many options" they had in dealing with such cases. Noting that the Prison Litigation Reform Act of 1996 had reduced the number of prisoner-filed civil rights suits by 31 percent in just one year (from 42,215 to 28,365), Justice Stevens said that for district court judges, "broad discretion in the management of the fact finding process may be more useful and equitable to all the parties than the categorical rule imposed by the Court of Appeals."

Other Opinions

Justice Kennedy's brief concurring opinion expressed concern for the way frivolous and "farcical" suits show "disdain for the judicial system," but he agreed with the Court that far-reaching solutions need to come from Congress, not from the courts. Chief Justice Rehnquist, joined by Justice O'Connor, offered the view that the Court's ruling had set a precedent that was at odds with

and undermined *Harlow,* in that the rule did not apply qualified immunity "across the board." He proposed extending *Harlow*'s qualified immunity to cases where the plaintiff fails to objectively establish that the official's reason for his or her action is merely a pretext. Justice Scalia's dissenting opinion, joined by Justice Thomas, indicated a preference for granting qualified immunity to all officials whose conduct measured objectively is valid, even if their intentions are otherwise.

Impact

The court of appeals' new rule would have severely limited plaintiffs' abilities to penetrate defendants' first line of defense in cases involving wrongful actions. By rejecting that rule, the Supreme Court maintained the balance between a plaintiff's right to seek redress for alleged violations of federal rights by a government employee and the government employee's need for protection against frivolous law suits. However, the ruling fails to keep the Constitution from, in Justice Scalia's words, "degenerating into a general tort law."

Related Cases

Monroe v. Pape, 365 U.S. 167 (1961).
Nixon v. Fitzgerald, 457 U.S. 731 (1982).
Harlow v. Fitzgerald, 457 U.S. 800 (1982).

Bibliography and Further Reading

Biskupic, Joan, and Elder Witt, eds. *Congressional Quarterly's Guide to the U.S. Supreme Court,* 3rd ed. Washington, DC: Congressional Quarterly, Inc., 1996.

SAMMY'S V. CITY OF MOBILE

Legal Citation: 140 F.3d 993 (1998)

Appellant
Sammy's of Mobile, Alabama

Appellee
City of Mobile, Alabama

Appellant's Claim
That a city ordinance prohibiting establishments that featured nude dancing from selling alcohol was unconstitutional.

Chief Lawyer for Appellant
Donald M. Briskman

Chief Lawyer for Appellee
Roderick P. Stout

Judges for the Majority
Stanley F. Birch, James C. Hill (writing for the majority)

Judges Dissenting
Phyllis A. Kravitch

Place
Atlanta, Georgia

Date of Decision
8 May 1998

Decision
The court ruled in favor of the city of Mobile and its ordinance.

Significance
This ruling affirmed the reasoning behind laws that prohibit alcohol from being served at establishments where there is also entertainment of a sexual or explicit nature. The Eleventh Circuit Court in Atlanta, Georgia, found that this particular ordinance was not in violation the First Amendment's clause regarding freedom of speech.

The Origins of the Case

In a prior decision for *Sammy's v. City of Mobile,* an Alabama court had ruled in the city's favor. It upheld an ordinance passed by Mobile's lawmaking body that prohibited establishments that served alcohol from offering topless or nude entertainment. The bars in Mobile that featured such activity then gave up their liquor licenses with the enactment of the ordinance. But a handful of clubs sued the city, led by a venue called "Sammy's," claiming the ordinance was unconstitutional. The decision of the U.S. District Court for the Southern District of Alabama was appealed to the Court of Appeals of the Eleventh Circuit. Part of the arguments in the trial hinged upon whether nude dancing was a form of "expressive conduct," and as such would be protected under the free speech clause of the First Amendment.

Ordinance No. 03-003

Elected legislative leaders of Mobile, Alabama, passed an ordinance enacted in February of 1996. This ordinance prohibited topless as well as nude dancing in any establishment that also possessed a liquor license to sell alcohol for consumption on the premises. The statute declared that the presence of both nude dancing and public consumption of alcohol "encourages undesirable behavior and is not in the interest of the public health, safety, and welfare."

Sammy's was the name of one such Mobile establishment that offered "exotic dancing" as well as alcoholic beverages. The Candy Store was another venue involved in this case. When the new ordinance went into effect, Sammy's voluntarily gave up its liquor license, and continued to feature topless and nude dancing. The Candy Store, however, did not surrender its liquor license, and served drinks to customers who were there to watch the women perform. Law enforcement authorities had not yet raided The Candy Store for this violation, but had indicated a tentative plan to do so.

Sammy's sued the city of Mobile in an Alabama state court for "injunctive relief"—the invalidation of the ordinance. The Candy Store filed suit in federal district

The exterior of Sammy's in Mobile, Alabama. © AP/Wide World Photos.

court that requested both injunctive relief and damages. The two cases were combined and heard in federal district court, which ruled in favor of the city. The court found the law did not violate the First Amendment. The case was appealed, and in the spring of 1998 the Court of Appeals for the Eleventh Circuit heard arguments from both sides on the matter.

Arguments Focused on Freedom of Expression

Attorneys for Sammy's argued that the Mobile ordinance banning topless dancing in places that sold liquor was invalid for a number of reasons. Primarily, it asserted that it was in conflict with the Free Speech Clause of First Amendment, which holds:

> Congress shall make no law respecting an establishment of religion, or prohibiting the free exercise thereof; or abridging the freedom of speech, or of the press; or the right of the people peaceably to assemble, and to petition the government for a redress of grievances.

In other words, a law that prohibited an establishment that featured nude or topless dancing from serving alcohol was actually a restriction on the nude and topless dancing. As one justice pointed out, "the Constitution does confer a right to be free from government regulation that prohibits expressive conduct on the basis of content." The legal team for The Candy Store put forth a similar case. They argued that dancing of all forms was a form of expressive conduct and could not be restricted.

Past Legal Decisions Cited

Several cases were used as precedent to decide in favor of the city of Mobile and the constitutionality of its ordinance. Firstly, there was the U.S. Supreme Court decision *California v. LaRue* (1972) that affirmed the right of the state to prohibit the sale of alcohol under certain conditions. The circuit court also used the Barnes-O'Brien test, named after two U.S. Supreme Court decisions, *United States v. O'Brien* (1968) and *Barnes v. Glen Theatre, Inc.* (1991).

The Barnes-O'Brien test is used to determine whether a law is in violation of the First Amendment. It consists of a four-part test: Is the law in question "within the constitutional power of the government"? Does it further "an important or substantial government interest"? Is the government's aim in the particular ordinance "unrelated to the suppression of free expression"? And, finally the Barnes-O'Brien test renders the law valid "if the incidental restriction on alleged First Amendment freedoms is no greater than is essential to the furtherance of that interest."

In the case of Sammy's and The Candy Store, the city of Mobile argued that it was not attempting to censor nude dancing, but rather aimed to curtail its possible secondary effects. Public safety records and investigations had shown that there was indeed a justifiable line of reasoning for Mobile's ordinance. Under the Barnes-O'Brien test, the ordinance was determined to be within the realm of the city's powers, and that it furthered the city's interest in reducing undesirable behavior resulting from the mix of nude dancing and alcohol consumption. More significantly, the court determined that Mobile's new law was not a judgment against nude dancing, since it did not restrict the practice in any way. The actual case of *Barnes* was cited by Justice Hill in his decision. "The [U.S. Supreme] Court rejected the argument that merely because nude dancing may have some expressive content, an ordinance prohibiting such dancing must be aimed at the suppression of that content," Hill wrote in his opinion. ". . . In prohibiting nude dancing where liquor is sold, the ordinance restricts only the place or manner of nude dancing without regulating any particular message it might convey."

As Justice Hill wrote, Mobile's ordinance "does not seek to ban bars or nude dancing. Everyone can still buy a drink and watch nude dancing in Mobile. They cannot, however, do both in the same place. The dissent seems to believe this may violate the rights of the people of Mobile, but we are unaware of any constitutional right to drink while watching nude dancing."

Related Cases

United States v. O'Brien, 391 U.S. 367 (1968).
California v. LaRue 409, 409 U.S. 109 (1972).
Barnes v. Glen Theatres, Inc., 501 U.S. 560 (1991).

FISTER V. MINNESOTA NEW COUNTRY SCHOOL

Legal Citation: 149 F.3d 1187 (1998)

Appellant
William Timothy Fister, guardian and parent on behalf of Mary Fister

Appellee
Minnesota New Country School

Appellant's Claim
That the Eighth District Court erred in its ruling for the appellee, and that the school had denied the student her First Amendment right to freedom of speech.

Circuit Judges
Pasco M. Bowman, Roger L. Wollman, Morris Sheppard Arnold

Place
Minneapolis, Minnesota

Date of Decision
11 May 1998

Decision
The court found that the disciplinary action taken by the school did not restrict the First Amendment rights of Mary Fister, and so upheld the ruling of the district court.

Significance
The case can be seen as a blow to the First Amendment rights of students in the ongoing battle over whether students have the same right to free speech as adults. But because the case involved not political expression, but personal comment about another student, its impact is likely to be limited.

In August of 1995, Mary Fister was a 12-year-old student at the Minnesota New Country School, a charter school in Le Sueur, Minnesota. Mary and other students in a nature studies class were exploring the Minnesota River when they discovered a population of deformed frogs. The discovery was widely reported in the area and nationally; Mary Fister planned to report the discovery in an article to be posted on the Internet. For the article, Fister collected quotations from fellow students. One student's parents objected to Fister's quoting their son, and sent a letter to her:

> Dear Mary: It has come to our attention you have been soliciting information and quotes from our son . . . regarding the frogs, his feelings about the frogs, and the research surrounding them. As . . . parents, we do not want you using information or quotes given to you by our son for publication.

As an experimental school, the Minnesota New Country School allowed students a degree of freedom, including providing special work spaces for each child. The work space included a desk and locker, and a divider which served as a display space. Fister posted the letter from the other student's parents on her divider, with a sign that read, "Making a mountain out of a molehill." The student and his mother complained to the school, stating that they felt the posting was harassment; the school insisted that Fister take down the letter and sign. When Fister re-posted the letter, the school cited a policy which specified that "[f]ighting, threatening language, other endangerment or harassment . . . [is] grounds for suspension and/or expulsion." Fister was suspended three times, and then expelled for one year after a hearing by the school. Fister protested the expulsion, and took the case to the Eighth District Court.

Fister argued that, based on the decision in *Tinker v. Des Moines Independent Community School District* (1969), her school had violated the First Amendment's Freedom of Speech Clause. In *Tinker,* three students wore black armbands to school to protest the war in Vietnam. They were asked to remove the armbands, and when they refused, they were suspended. The Supreme Court ruled in the students' favor, stating, "A prohibition against expression of opinion, without any evidence that the rule is necessary to avoid substantial interference with school discipline or the rights of others, is not permissible under the First and Fourteenth Amendments." The Court also said in its majority opinion, "First Amendment rights are available to teachers and students, subject to application in light of the special characteristics of the school environment." Fister saw her posting as a form of speech protected by the First Amendment, and argued that the school had, in fact, prohibited her expression just as the Des Moines School District had done in *Tinker.*

Another related case in the discussion of students' right to free speech, also relied upon by Fister, was *Hazelwood School District v. Kuhlmeier* (1988). In that case, the U.S. Supreme Court ruled that a principal "acted reasonably" when he deleted certain objectionable articles about pregnancy, divorce, and related issues from the student newspaper. But while *Hazelwood* limited students' freedom of speech, it did set a precedent by acknowledging that schools could create a public forum—"School facilities may be deemed to be public forums only if school authorities have by policy or by practice opened the facilities"—in which speech could not be limited. Fister argued that her school had created just such a forum, and then violated First Amendment freedoms by censoring her speech.

But both the Eighth District Court and the Court of Appeals for the Eighth District disagreed with Fister's arguments. Although *Tinker* protected students' speech, it stipulated that the students in that case "were not disruptive and did not impinge upon the rights of others." In Fister's case, teachers, students, and parents found her actions harassing and disruptive; the courts agreed. The court reasoned that such actions are not protected by the First Amendment. And in response to Fister's argument that the school had created a public forum, and then denied her access to it, the courts found that "because students were not permitted indiscriminate use of their display boards," no public forum existed. The school restricted what types of things could be shown on the boards, including, as the court said in its written opinion, "postings critical of other students or perceived by other students as harassing." Both courts found that the school acted reasonably by expelling Mary, and did not violate the First Amendment.

While this case, like *Hazelwood,* restricted the rights of students, its significance in the overall debate about students' free speech is limited. Because it involved student interaction, it is different from both *Tinker* and *Hazelwood,* which were about peaceful, and political, expression.

Related Cases
Tinker v. Des Moines Independent Community School District, 393 U.S. 503 (1969).
Hazelwood School District v. Kuhlmeier, 484 U.S. 260 (1988).

Bibliography and Further Reading
"Expelled for a Year for Posting a Letter," http://www.gac.edu/~mfister/.

Fister v. Minnesota New Country School, No. 97-2596, http://www.wulaw.wustl.edu/8th.cir/Opinions.

ARKANSAS EDUCATIONAL TELEVISION COMMISSION V. FORBES

Legal Citation: 118 S.Ct. 1633 (1998)

Petitioner
Arkansas Educational Television Commission

Respondent
Ralph P. Forbes

Petitioner's Claim
Arkansas Educational Television Commission excluded Ralph P. Forbes from participating in their television debate between major political party candidates as an exercise of editorial judgment because Forbes's status as an independent political candidate made him politically unviable and, therefore, not newsworthy.

Chief Lawyer for Petitioner
Richard D. Marks

Chief Lawyer for Respondent
Kelly J. Shackleford

Justices for the Court
Stephen Breyer, Anthony M. Kennedy (writing for the Court), Sandra Day O'Connor, William H. Rehnquist, Antonin Scalia, Clarence Thomas

Justices Dissenting
Ruth Bader Ginsburg, David H. Souter, John Paul Stevens

Place
Washington, D.C.

Date of Decision
18 May 1998

Decision
Arkansas Educational Television Commission's (AETC) exclusion of Forbes from the debate was a reasonable, viewpoint-neutral exercise of journalistic discretion consistent with the First Amendment.

Significance
This case is about a political candidate's First Amendment rights of free speech during media coverage of the electoral process. In a 6-3 decision, the U.S. Supreme Court ruled that a public television station can exercise editorial prerogative to exclude from debate a qualified fringe candidate whom the station believed could not win the election. Broadcasters, journalists, educators, and civil libertarians followed this case closely for at issue was also whether a public radio station always constitutes a public forum, in which there are very few controls on who may speak, or remains part of the free press and is therefore subject to journalistic standards alone. This troublesome question of how to balance First Amendment rights when the government—in the form of a state-affiliated broadcast network—is the speaker led the court to develop guidelines for a "public forum doctrine" in its decision.

The Events

In 1992 Ralph P. Forbes, a former American Nazi Party member, garnered enough signatures to become a viable (legally qualified) candidate for a congressional seat in the Third District of Arkansas. Arkansas Educational Television Commission decided to hold a debate on the government-funded Arkansas Education Television Network (AETN) between the Democratic and Republican party candidates. It denied Forbes's request to join the October debate.

Forbes sued AETC in federal court, claiming his First Amendment rights of free speech were violated by the exclusion. The federal court denied Forbes's request to join the debate; the debate proceeded between the two candidates. Forbes did not win the seat in the 3 November 1992 election.

In 1993, the federal district court dismissed Forbes's First Amendment claims. Forbes appealed in the Eighth Circuit U.S. Court of Appeals *Arkansas Educational Television Commission v. Forbes* (94-490), and on 28 April 1994, the court ruled in his favor.

Arkansas Educational Television Commission appealed the Eighth Circuit decision in the U.S. Supreme Court, but failed to get a hearing, so a jury trial was held in 1995, in federal district court. The jury determined that Forbes was excluded from the debate because he was a fringe candidate and not because of his political views. They ruled in favor of the AETN.

The Eighth Circuit Court then reversed the jury's ruling on 21 August 1996, on the grounds that the district court made an incorrect judgment that AETC was a non-public forum. It ruled in favor of Forbes, and ordered that a jury determine an entitlement of damages.

In November of 1996, AETC appealed to the U.S. Supreme Court. On 17 March 1997, the Court agreed to hear the case's oral arguments on 8 October. On 18 May 1998 the court ruled in favor of AETC.

Editorial Discretion, or Government Censorship?

Forbes claimed the moral high ground in his statement that AETC violated his First Amendment right to free speech and suggested the decision of AETC (considered a government-sponsored voice) was based on its disagreement with his political views. AETC's response was also based on the First Amendment, claiming editorial prerogative. Susan Howarth, AETC's executive director, denied Forbes's accusation of discrimination, listing the following reasons to prove the decision to exclude him was not only reasonable, but demonstrated journalistic responsibility:

> . . . the news organizations also did not consider him a serious candidate; . . . the Associated Press and a national election result reporting service did not plan to run his name in results on election night; . . . Forbes apparently had little, if any, financial support, failing to report campaign finances to the Secretary of State's Office or to the Federal Election Commission.

In the 6-3 decision for AETC, Justice Kennedy also addressed an important, related issue. Several *amicus* briefs in support of AETC voiced the concern that, faced with the choice between an unwieldy open-microphone situation for any political debate, or no political debate programming at all, public broadcasters and even educational facilities might opt for lack of controversy and choose the latter.

> Were it faced with the prospect of cacophony on one hand, and First Amendment liability, on the other, a public television broadcaster might choose not to air candidates' views at all . . . These concerns are not speculative. As a direct result of the court of appeals decision in this case, the Nebraska Educational Television Network cancelled a scheduled debate between candidates in Nebraska's 1996 United States Senate race.

The American Civil Liberties Union (ACLU) sided with Forbes on the grounds that the forum of political debate was unique, not only because the forum was public, but because the stakes were so high. Other *amicus* briefs from groups supporting Forbes stated that all parties should be given the widest audience possible because television is the major venue for information regarding political campaigns.

The Importance of Public and Nonpublic Forums

The extent of political candidates' First Amendment rights of free speech depends partially on where the candidates speak, and who, if anyone, controls their access to the public ear. A private, invitation-only party differs greatly from a call-in news and talk radio show. In his discussion of the unique situation that a candidate debate poses, Justice Kennedy stated that "the spe-

cial characteristics of candidate debates supports the conclusion that the AETC debate was a forum of some type. The question of what type must be answered by reference to our public forum precedents." He explained:

> . . . [T]raditional public fora are open for expressive activity regardless of the government's intent. The objective characteristics of these properties require the government to accommodate private speakers. The government is free to open additional properties for expressive use by the general public or by a particular class of speakers, thereby creating designated public fora. Where the property is not a traditional public forum and the government has not chosen to create a designated public forum, the property is either a nonpublic forum or not a forum at all . . . The parties agree the AETC debate was not a traditional public forum . . . Under our precedents, the AETC debate was not a designated public forum . . . Here, the debate did not have an open-microphone format.

Impact

The implications of this case were far-reaching, and demonstrate not only the full range of action possible through the law courts, but the delicate balance that exists between points of law and the Constitution. Arguing this case were not only the parties involved. Joint briefs were filed by no fewer than 20 states, the Federal Communications Commission (FCC), the Association of America's Public Television Stations (APTS), the Commission on Presidential Debates, the ACLU, and Acting Solicitor General Walter Dellinger.

Related Cases

Columbia Broadcasting System, Inc. v. Democratic National Committee, 412 U.S. 94 (1973).

FCC v. League of Women Voters of California, 468 U.S. 364 (1984).

Turner Broadcasting System, Inc. v. FCC, 512 U.S. 622 (1994).

Bibliography and Further Reading

Biskupic, Joan. "High Court Agrees to Review Ruling on Political Debates," *Washington Post,* March 18, 1997, p. 8.

Biskupic, Joan. "Justices Question Barring Fringe Candidates From Debates on Public TV," *Washington Post,* October 8, 1997, p. 15.

Fleming, Heather. "Court Forces Open TV Congressional Debate." *Broadcasting & Cable,* Sep. 23, 1996, p. 18.

FREEDOM OF THE PRESS

The Press

At the time the Constitution was written, the term "press" referred to the printing of newspapers, books, and leaflets. However, with the advance of technology through time a much broader application has evolved involving the broadcast media, such as radio and television, and online computer information systems. Specific reference to press in the Constitution was an acknowledgment of the critical role the press played in early American society. Though press was mentioned separately from speech in the First Amendment, the two terms became essentially coequal. Initially, the press referred to the institutional press, which some considered to deserve greater freedoms from government regulation than other forms of publication. However, recognition grew that every citizen had a right to publish what sentiments they pleased before the public. Thus, press became steadily broadened until the 1990s when the concept of "publishing" itself became challenged by new online technologies.

The Origins of Free Press Concerns

The printing of thoughts and ideas began thousands of years ago with the carving of designs into wet clay. Though paper was invented in China in the twelfth century, modern printing did not begin until about 500 years ago. In response to the Renaissance interest in learning, German Johannes Guttenberg pioneered the use of movable type and began the printing of books. However, even before there was a press and printing, rulers and church leaders commonly restricted the writing and distribution of certain material. Written by hand, books considered contrary to church teachings or a threat to social order were banned or burned.

Shortly after the introduction of printing in the fifteenth century, early printers were required to obtain a license from the government or a religious group to publish material. By the mid sixteenth century, anyone in England found with unapproved books critical of the government could face execution. In 1585 Queen Elizabeth created new regulations concerning the printing of books. Printing could only occur at presses in Oxford, Cambridge, and London and all materials to be printed required approval beforehand by the Archbishop of Canterbury or the Bishop of London. Imprisonment and destruction of the printing equipment was punishment for any violations. English control of the press continued into the seventeenth century as part of common law recognizing the right of government to impose criminal penalties on those maliciously criticizing the government, known as the "sedition libel doctrine." By the mid-seventeenth century, arguments against licensing mounted and by 1700 freedom from censorship grew as a recognized natural right, free of prior restraints but not absolute freedom from punishment after publication.

Printing was introduced in the American colonies in 1639 in Cambridge, Massachusetts and rapidly spread but under strict controls. In 1735, the trial of colonist newspaper publisher John Peter Zenger, charged with criticizing the British government, attracted widespread attention. By 1765, over 30 newspapers were published in the colonies. After conclusion of war with France in 1763, Britain decided to tighten its control on the colonies and station troops in America. To finance the expense, the British Parliament in 1765 passed the Stamp Act placing a tax on newspapers. The act, the first of several unpopular tax measures imposed by Britain in the decade between 1765 and 1775, helped forge colonial opposition to British rule and directly led to the Revolutionary War.

The framers of the Constitution viewed freedom of press as a key means of ensuring participatory democracy. Freedom of speech and religion would become meaningless without the freedom to publish such thoughts. Thus, the right to publish freely served as a protection of other constitutional freedoms, a watchdog over threats to the other rights. The Constitution was written to express that "Congress shall make no law . . . abridging the freedom . . . of the press." However, few details were provided about how to apply the press clause. It had been generally accepted that any form of government censorship, or prior restraint, was prohibited. Punishment of published material, such as seditious libel, was allowed with recognition that to preserve peace and order, abuses by people of their freedom must be addressed in some manner.

The Press and Prior Restraints

Throughout history the most severe restrictions placed on the press has occurred during times of social stress, particularly during wars. The first restrictions by Congress on the press was through the Sedition Act of 1798, based on English common law, which prohibited malicious criticism of the government or government officials. Several editors were tried and convicted before the highly controversial law was allowed to expire in 1801. The convictions were subsequently pardoned and no legal challenges resulted. The Civil War in the early 1860s also brought press censorship through martial law. Again, no legal cases resulted. World War I brought a new set of federal and state sedition laws. Several newspaper editors were convicted under the laws and legal challenges this time did result. The Supreme Court uniformly rejected freedom of the press claims. Importantly among these rulings was the finding in *Gitlow v. New York* (1925) that First Amendment press protections applied to state laws as well as federal in the form of personal rights and liberties protected by the due process clause of the Fourteenth Amendment. In another of the sedition cases Justice Oliver Wendell Holmes established the "marketplace of ideas" metaphor which proved influential in supporting press freedoms throughout the twentieth century.

As with speech, the government has restricted the press through both prior restraints and through punishment after publication. Prior restraints have taken the form of censorship, taxation, and licensing. Punishment has been applied to publishers deliberately printing false and defamatory material about public and private individuals. Several aspects of press freedom were addressed by the courts since the World War I era sedition cases.

A prior restraint doctrine was first elaborated by the Supreme Court in the 1931 *Near v. Minnesota* ruling. The Court for the first time struck down a state law as an unconstitutional prior restraint on the press. The Court identified four situations where government censorship through prior restraint might be warranted: (1) protection of crucial war information; (2) banning obscene materials; (3) preventing the incitement of violence against the community or overthrow of the government; and, (4) protecting privacy. The obscenity prohibition was upheld in *Kingsley Books v. Brown* (1957) by supporting state law that allowed public officials to seek injunctions against the sale of materials considered obscene. The issue of civil or criminal liability regarding libel did not come to the Court until *New York Times Company v. Sullivan* (1964). The Court provided some protection to the press by holding that public officials must prove "actual malice" to recover libel damages. Later, the Court decreased press protection when non-public figures were suing. The most celebrated prior restraint decision regarding national security was *New York Times v. United States*

(1971). The Court refused to block newspapers from publishing previously classified foreign policy information on the Indochina war but did leave open that national security considerations remained a legitimate cause for prior restraint. As a result criticism by the press greatly influenced public opposition to the Vietnam War.

Regarding privacy, the Court set limits on private damage suits against the press for invasion of privacy. In 1975, the Court in *Cox Broadcasting Corp. v. Cohn* overturned a Georgia state law prohibiting publication of rape victims' names already found in public records. But the Court noted states could pass laws keeping such information out of public records. Later, in 1989, the Court overturned a lower court's award of civil damages under a state law prohibiting disclosure of rape victim's name in *Florida Star v. B. J. F.* in a case where the victim's name was mistakenly and illegally placed in the public record. Regarding the old issue of newspaper taxation, the Court held in *Minnesota Star v. Minnesota Commissioner of Revenue* (1983) and later cases that any taxes must be equally applied to all, not singling out publishers.

News Gathering

Another area addressed by the Court involved press claims that to effectively perform their duties for the public, government must provide special access to proceedings and institutions. However, the Court did not recognize such a general constitutional right of access except in criminal trials. The Court also did not recognize a journalist's privilege to withhold information in protecting news sources. Three cases addressed by the Court in 1972 involved reporters challenging subpoenas to testify before grand juries. In all, reporters claimed the promise of confidentiality was imperative to their information gathering activities. Significantly, the Court ruled in *Branzburg v. Hayes* (1972) that journalists do not have such privileges beyond ordinary citizens. A public interest in law enforcement prevailed over press rights. In *Zurcher v. The Stanford Daily* (1978) the Court also upheld police use of search warrants rather than subpoenas against news organizations. As a result, in 1980 Congress passed a law prohibiting newsroom searches by government officials except under special circumstances.

Access to public facilities was the topic of two Supreme Court cases in 1974, in *Pell v. Procunier* and *Saxbe v. Washington Post*. The Court rejected press claims to a special right of access by upholding rules restricting reporters' access to inmates, like citizens. The finding was further affirmed in the 1978 *Houchins v. KQED* ruling. The Court essentially held that the First Amendment does not require the government to allow special access not available to the public. Yet, the press does have an important societal role in keeping the public informed. The first issue addressed by the Court in press access to criminal trial proceedings involved protecting a defendant's right to a fair trial. In the 1960s and 1970s, many judges issued "gag orders" forbidding the press to publish certain information. In 1976 *Nebraska Press Association v. Stuart* the Court overturned a gag order. Some courts responded by closing pretrial hearings to minimize publicity. However, in 1980 in *Richmond Newspapers, Inc. v. Virginia* the Court ruled that except in rare cases, criminal trials must be open to the press. In 1986 the Court extended the right to pretrial hearings in *Press-Enterprise Co. v. Superior Court of California*. The entire criminal judicial system was opened to public scrutiny.

The Electronic Age

Though First Amendment press protections were eventually extended to broadcasting and cable television media, the courts recognized a government regulatory role because of the limited number of broadcast frequencies available. In 1943 the power of the Federal Communications Commission (FCC) to determine who receives broadcast licenses was upheld. However, the FCC was required to apply neutral criteria not based on an applicant's viewpoints. In the late 1940s the FCC established a "fairness doctrine" requiring broadcasters to cover public issues and allow various views to be aired. Broadcasters challenged this rule as government interference of content and a First Amendment violation. In 1969 *Red Lion Broadcasting Co. v. Federal Communications Commission* the Court upheld the rule, but by 1987 the FCC discarded the "fairness doctrine."

Earlier in the 1960s, the FCC had entered the realm of regulating cable television by requiring cable companies to serve local community needs. In the mid-1970s the FCC required new cable systems to allocate channels for public, educational, and local government use but these requirements were not supported by the Court in a 1979 decision. In 1986 *City of Los Angeles v. Preferred Communications, Inc.* the Court extended First Amendment protection to the cable franchising process. Most of the same constitutional guarantees of newspapers and magazines were extended to cable TV in a cable television's "Bill of Rights" in 1994 *Turner Broadcasting System v. Federal Communications Commission,* though later in 1997 the Court in *Turner Broadcasting System v. Federal Communications Commission II* added some restrictions.

The Press and Private Ownership

Commercialization of the press began in the early twentieth century, eventually leading to corporate ownership of the media. Increasingly the line blurred between political and commercial activities and between public and commercial. Beginning in the 1970s, the courts increasingly extended First Amendment protections to corporate and commercial activities, regardless of their relationship to political debate, consistent with the "marketplace of ideas" doctrine expressed earlier in the century. This broadening, according to critics, opened the door to censorship of the press by shareholders and investors of corporations who own news organizations. Concern over government restriction of the press had shifted significantly to concern over corporate censorship. The marketplace had became a commercial marketplace. In the 1990s the Court continued to witness a number of cases seeking to prohibit government regulation of political campaign spending, commercial broadcasting, and commercial speech. Favorable decisions toward the expanded rights came from an increasingly conservative Supreme Court with support of the political right and business community. People feared that the First Amendment had become a tool for protecting corporate commercial interests rather than the exchange of political ideas.

By the 1990s, distinct changes in public opinion regarding the press' responsibility were being registered in polls. Central to the trend was a distinct lack of trust in the press' fairness through perceived excessive news coverage on some subjects, corporate motives for news ratings and circulation, and respect for personal privacy. The public feared the press role to inform and educate was lost. At the same time, emergence of an interactive media such as talk shows also allowed citizens to participate in the press rather than merely be consumers, led to an even greater exchange of information and opinion. Critical opinions of the government free of censorship or fear of retaliation constituted a major part of exchanges. Others kept vigilance over government intrusions in the press. The American Booksellers Foundation for Freedom of Expression in 1998 assessed threats to freedom of the press through three events: publication of a murder-manual book (*Hit Man: A Technical Manual for Independent Contractors*) which a 1997 court ruling held was outside First Amendment protections; the subpoena of Monica Lewinsky's bookstore purchases by a governmental special investigator; and, indictments against a major national bookstore chain for selling books containing nude photographs of children. Aiding this diversity of free press concerns was the fact that the Court had never developed a comprehensive theory regarding the freedom of press. Though the United States enjoyed the greatest freedoms for the press in the world, serious issues were in need of resolution as the twentieth century drew to a close.

See also: **Freedom of Speech, Libel, Obscenity, Privacy**

Bibliography and Further Reading

Asante, Clement E. *Press Freedom and Development: A Research Guide and Selected Bibliography.* Westport, CT: Greenwood Press, 1997.

Barendt, Eric (ed.). *Media Law.* New York: New York University Press, 1993.

Coetze, J. M. *Giving Offense: Essays on Censorship.* Chicago: University of Chicago Press, 1996.

Fiss, Owen M. *Liberalism Divided: Freedom of Speech and the Many Uses of State Power.* Boulder, CO: Westview Press, 1996.

Hindman, Elizabeth B. *Rights vs. Responsibilities: The Supreme Court and the Media.* Westport, CT: Greenwood Press, 1997.

Keane, John. *The Media and Democracy.* Cambridge: Polity, 1991.

Schwartz, Bernard. *Freedom of the Press.* New York: Facts on File, 1992.

Wagman, Robert J. *The First Amendment Book: Celebrating 200 Years of Freedom of the Press and Freedom of Speech.* New York: World Almanac, 1991.

GOMPERS V. BUCK'S STOVE & RANGE COMPANY

Legal Citation: 221 U.S. 418 (1911)

Petitioners
Samuel Gompers, et al.

Respondent
Buck's Stove & Range Company

Petitioners' Claim
That even though they violated the terms of an injunction, the actions of Gompers and others in the American Federation of Labor were protected under the First Amendment.

Chief Lawyers for Petitioners
Alton B. Parker, Jackson H. Ralston

Chief Lawyers for Respondent
J. J. Darlington, Daniel Davenport

Justices for the Court
William Rufus Day, John Marshall Harlan I, Oliver Wendell Holmes, Charles Evans Hughes, Joseph Rucker Lamar (writing for the Court), Horace Harmon Lurton, Joseph McKenna, Willis Van Devanter, Edward Douglass White

Justices Dissenting
None

Place
Washington, D.C.

Date of Decision
15 May 1911

Decision
The Court would not consider the free speech argument, but reversed two lower courts' findings of criminal contempt on a technicality.

Significance
The Supreme Court did not analyze the constitutional question raised under the First Amendment, concluding that the injunction did not, by its terms, restrict or restrain any forms of publication (or speech). Therefore, there was no question on appeal as to an "abridgment" of free speech. Instead, the Court considered whether a lower court had the power to issue an anti-boycott injunction, even if the boycott itself was in the form of written or spoken words or statements. The Court held that such words or statements were not protected speech under the First Amendment, but were unified "verbal acts" (under an alleged conspiracy to act together to harm Buck's company). As such, they were subject to injunctive restraint, if the boycott would result in property being irreparably damaged or commerce being illegally restrained.

Historical Backdrop

During the 1800s, many laborers and workers organized and formed unions to strengthen their bargaining power to negotiate for better working conditions and wages. Courts were reluctant to restrict or restrain these efforts, in consideration of First Amendment protections of freedom of speech (e.g., the right to speak out against unfair conditions) and freedom of association (e.g., the right to join with others to speak out against unfair conditions). However, courts also needed to weigh or balance conflicting individual freedoms, particularly where certain freedoms of expression might result in harm or damage to the property rights of others.

With the rise in interstate commerce, individual labor unions began to form voluntary associations with others under the umbrella organization of the American Federation of Labor (AF of L, later AFL). This enhancement of bargaining power for individual laborers was intimidating to manufacturers and producers, who formed their own professional affiliations and associations, in a reciprocal effort to maintain equal bargaining power.

Testing the Waters

The AFL published its own newspaper, the *American Federationist*, of which Samuel Gompers was editor (as well as president of the AFL). John Mitchell was AFL vice president and Frank Morrison was manager of circulation for the paper, which had a broad readership of both the public and federation members. Following a labor dispute with Buck's Stove & Range Company over hours of work, workers began a boycott, and the *Federationist* published the name of Buck's company on "Unfair" and "We Don't Patronize" blacklists.

Buck's filed an action in the trial court for the District of Columbia, alleging, among other things, that Gompers and others had entered into an illegal boycott to restrain Buck's business and had threatened other merchants not to deal with Buck's, causing irreparable damage to its business. After lengthy arguments, the trial court agreed with Buck's and issued a lengthy temporary injunction, prohibiting Gompers and the others from engaging in any boycott ". . . for the purpose of, or tending to, any injury to or interference with the

---

Unions

The first efforts to organize employees into unions were met with fierce resistance by employers. The U.S. legal system played a part in the resistance, indicting boot and shoemakers in *Commonwealth v. Pullis* (1806) for conspiring to raise their wages. The first national labor federation to remain active for more than a few years was the Noble Order of the Knights of Labor. It was established in 1869 and had set as goals the eight-hour workday, equal pay for equal work, and the abolition of child labor. The Knights of Labor grew to 700,000 members by 1886, but went into decline that year with a series of failed strikes. By 1900 it had disappeared.

Unions flourished and were at their strongest following World War II. By 1955, the American Federation of Labor (AFL) and Congress of Industrial Organizations (CIO) joined forces to become AFL-CIO. It is now one of the largest unions in this country with a membership of 15 million.

Over 70 unions fall under the protective umbrella of AFL-CIO, which calls itself the "voice of working American men and women."

Source(s): *West's Encyclopedia of American Law,* Volume 6. Minneapolis/St. Paul, MN: The West Group, 1998.

---

complainant's business." Following additional taking of evidence and hearing arguments, the trial court made the injunction permanent on 23 March 1908. The defendants in that action (Gompers, Mitchell, Morrison, and others) appealed the matter. However, before any appellate decision was rendered, Buck's filed another petition in equity with the trial court, asking the court to find the defendants in the original action guilty of violating the terms of the injunction and to punish them for contempt. The petition cited several examples of speech and editorials, published subsequent to the court's earlier decision, which Buck's believed to be in violation of the anti-boycott injunction. Following a "show cause" order to the defendants, the trial court again agreed with Buck's and found that Gompers, Mitchell, and Morrison had disobeyed the terms of the injunction, and further found them guilty of contempt, sentencing them to several months imprisonment. The defendants again appealed.

The Court of Appeals for the District of Columbia affirmed the lower court's decision, but made some changes to the language of the injunction. From this, both sides appealed to the Supreme Court. However, again prior to decision, both sides resolved many issues between them, and only Gompers's appeal became part of the Supreme Court's decision. Essentially, the petitioners argued that: (1) they had not been in contempt of the trial court's order; (2) the statements they made or published were not violative of the injunction; and (3) *arguendo,* even if it appeared that their statements violated the injunction, the trial court could not abridge their freedom of speech or of the press under the First Amendment; therefore, the injunction was invalid and there could be no contempt.

The Court's Analysis

Writing the opinion for the majority, Justice Lamar first addressed the constitutional issue posed by the peti-

tioners, stating that the terms of the injunction did not restrain speech or press, as they had argued. Instead, he reasoned, the real issue posed was whether a lower court in equity had the power to impose an injunction on the continuance of a boycott, which, "by words and signals, printed or spoken, caused or threatened irreparable damage." He referred to several federal laws (including the Sherman Anti-Trust Act) and prior Supreme Court cases which clearly upheld courts' powers to enjoin a boycott where interstate commerce was restrained or property was irreparably damaged. He again reasoned that if the restraint of trade could be enjoined, but the means through which the restraint was accomplished could not be enjoined, it would render all the laws "impotent."

Lamar then briefly discussed the difference between an individual's right of speech and association versus the rights of a "multitude of members" who have acquired vast power by uniting, such as in a labor organization. In those circumstances, Lamar explained, ". . . it is the duty of government to protect the one against the many, as well as the many against the one." Accordingly, a court's protective and restraining powers extended, "to every device whereby property is irreparably damaged or commerce is illegally restrained."

The opinion further distinguished between an individual's words or signals, and those of an unlawful conspiracy among persons to act together against a business. Such a conspiracy, Lamar noted, ". . . gives the words 'Unfair,' 'We Don't Patronize,' or similar expressions, a force not inhering in the words themselves, and therefore exceeding any possible right of speech which a single individual might have. Under such circumstances they become what have been called 'verbal acts,' and as much subject to injunction as the use of any other force whereby property is unlawfully damaged." Lamar then stated that when the facts in a case warranted it, a court with proper jurisdiction over the parties and the subject matter indeed had the power to grant an injunction.

The remainder of the opinion focused on the appropriateness of the remedy. After a lengthy discussion of the differences between civil and criminal contempt, Lamar concluded that, not only did the lower courts' determination (that this case was one of criminal contempt) require reversal, but also that Buck's was not entitled to "any compensation or relief" because the offending contempt was against the court, not Buck's. Therefore, the contempt proceedings instituted by Buck's were ordered dismissed, but the opinion left open the right of the original trial court to institute its own contempt proceedings against Gompers, et al. for any contempt committed against it.

Impact

Again, the issue here was not the right of free speech, but rather, whether one could use the protections of free speech to accomplish an otherwise illegal act, objective, or purpose. This case has been relied on as authoritative in dozens of subsequent cases seeking to quash boycotts. Most forms of boycotting remain illegal under the Sherman Anti-Trust Act. However, non-violent, politically-motivated economic boycotts which seek to secure constitutional rights are generally protected. Boycotts are to be distinguished from "pickets," wherein employees and workers may peacefully protest at their place of employment, and make known to the public their grievances against their employer.

Related Cases

Ex Parte Rowland, 104 U.S. 604 (1882).
Tinker v. Des Moines School District, 393 U.S. 503 (1969).
NAACP v. Claiborne Hardware Company, 458 U.S. 886 (1982).
Waters v. Churchill, 511 U.S. 661 (1994).
Madsen v. Women's Health Center, 513 U.S. 753 (1994).

Samuel Gompers. © AP/Wide World Photos.

Bibliography and Further Reading

Hall, Kermit L., ed. *Oxford Companion to the Supreme Court of the United States.* New York: Oxford University Press, 1992.

Mill, John Stuart. *On Liberty.* London, England: Oxford University Press, 1859.

Wade, Edwin L. *Constitution 2000.* Chicago, IL: Let's Talk Sense Publishing Company, 1995.

NEAR V. MINNESOTA

Legal Citation: 283 U.S. 697 (1931)

Appellant
J. M. Near

Appellee
State of Minnesota, ex rel. Floyd B. Olson, County Attorney of Hennepin County

Appellant's Claim
That a state "gag law" preventing publication of his newspaper constitutes prior restraint prohibited by the First Amendment.

Chief Lawyers for Appellant
Weymouth Kirkland, T. E. Latimer

Chief Lawyers for Appellee
James E. Markham, Arthur L. Markve

Justices for the Court
Louis D. Brandeis, Oliver Wendell Holmes, Charles Evans Hughes (writing for the Court), Owen Josephus Roberts, Harlan Fiske Stone

Justices Dissenting
Pierce Butler, James Clark McReynolds, George Sutherland, Willis Van Devanter

Place
Washington, D.C.

Date of Decision
1 June 1931

Decision
The Supreme Court struck down the gag law.

Significance
Near was one of the most important cases concerning freedom of the press that the Court ever decided. Afterward, it was clear that the prohibition against prior restraint—the very heart of the First Amendment—applied to states as well as the federal government.

In 1925, Minnesota passed a statute, also known as the Minnesota Gag Law, which permitted a judge, acting without a jury, to stop publication of any newspaper, magazine, or other periodical publication the judge found "obscene, lewd, and lascivious" or "malicious, scandalous, and defamatory." The law provided that a periodical could be permanently enjoined from future publication.

The Minnesota Gag Law was a response to the spread of "yellow journalism"—sensationalistic news accounts—across the country in the 1920s. In general, the law was regarded approvingly, and the American public watched to see how Minnesota would proceed.

The law was first applied to the *Saturday Press,* a weekly newspaper published in Minneapolis by the controversial J. M. Near. Actually, Near's paper was controversial, too, although its muckraking accounts of corruption in city politics were largely accurate. Near himself was far more disreputable: he was anti-Catholic, anti-Jewish, anti-black, and anti-labor. Still, journalists and the American Civil Liberties Union (ACLU) rallied to his cause when Floyd B. Olson, the county attorney, tried to use the gag law to close down the *Saturday Press.* (The state of Minnesota sued on his behalf, or "ex relation.")

Near's defenders were concerned because the gag law constituted a form of prior restraint, an attempt by government to prohibit communication of information before publication. In essence, prior restraint amounts to the kind of censorship specifically ruled out by First Amendment guarantees of freedom of speech and press.

After the Minnesota Supreme Court upheld the injunction preventing publication of the *Saturday Press,* the conservative Chicago publisher, Colonel Robert R. McCormack, substituted his legal staff for the ACLU's. Near then appealed his case to the U.S. Supreme Court.

Although the vote was close, the opinion of the Court written by Chief Justice Hughes came out squarely against the gag law. In the minds of the majority, there was no question but that the First Amendment ruled out prior restraint, at the state as well as the federal level:

Prior Restraint

Prior restraint is one way governments have sought to restrict the publication of materials determined objectionable by censoring them before publication. One such Minnesota law prohibiting printing materials viewed as "malicious" or "scandalous" was found unconstitutional by the U.S. Supreme Court. This sort of censorship is unusual in the United States as well as other democratic nations.

Censorship of this type has roots in English law; Henry VIII instituted such a censorship law in England in 1534. In England, this law was challenged in 1644 by John Milton's essay, *Areopagitica*; the law was repealed in 1695. However, the English government still had the power to prosecute the publishers of materials who criticized government practices, regardless of the truth or falsity of the statements, on the basis of "seditious libel."

These same laws and practices were applied to early American colonists by the British. In colonial America, a landmark 1735 decision cleared John Peter Zenger of charges of publishing libelous statements criticizing programs of the colonial governor because Zenger's accusations were true. Using the truth of statements as a defense against libel did not become acceptable in England until 1868.

Source(s): Cornell.http://supct.law.cornell.edu/supct/.
First Amendment Center—Press.http://www.fac.org/press/press97.htm.

This statute . . . raises questions of grave importance transcending the local interests involved in the particular action. It is no longer open to doubt that the liberty of the press and of speech is within the liberty safeguarded by the due process clause of the Fourteenth Amendment from invasion of state action.

In fact, said Hughes, "it is the chief purpose of the guaranty [of a free press] to prevent previous restraints upon publication." The ban on prior restraint goes right to the heart of the First Amendment.

Speaking for the four dissenters, Butler argued otherwise. In his view, the majority's decision would put unprecedented restrictions on states, which had traditionally used their police powers to promote public welfare. Prohibiting publication of scandalous or defamatory claims such as those allegedly published by the *Saturday Press* surely fell within this purview.

The view of the majority in *Near*, however, was quickly adopted by the American people. The principle it set forth has prevented journalists from being censored by politicians and prosecutors and, in fact, permitted the press to act as a public watchdog. There is a straight line connecting J. M. Near's criticism of police corruption in Minneapolis in the 1930s to the *New York Times*'s publication of the "Pentagon Papers" in 1971. Had it not been for *Near v. Minnesota*, the American people might never have learned the truth about the federal government's undertaking of the war in Vietnam.

Related Cases

Adkins v. Children's Hospital, 261 U.S. 525 (1923).
Gitlow v. New York, 268 U.S. 625 (1925).
Whitney v. California, 274 U.S. 357 (1927).
Stromberg v. California, 283 U.S. 359 (1931).
New York Times v. United States, 403 U.S. 713 (1971).

Bibliography and Further Reading

Blanchard, Margaret A. *Revolutionary Sparks: Freedom of Expression in Modern America.* New York, NY: Oxford University Press, 1992.

Johnson, John W., ed. *Historic U.S. Court Cases, 1690-1990: An Encyclopedia.* New York: Garland Publishing, 1992.

Levy, Leonard Williams. *Emergence of a Free Press.* New York, NY: Oxford University Press, 1985.

Murphy, Paul L. *The Shaping of the First Amendment, 1791 to the Present.* New York, NY: Oxford University Press, 1992.

GROSJEAN V. AMERICAN PRESS CO.

Legal Citation: 297 U.S. 233 (1936)

Appellant
Alice Lee Grosjean, Supervisor of Public Accounts for the State of Louisiana

Appellee
American Press Co.

Appellant's Claim
That a state law imposing an advertising sales tax on large-circulation newspapers violates the principle of freedom of the press.

Chief Lawyers for Appellant
Charles J. Rivet and Gaston L. Porterie

Chief Lawyers for Appellee
Esmond Phelps and Elisha Hanson

Justices for the Court
Louis D. Brandeis, Pierce Butler, Benjamin N. Cardozo, Charles Evans Hughes, James Clark McReynolds, Owen Josephus Roberts, Harlan Fiske Stone, George Sutherland (writing for the Court), Willis Van Devanter

Justices Dissenting
None

Place
Washington, D.C.

Date of Decision
10 February 1936

Decision
The Supreme Court struck down the Louisiana tax.

Significance
Although the Supreme Court subsequently ruled that the press is subject to various types of nondiscriminatory economic regulation, in *Grosjean*, it made clear its condemnation of any attempt at prior restraint of the press that posed as taxation.

In 1934, the state of Louisiana passed an act imposing a license tax for the privilege of selling advertising. The tax applied only to newspapers with a circulation of more than 20,000 copies per week. Of the 163 newspapers published in the state at the time, only 13 fit this description, and all 13 were vocal opponents of the policies of former Louisiana Governor Huey Long, who had fostered the licensing tax. When the District Court of the United States for the Eastern District of Louisiana upheld the tax, the publishers of the 13 large-circulation papers brought suit against the state tax supervisor in the U.S. Supreme Court.

Court Strikes Down Tax As Unconstitutional Prior Restraint

The Supreme Court unanimously declared that the tax was a violation of the First Amendment guarantee of freedom of the press, which was applicable to state governments because of the Due Process Clause of the Fourteenth Amendment. The purpose of the tax, said the Court, was not to raise revenue for Louisiana, but to silence criticism of state government. In this, the license tax resembled certain "taxes on knowledge" imposed by the British Parliament in the eighteenth century on newspapers critical of the Crown. The knowledge taxes, noted the Court, were one of the sparks that set off the Revolutionary War:

> [T]hese taxes constituted one of the factors that aroused the American colonists to protest against taxation for the purposes of the home government . . . the revolution really began when, in 1765, that [British] government sent stamps for newspaper duties to the American colonies . . . in the adoption of the English newspaper stamp tax and the tax on advertisements, revenue was of subordinate concern . . . the dominant and controlling aim was to prevent, or curtail the opportunity for, the acquisition of knowledge by people in respect of their governmental affairs.

Taxes on knowledge, like the Louisiana license tax, were imposed on those newspapers with the widest readership. Both taxes resulted in what amounted to state-sponsored censorship.

Pro and Con: Taxing Newspapers

Special taxes imposed upon newspapers by state or federal governments may be unconstitutional. Newspapers are subject to taxes, as are any other type of business. Some states assert a right to impose an additional tax, applicable only to newspapers. For example, in Louisiana a 1934 law imposed a tax upon newspapers that sold over 20,000 copies per week. The tax was connected to the gross revenue the newspaper received from advertisements.

This sort of taxation, uniquely applied to newspapers, has a long history of misuse in this country. The British crown tried to restrict American colonists' freedom of press by imposing such a tax with the Stamp Act. The First Amendment prohibits the government from imposing restrictions upon the press, and this sort of tax is clearly designed for that purpose. The U.S. Supreme Court ruled this sort of tax unconstitutional.

Source(s): Cornell. http://supct.law.cornell.edu/supct/.

The prohibition on prior restraint of the press thus became one of the building blocks of the American democracy, enshrined in the First Amendment. One of the primary targets of the First Amendment was such "odious methods" of government censorship as discriminatory taxes on the press, clearly intended to prevent free public discussion of matters pertinent to the exercise of individual rights.

Louisiana's once governor, Huey P. Long, has been called a democrat and a demagogue, a populist and a fascist. Even after he left the governorship in 1930 to assume a seat in the U.S. Senate, Long continued to use his political machine to control the executive, legislative, and judicial branches of Louisiana government. His policy was "the end justifies the means," and he used it to rationalize his nearly dictatorial use of the legislature to achieve his political ends. For many, he bore a strong resemblance to the absolute monarchs whose arbitrary exercise of power had so alienated the American colonists. After Long was assassinated in 1935, Robert Penn Warren wrote a novel based on his career called *All the King's Men* (1946).

After *Grosjean*, the Supreme Court upheld other, nondiscriminatory taxation of newspapers. What the Court made clear in the earlier case, however, is that abuses of power—in *Grosjean* the legislative taxing power—intended to circumvent the First Amendment will not be tolerated at the federal or the state level. The founding fathers framed their intolerance of such abuses in clear language when they wrote: "Congress shall make no law . . . abridging the freedom of speech, or of the press."

Related Cases
Minneapolis Star and Tribune Company v. Minnesota Commissioner of Revenue, 460 U.S. 575 (1983).

Bibliography and Further Reading
Bollinger, Lee C. *Images of a Free Press*. Chicago, IL: University of Chicago Press, 1991.

Schwartz, Bernard. *Freedom of the Press*. New York, NY: Facts on File, 1992.

Warren, Robert Penn. *All the King's Men*. New York, NY: Harcourt, Brace, 1946.

Huey Long, 1933. © Corbis-Bettmann.

LOVELL V. CITY OF GRIFFIN

Legal Citation: 303 U.S. 444 (1938)

Petitioner
Alma Lovell

Respondent
City of Griffin, Georgia

Petitioner's Claim
A city ordinance prohibiting distribution of any kind of literature within the city limits without permission of the city manager violates the First and Fourteenth Amendments.

Chief Lawyer for Petitioner
O. R. Moyle

Chief Lawyers for Respondent
Hughes Spalding and Sumter M. Kelley

Justices for the Court
Hugo Lafayette Black, Louis D. Brandeis, Pierce Butler, Charles Evans Hughes (writing for the Court), James Clark McReynolds, Stanley Forman Reed, Owen Josephus Roberts, Harlan Fiske Stone

Justices Dissenting
None (Benjamin N. Cardozo did not participate)

Place
Washington, D.C.

Date of Decision
28 March 1938

Decision
The city ordinance was invalidated on its face under the First Amendment, and the defendant's conviction was reversed.

Significance
This decision made it clear that municipalities could not enact ordinances prohibiting the distribution of literature on public streets at all times, at all places, and under all circumstances without the city's permission. Such an ordinance was an unconstitutional censorship or prior restraint upon First Amendment freedoms. The decision also made clear that a facially unconstitutional ordinance could be ignored. The defendant was not required to apply for a permit before challenging the ordinance in court. This decision limited the scope of local governments' power to regulate the distribution of literature in public places that previously had been taken for granted.

Printed publications, including pamphlets, leaflets, and handbills, have been historic weapons in the defense of liberty. They have been used in the United States since pre-Revolutionary times to disseminate information to the public, including controversial and unpopular political, social, and religious ideas. For years legislatures, local authorities, and the courts have grappled with claims of the right to disseminate ideas in public places as against claims of an effective power in government to keep the peace and to protect other interests of a civilized community. Beginning in the 1930s, the Jehovah's Witnesses became involved in a lengthy series of Supreme Court decisions expanding the rights of religious proselytizers and other advocates to use the streets and parks to broadcast their ideas.

In 1938, a Jehovah's Witness, Alma Lovell, was charged in a Georgia state court with violating a city ordinance requiring written permission from the city manager to distribute "circulars, handbooks, advertising or literature of any kind" within the city limits. Under the ordinance, distributing literature without permission was deemed a nuisance and was punishable as an offense against the city. Lovell violated the ordinance by distributing, without prior permission, a religious pamphlet and magazine setting forth the gospel of the "Kingdom of Jehovah." Lovell had not applied for a permit because she regarded herself as sent "by Jehovah to do His work" and considered that applying for permission would be "an act of disobedience to His commandment."

At trial Lovell moved to dismiss it the charge, contending that the ordinance abridged the freedom of the press and prohibited the free exercise of her religion in violation of the First Amendment to the U.S. Constitution. As a result, the ordinance also violated the Fourteenth Amendment, which prohibited states from denying U.S. citizens the fundamental personal rights and liberties protected under the Constitution. According to the Lovell, the ordinance abridged the freedom of the press because it absolutely prohibited distribution of any kind of literature within the city limits without the city manager's permission. The Lovell also claimed that the ordinance prohibited the free exercise of religion by prohibiting her from distributing literature about her religion. Lovell was convicted and sentenced to a $50 fine or 50 days in jail if the fine was not paid. The superior court of the county refused her petition for review. The Georgia Court of Appeals overruled the defendant's objections, sustained the constitutional validity of the ordinance, and affirmed the judgment of the superior court. The Supreme Court of Georgia subsequently denied an application for *certiorari,* and an appeal was made to the U.S. Supreme Court.

A Substantial Federal Question

The U.S. Supreme Court accepted the case after determining that the appeal presented a substantial federal question within its jurisdiction. The question that the Court found adequately presented was whether the ordinance violated the freedom of speech and of the press. The Court decided not to review the issue of free exercise of religion because the issue had been previously presented to the Court and dismissed for want of a substantial federal question in *Coleman v. City of Griffin.*

Ordinance Is Unconstitutional Prior Restraint

In an opinion authored by Chief Justice Hughes, the Supreme Court ruled that the ordinance was unconstitutional on its face and reversed Lovell's conviction. By ruling that the ordinance was unconstitutional "on its face," the Court limited its analysis to the language used in the ordinance, i.e., the "face" of the ordinance, and did not consider how the ordinance was applied. The Court ruled that, because the ordinance prohibited distribution of any kind of literature in any manner, at any place, and at any time without a permit from the city manager, the ordinance was an unconstitutional prior restraint in violation of the First Amendment. Previous Supreme Court decisions had upheld the power of local authorities to vest in a single official the discretion to issue permits or licenses, including a permit to speak in a public commons (*Davis v. Massachusetts* [1897]). This decision placed some limits on this power.

Before looking at the ordinance itself, the Supreme Court set forth two legal principles: (1) that freedom of speech and freedom of the press, protected under the First Amendment from infringement by Congress, are among the fundamental personal rights and liberties which are protected by the Fourteenth Amendment from invasion by state action; and, (2) that municipal ordinances adopted under state authority constitute state action and are within the prohibition of the Fourteenth Amendment.

The Supreme Court next reviewed the language of the ordinance and concluded that, "The ordinance in its broad sweep prohibits the distribution of 'circulars, handbooks, advertising, or literature of any kind.' It manifestly applies to pamphlets, magazines, and periodicals . . . The ordinance embraces 'literature' in the widest sense." The Court also concluded that the ordinance was ". . . comprehensive with respect to the method of distribution. It covers every sort of circulation 'either by hand or otherwise.' There is thus no restriction in its application with respect to time or place."

The Court pointed out that there was no language in the ordinance suggesting that the city was concerned with literature that was obscene or offensive to public morals or that advocated unlawful conduct. There was also no language suggesting that the ordinance was concerned with distribution methods that might be regarded as "inconsistent with the maintenance of public order, or as involving disorderly conduct, the molestation of inhabitants, or the misuse or littering of the streets." According to the Court, the ordinance prohibited the distribution of "literature of any kind at any time, at any place, and in any manner without a permit from the city manager."

Because of the unrestrained reach of its language, the Court found the ordinance invalid on its face. The Court concluded that, regardless of the reasons the city had for adopting the ordinance, "its character is such that it strikes at the very foundation of the freedom of the press by subjecting it to license and censorship." Viewing the struggle for the freedom of the press from an historical perspective, the Court stated,

> [t]he struggle for the freedom of the press was primarily directed against the power of the licensor. It was against that power that John Milton directed his assault by his 'Appeal for the Liberty of Unlicensed Printing.' And the liberty of the press became initially a right to publish 'without a license what formerly could be published only with one.' While this freedom from previous restraint upon publication cannot be regarded as exhausting the guaranty of liberty, the prevention of that restraint was a leading purpose in the adoption of the constitutional provision.

According to the Court, enforcing the ordinance would "restore the system of license and censorship in its baldest form."

'Press' Includes Pamphlets

The fact that Lovell was distributing pamphlets, rather than newspapers or periodicals was irrelevant to the Court. Since the "press" connotes every sort of publication that affords a vehicle of information and opinion, liberty of the press necessarily embraces pamphlets and leaflets. The fact that the ordinance regulated only distribution and not publication also could not save it. Liberty of press includes by necessity liberty to circulate as well as publish. Without circulation, publication would be of little value. In view of the facial unconstitutionality of the ordinance, the Court concluded its opinion by ruling that defendant was not required to apply for a permit under the ordinance in order to challenge the ordinance in answer to the charge against her.

Impact

This decision was the first in a long line of Supreme Court cases that struck down city ordinances requiring prior permission of an official in order to distribute literature within the limits of that city. The following year, in *Schneider v. State* (1939), the Supreme Court invalidated three of four ordinances from New Jersey, California, Wisconsin, and Massachusetts, each forbidding distribution of leaflets. Between 1938 and 1955, Jehovah's Witnesses alone won numerous U.S. Supreme Court cases based on claims that their freedom of speech, press, assembly, or worship were violated by laws and ordinances regulating, among other things, distribution and sales of literature, peddling, charitable solicitations, preaching in public parks, door bell ringing, and the use of "fighting words." As late as 1985, in *Lowe v. SEC*, the reasoning of *Lovell* was used by the Supreme Court in deciding whether an injunction against the publication of an investment newsletter was an unconstitutional prior restraint.

Related Cases

Davis v. Massachusetts, 167 U.S. 43 (1897).

Near v. Minnesota, 283 U.S. 697 (1931).

Coleman v. City of Griffin, 302 U.S. 636 (1937).

Hague v. C.I.O., 307 U.S. 496 (1939).

Schneider v. State, 308 U.S. 147 (1939).

Cantwell v. Connecticut, 310 U.S. 296 (1940).

Cox v. New Hampshire, 312 U.S. 569 (1941).

Jamison v. Texas, 318 U.S. 413 (1943).

Everson v. Board of Education of Ewing Township, 330 U.S. 1 (1947).

Niemotko v. Maryland, 340 U.S. 268 (1951).

Shuttlesworth v. Birmingham, 394 U.S. 147 (1969).

Lowe v. SEC, 472 U.S. 181 (1985).

Bibliography and Further Reading

Braden, Charles. *These Also Believe.* New York: The Macmillan Company, 1949.

McCoy, Ralph E. *Freedom of the Press, An Annotated Bibliography.* Electronic Ed. CNI/AAUP Project, Library Affairs, SIUC. 10 January 1995. http://www.lib.siu.edu

Owen, Ralph D., "Jehovah's Witnesses and Their Four Freedoms," *University of Detroit Law Journal,* March, 1951.

NEW YORK TIMES COMPANY V. UNITED STATES

Legal Citation: 403 U.S. 713 (1971)

Petitioner
United States

Respondent
The New York Times Company

Petitioner's Claim
That the government's efforts to prevent the *New York Times* from publishing certain Vietnam War documents known as the "Pentagon Papers" were justified because of the interests of national security.

Chief Lawyers for Petitioner
Alexander M. Bickel, William E. Hegarty

Chief Lawyers for Respondent
Daniel M. Friedman, Erwin N. Griswold, Robert C. Mardian

Justices for the Court
Hugo Lafayette Black (writing for the Court), William J. Brennan, Jr., William O. Douglas, Thurgood Marshall, Potter Stewart, Byron R. White

Justices Dissenting
Harry A. Blackmun, Warren E. Burger, John Marshall Harlan II

Place
Washington, D.C.

Date of Decision
30 June 1971

Decision
The government cannot restrain the *New York Times* from publishing the Pentagon Papers.

Significance
In *New York Times Company v. United States*, the Supreme Court held that the government must meet a heavy burden of justification before it can restrain the press from exercising its First Amendment right to publish.

In the spring of 1971, the Vietnam War was still raging despite the fact that popular opinion was against President Richard Nixon's administration's efforts to keep the United States in the conflict. Opposition to the war spread throughout the armed forces themselves and into what has been called the military-industrial complex. This opposition sentiment affected one man in particular, a former employee of the U.S. Department of Defense who had also worked for the Rand Corporation, an important military contractor. His name was Daniel Ellsberg.

Ellsberg and a friend, Anthony Russo, Jr., stole a copy of a massive, 47-volume study prepared by the Department of Defense titled "History of U.S. Decision-Making Process on Vietnam Policy." The study had more than 3,000 pages, supplemented with 4,000 more pages of source documents. Ellsberg and Russo also stole a one-volume study titled "Command and Control Study of the Gulf of Tonkin Incident," prepared in 1965. These studies were essentially a massive history of American involvement in Vietnam since World War II, and were classified "TOP SECRET-SENSITIVE" and "TOP SECRET" respectively.

Ellsberg and Russo passed these studies on to two newspapers, the *New York Times* in New York City and the *Washington Post* in Washington, D.C. Neither paper was involved in the theft of government documents. In its Sunday, 13 June 1971 edition, the *Times* began a series of articles containing excerpts from the studies, which were dubbed the "Pentagon Papers." The *Times* published more articles on 14 and 15 June.

The Government Moves to Stop the Leak

On 15 June 1971 the government asked the U.S. District Court for the Southern District of New York to restrain the *Times* from publishing any more of the Pentagon Papers. The court refused to issue an injunction against the *Times* but did grant a temporary restraining order against the *Times* while the government prepared its case. On June 18, the *Post* also published portions of the Pentagon Papers, and the government promptly began proceedings in the District of Columbia to restrain that paper as well. The focus of the Pentagon Papers dispute, however,

---

The Pentagon Papers

The Pentagon Papers was a voluminous study secretly conducted for the U.S. Defense Department, from 1967 to 1969. Its official name was the *History of the U.S. Decision-Making Process on Viet Nam Policy.* This classified document was highly critical of the policies employed by the United States in Southeast Asia, which subsequently contributed to the Vietnam War.

In 1971, Daniel Ellsberg released the study to the *New York Times,* which along with the *Washington Post* began publishing portions of the material through a series of articles. Citing national security issues, the U.S. Department of Justice ordered the papers to cease publication of the material. However, this edict was overturned by the U.S. Supreme Court asserting that

Freedom of the Press rights overrode national security interests.

Circulation of *The Pentagon Papers* in the newspapers resumed. Later in 1971, the study was organized and published in book form. Daniel Ellsberg, the individual responsible for release of the information, was indicted on charges of theft, espionage, and conspiracy. These charges were ultimately dropped after the discovery that some of President Richard Nixon's staff had broken into Ellsberg's psychiatrist's office.

Source(s): Cornell. http://supct.law.cornell.edu/supct/ Grolier Electronic Publishing, Inc., 1995.

---

remained with the legal proceedings against the *Times* in New York City.

On 18 June 1971 the district court held a hearing. The government presented five experts on national security, who testified that publication of the Pentagon Papers would compromise the war effort. The next day, district court Judge Murray I. Gurfein issued his decision, in which he again refused to issue an injunction against the *Times:*

> I am constrained to find as a fact that the . . . proceedings at which representatives of the Department of State, Department of Defense and the Joint Chiefs of Staff testified, did not convince this Court that the publication of these historical documents would seriously breach the national security. It is true, of course, that any breach of security will cause the jitters in the security agencies themselves and indeed in foreign governments who deal with us . . . Without revealing the content of the testimony, suffice it to say that no cogent reasons were advanced as to why these documents except in the general framework of embarrassment previously mentioned, would vitally affect the security of the Nation.

Gurfein did, however, prevent the *Times* from publishing any more of the Pentagon Papers while the government hurried to file its appeal with the U.S. Court of Appeals for the Second Circuit (which covers New York). Once the appeal was filed, Circuit Judge Irving R. Kaufman continued the temporary restraint against the *Times* until the government could argue its case, which happened 22 June 1971. Usually, only three circuit judges hear an appeal, but in an unusual procedure all eight second circuit judges were on the bench

that day. They listened to the government's claim that the Pentagon Papers' release would hurt national security, and the *Times'* defense that the First Amendment protected its publication of the excerpts.

The next day, 23 June, the appeals court refused to give the government the injunction it wanted. On 24 June, the government filed a petition with the Supreme Court. On 25 June, the Court ordered the government and the *Times* to appear before the Court in Washington on the 26 June for a hearing.

Supreme Court Throws Out Government's Case

The Pentagon Papers' case was a litigation whirlwind, beginning on 15 June 1971 and ending just over two weeks later, after having traveled through three courts, when the Supreme Court issued its decision on 30 June 1971. By 6-3 vote, the Court slammed the door shut on the government's attempt to stop the *Times* from publishing the Pentagon Papers, with Justice Black stating:

> In seeking injunctions against these newspapers and in its presentation to the Court, the Executive Branch seems to have forgotten the essential purpose and history of the First Amendment . . .

> Yet the Solicitor General argues . . . that the general powers of the Government adopted in the original Constitution should be interpreted to limit and restrict the specific and emphatic guarantees of the Bill of Rights . . . I can imagine no greater perversion of history. Madison and the other Framers of the First Amendment, able men that they were, wrote in language they earnestly believed could never be misun-

derstood: "Congress shall make no law . . . abridging the freedom . . . of the press . . ." Both the history and language of the First Amendment support the view that the press must be left free to publish news, whatever the source, without censorship, injunctions, or prior restraints.

Not only did the Court reject the government's national security argument, but it criticized in no uncertain terms the Nixon administration's attempt to subvert the First Amendment. The role of the federal courts in the division of powers set up by the Constitution, namely as the judicial branch of government charged with the responsibility of protecting individual rights, was also reaffirmed:

> Our Government was launched in 1789 with the adoption of the Constitution. The Bill of Rights, including the First Amendment, followed in 1791. Now, for the first time in the 182 years since the founding of the Republic, the federal courts are asked to hold that the First Amendment does not mean what it says, but rather means that the government can halt the publication of current news of vital importance to the people of this country.

Chief Justice Burger and Justices Blackmun and Harlan dissented, arguing that the Court should defer to the executive branch's conclusion that the Pentagon Papers leak threatened national security.

The Court also dismissed the government's legal actions against the post. The Pentagon Papers proceedings were not over yet, however. The government obtained a preliminary indictment against Ellsberg on 28 June 1971 for violating criminal laws against the theft of federal property. More formal indictments came against Ellsberg, and Russo as well, on 30 December 1971. In addition to theft, the government charged Ellsberg and Russo with violations of the federal Espionage Act.

Government Thwarts Own Prosecution of Ellsberg

The criminal prosecution involved 15 counts of theft and espionage against Ellsberg and Russo. Ellsberg faced a possible 105 years in prison and $110,000 in fines if convicted. Russo faced a possible 25 years in prison and $30,000 in fines if convicted. The two men were tried in the U.S District Court for the Central District of California, which includes Los Angeles, where they were alleged to have stolen the Pentagon Papers.

The judge was William Matthew Byrne, Jr. Pretrial procedural activities stalled the trial for over three months, but jury selection finally began in June of 1972. It took until July for a jury to be formed and the trial to begin, but the trial was halted almost immediately after it began when it was revealed that the government had been secretly taping the defendants' confidential communications. Supreme Court Justice Douglas, who was responsible for hearing emergency appeals from the Ninth Circuit, which includes Los Angeles, ordered the trial halted until October.

In fact, it was not until 17 January 1973 that the Ellsberg and Russo trial resumed. A whole new jury had to be selected. Further, the case was now overshadowed by the Watergate scandal. On 3 September 1971 G. Gor-

Daniel Ellsberg, 1971.
© AP/Wide World Photos.

don Liddy and E. Howard Hunt, Jr. led a group of Cuban exiles in a break-in of the offices of Dr. Lewis Fielding, which were located in Beverly Hills, California. Fielding was Ellsberg's psychoanalyst, and the White House-sponsored break-in team was hoping to discover the identity of other Ellsberg accomplices from Fielding's files. The break-in was a total failure: there was nothing in Fielding's files.

When news of the government-sponsored bugging of the Democratic Party's headquarters in the Watergate hotel and office complex in Washington broke sometime later, it was only a matter of time before the special Watergate prosecutors learned of the Fielding break-in. This information was publicly revealed 26 April 1973, after the Ellsberg and Russo trial had been dragging on for months without any sign of an imminent conclusion.

At first, Byrne did not want to consider dismissing the charges against Ellsberg and Russo. The government had invested a great deal of time and money in the prosecution. Then, after 26 April there were further revelations that the government had been conducting more illegal wiretaps of Ellsberg's conversations than had previously been admitted. In disgust, Byrne dismissed the entire criminal prosecution against Ellsberg and Russo on 11 May 1973.

Byrne's final dismissal of the charges against Ellsberg and Russo ended the Pentagon Papers affair. The significance of the entire episode is embodied in the Supreme Court's rejection of the government's attempt to prohibit the *Times* from publishing the news. Although the government will not necessarily always lose a case based on the alleged interests of national security, under *New York Times Company v. United States* it must meet a heavy burden of justification before it can restrain the press from exercising First Amendment rights.

Related Cases
Schenck v. United States, 249 U.S. 47 (1919).
Near v. Minnesota, 283 U.S. 697 (1931).
DeJonge v. Oregon, 299 U.S. 353 (1937).
Hirabayashi v. United States, 320 U.S. 81 (1943).
Yates v. United States, 354 U.S. 298 (1957).
Roth v. United States, 354 U.S. 476 (1957).
New York Times v. Sullivan, 376 U.S. 254 (1964).
Freedman v. Maryland, 380 U.S. 51 (1964).

Bibliography and Further Reading
Johnson, John W., ed. *Historic U.S. Court Cases, 1690–1990: An Encyclopedia.* New York: Garland Publishing, 1992.

Meiklejohn Civil Liberties Instituted. *Pentagon Papers Case Collection: Annotated Procedural Guide and Index.* Berkeley, CA: Meiklejohn Civil Liberties Institute, 1975.

Salter, Kenneth W. *The Pentagon Papers Trial.* Berkeley, CA: Editorial Justa Publications, 1975.

Schrag, Peter. *Test of Loyalty: Daniel Ellsberg and the Rituals of Secret Government.* New York: Simon & Schuster, 1974.

Ungar, Sanford J. *The Papers & the Papers: an Account of the Legal and Political Battle over the Pentagon Paper.* New York: Columbia University Press, 1989.

BRANZBURG V. HAYES

Legal Citation: 408 U.S. 665 (1972)

Appellant
Paul M. Branzburg

Appellee
John P. Hayes, Judge

Appellant's Claim
That the First Amendment's guarantee of freedom of the press provides the press with a privilege protecting the confidentiality of media sources.

Chief Lawyer for Appellant
Edgar A. Zingman

Chief Lawyer for Appellee
Edwin A. Schroering, Jr.

Justices for the Court
Harry A. Blackmun, Warren E. Burger, Lewis F. Powell, Jr., William H. Rehnquist, Byron R. White (writing for the Court)

Justices Dissenting
William J. Brennan, Jr., William O. Douglas, Thurgood Marshall, Potter Stewart

Place
Washington, D.C.

Date of Decision
29 June 1972

Decision
The Supreme Court ruled against a special First Amendment privilege that would allow the press to refuse to answer grand jury questions concerning news sources.

Significance
The decision in *Branzburg v. Hayes* gave rise to considerable controversy and the implementation of several state laws shielding the press from grand jury inquiry.

Paul Branzburg, a reporter with the *Louisville Courier-Journal,* was subpoenaed to appear before a grand jury to testify about his story concerning the manufacture of hashish. He appeared, but he refused to answer questions about the individuals who had supplied him with information for his story. Branzburg's sources agreed to talk to the reporter only with the understanding that Branzburg would not reveal their identities. Citing a state reporters' privilege law and the First Amendment, Branzburg refused to obey an order issued by Kentucky trial court judge J. Miles Pound (the respondent in this case, John J. Hayes, was Pound's successor) that required the reporter to answer the grand jury's questions. When the Kentucky Court of Appeals denied Branzburg's petition to have the judge's order suppressed, Branzburg applied to the U.S. Supreme Court for a review of this decision.

The Supreme Court agreed to consider Branzburg's case (which also concerned a second, similar order to reveal confidential sources) with those of television journalist Paul Pappas, who declined to testify before a Massachusetts grand jury about his piece on the radical Black Panthers group, and Earl Caldwell, a *New York Times* reporter who refused to appear before a federal grand jury in California to testify about his coverage of the Black Panthers. The Court divided sharply on the issue of whether or not the First Amendment affords the press a special testimonial privilege. Writing for the five members who voted against such an interpretation of the First Amendment, Justice White asserted that the press's responsibility to provide evidence of criminal activity to grand juries is no different from that of any other citizen. Justice Douglas, writing in dissent, argued that a newsman has an unqualified right not to appear before a grand jury. Justice Stewart, writing for himself and Justices Brennan and Marshall, assumed a position between these two extremes.

Dissent Proposes Qualified Protection for Confidential News Sources

Justice Stewart's dissenting opinion stressed the importance of confidentiality to the news-gathering process:

> [W]e have held that the right to publish is central to the First Amendment and basic to the

Pro and Con: Naming Media Sources

The issue of journalists' and other media personnels' privilege in not naming sources of information has been tested in cases at the state level and in the U.S. Supreme Court.

The High Court asserted that journalists must appear and testify in response to subpoenas issued by grand juries. In cases of criminal matters, journalists have no greater privilege to withhold critical evidence than any other citizen. If they refuse to cooperate, sanctions or charges of contempt may be imposed. The "public interest" to deal with criminal matters takes priority over privileges protecting journalists' sources.

Journalists have protection against being forced to reveal sources of information under Shield Laws in some states. The media has also used the First Amendment's right to free press in support of withholding identities of sources. Congress also passed a law called the Federal Rule of Evidence 501, that qualifies the circumstances under which a reporter may avoid naming sources.

Source(s): Cornell. http://supct.law.cornell.edu/supct/
West's Encyclopedia of American Law. Volume 2. Minneapolis, MN: West Publishing, 1998.

existence of constitutional democracy . . . A corollary of the right to publish must be the right to gather news. The full flow of information to the public protected by the free-press guarantee would be severely curtailed if no protection whatever were afforded to the process by which news is assembled and disseminated . . . The right to gather news implies, in turn, a right to a confidential relationship between a reporter and his source.

Justice Stewart went on to say that the only way to protect the vital concept of confidentiality is to put limits on the grand jury's subpoena power. He proposed that in order to compel a journalist to appear before a grand jury the government must show: (1) probable cause to believe the journalist has information clearly relevant to a probable crime; (2) that this information cannot be obtained through some other means that is less destructive to First Amendment rights; and (3) a compelling and overriding interest in the information.

Branzburg sparked considerable public debate, and a number of states—taking up Justice White's sugges-

tion that only legislatures could establish a testimonial privilege for reporters—implemented press shield laws. The federal government has never followed suit, however, and nearly twenty years after *Branzburg*, in *Cohen v. Cowles Media Co.* (1991), the Supreme Court once again denied a claim of a special press privilege against compelled testimony grounded in the First Amendment.

Related Cases
Cohen v. Cowles Media Co., 501 U.S. 663 (1991).

Bibliography and Further Reading
The First Amendment Reconsidered: New Perspectives on the Meaning of Freedom of Speech and Press. New York: Longman, 1982.

Fuentes, Annette. "The Subpoena Club: Survey of News Organizations by Reporters Committee for Freedom of the Press." *Columbia Journalism Review.* March-May, 1992, pp. 8-9.

Scarce, Rik. "Confidential Sources." *The Progressive.* October, 1993, p. 38.

COLUMBIA BROADCASTING SYSTEM v. THE DEMOCRATIC NATIONAL COMMITTEE

Legal Citation: 412 U.S. 94 (1973)

Petitioner
Democratic National Committee (DNC) and the Business Executives' Move for Vietnam Peace (BEM)

Respondent
Columbia Broadcasting System, Inc.

Petitioner's Claim
That CBS's refusal to sell advertising time to the plaintiffs for expressing controversial views violated First Amendment rights.

Chief Lawyer for Petitioner
J. Roger Wollenberg

Chief Lawyer of Respondent
Thomas R. Asher

Justices for the Court
Harry A. Blackmun, Warren E. Burger (writing for the Court), William O. Douglas, Lewis F. Powell, Jr., William H. Rehnquist, Potter Stewart, Byron R. White

Justices Dissenting
William J. Brennan, Jr., Thurgood Marshall

Place
Washington, D.C.

Date of Decision
29 May 1973

Decision
The general policy of refusing to sell any editorial advertising time did not violate the First Amendment or the Federal Communications Act of 1934.

Significance
This case set the precedent that broadcasters were not required by the Constitution to accept editorials in the form of ads.

One of the things that sets the United States apart from other countries is the wide range of freedoms its citizens enjoy. Among those freedoms, one of the most precious is the freedom of speech as expressed in the Constitution's First Amendment. This amendment takes away from the U.S. government the authority to tell its residents what to say, how to say it, to whom they can say it, and much more.

Broadcasting, because of its pervasiveness, presented a large problem for the government. Ideas, previously concentrated in smaller, easily controlled areas, were now available to most of the country. There was much debate about how much information should be allowed to be transmitted across the airwaves and through television sets, and how much should be stopped from being communicated at all. The Supreme Court, in the center of this controversy, ruled that one of the purposes of the First Amendment was to allow for uninhibited ideas, allowing truth to ultimately shine through. They took a rather liberal approach to this problem.

Later, the Federal Communications Commission developed the "fairness doctrine," which Congress later legislated into law (and even later repealed). The "fairness doctrine" was to help maintain freedom of speech through the airwaves by requiring broadcasters "to afford reasonable opportunity for the discussion of conflicting views on issues of public importance."

However, with so many different citizens representing so many different views, individual freedoms sometimes clashed. When this happens, it is not always evident—even to the U.S. Supreme Court—in which direction constitutional compliance lies. It is within this problem that the *Columbia Broadcasting System v. The Democratic National Committee* case arose.

In January of 1970, Business Executives' Move for Vietnam Peace (BEM) filed a complaint with the Federal Communications Commission that a Washington, D.C. radio station—WTOP—had refused to sell it broadcast time for a series of one-minute spot announcements that expressed BEM's views on the Vietnam War.

Many broadcasters had a policy of refusing to sell announcement time to individuals and groups for

Is Ad Space/time Public?

Congress conferred considerable power on the Federal Communications Commission (FCC) in decisions involving the airwaves. The FCC's Fairness Doctrine is an important policy applied to issues connected with how much air time must be allotted to allow ample coverage of conflicting points of view. The Doctrine mandates that equal amounts of air time must be provided. It does not, however, force broadcasters to accept any and all advertising and/or editorial pieces.

Neither the FCC, the Communications Act, nor the First Amendment requires broadcasters to provide anyone and everyone access to the airwaves. As with newspaper content, the broadcaster has the right to manage the editorial content of the programming. Advertising and editorial pieces may be refused airtime provided that the duty is met to provide equal representation of controversial issues.

Source(s): www.law.vill.edu/Fed-Ct/Supreme/Flite/opinions/412US94.html

expressing their different views on controversial topics. WTOP—like many other stations—maintained that it already covered important topical issues, including Vietnam, broadly and fairly. Therefore, said the station, it did not have to accept BEMs "paid for" editorials. WTOP demonstrated that it had already broadcast the views of Vietnam policy critics on numerous occasions, and did not need or want the BEM's broadcasts.

BEM challenged WTOP's fairness in regard to Vietnam, but it couldn't muster any evidence demonstrating its claim. In May of the same year, the DNC asked the FCC to rule that, in general, a broadcaster could not refuse to sell advertising to responsible parties for soliciting funds or commenting on public issues. According to the DNC, this was covered by the Constitution's First Amendment, and the Communications Act. After due consideration, the FCC rejected the demands of the BEM and the DNC, stating broadly that WTOP had violated neither First Amendment rights nor the Federal Communications Act of 1934.

The U.S. Court of Appeals for the District of Columbia Circuit, reversed the FCC's decision, saying that, indeed the station's policy of refusing paid editorial advertisements violated the First Amendment as long as the station accepted other forms of paid advertising.

When the U.S. Supreme Court heard this case, Justice Burger ruled that broadcasters were not required by the Constitution to purchase and broadcast editorial advertising, and six other members joined in different points on his opinion. His point was that such an arrangement would not necessarily further the public interest nor the free exchange of ideas because the plat-

form would be weighted towards those who could spend the most for the most amount of editorial advertising time.

Furthermore, he was concerned that such a decision would add to government's control over the content of public debates, and that it could allow the airwaves to be monopolized by people and organizations of one political persuasion, creating, in effect, a true "captive audience." The Court put emphasis on the limited space and time of broadcasting, saying that, "[what] is essential is not that everyone shall speak, but that everything worth saying shall be said."

Justices Brennan and Marshall dissented, saying that since the broadcast media are so pervasive, deciding flatly to deny public access to broadcasting limits and hampers a free and open public debate severely.

Related Cases
Red Lion Broadcasting Co. v. FCC, 395 U.S. 367 (1969). *Miami Herald Publishing Company v. Tornillo*, 418 U.S. 241 (1974).

Bibliography and Further Reading
Franklin, Marc A. and David A. Anderson. *Cases and Materials on Mass Media Law*. The Foundation Press, Inc. 1990.

Lieberman, Jethro K. *The Evolving Constitution*. Random House: 1992.

Seidman, Louis M., Gerald R. Stone, Cass R. Sunstein, and Mark V. Tushnet. *Constitutional Law*. Little, Brown and Company: 1986.

MIAMI HERALD PUBLISHING COMPANY V. TORNILLO

Legal Citation: 418 U.S. 241 (1974)

Appellant
The Miami Herald Publishing Company, Division of Knight Newspapers, Inc.

Appellee
Pat L. Tornillo, Jr.

Appellant's Claim
That the *Miami Herald* did not have to print Tornillo's response to critical editorials published by the paper during his campaign for public office.

Chief Lawyer for Appellant
Daniel P. S. Paul

Chief Lawyer for Appellee
Jerome A. Barron

Justices for the Court
Harry A. Blackmun, William J. Brennan, Jr., Warren E. Burger (writing for the Court), William O. Douglas, Thurgood Marshall, Lewis F. Powell, Jr., William H. Rehnquist, Potter Stewart, Byron R. White

Justices Dissenting
None

Place
Washington, D.C.

Date of Decision
25 June 1974

Decision
The *Miami Herald* did not have to print Tornillo's rebuttal.

Significance
In a unanimous decision, the Supreme Court ruled that the *Miami Herald*'s First Amendment freedom of the press rights would be violated if they were forced to print Tornillo's response.

Prior to becoming a candidate for Florida's House of Representatives in 1972, Pat Tornillo was the Executive Director of the Classroom Teacher's Association. On 20 and 29 September 1972, The *Miami Herald* published two editorials criticizing Tornillo's record as director of the association. Specifically, the paper took issue with a teacher's strike spearheaded by Tornillo in 1968. The first editorial about the strike reprinted in the Court transcripts said in part:

> Call it whatever you will, it was an illegal act against the public interest and clearly prohibited by the statutes. We cannot say it would be illegal but certainly it would be inexcusable of the voters if they sent Pat Tornillo to . . . the House of Representatives.

According to Florida Statute 104.38, known as right to reply, the *Miami Herald* was required to provide Tornillo with equal space in the paper to rebut the criticisms. The editors refused, and Tornillo filed a suit against the *Miami Herald* seeking damages of more than $5,000. The Florida Circuit Court ruled that the right to reply statute violated the First Amendment guarantee to free press because it dictated what newspaper editors must print. Further, the decision stated that even if the right to reply was found constitutional, Tornillo would not be eligible for damages. The Florida Supreme Court reversed on appeal, finding the right to reply compatible with the First Amendment. The state supreme court however, upheld Tornillo's ineligibility for damages.

Appeal Goes to the U.S. Supreme Court

The *Miami Herald* appealed the Florida Supreme Court's reversal before the U.S. Supreme Court on 17 April 1974. Led by chief defense lawyer Jerome A. Barron, the paper argued that the right to reply statute was indeed unconstitutional according to the First Amendment. Attorney Daniel P. S. Paul argued that a strict interpretation of the First Amendment prevented the private individual from responding to press criticism. Whereas the press was easily accessible in 1791 when the amendment was ratified, the trend toward media monopolies in the modern age prohibits common people from par-

"Free Press" Refers to Press Only

The First Amendment guarantees "Congress shall make no law . . . abridging the freedom . . . of the press." While freedom of the press prohibits Congress from imposing restrictions upon the press, it does not guarantee anyone and everyone a forum for his or her opinions. The assurance does not provide for unfettered access by anyone wishing to editorialize. Newspapers were seen as a vital tool of democratic action by the framers of the Constitution. The intention was to prohibit the government from limiting the press in its power of editorial decision making.

At least one state has attempted to infringe upon newspapers' editorial decision making with a statute referred to as a "Right of Reply" law. The U.S. Supreme Court has struck down such statutes as unconstitutional because these type of regulations would allow the government to dictate what must be printed in the newspaper. In order to sustain a free press, the newspapers, not the government, nor the public, must maintain authority over decisions of editorial content, and not be forced to publish opinions that they would otherwise reject.

Source(s): Flite. http://www.law.vill.edu/FedCt/Supreme/Flite/opinions/418US241.htm.
Cornell. http://supct.law.cornell.edu/supct/.
Grilliot, Harold J. and Frank A. Schubert. *Introduction to Law and the Legal System.* Fifth edition. Boston, MA: Houghton Mifflin Co., 1992.

ticipating in public debate. This is mostly due to "economic factors which have . . . made entry into the marketplace of ideas served by the print media almost impossible," the trial transcripts stated. Therefore Paul argued, governmental intervention, such as the right to reply statute, is necessary to ensure a wider debate.

The *Miami Herald*'s counsel embraced Tornillo's argument regarding the need for wider debate as ammunition for their own case. Upholding the right to reply statute, they reasoned, would constrict rather than broaden debate on public issues as newspapers would shy away from controversial topics. In effect, reluctance to critically analyze issues, especially regarding politics and candidates for public office, would overshadow editorial judgment. Moreover, if the government were permitted to enforce the right to reply statute, a precedent would be set for intervening in other editorial decisions. This intervention, the *Miami Herald* pointed out, is exactly what the First Amendment was designed to protect against.

In a unanimous decision written by Chief Justice Burger, the Supreme Court found Florida's right to reply statute unconstitutional according to the First Amendment. In his opinion Justice Burger cited *Associated Press v. United States* (1945) as the first case which addressed government's reluctance to interfere in the affairs of a newspaper. He quoted that forcing a newspaper to print something that "'reason' tells them should not be published" violated free press guarantees. Furthermore, telling the *Miami Herald* what it must print is no different from telling them what not to print. Coupled with this argument was the point that enforcing the right to reply statute would incur printing costs and limit column space, effectively preventing the editors from printing other items that they may deem more important. In conclusion, Justice Burger wrote:

> A newspaper is more than a passive receptacle or conduit for news, comment, and advertising. The choice of material to go into a newspaper, and the decisions made as to limitations on the size and content of the paper, and treatment of public issues and public officials— whether fair or unfair—constitute the exercise of editorial control and judgment.

Although the U.S. Supreme Court decided the right to reply statute was unconstitutional, this does not prohibit public officials from contesting personal attacks printed by a newspaper. The print media is still beholden to libel laws that prevent them from publishing unsubstantiated, slanderous reports. However, Justice White expressed concern in his concurring opinion that proving libel was becoming increasingly difficult. Indeed, in *Gertz v. Robert Welch, Inc.* which was announced the exact day of the *Miami Herald Publishing Company v. Tornillo* decision, the Court disabled most of the protection afforded by the individual against libel. White warned that this was a dangerous development in a world where the power of the media monopoly remains unchecked.

Related Cases
Associated Press v. United States, 326 U.S. 1 (1945).
Gertz v. Robert Welch, 418 U.S. 323 (1974).

Bibliography and Further Reading
Hall, Kermit L., ed. *The Oxford Companion to the Supreme Court of the United States.* New York: Oxford University Press, 1992.

COX BROADCASTING CORP. V. COHN

Legal Citation: 420 U.S. 469 (1975)

Appellant
Cox Broadcasting Corp.

Appellee
Martin Cohn

Appellant's Claim
That a television station, newspaper, or other media outlet has the right to make public the name of a crime victim, if it was obtained through standard access to public documents.

Chief Lawyer for Appellant
Kirk McAlpin

Chief Lawyer for Appellee
Stephen A. Land

Justices for the Court
Harry A. Blackmun, William J. Brennan, Jr., Warren E. Burger, William O. Douglas, Thurgood Marshall, Lewis F. Powell, Jr., Potter Stewart, Byron R. White (writing for the Court)

Justices Dissenting
William H. Rehnquist

Place
Washington, D.C.

Date of Decision
3 March 1975

Decision
Struck down the Georgia statute that permitted the late victim's parent to sue for damages.

Significance
This 1975 ruling settled a case involving a Georgia law that banned news organizations from publishing, airing or otherwise making known the names of victims of sexual assault in conjunction with reporting the crime's prosecution. The High Court determined the law was unconstitutional, in violation of the First Amendment to the U.S. Constitution guaranteeing freedom of the press; it also found it in conflict with the terms of the Fourteenth Amendment guaranteeing the privileges of citizens. With this ruling the Court was tacitly indicating that an ordinary citizen (as opposed to a public figure) has little protection from intrusions by the media under certain circumstances. More significantly, though the High Court struck down a Georgia law that was essentially a holdover from an archaic era designed to protect victims of sexual assault. Several years later there would be a call to revive such statutes after a well-publicized rape case incited a national debate about the naming of victims in the press.

The Circumstances

In 1971 a 17-year-old Georgia high school student named Cynthia Leslie Cohn died of suffocation after being sexually assaulted by six teenaged boys in Sandy Springs. Because of the shocking nature of the crime, intense media coverage was given to the criminal proceedings. When five of the defendants went to trial in April of 1972, Atlanta television station WSB-TV assigned Thomas Wassell to cover the trial. During a court recess, Wassell approached the court clerk, asked to see the indictment against the defendants, and was handed the documents, "in open court," as Wassell noted in his testimony. "Moreover, no attempt was made by the clerk or anyone else to withhold the name and identity of the victim from me or anyone else and the said indictments apparently were available for public inspection upon request." Later that night, on the WSB evening news, Cohn's identity was made public.

In May of 1972, the deceased victim's father, Martin Cohn, brought suit against WSB and its owner, the Cox Broadcasting Corp. At the time, a Georgia law existed that made it a misdemeanor to broadcast or print the name of a rape victim. Other states, mostly in the South, also shielded victims of sexual assault through similar statutes, but most news organizations followed their own code of conduct and did not print or broadcast such information. This was in deference to the trauma the victim had already undergone—with the underlying assumption that to make the victim's identity known might further stigmatize her, and to do so in print or on television served no purpose other than sensationalism.

In his suit against Cox, Martin Cohn claimed that when WSB aired his murdered daughter's name, his family's right to privacy was violated. He requested criminal prosecution of the company on misdemeanor charges and the awarding of damages in compensation for the ensuing emotional trauma. A trial court ruled in Cohn's favor, but postponed the damages segment of the case until a jury trial at a later date. Lawyers for Cox Broadcasting appealed the decision, but the Georgia Supreme Court upheld lower court's decision. In turn, Cox Broadcasting brought legal action challenging the law. It petitioned the U. S. Supreme Court to review the legality of the Georgia statute. The case was

Pro and Con: Publishing Crime Victims' Names

Controversies arise about the publication of a crime victim's name in the print and broadcast media every day.

State laws may prohibit the publication of crime victims' names as a means of protecting individual privacy. They may address print and broadcast media. A statute may even allow for sanctions against the offending party if the law is violated. Individuals seeking redress under such statutes assert a violation of their privacy rights.

The First and Fourteenth Amendment, however, prevent the imposition of such restrictions and fines when the information has been obtained from public records, for example, from court proceedings. As with other issues regarding the maintenance of a spirited press, the Supreme Court supports publication of information obtained from public records, over individuals' privacy rights.

Source(s): Findlaw. http://www.findlaw.com/casecode/
supreme.html

argued before the High Court in November of 1974, and the decision was rendered on 3 March 1975.

At Issue: Privacy

The Supreme Court's acceptance of the case to the docket signified a new willingness to examine issues involving privacy and the media. There were several prior decisions applicable in the *Cox* case. One involved what is known in legal circles as the "Sullivan Standard." In a 1964 U.S. Supreme Court decision on libel, *New York Times v. Sullivan,* the Court asserted that a public person could not claim damages from a media organization for a unflattering news story—unless the plaintiff could first prove it was false, and that the newspaper knew it was false or acted in reckless disregard for the truth. In the *Cox* case, Martin Cohn could not dispute the fact that Wassell, on behalf of WSB, had reported something that was "false," in this case the name of his daughter. Furthermore, the gleaning of Cynthia Cohn's name did not occur under deceptive or otherwise illegal pretenses.

At Issue: Censorship

The crux of the arguments presented by Cox Broadcasting's attorneys involved the right to make the details of criminal proceedings known to the public. It was, of course, permissible for the press to report on just such government proceedings—in the 1947 *Craig v. Harney* decision, Justice William O. Douglas wrote in his opinion that "a trial is a public event. What transpires in the court room is public property." Wassell had learned Cohn's name when inspecting the indictment at the trial court for his story. The indictment was part of the public record, and because it was a public document it was indeed information that any citizen might obtain by going to the prosecutor's offices and requesting to inspect it.

Furthermore, the Supreme Court—as with many of the judicial bodies in the United States—usually backed

away from restricting the freedom of the press in cases not involving libel. The First Amendment, guaranteeing news organizations the right to report on matters of public interest without fear of censorship, was a near-sacrosanct element of the democratic traditions of the United States. According to some legal analysts, to restrict or otherwise punish the media for reporting truthful information (as the Georgia statute did) would incur what was called the "chilling effect." This referred to self-censorship or journalistic timidity should *any* legal constraint bind the media. This, in turn, would diminish the press's crucial role in a democratic society as a disseminator of information.

The Court's Decision

In a 6-1 vote, the High Court overturned the Georgia law that prohibited news outlets from broadcasting or printing the name of a rape victim, deeming it a violation of the First Amendment. Furthermore, it also held that a suit for damages on the basis of invasion of privacy—which Cohn had requested—in this case was not applicable. In his opinion, Justice White wrote that states may not impose laws that interfere with freedom of the press, and that court proceedings, moreover, were an especially protected area of public record. Noting that press coverage of trials was an integral part of the judicial system's fairness, White asserted that he and the other justices

> are reluctant to embark on a course that would make public records generally available to the media but forbid their publication if offensive to the sensibilities of the supposed reasonable man. Such a rule would make it very difficult for the media to inform citizens about the public business and yet stay within the law . . . Once true information is disclosed in public court documents open to public inspection, the press cannot be sanctioned for publishing it. In this instance as in others reliance must

rest upon the judgment of those who decide what to publish or broadcast.

The only dissenting vote in the opinion was from Justice Rehnquist, who wrote that the High Court did not have jurisdiction over the case, in part because the damages suit had not yet made it to court.

Impact

The Supreme Court decision in *Cox Broadcasting Corp. v. Cohn* effectively nullified the Georgia statute, but the issue was far from settled. "[T]he reality of the law," wrote Martin Arnold in the *New York Times* a few days after the ruling, "is such that lawyers who defended newspapers in privacy cases will now bring appeals based on the broader words of the ruling, hoping finally to inch the Court toward absolutely guaranteeing the press the right to print whatever information it wants."

Ironically, the *New York Times* considered the standard-bearer of American journalism, achieved infamy for doing just that in 1991, when it published the name of a rape victim in a highly-publicized trial. This incited a national debate on what became known as the "identity-disclosure" issue. Though there had been great strides in victims' rights legislation since the *Cox* decision, in 1991 it was still standard media practice to keep the names of victims of sexual assault private. This incident launched a court case in which the *Cox* decision was cited, but it was not entirely applicable since the *Times* and other news sources had not obtained the name through open public records.

I'm Not A Blue Blob. I'm A Person.

In the spring of 1991 a member of the Kennedy political family, William Kennedy Smith was accused of sexual assault in Palm Beach, Florida. When the criminal case came to trial later that year, television coverage of the proceedings initially obscured the female victim's face with a blue blob. Then, a local tabloid published her name after a foreign newspaper had done so, under the lurid headline "Kennedy Rape Gal Exposed." Soon, the *New York Times* and a number of other media outlets were publishing her name in their accounts of the case; in one article the *Times* sketched an account of her less-than-storybook life under the headline "Leap Up Social Ladder for Woman in Rape Inquiry." The paper also used the opportunity to disclose many unsavory details about the victim's character, insinuating that she was perhaps less a victim of rape than a publicity-seeking "perpetrator." Then the accuser appeared on a nationally broadcast news magazine to discuss the situation, which left her further open to criticism.

In the case of the Florida tabloid paper that first mentioned the victim's name in the Kennedy trial, that state overturned a law still on the books, as the Georgia one had been, that made it a misdemeanor to publish the name of a rape victim. Some argued that such laws belonged to the past, and to shield victims' identities only further reinforced stereotypes about the crime itself as well as the perceived stigmatization of such victims by society at large. However, in light of the media coverage of the Kennedy trial, many women were of a different opinion. A 1992 survey by the National Victim Center found that 68 percent of 4,000 women polled said that "victims would be less likely to report rapes if they felt their names would be disclosed by the news media"—in other words, perhaps more women who were victims of assault would step forward if they felt a law shielded them, that they would not become part of a sensationalized media event as the woman who had accused Kennedy had become. Writing in *Editor & Publisher*, Bruce S. Ticker opposed any such ban,

---

New Bedford Rape Trial

On 6 March 1983, a gang rape took place in Big Dan's Tavern in New Bedford, Massachusetts. The resulting trial convicted four men of aggravated rape, spurring national debate as to whether a woman's independent or compromising behavior made her partially responsible for sexual crimes committed against her.

The aggravated rape of a 21-year-old mother of two had some questioning why the woman was in the bar in the first place. She had been the only female in the establishment, consuming three drinks and flirting. Two men forcibly raped her on the pool table, two others had attempted to force the woman into oral sex, while two other men were acquitted of cheering and restraining the bartender.

The case attracted national interest of women's groups supporting the victim, while others rallied behind the defendants asserting that the woman should have been at home in the first place. Characterized by Susan Brownmiller, author of the landmark book *Against Our Will: Men, Women and Rape*, as a "public morality play," the trial was broadcast live on CNN, discussed in op-ed pages and homes across America, and monitored daily by both the Coalition Against Sexist Violence and the Committee for Justice (founded to support the accused).

Source(s): Knappman, Edward W., ed. *Great American Trials.* Detroit, MI: Visible Ink Press, 1994.

---

theorizing, "if lawmakers can prohibit the media from making one fact public, could this open the door to more official censorship . . . It would be no surprise if some authorities used a ban to deny reporters unrelated information, some of which even victims-rights advocates might want published to raise awareness about rape." A 1995 Florida law that prohibited the disclosure of victims' identities in the media, part of the Crime Victims Protection Act, was also challenged in court on constitutional grounds.

Related Cases

Craig v. Harney, 331 U.S. 367 (1947).
New York Times v. Sullivan, 376 U.S. 254 (1964).

Bibliography and Further Reading

Editor & Publisher, May 18, 1991, pp. 49-52; May 25, 1991, p. 32; August 13, 1994, p. 48.

Johnson, John W., ed. *Historic U.S. Court Cases, 1690–1990: An Encyclopedia.* New York: Garland Publishing, 1992.

Ms., July/August 1991, pp. 102-103.

New York Times, March 4, 1975; March 6, 1975.

Time, December 30, 1991, p. 61.

Village Voice, December 21, 1991.

TIME, INC. V. FIRESTONE

Legal Citation: 424 U.S. 448 (1976)

Petitioner
Time, Inc., publisher of *Time* magazine

Respondent
Mary Alice Firestone

Petitioner's Claim
That the finding of libel was inappropriate because the respondent was a public figure.

Chief Lawyer for Petitioner
John H. Pickering

Chief Lawyer for Respondent
Edna L. Caruso

Justices for the Court
Harry A. Blackmun, Warren E. Burger, Lewis F. Powell, Jr., William H. Rehnquist (writing for the Court), Potter Stewart

Justices Dissenting
William J. Brennan, Jr., Thurgood Marshall, Byron R. White (John Paul Stevens did not participate)

Place
Washington, D.C.

Date of Decision
2 March 1976

Decision
That Firestone was not a public figure for the purposes of this trial; case remanded to state court for determination of whether defendant was at fault.

Significance
The Court was agreed to accept the principles of the *Gertz v. Robert Welch, Inc.* (1974) verdict of two years earlier, which held that the nature of the person being allegedly defamed, rather than the nature of the issue which the defamation pertained to, would determine whether the plaintiff was a public figure and how much protection he or she was entitled to in matters of libel.

Russell Firestone, scion of a wealthy industrial family, married Mary Alice Firestone in 1961. The couple separated in 1964, and Mary Alice filed a complaint for separate maintenance. Russell countered with a suit for divorce on grounds of extreme cruelty and adultery. The divorce was granted by a Florida Circuit Court judge, whose decision read in part:

> According to certain testimony in behalf of the defendant, extramarital escapades of the plaintiff (Mary Alice) were bizarre and of an amatory nature which would have made Dr. Freud's hair curl. Other testimony, in plaintiff's behalf, would indicate that defendant (Russell) was guilty of bounding from one bedpartner to another with the erotic zest of a satyr. The court is inclined to discount much of this testimony as unreliable. Nevertheless, it is the conclusion and finding of the court that neither party is domesticated, within the meaning of that term as used by the Supreme Court of Florida . . . In the present case, it is abundantly clear from the evidence of marital discord that neither of the parties has shown the least susceptibility to domestication, and that the marriage should be dissolved.

The divorce had attracted a good deal of media attention in Palm Beach, and somewhat less in the national media, but Mary Alice did hold a number of press conferences during the course of the trial. Upon the announcement of the verdict, *Time* magazine ran a short announcement of the divorce in its "Milestones" department, saying that it was granted on the grounds for which it was sought: extreme cruelty and adultery. This was based on a newspaper account, a wire story, and information the magazine received from a stringer and a bureau chief. Mary Alice asked for a retraction, and when the magazine refused, she sued for libel, claiming the divorce was not stipulated on those points.

As is often the case with libel trials, there were several complicating points with the *Firestone* case. One was whether or not the divorce had, in fact, been granted on the grounds for which it was sought. The

Florida Supreme Court called the report a "flagrant example of journalistic negligence," noting that there was no possible way the divorce could have been granted on grounds of adultery, because alimony was granted to Mary Alice, whereas alimony would not be granted under Florida law if a divorce was granted on those grounds. The divorce was granted, however, on the concept of "lack of domestication between the two parties," a concept that heretofore had no basis in Florida law and could have been considered a judicial error. Justice Powell in a concurring opinion and Justice Brennan in a dissent both entertained the idea that the divorce decree was worded ambiguously enough that an interpretation that the divorce was granted on the grounds of adultery was not wholly unreasonable. The Court decided, however, as the two Florida courts had before it, that *Time*'s account was inaccurate.

Another question which the Court addressed was that of fault. Previous Supreme Court rulings had decreed that the media be given some room for understandable and honest mistakes, so that self-censorship not hamper the free communication of information and ideas. Florida law made no mention of fault being necessary for a finding of libel, and the state courts made no mention in their judgments, but freedom of the press being a constitutional issue, the federal criteria overrode the state rules. It was for this reason the case was remanded to the state courts for the matter of fault to be considered.

The issue of fault, however, was contingent upon the matter for which the case was most significant: the question of whether the allegedly libeled individual was a public figure or a private figure. The Court was fragmented in its evaluation of the *Firestone* case—it produced no fewer than five opinions among the eight justices hearing the case—but seven of the eight judges agreed on the answer to this question. Mary Alice Firestone was not a public figure, the Court decreed, and in so doing clarified a point with which it had been struggling for some years.

In 1964, with the *New York Times v. Sullivan* decision, the Supreme Court coined the concept of "actual malice." In what was seen as a victory for freedom of the press, the judgment held that for a libel case against a public official to be won, the offending party must

print false and damaging information with the knowledge of the information's falsity, or with reckless disregard for whether it was true or not. This gave leeway to the press, so that it does not need to constantly second-guess itself for fear of being sued for an honest mistake, but the decision did not explicitly address the question of when these rules would apply, based on the status of the litigants as public or private figures.

In 1967 the Court expanded the New York Times rule to cover public figures, such as celebrities or political activists, who were not public officials. In 1974 with the *Gertz* case the Court did some important fine-tuning of these criteria. It decided that individuals who were well-known enough to have access to the media, and thus the ability to correct erroneous reports adequately, would have to prove actual malice, as would individuals who deliberately thrust themselves into the public eye to influence some public issue. This moved the Court away from a trend in which it was trying to apply the actual malice rules depending on whether a libel case involved a "public issue," hence the shifting of the focus from the issue to the individual. The *Gertz* decision found the Court heavily split, however, and created some doubt as to how future cases would be decided.

The *Firestone* decision, then, unified the Court on this point. The actual malice standard must be met for plaintiffs to receive damages if they are deemed public figures, whereas private individuals may receive damages with merely a finding of fault. *Firestone* was a major step toward clarifying an issue the Court had been wrestling with for a long time.

Related Cases
New York Times Co. v. Sullivan, 376 U.S. 254 (1964).
Gertz v. Robert Welch, Inc., 418 U.S. 323 (1974).
Cox Broadcasting Corp, v. Cohn, 420 U.S. 469 (1975).

Bibliography and Further Reading
Brooklyn Law Review, Summer, 1976, p. 123.

Creighton Law Review, Vol. 10, No. 2, p. 351.

DePaul Law Review, Summer, 1977, p. 863.

*Mercer Law Review,*Vol. 38, p. 809.

NEBRASKA PRESS ASSOCIATION V. STUART

Legal Citation: 427 U.S. 539 (1976)

Petitioner
Nebraska Press Association

Respondent
Judge Hugh Stuart

Petitioner's Claim
The gag order violates freedom of press.

Chief Lawyer for Petitioner
E. Barrett Prettyman, Jr.

Chief Lawyer for Respondent
Harold Mosher, Assistant Attorney General of Nebraska

Justices for the Court
Harry A. Blackmun, William J. Brennan, Jr., Warren E. Burger (writing for the Court), Thurgood Marshall, Lewis F. Powell, Jr., William H. Rehnquist, John Paul Stevens, Potter Stewart, Byron R. White

Justices Dissenting
None

Place
Washington, D.C.

Date of Decision
30 June 1976

Decision
Reversed the gag order.

Significance
The Court decided that allowing the press to report events surrounding the trial would not interfere with the defendant's right to a fair trial.

On 19 October 1975, Erwin Simants was arrested and arraigned in Nebraska for the murders of six members of the Kellie family. The Kellie family lived in Sutherland, Nebraska, a community with only 850 people.

Soon after Simants was arrested, the media, including local, regional, and national reporters became interested in the story. Simants' attorney as well as the prosecuting attorney asked the judge at the Lincoln County Court to issue the "gag order." The two lawyers asked for the order because they both wanted Simants to get a fair trial. If the news media were allowed to publish or broadcast information related to the case, they stated, Simants would not receive a fair trial. This information related to the case included details about a confession Simants made, details about a note Simants wrote on the night of the murders, and aspects of the medical testimony and the alleged sexual assaults of the victims.

The county court granted the "gag order." Several days later, members of the news media including publishers, individual reporters and press and broadcast associations asked the county court to remove the "gag order." The arguments were heard in district court and again, on appeal, in the Nebraska Supreme Court—both upholding the county court's decision to keep the "gag order." In keeping the "gag order" the Nebraska Supreme Court quoted the 1971 case *New York Times Company v. United States* explaining that a "gag order" that restrains publication must be balanced against the importance of a person's right to a fair trial by an impartial jury. The Nebraska Supreme Court decided that there was enough publicity surrounding the Simants case to prevent the defendant from having a fair trial.

It is important to note that the "gag order" would end once the jury had been selected. Even though the case was not heard by the U.S. Supreme Court until after the jury had been selected in the Simants murder trial, the High Court chose to rule on it. The Supreme Court justices were faced with the problem that results from a conflict between First Amendment rights—freedom of the press—and Sixth Amendment rights—the right to a fair trial. America had experienced this conflict several times in its history. Going back as far as when John Adams defended British soldiers who fired

The "Little Lindbergh Law"

Section 209 of the California Penal Code was nicknamed the "Little Lindbergh Law." It was California's version of the Federal Kidnapping Act of 1932, better known as the Lindbergh Law.

The Lindbergh Law, of course, was named after Charles A. Lindbergh, famous for his pioneering solo flight across the Atlantic in 1927. Thereafter Lindbergh enjoyed a degree of admiration and notoriety. When tragedy struck Lindbergh, the world took notice.

Charles, Jr., son of Lindbergh and his wife Anne, was kidnapped and murdered in 1932. Bruno Hauptmann was later caught, convicted, and executed for the crime, but the trial was such a media circus that cameras were banned from courtrooms, a prohibition that would last until the 1970s.

Source(s): *West's Encyclopedia of American Law.* St. Paul, MN: West Group, 1998.

upon a crowd of demonstrators in Boston, the justices knew the power of people's passions to influence. Still, the justices voted against the "gag order" for several reasons. Echoing the eight other justices who voted to reject the "gag order," Chief Justice Burger, delivered the Court's ruling. Burger noted that there is nothing that prohibits the press from reporting on events taking place in a courtroom. He further explained that because of developments in handling the press during the *Hauptmann* case, and in years to come, there were guidelines in place so a judge could handle any problems and a defendant would get a fair trial. He said the Supreme Court's job in the *Nebraska* case was not to write a code but to deal with the legal aspect of the case. Citing many cases, including *Irvin v. Dowd* (1961), *Rideau v. Louisiana* (1963), *Estes v. Texas* (1965), and *Sheppard v. Maxwell* (1977), Burger stated that taken together these cases demonstrate that even widespread pretrial publicity does not lead to a defendant's unfair trial. Therefore, the U.S. Supreme Court ruled to reverse the lower court rulings. The ruling was based on the fact that all nine justices believed Judge Stuart's "gag rule" to be a denial of the news media's rights under the First Amendment to the U.S. Constitution—freedom of the press. The justices further suggested that the news media may even guard against miscarriages

of justice by publishing and broadcasting extensive details about a case.

Related Cases

Near v. Minnesota, 283 U.S. 697 (1931).
Grosjean v. American Press Co., 297 U.S. 233 (1936).
Irvin v. Dowd, 366 U.S. 717 (1961).
NAACP v. Button, 371 U.S. 415 (1963).
Rideau v. Louisiana, 373 U.S. 723 (1963).
Estes v. Texas, 381 U.S. 532 (1965).
Duncan v. Louisiana, 391 U.S. 145 (1968).
New York Times Company v. United States, 403 U.S. 713 (1971).
Miami Herald Publishing Company v. Tornillo, 418 U.S. 241 (1974).
Sheppard v. Maxwell, 384 U.S. 333 (1977).

Bibliography and Further Reading

Chandler, Ralph C., Richard A. Enslen, and Peter G. Renstrom. *The Constitutional Law Dictionary,* Volume 3: *The Sixth Amendment.* Santa Barbara: ABC-Clio, Inc., 1987.

Hall, Kermit L. ed. *The Oxford Companion to the Supreme Court of the United States.* New York: Oxford University Press, 1992.

ZURCHER V. THE STANFORD DAILY

Legal Citation: 436 U.S. 547 (1978)

Petitioner
James Zurcher, Chief of Police of Palo Alto

Respondent
The Stanford Daily

Petitioner's Claim
The Fourth and Fourteenth Amendments did not prohibit third party search warrants, even if the third party is not suspected of a crime, and the First Amendment does not protect newspapers from such searches.

Chief Lawyer for Petitioner
Robert K. Booth

Chief Lawyer for Respondent
Jerome B. Falk, Jr.

Justices for the Court
Harry A. Blackmun, Warren E. Burger, Lewis F. Powell, Jr., William H. Rehnquist, Byron R. White (writing for the Court)

Justices Dissenting
Thurgood Marshall, John Paul Stevens, Potter Stewart, (William J. Brennan, Jr., did not participate)

Place
Washington, D.C.

Date of Decision
31 May 1978

Decision
Reversed a district court's ruling that a state is prevented by the Fourth and Fourteenth Amendments from issuing a search warrant to a third party not suspected of a crime.

Significance
The Court ruled that the First Amendment would not protect newspapers and other media outlets from third party search warrants and that such search warrants were not overly intrusive into the daily operations of newspapers.

What the First Amendment Protects and What the Fourth and Fourteenth Amendments Prohibit

On 9 April 1971, after a telephone call from the director of Stanford University Hospital to remove demonstrators, officers from the Palo Alto Police Department and the Santa Clara County Sheriff's Department responded to the call. The demonstrators had occupied the hospital's administrative offices for a day-and-a half. Once at the hospital, officers were unable to persuade the demonstrators to leave. As officers forced their way into a corridor at the west end of the hospital, demonstrators sprang through the doors at the east end and attacked a group of nine officers with sticks and clubs. All of the officers were injured. The officers were only able to identify two assailants. One officer, however, did see a photographer taking pictures at the east doors. No police photographers were present at the east doors and other possible eyewitnesses such as reporters and bystanders were stationed on the west side.

Two days after the melee, a special edition of the *Stanford Daily*, the university's student newspaper, published articles and photographs on the incident. The byline credit on the photographs was a *Daily* staff member and suggested that he was positioned at the east end of the hospital hallway, which enabled him to photograph the attack on the officers. One day after the *Daily* published the article and the photos, the Santa Clara County district attorney's office obtained a search warrant to search the *Daily*'s offices for negatives, film and pictures of the demonstrations. The warrant made no suggestion that the newspaper or any staff member was involved with the criminal activity at the hospital. Four police officers search the *Daily*'s offices later that same day. Some members of *Daily* staff were present at the time the search was executed. Staff members later claimed that police had gone beyond the limits of the search warrant, which the police officers denied.

A month after the search took place, the *Daily* and several staff members initiated a civil action in the U.S. District Court for Northern District of Columbia seeking declaratory and injunctive relief. The defendants in the suit included the chief of police, the district attorney and the judge who issued the search warrant. The

The Privacy Protection Act

The Privacy Protection Act of 1980 adds further strength to the media's Freedom of Press rights under the First Amendment. Specifically, the act provides guidelines that must be followed by law enforcement officials seeking access to information in the possession of the media. The act imposes parameters upon authorities in connection to searches of newspapers when they are a "third party" to a crime. This means the media may have information pertaining to a criminal activity, but are not directly involved.

In most cases, a search warrant must be obtained first if newspaper staff are not suspected of criminal activity. Certain requirements must be met before a judge will issue a search warrant. There must be "reasonable cause" for the request of a search warrant. He or she must be convinced that evidence is located at the site addressed by the search warrant before issuance. An exception is made for the requirement of a search warrant if there's suspicion of criminal activity by newspaper personnel. Materials may also be seized if authorities have a legitimate belief that evidence may be destroyed, or to prevent death or serious injury to an individual.

Source(s): Cornell. http://supct.law.cornell.edu/supct/ Privacy Protection Act, http://stasi.bradley. edu/privacy/PPA.html

Stanford Daily claimed that the search was unconstitutional because it violated its rights under the First, Fourth and Fourteenth Amendments. The district court denied the request for an injunction, but granted declaratory relief. The district court held that third party search warrants were unconstitutional under the Fourth and Fourteenth Amendments. The court reasoned that when the third party was a newspaper that the First Amendment issues were pertinent and that a search warrant was legal "only in the rare circumstance where there is a clear showing that (1) important materials will be destroyed or removed from the jurisdiction; and (2) a restraining order would be futile." An appeals court affirmed the district court's ruling.

Justice White, writing for the majority, took issue with the district court's analysis of what was constitutional under the Fourth Amendment.

> It is an understatement to say that there is no direct authority in this way or any other federal court for the District Court's sweeping revision of the Fourth Amendment. Under existing law, valid warrants may be issued to search any property, whether or not occupied by a third party, at which there is probable cause to believe that fruits, instrumentalities, or evidence of a crime will be found. Nothing on the face of the amendment suggests that a third-party search warrant should not normally issue.

Justice White reasoned that the whether the third party was suspected of criminal activity was irrelevant. The only issue was whether there was "reasonable cause to believe that the specific things to be searched for and seized are located on the property to which entry is sought."

The district court had also concluded that a search would be "physically disruptive" to newsroom operations; that it could potentially endanger any relationship with confidential sources; that such searches would expose the internal operations of a daily newspaper, and that the press would engage in self-censorship rather than risk certain information being sought by police. White wrote: "Properly administered, the preconditions for a warrant—probable cause, specificity with respect to the place to be searched and the things to be seized, and overall reasonableness—should afford sufficient protection against the harms that are assertedly threatened by warrants for searching newspaper offices." Finally, Justice White reasoned that to obtain a search warrant required meeting certain standards that would eliminate any undue burden to the press.

Justice Stewart in a dissenting opinion joined by Justice Marshall believed that the search of the *Daily's* offices violated the First and Fourteenth Amendments' guarantee of a free press. Justice Stewart agreed with the district court's reasoning that search warrants would place an extraordinary burden on the operations of a daily newspaper. He wrote: "Policemen occupying a newsroom and searching it thoroughly for what may be an extended period of time will inevitably interrupt its normal operations, and thus impair or even temporarily prevent the processes of newsgathering, writing, editing, and publishing." He found the potential breach to confidential sources even more hazardous. "Protection of those sources is necessary to ensure that the press can fulfill its constitutionally designated function of informing the public, because important information can often be obtained only by an assurance that the source will not be revealed." Ultimately, he feared that such searches would result in "a diminishing flow of potentially important information to the public." Justice Stewart concluded that warrants should only be issued when a magistrate finds probable cause and determines that attaining information through the less-intrusive means of delivering a subpoena is impossible. The benefit of a subpoena from the press's standpoint regards the fact that with a subpoena the newspaper would be able to challenge the request before the search was conducted. In situations involving a warrant, the newspaper would not be able to respond until after a search when "the constitutional protection of the newspaper has been irretrievably invaded," Justice Stewart wrote.

Impact

As a direct result of the Court's decision Congress passed the Privacy Protection Act in 1980. It required all law enforcement officers, local, state and federal, to use subpoenas when attempting to gain potential evidence from the media. The only time a search warrant can be used is when there is sufficient evidence to suggest that the materials will be destroyed if a subpoena is issued.

Related Cases

Branzburg v. Hayes, 408 U.S. 665 (1972).

Minneapolis & Tribune Co. v. Minnesota Comm'r of Revenue, 460 U.S. 575 (1983).

Arkansas Writers' Project, Inc. v. Ragland, 408 U.S. 221 (1987).

Leathers v. Medlock, 499 U.S. 439 (1991).

Cohen v. Cowles Media Co., 501 U.S. 633 (1991).

Bibliography and Further Reading

Biskupic, Joan, and Elder Witt. *Guide to the U.S. Supreme Court*, 3rd ed. Washington, DC: Congressional Quarterly Inc., 1997

Corrigan, Don. "Police Try to Seize Tapes Violates Law, Court Rules." *St. Louis Journalism Review*, March 1995, p. 5.

Davis, John E. "Law Office Searches: The Assault on Confidentiality and the Adversary System." *American Criminal Law Review*, Summer 1996, pp. 1251.

Gunther, Gerald and Kathleen Sullivan. *Constitutional Law*, 13th ed. New York: The Foundation Press Inc., 1997.

HOUCHINS V. KQED

Legal Citation: 438 U.S. 1 (1978)

Petitioner
Thomas L. Houchins, Sheriff of the County of Alameda, California

Respondent
KQED, Inc.

Petitioner's Claim
That the news media has no special constitutional right of access to a county jail beyond that of the public to interview, photograph, and sound record inmates and the facility for publication and broadcasting purposes.

Chief Lawyer for Petitioner
Kelvin H. Booty, Jr.

Chief Lawyer for Respondent
William Bennett Turner

Justices for the Court
Warren E. Burger (writing for the Court), William H. Rehnquist, Potter Stewart, Byron R. White

Justices Dissenting
William J. Brennan, Jr., Lewis F. Powell, Jr., John Paul Stevens (Harry A. Blackmun and Thurgood Marshall did not participate)

Place
Washington, D.C.

Date of Decision
26 June 1978

Decision
Upheld Houchins's claim and overturned and remanded [sent back] the two lower courts' findings that the news media has substantially unrestricted access rights to Alameda County Jail facilities.

Significance
The ruling established that although the press has no greater access rights to government information than the public, both the press and public must be provided some degree of controlled access. While the Supreme Court routinely rules on freedom of the press issues regarding publication of information held by the news media, Congress is identified as the proper branch of government to establish limits on press access to government information. Though the press plays a critical role in the democratic system, limitations on news gathering do exist to safeguard certain government activities.

In 1972 District Court Judge Zirpoli found "shocking and debasing conditions . . . [which] constituted cruel and unusual punishment" at the Alameda County Jail in Santa Rita, California. To answer negative press coverage, jail administrators later that year conducted a carefully supervised public tour of selected parts of the facilities normally not accessible. In March of 1975 a prisoner in the Little Greystone portion of the jail committed suicide. A psychiatrist attributed the suicide to the conditions of the facility. KQED, a San Francisco Bay area licensed television and radio broadcasting company, requested permission to inspect and take pictures within the Little Greystone portion of the facility. After the jail refused permission, KQED, joined by others, filed suit in U.S. district court claiming jail authorities violated their First Amendment rights by refusing access to the news media and not providing for any means of public inspection. KQED asserted that television coverage of facility conditions would be the most effective means of informing the public of jail practices. Shortly after KQED filed the lawsuit, Houchins, sheriff of Alameda County, announced a new monthly public tour program through selected parts of the facility, excluding Little Greystone. Media would be treated as public and could not photograph or record within the facility. As in the 1972 tour, inmates were generally kept from view.

The district court ruled in favor of KQED holding that neither KQED news personnel nor other news media representatives could be barred from the jail, including Little Greystone. The district court also ruled that news personnel could use photographic and sound equipment and conduct interviews "at reasonable times and hours." Sheriff Houchins appealed to the U.S. court of appeals which concurred with the district court's ruling by asserting a public and media First Amendment right of access to prisons and jails. Houchins next appealed to the U.S. Supreme Court.

Freedom to Gather News

Founders of the United States strongly believed an informed public was crucial to the proper functioning of a democracy. They considered the press critically important in serving a reporting function. Therefore, the First Amendment prohibits government actions

Talk Radio in the United States

Today, the right to a free and unfettered press includes other print media, as well as broadcasts over radio and television, in movies, and through electronic information. Broadcast media may have more governmental control than the print media, but it still enjoys tremendous latitude in the discretion and choice of programming.

Radio talk show commentators and listeners calling the shows have the opportunity to discuss their opinions on various subjects. Shows offer discussion of current political issues, sports, psychology, and other topics of interest to the public. The ability to verbalize an opinion or subject that is controversial goes to the heart of citizens' First Amendment rights to free press and speech.

Talk shows serving as a forum for political discussion allowing for varying points of view, without government censorship, are another means of sustaining a vigorous exchange of information. This was the original intent of the Constitution's prohibition against government interference with the press. The framers of the Constitution supported the expression of conflicting points of view, even if in opposition to governmental policies. They viewed this as a critical element in a democracy.

Source(s): First Amendment Center—Press, http://www.fac.org/press/press97.htm.
Grolier Electronic Publishing, Inc., 1995.

---

from "abridging the freedom of . . . the press." This "Press Clause" has since served an important social function by ensuring a free flow of information to the general public. With the dramatic growth of the federal government during the 1930s and 1940s, the press assumed an even greater role after World War II in maintaining vigilance over government activities.

Demands for access to government information correspondingly increased beyond that enjoyed by the general public. However, through the 1960s, while the courts established considerable freedom from restraints on the publication of information, they did not so readily recognize such freedom in news gathering. The topic of news media access to government information surged to national prominence in 1971 over controversy related to publication of the Pentagon Papers by the *New York Times* and *Washington Post*. The 7,000 pages of confidential documents revealing U.S. policies toward Vietnam was the subject of *New York Times Company v. United States* (1971). In that case, the Court acknowledged a broad press right to publish information it obtained, while holding the government to a very strict standard in limiting press access to restricted information. Later in the 1970s in the *Pell v. Procunier* (1974) and *Nixon v. Warner Communications, Inc.* (1978) cases, the Court held that no special rights existed for media access to either criminal trials or prisons.

Houchins argued before the Court that broader access by the media would infringe on inmate privacy, create jail "celebrities" who could then generate problems within the jail, disrupt jail operations, and compromise security in general. Houchins noted other means available to inform the public, such as prison mail, personal visitations, and phone calls. Consenting inmates awaiting trial were also available for interview.

KQED countered that the First Amendment guaranteed a special right to gather news including access to government-controlled sources of information, such as interviewing inmates or photographing inside jail facilities. They argued such access was imperative for the public to be informed of governmental actions. KQED stressed the newly instituted monthly tours did not satisfactorily address access issues due to certain imposed restrictions.

Chief Justice Burger, in delivering the 4-3 majority opinion of the Court, referred back to *Pell* in which the Court held, "newsmen have no constitutional right of access to prisons or their inmates beyond that afforded to the general public." Though the role of the news media is important, they could not be granted greater access than the public, contrary to the district court finding. Burger wrote that the First Amendment does not provide a "guarantee of a right of access to all sources of information within government control." More generally, in the *Branzburg v. Hayes* (1972) case, the Court held that "the First Amendment does not guarantee the press a constitutional right of special access to information not available to the public generally." No "unrestrained right to gather information" exists. In fact, Burger highlighted that some forms of governmental information must be withheld from the public so that government may be able to effectively function. Foreign diplomacy and maintenance of effective national defense require confidentiality and secrecy. Without access restrictions, the United States would not be able to maintain mutual trust with other nations and communications would be significantly hampered. Other examples of exclusion include grand jury hearings, and, on occasion, executions and court trials where privacy interests of prisoners, witnesses, jurors, or litigants are important. In many situations it is more appropriately a public official's responsibility to gather and provide information, not the news media's. However, Burger added that *Pell* did not imply that equal access by the public and press could constitute no access. In fact, the level of access should be substantial.

The majority firmly believed limits to access rights are more appropriately a subject for Congress to define. As established in *Grosjean v. American Press Co.* (1936), the focus of the Press Clause is the right to communicate information once it is obtained. Burger also stressed an equal weight is given to the public's constitutional right to receive such information. Burger listed various means the public has to gain information about public penal facilities, including citizen committee reports, prison board inspections, health and fire inspectors, grand jury investigations, inmate letters, lawyer interviews, former inmates, prison visitors, and jail personnel.

The Press Serves the Public

In dissent, joined by Justices Brennan and Powell, Justice Stevens wrote that KQED was entitled to greater access than the public but to some measured degree less than that established by the lower court decisions. He described distinct differences between news media and the public, particularly that the former serves to inform the latter. U.S. society depends heavily on the press. For this reason "the First Amendment speaks separately of freedom of speech and freedom of the press." Stevens also noted the "unique function" prisons "perform in a democratic society [as] . . . an integral component of the criminal justice system." Not only does the public have a right to information regarding a trial, but equally a right in knowing how a convicted person is treated while serving a sentence. For example, Stevens noted the Santa Rita's inmate population is predominantly black and the National Association for the Advancement of Colored People (NAACP) largely depends on the news media to keep informed of their treatment. In addition, an inmate does retain "constitutional protections against cruel and unusual punishment." Therefore, the media should have "a more flexible and frequent basis" of access in order "to keep the public informed." However, access provided by the lower courts findings was too broad. Press access must be more carefully constructed. This concern is particularly relevant for facilities such as Santa Rita where some inmates are detainees awaiting trial and enjoy the same constitutional rights to privacy as common citizens until convicted.

Impact

Despite the Court's shift to a more conservative political orientation in the 1980s and 1990s, including a more restrictive view of constitutional rights, the press enjoyed as much freedom as ever. However, the importance of the *Houchins* case is the finding that the media's right of access to government information is no greater than the public's. Yet many agree with Justice Stevens that since the press serves to inform the public, its access should be greater. The press plays an important role not just in reporting information, but also in sifting through large quantities of information during its research. The Freedom of Information Act (FOIA), passed by Congress in 1988, served to provide public access to considerable amounts of government information. No comparable measure provides access to government facilities, such as prisons.

In regard to prison access, the national media watchdog group Fairness and Accuracy in Reporting (FAIR) focused in part on press censorship issues. FAIR identified three states in 1996 attempting to substantially restrict access of journalists to state prisons. Illinois banned one-to-one interviews with death row inmates. Virginia barred prison tours, photographs, and face-to-face inmate interviews. In addition to an interview ban, California sought to eliminate confidential mail privileges between inmates and members of the media. FAIR asserted that such actions not only gags the mouths of inmates—contrary to their First Amendment rights—but violates the news media's and public's constitutional rights of access as well.

The dispute over media access to government information increased through the 1990s as competition among the media grew. The rise in popularity of sensationalist television tabloid shows also contributed to the push for greater access. There remains no clear principle for courts to apply in determining the appropriateness of access in specific cases. Legal scholars suggested several key principles to safeguard press access rights to government information. The principles involved protecting the news media from: (1) preferential treatment; (2) denial of access where traditionally allowed; and (3) access policy that seems to arbitrarily change without sufficient reason. Some contend that balancing, on a case-by-case basis, the right of press access against government interest in confidentiality, places the Court in undesirable situations as the *Houchins* case demonstrated.

Related Cases

Grosjean v. American Press Co., 297 U.S. 233 (1936).

New York Times Company v. United States, 403 U.S. 713 (1971).

Branzburg v. Hayes, 408 U.S. 665 (1972).

Pell v. Procunier, 417 U.S. 817 (1974).

Nixon v. Warner Communications, Inc., 435 U.S. 589 (1978).

Cohen v. Cowles Media Co., 501 U.S. 663 (1991).

Bibliography and Further Reading

Boylan, James. "Punishing the Press: the Public Passes some Tough Judgements on Libel, Fairness, and Fraud." *Columbia Journalism Review,* March-April 1997, p. 24.

Olson, Tod. "Pentagon Papers." *Scholastic Update.* 12 April 1996, Vol. 128, no. 13.

Rothshild, Matthew. "Barring the Doors." *The Progressive.* September 1996.

Schwartz, Bernard. *Freedom of the Press: Constitutional Issues.* New York: Facts on File, Inc., 1992.

SMITH V. DAILY MAIL PUBLISHING CO.

Legal Citation: 443 U.S. 97 (1979)

Petitioner
Smith, Prosecuting Attorney and Circuit Judges of Kanawha County, West Virginia

Respondent
Daily Mail Publishing Co., et al.

Petitioner's Claim
That two newspapers violated West Virginia state law by publishing, without prior approval of juvenile court, the name of a juvenile charged with a crime.

Chief Lawyer for Petitioner
Cletus B. Hanley

Chief Lawyer for Respondent
Floyd Abrams

Justices for the Court
Harry A. Blackmun, William J. Brennan, Jr., Warren E. Burger (writing for the Court), Thurgood Marshall, William H. Rehnquist, John Paul Stevens, Potter Stewart, Byron R. White

Justices Dissenting
None (Lewis F. Powell, Jr., did not participate)

Place
Washington, D.C.

Date of Decision
26 June 1979

Decision
Affirmed West Virginia Supreme Court of Appeals finding that a West Virginia law prohibiting publication of a lawfully obtained identification of a juvenile offender violated the First and Fourth Amendments.

Significance
The Supreme Court found that two local newspapers could not be prosecuted for publishing the identity of a juvenile defendant. The Court held that if a newspaper obtains truthful information about a matter of public importance then the state can not constitutionally punish its publication, unless the state identifies an exceptional need to restrict the information. The argument of compelling interest to protect a juvenile for future rehabilitation purposes was not considered sufficient by the Court. In fact, the Court held under a "lawfully obtained" standard that states would rarely be able to demonstrate sufficient interest to restrict publication of truthful information. The practice of concealing juvenile offenders' identities was increasingly questioned by the public during a period of rising youth violence in the 1990s.

In February of 1978 a 14-year-old student shot and killed a 15-year-old classmate at Hayes Junior High School in St. Albans, West Virginia. Several eyewitnesses identified the alleged assailant arrested shortly after the shooting. Reporters and photographers for two nearby Charleston newspapers arrived shortly after the shooting to cover the incident. The reporters of both papers obtained the assailant's name at the scene through interviews with witnesses, police, and an assistant prosecuting attorney. The Charleston *Daily Mail* published a news article on the incident that same evening, but did not reveal the alleged juvenile offender's name as directed by state law. The *Charleston Gazette,* however, chose to include the assailant's name in their morning edition the following day. Meanwhile, at least three local radio stations broadcast the name of the assailant on the day of the crime and the following day. With the name of the assailant then public knowledge, the *Daily Mail* included the name in their next evening edition.

Three weeks later a grand jury indictment was issued against both newspapers alleging the papers knowingly published the name of the youth without state-required court approval. In response, the two papers filed a petition with the West Virginia Supreme Court of Appeals to stop legal action claiming the law violated their constitutional rights. The court concurred the state showed no compelling reason that state's interest in protecting the juvenile's identity outweighed the constitutional protections of press freedom. The court thus held the law requiring written permission by a juvenile court judge prior to publishing a juvenile's identity posed a "prior restraint" on free speech. The court thus prohibited the prosecuting attorney and county circuit court judges from pursuing prosecution of the two newspapers. The case was taken by the Supreme Court in 1978.

The newspapers continued their argument before the Supreme Court that state law operated as a "prior restraint" on speech. They considered having to ask permission of a judge an unconstitutional restraint. They also argued "the State's interest in the anonymity of a juvenile offender is not sufficient" to justify the restriction. In contrast, Smith argued that the state's interest in keeping the juvenile's name confidential was sufficient to impose restrictions. The stigma the juvenile would endure for the remainder of his life would significantly hamper rehabilitation measures and greatly restrict future employment opportunities.

Juvenile Protection and State Regulation of the Press

The Supreme Court had previously addressed the specific question of protecting juvenile defendant identities and the larger question of state regulation of the press. The Court ruled in *Oklahoma Publishing Co. v. District Court* (1977) against a lower court injunction barring publication of the name and photograph of an accused juvenile defender in a murder case. Basis for the decision was that reporters and public had been allowed access to a court hearing on the case. The Court held that since the juvenile's identity was already "in the public domain" the lower court could not constitutionally restrict publication. A year later in *Landmark Communications, Inc. v. Virginia* (1978), the Court established standards for assessing when a state's interest outweighs constitutional press protections. In that case, the Court unanimously ruled in favor of the press for publishing information on confidential state judicial review commission proceedings about alleged judge misconduct. The Court held that the state could not criminally prosecute the press for publishing such information, despite its compelling interest in maintaining confidentiality of judicial review.

In assessing the appropriateness of a state's restriction on publication of truthful information by the press, the Court routinely considers a series of questions. First, the state is responsible for demonstrating compelling interest in suppressing publication of certain information. Is the restriction necessary to achieve a specific objective? Secondly, if the Court agrees with the state on compelling interest, it then assesses effectiveness of the restriction. Does it really serve the purpose for which it was intended? Lastly, if the intended purpose is served to at least some degree, is the restriction sufficiently narrow to restrict no more speech than absolutely necessary? To assess this last question, the Court must conceive of different restrictions that would accomplish the same objective while imposing less of a restriction on freedom of speech and press.

In applying these questions, the Court ruled in favor of the two newspapers in a 8-0 vote. Chief Justice Burger, writing for the Court, acknowledged that state law giving prior approval authority to juvenile court judges is "less oppressive" than a total ban. But the Court determined that assessing the constitutionality of West Virginia's state law was unnecessary because the need for withholding the juvenile's identity was not sufficiently demonstrated. The Court considered the law overly "burdensome" because Smith did not

adequately demonstrate other alternatives existed to restrict publication of minors' names rather than resorting to criminal prosecution. Burger added that the West Virginia law was indeed unconstitutional by treating various forms of the press separately. The state law addresses only newspapers, not electronic media or other forms of publication.

Though writing in concurrence, Justice Rehnquist disagreed with the primary findings of the Court. He believed the claim for preserving the identity of the juvenile was sufficient to outweigh freedom of press concerns. He asserted the effect of such restrictions would be "minimal." Rehnquist wrote that the "hallmark of our juvenile justice system . . . [is that] youths . . . have been shielded from publicity." The main objective of the juvenile system is to rehabilitate and protect. He wrote, "Publication of the names of juvenile offenders may seriously impair the rehabilitative goals . . . The press is free to describe the details of the offense and inform the community of the proceedings against the juvenile." He did not see the general need for including names as well. The state law under question allowed a judge to grant permission where it may be warranted. Rehnquist agreed, though, that punishment after publication was likely the primary means for the state to enforce such restrictions. Though disagreeing with the other justices on these points, Rehnquist concluded the law was simply invalid due to its discrimination between electronic and print media.

Impact

Rights granted to the press in the Constitution are unique as the only rights granted to an institution rather than the individual. The Court must balance press freedom from government intervention on one hand, with public interest in privacy and confidentiality on the other, while ensuring the press serves its social role responsibly. Though the Court ruled in *Smith* that publication of truthful information gathered legally is protected by the Constitution, truthful information could be restricted in situations involving substantial state interest to restrict certain publication. In effect, the states find almost insurmountable standards in suppressing truthful information no matter how lawfully obtained. In *Florida Star v. B. J. F.* (1989) the casual mistakes by police clerks led to the continued endangerment of a crime victim because the press published the leaked information. Yet the Court ruled in favor of the press when the victim sued the press for damages. In *Globe Newspaper Co. v. Superior Court for the County of Norfolk* (1982) the Court ruled a state law unconstitutional that excluded the press and public from trials concerning sex offenses against juvenile victims. The Court ruled the restriction did not adequately serve the compelling interest of the state in protecting minors from additional trauma since the effects of press coverage would vary from case to case. Many believed the Court provided the press excessive access and authority to publish sensitive information.

A series of Court findings led to the creation of a rigid "lawfully obtained" standard regarding press publication rights. The standard posed major ramifications in the electronic information era that mushroomed in the 1990s with advanced computer technologies and vast databases. A source for just about any type of information can be discovered lawfully by a diligent reporter, and the Court has liberally judged almost everything as "newsworthy."

Legal scholars argued that more appropriate standards would involve whether the person was a public figure or private individual and a more strict interpretation of newsworthiness. Using these criteria for assessing the appropriateness of news publication could better serve public and privacy protection interests. Opponents to the "legally obtained" standard assert that some rare situations have occurred in which illegally obtained information was legally published for the benefit of the public as decided in the *New York Times Company v. United States* decision. Advocates for the press in support of the "lawfully obtained" standard believe that truth is the ultimate defense for publishing information. Variables, such as judgements regarding the appropriateness of material, they believe are subject to the changing values and personal tastes

of judges. By the late 1990s, several bills aimed at restricting the flow of intimate personal data were considered.

Related Cases

Oklahoma Publishing Co. v. District Court, 430 U.S. 308 (1977).

Landmark Communications, Inc. v. Virginia, 345 U.S. 829 (1978).

Globe Newspaper Co. v. Superior Court for the County of Norfolk, 457 U.S. 596 (1982).

Florida Star v. B. J. F., 491 U.S. 524 (1989).

Bibliography and Further Reading

American Bar Association Juvenile Justice Center. http://www.abanet.org/crimejust/juvjus/home.html

Hindman, Elizabeth B. *Rights vs. Responsibilities: The Supreme Court and the Media.* Westport, CN: Greenwood Press, 1997.

National Center for Juvenile Justice. http://www.ncjj. org

Rubenstein, Bruce. "Truth and Consequences: Is Juvenile Privacy a Necessary Protection or a Gross Injustice to Victim and Offender Alike." *MPLS-St. Paul Magazine.* October, 1995.

The Center on Juvenile and Criminal Justice. http://www.cjcj.org

GLOBE NEWSPAPER CO. V. SUPERIOR COURT FOR THE COUNTY OF NORFOLK

Legal Citation: 457 U.S. 596 (1982)

Appellant
Globe Newspaper Company

Appellee
Superior Court for the County of Norfolk, Massachusetts

Appellant's Claim
That it had the right to attend the rape trial in which the three witnesses claiming to be raped were 16 and 17 years old, despite a Massachusetts state law mandating that all sex-crime trials involving victims under 18 be closed to the public.

Chief Lawyer for Appellant
James F. McHugh

Chief Lawyer for Appellee
Mitchell J. Sikora, Jr., Assistant Attorney General of Massachusetts

Justices for the Court
Harry A. Blackmun, William J. Brennan, Jr. (writing for the Court), Thurgood Marshall, Sandra Day O'Connor, Lewis F. Powell, Jr., Byron R. White

Justices Dissenting
Warren E. Burger, William H. Rehnquist, John Paul Stevens

Place
Washington, D.C.

Date of Decision
23 June 1982

Decision
The Massachusetts state law was too broadly written and was therefore unconstitutional; although states did have the right to occasionally close trials to the press and the public, the laws permitting such closure had to allow for a case-by-case review rather than summarily closing all trials of a certain type.

Significance
The *Globe* case established broad rights of the press to cover trials of all types. However, in 1991, three states passed legislation restricting public disclosure of the identity of rape victims, opening the possibility that the rights of public access to criminal proceedings may again be narrowed.

In 1979, three young women in Massachusetts accused a man of "forcible rape and forced unnatural rape." At the time, two of the girls were 16 and one was 17. The girls had agreed to testify, but, as the prosecutor explained in a lobby conference before the trial, they were concerned about privacy. They were willing to have the press attend the trial, but they wanted guarantees about what would actually appear in the newspapers.

> Each . . . indicated that they had the same concerns and basically they are privacy concerns. The difficulty of obtaining any kind of guarantee that the press would not print their names or where they go to school or any personal data or take pictures of them or attempt to interview them, those concerns come from their own privacy interests, as well as the fact that there are grandparents involved with a couple of these victims who do not know what happened and if they were to find out by reading the paper, everyone was concerned about what would happen then.

Massachusetts state law required that all sex-crime trials involving victims under age 18 to be closed to the public, including the press. But the Globe Newspaper Company did not agree with this law. It moved to have the closure revoked. After a long court battle, the case finally made it to the Supreme Court. Although by then, the trial in question was long over (with the defendant found not guilty), the Court decided that this was an issue that would certainly come up again. Accordingly, the Court decided to review the case in order to set future precedents.

The Right to Privacy vs. the Public's Right to Know

The Court decided to strike down the Massachusetts law in the name of the First Amendment. Justice Brennan, who wrote the majority decision, agreed that some trials could be closed to the public and/or the press. However, as Brennan wrote, the Massachusetts law was simply too broad.

Brennan found two major arguments behind the reasoning for the Massachusetts law: that minors should

Was the Change of Venue Justified?

Judge Richard Matsch, presiding over the federal trial of Timothy McVeigh and Terry Nichols in the Oklahoma City bombing, decided on a change of venue—that is, to move the site of the trial from Oklahoma City to Denver. He believed that the defendants could not receive a fair trial from an impartial jury in Oklahoma City, site of the 19 April 1995 bombing, which killed 168.

From the standpoint of the defense, Matsch's decision was laudable. It was important to create an opportunity for a fair trial, and their defense believed it would have been difficult to find 12 people in Oklahoma City without an opinion about the bombing.

A number of observers, including Jo Thomas of the *Minneapolis Star Tribune*, criticized Matsch's decision. He cited the cost to the federal government of transporting and housing families of victims. Attorney Robert Precht, who represented Mohammed Salameh in the World Trade Center bombing trial, called the change of venue a "mistake." In his view, the people of Oklahoma City "wanted to show that they could be fair in a case like this."

Source(s): Thomas, Jo. "Change of Venue: Is Impartial Jury Possible?," Minneapolis *Star Tribune*, 23 February 1996, p. 8A.

---

be spared the humiliation of having to testify publicly about a traumatic sexual crime, and that more minors would be likely to come forward to report sexual crimes if they knew their privacy would be protected.

Brennan disagreed with the second argument. He pointed out that no one had offered any empirical evidence that protecting privacy did in fact encourage more crime victims to come forward. Moreover, he said, many people are unwilling to face the publicity of a criminal trial, not just victims of sex crimes who are minors. The Massachusetts law had no reason for singling out one type of trial to close on that basis.

Brennan added that the Massachusetts law did not guarantee absolute secrecy about a rape trial. In the *Globe* case, for example, the names of the victims were already in the public record. The press could have published their names even if no reporters had been allowed at the trial. Likewise, the press would have had access to the trial transcripts and could have published what it wished of their testimony. If victims were worried about publicity, the Massachusetts law would not allay their concerns; therefore, the law was restrictive for no good reason.

Protecting Minors from Trauma

Brennan was sympathetic with the wish to protect young victims of sex crimes from further trauma. But he said that a law more "narrowly tailored" was needed. "Although the right of access to criminal trials is of constitutional stature, it is not absolute," he wrote. "But the circumstances under which the press and public can be barred from a criminal trial are limited; the State's justification in denying access must be a weighty one."

Although Brennan did not spell out how to decide which trials should be closed, he did offer the following factors to consider:

. . . the minor victim's age, psychological maturity and understanding, the nature of the crime, the desires of the victim, and the interests of parents and relatives.

For example, Brennan wrote, some minors might not mind testifying with reporters in the courtroom, therefore there would be no reason why the public should be denied access to their trials. Some minors might even want the public to know "what a heinous crime the defendant had committed." Yet the broadly written Massachusetts law would close these trials as well as those in which minors had a genuine wish for privacy.

An Informed Discussion of Governmental Affairs

At first glance, it might be hard to understand why Brennan was so concerned with keeping trials open to the public, especially in cases where it might make people who had already suffered feel even more uncomfortable. But Brennan's arguments were based on the belief that the public must know what goes on at trials if it is to understand how the government works and what the government is doing. He wrote:

Underlying the First Amendment right of access to criminal trials is the common understanding that "a major purpose" of that Amendment was to protect the free discussion of governmental affairs. By offering such protection, the First Amendment serves to ensure that the individual citizen can effectively participate in and contribute to our republican system of self-government. Thus to the extent that the First Amendment embraces a right of access to criminal trials, it is to ensure that this constitutionally protected "discussion of governmental affairs" is an informed one.

Of course, the First Amendment does not explicitly say that the press has the right to attend criminal trials. But, Justice Brennan wrote, the First Amendment guarantees not just the rights it actually lists, but also those rights that are necessary to exercise the rights that it lists. For people to meaningfully exercise their First Amendment right to political speech, they have to know what their government is doing. To know what their government is doing, they have to read about it in a free press. Therefore, press coverage of governmental activities—including trials—is guaranteed by the First Amendment, and the state needs a "compelling reason" to limit that guarantee.

The Consequences of the *Globe* Decision

As a result of the *Globe* decision, federal courts have found many instances in which the public has the right to know about various aspects of the criminal justice system. Courts have affirmed public access to the examination of jurors, preliminary hearings, hearings to suppress, plea hearings, change of venue hearings, and documents submitted at hearings. The public has somewhat less access to proceedings that involve minors and to information about ongoing criminal investigations.

However, in the wake of the 1991 rape trial of William Kennedy Smith, in which the media publicized the name of Smith's alleged rape victim, Alaska, Louisiana, and New York all passed laws making it a crime to publicly disclose the identities of sex-crime victims. The focus of these laws has not been to restrict the press, but rather to cut off public access to identifying information in police and trial records.

Related Cases

Branzburg v. Hayes, 408 U.S. 665 (1972).
Cox Broadcasting Corp. v. Cohn 420 U.S. 469 (1975).
Federal Communications Commission v. Pacific Foundation, 438 U.S. 726 (1978).
Gannett Co. v. Depasquale, 443 U.S. 368 (1979).
Richmond Newspapers, Inc. v. Virginia, 448 U.S. 555 (1980).
Bose Corp. v. Consumer's Union of the United States, Inc., 466 U.S. 485 (1984).
Federal Communications Commission v. League of Women Voters of California, 468 U.S. 364 (1984).

Bibliography and Further Reading

Burrows, Karen B. "First Amendment: The Right of Access to Criminal Trials Extended." *Journal of Criminal Law and Criminology,* Winter, 1982, Vol. 73, no. 4, pp. 1388-1407.

Hutt, Sarah Henderson. "In Praise of Public Access: Why the Government Should Disclose the Identities of Alleged Crime Victims." *Duke Law Journal,* Vol. 41, pp. 368-414.

Lassiter, Christo. "TV or not TV—That is the Question." *Journal of Criminal Law and Criminology,* spring 1996, pp. 928.

Young, Rowland L. "Freedom of the Press . . . Access to Trials." *ABA Journal,* October 1982, Vol. 68, No. 10, p. 1301.

MINNEAPOLIS STAR V. MINNESOTA COMMISSIONER OF REVENUE

Legal Citation: 460 U.S. 575 (1983)

Appellant
Minneapolis Star & Tribune Company

Appellee
Minnesota Commissioner of Revenue

Appellant's Claim
That a state special tax assessment on ink and paper used in publication of the *Star Tribune* newspaper violated freedom of the press.

Chief Lawyer for Appellant
Lawrence C. Brown

Chief Lawyer for Appellee
Paul R. Kempainen, Special Assistant Attorney General of Minnesota

Justices for the Court
Harry A. Blackmun, William J. Brennan, Jr., Warren E. Burger, Thurgood Marshall, Sandra Day O'Connor (writing for the Court), Lewis F. Powell, Jr., John Paul Stevens, Byron R. White

Justices Dissenting
William H. Rehnquist

Place
Washington, D.C.

Date of Decision
29 March 1983

Decision
Upheld the *Minnesota Star*'s claim and overturned the Minnesota Supreme Court's decision that the special tax did not violate the newspaper's constitutional protections.

Significance
The ruling found that state tax systems cannot treat the press differently than any other business unless substantial justification exists. The state of Minnesota could demonstrate no compelling reason to justify imposing a special use tax on a select few newspaper publishers. Therefore, the tax was in violation of the First Amendment's Press Clause. The ruling was unique in subjecting state laws to strict scrutiny based on mere potential for censorship.

In 1967, the Minnesota state legislature established a general system of taxation including a sales tax on the retail sale of most goods and a use tax applied to certain personal property for which a sales tax did not apply. Initially, the *Star Tribune* newspaper, published by the Minneapolis Star & Tribune Co., was exempted from the sales and use taxes as were other news periodicals. But in 1971, the state legislature revised the tax system by imposing a use tax solely on the cost of paper and ink products used in their publication. In 1974, the legislature further revised the law by exempting the first $100,000 worth of ink and paper used by a publication in a calendar year. In effect, the special use tax applied only to the publications with largest circulations. As a consequence, only 14 of the 388 circulation newspapers in Minnesota were assessed use taxes in 1974. The *Star Tribune,* having the largest circulation in the state, paid approximately two-thirds of the total amount of ink and paper tax assessed statewide.

The *Star Tribune* subsequently filed a lawsuit challenging the constitutionality of both the use tax and its exemptions. The newspaper also sought a refund for use taxes paid for 1974 expenses and part of 1975. In 1981 the Minnesota Supreme Court held that the use tax did not violate the Constitution due to the lack of any censorship intent by the state.

Equal Treatment of the Press

Taxation of the press has long been a major issue in the United States. Opposition to unfair taxation policies of Britain played a central role in the American Revolution and greatly influenced the writing of the U.S. Constitution. The British government policy of using taxes to control the press and inhibit access of information to the general population profoundly influenced colonial America. Framers of the U.S. Constitution argued that the press should serve a unique role by keeping the public informed and arousing sentiment on key issues. The press should serve to restrain government and keep it under control. Consequently, the writers of the First Amendment inserted the "Press Clause," which states that government actions are prohibited from "abridging the freedom of . . . the press." Some even described the news media as the "fourth branch" of the U.S. government by providing yet another check on its powers. This public purpose is the essence of the First Amendment protection. Oddly, the issue of the First Amendment's Press Clause was rarely addressed by the Supreme Court prior to the 1936 *Grosjean v. American Press Co.* case. The focus of that case was on obvious censorship by a state attempting to limit circulation of a select group of newsletters through a special tax on their advertising revenue. The *Star Tribune* contended that the Minnesota special use tax should be voided based on precedence the Court established in the *Grosjean* case.

In response, the state of Minnesota argued their use tax was not actually "special," but part of the ordinary tax system. In fact, the system financially favored publishers because they actually paid much less tax to the state through the special use tax than if subjected to the general sales tax.

Justice O'Connor, writing for the 8-1 majority, wrote that the special use tax imposed by Minnesota on the *Star Tribune* indeed singled out the press for special treatment. The ordinary tax system focused primarily on retail sales of goods. In contrast, the state was taxing publishers on materials purchased wholesale to produce a newspaper, which "is without parallel in the State's tax scheme." However, O'Connor found *Grosjean* not a relevant precedent since "censorship" was the motive in that case. Even though Minnesota's intent was solely to raise revenue without intent to censor or suppress the newspaper, the state was still found in clear violation of the Press Clause. The Court found that Minnesota presented no compelling public or government interest to impose a different method of taxation on the press instead of the general sales tax. Though imposition of a special use tax rather than the general sales tax actually favored the press, the Court found differential treatment between the news media and other businesses could be abused with less favorable results in the future. In 1963, the Court wrote in *National Association for the Advancement of Colored People v. Button,* that simply the "threat of sanctions [censorship] may deter [the] exercise [of First Amendment rights] almost as potently as the actual application of sanctions."

On a second point, O'Connor found the statute not only singled out the press in general, but even a select group of publishers. The special tax actually applied to only a few large publishers due to the $100,000 exemption. Even fewer paid a substantial amount. The Court ruled that the press should not only be treated equal to other business entities, but equal to other press organizations as well. In essence, the First Amendment allows regulation of the press, but not differential treatment in any form. O'Connor wrote, "we think that recognizing a power in the State not only to single out the press but also to tailor the tax so that it singles out a

few members of the press presents such a potential for abuse that no interest suggested by Minnesota can justify the scheme." O'Connor continued, "the tax begins to resemble more a penalty for a few of the largest newspapers than an attempt to favor struggling smaller enterprises." In concurrence, Justice Byron White wrote that the $100,000 exemption was sufficient alone to rule a constitutional violation. He believed the other findings by the Court, such as a tax posing a threat by financially favoring the press, were questionable and need not be addressed.

Importantly, the Court majority in *Minneapolis Star* established that tax schemes did not have to involve censorship in order for them to be ruled in violation of the First Amendment. As in race, age, and gender discrimination, discrimination among media members or between the media institution and other businesses is prohibited under the First Amendment, regardless of whether censorship was a motive or not.

Benefit or Burden?

In dissent, Justice Rehnquist questioned the Court's rationale in determining that a tax system financially favoring the press poses a threat. He could not see how freedom was diminished by Minnesota's actions. He then calculated the cost of imposing the standard state sales tax, as suggested by the majority, rather than the special use tax. The *Star Tribune* would have paid over $3.6 million for the period a refund was sought, rather than the $1.2 million actually paid. Rehnquist was also troubled by the Court asserting itself into a state legislature's business. The Court had traditionally avoided involvement in the development of states' tax schemes, particularly where an inappropriate burden did not clearly exist. In sum, Rehnquist found the Court's decision, based on an "unprecedented" application of a "differential treatment" standard, a very hollow victory for the *Star Tribune.*

Impact

The 1983 *Minnesota Star* decision alerted states that taxation policies must treat the press very carefully. The case further validated the special institutional role of the press in American society. Through the 1980s, state courts strictly applied the *Minnesota Star* decision to a number of cases, creating problems with various states' revenue raising efforts. Two other Supreme Court cases involving state taxation of the media followed *Minnesota Star. Arkansas Writers' Project, Inc. v. Ragland* (1987) and *Leathers v. Medlock* (1991) focused on taxes imposed on the media in Arkansas. In the *Medlock* case, the Court developed a three-part test to judge cases involving differential taxation of the news media. The test incorporated the *Minnesota Star* finding that a tax must be applied equally to all. The other two parts question if a tax is inappropriately based on the subject matter of the particular news media and if the tax is targeted at only a small group of the media. If a tax scheme initially fails any of the three parts, then the tax legislation must be subjected to close scrutiny to determine if it poses an intolerable threat of state censorship.

Many defenders of press freedom worried, however, that the scope and impact of *Minnesota Star* was greatly reduced by *Medlock*. The latter decision reemphasized the primary concern over censorship motives by holding that differential taxes must be shown to actually pose a significant danger of censorship. The Court found that differential taxation involving the news media does not alone implicate the First Amendment violation. As a result, a Court test for violation of the First Amendment became increasingly stringent again. To many, the *Medlock* decision significantly detracted from the gains in freedom of the press protection offered by *Minnesota Star* by giving states greater control over regulation of the news media.

The *Minnesota Star* decision also established precedence for deliberating cases involving cable television as mass media technologies evolved through the 1980s. Issues regarding differential treatment of the various forms of communications media, such as traditional print media, broadcast media, and cable media were raised. Application of the First Amendment Press Clause to restrictions placed on these various forms of communication continued to be an issue through the 1990s, as demonstrated in *Turner Broadcasting System v. Federal Communications Commission*.

In conformance with Rehnquist's dissenting opinion in the *Minnesota Star* case, some believe the courts should concentrate on infringements of a more substantial and direct nature. They believe "incidental burdens" on fundamental constitutional rights are contained in most state and federal legislation. Therefore, the court system could become excessively mired in less meaningful cases. As a result, the politically conserva-

tive Supreme Court began developing more stringent limiting principles in the 1990s, such as the *Medlock* test. These decisions serve to limit the Court's role in state and federal legislative review.

Tax systems are a primary means states have to regulate business, raise revenue, and provide special support to particular industries important to their region. Consequently, the Court has held that states are fairly free to tax as they see fit. As established by *Minnesota Star,* state tax schemes will normally not be challenged unless they treat the news media differently than other businesses. Legal scholars are concerned about the implications of the *Medlock* case. They contend more factors than just reliance on censorship motives should be used to determine if a differential tax system applied to the news media warrants judicial scrutiny. Based on the *Minnesota Star* decision, it is imperative that states tax the press in the least discriminatory manner possible.

Related Cases

Grosjean v. American Press Co., 297 U.S. 233 (1936).
National Association for the Advancement of Colored People v. Button, 371 U.S. 415 (1963).
Arkansas Writers' Project, Inc. v. Ragland, 481 U.S. 221 (1987).
Leathers v. Medlock, 499 U.S. 439 (1991).
Turner Broadcasting System v. Federal Communications Commission, 520 U.S. 180 (1994).

Bibliography and Further Reading

Biskupic, Joan, and Elder Witt, eds. *Congressional Quarterly's Guide to the U.S. Supreme Court,* 3rd ed. Washington, DC: Congressional Quarterly, Inc., 1996.

Hawke, Anne and Kevin Donnelly. "Paparazzi." *The Quill.* September 1998, p. 19.

Schwartz, Bernard. *Freedom of the Press: Constitutional Issues.* New York: Facts on File, Inc., 1992.

PHILADELPHIA NEWSPAPERS INC. v. HEPPS

Legal Citation: 475 U.S. 767 (1986)

Appellant
Philadelphia Newspapers, Inc., et al.

Appellee
Maurice S. Hepps, et al.

Petitioner's Claim
That, due to First Amendment freedom of the press protections, a private individual in cases of public interest is responsible to prove accusations of criminal activity printed by a newspaper were false to win a defamation award.

Chief Lawyer for Appellant
David H. Marion

Chief Lawyer for Appellee
Ronald H. Surkin

Justices for the Court
Harry A. Blackmun, William J. Brennan, Jr., Thurgood Marshall, Lewis F. Powell, Jr., Sandra Day O'Connor (writing for the Court)

Justices Dissenting
Warren E. Burger, William H. Rehnquist, John Paul Stevens, Byron R. White

Place
Washington, D.C.

Date of Decision
21 April 1986

Decision
Reversed the Pennsylvania Supreme Court and found that for a private individual to establish defamation by the press they are required to prove untruthfulness of the news articles.

Significance
The Supreme Court found that for topics of public interest First Amendment protections of the press outweigh libel common law even in cases involving private citizens. The private individual, not the press, must prove the falseness of alleged smear statements. The finding held that private individuals and public personalities face the same rigorous standards for winning defamation suits against the press. Due to the continual altering of libel law by the Court since the 1960s, an individual's ability to legally protect their reputation has been greatly limited leading toward political efforts to substantially restructure libel law. This case was one of the more important procedural rulings by the Court favoring the news media in defamation suits.

General Programming, Inc. (GPI) franchised a chain of stores in the Philadelphia area known as "Thrifty" specializing in beer, soft drink, and snacks sales. Maurice S. Hepps was GPI's principal stockholder. Between May of 1975 and May of 1976, the *Philadelphia Inquirer,* owned by Philadelphia Newspapers, Inc., published a series of five articles linking Hepps and GPI to organized crime. The articles claimed GPI used criminal associations to influence the Pennsylvania legislature and the State Liquor Control Board. Hepps filed suit in a state court against Philadelphia Newspapers claiming their reputations were harmed.

Freedom to Defame

Defamation is the smearing of someone's reputation either by speaking (slander) or by writing (libel). Common law normally assumes statements determined defamatory through malice (hateful intent) or "careless indifference" are false until the speaker proves them truthful. No simple guidelines identifying what constitutes defamation exist due largely to infinite possibilities. Consequently, the Supreme Court's interpretation of how libel law applies to private individuals has been inconsistent with sharply divided votes.

The Supreme Court has struggled greatly over the issue of media responsibility in reporting the truth. Libel law did not become a subject under Court scrutiny until 1964. In the landmark *New York Times v. Sullivan* (1964) case the Court established that a public person (meaning actors, sports figures, government officials, and politicians) must prove the media acted with malice, not just using false information, to win a libel case. The Court identified an intense "national commitment to the principle that debate on public issues should be uninhibited, robust, and wide-open" including "sharp attacks." This test became known as the "actual malice standard" and brought civil libel law under constitutional protection. In *Time, Inc. v. Hill* (1967) the Court extended the actual malice standard to private citizens when incidentally involved as victims in crimes of public interest.

With some change in justices on the bench, the Court later reversed its direction. The Court ruled in

Shield Laws

Shield laws protect journalists from revealing sources of their information. The intent is to extend this privilege to journalists as a means of supporting a vital press in the United States. The first state enacting such a law was Maryland, in 1898. Half of the states had adopted similar laws by 1973. In 1975, Congress passed the Federal Rule of Evidence 501, which qualifies the privilege granted to journalists under state laws.

Shield laws can create controversies at times. Seeking to protect his or her sources, an issue may arise if a journalist is subpoenaed by a grand jury seeking testimony. The First Amendment rights guarantee free press, and shield laws may afford additional protection not to reveal sources. Conflicts occur between a journalist's right not to reveal sources and the government's right to information that relates to criminal activity. The U.S. Supreme Court has ruled that reporters must answer questions put forth by a grand jury. The First Amendment provides journalists no right to exception from testifying. In cases like this, "public interest" has priority.

Source(s): *West's Encyclopedia of American Law*, Vol 2. New York: West Publishing, 1998.

Gertz v. Welch (1974) that the actual malice standard did not always apply when a private citizen was suing the media for defamation. A distinction between public and private parties was based on a private citizen's lesser access to media sources for response, and that a private citizen does not normally seek public attention. The Court also determined that press freedom should be weighed against public interest when private citizens were the focus of the press. But the states were left to individually define how to balance concerns of private citizen defamation with that of press censorship.

Pennsylvania state law required a private individual alleging defamation by the press to prove carelessness or malice, however, it was the press responsibility to prove truthfulness of a defamatory statement. In presenting arguments, Hepps offered considerable testimony that the *Inquirer's* statements were false leaving the *Inquirer* to prove their truthfulness. In rebuttal, the *Inquirer* took advantage of Pennsylvania's "shield law" on several occasions to avoid revealing information sources. Unexpectedly, the court decided the state defamation law requiring the *Inquirer* to prove truthfulness of its statements was unconstitutional and instructed the jury that Hepps had responsibility to prove the published statements false. The jury decided in favor of Philadelphia Newspapers.

Hepps appealed the verdict and court proceedings to the Pennsylvania Supreme Court. In 1982 the court, ruling in his favor, determined that Hepps only needed to prove malice by the press to decide the defamation question and that proving truthfulness was not necessary. The court added that requiring the publisher to prove truthfulness as required in the Pennsylvania state law "did not unconstitutionally inhibit free debate" as the lower court had found. The case was sent back for retrial. The U.S. Supreme Court then assumed the case.

Chilling Effect

The Court was once again asked "to define the proper (balance) between the law of defamation and the freedoms of speech and press protected by the First Amendment." The Court first determined this case involved a private citizen, but topics of public interest. Therefore, based on precedence of the *New York Times* decision, constitutional rule prevailed over common law in this case. Proving truthfulness was not the publisher's responsibility. Justice O'Connor, writing for the 5-4 majority, found that "where a newspaper publishes speech of public concern, a private-figure plaintiff cannot recover damages without also showing that the statements at issue are false." When truth is uncertain, as may often be the case, the Constitution requires favoring the protection of speech. O'Connor wrote, "the common-law presumption that defamatory speech is false cannot" apply. In addition, the Pennsylvania shield law places even a greater burden on Hepps to prove defamation and falseness because the *Inquirer's* sources could not be identified or specifically questioned. In concurrence, Justice Brennan noted that the Constitution directly restricts only government actions limiting free speech. However, such restrictions must apply to private citizens as well when matters of public interest are involved. Burger wrote the press should not fear prosecution from private citizens in matters of public interest. Such fear serves as a "chilling effect" on free speech, meaning the press might be fearful of printing important public information if they were not absolutely sure it was truthful. A private citizen must clearly prove statements are false before recovering damages from the media for defamation. O'Connor noted a likely consequence of this strict standard set by *Hepps* was that some false statements about private individuals may receive protection by the Constitution in order to protect speech providing important information to the public.

Private Citizens and Public Figures

Justice Stevens, joined in dissent by Chief Justice Burger and Justices White and Rehnquist, sharply disagreed that private citizens should be treated the same as public and governmental figures. They should not be required to prove defamatory statements are also false. Stevens wrote the media should be clearly held responsible for false or irresponsible statements and the common defamation law of Pennsylvania should prevail. In many situations, a private citizen would not be able to disprove accusations about his past are false due to loss of records, death of possible witnesses, or other developments through time. Stevens believed the decision was a blatant misuse of previous rulings by equating public figure cases to those involving private citizens. In fact, he pointed out that in *Gertz* the Court actually considered and rejected the notion that private citizens must the bear the same responsibilities for proving truthfulness of statements as public persons.

By placing so little importance on protecting individual reputation, Stevens lamented the only victors in the decision would be publishers "who act negligently or maliciously." Prevention of false information serves an important public purpose as the McCarthy era of the 1950s demonstrated when government officials and the press falsely accused citizens of communist connections. Stevens charged the Court in essence granted the press a constitutional license to defame through character assassination. He concluded, "deliberate, malicious character assassination is not protected by the First Amendment" but truthful statements are.

Impact

Since 1964 the Supreme Court dramatically revised common libel law. The Court regularly rejected the common law balancing between First Amendment speech protections and privacy in favor of rigidly protecting the press. This decision, further expanded in *Hustler Magazine Inc. v. Falwell* (1988), had far reaching implications. Even where defamatory statements are false, a private individual can rarely win damages from the media if the topic is of public interest as liberally interpreted by the courts.

The increasingly conservative social climate of the 1980s and 1990s marked an era of government placing greater responsibility on individuals and institutions to conduct themselves properly. Basic court rules applied to the press were not to knowingly print false information, to provide an open discussion on public issues, and to act with reasonable care. But still no single standard was formally established for media responsibility in telling the truth.

Due to the substantial changes in libel law introduced by the Supreme Court, many became dissatisfied with the status of libel law in general. Libel law in the 1990s provided little protection for individuals' reputations, yet left the press open to occasional large damage awards that were not overturned in appeals courts. As a result, libel cases were still considered the single largest threat in the 1990s to press freedom. The high expense of legal defense alone posed a "chilling effect" on press freedom, if not actual adverse court rulings.

Libel law reform received considerable attention beginning in the 1960s. Some argued for abolishing libel law altogether, claiming history showed private citizens rarely suffered actual damage. Public opinion would thus serve as the judge of truth rather than the courts. Proponents for revising rather than abolishing libel law claimed some form of reputation protection is important for a civilized society. Justice Potter Stewart wrote in the 1966 case of *Rosenblatt v. Baer,* "The right of a man to the protection of his own reputation from unjustified invasion . . . [is] our basic concept of the essential dignity and worth of every human being— a concept at the root of any decent system of ordered liberty." Legislative solutions, including the proposed Uniform Defamation Act in the early 1990s, gained little organized support. The press institution provided organized opposition despite some proposals limiting monetary damage payments. Many reform efforts attempted to replace the requirement of proving malice with a system involving public retractions or a quicker system of judging truthfulness. In the meantime, the public gained greater appreciation of the contention between press freedom and defamation worries in accepting that some false statements may receive protection from the First Amendment to safeguard "the greater marketplace of ideas."

Related Cases

NAACP v. Button, 371 U.S. 415 (1963).
New York Times v. Sullivan, 376 U.S. 254 (1964).
Rosenblatt v. Baer, 383 U.S. 75 (1966).
Time, Inc. v. Hill, 385 U.S. 374 (1967).
Gertz v. Welch, 418 U.S. 323 (1974).
Hustler Magazine Inc. v. Falwell, 485 U.S. 46 (1988).

Bibliography and Further Reading

"Defamation on the Internet."*Forbes,* October 20, 1997.

Hindman, Elizabeth B. *Rights vs. Responsibilities: The Supreme Court and the Media.* Westport, CN: Greenwood Press, 1997.

Kane, Peter E. *Errors, Lies, and Libel.* Carbondale: Southern Illinois University Press, 1992.

Soloski, John, and Randall P. Bezanson, eds. *Reforming Libel Law,* New York: Guilford Press, 1992.

Wall Street Journal, February 25, 1998.

Wiesen, Daryl L. "Following the Lead of Defamation: A Definitional Balancing Approach to Religious Torts."*Yale Law Journal,* October 1995, p. 291.

HAZELWOOD SCHOOL DISTRICT V. KUHLMEIER

Legal Citation: 484 U.S. 260 (1988)

Petitioners
Hazelwood School District in St. Louis County, Missouri; various school officials; Robert Eugene Reynolds, principal of Hazelwood East High School; Howard Emerson, a teacher in the district

Respondents
Three former Hazelwood East students who were staff members of *Spectrum,* the school newspaper

Petitioners' Claim
That the Court should overturn a lower court decision holding that the students' First Amendment rights were violated when the principal removed two pages from their school newspaper before allowing it to go to press.

Chief Lawyer for Petitioners
Robert P. Baine, Jr.

Chief Lawyer for Respondents
Leslie D. Edwards

Justices for the Court
Anthony M. Kennedy, Sandra Day O'Connor, William H. Rehnquist, Antonin Scalia, John Paul Stevens, Byron R. White (writing for the Court)

Justices Dissenting
Harry A. Blackmun, William J. Brennan, Jr., Thurgood Marshall

Place
Washington, D.C.

Date of Decision
13 January 1988

Decision
The students' rights were not violated by the removal of the two pages from their newspaper, because student newspapers published under the auspices of a journalism class are a part of the school curriculum, rather than a "public forum."

Significance
This decision was seen as restricting students' First Amendment rights by giving school officials wide latitude to control student expression that might be seen as sponsored by the school.

The Journalism II students at Hazelwood East High School were proud of their school paper, *Spectrum.* In the 1982-1983 school year, the paper had a circulation of over 4,500, which included students, school personnel, and members of the community. According to the Curriculum Guide, Journalism II and the publishing of the paper itself was supposed to teach "the legal, moral and ethical restrictions imposed on journalists within the school community" and the "responsibility and acceptance of criticism for articles of opinion." Students worked under the supervision of a faculty member, and they received grades and credit for completing the course.

Just as the 13 May 1983 issue was about to come out, Principal Robert Eugene Reynolds pulled two pages from the paper. As was usual, the faculty advisor, Howard Emerson, had shown Reynolds the paper before it came out. Reynolds was concerned about two articles. One described three Hazelwood East students' experiences with pregnancy. The other discussed the impact of divorce on Hazelwood students.

Privacy and the Right to Respond

Although the story about pregnancy had used false names, Reynolds believed that it might be too easy to identify the students and their boyfriends, thus violating their right to privacy. He also believed that the discussion of sexual activity and birth control in the article would not be appropriate reading matter for the younger students at the school.

The story about divorce included a student's complaint that her father had not spent "enough time with my mom, my sister and I" before the divorce, along with her perception that her father "was always out of town on business or out late playing cards with the guys" and "always argued about everything" with her mother. Reynolds was upset that the student was identified by name, because he thought her parents, particularly her father, should then have been given the chance to respond to this criticism. He did not realize that the student's name had in fact been deleted from the final version of the article.

It might have been possible to fix the problems in the articles, to delay publication, or to have solved the

---

School Paper Censorship

Do school students have the same rights of free press and speech while engaged in school activities? Can school officials control the content of school newspapers?

Students may believe the Constitution guarantees them these rights in and out of school. They may assert these rights in disagreements with school officials in connection to the publication of material in a school sponsored newspaper or in the language they use in school. Student newspaper staff members may attempt to assert their rights to determine the editorial content of their paper, citing the rights public newspapers have to control what they do and do not publish.

Student newspapers may not be viewed in the same light as a public newspaper, since the school newspaper is not usually a vehicle for public communication. Also, a school publication is generally produced in conjunction with classwork and subsequently may be considered part of the curriculum. While school authorities cannot censor students' speech beyond school, they do have the right to ensure that students' speech and publications meet certain standards and do not conflict with the educational purposes of the school.

Source(s): Cornell. http://supct.law.cornell.edu/supct/

---

problems in some other way, but the teacher who had run the paper all year had left to take a job in private industry, and Emerson, the new teacher, either was not aware of all the options or did not think to mention them to the principal. So Reynolds, believing he had to act quickly, removed not just the two offending articles, but the entire page that each was on, even though he had no objection to the other articles on the two pages.

The students who ran the paper were furious. They claimed that their First Amendment rights to free speech and free press had been violated. They took their case to court. Eventually, their case was reviewed by the Supreme Court.

At the Schoolhouse Gate

In the famous decision *Tinker v. Des Moines Independent Community School District* (1969), the Court held that students in public schools do not "shed their constitutional rights to freedom of speech or expression at the schoolhouse gate." Justice White, writing for the majority, even cited this decision in his own ruling. Yet White ruled against the Hazelwood students, asserting that the principal had had a perfect right to pull the articles, and that, given the time pressure he was under, he had acted reasonably to delete the other articles on the same page, since he believed that was the only way that the paper could come out in time. White's opinion was very clear:

> First Amendment rights of students in the public schools are not automatically coextensive with the rights of adults in other settings, and must be applied in light of the special characteristics of the school environment. A school need not tolerate student speech that is inconsistent with its basic educational mission, even though the government could not censor similar speech outside the school.

Therefore, White reasoned, a school newspaper could not be seen as the kind of public forum that, say, an empty classroom was. If a school opened its doors to the community, allowing it to rent classroom space for a public meeting, then the school should not be able to decide what was said or done at that meeting. A class held in that classroom was not a public forum, but rather a part of the school curriculum. Certainly, White thought, schools had the right to control what was taught under their sponsorship.

White's ruling rested on the premise that the *Spectrum* was really part of the Journalism II class. If it had been an underground newspaper printed and circulated by students with no school involvement, it would have had a different legal standing. Indeed, White pointed out, the offending pages of the school paper had been copied and circulated by the students, and the school had taken no action. The school was not trying to control what students read or how they expressed themselves. It was simply trying to teach students how to be good journalists.

Moreover, White said, schools had the right to refuse support to student expression that did not fit the values of the school. If the principal thought that the *Spectrum* did not do a good job of representing Hazelwood East in the larger community—if he worried, for example, that parents might be offended at the sexual content of some of the articles or that they might not want their younger children to read about birth control—then the principal had every right to exercise "editorial control" over "the style and content of student speech . . . so long as his actions are reasonably related to legitimate pedagogical concerns."

A Better Civics Lesson

Justices Brennan, Marshall, and Blackmun all dissented vehemently from the Court's majority opinion. Bren-

Principal Robert E. Reynolds holds a copy of the Hazelwood East High School newspaper. © Corbis-Bettmann.

nan wrote the dissent, in which he argued that "school officials may censor only such student speech as would 'materially disrup[t]' a legitimate curricular function." In other words, he maintained, the majority wanted to give school officials power over student speech in order to promote educational goals. The dissenters would allow school officials restrictive power only to prevent students from actively disrupting a class or other school function.

Brennan was scornful about the principal's supposed right to shield impressionable high school students from unsuitable material. Although he agreed that educators had a right, even a duty, to supervise curriculum, he said that this was not "a general warrant to act as 'thought police' stifling discussion of all but state-approved topics and advocacy of all but the official position."

Related Cases

Tinker v. Des Moines Independent Community School District, 393 U.S. 503 (1969).
Grayned v. City of Rockford, 408 U.S. 104 (1972).
Federal Communications Commission v. League of Women's Voters, 468 U.S. 364 (1984).

Bethel School District No. 403 v. Fraser, 478 U.S. 675 (1986).

Bibliography and Further Reading

Brasher, Richard M. "Commentary: A Return of Control to the Educators or a Beginning of the Orwellian Nightmare?" *Journal of Law and Education.* spring, 1988, Vol. 17, no. 2, pp. 320-326.

Gill, Ann M. "In the Wake of Fraser and Hazelwood." *Journal of Law and Education.* summer, 1991, Vol. 20, no. 3, pp. 253-326.

Kaplan, Joel. "Hazelwood Decision Continues to Haunt High School." *Editor & Publisher,* 7 May 1994, p. 48.

Kerber, Ross. "Kids Say the Darnedest Things: Student Web Sites Present Schools with Difficult Free-Speech Issues." *The Wall Street Journal,* 17 November 1997, p. R12.

Stewart, Malcolm. "The First Amendment, the Public Schools, and the Inculcation of Community Values." *Journal of Law and Education.* winter, 1989, Vol. 18, no. 1, pp. 23-92.

Tidwell, James A. "Chalk Talk." *Journal of Law and Education.* spring, 1988, Vol. 17, no. 2, pp. 320-326.

HUSTLER MAGAZINE INC. V. FALWELL

Legal Citation: 485 U.S. 46 (1988)

Petitioners
Hustler Magazine, Inc., et al.

Respondent
Jerry Falwell

Petitioners' Claim
Under the First Amendment to the U.S. Constitution, a public figure cannot recover damages for intentional infliction of emotional distress caused by a magazine's publication of an advertisement parody that used the figure's name and likeness.

Chief Lawyer for Petitioners
Alan L. Isaacson

Chief Lawyer for Respondent
Norman Roy Grutman

Justices for the Court
Harry A. Blackmun, William J. Brennan, Jr., Thurgood Marshall, Sandra Day O'Connor, William H. Rehnquist (writing for the Court), Antonin Scalia, John Paul Stevens, Byron R. White

Justices Dissenting
None (Anthony M. Kennedy did not participate)

Place
Washington, D.C.

Date of Decision
24 February 1988

Decision
Held that a public figure cannot recover for emotional injury caused by publication of a parody that could not be reasonably taken as a statement of fact.

Significance
The Court applied the actual malice standard set out in *New York Times v. Sullivan*, which requires that a false statement must be published with knowledge of or reckless disregard for the truth. It found the parody to be a statement of opinion, protected by the First Amendment.

The November 1983 issue of *Hustler* magazine featured a parody of an advertisement for Campari liquor. The layout used a caricature of the Rev. Jerry Falwell, a well-known minister and conservative political activist, which was titled "Jerry Falwell talks about his first time," a take-off on the Campari ad campaign. The text of the advertisement implied that Falwell's first sexual experience was a drunken rendezvous with his mother in an outhouse. The ad also presented Falwell as a hypocrite, who preached only when drunk. A small print statement informed the reader that this was an "ad parody-not to be taken seriously" and the table of contents also listed it as a parody.

Falwell sued *Hustler* and its publisher, Larry Flynt, for invasion of privacy, libel, and intentional infliction of emotional distress. The trial court rejected the privacy allegation, but allowed the jury to decide the libel and emotional distress claims. The jury found that the parody was not reasonably believable and ruled that the magazine had therefore not libeled Falwell. However, it ruled that Falwell had suffered emotional distress, and awarded him $100,000 for compensatory (actual) damages and $100,000 in punitive damages.

Hustler and Flynt appealed to the U.S. Court of Appeals for the Fourth Circuit, which upheld the jury verdict. The Fourth Circuit found that while actual malice was required for a libel case, a lesser standard was allowed for emotional distress claims. It said the question was whether the ad "was sufficiently outrageous to constitute intentional infliction of emotional distress," regardless of whether it was an opinion. The Supreme Court granted review of the case.

The High Court disagreed with the appeals court, finding that the expression of opinions on matters of public interests was of "fundamental importance" under the First Amendment. It compared the parody to political cartoons, though noting as an aside that it was "a distant cousin . . . and a rather poor relation at that." However, quoting its 1978 decision in *FCC v. Pacifica Foundation*, the Court said: "[T]he fact that society may find speech offensive is not a sufficient reason for suppressing it. Indeed, if it is the speaker's opinion that gives offense, that is a reason for according it constitutional protection."

Political Cartoons or Parodies

Political Cartoons characterizing public figures in a negative manner may find protection under the Constitution. The U.S. Supreme Court has reiterated these protections in various decisions. Whereas a private individual may have greater recourse in defamation suits, public figures and officials may be used as the butt of jokes with greater freedom.

In cases involving political cartoons or parodies, a major factor used to deny public figures damages in libel suits, is the fact that the cartoon is clearly understood not to be true. The intent is to poke fun at or satirize the object in the cartoon or some behavior he or she exhibits. The cartoon may be considered offensive or outrageous by some, but this judgment is subjective in nature. The U.S. Supreme Court asserted that open discourse in the press about issues of public concern takes priority over protection to public figures from the "emotional distress" caused by political cartoons and the like.

Source(s): Cornell. http://supct.law.cornell.edu/supct/

The Court strongly rejected arguments that the particular outrageousness of the parody should affect its protection under the First Amendment. The intent to cause emotional distress may be a serious injury in other situations, the Court said, but it would chill public debate to allow recovery for it in situations involving public discourse. Quoting from its 1964 decision in *Garrison v. Louisiana,* the Court declared, "Debate on public issues will not be uninhibited if the speaker must run the risk that it will be proved in court that he spoke out of hatred; even if he did speak out of hatred, utterances honestly believed contribute to the free interchange of ideas and the ascertainment of truth."

The Court noted that in the 1964 decision in *New York Times v. Sullivan* it held that a speaker cannot be held liable for even a false statement about a public figure unless that statement was made "with knowledge that it was false or with reckless disregard of whether it was false or not." The *Sullivan* case severely limited the rights of public figures under libel and slander laws, because of the importance of the First Amendment. However, as the Court noted, the jury in this case found that the parody was clearly not intended to be taken as fact. For that reason, the publisher would not be liable for making knowingly false statements.

Related Cases
New York Times v. Sullivan, 376 U.S. 254 (1964).
Garrison v. Louisiana, 379 U.S. 64 (1964).
FCC v. Pacifica Foundation, 438 U.S. 726 (1978).

Bibliography and Further Reading
Alexander, Larry. "Banning Hate Speech and the Sticks and Stones Defense." *Constitutional Commentary,* Spring 1996, pp. 71–100.

Johnson, John W., ed. *Historic U.S. Court Cases, 1690–1990: An Encyclopedia.* New York: Garland Publishing, 1992.

Smolla, Rodney A. *Jerry Falwell v. Larry Flynt: The First Amendment on Trial.* Champaign: University of Illinois Press, 1990.

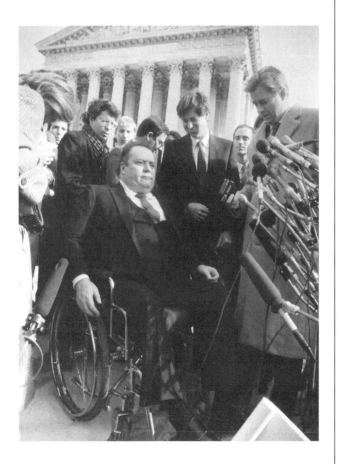

Larry Flynt (center) with his lawyer outside the U.S. Supreme Court, 1987. © AP/Wide World Photos.

COHEN V. COWLES MEDIA CO.

Legal Citation: 501 U.S. 663 (1991)

Petitioner
Dan Cohen

Respondent
Cowles Media Co., DBA Minneapolis Star & Tribune Co., et al.

Petitioner's Claim
That the First Amendment does not prevent a plaintiff from recovering damages under a state law of general applicability when a newspaper breaches a promise of confidentiality to the plaintiff.

Chief Lawyer for Petitioner
Elliot C. Rothenberg

Chief Lawyer for Respondent
John D. French

Justices for the Court
Anthony M. Kennedy, William H. Rehnquist, Antonin Scalia, John Paul Stevens, Byron R. White (writing for the Court)

Justices Dissenting
Harry A. Blackmun, Thurgood Marshall, Sandra Day O'Connor, David H. Souter

Place
Washington, D.C.

Date of Decision
24 June 1991

Decision
Reversed and remanded the Minnesota Supreme Court's decision that enforcement of a promise of confidentiality would violate the First Amendment rights of the publishers of the *Pioneer Press* and *Star Tribune*.

Significance
In a decision that jarred the American news media, the Court ruled that the First Amendment does not protect journalists from being sued, under general-application laws, by a confidential source when that source's identity is revealed without consent. This ruling troubled constitutional analysts as well as the general press. Legal scholars feared it paved the way for future weakening of First Amendment protections. Some media commentators foresaw unprecedented restrictions on the news-gathering process and editorial control. Although there is evidence that news organizations did not extensively alter their confidentiality policies and procedures after *Cohen,* many did reconsider them in its wake.

The Sacred Trust Between Reporter And Source

Protecting the anonymity of confidential news sources in exchange for information is an established journalistic tradition in the American press. It is common practice in the news industry and accepted by most citizens as a necessary journalistic tool. Although the U.S. Supreme Court has recognized that freedom of speech and of the press may be constitutionally limited, prior to 1991 it had voiced little about how news organizations obtained information. This 5-4 decision, however, changed that.

Dan Cohen was the public relations director for the Independent-Republican candidate in the 1982 Minnesota governor's race. In exchange for a promise that he would remain anonymous, Cohen offered information about an opposing candidate to reporters from two Minnesota newspapers. The reporters promised confidentiality, so Cohen provided them with copies of two public court records that showed that the Democratic-Farmer-Labor candidate, Marlene Johnson, had been charged with unlawful assembly in 1969 and convicted of petit theft in 1970. Johnson was soon afterward interviewed for her explanation. Subsequently, Cohen's source for the records was discovered, which revealed that the charges of unlawful assembly had been dismissed and the 1970 conviction had been vacated. After some debate, the editors of each newspaper decided to publish Cohen's name and his connection to the Independent-Republican campaign in their stories on Johnson. Republican campaign officials denied any part in the affair, and Cohen was fired the day the stories were printed.

Cohen then sued the newspapers' publishers for fraudulent misrepresentation and breach of contract in a Minnesota state court. In that trial, the publishers argued that Cohen's lawsuit was prohibited by the First Amendment since it violated the right of freedom of the press. The jury, however, found in Cohen's favor and awarded him $200,000 in compensatory damages and $500,000 in punitive damages. On appeal, the Minnesota Court of Appeals found that Cohen had not proven fraud. It reversed the punitive damages award, as fraud was the only claim that would provide for that kind of award. The court did, however, uphold the breach of contract judgment and the compensatory damage award.

The case went on to the Minnesota Supreme Court. During the oral arguments, one justice raised a question regarding equitable estoppel, in which one party is prevented from asserting his rights against another because the second party justifiably depended upon the conduct of the first and would suffer injustice if the first party was allowed to break the contract. This argument had not been presented before either of the previous courts by either Cohen or the publishers. Nevertheless, the Minnesota Supreme Court addressed the question of whether Cohen had a case based on a promissory estoppel, theory. This principle allows for a non-contractual promise to be made enforceable to avoid an injustice. It is used where, although there may not be a binding contract, because one party has relied on the promise of the other, it would be unjust not to enforce the agreement. As they began their analysis, the court stated that to avoid injustice, the First Amendment rights to a free press must be weighed equally with Cohen's right to have the promise of confidentiality enforced. The court ultimately found that, "in this case, enforcement of the promise of confidentiality under a promissory estoppel theory would violate the defendants' First Amendment rights." The court reversed the compensatory damages award. The U.S. Supreme Court later granted *certiorari,* or commanded the lower court to forward the record of its proceedings for review, to consider the case's relationship to the First Amendment.

The Press Is Subject To The Same Laws As All Citizens

The Supreme Court considered three principal questions. First, the publishers argued that the case should be dismissed because the promissory estoppel theory had not been argued in the lower courts. The Court quickly disagreed, citing several precedents which defended its jurisdiction regardless of whether or not a party had raised a federal law issue in a lower court. The second and most important issue was whether the First Amendment prevents a plaintiff from using a state promissory estoppel law to recover damages when a newspaper breaks a promise of confidentiality to the plaintiff. Writing for the majority, Justice White began by establishing that promissory estoppel is a state law doctrine that creates legal responsibilities which, though not expressly assumed by the parties, were still enforceable in Minnesota state courts. Thus, a promissory estoppel cause of action "involves state action within the meaning of the Fourteenth Amendment, and therefore triggers the First Amendment protections."

However, he reasoned, the doctrine was applicable to all Minnesota citizens, not just to the press specifically. Thus, he said, the First Amendment did not

require that a stricter scrutiny be applied to the enforcement of promissory estoppel against the press than would be applied to anyone else. The respondents had argued that publication of legally gathered, truthful news about public concerns was not punishable by the state. But Justice White concluded that the First Amendment did not insulate the press from any law which in any way limited its right to report the truth. In defense of this conclusion, he cited several prior decisions which had found that members of the press were subject to the same laws as all citizens. These decisions, Justice White wrote, supported the notion that

> the publisher of a newspaper has no special immunity from the application of general laws. He has no special privilege to invade the rights and liberties of others.

Furthermore, he wrote, compensatory damages were not punishment in the criminal sense, but were "constitutionally indistinguishable from a generous bonus paid to a confidential news source."

Finally, Justice White maintained that any limitations on the press's right to report the truth resulting from the application of a general law like promissory estoppel were "incidental, and constitutionally insignificant." Therefore, he concluded, the First Amendment did not forbid the application of that law to the press. The final question before the Court was whether it should restore Cohen's damages award. The Court rejected the request. The issues of Cohen's verdict and the interpretation of Minnesota State Constitution, it felt, were matters for the Minnesota Supreme Court to address. On remand in 1992, Cohen's $200,000 jury award was reinstated to him by the Minnesota Supreme Court under promissory estoppel.

The Press' Freedom Is The Public's Right

In his dissenting opinion, Justice Blackmun disagreed with the line of decisions which the majority used as the "controlling precedent." He supported the Minnesota Supreme Court in basing its decision "not on the identity of the speaker, but on the speech itself." He pointed out that it was important to think of this case in a "classic First Amendment context, . . . namely a political source in a political campaign." He also disagreed with the majority opinion that the famous case of *Hustler Magazine Inc. v. Falwell* (1988) was not comparable to this case. In that case, he wrote, the Court had found the First Amendment did apply to a claim involving a state law of general applicability, because the law was used to "penalize the expression of opinion."

Justice Souter also wrote a dissenting opinion. In contrast to the majority, he centered on the necessity of weighing the specific issues at hand—the state's interest in enforcing a newspaper's promise, and the greater public interest in "unfettered publication of the information revealed in this case." The real character of the right of freedom of the press, he wrote, lies ultimately in that it is the public's right, not simply the media's. He reasoned that the exercise of that right must be measured according to how well it empowers public discussion; how well it makes for a "better informed, and thus more prudently self-governed" society. He conceded that in another situation, a breach of a confidentiality promise might not be constitutionally protected. However, he felt the "First Amendment value" of the information in this case outweighed the state's interest in enforcing a promise.

Impact

In the months after it was handed down, this ruling inspired other courts to distinguish between media content and media news-gathering when determining what was protected under the First Amendment. It also brought calls of alarm from academic, legal, and media observers. In law journals, some writers criticized the justices' reasoning regarding when and how to apply First Amendment protections. Certain media and communications critics feared that opening the door for confidential sources to legally enforce reporter-source agreements would have a "chilling effect" on the newsgathering process. It was predicted that journalists would be less likely to make use of anonymous source information, hindering the free flow of speech and information in the media. In 1994 a study of 106 large daily American newspapers was conducted to ascertain how the *Cohen* case affected their use of anonymous information. It found that most editors were aware of the case and the significance of the decision. It also discovered that as a result of the ruling most newspapers reviewed their confidential source policies, but less than 20 percent changed them. The study concluded that either editors did not see the *Cohen* decision as a threat, or they felt their existing policies would hold up well in court against the criteria set by it.

Related Cases

New York Times v. Sullivan, 376 U.S. 254 (1964).
Branzburg v. Hayes, 408 U.S. 665 (1972).
Smith v. Daily Mail Publishing, 443 U.S. 97 (1979).
Hustler Magazine Inc. v. Falwell, 485 U.S. 46 (1988).

Bibliography and Further Reading

Bunker, Matthew D. "Legally Enforceable Reporter—Source Agreements: Chilling News Gathering at the Source?" *Journalism Quarterly,* Vol. 70, no. 4, 1993.

Davis, Charles N. "How Newspaper Editors Feel about Confidential Sources in the Wake of Cohen v. Cowles." *Newspaper Research Journal,* Vol. 17, nos. 3-4, 1996.

Monday, Gregory F. "Cohen v. Cowles Media Is Not a Promising Decision." *Wisconsin Law Review,* No. 4, 1992.

Srinivasan, Srikanth. "Incidental Restrictions of Speech and the First Amendment." *Constitutional Commentary,* Winter 1995, pp. 401.

Vermeule, C. Adrian. "Confidential Media Sources and the First Amendment." *Harvard Journal of Law & Public Policy,* Vol. 15, no. 1, 1992.

THE INTERNET

An estimated 44 million individuals participate in the Internet, and the audience is doubling each year. On each day in 1997, 71,000 new users logged on. Sixty percent of Internet content originates in the United States. Those interested in regulation efforts include the government, which swears to protect children from inappropriate material, parenting groups who are concerned about what their children may encounter, First Amendment free speech watchdogs who are concerned about preserving the unrestricted state of the cybercommunity, and the average curious individual who may just want to click on some pretty raunchy content. As a general rule, the Constitution forbids the government from silencing speakers because of their particular message. The Federal Communication Commission (FCC) is empowered to "describe" measures it believes to be "reasonable, effective, and appropriate" to block minors' access, but it cannot "approve, sanction, or permit, the use of such measures."

Obscenity Issues

Several cases serve as guides for regulating Internet content. A federal statute passed in 1993 prohibits persons from making indecent comments, requests, and suggestions by telephone. The Supreme Court had struck down an earlier version which aimed to protect minors from dial-a-porn messages. The Court concluded that a blanket ban on indecency in telephone communications exceeded what was needed, and that restrictions on the content of protected speech in media other than broadcast media must advance a compelling state interest and be accomplished by the least restrictive means. Regulations for the Internet will need to comply similarly. In *Bolger v. Youngs Drug Prod. Corp.* and *Federal Communications Commission v. Pacifica Foundation,* the Supreme Court demonstrated a commitment to free speech concerning ads and commercial speech, and that any restriction must be narrowly tailored.

The Communications Decency Act & CDA II

Described as a deregulation measure, the Telecommunications Act of 1996 imposed sweeping content regu-

lations on electronic media. Sections 502 and 507 of the act were known as the Communications Decency Act (CDA). The CDA made it a crime to distribute obscene material using the Internet, punishable by two years in jail and a $250,000 fine. The restriction of such material would be based on contemporary community standards. But the CDA also applied to indecent material which is constitutionally protected.

The CDA was drafted after the emergence of the graphics-based World Wide Web and public reactions to surfing across sexually explicit images. But the Supreme Court struck the CDA down as unconstitutionally vague and unenforceable. In September of 1998, the House passed the Children's Online Protection Act (COPA), dubbed the CDA II, that would ban open display of the majority of sexually explicit materials on the Internet. COPA would ban commercial Web sites from carrying materials harmful to minors without first placing those materials in an area that can be accessed only by persons over 18 years of age.

Community Standards

Restrictions of adult materials have traditionally been based on contemporary community standards. Web pages are likely to be determined to be commercial speech that the Constitution permits the states to regulate. Of course, obscenity and child pornography are not protected speech in any form, anywhere. To evaluate if a work is obscene, the Court developed the Miller test, a three part evaluation that resulted from *Miller v. California* (1973). The test stands to question three aspects of a work: 1) Would the "average person," using standards common to the time and place, find that the work in question appeals to sexual desires?; 2) Does the work use clearly offensive means to show desirable sexual conduct in a way specifically prohibited by law?; 3) Does the work "taken as a whole, [lack] literary, artistic, political or scientific value?" The first time the Miller test was applied to the Internet was a federal obscenity case involving material disseminated on a computer bulletin board service in 1996. In *United States v. Thomas* (1996) a California couple was convicted for distributing obscenity in Tennessee. The content failed to meet local community standards in Tennessee. The

Thomases appealed, saying that Internet users form their own community. The Sixth Circuit Court of Appeals rejected the idea of a cyber community.

Another solution is filtering software set to block offensive words. But after the courts struck down the CDA, Florida and Massachusetts libraries ordered such governing software and adults protested bitterly that they were being denied First Amendment rights when library Internet access was reduced to a child's content availability.

In 1996, the Child Pornography Protection Act became law, changing the definition of child pornography to include computer-generated images because software programs allow pornographers to create erotic material without using live humans. This bill makes no distinction between the legal consequence of distributing computer-generated child pornography and regular child pornorgraphy.

Ten states have proposed to make it illegal to transmit indecent material to minors. Twenty-three states have created laws making possession of child pornography a felony regardless of intent to distribute. Of these, only one law predated the emergence of the Web in 1994.

Defamation

The Internet has evolved as a community where there is a profound lack of mutual respect as demonstrated by flame wars and railing in forum discussions. Anonymity has contributed to the public trashing of others as if libel laws are suspended. They are not. The laws that apply to written speech still apply online. Saying things that defame, libel or invade the privacy of others is grounds for legal action.

Business fraud, false advertising and forgery are also problems. For example, in 1996 a forger posted an ad for child pornography in thousands of newsgroups and gave the name and address of an innocent man. In the early 1990s a Prodigy subscriber was hit with a $100 million libel suit for comments posted in a financial forum. It turned out someone else had used the Prodigy member's account, so the lawsuit was aimed at Prodigy. Authenticating the source of a message is difficult.

Privacy Issues

The technology of the Internet provides a great possibility for the invasion of individual privacy. The Clinton Administration policy is to have consumer groups and the electronic commerce industry develop privacy policies that are enforced by private non-profit organizations. But Lori Fena, executive director of the non-profit Electronic Frontier Foundation, cautions that privacy is being invaded. Researchers can use autonomous agents like Web spiders and robots to gather data with-

out permissions. Users reveal information voluntarily and involuntarily. Voluntary revelations come in the form of surveys and registrations filled out by the individual. Involuntary revelations come from software developers ability to track the user using "cookies," information files that are deposited on the hard drive of the Internet visitor. Cookies "tell" the web site when the visitor returns. Cookies also track what other sites the person visits, providing information on interests and online habits that can be compiled into profiles of hobbies, buying habits, financial status, health, and who they associate with online.

The Federal Trade Commission disagrees with the Clinton Administration that business can regulate itself. Internet businesses are asked to tell consumers that they are collecting personal information, what they are going to do with it, and how consumers can refuse. In 1997, the FTC searched the Internet for privacy problems. Code named the "Big Surf," the investigation reported that 90 percent of the 1,400 sites examined collected personal information from visitors, but only 14 percent disclosed how this information would be used. The FTC is expected to draft a bill calling for clear Internet privacy standards. Presently, the FTC files charges against companies who promise not to give out personal information collected online but do so.

E-mail Privacy

Telephone conversations in the workplace are usually private, but e-mail is not. Courts have ruled in favor of an employer's right to read without consent or notice any e-mail that passes through a company-owned system because employers can be held liable for an employee's criminal activity on communication systems such as e-mail and voicemail. Even e-mail files that have been deleted can be re-obtained in the company's directory. According to law, the employer is the sole copyright holder of the texts its personnel generate while employed by the company.

Existing state and federal electronic surveillance laws govern e-mail confidentiality. In 1986, Congress amended the Electronic Communications Privacy Act to include electronic communication in order to protect electronic communication from hackers and to protect the privacy of particular messages in transference over public service systems. But there is uncertainty about its interpretation in regard to employee e-mail.

Encryption

Data scrambling, or encryption, allows secure electronic commerce such as credit card information to be sent through the Internet. Use of encryption is not regulated within the US, but the export of encryption software has been banned. In late 1998, the United States relaxed export restrictions for some encryption products.

Copyright Law and the Electronic Rights Clause

Digital technology and electronic networks make global piracy likely. The law provides the copyright owner with the exclusive right to reproduce, display work publicly, or permit someone else to reproduce copyrighted works. But individuals can post a copy of an article to a bulletin board or archive where anyone can download it. A published article can ordinarily be resold by the author, but once posted online, it is free to all.

In 1995, the *New York Times* began a policy of assuming the rights to freelance work in all formats for all times without additional compensation. The Authors Guild, the American Society of Journalists and Authors, and the National Writers Union joined forces to fight rights-grabbing contracts. In 1995, the Author's Registry was created, with over 50,000 writers, 95 literary agencies and 30 groups aligned to establish a new and convenient way for publishers to pay for electronic rights.

Senator John Ashcroft of Missouri has introduced legislation that addresses copyright issues raised by the Internet. His legislation would create a take-down notice procedure for handling materials that infringe copyright. But copyright is not simply a U. S. problem. The World Intellectual Property Organization created the WIPO Copyright Treaty and the WIPO Performances and Phonograms Treaty in 1996 to address these issues throughout the international community. The treaties have been submitted to the U.S. Senate for ratification and are under consideration.

Fair Use and Unfair Competition

Copyright was designed as incentive for authors to create new works from which to profit. Fair use is a provision of copyright law that allows a limited amount of copying for educational purposes, so long as that use does not diminish the market value of the work for the creator, or allow the second party to profit from someone else's work. Photographers and song writers have found a technology allowing "digital watermarks" so their work displayed in cyberspace can be identified and protected from unlawful use. When someone downloads a digitally marked photograph, for example, he can click on the copyright symbol and be connected to the company holding copyright information. The company can check on illegal use of the photograph by sending web crawlers to search the web for the imbedded mark and report the location of photos to the company with a database of legal users of the photograph.

Audio watermarks are even more remarkable. They remain intact even when the sound is transformed from digital to analog for radio broadcast, so that monitoring equipment hears the mark and reports the artist and song back to the company.

When The New York Times entered a contractual arrangement with Barnes & Noble to link book reviews in the online newspaper to the online bookstore source, 26 independent bookstores and the American Booksellers Association protested the partnership as an unfair business practice and filed suit claiming the deal put them at a competitive disadvantage and posed a threat to their survival. But, *Advertising Age* editors say such arrangements are a proper use of the new technology, and that critics are engaging in "a misguided effort to apply rigid, print-driven rules to fluid cyberspace." The use of the links serves the readers.

Trademark Law

A trademark is any word, symbol or device, or a combination of the three, that identify an individual's or company's goods or services. Trademarks are registered with the Patent and Trademark Office, but must be protected by the owner. Letters, threats of lawsuits and legal actions are used to stop other people from using the mark. No government agency opposes trademark violation. If public use of the mark is unopposed, the trademark becomes generic and can no longer be claimed exclusively by the individual or company.

In cyberspace, trademark protection has taken strange turns. One area is the domain name for Web sites. In 1992, a Virginia-based firm called Network Solutions won a government contract for a monopoly on Internet name registration. Domain names were handed out on a first-come, first-served basis, and many companies found they were unable to buy their own name for a domain because it had already been sold. In June of 1998, the U. S. government issued a policy paper calling for a non-profit organization to take over domain name management because a corporate name is valuable and third parties should not be allowed to claim or abuse it. The Clinton Administration plans to end federal financing for the management of Internet domain names.

In August of 1998, a Los Angeles judge ruled that one company, Mailbank, did not have the right to register the domains of avery.net and dennisn.net since they were the trade names of office supply venders.

Courts are deciding if trademark infringement is possible when it is invisible, such as when hidden meta tags direct search engines to list a different site from what the consumer expects. For example, Chrysler Corporation has filed against two New York Internet companies, accusing them of trademark infringement for sending would-be customers to a pornographic site. CNN filed suit in Atlanta accusing The Net, Inc., of diluting its trademark and tarnishing its name because The Net uses a Web address similar to CNN's to sell pornography. In 1997, *Playboy* won a judgment forcing site operators to remove words from their meta tags that made search engines send would-be *Playboy* visitors elsewhere.

Online Sale of Software

Most software comes with so called shrink-wrap licenses which are legal contracts that end with a button that reads "I accept." Consumers must click in order to install the software, thereby agreeing to the contract. States are in process of passing legislation known as Article 2B of the Uniform Commercial Code (UCC 2B) making these contracts binding even when they are incomprehensible. UCC 2B may outlaw the right to make back-up copies of software without permission from the manufacturer.

Secure Payment

The Internet has become a 24-hour shopping mall, with first quarter ad revenue for 1998 at $350 million. Recently, a company got federal approval to let online investors buy shares in its mutual funds with credit cards. In late 1998, the first Internet bank was granted a national charter by federal regulators. Paper checks are used for 50 percent of online payments and credit cards pay the rest. Yet merchants and credit card companies need to agree on payment standards for online card use. New payment options beyond the credit card have emerged, such as electronic wallets—browser-linked applications that manage a consumer's payment accounts and digital certificates, and Echecks—secure checks send via e-mail. Protecting payment is key, and an inexpensive new chip introduced in 1998 that reads fingerprints for identification may solve the problems of fraud and theft without new legislation.

See also: Freedom of Speech, Obscenity

Bibliography and Further Reading

Harper, Christopher. *And That's the Way it Will Be: News and Information in a Digital World*. NY: New York University Press, 1998.

Platt, Charles. *Anarchy Online: Net Sex Net Crime*. NY: Harper Prism, 1997.

Provenzo, Eugene F., Jr. *The Educator's Brief Guide to the Internet and the World Wide Web*. NY: Eye on Education, 1997.

CUBBY, INC. V. COMPUSERVE, INC.

Legal Citation: 776 F.Supp. 135 (1991)

Plaintiff
Cubby, Inc., and Richard G. Blanchard

Defendant
CompuServe Inc.

Plaintiff's Claim
That CompuServe was liable for defamatory statements published in the newsletter, *Rumorville*, against rival newsletter, *Skuttlebut*.

Chief Lawyer for Plaintiff
Leo Kayser

Chief Defense Lawyer
Leslie Mullady

Judge
Peter K. Leisure

Place
New York, New York

Date of Decision
29 October 1991

Decision
The court ruled in favor of CompuServe finding that the Internet service provider was not liable for the statements printed in the newsletter transmitted through its system.

Significance
The case applied traditional libel law, originally developed for the printed and broadcast medium, to the Internet for the first time. The court extended protections traditionally held by information distributors, such as newsstands and bookstores, to the newly emerging industry of internet providers. As a result, the court extended First Amendment rights to Internet publishers and set a precedent for the regulation of Internet activity.

American courts have long recognized the First Amendment protections of the free flow of speech as they relate to the distributors of information. As the U.S. Supreme Court made clear in *Smith v. California* (1959), requirements for distributors, such as book sellers or news vendors, to know the contents of every material they sell would place an undue burden on distributors, and an impediment to the free flow of speech. The emergence of online computer service companies by the 1990s, including CompuServe, America Online, and Prodigy, and thousands of electronic bulletin board operators using the service companies created new forms of tort liability ranging from defamation to trademark and copyright issues. The Internet services provide online general information, or electronic library, available to subscribers who pay a membership fee. Included are thousands of information sources including special-interest bulletin boards, interactive online "chat rooms," and databases on various topics. Unlike electronic mail (e-mail) that is usually directed to specific addresses, bulletin boards and newsgroups can reach a much larger audience. The providers exert various levels of control over the material that passes through their systems, from none to some filtering.

Liability has historically grown as communications technology grew. The Internet not only greatly altered how individuals communicated, but also how libel could occur due to its broad reach and the anonymous nature of many participants. As a result, the nation's insurance market scrambled to develop policies for online service providers and other entities operating on the Internet to financially protect them from defamation, invasion of privacy, and copyright infringement claims. The record of case law and legislation concerning cyberspace was still young at the inception of the 1990s. Little guidance existed on how much knowledge and editorial control by a provider was needed to establish liability.

CompuServe of Columbus, Ohio offered, as one of its many computer services, access to CompuServe Information Service (CIS) which provided thousands of information sources for subscribers. Within CIS, subscribers could access the Journalism Forum, and within this Forum was the newsletter *Rumorville*, which con-

---

Regulation of the Internet

The Internet, a powerful, new, unregulated, electronic communication medium, grew rapidly in the 1990s. By 1995, 24 million people subscribed to Internet providers. Internet technology allows worldwide transmission of written text and digitized images. Concerns over what was transmitted across the net escalated. The related debate focused on creating controls versus freedom of ideas.

Pornography is one major concern. Regulation proponents contend distribution of obscene or indecent material to children must be halted. Civil libertarians counter with a defense of freedom of speech and ideas. Furthermore, attempts at regulation usually restrict more than intended.

Some maintain online providers must review all material posted on the Internet. Opponents argue that it is unreasonable for providers to be held libel for everything that flows though their hardware.

Another issue is "content filtering." Filtering allows individuals to block out material. Proponents advocate the ability to block out at the receiving end. Opponents say that not only individuals but employers, organizations, and even entire service providers could block out materials, causing obtrusive barriers in freewheeling Internet communication.

Source(s): Marshall, Joshua M. "Will Free Speech Get Tangled in the Net?" *The American Prospect,* January-February 1998.

---

tained information about broadcast journalism and journalists. The Journalism Forum was produced for CompuServe by Cameron Communications, Inc. (CCI). CCI in turn contracted with Don Fitzpatrick Associates (DFA) to create the newsletter *Rumorville,* which was loaded into CIS as part of the Journalism Forum and made immediately available to CIS subscribers.

With the intent to compete with *Rumorville,* Cubby, Inc. developed and offered *Skuttlebut,* a subscription newsletter which also contained information about television and radio journalism. *Rumorville* soon published remarks, including "a suggestion that the individuals at *Skuttlebut* gained access to information first published by *Rumorville* 'through some back door' . . . and a description of *Skuttlebut* as a 'new start-up scam.'" *Rumorville* also published a statement that the creator of *Skuttlebut,* Robert Blanchard, was "'bounced' from his previous employer, WABC." Based on these statements, Cubby accused CompuServe of libel, business disparagement, and unfair competition.

In defense, CompuServe chose not to address the allegedly defamatory nature of the statements but rather CompuServe's liability for those statements. The key issue became CompuServe's relation to *Rumorville.*

Cubby claimed that CompuServe acted as a "republisher" of the defamatory statements. In *Cianci v. New Times Publishing* (1980), the responsibility of the republisher was defined as, "One who repeats or otherwise republishes defamatory matter is subject to liability as if he had originally published it." But Judge Peter K. Leisure, writing for the court, agreed with CompuServe that the company was not a republisher, but rather a distributor. A distributor, such as a library, bookseller, or news vendor, holds different rights and responsibilities than a publisher or republisher. In *Lerman v. Chuck-*

leberry Publishing (1981), Leisure noted that, "New York courts have long held that vendors and distributors of defamatory publications are not liable if they neither know nor have reason to know of the defamation." Leisure considered CIS to be a resource for many different information sources, hence a distributor of those sources. In a sense, CIS was an electronic library. Because Cubby did not claim that CompuServe had knowledge of the defamatory statements, and CompuServe did not review the information before it was posted in the Journalism Forum, the company could also not be held liable as a distributor.

Leisure explained,

> CompuServe and companies like it are at the forefront of the information industry revolution. High technology has markedly increased the speed with which information is gathered and processed; it is now possible for an individual with a personal computer, modem, and telephone line to have instantaneous access to thousands of news publications from across the United States and around the world. While CompuServe may decline to carry a given publication altogether, in reality, once it does decide to carry a publication, it will have little or no editorial control over that publication as part of a forum that is managed by a company unrelated to CompuServe.

Leisure extended those First Amendment protections previously established in *Smith v. California* to Internet information providers by writing,

> Technology is rapidly transforming the information industry. A computerized database is the functional equivalent of a more traditional

news vendor, and the inconsistent application of a lower standard of liability to the electronic news distributor such as CompuServe than that which is applied to a public library, book store, or newsstand would impose an undue burden on the free flow of information.

Because of all these factors, the court dismissed the charges in a summary judgment.

Impact

The *Cubby* case highlighted the beginning struggle by the courts to assess accountability for illegal conduct on the Internet. The *Cubby* decision strengthened the legitimacy of online servers as publishers and distributors of information. The decision better defined the roles of on-line services, and extended to these services the same First Amendment protections enjoyed by other forms of journalism and expression.

In determining whether CompuServe was like a publisher or a common carrier, like telephone companies, the court determined the latter. However, Internet libel law was still in its infancy as the 1990s progressed. Surprisingly, the number of Internet libel cases did not skyrocket through the 1990s as some anticipated.

As the electronic media market grew, still more definition of liability and on-line libel was needed. In the case of *Stratton Oakmont v. Prodigy Services Co.* (1995), the New York Supreme Court found that Prodigy was liable for statements published on a bulletin board it supported. Critics charged that the courts in essence rewarded companies, such as CompuServe in the *Cubby* case, who exert little control over the material they transmit by greatly limiting their liability for the nature of material transmitted. Whereas, a server such as Prodigy is charged with much greater liability because they attempted to screen materials submitted for transmittal.

Quickly, Congress passed the 1996 act to regulate the material transmitted on the Internet and limit the liability of service providers such as CompuServe and Prodigy. The Supreme Court in *Reno v. American Civil Liberties Union* (1997) struck down parts of the law regulating Internet content on First Amendment freedom of speech grounds, but the section of the law addressing server liability remained valid. The courts in *Zeran v. America Online* (1997) provided an even broader interpretation of the immunity to prosecution that the service providers hold. Additional questions of Internet service provider liability for libel arose in 1997 when White House aide Sidney Blumenthal field suit against America Online and a columnist employed by AOL, Matt Drudge. The courts dismissed AOL from the suit based on immunity from the Communications Decency Act and Drudge claimed constitutional protection, which journalists have in reporting on public figures.

A wide range of defamation and other liability issues continued to confront online service providers and their users through the 1990s. Strong interest over legislatively regulating the Internet and protecting innocent individuals from defamation continued as the decade came to a close.

Related Cases

Smith v. California, 361 U.S. 147 (1959).
Cianci v. New Times Publishing Co., 639 F 2d 54 (1980).
Lerman v. Chuckleberry Publishing, Inc., 521 F.Supp. 228 S.D.N.Y. (1981).
Statton Oakmont, Inc. v. Prodigy Services, Co., WL 323710 N.Y.S.C. (1995).
Zeran v. America Online, Inc., 129 F.3d 327 (1997).

Bibliography and Further Reading

Cameron, Donald M., and Smith Lyons, editors. Defamation on the Internet. Website, http://www.jurisdiction.com.

Godwin, Mike. *Cyber Rights: Defending Free Speech in the Digital Age.* New York: Times Books, 1998.

Rose, Lance. *NetLaw: Your Rights in the Online World.* Berkeley, CA: Osborne McGraw-Hill, 1995.

Stuckey, Kent D. *Internet and Online Law.* New York: Law Journal Seminars Press, 1996.

CYBER PROMOTIONS, INC. V. AMERICA ONLINE, INC.

Legal Citation: 948 F.Supp. 456 (1996)

Plaintiff
Cyber Promotions, Inc.

Defendant
America Online, Inc.

Plaintiff's Claim
That the defendant's blocking of e-mail advertisements sent by the plaintiff to the defendant's customers violated the plaintiff's right to free speech under the First Amendment.

Chief Lawyer for Plaintiff
Ralph A. Jacobs

Chief Defense Lawyer
Ronald P. Schiller

Judge
Charles R. Weiner

Place
Philadelphia, Pennsylvania

Date of Decision
4 November 1996

Decision
That because the defendant was a private company, rather than a public actor, its blocking of the plaintiff's e-mail advertisements did not violate the First Amendment; the First Amendment only prevents public officials from restricting freedom of speech, not private actors.

Significance
The court's decision recognized that private on-line service providers have nearly absolute power to control the information which is sent over their on-line systems, without regard to the First Amendment. Thus, on-line service providers are free to impose whatever type of restrictions they please on the dissemination of information over their systems following the court's decision.

During the late 1980s and early 1990s, the proliferation of computers and computer technologies lead to the development of the Internet. The Internet, a vast, complex network of interconnected computers, allows millions of computer users to communicate with each other and to access information from around the world on virtually any topic. There are a number of ways to access the Internet. For example, many universities provide Internet access to students and faculty, and some employers provide such access to their employees. However, a large number of people access the Internet through the use of private on-line companies. A person can subscribe to the on-line company and pay a monthly fee for the service. When the user connects to the on-line company, the user is given access to whatever amenities the on-line company may have. For example, the on-line company may provide electronic mail services, its own newsgroups, information services, and "chat rooms." These companies also generally provide access to the Internet.

America Online, Inc. (AOL) is one such private on-line company. Cyber Promotions, Inc., an Internet advertiser, sent unsolicited electronic mail advertisements to AOL subscribers via the Internet. On 26 January 1996, AOL sent a letter to Cyber Promotions advising it that AOL was unhappy with Cyber Promotions' dissemination of these unsolicited e-mails to AOL subscribers. When Cyber Promotions refused to stop the practice, AOL sent a number of "e-mail bombs" to Cyber Promotions' Internet service providers. AOL accomplished this by sending all unsolicited e-mail messages, which were addressed to AOL subscribers but not delivered, back to Cyber Promotions' service providers. These "bombs" disabled Cyber Promotions' service providers because their sheer bulk overwhelmed the capabilities of the service providers.

In response, Cyber Promotions filed a lawsuit in the U.S. District Court for the Eastern District of Pennsylvania, alleging that as a result of AOL's "e-mail bombs" two Internet service providers canceled their relationship with Cyber Promotions, and thus AOL interfered with its business relationships. Thereafter, AOL filed its own lawsuit in the U.S. District Court for the Eastern District of Virginia, alleging various counts of computer fraud and trademark infringement. The Virginia court transferred the second case to the Pennsylvania court, which consolidated the two lawsuits. The Pennsylvania court then directed the parties to file legal briefs addressing whether Cyber Promotions has a right to send unsolicited e-mail messages to AOL subscribers, or conversely whether AOL has a right to block such e-mail.

Private Restriction on Internet Speech Is Valid

The First Amendment prohibits the government from "abridging the freedom of speech." AOL argued that, because it is a private company and not a government actor, it was free to prohibit Cyber Promotions' e-mails. Cyber Promotions, on the other hand, argued that although AOL is a private actor, its conduct had character of governmental, or state action. As the Supreme Court explained in the 1974 case of *Jackson v. Metropolitan Edison Co.*, there are three tests under which a purely private action may be deemed "state action" for purposes of determining whether the conduct is prohibited by the Constitution. Judge Charles Weiner rejected Cyber Promotions' arguments that any of these three tests converted AOL's action into a governmental restriction on free speech prohibited by the First Amendment.

The first test is known as the "exclusive public function" test. Under this test, conduct of a private actor may be deemed to constitute state action where the private actor is exercising powers typically exercised by the government. For example, where a state government contracts with a private company to administer the state's prisons, then the actions of the private company will be deemed to constitute state action because

the running of prisons is normally a power exercised by the state. Judge Weiner concluded that AOL did not exercise any such powers with respect to the Internet. Indeed, he noted, no entity seems to exercise any control over the Internet. He reasoned that, although AOL opened its system to the public, which can send e-mails into the AOL system, it did not do so by exercising any traditional governmental powers. Thus, AOL's provision of Internet e-mail access did not meet the exclusive public function test.

Judge Weiner also rejected Cyber Promotions' claim that AOL's conduct constituted state action under the second test explained in *Jackson*. Under this second test, called the "symbiotic relationship" or "joint participation" test, a private actor's conduct will be deemed state action where the state has so insinuated itself into the private actor's conduct that the public and private actors are acting together in furtherance of a common goal. Cyber Promotions argued that, because AOL filed a lawsuit asking the court to prohibit it from sending the unsolicited e-mails, AOL and the court which was unquestionably a state actor were engaged in a joint enterprise to restrict Cyber Promotions' free speech rights. Judge Weiner rejected this argument, noting that the mere fact that a private party seeks to enforce its private rights in court does not transform its actions into state action. Cyber Promotions offered no other evidence of concerted action between AOL and a government actor. Thus, Judge Weiner concluded that AOL could not be considered a state actor under the joint participation test.

Finally, Judge Weiner rejected Cyber Promotions' claim that AOL was a state actor under the third test

American Online Headquarters in Chantilly, Virginia, 1997. © Photograph by Willia Philpott. AP/Wide World Photos.

explained by the *Jackson* Court. This third test, known as the "government compulsion" test, converts private action into state action where the state has coerced or strongly encouraged the state actor to engage in the allegedly unconstitutional conduct. Judge Weiner noted that, as with the second test, Cyber Promotions presented no evidence that any governmental actor encouraged or participated in AOL's e-mail bombings. Thus, AOL's conduct could not be deemed state action under the government compulsion test. Thus, Judge Weiner concluded that, because AOL is a private company, Cyber Promotions has no First Amendment right to send unsolicited e-mail over AOL's e-mail system. Therefore, AOL did not infringe on Cyber Promotions' First Amendment free speech rights by blocking these e-mails and delivering them back to Cyber Promotions.

Impact

Shortly after he issued his decision, a judge in the U.S. District Court for the Northern District of Ohio adopted Judge Weiner's reasoning. In *Compuserve Inc. v. Cyber Promotions, Inc.,* that court rejected a similar claim by Cyber Promotions, relying extensively on Judge Weiner's opinion. Thus, it is apparent that private on-line service providers are free to regulate the type of speech which is disseminated over their on-line systems without regard to the First Amendment. Given that other courts have struck down a number of different restrictions on Internet speech enacted by the state and federal governments, the courts are in large part coming to the conclusion that the Internet is best left alone to allow Internet users to police their own system.

Related Cases

Jackson v. Metropolitan Edison Co., 419 U.S. 345 (1974).
Lugar v. Edmondson Oil Co., 457 U.S. 922 (1982).
Edmonson v. Leesville Concrete Co., 500 U.S. 614 (1991).
Turner Broadcasting Systems, Inc. v. Federal Communications Commission, 512 U.S. 622 (1994).
Reno v. American Civil Liberties Union, 514 U.S. 844 (1997).
Compuserve Inc. v. Cyber Promotions, Inc., 962 F.Supp. 1015 (1997).

Bibliography and Further Reading

Alexander, Lawrence A. *Whom Does the Constitution Command?: A Conceptual Analysis with Practical Implications.* New York: Greenwood Press, 1988.

Beeferman, Larry W. *Images of the Citizen and State: Resolving the Paradox of Public and Private Power in Constitutional Law.* Lanham, MD: University Press of America, 1996.

Emord, Jonathan W. *Freedom, Technology, and the First Amendment.* San Francisco: Pacific Research Institute for Public Policy, 1991.

Nimmer, Raymond T. *The Law of Computer Technology.* Boston: Warren Gorham Lamont, 1992.

AMERICAN LIBRARIES ASSOCIATION V. PATAKI

Legal Citation: 969 F.Supp. 160 (1997)

Plaintiff
American Libraries Association, et al.

Defendant
George Pataki, Governor of the State of New York, et al.

Plaintiff's Claim
That a New York law prohibiting the dissemination of obscene materials to children through a computer placed impermissible burdens on commerce between the states, and was thus unconstitutional.

Chief Lawyer for Plaintiff
Jeanne Lahiff, Assistant Attorney General of the State of New York

Chief Defense Lawyer
Michael K. Hertz

Judge
Loretta A. Preska

Place
New York, New York

Date of Decision
20 June 1997

Decision
That the New York statute placed substantial burdens on the free flow of commerce and conflicted with generally applicable federal laws, and thus was unconstitutional.

Significance
By invalidating New York's attempt to regulate Internet communications, the court made it clear that the broad, national character of the Internet renders such communications susceptible only to regulation by the federal government. Thus, state attempts to regulate Internet communications will always be invalid. Viewed in conjunction with the Supreme Court's decision in *Reno v. American Civil Liberties Union* (1997) which struck down a law similar to the New York law on the ground that it violated the First Amendment right to free speech, the Court's decision was a welcome relief to Internet uses who feared increasing government regulation of this rapidly expanding area of communication.

Article I, section 8 of the U.S. Constitution describes the powers of the U.S. Congress. Clause 3 of this section, generally referred to as the Commerce Clause, in part grants Congress the power to "regulate Commerce . . . among the several states." Although the Commerce Clause speaks in terms of a positive grant of power to the federal government, the Commerce Clause has long been recognized to carry an implicit negative component prohibiting the state government from regulating interstate commerce in certain respects, notably where the state regulation would burden the free flow of commerce from state to state. This "Negative Commerce Clause" was first recognized by Justice Thomas Johnson in *Gibbons v. Ogden* (1824). Specifically, the Supreme Court has recognized three types of state laws or regulations which are prohibited by the negative aspect of the Commerce Clause: (1) regulations which are aimed directly at prohibiting interstate commerce; (2) regulations which unduly burden interstate commerce; and (3) regulations aimed at aspects of commerce which by their very nature require uniform treatment throughout the United States. In *American Libraries Association v. Pataki*, the court system considered the extent to which the negative aspect of the Commerce Clause prohibited the state of New York from imposing restrictions on the types of material received over the Internet.

During the late 1980s and early 1990s, the proliferation of computers and computer technologies led to the development of the Internet. The Internet, a vast, complex network of interconnected computers, allows millions of computer users to communicate with each other and to access information from around the world on virtually any topic. Among these various categories of information, a large amount of material dealing with topics from drugs to pornography to weaponry is transmitted over the Internet. New York, along with a number of other states and the federal government, sought to limit the extent to which such material was sent and received over the Internet. Specifically, New York passed a law making it a crime to knowingly send over any computer communications system any sexually explicit material to a minor.

The American Library Association, along with a number of other library associations, bookstore associations,

Ralph Nader

Born in 1934 in Winsted, Connecticut, Ralph Nader is an attorney and consumer rights advocate who is considered to be the founding father of the consumer rights movement. In the 1980s Nader campaigned against car insurance rates in California and a 50 percent wage increase for members of Congress. His success with these two high profile issues stand as vivid illustrations of the consumer rights movement which Nader is associated. Nader is the founder of the Center for Responsive Law, Public Interest Research Group, Center for Auto safety, Clean Water Action Project, the Disability Rights Center, and the Project for Corporate Responsibility.

Nader has been most influential in the area of public safety. He has written numerous books on the subject of consumer protection the most notable of which is *Unsafe at Any Speed* in 1965. The book resulted in the discontinuation of GM's *Corvair* which Nader reported was dangerous in high speed turns. He was also instrumental in the formation of the Environmental Protection Agency (EPA) (1970), the Freedom of Information Act (1974), and the Occupational Safety and Health Administration (OSHA) (1976). During the deregulating Reagan era the term "Naderism" was coined to characterize the consumer rights movement as an extreme.

Source(s): *Current Biography*, 1986 p. 402.

Internet service providers, and publishers filed a lawsuit in the U.S. District Court for the Southern District of New York, claiming that New York had no power to regulate interstate transmission of material over the Internet, and thus the law was an unconstitutional violation of the negative aspect of the Commerce Clause. The plaintiffs asked the court to enter a preliminary injunction preventing the state from enforcing the law. The court concluded that the New York statute violated the negative aspect of the Commerce Clause, and thus the plaintiffs were entitled to an injunction preventing the state from enforcing the law.

Negative Commerce Clause Applies to Internet

Judge Loretta Preska began her analysis by noting that while the Internet is certainly an innovative technological field, "the innovativeness of the technology does not preclude the application of traditional legal principles provided that those principles are adaptable to cyberspace." Judge Preska first concluded that the Internet, and the New York law, relate to "commerce" under the Commerce Clause. She noted that people engage in commercial transactions over the Internet, and even those who use the Internet for purely non-commercial reasons often do so through a commercial Internet service. Thus, Judge Preska applied the traditional legal principles related to the negative aspect of the Commerce Clause and concluded that the New York law violated the Commerce Clause in three ways.

First, Judge Preska concluded that the New York statute was impermissible under the negative aspect of the Commerce Clause because it regulates conduct which occurs wholly outside of New York. She rejected New York's argument that the statute sought only to regulate the conduct of New York residents sending indecent material over the Internet, reasoning that the very nature of the Internet precludes such an argument. She concluded that "[t]he Internet is wholly insensitive to geographic distinctions." She based this conclusion

George Pataki, 1995. © Archive Photo/Dipeso.

Mayhem Manuals

The explosion in Internet usage has raised new questions about whether all information therein has a guarantee of Freedom of the Press under the First Amendment. The Constitution guaranteed a free and uncensored press; later expansions provide similar coverages to other print and broadcast media. The 1986 Communication Privacy Act protects individual privacy rights in using email, bulletin boards, and other electronic media.

The devastation caused by the Oklahoma City bombing increased awareness that the Internet was itself a tool used by hate groups and others advocating violence and anarchy. Materials detailing how to construct bombs, such as a 93 page "mayhem manual," are available on the Internet, as well as in print. During a Senate Subcommittee debate on Terrorism, Narcotics, and International Operations, Senators discussed ways that public safety might be maintained without censorship. Up for debate was whether censorship was permissible in cases such as bomb building manuals. Further, if censorship of such materials was imposed, whether it was feasible to monitor and control such information considering the vastness of the Internet. Senator Arlen Specter noted a 1969 U.S. Supreme Court decision that stated, "Speech could not be punished unless it was 'an incitement to imminent lawless action.'"

Source(s): Hernandez, Debra Gersh. "Mayhem Online." *Editor & Publisher,* 24 June 1995, p. 34.

on several factors. For example, she noted that there is no way for a person posting an Internet web page to screen who is accessing the web page based on the location of the user, thus making it impossible for a web poster outside of New York to block a minor in New York from accessing the material. Similarly, people communicating through newsgroup postings or "chat rooms"—both of which involve forms of group electronic discussions—have no way of knowing the location of the other people participating in the discussion. Further, it is possible, and quite frequent, for people communicating via chat rooms or electronic mail to mask the location from which they are communicating. Finally, electronic mail may be routed through New York even though both the sender and recipient are outside New York, or conversely may be routed through another state even though both the sender and recipient are in New York. Thus, Judge Preska concluded, "[t]he New York Act . . . cannot effectively be limited to purely intrastate communications over the Internet because no such communications exist. No user could reliably restrict her communications only to New York recipients."

Next, Judge Preska concluded that, even if the New York law was interpreted as involving only an incidental burden on interstate commerce rather than a direct burden, the statute violated the negative aspect of the Commerce Clause because the burdens the law places on commerce between the states outweigh the benefits received by the state from the law. In the 1970 case of *Pike v. Bruce Church, Inc.* the Court set forth a balancing test for analyzing laws which only indirectly burden interstate commerce. Under this test, the state law "will be upheld unless the burden imposed on commerce is clearly excessive in relation to the putative local benefits." Applying this test in *American Libraries*

Association, Judge Preska agreed with the state that the protection of children from receiving indecent materials is a legitimate purpose for the state to pursue. Nevertheless, she concluded that the benefits of the law are not overwhelming. She reasoned that it was unlikely that out of state senders of such material would be prosecuted in New York under the law. She also noted that New York has other, more effective laws designed to protect children from sexual exploitation. On the contrary, Judge Preska concluded that the New York law substantially burdens interstate commerce because it "casts its net worldwide" and is likely to deter people from sending communications which may not be banned by the law if the person is unsure of the extent of the law. Thus, she concluded, as a second basis for striking down the New York law, that "[t]he severe burden on interstate commerce resulting from the New York statute is not justifiable in light of the attenuated local benefits arising from it."

Finally, Judge Preska concluded that the Internet was the type of commerce which, by its very nature, demanded uniform, national regulation and not inconsistent regulation by the states. Relying on Supreme Court cases noting that certain aspects of commerce, such as highway and railway regulations, must be uniform across the United States if an efficient economic system is to be maintained, Judge Preska noted that "effective regulation [of the Internet] will require national, and more likely global, cooperation. Regulation by any single state can only result in chaos, because at least some states will likely enact laws subjecting Internet users to conflicting obligations." Accordingly, the need for uniform national regulation of the Internet provided a third basis for concluding that the New York law violated the negative aspect of the Commerce Clause.

Impact

The court's decision in *American Libraries Association* is extremely important. If followed by other federal courts, the decision means that only Congress, and not the states, will be able to regulate the flow of information over the Internet. This impact is particularly important given the Supreme Court's subsequent holding in the 1997 case of *Reno v. American Civil Liberties Union*. In *American Libraries Association*, Judge Preska did not reach the plaintiffs' argument that the New York statute violated the First Amendment's guarantee of free speech, because the law was unconstitutional under the Commerce Clause. In *Reno*, the Court invalidated a federal law regulating indecent material over the Internet which was similar to the New York law on the ground that it violated the right to free speech. Thus taken together, *American Libraries Association* and *Reno* provide broad protections for Internet users. Under these decisions, only the U.S. Congress, and not the states, may regulate the Internet, and Congress must do so in a way which does not violate the First Amendment.

Related Cases

Gibbons v. Ogden, 22 U.S. 1 (1824).

Price v. Bruce Church, Inc., 397 U.S. 137 (1970).

Healy v. The Beer Institute, 491 U.S. 324 (1989).

Reno v. American Civil Liberties Union, 512 U.S. 844 (1997).

Bibliography and Further Reading

American Civil Liberties Union, and Electronic Privacy Information Center, First Amendment http://www.firstamendment.org.

Corwin, Edward S. *The Commerce Power vs. States Rights.* Princeton, NJ: Princeton University Press, 1936.

Emord, Jonathan W. *Freedom, Technology, and the First Amendment.* San Francisco: Pacific Research Institute for Public Policy, 1991.

Frankfurter, Felix. *The Commerce Clause Under Marshall, Taney & Waite.* Chicago: Quadrangle Press, 1964.

Gavit, Bernard C. *The Commerce Clause of the United States Constitution.* New York: AMS Press, 1970.

Nimmer, Raymond T. *The Law of Computer Technology.* Boston: Warren Gorham Lamont, 1992.

ZERAN V. AMERICA ONLINE, INC.

Legal Citation: 129 F. 3d 327 (4th Cir. 1997)

Appellant
Kenneth M. Zeran

Appellee
America Online, Inc. (AOL)

Appellant's Claim
That AOL's delay in responding to notification of defamatory messages posted on their Internet system constituted libel in violation of the First Amendment.

Chief Lawyer for Appellant
John Saul Edwards

Chief Lawyer for Appellee
Patrick Joseph Carome

Judges
Chief Judge Wilkinson (writing for the court), Circuit Judge Russell, and U.S. District Judge Boyle

Place
North Carolina

Date of Decision
12 November 1997

Decision
Upheld district court decision that AOL was free of liability for anonymous third party postings on their system.

Significance
The decision meant Internet service providers (ISP) were not responsible as publishers or distributors for what their subscribers wrote, even when receiving notice of potential defamatory language from other parties. The ruling sent a clear message that Section 230 of The Communications Decency Act of 1996 designed to protect ISPs could withstand legal challenge and protect the newly emerging medium of the Internet from unwarranted government intrusion on freedom of speech. However, the decision raised issues concerning the applicability of traditional libel law to the high speed, high volume world of electronic communications. Victims of malicious defamation were essentially left without legal recourse for remedies.

The Internet, with its instantaneous communications and global reach, created unique legal pressures on the First Amendment right of free speech. The Internet, a new bastion of instant and uncensored expression, became a convenient vehicle for material of potentially obscene or defamatory nature. Many citizens, including those with children vulnerable to predators using the World Wide Web and members of minority groups who were targets of hate and racist commentary, were justifiably concerned. Questions of censorship and liability arose which heightened concerns over preserving the constitutional rights of free speech within this new technological framework.

The first case addressing Internet Service Provider (ISP) liability for third-party posted defamation statements was *Cubby, Inc. v. CompuServe, Inc.* in 1991. However, that case involved a known author and the service provider, CompuServe, won its case by claiming lack of editorial control, hence no liability for the particular messages. Then, in *Stratton Oakmont v. Prodigy Services, Inc.* (1995) the court ruled against the ISP, Prodigy. Because Prodigy placed some controls over what could be posted on its system, the court considered Prodigy a publisher and, therefore, responsible for the content of posted statements. The *Stratton* decision sent shock waves through the Internet industry and potentially set the stage for considerable online defamation lawsuits. No clear-cut guidelines existed for ISPs to avoid liability for defamation. Congress quickly responded. On 8 February 1996, Congress passed the Communications Decency Act of 1996 (CDA) to address these issues and others. Section 230 of the act, intending to promote unfettered free speech on the Internet and encourage self-regulation by ISPs, placed liability for obscene and defaming statements solely on the original authors. The intent of Section 230 was to allow ISPs to exert control without incurring liability so that speech not protected by the First Amendment could be filtered out.

A Nightmare in Seattle

Kenneth M. Zeran operated a home-based business in Seattle, Washington, that depended on his telephone for access to the public. On 25 April 1995, six days after the bombing of the federal building in Oklahoma City, an unidentified person posted a message on an AOL bulletin board advertising "Naughty Oklahoma T-Shirts." The shirts featured offensive slogans related to the bombing. The name "Ken" and Zeran's Seattle telephone number were given as the contact for those interested in purchasing the shirts. Zeran, immediately inundated with calls that included derogatory messages and death threats, called AOL and explained his problem. AOL responded that the posting would be removed, but as a matter of policy AOL would not post a retraction.

The next day, another posting advertised additional shirts with new slogans, again offering Zeran's number as a contact and encouraging interested parties to continue to call back due to high demand. The postings continued for four days, with new items and slogans being added to the offering. By 30 April, Zeran was receiving abusive phone calls about every two minutes, some containing death threats.

During this time, a copy of the first AOL posting was sent to the Oklahoma City radio station KRXO. On 1 May a KRXO announcer read the message on the air, attributed the authorship to "Ken" at Zeran's phone number, and urged listeners to call the Seattle number. Zeran was inundated with calls from Oklahoma City that contained violent language and death threats.

Zeran notified the local police and the Seattle FBI, and remained in contact with AOL and KRXO regarding the incidents. AOL assured Zeran that the subscriber's account would soon be closed. Local police began surveillance of Zeran's home to protect him. Finally, an Oklahoma City newspaper exposed the AOL postings as a hoax, and KRXO made an on-air apology. By 14 May 1995 the number of abusive calls to Zeran subsided to 15 a day. In January of 1996 Zeran filed suit against KRXO in the U.S. District Court for the Western District of Oklahoma and in April, he filed a separate suit in the same court against AOL. He could not bring action against the party who posted the messages because of AOL's failure to maintain adequate records of its subscribers.

Zeran alleged AOL was liable for defamatory speech initiated by a third party. Zeran argued that once notified, AOL had an obligation to remove the messages, notify other subscribers that they were false, and to screen against future postings. AOL used Section 230 of CDA as its defense. The case was transferred to the Eastern District of Virginia which ruled in favor of AOL. Zeran appealed to the U.S. Court of Appeals.

Distributors as Publishers

In the court of appeals decision, Chief Judge Wilkinson elaborated on the lower court's decision by noting that Section 230 of CDA, "precludes courts from entertaining claims that would place a computer service provider in a publisher's role. Thus, lawsuits seeking to hold a service provider liable for its exercise of a publisher's traditional editorial functions—such as deciding whether to publish, withdraw, postpone or alter content—are barred."

However, Zeran argued the law of torts distinguishes distributors from publishers and holds them liable for defamatory material when they have knowledge of their existence. Thus, AOL acted as a distributor as well as a publisher. AOL had been notified, yet the messages were still posted, and the subscriber's access was not closed down in a timely manner. AOL was like a book seller or news vendor who continued to offer offending material for sale after they were notified of the nature of the publications on their shelves. Zeran contended that because a common law distinction existed between distributors and publishers, two different forms of liability applied. AOL was liable as a distributor which was not protected by Section 230.

Wilkinson disagreed with Zeran's logic. Wilkinson noted that even if Zeran had "satisfied the requirements for imposition of distributor liability, this theory of liability is merely a subset, or a species of publisher liability, and is therefore also foreclosed by 230." In essence, and ironically, Zeran's argument placed AOL as a publisher, hence protected by Section 230. Wilkinson continued, "Because the publication of the statement is a necessary element in a defamation action, only one who publishes can be subject to this form of tort liability . . . In this case, AOL is legally considered to be a publisher. Even distributors are considered to be publishers for the purposes of defamation law."

Judge Wilkinson brought two other important points to light in his decision. First, Section 230 sought to address the problems of both censorship and liability given the sheer volume of traffic on the Internet. Wilkinson wrote, "Interactive computer services have millions of users. The amount of information communicated . . . is, therefore, staggering. The spectre of tort liability in the area of such prolific speech would have an obvious chilling effect. It would be impossible for service providers to screen each of their millions of postings for possible problems."

The second point was that 230 sought to encourage service providers to self-regulate the dissemination of offensive material, both by advertising their philosophy, and by choosing to remove offensive material when notified of its presence.

> Congress enacted 230 to remove disincentives to self-regulation posed by the *Statton Oakmont* decision. Under that court's holding, computer service providers who regulated the dissemination of offensive material . . . risked subjecting themselves to liability, because [it] cast the service provider in the role of a publisher.

The CDA also stopped third parties from indulging in what Wilkinson called "a no-cost means to create future lawsuits." If an ISP was unprotected, any subscriber could notify them that a message they found was offensive, and legally defamatory. The fact of notice would make the ISP responsible for publishing the message. Wilkinson wrote, "Thus, like strict liability, liability upon notice has a chilling effect on the freedom of Internet speech."

Impact

Zeran next appealed to the Supreme Court, but the Court in 1998 refused to hear the case leaving the lower courts' decisions stand. To enhance its public image following the decision, AOL began conducting background checks of the key individuals involved in its various information forums. The checks were an attempt to increase accountability in a largely anonymous communications medium.

The speed, the volume, and the global access of the Internet has international implications legally as well as socially. The Internet has also become an important player in the globalizing commerce. One cautionary note was offered by Chris Hansen, senior staff counsel to the American Civil Liberties Union. Hansen believed that although it was good that ISPs were not treated as though they had to review every message on their site and decide on its defamatory nature, it was wrong that ISPs were free to apply whatever censorship they wished.

With the Internet, false statements highly damaging to peoples' reputations or their businesses could be easily transmitted anonymously to thousands of readers. Critics charged the *Zeran* decision left individuals with almost no legal recourse to correct the injury caused. They claimed the courts went well beyond the literal meaning of the CDA and safeguarded speech not commonly protected by the First Amendment. ISPs received greater protection than any other entity in communications, essentially all the immunity of a common carrier without any regulatory accountability carriers normally bear.

The Supreme Court clearly ruled in *Reno v. American Civil Liberties Union* (1997) that protection of free speech in cyberspace was of paramount importance. Courts began to struggle with protecting individuals from defamatory statements and right to privacy. Over 130 bills were pending before Congress addressing the regulation of speech on the Internet by the end of 1997. Many believed that libel law in general was ineffective, and its application to the Internet only compounded the shortcomings, neither protecting the authors of statements nor the subjects of those statements.

Identifying customers using pseudonyms to post critical comments on the Internet became an important issue in a 1998 Canadian case. A Canadian court ordered two Canadian Internet service providers to identify names of libel suspects allegedly posting anonymous critical comments about Philip Services Corporation of Canada, a recycling company suffering major financial losses in 1997. The ruling could force ISPs to notify users that their privacy cannot be guaranteed, or else the providers could be vulnerable to liability.

Related Cases

Cubby, Inc. v. CompuServe, Inc., 776 F.Supp. 135 S.D.N.Y. (1991).

Statton Oakmont, Inc. v. Prodigy Services, Co., WL 323710 (N.Y. Sup. Ct. 1995).

Reno v. American Civil Liberties Union, 512 U.S. 824 (1997).

Doe v. America Online, Inc., No. CL 97-63 (Fla Cir. Ct. 1997).

Bibliography and Further Reading

American Civil Liberties Union. Website, http://www.aclu.org.

Guenther, Nancy W. Good Samaritan to the Rescue: America Online Free from Publisher and Distributor Liability for Anonymously Posted Defamation. *Communications and the Law,* Vol. 20: pp. 35-95, 1998.

Keeton, W. Page, editor. *Prosser and Keeton on the Law of Torts.* (5th ed.). St. Paul, MN: West Publishing Co., 1984.

AMERICAN CIVIL LIBERTIES UNION V. MILLER

Legal Citation: 96CV.2475MH (1997)

Plaintiffs
American Civil Liberties Union of Georgia (ACLU), The AIDS Survival Project, The Atlanta Free Thought Society, Atlanta Veterans Alliance, Community ConneXion, Electronic Frontier Foundation, Electronic Frontiers Georgia, Representative Mitchell Kaye, Ken Leebow, Bruce Mirken, Bonnie L. Nadri, Josh Riley, John Troyer, and Jonathan Wallace

Defendants
Zell Miller, Governor of Georgia, and Michael Bowers, Georgia State Attorney General

Plaintiffs' Claim
That Georgia's Computer Systems Protection Act is vague and overbroad, violating the First and Fourteenth amendments' rights to free expression and association, the Fifth Amendment's right to privacy, and the Commerce Clause.

Chief Lawyer for Plaintiffs
Ann Beeson

Chief Defense Lawyer
David A. Runion

Judge
Marvin H. Shoob

Place
Atlanta, Georgia

Date of Decision
7 August 1997

Decision
Ruled in favor of the ACLU and granted a preliminary injunction against enforcement of the Georgia Interstate Fraud Statute.

Significance
The ruling posed a wide impact on the way legislators could craft laws regulating the Internet. The decision upheld the right of constitutionally-protected free speech over the Internet and, in doing so, this judgment carried important implications. Pointing out that similar restrictions were not applied to print publications, the court underscored both the inappropriateness of such censorship and the parallel nature of print and Internet media.

The Internet began in the late sixties as a military experiment linking various computer networks. By the 1990s commercial use by private business had mushroomed reaching millions of people globally. The expansive use brought extensive concerns over protection of its users from crime, obscenity, and defamation. During 1996, in the wake of the U.S. Congress' passage of the Communications Decency Act, states considered legislation to regulate online speech. Georgia state legislators approached Internet regulation differently by crafting an act preventing online users from using false names or pseudonyms. That statute, voted into law by the state legislature on 1 July 1996, called for criminal sanctions of up to 12 months in jail and/or up to $1,000 fine for violations.

Legal Action Created Politically Diverse Group of Plaintiffs

Among those objecting to Georgia's legislation were the ACLU, Electronic Frontiers Georgia, Electronic Founders Foundations, as well as politically conservative Georgia State Representative, Mitchell Kaye. The diversity of co-plaintiffs was highlighted by the participation of the Atlanta Veterans Alliance—a Georgia-based organization for gay, lesbian, bisexual, and transgendered veterans. Although politically opposites, the various parties nonetheless agreed that the statute was unconstitutionally vague and overbroad because it barred online users from using pseudonyms or communicating anonymously over the Internet. At a joint press conference held by the plaintiffs in Atlanta, Rep. Kaye explained he became involved after his private web site came under attack by some members of the Georgia House of Representatives. Kaye maintained they felt threatened because his site featured voting records along with political commentary not always flattering. At the conference, Teresa Nelson, executive director of the ACLU of Georgia, announced the ACLU would take the lead in filing a complaint requesting a preliminary injunction to prevent enforcement of Georgia's newly-passed Internet fraud statute.

The complaint filed by the ACLU in September of 1996, claimed that, "The law makes it a crime to use a name that 'falsely' identifies a speaker on the Internet,

---

Should Copyright Law Apply to the Internet?

Copyrights protect the original creative expression of authors, movie makers, and songwriters. Copyrights give authors exclusive rights to reproduce and distribute their work for financial gain. However, an estimated $2 billion in royalty fees were lost in 1997 through internet transmissions. Should copyright laws apply to this new electronic international medium? Most agree they should, but the debate focuses on who is responsible for preventing such violations.

The authors, or "content providers" as known in the computer age, argue "access providers," including commercial online services such as America Online and internet browsers, should be held responsible for the transmission of copyrighted materials. Those actually doing the pirating are often hobbyists with little money or live in foreign countries out of reach of U.S. authorities.

Access providers claim little capability to prevent copyright infringements before their occurrence. They contend a requirement to inform their users of copyright laws and remove copywritten materials from their systems as soon as identified should be their basic responsibilities. Like video recorder distributors of the 1980s, they should not be held responsible for how someone uses their hardware and software. Such restrictions would stifle creativity and threaten privacy. Congress passed the Online Copyright Infringement Liability Limitation Act of 1998 to begin addressing these concerns.

Source(s): Patents, Trademarks, Copyrights: Intellectual Property in a Global Economy *Congressional Digest*, vol. 75. Washington, DC: Congressional Digest Corp., December 1996.

---

without distinguishing whether the person communicating had any intent to deceive or defraud or simply wanted to keep his or her identity unknown." The ACLU argued the act did not define important terms like "use" nor was the statute clear about using trade names, logos, or other trademark symbols commonly used to link web sites to one another.

The ACLU stressed the importance of anonymous Internet communications explaining that false names or pseudonyms eliminated the potential for discrimination and harassment according to gender or ethnicity. The ACLU argued, "It is a necessary security measure. The personal safety of human rights dissidents, domestic violence victims, and whistle-blowers would be compromised if they could not communicate anonymously."

On 30 January 1997, the case was argued before Marvin H. Shoob, Senior Judge of the U.S. District Court for the Northern District of Georgia. The crux of the state's argument was that, as written, the statute was meant to be interpreted to only forbid fraudulent transmissions over the Internet. The intent of the statute was to prevent misappropriation of the identity of another person or entity for improper purposes.

The State of Georgia argued a motion to dismiss for two reasons. First, since no one individual or organization named as plaintiffs had been prosecuted or even threatened with prosecution, no "live controversy" actually existed. For that reason, Georgia argued, the plaintiffs had no legal grounds to bring suit. The state further argued that the court should refrain from exercising its jurisdiction because of the claim that the law was ambiguous. Because of that claim, Georgia contended the Georgia Supreme Court should have the

opportunity to issue an interpretative ruling in order to clarify the law.

Conversely, in their motion for the court to issue a preliminary injunction against enforcement of the Georgia statute, the ACLU focused arguments in two directions. As written, the broad and nonspecific language of the act would impose unconstitutional restrictions on the content of speech. First, the language of the law prohibited any communications using names that would "falsely identify" a user. The ACLU contended such a restriction would prevent the widespread and common practice over the Internet of using anonymous names or pseudonyms in discussion groups, email, and the publishing of Internet documents. Secondly, the ACLU argued that the act prohibited communications using trade names, logos, and other images without permission. They maintained such a restriction effectively precluded the use of hyperlinks between web pages, the primary means by which Internet users easily navigate the World Wide Web and access information from Internet sites.

Jurisdiction a Question of Precedent

In issuing his decision, Judge Shoob, first needed to establish whether it was appropriate for the U.S. District Court to make a ruling. In that regard, Shoob pointed out that in cases addressing First Amendment issues, the rules of standing are relaxed, especially if citizens might engage in self-censorship under threat of potential prosecution. Quoting from *Virginia v. American Booksellers Association* (1988), Judge Shoob noted, "The statute's alleged danger is, in large measure, one of self-censorship; a harm that can be realized even

Zell Miller, Governor of Georgia, in 1998. © Photograph by Charles Rex Arbogast. AP/Wide World Photos.

without an actual prosecution." Further, Shoob expressed that if he failed to make a ruling, the delay might impose "a chilling effect" on First Amendment-protected free speech. The concept of "chilling effect" relates to individuals deciding not to put forth views for fear of criminal prosecution. Because of these pressing constitutional issues, the court should hear the case.

By specifically upholding the right of the plaintiffs to bring suit, the court directly addressed the heart of Georgia's motion to dismiss. In their initial complaint, the ACLU pointed out that many intended to continue engaging in what they considered constitutionally protected conduct which the law seemed to prohibit. Thus, citing *Graham v. Butterworth* (1993) as precedence, Shoob ruled that individuals, indeed, faced a credible threat of prosecution even though they had not yet been prosecuted or threatened with prosecution.

Shoob cited four reasons why ACLU would likely succeed on the merits of their claim. First, Shoob did not agree with Georgia's argument that because language of the act was imprecise, the case therefore warranted dismissal so a ruling could be sought from a state court. Instead, Shoob found that the plaintiffs' complaint succeeded precisely because the statute addressed content-based restrictions that were "not narrowly

tailored to achieve the state's purported compelling interest" to restrict Internet communications. Specifically, Shoob cited language of the act which he maintained only generally defined as illegal "transmissions which 'falsely identify' the sender but were not 'fraudulent' within the specific meaning of the (Georgia) criminal code." Shoob held that, "The statute was not drafted with the precision necessary for laws regulating speech" and was, therefore, constitutionally invalid.

While the state maintained that the law only applied to individuals who misappropriated the identity of another entity or person, ACLU argued that the language of the act did not specifically state that intent. Shoob agreed with ACLU noting that, by law, the court must only follow the literal language of the statute. The language of the act, therefore, contained nothing "from which a reasonable person would infer such a requirement."

A Question of First Amendment Rights

As written, the overly-broad wording of the act did not only apply to people who misappropriated the identity of another person. The ACLU argued persuasively that the statute prohibited protected free speech such as the use of a pseudonym for protection from discrimination, harassment, or invasion of privacy. Moreover, under the Federal Trademark Dilution Act, Congress provided for the non-commercial use of trade names and logos (such as education, news, or commentary). The language of the Georgia statute, however, prohibited such use.

Judge Shoob feared the act could lead to selective prosecution of minorities or unpopular opinions. Lastly, he found that the act infringed on free expression because some individuals in their confusion, may have altered their conduct and behavior over the Internet in spite of the belief that such activities were inherently legal, in a form of self-censorship. For that reason, Shoob believed their constitutionally protected free speech under the First Amendment had been abridged.

In summarizing his decision, Judge Shoob disagreed with the state of Georgia that specific legislation was needed to specifically prevent Internet fraud. Instead, he cited several Georgia statutes already in place that not only addressed fraud and deception but were less restrictive measures. Moreover, besides failing to adequately define what constituted a specific category of Internet-based fraud or deception, the judge noted that Georgia's legislation had not addressed similar practices in print media. Thus, Judge Shoob issued his preliminary injunction enjoining the state of Georgia from enforcing the Georgia law. This temporary injunction became final on 7 August 1997 since the state of Georgia failed to refile their case or appeal the federal court's decision.

Impact

The court ruling in essence established a right to communicate on the Internet and underscored the complexity of balancing trademark rights and freedom of speech. While Judge Shoob narrowed his ruling to specifically focus on the protection of the Internet under First Amendment free speech rights, his ruling had the effect of stemming the rush among state legislatures in the United States to regulate Internet activity. The ruling specifically relied on existing legislation that was initially crafted to address fraud and deception in print; in so doing, the similar nature of publishing and communications in both print and Internet media was established.

However, the Internet holds some very unique qualities as well, not seen in other media. The system is neither owned nor controlled by a government or any private organization. In essence, those who use it actually control the content and guidelines for use. Despite public pressures to regulate cyberspace, courts initially demonstrated a great reluctance to impose limitations. The *Miller* decision appeared to recognize these differences in that trademark restrictions may not apply as fully on the Internet as elsewhere. Therefore, the ability of trademark owners to control their use on the Internet is limited. Over 130 bills were before Congress by the end of 1997 and each state was evaluating how to follow the lead of the short-lived Communications Decency Act that the Supreme Court largely ruled invalid in *Reno v. American Civil Liberties Union* (1997). Proposals for state legislation assigning some liability to Internet service providers were developed that would establish procedures for plaintiffs to follow in proving harm.

The ability of states to regulate Internet activity was further questioned in *American Libraries Association v. Pataki* (1997) striking down a New York law due to the burden it placed on interstate commerce through cyberspace. The court held that development of the Internet should not be paralyzed by inconsistent legislation from various states. The *Miller* and *Reno* cases combined provide a strong constitutional protection to activities over the Internet and limit states' abilities to impose restrictions.

Related Cases

Virginia v. American Booksellers Association, 484 U.S. 383 (1988).

American Libraries Association v. Pataki, 969 F.Supp. 160 (1997).

Reno v. American Civil Liberties Union, 512 U.S. 844 (1997).

Bibliography and Further Reading

ACLU Cyber Liberties. Website, http://www.star.org/oraclu/news/liberty2.htm.

American Civil Liberties Union. Website, http://www.aclu.org.

American Library Association. Website, http://www.ala.org.

Lee, Lewis C., and J. Scott Davidson, eds. *Intellectual Property for the Internet.* New York: Wiley Law Publications, 1997.

Libel, Slander, and Defamation

A person who writes or publishes false information about another person, a group of people, or an organization like a corporation that injures their reputation may be found guilty of libel. Frequently, such conduct is not protected by the First Amendment constitutional guarantees of freedom of expression. The U.S. judicial system has in a number of circumstances reinforced the notion that freedom of speech or the press is not absolute. Citizens, in exercising their freedoms under the Constitution, still hold a responsibility to not infringe on the rights of others, including the right of privacy and pursuit of happiness. The latter includes unjustly harming another's reputation such that one cannot freely function in society. When false statements causing injury are spoken rather than written, it is more commonly known as slander. Libel and slander are the two forms of defamation. If a person wishes to sue for defamation, they must petition under libel or slander laws, which are very similar.

Libel in History

Following introduction of the printing press in the 1400s, the English government tightly regulated what was published. Execution was possible for writing or printing libelous material about the church or government. Through evolving English common law in the 1600s, a person publishing malicious statements about government or government figures could be prosecuted under sedition libel laws. Punishment for publication through such laws replaced blatant censorship rules by the 1700s. English libel law was rigidly enforced in the young American colonies, largely aimed at restricting criticisms of the king and government. In the eighteenth century, as the United States was being formed, freedom of expression was poorly protected in England. The lack of clear standards spelled out in a constitution left individuals open to the whims of those in political power.

As a result, the framers of the American Constitution eagerly recognized freedom of the press and speech in the First Amendment. The amendment reads, "Congress shall make no law . . . abridging the freedom of speech, or of the press." No mention of libel law was included but soon Congress passed a sedition libel law in 1789. Instantly the subject of great criticism, it was allowed to expire and President Thomas Jefferson pardoned all those who had been convicted under the law.

From Common to Constitutional Law

For much of the nation's history, the First Amendment freedom of speech and press guarantees did not apply to cases involving libel or slander charges. Libel law was left to the states, and courts applied common law when hearing cases. Libel cases often involved both criminal and civil damages but the more typical cases involved civil suits between individuals. The speaker, if found guilty of libel, could face criminal penalties while the victim could receive a civil damage award. Defamatory statements harming a person's reputation through malice (hateful intent) were automatically considered untruthful statements until the speaker proved their truthfulness. The U.S. Supreme Court even issued rulings supporting this supremacy of state law for libel. In *Chaplinsky v. New Hampshire* (1942), the landmark decision exempting "fighting words" from constitutional protection, the Court held that at no time was libelous expression critical for expressing opinion and therefore should not be protected by the Constitution. A decade later in *Beauharnais v. Illinois* (1952), the Court reaffirmed the lack of constitutional protection for libel in its only case involving group libel laws. The strongly split decision sustained an Illinois state law prohibiting the defamation of groups of people based on their race, color, or religion. Such laws were considered in the public's interest to restrict racial and religious intolerance. The constitutionality of group libel laws remained suspect through the remainder of the twentieth century.

Only a dozen years after *Beauharnais,* the Court, operating under the guidance of Chief Justice Earl Warren, dramatically changed direction. In *New York Times v. Sullivan* (1964), the Warren Court decided some forms of libelous speech were important for political debate. A distinction was drawn between common citizens and public officials. The justices asserted that a requirement to prove absolute truth of statements made regarding a public official could significantly limit debate about public policy and government actions, quite contrary to the intent of the First Amendment. Therefore, the Court created a higher standard for public officials to recover damages for libelous statements and limited officials to only collect civil damages. To do so, the official must prove malice by the speaker or writer or a "reckless disregard" as to the truthfulness of the statement. The decision established the demanding "actual malice standard." The decision in *Garrison v. Louisiana* (1964) extended the actual malice standard to criminal libel cases as well.

After *Sullivan,* the Court continued revising libel common law by rigorously protecting the press. The Court used three decisions in 1967 to clarify the *Times* decision. In *Associated Press v. Walker* (1967) and *Curtis Publishing Company v. Butts* (1967), the Court greatly expanded the definition of public official to include public figures in general, including prominent business leaders, entertainers and sports figures. By becoming public figures, individuals in essence surrendered certain rights to privacy. In *Time, Inc. v. Hill* (1967) the Court further expanded the malice standard to apply to private individuals who were not public figures but were involved in events of public interest. This change was designed to free the media in reporting events with considerably less fear of lawsuit. The decision was soon reaffirmed in *Rosenbloom v. Metromedia* (1971).

Following *Rosenbloom,* many believed the Court had gone too far in restricting a private individual's ability to challenge the media when defamatory statements were published about them. The media was becoming too unaccountable. As membership on the Supreme Court changed in the 1970s, the Court weakened the actual malice standard. The Court in *Gertz v. Welch* (1974) again focused primarily on the status of the alleged libel victim, whether they were public figures or not, and not on the nature of the event at issue. Public figures were considered those who intentionally placed themselves before the public, excluding those who inadvertently became caught up in public situations. The ruling returned greater First Amendment protections to private individuals when suing the media for defamation. A part of the Court's reasoning was that public figures had greater access to the media for responding to false statements about them. Also, lower courts were no longer left with the burden of deciding which events were of public interest and which were not. In suits against the media, private individuals were still required to prove negligence to win their case. Consequently, individuals who willingly became involved in public controversies were still required to satisfy the actual malice standard in proving defamation for false statements by others. In *Philadelphia Newspapers Inc. v. Hepps* (1986), the Court went further in protecting the press by ruling that any private individual must bear the burden of proving the falseness of statements when suing the media. If

defamatory statements related strictly to a private matter, the standard would not apply.

Just when somewhat of a trend was becoming established in Court rulings after 1971 that libel was constitutionally protected in increasingly fewer situations, the Court surprisingly expanded protections further in *Hustler Magazine Inc. v. Falwell* (1988). The Court ruled unanimously, which was highly unusual for a libel case, that even when a private individual proves the published statements about them are false, they can still not collect damages if the particular topic was of public interest. The Court provided a surprisingly broad interpretation for determining what a public needs to know. Only three years later, the Court in *Masson v. New Yorker Magazine* (1991) addressed the issue of when an author altered a quote attributed to a public figure to enhance their story. Again, the Court held that malice must be proven to win damages by the public figure.

Libel in the Late 1990s

By the end of the 1990s, alleged libel victims were required to satisfy certain conditions in seeking recovery of damages: 1) Did the speaker actually convey the defamatory statement to others; 2) was reference to the victim clear; 3) could the victim demonstrate some actual injury? In other words, at least one other person must have heard or read the comment and perceived it as defamatory and not in jest. In comparison to libel, proving slander required stronger proof of damages unless the statements refer to criminal or sexual behavior, disease, or business and professional references. Of course, many contended that the added requirement for public figures to prove actual malice was almost insurmountable to successfully sue for damages.

On the other hand, those accused of making libelous statements also had certain standards to satisfy in proving innocence. These factors included proving the defamatory statement was true, showing the target of the statement consented to it being published, publication was accidental, or if a privilege exists which provided immunity to the speaker. Those exempt, or privileged, from libel liability, included attorneys, judges, jurors, witnesses, and others conducting some relevant public business.

Liability for making libelous statements also extended to others who repeated or republished statements they knew were defamatory. This liability also extended to libraries, bookstores, and others who distributed materials. It was more limited for telephone companies and Internet service providers. While in common law only living persons could be defamed, some state laws also protected the deceased as well.

The Ongoing Libel Dilemma

With the increasing complexity of libel law through the latter part of the twentieth century, some legal experts argued that libel law should be abolished. Justice Hugo Black stated in an interview in 1962 that he firmly believed the First Amendment intended to prohibit all libel or defamation laws. The Supreme Court had been inconsistent through the years in its findings concerning libel cases, and even had seen justices concurring on the same opinion but strongly disagreeing over the reasons for their finding. Difficulty was often experienced in determining if a person was a public figure, or what the truth may be behind essentially political opinions. In addition, studies indicated libel law complexities frequently led to jury confusion and courts ruling in favor of the alleged victims with minimal evidence their reputations had been damaged.

The meteoric rise of the electronic communications era through the 1990s only added further libel law concerns. When a libelous statement could reach millions of people around the world in an instant, after-the-fact punitive measures offered little protection. Claims were made that people's reputations were rarely protected by libel law, yet the press and others were left vulnerable to large and expensive lawsuits. Libel claims were the most common legal problems facing journalists with court decisions highly unpredictable. The threat of such lawsuits posed a "chilling effect" on publishers to print information they were not absolutely sure was true, especially for the smaller publishers with less cash reserves to sustain high court costs. Libel cases could labor along for years consuming a good deal of staff time and energy. Some contended that the press should enjoy full immunity from libel laws so as not to restrict debate over political issues. Without libel law, the public aided by the press, rather than the courts, would determine the accuracy of defamatory statements.

Libel law proponents still believed the ability of individuals to protect their reputation was basic to freedom and public order. However, libel law as it existed in the late twentieth century protected neither the media nor targeted individuals. Numerous reform proposals through the 1990s were offered but little progress was made. Some key proposals, such as the Uniform Defamation Act, eliminated monetary awards for damages in favor of more straightforward declaratory judgements by the court, called for formal retractions of defamatory statements if found guilty, removed the actual malice standards for public figures, and placed the responsibility on alleged victims for proving defamatory statements false with clear and convincing evidence. If the alleged victim could not prove the falseness of statements, then the individual would have to pay the legal expenses of those accused of libel within reason. Few states had adopted such laws by the late 1990s as the search for more effective ways of protecting reputations from unjust comments persisted.

Bibliography and Further Reading

Hindman, Elizabeth B. *Rights vs. Responsibilities: The Supreme Court and the Media.* Westport, CT: Greenwood Press, 1997.

Kane, Peter E. *Errors, Lies, and Libel.* Carbondale: Southern Illinois University Press, 1992.

Kaplan, M. Lindsay. *The Culture of Slander in Early Modern England.* New York: Cambridge University Press, 1997.

Kim, Gyong Ho, and Anna R. Paddon. "Uniform Correction or Clarification of Defamation Act: An Alternative to Libel Suits." *Communications and the Law,* September 1998.

Lewis, Anthony. *Make No Law: The Sullivan Case and the First Amendment.* New York: Random House, 1991.

Sack, Robert D. *Libel, Slander, and Related Problems.* New York: Practicing Law Institute, 1994.

Soloski, John, and Randall P. Bezanson, eds. *Reforming Libel Law.* New York: Guilford Press, 1992.

REYNOLDS V. PEGLER

Legal Citation: 223 F.2d 429 (1954)

Plaintiff
Quentin Reynolds

Defendants
Westbrook Pegler, The Hearst Corporation, and Hearst Consolidated Publications

Plaintiff's Claim
That a certain column published by the defendants on 29 November 1949 libeled the plaintiff.

Chief Lawyers for Plaintiff
Walter S. Beck, Paul Martinson, Louis Nizer

Chief Defense Lawyer
Charles Henry

Judge
Edward Weinfeld

Place
New York, New York

Date of Decision
22 July 1954

Decision
Against all defendants: Reynolds awarded $1 in compensatory damages and $175,000 in punitive damages.

Significance
The lopsided award of a huge amount of punitive damages in connection with an award of only nominal compensatory damages was the largest in history at the time. The decision sent a clear signal to the publishing industry that it would be held accountable for the libelous acts of its writers and reporters.

William Randolph Hearst, the publishing magnate, built an empire by publishing newspapers that had stories the public wanted to read. Hearst made sure that his papers had the best editors, writers and reporters money could buy. One of Hearst's favorite writers was Westbrook Pegler, who wrote articles for the King Features Syndicate of The Hearst Corporation, which in turn sold the articles to other Hearst papers. In particular, King Features sold Pegler articles to the *New York Journal-American*, a New York City newspaper owned by Hearst Consolidated Publications.

Hearst died in 1945, nearly 90 years old, but Pegler remained with the Hearst organization. Pegler's articles could be very vindictive and biting, and in 1949 Pegler was accused of using his writing ability to hurt an old friend. On 20 November 1949 a writer for the New York Herald Tribune Book Review named Quentin Reynolds wrote a review of Dale Kramer's book *The Heywood Broun His Friends Recall*. Heywood Broun, himself a writer, had once been a friend of Pegler but, during the 1930s, the two men had a falling-out. In 1939, Pegler wrote a scathing attack on Broun's works. According to Kramer, Broun was so upset by Pegler's attack that Broun was unable to recover from a minor illness and died.

Despite the fact that the events described in Kramer's book were over ten years old, Pegler took offense at Reynolds' review. On 29 November 1949 Pegler's article, "On Heywood Broun and Quentin Reynolds," was published in the Journal-American. Pegler's article had little to do with any critique of Reynolds' review, and was instead a wholesale assassination of Reynolds' character. Without any substantiation, Pegler said, that Reynolds and his girlfriend made a habit of appearing nude in public; that on the way to Heywood Broun's funeral Reynolds had proposed marriage to the widow, Connie Broun; that Reynolds had been a profiteer during World War II; that while working as a war correspondent in London, Reynolds had been a coward; and so forth. Pegler also called Reynolds a degenerate who associated with Communists, blacks and others Pegler regarded as undesirables.

Libel: Are Large Settlements Deterrents?

Financial awards in libel cases have become astronomical in recent years. Does the potential high cost of libel suits prevent publishers from printing controversial material?

The potential financial damage such a suit could cost a publisher or broadcaster must make many think twice about publishing certain material. A jury awarded former Texas district attorney, Victor Feazell, $58 million in a suit against a television station. Feazell announced after the decision that, "This verdict sends a message to the rest of the media to get your facts straight." Settling libel cases involving millions of dollars could literally put small publishers and broadcasters out of business. Companies like the MMR Group, who in 1997 sued Dow Jones & Co. for libel and won a settlement for $220.7 million, may never see their settlement money after the multiple appeals that big companies can afford to file.

Conversely, since the 1964 decision of *New York Times v. Sullivan*, public officials and public figures have had a greater burden upon them to prove the falsity of information, or that the material was published with a "reckless disregard" for the truth. Large media organizations with deep financial pockets, may be less likely to hesitate than smaller ones in publishing questionable information.

Source(s): Pressman, Steven. "An Unfettered Press. Libel Law in the United States." http://www.usia.gov/usa/infousa/media/unfetter/press08.htm

Reynolds Sues for Libel

After the publication of Pegler's article, Reynolds sued Pegler, The Hearst Corporation and Hearst Consolidated Publications for libel. Reynolds' lawyers were Walter S. Beck, Paul Martinson, and Louis Nizer. The defendants' chief lawyer was Charles Henry, and the judge was Edward Weinfeld. The trial began on May 10, 1954.

Aware that truth was a defense to the charge of libel, Nizer showed that Pegler's allegations in the article could not possibly be true. Nizer presented witnesses who testified that Reynolds could not have proposed to Connie Broun because she had been asleep and in the company of others all the way to the funeral, that Reynolds had not been a war profiteer, that Reynolds' war record in fact showed considerable heroism rather than cowardice, and so on. Weinfeld was convinced, and he instructed the jury that they were to take it as a given that Pegler's article was libelous:

> [T]hat column read in its entirety, I charge you as a matter of law, is defamatory.

Henry tried his best to present plausible justifications for Pegler's accusations, but his excuses came across sounding rather thin. For example, Henry tried to explain away Pegler's charge that Reynolds had proposed to Connie Broun as possibly referring to the same high-minded spirit as Moses's ancient laws, which in biblical times placed:

> . . . upon a brother the duty of proposing to his dead brother's widow.

The jury was not convinced. On 22 July 1954 the jurors returned a guilty verdict against all three defendants. Given the nature of Pegler's article and Weinfeld's instructions, this verdict was not surprising. What was surprising, however, was the amount of damages the jury awarded to Reynolds, which were of two types. The first type was the compensatory damages, which represented compensation to Reynolds for the damage,

Columnist Westbrook Pegler, 1951. © AP/Wide World Photos.

Matthew Heywood Broun. © Corbis-Bettmann.

emotional and otherwise, caused by Pegler's vicious public attack on his character. As is common in such cases, the dollar value of the damage done was hard to determine and so the jury gave a nominal award of just one dollar. The second type of damages was punitive, which represented the punishment that the jury saw fit to impose on the defendants for having published the article.

The amount of punitive damages rocked the publishing industry, for at the time it was the largest award of its kind in American history. The jury awarded Reynolds $100,000 against Pegler, $50,000 against The Hearst Corporation, and $25,000 against Hearst Consolidated Publications, for a total of $175,000 in punitive damages. Although the size of the award was unprecedented, it was financially a drop in the bucket to the massive Hearst organization. The disturbing part, however, was that publishers could now be held financially liable for the libels and other unlawful acts of their writers. The defendants promptly appealed.

On 16 and 17 February 1955 the U.S. Court of Appeals for the Second Circuit heard the parties' arguments. The court issued its decision on 7 June of the

same year. The court not only upheld the verdict against Pegler and the other defendants, but it reaffirmed the principle that publishers could be held accountable for the acts of their writers:

> The mere fact that there was no proof of personal ill-will or animosity on the part of any of the corporate executives toward plaintiff does not preclude an award of punitive damages. Malice may be inferred from the very violence and vituperation apparent upon the face of the libel itself, especially where, as here, officers or employees of each corporate defendant had full opportunity to and were under a duty to exercise editorial supervision for purposes of revision, but permitted the publication of the column without investigation, delay or any alteration whatever of its contents. The jury may well have found on this evidence a wanton or reckless indifference to plaintiff's rights.

Thus, the court was telling the Hearst companies in particular and the publishing industry in general that if writers like Pegler wrote vicious and personal articles, the publishers would be held liable if they did not exercise proper editorial control over potentially defamatory material. The defendants exercised their final avenue of appeal, namely a petition for a writ of *certiorari* to the Supreme Court, which was denied on 10 October 10, 1955.

The case of *Reynolds v. Pegler,* with its stupendous award of punitive damages in relation to the nominal compensatory damages, sent a danger signal throughout the publishing industry. This new awareness of potential liability changed forever the relationship between publishers, writers, and reporters. From this date forward, publishers and editors would take greater care to make sure that their publications were accurate and nondefamatory.

Related Cases

New York Times Co. v. Sullivan, 376 U.S. 254 (1964).

Westmoreland v. CBS, 770 F. 2d 1168 (1984).

Hustler Magazine v. Falwell, 485 U.S. 46 (1988).

Bibliography and Further Reading

Farr, Finis. *Fair Enough: The Life of Westbrook Pegler.* New Rochelle, NY: Arlington House Publishers, 1975.

Nizer, Louis. *My Life in Court.* Garden City, NY: Doubleday & Co., 1961.

Pilat, Oliver Ramsay. *Pegler, Angry Man of the Press.* Boston: Beacon Press, 1963.

Reynolds, Quentin. *By Quentin Reynolds.* New York: McGraw-Hill, 1963.

NEW YORK TIMES V. SULLIVAN

Legal Citation: 376 U.S. 254 (1964)

Appellant
The New York Times Company

Appellee
L. B. Sullivan

Appellant's Claim
That the Supreme Court of Alabama's affirmation of a libel judgment against the *Times* violated the free speech and due process rights as defined by the First and Fourteenth Amendments of the Constitution and certain Supreme Court decisions; also, that an advertisement published in the *Times* was not libelous and the Supreme Court should reverse the decision of the Alabama trial court.

Chief Lawyers for Appellant
Herbert Brownell, Thomas F. Daly and Herbert Wechsler

Chief Lawyers for Appellee
Sam Rice Baker, M. Roland Nachman, Jr. and Robert E. Steiner III

Justices for the Court
Hugo Lafayette Black, William J. Brennan, Jr. (writing for the Court), Tom C. Clark, William O. Douglas, Arthur Goldberg, John Marshall Harlan II, Potter Stewart, Earl Warren, Byron R. White

Justices Dissenting
None

Place
Washington, D.C.

Date of Decision
9 March 1964

Decision
The Alabama courts' decisions were reversed.

Significance
The U.S. Supreme Court limited for the first time states' authority to award libel damages based on individual state laws and defined "actual malice" as a national standard for determining libel cases involving public figures.

On 23 March 1960 an organization calling itself the "Committee to Defend Martin Luther King and the Struggle for Freedom in the South" paid the *New York Times* to publish a certain advertisement. The ad took up one full page and was a call for public support and money to defend Reverend Martin Luther King, Jr. and the civil rights struggle in the South. Bearing the caption "Heed Their Rising Voices" in large, bold print, the ad was published in the 29 March 1960 edition of the *Times*.

The ad criticized several Southern jurisdictions, including the city of Montgomery, Alabama, for breaking up various civil rights demonstrations. No individual was mentioned by name. Further, the ad declared that "Southern violators of the Constitution" were determined to destroy King and his movement. The reference was to the entire South, not just Montgomery and other localities, and again no individual was mentioned by name.

Over 600,000 copies of the 29 March 1960 *Times* edition carrying the ad were printed. Only a couple hundred went to Alabama subscribers. Montgomery City Commissioner L.B. Sullivan learned of the ad through an editorial in a local newspaper. Incensed, on 19 April 1960 Sullivan sued the *Times* for libel in the Circuit Court of Montgomery County, Alabama. Sullivan claimed that the ad's reference to Montgomery and to "Southern violators of the Constitution" had the effect of defaming him, and he demanded $500,000 in compensation.

On 3 November 1960 the circuit court found the *Times* guilty and awarded Sullivan the full $500,000 in damages. The Alabama Supreme Court affirmed the circuit court judgment on 30 August 1962. In its opinion, the Alabama Supreme Court gave an extremely broad definition of libel:

> Where the words published tend to injure a person libeled by them in his reputation, profession, trade or business, or charge him with an indictable offense, or tends to bring the individual into public contempt [they] are libelous per se . . . We hold that the matter

Actual Malice Standards

Until 1964, each state used its own standards to determine what was considered libelous. This changed after the U.S. Supreme Court decision of *New York Times v. Sullivan.* This landmark case established the criteria that would be used nationwide when determining libel cases involving public officials.

The Court stated that "actual malice" must be shown by the publishers of alleged libelous material, when the falseness of the material is proven. Justice William J. Brennan, Jr., author of the decision, clarified this further. He stated that to show malice in a libel case, information had to have been printed despite "knowledge" of its falsity, or "with reckless disregard of whether it was false or not."

This standard was later broadened by the High Court to include not only public officials, but also "public figures." This includes well known individuals outside of public office who receive media attention, such as athletes, writers, entertainers, and others who have celebrity status.

Source(s): Cornell. http://supct.law.cornell.edu/supct/
http://www.usia.gov/usa/infousa/media/u
nfetter/press08.htm

complained of [by Sullivan] is, under the above doctrine, libelous per se.

Supreme Court Protects the Press

On 9 March 1964, the Supreme Court unanimously reversed the Alabama courts' decisions, holding that Alabama libel law violated the *Times*'s First Amendment rights. Justice Brennan stated for the Court that:

> We hold that the rule of law applied by the Alabama courts is constitutionally deficient for failure to provide the safeguards for freedom of speech and of the press that are required by the First [Amendment] in a libel action brought by a public official against critics of his official conduct.

The Court was in fact only recognizing what Alabama's own newspapers had been saying, namely that Alabama's libel law was a powerful tool in the hands of anti-civil rights officials. The *Montgomery Advertiser* had even printed an edition (before the *Sullivan* case went to the Court) with the headline "STATE FINDS FORMIDABLE LEGAL CLUB TO SWING AT OUT-OF-STATE PRESS," reporting that "State and city authorities have found a formidable legal bludgeon to swing at out-of-state newspapers whose reporters cover racial incidents in Alabama." The Court's decision invalidated Alabama's overly broad libel law so that it could not be used anymore to threaten freedom of the press.

Next, Justice Brennan stated what the Court had determined was the proper basis of libel law under the First Amendment in cases involving publications concerning public officials:

> The constitutional guarantees require, we think, a federal rule that prohibits a public official from recovering damages for a defamatory falsehood relating to his official conduct unless he proves that the statement was made with "actual malice."

Sullivan had not proven that the *Times* acted with actual malice, so even if Alabama's libel law was not unconstitutional, his lawsuit still had to be rejected. The Court defined actual malice as: ". . . knowledge that it was false or with reckless disregard of whether it was false or not."

In certain libel lawsuits after *New York Times v. Sullivan,* the Court expanded the First Amendment's protection. For any "public figure" to sue for libel, he would have to prove actual malice. The Court has said that public figures include anyone widely known in the community, not just public officials. Further, anyone accused of libel is protected by this actual malice requirement, not just newspapers like the *Times*. The *Sullivan* case was a tremendous advance for personal as well as press freedom of speech, and it prevented legitimate criticism and social commentary from being suppressed by the threat of damaging libel lawsuits. *Sullivan* has not, however, become a license to print anything that the papers see fit: as in *Reynolds v. Pegler,* defendants who do act with actual malice are subject to severe penalties.

Related Cases

*Stromberg v. California,*283 U.S. 359 (1931).
DeJonge v. Oregon, 299 U.S. 353 (1937).
Lovell v. Griffin, 303 U.S. 444 (1938).
Terminiello v. Chicago, 337 U.S. 1 (1949).
Roth v. United States, 354 U.S. 476 (1957).
Speiser v. Randall, 357 U.S. 513 (1958).
NAACP v. Button, 371 U.S. 415 (1963).

Bibliography and Further Reading

Bain, George. "A Question of Honor, Malice and Rights." *Maclean's.* October 1984, p. 64.

Friedman, Robert. "Freedom of the Press: How Far Can it Go?" *American Heritage*. October/November 1982, pp. 16-22.

Hopkins, W. Wat. *Actual Malice: Twenty-Five Years After Times v. Sullivan*. New York: Praeger, 1989.

Johnson, John W., ed. *Historic U.S. Court Cases, 1690–1990: An Encyclopedia*. New York: Garland Publishing, 1992.

Lewis, Anthony. *Make No Law: the Sullivan Case and the First Amendment*. New York: Random House, 1991.

Winfield, Richard N. *New York Times v. Sullivan : the Next Twenty Years*. New York: Practicing Law Institute, 1984.

ROSENBLATT V. BAER

Legal Citation: 383 U.S. 75 (1966)

Petitioner
Mr. Rosenblatt

Respondent
Mr. Baer

Petitioner's Claim
That by finding Rosenblatt negligent in a civil libel case involving public affairs, a New Hampshire state court violated his freedom of speech, and limited public discussion.

Chief Lawyer for Petitioner
Arthur H. Nighswander

Chief Lawyer for Respondent
Stanley M. Brown

Justices for the Court
William J. Brennan, Jr. (writing for the Court), Tom C. Clark, William O. Douglas, Potter Stewart, Hugo Lafayette Black, Earl Warren, Byron R. White

Justices Dissenting
John Marshall Harlan II, Abe Fortas

Place
Washington, D.C.

Date of Decision
21 February 1966

Decision
Overturned state court's ruling, deciding that Rosenblatt's article was not libelous, and that finding it so would limit free discussion matters of public interest.

Significance
The ruling contributed to the Court's consideration of the question of libel, especially when the figures and events involved were public figures. The important question considered in this case was how much protection against defamation a public official could be granted, before that protection impeded freedom of speech.

Baer was employed by Belknap County in New Hampshire to supervise a recreation facility, mostly functioning as a ski resort; he reported to three elected commissioners. During the 1950s, the management and development of the area were publicly criticized. Some local observers argued that the Baer and the commissioners were not using the area in a way that exploited its full potential. In response to these criticisms, in 1959 control of the area was transferred to a special new commission, and Baer was replaced as supervisor.

Rosenblatt regularly wrote an unpaid column for the *Laconia Evening News,* in which he voiced his opinions about local politics, including criticism about the management of the recreation area. In one of his columns, approximately six months after the shift in management, Rosenblatt wrote in praise of the new management, which he claimed was producing results "literally hundreds of per cent BETTER than last year." In the same article, he posed the questions "What happened to all the money last year? and every other year?" Baer brought a civil libel case against Rosenblatt, and argued before a state court in New Hampshire that these statements implied mismanagement and even hinted at criminal behavior on his part, as supervisor of the area. The jury in the civil case awarded Baer damages, agreeing that he had been libeled by Rosenblatt

The U.S. Supreme Court overturned the ruling. The decision was based largely on *New York Times v. Sullivan* (1964) which the Court had recently decided. In that case, the Court found that states could not impede on freedoms of speech guaranteed by the First and Fourteenth Amendments, and that damages could only be awarded a public official if he or she could prove that criticisms of official conduct written made with "actual malice." The question of whether Baer was actually a public official did not have to be directly addressed by the Court in this case; he was employed by, and acting on behalf of, a governmental agency, and so could be considered a public official.

According to this precedent, then, the case before the Court had to address certain questions: whether Baer was actually a public official, whether the statements in question referred directly to Baer (although they did not mention his name), and whether Rosenblatt wrote with actual malice.

The determination of public official status had been addressed by the Court in *New York Times v. Sullivan* and *Garrison v. Louisiana* (1964).

Regarding the question of whether the statements referred directly to Baer, the U.S. Supreme Court decided that the trial judge had been wrong to direct the jury that as member of a small group, Baer could be granted damages if the comments cast suspicion on all members of that group. When applied to governmental bodies, this proof is insufficient; Baer must prove that the comments were directed specifically at him. To apply the small group scenario to public officials, the Court stated, was to "invite the spectre of prosecutions for libel on government, which the Constitution does not tolerate in any form." For example, if a journalist criticized the actions of a town planning board, and any member of that board could bring a civil libel suit against the journalist, the freedom to criticize or question the official actions of public officials would be seriously limited. Instead, a public official must prove that allegations of misconduct are directed at him or her specifically.

The final question, that of whether Rosenblatt wrote with actual malice, also did not have to be directly addressed by the Court. Instead, the justices had only to look at the instructions the trial judge gave the jury in the state civil libel case to determine that the basis for the decision was incorrect, and the judgement had to be overturned. The trial judge explained malice as "ill will, evil motive, intention to injure . . .;" but in a libel case involving public officials, actual malice must be proved: that the statements were false, and that they were published either with the knowledge that they were false, or with reckless disregard as to whether or not they were true. If these requirements proving malice did not exist, it would again be possible to limit the freedom to criticize the government with the threat of libel cases.

At the heart of this case is the tension between protecting the reputations of individuals against defamation, and the constitutional protection of freedom of speech and the freedom to criticize the actions of the government. In this case, as in the others it is based on, the Court limited the protection of individuals who are public officials, because "criticism of those responsible for government operations must be free, lest criticism of government itself be penalized." Ultimately, the Court decided, it is the freedom of speech granted in the First and Fourteenth Amendments which must be given priority. This ruling reflects "a profound national commitment to the principle that debate on public issues should be uninhibited, robust, and wide-open," a commitment that supersedes individual protections against libel.

Related Cases
Thornhill v. Alabama, 310 U.S. 88 (1940).
New York Times v. Sullivan, 376 U.S. 254 (1964).
Garrison v. Louisiana, 379 U.S. 64 (1964).
Herbert v. Lando, 441 U.S. 153 (1979).

Bibliography and Further Reading
Biskupic, Joan, and Elder Witt. *Guide to the U.S. Supreme Court*. Washington, DC: Congressional Quarterly, Inc., 1997.

CURTIS PUBLISHING CO. V. BUTTS

Legal Citation: 388 U.S. 130 (1967)

Petitioner
Curtis Publishing Company

Respondent
Wally Butts

Petitioner's Claim
That the ruling in *New York Times v. Sullivan* (1964) allowing public officials to sue for libel only if they can prove actual malice or reckless disregard for the truth should be extended to public figures as well.

Chief Lawyers for Petitioner
Herbert Wechsler, William Rogers

Chief Lawyers for Respondent
Allen Lockerman, Clyde J. Watts

Justices for the Court
Tom C. Clark, Abe Fortas, John Marshall Harlan II (writing for the Court), Earl Warren

Justices Dissenting
Hugo Lafayette Black, William J. Brennan, Jr., William O. Douglas, Byron R. White

Place
Washington, D.C.

Date of Decision
12 June 1967

Decision
This ruling is based on two cases, *Curtis Publishing Co. v. Butts* and *Associated Press v. Walker*. In *Curtis*, the Court ruled that Butts was defamed and the libel judgment was upheld. In *Associated Press v. Walker* the court determined that under *New York Times v. Sullivan* Walker was not libeled.

Significance
The *New York Times v. Sullivan* ruling of "actual knowledge or reckless disregard for the truth" test for public officials to prove defamation was extended to public figures. The Court agreed that both Butts and Walker were public figures; however, only Butts's case under the extension of the *New York Times* ruling was actually defamation.

Two Cases of Libel?

After an article published in the *Saturday Evening Post* accused Wally Butts of attempting to fix a football game in 1962 between the University of Georgia and the University of Alabama he sued Curtis Publishing Company for libel. When the article was published, Butts was the athletic director and formerly the coach of the University of Georgia's football team. He was a well-known figure within the coaching ranks, and was up for a job with a professional football team.

The primary source for the article was George Burnett, an Atlanta insurance salesman. Burnett had accidentally overhead a telephone conversation, a week before the football game, between Butts and the coach of Alabama's football team, Paul Bryant. Burnett made notes of the conversation during which Butts revealed Georgia's game plans even naming specific players and plays. Butts sued for libel and sought $5 million in compensatory and $5 million in punitive damages. The trial was finished before the Court ruled in the *New York Times v. Sullivan*. Curtis's only defense was truth.

The trial focused on whether the article was true and the accuracy of the reporting. Burnett overheard a conversation between Butts and Bryant; however what he heard was a matter of debate. Butts claimed the conversation was confined to general football talk and would have yielded little useful information to any opposing coach. In preparation of the article it was revealed that the magazine had "departed greatly from the standards of good investigation and reporting." The jury returned a verdict for $60,000 in general damages and $3 million in punitive damages. The trial court reduced the award to $460,000. A short time later, the Court announced the *Sullivan* decision and Curtis motioned for a new trial. The trial court rejected the motion on two grounds. First, it held that *New York Times* was not applicable because Butts was not a public official; and second, there was plenty of evidence for the jury to have concluded that there was a reckless disregard for the truth. Curtis appealed the ruling to the Court of Appeals for the Fifth Circuit, but the judgment was affirmed. A rehearing was denied and the Supreme Court granted *certiorari*.

A second case in which the press used the accuracy of their reporting as a defense was *Associated Press v. Walker*. The case resulted from a press report on a riot that resulted in James Meredith, a black student, trying integrate the University of Mississippi under a court decree. The report accused retired general Edwin Walker of leading a charge against the federal marshals and described Walker as encouraging the use of violence and even advising the rioters on how to avoid the harmful side effects of tear gas. Walker was a private citizen at the time of the riot and press report. He had a long and distinguished career in the U.S. Army and had been in command of general troops during the school confrontation in Little Rock, Arkansas in 1957. Walker resigned his army post to become more politically active and had received some publicity over his views on integration. He sued for libel in the state courts of Texas seeking $2 million in compensatory and punitive damages.

Associated Press used the accuracy of its report as well as constitutional defenses. Walker disputed the facts in the wire story. He said he was indeed on the campus, but that he had tried to keep the crowd from rioting and urged them to remain peaceful. He denied taking part in the charge against federal marshals. The reporter was at the riot. There was no evidence suggesting that the article was not prepared properly or any personal prejudice or incompetence on the part of the reporter or Associated Press.

The jury was told that it could award compensatory damages if the article was false and that punitive damages could be awarded if the report was motivated by "ill will, bad or evil motive, or that entire want of care which would raise the belief that the act or omission complained of was the result of a conscious indifference to the right or welfare of the person to be affected by it." The jury returned a verdict of $500,000 in compensatory damages and $300,000 in punitive damages. The trial judge found no evidence of actual malice and refused to enter the punitive award. The trial judge said that the lack of malice would require a verdict for the Associated Press, if *New York Times* was applicable, but he concluded that it was not applicable since there were "no compelling reasons of public policy requiring additional defenses to suits for libel. Truth alone should be an adequate defense." Both sides appealed, and the Texas Court of Civil Appeals affirmed the compensatory damages and the dismissal of punitive damages. The Supreme Court of Texas denied writ of error and the U.S. Supreme Court granted *certiorari*.

The Supreme Court decided to extend the *New York Times* ruling to public figures, but was sharply divided in its reasoning. The majority, after determining that both Butts and Walker were public figures, reasoned that as public figures they could recover damages once it was proven that the standards of traditional report-

ing were not followed. They found that standard was satisfied in *Butts*, but not in *Walker*. The Court further reasoned that unlike the case of *Walker*, there was no breaking news involved in the case of *Butts*, which meant that the *Saturday Evening Post* had plenty of time to verify the facts in the article. Even with the lack of time constraints, the Court concluded that the reporting of the Butts story was sloppy. In fact, the *Saturday Evening Post* was aware that Burnett was on probation for writing bad checks, but published the story without corroborating it. No other magazine personnel reviewed Burnett's notes before publication, and the individual supposedly with Burnett when he overheard the phone call was not interviewed. The writer assigned to the story was not a football expert and no attempt was made to have an expert review the story before publication. "In short, the evidence is ample to support a finding of highly unreasonable conduct constituting an extreme departure from the standards of investigation and reporting ordinarily adhered to by responsible publishers."

Justice Warren, in a separate opinion agreeing with result but disagreeing with the reasoning, placed more emphasis on the status of both Walker and Butts as public figures and reasoned that should be the major thrust behind the Court's ruling. The majority opinion recognized this distinction, but focused more on the quality of reporting and whether it substantially deviated from acceptable journalistic practices. "To me, differentiation between 'public figures' and 'public officials' and adoption of separate standards of proof for each have no basis in law, logic, or First Amendment policy. Increasingly in this country, the distinctions between governmental and private sectors are blurred," Warren wrote. Under the *Times* rule it was clear that Walker had not proven malice, and that the *Butts* case showed a "degree of reckless disregard for the truth."

Justice Black joined by Justice Douglas wrote yet another opinion agreeing with the result in *Walker*, but dissenting with the majority in *Curtis Publishing Co. v. Butts*. Urging a broader press immunity, he argued that *Sullivan* failed to adequately protect the press from libel judgments. He would have reversed the *Butts* ruling because the article was a matter of public interest. Justice Brennan joined by Justice White agreed with *Walker*, but dissented in *Butts*. Brennan reasoned that the jury instructions did not follow the standard for malice and therefore the ruling should be reversed and remanded for a new trial. He further reasoned that the jury should have an opportunity to determine if the *New York Times* standard was met.

Impact

In the tumultuous events that shaped the 1960s and the early 1970s, the Court's ruling went a long way to ensure the press could cover stories without fear of lawsuits for inaccuracies that can occur when reporting on deadline. The rulings also helped pave the way for the hard hitting investigative journalism that allowed newspapers and television news broadcasts to pursue Watergate and publish the Pentagon Papers. The Court has consistently protected the rights of a free press, some would argue to the detriment of the individual, particularly when dealing with public figures.

Related Cases

New York Times v. Sullivan, 376 U.S. 254 (1964).
Rosenbloom v. Metromedia, 403 U.S. 29 (1971).
Gertz v. Robert Welch, Inc., 418 U.S. 323 (1974).

Time, Inc. v. Firestone, 424 U.S. 448 (1976).
Hutchinson v. Proxmire, 443 U.S. 111 (1979).

Bibliography and Further Reading

Biskupic, Joan, and Elder Witt. *Guide to the U.S. Supreme Court,* 3rd ed. Washington, DC: Congressional Quarterly Inc., 1997.

Gunther, Gerald, and Kathleen Sullivan. *Constitutional Law* 13th ed. New York: The Foundation Press Inc., 1997.

Hall, Kermit L., ed. *The Oxford Companion to the Supreme Court of the United States.* New York: Oxford University Press, 1992.

ROSENBLOOM V. METROMEDIA

Legal Citation: 403 U.S. 29 (1971)

Petitioner
George Rosenbloom

Respondent
Metromedia, Inc.

Petitioner's Claim
A radio station that broadcast defamatory information about a private individual has committed libel, since the news was not about a public figure or public official.

Chief Lawyer for Petitioner
Ramsey Clark

Chief Lawyer for Respondent
Bernard G. Segal

Justices for the Court
Hugo Lafayette Black, Harry A. Blackmun, William J. Brennan, Jr. (writing for the Court), Warren E. Burger, Byron R. White

Justices Dissenting
John Marshall Harlan II, Thurgood Marshall, Potter Stewart (William O. Douglas did not participate)

Place
Washington, D.C.

Date of Decision
7 June 1971

Decision
Upheld an appeals court ruling that even though a news broadcast contains information about a private citizen it is not libel unless the plaintiff can demonstrate a reckless disregard for the truth or malicious intent.

Significance
News about an individual who is not a public official or public figure, but was of interest to the general public falls under *New York Times v. Sullivan* (1964), which means evidence of a reckless disregard for the truth or malicious intent has to be proven for libel.

In the fall of 1963, George Rosenbloom, a distributor of nudist magazines in the Philadelphia area, was arrested as part of a crackdown on obscene materials. He was released on bail. Three days later, on 4 October, police searched Rosenbloom's home and a barn he used as a warehouse after obtaining a warrant. Magazines and books were seized by the police. Rosenblum surrendered to police, and was arrested yet again.

After the second arrest, the police captain informed two radio stations, a wire service and the local newspaper about the raid on Rosenblum's home and his arrest. Radio station, WIP, which Metromedia owned, broadcast the following story twice:

> The Special Investigations Squad raided the home of George Rosenbloom in the 1800 block of Vesta Street this afternoon. Police confiscated 1,000 allegedly obscene books at Rosenbloom's home and arrested him on charges of possession of obscene literature. The Special Investigations Squad also raided a barn in the 20 Hundred block of Welsh Road near Bustleton Avenue and confiscated 3,000 obscene books. Capt. Ferguson says he believes they have hit the supply of main distributor of obscene material in Philadelphia.

On the third report, "reportedly" was added before obscene. The information was repeated several times, but also with "allegedly" or "reportedly" before obscene.

Two weeks later, Rosenbloom sued city and police officials and several local media outlets claiming that the materials he distributed were not obscene. He sought to stop the police from interfering in his business and to end the publicity. WIP then reported on the lawsuit. After being informed of the news reports, Rosenbloom visited the radio station. Rosenbloom spoke with a part-time newscaster at the station over a telephone in the lobby and told him that his materials were not obscene. Rosenbloom informed the newscaster that his magazines were "found to be completely legal and legitimate by the U.S. Supreme Court." The newscaster said that the district attorney described the magazines as obscene. Rosenbloom said he had a statement from the same district attorney calling the magazines legal. Rosenbloom said the newscaster ended the conversation by hanging up the telephone. Rosenbloom, however, did not request a retraction or a correction.

In May of 1964, Rosenbloom was acquitted of criminal obscenity charges by a state court jury. After his acquittal, Rosenbloom sued for libel in federal court. He said that his acquittal on criminal charges proved that he was libeled. He said that broadcasts about his lawsuit for injunctive relief were false and defamatory because the radio station described him and his associates as "smut distributors" and "girlie-book peddlers," among other defamatory language. The radio station used truth and privilege as a defense. The station's news director testified that the only source for these reports was the police captain, who then testified that the information was accurately reported.

The jury was instructed that under Pennsylvania law four conditions had to be met to prove libel: at least one of the broadcasts had to be defamatory, that a reasonable listener would conclude that the statements were about Rosenbloom; that the radio station "had forfeited its privilege to report official proceedings fairly and accurately, either because it intended to injure the plaintiff personally or because it exercised the privilege unreasonably and without reasonable care;" and finally, that the reporting was false. The jury was also told that Rosenbloom had to prove the first three, but the radio station had to prove that the reporting was true. The jury awarded Rosenbloom $25,000 in general damages and $725,000 in punitive damages. The award was reduced to $250,000 by the district court. The court of appeals reversed reasoning that the reports were breaking news and of interest to the public, and while Rosenbloom was not a public official or public figure that *New York Times v. Sullivan* was applicable.

In upholding the appeals court ruling, Justice Brennan explained that if a news item is of public or general interest it does not lose its news value because a private individual is involved. The priority is not whether an individual is well-known, but if the information is of interest and importance to the community. "We honor the commitment to robust debate on public issues, which is embodied in the First Amendment, by extending constitutional protection to all discussion and communication involving matters of public or general concern, without regard to whether the persons involved are famous or anonymous," Brennan wrote. Rosenbloom argued that the private individual does not have the resources available to him to counter an inaccurate or defamatory report. Additionally, he claimed that unlike the public figure, the private individual had not thrust himself into the spotlight. Brennan believed however, that even a public figure was at

a disadvantage to counter or rebut a defamatory report because it was not breaking news and undoubtedly would not receive the same coverage as the initial report. Brennan further reasoned that in a free society no one is truly a private person. "The idea that certain public figures have voluntarily exposed their entire lives to public inspection, while private individuals have kept theirs carefully shrouded from public view is, as best, a legal fiction."

In a separate opinion, Justice Black agreed with the majority's decision, but would have taken it a step further. He believed that under the First Amendment no one can recover libel judgments against the media, even if the media outlet is aware that the statements are false. Black believed that the purpose of the First Amendment was to protect the media from "the harassment of libel judgments." Justice White, concurred in judgment, but disagreed with the other justices in their reasoning because it infringed too greatly on state libel laws. White reasoned that it would make little sense to report on the actions of the police without providing details to the public about whom and why the arrests were made. He felt that *New York Times v. Sullivan*, not only protected the media when they criticized public officials or figures, but when they praised them as well.

In separate dissenting opinions, Justice Harlan and Marshall disagreed with extending the *New York Times v. Sullivan* protection to private individuals. Justice Marshall, joined by Justice Stewart, believed that trying to determine what is of general interest to the public is problematic. "Courts, including this one, are not anointed with any extraordinary prescience." Additionally, Marshall predicted that since the courts will have to balance the individual's rights against defamation against the rights of a free press that courts would regularly be engaged in "a constant and continuing supervision of defamation litigation throughout the country."

Impact

The rights of a free press versus the right of a private individual is bound to strain constitutional limits. While the Court in this case was willing to defer to a free press those dissenting seem to recognized the potential slippery slope involved. In fact, three years later in *Gertz v. Robert Welch, Inc.* (1974) the Court abandoned *Rosenbloom* and held that an individual should be able to recover for libel damages without using the *New York Times v. Sullivan* standard.

Related Cases

New York Times v. Sullivan, 376 U.S. 254 (1964).
Curtis Publishing Co. v. Butts., U.S. (1967).
Gertz v. Robert Welch, Inc., 418 U.S. 323 (1974).

Time, Inc. v. Firestone, 424 U.S. 448 (1976).
Hutchinson v. Proxmire, 443 U.S. 111 (1979).

Bibliography and Further Reading

Biskupic, Joan and Elder Witt. *Guide to the U.S. Supreme Court,* 3rd edition. Washington, DC: Congressional Quarterly Inc., 1997.

Gunther, Gerald and Kathleen Sullivan. *Constitutional Law,* 13th edition. New York: The Foundation Press Inc., 1997.

Hall, Kermit L., ed. *The Oxford Companion to the Supreme Court of the United States.* New York: Oxford University Press, 1992.

WESTMORELAND V. CBS, INC.

Legal Citation: 596 F.Supp. 1170 (1984)

Plaintiff
General William C. Westmoreland

Defendant
CBS, Inc., Mike Wallace, George Crile, Sam Adams, Van Gordon Sauter

Plaintiff's Claim
That a television documentary broadcast by CBS concerning the conduct of the Vietnam War libeled Westmoreland.

Chief Lawyers for Plaintiff
Dan M. Burt, David M. Dorsen

Chief Defense Lawyers
David Boies, Stuart W. Gold

Judge
Pierre N. Leval

Place
New York, New York

Date of Decision
18 February 1985

Decision
The case was settled out of court before going to the jury.

Significance
The case affirmed stringent standards set for public figures to successfully seek libel damages through litigation. Public figures must prove actual malice. Despite evidence of press misconduct in this and a similar contemporaneous case involving Israeli leader Ariel Sharon, both plaintiffs lost. This case received significant national publicity and underscored the many problems with libel law in the United States. A number of national reforms were proposed following the case through the nineties.

The Vietnam War obscurely began in 1957 with limited U.S. military support provided to South Vietnam. U.S. involvement escalated dramatically following the 1964 Gulf of Tonkin naval incident. The war effort steadily grew through the next several years as public and Congressional support began to gradually diminish. Finally, a turning point in the war occurred in January of 1968 when North Vietnamese forces invaded the city of Hue and other South Vietnam cities including Saigon. Known as the Tet Offensive, the North Vietnamese were at first successful in capturing Hue but U.S. forces counterattacked repelling the North Vietnamese forces. The U.S. victory was costly as fighting had been intense throughout the region. The battles dramatized to the American people the likely futility in winning the war on the battlefield without at least incurring a great deal of human loss on both sides, and a great deal of expense. The Tet Offensive consequently forced major changes in U.S. policy in Vietnam leading to the initiation of peace talks with North Vietnam. President Lyndon Johnson refused to send additional troops to the 500,000 already there, and announced he would not seek reelection for president. Controversy concerning the U.S. preparedness for the battle and estimation of enemy troop strength erupted publicly. The war still raged on until 1975 making it the longest and most costly war in U.S. history.

General William C. Westmoreland was U.S. commander in Vietnam from 1964 to 1968 during the Tet Offensive. Born in South Carolina in 1914, Westmoreland graduated from the U.S. Military Academy in 1936 and commanded artillery forces in North Africa, Sicily, and northern Europe during World War II and led a paratroop regiment during the Korean War. He became a lieutenant general in 1963. During the Vietnam War Westmoreland instituted a policy of "search and destroy" which placed priority over the number of enemy killed over amount of territory gained. Later in 1968 following the Tet Offensive Westmoreland was transferred back to the United States serving as Army chief of staff before retiring in 1972.

On 23 January 1982 CBS Television aired a documentary entitled "The Uncounted Enemy: A Vietnam Deception." The narrator, Mike Wallace, took an

Out of Court Settlements

In general, an out of court settlement may be reached in many types of civil cases, including but not limited to libel suits. The terms of agreement may be private or public, depending upon the parties involved. In some cases, money may be accepted in return for not going forward with a pending law suit, or one already in process. An out of court settlement also ends any potential future litigation, meaning an appeal cannot later be filed. This sort of settlement is made without input or agreement by the courts. The terms of the agreement are determined by the parties involved, and may be reached at various points in court proceedings.

Source(s): *West's Encyclopedia of American Law.* Volume two. New York: West Publishing, 1998.

aggressive investigative approach in preparing the documentary. The theme of the program was that the effects of infamous Tet Offensive, which took American forces by surprise and caused much loss of life, could have been avoided if the actual size of North Vietnam's troop strength had been more accurately estimated. The documentary placed much of the blame on General Westmoreland for the Tet Offensive successes by the North Vietnamese. Wallace accused Westmoreland of juggling enemy troop figures to produce an artificially low count in order to please then-President Lyndon Johnson. During the course of the interview Wallace made Westmoreland appear uncertain and less than truthful about enemy troop estimates.

Incensed after the program was televised, Westmoreland strenuously denied the allegations raised about his conduct. The Capitol Legal Foundation, offering to represent Westmoreland for free, filed a $120 million libel suit on 13 September 1982. The suit, originally filed in South Carolina, was transferred to the Federal Court of the Southern District of New York.

CBS immediately moved for a summary judgement claiming immunity from libel under the precedent established in *New York Times v. Sullivan* (1964) since they were the press making commentary on a public figure. CBS claimed they believed all of their statements on the program to be true. CBS asserted Westmoreland, being a high-ranking public figure, had sufficient opportunities through the media to respond to allegations concerning performance of his duty in Vietnam. CBS further claimed the libel lawsuit essentially constituted "unconstitutional prosecution for seditious libel of the government" by forcing CBS to sustain legal expenses to defend the program. CBS also claimed to have been voicing an opinion on the program, but Judge Leval considered accusations of governmental conspiracy in misrepresenting facts too serious of an allegation to constitute merely an opinion. CBS further noted that it would be difficult to prove malice. Sam Adams, a consultant for CBS and former CIA intelligence analyst in 1967-68, had initially presented his allegations in 1967, and another CBS associate, George

Crile, joined the debate in 1975 eventually leading CBS to initiate further research leading to the broadcast program. CBS claimed its investigation lasted a year and interviewed over 80 individuals many of whom participated in the events.

Westmoreland, however, charged the investigation was biased based on the way questions were framed and interviewees chosen. Most seriously, Westmoreland charged CBS dishonestly edited interview tapes, taking statements out of context to support their opinions, thus constituting reckless misstatements of evidence. Westmoreland contended these distortions indicated malice.

In September of 1984 Judge Pierre N. Leval ruled Westmoreland had raised sufficient questions of "reckless falsity" to make inappropriate a summary judgement on CBS' behalf. Leval wrote the case should proceed to trial.

Testimony was presented through the ensuing months, in some instances by some former high-ranking military officials supporting CBS allegations. Westmoreland and CBS ultimately settled their case out of court on 18 February 1985 with both sides agreeing to pay their own legal fees. Westmoreland received none of the $120 million claim but instead issued a joint public statement with CBS claiming that CBS "never intended to assert . . . General Westmoreland was unpatriotic or disloyal in performing his duties as he saw them." In essence, CBS stood by its program in the end.

Impact

At the same time the Westmoreland case was pending, another prominent military figure was also pursuing a libel lawsuit. Israeli general Ariel Sharon sued Time, Inc., which published *Time* magazine, for having printed an article on 14 February 1983 that accused Sharon of encouraging certain Lebanese militia forces to massacre some Palestinians in 1982. This case was the first occasion a major foreign official had attempted to use the U.S. court system to sue for libel for statements concerning their official actions. The case was tried from November of 1984 to January of 1985 in New York, City

William Westmoreland stands with his lawyer Dan Burt (left) at a press conference, 1982. © AP/Wide World Photos.

before Judge Abraham D. Sofaer. A jury found Time not guilty due to lack of actual malice, and Sharon dropped his case. However, jury members made a special point of stating that they thought *Time* had acted "negligently and carelessly" in preparing the article.

Generals Westmoreland and Sharon faced similar obstacles in their cases. Despite strong evidence of press misconduct, under the standard set by *New York Times v. Sullivan* they could not meet the difficult showing of proof required of public figures to win libel suits. Many in foreign countries were astounded by the stiff standards in U.S. courts. Even though statements were found to be defamatory and false in the *Sharon* case, they still were not considered libelous under the *Sullivan* standard. In the *Sharon* case, and other cases involving foreign officials, the press may not be able to successfully gain access to documents and witnesses because the lack of cooperation of that government. In the *Sharon* case, *Time* came away victorious but embarrassed and poorer.

Immediate fears from the *Westmoreland* and *Sharon* cases was that more foreign and U.S. officials would begin using the court system for political vindication. Regardless of whether the official won their libel case, trial publicity could well serve the political purpose and at the same time led to considerable legal expenses by the press in defending their publication.

During the late 1970s and early 1980s libel litigation exploded with damage awards and legal expenses reaching into the millions of dollars with the *Westmoreland* case being a key example. However, the record showed

few individuals pursuing libel claims against the press actually received awards or any vindication of their reputation. Success in winning a libel suit was slim, and even if damages were awarded, the monies often went toward high legal fees.

The landmark case of *New York Times v. Sullivan* compelled public figures to prove a reporter wrote defamatory statements either in the belief that it was false or with reckless disregard whether it was true or not. Such a standard is tough to achieve. Many considered libel law as it had evolved into the 1990s a legal disaster, though still the most common legal problem facing journalists. The law rarely satisfactorily protects either the First Amendment rights of the journalists or to vindicate the subject of the statements. In addition, court decisions since the 1960s have been viewed as inconsistent and increasing the complexity of demonstrating proof of harm and malice. The *Westmoreland* case highlighted instances where millions of dollars were spent in attorney's fees by both sides, and yet never went to jury for a decision.

Proposals to reform libel law included the 1993 proposed Uniform Correction or Clarification of Defamation Act by the National Conference of Commissioners on Uniform State Laws. Intent of the proposed law was to provide a speedier and less costly remedy for defamatory disputes. However, by 1998 only one state had adopted the law. Critics of the law claimed it could well be unconstitutional on freedom of the press grounds. A publication may be forced to publish a correction or clarification of the original statement and reporters may be forced to reveal confidential sources of information. By the end of the nineties no national standard for libel had been adopted and the advent of Internet libel cases introduced even more chaos into the realm of libel law. As the century closed, expensive libel suits and ineffective means of protecting reputations persisted.

Regarding the *Westmoreland* and *Sharon* cases, many believed public figures should not be able to sue for libel in instances involving events in which they were involved. These issues constitute political debates and are not the kind issues to be decided by juries. In Westmoreland's case, he was a high-ranking policy-making official who should be openly subject to public scrutiny.

Related Cases

New York Times Co. v. Sullivan, 376 U.S. 254 (1964).
Rosenblatt v. Baer, 393 U.S. 75 (1966).
Curtis Publishing Co. v. Butts, 388 U.S. 130 (1967).
Rosenbloom v. Metromedia, 403 U.S. 29 (1971).
Sharon v. Time, Inc., 599 F.Supp. 538 (S.D.N.Y. 1984).

Bibliography and Further Reading

Adler, Renata. *Reckless Disregard: Westmoreland v. CBS, Sharon v. Time.* New York: Knopf, 1986.

Benjamin, Burton. *Fair Play: CBS, General Westmoreland, and How a Television Documentary Went Wrong.* New York: Harper & Row, 1988.

DeMailo, Alfred S., and Peter W. Brush. "Tet: First In . . . And Last Out." *American Heritage,* July-August 1993.

Johnson, John W., ed. *Historic U.S. Court Cases, 1690-1990: An Encyclopedia.* New York: Garland Publishing, 1992.

Kim, Gyong Ho, and Anna R. Paddon. "Uniform Correction or Clarification of Defamation Act: An Alternative to Libel Suits." *Communications and the Law,* Vol. 20, no. 3, pp. 53-65.

Roth, M. Patricia. *The Juror and the General.* New York: William Morrow & Co., 1986.

OBSCENITY

Pornography and Obscenity

Often used interchangeably, the terms pornography and obscenity in fact have different meanings. Pornography, derived from the Greek for "writing about prostitutes," refers to literature, photographs, or depictions of scenes of sexual behavior that are erotic or lewd and designed to arouse sexual interest. Obscenity, derived from the Greek for "filth," is a more narrowly defined legal term to describe written and visual materials, as well as speech and behavior, all of an explicitly sexual nature, which are not protected by the free speech provisions of the First Amendment. While some forms of pornography are considered legally obscene, others are not. Pornography is divided into two types, soft core and hard core. Soft-core pornography, which usually falls under free speech rights, generally involves the depiction of nudity and limited, simulated sexual behavior. Hard-core pornography, by contrast, is a more graphic, realistic depiction of sexual acts, including intercourse, sodomy, and sadism. It is the realm of hard-core pornography that often comes under purview of the courts in determining obscenity.

Pornography, Obscenity, and the Law

Pornographic and obscene materials have a long history, from the *Kama Sutra,* the ancient Indian sex manual, to depictions on Greek vases, to the celebrated profligacy of John Cleland's *Fanny Hill* in eighteenth-century England, and the Marquis de Sade's writings in France of the same period. Society's stance regarding pornography is a relativistic one, differing from one culture to the next and from one historical epoch to another. As early as 1711, the government of Massachusetts got into the censorship game by banning publication of "wicked, profane, impure, filthy and obscene material," thus begging the question that has bedeviled the censorship debate up to modern times: Who determines what is obscene?

Initially, obscenity offenses fell under laws proscribing blasphemy or disorderly conduct, but in 1815 the Pennsylvania Supreme Court began the long and laborious process of exactly defining what sort of pornography might be considered obscene. In *Commonwealth v. Sharpless,* that court ruled that a merchant could not exhibit a picture of a nude couple for profit. Two Boston booksellers were convicted in 1821 for selling copies of *Fanny Hill,* further defining the limits of obscenity. And in 1843, the first federal obscenity law was passed in the United States, to regulate the sale of racy French postcards.

Throughout the nineteenth century and well into the twentieth, U.S. courts based their rulings in obscenity cases on a decision handed down by a British court in 1868. That case, *Regina v. Hicklin* found as obscene those materials whose tendency was to "deprave and corrupt those whose minds [were] open to such immoral influences, and into whose hands a publication of this sort may fall." Thus from the outset, the assumption was made that pornography could have a negative effect on the user. In 1873, Congress passed the first general anti-obscenity act, the Comstock Act, named after an anti-porn crusader who had founded the New York Society for the Suppression of Vice. Taken in tandem, *Hicklin* and the Comstock Act provided a narrowly defined range of pornography which would automatically fall into the category of obscene materials and were thus not protected by First Amendment rights. The first challenge to such a narrow definition came in 1913 from Supreme Court Justice Learned Hand who argued that such restrictions on passages taken out of context of the entire work would in effect reduce adults to the reading level of children, an argument later echoed by Justice Felix Frankfurter.

New challenges also came from changing literary and artistic tastes, as well as an increasingly sophisticated public. Book bannings and burnings continued, and the motion picture industry instituted its own self-censorship guidelines with the Hays Code banning obscenity in "word, gesture, reference, song, joke or by suggestion." The movie industry in particular has had as sketchy history *vis-a-vis* First Amendment rights. In 1915, the Supreme Court ruled that films did not fall under free speech rights because they were seen as diversionary entertainment and "a business pure and simple." Not until 1952 did the Court reverse itself in this. Meanwhile, however, a more relaxed interpretation of other forms of expression was seen, evidenced by the 1933 New York court rule determining that

James Joyce's *Ulysses* was not obscene as it was not written merely with pornographic intent to "stir the lustful thoughts" of the reader. Still it was not for almost another quarter of a century before the U.S. Supreme Court ruled for the first time on an obscenity case.

Upholding the conviction of a New York bookseller, the Court provided its first definition of obscenity in *Roth v. United States* (1957). Writing for the majority, Associate Justice William J. Brennan, Jr., noted that obscenity depends on "whether to the average person, applying contemporary community standards, the dominant theme of the material taken as a whole appeals to the prurient interests." *Roth* also used as a measure for obscenity the fact that the "material is utterly without redeeming social value." Using these new guidelines, court cases involving the works of D. H. Lawrence, Henry Miller and others tested the liberality of the law. The Court further refined its definition of obscene materials in the 1959 case, *Kingsley International Pictures v. Regents of the State of New York,* in which it was found that there could be no such thing as "ideological obscenity," and in *Ginzburg v. United States,* where it was found that "the conduct of the defendant is the central issue, not the obscenity of a book or picture." In *Stanley v. Georgia* (1969), the Supreme Court declared that "the mere private possession of obscene matter cannot constitutionally be held a crime."

In 1966, the Supreme Court decided that *Fanny Hill* was not obscene, ushering in a new era of permissiveness. Films, both foreign and domestic, pushed the limits of what was once considered obscene, and *Midnight Cowboy* became the first mainstream film with an X rating. A presidential commission on obscenity and pornography reported in 1970 that there was no proof that pornography was harmful or linked to violence, and the commission recommended the repeal of laws prohibiting the sale of such materials to consenting adults.

Action breeds reaction. As hard-core pornography added more Xs to its rating, voices of opposition arose. The Nixon White House rejected out of hand the findings of a former president's pornography commission. The courts became filled with obscenity cases, and in 1973 the Supreme Court established in *Miller v. California* the test for obscenity still in use today. *Miller* built on *Roth,* employing a three-part guideline for the determination of obscenity: "a) whether the average person, applying contemporary community standards would find that the work, taken as a whole, appeals to the prurient interest; b) whether the work depicts or describes, in a patently offensive way, sexual conduct specifically defined by the applicable law; and c) whether the work, taken as whole, lacks serious literary, artistic, political, or scientific value." This last guideline was a rejection of *Roth*'s "utterly without redeeming social value" and thus a stricter measure.

Miller v. California also narrowed the concept of "constant obscenity" found in *Roth* to a variable one which could be determined by district attorneys and juries in each community. In addition, *Miller v. California* also defined specific pornographic depictions which the Court found not protected by the First Amendment, including "patently offensive representations or descriptions or ultimate sexual acts, normal or perverted, actual or simulated," and "patently offensive representations or descriptions of masturbation, excretory functions and lewd exhibitions of the genitals."

Further obscenity definitions and restrictions set in with the Reagan administration and its alliance with the fundamentalist right. In 1982 in *New York v. Ferber,* the Supreme Court ruled that authorities can prohibit sexually explicit materials involving children without showing that such material is obscene. The 1984 Child Protection Act provided the Postal Inspection Service with new investigative powers against child porn, thus setting the stage for what has become one of the major battlefields in the anti-pornography fight. The government, through the Justice Department, has vigorously prosecuted purveyors and consumers of child porn, though some of its efforts have been proven overly zealous, as witnessed in the Supreme Court decision of 1992, *Jacobson v. United States,* in which a conviction for possession of child pornography was reversed because of entrapment measures on the part of the post office investigators.

The Meese Commission and the Pornography Debate

The Reagan administration continued its war on pornography by convening in 1985 the Meese Commission to study the effects of pornography on society in general and women in specific. With a budget of $500,000 and over 200 witnesses, the Meese Commission set out to prove the deleterious effects that obscenity has on the body politic. The results of the *Final Report* concluded that pornography harms the individual and society. An interesting by-product of the commission's work was the formation of an unlikely alliance between political conservatives, fundamentalists, and radical feminists. Religious critics of pornography claim that the viewing of pornographic material ultimately warps the user's view of sex, and that users become dissatisfied with their real-life sex partners. Some psychologists also claim that pornography becomes addictive, forcing the user to search for ever more shocking forms of sexual titillation. The feminist writer, Andrea Dworkin, and law professor, Catherine A. McKinnon, testified before the commission, adding fuel to the argument of the link between pornography and rape. Dworkin's view of the sex-object role in which pornography places women was clearly stated in her book, *Pornography: Men Possessing Women.* McKinnon had also previously fought pornography as a form of sex discrimination, taking the debate to another legal level.

However, the inevitable backlash set in with the findings of the Meese Commission: many feminists disagreed with Dworkin's and McKinnon's position, arguing that a crackdown could hit all sexually oriented literature and presentations, pornographic or not. And other social scientists and researchers noted that the link between pornography and violence to women was not so simplistic as described in the commission report, with some even taking the position that pornography could work as preventative to such violence, allowing a fanciful resolution to aggressive tendencies. Studies thus far have been inconclusive in directly connecting, for example, the viewing of hard-core pornography with rape, and the harmful, addictive effects of pornography on users has also been challenged by scholars.

Electronic Pornography

Increasingly, with advanced technologies, the delivery of pornography and thus its control has reached new levels of sophistication. In addition to cable television, dial-a-porn companies, and home videos, the growth of the Internet has created an entirely new medium for the dissemination of any message, including pornographic ones. Parent groups and religious groups have banned together to lobby for control of such media. Such pressure bore early fruit in the music industry with the Washington, D.C.-based Parents' Music Resource Center headed by Tipper Gore. By 1990 the group had managed to label 93 major music releases with the "Parental Advisory: Explicit Lyrics" warning. However, critics of such measures point out that these warning labels only whet the appetites of kids for such products.

The use of 900 numbers for phone sex has also come under close scrutiny, as many of the users of such services are under age. In 1989, the Supreme Court ruled in *Sable Communications of California Inc. v. FCC* that a ban on dial-a-porn obscenity was constitutional. However, in the same finding, it was decided that a ban on indecency was not constitutional. Thus, if government wanted to protect minors from such phone communication, narrowly defined laws would have to be adopted that would not at the same time violate the free speech rights of adults to the same services.

Television, too, has had its critics, of both the sex and violence portrayed on the airwaves. One study has shown that in a typical week of viewing, teens can see about 57 sexual behaviors on afternoon television. During prime time the viewer could witness 143 per week. New rating systems have been devised by the industry, under pressure from parent groups and with the implicit threat of possible government intervention if nothing was done. Initially, six categories of parental

guidance were developed: TV-Y, TV-Y7, TV-G, TV-PG, TV-14, and TV-M. However, such designations were found to be so cumbersome, that new pressure was brought to bear in 1997, and the television industry, with the exception of NBC, agreed on a new rating system: S for sex, V for violence, L for foul language, and D for suggestive dialogue. Critics of the guidelines say that such labeling goes too far into the realm of censorship, giving no indication of the context of such elements, and scaring potential advertisers away from shows that deal with realistic contemporary content. Such measures are in a way merely stop-gap, however, for in 1995 Congress passed a provision for a so-called V-chip, which, inserted in new televisions, would allow for the automatic blocking of undesirable types of programming.

The Internet has also come in for its share of criticism over the availability of pornography. Not only content has been criticized, but also its ready availability for users of all ages. The worldwide nature of such material as well as the ability to download images makes the system virtually impossible to censor. In a landmark case in 1997 the Supreme Court invalidated a Clinton administration piece of legislation regulating cyberspace. In *Reno v. American Civil Liberties Union* the Court decided that sending "indecent" or "offensive" material to a minor through the Internet can not be a crime, as such transmission is protected under the First Amendment. Thus for the time being, censorship of the Internet has been averted.

The Ongoing Pornography Debate

Polls indicate that Americans are divided over the effects of pornography on society, but also demonstrate that the public generally shies away from outright censorship. *Miller v. California,* with its variable obscenity argument, opened the door to local standards and therefore litigation, and such local standards are still in the process of being formed. One difficulty with such standards is the evolving nature of society itself. In an information-based society such as ours, new thresholds are reached on a seemingly daily basis regarding what is considered pornographic. The conflict between free speech and censorship in a democratic society is one that will not go away, but rather one that is integrally linked to the political processes and health of the nation.

See also: **Freedom of Speech, Internet, Privacy**

Bibliography and Further Reading

Donnerstein, Edward I., and others. *The Question of Pornography: Research Findings and Policy Implications.* New York: Free Press, 1987.

Downs, Donald Alexander. *The New Politics of Pornography.* Chicago: University of Chicago Press, 1989.

Easton, Susan M. *The Problem of Pornongraphy: Regulation and the Right to Free Speech*. New York: Routledge, 1994,

Gorman, Carol. *Pornography*. New York: Franklin Watts, 1988.

Gubar, Susan, and Joan Hoff, editors. *For Adult Users Only: The Dilemma of Violent Pornography*. Bloomington: Indiana University Press, 1989.

Stoller, Robert J. *Porn: Myths for the Twentieth Century*. New Haven: Yale University Press, 1991.

Strossen, Nadine. *Defending Pornography: Free Speech, Sex, and the Fight for Women's Rights*. New York: Scribners, 1995.

UNITED STATES V. ONE BOOK CALLED *ULYSSES*

Legal Citation: 5 F.Supp. 182 (1933)

Plaintiff
State of New York

Defendant
One Book Entitled *Ulysses* by James Joyce

Plaintiff's Claim
The book violated national standards for obscenity.

Chief Lawyers for Plaintiff
Nicholas Atlas, Samuel C. Coleman, Martin Conboy

Chief Defense Lawyers
Morris L. Ernst, Alexander Lindey

Judge
John M. Woolsey

Place
New York, New York

Date of Decision
26 November 1933

Decision
The book was ruled not obscene.

Significance
Judge John Woolsey's decision in the *Ulysses* case marked a notable change in the policies of the courts and legislative bodies of the United States toward obscenity. Before this decision, it was universally agreed that a) laws prohibiting obscenity were not in conflict with the First Amendment of the U.S. Constitution and b) the U.S. Post Office and the U.S. Customs Service held the power to determine obscenity. *Ulysses* became the major turning point in reducing government prohibition of obscenity.

Friends of James Joyce had warned him that *Ulysses* would run into trouble with American postal and customs officials. As early as 1919 and 1920, when the *Little Review* serialized some of the book, the U.S. Post Office confiscated three issues of the magazine and burned them. The publishers were convicted of publishing obscene material, fined $50 each, and nearly sent to prison.

After that decision, several American and British publishers backed off from considering publishing the book in its entirety. Joyce, visiting his friend Sylvia Beach's Parisian bookstore, Shakespeare and Company, despaired of finding a publisher. Beach then asked if Shakespeare and Company might "have the honor" of bringing out the book. Thus *Ulysses* was first published in 1922 in Paris and instantly became an object of smuggling pride and a valuable collector's item when successfully transported past British and American customs agents. By 1928, the U.S. Customs Court officially listed *Ulysses* among obscene books to be kept from the hands and eyes of American readers.

Meantime, such literary figures as T. S. Eliot, Virginia Woolf, and Ezra Pound had acclaimed the Joyce work as already a classic. In Paris, Bennett Cerf, who with Donald S. Klopfer had successfully put the Random House publishing firm on its feet by establishing the Modern Library, told Joyce he would publish the book if its publication could be legalized.

Two Percent for Life

Cerf engaged Morris L. Ernst, America's leading lawyer in obscenity cases. Ernst's fee, contingent upon winning the case, was a five percent royalty on the first 10,000 published copies, then two percent for life on all subsequent printings.

Ernst and his associate, Alexander Lindey, carefully planned their strategy. Early in 1932, they had a copy of the book mailed across the sea, expecting customs to seize it. It arrived untouched.

"So we had a friend bring a copy in," wrote Klopfer many years later, "and we went down to the dock to welcome him! The Customs man saw the book and didn't want to do anything about it, but we insisted

Did Censorship Help *Ulysses*?

James Joyce's *Ulysses*, is far more than an obscenity case. The tale of a single day in the life of Dublin, Ireland, it is modelled after Homer's Odyssey; only in Joyce's version, Odysseus or Ulysses is reborn as Leopold Bloom, a mild-mannered Jewish advertising salesman whose wife regularly cheats on him with younger men.

It was chiefly the parts involving Molly, Leopold's wife—passages involving references to sexual acts—which raised the censors' hackles. But considering the densely layered texture of Joyce's book, which is not so much a story as a celebration of various literary techniques in symbols, it is hard to imagine how anyone other than a serious reader ever got to the questionable portions.

Ulysses was never the sort of book likely to be read by the general public: so difficult is the narrative that Joyce scholars recommend the use of a guidebook.

How did the book acquire such a reputation that it was banned in America for many years? Simply through the attentions of censors—who have added immeasurably to the notoriety of a book that would otherwise be largely unknown in non-literary circles.

Source(s): Gilbert, Stuart. *James Joyce's Ulysses: A Study by Stuart Gilbert.* New York: Vintage, 1955.

---

and got his superior over, and finally they took the book and wouldn't allow us to bring it into the U.S. because it was both obscene and sacrilegious." That copy was sent by customs to the U.S. attorney for libel proceedings. One meaning of the word "libel" is "the publication of blasphemous, treasonable, seditious, or obscene writings or pictures."

Ernst then got the U.S. attorney to agree to have the issue tried before a single judge—thus avoiding the potential pitfalls of a jury trial.

Finally, Ernst managed to keep postponing the case until it came before one particular judge: John M. Woolsey. The judge was known to Ernst as a cultivated gentleman who wrote elegant decisions and who loved old books and antique furniture.

The judge further postponed hearing the case to give himself time to read *Ulysses* and other books that had been written about it. But at last, on 25 November, in a jam-packed small hearing room that seated fewer than 50 people, the hearing began. One of the prosecuting attorneys turned to Morris Ernst. "The government can't win this case," he said. Ernst asked why. "The only way to win," said the prosecutor, "is to refer to the great number of vulgar four-letter words used by Joyce. But I can't do it." Why not, asked Ernst.

"Because there is a lady in the courtroom."

"But that's my wife," said Ernst. "She's a school-teacher. She's seen all these words on toilet walls or scribbled on sidewalks by kids who enjoy them because of their being taboo."

The government's case against Joyce's book made two distinct objections. First was the use of four-letter words not mentionable in polite company. Ernst set out to prove that standards of obscenity change, and that by the standards of 1933, Joyce's choice of words did not make the work obscene. To help make his point, Ernst traced the etymologies of a number of four-letter words. Of one particularly abhorrent word, he said, "Your Honor, it's got more honesty than phrases that modern authors use to connote the same experience."

"For example, Mr. Ernst?"

"Oh—'they slept together.' It means the same thing."

"That isn't usually even the truth," said Judge Woolsey.

At that moment, Ernst later remarked, he knew "the case was half won."

The second objection was to the frankness of the unconscious stream of thought that Joyce portrayed in such characters as Molly Bloom. This was (as Ernst later put it) Joyce's "dramatic incisive attempt to record those thoughts and desires which all mortals carry within themselves."

The judge asked Ernst if he had read through Joyce's entire book. "Yes, Judge," he replied. "I tried to read it in 1923 but could not get far into it. Last summer, I had to read it in preparation for this trial. And while lecturing in the Unitarian Church in Nantucket on the bank holiday . . ."

"What has that to do with my question 'Have you read it?'"

"While talking in that church I recalled after my lecture was finished that while I was thinking only about the banks and the banking laws I was in fact, at that same time, musing about the clock at the back of the church, the old woman in the front row, the tall shutters at the sides. Just as now, Judge, I have thought I was involved only in the defense of the book—I must admit at the same time I was thinking of the gold ring around your tie, the picture of George Washington behind your bench and the fact that your black judicial robe is slipping off your shoulders. This double stream of the mind is the contribution of Ulysses."

The judge rapped on the bench. "Now for the first time I appreciate the significance of this book. I have listened to you as intently as I know how. I am disturbed by the dream scenes at the end of the book, and still I must confess, that while listening to you I have been thinking at the same time about the Hepplewhite furniture behind you."

"Judge," said Ernst, "that's the book."

"His Locale Was Celtic and His Season Spring"

On December 6, Judge Woolsey delivered his opinion on *United States v. One Book Called Ulysses*:

> I hold that *Ulysses* is a sincere and honest book, and I think that the criticisms of it are entirely disposed by its rationale . . . The words which are criticized as dirty are old Saxon words known to almost all men, and, I venture, to many women, and are such words as would be naturally and habitually used, I believe, by the types of folk whose life, physical and mental, Joyce is seeking to describe. In respect of the recurrent emergence of the theme of sex in the minds of his characters, it must always be remembered that his locale was Celtic and his season Spring . . .
>
> I am quite aware that owing to some of its scenes *Ulysses* is a rather strong draught to ask some sensitive, though normal, persons to take. But my considered opinion, after long reflection, is that whilst in many places the effect of *Ulysses* on the reader undoubtedly is somewhat emetic, nowhere does it tend to be an aphrodisiac. *Ulysses* may, therefore, be admitted into the United States.

Ten minutes after the judge completed his statement, Random House had typesetters at work on *Ulysses*.

The government appealed Woolsey's decision to the Circuit Court of Appeals, where Judge Learned Hand and his cousin, Judge Augustus Hand, affirmed the judgment. Judge Martin Manton dissented.

Morris L. Ernst. © AP/Wide World Photos.

Bibliography and Further Reading

Anonymous. *The Obscenity Report* (report to the President's Task Force on Pornography and Obscenity). New York: Stein and Day, 1970.

Esterow, Milton. "Perspective: United States of America v. One Book Called *Ulysses*." *Art News*. September 1990, pp. 189-190.

Moscato, Michael, and Leslie LeBlanc. *The United States of America v. One Book Entitled ULYSSES* by James Joyce. Frederick, MD: University Publications of America, 1984.

Oboler, Eli M. *The Fear of the Word: Censorship and Sex.* Metuchen, NJ: Scarecrow Press, 1974.

HANNEGAN V. ESQUIRE

Legal Citation: 327 U.S. 146 (1946)

Petitioner
Robert Hannegan, U.S. Postmaster General

Respondent
Esquire, Inc.

Petitioner's Claim
That Esquire, Inc. was not entitled to second class postal delivery, as the material published in the magazine was not contributing to the public good or public welfare.

Chief Lawyer for Petitioner
Marvin C. Taylor

Chief Lawyer for Respondent
Bruce Bromley

Justices for the Court
Hugo Lafayette Black, Harold Burton, William O. Douglas (writing for the Court), Felix Frankfurter, Frank Murphy, Stanley Forman Reed, Wiley Blount Rutledge, Fred Moore Vinson

Justices Dissenting
None (Robert H. Jackson did not participate)

Place
Washington, D.C.

Date of Decision
4 February 1946

Decision
Decided for Esquire, Inc., allowing the magazine to retain rights to second class postal service and refusing the Postmaster broad powers of censorship.

Significance
The ruling limited the postmaster general's powers of censorship, and reinforced the freedom of circulation in the mail system. The Court's decision made clear that materials that were not considered obscene could not be excluded from normal postal services, whether or not they were thought by any individual, even the postmaster, to be contributing to the public good.

Second class mailing rates are considered a kind of subsidy from the government, allowing periodicals such as newspapers and magazines cheaper rates of postage. The goal for these special rates is to allow the broad circulation of periodicals, which will contribute to the education of the public. The Classification Act of 1879, which set up the second class postage system, required that periodicals receiving the special postage rate "be originated and published for the dissemination of the information of a public character, or devoted to literature, the sciences, arts, or some special industry, and having a legitimate list of subscribers."

The postmaster general issued a citation against *Esquire* magazine, called "the Magazine for Men," designating a board to determine whether the magazine's permit for second class distribution be revoked. Although the board recommended that the magazine be allowed to continue receiving the special postage rates as before, the postmaster revoked the permit anyway. He cited recurring items in the magazine that he found strongly objectionable; these included jokes, cartoons, and articles with sexual content.

It is important to note that the postmaster was not claiming that the magazine was actually obscene, because obscene material does not receive protection from the First Amendment, and cannot legally be mailed, as the Court determined in *Ex parte Jackson* (1877). Instead, the postmaster was arguing that the material in *Esquire* did not deserve to receive the special, discount rate of postage because the magazine did not contribute to the public good, and because it contained material that was "morally improper and not for the public welfare." This determination was not indisputably held by the general public; the Court considered testimony from several witnesses, whose opinions of the material ranged from "highly objectionable" to finding no basis for objection.

The Court determined that what the postmaster was really questioning in this case was not whether Esquire, Inc. abided by the requirements set forth in the Classification Act of 1879, but whether the content was of suitable quality—i.e., whether the magazine was good or bad. The Court understood this as a question of whether the postmaster should be granted powers of censorship.

Hank Greenberg (right),
first baseman for the
Detroit Tigers, presents
President Truman with a
baseball. Looking on is
Postmaster General
Robert Hannegan.
© UPI/Corbis-Bettmann.

Granting these powers would allow the postmaster to determine what was fit to be distributed, not just regarding questions of sexual content, but also of political opinion. This same issue was addressed in *United States ex rel. Milwaukee Social Democratic Publishing Co. v. Burleson* (1921), but with respect to political motivations.

In the *Esquire* case, the Court decided that these powers of censorship were decidedly beyond the call of the job of the postmaster general. Justice Douglas wrote in the Court's opinion,

> Under our system of government there is an accommodation for the widest varieties of tastes and ideas. What is good literature, what has educational value, what is refined public information, what is good art, varies with individuals as it does from one generation to another . . . A requirement that literature or art conform to some norm prescribed by an official smacks of an ideology foreign to our system.

The Court decidedly supported the freedom of circulation, and rejected the idea that a public official should have the kind of control over a publication's content as the postmaster was seeking.

The ruling in this case, however, does not represent a unified approach to the question of censorship throughout the history of the U.S. government. During times of war, circulation of publications that violate espionage laws have been limited. The Court upheld the right of the postmaster to exercise some censorship in *United States ex rel. Milwaukee Social Democratic Publishing Co. v. Burleson*. In this case, the Court upheld the withdrawal of second class rates from the *Milwaukee Leader*, a Socialist newspaper. Obscene materials have continued to be subjected to circulation limitations, even as public standards and concerns change.

Related Cases
Ex parte Jackson, 96 U.S. 727 (1877).
United States ex rel. Milwaukee Social Democratic Publishing Co. v. Burleson, 255 U.S. 407 (1921).
Lamont v. Postmaster General, 381 U.S. 301 (1965).

Bibliography and Further Reading
Biskupic, Joan, and Elder Witt, eds. *Guide to the U.S. Supreme Court.* Washington, DC: Congressional Quarterly, Inc., 1997.

Konvitz, Milton R., ed. *Bill of Rights Reader,* 5th ed. Ithaca, NY: Cornell University Press, 1973.

ROTH V. UNITED STATES

Legal Citation: 354 U.S. 476 (1957)

Appellant
Samuel Roth

Appellee
United States

Appellant's Claim
That publication of "obscene" material is protected by the First Amendment.

Chief Lawyers for Appellant
David von G. Albrecht and O. John Rogge

Chief Lawyer for Appellee
Roger D. Fisher

Justices for the Court
William J. Brennan, Jr. (writing for the Court), Harold Burton, Tom C. Clark, Felix Frankfurter, Earl Warren, Charles Evans Whittaker

Justices Dissenting
Hugo Lafayette Black, William O. Douglas, John Marshall Harlan II

Place
Washington, D.C.

Date of Decision
24 June 1957

Decision
The Supreme Court upheld both state and federal laws punishing the sale and distribution of publications of material judged to be obscene or indecent.

Significance
In *Roth*, the Supreme Court for the first time defined obscenity, which it described in terms of the First Amendment.

Samuel Roth ran a business in New York City that published and sold books, magazines, and photographs. He advertised his wares in circulars and other advertisements which he mailed to potential customers. He was convicted in federal district court of mailing obscene material in violation of a federal obscenity statute. After the circuit court upheld his conviction, Roth took his case to the U.S. Supreme Court.

In another case decided with *Roth*, David S. Alberts, who ran a mail order business in Los Angeles, was convicted in state court of selling obscene and indecent books and publishing an obscene advertisement of them. A California appellate court upheld his conviction for having violated a state obscenity law. Like Roth, Alberts appealed to the U.S. Supreme Court.

Both men questioned the constitutionality of obscenity laws which they said conflicted with First Amendment guarantees of free speech and a free press. The United States had, since the early nineteenth century, had criminal obscenity laws on the books. Because no question had been raised about a potential conflict between these laws and the first component of the Bill of Rights, they were regularly enforced. As a consequence, works of obvious literary merit alleged to be obscene, such as Theodore Dreiser's 1925 novel *An American Tragedy,* had no constitutional protection. In *Roth* the Court was obliged to confront the question of whether or not obscenity was actually protected by the First Amendment.

Supreme Court Defines Obscenity

Justice Brennan began his opinion for the Court by noting that as far back as the colonial period, certain types of speech, including libel, blasphemy, and profanity, had been deemed unlawful. Based on his survey, Brennan initially concluded: "In light of this history, it is apparent that the unconditional phrasing of the First Amendment was not intended to protect every utterance." Obscenity, Brennan declared, is like other types of unprotected speech in that it is "utterly without social importance." But what exactly is obscenity? For the first time Brennan struggled to define it:

> [S]ex and obscenity are not synonymous. Obscene material is material which deals with

sex in a manner appealing to prurient interest. The portrayal of sex, e.g., in art, literature, and scientific works, is not itself sufficient reason to deny material the constitutional protection of freedom of speech and press . . . [Something is obscene if] to the average person, applying contemporary community standards, the dominant theme of the material taken as a whole appeals to the prurient interest.

Using Brennan's new standard, the laws, both federal and state, used to convict Roth and Alberts were upheld, as were the men's convictions. The test introduced in *Roth* proved to be highly controversial. On the one hand, it did away with the practice of prosecuting obscenity by using selected excerpts for a work that selective members of society found offensive. After *Roth*, unprotected obscenity could only be judged by the "average person" considering the work "taken as a whole." On the other hand, Brennan's test did not require a showing that any particular harm had been done. Other types of unprotected speech, such as libel, can be barred only after such proofs have been made in court.

Part of the problem with the *Roth* test for obscenity was that its focus remained undefined. In *Memoirs v. Massachusetts* (the 1966 *Fanny Hill* case), Brennan revised his test. The standard then became whether or not the material being judged was "patently offensive" and had even minimal social value. This standard was deemed too lax, and in *Miller v. California* (1973), the Court once again revised its test for obscenity. Ever since *Miller*, material is judged obscene if: 1) an average person, applying community standards, finds the work's predominant theme to be prurient; 2) it depicts sexual conduct in a plainly offensive way; and 3) taken as a whole, it lacks serious literary artistic, political, or scientific value.

In *Paris Adult Theatre v. Slaton District Attorney* (1973), a companion case to *Miller*, Justice Brennan concluded that the Court was unable to come up with a truly workable definition of obscenity. Therefore, the whole attempt to regulate obscenity was for him unconstitutionally vague. Additionally, feminists have criticized the Court's attempts to define obscenity because these efforts fail to account for the violent treatment of women and children that is a common feature of pornography. Nonetheless, *Miller* remains the law, and obscenity remains outside the protection of the First Amendment.

Related Cases
Near v. Minnesota, 283 U.S. 697 (1931).
Memoirs v. Massachusetts 383 U.S. 413 (1966).
Miller v. California, 413 U.S. 15 (1973).
Paris Adult Theater v. Slaton District Attorney, 413 U.S. 49 (1973).

Bibliography and Further Reading
DeGrazia, Edward. *Girls Lean Back Everywhere: The Law of Obscenity and the Assault on Genius.* New York, NY: Random House, 1992.

Easton, Susan. *The Problem of Pornography: Regulation and the Right to Free Speech.* New York: Rutledge, 1994.

Gewirtz, Paul. "On 'I Know It When I See It.'" *Yale Law Journal,* January 1996, pp. 1023.

Gurstein, Rochelle. *The Repeal of Reticence: A History of America's Cultural and Legal Struggles over Free Speech, Obscenity, Sexual Liberation, and Modern Art.* New York, NY: Hill and Wang, 1996.

Johnson, John W., ed. *Historic U.S. Court Cases, 1690–1990: An Encyclopedia.* New York: Garland Publishing, 1992.

JACOBELLIS V. OHIO

Legal Citation: 378 U.S. 184 (1964)

Appellant
Nico Jacobellis

Appellee
State of Ohio

Appellant's Claim
That under the First and Fourteenth Amendments, he should not have been punished for showing *The Lovers,* a film deemed obscene under Ohio State law.

Chief Lawyer for Appellant
John T. Corrigan

Chief Lawyer for Appellee
Ephraim London

Justices for the Court
Hugo Lafayette Black, William J. Brennan, Jr. (writing for the Court), William O. Douglas, Arthur Goldberg, Potter Stewart, Byron R. White

Justices Dissenting
Tom C. Clark, John Marshall Harlan II, Earl Warren

Place
Washington, D.C.

Date of Decision
22 June 1964

Decision
The film was not obscene and Jacobellis' conviction should be overturned.

Significance
This was a landmark case that helped define the legal standards for determining obscenity.

In 1964, movie theater manager Nico Jacobellis was convicted of exhibiting an obscene movie, Louis Malle's *Les Amants,* "The Lovers." The advertising for the film made it sound quite daring:

> "When all conventions explode . . . in the most daring love story ever filmed!" "As close to authentic amour as is possible on the screen." "The frankest love scenes yet seen on film." "Contains one of the longest and most sensuous love scenes to be seen in this country."

Yet to most critics and filmgoers, the film was nothing more than a sensitive love story, directed by the renowned French director Louis Malle and starring the internationally famous actress Jeanne Moreau. In the words of the Supreme Court decision:

> "The Lovers" involves a woman bored with her life and marriage who abandons her husband and family for a young archaeologist with whom she has suddenly fallen in love. There is an explicit love scene in the last reel of the film, and the State's objections are based almost entirely upon that scene. The film was favorably reviewed in a number of national publications, although disparaged in others, and was rated by at least two critics of national stature among the best films of the year in which it was produced.

Although the film was shown in some 100 U.S. cities, including Columbus and Toledo, Ohio, Jacobellis was prosecuted for showing it in Cleveland Heights, a middle-class suburb of Cleveland.

Defining Obscenity

In a 6-3 decision, the Supreme Court decided that Jacobellis had been wrongly convicted. By no stretch of the imagination could *The Lovers* be called obscene. Yet *Jacobellis* displayed the wide diversity of opinion about what constitutes obscenity and who should judge.

Justice Brennan announced the judgment of the Court and was joined in his opinion by Justice Goldberg. Brennan reiterated that obscenity is not covered by the First Amendment's protection of free speech.

Banned Films

Banned Films: Movies, Censors and the First Amendment, lists 122 films which, for "political, religious, moral, [or] sexual reasons," were the focus of censorship cases between 1908 and 1981. In *The Encyclopedia of Censorship,* published eight years later, only five more films were listed, suggesting that the bulk of these legal actions took place earlier in the history of film rather than later.

The first case noted by the authors involved the films *Night Riders* and *The James Boys in Missouri,* both banned in Chicago in 1908. Though both films depicted "the American historical experience," according to their promoters, the authorities found in them evidence of immorality.

A sampling of some other banned films include: *The Birth of a Nation* (1915), whose racist themes would "invite race hatred and race riots"; *Tomorrow's Children* (1937), a film that depicts sterilization and corrupt public officials; *Victory in the West* (1941), a German newsreel celebrating Nazi victories in France and the Low Countries; *Curley* (1949), a *Little Rascals*-style Hal Roach film banned in Memphis because it showed white children and black children in school together; and *The Man with the Golden Arm* (1956), which portrayed drug addiction.

Source(s): Grazia, Edward de and Roger K. Newman. *Banned Films: Movies, Censors and the First Amendment.* New York: R. R. Bowker, 1982.

Therefore, it was legal to pass laws against obscenity and to prosecute people for distributing it. The problem came in determining just what counted as obscene material.

Some people, wrote Brennan, wanted obscenity to be treated "as a purely factual judgment" that could be decided by a jury or at least by state and the lower federal courts. In this view, the Supreme Court's role in obscenity cases would be limited only to judging whether sufficient evidence supported the lower court's ruling—in other words, asking only whether the lower court proceeded in a constitutional manner, without regard to its actual judgment.

"The suggestion is appealing," continued Brennan, "since it would lift from our shoulders a difficult, recurring, and unpleasant task"—having continually to review materials and decide whether they were obscene. Unfortunately, Brennan wrote, the Court had to be involved in specific decisions. Otherwise, it was far too likely that work deserving of First Amendment protections would be ruled obscene and lose its constitutional safeguard.

Brennan referred to a 1957 decision, *Roth v. United States,* as the most recent working definition of obscenity available:

> . . . obscenity is excluded from constitutional protection only because it is "utterly without redeeming social importance," and . . . "the portrayal of sex, e.g., in art, literature and scientific works, is not itself sufficient reason to deny material the constitutional protection of freedom of speech and press."

The Court would not, moreover, "weigh" the social importance of a work against its obscene qualities. If

a work had any "social importance" whatsoever, it deserved constitutional protection.

Brennan went on to write that the *Roth* standard required material to be considered obscene only if it went "substantially beyond customary limits of candor in description or representation of such matters."

Finally, Brennan examined the *Roth* decision's idea that obscenity be judged by "contemporary community standards." He stressed that "community" in this context meant "society at large . . . the public, or people in general." Otherwise, wrote Brennan, a work might be considered obscene in one community while being permitted in another. This would make it virtually impossible for publishers and film distributors to know how to distribute work nationally. The probable effect would be to "restrict the public's access to forms of the printed word which the State could not constitutionally suppress directly."

Other Opinions: "I Know It When I See It"

Justices Warren and Clark dissented. They believed that community standards of the local area in which the work was being prosecuted should be invoked. And Justice Harlan, another dissenter, believed that while federal laws had to define obscenity very narrowly, states had somewhat more latitude in making these judgments.

However, the dissenters were not the only ones to express individual opinions in this controversial case. Those who agreed with the majority decision also wrote their own opinions about it. Justice Black, for example, joined by Justice Douglas, wrote a "First Amendment absolutist" opinion. The justices felt that any conviction of anyone for exhibiting a movie "abridges freedom of the press as safeguarded by the First Amend-

Justice Potter Stewart. © Photograph by Chase LTD. Collection of the Supreme Court of the United States.

ment." Since the Fourteenth Amendment meant that state laws, too, had to follow the First Amendment, no laws against obscenity were possible under the Constitution.

Justice Goldberg wrote a separate opinion, stressing that the love scene in the movie was "so fragmentary and fleeting that only a censor's alert would make an audience conscious that something 'questionable' is being portrayed." Perhaps, wrote Goldberg sarcastically, the exhibitors of the movie could be prosecuted—but only if the "exaggerated character of the advertising rather than the obscenity of the film is to be the constitutional criterion."

But the most famous opinion in the *Jacobellis* case came from Justice Stewart, who said that the only unprotected material in his opinion was "hard-core pornography." Stewart expressed his concern that such material was impossible to define. "But I know it when I see it," he wrote, coining a phrase that was to become widely quoted in both admiring and disparaging terms.

Consequences of *Jacobellis*

Justice Stewart's notion of knowing obscenity when he saw it has been quoted in more than 150 court decisions. Eventually, Stewart's frustration with the general inability to define obscenity led him to join Justice Brennan in the belief that obscene material should not be suppressed, because of the difficulty of suppressing only it and not permissible material as well. By 1973, Justices Stewart, Brennan, and Marshall were all arguing that the state should regulate only the distribution of obscene material to children and unconsenting adults, leaving consenting adults to enjoy obscene material if they chose.

Related Cases

Roth v. United States, 354 U.S. 476 (1957).
Kingsley Pictures Corp. v. Regents of the University of the State of New York, 360 U.S. 684 (1959).
Manual Enterprises, Inc., v. Day, 370 U.S. 478 (1962).
Bantam Books Inc. v. Sullivan, 372 U.S. 58 (1963).
Miller v. California, 413 U.S. 15 (1973).
Jenkins v. Georgia, 418 U.S. 153 (1974).

Bibliography and Further Reading

Emerson, Thomas I., David Haber, and Norman Dorsen. *Political and Civil Rights in the United States,* 3rd ed. Boston: Little Brown & Co., 1967.

Gewirtz, Paul. "On 'I Know It When I See It.'" *Yale Law Journal,* Vol. 105, no. 4, January 1996, pp. 1023-1047.

Konvitz, Milton R. *Expanding Liberties.* Westport, CT: Greenwood Press, 1966.

Regan, John J., C.M. "The Supreme Court, Obscenity and Censorship." *Catholic World,* Vol. 200, December 1964, pp. 142-148.

MEMOIRS V. MASSACHUSETTS

Legal Citation: 383 U.S. 413 (1966)

Petitioner
A Book Named "John Cleland's Memoirs of a Woman of Pleasure," G. P. Putnam's Sons

Respondent
William I. Covin, Assistant Attorney General of Massachusetts

Petitioner's Claim
That the book *John Cleland's Memoirs of a Woman of Pleasure*, better known as *Fanny Hill*, was entitled to protection under the First and Fourteenth Amendments, and that the Massachusetts Supreme Judicial Court erred when it found that a book which appealed to the prurient interest was not required to be completely worthless to be ruled obscene.

Chief Lawyer for Petitioner
Charles Rembar

Chief Lawyer for Respondent
William I. Cowin

Justices for the Court
Hugo Lafayette Black, William J. Brennan, Jr. (writing for the Court), William O. Douglas, Abe Fortas, Potter Stewart, Earl Warren.

Justices Dissenting
Tom C. Clark, John Marshall Harlan II, Byron R. White

Place
Washington, D.C.

Date of Decision
21 March 1966

Decision
The Supreme Court found that the book was not obscene, and that the First and Fourteenth Amendments prevented Massachusetts from prohibiting its publication or distribution. However, the justices did not agree on why the book constituted protected speech, and no majority opinion was delivered.

Significance
The case added to the debate among First Amendment scholars concerning definitions of obscenity and the authority to deem printed materials as works without merit.

Lower Court Found *Fanny Hill* Obscene

John Cleland wrote *Memoirs of a Woman of Pleasure* in about 1750. In the 1960s, the attorney general of Massachusetts filed a suit against the book itself to declare it obscene, an unusual proceeding permitted under Massachusetts law. Publisher G. P. Putnam's Sons, who had published the book, intervened in the suit. A hearing was held before a trial judge, who reviewed the book and took evidence from experts to assess its literary, cultural, and educational character. The trial judge found the book obscene and therefore not entitled to the protection of the First and Fourteenth Amendments. The Massachusetts Supreme Judicial Court affirmed the trial court's ruling.

Justice Douglas noted in his opinion that *Fanny Hill* was "concededly . . . an erotic novel." As described by Douglas, the book is the story of a young girl who becomes a prostitute in London, but eventually abandons that life to marry her first lover. He noted that expert witnesses at the trial introduced "considerable and impressive testimony to the effect that this was a work of literary, historical, and social importance." Rev. John R. Graham observed, in a speech appended to Douglas's opinion, that the book was feared more because it raised serious questions about what is, and is not, moral, rather than because of its sexual scenes. Douglas noted that the book had survived for over 200 years despite many efforts to ban it, and that libraries and universities sought to purchase copies when it was published. However, Justice Clark said in his opinion that the book was solely about sex, noting the explicitness of the sexual activities portrayed in it.

The case was decided along with two other obscenity cases, *Ginzburg v. United States* and *Mishkin v. New York*. Both of those cases involved criminal charges, and in both cases the Supreme Court upheld convictions for violation of obscenity laws. In those cases, Justices Brennan, Warren, and Fortas agreed with the dissenters in the *Fanny Hill* case that the materials in question were obscene. In his opinion, Brennan set out the three point test the Court had defined in its earlier decision in *Roth v. United States*: "(a) the dominant theme of the material taken as a whole appeals to a prurient interest in sex; (b) the material is patently offensive because it affronts

Banned Books

The 1994 book *Banned in the U.S.A.*, offers a list of the 50 books most often banned or challenged in the 1990s. In the number-one slot is *Impressions* by Jack Booth and others (1984-87), a series of language-arts textbooks for children from kindergarten through sixth grade. Used in 34 states, it has been the basis of numerous challenges from parents who hold that it teaches "witchcraft, mysticism, and fantasy [along with] themes of rebellion against parents and authority figures."

The remainder of the top-five list includes *Of Mice and Men*, by John Steinbeck (1937), challenged mainly on the basis of the profanity contained in it; *The Catcher in the Rye*, by J. D. Salinger (1951); *The Adventures of*

Huckleberry Finn, by Mark Twain (1885), for its racial epithets; and *The Chocolate War*, by Robert Cormier (1974), because it portrays school and church in a negative light.

A significant number of books on the list have won Newbery, National Book, Pulitzer, or even Nobel prizes: *A Wrinkle in Time*, by Madeleine L'Engle, *I Know Why the Caged Bird Sings*, by Maya Angelou, and *One Hundred Years of Solitude*, by Gabriel Garcia Marquez.

Source(s): Foerstel, Herbert N. *Banned in the U.S.A: A Reference Guide to Book Censorship in Schools and Public Libraries.* Westport, CT: Greenwood, 1994.

---

contemporary community standards relating to the description or representation of sexual matters, and (c) the material is utterly without redeeming social value."

Justice Douglas Noted Definition of Obscene Objective

Brennan concluded that the Massachusetts court misinterpreted the social value standard, noting that it erred in determining that a book could be considered obscene even if it were not "unqualifiedly worthless." Brennan wrote that "[E]ach of the three federal constitutional criteria is to be applied independently." He added that the "social value can neither be weighed against nor canceled by its prurient appeal or patent offensiveness." Brennan also suggested, however, that it might be possible to find that a book that would otherwise be constitutionally protected would have no redeeming social importance if it were sold only to exploit its prurient appeal. However, he added that the decision before the Court was based solely on an abstract review of the book, and not on the circumstances of its publication.

Douglas disagreed with Brennan on the idea that it might be possible to ban a book based on the way it was sold. He observed that it was "inexplicable how a book that concededly has social worth can nonetheless be banned because of the manner in which it is advertised and sold. However florid its cover, whatever the pitch of its advertisements, the contents remain the same."

Douglas also questioned the wisdom of leaving the review of books for obscenity in the hands of judges, noting that a majority of judges in Massachusetts found the book obscene, while a majority in New York did not. "It substitutes majority rule where minority tastes or viewpoints were to be tolerated," he said. He also noted that there is no definition of obscene in the common law, no unity in the definitions of what is, and is

not, obscene. He concluded that the First Amendment "demands more than a horrible example or two or the perpetrator of a crime of sexual violence, in whose pocket is found a pornographic book, before it allows the Nation to be saddled with a regime of censorship." The First Amendment, he added, does not give the government power over the expression of ideas.

In his dissent in the companion cases of *Mishkin* and *Ginzburg,* which he listed as his reason for concurring in the result, Black stated firmly that the First Amendment, which was made applicable to the individual states by the Fourteenth Amendment, gives the states "no power at all . . . to make the expression of views a crime." In his interpretation, the wording of the First Amendment means literally what it says: governments can pass "no law" that restricts the freedom of speech or the press. While Black held to his opinion that the First Amendment completely prohibits censorship, he noted that the Court was an inappropriate organization for deciding what is, and is not, obscene. Black wrote: "If censorship of views about sex or any other subject is constitutional, then I am reluctantly compelled to say that I believe the tedious, time-consuming and unwelcome responsibility for finally deciding what particular discussions or opinions must be suppressed in this country should . . . be vested in some governmental institution or institutions other than this court."

Stewart's dissent in the two companion cases, cited as his concurring opinion in *Fanny Hill,* stated simply that "[h]owever tawdry those books may be, they are not hard-core pornography."

Dissenting Justices Find Differing Conclusions

Clark, writing in dissent, argued that the other justices had misinterpreted *Roth*. Quoting from *Roth*, he said the test for obscenity was, "whether, to the average person, applying contemporary community standards, the dominant theme of the material, taken as a whole, appeals to prurient interests." Clark also noted that he found the book, "too much even for me." He suggested that allowing "utterly without redeeming social value" to be the deciding factor would allow the "smut artist free rein."

Clark also examined the book and testimony. He concluded that it had "no substance," adding that the "sole response evoked by the book is sensual." He also suggested that the idea that pornographic materials may cause antisocial behavior should be incorporated into the social value test.

Harlan's dissent argued that the First Amendment permitted federal suppression of hard core pornography. While he agreed that *Fanny Hill* did not meet that definition, he said that the application of the First Amendment by the states allowed for a looser definition. Under his view, states could prohibit obscene material if they applied "criteria rationally related to the accepted notion of obscenity," and reached "results not wholly out of step with current American standards."

White concluded in his dissent that the social value test should not be applied separately from a determination of whether the book appealed to the prurient interest.

Impact

Six justices of the Supreme Court agreed that *Fanny Hill* was not obscene and that its publication and distribution was protected by the First and Fourteenth Amendments. However, their lack of agreement on why publication should be permitted left the law on obscenity unclear. Justice Brennan applied the obscenity test set in *Roth v. United States* (1957) requiring that a book appeal to the prurient interest, be patently offensive, and "utterly without redeeming social value," and determined that the book was not obscene. Justice Douglas concluded that the First Amendment does not make an exception for obscenity. Justices Black and Stewart referred to their dissenting opinions in two companion cases, *Ginzburg v. United States* (1966) and *Mishkin v. New York* (1966), in which works were found obscene. Black said the Court had no constitutional power to censor speech. Stewart said the material in question was not obscene. Their diverse opinions on the manner reveal the difficult nature of cases involving obscenity, an issue that would receive further attention in cases in later years.

Related Cases

Roth v. United States, 354 U.S. 476 (1957).
Ginzburg v. United States, 383 U.S. 463 (1966).
Mishkin v. New York, 383 U.S. 502 (1966).

Bibliography and Further Reading

Biskupic, Joan, and Elder Witt, eds. *Congressional Quarterly's Guide to the U.S. Supreme Court,* 3rd ed. Washington, DC: Congressional Quarterly, Inc., 1996.

Johnson, John W., ed. *Historic U.S. Court Cases, 1690–1990: An Encyclopedia.* New York: Garland Publishing, 1992.

Konvitz, Milton R., ed. *Bill of Rights Reader,* 5th ed. Ithaca, NY: Cornell University Press, 1973.

Time, April 1, 1966.

STANLEY V. GEORGIA

Legal Citation: 394 U.S. 557 (1969)

Appellant
Robert Eli Stanley

Appellee
State of Georgia

Appellant's Claim
A Georgia state law criminalizing the possession of obscene material in one's home is unconstitutional because it violates the freedom of speech clause in the First Amendment.

Chief Lawyer for Appellant
Wesley R. Asinof

Chief Lawyer for Appellee
J. Robert Sparks

Justices for the Court
Hugo Lafayette Black, William J. Brennan, Jr., William O. Douglas, Abe Fortas, John Marshall Harlan II, Thurgood Marshall (writing for the Court), Potter Stewart, Earl Warren, Byron R. White

Justices Dissenting
None

Place
Washington, D.C.

Date of Decision
7 April 1969

Decision
Reversed a Georgia Supreme Court decision that upheld the constitutionality of a Georgia state statute that criminalized the private possession of obscene material.

Significance
With *Stanley v. Georgia* the Court established boundaries over which state and federal laws could criminalize private ownership of pornographic or obscene material. The Court ruled that the First Amendment protects the right of what an individual reads or watches in the privacy of his home.

Obscene Materials, Privacy and the First Amendment

Appellant Stanley was being investigated for operating an illegal gambling operation in his home. Federal and state law enforcement officers obtained a search warrant and were searching Stanley's home, but uncovered little to prove a bookmaking operation. However, law enforcement authorities discovered three reels of eight-millimeter film in a desk drawer. Using a projector and screen found in Stanley's living room, they watched the films. The state law enforcement officer determined that the movies were obscene. Stanley was charged with possession of obscene material and was arrested. He was later indicated for "knowingly hav[ing] possession of obscene matter," which violated the state's law. Stanley was tried by a jury and convicted. The Supreme Court of Georgia affirmed the conviction.

In his opinion, Justice Marshall dealt solely with Stanley's argument that the Georgia obscenity statute violated the First Amendment. He wrote:

> If the First Amendment means anything, it means that a State has no business telling a man, sitting alone in his own house, what books he may read or what films he may watch. Our whole constitutional heritage rebels at the thought of giving government the power to control men's minds.

Attorneys for the state argued that law was derived from the dangers of viewing obscene material that it could lead to "deviant sexual behavior or crimes of sexual violence." Justice Marshall dismissed this concern. ". . . the State may no more prohibit mere possession of obscene matter on the ground that it may lead to antisocial conduct than it may prohibit possession of chemistry books on the ground that they may lead to the manufacture of homemade spirits." Finally, the Court addressed the argument that banning private possession of pornographic material was the only way to prevent distribution of such material. While the Court acknowledged that it may be difficult to make a case against the "intent to distribute or in producing evidence of actual distribution," that was not a good reason to violate the sanctity and privacy of an individual's home. Justice Marshall wrote:

> We are not convinced that such difficulties exist, but even if they did we do not think that they would justify infringement of the individual's right to read or observe what he pleases. Because that right is so fundamental to our scheme of individual liberty, its restriction may not be justified by the need to ease the administration of otherwise valid criminal laws.

Justice Stewart in a concurring opinion reasoned that the majority while correct in reversing the conviction had over looked that the obscene material was illegally obtained. Before the criminal trial, Stanley had filed a motion to suppress the films because they were obtained in violation of the Fourth and Fourteenth Amendments, against unreasonable searches and seizures. The Georgia Supreme Court ruled that the seizure of the materials was indeed legal.

> This record presents a bald violation of that basic constitutional rule. To condone what happened here is to invite a government official to use a seemingly precise and legal warrant only as a ticket to get into a man's home, and, once inside, to launch forth upon unconfined searches and indiscriminate seizures as if armed with all the unbridled and illegal power of a general warrant.

Impact

Two years later in *United States v. Reidel* (1971), the Court did not extend the same rights to the distribution of pornographic material. While the Court acknowledged the First Amendment right for an individual to have obscene material distributing such material was not afforded the same protections because that material could be sent to children. In later cases the Court has said that obscene materials are not protected by the First Amendment, but any such statutes must be limited.

Related Cases

Roth v. United States, 354 U.S. 476 (1957).
Kingsley Int'l Pictures Corp. v. Regents, 360 U.S. 684 (1959).
United States v. Reidel, 402 U.S. 351 (1971).
Miller v. California, 413 U.S. 15 (1973).
Paris Adult Theatre v. Slaton, 413 U.S. 49 (1973).
Hamling v. United States, 418 U.S. 87 (1974).
Jenkins v. Georgia, 418 U.S. 153 (1974).
Smith v. United States, 431 U.S. 291 (1977).
Pope v. Illinois, 481 U.S. 497 (1987).

Bibliography and Further Reading

Biskupic, Joan, and Elder Witt. *Guide to the U.S. Supreme Court,* 3rd ed. Washington, DC: Congressional Quarterly Inc., 1997.

Gunther, Gerald, and Kathleen Sullivan. *Constitutional Law,* 13th ed. New York: The Foundation Press Inc., 1997.

MILLER V. CALIFORNIA

Legal Citation: 413 U.S. 15 (1973)

Appellant
Marvin Miller

Appellee
State of California

Appellant's Claim
That the state of California's definition of obscenity conflicted with that set forth by the U.S. Supreme Court, and that the Appellant's conviction in California State Court should be overturned.

Chief Lawyer for Appellant
Burton Marks

Chief Lawyer for Appellee
Michael R. Capizzi

Justices for the Court
Harry A. Blackmun, Warren E. Burger (writing for the Court), Lewis F. Powell, Jr., William H. Rehnquist, Byron R. White

Justices Dissenting
William J. Brennan, Jr., William O. Douglas, Thurgood Marshall, Potter Stewart

Place
Washington, D.C.

Date of Decision
21 June 1973

Decision
The Supreme Court vacated and remanded the case, effectively affirming the lower courts' verdict.

Significance
Established a new definition of obscenity, replacing a standard of lewd materials "utterly without redeeming social value" with one of materials judged to be obscene by "the average person, applying contemporary community standards."

The First Amendment to the U.S. Constitution states that "Congress shall make no law respecting an establishment of religion, or prohibiting the free exercise thereof; or abridging the freedom of speech or the press; or the right of the people peaceably to assemble, and to petition the government for a redress of grievances." This seemingly straightforward text lends itself to a variety of interpretations and its exact meaning has been the subject of many Supreme Court decisions, particularly with regard to freedom of speech. Freedom of speech has been found to have certain limits in carefully constrained circumstances, for instance that corporations may not make untruthful claims about their products, but its limits when applied to individual expression are much harder to define. The publication and distribution of sexually explicit materials has also been limited by Court action.

Marvin Miller was convicted in a California State court of knowingly distributing obscene matter, a misdemeanor under state law. During Miller's trial, the presiding judge instructed the jury to determine whether or not the materials in question were obscene by applying "contemporary community standards in California."

Miller appealed the case on the grounds that the instructions to the jury did not reflect the standard for judging materials to be obscene put forth in *Memoirs v. Massachusetts,* a case decided by the U.S. Supreme Court in 1966. In that decision the Court ruled that, to be obscene in the eyes of the law, materials must: be taken as a whole appeal to a lewd interest in sex; be patently offensive by affronting contemporary community standards; and be "utterly without redeeming social value." The case reaffirmed a long-standing determination that obscene materials are not to be afforded First Amendment protection. Miller's attorneys maintained that since freedom of speech issues are by definition constitutional, only a national standard could be applied when determining the obscenity of materials. The Appellate Department, Superior Court of California, County of Orange, affirmed the lower court's ruling, and Miller appealed the case to the Supreme Court where arguments were heard on 18-19 January and 7 November 1972.

The Miller Standard for Obscenity

Chief Justice Warren Burger, writing for the majority in *Miller*, established a three-part standard for obscenity. According to the Miller standard, a judge should ask him or herself three questions. First of all, would "the average person," using standards common to the time and place find that a given movie, book, or other work appeals to sexual desires? Second, does the movie, book, or other work use clearly offensive means to show or describe sexual conduct in a way specifically prohibited by state law? And third, does the movie, book, or other work, "taken as a whole, [lack] literary, artistic, political, or scientific value"?

Elsewhere in his majority opinion, Burger declared flatly that the First Amendment does not protect obscene material as a form of free speech; to be protected, it must be shown to serve some purpose other than appealing to sexual interests. In this he reaffirmed the Court's holding in *Roth v. United States* (1957), and built on the three-part obscenity test established by Justice William J. Brennan in *Memoirs v. Massachusetts* (1966), a set of questions revolving around whether "(a) the dominant theme of the material taken as a whole appeals to a prurient interest in sex; (b) the material is patently offensive because it affronts contemporary community standards relating to the description or representation of sexual matters; and (c) the material is utterly without redeeming social value."

Source(s): Levy, Leonard W. *Encyclopedia of the American Constitution.* New York: Macmillan, 1986.

The Court vacated and remanded, in effect upholding the lower courts' verdicts. Chief Justice Burger delivered the opinion of the Court, with Justices Brennan, Douglas, Marshall, and Stewart dissenting. The majority concluded that the standard for defining obscenity set forth in *Memoirs v. Massachusetts* was too rigorous, given the difficulty in deciding that anything is *utterly* without "redeeming social value." The Court therefore determined to reinstate a somewhat modified version of the previous standard for judging the obscenity of materials as set forth in *Roth v. United States,* a case decided in 1957. The new standard for judging materials to be obscene was set forth as follows:

> (a) whether "the average person, applying contemporary community standards" would find that work, taken as a whole, appeals to prurient interest, (b) whether the work depicts or describes, in a patently offensive way, sexual conduct specifically defined by the applicable state law . . . (3) the test of "utterly without redeeming social value" articulated in Memoirs, supra, is rejected as a constitutional standard, (4) the jury may measure the essentially factual issues of prurient appeal and patent offensiveness by the standard that prevails in the forum community, and need not employ a "national standard."

Miller v. California marked a retreat by the Court from its broad interpretation of First Amendment protection of free speech that had been articulated in *Roth v. United States*. In a sign of things to come, the Court reverted to an older, more conservative standard for determining the obscenity of materials while also transferring responsibility from national bodies to communities.

Related Cases
Roth v. United States, 354 U.S. 476 (1957).
Memoirs v. Massachusetts, 383 U.S. 413 (1966).

Bibliography and Further Reading
Bartlett, Jonathan, editor, *The First Amendment in a Free Society.* New York: H. W. Wilson, 1979.

Jasper, Margaret C. *The Law of Obscenity and Pornography.* Dobbs Ferry, NY: Oceana Publications, 1996.

Johnson, John W., editor, *Historic U.S. Court Cases, 1690–1990: An Encyclopedia.* New York: Garland Publishing, 1992.

Michael R. Capizzi, 1998. © AP/Wide World Photos.

PARIS ADULT THEATRE V. SLATON DISTRICT ATTORNEY

Legal Citation: 413 U.S. 49 (1973)

Petitioner
Paris Adult Theatre, et al.

Respondent
Lewis R. Slaton, District Attorney, et al.

Petitioner's Claim
That the adult films that they were showing were protected under First Amendment Rights.

Chief Lawyer for Petitioner
Thomas E. Moran

Chief Lawyer for Respondent
Robert Eugene Smith

Justices for the Court
Harry A. Blackmun, Warren E. Burger (writing for the Court), Lewis F. Powell, Jr., William H. Rehnquist, Byron R. White

Justices Dissenting
William J. Brennan, Jr., Potter Stewart, Thurgood Marshall, William O. Douglas

Place
Washington, D.C.

Date of Decision
21 June 1973

Decision
The Court ruled that obscene films did not automatically get First Amendment protection simply because they are shown for adults only.

Significance
The legal push and pull that has existed since the inception of the motion picture between freedom of speech and the right of a jurisdiction to regulate what is shown to its constituents is given clarity in this case. The Court's decision that pornography is not protected under the First Amendment simply because the existence and viewing of pornography by adults is legal is the most straightforward stance taken by the government on this issue by this time.

In 1973, the U.S. Supreme Court had a flurry of pornography cases on its docket and a growing unease regarding the way that obscenity was legally defined. Some members of the Court pushed to abolish all bans on pornographic material due to the difficulties encountered in enforcing them or even in determining what constituted obscene material. Still, the more conservative members lobbied instead for a stricter definition of pornography and for rights to be given to individual states to ban works that it felt would be considered offensive to those who lived there. Justice Brennan wrote:

> As a result of our failure to define standards with predictable application to any given piece of material, there is no probability of regularity in obscenity decisions by state and lower federal Courts. That is not to say that these Courts have performed badly in this area or paid insufficient attention to the principles we have established. The problem is, rather, that one cannot say with certainty that material is obscene until at least five members of this Court, applying inevitably obscure standards, have pronounced it so. The number of obscenity cases on our docket gives ample testimony to the burden that has been placed upon this Court.

One of these cases began on 28 December 1970 when the Paris Adult Theatres (two theatres linked with a shared lobby and box office) in Atlanta, Georgia, were showing the films "Magic Mirror" and "It All Comes Out in the End." The theatres billed themselves as "adult theatres" and had signs outside says "Adults Only," "You Must be 21 and Able to Prove It," and "If the Nude Body Offends You, Do Not Enter." Although there were no signs outside giving further information about the particular films that were being shown, it seemed clear that these were indeed films of a graphic sexual nature.

Two criminal investigators paid $3 each to enter the theatre. The district attorney's office filed a complaint against each of the films seeking to have them declared obscene and to have them banned from being shown. The complaints charged that the films constituted

Regulation—Or Censorship?

The first documented protest of a motion picture occurred on 28 April 1894—exactly two weeks after Thomas Edison conducted his first public demonstration of the kinetoscope, an early device for viewing motion pictures.

Since the 1930s, Hollywood has—with varying degrees of commitment—abided by voluntary codes regarding acceptable and unacceptable types of films. Television, because it is available to anyone with access to a TV set, has even more strict standards, and in the 1990s it adopted a ratings system not unlike that which governs motion pictures. Meanwhile, as America moved into the twenty-first century, legislators and civil libertarians debated regulation of the Internet.

But when does regulation become censorship? Certainly most people would agree that it is improper to expose a minor to scenes of explicit sex or violence; however, efforts at regulation could result in preventing adults from gaining access to a particular movie, program, or Web site. Which is a more important liberty: the right of adults to be adults, or the right of children to remain children? Many are concerned that the authorities use sex or violence as an excuse to ban a movie they find objectionable for ideological reasons. Conversely, some fear that filmmakers cynically use tacked-on "messages" to justify cinematic orgies.

Source(s): Green, Jonathon. *The Encyclopedia of Censorship.* New York: Facts on File, 1990.

---

a flagrant violation of Georgia Code Section 26-2101 in that the sole and dominant theme(s) of the said motion picture film[s] considered as a whole and applying contemporary community standards [appeal] to the prurient interest in sex, nudity and excretion, and that the said motion picture film[s are] utterly and absolutely without any redeeming social value whatsoever, and [transgress] beyond the customary limits of candor in describing and discussing sexual matters.

The district attorney's office could have brought criminal charges against the theatre since they were "knowingly distributing obscene material." Instead, they sought only to have the films judged obscene and to stop the theatres from showing them. Both sides waived their rights to a jury trial and agreed that the findings of the court on whether the films were obscene or not would be the final decision. It was never stipulated by the state whether they would pursue further legal action should the films be deemed obscene. When the complaint was filed, a hearing was set and the court barred the theatre from "concealing, destroying, altering or removing" the movies, but not, surprisingly, from showing them.

The court viewed the films along with photos showing the signs outside the theatre banning minors and stating the nature of the films. They interviewed witnesses and heard nothing to lead them to believe that minors were allowed in, although they also found no system in place to bar them. The court found that the films were indeed obscene "[a]ssuming that obscenity is established by a finding that the actors cavorted about in the nude indiscriminately," but also found that the theatre had a right to show them so long as

they did not allow minors into the theatre and they stated up-front, the nature of the films.

In appeal to the Supreme Court of Georgia, the decision was reversed based on *United States v. Reidel.* The court stated:

In [*Reidel*] the Supreme Court expressly held that the government could constitutionally prohibit the distribution of obscene materials through the mails, even though the distribution by limited to willing recipients who state that they are adults, and further, that the constitutional right of a person to possess obscene material in the privacy of his own home, as expressed in the *Stanley* case, does not carry with it the right to sell and deliver such material . . . Those who choose to pass through the front door of the defendant's theater and purchase a ticket to view the films and who certify thereby that they are more than 21 years of age are willing recipients of the material in the same legal sense as were those in the *Reidel* case, who, after reading the newspaper advertisements of the material, mailed an order to the defendant accepting his solicitation to sell them the obscene booklet there.

In other words, while the patrons of the theatre had every right to watch the films under the First Amendment, the theatre was not similarly protected to show them.

The theatre appealed the decision to the U.S. Supreme Court, which upheld the decision that the distribution of pornographic material is not protected under the First Amendment. Writing for the majority,

Chief Justice Burger wrote "The films in this case leave little to the imagination. It is plain what they purport to depict, that is, conduct of the most salacious character. We hold that these films are also hard core pornography, and the showing of such films should have been enjoined since their exhibition is not protected by the First Amendment."

Further, the Court agreed with the Georgia Supreme Court when it ruled that just because the theatre barred minors, that still did not given them legal protection to show obscene material. Berger wrote "In particular, we hold that there are legitimate state interests at stake in stemming the tide of commercialized obscenity, even assuming it is feasible to enforce effective safeguards against exposure to juveniles and passersby." The possible link between pornography and violence was enough, he wrote, to warrant states to act to protect the social climate in their jurisdiction. Acting as a type of parent, Burger concluded that sometimes, government needs to step in to protect the rights of the many over the wishes of the few. "Such laws are to protect the weak, the uninformed, the unsuspecting, and the gullible from the exercise of their own volition. Nor do modern societies leave disposal of garbage and sewage up to the individual 'free will,' but impose regulation to protect both public health and the appearance of public places."

Still, it was not the existence of the films or of the rights of an individual to watch them that was the focus of the Court's debate, but whether the theatre was guaranteed the right to show them. Justice Burger wrote:

> Conduct or depictions of conduct that the state police power can prohibit on a public street do not become automatically protected by the Constitution merely because the conduct is moved to a bar or a 'live' theatre stage, any more than a 'live' performance of a man and woman locked in a sexual embrace at high noon in Times Square is protected by the Constitution because they simultaneously engage in a valid political dialogue.

The more liberal members of the Court did not feel that the case was so clear-cut however. Writing for the minority, Justice Douglas disagreed that obscene material was not protected under the First Amendment simply because it was judged to be obscene. And he was not even comfortable that a piece of work could be judged obscene categorically. He wrote:

> Art and literature reflect tastes; and tastes, like musical appreciation, are hardly reducible to precise definitions. That is one reason I have always felt that 'obscenity' was not an exception to the First Amendment. For matter of taste, like matter of belief, turn on the idio-

syncrasies of individuals. They are too personal to define and too emotional and vague to apply . . .

The dissenting opinion was that people are often offended by many things. Actions taken by the government, articles and opinions read in newspapers, ideas put forth on television all run the risk of offending segments of the population. That a group of people take offense at them, does not make them obscene or wrong. Justice Douglas further wrote:

> There are regimes in the world where ideas 'offensive' to the majority (or at least to those who control the majority) are suppressed. There, life proceeds at a monotonous pace. Most of us would find that world offensive. One of the most offensive experiences in my life was a visit to a nation where bookstalls were filled only with books on mathematics and books on religion.

Douglas continued to say that he had never found himself to be coerced into reading or viewing something that he found offensive. Understandably, one might ban their children from viewing something that they found unfit, but he found that it was not in the government's place to judge the "tastes or beliefs" of an individual so long as it did not result in actions that infringed on the rights of another. In fact, he wrote that the entire nature of the First Amendment rested on the fact that an individual had the freedom to choose his own beliefs.

> When man was first in the jungle he took care of himself. When he entered a societal group, controls were necessarily imposed. But our society—unlike most in the world—presupposed that freedom and liberty are in a frame of reference that makes the individual, not government, the keeper of his tastes, beliefs, and ideas. That is the philosophy of the First Amendment; and it is the article of faith that sets us apart from most nations in the world.

Nonetheless, the Court's decision took the stance that material is covered by the First Amendment when the content of that material is not of an obscene nature. That the distribution of this material and any measures taken to insure that its audience is not inappropriate was determined inconsequential, set a strong precedent for the rights of states to decide what they best feel serves their jurisdictions as well as for a conservative leaning on the meaning of free speech.

Related Cases
Roth v. United States, 354 U.S. 476 (1957).
Redrup v. New York, 386 U.S. 767 (1967).

Bibliography and Further Reading

Cushman, Robert F. *Leading Constitutional Decisions* Prentice Hall. 1977.

"Hard-Nosed About Hard-Core." *Time,* July 2, 1973.

Johnson, John W., ed. *Historic U.S. Court Cases, 1690–1990: An Encyclopedia.* New York: Garland Publishing, 1992.

JENKINS V. GEORGIA

Legal Citation: 418 U.S. 153 (1974)

Appellant
Billy Jenkins

Appellee
State of Georgia

Appellant's Claim
That he had been wrongfully convicted under a Georgia state obscenity statute that had made it illegal for him to show the film *Carnal Knowledge*.

Chief Lawyer for Appellant
Louis Nizer

Chief Lawyer for Appellee
Tony H. Hight

Justices for the Court
Harry A. Blackmun, William J. Brennan, Jr., Warren E. Burger, William O. Douglas, Thurgood Marshall, Lewis F. Powell, Jr., William H. Rehnquist (writing for the Court), Potter Stewart, Byron R. White

Justices Dissenting
None

Place
Washington, D.C.

Date of Decision
24 June 1974

Decision
That the film *Carnal Knowledge* was not obscene under the constitutional standards that the Court had recently announced in *Miller v. California*, and that Jenkins' conviction should be reversed.

Significance
Chief Justice Rehnquist wanted to establish a consistent standard for obscenity, so that the Supreme Court would not have to review so many individual cases; however, *Jenkins v. Georgia* made it clear that the Court had not yet discovered such a standard. Some of the justices, who were critical of all anti-obscenity laws, saw this case as proof that the Court would never be able to set forth a consistent standard.

One of the most important rights set out in the U.S. Constitution is freedom of speech. This right is guaranteed by the First Amendment, which says, "Congress shall make no law . . . abridging the freedom of speech . . ." However, people interpret the First Amendment in different ways. Some people believe that "no law" means just that—no law. Others believe that some kinds of speech, or "expression," can be limited. For example, they believe that the First Amendment allows laws against obscenity. *Jenkins v. Georgia* illustrates how difficult it is to create laws that will prevent obscenity while still preserving the First Amendment.

"I Know It When I See It"

For many years, the ruling definition on obscenity was summed up in a famous comment made by Justice Stewart in 1964. Stewart explained that while obscenity was difficult to define precisely, "I know it when I see it."

The problem was that for Stewart or any other Supreme Court justice to see it, the obscene book, film, or photograph had to become the subject of a court case in which someone protested a local obscenity law and took his or her protest to the Supreme Court. This meant that people whose work was not necessarily obscene—serious filmmakers, writers, or photographers who wanted to deal with sexuality or to portray nudity—felt a "chilling effect." This is when fearing to be charged with obscenity, they might censor themselves and thereby lose their First Amendment rights to free expression. Moreover, commercial filmmakers and other artists who wanted to stay within the law did not exactly know where to draw the line.

Stewart's decision did at least define what was not obscene: any work that had "redeeming social value." His decision held sway for the liberal Warren Court of the 1960s. Then, in 1973, the more conservative Burger Court offered a sterner ruling. In the landmark decision *Miller v. California*, the Court changed the standards: now, rather than "redeeming social importance," a work had to have "literary, artistic, political or scientific value." Juries were encouraged to find obscene any work that would be considered "patently offensive" according to "contemporary community standards."

Friend of the Court

Amicus curiae is the Latin translation for the phrase "friend of the court." An *Amicus curiae* is a private or public individual or organization with a strong interest or strong viewpoint on a subject before a court. An *Amicus curiae* is not a party to the action or lawsuit, but acts as an interested third party calling the court's attention to some matter of the law which is in doubt or which might otherwise escape the court's attention.

An *amicus curiae* files a brief with consent of the other litigants (participants in the lawsuit), with permission of the court, or at the request of the court. Briefs are commonly filed in cases of broad and wide ranging matters of interest and controversy.

The Supreme Court frequently requests the U.S. Solicitor General, appointed by the president and whose office represents the position of the federal government, to submit briefs. Special interest groups also file thousands of briefs yearly to urge a particular result on behalf of third parties who may be affected by the court's decision. Similarly, state's attorney generals or legislators also regularly file briefs expressing a state's views on an issue.

Source(s): Witt, Elder, editor. *The Supreme Court A to Z. CQ's Encyclopedia of American Government.* Washington, DC: Congressional Quarterly, Inc., 1993.

An "Obscenely Boring" Film

Miller gave a few more explicit guidelines for obscenity: "representations or descriptions or ultimate sexual acts, normal or perverted, actual or simulated," and "representations or descriptions of masturbation, excretory functions, and lewd exhibition of the genitals." The goal of *Miller,* as Justice Rehnquist explained in *Jenkins v. Georgia,* was to make questions about what was obscene "essentially questions of fact"—not questions of opinion.

Meanwhile, across the United States, people continued to be convicted of obscenity charges. There was enough uncertainty about exactly what was considered obscene that many of these cases were appealed to higher and higher courts. Eventually, one of those cases made it to the U.S. Supreme Court.

On 13 January 1972, theater manager Billy Jenkins was showing a film called *Carnal Knowledge* in a little movie house in Albany, Georgia. While the film was playing, local law-enforcement officers seized it and used it to charge Jenkins with distributing obscene material. Jenkins was fined $750 and sentenced to 12 months probation.

Carnal Knowledge was a mainstream Hollywood film that had already played in 29 towns in Georgia. The movie was directed by Mike Nichols, written by Jules Feiffer, and starred Jack Nicholson, Art Garfunkel,

Jack Nicholson and Ann-Margret in the 1971 film **Carnal Knowledge**. © Archive Photos.

Banned Films

On 14 April 1894, Thomas Edison put on the first-ever public demonstration of his kinetoscope, an early motion-picture viewing device. Two weeks later, on 28 April, an Atlantic City protest against a peep show called *Dolorita in the Passion Dance* became the first attempt to ban a motion picture. Since then, movies and morality have often been at odds with one another.

In 1913, Ohio became the first state to attempt a ban on a film, and two years later the U.S. Supreme Court upheld local censorship in *Mutual Film Corporation v. Industrial Commission of Ohio*.

The United States, unlike most other countries, has no system of national censorship; rather, since the 1930s Hollywood, through the Motion Picture Produc-

ers and Distributors Association (later renamed the Motion Picture Association of America, or MPAA) has been self-regulating. By the early 1960s, however, the old guidelines had broken down, and in response to growing concerns over sex and violence in films, MPAA joined with associations representing theatre owners and film distributors to establish the Classification and Rating Administration (CARA). The latter reviews films and gives them ratings that range from G, meaning that they are suitable for general audiences of all ages, to X, films suitable only for persons 17 years of age or older.

Source(s): Green, Jonathon. *The Encyclopedia of Censorship.* New York: Facts on File, 1990.

Candice Bergen, and Ann-Margret. The film had made several "Ten Best" lists when it came out in 1971, and Ann-Margret had even been nominated for an Oscar. The movie was a portrait of two men who meet at college in the 1950s and continue as friends and romantic rivals throughout the liberated 1960s, each engaging in more and more sexual encounters that become less and less satisfying.

In his majority opinion for *Jenkins,* Rehnquist made it clear that the movie could in no way be viewed as obscene.

> While the subject matter of the picture is, in a broader sense, sex, and there are scenes in which sexual conduct including "the ultimate sexual act" is to be understood to be taking place, the camera does not focus on the bodies of the actors at such times. There is no exhibition whatever of the actors' genitals, lewd or otherwise, during these scenes. There are occasional scenes of nudity, but nudity alone is not enough to make material legally obscene under the *Miller* standards

At the first screening of the film for the nine justices, Justice White put it more succinctly. "The only thing obscene about this movie is that it is obscenely boring," he complained.

Defining Obscenity

Clearly, the Court had no choice but to overturn Jenkins' conviction. "It would be a serious misreading of *Miller,*" Rehnquist warned, "to conclude that juries have unbridled discretion in determining what is 'patently offensive' . . ."

Justice Brennan, who had long objected to obscenity laws on the grounds that they almost all violated the First Amendment, added an opinion to the case that was basically a way of saying, "I told you so." Brennan pointed out that *Miller,* which was supposed to render obscenity questions into mere questions of fact, had obviously failed. Clearly, local juries would give their own opinions—as they had done in finding *Carnal Knowledge* obscene—and then the Supreme Court would have to come along and correct these problematic, perhaps even absurd, decisions. Thus, wrote Brennan, ". . . the Court's new formulation does not extricate us from the mire of case-by-case determinations of obscenity."

Reactions to the case from movie-makers was likewise mixed. "It appears clear that the freedom of the filmmaker to tell an honest story without hard-core pornography has been upheld," said Jack Valenti, president of the Motion Picture Association. But Peter M. Fishbein, attorney for the National Association of Theater Owners, objected. "There's a long spectrum from *Carnal Knowledge* to a stag movie, and we are disappointed that the Supreme Court hasn't clarified standards for the area in between."

In determining the final results of *Jenkins v. Georgia,* it is helpful to look at the *amicus curiae* (friend of the court) briefs that were filed in support of each side. Those urging that the Georgia obscenity law be struck down included the National Association of Theatre Owners, the Adult Film Association of America, the Directors Guild of America, the American Library Association, the American Booksellers Association, the Council for Periodical Distributors Association, the Association of American Publishers, and the Authors League of America. The one brief supporting the obscenity law was filed by Charles H. Keating, Jr., the anti-pornography crusader who later targeted Larry Flynt and *Hustler* magazine, and who later still was involved in the savings and loan scandal.

Related Cases

Roth v. United States, 354 U.S. 476 (1957).
Kingsley Pictures Corp. v. Regents of the University of the State of New York, 360 U.S. 684 (1959).
Manual Enterprises, Inc. v. Day, 370 U.S. 478 (1962).
Bantam Books Inc. v. Sullivan, 372 U.S. 58 (1963).
Jacobellis v. Ohio, 378 U.S. 184 (1964).
Miller v. California, 413 U.S. 15 (1973).

Bibliography and Further Reading

"Clearing the Calendar." *Time*, 8 July 1974, pp. 57-58.

"Effect of High-Court Rulings on Obscenity Press Freedom." *U.S. News & World Report*, 8 July 1974, p. 25.

"Obscenity: Balancing Act." *Newsweek*, 8 July 1974, pp. 78-79.

Woodward, Bob and Scott Armstrong, *The Brethren: Inside the Supreme Court*, New York: Simon & Schuster, 1979.

YOUNG V. AMERICAN MINI THEATRES, INC.

Legal Citation: 427 U.S. 50 (1976)

Petitioner
Coleman A. Young, Mayor of the City of Detroit

Respondent
American Mini Theatres, Inc.

Petitioner's Claim
That city zoning ordinances attempting to prevent concentration of sexually oriented businesses did not violate the First Amendment guarantee of free speech.

Chief Lawyer for Petitioner
Maureen Pulte Reilly

Chief Lawyers for Respondent
Stephen M. Taylor and John H. Weston

Justices for the Court
Warren E. Burger, Lewis F. Powell, Jr., William H. Rehnquist, John Paul Stevens (writing for the Court), Byron R. White

Justices Dissenting
Harry A. Blackmun, William J. Brennan, Jr., Thurgood Marshall, Potter Stewart

Place
Washington, D.C.

Date of Decision
24 June 1976

Decision
The Supreme Court upheld the ordinance as constitutional.

Significance
Young marked the beginning of a new era in Supreme Court rulings on speech, in which the Court began to distinguish certain types of legal speech as offensive and therefore subject to varying degrees of restriction.

In 1972, the city of Detroit, Michigan, passed two amendments to its "Anti-Skid Row Ordinance" dating from a decade earlier. The amendments provided that a theater showing so-called "adult" films could not be located within 1,000 feet of another such establishment or within 500 feet of a residential area. American Mini Theatres, which operated two theaters that exclusively showed sexually explicit but legal films, challenged the 1972 ordinances. After the federal district court upheld the zoning laws, the Sixth Circuit Court of Appeals, finding that the ordinances constituted prior restraints on constitutionally protected forms of speech, overturned this decisions. The mayor of Detroit then petitioned the U.S. Supreme Court for review of this decision.

The federal appellate court had based its ruling on a 1975 case, *Erznoznik v. City of Jacksonville,* in which the Supreme Court held that all sexually-oriented material not judged to be obscene should receive full First Amendment protection. Because the Detroit ordinances did not require that a determination of obscenity be made before the city banned outlets for questionable material from certain areas, the court was obliged to give establishments like American Mini Theatres the benefit of the doubt.

Supreme Court Holds That Government Can Restrict Certain Types of Offensive Speech

Justice Stevens wrote for only a plurality of the Court; four of the nine justices voted against him, and Justice Powell wrote out his own reasons for supporting the Detroit zoning ordinances. It is hardly surprising that *Young* proved to be such a contentious case. In declaring that some degree of restriction of otherwise legal speech did not violate the First Amendment, Stevens was breaking new ground. He gave three reasons for upholding Detroit's zoning restrictions: first, they did not entirely ban sexually explicit material; second, most people found such material highly offensive; and third, this was not the type of speech whose content merited full First Amendment protection:

> [E]ven though we recognize that the First Amendment will not tolerate the total sup-

City Ordinances and Nude Dancing

In the 1990s, cities and towns across the United States began to combat the spread of nude dancing and other facets of the "adult entertainment" industry. Bills under consideration by a local council in the greater New York City area in 1993, for instance, included measures designating nude-dancing clubs and adult video stores as "public nuisances" which must be located 500 feet or more from the nearest residential area. Marjorie Heins of the Arts Censorship Project and Jon Cummings of the American Civil Liberties Union (ACLU), assessing this proposal in *Newsday*, noted that this strategy was a departure from "a recent wave of efforts in other states to outlaw nude dancing entirely."

In metropolitan Atlanta and a number of other cities, communities have taken a different approach, outlaw-

ing the sale of alcohol at nude dancing clubs. Ostensibly this is due to claims of higher crime rates surrounding strip clubs that serve alcohol, but a study by Fulton County, Georgia police found that the police actually received fewer calls for service at nude-dancing clubs than at regular bars which serve alcohol. Nonetheless, the prohibition of alcohol sales, some community leaders hold, will help to reduce the allure of nude dancing.

Source(s): Marjorie Heins and Jon Cummings, "New York Forum about Nude Clubs: Stripping the First Amendment." *Newsday,* 13 May 1993.

Carlos Campos, "Nudity and Alcohol: Study Disputes Blight Claims." *Atlanta Journal and Constitution,* 27 November 1997.

pression of erotic materials that have some arguably artistic value, it is manifest that society's interest in protecting this type of expression is of a wholly different, and lesser, magnitude than the interest in untrammeled political debate . . . Few of us would march our sons and daughters off to war to preserve the citizen's right to see "Specified Sexual Activities" exhibited in the theaters of our choice.

Justice Stevens's discriminating approach to the First Amendment has proven to be a genuine departure for the Court, which had previously held that speech was either fully protected or unprotected. The Court has, however, always had difficulty defining what constitutes legally obscene and therefore unprotected expression. Previously, in *Miller v. California* (1973), the Court defined obscenity as material whose prominent theme is lewd according to community standards, depicts sexual activity in a patently offensive way, and, taken as a whole, "lacks serious literary, artistic, political, or scientific value." In general, this test requires the Court to make an evaluation in each case. Attempts to ban whole categories of sexually explicit speech, such as a push by feminists in the 1980s to ban pornography, have been unsuccessful. But limited restrictions that do not rise to the level of outright prohibition have been tolerated in the area of obscenity and pornography since *Young.*

Related Cases

DeJonge v. Oregon, 299 U.S. 353 (1937).
Terminiello v. Chicago, 337 U.S. 1 (1949).
NAACP v. Button, 371 U.S. 415 (1963).
New York Times Co. v. Sullivan, 376 U.S. 254 (1964).

Cohen v. California, 403 U.S. 15 (1971).
Miller v. California, 413 U.S. 15 (1973).
Broadrick v. Oklahoma, 413 U.S. 601 (1973).
Erznoznik v. City of Jacksonville, 422 U.S. 205 (1975).

Coleman A. Young, Mayor of Detroit, 1981. © AP/Wide World Photos.

Bibliography and Further Reading

Greenawalt, Kent. *Fighting Words: Individuals, Communities, and Liberties of Speech.* Princeton, NJ: Princeton University Press, 1995.

Hixson, Richard F. *Pornography and the Justices: The Supreme Court and the Intractable Obscenity Problem.* Carbondale: Southern Illinois University Press, 1996.

Jasper, Margaret C. *The Law of Obscenity and Pornography.* Dobbs Ferry, NY: Oceana Publications, 1996.

NEW YORK V. FERBER

Legal Citation: 458 U.S. 747 (1982)

Petitioner
State of New York

Respondent
Paul Ira Ferber

Petitioner's Claim
That a state law restricting the sales and distribution of films and photographs containing children in sexually explicit scenes does not violate the First Amendment's protection of free speech.

Chief Lawyer for Petitioner
Robert M. Pitler

Chief Lawyer for Respondent
Harold Price Fahringer

Justices for the Court
Harry A. Blackmun, William J. Brennan, Jr., Warren E. Burger, Thurgood Marshall, Sandra Day O'Connor, Lewis F. Powell, Jr., William H. Rehnquist, John Paul Stevens, Byron R. White (writing for the Court)

Justices Dissenting
None

Place
Washington, D.C.

Date of Decision
2 July 1982

Decision
Upheld the state of New York's claim and overturned a lower court's decision prohibiting the restriction of nonobscene materials by a state law.

Significance
The ruling created a new category of speech, child pornography, not protected by the First Amendment's Free Speech Clause. The state successfully argued its interest that protecting the physical and psychological well-being of children far outweighed any social value of materials containing sexually explicit scenes involving juveniles. The addition of a new category of speech excluded from constitutional protection stirred considerable controversy. Creating such speech categories, though sending strong social messages, actually limits the courts' constitutional role in reviewing actions of the other two branches of government. Despite these concerns, additional categories, including pornography in general and hate speech, were later proposed for exclusion from First Amendment protection.

There has been broad recognition that free speech requires additional restrictions where children are involved. During the 1970s exploitative use of children in pornography rose sharply. In response, by 1982 almost all states and Congress passed laws banning child pornography. One of the first states to act, New York established a law in 1977 making the use of children less than 16 years old in "sexual or simulated sexual performances" a felony. The material did not have to be legally obscene to be prohibited. Materials are legally obscene when, taken as a whole, they can be considered offensive and lacking serious value of any type.

Soon after the law passed, undercover police officers arrested Paul Ferber, an adult bookstore owner in New York City, after selling them two films containing sexually explicit scenes of underage boys. Though a jury in a New York lower court did not find the films legally obscene, it convicted Ferber under the New York statute banning child pornography. The Appellate Section of the New York Supreme Court affirmed the conviction, but the New York Court of Appeals reversed it. The appeals court ruled that the material should have First Amendment protection since a jury did not find it obscene. The court found that "nonobscene adolescent sex" was too narrow a form of speech to be singled out for exclusion from First Amendment protection. The U.S. Supreme Court then accepted the case to decide this difficult constitutional issue.

Speech Unworthy of Protecting

In a series of decisions the Supreme Court identified "fighting words," group libel, and obscenity as types of speech that lack any social benefit and deserve automatic exclusion from constitutional protection. In the 1942 *Chaplinsky v. New Hampshire* case, the Court ruled that fighting words are "those which by their very utterance inflict injury or tend to incite an immediate breach of the peace." Later cases added the importance of the circumstance in which the words are spoken. In the 1952 *Beauharnais v. Illinois* case, the Court held that speech attacking a class of people, such as a racial minority, constituted group libel and was not protected by the First Amendment.

A definitive Supreme Court ruling regarding obscenity did not occur until 1957 in *Roth v. United States*. In defining obscene, the Court held that obscenity was a category of speech "utterly without redeeming social importance." Obscenity could not be sex alone, but sex portrayed in the most indecent manner. The Court, in establishing a new category of speech unprotected by the First Amendment, proclaimed obscenity as unworthy of any level of acceptability. In *Miller v. California* (1973), the Court revised *Roth* by establishing a test to determine if certain material was obscene and to balance states' interests in restricting pornography with speech censorship. The test involved determining if the speech was: (1) improper based on state or local "contemporary community standards" rather than on national standards under *Roth*; (2) obviously sexually offensive as banned by the law; and, (3) of no serious political, scientific, literary, or artistic value.

The Court considered state laws restricting speech based on content, such as fighting words, group libel, and obscenity, appropriate only when the restrictions were very specifically defined and applied. The Court considered speech not included in these categories protected unless presenting a "clear and present danger" of substantial harm to someone.

A New Speech Category

In *Ferber*, the Court ruled for the first time on a law restricting depictions of sexual activity involving children. Justice White, writing for the unanimous Court, found the Miller test irrelevant when considering child pornography. White stated "it is evident . . . that a State's interest in safeguarding the physical and psychological well-being of a minor is compelling." In stating why child pornography should comprise a new form of unprotected expression under the Constitution, the Court found that child pornography was always child abuse and did not warrant any level of protection. White wrote "the use of children as subjects of pornographic materials is harmful to the physiological, emotional and mental health of the child." White added, "It is irrelevant to the child whether or not the material has literary, artistic, political or scientific value." However, he wrote that child nudity "without more" did "constitute protected expression." White concluded that New York had considerable flexibility to regulate child pornography and the law was valid.

Though concurring, Justice O'Connor was concerned that future state laws inappropriately restricting speech would be shielded from court review by creation of the new speech category. Medical photographs and photographs of ceremonial rites in other cultures could be improperly restricted. To this concern Justice Stevens responded in his concurrence that the "First Amendment affords some forms of speech more protection from governmental regulation than other forms of

speech," and that child pornography ranks "near the bottom of this hierarchy." For speech so marginal, Stevens wrote, concern about the overly broad aspects of laws restricting such offensive speech need not be addressed by the Court.

Impact

Though Court decisions on obscenity often seemed vague and contradictory, the Court made a clear statement on child pornography. Free from fears of violating the First Amendment by placing tough restrictions on child pornography, Congress passed the Child Protection Act of 1984 shortly after the decision. Where *Ferber* focused primarily on distribution of child pornography, the issue of personal possession soon arose. In the 1990 *Osborne v. Ohio* case, the Court found an Ohio law banning the possession of child pornography for other than very specific medical, educational, governmental, religious, or other identified purposes was constitutionally valid. The Court "cannot fault Ohio for attempting to stamp out this vice at all levels of the distribution chain." Similarly, the Court in 1994, held in *United States v. X-Citement Video* that distributors are responsible for knowing if minors are used in materials they sell.

Questions of obscenity and regulation of pornography escalated with the rise of the Internet in the early 1990s. Prohibition of child pornography was one of the first issues tackled by the Clinton administration in 1993. By the mid-1990s Congress attempted to ban child pornography on the Internet through the Communications Decency Act of 1996, but the courts found language defining child pornography as "an image that appears to be a minor engaging in sex" too vague. As a consequence, a special Senate hearing in April of 1997 focused on proliferation of child pornography on the Internet and protecting children using computers from online sexual predators. With the global reach of the Internet, the relevance of *Miller*'s "community standards" appeared to breakdown. To update the standard, sociologists attempted to determine the "international community's" opinion on electronic erotica.

The key legal issues raised by *Ferber* was the creation of another speech category not protected by the First Amendment. Many, like O'Connor, feared use of these categories could lead to greater restrictions for additional types of speech. For that reason, many legal scholars believed using collective categories, rather than judging each case on its own merit, reversed the basic principles of constitutional law. Unprotected speech categories resulted in making it the speaker's responsibility to justify the social value of his speech. To contrast, protected speech places the burden of proof with the state government when restricting speech. The use of categories resulted in government restrictions which were free from rigorous judicial examination. The Court was accused of dodging the constitutional and socially important duties it was created to perform, such as deciding the appropriateness of government restriction on individual rights. Because of the variability of speech in unlimited possible settings, many believed the Court should seek to resolve speech issues and establish principles by carefully reviewing each case separately on its own merits. In effect, First Amendment exclusions eliminated from judicial review the marginal forms of speech that the courts should most likely focus on. The Court would only be judging forms of speech it felt more comfortable hearing. Free speech advocates claimed the unpopularity of a particular speech should command more review and possible protection by the Court, not less. In fact, many claimed any legislation developed over such an emotional subject as child pornography should receive the closest judicial review of all.

In contrast, those supporting use of speech categories claimed that case-by-case court review led to unpredictable results and confusion for states and the media. Other possible speech categories proposed since *Ferber* included hate speech and pornography in general. Both were based on the perceived connection of these marginal forms of speech to violence. Pornography was portrayed as a form of discrimination against women by shaping social attitudes and hindering equality of the sexes. The need for censorship was identified. However, in 1985 *American Booksellers Association v. Hudnut,* the Court rejected the notion that pornography was a form of discrimination against women and declined to create another speech category excluded from First Amendment protection.

Many feared the number of categories of speech free from First Amendment protections would continue to grow. If so, then popular majority views and social trends that drive creation of state laws restricting individual rights would not be subjected to court review. Clearly, the New York law prohibiting child pornography would have been ruled unconstitutionally valid without creation of a speech category. With quickly evolving new electronic media in the late 1990s, many claimed Court review of tough speech issues was needed more than ever.

Related Cases

Chaplinsky v. New Hampshire, 315 U.S. 568 (1942).
Beauharnais v. Illinois, 343 U.S. 250 (1952).
Roth v. United States, 354 U.S. 476 (1957).
Miller v. California, 413 U.S. 15 (1973).
Hudnut v. American Booksellers Association, 475 U.S. 1001 (1985).
Osborne v. Ohio, 495 U.S. 103 (1990).
United States v. X-Citement Video, Inc., 513 U.S. 64 (1994).

Bibliography and Further Reading

Delgado, Richard, and Jean Stefancie. *Must We Defend Nazis? Hate Speech, Pornography, and the New First Amendment.* New York: New York University Press, 1997.

Hixson, Richard F. *Pornography and the Justices: The Supreme Court and the Intractable Obscenity Problem.* Carbondale: Southern Illinois University Press, 1996.

Kimmel, Michael S., and Annulla Linders. "Does Censorship Make a Difference? An Aggregate Empirical Analysis of Pornography and Rape." *Journal of Psychology and Human Sexuality,* Vol. 8, no. 3, 1996, pp. 1-20.

Thomas, Daphyne S. "Cyberspace Pornography: Problems with Enforcement." *Internet Research,* Vol. 7, no. 3, 1997, pp. 201–7.

MASSACHUSETTS V. OAKES

Legal Citation: 491 U.S. 576 (1989)

Petitioner
State of Massachusetts

Respondent
Douglas Oakes

Petitioner's Claim
That the conviction of Oakes, who took photographs of his partially nude stepdaughter, should be upheld under a Massachusetts law prohibiting adults from "posing or exhibiting nude minors for purposes of visual representation or reproduction in any book, magazine, pamphlet, motion picture, photograph, or picture."

Chief Lawyer for Petitioner
James M. Shannon, Massachusetts Attorney General

Chief Lawyer for Respondent
Richard J. Vita

Justices for the Court
Harry A. Blackmun, Anthony M. Kennedy, Sandra Day O'Connor (writing for the Court), William H. Rehnquist, Antonin Scalia, Byron R. White

Justices Dissenting
William J. Brennan, Jr., Thurgood Marshall, John Paul Stevens

Place
Washington, D.C.

Date of Decision
21 June 1989

Decision
The Court send Oakes's case back to a lower court to determine if his conviction should be upheld under the original statute.

Significance
The Supreme Court came to some important conclusions about the concept of "overbreadth"—the idea that a statute is so broad and sweeping in what it calls illegal, it might have a "chilling effect," discouraging speech or activity that is actually protected under the Constitution.

One afternoon in 1984, Douglas Oakes took ten color photographs of his 14-year-old stepdaughter, L. S. He photographed her in the basement of the home where he, she, and her mother lived together, with L. S. wearing nothing but red-and-white-striped bikini bottoms and a red scarf that only partially covered her breasts. As Justice Scalia later described them, the photographs were "sexually provocative . . . of the type frequently found in magazines displayed by storekeepers in sealed cellophane wrappers."

Indeed, as L. S. testified at Oakes' trial, her stepfather told her that he "wanted to make her big for *Playboy.*" When L. S. saw the developed photographs, she tore them up and threw them in the woods, but, according to her testimony, Oakes made her find them and give them back. L. S. also testified that Oakes had taken the pictures while her mother was away. The case against Oakes began because of the complaint L. S. made against him.

Overbroad or Not?

Oakes was sentenced to ten years in prison for violating a Massachusetts statute that read, in part:

> Whoever with knowledge that a person is a child under eighteen years of age . . . hires, coerces, solicits, or entices, employs, procures, uses, causes, encourages, or knowingly permits such child to pose or be exhibited in a state of nudity or to participate or engage in any live performance or in any act that depicts, describes, or represents sexual conduct for purpose of visual representation or reproduction in any book, magazine, pamphlet, motion picture film, photograph, or picture shall be punished . . .

The law went on to specify the punishment: ten to 20 years in prison, a fine of $10,000 to $50,000, or both. The law also specified that a person would not be prosecuted if such pictures were intended for a scientific or medical purpose, or for "an educational or cultural purpose for a bona fide school, museum, or library."

Oakes appealed, and the Massachusetts Supreme Court reversed his conviction. They found that Oakes's posing L. S. for the semi-nude photographs was a kind of self-expression, or "speech," and was therefore guaranteed under the First Amendment, which protects freedom of speech. The majority also found that the Massachusetts statute was overbroad.

As it is used in U.S. constitutional law, a statute is overbroad if it prohibits not just actions that might reasonably be considered illegal, but also actions that are protected by the U.S. Constitution. In the case of the Massachusetts statute, the prohibition against posing under-aged children in "any act that depicts . . . sexual conduct" might be considered illegal. However, the act also prohibited posing under-aged children "in a state of nudity." The Massachusetts Supreme Court thought this was going too far. In their view, the statute "criminalized conduct that virtually every person would regard as lawful, [making] a criminal of a parent who takes a frontal view picture of his or her naked one-year-old running on a beach or romping in a wading pool."

Overbroad statutes have one very special feature. Whereas most laws can be challenged in court only on the grounds that they are directly affecting the plaintiff, an overbroad law can be challenged on the grounds that it might adversely affect someone else. In other words, Oakes could challenge the Massachusetts law not on the grounds that he had been hurt by it, but on the grounds that such a law posed a danger to free speech. Even if Oakes had been committing an act that a better-written law could condemn, he was still free to challenge the law on the grounds that another, more innocent person would be unduly hurt by the law.

Creating a "Chilling Effect"

Before the Supreme Court had time to review Oakes' case, the Massachusetts state legislature revised the law. They specified that only nudity photographed "with lascivious intent" was illegal, and they removed the exemptions for medical, scientific, and artistic purposes. The Supreme Court agreed that this new law was not overbroad. Unlike the original statute, it would not have what is known as a "chilling effect"—that is, it would not keep people from exercising their constitutional rights of free expression for fear of being arrested.

But the important question of what to do with Oakes still remained. His challenge to the original statute had been based on the premise that the statute was overbroad, that it did have a chilling effect on the free speech of others. By rewriting the law, the Massachusetts legislature had removed that chilling effect. On the question of whether or not Oakes's case would still be considered, the Court was divided. A plurality of justices—enough to carry the vote but less than a majority—agreed to remand Oakes's case back to a lower court. The lower court would then be free to reconsider Oakes's case.

However, some justices strongly disagreed. They felt that part of the point of calling a law overbroad was to discourage legislatures from passing such sweeping legislation. If the Massachusetts legislature was not penalized

by losing the chance to convict Oakes, the justices feared it would not learn to restrain itself in the future. As Justice Scalia wrote in his partial dissent, if no valid convictions are lost when an overbroad law is thrown out, "then legislatures would have significantly reduced incentive to stay within constitutional bounds in the first place."

In other words, some of the justices felt that unless legislatures lose something by writing overly broad laws—as in this case, they might lose the chance to convict Douglas Oakes—they might tend to write broad, sweeping laws and just wait for the courts to narrow them. Meanwhile, the overbroad laws would have a chilling effect, and many law-abiding citizens would have their constitutional rights restricted.

Dissension in the Court

The Supreme Court justices disagreed on just about every aspect of the case. Some wanted to remand Oakes back to a lower court; others disagreed. Some considered the original Massachusetts statute overbroad; others thought the original law was perfectly appropriate. The one question that won a majority of the Court was the issue of overbreadth. Five justices could agree that in order to preserve our constitutional freedoms, defendants had to be able to object to a law not just because it restricted them, but also because it might have a chilling effect on others.

The result of this agreement is that legislatures now have to be more careful not to write overly broad laws. They must take more trouble to respect everyone's constitutional rights, especially First Amendment rights to free speech. That respect for rights is the most important legacy of *Massachusetts v. Oakes*.

Related Cases
Ginsberg v. New York, 390 U.S. 629 (1968).
Broadrick v. Oklahoma, 413 U.S. 601 (1973).
Bigelow v. Virginia, 421 U.S. 809 (1975).
New York v. Ferber, 458 U.S. 747 (1982).

Bibliography and Further Reading
Anhang, George. "Separation of Powers and the Rule of Law: On the Role of Judicial Restraint in 'securing the blessings of liberty.'" *Akron Law Review,* fall 1990, Vol. 24, No. 2, pp. 211-227.

Lu, Christopher P. "The Role of State Courts in Narrowing Overbroad Speech Laws after *Osborne v. Ohio.*" *Harvard Journal on Legislation,* winter 1991, Vol. 28, No. 1, pp. 253-268.

Moran, Tim. "First Amendment Overbreadth Doctrine." *Harvard Civil Rights-Civil Liberties Law Review,* winter 1990, Vol. 25, no. 1, pp. 221-239.

Prentiss, David M. "The First Amendment Overbreadth Doctrine and the Nature of the Judicial Review Power." *New England Law Review,* spring 1991, Vol. 25, No. 3, pp. 989-1017.

OSBORNE V. OHIO

Legal Citation: 495 U.S. 103 (1990)

Appellant
Clyde Osborne

Appellee
State of Ohio

Appellant's Claim
That an Ohio law banning the possession of child pornography violated the First Amendment.

Chief Lawyer for Appellant
S. Adele Shank

Chief Lawyer for Appellee
Ronald J. O'Brien

Justices for the Court
Harry A. Blackmun, Anthony M. Kennedy, Sandra Day O'Connor, William H. Rehnquist, Antonin Scalia, Byron R. White (writing for the Court)

Justices Dissenting
William J. Brennan, Jr., Thurgood Marshall, John Paul Stevens

Place
Washington, D.C.

Date of Decision
18 April 1990

Decision
The Court upheld the constitutionality of the Ohio law, but ordered Osborne to be retried because of procedural errors during the trial.

Significance
The Court made an exception to an earlier ruling that said individuals have First Amendment protection to possess obscenity in their homes. States have a right to fight the production and distribution of child pornography by making its possession illegal.

Ideas and images are protected as free speech under the First Amendment, but the Supreme Court has long held that the constitutional protection of speech is not absolute. Obscenity is one type of expression that states can regulate. The Court has made a distinction between pornography and obscenity. Although both usually involve sexual images, pornography is protected, but obscenity is not. The toughest legal issue, however, has been defining what constitutes obscene material.

In *Miller v. California* (1973), the Court established a three-part test to determine when expression is not protected. Material is obscene if a typical member of the community would find it prurient, if it depicts sexual activity in a patently offensive way, and if the work, taken as whole, has no literary, artistic, political, or scientific value. Material that fits all three qualifications could be banned. But four years before the *Miller* ruling the Court had said that although some material might be obscene and illegal, the mere possession of it was not.

The decision in *Stanley v. Georgia* (1969) overturned a Georgia law that made it a crime to possess obscene materials. The Court used both free speech and right-to-privacy arguments to strike down the law. But as Clyde Osborne learned years later, the *Stanley* decision, like First Amendment protection in general, was not absolute.

Osborne's Pictures

Osborne received through the mail four pictures of a naked 14-year-old boy in sexually suggestive poses. Acting on a tip from a postal inspector, the Columbus, Ohio police obtained a search warrant, raided Osborne's home, and found the pictures. The police arrested him under an Ohio law prohibiting the possession of any material featuring a naked minor, if the suspect is not the child's parent or if the parents have not given written consent for the child to appear in the material. (The law exempted material with artistic, scientific, educational, or other merit.)

At Osborne's trial, his lawyer contested that the law was overbroad and vague. "Judge, if you had some nude photos of yourself when you were a child, you would probably be violating the law." The judge, however, disagreed. Osborne was convicted and sentenced to six months in prison. He appealed twice, to an appellate court and the Ohio Supreme Court, still arguing that the Ohio law was overbroad, and that his First Amendment rights had been denied. Both courts denied his appeal, though the Ohio Supreme Court's ruling narrowed the law's focus. Now the law applied to material showing a "lewd exhibition" of nudity or "graphic focus" on the genitals. But even then, Osborne's pictures were illegal.

When the case reached the Supreme Court, Osborne's attorney, S. Adele Shank, pointed to the precedent set in *Stanley* regarding the possession of obscene material. She again attacked the vagueness of the Ohio law. The Court, however, voting 6-3, upheld Osborne's conviction.

At the start of his decision, Justice White warned not to read the *Stanley* ruling too broadly. Quoting the decisions in that case, he wrote, "We did not 'mean to express any opinion on states making criminal possession of other types of printed, filmed, or recorded materials . . . In such cases, compelling reasons may exist for overriding the right of the individual to possess those materials.'" Osborne's case, the majority found, was clearly one of those instances.

Child pornography, the Court said, was vastly different from material featuring adults. The Court had already ruled, in *New York v. Ferber* (1982), that states could prohibit the manufacture and distribution of nonobscene child pornography. Believing child pornography adversely affects the models featured, the Court did not hesitate to limit the freedom granted in *Stanley*.

> Given the importance of the State's interest in protecting the victims of child pornography, we cannot fault Ohio for attempting to stamp out this vice at all levels in the distribution chain. According to the State, since the time of our decision in Ferber, much of the child pornography market has been driven underground; as a result, it is now difficult, if not impossible, to solve the child pornography problem by only attacking production and distribution.

White also found that the original Ohio statute was probably not overbroad, given its exemptions for materials with some merit. The state supreme court helped clarify the vagueness issue when it added the clause about lewd exhibitions and graphic focus. But the Court did find one point in Osborne's favor: the trial judge had violated Osborne's due process by giving the jury faulty instructions. Osborne was entitled to a new trial, but the law by which he had been convicted was constitutional.

The Subjectivity of Words

One of the problems with almost all of the Supreme Court decisions regarding obscenity has been defining the concepts of obscenity and pornography. They are abstract and subjective, based on, among other things, the moral and social beliefs of the person or body defining them. In his dissent from *Osborne*, Justice Brennan focused on this point.

Brennan found the Ohio statute overbroad, both as originally written and then modified by the state supreme court. The statute might outlaw a photo of a model wearing transparent clothing or a replica of Michelangelo's famous statue of David, which prominently displays his genitals. Brennan wrote:

> It might be objected, that many of these depictions of nudity do not amount to "lewd exhibition." But in the absence of *any* authoritative definition of that phrase by the Ohio Supreme Court, we cannot predict which ones . . . Indeed, some might think that *any* nudity, especially that involving a minor, is by definition "lewd," yet this Court has clearly established that nudity is not excluded automatically from the scope of the First Amendment. The Court today is unable to even hazard a guess as to what a "lewd exhibition" might mean.

The issue of child pornography remains highly visible, thanks largely to computers and the Internet. There have been numerous reports of child pornographers using the Internet to spread their product. Electronic media have made traditional notions about the distribution and even "possession" of obscene materials obsolete, though the Court has yet to address First Amendment issues and the Internet.

Related Cases

Stanley v. Georgia, 394 U.S. 557 (1969).
Miller v. California, 413 U.S. 15 (1973).
New York v. Ferber, 458 U.S. 747 (1982).
Massachusetts v. Oakes, 491 U.S. 576 (1989).

Bibliography and Further Reading

Goodman, Allison C. "Two Critical Evidentiary Issues in Child Sexual Abuse Cases." *American Criminal Law Review*, Spring 1995, pp. 855.

Hall, Kermit L., ed. *The Oxford Companion to the Supreme Court of the United States.* New York: Oxford Press, 1992.

The New York Times. 19 April 1990.

The Washington Post. 19 April 1990.

CINCINNATI V. CINCINNATI CONTEMPORARY ARTS CENTER

Legal Citation: 566 N.E.2d 214 (1990)

Plaintiff
State of Ohio

Defendants
Dennis Barrie and the Cincinnati Contemporary Arts Center

Plaintiff's Claim
That the exhibition of photographs by the artist Robert Mapplethorpe was obscene.

Chief Lawyers for the Plaintiff
Richard A. Castellini, Frank H. Prouty, Jr., and Melanie J. Reising

Chief Defense Lawyers
Marc D. Mezibov and H. Louis Sirkin

Judge
F. David J. Albanese

Place
Cincinnati, Ohio

Date of Decision
5 October 1990

Decision
The jury found the five photographs in question not to be obscene.

Significance
The acquittal of the Mapplethorpe defendants was a major reaffirmation of First Amendment freedom of speech protection in the realm of homosexual art.

In the spring of 1990, the Contemporary Arts Center (CAC) in Cincinnati, Ohio held an exhibit of photographs by the late artist Robert Mapplethorpe. The exhibit was controversial from the start because of the openly homosexual nature of much of Mapplethorpe's work and was well covered in the Cincinnati press. There was a great deal of negative public reaction, and rumors spread that the city of Cincinnati would attempt to close down the exhibit under Ohio's obscenity statute, which makes it illegal for any person to "Promote . . . display . . . or exhibit . . . any obscene material."

The CAC's director, Dennis Barrie, attempted a preemptive strike aimed at heading off an obscenity prosecution. The CAC filed an action for a declaratory judgment, which is a type of civil lawsuit, on 27 March 1990 in Hamilton County (which includes Cincinnati) Municipal Court. CAC asked the court to declare the exhibit not obscene, but on 6 April 1990 the court refused and dismissed the action. The next day, the Hamilton County Grand Jury indicted CAC and Barrie for criminal violations of the Ohio obscenity statute.

Of the approximately 175 pictures in the exhibit, seven were particularly controversial and were the focus of the ensuing trial. Two pictures were of naked minors, one male and one female, with a "lewd exhibition or graphic focus on the genitals." The other five were of adult men engaged in unusual sadomasochistic poses.

Obscenity or Art?

The prosecutors had to convince the jury that the seven pictures were legally obscene, as "obscene" was defined by the Supreme Court in the 1973 case *Miller v. California.* Miller stated that material is obscene only if: (1) the average person, applying contemporary community standards, would find that the material as a whole appeals to the prurient interest; (2) the material depicts or describes sexual conduct in a patently offensive way; and (3) the material, as a whole, lacks serious literary, artistic, political or scientific value.

Both the prosecution and the defense wanted Albanese, rather than the jury, to make the decision on particular elements of the Miller test. Prosecutor Prouty argued that Albanese should determine what community standards were:

The NEA and Sexually Explicit Art

Congress established the National Endowment for the Arts (NEA) in 1965 as an institution to distribute grant monies to artists and arts organizations. Beginning in 1989, with a controversy over an NEA-funded exhibit of photographs by the late Robert Mapplethorpe, the NEA has been at the center of a controversy over publicly funded art.

On one side are those who profess themselves proponents of free speech and/or the arts, who hold that attempts to withhold funding for artwork such as Mapplethorpe's constitutes a type of censorship. On the other side are those who position themselves as defenders of public morality, who claim that the government has no business funding Mapplethorpe's photographs. To some, public funding of the arts constitutes yet another form of government intrusion into the lives of its people; to others, the refusal to fund sexually explicit art is itself a form of intrusion.

In medieval times and during the Renaissance, artists had patrons—initially kings and cardinals, and later wealthy individuals—who funded their creations. The twentieth century has seen a return to the patronage system, in the form of government funding. Many consider the government's ability to make such determinations just a product of the modern-day patronage system.

Source(s): "Governmental Patronage," Sinclair Community College. http://www.sinclair.edu

We're not required to show community standards because the court [Albanese] becomes the community.

For the defense, Mezibov argued that Albanese and not the jury should decide whether the pictures had serious artistic value:

It would be inappropriate, it would be wrong, I submit, for lay people to guess and to speculate as to what constitutes serious artistic value.

Albanese, however, decided to leave all three elements of the Miller test to the jury, holding that, "The court will not substitute its judgment for that of the jury."

To prove the defense's claim that the seven pictures had serious artistic value, therefore, Mezibov and Sirkin brought in several art experts to testify. Although the pictures were of scenes such as one man urinating into another man's mouth, the art experts called them the work of "a brilliant artist," with "symmetry" and "classic proportions."

Apparently, the defense's experts convinced the jury. On 5 October 1990, the eight jurors found CAC and Barrie not guilty of the charges of displaying obscene material. Under Ohio law, the case ended then and there, because the state is prohibited from appealing a jury verdict. Coincidentally, the Mapplethorpe obscenity trial ended only two days after another widely publicized obscenity trial, namely the conviction in Florida of a music store owner for selling records by the rap group 2 Live Crew. Although CAC and Barrie were vindicated, the victory was expensive: The trial cost CAC over $200,000 in costs and attorneys' fees.

The acquittal of the Mapplethorpe defendants reaffirmed the obscenity principles of *Miller v. California* and the protection of the First Amendment in a new area. This new area was the field of gay rights and the right of homosexual artists to express themselves. As Mezibov said after the trial:

Yes, we have a Bill of Rights. But it's meaningless unless you fight for it.

Related Cases
Kois v. Wisconsin, 408 U.S. 229 (1972).
Miller v. California, 413 U.S. 15 (1973).

Bibliography and Further Reading
Cembalest, Robin. "Who Does it Shock? Why Does it Shock?" *Artnews*. March 1992, p. 32-33.

"The Obscenity Trial: How They Voted to Acquit." *Artnews*. December 1990, pp. 136-141.

Gurstein, Rochelle. "Current Debate: High Art or Hard-Core? Misjudging Mapplethorpe: the Art Scene and the Obscene." *Tikkun*. November-December 1991, pp. 70-80.

Herbert, Wray. "Is Porn Un-American?" *U.S. News & World Report*, July 3, 1995, p. 51.

Light, Judy. "Jury Acquits Museum in Landmark Art Trial." *Dancemagazine*. December 1990, pp. 12-13.

Merkel, Jayne. "Art on Trial." *Art in America*. December 1990, pp. 41-46.

Parachini, Allan. "Year of the Censor; How Photography Became the Focus of Fear and Loathing." *American Photo*. November-December 1990, pp. 39-42.

RENO V. AMERICAN CIVIL LIBERTIES UNION

Legal Citation: 512 U.S. 844 (1997)

Petitioner
Janet Reno, U.S. Attorney General

Respondent
American Civil Liberties Union

Petitioner's Claim
A federal district court erred in finding two provisions of the Communications Decency Act of 1996 unconstitutional under the First Amendment.

Chief Lawyer for Petitioner
Seth P. Waxman

Chief Lawyer for Respondent
Bruce J. Ennis

Justices for the Court
Stephen Breyer, Ruth Bader Ginsburg, Anthony M. Kennedy, Antonin Scalia, John Paul Stevens (writing for the Court), David H. Souter, Clarence Thomas

Justices Dissenting
Sandra Day O'Connor, William H. Rehnquist

Place
Washington, D.C.

Date of Decision
26 June 1997

Decision
The provisions of the Communications Decency Act prohibiting indecent transmissions and patently offensive displays are unconstitutional because they abridge the freedom of speech protected by the First Amendment.

Significance
In this, the first ruling by the Supreme Court on legal issues raised by the Internet, the Court determined that online communication differed significantly from broadcasting and should therefore be subject to less regulation. It found that two regulations intended to protect minors from pornography were unconstitutionally vague.

Congress adopted the Communications Decency Act (CDA) as part of the Telecommunications Act of 1996, a law regulating many aspects of the telecommunications business, including the Internet. The CDA included two provisions designed to prevent persons under 18 from viewing pornographic materials on the Internet. The first provision, 47 U.S.C. sec. 223(a), prohibited the knowing transmission of obscene or indecent messages to persons under 18, regardless of who initiated the communication. The second section, 47 U.S.C. sec. 223(d) prohibited "sending or displaying patently offensive messages" to persons under 18. Both set out criminal penalties, including prison terms of up to two years.

Two affirmative defenses were also allowed. One provided an exception for people who take "good faith, reasonable, effective, and appropriate actions" to prevent minors from seeing such material. The other covered methods of restricting access, such as age verification services.

Two suits challenging the law were filed by the American Civil Liberties Union and a number of other organizations including several major Internet service providers; organizations representing journalists, booksellers, publishers, editors, libraries, and writers; and several groups providing educational materials on sex and sexually transmitted diseases. A federal district judge granted a temporary restraining order in February 1996 against sec. 223(a) on the grounds that the word "indecent" was too vague. The two cases were consolidated and brought before a panel of three federal district judges. The three judge panel granted a preliminary injunction against both provisions, permitting only the language prohibiting obscene communications in sec. 223(a) to stand. The federal government appealed the case directly to the U.S. Supreme Court.

Perhaps the most significant part of the High Court's ruling distinguished the Internet from the broadcast industry. In finding that the 1978 decision in *FCC v. Pacifica Foundation* did not apply to this case, the Court noted that the broadcast medium had been subject to extensive regulation for many years, while the Internet has not been regulated. It also noted that the Internet was not as "invasive" as radio and television. An Inter-

---

America's First Female Attorney General

On 11 February 1993, Janet Reno became the first female attorney general in American history. Over the preceding years, she had built a successful career as state attorney in Dade County, Florida, where she had enjoyed the support of both Republicans and Democrats. After having been sworn in by President Bill Clinton as America's chief law enforcement officer—other than the president himself—she faced vast new challenges in the form of nationwide concerns over crime, outbreaks of terrorism, and other issues.

Born on 21 July 1938, in Miami, Reno grew up on a 20-acre farm near the Everglades. Both of her parents were journalists, and her mother was known as an eccentric whose leisure-time activities included wrestling alligators. Reno attended Coral Gables High School, and later Cornell University, where she earned

her law degree in 1960. She graduated from law school at Harvard University in 1963.

After working in private practice for several years, Reno in 1971 was appointed to a position with the judiciary committee of Florida's legislature. In 1978 she was elected to the state attorney's position, and over the coming years she dealt with local turmoil that included race riots in Miami's Liberty City, and massive upheaval brought by the arrival of thousands of Cuban refugees during the 1980s.

Reno became Clinton's attorney general after two of the president's earlier nominees failed to win the approval of Congress.

Source(s): *Webster's Dictionary of American Women.* New York: Merriam-Webster, 1996.

---

net user rarely finds material accidently, the Court said, and most indecent material is preceded by warnings to that effect. Conversely, it noted, broadcasts are sent to a wide audience that can easily include children. The program at issue in the *Pacifica* case involved an afternoon broadcast of a radio monologue called "Filthy Words."

The Court concluded that use of the Internet was more similar to that of prerecorded sexually explicit telephone messages. In *Sable Communications of California Inc. v. FCC,* the High Court found a law prohibiting such services unconstitutional when applied to indecent messages, though it allowed it when applied to obscene ones. Quoting from its opinion in "Sable", the Court said, "Placing a telephone call is not the same as turning on a radio and being taken by surprise by an indecent message." The Court also noted that the Internet, unlike the broadcast medium, was a scarce commodity, and therefore did not require the same extensive regulation.

The Court also noted another strong distinction between the material regulated by the CDA and other laws regulating indecent and obscene materials: the right of parents to determine what their children should see. In another case cited by the government in support of the constitutionality of the CDA, *Ginsberg v. New York,* the High Court upheld a law that prohibited selling materials to minors that were deemed obscene for children though not obscene for adults. In distinguishing this case, the Court noted that, under the New York law, parents could provide these materials to their children. In contrast, under the CDA parental consent would not make the material available. The Court also rejected as precedent a 1986 decision, *Renton v. Play-*

time Theatres, noting that the law upheld in that case was primarily a zoning ordinance that prohibited adult movie theaters in certain neighborhoods. That law was aimed at crime associated with such theaters, rather than speech regulation, the Court said.

Since the CDA clearly regulated the content of speech, and set out criminal penalties, the Court found the ambiguity of its language presented major First Amendment problems. Given the vagueness of terms such as "indecent" and "patently offensive as measured by contemporary community standards," the Court said serious questions arose. "Could a speaker confidently assume that a serious discussion about birth control practices, homosexuality, the First Amendment issues raised by the Appendix to our *Pacifica* opinion, or the consequences of prison rape would not violate the CDA?" the Court asked, adding "This uncertainty undermines the likelihood that the CDA has been carefully tailored to the congressional goal of protecting minors from potentially harmful materials."

The Court concluded that the CDA differed markedly from the obscenity test set out in 1973 in *Miller v. California,* the case that established the definition of obscenity. *Miller* requires that a work appeal to prurient interests, describe sexual content offensively and as "specifically defined by the applicable state law," and have no "literary, artistic, political or scientific value." The CDA does not meet that specificity test, and adds "excretory activities," a term not used in *Miller.* The Court also noted that while *Miller* set out the term "contemporary community standards," it did not apply that term to the literary, artistic, and other values that a work might have. The CDA's vague terms do not include such protections. "In contrast to *Miller* and our

Janet Reno, U.S. Attorney General, 1997. © Corbis-Bettmann.

install that prevents children from accessing certain sites would soon be widely available. Concluding that the CDA puts an "unacceptably heavy burden on protected speech," the Court left intact only the provisions prohibiting obscene speech. In closing, the Court noted that the "interest in encouraging freedom of expression in a democratic society outweighs any theoretical but unproven benefit of censorship."

Related Cases

Ginsberg v. New York, 390 U.S. 629 (1968).
Miller v. California, 413 U.S. 15 (1973).
FCC v. Pacifica Foundation, 438 U.S. 726 (1978).
Renton v. Playtime Theatres, 475 U.S. 41 (1986).
Sable Communications of California Inc. v. FCC, 492 U.S. 115 (1989).

Bibliography and Further Reading

Emord, Jonathan W. *Freedom, Technology, and the First Amendment.* San Francisco: Pacific Research Institute for Public Policy, 1991.

Kende, Mark S. "The Supreme Court's Approach to the First Amendment in Cyberspace." *Constitutional Commentary,* winter 1997, pp. 465-480.

Levendosky, Charles. "Freeing the Net: Supreme Court's Ruling a Victory for Town Criers on the Computer." *Cleveland Plain Dealer.* July 13, 1997, p. 1E.

Nimmer, Raymond T. *The Law of Computer Technology.* Boston: Warren Gorham Lamont, 1992.

Podgers, James. "Internet Regulation, Round Three." *ABA Journal,* March 1998, p. 99.

Schroeder, Theodore. *"Obscene" Literature and Constitutional Law: A Forensic Defense of Freedom of the Press.* New York: Da Capo Press, 1972.

Simon, Glenn E. "Cyberporn and Censorship." *Journal of Criminal Law and Criminology,* Spring 1998, pp.1015–1048.

other previous cases, the CDA thus presents a greater threat of censoring speech that, in fact, falls outside the statute's scope," the Court said. It added, "We are persuaded that the CDA lacks the precision that the First Amendment requires when a statute regulates the content of speech."

The Court also noted that it would be "prohibitively expensive" for website owners to verify that their users were adults. It also noted that software for parents to

PRIVACY

The citizens of the United States expect to enjoy their privacy. Indeed, few rights are as commonly taken for granted as that of privacy in this highly individualistic society. Yet the recognition of a constitutional right to privacy is fairly recent. Only since the late twentieth century has it been explicitly recognized, protected, and ultimately expanded. This may seem ironic in light of the many freedoms guaranteed by the Bill of Rights, but the Constitution makes no mention of privacy. In fact, the right had to be identified by the U.S. Supreme Court in a series of controversial, groundbreaking decisions. Its existence is due to the continual interpretation of the law, which in turn reflects sweeping changes in modern life. Today, federal and state privacy laws protect individuals from the intrusion of government, business, and other citizens.

Until the late nineteenth century, few people spoke of privacy rights. No court or law had expressly mentioned the idea. A new view began to emerge with the publication of "The Right to Privacy," a *Harvard Law Review* article written in 1890 by the scholars Samuel D. Warren and Louis D. Brandeis. They argued that privacy should exist as a common law right, particularly to protect the average person from public humiliation in newspapers. One of history's great champions of civil liberties, Brandeis became a Supreme Court justice, and later wrote a famous dissenting opinion that placed privacy at the very heart of the Constitution. "The makers of our Constitution . . . sought to protect Americans in their beliefs, their thoughts, their emotions and their sensations," he stated in *Olmstead v. United States* (1928). "They conferred as against the Government, the right to be let alone—the most comprehensive of the rights of man and the right most valued by civilized men."

Almost four decades passed before this idea took hold. The period between the 1930s and 1960s showed a relentless official disregard for privacy, as wartime and Cold War passions led the government on crusades that involved spying on unpopular groups and hauling witnesses before congressional panels. During the 1950s, the refusal to answer questions of the House Committee on Un-American Activities (HUAC), for instance, often resulted in prosecution for contempt of Congress. In *Watkins v. United States* (1957), an important early

step in limiting government intrusion into privacy, the Supreme Court overturned the conviction of a man who had refused to answer some questions about his past political views and associations. Congress, it held, has no general authority to expose the private affairs of individuals without justification, but instead must respect the freedoms of speech, press, religion, political belief, and association.

During the post-war years, government cared deeply about what people did in their bedrooms. States tightly restricted intimate personal choices with laws governing sexual practices, birth control, and abortion. Even as social values and mores began changing in the midst of the sexual revolution, legal progress toward privacy rights was slow. Echoes of Brandeis' call for privacy could be heard occasionally, as in Justice William O. Douglas' dissent in *Public Utilities Commission v. Pollak* (1952), opining, "The right to be let alone is indeed the beginning of all freedoms." And in *Poe v. Ullman* (1961), Justice John Marshall Harlan II dissented from a decision allowing a state to ban contraceptive sales, calling the law "an intolerable invasion of privacy."

By 1965, privacy's time had come. In *Griswold v. Connecticut* (1965), the Supreme Court struck down a state law that forbade married couples from using contraceptives. Writing the majority opinion now, rather than a mere dissent, Justice Douglas acknowledged that the Constitution made no mention of privacy. But he located such a right in the combination of liberties guaranteed by the Bill of Rights. Together, he wrote, the First, Third, Fourth, Fifth and Fourteenth Amendments have *penumbras*—a term from astronomy meaning partial illumination around a shadow. These penumbras were "formed by emanations from those guarantees that help give them life and substance." Metaphorically, Douglas meant that the right to privacy could be inferred from the amendments even if they did not explicitly state it.

In a quick succession of cases, the scope of the new constitutional right became clear. It was even broader than the *Griswold* decision had suggested. Family planning issues again provided the focus. In *Eisenstadt v. Baird* (1972), the Supreme Court threw out a state law that prohibited selling contraceptives to unmarried persons. Intimate personal decisions, the opinion stressed, could not be dictated by the government. "If the right of privacy means anything," wrote the Court, "it is the right of the individual, married or single, to be free from unwarranted governmental intrusion into matters so fundamentally affecting a person." Within two years, the development of this idea produced the decision in *Roe v. Wade* (1974), establishing the right of a woman to abortion. While noting that the right to privacy is not absolute, the *Roe* decision found that it is "broad enough to encompass a woman's decision whether or not to terminate her pregnancy."

The privacy decisions ignited controversies that still burn today. Apart from moral objections to contraception and abortion, there has been ongoing legal debate over constitutional interpretation. The debate hinges upon whether the Constitution should be interpreted flexibly or strictly in light of what the framers intended. Liberal legal scholars and proponents of civil liberties hail the privacy decisions, seeing them as reflecting the robust ability of constitutional law to adapt to modern life. Conservative critics, who have often sneered at the privacy decisions, demand that interpretation closely follow the text of the Constitution. In one critical essay in 1986, Supreme Court nominee Robert H. Bork blasted the Court for dictating, "without guidance from the Constitution, which liberties or gratifications may be infringed by majorities and which may not." The debate is far from academic, as it informs the future course of the Court on issues such as abortion rights, often challenged in the 1980s and 1990s.

Although privacy rights grew out of decisions on family planning issues, the right to privacy in sexual matters is far from universal. Several states retain age-old laws that criminalize consensual sex between unmarried adults, though these are seldom enforced. However, states have long prosecuted gay men under sodomy statutes that ban anal and oral sex. Once commonplace, these laws remain on the books in 19 states. Between the 1960s and 1990s, many legislatures repealed them, and four courts ruled that their laws violated state constitutions. However, this trend was not followed by the Supreme Court in *Bowers v. Hardwick* (1986). In *Bowers,* a gay man challenged his conviction under a Georgia statute outlawing sodomy, which occurred after a policeman entered a private home and found him engaged in consensual sex with another man. Allowing the law to stand, the Court held that there was no constitutional right for homosexuals to engage in sodomy.

Another critical area for the privacy of gays and lesbians is military service. In the 1990s, the federal government addressed the military's long-standing refusal to allow them in its ranks. Instead of mandating that the armed services change their rules entirely, the Clin-

ton administration attempted to safeguard sexual preference by keeping it private. Its so-called "Don't Ask, Don't Tell" policy, calling for servicepeople to hide their sexuality and for officials not to try to expose it, came under attack from all sides. Neither gays and lesbians nor the military considered the policy workable.

The ownership of pornography has enjoyed more constitutional protection than sex itself. Legal battles over pornography, which depicts sexual acts, have stretched across U.S. history. Generally, pornography is protected under the First Amendment, although the sale and distribution of obscene materials can be prosecuted under a community standards test. Even so, individuals can possess obscene materials in their own home, a right recognized in *Stanley v. Georgia* (1969). In a ringing defense of free thought as a fundamental form of privacy, *Stanley* struck down a Georgia statute punishing the mere possession of obscenity. Government, the Court determined, "has no business telling a man, sitting alone in his own house, what books he may read or what films he may watch." There are limits, however, involving privacy and pornography. The right outlined in *Stanley* does not translate into the right to receive, transport or distribute obscene materials in interstate commerce. Nor does it extend at all to child pornography, which has no constitutional protection.

In criminal law, the Fourth Amendment protects citizens against violations of their privacy by the police and prosecutors. Its ban on "unreasonable searches and seizures" has roots in the experience of colonial America prior to the Revolution, when British authorities were wont to suddenly break down the door in making arrests. In the twentieth century, the amendment has restricted how and when the police may stop, arrest, search, or take the property of an individual or business, thus, in theory, preventing arbitrary actions by the government. Police generally need a search warrant, issued by a court, before they can enter a private residence. To deter police heavy-handedness, violations of the Fourth Amendment can result in evidence being thrown out of court under the so-called "exclusionary rule," a safeguard that has applied to the states since *Mapp v. Ohio* (1961). The rule is extremely controversial, as it often leads to criminal cases being dismissed. Limits on the rule appeared in *United States v. Leon* (1984), which allows for a good faith exception when police make reasonable mistakes. Indeed, in the 1980s, the trend of Supreme Court decisions was to constrain Fourth Amendment protections by allowing greater latitude to police to conduct searches without warrants, whether on buses, through aerial surveillance, or in people's garbage.

Testimony in court comes under a specific protection of privacy. The Fifth Amendment allows criminal defendants to keep secret any information that might help lead to their conviction, known as the right to avoid self-incrimination. Thus a person is protected from having to testify against him or herself and the government must, as the Court held in *Tehan v. United States* (1966), "shoulder the load." Testimony against others is mandatory once a witness is called, but certain notable exceptions exist that safeguard privacy. Known as privileges, these include confidential communications between a husband and wife, an attorney and a client, a doctor and a patient, and a priest and penitent.

Civil litigation often involves privacy claims. Under the common law of torts, five discrete rights of privacy are recognized. Individuals may sue when their solitude is intruded upon in an offensive manner, when private information is made public in an objectionable fashion, when information is made public that places them in a false light, when their name or likeness is appropriated without consent, and, in the case of businesses, when competitors steal trade secrets. Many of these claims arise in lawsuits against the media. Notably, public officials and celebrities have less likelihood than private citizens of recovering in such cases, unless they can prove that information was published with knowledge of its falsity or in reckless disregard for its truth, as in the case *Time, Inc. v. Hill* (1967). And in litigation between private citizens, not all invasions of privacy hold up in court, but generally only those in which the intrusion is highly unreasonable and offensive.

State and federal legislation protecting privacy has existed since the late 1960s. Numerous laws forbid snooping and dissemination of personal information. Electronic surveillance by individuals and the police is regulated by the federal Omnibus Crime Control and Safe Streets Act of 1968, which requires police to obtain search warrants before conducting wiretapping and forbids private parties from using information obtained without another person's consent. The Privacy Protection Act of 1974 and the Freedom of Information Act limit the government to using fair practices in the collection, use, and disclosure of data about its citizens, while also allowing people to see what the government knows about them, correct mistakes, and add details. A similar right is found in the Family Educational Rights and Privacy Act of 1974, which permits parents access to their children's scholastic records. Under the Fair Credit Reporting Act of 1970, credit records can only be given out to third parties for legitimate business purposes, and credit bureaus must maintain accurate reports, allow consumers to challenge inaccuracies, and make no use of their records for marketing.

Bibliography and Further Reading

ACLU. "The Year in Civil Liberties, 1997." Unsigned article. www.aclu.org, 1998

ACLU. "Briefing Paper No. 18: Lesbian and Gay Rights." Unsigned article. www.aclu.org, 1998

ACLU. "Do You Know Where Your Data Is?" Unsigned article. www.aclu.org, 1998

Beattie, James R. Jr. "Privacy in the First Amendment: Private Facts and the Zone of Deliberation." *Vanderbilt Law Review,* May 1991

Hall, Kermit L., ed. *The Oxford Companion to the Supreme Court of the United States.* New York: Oxford University Press, 1992

Schwartz, Bernard. *A History of the Supreme Court.* New York: Oxford University Press, 1993

West's Encyclopedia of American Law. St. Paul: West Group, 1998

Zimmerman, Diane L. "Requiem for a Heavyweight: A Farewell to Warren and Brandeis's Privacy Tort." *Cornell Law Review,* March 1983

JACOBSON V. MASSACHUSETTS

Legal Citation: 197 U.S. 11 (1905)

Appellant
Commonwealth of Massachusetts

Appellee
Henning Jacobson

Appellant's Claim
That a state statute authorizing compulsory vaccination and delegating to a municipality the authority to determine when compulsory vaccination was necessary was constitutional.

Chief Lawyers for Appellant
George Fred Williams and James A. Halloran

Chief Lawyers for Appellee
Frederick H. Nash and Herbert Parker

Justices for the Court
Henry Billings Brown, William Rufus Day, Melville Weston Fuller, John Marshall Harlan II (writing for the Court), Oliver Wendell Holmes, Joseph McKenna, Edward Douglass White

Justices Dissenting
David Josiah Brewer, Rufus Wheeler Peckham

Place
Washington, D.C.

Date of Decision
20 February 1905

Decision
Upheld the constitutionality of the statute, and affirmed defendant's conviction and fine for refusing to be vaccinated.

Significance
In this decision, the Supreme Court addressed for the first time the issue of compulsory vaccination. The decision upheld the right of a state under its police power to provide for compulsory vaccination and to delegate to a municipality the authority to determine when compulsory vaccination was necessary. The decision was welcomed by states in an era when smallpox epidemics were common.

In the fourteenth century, when the bubonic plague was sweeping through England, the English government attempted to control the spread of the disease by passing public health laws imposing quarantines and requiring the burning of victims' household goods and the mandatory cleaning of city gutters. Failure to comply could result in criminal punishment, e.g., the searing of an ear lobe with a hot iron to brand the law breaker. In the nineteenth century, the concern was not the plague, but smallpox, a highly contagious and deadly disease. In 1796, the British physician Edward Jenner discovered a vaccination for smallpox, and vaccination became compulsory in Britain in 1853. Medical studies during the last half of the nineteenth century reported a significant reduction in the prevalence of the disease, and in mortality, amongst vaccinated populations. In the United States, by the early 1900s, most states had passed public health laws authorizing compulsory smallpox vaccination of all inhabitants in the event of an outbreak. Although by 1900, most physicians and most of the public had accepted vaccination as a effective preventative measure, this acceptance was not unanimous. Some physicians and some of the public objected to vaccination on health or philosophical grounds.

In 1902, the board of health of the city of Cambridge, Massachusetts adopted a regulation requiring all inhabitants of the city to be vaccinated against smallpox. A Massachusetts statute authorized the board of health to impose compulsory vaccination if it were necessary for public health or safety. Henning Jacobson, an inhabitant of the city, refused to be vaccinated, and the city filed criminal charges against him. A jury convicted Jacobson after the trial judge excluded his offers of proof and rejected his requested jury instructions. Jacobson offered to prove that vaccination did not prevent smallpox and instead harmed the person vaccinated and that he and his son had reacted adversely to vaccinations in the past. His requested jury instructions asserted that compulsory vaccination violated the U.S. Constitution. On appeal, the supreme judicial court of Massachusetts sustained the conviction, ordering Jacobson jailed until he paid a $5.00 fine. Jacobson appealed to the U.S. Supreme Court.

The National Childhood Vaccine Injury Act

Even though vaccines are intended to prevent illness, sometimes illness itself results when a patient, because of an allergy or for other reasons, responds adversely to a vaccination. Such a reaction can even be fatal, or at least permanent in its damage—a tragedy under any circumstances, but particularly in the case of a child. Such was the situation for Billy McCarren, whose parents alleged in a 1994 lawsuit that he contracted residual seizure disorder (RSD) and encephalopathy after being administered a diphtheria vaccination in 1990.

Situations such as Billy's had led Congress to pass the National Childhood Vaccine Injury Act in 1986. Among other things, the legislation requires physicians and other health-care providers who administer vaccines to keep permanent immunization records, and to report

to the Department of Health and Human Services (HHS) any adverse reaction suffered as a result of a vaccination. The act also provided for a Vaccine Adverse Events Reporting System (VAERS), which has its own 800-number hotline.

The McCarrens and many others have filed suit for compensation by that fund, only to have their claims denied. The CDC, while noting that three-quarters of its petitioners are the families of injured or dead children, counters that denied claimants such as Billy McCarren do not show "recognized vaccine injuries" as stipulated by the act.

Source(s): Centers for Disease Control (CDC). http://www.cdc.gov

Compulsory Vaccination Lawful

In a 7-2 decision, the U.S. Supreme Court affirmed the conviction, upholding the right of the city to impose and enforce compulsory smallpox vaccination on all its inhabitants, including those who objected. On appeal, the Court limited its discussion to Jacobson's claim that compulsory vaccination violated the Fourteenth Amendment. With respect to this claim, Jacobson argued that

his liberty is invaded when the state subjects him to fine or imprisonment for neglecting or refusing to submit to vaccination; that a compulsory vaccination law is unreasonable, arbitrary, and oppressive, and, therefore, hostile to the inherent right of every freeman to care for his own body and health in such way as to him seems best; and that the execution of such a law against one who objects to vaccination, no matter for what reason, is nothing short of an assault upon his person.

Before deciding whether the compulsory vaccination statute violated the Fourteenth Amendment, the Court had to determine the scope and meaning of the statute. To do this, the Court looked to the opinion of the supreme judicial court of Massachusetts. Quoting extensively from that opinion, which upheld the exclusion of offers of proof that vaccination was ineffective and dangerous, the Supreme Court defined the scope of the statute to require. As a general rule, adults not under the guardianship and remaining within the limits of the city had to submit to the compulsory vaccination regulation adopted by the board of health.

The Supreme Court then addressed the issue of the statute's constitutional validity. The Court recognized the state's authority under its police power to enact

state health laws and to vest power in local governments to administer those laws. "Police power" is the power that the state did not surrender to the federal government under the Constitution when it became a member of the Union. This power is limited only by the condition that any local law not infringe upon any constitutional right. The constitutional right Jacobson claimed compulsory vaccination violated was his "liberty" to care for his own body and health in the way that seemed best to him. The Court rejected Jacobson's broad definition of "liberty," saying

[Liberty] does not import an absolute right in each person to be, at all times and in all circumstances, wholly freed from restraint. There are manifold restraints to which every person is necessarily subject for the common good . . . Real liberty for all could not exist under the operation of a principle which recognizes the right of each individual person to use his own, whether in respect of his person or his property, regardless of the injury that may be done to others . . . [Liberty] is not unrestricted license to act according to one's own will. It is only freedom from restraint under conditions essential to the equal enjoyment of the same right by others. It is, then, liberty regulated by law.

Applying these legal principles to the case before it, the Court ruled first that the state did not act unreasonably or arbitrarily in allowing the city board of health to determine that compulsory vaccination was necessary. Moreover, the city did not act arbitrarily in deciding that conditions in the city warranted compulsory vaccination. At the time the regulation was adopted, evidence indicated that smallpox was prevalent and increasing in the city, and most of the medical profession and the public believed that vaccination would stop the spread of the disease. As to the rights of an individual who objects to vaccination, the Court stated, "it was the duty of the constituted authorities primarily to keep in view the welfare, comfort, and safety of the many, and not permit the interests of the many to be subordinated to the wishes or convenience of the few." The power of the public to guard itself against imminent danger does not depend "in every case involving the control of one's body upon [a person's] willingness to submit to reasonable regulations established by the constituted authorities, under the sanction of the state, for the purpose of protecting the public collectively against such danger."

Court Defers to Legislature

The Court ultimately ruled that neither the statute nor the methods employed by the city were unconstitutional, and that application of the statute to Jacobson did not violate his Fourteenth Amendment rights. Underlying the Court's ruling was the Court's unwillingness to second-guess the state legislature, the board of health, and the medical profession as to the efficacy and safety of the smallpox vaccine. Conceding that some reputable physicians did not believe that vaccination prevented smallpox, the Court nonetheless took judicial notice of the fact that, for generations, the mass of the people, as well as most members of the medical profession had accepted vaccination as a preventive of smallpox. The Court said,

> Since, then, vaccination, as a means of protecting a community against smallpox, finds strong support in the experience of this and other countries, no court, much less a jury, is justified in disregarding the action of the legislature simply because in its or their opinion that particular method was—perhaps, or possibly—not the best either for children or adults.

Exemption for Unfit Adult?

Although the Massachusetts statute exempted children whom a physician declared "unfit" for vaccination, it provided no exemption for adults. Jacobson claimed that the city ordinance was broad enough to require a person to submit to compulsory vaccination even when his physical condition might be such as to render such treatment dangerous to life and even cruelly oppressive. The Court held that Jacobson's case presented no such situation. Although Jacobson claimed that he had, as a child, reacted adversely to a vaccination and his son had experienced the same reaction, he did not offer to prove that as an adult, he was not a fit subject for vaccination. However, the Court took great pains to point out the limits of its ruling by acknowledging the possibility that in another case an adult might be entitled to an exemption. The Court said,

We are not inclined to hold that the statute establishes the absolute rule that an adult must be vaccinated if it be apparent or can be shown with reasonable certainty that he is not at the time a fit subject of vaccination, or that vaccination, by reason of his then condition, would seriously impair his health, or probably cause his death.

Impact

The *Jacobson* decision is rich in law. It has been used in many subsequent Supreme Court decisions to support rulings on a wide range of issues, including the scope and limits of police power, the right of privacy under the Fourteenth Amendment, and the power of the judiciary to review legislative action. In *Zucht v. King*, (1922), the Supreme Court dismissed a challenge to an ordinance requiring vaccination for public school admittance on the ground that *Jacobson* had conclusively decided the issue.

In 1980, the World Health Organization declared smallpox extinct, attributing the extinction to worldwide efforts and the promotion of vaccination. Today, because state laws have for years required all children to be immunized before attending school, few adults are unvaccinated. However, some people, including physicians, still believe that vaccinations are not always effective and may produce adverse side effects or consequences. As a result, compulsory vaccination or immunization is still not free of controversy. As a result, some states allow medical, religious, and even philosophical exemptions from immunizations. In 1986, Congress passed the National Childhood Vaccine Injury Act to provide compensation for vaccine-related injuries and deaths.

Related Cases

Zucht v. King, 260 U.S. 174 (1922).
Buck v. Bell, 274 U.S. 200 (1927).
Prince v. Massachusetts, 321 U.S. 158 (1944).
Griswold v. Connecticut, 381 U.S. 479 (1965).
Roe v. Wade, 410 U.S. 113 (1973).
Cruzan v. Director, MDH, 497 U.S. 261 (1990).
Washington v. Glucksberg, 512 U.S. 702 (1997).

Bibliography and Further Reading

Gostin, Lawrence O., and Zita Lazzarini. "Childhood Immunization Registries." *JAMA, The Journal of the American Medical Association,* Dec. 13, 1995, pp. 1793.

Janus, Eric S. "Preventing Sexual Violence: Setting Principled Constitutional Boundaries on Sex Offender Commitments." *Indiana Law Journal,* Vol. 72, no. 1, Winter 1996.

Malloy, Suzanne M., "Mandatory HIV Screening of Newborns: A Proposition Whose Time Has Not Yet Come." *American University Law Review,* April, 1996.

MEYER V. NEBRASKA

Legal Citation: 262 U.S. 390 (1923)

Appellant
Robert T. Meyer

Appellee
State of Nebraska

Appellant's Claim
That the state denied him due process, as protected by the Fourteenth Amendment, when it convicted him for teaching the German language.

Chief Lawyer for Appellant
Charles E. Sandall

Chief Lawyer for Appellee
Mason Wheeler

Justices for the Court
Louis D. Brandeis, Pierce Butler, Oliver Wendell Holmes, Joseph McKenna, James Clark McReynolds (writing for the Court), Edward Terry Sanford, George Sutherland, William Howard Taft, Willis Van Devanter

Justices Dissenting
None

Place
Washington, D.C.

Date of Decision
4 June 1923

Decision
The Court reversed a lower court decision and found for the appellant.

Significance
For the first time, the Supreme Court hinted that the right to privacy was implied in the Due Process Clause of the Fourteenth Amendment. Although this case dealt with Meyer's right to teach German, and parents' rights to have their children learn the language, *Meyer* was later used as a precedent to uphold contraceptive and abortion rights.

During and after World War I, a wave of "100 percent Americanism" swept the United States. Immigrants, especially Germans, were looked at with suspicion, and businesses and civic groups promoted the teaching of English and American values. Sauerkraut was renamed "liberty cabbage," and in Nebraska, angry citizens burned books written in German. In the context of that patriotic fervor, the state of Nebraska passed the Foreign Language Statute. The 1919 law prohibited an instructor from using a modern foreign language or teaching a foreign language to students in grades one through eight. Any teacher violating the law was subject to a fine or jail term of not more than 30 days.

Robert Meyer was a teacher in Hamilton County, Nebraska, at the Lutheran Zion Parochial School. In his class, Meyer used a collection of Bible stories written in German to teach reading to ten-year olds. The state found out and charged him on 25 May 1920, for violating the language law. Meyer was convicted in the district court of Hamilton. He then appealed to the Nebraska Supreme Court, claiming his right to teach had been denied, a right guaranteed under the Due Process Clause of the Fourteenth Amendment.

The Nebraska court ruled that Meyer violated the statute. The law was a valid exercise of the state's police power, and it did not infringe on Meyer's Fourteenth Amendment rights. In its decision, the court reflected the anti-immigrant feelings of the time:

> The salutary purpose of the statute is clear. The legislature has seen the baneful effects of permitting foreigners who had taken residence in this country, to rear and educate their children in the language of their native land. The result of that condition was found to be inimical to our own safety. To allow the children of foreigners who had emigrated here, to be taught from early childhood in the language of the country of their parents, was to rear them with that language as their mother tongue . . . The obvious purpose of this statute was that the English language should be and become the mother tongue of all children reared in this state.

Academic Freedom and the Constitution

In 1915, the American Association of University Professors (AAUP) adopted a statement establishing certain guidelines for academic freedom. The AAUP, together with the Association of American Colleges, in 1940 produced a revision to the earlier statement, which it published as *Statement of Principles on Academic Freedom and Tenure*. The statement, which called for freedom in the realms of research, publication, and teaching, has been incorporated into the charters of numerous colleges, and has been endorsed by more than 100 academic organizations.

Academic freedom emerged as a significant issue in the 1950s for a number of reasons, not the least of which was the effort led by Senator Joseph McCarthy to iden-

tify and censure persons with Communist sympathies. In *Sweezy v. New Hampshire* (1957), the Supreme Court reversed a contempt conviction against a Marxist academician who refused to answer questions regarding his political sympathies. Justice Felix Frankfurter, concurring in the opinion, quoted with approval a statement by anti-Apartheid South African scholars regarding "'the four essential freedoms of a university'—to determine for itself on academic grounds who may teach, what may be taught, how it shall be taught, and who may be admitted to study."

Source(s): Levy, Leonard W. ed. *Encyclopedia of the American Constitution.* New York: Macmillan, 1986.

From Language to Personal Liberty

The Supreme Court heard Meyer's case on 23 February, 1923. In a 7-2 decision, the Court overturned the Nebraska court's affirmation of the verdict. For the Court, Justice McReynolds noted that Meyer taught German as part of his occupation. Under the Fourteenth Amendment, Meyer had a right to work as a teacher, and the parents of his students had the right to have their children taught using German. The justice also pointed out that the state's exercise of its police power was subject to judicial review.

In this case, the Court believed the state of Nebraska had infringed on personal liberty, even if the intent of the language law had a desirable end: ensuring all children learned English. The Constitution, McReynolds added, protected everyone, even people who speak a foreign language, and the laudable goal of promoting English "cannot be promoted by prohibited means."

The decision had the immediate effect of restricting a state's ability to control completely the curriculum taught in a private school. But *Meyer*'s broader significance came from the reasoning McReynolds used to support the Court's verdict. McReynolds wrote that the Court had not specifically spelled out the liberty guaranteed under the Fourteenth Amendment, and he started to do so:

> Without doubt, it [liberty] denotes not merely freedom from bodily restraint, but also the right of the individual to contract, to engage in any of the common occupations of life, to acquire useful knowledge, to marry, to establish a home and bring up children, to worship God according to the dictates of his own conscience, and, generally, to enjoy those privi-

leges long recognized at common law as essential to the orderly pursuit of happiness by free men . . . The established doctrine is that this liberty may not be interfered with, under the guise of protecting the public, by legislative action which is arbitrary or without reasonable relationship to some purpose within the competency of the state to effect.

Greater Impact for the Future

In the words of the *Oxford Companion to the Supreme Court,* the *Meyer* decision "languished in doctrinal obscurity for forty years." But starting in the 1960s, the decision's notion of protected personal liberty helped shape the idea of a right to privacy. The Court held that the right to privacy was implied in the Fourteenth Amendment and in McReynolds' assertion that marriage, child-rearing, and other personal pursuits were fundamental, guaranteed liberties under that amendment. In *Griswold v. Connecticut* (1965), the Court said privacy rights allowed a married couple to use contraception without government interference. In another landmark case, *Roe v. Wade* (1973), Justice Harry Blackmun again cited the *Meyer* decision and the protection it extended to personal, private liberty. A woman's right to privacy, *Roe* held, allows her to have an abortion if she chooses.

Related Cases

Griswold v. Connecticut, 381 U.S. 479 (1965).
Roe v. Wade, 410 U.S. 113 (1973).

Bibliography and Further Reading

Choper, Jess H, Yale Kasimir, and William B. Lockhart. *Constitutional Rights and Liberties.* St. Paul: West Publishing Company, 1975.

Hall, Kermit L., ed. *The Oxford Companion to the Supreme Court of the United States.* New York: Oxford Press, 1992.

Norton, Mary Beth, et al. *A People & A Nation: A History of the United States,* Vol. 2. Boston: Houghton Mifflin Company, 1982.

Nowak, John E., Ronald D. Rotunda, and J. Nelson Young, *Constitutional Law,* 2nd ed. St. Paul: West Publishing Company, 1984.

Witt, Elder, ed. *The Supreme Court A to Z.* CQ's Encyclopedia of American Government. Washington, DC: Congressional Quarterly, Inc., 1993.

PIERCE V. SOCIETY OF SISTERS

Legal Citation: 268 U.S. 510 (1925)

Appellant
Walter M. Pierce, Governor of Oregon

Appellees
Society of Sisters of the Holy Names of Jesus and Mary, Hill Military Academy

Appellant's Claim
That an Oregon law requiring students between eight and sixteen years old to attend public schools did not violate the Fourteenth Amendment.

Chief Lawyers for Appellant
George E. Chamberlain, Albert H. Putney

Chief Lawyer for Appellees
William D. Guthrie

Justices for the Court
Louis D. Brandeis, Pierce Butler, Oliver Wendell Holmes, James Clark McReynolds (writing for the Court), Edward Terry Sanford, Harlan Fiske Stone, George Sutherland, William Howard Taft, Willis Van Devanter

Justices Dissenting
None

Place
Washington, D.C.

Date of Decision
1 June 1925

Decision
The Court affirmed a lower court's injunction prohibiting enforcement of the Oregon law.

Significance
Following up on its 1923 decision in *Meyer v. Nebraska*, the Court said parents have the right to choose how their children are educated, though the states can compel children to attend some kind of school and set minimum standards for private schools. As with *Meyer*, the *Pierce* decision was later used to help craft an unwritten constitutional right to privacy.

After World War I, some states concerned about the influence of immigrants and "foreign" values looked to public schools for help. The states drafted laws designed to use schools to promote a common American culture. But in their patriotic zeal, the states sometimes trampled on the constitutional rights of their citizens. Oregon was one of the states that tried to dictate how children should be educated, but the Supreme Court thwarted the effort.

In 1922, Oregon voters approved an initiative that required all students between eight and sixteen years old—with limited exceptions—to attend public schools. Parents or legal guardians who disobeyed the law faced arrest on misdemeanor charges. The drive for the Compulsory Education Act was led by the Ku Klux Klan and the Scottish Rite Masons, and it reflected anti-immigrant and anti-Catholic sentiments. The law's supporters did not want students of different religious or ethnic backgrounds studying together in private schools. The law was supposed to take effect on 1 September 1926, but private schools were already feeling its effects, as parents removed their children or stopped enrolling new students. Two organizations, the Society of the Sisters of the Holy Names of Jesus and Mary, and the Hill Military Academy, filed for injunctions against the Compulsory Education Act.

The Society of Sisters was a Roman Catholic order that took care of orphans and operated a number of parochial schools. Many of its students were between ages eight and sixteen. Hill was a private military academy that also taught students between those ages. Both schools argued that the education law denied them property—their income from tuition—without due process. Both schools also claimed the compulsory school law infringed on the liberty of parents to choose the school they desired for their children. The state of Oregon, however, planned to enforce the law, leading to the request for an injunction. A number of religious groups supported the request, which was granted by a federal district court. The state then appealed the ruling to the U.S. Supreme Court.

A Recent Precedent Sets the Way
The Court voted unanimously to affirm the injunction and strike down the Oregon law. Justice McReynolds

drew on the reasoning used in *Meyer v. Nebraska* (1923). In that case, the Court struck down a Nebraska law prohibiting teachers from using a foreign language in the classroom. In that instance, the Court said parents had a right to raise their children as they saw fit, and this applied to the kind of schooling they chose. The same principle, the appellees had argued, was at work in *Pierce,* and McReynolds agreed:

> The fundamental theory of liberty upon which all governments in this Union repose excludes any general power of the state to standardize its children by forcing them to accept instruction from public teachers only. The child is not the mere creature of the state; those who nurture him and direct his destiny have the right, coupled with the high duty, to recognize and prepare him for higher obligations.

McReynolds agreed with the appellees' second point as well. The Oregon law denied private schools their right to property by destroying their business. By forcing students to attend public schools the state would, in practice, shut down private schools geared toward students between the ages of eight and sixteen.

The Court's decision recognized that states could compel some form of minimum education, and had an interest in regulating schools. The state could inspect a school building to ensure it was sound, require teachers to have high moral character, and insist certain courses be taught, but restricting education to public schools was unconstitutional.

Although *Pierce* involved a Catholic organization, and parochial schools were an implied target of the Compulsory Education Act, the Court did not address any First Amendment issues regarding the establishment or prohibition of religion. At the time, the Court had not made the Establishment Clause applicable to the states. It would be another 15 years before that constitutional protection applied to state law in *Cantwell v. Connecticut,* (1940). But in *Pierce,* the Court used an economic interpretation, common at the time, of the Due Process Clause of the Fourteenth Amendment. This "substantive" due process was often invoked to the advantage of American corporations when states tried to regulate their behavior. In this case, the economic reasoning was paired with the protection of individual liberty.

The decision in *Pierce* also reinforced a new concept introduced in *Meyer,* an implied constitutional right to privacy. In this case, the right extended to how parents raise their children. Forty years later, some members of the Supreme Court used the concept to defend contraceptive rights in *Griswold v. Connecticut* (1965), and then a woman's right to have an abortion in *Roe v. Wade* (1973). Legal expert Mark Yudof wrote, "If, as some scholars have asserted, America has an 'unwritten constitution,' *Pierce* is a critical example of its invocation."

Related Cases
Truax v. Raich, 239 U.S. 33 (1915).
Meyer v. Nebraska, 262 U.S. 390 (1923).
Cantwell v. Connecticut, 310 U.S. 296 (1940).
Griswold v. Connecticut, 381 U.S. 479 (1965).
Roe v. Wade, 410 U.S. 113 (1973).

Bibliography and Further Reading

Choper, Jess H, Yale Kasimir, and William B. Lockhart. *Constitutional Rights and Liberties.* St. Paul: West Publishing Company, 1975.

Hall, Kermit L, ed. *The Oxford Companion to the Supreme Court of the United States.* New York: Oxford Press, 1992.

Levine, Samuel J. "Unenumerated Constitutional Rights and Unenumerated Biblic Preliminary Study in Comparative Hermeneutics." *Constitutional Commentary,* fall 1998, p. 511.

New York Times, June 1-2, 1925.

Nowak, John E., Ronald D. Rotunda, and J. Nelson Young. *Constitutional Law,* 2nd edition. St. Paul: West Publishing Company, 1984.

Witt, Elder, ed. *The Supreme Court and Individual Rights.* Washington, DC: Congressional Quarterly, Inc., 1979.

OLMSTEAD V. UNITED STATES

Legal Citation: 277 U.S. 438 (1928)

Petitioners
Roy Olmstead, et al.

Respondent
United States

Petitioners' Claim
That the government's use of evidence obtained through illegal wiretaps violated his Fourth Amendment protection against illegal search and seizure and his right under the Fifth Amendment not to incriminate himself.

Chief Lawyer for Petitioners
John F. Dore

Chief Lawyers for Respondent
John G. Sargent, U.S. Attorney General; Michael J. Doherty

Justices for the Court
James Clark McReynolds, Edward Terry Sanford, George Sutherland, William Howard Taft (writing for the Court), Willis Van Devanter

Justices Dissenting
Pierce Butler, Louis D. Brandeis, Oliver Wendell Holmes, Harlan Fiske Stone

Place
Washington, D.C.

Date of Decision
4 June 1928

Decision
The Supreme Court upheld the use of wiretaps.

Significance
In this, the first Supreme Court case to consider the legality of wiretaps, the Court found that because they did not involve private property, they did not violate the ban on illegal search and seizure. Later the Court would overrule *Olmstead.*

In January of 1919, the states ratified the Eighteenth Amendment to the Constitution, which instituted a nationwide prohibition on alcoholic beverages. Later that year, Congress passed the National Prohibition Enforcement Act, also called the Volstead Act, which prohibited the manufacture and distribution of intoxicating beverages. Roy Olmstead, along with two others, was accused of violating the Volstead Act by conspiring to transport and sell liquor. The U.S. District Court for the Western District of Washington allowed the government to introduce evidence obtained through use of wiretaps placed in the defendants' homes and offices. This evidence proved convincing, and the defendants were convicted. After appeals to the Ninth Circuit Court of Appeals failed, they applied to the U.S. Supreme Court for review of their convictions.

Olmstead and his co-conspirators charged that the evidence used to convict them had been illegally obtained and therefore should not have been admitted at trial. They claimed that the government had violated their Fourth Amendment protection from illegal search and seizure and their Fifth Amendment protection against compelled self-incrimination.

Court Rules that Wiretapping Does Not Constitute Illegal Search and Seizure

Writing for the Court, Chief Justice Taft addressed both of Olmstead's constitutional claims. The Fifth Amendment argument was dismissed outright:

> There is no room in the present case for applying the Fifth Amendment, unless the Fourth Amendment was first violated. There was no evidence of compulsion to induce the defendants to talk over their many telephones. They were continually and voluntarily transacting business without knowledge of the interception. Our consideration must be confined to the Fourth Amendment.

The Fourth Amendment, Taft maintained, did not apply in this case either. The government agents investigating the case did not actually invade Olmstead's home, so there could be no question of illegal search

John Garibaldi Sargent,
U.S. Attorney General.
© Corbis Corporation.

and seizure. Somewhat disingenuously, Taft added: "the courts [do not] have a discretion to exclude evidence, the admission of which is not unconstitutional, because unethically obtained."

Writing in dissent, Brandeis argued that, to the contrary, the Fourth and Fifth Amendments, working together, served to protect an implicit right to privacy. It was not necessary for federal agents to trespass physically on the petitioners' property to violate their constitutional rights. Further, Brandeis stated, letting in evidence obtained by wiretapping sanctions criminal behavior on the part of the government.

Later Supreme Court decisions would uphold Brandeis's point of view. The so-called exclusionary rule, prohibiting introduction in criminal trials of illegally obtained evidence, was extended to federal criminal prosecutions in *Nardone v. United States* (1937). In *Katz v. United States* (1967), the Court overruled *Olmstead* outright. Congress, too, passed legislation that outlawed government wiretapping. The 1934 Federal Communications Act prohibited interception of communications, and the Crime Control and Safe Street Act of 1968 permitted the use of wiretaps only when

authorized by a federal judge under certain specific circumstances.

Brandeis's advocacy for a right to privacy began with an 1890 law review article in which he and coauthor Samuel Warren posited that although such a right appears nowhere in the Constitution, the nation's foundation document nevertheless supports it. The Supreme Court has rejected the notion Brandeis advanced in *Olmstead* that invasion of privacy can be a defense in criminal prosecutions. But the Court has endorsed a right to privacy in other areas of the law, most notably with regard to contraception and abortion.

Related Cases

Weeks v. United States, 232 U.S. 383 (1918).
Village of Euclid v. Ambler Realty Co., 272 U.S. 365 (1926).
Buck v. Bell, 274 U.S. 200 (1927).
Katz v. United States, 389 U.S. 347 (1967).

Bibliography and Further Reading

Gasque, Aubrey. *Wiretapping: A History of Federal Legislation and Supreme Court Decisions.* New York, NY: International Academy of Trial Lawyers, 1962.

Wiretapping in America

In 1991 and 1992, there were 1,078 state-authorized wiretaps around the United States, according to *Wiretap Report 1991 and 1992*, issued by the Administrative Office of the U.S. Courts. This was in addition to 696 wiretaps authorized by the federal government.

Of the 50 states, 13 have no statute authorizing wiretaps. Twelve others, despite existing wiretap legislation, had no documented wiretapping cases during 1991 and 1992. Among these 12 states are Illinois, Louisiana, Hawaii, and Ohio, all of which are populous, thus making the absence of wiretaps surprising—unlike, for instance, in the case of North and South Dakota, which are also among the 12. In addition, the District of Columbia had no wiretaps, although Washington, D.C., Mayor Marion Barry was convicted on drug charges in 1991 after federal agents videotaped him smoking crack cocaine.

The states in the bottom half of the "top ten" had only a handful of wiretaps, ranging from 14 in Texas to 26 in Georgia. Maryland, at No. 5 on the list, had 41. But the vast majority of all state-authorized wiretaps—nearly 80 percent—took place in just four states. Pennsylvania had 153, and Florida 159. Fully half of all wiretaps took place in New Jersey (209) and New York (333), both leading areas of operation for organized crime.

Source(s): Morgan, Kathleen O'Leary, et al., eds. *Crime State Rankings 1994.* Lawrence, KS: Morgan Quitno, 1994.

Johnson, John W., ed. *Historic U.S. Court Cases, 1690–1990: An Encyclopedia.* New York: Garland Publishing, 1992.

Murchison, Kenneth M. *Federal Criminal Law Doctrines: The Forgotten Influence of National Prohibition.* Durham, NC: Duke University Press, 1994.

Regan, Priscilla M. *Legislating Privacy: Technology, Social Values, and Public Policy.* Chapel Hill: University of North Carolina Press, 1995.

WATKINS V. UNITED STATES

Legal Citation: 354 U.S. 178 (1957)

Petitioner
John T. Watkins

Respondent
United States

Petitioner's Claim
That Congress does not have unlimited power to investigate the private lives of individual citizens.

Chief Lawyer for Petitioner
Joseph L. Rauh, Jr.

Chief Lawyer for Respondent
J. Lee Rankin, U. S. Solicitor General

Justices for the Court
Hugo Lafayette Black, William J. Brennan, Jr., William O. Douglas, Felix Frankfurter, John Marshall Harlan II, Earl Warren (writing for the Court)

Justices Dissenting
Tom C. Clark (Harold Burton and Charles Evans Whittaker did not participate)

Place
Washington, D.C.

Date of Decision
17 June 1957

Decision
The Supreme Court ruled that the congressional power of investigation is not unlimited and should not intrude upon law enforcement, a function of the executive branch, or try cases, thus assuming a judicial role.

Significance
Watkins was one of the decisions in favor of persons accused of communist affiliations handed down on "Red Monday" by the liberal Court headed by Chief Justice Warren. These decisions signaled a change not only in the attitude of the Supreme Court, but an abatement of the anti-communist hysteria that had gripped the nation since the end of the Second World War.

The House Un-American Activities Committee (HUAC) was first established in 1938 for the purpose of investigating Nazi, fascist, communist and other "un-American" organizations. In 1945, towards the end of World War II, it was given permanent status. HUAC reached the pinnacle of its power in the early 1950s, during a period known as the Red Scare, when Senator Joseph McCarthy of Wisconsin, playing on fears generated by Soviet post-war expansionism, whipped up public hysteria about an international communist conspiracy. McCarthy and HUAC became notorious, however, for their attempts to unmask domestic communists. McCarthy was eventually discredited in 1954, and by the time the Supreme Court decided *Watkins,* paranoia about communist infiltration had quieted somewhat.

John T. Watkins was a labor union official. His name had been mentioned by two witnesses who appeared earlier before HUAC and agreed to "name names" of others with allegedly communist affiliations. Both witnesses claimed that Watkins had recruited them into the Communist Party in 1943. Watkins himself testified that he had never been a member of the Communist Party, but that from 1942 to 1947, he had cooperated with the party and made contributions to communist causes. He agreed to answer any questions the committee might have about him and any others he knew to be Communist Party members. Watkins declined, however, to answer questions about individuals who, although they might have been party members in past, no longer held that status.

Watkins was convicted of contempt of Congress, and this conviction was affirmed by the Court of Appeals for the District of Columbia. Watkins then petitioned the U.S. Supreme Court for review of this decision.

Supreme Court Rules that Congressional Power of Investigation Is Not Unlimited

Watkins was one of four decisions the Court handed down in what came to known as "Red Monday." In all four, the Court ruled against governmental attempts to prosecute alleged communists. *Watkins* was especially significant because of the limits it placed on Congress's power to investigate individual citizens. Writing for the

UAW attorney Joseph L. Rauh, Jr., 1958. © UPI/Corbis-Bettmann.

Court, Chief Justice Warren clearly indicated that HUAC had overstepped its bounds:

> [B]road as is this [congressional] power of investigation, it is not unlimited. There is no general authority to expose the private affairs of individuals without justification in terms of the functions of the Congress . . . Nor is the Congress a law enforcement or trial agency. These are functions of the executive and judicial departments of government. No inquiry is an end in itself; it must be related to, and in furtherance of the Congress.

For good measure, Warren included a reprimand to those legislators, like Senator McCarthy, who were manipulating people's lives—as well as the public's fears—to advance their own political careers: "Investigations conducted solely for the personal aggrandizement of the investigators or to 'punish' those investigated are indefensible."

The Red Monday decisions caused a revolt among conservative legislators. One senator, William Jenner, even introduced a bill to take away the Court's power to hear cases involving alleged subversives. Facing such protest, two members of the Court, Justices Frankfurter and Harlan, retreated from their previous stance. In various cases heard over the next three years, there were enough votes to uphold convictions of Communist Party members. This reversal did not last long, however. With the retirement of Frankfurter in 1962, the Warren Court resumed its liberal posture.

Related Cases
Kilbourn v. Thompson, 103 U.S. 168 (1881).
American Communications Association v. Douds, 339 U.S. 382 (1950).

Bibliography and Further Reading

Beck, Carl. *Contempt of Congress: A Study of the Prosecutions Initiated by the Committee on Un-American Activities.* New Orleans, LA: Hauser Press, 1959.

Goodman, Walter. *The Committee: The Extraordinary Career of the House Committee on Un-American Activities.* New York, NY: Farrar, Straus & Giroux, 1968.

Johnson, John W., ed. *Historic U.S. Court Cases, 1690-1990: An Encyclopedia.* New York: Garland Publishing, 1992.

O'Reilly, Kenneth. *Hoover and the Un-Americans: The FBI, HUAC, and the Red Menace.* Philadelphia, PA: Temple University Press, 1983.

GRISWOLD V. CONNECTICUT

Legal Citation: 381 U.S. 479 (1964)

Appellants
Charles Lee Buxton, Estelle T. Griswold

Appellee
State of Connecticut

Appellants' Claim
That Connecticut's birth-control laws violated its citizens' constitutional rights.

Chief Lawyers for Appellants
Tom Emerson, Fowler Harper, Harriet Pilpel, Catherine Roraback

Chief Lawyer for Appellee
Joseph B. Clark

Justices for the Court
William J. Brennan, Jr., Tom C. Clark, William O. Douglas (writing for the Court), Arthur Goldberg, John Marshall Harlan II, Earl Warren, Byron R. White

Justices Dissenting
Hugo Lafayette Black, Potter Stewart

Place
Washington, D.C.

Date of Decision
11 May 1964

Decision
Reversed Griswold's and Buxton's lower court convictions for providing contraceptive information to married couples and struck down all state laws forbidding the use of contraceptives by such couples.

Significance
The decision articulated a constitutional "right to privacy," which would later be interpreted as protecting the right of unmarried persons to use birth control in *Eisenstadt v. Baird* (1972), and the right of women to terminate their pregnancies in *Roe v. Wade* (1973).

Connecticut's anti-contraceptive law, passed in 1879, was simple and unambiguous:

> Any person who uses any drug, medicinal article or instrument for the purpose of preventing conception shall be fined not less than fifty dollars or imprisoned not less than sixty days nor more than one year or be both fined and imprisoned. (General Statutes of Connecticut, Section 53–32.)

> Any person who assists, abets, counsels, causes, hires or commands another to commit any offense may be prosecuted and punished as if he were the principal offender. (Section 54–196.)

The Planned Parenthood League of Connecticut first brought the law before the U.S. Supreme Court in 1942, with a physician as appellant. The Court ruled that the doctor lacked standing to sue, since his patients—and not he—suffered injury due to his inability to legally prescribe birth control. In June of 1961, declining to rule in a suit brought by several women, the Supreme Court called the normally unenforced law "dead words" and "harmless empty shadows." Estelle T. Griswold, executive director of the Planned Parenthood League of Connecticut, and Dr. C. Lee Buxton, chairman of Yale University's obstetrics department, decided to test the "death" of the 1879 law: On 1 November 1961, they opened a birth-control clinic in New Haven. Dr. Buxton cited the June decision and explained to the press: "This leads me to believe that all doctors in Connecticut may now prescribe child spacing techniques to married women when it is medically indicated."

1879 Law Alive and Well

Griswold and Buxton were arrested and their center closed on 10 November 1961. On 8 December 1961, the opening day of the Sixth Circuit Court trial, defense attorney Catherine G. Roraback argued that Connecticut's birth-control law violated their clients' constitutional right to freedom of speech. Judge J. Robert Lacey, saying he wished to study the defense's brief, continued the case indefinitely.

The Right to Privacy

Since *Griswold* and, even more significant, *Roe v. Wade* (1973), it has been commonplace to refer to a "right to privacy." But just as people tend to erroneously attribute to the Bible statements such as "The Lord helps them that help themselves," there is no reference to a "right to privacy" in the Constitution. Nonetheless, many would say that the above expression is consistent with the Bible, and likewise the idea of a right to privacy is certainly consistent with the Constitution.

Using *Griswold* as their model, Linda Coffee and Sarah Weddington, legal counsel for the petitioner in *Roe*, based their argument on the idea that the Ninth Amendment offers a protection of "the right to pri-

vacy" in its reservation for the people of all rights not otherwise enumerated. The actual location of this right in the Constitution may have been problematic, Justice Harry Blackmun suggested when he delivered the Court's opinion, but the existence of the right itself was not: "This right of privacy, whether it be found in the Fourteenth Amendment's conception of personal liberty and restrictions on state action . . . or . . . in the Ninth Amendment's reservation of rights to the people, is broad enough . . ."

Source(s): Garrow, David J. *LibertyF and Sexuality: The Right to Privacy and the Making of Roe v. Wade.* New York: Macmillan, 1994.

On 2 January 1962, the trial took place. It lasted only six hours. Julius Martez was the Sixth Circuit Court prosecutor who had requested warrants for Griswold's and Buxton's arrests. He now called his witnesses. John A. Blasi, a New Haven police detective who had entered the clinic on its third day of operation, testified that six women were in the waiting room at the time; that Estelle Griswold freely told him that the facility was, indeed, a birth-control clinic; and that Griswold had offered him contraceptive information and devices. Another detective offered similar testimony.

Dr. Buxton testified that he and his medical colleagues believed that "this type of advice" played a crucial part in women's health care.

Prosecutor Martez said that Griswold and Buxton had broken the law and that the Connecticut legislature, not the court, was the proper forum for anyone objecting to the 82-year-old statute.

Judge Lacey agreed with Martez. He described the statute as "absolute," and he emphasized that it had been upheld three times by the Connecticut Supreme Court of Errors. Rejecting defense attorney Catherine Roraback's free speech argument, he characterized the prohibition of a physician's prescription of birth-control devices as a "constitutional exercise of the police powers of the State of Connecticut." Griswold and Buxton were then convicted of violating Connecticut's birth control law, and each was fined $100.00.

Ten days later, defense attorneys Roraback and Harriet Pilpel filed their clients' appeal with the Appellate Division of the Sixth Connecticut Circuit Court. A three-judge panel heard the case 19 October 1962 and upheld Griswold's and Buxton's convictions on 18 January 1963. However, citing questions "of great public importance," it certified the case for a review by the State Supreme Court of Errors.

That court upheld the convictions on 11 May 1964. Associate Justice John Comley's opinion declared: "We adhere to the principle that courts may not interfere with the exercise by a state of the police power to conserve the public safety and welfare, including health and morals."

On to the Supreme Court

The first action Planned Parenthood took in preparing *Griswold v. Connecticut* for the U.S. Supreme Court was to replace its female attorneys, Roraback and Pilpel, with two male attorneys: Fowler Harper and, upon his death, Thomas I. Emerson, both professors at Yale Law School.

Oral argument began before the Supreme Court on 29 March 1964. Ethel Kennedy (wife of Senator Robert F. Kennedy) and Joan Kennedy (wife of Senator Edward Kennedy), both Catholic and with 11 children between them, were in the audience.

Emerson argued that Connecticut's birth-control law deprived his clients and their clinic's patients of the First Amendment right to free speech and of their right to liberty, which according to the Fourteenth Amendment, could not be abridged without "due process of law." Moreover, he claimed that his clients had a right to privacy, which was guaranteed by the Ninth Amendment to the Constitution: "The enumeration in the Constitution, of certain rights, shall not be construed to deny or disparage others retained by the people."

Emerson characterized the Connecticut law as an effort to erect "a principle of morality" by declaring it "immoral to use contraceptives even within the married relationship." This was, he continued, a "moral judgment" that did not "conform to current community standards."

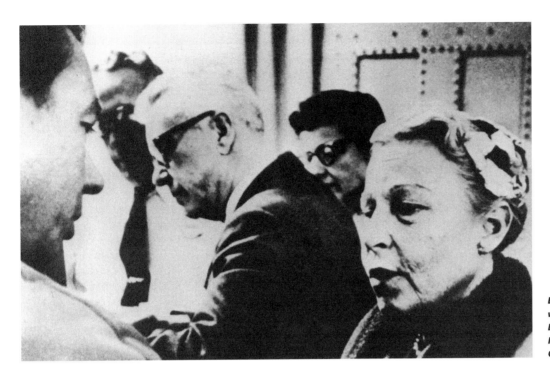

Estell T. Griswold speaks with Dr. Charles Lee Buxton. © Planned Parenthood of Connecticut.

Both Emerson and Connecticut's attorney, Thomas Clark, were questioned about the presumed "under-the-counter" availability of birth-control devices in Connecticut. Clark classified it with clandestine bookmaking on racehorses—available, but not in the open. Emerson said the devices were simply termed "feminine hygiene" items. Clark was then asked whether it was permissible to prescribe contraceptives to prevent the spread of disease. Clark called this a "ludicrous argument" and explained that sexually transmitted disease was not present in married couples, who were claimed as clients of the Planned Parenthood clinic. As the *New York Times* summarized Clark's reasoning, "Connecticut requires applicants for marriage licenses to take venereal disease tests, and . . . Connecticut also has laws against fornication and adultery. Thus, [Clark] indicated, there would be no reason to believe that any such disease would spread."

The next day, Justice Stewart asked Clark to explain the purpose of the statute. "To reduce the chances of immorality," he said. "To act as a deterrent to sexual intercourse outside marriage."

Justice Stewart replied, "The trouble with that argument is that on this record it [the clinic] involves only married women."

A little later in the questioning, Clark declared that Connecticut had the right to guarantee its own "continuity" by prohibiting contraceptives.

Justice Goldberg returned to the statute's alleged role in preventing intercourse outside of marriage, and he asked why Connecticut's laws banning fornication and adultery were not sufficient. Clark replied that "it's easier to control the problem" with the addition of anti-birth control laws.

Decision Reverses Convictions

The Supreme Court, in a 7-2 ruling, reversed Griswold's and Buxton's convictions, invalidated the 1879 law, and enunciated a constitutional "right to privacy." The majority opinion, written by Justice Douglas, declared that the "specific guarantees in the Bill of Rights have penumbras, formed by emanations from those guarantees that help give them life and substance" and cited the Constitution's First, Third, Fourth, Fifth, Ninth, and Fourteenth Amendments. The Ninth Amendment, Douglas quoted in its entirety: "The enumeration in the Constitution, of certain rights, shall not be construed to deny or disparage others retained by the people." The enforcement of the Connecticut birth-control law would require gross violation of privacy, which was presumably a right "retained by the people." "Would we allow the police to search the sacred precincts of marital bedrooms for telltale signs of the use of contraceptives?" Douglas asked. He characterized such action as "repulsive to the notions of privacy surrounding the marriage relationship" and reversed the lower court convictions.

Justices Black and Stewart issued dissenting opinions. Black wrote:

> The Court talks about a constitutional "right of privacy" as though there is some constitutional provision or provisions forbidding any law ever

to be passed which might abridge the "privacy" of individuals. But there is not . . . I cannot rely on the Due Process Clause [of the Fourteenth Amendment] or the Ninth Amendment or any mysterious and uncertain natural law concept as a reason for striking down this state law.

Griswold, Applied Outside the Marital Bedroom

Before *Griswold,* the Ninth Amendment had usually been interpreted as reserving to the state government any right not specifically granted to the federal government; Douglas' literal interpretation, that the Ninth Amendment reserved such rights *to the people,* formed the basis of two other successful challenges to state reproduction laws.

In *Eisenstadt v. Baird* (1972), single people won the right to purchase and use contraceptives. Justice Brennan, a concurring justice in *Griswold,* delivered the majority opinion:

> If under *Griswold* the distribution of contraceptives to married persons cannot be prohibited, a ban on distribution to unmarried persons would be equally impermissible. It is true that in *Griswold* the right of privacy in question inhered in the marital relationship. Yet the marital couple is not an independent entity with a mind and heart of its own, but an association of two individuals each with a separate intellectual and emotional makeup. If the right of privacy means anything, it is the right of the *individual,* married or single, to be free from unwarranted governmental intrusion into matters so fundamentally affecting a person as the decision whether to bear or beget a child.

The following year, in its controversial *Roe v. Wade* decision, the Court held that the "right of privacy . . . is broad enough to encompass a woman's decision whether or not to terminate her pregnancy."

Related Cases

Lochner v. New York, 198 U.S. 45 (1906).
Truax v. Raich, 239 U.S. 33 (1915).
Meyer v. Nebraska, 262 U.S. 390 (1923).
Pierce v. Society of Sisters, 268 U.S. 510 (1925).
West Coast Hotel v. Parrish, 300 U.S. 379 (1937).
Adler v. Board of Education, 342 U.S. 485 (1952).
NAACP v. Alabama, 357 U.S. 449 (1958).
NAACP v. Button, 371 U.S. 415 (1963).

Bibliography and Further Reading

Carey, Eve and Kathleen Willert Peratis. *Woman and the Law.* Skokie, IL: National Textbook Co. in conjunction with the American Civil Liberties Union, New York, 1977.

Countryman, Vern, ed. *The Douglas Opinions.* New York: Random House, 1977.

Cushman, Robert F. *Cases in Constitutional Law,* 6th ed. Englewood Cliffs, NJ: Prentice Hall, 1984.

Davis, Flora. *Moving the Mountain: The Women's Movement in America Since 1960.* New York: Simon & Schuster, 1991.

Faux, Marian. *Roe v. Wade.* New York: Macmillan Co., 1988.

New York Times. 27 October 1961; 4 November 1961; 11 November 1961; 13 November 1961; 25 November 1961; 2 December 1961; 9 December 1961; 3 January 1962; 13 January 1962; 20 October 1962; 18 January 1963; 17 May 1963; 19 May 1963; 12 May 1964; 9 December 1964; 30 March 1965; 31 March 1965; 8 June 1965; 9 June 1965; 10 June 1965; 13 June 1965; and 15 June 1965.

LOVING V. COMMONWEALTH OF VIRGINIA

Legal Citation: 388 U.S. 1 (1967)

Appellants
Mildred Jeter Loving, Richard Perry Loving

Appellee
Commonwealth of Virginia

Appellants' Claim
That Virginia miscegenation statutes violate the equal protection and the Fourteenth Amendment's due process clauses.

Chief Lawyer for Appellants
Bernard S. Cohen

Chief Lawyer for Appellee
R. D. McIlwaine III

Justices for the Court
Hugo Lafayette Black, William J. Brennan, Jr., William O. Douglas, Abe Fortas, John Marshall Harlan II, Potter Stewart, Earl Warren (writing for the Court), Byron R. White

Justices Dissenting
None (Thurgood Marshall did not participate)

Place
Washington, D.C.

Date of Decision
12 June 1967

Decision
The previous convictions were reversed.

Significance
This case established that under the Equal Protection Clause, a state cannot regulate marriages because the partners are of different skin color, religions or national origins.

When the Fourteenth Amendment was drafted it was designed to ensure all Americans the same civil rights and equal protection under the law. But it went further than that. It took the power away from the individual states to withhold equal protection of the laws.

Therefore, the Fourteenth Amendment voided state laws which wholly discriminated against any race. It warned against the passage of laws which appeared fair and equal, but that were not expected to be upheld in a fair and equal manner. "Though the law itself be fair on its face and impartial in appearance, yet, if it is applied and administered by public authority with an evil eye and an unequal hand, so as practically to make unjust and illegal discriminations between persons in similar circumstances, material to their rights, the denial of equal justice is still within the prohibition of the Constitution." These principles were called into question in the case of *Loving v. Commonwealth of Virginia*.

Mildred Jeter and Richard Loving, two Virginia residents, got married in June of 1958, in the District of Columbia, according to its laws. Shortly after that, the couple moved back to Virginia and established their household in Caroline County. During the October of 1958 term of the Circuit Court of Caroline County, a grand jury issued an indictment for the Lovings' arrest.

Mildred Jeter was an African American woman and Richard Loving was Caucasian. They were charged with violating Virginia's law forbidding interracial marriages. At the time, Virginia was one of 16 states that prohibited and punished interracial marriages. These statutes had a tradition almost as old as America itself. Virginia has had miscegenation penalties since colonial times, arising as a consequence of slavery.

The statutory scheme at the time of the Lovings' offense dated from the adoption of the Racial Integrity Act of 1924. The kernel of this act was the absolute prohibition of a white person marrying anyone other than another white person.

The Lovings were convicted and sentenced under two Virginia statutes. Section 20-58 of the Virginia Code prohibited interracial couples from being married out of state and then returning to Virginia. Section 20-59 defined the penalty for miscegenation, stating

Interracial Marriage

The U.S. Bureau of the Census in 1980 counted 49,714,000 married couples in the United States. Of these, 97 percent or 48,264,000 were "same race couples." About 1.3 percent, or 651,000 couples, were designated as interracial couples, with either a black person married to a white person, a black person married to someone of another race, or a white person married to someone of another race. (In addition to same-race or interracial couples, the Census Bureau counted 799,000 in the category of "all other couples," meaning that neither partner was white or black.)

Of the 651,000 interracial couples noted by the Census Bureau in 1980, the overwhelming majority—69 percent—was composed of whites married to someone of another race. The smallest category, amounting to a little more than 5 percent, was made up of blacks married to someone of another race. Just over one-quarter of the interracial couples were black-white marriages, of which three-quarters (122,000) were couples with a black husband and a white wife, as opposed to just 45,000 couples with a white husband and black wife.

Sixteen years later, Census Bureau estimates for 1996 revealed several changes. The number of married couples nationwide had grown by almost 10 percent, to 54,664,000, but the number of interracial marriages had almost doubled, to 1,260,000.

Source(s): *Statistical Abstract of the United States 1997.* Washington, DC: U.S. Government Printing Office, 1997.

that those who are guilty of this "crime," are felons and "shall be punished by confinement in the penitentiary for not less than one nor more than five years."

On 6 January 1959, the Lovings pleaded guilty to the charge and were sentenced to one year in jail. The trial judge suspended the sentence for a period of 25 years on the condition that the Lovings leave the state and not return to Virginia together for a period of 25 years. He stated in an opinion that:

> Almighty God created the races white, black, yellow, malay and red, and he placed them on separate continents. And, but for the interference with his arrangement, there would be no cause for such marriage. The fact that he separated the races shows that he did not intend for the races to mix.

After their convictions, the Lovings moved to the District of Columbia. On 6 November 1963, they filed a motion in the state trial court to vacate the judgment and set aside the sentence on the grounds that the violated statutes ran counter to the Fourteenth Amendment.

Richard and Mildred Loving, 1967.
© AP/Wide World Photos.

When the motion hadn't been decided by 28 October 1964, the Lovings began a class action in the U.S. District Court for the Eastern District of Virginia. They requested that a three-judge court convene to declare the Virginia anti-miscegenation statutes unconstitutional and to keep state officials from enforcing their convictions.

On 22 January 1965, the state trial judge denied the motion to vacate the sentences, and the Lovings perfected an appeal to Virginia's Supreme Court of Appeals. On 11 February 1965, the three-judge district court decided to allow the Lovings to present their constitutional claims to the highest state court.

The Virginia Supreme Court of Appeals upheld the constitutionality of the anti-miscegenation statutes and, after modifying the sentence, affirmed the convictions. This court cited its 1955 decision in *Naim v. Naim* where the state court concluded that it was legitimate for the state "to preserve the racial integrity of its citizens," and to prevent "the corruption of blood," "a mongrel breed of citizens," and "the obliteration of racial pride." The state also argued that in this case the Fourteenth Amendment's Equal Protection Clause did not hold because both the white and African American participants are punished equally. Therefore, there is no "invidious discrimination against race."

The U.S. Supreme Court felt otherwise. It decided that marriage is one of the "basic civil rights of man." Therefore, to deny the Lovings this basic freedom based on the racial classification that these state statutes implied, deprived them of a freedom of choice. Chief Justice Warren held that "miscegenation statutes adopted by Virginia to prevent marriages between persons solely on basis of racial classification violate equal protection and due process clauses of Fourteenth Amendment." The Court furthermore ruled that people whose skins are colored differently have the freedom to choose whether or not to marry. The state has no power over them. In a unanimous decision, the Supreme Court reversed the Lovings' convictions and thereby struck down *all* state miscegenation laws.

Related Cases

Pace v. Alabama, 106 U.S. 583 (1883).
Maynard v. Hill, 125 U.S. 190 (1888).
Meyer v. Nebraska, 262 U.S. 390 (1923).
Skinner v. Oklahoma, 316 U.S. 535 (1942).

Bibliography and Further Reading

Johnson, John W., ed. *Historic U.S. Court Cases, 1690–1990: An Encyclopedia.* New York: Garland Publishing, 1992.

Lieberman, Jethro K. *The Evolving Constitution.* New York: Random House, 1992.

Seidman, Louis M., Gerald R. Stone, Cass R. Sunstein, and Mark V. Tushnet. *Constitutional Law.* Boston: Little, Brown and Company, 1986.

KATZ V. UNITED STATES

Legal Citation: 389 U.S. 347 (1967)

Petitioner
Charles Katz

Respondent
United States

Petitioner's Claim
That evidence obtained by a wiretap on a public phone violated the Fourth Amendment's prohibition of unreasonable search and seizure and should have been ruled inadmissible.

Chief Lawyers for Petitioner
Harvey A. Schneider and Burton Marks

Chief Lawyer for Respondent
John S. Martin, Jr.

Justices for the Court
William J. Brennan, Jr., William O. Douglas, Abe Fortas, John Marshall Harlan II, Thurgood Marshall, Potter Stewart (writing for the Court), Earl Warren, Byron R. White

Justices Dissenting
Hugo Lafayette Black

Place
Washington, D.C.

Date of Decision
17 October 1967

Decision
Placing a wiretap on a public phone violates the Fourth Amendment.

Significance
Investigations to obtain information about a suspect's private activities, even if those activities are conducted in public places or are obtained via electronic media or means, are subject to the same standards of judicial process as searches of a suspect's private property.

Charles Katz was convicted of transmitting gambling information by telephone from Los Angeles, California to Miami, Florida; and Boston, Massachusetts. At his trial in U.S. District Court for the Southern District of California, Katz objected to the use of information obtained by an electronic surveillance device placed on a public phone he used to transact business. Following his conviction, Katz's case was appealed to the Court of Appeals for the Ninth Circuit, where the district court's decision was upheld.

Katz's appeal was denied on the basis of the precedent established in the case of *Olmstead v. United States* in 1928. In this case, a group of individuals were convicted in U.S. district court of illegally possessing, transporting, and importing intoxicating liquors during Prohibition. Government evidence leading to these convictions was obtained by wiretapping the plaintiffs' telephones. The plaintiffs argued that the evidence was obtained in violation of the Fourth Amendment prohibition of unreasonable search and seizure, and appealed their case to the U.S. Supreme Court where their convictions were upheld. At the time, Chief Justice William Howard Taft delivered the Court's opinion, stating that the language of the Fourth Amendment ". . . can not be extended and expanded to include telephone wires reaching the whole world from the defendant's house or office. The intervening wires are not part of his house or office, any more than are the highways along which they are stretched . . ." He clarified his position by adding that a defendant's Fourth Amendment rights will not be violated ". . . unless there has been an official search and seizure of his person or such a seizure of his papers or his tangible material effects or an actual physical invasion of his house 'or curtilage' for the purpose of making a seizure." In Katz's case, law enforcement agents had scrupulously adhered to existing standards for applying wiretaps, but did not seek judicial approval (a warrant) for conducting a search and did not report the results of their search to a magistrate.

In seeking to persuade the Court to overturn *Olmstead v. United States,* Katz's attorneys argued that a public telephone should be considered a constitutionally protected area and, as such, that the surreptitious

The Pros and Cons of Wiretapping

In 1928, the Supreme Court in *Olmstead v. United States* ruled that neither the Fourth nor the Fifth Amendments prevented law-enforcement authorities from conducting wiretapping of a criminal suspect. But with *Katz* the Court found within the Fourth Amendment grounds for an expectation of privacy. These two decisions suggest the polarities surrounding wiretapping, and indeed any number of other constitutional questions: the right of privacy on the other hand, and the need to preserve public order on the other.

Though the Constitution contains no explicit mention of a "right to privacy," the idea is implied throughout the document, as it is in the rights to "liberty . . . and the pursuit of happiness" referred to in the Declaration of Independence.

Because of justified public fears concerning the power of government to invade private lives, Congress has passed a number of measures to limit wiretapping. Yet the practice clearly has legitimate uses, under strict probable-cause guidelines: the FBI's virtual destruction of the Gotti crime family, and by extension most of the Mafia, was due in large part to bugs on Cosa Nostra meetings during the 1980s and early 1990s.

Source(s): Levy, Leonard W., ed. *Encyclopedia of the American Constitution.* New York: Macmillan, 1986.

recording of conversations held in a phone booth would violate the right to privacy of the booth's user. They also raised the question of whether actual ". . . physical penetration of a constitutionally protected area is necessary before a search and seizure can be said to violate the Fourth Amendment . . ." The government's attorneys argued that the law enforcement agents monitoring Katz acted as they did due to their understanding of *Olmstead,* and that in any case the wiretapping of a public telephone should be viewed as exempt from advance authorization by a magistrate.

Although the Court did not agree with the arguments put forward by Katz's attorneys, they did rule to overturn his conviction with Justice Black the lone dissenter. Justice Stewart delivered the Court's opinion, holding that the "Fourth Amendment protects people, not places," and therefore the fact that Katz's conversations occurred in a public phone booth was irrelevant. He further offered that what a person ". . . seeks to preserve as private, even in an area accessible to the public, may be constitutionally protected . . . wherever a man may be, he is entitled to know that he will remain free from unreasonable searches and seizures." The Court had already stated, in an earlier case, *Beck v. Ohio,* that omission of judicial authorization of a proposed search or seizure "bypasses the safeguards provided by an objective predetermination of probable cause, and substitutes instead the far less reliable pro-

cedure of an after-the-event justification for the . . . search, too likely to be subtly influenced by the familiar shortcomings of hindsight judgement."

Katz removed many constitutional questions raised by *Olmstead,* which had seemed to draw distinctions between places and media with regard to the applicability of the Fourth Amendment. After *Katz,* it was clear that the Fourth Amendment prohibition of unreasonable search and seizure was equally applicable to physical searches and monitoring of electronic media.

Related Cases
Olmstead v. United States, 277 U.S. 438 (1928).
Beck v. Ohio, 379 U.S. 89 (1964).
United States v. U.S. District Court for the Eastern District of Michigan, 407 U.S. 297 (1972).
Arkansas v. Sanders, 442 U.S. 753 (1979).
California v. Ciraolo, 476 U.S. 207 (1986).
California v. Greenwood, 486 U.S. 35 (1988).

Bibliography and Further Reading
Ferguson, Robert W. *Legal Aspects of Evidence.* New York: Harcourt Brace Jovanovich, 1978.

Friedman, Phillip. *Inadmissible Evidence.* New York: Ivy Books, 1993.

Landynski, Jacob W. *The Living U.S. Constitution.* New York: New American Library, 1983.

UNITED STATES V. U.S. DISTRICT COURT

Legal Citation: 407 U.S. 297 (1972)

Petitioner
United States

Respondent
U.S. District Court for the Eastern District of Michigan

Petitioner's Claim
That the government's petition for a writ of *mandamus* compelling the district court judge to vacate his disclosure order in a criminal case involving evidence obtained by electronic surveillance be granted.

Chief Lawyer for Petitioner
Robert C. Mardian

Chief Lawyer for Respondent
William T. Gossett

Justices for the Court
Harry A. Blackmun, William J. Brennan, Jr., Warren E. Burger, William O. Douglas, Thurgood Marshall, Lewis F. Powell, Jr. (writing for the Court), Potter Stewart, Byron R. White

Justices Dissenting
None (William H. Rehnquist did not participate)

Place
Washington, D.C.

Date of Decision
19 June 1972

Decision
That the U.S. district court was correct in ordering disclosure of a defendant's conversations obtained by electronic surveillance and used as evidence in his criminal trial.

Significance
Affirmed the primacy of Fourth Amendment prohibition against unreasonable search and seizure in matters believed by the government to affect national security.

The late 1960s and early 1970s were a turbulent period in American history. Resistance to U.S. involvement in the Vietnam War was at its peak, and many radical opponents of the war turned to violent means to express their discontent. Law enforcement bodies sought to counter social unrest by seeking increased freedom from judicial review in criminal investigations through measures such as the Omnibus Crime Control and Safe Streets Act of 1968. Although the act affirmed the necessity of judicial review of all electronic surveillance undertaken in criminal investigations per *Katz v. United States* (1967), it also stated in Title III that nothing ". . . contained in this chapter be deemed to limit the constitutional power of the President to take such measures as he deems necessary to protect the United States against overthrow of the Government by force or other unlawful means, or against any other clear and present danger to the structure or existence of the Government."

Against this backdrop of unrest and apparently broadened police powers, the United States brought criminal charges against well-known dissidents John Sinclair, Lawrence Plamondon, and John Forrest for conspiracy to destroy government property. Plamondon was also charged with the bombing of an office of the Central Intelligence Agency in Ann Arbor, Michigan. Some of the evidence used to bring the defendants to trial had been obtained by electronic surveillance without benefit of a warrant, and the defendants moved to compel the government to disclose selected surveillance information and to conduct a hearing to determine the admissibility of the surveillance data obtained without judicial approval. Their motion was sustained, and the government countered by petitioning for a writ of *mandamus* compelling the district judge to vacate his disclosure order. The government also obtained an affidavit from the U.S. attorney general stating that he had approved of the electronic surveillance of Plamondon and that the surveillance was lawful under the provisions of the Omnibus Crime Control and Safe Streets Act allowing the president to investigate without judicial oversight in cases of clear and present danger to the sovereignty of the United States. The Supreme Court agreed to hear the case on *certiorari*, and arguments were presented on 24 February 1972.

Writ of *Mandamus*

Mandamus, pronounced "man-DAME-us," is from the Latin *mandare,* meaning "We enjoin" or "We command." A *mandamus,* or writ of mandamus, is an order from a higher court or authority to a lower court or authority, enjoining it to perform a specific act or duty.

In American constitutional history, writ of *mandamus* made an early and significant appearance in *Marbury v. Madison* (1803), the first important decision by the Supreme Court.

Generally, the decisions of a lower court made in the course of a continuing case will not be reviewed by higher courts until there is a final judgement in the case. On the federal level, appellate review of lower court decisions should be postponed until after a final judgement has been made in the lower court. A writ of mandamus offers one exception to this rule. If a party to a case is dissatisfied with some decision of the trial court, the party may appeal the decision to a higher court with a petition for a writ of mandamus before the trial proceeds. The order will be issued only in exceptional circumstances.

Source(s): *West's Encyclopedia of American Law,* Volume 7. Minneapolis, MN: West Publishing, 1998.

Government attorneys based their case on the national security provisions of the Omnibus Crime Control and Safe Streets Act, maintaining that the surreptitious recording of the defendant's conversations was approved by the attorney general without consulting a neutral magistrate because the defendant's planned actions threatened national sovereignty. Furthermore, they asserted that disclosure to a magistrate of certain aspects of domestic surveillance could compromise security activities and "... create serious potential dangers to the national security and to the lives of informants and agents." Attorneys for Plamondon and the district court merely reasserted their contention that the evidence was illegally obtained and in fact tainted all other evidence legally gained in investigations surrounding the case.

In ruling against the United States in this case, the Court opted for a narrow view of the questions raised, stipulating that its decision in no way impacted the actions of national security personnel investigating activities of foreign nationals. Justice Powell, delivering the opinion of the Court, held that neither the Omnibus Crime Control and Safe Streets Act nor the Fourth Amendment allow the warrantless interception of private communications. With regard to the influence of national security questions on Fourth Amendment rights, the Court maintained that:

> Security surveillances are especially sensitive because of the inherent vagueness of the domestic security concept, the necessarily broad and continuing nature of intelligence gathering, and the temptation to utilize such surveillances to oversee political dissent. We recognize, as we have before, the constitutional basis of the President's domestic security role, but we think it must be exercised in a manner compatible with the Fourth Amendment.

The decision also implied that Title III, which covered criminal investigations, should not be applicable to domestic security matters, and suggested that Congress consider establishing standards of judicial oversight of domestic security investigations that would be "reasonable both in relation to the legitimate need of Government for intelligence information and the protected rights of our citizens." Finally, the Court asserted that use of approved warrant procedures could not be considered a threat to investigative operations or security.

The *United States v. U.S. District Court* case upheld and expanded the protection against unwarranted monitoring of electronic communications afforded by *Katz v. United States.* The decision closed the apparent loophole offered by Title III of the Omnibus Crime Control and Safe Streets Act and mandated the acquisition of warrants from a neutral magistrate even by investigations seeking information on perceived threats to national security.

Related Cases

Cox v. New Hampshire, 312 U.S. 569 (1941).
Miranda v. Arizona, 384 U.S. 436 (1966).
Katz v. United States, 389 U.S. 347 (1967).
Terry v. Ohio, 392 U.S. 1 (1968).
United States v. Nixon, 418 U.S. 683 (1974).

Bibliography and Further Reading

Deegan, Paul J. *Search and Seizure.* Minneapolis: Abdo and Daughters, 1987.

Landynski, Jacob W. *The Living U.S. Constitution.* New York: New American Library, 1983.

McWhirter, Darien A. *Search, Seizure and Privacy.* Phoenix: Oryx Press, 1994.

Waddington, Lawrence C. *Arrest, Search and Seizure.* Beverly Hills: Glencoe Press, 1974.

DAVIS V. ALASKA

Legal Citation: 415 U.S. 308 (1974)

Petitioner
Joshaway Davis

Respondent
State of Alaska

Petitioner's Claim
By being prohibited from cross-examining a prosecution witness regarding the witness's status as a juvenile offender (under a state law protecting the anonymity of juvenile offenders), petitioner was denied his right to confront witnesses under the Sixth (and Fourteenth) Amendments.

Chief Lawyer for Petitioner
Robert H. Wagstaff

Chief Lawyer for Respondent
Charles M. Merriner

Justices for the Court
Harry A. Blackmun, William J. Brennan, Jr., Warren E. Burger (writing for the Court), William O. Douglas, Thurgood Marshall, Lewis F. Powell, Jr., Potter Stewart

Justices Dissenting
William H. Rehnquist, Byron R. White

Place
Washington, D.C.

Date of Decision
27 February 1974

Decision
A defendant's right to confront and cross-examine witnesses outweighs a state's interest in protecting the anonymity of a juvenile offender when the juvenile is a witness for the prosecution in a criminal case.

Significance
Further reinforces the importance of Sixth Amendment protections for criminal defendants.

The Facts of the Case

Joshaway Davis was charged with burglary of a bar and theft of a safe containing more than $1,000. Green, a witness for the prosecution, testified that he had seen Davis, holding a crowbar, and another man standing by Davis's car near the site where the pried-open, empty safe was later found (which was the property of Green's stepfather). There was other evidence that pointed to Davis as the thief—paint chips and insulation matching that of the stolen safe were found in his car—but Green's testimony was important as direct, eyewitness evidence linking Davis to the place where the safe was discovered shortly after the crime.

Green, a minor, was himself on probation at the time for the burglary of two cabins. Before the trial of Davis for grand larceny and burglary, the prosecutor asked for and obtained a protective order prohibiting any reference during cross-examination to Green's status as a juvenile offender under an Alaska state law protecting the identities of minors charged with crimes, despite the opposition of Davis's counsel.

Davis's counsel wanted to discredit Green's testimony by showing that as a probationer he was subject to police pressure to testify in the manner they desired. At trial, although prohibited from bringing up Green's status as a juvenile offender, he questioned Green regarding his state of mind: was he "upset" when he heard about the discovery of the safe near his home? Did he feel "uncomfortable" about it? Did he "suspect for a moment that the police might somehow think that [he] was involved in this"? After eliciting from Green the fact that Green had been driven to the police station and that he had been questioned by two investigators, Davis's counsel asked, "Had you been questioned like that before by any law enforcement officers?" to which Green replied, "No." At this point the prosecution objected, and the judge sustained the objection, cutting off further inquiry in that direction.

Davis was convicted of burglary and grand larceny, and he appealed to the Alaska Supreme Court on grounds that the limits on his cross-examination of Green violated his Sixth Amendment right to confront witnesses against him, the crux of which is the right

---

Separate Rights for Juveniles?

If persons under the age of 18 are to enjoy the same rights as adults, is it fair that they should have privileges denied to adults, included anonymity for juvenile offenders? Australia, which like the United States has a legal system based in part on English common law, appears to think not: in 1996 the government of New South Wales began considering removal of the time-honored juvenile right to anonymity as a means of curbing crime among youths.

The Australian measure is in keeping with rising concerns among Americans regarding kids and crime. As the newspapers are filled with stories of juvenile murderers, numerous jurisdictions in the United States have adopted measures to treat underage killers as adults.

Is this an appropriate response? Many would say that if a child can commit the crime of an adult, he should serve the time of an adult. Others emphasize the fact that youths possess a lesser degree of judgment than adults, and may not know as clearly what they are doing when they commit a crime—even murder. Still others say that an increase in juvenile crime is a sign of deep societal problems that cannot be dealt with simply by a change of laws.

Source(s): Levy, Leonard W. ed. *Encyclopedia of the American Constitution.* New York: Macmillan, 1986.

---

to cross-examine them and, if desired, to impeach their credibility. The Alaska Supreme Court upheld the decision of the lower court, stating that "counsel for the defendant was able adequately to question [Green] in considerable detail concerning the possibility of bias or motive." Because of this the "jury . . . was afforded the opportunity to pass on [Green's] credibility"; thus there was no need to rule on any possible conflict of the state's protection of Green as a minor and Davis's Sixth Amendment right to confront witnesses against him.

The requisite number of justices did see the necessity of adjudicating a conflict of rights in this instance, however, and the U.S. Supreme Court granted *certiorari.* In a 7-2 decision the Court reversed Davis's conviction, ruling that the state of Alaska had prevented him from effective cross-examination of Green in violation the Sixth Amendment.

The Majority Decision

Chief Justice Burger began by stating that the Sixth Amendment has always been construed to include not only a defendant's right to be physically present during the testimony of witnesses against him but to include cross-examination of those witnesses. This is in the interest of the state as well as that of a defendant because such questioning "is the principal means by which the believability of a witness and the truth of his testimony are tested." This goes beyond simple examination of possible inaccuracy of fact or memory: "the cross-examiner has traditionally been allowed to . . . discredit the witness." Presenting "possible biases, prejudices, or ulterior motives" is material to the credibility of the witness and is "a proper and important function of the constitutionally protected right of cross-examination."

Although defense counsel attempted to demonstrate bias on Green's part, he was prohibited from presenting a record of fact that would have supported his contention and indeed would have presented another reason for the jurors to question Davis's truthfulness: his position as a juvenile offender on probation rendered him vulnerable to police pressure. Without such knowledge the jury could have concluded that there was no basis to the defense's imputations of bias. Davis's counsel could have questioned Green more effectively regarding his possible worry that the police might have suspected Green himself of the burglary and perhaps, more importantly, also could have effectively brought forth the issue of possible police pressure on Green, resulting in a fear of jeopardizing his probationary status if he did not cooperate with them.

The "accuracy and truthfulness of Green's testimony were key elements in the State's case," but nonetheless it was not necessary for the petitioner to prove that had the cross-examination not been restricted the jury would have made a different judgment of Green's credibility. The jurors were "entitled to have the benefit of the defense theory before them" but were not given the opportunity to hear facts that may have affected their evaluation of Green's testimony. Davis "was thus denied the right of effective cross-examination."

Recognizing the legitimacy of state interest in the protection of minors, the Court did not attack the constitutionality of the Alaska state law itself; rather, the majority argued that the state's interest in protecting Green "must fall before the right of petitioner to seek out the truth in the process of defending himself." Had the state wished to, it could have abstained from presenting Green as a witness.

Justice Stewart, in a brief concurring opinion, noted that the balancing of rights in this specific case resulting in a ruling for the petitioner did not mean that in every case the right to discredit a witness by making reference to "past delinquency adjudications or criminal convictions" during cross-examination was automatically conferred.

Although it was not addressed in the Court's decision, the petitioner had also cited in his claim the Fourteenth Amendment, which made the protections of the Bill of Rights applicable to the states.

The Dissent

Justice White issued a dissenting opinion, joined by Justice Rehnquist. They declared that "there [was] no constitutional principle at stake here." Trial courts have the power to "control or limit cross-examination," and appellate courts may uphold controls. The Supreme Court "insists on second-guessing" the judgment of trial judges and appellate courts. White and Rehnquist believed that such "second-guessing" was unlikely to result in superior judgments, given "fact-bound cases and a cold record."

Impact

The decision in *Davis* further stressed the importance of the Sixth Amendment right of criminal defendants to confront and cross-examine their accusers. The case has often been referred to in efforts to impeach the testimony of witnesses during cross examination. The important ruling in *Davis* was that discrediting a witness by revealing their motives is inherent to an individual's Sixth Amendment right to a fair trial. In *Delaware v. Van Arsdall* (1986) the sanctity of the Confrontation Clause stressed in *Davis* was reaffirmed. The ruling in *Davis* also undermined the ability of states to protect the anonymity of juvenile offenders. In *Smith v. Daily Mail Publishing Co.* the Court cited *Davis* (1979) ruling that a state cannot prohibit the "truthful publication of an alleged juvenile delinquent's name."

Davis has been also been a popular citation in child abuse and rape cases. In a *Western New England Law Review* article, Jason M. Price wrote: "Courts usually employ . . . *Davis* in interpreting rape shield statutes to allow sexual history evidence related to victim's motive to fabricate." In *Olden v. Kentucky* (1988) the Court employed *Davis* to allow the cross examination of a witness whose testimony had significant bearing on the truthfulness of the events. In this case, what appeared to be rape on the surface, turned out to be an extramarital affair upon cross examination.

Related Cases

Alford v. United States, 282 U.S. 687 (1931).
Pointer v. Texas, 380 U.S. 400 (1965).
Olden v. Kentucky, 488 U.S. 227 (1988).
Idaho v. Wright, 497 U.S. 805 (1990).

Bibliography and Further Reading

Biskupic, Joan, and Elder Witt, eds. *Congressional Quarterly's Guide to the U.S. Supreme Court*, 3rd ed. Washington, DC: Congressional Quarterly, Inc., 1996.

Price, Jason M. "Sex, Lies, and Rape Shield Statutes: The Constitutionality of Interpreting Rape Shield Statutes to Exclude Evidence Relating to the Victim's Motive to Fabricate." *Western New England Law Review*, Vol. 18, no. 541, 1996.

PAUL V. DAVIS

Legal Citation: 424 U.S. 693 (1976)

Petitioner
Edgar Paul

Respondent
Edward Charles Davis III

Petitioner's Claim
A published flyer which contained the name and picture of the respondent who was charged (but not convicted) for "shoplifting" did not violate privacy as provided by Fourteenth Amendment due process guarantees.

Chief Lawyer for Petitioner
Carson P. Potter

Chief Lawyer for Respondent
Daniel T. Taylor

Justices for the Court
Harry A. Blackmun, Warren E. Burger, Lewis F. Powell, Jr., William H. Rehnquist (writing for the Court), Potter Stewart

Justices Dissenting
William J. Brennan, Jr., Thurgood Marshall, Byron R. White (John Paul Stevens did not participate)

Place
Washington, D.C.

Date of Decision
23 March 1976

Decision
Deprivation of constitutional rights under the Fourteenth Amendment's due process of law did not occur through an official distribution of defamatory pamphlets regarding the respondent's alleged shoplifting because reputation alone did not implicate "liberty" and "property" elements of the Due Process Clause.

Significance
After the publication of the "Active Shoplifters" pamphlets, the respondent (for whom shoplifting charges were dropped) claimed he was denied protection under the due process of law and his reputation was besmirched. Regardless, the Supreme Court found that it was inappropriate to invoke constitutional rights because state law torts should have been invoked for redress. A "mere defamation" without precise delineation of what rights an individual was deprived could not be recognized as a violation of "liberty" or "property" as guaranteed by the Due Process Clause contained in the Fourteenth Amendment. Thus, the U.S. Supreme Court clarified that unless an individual could distinctly identify injury that resulted in diminishment of specific constitutional rights, defamation alone did not sufficiently justify constitutional protection.

The respondent, Edward Davis was arrested in Louisville, Kentucky, during the summer of 1971 for shoplifting. He protested his arrest and, after several months, charges against him were "filed away with leave to reinstate." Final action on his "shoplift" charge was left unsettled for more than one year. Ultimately, in December of 1972, charges relating to the incident were dropped by the Louisville Police Court. However, Davis' troubles, relative to that misadventure, had just started.

Due to heightened risk of shoplifting during the Christmas season, Edgar Paul, Chief of Police of Louisville, Kentucky, in concert with Jefferson County law enforcement officials, initiated action to alert local merchants to thieves. Pamphlets were distributed in the Louisville metropolitan area that identified "active shoplifters." Flyers contained the alphabetically arranged mug shot photos of persons arrested for shoplifting, including the photo of Edward Davis. Flyers included information, compiled by the police departments of the Jefferson County and City of Louisville, about persons arrested for shoplifting during a two-year period, from 1971 to 1972. The flyers suggested that to ensure adequate protection, security personnel should watch for individuals whose pictures were published in the flyers.

Charges against Davis were dismissed just six days after circulation of the flyers had begun. He immediately objected and filed a lawsuit against police authorities in the District Court for the Western District of Kentucky (under 42 U.S.C 1983 which provides remedy when position was abused by any official). Davis opted to not file suit in the state courts of Kentucky because he contended that government (city and county) law enforcement officials contributed to the loss of his rights. In his lawsuit, Davis sought a court order (injunction) to bar distribution of the pamphlets.

The district court ruled that (under 28 U.S.C. 1343) "the facts alleged in this case do not establish that plaintiff has been deprived of any right secured to him by the Constitution of the United States." On appeal, the Court of Appeals for the Sixth Circuit found merit in the respondent's (Davis) assertion that he was deprived of his constitutional rights. They cited *Wisconsin v. Con-*

Megan's Law: Is It Okay to Tell?

Should communities be warned of the possibility of convicted child molesters and rapists moving into their neighborhoods? That question is at the center of the controversy surrounding "Megan's Law," a New Jersey statute that has been emulated by a number of other states. The name of the law comes from that of seven-year-old Megan Kanka, raped and murdered by a child molester who lived across the street from her and who had served six years for two counts of child sexual abuse. When the community found out, it was too late; hence Megan's Law, which requires that released sex offenders register with local authorities before moving in to a neighborhood.

Advocate Bonnie Steinbock, stated that "the paramount issue is the protection of children, that their

rights to be safe from violent sexual assault certainly outweigh the rights of sexual predators not to be stigmatized." Nonetheless, she took issue with the fact that the law may encourage "vigilantism." A particularly tragic incident occurred in Warren County, New Jersey, when a father and son broke into the house of a known molester and beat to death a man they found there—a man who happened to be innocent.

Source(s): Steinbock, Bonnie. "Megan's Law: Community Notification of the Release of Sex Offenders." *Criminal Justice Ethics*, 22 June 1995.

---

stantineau (1971) as a related case which justified the respondent's claim under another statute, 42 U.S.C 1983 (related to redress in cases when a state's law abridges constitutional rights). The appellate court held the respondent had "alleged fact that constitute(d) a denial of due process of law."

Due Process Clause Invoked

Respondent's main argument was that the pamphlet violated his privacy and liberty under the Due Process Clause of the Fourteenth Amendment. Davis particularly objected to the title, "Active Shoplifters." He contended that inclusion of his photo and name in the pamphlet was inappropriate; police action intruded on his privacy and jeopardized his personal autonomy. Davis contended that classifying him as an "active shoplifter" ruined his reputation and limited future employment opportunities. He also maintained that police authorities defamed him by characterizing him as a criminal and that reason alone sufficiently justified bringing suit without having to prove specific damages.

The U.S. Supreme Court found the respondent's interpretation of the Fourteenth Amendment was incorrect. Five justices for the majority opinion reasoned it was inappropriate to hold that arrest by law officials and later publication of that fact entitled a person to claims under 42 U.S.C 1983. The justices also pointed out that attacks on a person's "good name" did not equate to "liberty" or "property" deprivations actionable under 42 U.S.C 1983. The majority opinion explained that every legally performed action which might be recognizable as injury by state officials could not be regarded as a violation of the Fourteenth Amendment. Moreover, injury by governmental employees did not invoke protection under the Due Process Clause

unless claims first invoked state-law torts. Citing *Screws v. United States* (1945), the Court held that "violation of local law does not necessarily mean that the federal rights have been invaded." Only when action by government officials resulted in deprivation of *specific rights* guaranteed by the Constitution could the issue of a rights violation be considered. Furthermore, the justices stressed that there must always be a clearly understandable right which was forfeited to reasonably expect protection under the Fourteenth Amendment. Thus, procedural guarantees established under due process of law were not related to privacy expectations. According to previous cases where state law torts were available as remedy, they explained that constitutional provisions under the Fourteenth Amendment were not litigated.

No Violation of Fourteenth Amendment Rights Found

The Court found that without first invoking state tort law/remedies, it was inappropriate to petition federal courts for constitutional protection under the Fourteenth Amendment. The Court thus rejected the decision of the appellate court that taint of a person's reputation required action under 42 U.S.C 1983 and invoked the Due Process Clause. A "stigma" on someone's good name did not entitle the respondent to claim violation of his right to "liberty" and "property" (which were entitled under the Fourteenth Amendment). Further, no provision in the Constitution stipulated that defamation by the government implicated procedural protection under due process of law.

On behalf of the majority, Justice Rehnquist wrote: "we think that weight of our decisions establishes no constitutional doctrine converting every defamation by public official into a deprivation of liberty within the meaning of the Due Process Clause of the Fifth and Fourteenth Amendment." He explained that the respondent's claim was unlike *Wisconsin v. Constantineau* (1971) and also *Anti-Fascist Committee v. McGrath* (1961) wherein the Court held that governmental action deprived individuals of particular rights which previously existed before the state's illegal action (e.g., in *Constantineau* the plaintiff was deprived of "the right to purchase or obtain liquor on common with the rest of citizenry.") Defamation alone in *Constantineau* and *McGrath* was not the primary factor under which those decisions were rendered but rather the consideration that the "alteration of legal status" was directly attributed to the exercise of unacceptable practice by the state. Further, the majority opinion emphasized that the respondent's petition for protection under the Constitution was not proper because his claim that defamation could restrict his opportunities for employment or "damage his standing and associations in his community" was not valid since the respondent's employment was not terminated.

Although the U.S. Supreme Court majority did not find fault in the respondent's objection to being defamed, they held that publication of pamphlets did not entitle him to claim that he was denied any particular constitutional privilege. They concluded that Davis's privacy was not violated by any recognizable right identified in the constitution such as marriage, procreation, contraception, education, etc. Consequently, no previous decisions about privacy were applicable to the respondent's case. Furthermore, the Court believed that the publication of the flyers was defensible because nothing more was alleged than the fact that the respondent was arrested because of "shoplifting." He was not deprived of any freedom that could be perceived within the domain of privacy that could be secured under the Fourteenth Amendment. In fact, because respondent had been charged for shoplifting, the Court reasoned that his constitutional rights were not violated and actionable under the provisions of 42 U.S.C 1983.

Minority Opinion

Three justices disagreed with the findings of the majority. The dissenting opinion reasoned that the decision justified the conduct of police officials although their intrusive action defamed and stigmatized the respondent as a criminal. Justice Brennan, writing for the minority, reasoned publication of the pamphlets constituted an illegitimate and improper enforcement of law that assaulted constitutional safeguards. According to 42. U.S.C. 1983, citizens of every state were entitled to redress if harmful wrongdoing was the result of law enforcement and such wrong doing deprived them from protection guaranteed by the Constitution. (The

majority rejected the respondent's complaint because they reasoned that a recognizable claim under 42. U.S.C. 1983 had to involve forfeiture of a specific constitutional right resulting in deprivation according to the letter of law.) Brennan disagreed that the conduct of police officials was, as the majority reasoned, "purposeful" and performed as "official practice." The respondent was labeled as a criminal without regard to constitutional safeguards. He had never been convicted and his only offense was a single arrest. His "shoplifting" charge was dropped and he was not convicted for the offense. The minority opinion, therefore, maintained police unacceptably harmed the respondent by the distribution of 1000 pamphlets which characterized the respondent as a thief, active in shoplifting.

Justices for the minority disagreed that "mere defamation" could not be recognized as a legitimate claim under the Fourteenth Amendment. They found as improper the Court's rationalization that interest in reputation could not be considered infringement of "life, liberty and property" provisions in the Fourteenth Amendment. In his written opinion, Justice Brennan held "the enjoyment of one's good name and reputation has been recognized repeatedly in our cases as being among the most cherished of right enjoyed by a free people, and therefore as falling within the concept of personal liberty." Constitutional law provided measures to ensure no guilt could be assumed on the basis of arbitrary actions and that consequences of such conduct had to be correctable as a matter of due process of law. The publication of the flyers, then, had to be recognized as an action that negatively affected the respondent's personal interest in reputation. He had justifiable reason, therefore, to expect constitutional protection.

Impact

The U.S. Supreme Court held that the respondent's constitutional right to privacy was not affected by what they (tacitly) acknowledged was a defamatory publication. The salient consideration which arbitrated their finding was that no violation of the Fourteenth Amendment occurred because law enforcement had published an official record of fact which stated that the respondent was arrested for shoplifting. The respondent claimed that he was entitled to protection under due process because state officials stigmatized him and impeached his reputation; however, the U.S. Supreme Court held that the Due Process Clause was not invokable in every case wherein the state might be named as litigant. Moreover, constitutional protection need not automatically be invoked when state torts provided means for redress. Finally, the Court clarified for lower courts that with respect to issues of defamation, constitutional protection could be extended only when the expectation of privacy was abridged as one of the liberties guaranteed (marriage, reproduction, contraception, education) under the Fourteenth Amendment.

Related Cases

Screws v. United States, 325 U.S. 91 (1945).
Joint Anti-Fascist Refugee Comm. v. McGrath, 341 U.S. 123 (1951).
Wieman v. Updegraff, 344 U.S. 183 (1952).
Monroe v. Pape, 365 U.S. 167 (1961).
Wisconsin v. Constantineau, 400 U.S. 433 (1971).

Bibliography and Further Reading

FindLaw, Inc. *Supreme Court Cases Online.* http://laws.findlaw.com.

Northwestern University. *Oyez, oyez, oyez—A U.S. Supreme Court Database.* http://court.it-services.nwu.edu/oyez.

Oxford University Press. *The Oxford Companion to the Supreme Court of the United States.* 1992.

WHALEN V. ROE

Legal Citation: 429 U.S. 589 (1977)

Appellant
Whalen, Commissioner of Health New York

Appellees
Roe, et al.

Appellant's Claim
A New York state law requiring that the names of prescription drug users be sent to a computer for record-keeping did not violate the constitutional right to privacy under the Fourteenth Amendment.

Chief Lawyer for Appellant
A. Seth Greenwald

Chief Lawyer for Appellees
Michael Lesch

Justices for the Court
Harry A. Blackmun, William J. Brennan, Jr., Warren E. Burger, Thurgood Marshall, Lewis F. Powell, Jr., William H. Rehnquist, John Paul Stevens (writing for the Court), Potter Stewart, Byron R. White

Justices Dissenting
None

Place
Washington, D.C.

Date of Decision
22 February 1977

Decision
The Court upheld a New York State law requiring that the names of prescription drug users be sent to a computer for record-keeping.

Significance
In *Whalen v. Roe* the Court established that liberty within itself was not a fundamental right guaranteed to all. If the state, as was the case with the New York's drug prescription registry, could make a rational showing for the law then it was not unconstitutional.

Prescription Drugs and the Patients' Right to Privacy

In response to escalating abuse of both lawful and illegally obtained drugs, the New York State legislature in 1970 established a commission to review the state's drug control laws. The commission found much lacking with the state's drug control laws. For example, it was impossible to stop the use of stolen or altered prescription drugs. Additionally, there was no way to prevent unethical pharmacists from continuously refilling prescriptions, to keep users from obtaining prescriptions from more than one doctor, or to stop doctors from over prescribing drugs. Before adopting the central registry for drug prescriptions, the commission spoke with enforcement officials in California and Illinois where similar systems were in place.

The New York law placed potentially harmful drugs in five categories. Drugs such as heroin, for example, which was abused and had no discernible medical value, were Schedule I and cannot be prescribed. Drugs in Schedules II through V had a lower potential for abuse and had legitimate medical use. The law required that all prescriptions for Schedule II drugs be prepared by a physician on an official form providing three copies. The completed form identified the prescribing physician, the dispensing pharmacy, the drug, its dosage, and the name, address, and age of the patient. Under the statute, the physician kept one copy of the form, the pharmacist the second, and the third was retained by the New York State Department of Health. Schedule II prescriptions were limited to a 30-day supply, and could not be refilled.

The district court found that each month about 100,000 Schedule II forms were sent to the Department of Health in Albany, New York. Once in Albany, the forms were sorted, coded, logged, and then recorded on magnetic tapes for processing by the computer. Under the statute, the forms were stored for five years and then destroyed. The computer information was kept in a locked cabinet. The computer tapes were run "offline," which meant that no other terminals could read or record the information. The statute prohibited disclosure of the patients' identity. Violating the statute was punishable by up to one year in prison and a $2,000 fine. When the statute was challenged in court, 17 Department of Health employees had access to the files and 24 investigators were authorized to investigate the dispensing by using the information stored in the computer. Nearly, two years after the statute was passed, the computer registry had been used in only two investigations.

Just days before the law went into effect, a group of patients receiving Schedule II drugs on a regular basis, doctors prescribing the Schedule II drugs, and two physician's associations challenged the constitutionality of the law in court. A three-judge district court held a one-day trial. At the brief trial, the appellees presented evidence that some individuals in need of Schedule II drugs would avoid treatment fearful of being identified as a drug addict. The district court ruled that "the doctor-patient relationship is one of the zones of privacy accorded constitutional protection." Additionally, the court concluded that the statute invaded that privacy with "a needlessly broad sweep." The district court concluded that the state was unable to prove the need for the patient-identification requirement over the 20-months the statute was in effect.

In a unanimous opinion, the Supreme Court reasoned that "the district court's finding that the necessity for the requirement had not been proved is not, therefore, a sufficient reason for holding the statutory requirement unconstitutional." The appellees argued and the district court agreed that the statute violated a constitutionally protected "zone of privacy." Yet, Justice Stevens writing for the majority, reasoned that cases involving a "zone of privacy" traditionally included an individual trying to prevent disclosure of a personal matter and independence in making certain kinds of decisions, but that the New York statute did not violate these interests. He wrote:

> The mere existence in readily available form of the information about patients' use of Schedule II drugs creates a genuine concern that the information will become publicly known and that it will adversely affect their reputations. This concern makes some patients reluctant to

use and some doctors reluctant to prescribe such drugs even when their use is medically indicated. It follows, they argue, that the making of decisions about matters vital to the care of their health is inevitably affected by the statute. Thus, the statute threatens to impair both their interest in the nondisclosure of private information and their interest in making important decisions independently. We are persuaded, however, that the New York program does not, on its face, pose a sufficiently grievous threat to either interest to establish a constitutional violation.

Impact

The Court established a tier system for determining constitutionally protected areas of privacy and areas in which the state could intrude upon that zone. Prior to *Whalen v. Roe* in cases such as *Roe v. Wade* and *Griswold v. Connecticut* the Court concluded that individuals have a right to make a decision. In *Roe,* for instance, a woman's right to terminate a pregnancy was a fundamentally protected constitutional right. Yet, preventing one's name from being included in a computerized drug registry was not a constitutionally protected right. Just a year before the ruling in *Whalen v. Roe,* the Court in *Kelley v. Johnson* upheld a police department regulation regulating the length and style of a policeman's haircut. The Court reasoned that there was no fundamental right for police officers to wear their hair any way they wanted.

Related Cases
Kelley v. Johnson, 425 U.S. 238 (1976).
Youngberg v. Romeo, 457 U.S. 307 (1982).
Roberts v. United Jaycees, 468 U.S. 609 (1984).
Cruzan v. Director, Missouri Dept. of Health, 497 U.S. 261 (1990).

Bibliography and Further Reading
Gunther, Gerald and Kathleen Sullivan. *Constitutional Law,* 13th edition. New York: The Foundation Press Inc., 1997.

DOE V. MCMILLAN

Legal Citation: 412 U.S. 306 (1979)

This case revolved around a 450-page report submitted to the Speaker of the House by a Special Select Subcommittee on the District of Columbia. The report included a section on disciplinary problems in the Washington D.C. school system and contained absence sheets, lists of absentees, copies of test papers, and documents relating to disciplinary problems of certain specifically named students. When the report was made public, a group of parents of these school children sued for damages, claiming an invasion of privacy. The defendants they targeted included members of the House committee, committee employees, a committee investigator, the Public Printer, the Superintendent of Documents, and various employees of the school system. The case first went to U.S. District Court.

The Lower Court Rulings

The District Court sided with the defendants, dismissing all action by the parents. The U.S. Court of Appeals affirmed this decision, arguing that the House members and their staff were immune from lawsuits under the Speech or Debate Clause of the U.S. Constitution, while the District of Columbia officials and the legislative employees were protected by the official immunity doctrine. Not content with this decision, the parents then appealed to the U.S. Supreme Court.

The Supreme Court Ruling

On 29 May 1973 the Supreme Court issued its decision. By a narrow vote of 5-4, it affirmed the ruling of the Court of Appeals—but only with regard to the congressmen, congressional staff, and committee employees. Justice White wrote the majority opinion, in which he was joined by Justices Marshall, Brennan, and Douglas. The remaining justices, Chief Justice Burger, Justice Blackmun, and Justice Rehnquist, agreed with parts of the majority opinion but dissented on some points. The majority opinion rested on two main points.

Legislative Acts Immune From Suit

The Speech or Debate Clause of the U.S. Constitution grants members of Congress absolute immunity from civil suits arising from legislative activity. In this case, the Supreme Court held that none of the activity conducted by the congressmen or their staffs—from prepar-

Petitioner
John Doe

Respondent
John L. McMillan

Petitioner's Claim
That U.S. Representatives, their staffs, and Government Printing Office officials should all be held liable for the distribution of a report defaming Washington, D.C. school children.

Chief Lawyers for Petitioner
Fred M. Vinson, William C. Cramer, David P. Sutton

Chief Lawyer for Respondent
Michael Valder

Justices for the Court
William J. Brennan, Jr., William O. Douglas, Thurgood Marshall, Lewis F. Powell, Jr., Potter Stewart, Byron R. White (writing for the Court)

Justices Dissenting
Harry A. Blackmun, Warren E. Burger, William H. Rehnquist

Place
Washington, D.C.

Date of Decision
29 May 1973

Decision
The House members and their staff retain absolute immunity for their actions, but Government Printing Office officials do not.

Significance
Doe v. McMillan set important limits on immunity from civil liability for government officials.

Absolute Immunity

Although *McMillan* did not hinge on it, issues involving absolute immunity often relate to the Civil Rights Act of 1871. The Civil Rights Act, adopted during the violent days of Reconstruction, stated in part that "Every person who, under color of any statute . . . of any State or Territory . . . subjects, or causes to be subjected, any citizen of the United States . . . to the deprivation of any rights, privileges, or immunities secured by the Constitution and laws, shall be liable to the party injured in an action at law . . ."

This language proved problematic for a number of reasons, including the issue that led to the placement of absolute immunity provisions not in the legislation itself, but within courtrooms that reviewed these claims. In any number of instances, an official acting in a legitimate capacity must deprive another citizen of rights: for instance, a judge who sentences a man to prison for a crime is certainly depriving that man—even if his guilt is proven beyond all reasonable doubt—of his right to freedom. Therefore in a series of decisions over the next century, the Supreme Court provided absolute immunity for legislators, judges, and various other types of officials, as long as they are acting in their prescribed official capacities.

Source(s): *West's Encyclopedia of American Law* St. Paul, MN: West Group, 1998.

ing the report to referring it to the House Speaker to voting for its publication—went beyond the bounds of legislative activity. Therefore, they could not be sued for invasion of privacy:

> Petitioners argue that including in the record of the hearings and in the report itself materials describing particular conduct on the part of identified children was actionable because unnecessary and irrelevant to any legislative purpose [*sic*] . . . Although we might disagree with the Committee as to whether it was necessary, or even remotely useful, to include the names of individual children in the evidence submitted to the Committee and in the Committee Report, we have no authority to oversee the judgment of the Committee in this respect or to impose liability on its Members if we disagree with their legislative judgment. The acts of authorizing an investigation pursuant to which the subject materials were gathered, holding hearings where the materials were presented, preparing a report where they were reproduced, and authorizing the publication and distribution of that report were all "integral part[s] of the deliberative and communicative processes by which Members participate in committee and House proceedings with respect to the consideration and passage or rejection of proposed legislation or with respect to other matters which the Constitution places within the jurisdiction of either House." . . . As such, the acts were protected by the Speech or Debate Clause.

Dissemination of Report Not Immune

Next, the Court addressed the other defendants named in the suit: the Superintendent of Documents and the Public Printer. It held that these officials were not immune from suit, because their actions in disseminating the report were not protected under the Speech or Debate Clause:

> [W]e cannot accept the proposition that in order to perform its legislative function Congress not only must at times consider and use actionable material but also must be free to disseminate it to the public at large, no matter how injurious to private reputation that material might be.

Finally, the Court considered the Court of Appeals ruling that the persons who disseminated the report were immune from suit under the "official immunity doctrine," which protects public officials from bothersome lawsuits. This claim was dismissed as well:

> Congress has conferred no express statutory immunity on the Public Printer or the Superintendent of Documents. Congress has not provided that these officials should be immune for printing and distributing materials where those who author the materials would not be . . . We conclude that, for the purposes of the judicially fashioned doctrine of immunity, the Public Printer and the Superintendent of Documents are no more free from suit in the case before us than would be a legislative aide who made copies of the materials at issue and distributed them to the public at the direction of his superiors.

In conclusion, the Supreme Court ruled:

> Because we think the Court of Appeals applied the immunities of the Speech or Debate Clause and of the doctrine of official immunity too

broadly, we must reverse its judgment and remand the case for appropriate further proceedings.

Related Cases

Tenney v. Brandhove, 341 U.S. 367 (1951).
Barr v. Matteo, 360 U.S. 564 (1959).
Gravel v. United States, 408 U.S. 606 (1972).

Bibliography and Further Reading

Biskupic, Joan, and Elder Witt, eds. *Congressional Quarterly's Guide to the U.S. Supreme Court,* 3rd ed. Washington, DC: Congressional Quarterly, Inc., 1996.

A Reference Guide to the U.S. Supreme Court. New York, NY: Sachem Publishing Associates, Inc., 1986.

CHANDLER V. FLORIDA

Legal Citation: 449 U.S. 560 (1981)

Appellant
Noel Chandler

Appellee
State of Florida

Appellant's Claim
Televising trials without approval from the defendant denies that individual his due process rights and guarantees an unfair trial.

Chief Lawyer for Appellant
Joel Hirschhorn

Chief Lawyer for Appellee
Jim Smith

Justices for the Court
Harry A. Blackmun, William J. Brennan, Jr., Warren E. Burger (writing for the Court), Thurgood Marshall, Lewis F. Powell, Jr., William H. Rehnquist, Potter Stewart, Byron R. White

Justices Dissenting
None (John Paul Stevens did not participate)

Place
Washington, D.C.

Date of Decision
26 January 1981

Decision
Affirmed a Florida court's ruling that televising trials did not infringe upon the defendant's right to a fair and impartial trial.

Significance
Reinterpreted the Court's ruling in *Estes v. Texas* (1964), and paved the way for live television coverage of trials without fear of infringing on the defendant's or victim's right to privacy.

Cameras in the Courtroom

In July of 1977, two Miami Beach police officers, Noel Chandler and Robert Granger were charged with conspiracy to commit burglary, grand larceny and possession of burglary tools. During the burglary an amateur radio operator overheard and recorded conversation between Chandler and Granger over their police radio during the alleged burglary. Around the same time, the Florida Supreme Court approved a one-year pilot program that allowed televised coverage of all court proceedings in Florida as long as they did not infringe upon the rights of the accused. Additionally, under the pilot program, court proceedings could be covered by television stations and other electronic media outlets without the permission of the accused.

In a pre-trial motion, Chandler and Granger tried to have the pilot program declared unconstitutional. The trial court deferred to the Florida Supreme Court but it declined to rule claiming that the issue was not relevant to the charges against Chandler and Granger. The defendants continued to try to bar electronic coverage however they were unsuccessful. Potential jurors were asked whether the presence of television cameras in the courtroom would impair or hamper their ability. Each juror selected stated that such coverage would not hamper them. The jury selection process was covered by television camera. A defense motion to sequester the jury because of the television camera was denied. Jurors were told not to watch local news. The court denied request by the defense that jurors be barred from watching any television news broadcasts. A television camera recorded the testimony of the state's key witness and closing arguments. The jury found Chandler and Granger guilty on all counts. The defendants motioned for a new trial asserting that the television coverage had denied them a "fair and impartial trial." The Florida District Court of Appeals upheld the convictions and the Florida Supreme Court denied review.

Does the Constitution Forbid Televised Coverage of Trials?

In positioning their case Chandler and Granger relied upon *Estes v. Texas*. In his opinion, Justice Burger wrote that the appellants had misinterpreted the Court's ruling

Televised Trials

The 1980s saw the rise of televised trials in state and county courtrooms, coupled with a growing national interest in law-related TV shows such as *Unsolved Mysteries* and *America's Most Wanted*. These facts led in part to the establishment in 1991 of Court TV, a commercial cable network that presents legal information in an easy-to-understand format. But the true watershed with regard to popular interest in courtroom proceedings came with the 1995 trial of O. J. Simpson for the murders of his estranged wife Nicole Brown and her friend Ron Goldman.

To many observers, what they saw when the cameras went into the courtroom was not pleasant. "Lawyers in the O. J. trial pandered to the camera," wrote *Detroit News* television commentator Tim Kiska, "grieving parents wept at emotional press conferences, and an electronic 'village' of countless cameras sprung up outside of the Los Angeles courthouse." When U.S. District Judge Richard Matsch kept cameras out of his courtroom during the 1997 trials of Oklahoma City bombing suspects Timothy McVeigh and Terry Nichols, he was no doubt influenced by the Simpson example.

Source(s): Kiska, Tim. "O. J.'s Pandering Lawyers Jeopardize Future of Cameras in the Courtroom." *Detroit News*, 5 October 1995.

Estes is not to be read as announcing a constitutional rule barring still photographic, radio, and television coverage in all cases and under all circumstances. It does not stand as an absolute ban on state experimentation with an evolving technology, which, in terms of modes of mass communication, was in relative infancy in 1964, and is, even now, in a state of continuing change.

While acknowledging that trials that generated a lot of publicity may infringe upon the defendant's right to a fair trial, Burger concluded that was no reason to ban television coverage of trials.

Dangers lurk in this, as in most experiments, but unless we were to conclude that television coverage under all conditions is prohibited by the Constitution, the states must be free to experiment. We are not empowered by all the Constitution to oversee or harness state procedural experimentation; only when the state action infringes fundamental guarantees are we authorized to intervene. We must assume state courts will be alert to any factors that impair the fundamental rights of the accused.

Justice Stewart while agreeing with the result took issue with the majority's reasoning. Stewart agreed with the appellant's interpretation of *Estes v. Texas* that it banned all television coverage of criminal trials as unconstitutional, and he concluded that it should be overruled. While the majority opinion recognized that technological advances would make televised trials less intrusive, Stewart argued that even if technological advances made televising trials less physically disruptive that cameras and recording devices by their mere presence make the process impartial.

The Court in *Estes* found the admittedly unobtrusive presence of television cameras in a criminal trial to be inherently prejudicial, and thus violative of due process of law. Today the Court reaches precisely the opposite conclusion. I have no great trouble in agreeing with the Court today, but I would acknowledge our square departure from precedent.

Justice White wrote a separate opinion that agreed with the majority's ruling, but also took exception to the reasoning. He thought that *Estes* should be overturned.

Although the Court's opinion today contends that it is consistent with *Estes,* I believe that it effectively eviscerates *Estes*. The Florida rule has no exception for the sensational or widely publicized case. Absent a showing of specific prejudice, any kind of case may be televised as long as the rule is otherwise complied with.

Impact

The Court's ruling, in a way, made the Court TV network, a 24-hour network devoted to covering trials and legal news, possible. Yet, while the televising of state criminal procedures has become standard, television cameras are rarely allowed in federal courts. The Supreme Court has continuously refused to allow any of their proceedings to be televised. Some, have once again, come to question the wisdom of placing cameras in the courtroom after such highly publicized trials as the murder case of O. J. Simpson, who was charged with murdering his wife and her male companion. The nation was obsessed with the case and many believed that the attorneys and even the judge presiding over the case were impacted by the presence of the television cameras. After the Simpson trial concluded some state judges refused to allow television cameras in their courtroom fearful of creating a circus-like atmosphere. The presence of television cameras in courtrooms continues to generate debate.

Related Cases

Estes v. Texas, 381 U.S. 532 (1964).
Sheppard v. Maxwell, 384 U.S. 333 (1966).
Furman v. Georgia, 408 U.S. 238 (1972).
Murphy v. Florida, 421 U.S. 794 (1975).
Nixon v. Warner Communications Inc, 435 U.S. 589 (1978).

Bibliography and Further Reading

Biskupic, Joan and Elder Witt, eds. *Congressional Quarterly's Guide to the U.S. Supreme Court,* 3rd ed. Washington, DC: Congressional Quarterly, Inc., 1996.

Brill, Steven. "Cameras Belong in the Courtroom." *USA Today (Magazine),* July 1996, pp. 52.

Lassiter, Christo. "TV or not TV—That is the Question." *Journal of Criminal Law and Criminology,* Spring 1996, pp. 928.

Shoop, Julie Gannon, and Christo Lassiter. "Cameras in the Courtroom?" *Trial,* March 1995, pp. 68.

Tanick, Marshall H. "Burger Rulings Caused the Simpson Circus." *The National Law Journal,* August 28, 1995, p. A19.

GRUSENDORF V. CITY OF OKLAHOMA CITY

Legal Citation: 816 F.2d 539 (10th Cir. 1987)

Appellant
Greg Grusendorf

Appellee
City of Oklahoma City, Oklahoma

Appellant's Claim
That city regulation which prohibited firefighter trainees from smoking both on duty and off duty violated his constitutional right to privacy.

Chief Lawyer for Appellant
Steven M. Angel

Chief Lawyer for Appellee
Diane Davis Huckins

Judges for the Court
James E. Barrett (writing for the court), Bruce S. Jenkins, Deanell Reece Tacha

Judges Dissenting
None

Place
Denver, Colorado

Date of Decision
17 April 1987

Decision
The city regulation was reasonably related to the city's legitimate interest in protecting the health and safety of its firefighters, and thus was constitutional.

Significance
The court's decision cleared the way for city and state governments to impose restrictions on the conduct of their employees outside of work, so long as those restrictions are related in some way to the performance of the employee's job. Particularly with respect to public safety employees, such as police officers and firefighters, the court's decision essentially approved a wide range of government restrictions on the off-work conduct of public employees.

In the early 1980s, as the medical community and the public became more aware of the dangers associated with smoking, private and public employers began to institute severe restrictions on the ability of employees to smoke. In October of 1984 Greg Grusendorf was hired as a firefighter trainee by the Oklahoma City Fire Department, which had a policy prohibiting firefighter trainees from smoking either on or off duty. In December of 1984, while at lunch with other trainees, Grusendorf partially smoked a cigarette. The incident was observed by another city employee, who reported the incident to the fire chief. Grusendorf was fired, pursuant to the city's anti-smoking policy.

Because the city is a public entity, it is bound by the terms of the Due Process Clause of the Fourteenth Amendment to the U.S. Constitution, which provides that the government may not "deprive any person of life, liberty, or property, without due process of law." Although the Fourteenth Amendment speaks of the fairness of the "process" used to deprive someone of their rights, the Supreme Court has held that the amendment protects against any deprivation of certain "fundamental" rights, regardless of the procedures used by the government, a concept known as "substantive due process." These "fundamental" rights include the rights mentioned in the first ten amendments to the Constitution, such as the right to free speech, and certain rights concerning privacy and personal autonomy, such as marriage and procreation.

Grusendorf filed a lawsuit against the city in the U.S. District Court for the Western District of Oklahoma, claiming that the city's anti-smoking policy, as applied to his activities when he was off-duty, violated his substantive due process rights under the Due Process Clause. The district court granted the city's motion to dismiss Grusendorf's suit, and Grusendorf appealed the decision to the U.S. Court of Appeals for the Tenth Circuit.

Tenth Circuit Finds City's Policy Reasonable

Grusendorf argued that the city's anti-smoking policy violated his liberty and privacy rights under the Fourteenth Amendment. He claimed, based on U.S. Supreme Court cases recognizing various privacy rights, that under the Fourteenth Amendment he has a right to be left alone in the conduct of his private life, which includes the right to smoke. The city, on the other hand, argued that its anti-smoking policy did not implicate any privacy rights, because the Supreme Court has limited the scope of privacy rights protected by the Due Process Clause to privacy rights of an intimate, personal nature, such as the right to abortion, to educate one's children, and to marriage.

The court partially disagreed with the city's position. The court noted that although smoking does not implicate the same privacy concerns that marriage, procreation, and child-rearing do, the city's policy extended far beyond the workplace and regulated Grusendorf's conduct in his own home. The court reasoned that in the 1976 case of *Kelley v. Johnson* the Supreme Court assumed, without ultimately deciding the issue, that a public employee has a privacy interest in matters of personal appearance, and concluded that smoking was similar to personal appearance. Thus, the court of appeals assumed that Grusendorf had a privacy interest in smoking outside of work.

Nevertheless, the court concluded that the city's anti-smoking policy did not violate Grusendorf's right to privacy. In *Kelley,* the Supreme Court concluded that a city policy relating to the personal appearance and activities of public safety employees, such as police officers and firefighters, does not violate an employee's privacy rights unless the employee shows "that there is no rational connection between the regulation . . . and the promotion of safety of persons and property." Applying this test, the court of appeals concluded that the city's anti-smoking policy was rationally related to protecting property and personal safety. The court reasoned that cigarette smoking is hazardous to health, and that the city has an interest in making sure that its firefighters are in good health and physical conditioning. The court also reasoned that firefighters face health risks due to smoke inhalation, and that smok-

ing can increase these risks. Accordingly, the court concluded that the city's anti-smoking policy did not violate Grusendorf's privacy rights.

Impact

The court's decision was important in defining the scope of rules which employers may impose on their employees. Certainly, both public and private employers are free to impose a wide range of rules relating to an employee's conduct in the workplace. The *Grusendorf* decision, however, also cleared the way for at least public employers to impose restrictions on an employee's conduct outside of work, so long as those restrictions are related to the employee's job. Also, the decision was part of a larger debate throughout the 1980s and intensifying in the 1990s concerning the rights of smokers.

Related Cases

Griswold v. Connecticut, 381 U.S. 479 (1964).
Roe v. Wade, 410 U.S. 113 (1973).
Kelley v. Johnson, 425 U.S. 238 (1976).

Bibliography and Further Reading

Dworkin, Terry Morehead. "It's My Life—Leave Me Alone." *American Business Law Journal,* fall 1997, pp. 47–103.

Geyelin, Milo. "The Job is Yours—Unless You Smoke." *Wall Street Journal,* April 21, 1989, p. A16.

Koenig, Bill. "Privacy at Work: A 90's Debate." *Indianapolis Star,* November 8, 1988, p. B1.

Rabin, Robert L. and Stephen D. Sugarman, eds. *Smoking Policy: Law, Politics and Culture.* New York: Oxford University Press, 1993.

Staimer, Marcia. "Do Workers Have Private Lives?" *USA Today,* May 31, 1991, p. A1.

NATIONAL TREASURY EMPLOYEES UNION V. VON RAAB

Legal Citation: 489 U.S. 656 (1989)

Petitioner
National Treasury Employees Union

Respondent
William Von Raab, Commissioner, U.S. Custom Service

Petitioner's Claim
Chemical drug testing of U.S. Customs Service employees (considered a "search") was constitutionally intrusive and irregular under the provisions of the Fourth Amendment.

Chief Lawyer for Petitioner
Lois G. Williams

Chief Lawyer for Respondent
Charles Fried

Justices for the Court
Harry A. Blackmun, Anthony M. Kennedy (writing for the Court), Sandra Day O'Connor, William H. Rehnquist, Byron R. White

Justices Dissenting
William J. Brennan, Jr., Thurgood Marshall, Antonin Scalia, John Paul Stevens

Place
Washington, D.C.

Date of Decision
21 March 1989

Decision
The Fourth Amendment rights of U.S. Customs Service employees were not violated by drug screening for employees serving in or applicants applying for positions in which they might perform "sensitive tasks" or for employees applying for promotion to sensitive positions.

Significance
The Supreme Court found the requirement to submit a urine sample as a condition of performing Customs Service duties appropriate. The procedure targeted new applicants and three categories of Customs Service employees—those who dealt with interception of illegal drugs, carried firearms, and operated with sensitive information. The Court disagreed with the petitioners who cited the Constitution's Fourth Amendment as protection against employee drug testing. Governmental interest superseded the "sanctity of privacy" because of a growing social problem of drug abuse made necessary the institution of drug-free programs to preserve reliability and efficient performance of duties by mentally and physically fit officers.

The mission of the U.S. Customs Service is to control, observe, and make sure that illicit effects do not enter the country. One primary duty, interdiction of drug traffic and seizure of contraband, brings employees into direct, daily contact with drug-related criminal operations. Sometimes their duties carry the high risk of using firearms. In December of 1985, Commissioner of Customs William Von Raab prepared a drug screening program for personnel whom he recognized as employees with sensitive tasks. Drug tests were demanded for employees who were directly exposed to activities where there was a potential for corruption, for employees that might have to use firearms, and for high level positions with access to classified information. Although he expressed that drug abuse among Customs Service employees most likely was not widespread, he also acknowledged that "no segment of society is immune from threat of illegal drug use."

In May of 1986, implementation of drug testing started at the U.S. Customs Service. Urinalysis was required for new applicants for certain positions and for some employees already in the service. The program for urinalysis was established with all precautions to ensure accuracy of testing. All applicants for Custom Service positions were notified about the drug screening as a condition of employment. Current employees could choose when and where to submit urine for analysis. On reporting for the test, employees were indirectly observed by monitors of the same sex to avoid possibilities of adulteration of the specimen or substitution of a sample from another person. Laboratory analysis of urine was used to determine presence of marijuana, cocaine, opiates, amphetamines, and phencyclidine. Verified positive results were delivered to a Medical Review Officer, and agency employees who tested positive were not permitted to continue their duties. All results of testing remained within the agency and could not be given to other agencies or law enforcement officials.

Believing that their rights under the Fourth Amendment were violated, the National Treasury Employees Union (on behalf of their Customs Service membership) filed suit objecting to the drug screening program. The U.S. District Court for the Eastern District of Louisiana accepted their arguments; ruling in favor of the petitioners, the court reasoned that "the drug testing plan constitutes an overly intrusive policy of searches and seizures without probable cause or reasonable suspicion, in violation of legitimate expectations of privacy." On appeal, the U.S. Court of Appeals disagreed and found that although requirements for urinalysis could be viewed as an intrusion into Fourth Amendment privacy rights, the government's interests outweighed the petitioners' expectation and right to privacy. The appellate court thus vacated the lower court's ruling citing as their rationale that "drug use by covered employees casts substantial doubt on their ability to discharge their duties honestly and vigorously." Moreover, the appellate court felt the scope of the Customs Service drug detection program was of limited intrusiveness (there was no visual observation of the act of urination).

When on appeal to the U.S. Supreme Court, petitioners argued that constitutionally-guaranteed Fourth Amendment rights meant that the government's interest should not be considered a justified intrusion on their reasonable expectation of privacy. Counsel for the National Treasury Employees Union did not minimize the significance of governmental efforts to establish measures to prevent irrational use of firearms or compromise of important and classified information. However, their main argument contended that no significant indicators showed an existence of a drug abuse problem among employees; therefore, chemical testing was not justified. (The respondent's brief indicated that results of the drug screening program proved only 5 of 3,600 employees tested positive.) Furthermore, the petitioner's attorney contended that the testing mechanism was not properly constructed, because drug abusers could simply abstain from drug use for a period of time to avoid detection or could switch their urine specimen with a "clean" sample from a friend.

Attorneys for the respondent countered by arguing that there existed a great social problem of drug abuse in the country. Quoting Commissioner Von Raab from a memorandum, counsel reasoned that "Implementation of the drug screening program would set an important example in our country's struggle with the most serious threat to our national health and security." Moreover, there was an absolute incongruity between regular performance of duty and enjoying drugs, especially when Customs Service employees could be tempted by smugglers, blackmailed, or exposed to dangerous situations where physical conditions must be perfectly controlled. Considering that the service's mission was a "first line of defense," requirements for chemical testing were justified. Soon after the U.S. Court of Appeals ruling, the U.S. Department of Health and Human Services instituted procedures for drug screening programs for federal employees which equally applied to the U.S. Customs Service.

The U.S. Supreme Court affirmed almost all opinions of the Appellate Court. The majority opinion held it was admissible to require federal employees to submit urine samples for drug testing, specifically incumbents who were directly involved in drug interdiction and those who carried firearms. The Court based its decision on the precedent set in *Skinner v. Railway Labor Executives' Assn.* (1989). In that case, the Court specified that the government's purpose must be reasonable and that the intrusion must justifiably outweigh an individual's privacy rights under the Fourth Amendment. The Court determined that in the matter of drug testing of Customs Service employees, individual privacy was overshadowed by the respondent's purpose, namely, the governmental interest could be justified as being beyond the "normal need of law enforcement." The Customs Service had a "substantial interest" in ensuring that drug abusers were not operating in demanding positions where mental unreliability could endanger effective duty performance. Justices for the majority did not find merit in the petitioner's contention that the "probable cause standard" should prevent testing. Instead the majority opined that Fourth Amendment privacy rights could be abridged "where the Government seeks to prevent development of hazardous conditions." Further, the Court emphasized that duties of Customs Service agents were often hazardous and risky and that officers were often a target for blackmail or bribery. Thus, the service's interest in drug screening reflected a well-founded need to ensure physical fitness and reliability of their personnel.

The justices pointed out that there existed a national and public interest to ensure enforcement of measures that could bar individuals with impaired perception that might negatively affect their conduct and imperil their own safety, the safety of other employees, and the public at large. The U.S. Supreme Court found that public employees must be aware of certain circumstances when privacy expectations were diminished by the government's interest when the safety and integrity of borders were concerned. Moreover, although few employees were detected as drug positive, the Court did not consider this reason to stop chemical testing. They stressed that the preventative measure of imposing testing requirements helped preclude dealing with employees who were addicts. The possible harm of such individuals actively operating as agents justified the testing program despite infrequent cases of drug abuse among Customs employees. Further, the justices thus found as "meaningless" the petitioners' questioning of the accuracy and reliability of techniques and precautions taken to preclude manipulation with urine samples. First, there was no real basis to reason that drug testing protocol was ineffective, and, second, the "fade-away effect" of drugs would likely incriminate a drug user even if that person refrained from taking drugs for a period of time.

The U.S. Supreme Court remanded the case, so that the Court of Appeals could make a more specific determination as to which categories of employees were "required to handle classified material" and should be subject to drug testing. In previous cases, the Court recognized that there existed circumstances when, in order to protect "truly sensitive information," government had a compelling interest to establish restrictions to defend its "vital interest." But, the U.S. Supreme Court did not find evidence that categories of employees who deal with "sensitive information" were precisely identified and thus testing was administered to a broad number of employees without clearly defining what constituted an employee assigned to a "high level position." The Court directed the court of appeals to "examine the criteria used by the service in determining what materials are classified and decide whom to test under this rubric."

Although the majority presented compelling rationale for its decision, the decision was far from unanimous. Dissenting opinion was supported by four justices who believed that searches without "probable cause" were "unprincipled and unjustifiable." Minority opinion felt the intrusiveness of the Custom Service's drug testing plan was "offensive to personal dignity." Although the majority based its decision, in part, on *Skinner v. Railway Labor Executives' Assn.* (1989), dissenting justices felt there was no similarity between the two cases. (The Court previously held substance abuse testing valid in *Skinner* due to substantive evidence of "grave harm" caused by alcohol use among railroad employees.) There was neither evidence pointing to a history of employees engaging in drug abuse nor was there documentation of actual damage resulting from drug abuse by customs agents. They believed that arguments by the respondent were conjectural and not based on "plausible speculations," because results of testing showed that there were no reasonable expectations of drug abuse among service's employees. The dissenting justices reasoned that the majority opinion rested only on the symbolic value of their holding and expressed concern that accepting Fourth Amendment limitations supported by the majority opinion could inappropriately encourage "similar testing of private citizens who use dangerous instruments such as guns or cars or have access to classified information."

Impact

In a close decision of 5-4, the U.S. Supreme Court sought to identify how valid governmental interests could outweigh the guarantee of privacy rights under the Fourth Amendment. They found the rationale for maintaining a drug testing program for U.S. Customs Service employees was justified. The service manifested a bona fide concern regarding the safety and effectiveness of agents engaged in interdiction of illicit narcotics. The dissenting opinion presented equally compelling reservations regarding the potential for infringement on Fourth Amendment rights. The Court justified its decision on a just, theoretical basis that sought to address the problem of drug abuse in the workplace and uphold a governmental interest in using its power to compel their interests in the "war on drugs."

Related Cases

O'Connor v. Ortega, 480 U.S. 709 (1987).

Skinner v. Railway Labor Executives' Assn., 489 U.S. 602 (1989).

Bibliography and Further Reading

Anderson, Sean. "Individual Privacy Interests and the 'Special Needs' Analysis for Involuntary Drug and HIV Tests." *California Law Review,* January 1998, pp. 119–177.

Dripps, Donald A. "Drug Testing—Again." *Trial,* June 1997, p. 72.

LaFave, Wayne R. "Computers, Urinals, and the Fourth Amendment: Confessions of a Patron Saint." *Michigan Law Review,* August 1996, pp. 2553–2589.

Hall, Kermit L. *The Oxford Companion to the Supreme Court of the United States.* New York: Oxford University Press, 1992.

Richman, Roger. "Balancing Government Necessity and Public Employee Privacy: Reconstructing the Fourth Amendment through the Special Needs Doctrine." *Administration & Society,* May 1994, p. 99.

Shutler, Samantha Elizabeth. "Random, Suspicionless Drug Testing of High School Athletes." *Journal of Criminal Law and Criminology,* summer 1996, pp. 1265–1303.

PLANNED PARENTHOOD OF SOUTHEASTERN PENNSYLVANIA V. CASEY

Legal Citation: 505 U.S. 833 (1992)

Petitioner
Planned Parenthood of Southeastern Pennsylvania

Respondent
Robert P. Casey, Governor of Pennsylvania, et al.

Petitioner's Claim
That under the due process clause of the Constitution, the 1988 and 1989 amendments to the Pennsylvania abortion law were illegal.

Chief Lawyer for Petitioner
Kathryn Kolbert

Chief Lawyer for Respondent
Ernest D. Preate, Jr., Attorney General of Pennsylvania

Justices for the Court
Harry A. Blackmun, Anthony M. Kennedy (writing for the Court), Sandra Day O'Connor, David H. Souter, John Paul Stevens

Justices Dissenting
William H. Rehnquist, Antonin Scalia, Clarence Thomas, Byron R. White

Place
Washington, D.C.

Date of Decision
29 June 1992

Decision
Judicial respect for precedent required the Court to reaffirm *Roe v. Wade,* the Court's 1973 decision making abortion legal in the United States. The justices declared Pennsylvania's Abortion Control Act law constitutional in part and unconstitutional in part.

Significance
In the words of Pulitzer Prize winning historian David J. Garrow, "*Casey* was a watershed event in American history." It resolved a national dispute over abortion by upholding the essentials of *Roe v. Wade* while permitting Pennsylvania to regulate abortions as long as the state did not place an undue burden on women.

In 1989, the Supreme Court allowed the states more leeway in regulating abortions, with *Webster v. Reproductive Health Services.* In its aftermath, anti-abortion groups stepped up their campaign to harass abortion clinics throughout the nation. Radical, fringe antiabortion activists threw firebombs, videotaped the children of medical employees, threatened patients, poured glue in keyholes, and distributed posters identifying doctors and nurses as "baby killers."

In 1982, the growing pro-life movement was ready to test the Supreme Court's landmark 1973 decision in *Roe v. Wade,* which protects a woman's right to an abortion. That year, Pennsylvania passed the Abortion Control Act, followed by amendments in 1988 and 1989. Governor Robert P. Casey signed the last one in November of 1989, only four months after the *Webster* decision.

The Abortion Control Act required that women seeking abortions give their informed consent—clinics must provide them with state-scripted information about the abortion at least 24 hours before the procedure. The statute also required the informed consent of one parent in order for a minor to obtain an abortion, although it provided "judicial by-pass" steps for the teen to go to court for permission in special cases.

One section of the law required a wife seeking an abortion to sign a statement that she had notified her husband. The statute also imposed reporting requirements on clinics providing abortions. The regulations were lifted only in emergencies.

Before any of the provisions had taken effect, women's groups, clinics, and doctors challenged the law. Five abortion clinics and a doctor representing a class of physicians who provided abortion services went to court to have the law declared unconstitutional. The challenges to the 1988 and 1989 Abortion Control Acts merged into one case—*Planned Parenthood of Southeastern Pennsylvania v. Casey.*

Win Some, Lose Some

The district court declared the law unconstitutional except for one provision requiring physicians to tell women the age of her embryo or fetus. The case then went through two appeals—on 21 October 1991, and 30

Massachusetts's Abortion Consent Act

In 1974, the chief legislative body in Massachusetts passed an abortion consent act that became part of the commonwealth's legal code. The law states in part that a doctor cannot perform an abortion without written consent from the pregnant patient. The consent form should be in simple-to-understand language and contain information regarding the procedure the physician will have to perform in order to end the pregnancy, possible complications associated with the procedure, and available alternatives to abortion.

The act further provides that, if the pregnant woman is under 18 years of age, both she and her parents must sign the consent form. Finally, in a change adopted in 1980, the law permits a pregnant teen who cannot gain the consent of her parents, or elects not to seek it, to petition a judge to make such a determination.

Planned Parenthood opposed the informed-consent requirement in the state case of *Planned Parenthood of Massachusetts v. Belotti* (1987). As a result of its victory, the state struck down a requirement of a 24 hour waiting period before a woman signs a consent form, as well as a requirement that the physician inform the pregnant woman of the stage of the unborn child's development before terminating the pregnancy.

Source(s): Massachusetts General Laws Annotated, Chapter 112, Section 12S.

October 1992. The Court of Appeals, striking down the husband-notification provision, upheld the others. The stage was set for Supreme Court appeals by both sides.

The oral arguments began on 22 April, a month that brought 500,000 pro-choice women to the nation's capital. Kathryn Kolbert, an experienced American Civil Liberties Union (ACLU) lawyer, explained the fundamental issue for the plaintiffs:

> [Does] . . . government [have] the power to force a woman to continue or to end a pregnancy against her will? . . . Since . . . *Roe v. Wade,* a generation of American women . . . [have been] secure in the knowledge . . . their child-bearing decisions [are protected]. This landmark decision . . . not only protects rights of bodily integrity and autonomy, but has enabled millions of women to participate fully and equally in society.

Kolbert's opponent, Ernest D. Preate, Jr., followed her to the floor. He had spoken only a few words when Justice Blackmun, the 83-year old author of *Roe v. Wade,* interrupted, "Have you read *Roe*?" Preate replied, "Yes." Then, before Preate could finish his remarks, Justice O'Connor showered him with critical questions regarding the spousal notification clause. Justices Stevens and Kennedy continued her skeptical line of questioning, followed by Justice Souter.

Next, U.S. Solicitor General Kenneth W. Starr, representing the administration of President George Bush, came to the lectern to attack *Roe v. Wade.* According to historian David J. Garrow, Souter "pressed Starr to concede that if his position prevailed, states could outlaw *all* abortions, except perhaps those where a pregnancy directly threatened a woman's life." Souter questioned Starr about whether a complete ban on abortions would

meet the *Webster* case's "rational basis" standard. Starr answered that any law would have to include the life of the mother exception or else face "serious questions." Souter remarked in exasperation, "You're asking the Court to adopt a standard and I think we ought to know where the standard would take us."

Justice David H. Souter. © The Supreme Court Historical Society.

The Dark Horse

The final vote would rest on Souter's actions. From earlier conversations he suspected that O'Connor, Kennedy, and himself, could agree that the Pennsylvania law could be upheld *and* still leave *Roe* intact.

However, Chief Justice Rehnquist had already begun to draft the Court's opinion to overturn Wade, assuming the other judges agreed with him. Then, unexpectedly, Kennedy changed his mind, joining Souter and O'Connor in a compromise. Behind the scenes, Souter began working out the details of the middle ground.

In May, before Rehnquist had finished his opinion, Kennedy, Souter, and O'Connor met in Souter's chambers on the far southeastern corner of the main floor. Their private conversations led to a joint decision to uphold *Roe,* derailing Rehnquist's work. When they discovered the switch, Rehnquist and Scalia "were stunned," according to the *New York Times.* They had failed to capture the five votes they needed to overthrow *Roe.* Instead, Souter and his allies—along with Blackmun and Stevens—were voting to uphold the landmark decision.

On Monday morning, 29 June 1992, on the final day of the term, observers were unprepared for the results. In a rare action, O'Connor, Kennedy and Souter—on behalf of Blackmun and Stevens—delivered the opinion of the Court, upholding *Roe's* "essential holding."

The three then described "a realm of personal liberty which the government may not enter." Kennedy wrote, "At the heart of liberty is the right to define one's own concept of existence, of meaning, of the universe, and of the mystery of human life." In abortion, "the liberty of the woman is at stake in a sense unique to the human condition and so unique to the law." A woman's "suffering is too intimate and personal for the State to insist . . . upon its own vision of the woman's role, however dominant that vision has been in the course of our history and our culture."

However, the most original opinion came from Souter: "The ability of women to participate equally in the economic and social life of the Nation [for 20 years] has been facilitated by their ability to control their reproductive lives . . ." He noted that the Court's decision on *Roe* had a "dimension" that was present only when a decision "calls the contending sides of a national controversy to end their national division by accepting a common mandate rooted in the Constitution." However, he recognized that there were always going to be efforts to thwart putting such a decision into effect. Therefore, "only the most convincing justification under accepted standards of precedent could suffice to demonstrate that a later decision overruling the first was anything but a surrender to political pressure, and an unjustified repudiation of the principle on which the Court staked its authority in the first instance."

The majority held that the doctrine of *stare decisis—* the rule by which courts are slow to interfere with principles announced in former decisions—required that *Roe v. Wade* be affirmed in its "essential holding," recognizing a woman's right to choose an abortion. The Court also established that an "undue burden test," not *Roe's* "trimester" framework, be used in evaluating abortion restrictions before viability.

The Court accepted the Abortion Control Act except for the spousal notification provision, which did impose an undue burden and was therefore unconstitutional. Therefore, *Planned Parenthood of Southeastern Pennsylvania v. Casey* was affirmed in part, reversed in part.

Because of this decision by a Court widely thought to be conservative, a woman's right to an abortion today rests on even firmer legal foundations than before.

Related Cases

Roe v. Wade, 410 U.S. 113 (1973).

Webster v. Reproductive Health Services, 492 U.S. 490 (1989).

Bibliography and Further Reading

Benshoof, Janet. "Planned Parenthood v. Casey: the Impact of the New Undue Burden Standard on Reproductive Health Care." *The Journal of the American Medical Association,* 5 May 1993, p. 2249.

Garrow, David J. "Justice Souter Emerges." *New York Times Magazine,* 25 September 1994.

Garrow, David J. *Liberty and Sexuality: The Right to Privacy and the Making of Roe v. Wade.* New York: Macmillan, 1994.

Hoff, Joan. *Law, Gender, and Injustice: A Legal History of U.S. Women.* New York: New York University Press, 1991.

Joyce, Theodore, et al. "The Impact of Mississippi's Mandatory Delay Law on Abortions and Births." *The Journal of the American Medical Association,* 27, August 1997, p. 653.

Kassopm Nancy. "From Arguments to Supreme Court Opinions in Planned Parenthood v. Casey." *Political Science and Politics,* March 1993, p. 53.

Tribe, Lawrence. *American Constitutional Law,* 2d ed. Mineola, NY: The Foundation Press, 1988.

MADSEN V. WOMEN'S HEALTH CENTER, INC.

Legal Citation: 512 U.S. 753 (1994)

Petitioner
Judy Madsen, et al.

Respondent
Womens Health Center, Inc.

Petitioner's Claim
Portions of an injunction limiting the activities of abortion protesters violate First Amendment rights to free speech.

Chief Lawyer for Petitioner
Matthew D. Staver

Chief Lawyer for Respondent
Talbot D'Alemberte

Justices for the Court
Harry A. Blackmun, Ruth Bader Ginsburg, Sandra Day O'Connor, William H. Rehnquist (writing for the Court), David H. Souter, Clarence Thomas

Justices Dissenting
Anthony M. Kennedy, Antonin Scalia, John Paul Stevens

Place
Washington, D.C.

Date of Decision
30 June 1994

Decision
The injunction is upheld in part and reversed in part.

Significance
The mixed verdict could be viewed as a victory for either side, although petitioners prevailed on most parts of their claim.

In 1992 the operators of the Aware Woman Center for Choice, a facility that conducted abortion counseling and performed abortions at their clinic in Melbourne, Florida, were subjected to daily picketing and confrontation of their patients by Operation Rescue, a group opposed to abortion. A Florida state court issued an injunction prohibiting the protesters from (1) "physically abusing" persons entering or leaving the clinic; (2) entering the clinic; and (3) obstructing access to or exit from the clinic. Six months after the injunction was issued, the clinic operators claimed that access to the clinic was still being obstructed and that the activities of the protesters, which included singing, the use of bullhorns, the carrying of placards, and approaching those entering or leaving the clinic, had a physically harmful effect on patients of the clinic. Protesters also picketed in front of the homes of those who worked at the clinic.

In response the Court amended the original injunction, increasing the limits on the activities of the protesters. The amended injunction prohibited the protesters from (1) entering the clinic or clinic property; (2) "blocking, impeding, inhibiting, . . . or obstructing or interfering" with access to or exit from the clinic; (3) coming within 36 feet of the property line of the clinic; (4) using sound amplification equipment, including bullhorns, and making other loud noises such as singing or yelling from 7:30 a.m. to noon Monday through Saturday; and from displaying images "observable to . . . those inside the clinic"; (5) approaching any person going to the clinic while within 300 feet of the clinic, unless "such person indicates a desire to communicate"; persons not wishing to communicate may not be threatened or harassed; (6) demonstrating within 300 feet of the residences of clinic staff; this also applied to "those acting in concert" with the demonstrators; (7) harassing of persons entering or leaving the clinic or the residences of clinic staff; (8) harassing clinic staff; (9) inciting others to commit any of the prohibited acts.

Different members of the protest group appealed in two separate actions, one to the Florida Supreme Court and to the U.S. District Court of Appeals. The court of appeals issued a ruling that the injunction was unconstitutional on First Amendment grounds, as an "actual prohibition of speech" to prevent a "potential hindrance" of the exercise of abortion rights. Shortly after, the Florida Supreme Court held the injunction to be constitutional because it was "content-neutral" and served a legitimate government interest. The Supreme Court granted *certiorari* to resolve the two conflicting decisions.

Standards of Scrutiny

The Court has traditionally closely examined any government action which impairs or abridges any fundamental constitutional right. Exactly how closely the Court must examine the action or rule in question, however, depends on the specific facts at hand. According to precedent, the action is weighed according to one of two standards. "Strict scrutiny" entails the closest, most skeptical view of the government's intentions and the effects of the action on the rights of those affected. When First Amendment issues are at stake, strict scrutiny is necessary if the abridgment of speech hinges on its content; such abridgment is "content-based" and may be used by the government to suppress the expression of certain opinions. Such a rule must be "necessary to serve a compelling state interest and . . . narrowly drawn to achieve that end." (*Carey v. Brown,* [1980]). If the rule is "content-neutral," a less stringent standard prevails: it must be: "narrowly tailored to serve a significant government interest, and leave open ample alternative channels of communication (*U.S. Postal Service v. Council of Greenburgh Civic Associations,* [1981]).

The petitioners argued that the buffer zones (sections 3 and 5 of the injunction) and bans on noise and display of images (section 4) were unconstitutional content-based abridgments of free speech, in particular because they did not apply to abortion rights supporters who also demonstrated in the area. The consent requirement (section 6) was an unconstitutional prior restraint on speech; further, the inclusion of the phrase "and those acting in concert with them" was vague and overbroad. The rest of the injunction was not challenged.

The Majority Opinion

The majority upheld parts of the injunction and struck down others. The record of fact found by the lower court was accepted by the majority, which noted the petitioners "studiously refrained" from challenging it and to the Florida Supreme Court stated that the question at hand was one of law only. In making its decision, the Court first examined the injunction in order to determine what level of scrutiny to apply. They rejected the petitioners' contention that the injunction was content-based, finding that, while addressed to a specific group which held a certain view, it was addressed to that group because of their past conduct rather than its views: "There is no suggestion in this

record that Florida law would not equally restrain similar conduct directed at a target having nothing to do with abortion."

The majority declined to follow the path of strict scrutiny but was unsatisfied with intermediate scrutiny as well, noting that injunctions "carry greater risks of censorship and discriminatory application than do general ordinances." It thus took a middle road in examining the sections of the injunction in dispute, adopting the standard that to be constitutional they should "burden no more speech than necessary to serve a significant government interest." Applying this standard to the contested sections of the injunction, they found as follows: The 36-foot buffer zone (section 3) was not unduly burdensome in part. The majority noted that one petitioner admitted that protesters would still be only 10 or 12 feet away from the driveway of the clinic. Further, the protesters "can still be seen and heard from the clinic parking lots." The part of the zone that extended to the private property to the north and west of the clinic was too restrictive, however, since there was no evidence of protesters impeding access to the clinic while located on that property. The noise restrictions (section 4) were upheld on the ground that such limitation was necessary to protect the health of clinic patients, but the prohibition of "observable images" was found to be too broad an infringement of speech, since those inside the clinic could close the curtains if they were upset by any images displayed. Prohibiting the demonstrators from approaching clinic patients within 300 feet of the clinic (section 5) was struck down as overly burdensome; the First Amendment does not protect citizens from being confronted with speech they find offensive. The 300-foot buffer zone around residences (section 6) and the prohibition of use of sound amplification at those sites was struck down as overly broad. A "limitation on the time, duration, and number of pickets outside a smaller zone could have accomplished the desired result." The mention of parties acting "in concert with the petitioners was not held to be too broad or vague; in any case, because it named persons other than the petitioners, the petitioners lacked standing to challenge it.

Justice Souter issued a concurring opinion, which accepted the reasoning of the majority. He noted that petitioners themselves accepted a legitimate government interest of public safety, the free movement of traffic, and property rights. He wanted to clarify the holding regarding the "in concert" provision, declaring that it was "a matter to be taken up in individual cases, and not to be decided on the basis of protesters' viewpoints."

Stevens Dissents in Part

Justice Stevens dissented on the issue of the level of scrutiny to be applied to injunctions and on the majority disposition of the 300-foot buffer zone around the clinic. On the scrutiny issue, he stated that injunctions should be treated more leniently than legislation. The same regulation when enacted as statute might well be unconstitutional, but injunctions apply "solely to [specific parties] who, by engaging in illegal conduct, have been judicially deprived of some liberty—the normal consequence of illegal activity." Souter also rejected the majority finding regarding the 300-foot buffer zone, declaring that it proscribed conduct, not speech, noting that the trial judge found this necessary to protect clinic patients from stalking and shadowing by protesters.

Scalia Dissents

Scalia dissented from all parts of the majority opinion upholding the injunction. He also disagreed regarding the level of scrutiny to be applied to all such restrictions. All should be subjected to strict scrutiny because of the risk of suppression of unpopular points of view. His rejection of the injunction rested largely on his rejection of the trial court's finding of facts. This rejection was largely based on a videotape submitted by the respondents in which he found no egregious violation, in fact no violation, of the original injunction. In Scalia's opinion, the trial court judge found without evidence that protesters were blocking access to the clinic; the videotape showed a slowing of traffic and a delay of cars entering the parking lot that was the normal, inevitable result of congestion when a crowd gathers, not tortious behavior on the part of respondents. Since there was no violation of the original injunction, it was unnecessary to extend it further. He did not address the issue of violence in the antiabortion movement or the petitioners' acceptance of the trial court's finding of facts.

Impact

No contemporary issue is more contentious than abortion. In recent years there have been acts of vandalism, arson, invasions, and shootings (some fatal) by radical antiabortion activists. The Court apparently made its decision with this in mind. Some decried the decision; in a *Connecticut Law Tribune* article, Bruce Fein called it a "blunderbuss attack on free speech." In the *Maryland Journal of Contemporary Issues* Heather O'Connor called it "a step in the right direction," but said that other

precedents existed to support further action: "The Court had authority and opportunity to go further in protecting states' interests and the safety of women . . . The Court failed to do so, allowing the violence . . . to continue." The Court used the "*Madsen* test" in *Schenck v. Pro-Choice Network of Western New York* (1997) to limit injunctive restrictions on abortion protesters. So while upholding some protection for those seeking abortions and the clinics that perform them, *Madsen* is likely to be used to protect the protesters' rights.

Related Cases

Carey v. Brown, 447 U.S. 455 (1980).

United States Postal Service v. Council of Greenburgh Civic Associations, 453 U.S. 114 (1981).

International Society for Krishna Consciousness v. Lee, 505 U.S. 672 (1992).

Operation Rescue v. Women's Health Center, 626 So. 2d 664 (Fla. 1993).

Schenck v. Pro-Choice Network of Western New York, 519 U.S. 357 (1997).

Bibliography and Further Reading

Chemerinsky, Erwin. "Court Allows 'In Your Face' Abortion Protests." *Trial*, May 1997, p. 82.

Chemerinsky, Erwin. "Protecting Abortion Protesters and Patients." *Trial*, December 1994, p. 62.

Cole, David. "The Perils of Pragmatism." *The Recorder*, 29 August 1994.

Fein, Bruce. "Should Free Speech Depend on Who's Using the Bullhorn?" *Connecticut Law Tribune*, 18 July 1994.

Lenz, Timothy O. "The Restriction of Abortion Protesters in Florida." *Albany Law Review*, Vol. 59, 1996.

O'Connor, Heather. "First Amendment Rights Versus the Right to Choice: Madsen v. Women's Health Center, Inc." *Maryland Journal of Contemporary Issues*, spring/summer 1996.

Tepper, Arianne K. "In Your F.A.C.E: Federal Enforcement of The Freedom of Access to Clinic Entrances Act of 1993." *17 Pace Law Review*, 489, Spring 1997.

NORMAN-BLOODSAW V. LAWRENCE BERKELEY LABORATORY

Legal Citation: 135 F.3d 1260 (1998)

Appellant
Marya S. Norman-Bloodsaw, Vertis B. Ellis, and six other individuals

Appellee
Lawrence Berkeley Laboratory, Regents of the University of California, U.S. Department of Energy, and others

Appellant's Claim
That a public employer conducting medical tests on its employees to determine intimate medical conditions without their knowledge or consent violates the employees' constitutional right to privacy.

Chief Lawyer for Appellant
William C. McNeill III

Chief Lawyer for Appellee
Douglas H. Barton

Justices for the Court
Stephen Reinhardt (writing for the court), Thomas G. Nelson, Michael Daly Hawkins

Justices Dissenting
None

Place
San Francisco, California

Date of Decision
3 February 1998

Decision
The appeals court reversed a district court's ruling by finding the secret medical tests violated Title VII of the 1964 Civil Rights Act and state and federal constitutional privacy guarantees.

Significance
The ruling created a significant legal precedent protecting employees or job applicants from medical testing without their prior knowledge and approval. In an era of rising health care costs and insurance liabilities, more employers sought means for reducing their financial risks. The court reasserted an individual's right to privacy and freedom from discrimination based on a person's medical condition that may have no bearing on their ability to perform the work. Concerns over the privacy of genetic information led a dozen states to pass legislation prohibiting genetic discrimination in the workplace.

Developments in the late twentieth century in genetics, including genetic screening, and electronic data keeping introduced substantial new legal questions. Genetic screening is the examination of a person's genetic makeup to determine their tendency to acquire or carry certain diseases. Such screening first began to attract significant state and federal legislative action in the seventies. The Genetic Diseases Act of 1976 allowed for use of public funds to support voluntary genetic screening programs. States passed laws requiring the screening of school children for sickle cell anemia as well as voluntary premarital testing. Concerns mounted that genetic screening could lead to discrimination as certain genetic diseases were more prevalent in some ethnic groups than others, as well as gender differences. For this reason, many believed any form of compulsory testing would violate the search and seizure clause of the Fourth Amendment and the 1964 Civil Rights Act among other legal concerns. Supporters of the use of screening claimed legitimate state interests were involved in promoting quality of life of its citizens and minimizing drains on public funds.

Medical Secrecy in California

The Ernest Orlando Lawrence Berkeley National Laboratory is the oldest national research laboratory in the United States. Operated by the University of California in coordination with the U.S. Department of Energy, the laboratory conducted unclassified research on human genetic makeup, breast cancer, astrophysics, and nuclear science, among other subjects. For years hundreds of employees gave blood samples as part of routine tests for hiring and subsequently during employment. One such employee, Vertis Ellis, worked as an administrative assistant for Lawrence.

Late in 1994, Ellis opened the large envelope containing her medical records from work. Inside she found indications that the laboratory had conducted syphilis tests on her without her knowledge on several occasions during company exams over the previous 29 years. Upon inquiry to Lawrence, laboratory officials acknowledged testing the blood and urine samples of its employees for syphilis, the sickle cell trait, and pregnancy under the guidance and approval of the U.S.

Department of Energy but claimed most such testing had ceased. Neither Ellis nor others had either given authorization for such tests or received results.

In September of 1995, Marya S. Norman-Bloodsaw, Ellis, and six other employees filed a class action suit in district court on behalf of all past and present Lawrence employees subjected to such medical tests. Among those named in the suit were the laboratory, the Secretary of the U.S. Department of Energy, and the Regents of the University of California. The employees claimed that the testing of their blood and urine samples for syphilis, sickle cell trait, and pregnancy occurred without their knowledge or consent, and without any later notification that the tests had been conducted. The employees alleged several legal violations by Lawrence. First, they charged that Lawrence failed to provide adequate safeguards to protect the test results from being known to others. Secondly, that only black employees were tested for sickle cell trait and only female employees tested for pregnancy violated Title VII of the Civil Rights Act of 1964. Thirdly, the employees argued the testing violated the American with Disabilities Act (ADA) since the tests were neither job-related nor consistent with a business need. Most important constitutionally, the testing, collecting and maintaining the results of the testing, and failing to provide adequate safeguards against disclosure of the results violated their right to privacy under the federal and California constitutions.

In September of 1996, the district court in San Francisco ruled the statute of limitations negated all claims. The court also disagreed with the employees' arguments on their merits, including the lack of demonstration of harm under Title VII. Although the government had failed to identify any "undisputed legitimate governmental purpose" for the three tests, any intrusions resulting from the testing were only minimal. This finding was based on strong similarity between the subjects covered by the medical questionnaire and the three tests, and comparison to the "overall intrusiveness" of "a full-scale physical examination." The federal district judge found that the employees had no proof of any connection between the discontinued secret tests and their employment conditions, either in the past or future.

In dismissing the case, Judge Vaughn Walker concluded, "The three tests in question were administered as part of a comprehensive medical examination to which plaintiffs had consented." The employees next appealed to the U.S. Court of Appeals for the Ninth Circuit in San Francisco.

A Right to Personal Privacy

In reviewing the case, the appeals court considered the statute of limitations issue first. The district court had ruled that the limitations period began at the time the blood and urine samples were taken. However, Judge Stephen Reinhardt, writing for the court, asserted that the general federal rule for initiating limitation periods was based on when an individual becomes aware of an injury. Reinhardt disagreed with the district court's finding that the employees had reason to know of the actual nature of the medical tests simply by submitting to the examinations. Reinhardt reversed the district court's limitations finding.

Reinhardt then examined the issue of due process right to privacy under the U.S. Constitution. Reinhardt applied the "balancing test" to the facts of the case. He balanced the government's interest in conducting these particular tests against the employees' expectations of privacy. Reinhardt found no state compelling interests in tests which had little bearing on a person's ability to perform the work. Reinhardt also observed that the privacy interest in avoiding disclosure of personal information clearly included confidentiality of a person's medical record. Thus, Reinhardt reversed the district court decision to dismiss the claims on the ground that any privacy violation was minimal. Reinhardt held the tests were indeed search violations of the Fourth Amendment.

Reinhardt also examined the right to privacy issue under Article I of the California Constitution. Three elements must be established to bring a case under the California Constitution. These elements are presence of a legally protected privacy interest, a reasonable expectation of privacy by the individual under the circumstances, and conduct by the defendant amounting to a "serious invasion " of the protected privacy. The district court had previously ruled employees "could not proceed" with this allegation because of "undisputed facts" that the employees had completed a medical questionnaire at the time of the exam, consented to the pre-placement examination, and voluntarily given of blood and urine samples. Reinhardt ruled that the district court undervalued the seriousness of the tests and hence erred in dismissing the state constitutional privacy claim.

Reinhardt then considered the allegation of a Title VII violation of the Civil Rights Act of 1964. Reinhardt wrote that Title VII prohibits discrimination not only in the "terms" and "conditions" of ongoing employment, but also in the "terms" and "conditions" under which individuals may obtain employment. In this case, the laboratory required black employees to unknowingly undergo a test for the sickle cell trait and for women, to unknowingly undergo a pregnancy test. Reinhardt found that the employment of women and blacks at Lawrence Berkeley Laboratory was conditioned on unconstitutional invasions of privacy to which others were not subjected a violation of Title VII on the basis of race and sex discrimination.

On one point Reinhardt did agree with the district court. Reinhardt ruled that only those medical examinations occurring "on or after January 26, 1992," could potentially be violating the Americans with Disabilities Act (ADA). On that date the ADA had become applicable to public entities. Only two employees involved in the case had undergone testing after that date. Reinhardt held that the Americans with Disabilities Act did not limit the scope of such examinations to matters that are "job-related and consistent with business necessity." Therefore, dismissal of the ADA claims were proper.

Though Lawrence contended the case was moot because the issues involved were no longer occurring and the employees lacked any further interest in the tests outcome, Reinhardt asserted that mere voluntary discontinuation of allegedly illegal activity could not moot a case. Lawrence had even stated it might resume testing for intimate medical conditions at some time though not offering a reason why. Reinhardt concluded that a reasonable possibility existed that Lawrence would again conduct undisclosed medical testing of its employees for intimate medical conditions. Reinhardt granted an injunctive relief to the employees.

Impact

The ruling reinstated the Lawrence employees' case to proceed with their discrimination claims. The employees sought to require the laboratory to notify all persons that were tested, destroy the test results, and provide explanations of how the medical information was used. The U.S. Department of Energy soon after the decision changed its policies requiring that clear communication occur with all employees concerning the nature of medical exams used and their results.

The *Norman-Bloodsaw* decision ventured into a new area of law by recognizing a constitutional right to genetic privacy in the workplace. Previous cases defining the privacy interest in medical information had typically involved disclosures to "third" parties. However, this case dealt with the collection of information by unlawful means. An employer could not conduct tests for genetic information on its employees without their consent. The court indicated that some types of medical information were more private than others and that

genetic information should be treated differently from other forms of medical information. The ruling also broadened the concept of harm to the employee that was necessary to attain legal standing to file a lawsuit. The "stigmatizing" of the workplace through violation of an employees' constitutional rights was sufficient harm in itself. Previous rulings had focused on unauthorized release of such information to third parties.

Many feared genetic testing was increasingly becoming a condition of employment in corporate America. Interest in reducing health costs of the companies and illness-related absenteeism were the common objectives. By late 1998, denial of employment to individuals with certain genetic traits was legal in all but 12 states. Federal legislation prohibiting such genetic discrimination was stalled in Congress. Meanwhile, as the 20th century came to a close, the project to decode the human genetic structure neared completion. Genetic testing would be that much more informative. Fears mounted that widespread availability of personal genetic information would lead to insurance coverage and creditor issues. Organizations including the Council for Responsible Genetics and the National Breast Cancer Coalition increased their vigilance.

Related Cases

Schowengerdt v. General Dynamics Corp., 823 F.2d 1328 (9th Cir. 1987).
Yin v. California, 95 F.3d 864 (9th Cir. 1996).
Loder v. City of Glendale, 927 P.2d 1200 (Cal 1997).

Bibliography and Further Reading

Agre, Philip E., and Marc Rotenberg, eds. *Technology and Privacy: The New Landscape.* Cambridge, MA: MIT Press, 1997.

Boling, Patricia. *Privacy and the Politics of Intimate Life.* Ithaca, NY: Cornell University Press, 1996.

Rothstein, Mark A., ed. *Genetic Secrets: Protecting Privacy and Confidentiality in the Genetic Era.* New Haven, CT: Yale University Press, 1997.

Smith, Janna Malamud. *Private Matters: In Defense of the Personal Life.* Reading, MA: Addison-Wesley Pub., 1997.

RIGHT TO BEAR ARMS

Hot Topic

A mere 27 words in the Second Amendment of the Bill of Rights somehow manage to incite some of the most heated and occasionally violent debates over two centuries after its drafting. The Second Amendment provides: "A well regulated Militia, being necessary to the security of a free State, the right of the people to keep and bear Arms, shall not be infringed." Widely divergent contentions emerge from this sentence. Some believe that the Second Amendment provides an absolute, personal right to bear arms. Others argue that any right to bear arms is subordinate to ensuring public safety. A third argument contends that the Second Amendment simply restricts the powers of the national government and grants the states the right to maintain a militia separate from a federally-controlled army.

Most of the controversy surrounding the Second Amendment has arisen in the second half of the twentieth century, although that controversy has been played out much more frequently in the press than in the courts. The Second Amendment has been interpreted in a relatively small number of cases. Nevertheless, the United States Supreme Court has been virtually unwavering in its reading of the amendment. In essence, the Supreme Court historically has defined the Second Amendment as giving states the right to maintain a militia separate from a federally controlled army. The Court has never recognized an individual's unconditional right to own firearms, nor has any lower court so ruled. Courts have consistently held that the state and federal governments may lawfully regulate the sale, transfer, receipt, possession, and use of certain categories of firearms, as well as mandate who may and may not own a gun. Although the National Rifle Association (NRA) has repeatedly referred to a constitutional right to gun ownership, one has never been recognized, nor do the courts show the slightest indication of moving toward such a recognition.

History of the Right to Bear Arms

The first recorded instance of gun control was in England in 1671, a few years following its Civil War. The Game Act restricted hunting and gun ownership among the peasants while permitting the wealthy to maintain their weaponry and to own hunting lands. Persons below a certain income level were not allowed to keep weapons, even for self-defense. A few years later the English Bill of Rights included a right of Protestants to bear arms, and also denounced the abuse of standing armies. The colonists coming to America brought with them the English tradition of using arms for self-preservation and defense.

Self-preservation and defense quickly became crucial to the colonists. Firearms were needed for protection of life, and for sustenance. Colonists were imbued with a fear of standing armies because of the Boston Massacre, the seizure of arms and militia at Lexington, and other Revolutionary War incidents. Clearly, the Revolutionary War would have had a different outcome had individual citizens not taken up arms to fight the Red Coats.

Reflecting the times in which it was written, the Virginia Constitution, adopted in June of 1776, provided that "a well-regulated Militia, composed of the body of the people, trained to arms, is the proper, natural, and safe defence of a free State." It also acknowledged the danger of a standing army. Other colonies enacted similar provisions. Some constitutions from the late eighteenth century spoke of a "right" to bear arms, while others denominated it a "duty." This fear of standing armies and a tyrannical central government, as well as the fact that individual armed citizens were crucial to the American's victory in the Revolutionary War, provided the backdrop to the drafting of the Second Amendment.

Interpretation of the Second Amendment

The historical context of an amendment illuminates its text, but in the final analysis, its meaning is determined only upon examination of the specific words in the amendment. Only the Second Amendment starts with a "mini-preamble." For years scholars have debated as to whether "militia" was intended to be the subject of the sentence, and whether the comma before "shall" was grammatically necessary, or if it was a mistake.

The Second Amendment and a right to bear arms were first addressed in the 1875 case of *United States v. Cruikshank*. The case dealt with some Ku Klux Klansman convicted of conspiring to deprive two African Americans of the right to assemble, the right of free speech, and the right to keep and bear arms. The Supreme Court held that "bearing arms for a lawful purpose is not a right guaranteed by the Constitution . . . The Second Amendment declares that it shall not be infringed; but this . . . means no more than it shall not be infringed by Congress. This [amendment] has no other effect than to restrict the powers of the national government." *Cruikshank* began the precedent that continues to the present day: unlike most of the rest of the Bill of Rights, the Second Amendment has never been incorporated into the Fourteenth Amendment (it pertains only to federal power and has never been made applicable to the states through the Due Process Clause of the Fourteenth Amendment).

The 1886 case of *Presser v. Illinois* involved a challenge to an Illinois law barring paramilitary organizations from drilling or parading without a license. Although stating that "it is undoubtedly true that all citizens capable of bearing arms constitute the reserved military force or reserve militia of the United States," and "states . . . cannot prohibit the people form keeping and bearing arms," the Supreme Court found that the challenged activity "is not an attribute of national citizenship." *Presser* confirmed that the Second Amendment's meaning is to prevent the federal government from infringing upon the right of the state to form militias, and unequivocally rejected the idea of a citizen-created militia. Two more late-nineteenth century cases, *Miller v. Texas,* and *Robertson v. Baldwin,* essentially reiterated these points.

Although debate surges unabated around the right to bear arms, the Supreme Court has only once addressed the issue in the twentieth century. In *United States v. Miller* (1934), two men challenged their convictions for transporting an unregistered 12-gauge sawed off shot gun across state lines, a violation of the National Firearms Act. The Supreme Court ruled that the Second Amendment does not guarantee the right to keep and bear a double-barreled, sawed off, 12-gauge shot gun, because its possession did not have "some reasonable relationship to the preservation or efficiency of a well-regulated militia."

The Supreme Court has shown no indication of revisiting these early cases, and the lower courts have generally followed precedent. In one widely-publicized case in the United States Court of Appeals, *Quilici v. Village of Morton Grove* (1982), a town's ban of handguns was found to be constitutional. The Supreme Court declined to accept an appeal of the case.

Gun Control Legislation

It is impossible to determine the number of firearms in the United States because many guns are unregistered. Nevertheless, the Bureau of Alcohol, Tobacco, and Firearms (ATF) estimated that private citizens owned more than 220 million firearms by 1995. Depending on where one lives, a person may only be forbidden from carrying a concealed handgun, or may be forbidden from owning a handgun at all.

Congressional power to regulate firearms stems from the Commerce Clause of the Constitution. The Commerce Clause empowers the federal government to regulate commercial activity between the states and commerce with foreign countries. Generally speaking, states and the federal government have successfully (1) denied certain individuals, i.e., convicted felons and the mentally incompetent, the right to own firearms; (2) required licenses and made owners pass a firearms safety examination (3) made illegal the possession and transfer of certain firearms; and (4) required registration for certain classes of firearms.

The National Firearms Act of 1934, still in effect today, was passed to hinder acquisition of certain dangerous weapons, including machine guns and sawed-off shotguns. Key components of this legislation included heavy taxes on the manufacturing and distribution of firearms and required registration throughout production, distribution, and sale. The Federal Firearms Act of 1938 provided for federal licensing of firearms dealers, regulated firearm transportation across state lines by dealers, outlawed the transportation of stolen guns with the manufacturer's mark eradicated or changed, and outlawed firearms from being sent to fugitives, indicted defendants or convicted felons.

The National Firearms Act was later amended significantly by the Gun Control Act of 1968, passed in the wake of the assassination of President John F. Kennedy and others. The Gun Control Act also repealed the 1938 Federal Firearms Act. and replaced it with increased federal control. The Gun Control Act contained far-reaching provisions, pertaining to licensing, sales, buyer requirements, and the importation of non-sporting guns. For all its measures, the law did not forbid the importation of unassembled weapon parts. Gun control advocates were not satisfied and called for stricter laws; owners and dealers decried the Gun Control Act as burdensome and infringing on personal rights. Finally in 1986, the Firearm Owners' Protection Act (also known as the Gun Control Act of 1986) was passed, amending the 1968 law. The 1986 Gun Control Act imposed some new restrictions and extended prior ones, but in some instances it eased requirements of the 1968 law. Machine guns made after 19 May 1986 were banned from sale by the 1986 Firearms Owners Protection Act.

Hijacking fears prompted plastic guns or other undetectable firearms to be targeted and banned from manufacture, sale, import, transfer or possession by the Undetectable Firearms Act of 1988. Also in 1988, Congress required look-alike toy guns to have a "blaze orange plug inserted in the barrel." In late 1994, following two separate police shootings of youths with toy guns, three large toy retailers, including Toys 'R' Us, Inc., decided to stop selling look-alike guns. The Crime Act of 1994 banned the sale and possession of 19 assault-type firearms and certain high-capacity ammunition magazines.

The Gun-Free School Zone Act, passed in 1990, outlawed the knowing possession of firearms in school zones, and made it a crime to carry unloaded firearms within 1,000 feet of the grounds of any public or private school. This law was later held unconstitutional in 1995, in *United States v. Lopez*. The decision was based upon a determination that the law did not establish an adequate connection between commerce and gun-free school zones, as required by the Commerce Clause.

The 1982 assassination attempt on President Ronald Reagan eventually resulted in the Brady Handgun Violence Prevention Act of 1993. The Brady Bill imposed a five-day waiting period before a handgun may be taken home by a buyer. The law set a timetable for the expiration of the waiting period and provided for replacement of a computerized background checks. The law also mandated that local chief law enforcement officers conduct background checks on prospective handgun purchasers buying from federally licensed dealers. This part of the law was struck down by the Supreme Court in 1997 in *Printz v. United States* as unconstitutional under the Tenth Amendment.

Bibliography and Further Reading

Carter, Gregg Lee. *The Gun Control Movement*. New York: Twayne Publishers, and Prentice Hall International. 1997.

Gun Control—Restricting Rights or Protecting People? Wylie, TX: Information Plus. 1997.

Spitzer, Robert J. *The Politics of Gun Control*. Chatham, NJ: Chatham House Publishers, Inc. 1995.

Tribe, Laurence H. & Michael C. Dorf. *On Reading the Constitution*. Cambridge, MA and London, England: Harvard University Press (1991).

West's Encyclopedia of American Law (various sections). St. Paul, MN: West Publishing Co. 1997.

UNITED STATES V. MILLER

Legal Citation: 307 U.S. 174 (1939)

Appellant
United States

Appellees
Jack Miller, Frank Layton

Appellant's Claim
That the Western Arkansas District Court had erred in dismissing indictments against the appellees for violating the National Firearms Act of 1934.

Chief Lawyer for Appellant
Gordon Dean

Chief Lawyer for Appellees
None

Justices for the Court
Hugo Lafayette Black, Pierce Butler, Felix Frankfurter, Charles Evans Hughes, James Clark McReynolds (writing for the Court), Stanley Forman Reed, Owen Josephus Roberts, Harlan Fiske Stone

Justices Dissenting
None (William O. Douglas did not participate)

Place
Washington, D.C.

Date of Decision
15 May 1939

Decision
In favor of the government's appeal, reversing the lower court's dismissal of charges against Miller and Layton.

Significance
By declaring that a sawed-off shotgun had no reasonable relation to the terms of the Second Amendment, the Court set an important precedent for later cases involving firearms possession.

Sawed-Off Shotguns & The Second Amendment

When Jack Miller and Frank Layton were stopped in Siloam Springs, Arkansas, police found a double-barreled, 12-gauge shotgun in their possession. The gun, bought by the men in Claremore, Oklahoma, earned them an arrest for violating the National Firearms Act of 1934.

Prohibition ended in 1933, but memories of over a decade of gangland mayhem were still fresh a year later. Bank robberies and other violent federal offenses were still a concern when Congress passed The National Firearms Act on 23 June 1934. The law focused on machine guns, silencers, and all rifles and shotguns with barrels shorter than 18 inches. To sell or otherwise "transfer" such a weapon, the owner or manufacturer was required to register it and pay a $200 tax, in return for regulatory tax stamps. In effect, the law prohibited the interstate transportation of such weapons and their subsequent ownership. Penalties for violating the Firearms Act included a $2,000 fine and/or five years imprisonment.

Miller and Layton's shotgun had been sawed off. They were charged with transporting a shotgun whose barrel was less than 18 inches long across state lines without proper registration and without a federal tax stamp. Attorneys for the men filed a motion for demurrer, asking that the indictment be dismissed. The lawyers argued that the law under which Miller and Layton had been indicted violated their Second Amendment right to bear arms. The demurrer also alleged that the tax clauses of the Firearms Act were not genuine revenue collecting measures, but an attempt by the federal government to usurp police powers reserved to the states. The Western Arkansas District Court agreed. The indictments were dismissed and the two men were freed.

Preserving A Well-Regulated Militia

Federal authorities were unwilling to ignore this challenge, even though Miller and Layton quickly disappeared after gaining their freedom. The government's appeal of the decision to quash the indictment was

The Brady Bill

On 30 March 1981, would-be assassin John David Hinckley fired on President Ronald Reagan as he left a Washington, D.C. hotel. Reagan was not critically wounded; but his press secretary, James Brady, was paralyzed for life. As a result, Brady and his wife Sarah became active in the campaign for handgun control legislation, and because Brady was a former member of a conservative administration, the couple were particularly popular spokespeople for gun control—typically a liberal issue.

Congress, on 30 November 1993, passed the Brady Handgun Violence Prevention Act, popularly known as the "Brady Bill." The Brady Bill's provisions included a five-day waiting period for persons buying firearms; background checks on prospective firearms purchasers;

up to $200 million a year to upgrade states' criminal recordkeeping; federal court prosecution for gun theft; and a hike in fees for federal firearms licenses from $30 to $200.

Despite these measures, as *US News* reported, "If there's one thing supporters and opponents of the Brady Bill agree on . . . it is that the measure . . . won't stop the majority of criminals from obtaining firearms." Only 17 percent of firearms used by criminals, according to the magazine, are obtained through lawful means.

Source(s): Witkin, Gordon. "Gun Control's Limits." *US News & World Report*, 6 December 1993.

argued before the Supreme Court on 30 March 1939. Since Miller and Layton were not available despite being named as the appellees, only the government argument was heard. The Court quickly returned a decision in favor of the government on 15 May, agreeing unanimously that the Firearms Act neither violated the Second Amendment nor was an unconstitutional infringement of states' rights.

Like the defendants' lawyers and the Arkansas court, the Supreme Court decision focused on the Second Amendment, which states:

A well regulated militia, being necessary to the security of a free State, the right of the people to keep and bear Arms, shall not be infringed.

In his written decision, Justice McReynolds sketched the origins and importance of self-armed citizen militias in the early history of the American colonies. In the present case, however, McReynolds and other members of the Court rejected the idea that weapons named in the Firearms Act had any valid relation to the maintenance of military protection.

"In the absence of any evidence tending to show that the possession or use of a 'shotgun having a barrel of less than eighteen inches in length' at this time has some reasonable relationship to the preservation or efficiency of a well-regulated militia, we cannot say that the Second Amendment guarantees the right to keep and bear such an instrument," wrote McReynolds.

By this standard, the Court found that Congress had not violated the Second Amendment by passing the Firearms Act. "Certainly," McReynolds added, "it is not within judicial notice that this weapon is any part of the ordinary military equipment or that its use could contribute to the common defense."

The Court's decision that the charges against Miller and Layton were incorrectly dismissed had no effect on the indicted men, both of whom vanished long before their names appeared on the national legal battlefield. In a larger sense, however, the *Miller* decision became a benchmark for lower courts in deciding cases dealing with gun possession. By narrowly interpreting the Second Amendment right to gun ownership according to its relationship to a "well-regulated militia," the Court, for the first time, provided a framework within which regulatory firearms legislation could be drafted.

Related Cases
United States v. Smith, 341 F.Supp. 687 (1972).

Bibliography and Further Reading
Biskupic, Joan and Elder Witt. *Congressional Quarterly's Guide to the U.S. Supreme Court*, 3rd ed. Washington, DC: Congressional Quarterly, Inc., 1996.

McLenden, Regina. "Limits On the Federal Power To Regulate Firearms." *Public Law Research Institute, University of California, Hastings College of Law*. fall, 1994.

"Supreme Court Bars Sawed-Off Shotgun." *New York Times*, 16 May 1939, p. 15.

UNITED STATES V. LOPEZ

Legal Citation: 514 U.S. 549 (1995)

Petitioner
United States

Respondent
Alfonso Lopez, Jr.

Petitioner's Claim
That it was left to Congress to decide what seriously affects interstate commerce and Congress found the Gun-Free School Zone Act constitutional under the Commerce Clause.

Justices for the Court
Anthony M. Kennedy, Sandra Day O'Connor, William H. Rehnquist (writing for the Court), Antonin Scalia, Clarence Thomas

Justices Dissenting
Stephen Breyer, Ruth Bader Ginsburg, David H. Souter, John Paul Stevens

Place
Washington, D.C.

Date of Decision
26 April 1995

Decision
The Court stated that Congress had overstepped the bounds of the Commerce Clause; the act was deemed unconstitutional.

Significance
The decision dealt a large blow to Congress' attempts to cut down on school-related violence and improve the safety ratings of America's schools. However, the Violent Crime Control and Law Enforcement Act of 1994 was able to fill in some of the gaps left open by the striking down of the Gun-Free School Zone Act.

Alfonso Lopez, a 12th grade high school student, brought a concealed handgun and five rounds of ammunition into his high school in San Antonio, Texas. His weapon was discovered and he was charged under Texas law with firearm possession on school premises. The next day, the state charges were dismissed after he was charged with violating the Gun-Free School Zones Act of 1990, a federal law which forbids a person to possess a firearm in a place that he or she knows is a school zone. Lopez moved to have the charges dismissed on the grounds that the law was unconstitutional and Congress did not have the power to legislate with respect to public schools. The district court denied this motion and Lopez was found guilty and was sentenced to six months imprisonment, two years of supervised release, and a $50.00 fine.

Court of Appeals Ruling

Lopez appealed this decision to the Fifth Circuit Court of Appeals, again on the grounds that Congress had no constitutional authority to pass the Gun-Free School Zones Act. Attorneys for the United States government contended that the law was an appropriate use of power under the interstate Commerce Clause. The circuit court reversed the district court's decision and agreed with Lopez that the Gun-Free School Zones Act was invalid because it was beyond Congress' power under the Commerce Clause. The Court found the federal law unconstitutional.

Supreme Court Ruling

The only question before the U.S. Supreme Court was whether Congress had power to pass the Gun-Free School Zones Act of 1990. In a 5-4 decision, the U.S. Supreme Court affirmed the decision of the court of appeals, holding that the Gun-Free School Zones Act exceeds Congress' Commerce Clause authority. Justice Rehnquist delivered the opinion and Justices Stevens, Breyer, Souter and Ginsburg dissented.

The Court reasoned that possession of a gun in a local school zone is not an economic activity that might, through repetition elsewhere, have an impact on interstate commerce. The act was seen as a criminal

Federal Attempts at Gun Control—A Good Thing?

After the Supreme Court overturned the Gun Free School Zone Act of 1990 in *Lopez,* reactions were mixed. A comparison of articles that appeared in the *New Republic* and *USA Today,* for instance, might leave one wondering if the commentators were even talking about the same case. "The *Lopez* decision is good news for liberal constitutionalists," wrote the *New Republic*'s Jeffrey Rosen, who criticized "The mindless impulse to federalize crimes that the states are prosecuting perfectly well on their own . . . If any law falls outside the limits of Congress's power to 'regulate Commerce . . .' the Gun Free School Zones Act is it." To Herb Kohl in *USA Today,* however, "The Supreme Court's 5-4 decision . . . cripples Congress's power to fight violence in

our schools and raises questions about the federal government's ability to protect its citizens."

Meanwhile, the passage of the Violent Crime Control and Law Enforcement Act of 1994 gave pundits much more to debate with regard to the federal government's attempts to fight crime at the state and local level.

Source(s) Kohl, Herb. "Keep Schools Gun Free." *USA Today,* 3 May 1995.

Rosen, Jeffrey. "Fed Up: Gun Free School Zones Act of 1990 Justifiably Overturned by U.S. Supreme Court." *New Republic,* 22 May 1995.

statute, having nothing to do with commerce or economic activity, no matter how broad the definition of that term. The possession of a gun in a local school zone is not an essential part of larger economic activity. In addition, they claimed that Congress failed to sufficiently show the link between gun violence in schools with interstate commerce.

Rehnquist made the argument on the basis of history, referring to the fact that the Constitution "created a federal government of limited and enumerated powers." The Court found that some laws are too far removed from the powers granted to Congress to be able to be considered constitutional. Rehnquist also indicated that, although there had been some unclear rulings in the past on the nature of the Commerce Clause, the Gun-Free School Zones Act had no "substantial" impact on commerce.

Dissenting Opinion

Justice Breyer sought to explain Congress' rational basis for a connection between gun-related violence in schools and interstate commerce. His opinion held that such violence "significantly undermines the quality of education that is critical to economic prosperity" and that teaching and learning are linked to commerce, which is threatened by the presence of guns in schools.

Implications

The fact that the Supreme Court upheld the Fifth Circuit Court of Appeals' decision does not mean that gun laws will be more difficult to enforce; nor does it mean that guns should be allowed near schools. The main question in this case is not about guns or schools, but about how much authority the Congress has over issues usually legislated by the state. It is a question of the division of power between the federal and state governments, not of crime prevention.

The reason that the Gun-Free School Zone law was tried under the Commerce Clause is a traditionally broad interpretation of the clause to allow federal regulation of activities based on their relation to interstate commerce. Since guns often travel through more than one state in the path from manufacturer to purchaser, possession of guns may fall under this clause.

Some say that this ruling may simply signal to Congress that it must more carefully and explicitly detail how its legislation pertains to interstate commerce. Yet the impact of this decision could also be far reaching, affecting such laws as state environmental laws among others. Some commentators interpret this ruling to mean that Congress will not have the power to legislate with respect to local and non-economic activities. "At the very least, *Lopez* has introduced an element of instability in an area of the law previously considered 'settled.' Commerce Clause cases clearly merit close watching in the future."

Related Cases

Wickard v. Filburn, 317 U.S. 111 (1942).
Heart of Atlanta Motel v. United States, 379 U.S. 241 (1964).
Katzenbach v. McClung, 379 U.S. 294 (1964).
Maryland v. Wirtz, 392 U.S. 183 (1968).
League of Cities v. Usery, 426 U.S. 183 (1968).
Garcia v. San Antonio Metropolitan Transit Authority, 469 U.S. 528 (1985).
Gregory v. Ashcroft, 501 U.S. 452 (1991).

Bibliography and Further Reading

Aalberts, Robert. "Regulation of the Environment: The Future Remains with the Federal Government." *Real Estate Law Journal,* Vol. 24, no. 3, pp. iii-iv.

Epstein, Lee, and Thomas G. Walker. *Constitutional Law for a Changing America: A Short Course.* Washington, DC: Congressional Quarterly Press, 1996.

Epstein, Lee, and Thomas, G. Walker. *Constitutional Law for a Changing America: Institutional Powers and Constraints,* 1994-1995 Supplement. Washington, DC: Congressional Quarterly Press, 1995.

Katzmann, Robert A. "Guns, the Commerce Clause, and the Court." *Brookings Review,* Vol. 13, no. 3, summer, 1995, p. 52.

Legal Information Institute and Project Hermes. Syllabus, United States v. Lopez. Website: http://supct.law.cornell.edu/supct. November, 1997.

McClendon, Regina. "Limits on the Federal Power to Regulate Firearms." *Public Law Research Institute Report,* fall, 1994.

Sowell, Thomas. "Is the Constitution Superfluous?" *Forbes,* Vol. 155, no. 12, 5 June 1995, p. 61.

MUSCARELLO V. UNITED STATES

Legal Citation: 118 S.Ct. 1911 (1998)

Petitioners
Frank J. Muscarello, Donald Cleveland and Enrique Gray-Santana

Respondent
United States

Petitioners' Claim
That the United States violated the Second Amendment's right to bear arms by a broad interpretation of U.S. legal codes.

Chief Lawyers for Petitioners
Robert H. Klonoff and Norman S. Zallkind

Chief Lawyer for Respondent
James A. Feldman

Justices for the Court
Stephen Breyer (writing for the Court), Anthony M. Kennedy, Sandra Day O'Connor, John Paul Stevens, Clarence Thomas

Justices Dissenting
Ruth Bader Ginsburg, William H. Rehnquist, Antonin Scalia, David H. Souter

Place
Washington D.C.

Date of Decision
8 June 1998

Decision
The decision found in favor of the United States by ruling that the phrase "carries a firearm" applies to persons knowingly possessing and conveying firearms in a vehicle, including in a locked glove compartment or car trunk.

Significance
The decision was a rare ruling addressing Second Amendment Right to Bear Arms Clause. By affirming the courts' broad interpretation of firearms restrictions in two criminal cases, the Court strengthened the effectiveness of law enforcement in drug offenses. By the end of the 1990s, local and state governments were forming a united effort in passing more gun-control legislation and addressing the liability of firearms manufacturers and distributors in courts.

Despite extensive debate and legislative action regarding the regulation of firearm use since 1934, little has been resolved concerning the actual meaning of the Second Amendment of the Constitution. The amendment reads, "A well regulated Militia being necessary to the security of a free State, the right of the people to keep and bear Arms shall not be infringed." Some claimed the amendment protects individual rights to possess and transport guns. Others insisted it protected states' authority to maintain militia units which became the National Guard in later years. The Court in *United States v. Miller* (1939) ruled the amendment protected individuals, but only in the context of maintaining a militia capability for the state. The Court ruled in *Miller* that restrictions on sawed-off shotguns did not violate the Second Amendment because they are not the normal type of weapon a militia would need to be effective. The Court found no individual right to bear arms.

By the 1990s according to Department of Justice records over 40 percent of Americans had guns in their homes. Also, over 20,000 federal, state, and local laws regulating firearms were passed under police and commerce governmental powers. Passage of the 1993 Brady Act and 1994 assault weapons ban added further fuel to an already fierce debate over gun control. Then in a stunning reversal from earlier interpretations of broad federal powers under the Commerce Clause of the Constitution, the Court struck down a firearms-related law in *United States v. Lopez* (1995). For similar concerns over the limitation of federal authority, the Court next struck down key provisions of the Brady Act in *Printz v. United States* (1997).

Drugs and Guns

Through the years, Congress created a variable penalty with no set minimum sentence for persons who "transport," or "ship" or "receive," a firearm even when knowing it was to be used to commit a crime. However, a five year mandatory minimum sentence must be imposed upon individuals who "carry" a firearm "during and in relation to" a "drug trafficking crime." The mandatory sentence was intended to apply to anyone bringing a weapon with them, either actually on them or in their car, to the site of a drug sale.

The National Firearms Act

On 15 February 1933, Governor Franklin D. Roosevelt, scheduled to be sworn in as President of the United States on March 4, was speaking at Bay Front Park in Miami when an assassin fired five shots at the bandstand. Police wrestled the would-be assassin, Giuseppe Zingara, to the ground, and later found in his pocket a newspaper clipping regarding the assassination of President William McKinley thirty-two years before. "I'd kill every president," he later told police. But instead of killing the president-elect, his shots fatally wounded Chicago Mayor Anton Cermak.

The incident, along with widespread fears concerning the spread of gangland violence at the behest of Al Capone at others, led Congress to pass one of the nation's first significant pieces of gun-control legislation. This was the National Firearms Act of 1934, which placed taxes on—and therefore required the registration of—machine guns, sawed-off shotguns, and rifles.

A generation after the 1934 National Firearms Act, in 1968, assassination again led to the passage of a gun-control act. In that year, assassins shot and killed civil rights leader Martin Luther King, Jr. and presidential candidate Senator Robert F. Kennedy. As a result, Congress passed the Gun Control Act of 1968.

Source(s): Bacon, Donald C., et al., ed. *The Encyclopedia of the United States Congress.* New York: Simon & Schuster, 1995.

Frank J. Muscarello, unlawfully sold marijuana, which he carried in his truck to the place of sale. Police officers found a handgun locked in the truck's glove compartment. During plea proceedings, Muscarello admitted that he had "carried" the gun "for protection in relation" to the drug offense. Later, he claimed to the contrary, adding that, in any event, his "carrying" of the gun in the glove compartment did not fall within the scope of the word "carries" in the legal codes.

In a separate incident, Donald Cleveland and Enrique Gray-Santana traveled by car to a proposed drug-sale with several guns placed in a bag in the vehicle trunk. Their intent was to steal drugs from the sellers. Federal agents stopped them and in searching the car found the guns and drugs. They were placed under arrest.

All three individuals were later convicted of having "carried" guns as part of committing a drug trafficking offenses and sentenced to prison under the mandatory firearms sentence. In both cases an appeals courts reaffirmed the convictions. Both cases were then appealed to the Supreme Court pursuing the question as to whether the phrase "carries a firearm" applied only to the carrying of firearms on the person or if it also applied to individuals knowingly possessing and conveying firearms in a glove compartment or vehicle trunk. The Court combined the two cases, *Cleveland v. Unites States* with *Muscarello*, for consideration. The Court granted *certiorari* to determine if guns found in locked glove compartments or car trunks should not be considered under the mandatory sentencing or protected under the Second Amendment.

To Carry a Firearm

Muscarello argued the definition adopted by the courts blurred the legal distinction between the terms "carry" and "transport." The latter word was used prevalently elsewhere in "firearms" related legislation and federal regulations. He argued the Court's interpretation of the law would apply as well to passengers on buses, trains, or ships, who stored firearms in checked luggage. Muscarello claimed the law was ambiguous and should not be enforced.

By a narrow majority vote of 5-4, the Court affirmed the lower courts' findings in the First and Fifth Circuits. Justice Stephen Breyer, writing for the majority, wrote that the phrase "carries a firearm" applied to persons knowingly possessing and conveying firearms in a vehicle, including locked compartments of the car. Breyer found many of Muscarello's arguments unconvincing.

Breyer examined the ordinary English meaning of the phrase "carries a firearm." The parties to the case essentially agreed that Congress intended the ordinary meaning of the phrase. Though the word "carry" may have many different meanings, only two were found relevant in this decision. The primary meaning of "carry firearms" is that a person can carry a firearm in a wagon, car, truck, or other vehicle. Breyer noted the modern press, novels and newspapers commonly used "carry" in this way. Breyer wrote that though these examples do not relate directly to carrying guns, nothing is unique distinguishing weapons from other materials.

When the word carry was used to mean "bearing" or "packing," Breyer found the meaning was less clear. "Packing" a gun could apply, even if a person "carrying" the gun was stationary. However, Breyer found no reason to think that Congress intended to limit the word to this narrow meaning. Breyer wrote, "It is difficult to believe, however, that Congress intended to limit the statutory word to this definition imposing special punishment upon the comatose gangster while ignoring drug lords who drive to a sale carrying an arsenal of weapons in their van." It made no sense for a statute to penalize a person who walked with a gun in a bag to the site of a drug sale, but ignored an individual who drove to the same site with a gun in a bag in the car. Breyer asked "How persuasive is a punishment that is without effect until a drug dealer who has brought his gun to a sale (indeed has it available for use) actually takes it from the trunk (or unlocks the glove compartment) of his car?" Breyer found it difficult to hold that those who were prepared to sell drugs by placing guns in their cars were less dangerous, or less deserving of punishment, than those who carried handguns on their person.

Breyer concluded Congress intended the former, more common use of the word. Breyer found it not surprising that the federal circuit courts relied consistently on this common meaning of "carry" and not to the more limited interpretation.

Muscarello argued that the Court's broad interpretation of carry confused the term with transport. However, Breyer responded "that our definition does not equate carry and transport. Carry implies personal agency and some degree of possession, whereas transport does not have such a limited connotation and, in addition, implies the movement of goods in bulk over great distances." Therefore, "transport" was a broad category that included "carry" as well as other activities. Breyer found no violation of the person's right to "bear" arms.

In dissent, Justice Ruth Bader Ginsburg was joined by William Rehnquist, Antonin Scalia, and David Souter. Ginsburg disagreed with the majority's interpretation of "carries." Ginsburg argued the phrase "carrying a firearm" literally meant to bear a weapon in a manner ready for use. Carry commonly implied various meanings, but the meaning embraced by the Court she did not consider a reliable indicator of what Congress intended by "carries a firearm." She also noted discrepancies between the more general federal sentencing guidelines and the mandatory minimum sentence under the drug crime law. In Muscarello's case, the general guidelines recommended a 16 month maximum sentence, dramatically less than the five year minimum sentence. A significant difference when the Court was so divided over the intent of the more stringent code.

Impact

The Court's broad interpretation of a federal law applying a five year mandatory prison sentence to anyone who carries a firearm while trafficking in illegal drugs was welcomed by law enforcement. Public concern over the availability and use of firearms in American society continued following the *Muscarello* decision. Approximately 4 million firearms continued to be sold annually in the nation. Handguns were shown to be a key factor in the rise of violent juvenile crime, even while the overall crime rates declined. New tough measures to confiscate guns and put offenders behind bars who used guns seemed to make a difference in public safety.

By the end of 1998 following court successes against the tobacco industry, many local and state governments began to unite in a campaign to make gun manufacturers and distributors more accountable for the social and financial costs that guns pose. New restrictions were sought on the production and marketing of firearms through the pressing of product liability and public nuisance charges. Actions by the state and local governments rather than Congress avoided issues over limitations of federal power over gun control that 1990s Court rulings were establishing.

Related Cases
United States v. Miller, 301 U.S. 174 (1939).
United States v. Lopez, 514 U.S. 549 (1995).
Bailey v. United States, 516 U.S. 137 (1996).
Printz v. United States, 521 U.S. 98 (1997).
Cleveland v. United States, 106 F.3d 1056 (1998).

Bibliography and Further Reading
Davidson, Osha Gray. *Under Fire: The NRA and the Battle for Gun Control.* Iowa City: University of Iowa Press, 1998.

Kleck, Gary. *Targeting Guns: Firearms and Their Control.* New York: Aldine de Gruyter, 1997.

Lott, John R., Jr. "Gun Shy: Cities Turn from Regulation to Litigation in Their Campaign against Guns." *National Review,* 21 December 1998.

Polsby, Daniel D. *Firearms and Crime.* Oakland, CA: Independent Institute, 1997.

Zimring, Franklin. *American Youth Violence.* Oxford: Oxford University Press, 1998.

SYMBOLIC SPEECH

Symbolic speech is a facet of free speech, which protects a persons conduct or expressions about a particular issue. A large and enduring example of symbolic speech has been the issue of flag burning. Flag burning outrages many Americans. As an extreme form of political dissent, this act strikes at the nation's most cherished symbol and, by extension, its sense of heritage and pride. It is no wonder, then, that protection of the flag has been fiercely enshrined in state and federal law throughout the twentieth century. Protesters who occasionally break these laws do so to protest national policy and values, especially during times of crisis. Whatever their motives, society has been quick to punish them. Yet the thrust of Supreme Court doctrine over the century has favored dissenters, as the Court increasingly ruled that the Constitution protects even those types of protest that deeply offend popular and official beliefs. In doing so, it embraced the idea that certain expressive actions, as well as words, are protected by the First Amendment as forms of so-called symbolic speech. This trend ultimately led to its controversial 1989 ruling that anti-flag burning laws are unconstitutional.

Political dissent is as old as politics itself. In U.S. history, it has been present from the beginning, first in the wellsprings of the Revolutionary War and soon thereafter when disputes between the founders nearly thwarted passage of the Constitution. Ever since, the First Amendment's guarantee of free speech has been repeatedly tested. For those in power, tolerance for unpopular viewpoints has been in short supply. Government crackdowns have recurred many times, from suppression of labor protests in the 1800s, to massive roundups of suspected radicals in both world wars, to the systematic harassment of alleged communists in the Cold War era, and the beatings and jailings of Civil Rights and Vietnam War demonstrators. Dissenters have sometimes found the First Amendment's bold words to be cold comfort.

In this context, political treatment of the flag has had a relatively modern role. Legislation first appeared in the late nineteenth century, during a period of tumult as waves of immigration brought new arrivals. Fearful of change, the expanding nation regarded its flag protectively. In 1878, Congress considered a law proposing a ban on the flag in advertising, ultimately rejecting it because politicians wanted to use it in their own campaigns. Two decades later, protective measures were encouraged by organizations such as the American Flag Association, the Daughters of the American Revolution, and the hate group, the Ku Klux Klan. The actions of such would-be protectors of tradition begged the question: what did the nation's flag need to be protected against?

Pennsylvania's 1898 law making it a crime to damage the flag started a trend that would continue for thirty years. One by one, states added their own anti-desecration laws, as well as others banning the commercial use of the flag or the flying of other flags. In reality, there was no frequent attack upon the American flag, and, in any case, there did not have to be. Influencing these laws were the great upheavals of the early twentieth century. World War I and its aftermath saw the rise of political dissent and a harsh official reaction against it. The Bolshevik revolution in Russia produced the first so-called Red Scare in the United States, as local, state, and federal authorities hunted down, jailed, and deported suspected radicals, deemed "Reds" in a disparaging reference to the color of the Communist flag. During this time, Congress passed an anti-desecration law applying to the District of Columbia.

While lawmakers were busy trying to protect the flag, the Supreme Court gradually moved in another direction. Its earliest opinion gave little sign of how far it would go. *Halter v. Nebraska* (1917) held that a state could ban flag use in advertising, thus stopping a company from displaying the flag on its beer containers. The decision was made on the basis of property rights, however, rather than freedom of speech because, at this point in history, federal courts did not apply a constitutional test for speech rights to state cases. That situation changed only a few years later in *Gitlow v. New York* (1925), the landmark decision which began extending the First Amendment's protections to the states. As subsequent cases took this expansion further, states, accustomed to controlling speech as they saw fit, would face court challenges to their laws.

Perhaps coincidentally, one of the first and most important challenges concerned a state flag law. Dating to 1919, California's ban on displaying a red-colored flag was a product of the Red Scare, when lawmakers were anxious to protect citizens from anarchy and radicalism. One decade later, in 1929, such passions had hardly subsided. The Better American Federation, a citizen group, had convinced local police to raid a summer camp for working class children that was run by several groups, including Communists. Finding a red flag, police arrested staff members and a part-time teacher, Yetta Stromberg, who was later convicted. On appeal to the U.S. Supreme Court in *Stromberg v. California* (1931), she argued that the state law prohibited the symbol of a legal political party. The Court's 7-2 decision in her favor concluded that the statute was vague and interfered with constitutionally-protected speech. Dramatically, the Court for the first time ruled that a state law violated the First Amendment. And it held that a form of non-verbal speech—displaying a flag—enjoyed constitutional protection, too.

By the 1940s, wartime passions brought a new legal reaction. Flag saluting and recitation of the Pledge of Allegiance were seen by many as proof of patriotism. Those who refused to demonstrate their loyalty suffered prosecution and worse. In particular, the Jehovah's Witnesses, maintaining that flag saluting violated their religious beliefs, paid a high price for their children's refusal to take part in public school ceremonies, from school expulsions to physical assaults, burnings of their meeting places, and even threats by authorities to confiscate their children. In 1943, citing speech freedoms rather than religious rights, the Court declared that the purpose of the Bill of Rights was to place the exercise of controversial freedoms "beyond the reach of majorities and officials" (*West Virginia State Board of Education v. Barnette*). That same year, it ruled that Mississippi could not punish students for "refusal to salute, honor, or respect the national and state flags and governments."

Although court rulings embraced speech rights, the period which followed was dark for dissent. Throughout the 1950s and into the 1960s, the Cold War gave rise to anti-Communist hysteria, famously characterized by the witch hunts of Senator Joseph McCarthy and the House Un-American Activities Committee. Yet even as the government was preoccupied with finding so-called subversives, two major social movements were afoot. The Civil Rights movement pressed for equal rights for African Americans, and, by the mid-1960s, growing hostility to the U.S. war in Vietnam brought about outpourings of public protest. Widespread political dissent, on a scale not seen before, became popular. And as anti-war protests increased, the news media frequently carried an image both unfamiliar and disturbing to many Americans—the national flag being burned in demonstrations.

While avoiding any ruling on flag burning itself, the Supreme Court continued to define the limits of sym-

bolic speech. Generally, these decisions expanded protection. As state flag misuse laws failed to survive Court scrutiny, convictions under these laws were overturned. In *Street v. New York* (1968), the Court ruled that contemptuous words spoken about the flag were constitutionally protected. Two 1974 Court decisions set aside convictions for offensiveness that were based on wearing a flag patch on the seat of one's pants and taping a peace symbol onto a flag. Importantly, however, the Court said there were times when symbolic speech was not protected. This recognition emerged in response to anti-war demonstrators burning their military draft cards, the documents which, by law, they were required to carry in preparation for being called upon for military service. In *United States v. O'Brien* (1968), the Court distinguished between speech and the "nonspeech" action involved in this form of protest. When these two types of action were combined, the Court found, "a sufficiently important governmental interest in regulating the nonspeech element can justify limitations on First Amendment freedoms." The government's interest in running the military draft thus outweighed the protesters' speech rights. For future symbolic speech cases, the important test now would be how important an interest the government could assert.

Then, in 1989, came the bombshell. In *Texas v. Johnson*, the Court ruled that flag burning was constitutionally protected. The case grew out of a protest at the 1984 Republican National Convention in Dallas, where Gregory Lee Johnson was arrested for burning the flag and chanting, "America, the red, white, and blue, we spit on you." Convicted under state law, Johnson later won on appeal, after which Texas authorities appealed to the U.S. Supreme Court. The state's law forbade desecration which "the actor knows will seriously offend one or more persons." Texas offered two main justifications for its law: preventing violence and preserving the flag as a national symbol. Neither justification persuaded the Court. Johnson's action was expressive communication, it ruled, and government "may not prohibit the expression of an idea simply because society finds the idea itself offensive or disagreeable." The narrow 5–4 decision reflected a majority made up of liberals and conservatives. Anticipating the controversy it would provoke, Justice William J. Brennan Jr.'s opinion cautioned that people should not be surprised by the decision, as it grew out of the Court's earlier flag rulings. Brennan also explained the principle of liberty at stake: "We do not consecrate the flag by punishing its desecration, for in doing so we dilute the freedom that this cherished emblem represents."

Like earlier rulings on abortion and affirmative action, the decision ignited a political firestorm. Republicans and Democrats alike immediately began looking for a means to get around it. The former, led by President George Bush, demanded a constitutional amendment forbidding flag burning, while the latter pushed for legislation, arguing that only one vote on the Supreme Court was needed in order to produce a new ruling. Congress swiftly passed the Flag Protection Act of 1989, providing for the criminal prosecution of anyone who "knowingly mutilates, defaces, physically defiles, burns, maintains on the floor or ground, or tramples upon" the flag. Tailored carefully to skirt the issue of symbolic speech altogether, the law avoided the constitutional pitfalls which had sunk Texas' statute. Congress thereby hoped to have the law regarded in the same way as the draft card issue in *O'Brien.*

This legislative strategy failed. Civil liberties activists staged flag burnings in protest of the law and then won in court. In *United States v. Eichman* (1990), the Supreme Court invalidated the Flag Protection Act, once again by a 5–4 majority. The Court acknowledged the differences between the federal law and the Texas statute, yet found these to be superficial. Even though the federal law did not prohibit offensive treatment of the flag, the government's interest in suppression of free speech violated the First Amendment.

In the aftermath of the *Johnson* and *Eichman* decisions, political debate over flag burning has been as hot as ever. Free speech advocates strongly oppose any efforts to dictate flag treatment, fearing that such measures will ultimately constrain all speech rights. Politi-cians, backed by public opinion polls, have pressed for action. Stymied by the Supreme Court, federal lawmakers have looked to a constitutional amendment as their best hope. Such efforts ground to a halt in 1990 and 1995, but regained momentum in 1998. If an amendment were to pass Congress and be sent to the states for a vote, the approval process would take years. In any event, the deep tensions between liberty and authority, dissent and the status quo, mean the issue is unlikely ever to be truly settled.

See also: **Freedom of Speech**

Bibliography and Further Reading

American Civil Liberties Union. "History of Flag Protection." www.aclu.org, 1998

Collins, Randolph Marshall. "The Constitutionality of Flag Burning: Can Neutral Values Protect First Amendment Principles?" *American Criminal Law Review,* 1991

Dyroff, David. "Legislative Attempts to Ban Flag Burning." *Washington University Law Quarterly,* Fall 1991

Greenawalt, Kent. "O'er the Land of the Free: Flag Burning as Speech." *UCLA Law Review,* June 1990

Schwartz, Bernard. *A History of the Supreme Court.* New York: Oxford University Press, 1993

West's Encyclopedia of American Law. St. Paul: West Group, 1998

STROMBERG V. CALIFORNIA

Legal Citation: 283 U.S. 359 (1931)

Appellant
Yetta Stromberg

Appellee
State of California

Appellant's Claim
That the California Red Flag Law prohibits symbolic speech and therefore violates the First Amendment.

Chief Lawyer for Appellant
John Beardsley

Chief Lawyer for Appellee
John D. Richer

Justices for the Court
Louis D. Brandeis, Oliver Wendell Holmes, Charles Evans Hughes (writing for the Court), Willis Van Devanter, James Clark McReynolds, Owen Josephus Roberts, Harlan Fiske Stone, George Sutherland

Justices Dissenting
Pierce Butler

Place
Washington, D.C.

Date of Decision
18 May 1931

Decision
The Supreme Court overturned Stromberg's conviction.

Significance
Although the Court did not specifically address the free speech issues raised by *Stromberg,* the case is important in the development of First Amendment law. It marked the first time that the Supreme Court used the Fourteenth Amendment to stop a state effort to interfere with a right guaranteed by the First Amendment.

In the summer of 1929, 19-year-old Yetta Stromberg, a member of the Young Communist League, was a counsellor at a summer camp for ten- to 15-year-olds. The Pioneer Summer Camp was located in the foothills of the San Bernardino mountains and was a place where the campers learned, among other things, "class-consciousness, the solidarity of the workers and the theory that the workers of the world are of one blood and brothers all." As a part of her duties, Stromberg was responsible for supervising the daily camp ceremony of raising a red flag, which was a camp-made reproduction of the flag of the Soviet Union. Campers would then salute the flag and pledge allegiance to it and to "freedom for the working class."

At the time, California had on its books a so-called "red flag statute," making it a criminal offense to display such a banner, or anything which was "a sign, symbol, or emblem of opposition to organized government or . . . an invitation or stimulus to anarchistic action." Although it was adopted in 1919, the law had never been enforced. During the summer of 1929, however, the Pioneer Camp was targeted by the Better American Federation (BAF), a group dedicated to ridding California of dangerous elements. The BAF convinced the San Bernardino County sheriff to search the camp, where he discovered the red flag and arrested Stromberg and other camp supervisors. The "red flag statute" was used to indict Stromberg, who was convicted of a felony in state court. After a state appellate court upheld her conviction, Stromberg appealed to the U.S. Supreme Court, claiming that the California statute violated her First Amendment right to freedom of expression.

Court Overturns Conviction Under "Red Flag Law"

In the Supreme Court, Stromberg's lawyers argued that the flag was a symbol of a legitimate political party which had received 50,000 votes in the last election. In prohibiting display of the flag, California was unconstitutionally preventing Stromberg and others from exercising their right to freedom of expression under the First Amendment. Displaying the flag was, her lawyers claimed, a form of symbolic speech. What is

Anarchistic Legislation: Red Flag Laws

Following the end of the Bolshevik revolution in Russia in November of 1917, which closely coincided with the end of World War I, the United States began to worry about Communist activities within its borders. In 1919 on the first day of May, the communist labor day called May Day, American radicals in several Northeast cities staged rallies and conducted Red flag parades. The term red was synonymous with Communist and red flags symbolized rebellious discontent and revolution. In reaction, public sentiment against radicalism rose to a fever pitch. The general feeling was the Red flag would have to go for democracy to survive. To prevent reoccurrences of Red flag demonstrations, 32 states passed Red flag laws.

In California, state law established a felony crime to display a red flag or certain other articles as a symbol of opposition to organized government, as a stimulus to anarchistic (violent government overthrow) action, or as an aid to propaganda.

Intent on suppressing dissent, California in particular vigorously arrested and prosecuted individuals. Between 1919 and 1921, 500 persons were arrested and 264 convicted. The state frequently targeted socialists, Communist Labor party members, and the Industrial Workers of the World, a radical labor union.

Source(s): Murray, Robert K. *Red Scare: A Study of National Hysteria, 1919-1920.* New York: McGraw-Hill Book Company, 1964.

more, it was a form of symbolic political speech. Applying the test for prohibited speech developed by Justice Oliver Wendell Holmes in *Schenck v. United States* (1919), displaying the flag hardly represented a "clear and present danger."

Writing for the Court, Chief Justice Hughes largely sidestepped the First Amendment issues raised by *Stromberg*. Although the opinion of the seven-man majority followed the reasoning of the Holmes doctrine, Hughes used it to arrive at the conclusion that the California law was simply too vague to be constitutional:

> The state court recognized the indefiniteness and ambiguity of the clause. The court considered that it might be construed as embracing conduct which the State could not constitutionally prohibit . . . The maintenance of the opportunity for free political discussion to the end that government may be responsive to the will of the people and that changes may be obtained by lawful means . . . is a fundamental principle of our constitutional system. A statute which upon its face . . . is so vague and indefinite as to permit the punishment of the fair use of this opportunity is repugnant to the guaranty of liberty contained in the Fourteenth Amendment.

The Court overturned Stromberg's conviction. And two years later, California repealed its "red flag law." Although the outcome in *Stromberg* was not based on a free speech analysis, it is nonetheless a landmark in the history of First Amendment law. In this case, for the first time, the Supreme Court used the Fourteenth Amendment to protect citizens from state interference with free expression.

Related Cases
State v. Tuscano, 520 So.2d 1311 (1988).
State v. Grissom, 840 P.2d 1142 (1992).
Griggs v. State of Kansas, 814 F.Supp. 60 (1993).

Yetta Stromberg, 1931. © UPI/Corbis-Bettmann.

Bibliography and Further Reading

Haiman, Franklyn Saul. *"Speech Acts" and the First Amendment.* Carbondale: Southern Illinois University Press, 1993.

Klehr, Harvey. *The Heyday of American Communism: The Depression Decade.* New York, NY: Basic Books, 1984.

Lewy, Guenter. *The Cause That Failed: Communism in American Political Life.* New York, NY: Oxford University Press, 1990.

THORNHILL V. ALABAMA

Legal Citation: 310 U.S. 88 (1940)

Peititioner
Byron Thornhill

Respondent
State of Alabama

Petitioner's Claim
That an Alabama statute prohibiting all picketing, even peaceful labor demonstrations, violated his First Amendment right to freedom of speech.

Chief Lawyers for Petitioner
James J. Mayfield, Joseph A. Padway

Chief Lawyer for Respondent
William H. Loeb

Justices for the Court
Hugo Lafayette Black, William O. Douglas, Felix Frankfurter, Charles Evans Hughes, Frank Murphy (writing for the Court), Stanley Forman Reed, Owen Josephus Roberts, Harlan Fiske Stone

Justices Dissenting
James Clark McReynolds

Place
Washington, D.C.

Date of Decision
22 April 1940

Decision
The Supreme Court overturned the anti-picketing statute.

Significance
Thornhill was a recognition that President Franklin Roosevelt's New Deal reforms, which included the National Labor Relations Act, had made picketing and other public demonstrations a part of the American landscape.

In 1935, in *A.L.A. Schechter Poultry Corporation v. United States*, the Supreme Court struck down the National Industrial Relations Act, an important element in President Franklin Roosevelt's "First" New Deal program of economic and social reforms. Afterward, Roosevelt threatened to "pack" the Court with justices who would help him lift the country out of the Great Depression by supporting his legislative proposals. The court-packing plan did not pass, but it coincided with an about-face in the Court's attitude towards the New Deal.

Nowhere is the Court's re-orientation more apparent than in the area of labor relations. In 1937, with *National Labor Relations Board v. Jones & Laughlin Steel Corp.*, the Court upheld the legitimacy of the National Labor Relations Act (NLRA), the successor to the National Industrial Relations Act. Throughout the 1930s, the Court continued to uphold laws favoring organized labor. *Hague v. Committee for Industrial Organization* (1939) marked the first time the Supreme Court used the First Amendment to prevent the states from interfering with labor's attempts to organize local workers. *Thornhill* extended organized labor's First Amendment protections to include picketing.

Byron Thornhill was an employee of the Brown Wood Preserving Company of Tuscaloosa County, Alabama. During a strike by a local affiliate of the American Federation of Labor, Thornhill was arrested for picketing in front of the Brown Wood plant. He was charged with violating a state statute outlawing all forms of picketing. After his conviction was upheld on appeal, Thornhill petitioned the U.S. Supreme Court for review of his case.

Court Upholds Labor Pickets as Exercise of Freedom of Speech

Justice Murphy, who wrote the opinion of the Court, knew a great deal about strikes. Before coming to sit on the high bench, he had served as governor of Michigan, where his refusal to call in troops to deal with a sit-down strike by automotive workers cost him re-election. In *Thornhill*, he left little doubt about his support for organized labor:

> In the circumstances of our times the dissemination of information concerning the facts of

a labor dispute must be regarded as within that area of free discussion that is guaranteed by the Constitution . . . Labor relations are not matters of mere local or private concern. Free discussion concerning the conditions in industry and the causes of labor disputes appears to us indispensable to the effective and intelligent use of the processes of popular government to shape the destiny of modern industrial society.

For Murphy and seven other members of the Court, picketing was not only an exercise of freedom of expression, it also performed an educational function. The public's right to know about the state of industrial relations was as important as the picketers' right to express their dissatisfaction with their employers. The Alabama statute, which outlawed all picketing, was simply too broad to be constitutional. The Court struck it down and reversed Thornhill's conviction.

All the same, *Thornhill* did not endorse all aspects of picketing. States remained free to impose conditions on labor demonstrations in order to preserve the peace and privacy of its citizens. In later years, the Court would in fact cite *Thornhill* as authority for limiting labor activism that threatened economic production. In the 1940s, the Court came to emphasize the public interest in granting organized labor constitutional protections, rather than the workers' own fundamental rights.

The logical result of this reasoning came into focus with *American Communications Association v. Douds* (1950), in which the Court used the NLRA's mission of protecting the free flow of commerce to uphold legislation intended to rid labor of communist sympathizers.

Related Cases

Stromberg v. California, 283 U.S. 359 (1931).
Near v. Minnesota, 283 U.S. 697 (1931).
A.L.A. Schechter Poultry Corp. v. United States, 295 U.S. 495 (1935).
DeJonge v. Oregon, 299 U.S. 353 (1937).
National Labor Relations Board v. Jones and Laughlin Steel Corp., 301 U.S. 1 (1937).
Hague v. Committee for Industrial Organizations, 307 U.S. 496 (1939).
American Communications Association v. Douds, 339 U.S. 382 (1950).

Bibliography and Further Reading

Bracken, Harry M. *Freedom of Speech: Words Are Not Deeds.* Westport, CT: Praeger, 1994.

Gordon, Colin. *New Deals: Business, Labor, and Politics in America, 1920-1935.* New York, NY: Cambridge University Press, 1994.

Whitehead, John W. *The Right to Picket and the Freedom of Public Discourse.* Westchester, IL: Crossway Books, 1984.

UNITED STATES V. O'BRIEN

Legal Citation: 391 U.S. 367 (1968)

Petitioner
United States

Respondent
David Paul O'Brien

Petitioner's Claim
That a federal law prohibiting the destruction of draft cards is not a violation of the First Amendment's free speech guarantees.

Chief Lawyer for Petitioner
Erwin N. Griswold, U.S. Solicitor General

Chief Lawyer for Respondent
Marvin M. Karpatkin

Justices for the Court
Hugo Lafayette Black, William J. Brennan, Jr., Abe Fortas, John Marshall Harlan II, Potter Stewart, Earl Warren (writing for the Court), Byron R. White

Justices Dissenting
William O. Douglas (Thurgood Marshall did not participate)

Place
Washington, D.C.

Date of Decision
27 May 1968

Decision
The Supreme Court upheld the federal statute and O'Brien's conviction.

Significance
O'Brien saw the advent of a new test for determining the constitutionality of government regulation of "symbolic" speech.

On 31 March 1966, David O'Brien and three companions burned their selective service registration cards on the steps of the South Boston Courthouse. The purpose of their symbolic gesture was to protest the war in Vietnam, and a sizeable crowd–including several agents of the Federal Bureau of Investigation (FBI)–witnessed the act. Immediately afterward, some members of the crowd began attacking the draft card burners, and an FBI agent ushered O'Brien inside the courthouse to safety. The agent then advised O'Brien of his right to legal counsel and to silence, whereupon O'Brien announced that he had burned his draft card to demonstrate his beliefs and that he did so with the full knowledge that he was violating federal law. He gave his permission for the charred remains of his draft card to be photographed.

A federal statute made it a criminal offense to knowingly destroy or mutilate a Selective Service registration certificate. This law was used in the U.S. District Court for the District of Massachusetts to try and convict O'Brien. O'Brien did not contest the government's presentation of facts; indeed, he told the jury that he had burned his draft card with the specific intention of encouraging others to adopt his antiwar beliefs. Instead, O'Brien argued that the federal statute outlawing the destruction of draft cards was a violation of First Amendment free speech rights. Although the district court dismissed these arguments, the Court of Appeals for the First Circuit found that the federal law was unconstitutional. The government then petitioned the U.S. Supreme Court for review of this decision.

Court Upholds Constitutionality of Law Prohibiting Draft Card Burning

The Court voted 7-1 to uphold the federal law. Writing for the majority, Chief Justice Warren set out a new test for determining when government regulation of symbolic speech is permissible:

> We cannot accept the view that an apparently limitless variety of conduct can be labeled "speech" whenever the person engaging in the conduct intends thereby to express an idea . . . we think it clear that a government regulation

Draft Card Burning

As the 1960s progressed the war in Vietnam substantially escalated. Many Americans, believing the war immoral, criticized the Selective Service System which drafted young men into military service. Chanting "We Won't Go," more than 1,000 students gathered in New York City in May of 1964 to protest. Twelve burned their draft cards in a symbolic expression of opposition to the war.

In 1965 Congress passed an amendment to the Selective Service Act criminalizing the destruction or mutilation of draft cards. Penalties included fines up to $10,000 and five years in prison. That same year, David J. Miller of Manhattan publicly burned his draft card and became the first person convicted under the new law. Nevertheless, draft card burning continued as the

rate of draftees inducted into service accelerated between 1965 and 1967.

The demand for draftees began to decline in 1969, yet the reported violations of the Selective Service Act including draft card destruction actually increased. However, only 544 cases ended in imprisonment of the 31,831 reported violations. A national public movement to abolish the draft rapidly grew. Finally, in 1973 Congress ended the draft and established an all volunteer army.

Source(s): Dougan, Clark and Samuel Lipsman, *A Nation Divided: The Vietnam Experience.* Boston: Boston Publishing Company, 1984.

is sufficiently justified if it is within the constitutional power of the Government; if it furthers an important or substantial governmental interest; if the governmental interest is unrelated to the suppression of free expression; and if the incidental restriction on alleged First Amendment freedoms is no greater than is essential to the furtherance of that interest.

The Court found that the law met all of the above requirements. First, its purpose was to uphold the government's broad power to raise and support an army. Second, draft cards furthered the important government interest of knowing who was in the army and aiding communications with those persons. The law had no bearing on the repression of free speech. And lastly, the Court found that the reach of the law was no broader than was necessary to implement the Selective Service Act. O'Brien's act had violated the law and deliberately hindered the government's legitimate, constitutionally granted military mandate. O'Brien's conviction stood.

The *O'Brien* test, in which a regulation must only incidentally impinge on the content of speech and be narrowly tailored to achieve a legitimate government interest, has since been employed in cases concerning so-called "time, place, and manner" restrictions. Such restrictions are intended to control the potentially harmful side effects of speech, while remaining neutral as to the content of the speech. They can apply not only to pure speech, but to speech acts such as O'Brien's highly public draft card burning ceremony.

A man burns his draft card at an anti-Vietnam War demonstration in San Francisco, 1967. © Ted Streshinsky/Corbis.

Related Cases

McCray v. United States, 195 U.S. 27 (1904).

Selected Draft Law Cases, 245 U.S. 366 (1918).

Stromberg v. California, 283 U.S. 359 (1931).

Grosjean v. American Press Co., 297 U.S. 233 (1936).

Ex parte Quirin, 317 U.S. 1 (1942).

Gomillion v. Lightfoot, 364 U.S. 339 (1960).

Bibliography and Further Reading

Bosmajian, Haig A., comp. *Dissent: Symbolic Behavior and Rhetorical Strategies.* Boston, MA: Allyn and Bacon, 1972.

Bracken, Harry M. *Freedom of Speech: Words Are Not Deeds.* Westport, CT: Praeger, 1994.

Greenawalt, Kent, *Fighting Words: Individuals, Communities, and Liberties of Speech.* Princeton, NJ: Princeton University Press, 1995.

TINKER V. DES MOINES INDEPENDENT COMMUNITY SCHOOL DISTRICT

Legal Citation: 393 U.S. 503 (1969)

Petitioners
John P. Tinker, Mary Beth Tinker, Christopher Eckhardt

Respondent
Des Moines Independent Community School District

Petitioners' Claim
That it was a violation of free speech rights for their high school to suspend them for wearing black armbands to protest the Vietnam War.

Chief Lawyer for Petitioners
Dan Johnston

Chief Lawyer for Respondent
Allan A. Herrick

Justices for the Court
William J. Brennan, Jr., William O. Douglas, Abe Fortas (writing for the Court), Thurgood Marshall, Potter Stewart, Earl Warren, Byron R. White

Justices Dissenting
Hugo Lafayette Black, John Marshall Harlan II

Place
Washington, D.C.

Date of Decision
24 February 1969

Decision
The Supreme Court struck down the school regulation that resulted in the suspension.

Significance
Tinker is one of the most important Supreme Court cases to deal with the rights of public school students in the marketplace of ideas.

In December of 1965, a group adults met at the home of Mr. and Mrs. William Eckhardt. They discussed ways to protest the U.S. involvement in the Vietnam War. Some of their children were present, including 16-year-old Christopher Eckhardt, 15-year-old John Tinker, and 13-year-old Mary Beth Tinker. They decided to join the adults in wearing black armbands during the holiday season and to fast on 16 December and New Year's Eve. The principals of the Des Moines Public Schools became aware of this plan, and on 14 December, they jointly adopted a policy of prohibiting black armbands in their schools. Any student wearing one would be asked to remove it. If the student refused, he or she would be suspended until the armband was removed.

The Tinkers were aware that the school board had adopted this policy, but they went ahead and wore their armbands on 16 and 17 December. They were sent home, and they did not return to school until after New Year's Day, when they had originally planned to end their protest. In the meanwhile, they filed a complaint in U.S. district court, asking for an injunction preventing the school board from taking disciplinary action against them. When the district court ruled against them and an equally divided federal court of appeals upheld that decision, the Tinkers took their case to the U.S. Supreme Court.

Supreme Court Upholds Wearing of Black Armbands as Akin to "Pure Speech"

The Tinkers claimed that the school board had violated their First Amendment right to freedom of expression. Writing for the Court, Justice Fortas agreed:

> First Amendment rights, applied in light of the special characteristics of the school environment, are available to teachers and students. It can hardly be argued that either students or teachers shed their constitutional rights to freedom of speech or expression at the schoolhouse gate . . . Statutes to this effect . . . unconstitutionally interfere with the liberty of teacher, student, and parent.

Fortas went on to emphasize the fact that the Tinkers' behavior had been in no way disruptive of other

Student Protests, 1964-1967

During the turbulent 1960s the civil rights movement and the largely student-led Vietnam War protests expanded the ways of communicating political messages. Traditional forms of speech and press gave way to demonstrations. Sit-ins, marches, black arm bands, draft card burning, and flag desecration graphically presented the protester's political message.

The student protest movement began in 1964 at Berkeley, California. In what became known as the Free Speech Movement, students pressed issues against an academic bureaucracy out of touch with the problems of contemporary society. Students staged sit-ins, strikes, sang folk songs, and created slogans to identify the targets of their protests. By 1965, with escalating events in Vietnam coming to the forefront, students rallied in opposition to the war. "Make Love Not War" became a new slogan. The draft system of the Selective Service was the most visible target of the government war policy spurring draft card burnings, sit-ins, and picketing of local draft boards. From 1965 to 1967 the nature of the student protests slowly changed from peaceful demonstrations to more aggressive tactics including calls for outright revolution. During this time period student activism and protests dramatically increased on college campuses nationwide.

Source(s): Dougan, Clark and Samuel Lipsman. *A Nation Divided: The Vietnam Experience.* Boston: Boston Publishing Company, 1984.

students or of the school routine. Indeed, their wearing of black armbands had been an exercise of "First Amendment rights akin to pure speech.'"

The Tinkers were in fact engaging in symbolic political speech, the protection of which lies at the heart of the First Amendment. Fortas underscored this analysis by pointing to other instances when the school district had tolerated more conventional displays of political opinions, such as the wearing of campaign buttons. School officials had not even protested when a student showed up for classes wearing a Nazi iron cross. It was only when the Tinkers displayed their opposi-

tion to the Vietnam War—apparently an unpopular stance to assume in Des Moines, Iowa, in 1968—that the school board attempted to regulate a graphic representation of a political point of view. This reaction, the Court indicated, bore a resemblance to state censorship:

> In our system, state-operated schools may not be enclaves of totalitarianism. School officials do not possess absolute authority over students . . . In our system, students may not be regarded as closed-circuit recipients of only that which the State chooses to

Mary Beth and John Tinker display the armbands that are at the center of their Supreme Court case. © Corbis-Bettmann.

communicate. They may not be confined to the expression of those sentiments that are officially approved.

In his three and a half years on the Court bench, Justice Fortas was known for championing the rights of juveniles in such cases as *In re Gault* (1967). His clear sympathy with the relative powerlessness of school children was on display in *Tinker,* too. In marked contrast, in his long career as a justice of the Supreme Court, Justice Black had changed from a First Amendment absolutist to a neo-conservative on social issues. His disapproval of political activism in the schoolhouse was manifest in his dissenting opinion in *Tinker,* in which he declared that district officials were well within their rights in controlling how their schools were run.

In subsequent opinions, the Supreme Court has vacillated between the Fortas point of view and that of Justice Black. The Court continues to place a great deal of emphasis on the school's responsibility for conveying ethics and morality. In general, however, school officials are granted more latitude to regulate student behavior connected with school-sponsored activities, such as school newspapers.

Related Cases

Meyer v. Nebraska, 262 U.S. 390 (1923).
Pierce v. Society of Sisters, 268 U.S. 510 (1925).
Stromberg v. California, 283 U.S. 359 (1931).
West Virginia v. Barnette, 319 U.S. 624 (1943).
Shelton v. Tucker, 364 U.S. 479 (1960).
Engel v. Vitale, 370 U.S. 421 (1962).
Edwards v. South Carolina, 372 U.S. 229 (1963).
Cox v. Louisiana, 379 U.S. 536 (1965).
Keyishian v. Board of Regents, 385 U.S. 589 (1967).
In re Gault, 387 U.S. 1 (1967).
Airport Comm'rs v. Jews for Jesus, 482 U.S. 569 (1987).

Bibliography and Further Reading

Bogen, David S. *Bulwark of Liberty: The Court and the First Amendment.* Port Washington, NY: Associated University Press, 1984.

Bracken, Harry M. *Freedom of Speech: Words Are Not Deeds.* Westport, CT: Praeger, 1994.

Johnson, John W., ed. *Historic U.S. Court Cases, 1690-1990: An Encyclopedia.* New York: Garland Publishing, 1992.

Lane, Robert Wheeler. *Beyond the Schoolhouse Gate: Free Speech and the Inculcation of Values.* Philadelphia, PA: Temple University Press, 1995.

COHEN V. CALIFORNIA

Legal Citation: 403 U.S. 15 (1971)

Appellant
Paul Robert Cohen

Appellee
The State of California

Appellant's Claim
That wearing a jacket bearing a controversial opinion about the draft in a county courthouse constituted political speech protected by the First Amendment.

Chief Lawyer for Appellant
Melville B. Nimmer

Chief Lawyer for Appellee
Michael T. Sauer

Justices for the Court
William J. Brennan, Jr., William O. Douglas, John Marshall Harlan II (writing for the Court), Thurgood Marshall, Potter Stewart

Justices Dissenting
Hugo Lafayette Black, Harry A. Blackmun, Warren E. Burger, Byron R. White

Place
Washington, D.C.

Date of Decision
7 June 1971

Decision
The Supreme Court struck down Cohen's conviction for disturbing the peace.

Significance
Cohen extended the boundaries of First Amendment protection for speech which is potentially provocative or obscene.

Paul Robert Cohen was arrested in the Los Angeles County Courthouse, where he was roaming the corridors while wearing a jacket with "F*** the Draft" emblazoned across the back. Although he was making no noise at the time of his arrest, he was convicted under a state statute outlawing willful and malicious disturbance of the peace and sentenced to 30 days in jail. Although Cohen testified that he wore the jacket with full knowledge of what it said, he also stated that he did so to express the depth of his feeling about the war in Vietnam. Citing his First Amendment guarantee of free speech, he appealed his conviction to the Court of Appeals of California, then to the State Supreme Court. After both upheld his conviction, he appealed to the U.S. Supreme Court.

The Court first determined that Cohen had been convicted solely because of the words on his back, rather than any offensive conduct. In the words of the opinion of the Court, written by Justice Harlan, ". . . the only conduct' which the State sought to punish is the fact of the communication." The Court next had to ascertain whether or not these words—in the context in which they had received their expression—fell under any of the exceptions to First Amendment protection. Harlan conceded that while the expletive Cohen used may have been vulgar, it was not legally obscene. Neither did it constitute "fighting words" intended to incite a violent response—while the phrase might have been provocative, it was not aimed at anyone in particular.

Court Upholds First Amendment Protection for Nonverbal Aspects of Communication

Since the language on Cohen's jacket did not fall under any of the exceptions to First Amendment protection, California was prohibited from punishing him solely because of the content of that language. The only issue remaining in the case was whether or not the state had the power to preserve the cleanliness of public speech. But this, the Court said, the state could not do.

First, the principle contended for by the State seems inherently boundless. How is one to distinguish this from any other offensive word?

Surely the State has no right to cleanse public debate to the point where it is grammatically palatable to the most squeamish among us . . . one man's vulgarity is another's lyric . . . Additionally . . . much linguistic expression serves a dual communicative function: it conveys not only ideas . . . but otherwise inexpressible emotions as well . . . We cannot sanction the view that the Constitution, while solicitous of the cognitive content of individual speech, has little or no regard for that emotive function which . . . may often be the more important element of the overall message . . .

Cohen is thought of as a landmark case because it sought to protect speech which could be either provocative or obscene but which, taken in context, is neither. By prohibiting the manner of expression in a case such as this, government runs the impermissible risk of censoring the message. What remains unstated but still arguably implicit in the Court's opinion is that at the heart of Robert Paul Cohen's "speech" lies the expression of a political sentiment—strong disagreement with an unpopular war—which is the very type of speech the First Amendment was most clearly designed to protect.

Related Cases
Schenck v. United States, 249 U.S. 47 (1919).
Chaplinsky v. New Hampshire, 315 U.S. 568 (1942).
Edwards v. South Carolina, 372 U.S. 229 (1963).
Bethel School District v. Fraser, 478 U.S. 675 (1986).

Bibliography and Further Reading
Blanchard, Margaret A. *Revolutionary Sparks: Freedom of Expression in Modern America.* New York: Oxford University Press, 1992.

Greenawalt, Kent. *Fighting Words: Individuals, Communities, and Liberties of Speech.* Princeton, NJ: Princeton University Press, 1995.

Schauer, Frederick F. *Free Speech: A Philosophical Inquiry.* New York: Cambridge University Press, 1982.

TEXAS V. JOHNSON

Legal Citation: 491 U.S. 397 (1989)

Petitioner
State of Texas

Respondent
Gregory Lee Johnson

Petitioner's Claim
That the Texas statute against "desecration of venerated objects," in this instance burning an American flag, did not violate Gregory Lee Johnson's constitutional rights.

Chief Lawyer for Petitioner
Kathi Alyce Drew

Chief Lawyer for Respondent
William M. Kunstler

Justices for the Court
Harry A. Blackmun, William J. Brennan, Jr. (writing for the Court), Anthony M. Kennedy, Thurgood Marshall, Antonin Scalia

Justices Dissenting
Sandra Day O'Connor, William H. Rehnquist, John Paul Stevens, Byron R. White

Place
Washington, D.C.

Date of Decision
21 June 1989

Decision
The Texas statute was declared unconstitutional.

Significance
No matter how unpopular it is to burn an American flag, the First Amendment protects that and other forms of political expression and symbolic speech.

Gregory Lee Johnson, nicknamed "Joey," was a fervent supporter of an American communist movement known as the Revolutionary Communist Youth Brigade. When the Republican National Convention met in Dallas, Texas in 1984, Johnson decided to participate in a political demonstration called the "Republican War Chest Tour." The demonstration's purpose was to protest the policies of the Reagan Administration.

On 22 August 1984 Johnson, amidst a crowd of approximately 100 other demonstrators, unfurled an American flag. He splashed it with kerosene and set it on fire, while the other demonstrators chanted: "America, the red, white, and blue, we spit on you." After the flag burned, the demonstrators left, and one of the many shocked onlookers gathered the burnt remains for burial in his backyard. No one was hurt, and no property other than the flag was destroyed. Both the press and the police were at the scene of the flag burning, and when police reinforcements arrived shortly thereafter they arrested Johnson.

Johnson was prosecuted under a Texas law that made it illegal to "intentionally or knowingly desecrate . . . a state or national flag." Johnson was convicted in Dallas County Criminal Court No. 8 of desecration of a venerated object and sentenced to a year in prison and a $2,000 fine. The prosecutor blatantly asked the jury to convict Johnson for the political symbolism expressed by the flag-burning incident: "And you know that he's also creating a lot of danger for a lot of people by what he does and the way he thinks."

The Court of Appeals of Dallas, Texas affirmed Johnson's conviction on 23 January 1986. On 20 April 1988 the Texas Court of Criminal Appeals reversed the court of appeals and the trial court, and threw out Johnson's conviction. The court of criminal appeals rejected the state's argument that the antiflag-burning statute was a valid measure to preserve a symbol of national unity: "Recognizing that the right to differ is the centerpiece of our First Amendment freedoms, a government cannot mandate by fiat a feeling of unity in its citizens."

The state of Texas appealed to the U.S. Supreme Court. Johnson's attorney was William M. Kunstler, and the state's attorney was Kathi Alyce Drew. The par-

Flag Burning: Protected Expression or Desecration?

Political reaction quickly mounted to the Supreme Court's *Texas v. Johnson* decision and the striking down of the Flag Protection Act of 1989. The burning of an American flag had become a valid gesture of expressive freedom. A constitutional amendment prohibiting the desecration of the U.S. flag was introduced in Congress in 1995, and reintroduced again in 1997.

Amendment proponents led by the Citizens Flag Alliance (CFA) contended freedom of expression guarantees were never absolute, and the flag, a national symbol of U.S. society, deserved protection from desecration. CFA rebuffed the idea flag burning is "speech." Rather, they regarded it "conduct" outside constitutional protection. Proponents maintained the proposals did not restrict freedom of speech since persons could still freely speak or write their views on the government or flag.

Amendment opponents including the American Civil Liberties Union (ACLU) insisted the new amendment would restrict the First Amendment's freedom of expression guarantees. They saw the flag as a symbol standing for the freedom every American enjoys including the right to burn that symbol. The ACLU argued a flag burning ban would open the door for legislators to restrict other individual freedoms. Besides, the ACLU considered flag burning as a rare event not meriting a constitutional amendment.

Source(s): *West's Encyclopedia of American Law.* Minneapolis/St. Paul, MN: West Publishing, 1998.

ties argued their case before the Supreme Court on 21 March 1989.

Justice Brennan authored the decision for the majority of the court, which was issued on 21 June 1989. By a 5-4 vote the justices upheld the Texas Court of Criminal Appeals decision, stating that:

> The way to preserve the flag's special role is not to punish those who feel differently about these matters. It is to persuade them that they are wrong . . . We can imagine no more appropriate response to burning a flag than waving one's own, no better way to counter a flag-burner's message than by saluting the flag that burns, no surer means of preserving the dignity even of the flag that burned than by, as one witness here did, according its remains a respectful burial. We do not consecrate the flag by punishing its desecration, for in doing so we dilute the freedom that this cherished emblem represents.

The Supreme Court's decision sparked a vigorous but brief political uproar, culminating in President George Bush proposing an antiflag-burning constitutional amendment which quietly died. The lasting legacy of the *Johnson* case was to demonstrate the First Amendment protection of forms of political expression, extends even to those as unpopular and provocative as burning the national flag.

Related Cases
Stromberg v. California, 283 U.S. 359 (1931).
United States v. O'Brien, 391 U.S. 367 (1968).
United States v. Eichman, 496 U.S. 310 (1990).

Bibliography and Further Reading
Goldstein, Robert Justin. "This Flag is not for Burning: Snuffing out Symbolic Speech." *The Nation,* July 18, 1994, p. 84.

Gregory Johnson. © Corbis-Bettmann.

Grogan, David. "Unimpressed by the Freedom to Burn Old Glory Joey Johnson Still Wants a Revolution." *People,* 10 July 1989, pp. 98-100.

Jacoby, Tamar. "A Fight for Old Glory." *Newsweek,* 3 July 1989, pp. 18-20.

Johnson, John W., ed. *Historic U.S. Court Cases, 1690–1990: An Encyclopedia.* New York: Garland Publishing, 1992.

Simpson, Glenn. "Decision Unravels Flag's Very Fabric." *Insight,* 24 July 1989, pp. 8-13.

The Editors. "The Flag Again." *The Progressive,* February, 1989, p. 8.

The Editors. "Waiving the Flag." *The New Republic* 23 January 1989, pp. 7-8.

UNITED STATES V. EICHMAN

Legal Citation: 496 U.S. 310 (1990)

Appellant
United States of America

Appellee
Shawn D. Eichman

Appellant's Claim
That the 1989 Flag Protection Act does not violate the First Amendment guarantee of freedom of speech.

Chief Lawyer for Appellant
Kenneth W. Starr, U.S. Solicitor General

Chief Lawyer for Appellee
William M. Kunstler

Justices for the Court
Harry A. Blackmun, William J. Brennan, Jr. (writing for the Court), Anthony M. Kennedy, Thurgood Marshall, Antonin Scalia

Justices Dissenting
Sandra Day O'Connor, William H. Rehnquist, John Paul Stevens, Byron R. White

Place
Washington, D.C.

Date of Decision
11 June 1990

Decision
The Supreme Court struck down the Flag Protection Act as unconstitutional.

Significance
In *Eichman* a bare majority of the Court agreed that flag desecration laws would always be regarded as constitutionally suspect.

United States v. Eichman consolidated two appeals in flag burning cases arising out of the Flag Protection Act of 1989. In one case, the federal government prosecuted several individuals for deliberately setting fire to a number of American flags on the steps of the U.S. Capitol to protest the government's foreign and domestic policies. In the second case, others were prosecuted for deliberately setting fire to a U.S. flag in Seattle, Washington, to protest the Flag Protection Act. Based on the 1989 Supreme Court case of *Texas v. Johnson,* both the U.S. District Court for the District of Columbia and the U.S. District Court for the Western District of Washington held that the Flag Protection Act was unconstitutional. The government appealed both cases directly to the U.S. Supreme Court.

Congress passed the Flag Protection Act specifically to provide the Court with an opportunity to reconsider its decision in *Texas v. Johnson* (1989). In that case, Johnson burned an American flag during the Republican National Convention in Dallas, Texas, to protest the policies of President Ronald Reagan. Johnson was then convicted of having violated a Texas statute making it a crime to knowingly desecrate a state or national flag. A state appellate court overturned his conviction, and the U.S. Supreme Court upheld this decision. In his opinion for the Court, Justice Brennan wrote that the Texas law violated the core First Amendment protection for political speech, which cannot be censored solely because of its context. Brennan added that the state law went well beyond the "time, place, and manner" restrictions a state may place on expressive conduct.

Court Declares Federal Flag Protection Act Unconstitutional

In *Eichman,* the U.S. government contended that the Flag Protection Act was not intended to repress conduct *per se*; in contrast to the Texas law, the federal act was intended to prevent any form of flag desecration. Unlike the Texas statute, the Flag Protection Act did not contain a list of prohibited acts. Therefore, the government argued, the Court need not apply the highest standard of review when considering the constitutionality of the federal act.

Writing for the Court once again, Justice Brennan disagreed:

> Although the Flag Protection Act contains no explicit content-based limitation on the scope of prohibited conduct, it is nevertheless clear that the Government's asserted *interest* is "related 'to the suppression of free expression,'" and concerned with the content of such expression. The Government's interest in protecting the flag rests upon a perceived need to preserve the flag's status as a symbol of our nation and certain national ideals . . . implicated only when a person's treatment of the flag communicates [a] message to others that is inconsistent with those ideals. [Quoting *Texas v. Johnson*.]

For good measure, Brennan went on to imply that any flag desecration law would, by its very nature, be subject to the highest test in determining whether or not it passed constitutional muster. But the vote in *Eichman*, as in *Johnson*, was 5-4. Writing for the four dissenters in *Eichman*, Justice Stevens maintained that the Flag Protection Act was constitutional. He agreed with the government that the act still left protesters with many avenues besides flag desecration for conveying their dissent. As for the American flag, it "uniquely symbolizes the ideas of liberty, equality, and tolerance . . . The flag embodies the spirit of our national commitment to those ideals. The message thereby transmitted does not take a stand upon our disagreements, except to say that those disagreements are best regarded as competing interpretations of shared ideals."

Related Cases
Stromberg v. California, 283 U.S. 359 (1931).
United States v. O'Brien, 391 U.S. 367 (1968).
Texas v. Johnson, 491 U.S. 397 (1989).

Bibliography and Further Reading

Curtis, Michael Kent, ed. *The Constitution and the Flag.* New York: Garland Publishing, 1993.

Goldstein, Robert Justin. *Burning the Flag: The Great 1989-1990 American Flag Desecration Controversy.* Kent, OH: Kent State University Press, 1996.

Greenawalt, Kent. *Fighting Words: Individuals, Communities, and Liberties of Speech.* Princeton, NJ: Princeton University Press, 1995.

Luckey, John R. "Congressional Research Report October 1, 1998" *Flag Protection: A Brief History and Summary of Recent Supreme Court Decisions and Proposed Constitutional Amendment.* Bethesda, MD: Penny Hill Press, 1998.

BARNES V. GLEN THEATRE, INC.

Legal Citation: 501 U.S. 560 (1991)

Petitioner
Michael Barnes, Prosecuting Attorney of St. Joseph County, Indiana

Respondent
Glen Theatre, Inc.

Petitioner's Claim
Nude dancing is a form of expressive conduct that is not protected by the First Amendment.

Chief Lawyer for Petitioner
Wayne E. Uhl, Deputy Attorney General of Indiana

Chief Lawyer for Respondent
Bruce J. Ennis, Jr.

Justices for the Court
Anthony M. Kennedy, Sandra Day O'Connor, William H. Rehnquist (writing for the Court), Antonin Scalia, David H. Souter

Justices Dissenting
Harry A. Blackmun, Thurgood Marshall, John Paul Stevens, Byron R. White

Place
Washington, D.C.

Date of Decision
21 June 1991

Decision
Although they were unable to agree upon an opinion, a majority of the justices upheld the constitutionality of an Indiana statute outlawing public nudity, as the law applied to nude dancing performed as entertainment.

Significance
Barnes v. Glen Theatre, Inc. marked a retreat from the Court's previous view that nude dancing, to the extent it is not obscene, is a form of free expression protected by the First Amendment.

Two South Bend, Indiana, establishments wanted to provide totally nude dancing as entertainment. They brought suit in federal trial court to challenge a state law outlawing all public nudity. The law, as written, would require the dancers at the Glen Theatre to wear what amounted to "pasties" and "G-strings," requirements that would, the Glen Theatre claimed, violate the dancers' First Amendment right to free expression.

When Glen Theatre lost its case in the U.S. District Court for the Northern District of Indiana, it went on to appeal this decision in the U.S. Court of Appeals for the Seventh Circuit, which overturned the trial court's decision. The state prosecutor in turn petitioned the U.S. Supreme Court for a review of the appellate court's decision.

In the opinion of Chief Justice Rehnquist, who announced the judgment of the Court, the Indiana statute did not violate the First Amendment. Rehnquist stated that the intent of the law was not to prohibit nude dancing, but to prevent public nudity, which has nothing to do with free expression. The effects of the statute on the type of nude dancing proposed by Glen Theatre were only "incidental," and the "pasties" and "G-strings" requirements were not excessively burdensome. Therefore, the Indiana law was a permissible "time, place, or manner" restriction that did not focus on content and thus did not violate the First Amendment, which provided only minimal protection for nude dancing.

A decade earlier, in *Schad v. Borough of Mount Ephraim* (1981), the Supreme Court had held that nude barroom dancing was protected expressive conduct. But the statute in question in *Schad* had not been addressed to public nudity, merely to nude live entertainment. It could, therefore, be used to outlaw nudity in other forms of recreation, and the Court found it to be phrased in an overly broad fashion and therefore unconstitutional. The distinction between that law and the Indiana statute, according to Justice Rehnquist, was that while the former specifically addressed expression, the latter was a permissible exercise of a state's traditional police power, which authorizes regulation of activities as they affect the public's health, safety, and morals.

Nude Dancing—Form of Expression

Is nude dancing the type of expression with which the First Amendment is concerned? Does it constitute a form of protected symbolic speech or is it merely conduct without any expressive quality?

Proponents describe striptease as an ensemble of dance, music, and disrobing. Taken together the elements express erotic emotion and make a symbolic statement. Striptease conveys meaning and expression just as Balanchine's ballets and Titian's painting, *Venus with a Mirror*. Nude dancing is neither legally obscene nor forced on a captive audience. Therefore, if nude dancing is not protected, much of what is called art could also be left without expressive protection. Such aesthetic or personal value judgements should not play a role in setting First Amendment boundaries.

Opponents argue nude dancing is not performed by trained professional dancers and is generally not choreographed. The music is canned and dancers often sell drinks to customers afterward. Therefore, the expressive elements of the performance are phony and do not relay a message. The First Amendment protects expressions of ideas and is degraded when interpreted to protect the raw conduct of barroom striptease. Additionally, protecting nude dancing supports immorality and the secondary social harms which follow it.

Source(s): Blasi, Vincent. Six Conservatives in Search of the First Amendment: The Revealing Case of Nude Dancing. *William and Mary Law Review*, Vol. 33, 1992, pp. 611-665.

Dissenters Vote to Uphold Nude Dancing

Justice White's dissenting opinion, in which Justices Marshall, Blackmun, and Stevens joined, pointed out that far from being merely a restriction on "time, place, or manner," the Indiana law was intended to prevent customers in establishments such as Glen Theatre from being exposed to the sensuality and eroticism that were the essence of the dancers' expression.

> The sight of a fully clothed, or even partially clothed, dancer generally will have a far different impact on the spectator than that of a nude dancer, even if the same dance is performed. The nudity is itself an expressive component of the dance, not merely incidental "conduct." We have previously pointed out that "'[n]udity alone' does not place otherwise protected material outside the mantle of the First Amendment." . . . It cannot be said that the statutory prohibition is unrelated to expressive conduct.

The "time, place, or manner" rule is a doctrine that permits government to control the incidental effects of speech (or, in its broader sense, expression), so long as

the restrictions are neutral as to the content of the expression and do not excessively burden the articulation of its ideas. While the chief justice's argument seemed to address the right of individual states to govern themselves, Justice White's opinion was concerned with the intersection of obscenity and the First Amendment.

Related Cases
United States v. O'Brien, 391 U.S. 367 (1968).
Paris Adult Theatre v. Slaton, 413 U.S. 49 (1973).
Doran v. Salem, Inc., 422 U.S. 922 (1975).
Renton v. Playtime Theatre, Inc., 475 U.S. 41 (1986).
Bowers v. Hardwick, 478 U.S. 186 (1986).
Dallas v. Stanglin, 490 U.S. 19 (1989).

Bibliography and Further Reading
Hixson, Richard F. *Pornography and the Justices: The Supreme Court and the Intractable Obscenity Problem.* Carbondale: Southern Illinois University Press, 1996.

Tedford, Thomas L. *Freedom of Speech in the United States.* New York: Random House, 1985.

Van Alstyne, William W. *Interpretations of the First Amendment.* Durham, NC: Duke University Press, 1984.

GLOSSARY

A

Abandonment The surrender, relinquishment, disclaimer, or cession of property or of rights. Voluntary relinquishment of all right, title, claim, and possession, with no intention of reclamation.

The giving up of a thing absolutely, without reference to any particular person or purpose, such as vacating property with no intention of returning it, so that it may be appropriated by the next comer or finder. The voluntary relinquishment of possession of a thing by the owner with intention of terminating ownership, but without vesting it in any other person. The relinquishing of all title, possession, or claim, or a virtual, intentional throwing away of property.

Accessory Aiding or contributing in a secondary way or assisting in or contributing to as a subordinate.

In criminal law, contributing to or aiding in the commission of a crime. One who, without being present at the commission of an offense, becomes guilty of such offense, not as a chief actor, but as a participant, as by command, advice, instigation, or concealment; either before or after the fact of commission.

One who aids, abets, commands, or counsels another in the commission of a crime.

Accessory after the fact One who commits a crime by giving comfort or assistance to a felon, knowing that the felon has committed a crime, or is sought by authorities in connection with a serious crime.

Accomplice One who knowingly, voluntarily, and with common intent unites with the principal offender in the commission of a crime. One who is in some way involved with commission of a crime; partaker of guilt; one who aids or assists, or is an accessory. One who is guilty of complicity in a crime charged, either by being present and aiding or abetting in it, or having advised and encouraged it, though absent from place when it was committed. However, the mere presence, acquiescence, or silence, in the absence of a duty to act, is not enough, no matter how reprehensible it may be, to constitute one an accomplice. One is liable as an accomplice to the crime of another if he or she gave assistance or encouragement or failed to perform a legal duty to prevent it with the intent thereby to promote or facilitate commission of the crime.

Accord An agreement that settles a dispute, generally requiring a compromise or satisfaction with something less than what was originally demanded.

Acquittal The legal and formal certification of the innocence of a person who has been charged with a crime.

Action Conduct; behavior; something done; a series of acts.

A case or a lawsuit; a legal and formal demand for the enforcement of one's rights against another party asserted in a court of justice.

Actual authority The legal power, expressed or implied, that an agent possesses to represent and to bind into agreement the principal with a third party.

Actual damages Compensation awarded for the loss or the injury suffered by an individual.

Adjudication The legal process of resolving a dispute. The formal giving or pronouncing of a judgment or decree in a court proceeding; also the judgment or decision given. The entry of a decree by a court in respect to the parties in a case. It implies a hearing by a court, after notice, of legal evidence on the factual issue(s) involved. The equivalent of a determination. It indicates that the claims of all of the parties thereto have been considered and set at rest.

Administrative agency An official governmental body empowered with the authority to direct and supervise the implementation of particular legislative acts. In addition to *agency*, such governmental bodies may be called commissions, corporations (i.e., FDIC), boards, departments, or divisions.

Administrative law The body of law that allows for the creation of public regulatory agencies and contains all of the statutes, judicial decisions, and regulations that govern them. It is the body of law created by administrative agencies to implement their powers and duties in the form of rules, regulations, orders, and decisions.

Administrator A person appointed by the court to manage and take charge of the assets and liabilities of a decedent who has died without making a valid will.

Admissible A term used to describe information that is relevant to a determination of issues in any judicial proceeding so that such information can be properly considered by a judge or jury in making a decision.

Adultery Voluntary sexual relations between an individual who is married and someone who is not the individual's spouse.

Adversary system The scheme of American jurisprudence wherein a judge renders a decision in a controversy between parties who assert contradictory positions during a judicial examination, such as a trial or hearing.

Affidavit A written statement of facts voluntarily made by an affiant under an oath or affirmation administered by a person who is authorized to do so by law.

Affirmative action Employment programs required by federal statutes and regulations designed to remedy discriminatory practices in hiring minority group members; i.e., positive steps designed to eliminate existing and continuing discrimination, to remedy lingering effects of past discrimination, and to create systems and procedures to prevent future discrimination; commonly based on population percentages of minority groups in a particular area. Factors considered are race, color, sex, creed, and age.

Agent One who agrees and is authorized to act on behalf of another, a principal, to legally bind an individual in particular business transactions with third parties pursuant to an agency relationship.

Age of consent The age at which a person may marry without parental approval. The age at which a female is legally capable of agreeing to sexual intercourse, so that a male who engages in sex with her cannot be prosecuted for statutory rape.

Age of majority The age at which a person, formerly a minor or an infant, is recognized by law to be an adult, capable of managing his or her own affairs and responsible for any legal obligations created by his or her actions.

Aggravated assault A person is guilty of aggravated assault if he or she attempts to cause serious bodily injury to another or causes such injury purposely, knowingly, or recklessly under circumstances manifesting extreme indifference to the value of human life; or attempts to cause or purposely or knowingly causes bodily injury to another with a deadly weapon. In all jurisdictions, statutes punish such aggravated assaults as assault with intent to murder (or rob or kill or rape) and assault with a dangerous (or deadly) weapon more severely than "simple" assaults.

Alien Foreign-born person who has not been naturalized to become a U.S. citizen under federal law and the Constitution.

Alimony Payment a family court may order one person in a couple to make to the other when the couple separates or divorces.

Alimony pendente lite Temporary alimony awarded while separation and divorce proceedings are taking place. The award may cover the preparation for the suit, as well as general support.

Alternative dispute resolution Procedures for settling disputes by means other than litigation; i.e., by arbitration, mediation, or minitrials. Such procedures, which are usually less costly and more expeditious than litigation, are increasingly being used in commercial and labor disputes, divorce actions, in resolving motor vehicle and medical malpractice tort claims, and in other disputes that otherwise would likely involve court litigation.

Amendment The modification of materials by the addition of supplemental information; the deletion of unnecessary, undesirable, or outdated information; or the correction of errors existing in the text.

Amicus curiae [*Latin, Friend of the court.*] A person with strong interest in or views on the subject matter of an action, but not a party to the action, may petition the court for permission to file a brief, ostensibly on behalf of a party but actually to suggest a rationale consistent with his or her own views. Such amicus curiae briefs are commonly filed in appeals concerning matters of a broad public interest; i.e., civil rights cases. They may be filed by private persons or by the government. In appeals to the U.S. courts of appeals, an amicus brief may be filed only if accompanied by written consent of all parties, or by leave of court granted on motion or at the request of the court, except that consent or leave shall not be required when the brief is presented by the United States or an officer or agency thereof.

Amnesty The action of a government by which all persons or certain groups of persons who have committed a criminal offense—usually of a political nature that threatens the sovereignty of the government (such as sedition or treason)—are granted immunity from prosecution.

Annulment A judgment by a court that retroactively invalidates a marriage to the date of its formation.

Answer The first responsive pleading filed by the defendant in a civil action; a formal written statement that admits or denies the allegations in the complaint and sets forth any available affirmative defenses.

Apparent authority The amount of legal power a principal knowingly or negligently bestows onto an agent for representation with a third party, and which the third party reasonably believes the agent possesses.

Appeal Timely resort by an unsuccessful party in a lawsuit or administrative proceeding to an appropriate superior court empowered to review a final decision on the ground that it was based upon an erroneous application of law.

Appeals court *See* Appellate court or Court of appeal.

Appellate court A court having jurisdiction to review decisions of a trial-level or other lower court.

Appellate jurisdiction The power of a superior court or other tribunal to review the judicial actions of lower courts, particularly for legal errors, and to revise their judgments accordingly.

Apportionment The process by which legislative seats are distributed among units entitled to representation. Determination of the number of representatives that a state, county, or other subdivision may send to a legislative body. The U.S. Constitution provides for a census every ten years, on the basis of which Congress apportions representatives according to population. However, each state must have at least one representative. *Districting* is the establishment of the precise geographical boundaries of each such unit or constituency. Apportionment by state statute that denies the rule of one-person, one-vote is violative of equal protection laws.

Arbitration The submission of a dispute to an unbiased third person designated by the parties to the controversy, who agree in advance to comply with the award—a decision to be issued after a hearing at which both parties have an opportunity to be heard.

Arraignment The formal proceeding whereby the defendant is brought before the trial court to hear the charges against him or her and to enter a plea of guilty, not guilty, or no contest.

Arrest The detention and taking into custody of an individual for the purpose of answering the charges against him or her. An arrest involves the legal power of the individual to arrest, the intent to exercise that power, and the actual subjection to the control and will of the arresting authority.

Arrest warrant A written order issued by an authority of the state and commanding the seizure of the person named.

Arson At common law, the malicious burning or exploding of the dwelling house of another, or the burning of a building within the curtilage, the immediate surrounding space, of the dwelling of another.

Assault At common law, an intentional act by one person that creates an apprehension in another of an imminent harmful or offensive contact.

Assumption of risk A defense, facts offered by a party against whom proceedings have been instituted to diminish a plaintiff's cause of action or defeat recovery to an action in negligence, which entails proving that the plaintiff knew of a dangerous condition and voluntarily exposed himself or herself to it.

Attachment The legal process of seizing property to ensure satisfaction of a judgment.

Attempt An undertaking to do an act that entails more than mere preparation but does not result in the successful completion of the act.

Attractive nuisance doctrine The duty of an individual to take necessary precautions around equipment or conditions on his or her property that could attract and potentially injury children unable to perceive the risk of danger, such as an unguarded swimming pool or a trampoline.

Avoidance An escape from the consequences of a specific course of action through the use of legally acceptable means. Cancellation; the act of rendering something useless or legally ineffective.

B

Bail The system that governs the status of individuals charged with committing crimes from the time of their arrest to the time of their trial, and pending appeal, with the major purpose of ensuring their presence at trial.

Bait and switch A deceptive sales technique that involves advertising a low-priced item to attract customers to a store, then persuading them to buy more expensive goods by failing to have a sufficient supply of the advertised item on hand or by disparaging its quality.

Balancing A process sometimes used by the Supreme Court in deciding between the competing interests represented in a case.

Bankruptcy A federally authorized procedure by which a debtor—an individual, corporation, or municipality—is relieved of total liability for its debts by making court-approved arrangements for their partial repayment.

Battery At common law, an intentional unpermitted act causing harmful or offensive contact with the person of another.

Beneficiary An organization or a person for whom a trust is created and who thereby receives the benefits of the trust. One who inherits under a will. A person entitled to a beneficial interest or a right to profits, benefit, or advantage from a contract.

Bigamy The offense of willfully and knowingly entering into a second marriage while validly married to another individual.

Bilateral contract An agreement formed by an exchange of promises in which the promise of one party supports the promise of the other party.

Bill A declaration in writing. A document listing separate items. An itemized account of charges or costs. In equity practice, the first pleading in the action, that is, the paper in which the plaintiff sets out his or her case and demands relief from the defendant.

Bill of attainder A special legislative enactment that imposes a death sentence without a judicial trial upon a particular person or class of persons suspected of committing serious offenses, such as treason or a felony.

Bill of rights The first ten amendments to the U.S. Constitution, ratified in 1791, which set forth and guarantee certain fundamental rights and privileges of individuals, including freedom of religion, speech, press, and assembly; guarantee of a speedy jury trial in criminal cases; and protection against excessive bail and cruel and unusual punishment.

A list of fundamental rights included in each state constitution.

A declaration of individual rights and freedoms, usually issued by a national government.

Bill of sale In the law of contracts, a written agreement, previously required to be under seal, by which one person transfers to another a right to, or interest in, personal property and goods, a legal instrument that conveys title in property from seller to purchaser.

Black codes Laws, statutes, or rules that governed slavery and segregation of public places in the South prior to 1865.

Bona fide [*Latin, In good faith.*] Honest; genuine; actual; authentic; acting without the intention of defrauding.

Bona fide occupational qualification An essential requirement for performing a given job. The requirement may even be a physical condition beyond an individual's control, such as perfect vision, if it is absolutely necessary for performing a job.

Bonds Written documents by which a government, corporation, or individual—the obligator—promises to perform a certain act, usually the payment of a definite sum of money, to another—the obligee—on a certain date.

Booking The procedure by which law enforcement officials record facts about the arrest of and charges against a suspect, such as the crime for which the arrest was made, together with information concerning the identification of the suspect and other pertinent facts.

Breach of contract The breaking of a legal agreement that had been sealed by the signing of a written, legal contractual document.

Bribery The offering, giving, receiving, or soliciting of something of value for the purpose of influencing the action of an official in the discharge of his or her public or legal duties.

Brief A summary of the important points of a longer document. An abstract of a published judicial opinion prepared by a law student as part of an assignment in the case method study of law. A written document drawn up by an attorney for a party in a lawsuit or by a party appearing pro se that concisely states the (1) issues of a lawsuit; (2) facts that bring the parties to court; (3) relevant laws that can affect the subject of the dispute; and (4) arguments that explain how the law applies to the particular facts so that the case will be decided in the party's favor.

Broker An individual or firm employed by others to plan and organize sales or negotiate contracts for a commission.

Burden of proof The duty of a party to prove an asserted fact. The party is subject to the burden of persuasion—convincing a judge or jury—and the burden of going forward—proving wrong any evidence that damages the position of the party. In criminal cases the persuasion burden must include proof beyond a reasonable doubt.

Burglary The criminal offense of breaking and entering a building illegally for the purpose of committing a crime therein.

Bylaws The rules and regulations enacted by an association or a corporation to provide a framework for its operation and management.

C

Capacity The ability, capability, or fitness to do something; a legal right, power, or competency to perform some act. An ability to comprehend both the nature and consequences of one's acts.

Capital punishment The lawful infliction of death as a punishment; the death penalty.

Case law Legal principles enunciated and embodied in judicial decisions that are derived from the application of particular areas of law to the facts of individual cases.

Cause Each separate antecedent of an event. Something that precedes and brings about an effect or a result. A reason for an action or condition. A ground of a legal action. An agent that brings something about. That which in some manner is accountable for a condition that brings about an effect or that produces a cause for the resultant action or state.

A suit, litigation, or action. Any question, civil or criminal, litigated or contested before a court of justice.

Cause in fact The direct cause of an event. Commonly referred to as the "but for" rule, by which an event could not have happened but for the specified cause.

Cause of action The fact or combination of facts that gives a person the right to seek judicial redress or relief against another. Also, the legal theory forming the basis of a lawsuit.

Caveat emptor [*Latin, Let the buyer beware.*] A warning that notifies a buyer that the goods he or she is buying are "as is," subject to all defects.

Cease and desist order An order issued by an administrative agency or a court proscribing a person or a business entity from continuing a particular course of conduct.

Censorship The suppression or proscription of speech or writing that is deemed obscene, indecent, or unduly controversial.

Certiorari [*Latin, To be informed of.*] At common law, an original writ or order issued by the Chancery or King's Bench, commanding officers of inferior courts to submit the record of a cause pending before them to give the party more certain and speedy justice.

A writ that a superior appellate court issues on its discretion to an inferior court, ordering it to produce a certified record of a particular case it has tried, in order to determine whether any irregularities or errors occurred that justify review of the case.

A device by which the Supreme Court of the United States exercises its discretion in selecting the cases it will review.

Challenge for cause Request from a party that a prospective juror be disqualified for given causes or reasons.

Change of venue The removal of a lawsuit from one county or district to another for trial, often permitted in criminal cases where the court finds that the defendant would not receive a fair trial in the first location because of adverse publicity.

Charter A grant from the government of ownership rights in land to a person, a group of people, or an organization, such as a corporation.

A basic document of law of a municipal corporation granted by the state, defining its rights, liabilities, and responsibilities of self-government.

A document embodying a grant of authority from the legislature or the authority itself, such as a corporate charter.

The leasing of a mode of transportation, such as a bus, ship, or plane. A *charter-party* is a contract formed to lease a ship to a merchant in order to facilitate the conveyance of goods.

Chattel An item of personal property that is movable; it may be animate or inanimate.

Circumstantial evidence Information and testimony presented by a party in a civil or criminal action that permit conclusions that indirectly establish the existence or nonexistence of a fact or event that the party seeks to prove.

Citation A paper commonly used in various courts—such as a probate, matrimonial, or traffic court—that is served upon an individual to notify him or her that he or she is required to appear at a specific time and place.

Reference to a legal authority—such as a case, constitution, or treatise—where particular information may be found.

Citizens Those who, under the Constitution and laws of the United States, or of a particular community or of a foreign country, owe allegiance and are entitled to the enjoyment of all civil rights that accrue to those who qualify for that status.

Civil action A lawsuit brought to enforce, redress, or protect rights of private litigants (the plaintiffs and the defendants); not a criminal proceeding.

Civil death The forfeiture of rights and privileges of an individual who has been convicted of a serious crime.

Civil law Legal system derived from the Roman *Corpus Juris Civilis* of Emperor Justinian I; differs from a common-law system, which relies on prior decisions to determine the outcome of a lawsuit. Most European and South American countries have a civil law system. England and most of the countries it dominated or colonized, including Canada and the United States, have a common-law system. However, within these countries, Louisiana, Quebec, and Puerto Rico exhibit the influence of French and Spanish settlers in their use of civil law systems.

A body of rules that delineate private rights and remedies and govern disputes between individuals in such areas as contracts, property, and family law; distinct from criminal or public law.

Civil liberties Freedom of speech, freedom of press, freedom from discrimination, and other natural rights guaranteed and protected by the Constitution, which were intended to place limits on government.

Civil rights Personal liberties that belong to an individual owing to his or her status as a citizen or resident of a particular country or community.

Class action A lawsuit that allows a large number of people with a common interest in a matter to sue or be sued as a group.

Clause A section, phrase, paragraph, or segment of a legal document, such as a contract, deed, will, or constitution, that relates to a particular point.

Closing The final transaction between a buyer and seller of real property.

Closing argument The final factual and legal argument made by each attorney on all sides of a case in a trial prior to a verdict or judgment.

Code A systematic and comprehensive compilation of laws, rules, or regulations that are consolidated and classified according to subject matter.

Coercion The intimidation of a victim to compel the individual to do some act against his or her will by the use of psychological pressure, physical force, or threats. The crime of intentionally and unlawfully restraining another's freedom by threatening to commit a crime, accusing the victim of a crime, disclosing any secret that would seriously impair the victim's reputation in the community, or by performing or refusing to perform an official action lawfully requested by the victim, or by causing an official to do so.

A defense asserted in a criminal prosecution that a person who committed a crime did not do so of his or her own free will, but only because the individual was compelled by another through the use of physical force or threat of immediate serious bodily injury or death.

Cohabitation A living arrangement in which an unmarried couple live together in a long-term relationship that resembles a marriage.

Cohabitation agreement The contract concerning property and financial agreements between two individuals who intend to live together and to have sexual relations out of wedlock.

Collateral Related; indirect; not bearing immediately upon an issue. The property pledged or given as a security interest, or a guarantee for payment of a debt, that will be taken or kept by the creditor in case of a default on the original debt.

Collective bargaining agreement The contractual agreement between an employer and a labor union that governs wages, hours, and working conditions for employees which can be enforced against both the employer and the union for failure to comply with its terms.

Comity Courtesy; respect; a disposition to perform some official act out of goodwill and tradition rather than obligation or law. The acceptance or adoption of decisions or laws by a court of another jurisdiction, either foreign or domestic, based on public policy rather than legal mandate.

Commerce Clause The provision of the U.S. Constitution that gives Congress exclusive power over trade activities between the states and with foreign countries and Native American tribes.

Commercial paper A written instrument or document such as a check, draft, promissory note, or a certificate of deposit, that manifests the pledge or duty of one individual to pay money to another.

Commercial speech Advertising speech by commercial companies and service providers. Commercial speech is protected under the First Amendment as long as it is not false or misleading.

Common law The ancient law of England based upon societal customs and recognized and enforced by the judgments and decrees of the courts. The general body of statutes and case law that governed England and the American colonies prior to the American Revolution.

The principles and rules of action, embodied in case law rather than legislative enactments, applicable to the government and protection of persons and property that derive their authority from the community customs and traditions that evolved over the centuries as interpreted by judicial tribunals.

A designation used to denote the opposite of statutory, equitable, or civil; for example, a common-law action.

Common-law marriage A union of two people not formalized in the customary manner as prescribed by law but created by an agreement to marry followed by cohabitation.

Community property The holdings and resources owned in common by a husband and wife.

Commutation Modification, exchange, or substitution.

Comparable worth The idea that men and women should receive equal pay when they perform work that involves comparable skills and responsibility or that is of comparable worth to the employer; also known as pay equity.

Comparative negligence The measurement of fault in percentages by both parties to a negligence action, so that the award of damages is reduced proportionately to the amount of negligence attributed to the victim. In order to recover, the negligence of the victim must be less than that of the defendant.

Compelling state interest A basis of upholding a state statute, against constitutional challenges grounded on the First and Fourteenth Amendments, due to the important or "compelling" need for such state regulations. Often state laws implemented under a state's police power are deemed to have satisfied a compelling state interest and therefore will survive judicial scrutiny.

Compensatory damages A sum of money awarded in a civil action by a court to indemnify a person for the particular loss, detriment, or injury suffered as a result of the unlawful conduct of another.

Complaint The pleading that initiates a civil action; in criminal law, the document that sets forth the basis upon which a person is to be charged with an offense.

Conclusive presumption The presumption that a fact is true upon proof of another fact. Evidence to the contrary cannot refute the presumed fact. Proof of a basic fact creates the existence of the presumed fact, and that presumed fact becomes irrebuttable.

Concurrent jurisdiction The authority of several different courts, each of which is authorized to entertain and decide cases dealing with the same subject matter.

Concurrent powers The ability of Congress and state legislatures to independently make laws on the same subject matter.

Concurrent resolution An action of Congress passed in the form of an enactment of one house, with the other house in agreement, which expresses the ideas of Congress on a particular subject.

Concurring opinion An opinion by one or more judges that provides separate reasoning for reaching the same decision as the majority of the court.

Conditional Subject to change; dependent upon or granted based on the occurrence of a future, uncertain event.

Conditional acceptance A counter offer. Acceptance of an offer that differs in some respects from the original contract.

Condition precedent A stipulation in an agreement that must be performed before the contract can go into effect and become binding on the parties. In terms of estates, the condition must be performed before the estates can vest or be enlarged.

Condition subsequent A stipulation in a contract that discharges one party of any further liability or performance under an existing contract if the other party fails to satisfy the stipulation.

Confession A statement made by an individual that acknowledges his or her guilt in the commission of a crime.

Conflict of interest A term used to describe the situation in which a public official or fiduciary who, contrary to the obligation and absolute duty to act for the benefit of the public or a designated individual, exploits the relationship for personal benefit, typically pecuniary.

Consent Voluntary acquiescence to the proposal of another; the act or result of reaching an accord; a concurrence of minds; actual willingness that an act or an infringement of an interest shall occur.

Consent decree An agreement by the defendant to cease activities, alleged by the government to be unlawful, in exchange for the dismissal of the case. The court must approve the agreement before it issues the consent decree.

Consideration Something of value given by both parties to a contract that induces them to enter into the agreement to exchange mutual performances.

Consolidation The process of combining two or more parts together to make a whole.

Consolidation of corporations The formation of a new corporate entity through the dissolution of two or more existing corporations. The new entity takes over the assets and assumes the liabilities of the dissolved corporations.

Conspiracy An agreement between two or more persons to engage jointly in an unlawful or criminal act, or an act that is innocent in itself but becomes unlawful when done by the combination of actors.

Constituent An individual, a principal, who appoints another to act in his or her behalf, an agent, such as an attorney in a court of law or an elected official in government.

Constitution of the United States A written document executed by representatives of the people of the United States as the absolute rule of action and decision for all branches and officers of the government, and with which all subsequent laws and ordinances must be in accordance unless it has been changed by a constitutional amendment by the authority that created it.

Consumer An individual who purchases and uses products and services in contradistinction to manufacturers who produce the goods or services and wholesalers or retailers who distribute and sell them. A member of the general category of persons who are protected by state and federal laws regulating price policies, financing practices, quality of goods and services, credit reporting, debt collection, and other trade practices of U.S. commerce. A purchaser of a product or service who has a legal right to enforce any implied or express warranties pertaining to the item against the manufacturer who has introduced the goods or services into the marketplace or the seller who has made them a term of the sale.

Contempt An act of deliberate disobedience or disregard for the laws, regulations, or decorum of a public authority, such as a court or legislative body.

Content neutral The principle that the government may not show favoritism between differing points of view on a particular subject.

Contingent fee Payment to an attorney for legal services that depends, or is contingent, upon there being some recovery or award in the case. The payment is then a percentage of the amount recovered—such as 25 percent if the matter is settled, 30 percent if it proceeds to trial.

Continuance The adjournment or postponement of an action pending in a court to a later date of the same or another session of the court, granted by a court in response to a motion made by a party to a lawsuit. The entry into the trial record of the adjournment of a case for the purpose of formally evidencing it.

Contraband Any property that is illegal to produce or possess. Smuggled goods that are imported into or exported from a country in violation of its laws.

Contract implied in fact *See* Implied contract.

Contracts Agreements between two or more persons that create an obligation to do, or refrain from doing, a particular thing.

Contributing to delinquency A criminal offense arising from an act or omission that leads to juvenile delinquency.

Contributory negligence Negligence on the part of the plaintiff for failure to exercise reasonable care for his or her own safety, and which contributes to the negligence of the defendant as the actual cause of the plaintiff's injury.

Conversion Any unauthorized act that deprives an owner of personal property without his or her consent.

Copyright An intangible right granted by statute to the author or originator of certain literary or artistic productions, whereby, for a limited period, the exclusive privilege is given to the person to make copies of the same for publication and sale.

Corporations Artificial entities that are created by state statute, and that are treated much like individuals under the law, having legally enforceable rights, the ability to acquire debt and pay out profits, the ability to hold and transfer property, the ability to enter into contracts, the requirement to pay taxes, and the ability to sue and be sued.

Cosigner An obligor—a person who becomes obligated, under a commercial paper, such as a promissory note or check—by signing the instrument in conjunction with the original obligor, thereby promising to pay it in full.

Counsel An attorney or lawyer. The rendition of advice and guidance concerning a legal matter, contemplated form of argument, claim, or action.

Counterclaim A claim by a defendant opposing the claim of the plaintiff and seeking some relief from the plaintiff for the defendant.

Counteroffer In contract law, a proposal made in response to an original offer modifying its terms, but which has the legal effect of rejecting it.

Court below The court from which a case was removed for review by an appellate court.

Court of appeal An intermediate federal judicial tribunal of review that is found in thirteen judicial districts, called circuits, in the United States.

A state judicial tribunal that reviews a decision rendered by an inferior tribunal to determine whether it made errors that warrant the reversal of its judgment.

Court of claims A state judicial tribunal established as the forum in which to bring certain types of lawsuits against the state or its political subdivisions, such as a county. The former designation given to a federal tribunal created in 1855 by Congress with original jurisdiction—initial authority—to decide an action brought against the United States that is based upon the Constitution, federal law, any regulation of the executive department, or any express or implied contracts with the federal government.

Court of equity A court that presides over equity suits, suits of fairness and justness, both in its administration and proceedings. Courts of equity no longer exist due to the consolidation of law and equity actions in federal and state courts.

Court of general jurisdiction A superior court, which by its constitution, can review and exercise a final judgment in a case under its authority. No further judicial inspection is conducted, except by an appellate power.

Covenant An agreement, contract, or written promise between two individuals that frequently constitutes a pledge to do or refrain from doing something.

Credit A term used in accounting to describe either an entry on the right-hand side of an account or the process of making such an entry. A credit records the increases in liabilities, owner's equity, and revenues as well as the decreases in assets and expenses.

A sum in taxation that is subtracted from the computed tax, as opposed to a deduction that is ordinarily subtracted from gross income to determine adjusted gross income or taxable income. Claim for a particular sum of money.

The ability of an individual or a company to borrow money or procure goods on time, as a result of a positive opinion by the particular lender concerning such borrower's solvency and reliability. The right granted by a creditor to a debtor to delay satisfaction of a debt, or to incur a debt and defer the payment thereof.

Creditor An individual to whom an obligation is owed because he or she has given something of value in exchange. One who may legally demand and receive money, either through the fulfillment of a contract or due to injury sustained as a result of another's negligence or intentionally wrongful act. The term *creditor* is also used to describe an individual who is engaged in the business of lending money or selling items for which immediate payment is not demanded but an obligation of repayment exists as of a future date.

Criminal law A body of rules and statutes that defines conduct prohibited by the government because it threatens and harms public safety and welfare and that establishes punishment to be imposed for the commission of such acts.

Cross-examination The questioning of a witness or party during a trial, hearing, or deposition by the party opposing the one who asked the person to testify in order to evaluate the truth of that person's testimony, to develop the testimony further, or to accomplish any other objective. The interrogation of a witness or party by the party opposed to the one who called the witness or party, upon a subject raised during direct examination—the initial questioning of a witness or party—on the merits of that testimony.

Cruel and unusual punishment Such punishment as would amount to torture or barbarity, any cruel and degrading punishment not known to the common law, or any fine, penalty, confinement, or treatment so dispro-

portionate to the offense as to shock the moral sense of the community.

Custodial parent The parent to whom the guardianship of the children in a divorced or estranged relationship has been granted by the court.

D

Damages Monetary compensation that is awarded by a court in a civil action to an individual who has been injured through the wrongful conduct of another party.

Death penalty *See* Capital punishment.

Debtor One who owes a debt or the performance of an obligation to another, who is called the creditor; one who may be compelled to pay a claim or demand; anyone liable in a claim, whether due or to become due.

In bankruptcy law, a person who files a voluntary petition or person against whom an involuntary petition is filed. A person or municipality concerning which a bankruptcy case has been commenced.

Declaration of rights *See* Bill of rights.

Decree A judgment of a court that announces the legal consequences of the facts found in a case and orders that the court's decision be carried out. A decree in equity is a sentence or order of the court, pronounced on hearing and understanding all the points in issue, and determining the rights of all the parties to the suit, according to equity and good conscience. It is a declaration of the court announcing the legal consequences of the facts found. With the procedural merger of law and equity in the federal and most state courts under the Rules of Civil Procedure, the term *judgment* has generally replaced *decree*.

Decriminalization The passing of legislation that changes criminal acts or omissions into noncriminal ones without punitive sanctions.

Deed A written instrument, which has been signed and delivered, by which one individual, the grantor, conveys title to real property to another individual, the grantee; a conveyance of land, tenements, or hereditaments, from one individual to another.

De facto [*Latin,* In fact.] In fact; in deed; actually.

Defamation Any intentional false communication, either written or spoken, that harms a person's reputation; decreases the respect, regard, or confidence in which a person is held; or induces disparaging, hostile, or disagreeable opinions or feelings against a person.

Defendant The person defending or denying; the party against whom relief or recovery is sought in an action or suit, or the accused in a criminal case.

Defense The forcible repulsion of an unlawful and violent attack, such as the defense of one's person, property, or country in time of war.

The totality of the facts, law, and contentions presented by the party against whom a civil action or criminal prosecution is instituted in order to defeat or diminish the plaintiff's cause of action or the prosecutor's case. A reply to the claims of the other party, which asserts reasons why the claims should be disallowed. The defense may involve an absolute denial of the other party's factual allegations or may entail an affirmative defense, which sets forth completely new factual allegations. Pursuant to the rules of federal civil procedure, numerous defenses may be asserted by motion as well as by answer, while other defenses must be pleaded affirmatively.

De jure [*Latin,* In law.] Legitimate; lawful, as a matter of law. Having complied with all the requirements imposed by law.

Delegation of powers Transfer of authority by one branch of government in which such authority is vested to some other branch or administrative agency.

Deliberate Willful; purposeful; determined after thoughtful evaluation of all relevant factors; dispassionate. To act with a particular intent, which is derived from a careful consideration of factors that influence the choice to be made.

Delinquent An individual who fails to fulfill an obligation, or otherwise is guilty of a crime or offense.

Domestic partnership laws Legislation and regulations related to the legal recognition of non-marital relationships between persons who are romantically involved with each other, have set up a joint residence, and have registered with cities recognizing said relationships.

Demurrer An assertion by the defendant that although the facts alleged by the plaintiff in the complaint may be true, they do not entitle the plaintiff to prevail in the lawsuit.

Denaturalization The deprivation of an individual's rights as a citizen.

Deportation Banishment to a foreign country, attended with confiscation of property and deprivation of civil rights.

The transfer of an alien, by exclusion or expulsion, from the United States to a foreign country. The removal or sending back of an alien to the country from which he or she came because his or her presence is deemed inconsistent with the public welfare, and without any punishment being imposed or contemplated. The grounds for deportation are set forth at 8 U.S.C.A., sec. 1251, and the procedures are provided for in secs. 1252–1254.

Deposition The testimony of a party or witness in a civil or criminal proceeding taken before trial, usually in an attorney's office.

Desegregation Judicial mandate making illegal the practice of segregation.

Desertion The act by which a person abandons and forsakes, without justification, a condition of public, social, or family life, renouncing its responsibilities and evading its duties. A willful abandonment of an employment or duty in violation of a legal or moral obligation.

Criminal desertion is a husband's or wife's abandonment or willful failure without just cause to provide for the care, protection, or support of a spouse who is in ill health or impoverished circumstances.

Detention hearing A proceeding to determine the restraint to be imposed upon an individual awaiting trial, such as bail or, in the case of a juvenile, placement in a shelter.

Deterrent Anything that discourages or obstructs a person from committing an act, such as punishment for criminal acts.

Detriment Any loss or harm to a person or property; relinquishment of a legal right, benefit, or something of value.

Diplomatic immunity A principle of international law that provides foreign diplomats with protection from legal action in the country in which they work.

Directed verdict A procedural device whereby the decision in a case is taken out of the hands of the jury by the judge.

Direct examination The primary questioning of a witness during a trial that is conducted by the side for which that person is acting as a witness.

Direct tax A charge levied by the government upon property, which is determined by its financial worth.

Disaffirm Repudiate; revoke consent; refuse to support former acts or agreements.

Disbar To revoke an attorney's license to practice law.

Discharge To liberate or free; to terminate or extinguish. A discharge is the act or instrument by which a contract or agreement is ended. A mortgage is discharged if it has been carried out to the full extent originally contemplated or terminated prior to total execution.

Discharge also means to release, as from legal confinement in prison or the military service, or from some legal obligation such as jury duty, or the payment of debts by a person who is bankrupt. The document that indicates that an individual has been legally released from the military service is called a discharge.

Disclaimer The denial, refusal, or rejection of a right, power, or responsibility.

Discovery A category of procedural devices employed by a party to a civil or criminal action, prior to trial, to require the adverse party to disclose information that is essential for the preparation of the requesting party's case and that the other party alone knows or possesses.

Discretion Independent use of judgment to choose between right and wrong, to make a decision, or to act cautiously under the circumstances.

Discretion in decision making Discretion is the power or right to make official decisions using reason and judgment to choose from among acceptable alternatives.

Discrimination In constitutional law, the grant by statute of particular privileges to a class arbitrarily designated from a sizable number of persons, where no reasonable distinction exists between the favored and disfavored classes. Federal laws, supplemented by court decisions, prohibit discrimination in such areas as employment, housing, voting rights, education, and access to public facilities. They also proscribe discrimination on the basis of race, age, sex, nationality, disability, or religion. In addition, state and local laws can prohibit discrimination in these areas and in others not covered by federal laws.

Dishonor To refuse to accept or pay a draft or to pay a promissory note when duly presented. An instrument is dishonored when a necessary or optional presentment is made and due acceptance or payment is refused, or cannot be obtained within the prescribed time, or in case of bank collections, the instrument is seasonably returned by the midnight deadline; or presentment is excused and the instrument is not duly accepted or paid. Includes the insurer of a letter of credit refusing to pay or accept a draft or demand for payment.

As respects the flag, to deface or defile, imputing a lively sense of shaming or an equivalent acquiescent callousness.

Disinherit To cut off from an inheritance. To deprive someone, who would otherwise be an heir to property or another right, of his or her right to inherit.

Dismissal A discharge of an individual or corporation from employment. The disposition of a civil or criminal proceeding or a claim or charge made therein by a court order without a trial or prior to its completion which, in effect, is a denial of the relief sought by the commencement of the action.

Disposition Act of disposing; transferring to the care or possession of another. The parting with, alienation of, or giving up of property. The final settlement of a matter and, with reference to decisions announced by a court, a judge's ruling is commonly referred to as disposition, regardless of level of resolution. In criminal procedure, the sentencing or other final settlement of a criminal case. With respect to a mental state, denotes an attitude, prevailing tendency, or inclination.

Disposition hearing The judicial proceeding for passing sentence upon a defendant who was found guilty of the charge(s) against him or her.

Dispossession The wrongful, nonconsensual ouster or removal of a person from his or her property by trick, compulsion, or misuse of the law, whereby the violator obtains actual occupation of the land.

Dissent An explicit disagreement by one or more judges with the decision of the majority on a case before them.

Dissolution Act or process of dissolving; termination; winding up. In this sense it is frequently used in the phrase *dissolution of a partnership*.

Division of powers *See* Separation of powers.

Divorce A court decree that terminates a marriage; also known as marital dissolution.

Domicile The legal residence of a person, which determines jurisdiction for taxation and voting, as well as other legal rights and privileges. Considered to be the permanent residence of an individual, or the place where one intends to return after an absence, such as in the case of the president who physically lives in the White House, but has a domicile in his or her home state.

Double indemnity A term of an insurance policy by which the insurance company promises to pay the insured or the beneficiary twice the amount of coverage if loss occurs due to a particular cause or set of circumstances.

Double jeopardy A second prosecution for the same offense after acquittal or conviction or multiple punishments for the same offense. The evil sought to be avoided by prohibiting double jeopardy is double trial and double conviction, not necessarily double punishment.

Draft A written order by the first party, called the drawer, instructing a second party, called the drawee (such as a bank), to pay money to a third party, called the payee. An order to pay a certain sum in money, signed by a drawer, payable on demand or at a definite time, to order or bearer.

A tentative, provisional, or preparatory writing out of any document (as a will, contract, lease, and so on) for purposes of discussion and correction, which is afterward to be prepared in its final form.

Compulsory conscription of persons into military service.

A small arbitrary deduction or allowance made to a merchant or importer, in the case of goods sold by weight or taxable by weight, to cover possible loss of weight in handling or from differences in scales.

Due process of law A fundamental, constitutional guarantee that all legal proceedings will be fair and that one will be given notice of the proceedings and an opportunity to be heard before the government acts to take away one's life, liberty, or property. Also, a constitutional guarantee that a law shall not be unreasonable, arbitrary, or capricious.

Duress Unlawful pressure exerted upon a person to coerce that person to perform an act that he or she ordinarily would not perform.

Duty A legal obligation that entails mandatory conduct or performance. With respect to the laws relating to customs duties, a tax owed to the government for the import or export of goods.

E

Easement A right of use over the property of another. Traditionally the permitted kinds of uses were limited, the most important being rights of way and rights concerning flowing waters. The easement was normally for the benefit of adjoining lands, no matter who the owner was (an easement appurtenant), rather than for the benefit of a specific individual (easement in gross).

Emancipation The act or process by which a person is liberated from the authority and control of another person.

Embezzlement The fraudulent appropriation of another's property by a person who is in a position of trust, such as an agent or employee.

Eminent domain The power to take private property for public use by a state, municipality, or private person or corporation authorized to exercise functions of public character, following the payment of just compensation to the owner of that property.

Employment at will A common-law rule that an employment contract of indefinite duration can be terminated by either the employer or the employee at any time, for any reason; also known as terminable at will.

Encumbrance A burden, obstruction, or impediment on property that lessens its value or makes it less mar-

ketable. An encumbrance (also spelled incumbrance) is any right or interest that exists in someone other than the owner of an estate and that restricts or impairs the transfer of the estate or lowers its value. This might include an easement, a lien, a mortgage, a mechanic's lien, or accrued and unpaid taxes.

Entitlement An individual's right to receive a value or benefit provided by law.

Entrapment The act of government agents or officials that induces a person to commit a crime he or she is not previously disposed to commit.

Enumerated powers Authority specifically granted to a body of the national government under the U.S. Constitution, such as the powers granted to Congress in Article I, Section 8.

Equal Pay Act Federal law which mandates the same pay for all persons who do the same work without regard to sex, age, race or ability. For work to be "equal" within meaning of the act, it is not necessary that the jobs be identical, but only that they be substantially equal.

Equal protection The constitutional guarantee that no person or class of persons shall be denied the same protection of the laws that is enjoyed by other persons or other classes in like circumstances in their lives, liberty, property, and pursuit of happiness.

Equitable Just; that which is fair and proper according to the principles of justice and right.

Equitable action A cause of action that seeks an equitable remedy, such as relief sought with an injunction.

Equity The pursuit of fairness. In the U.S. legal system, a body of laws that seeks to achieve fairness on an individual basis. In terms of property, the money value of property in excess of claims, liens, or mortgages on the property.

Error A mistake in a court proceeding concerning a matter of law or fact which might provide a ground for a review of the judgment rendered in the proceeding.

Escrow Something of value, such as a deed, stock, money, or written instrument, that is put into the custody of a third person by its owner, a grantor, an obligor, or a promisor, to be retained until the occurrence of a contingency or performance of a condition.

Espionage The act of securing information of a military or political nature that a competing nation holds secret. It can involve the analysis of diplomatic reports, publications, statistics, and broadcasts, as well as spying, a clandestine activity carried out by an individual or individuals working under a secret identity for the benefit of a nation's information gathering techniques. In the United States, the organization that heads most activities dedicated to espionage is the Central Intelligence Agency.

Establishment Clause The provision in the First Amendment which provides that there will be no laws created respecting the establishment of a religion, inhibiting the practice of a religion, or giving preference to any or all religions. It has been interpreted to also denounce the discouragement of any or all religions.

Estate The degree, quantity, nature, and extent of interest that a person has in real and personal property. An estate in lands, tenements, and hereditaments signifies such interest as the tenant has therein. *Estate* is commonly used in conveyances in connection with the words *right, title,* and *interest,* and is, to a great degree, synonymous with all of them.

When used in connection with probate proceedings, the term encompasses the total property of whatever kind that is owned by a decedent prior to the distribution of that property in accordance with the terms of a will, or when there is no will, by the laws of inheritance in the state of domicile of the decedent. It means, ordinarily, the whole of the property owned by anyone, the realty as well as the personalty.

In its broadest sense, the social, civic, or political condition or standing of a person; or a class of persons considered as grouped for social, civic, or political purposes.

Estate tax The tax levied upon the entire estate of the decedent before any part of the estate can be transferred to an heir. An estate tax is applied to the right of the deceased person to transfer property at death. An "inheritance tax" is imposed upon an heir's right to receive the property.

Estoppel A legal principle that precludes a party from denying or alleging a certain fact owing to that party's previous conduct, allegation, or denial.

Euthanasia The merciful act or practice of terminating the life of an individual or individuals inflicted with incurable and distressing diseases in a relatively painless manner.

Eviction The removal of a tenant from possession of premises in which he or she resides or has a property interest, done by a landlord either by reentry upon the premises or through a court action.

Excise tax A tax imposed on the performance of an act, the engaging in an occupation, or the enjoyment of a privilege. A tax on the manufacture, sale, or use of goods or on the carrying on of an occupation activity, or a tax on the transfer of property. In current usage the term has been

extended to include various license fees and practically every internal revenue tax except the income tax (i.e., federal alcohol and tobacco excise taxes).

Exclusionary rule The principle based on federal constitutional law that evidence illegally seized by law enforcement officers in violation of a suspect's right to be free from unreasonable searches and seizures cannot be used against the suspect in a criminal prosecution.

Exclusive jurisdiction The legal authority of a court or other tribunal to preside over a suit, an action, or a person to the exclusion of any other court.

Exclusive power The authority held solely by one individual, such as the President, or one group, such as a regulatory committee.

Exclusive right The privilege that only a grantee can exercise, prohibiting others from partaking in the same.

Executive agreement An agreement made between the head of a foreign country and the President of the United States. This agreement does not have to be submitted to the Senate for consent, and it supersedes any contradicting state law.

Executive orders Presidential policy directives that implement or interpret a federal statute, a constitutional provision, or a treaty.

Executor The individual named by a decedent to administer the provisions of the decedent's will.

Ex parte [*Latin, On one side only.*] Done by, for, or on the application of one party alone.

Expatriation The voluntary act of abandoning or renouncing one's country and becoming the citizen or subject of another.

Expert witness A witness, such as a psychological statistician or ballistics expert, who possesses special or superior knowledge concerning the subject of his or her testimony.

Ex post facto laws [*Latin, "After-the-fact" laws.*] Laws that provide for the infliction of punishment upon a person for some prior act that, at the time it was committed, was not illegal.

Express Clear; definite; explicit; plain; direct; unmistakable; not dubious or ambiguous. Declared in terms; set forth in words. Directly and distinctly stated. Made known distinctly and explicitly, and not left to inference. Manifested by direct and appropriate language, as distinguished from that which is inferred from conduct. The word is usually contrasted with *implied.*

Express contract An oral or written contract where the terms of the agreement are explicitly stated.

Expressed power *See* Enumerated powers.

Express warranty An additional written or oral guarantee to the underlying sales agreement made to the consumer as to the quality, description, or performance of a good.

Extortion The obtaining of property from another induced by wrongful use of actual or threatened force, violence, or fear, or under color of official right.

Extradition The transfer of an accused from one state or country to another state or country that seeks to place the accused on trial.

F

Family court A court that presides over cases involving: (1) child abuse and neglect; (2) support; (3) paternity; (4) termination of custody due to constant neglect; (5) juvenile delinquency; and (6) family offenses.

Federal circuit courts The 12 circuit courts making up the U.S. Federal Circuit Court System. The twelfth circuit presides over the District of Columbia. Decisions made by the federal district courts can be reviewed by the court of appeals in each circuit.

Federal district courts The first of three levels of the federal court system, which includes the U.S. Court of Appeals and the U.S. Supreme Court. If a participating party disagrees with the ruling of a federal district court in its case, it may petition for the case to be moved to the next level in the federal court system.

Felon An individual who commits a crime of a serious nature, such as burglary or murder. A person who commits a felony.

Felony A serious crime, characterized under federal law and many state statutes as any offense punishable by death or imprisonment in excess of one year.

Fiduciary An individual in whom another has placed the utmost trust and confidence to manage and protect property or money. The relationship wherein one person has an obligation to act for another's benefit.

First degree murder Murder committed with deliberately premeditated thought and malice, or with extreme atrocity or cruelty. The difference between first and second degree murder is the presence of the specific intention to kill.

Forbearance Refraining from doing something that one has a legal right to do. Giving of further time for repayment of an obligation or agreement; not to enforce a claim at its due date. A delay in enforcing a legal right. Act by which a creditor waits for payment of debt due by a debtor after it becomes due.

Within usury law, the contractual obligation of a lender or creditor to refrain, during a given period of time, from requiring the borrower or debtor to repay the loan or debt that is then due and payable.

Foreclosure A procedure by which the holder of a mortgage—an interest in land providing security for the performance of a duty or the payment of a debt—sells the property upon the failure of the debtor to pay the mortgage debt and, thereby, terminates his or her rights in the property.

Forgery The creation of a false written document or alteration of a genuine one, with the intent to defraud.

Formal contract An agreement between two or more individuals in which all the terms are in writing.

Franchise A special privilege to do certain things that is conferred by government on an individual or a corporation and which does not belong to citizens generally of common right (i.e., a right granted to offer cable television service).

A privilege granted or sold, such as to use a name or to sell products or services. In its simplest terms, a franchise is a license from the owner of a trademark or trade name permitting another to sell a product or service under that name or mark. More broadly stated, a franchise has evolved into an elaborate agreement under which the franchisee undertakes to conduct a business or sell a product or service in accordance with methods and procedures prescribed by the franchisor, and the franchisor undertakes to assist the franchisee through advertising, promotion, and other advisory services.

The right of suffrage; the right or privilege of voting in public elections. Such a right is guaranteed by the Fifteenth, Nineteenth, and Twenty-fourth Amendments to the U.S. Constitution.

As granted by a professional sports association, franchise is a privilege to field a team in a given geographic area under the auspices of the league that issues it. It is merely an incorporeal right.

Fraud A false representation of a matter of fact—whether by words or by conduct, by false or misleading allegations, or by concealment of what should have been disclosed—that deceives and is intended to deceive another so that the individual will act upon it to her or his legal injury.

Freedom of assembly *See* Freedom of association.

Freedom of association The right to associate with others for the purpose of engaging in constitutionally protected activities, such as to peacefully assemble.

Freedom of religion The First Amendment right to individually believe and to practice or exercise one's belief.

Freedom of speech The right, guaranteed by the First Amendment to the U.S. Constitution, to express beliefs and ideas without unwarranted government restriction.

Freedom of the press The right, guaranteed by the First Amendment to the U.S. Constitution, to gather, publish, and distribute information and ideas without government restriction; this right encompasses freedom from prior restraints on publication and freedom from censorship.

Full Faith and Credit Clause The clause of the U.S. Constitution that provides that the various states must recognize legislative acts, public records, and judicial decisions of the other states within the United States.

Full warranty The guarantee on the workmanship and materials of a product. If the product is defective in any way, then the consumer is entitled to corrective action from the manufacturer, at no cost to the consumer, and within a reasonable amount of time.

Fundamental rights Rights which derive, or are implied, from the terms of the U.S. Constitution, such as the Bill of Rights, the first ten amendments to the Constitution.

G

Gag rule A rule, regulation, or law that prohibits debate or discussion of a particular issue.

Garnishment A legal procedure by which a creditor can collect what a debtor owes by reaching the debtor's property when it is in the hands of someone other than the debtor.

General partnership A business relationship with more than one owner where all parties manage the business and equally share any profits or losses.

Gerrymander The process of dividing a particular state or territory into election districts in such a manner as to accomplish an unlawful purpose, such as to give one party a greater advantage.

Good faith Honesty; a sincere intention to deal fairly with others.

Grandfather clause A portion of a statute that provides that the law is not applicable in certain circumstances due to preexisting facts.

Grand jury A panel of citizens that is convened by a court to decide whether it is appropriate for the government to indict (proceed with a prosecution against) someone suspected of a crime.

Grand larceny A category of larceny—the offense of illegally taking the property of another—in which the value of the property taken is greater than that set for petit larceny.

Grounds The basis or foundation; reasons sufficient in law to justify relief.

Guarantee One to whom a guaranty is made. This word is also used, as a noun, to denote the contract of guaranty or the obligation of a guarantor, and, as a verb, to denote the action of assuming the responsibilities of a guarantor.

Guaranty As a verb, to agree to be responsible for the payment of another's debt or the performance of another's duty, liability, or obligation if that person does not perform as he or she is legally obligated to do; to assume the responsibility of a guarantor; to warrant.

As a noun, an undertaking or promise that is collateral to the primary or principal obligation and that binds the guarantor to performance in the event of nonperformance by the principal obligor.

Guardian A person lawfully invested with the power, and charged with the obligation, of taking care of and managing the property and rights of a person who, because of age, understanding, or self-control, is considered incapable of administering his or her own affairs.

Guardian ad litem A guardian appointed by the court to represent the interests of infants, the unborn, or incompetent persons in legal actions.

H

Habeas corpus [*Latin, You have the body.*] A writ (court order) that commands an individual or a government official who has restrained another to produce the prisoner at a designated time and place so that the court can determine the legality of custody and decide whether to order the prisoner's release.

Hate crime A crime motivated by race, religion, gender, sexual orientation, or other prejudice.

Hearing A legal proceeding where issues of law or fact are tried and evidence is presented to help determine the issue.

Hearsay A statement made out of court that is offered in court as evidence to prove the truth of the matter asserted.

Heir An individual who receives an interest in, or ownership of, land, tenements, or hereditaments from an ancestor who had died intestate, through the laws of descent and distribution. At common law, an heir was the individual appointed by law to succeed to the estate of an ancestor who died without a will. It is commonly used today in reference to any individual who succeeds to property, either by will or law.

Homicide The killing of one human being by another human being.

Hung jury A trial jury duly selected to make a decision in a criminal case regarding a defendant's guilt or innocence, but who are unable to reach a verdict due to a complete division in opinion.

I

Immunity Exemption from performing duties that the law generally requires other citizens to perform, or from a penalty or burden that the law generally places on other citizens.

Impeachment A process used to charge, try, and remove public officials for misconduct while in office.

Implied consent Consent that is inferred from signs, actions, or facts, or by inaction or silence.

Implied contract A contract created not by express agreement, but inferred by law, based on the conduct of the parties and the events surrounding the parties' dealings.

Implied power Authority that exists so that an expressly granted power can be carried into effect.

Implied warranty A promise, arising by operation of law, that something that is sold will be merchantable and fit for the purpose for which it is sold.

Imprimatur [*Latin, Let it be printed.*] A licence or allowance, granted by the constituted authorities, giving permission to print and publish a book. This allowance was formerly necessary in England before any book could lawfully be printed, and in some other countries is still required.

Inalienable Not subject to sale or transfer; inseparable.

Inalienable rights Rights (i.e., life, liberty, and the pursuit of happiness) which cannot be ceded or transferred without permission from the individual who possesses them.

Incapacity The absence of legal ability, competence, or qualifications.

Income tax A charge imposed by government on the annual gains of a person, corporation, or other taxable unit derived through work, business pursuits, investments, property dealings, and other sources determined in accordance with the Internal Revenue Code or state law.

Incorporate To formally create a corporation pursuant to the requirements prescribed by state statute; to confer a corporate franchise upon certain individuals.

Indemnity Recompense for loss, damage, or injuries; restitution or reimbursement.

Indeterminate That which is uncertain or not particularly designated.

Indictment A written accusation charging that an individual named therein has committed an act or admitted to doing something that is punishable by law.

Indirect tax A tax upon some right, privilege, or corporate franchise.

Individual rights Rights and privileges constitutionally guaranteed to the people, as set forth by the Bill of Rights, the ability of a person to pursue life, liberty, and property.

Infants Persons who are under the age of the legal majority—at common law, 21 years, now generally 18 years. According to the sense in which this term is used, it may denote the age of the person, the contractual disabilities that nonage entails, or his or her status with regard to other powers or relations.

Information The formal accusation of a criminal offense made by a public official; the sworn, written accusation of a crime.

Inherent Derived from the essential nature of, and inseparable from, the object itself.

Inherent powers Implicit control, which by nature cannot be derived from another.

Inherent rights Rights held within a person because he or she exists. *See also* inalienable rights.

Inheritance Property received from a decedent, either by will or through state laws of intestate succession, where the decedent has failed to execute a valid will.

Inheritance tax A tax imposed upon the right of an individual to receive property left to him or her by a decedent.

Injunction A court order by which an individual is required to perform or is restrained from performing a particular act. A writ framed according to the circumstances of the individual case.

In loco parentis [*Latin, In the place of a parent.*] The legal doctrine under which an individual assumes parental rights, duties, and obligations without going through the formalities of legal adoption.

Inquisitorial system A method of legal practice in which the judge endeavors to discover facts while simultaneously representing the interests of the state in a trial.

Insanity defense A defense asserted by an accused in a criminal prosecution to avoid liability for the commission of a crime because, at the time of the crime, the person did not appreciate the nature or quality or wrongfulness of the act.

Insider In the context of federal regulation of the purchase and sale of securities, anyone who has knowledge of facts not available to the general public.

Insider trading The trading of stocks and bonds based on information gained from special private, privileged information affecting the value of the stocks and bonds.

Insurance A contract whereby, for a specified consideration, one party undertakes to compensate the other for a loss relating to a particular subject as a result of the occurrence of designated hazards.

Intangibles Property that is a "right," such as a patent, copyright, trademark, etc., or one that is lacking physical existence, like good will. A nonphysical, noncurrent asset that exists only in connection with something else, such as the good will of a business.

Intent A determination to perform a particular act or to act in a particular manner for a specific reason; an aim or design; a resolution to use a certain means to reach an end.

Intermediate courts Courts with general ability or authority to hear a case (trial, appellate, or both), but are not the court of last resort within the jurisdiction.

Intestate The description of a person who dies without making a valid will or the reference made to this condition.

Involuntary manslaughter The act of unlawfully killing another human being unintentionally.

Irrevocable Unable to cancel or recall; that which is unalterable or irreversible.

Item veto *See* Line item veto.

J

Joint committee Members of two houses of a state or federal legislature that work together as one group.

Joint resolution A type of measure that Congress may consider and act upon; the other types of measures being bills, concurrent resolutions, and simple resolutions, in addition to treaties in the Senate.

Judicial discretion Sound judgment exercised by a judge in determining what is right and equitable under the law.

Judicial review A court's authority to examine an executive or legislative act and to invalidate that act if it is contrary to constitutional principles.

Jurisdiction The geographic area over which authority extends; legal authority; the authority to hear and determine causes of action.

Jurisprudence From the Latin term *juris prudentia,* which means "the study, knowledge, or science of law;" in the United States, more broadly associated with the philosophy of law.

Jury In trials, a group of people selected and sworn to inquire into matters of fact and to reach a verdict on the basis of evidence presented to it.

Jury nullification The ability of a jury to acquit the defendant despite the amount of evidence against him or her in a criminal case.

Jus sanguinis The determination of a person's citizenship based upon the citizenship of the individual's parents.

Jus soli The determination of a person's citizenship based upon the individual's place of birth.

Just cause A reasonable and lawful ground for action.

Justifiable homicide The killing of another in self-defense or in the lawful defense of one's property; killing of another when the law demands it, such as in execution for a capital crime.

Juvenile A young individual who has not reached the age whereby he or she would be treated as an adult in the area of criminal law. The age at which the young person attains the status of being a legal majority varies from state to state—as low as 14 years old, as high as 18 years old; however, the Juvenile Delinquency Act determines that a youthful person under the age of eighteen is a "juvenile" in cases involving federal jurisdiction.

Juvenile court The court presiding over cases in which young persons under a certain age, depending on the area of jurisdiction, are accused of criminal acts.

Juvenile delinquency The participation of a youthful individual, one who falls under the age at which he or she could be tried as an adult, in illegal behavior. *See also* Delinquent child.

L

Landlord A lessor of real property; the owner or possessor of an estate in land or a rental property, who, in an exchange for rent, leases it to another individual known as the tenant.

Lapse The termination or failure of a right or privilege because of a neglect to exercise that right or to perform some duty within a time limit, or because a specified contingency did not occur. The expiration of coverage under an insurance policy because of the insured's failure to pay the premium.

The common-law principle that a gift in a will does not take effect but passes into the estate remaining after the payment of debts and particular gifts, if the beneficiary is alive when the will is executed but subsequently predeceases the testator.

Larceny The unauthorized taking and removal of the personal property of another by a person who intends to permanently deprive the owner of it; a crime against the right of possession.

Lease A contractual agreement by which one party conveys an estate in property to another party, for a limited period, subject to various conditions, in exchange for something of value, but still retains ownership.

Legal defense A complete and acceptable response as to why the claims of the plaintiff should not be granted in a point of law.

Legal tender All U.S. coins and currencies—regardless of when coined or issued—including (in terms of the Federal Reserve System) Federal Reserve notes and circulating notes of Federal Reserve banks and national banking associations that are used for all debts, public and private, public charges, taxes, duties, and dues.

Legation The persons commissioned by one government to exercise diplomatic functions at the court of another, including the ministers, secretaries, attachés, and interpreters, are collectively called the *legation* of their government. The word also denotes the official residence of a foreign minister.

Legislation Lawmaking; the preparation and enactment of laws by a legislative body.

Legislative intent The history of events leading to the enactment of a law that a court refers to when interpreting an ambiguous or inconsistent statute.

Liability A comprehensive legal term that describes the condition of being actually or potentially subject to a legal obligation.

Libel and slander Two torts that involve the communication of false information about a person, a group, or an entity, such as a corporation. Libel is any defama-

tion that can be seen, such a writing, printing, effigy, movie, or statue. Slander is any defamation that is spoken and heard.

Lien A right given to another by the owner of property to secure a debt, or one created by law in favor of certain creditors.

Limited liability partnership A form of general partnership that provides an individual partner protection against personal liability for certain partnership obligations.

Limited warranty A written performance guarantee that only covers workmanship or materials for a specified period of time.

Line item veto The power that governors in some states have to strike individual items from appropriation bills without affecting any other provisions.

Litigation An action brought in court to enforce a particular right. The act or process of bringing a lawsuit in and of itself; a judicial contest; any dispute.

Living will A written document that allows a patient to give explicit instructions about medical treatment to be administered when the patient is terminally ill or permanently unconscious; also called an advance directive.

Loan shark A person who lends money in exchange for its repayment at an interest rate that exceeds the percentage approved by law and who uses intimidating methods or threats of force in order to obtain repayment.

Lobbying The process of influencing public and government policy at all levels: federal, state, and local.

Lower court The court where a suit was first heard. *See also* Court below.

M

Magistrate Any individual who has the power of a public civil officer or inferior judicial officer, such as a justice of the peace.

Majority Full age; legal age; age at which a person is no longer a minor. The age at which, by law, a person is capable of being legally responsible for all of his or her acts (i.e., contractual obligations), and is entitled to the management of his or her own affairs and to the enjoyment of civic rights (i.e., right to vote). The opposite of minority. Also the *status* of a person who is a major in age.

The greater number. The number greater than half of any total.

Malfeasance The commission of an act that is unequivocally illegal or completely wrongful.

Malice The intentional commission of a wrongful act, absent justification, with the intent to cause harm to others; conscious violation of the law that injures another individual; a mental state indicating a disposition in disregard of social duty and a tendency toward malfeasance.

Malice aforethought A predetermination to commit an act without legal justification or excuse. A malicious design to injure. An intent, at the time of a killing, willfully to take the life of a human being, or an intent willfully to act in callous and wanton disregard of the consequences to human life; but *malice aforethought* does not necessarily imply any ill will, spite, or hatred towards the individual killed.

Malpractice The breach by a member of a profession of either a standard of care or a standard of conduct.

Mandate A judicial command, order, or precept, written or oral, from a court; a direction that a court has the authority to give and an individual is bound to obey.

Manslaughter The unjustifiable, inexcusable, and intentional killing of a human being without deliberation, premeditation, and malice. The unlawful killing of a human being without any deliberation, which may be involuntary, in the commission of a lawful act without due caution and circumspection.

Material Important; affecting the merits of a case; causing a particular course of action; significant; substantial. A description of the quality of evidence that possesses such substantial probative value as to establish the truth or falsity of a point in issue in a lawsuit.

Material fact A fact that is necessary in determining a case, without which there would be no defense. Disclosure of the fact is necessary for the reasonable person to make a prudent decision.

Mediation A settlement of a dispute or controversy by setting up an independent person between two contending parties in order to aid them in the settlement of their disagreement.

Mens rea [*Latin, Guilty mind.*] As an element of criminal responsibility, a guilty mind; a guilty or wrongful purpose; a criminal intent. Guilty knowledge and willfulness.

Merger The combination or fusion of one thing or right into another thing or right of greater or larger importance so that the lesser thing or right loses its individuality and becomes identified with the greater whole.

Minor An infant or person who is under the age of legal competence. A term derived from the civil law, which described a person under a certain age as *less than* so many

years. In most states, a person is no longer a minor after reaching the age of 18 (though state laws might still prohibit certain acts until reaching a greater age; i.e., purchase of liquor). Also, less; of less consideration; lower; a person of inferior condition.

Misdemeanor Offenses lower than felonies and generally those punishable by fine, penalty, forfeiture, or imprisonment other than in a penitentiary. Under federal law, and most state laws, any offense other than a felony is classified as a misdemeanor. Certain states also have various classes of misdemeanors (i.e., Class A, B, etc.).

Mistrial A courtroom trial that has been terminated prior to its normal conclusion. A mistrial has no legal effect and is considered an invalid or nugatory trial. It differs from a "new trial," which recognizes that a trial was completed but was set aside so that the issues could be tried again.

Mitigating circumstances Circumstances that may be considered by a court in determining culpability of a defendant or the extent of damages to be awarded to a plaintiff. Mitigating circumstances do not justify or excuse an offense but may reduce the severity of the charge. Similarly, a recognition of mitigating circumstances to reduce a damage award does not imply that the damages were not suffered but that they have been partially ameliorated.

Mitigation of damages The use of reasonable care and diligence in an effort to minimize or avoid injury.

Monopoly An economic advantage held by one or more persons or companies deriving from the exclusive power to carry on a particular business or trade or to manufacture and sell a particular item, thereby suppressing competition and allowing such persons or companies to raise the price of a product or service substantially above the price that would be established by a free market.

Moratorium A suspension of activity or an authorized period of delay or waiting. A moratorium is sometimes agreed upon by the interested parties, or it may be authorized or imposed by operation of law. The term also is used to denote a period of time during which the law authorizes a delay in payment of debts or performance of some other legal obligation. This type of moratorium is most often invoked during times of distress, such as war or natural disaster.

Mortgage A legal document by which the owner (buyer) transfers to the lender an interest in real estate to secure the repayment of a debt, evidenced by a mortgage note. When the debt is repaid, the mortgage is discharged, and a satisfaction of mortgage is recorded with the register or recorder of deeds in the county where the mortgage was recorded. Because most people cannot afford to buy real estate with cash, nearly every real estate transaction involves a mortgage.

Motion A written or oral application made to a court or judge to obtain a ruling or order directing that some act be done in favor of the applicant. The applicant is known as the moving party, or the movant.

Motive An idea, belief, or emotion that impels a person to act in accordance with that state of mind.

Murder The unlawful killing of another human being without justification or excuse.

N

National origin The country in which a person was born or from which his or her ancestors came. It is typically calculated by employers to provide equal employment opportunity statistics in accordance with the provisions of the Civil Rights Act.

Naturalization A process by which a person gains nationality and becomes entitled to the privileges of citizenship. While groups of individuals have been naturalized in history by treaties or laws of Congress, such as in the case of Hawaii, typically naturalization occurs on the individual level upon the completion of the following steps: (1) an individual of majority age, who has been a lawful resident of the United States for five years, petitions for naturalization; (2) the Immigration and Naturalization Service conducts an investigation to establish whether the petitioner can speak English and write English, has a general knowledge of American government and history, especially in regards to the principles of the Constitution, and is in good moral standing; (3) a hearing is held before a U.S. district court, or, when applicable, a state court of record; and (4) a second hearing is held after a period of at least thirty days when the oath of allegiance is administered.

Natural law The unwritten body of universal moral principles that underlie the ethical and legal norms by which human conduct is sometimes evaluated and governed. Natural law is often contrasted with positive law, which consists of the written rules and regulations enacted by government. The term *natural law* is derived from the Roman term *jus naturale*. Adherents to natural law philosophy are known as naturalists.

Necessary and Proper Clause The statement contained in Article I, Section 8, Clause 18 of the U.S. Constitution that gives Congress the power to pass any laws that are "necessary and proper" to carrying out its specifically granted powers.

Necessity A defense asserted by a criminal or civil defendant that he or she had no choice but to break the law.

Negligence Conduct that falls below the standards of behavior established by law for the protection of others against unreasonable risk of harm. A person has acted negligently if he or she has departed from the conduct expected of a reasonably prudent person acting under similar circumstances.

Negligence is also the name of a cause of action in the law of torts. To establish negligence, a plaintiff must prove that the defendant had a duty to the plaintiff, the defendant breached that duty by failing to conform to the required standard of conduct, the defendant's negligent conduct was the cause of the harm to the plaintiff, and the plaintiff was, in fact, harmed or damaged.

No-fault divorce Common name for the type of divorce where "irreconcilable" differences are cited as the reason for the termination of the marriage. Fault by either party does not have to be proven.

Nolo contendere [*Latin, I will not contest it.*] A plea in a criminal case by which the defendant answers the charges made in the indictment by declining to dispute or admit the fact of his or her guilt.

Nominal damages Minimal money damages awarded to an individual in an action where the person has not suffered any substantial injury or loss for which he or she must be compensated.

Nonprofit A corporation or an association that conducts business for the benefit of the general public without shareholders and without a profit motive.

Notary public A public official whose main powers include administering oaths and attesting to signatures, both important and effective ways to minimize fraud in legal documents.

Notice Information; knowledge of certain facts or of a particular state of affairs. The formal receipt of papers that provide specific information.

Nuisance A legal action to redress harm arising from the use of one's property.

Null Of no legal validity, force, or effect; nothing. The phrase "null and void" is used in the invalidation of contracts or statutes.

O

Obscenity The character or quality of being obscene; an act, utterance, or item tending to corrupt public morals by its indecency or lewdness.

Option A privilege, for which a person had paid money, that grants that person the right to purchase or sell certain commodities or certain specified securities at any time within an agreed period for a fixed price.

A right, which operates as a continuing offer, given in exchange for consideration—something of value—to purchase or lease property at an agreed price and terms within a specified time.

Ordinance A law, statute, or regulation enacted by a municipal corporation.

Original jurisdiction The authority of a tribunal to entertain a lawsuit, try it, and set forth a judgment on the law and facts.

Overbreadth doctrine A principle of judicial review that holds that a law is invalid if it punishes constitutionally protected speech or conduct along with speech or conduct that the government may limit to further a compelling government interest.

P

Palimony The settlement awarded at the termination of a non-marital relationship, where the couple lived together for a long period of time and where there was an agreement that one partner would support the other in return for the second making a home and performing domestic duties.

Pardon The action of an executive official of the government that mitigates or sets aside the punishment for a crime.

Parens patriae ["Parent of the country."] The principle that the state should provide for and protect the interests of those who cannot take care of themselves, such as juveniles or the insane. The term also refers to the state's authority to bring legal suits on behalf of its residents, such as antitrust actions.

Parental liability A statute, enacted in some states, that makes parents liable for damages caused by their children, if it is found that the damages resulted from the parents' lack of control over the acts of the child.

Parent corporation An enterprise, which is also known as a parent company, that owns more than 50 percent of the voting shares of its subsidiary.

Parole The conditional release of a person convicted of a crime prior to the expiration of that person's term of imprisonment, subject to both the supervision of the correctional authorities during the remainder of the term and a resumption of the imprisonment upon violation of the conditions imposed.

Parol evidence *Parol* refers to verbal expressions or words. Verbal evidence, such as the testimony of a witness at trial.

Parol evidence rule The principle that a finalized, written contract cannot be altered by evidence of contempo-

raneous oral agreements to change, explain, or contradict the original contract.

Partnership An association of two or more persons engaged in a business enterprise in which the profits and losses are shared proportionally. The legal definition of a partnership is generally stated as "an association of two or more persons to carry on as co-owners of a business for profit" (Revised Uniform Partnership Act sec. 101 [1994]).

Patent Open; manifest; evident.

Patents Rights, granted to inventors by the federal government, pursuant to its power under Article I, Section 8, Clause 8, of the U.S. Constitution, that permit them to exclude others from making, using, or selling an invention for a definite, or restricted, period of time.

Pawnbroker A person who engages in the business of lending money, usually in small sums, in exchange for personal property deposited with him or her that can be kept or sold if the borrower fails or refuses to repay the loan.

Payee The person who is to receive the stated amount of money on a check, bill, or note.

Peremptory challenge The right to challenge a juror without assigning, or being required to assign, a reason for the challenge.

Perjury A crime that occurs when an individual willfully makes a false statement during a judicial proceeding, after he or she has taken an oath to speak the truth.

Personal property Everything that is the subject of ownership that does not come under the denomination of real property; any right or interest that an individual has in movable things.

Personal recognizance *See* Release on own recognizance.

Petition A written application from a person or persons to some governing body or public official asking that some authority be exercised to grant relief, favors, or privileges.

A formal application made to a court in writing that requests action on a certain matter.

Petit jury The ordinary panel of twelve persons called to issue a verdict in a civil action or a criminal prosecution.

Petit larceny A form of larceny—the stealing of another's personal property—in which the value of the property that is taken is generally less than $50.

Plaintiff The party who sues in a civil action; a complainant; the prosecution—that is, a state or the United States representing the people—in a criminal case.

Plain view doctrine In the context of searches and seizures, the principle that provides that objects perceptible by an officer who is rightfully in a position to observe them can be seized without a search warrant and are admissible as evidence.

Plea A formal response by the defendant to the affirmative assertions of the plaintiff in a civil case or to the charges of the prosecutor in a criminal case.

Plea bargaining The process whereby a criminal defendant and prosecutor reach a mutually satisfactory disposition of a criminal case, subject to court approval.

Pleading Asking a court to grant relief. The formal presentation of claims and defenses by parties to a lawsuit. The specific papers by which the allegations of the parties to a lawsuit are presented in proper form; specifically, the complaint of a plaintiff and the answer of a defendant, plus any additional responses to those papers that are authorized by law.

Plurality The opinion of an appellate court in which more justices join than in any concurring opinion.

The excess of votes cast for one candidate over those votes cast for any other candidate.

Pocket veto A method of indirectly vetoing a bill due to a loophole in the Constitution. The loophole allows a bill that is left unsigned by the president or by the governor of a state at the end of a legislative session to be vetoed by default.

Police power The authority conferred upon the states by the Tenth Amendment to the U.S. Constitution which the states delegate to their political subdivisions to enact measures to preserve and protect the safety, health, welfare, and morals of the community.

Poll tax A specified sum of money levied upon each person who votes.

Polygamy The offense of having more than one wife or husband at the same time.

Power of attorney A written document in which one person (the principal) appoints another person to act as an agent on his or her behalf, thus conferring authority on the agent to perform certain acts or functions on behalf of the principal.

Precedent A court decision that is cited as an example or analogy to resolve similar questions of law in later cases.

Precinct A constable's or police district. A small geographical unit of government. An election district created for convenient localization of polling places. A county or municipal subdivision for casting and counting votes in elections.

Preferential treatment Consideration for an individual which is prioritized based on whether the person meets a certain requirement, such as residency. In employment, this type of consideration has been found to be a violation of fair employment practices.

Preliminary hearing A proceeding before a judicial officer in which the officer must decide whether a crime was committed, whether the crime occurred within the territorial jurisdiction of the court, and whether there is probable cause to believe that the defendant committed the crime.

Premarital agreement *See* Prenuptial agreement.

Premeditate To think of an act beforehand; to contrive and design; to plot or lay plans for the execution of a purpose.

Prenuptial agreement An agreement, made prior to marriage, between individuals contemplating marriage, to establish and secure property and other financial rights for one or both of the spouses and their children.

Preponderance of evidence A standard of proof that must be met by a plaintiff if he or she is to win a civil action.

Pre-sentence hearing A hearing commenced after the criminal trial judge examines the pre-sentence report and other relevant materials before passing sentence on the defendant.

Pre-sentence investigation Research that is conducted by court services or a probation officer relating to the prior criminal record, education, employment, and other information about a person convicted of a crime, for the purpose of assisting the court in passing sentence.

Pre-sentence report The written report of the pre-sentence investigation for the judge to evaluate before passing sentence on the defendant. Typically the report covers the following: description of the background, employment history, residency and medical history; information on the environment to which the defendant will return and the resources that will be available to him or her; the probation officer's view of the defendant; full description of the defendant's criminal record; and recommendations on sentencing.

Presentment A grand jury statement that a crime was committed; a written notice, initiated by a grand jury, that states that a crime occurred and that an indictment should be drawn.

In relation to commercial paper, presentment is a demand for the payment or acceptance of a negotiable instrument, such as a check. The holder of a negotiable instrument generally makes a presentment to the maker, acceptor, drawer, or drawee.

Pretrial motion A written or oral request made to the court before the trial to obtain a ruling in favor of the movant, such as a motion to dismiss or a motion to suppress evidence.

Preventive detention The confinement in a secure facility of a person who has not been found guilty of a crime.

Prima facie [*Latin,* On the first appearance.] A fact presumed to be true unless it is disproved.

Prima facie case A case that, because it is supported by the requisite minimum of evidence and is free of obvious defects, can go to the jury; thus the defendant is required to proceed with its case rather than move for dismissal or a directed verdict.

Primary liability In commercial law, the liability of a contract signer.

Principal A source of authority; a sum of a debt or obligation producing interest; the head of a school. In an agency relationship, the principal is the person who gives authority to another, called an agent, to act on his or her behalf. In criminal law, the principal is the chief actor or perpetrator of a crime; those who aid, abet, counsel, command, or induce the commission of a crime may also be principals. In investments and banking, the principal refers to the person for whom a broker executes an order; it may also mean the capital invested or the face amount of a loan.

Prior restraint Government prohibition of speech in advance of publication.

Privacy In constitutional law, the right of people to make personal decisions regarding intimate matters; under the common law, the right of people to lead their lives in a manner that is reasonably secluded from public scrutiny, whether such scrutiny comes from a neighbor's prying eyes, an investigator's eavesdropping ears, or a news photographer's intrusive camera; and in statutory law, the right of people to be free from unwarranted drug testing and electronic surveillance.

Private That which affects, characterizes, or belongs to an individual person, as opposed to the general public.

Private nuisance Anything that creates an unreasonable interference with the use and enjoyment of the property of an individual or small group.

Private property Property that belongs exclusively to an individual for his or her use. This tangible property can be possessed or transferred to another, such as a house or land.

Privilege An advantage, benefit, or exemption possessed by an individual, company, or class beyond those held by others.

Privileges and immunities Concepts contained in the U.S. Constitution that place the citizens of each state on an equal basis with citizens of other states with respect to advantages resulting from citizenship in those states and citizenship in the United States.

Probable cause Apparent facts discovered through logical inquiry that would lead a reasonably intelligent and prudent person to believe that an accused person has committed a crime, thereby warranting his or her prosecution, or that a cause of action has accrued, justifying a civil lawsuit.

Probate The court process by which a will is proved valid or invalid. The legal process wherein the estate of a decedent is administered.

Probate court Called Surrogate or Orphan's Court in some states, the probate court presides over the probate of wills, the administration of estates, and, in some states, the appointment of guardians or approval of the adoption of minors.

Probation A sentence whereby a convict is released from confinement but is still under court supervision; a testing or a trial period. It can be given in lieu of a prison term or can suspend a prison sentence if the convict has consistently demonstrated good behavior.

The status of a convicted person who is given some freedom on the condition that for a specified period he or she acts in a manner approved by a special officer to whom he or she must report.

An initial period of employment during which a new, transferred, or promoted employee must show the ability to perform the required duties.

Procedural due process The constitutional guarantee that one's liberty and property rights may not be affected unless reasonable notice and an opportunity to be heard in order to present a claim or defense are provided.

Product liability The responsibility of a manufacturer or vendor of goods to compensate for injury caused by a defective good that it has provided for sale.

Promissory note A written, signed, unconditional promise to pay a certain amount of money on demand at a specified time. A written promise to pay money that is often used as a means to borrow funds or take out a loan.

Property A thing or things owned either by government—public property—or owned by private individuals, groups, or companies—private property.

Property right A generic term that refers to any type of right to specific property whether it is personal or real property, tangible or intangible; i.e., a professional athlete has a valuable property right in his or her name, photograph, and image, and such right may be saleable by the athlete.

Pro se For one's own behalf; in person. Appearing for oneself, as in the case of one who does not retain a lawyer and appears for himself or herself in court.

Prosecute To follow through; to commence and continue an action or judicial proceeding to its ultimate conclusion. To proceed against a defendant by charging that person with a crime and bringing him or her to trial.

Prosecuting attorney An appointed or elected official in each judicial district, circuit, or county, that carries out criminal prosecutions on behalf of the State or people. Federal crimes are prosecuted by U.S. Attorneys.

Prosecution The proceedings carried out before a competent tribunal to determine the guilt or innocence of a defendant. The term also refers to the government attorney charging and trying a criminal case.

Protective order A court order, direction, decree, or command to protect a person from further harassment, service of process, or discovery.

Provision Anticipated accommodation(s) that may need to be made to fulfill an obligation in the event that something happens.

Proximate cause An act from which an injury results as a natural, direct, uninterrupted consequence and without which the injury would not have occurred.

Proximate consequence or result A consequence or result that naturally follows from one's negligence and is reasonably foreseeable and probable.

Proxy A representative; an agent; a document appointing a representative.

Public forum An open-discussion meeting that takes place in an area which is accessible to or shared by all members of a community.

Public hearing The due process of an individual before a tribunal to hear evidence and testimony in determination of the defendant's guilt or innocence.

Punitive damages Monetary compensation awarded to an injured party that goes beyond that which is necessary to compensate the individual for losses and that is intended to punish the wrongdoer.

Purchase To buy; the transfer of property from one person to another by an agreement, which sets forth the price and terms of the sale. Under the Uniform Commercial Code (UCC), taking by sale, discount, negotiation, mortgage, pledge, lien, issue, reissue, gift, or any voluntary transaction.

Q

Quiet enjoyment A covenant that promises that the grantee or tenant of an estate in real property will be able to possess the premises in peace, without disturbance by hostile claimants.

Quitclaim deed An instrument of conveyance of real property that passes any title, claim, or interest, that the grantor has in the premises but does not make any representations as to the validity of such title.

Quorum A majority of an entire body; i.e., a quorum of a legislative assembly.

Quota A quantitative boundary set for a class of things or people.

R

Rape A criminal offense defined in most states as forcible sexual relations with a person against that person's will.

Ratification The confirmation or adoption of an act that has already been performed.

Reapportionment The realignment in legislative districts brought about by changes in population and mandated in the constitutional requirement of one person, one vote.

Reasonable care The degree of caution that a rational and competent individual would exercise in a given circumstance. It is an subjective test used to determine negligence.

Reasonable person A phrase frequently used in tort and criminal law to denote a hypothetical person in society who exercises average care, skill, and judgment in conduct and who serves as a comparative standard for determining liability.

Rebut To defeat, dispute, or remove the effect of the other side's facts or arguments in a particular case or controversy.

Rebuttable presumption A conclusion as to the existence or nonexistence of a fact that a judge or jury must draw when evidence has been introduced and admitted as true in a lawsuit but that can be contradicted by evidence to the contrary.

Recall The right or procedure by which a public official may be removed from a position by a vote of the people prior to the end of the term of office.

Recognizance A recorded obligation, entered into before a tribunal, in which an individual pledges to perform a specific act or to subscribe to a certain course of conduct.

Redlining A discriminatory practice whereby lending institutions refuse to make mortgage loans, regardless of an applicant's credit history, on properties in particular areas in which conditions are allegedly deteriorating.

Redress Compensation for injuries sustained; recovery or restitution for harm or injury; damages or equitable relief. Access to the courts to gain reparation for a wrong.

Redress of grievances The right to request relief from the government for an injustice or wrong it has committed, as guaranteed by the First Amendment.

Referendum The right reserved to the people to approve or reject an act of the legislature, or the right of the people to approve or reject legislation that has been referred to them by the legislature.

Refugees Individuals who leave their native country for social, political, or religious reasons, or who are forced to leave as a result of any type of disaster, including war, political upheaval, and famine.

Regulation A rule of order having the force of law, prescribed by a superior or competent authority, relating to the actions of those under the authority's control.

Regulatory agency See Administrative agency.

Rehabilitation The restoration of former rights, authority, or abilities.

Release A contractual agreement by which one individual assents to relinquish a claim or right under the law to another individual against whom such a claim or right is enforceable.

Release on own recognizance The release of an individual who is awaiting trial without a bail bond. It is used in place of bail when the judge is satisfied that the defendant will appear for trial, given the defendant's past history, his or her roots in the community, his or her regular employment, the recommendation of the prosecutor, the

type of crime, and the improbability that the defendant will commit another crime while awaiting trial.

Remand To send back.

Remedy The manner in which a right is enforced or satisfied by a court when some harm or injury, recognized by society as a wrongful act, is inflicted upon an individual.

Removal The transfer of a person or thing from one place to another. The transfer of a case from one court to another. In this sense, removal generally refers to a transfer from a court in one jurisdiction to a court in another, whereas a change of venue may be granted simply to move a case to another location within the same jurisdiction.

Rent Control The system by which the federal, state, and local governments regulate rent rates by placing ceilings on the amount that private individuals can be charged for rent.

Replevin A legal action to recover the possession of items of personal property.

Replevy In regards to replevin, the return of goods to the original owner pending the outcome of the case. Also, the release of an individual on bail.

Repossession The taking back of an item that has been sold on credit and delivered to the purchaser because the payments have not been made on it.

Reprieve The suspension of the execution of the death penalty for a period of time.

Rescind To declare a contract void—of no legal force or binding effect—from its inception and thereby restore the parties to the positions they would have occupied had no contract ever been made.

Rescission The cancellation of a prison inmate's tentative parole date. The abrogation of a contract, effective from its inception, thereby restoring the parties to the positions they would have occupied if no contract had ever been formed.

Reservation A clause in a deed of real property whereby the grantor, one who transfers property, creates and retains for the grantor some right or interest in the estate granted, such as rent or an easement, a right of use over the land of another. A large tract of land that is withdrawn by public authority from sale or settlement and appropriated to specific public uses, such as parks or military posts. A tract of land under the control of the Bureau of Indian Affairs to which a Native American tribe retains its original title of ownership, or that has been set aside from the public domain for use by a tribe.

Reserve Funds set aside to cover future expenses, losses, or claims. To retain; to keep in store for future or special use; to postpone to a future time.

Residence Personal presence at some place of abode.

Resolution The official expression of the opinion or will of a legislative body.

Restraining order A command of the court issued upon the filing of an application for an injunction, prohibiting the defendant from performing a threatened act until a hearing on the application can be held.

Restrictive covenant A provision in a deed limiting the use of the property and prohibiting certain uses. A clause in contracts of partnership and employment prohibiting a contracting party from engaging in similar employment for a specified period of time within a certain geographical area.

Retainer A contract between attorney and client specifying the nature of the services to be rendered and the cost of the services.

Retribution Punishment or reward for an act. In criminal law, punishment is based upon the theory that every crime demands payment.

Reverse discrimination Discrimination against a group of people that is alleged to have resulted from the affirmation action guidelines applied for a different group of people who were historically discriminated against by the former group.

Revocation The recall of some power or authority that has been granted.

Rider A schedule or writing annexed to a document such as a legislative bill or insurance policy.

Right of legation *See* Legation.

Right-to-work laws State laws permitted by section 14(b) of the Taft-Hartley Act that provide in general that employees are not required to join a union as a condition of getting or retaining a job.

Robbery The taking of money or goods in the possession of another, from his or her person or immediate presence, by force or intimidation.

Rule of law Rule according to law; rule under law; or rule according to a higher law.

S

Sabotage The willful destruction or impairment of, or defective production of, war material or national defense

material, or harm to war premises or war utilities. During a labor dispute, the willful and malicious destruction of an employer's property or interference with his or her normal operations.

Sales agreement A present or future covenant that transfers ownership of goods or real estate from the seller to the buyer at an agreed upon price and terms.

Search warrant A court order authorizing the examination of a place for the purpose of discovering contraband, stolen property, or evidence of guilt to be used in the prosecution of a criminal action.

Second degree murder The unlawful taking of human life with malice, but without premeditated thought.

Secured transactions Business dealings that grant a creditor a right in property owned or held by a debtor to assure the payment of a debt or the performance of some obligation.

Security Protection; assurance; indemnification.

Security deposit Money aside from the payment of rent that a landlord requires a tenant to pay to be kept separately in a fund for use should the tenant cause damage to the premises or otherwise violate terms of the lease.

Sedition A revolt or an incitement to revolt against established authority, usually in the form of treason or defamation against government.

Seditious libel A written communication intended to incite the overthrow of the government by force or violence.

Segregation The act or process of separating a race, class, or ethnic group from a society's general population.

Self-defense The protection of one's person or property against some injury attempted by another.

Self-incrimination Giving testimony in a trial or other legal proceeding that could subject one to criminal prosecution.

Sentencing The post-conviction stage of a criminal justice process, in which the defendant is brought before the court for the imposition of a penalty.

Separate but equal The doctrine first enunciated by the U.S. Supreme Court in *Plessy v. Ferguson*, 163 U.S. 537, 16 S. Ct. 1138, 41 L. Ed. 256 (1896), establishing that different facilities for blacks and whites was valid under the Equal Protection Clause of the Fourteenth Amendment as along as they were equal.

Separation of church and state The separation of religious and government interest to ensure that religion does not become corrupt by government and that government does not become corrupt by religious conflict. The principle prevents the government from supporting the practices of one religion over another. It also enables the government to do what is necessary to prevent one religious group from violating the rights of others.

Separation of powers The division of state and federal government into three independent branches.

Settlement The act of adjusting or determining the dealings or disputes between persons without pursuing the matter through a trial.

Sexual harassment Unwelcome sexual advances, requests for sexual favors, and other verbal or physical conduct of a sexual nature that tends to create a hostile or offensive work environment.

Share A portion or part of something that may be divided into components, such as a sum of money. A unit of stock that represents ownership in a corporation.

Shield laws Statutes affording a privilege to journalists not to disclose in legal proceedings confidential information or sources of information obtained in their professional capacities.

Statutes that restrict or prohibit the use of certain evidence in sexual offense cases, such as evidence regarding the lack of chastity of the victim.

Shoplifting Theft of merchandise from a store or business establishment.

Silent partner An investment partner in a business who has no involvement in the management of the business.

Slander *See* Libel and slander.

Small claims court A special court, sometimes called conciliation court, that provides expeditious, informal, and inexpensive adjudication of small claims.

Sole proprietorship A form of business in which one person owns all the assets of the business, in contrast to a partnership or a corporation.

Solicitation Urgent request, plea or entreaty; enticing, asking. The criminal offense of urging someone to commit an unlawful act.

Sovereignty The supreme, absolute, and uncontrollable power by which an independent state is governed and from which all specific political powers are derived; the intentional independence of a state, combined with the right and power of regulating its internal affairs without foreign interference.

Specific performance An extraordinary equitable remedy that compels a party to execute a contract according to the precise terms agreed upon or to execute it substantially so that, under the circumstances, justice will be done between the parties.

Standing committee A group of legislators, who are ranked by seniority, that deliberate on bills, resolutions, and other items of business within its particular jurisdiction.

Stare decisis [*Latin, Let the decision stand.*] The policy of courts to abide by or adhere to principles established by decisions in earlier cases.

State courts Judicial tribunals established by each of the fifty states.

Status offense A type of crime that is not based upon prohibited action or inaction but rests on the fact that the offender has a certain personal condition or is of a specified character.

Statute An act of a legislature that declares, proscribes, or commands something; a specific law, expressed in writing.

Statute of frauds A type of state law, modeled after an old English law, that requires certain types of contracts to be in writing.

Statute of limitations A type of federal or state law that restricts the time within which legal proceedings may be brought.

Statutory Created, defined, or relating to a statute; required by statute; conforming to a statute.

Statutory law A law which is created by an act of the legislature.

Statutory rape Sexual intercourse by an adult with a person below a statutorily designated age.

Steering The process whereby builders, brokers, and rental property managers induce purchasers or lessees of real property to buy land or rent premises in neighborhoods composed of persons of the same race.

Stock A security issued by a corporation that represents an ownership right in the assets of the corporation and a right to a proportionate share of profits after payment of corporate liabilities and obligations.

Strict liability Absolute legal responsibility for an injury that can be imposed on the wrongdoer without proof of carelessness or fault.

Subcontractor One who takes a portion of a contract from the principal contractor or from another subcontractor.

Sublease The leasing of part or all of the property held by a tenant, as opposed to a landlord, during a portion of his or her unexpired balance of the term of occupancy.

Subpoena [*Latin, Under penalty.*] A formal document that orders a named individual to appear before a duly authorized body at a fixed time to give testimony.

Subsidiary Auxiliary; aiding or supporting in an inferior capacity or position. In the law of corporations, a corporation or company owned by another corporation that controls at least a majority of the shares.

Substantive due process The substantive limitations placed on the content or subject matter of state and federal laws by the Due Process Clauses of the Fifth and Fourteenth Amendments to the U.S. Constitution.

Substantive law The part of the law that creates, defines, and regulates rights, including, for example, the law of contracts, torts, wills, and real property; the essential substance of rights under law.

Suffrage The right to vote at public elections.

Summons The paper that tells a defendant that he or she is being sued and asserts the power of the court to hear and determine the case. A form of legal process that commands the defendant to appear before the court on a specific day and to answer the complaint made by the plaintiff.

Suppression or exclusion of evidence The dismissal of evidence put forth by the prosecution by a judge; often due to the unconstitutionality of the method of seizure of said evidence.

Supremacy clause The clause of Article VI of the U.S. Constitution that declares that all laws and treaties made by the federal government shall be the "supreme law of the land."

Supreme court An appellate tribunal with high powers and broad authority within its jurisdiction.

Surrogate mother A woman who agrees under contract to bear a child for an infertile couple. The woman is paid to have a donated fertilized egg or the fertilized egg of the female partner in the couple (usually fertilized by the male partner of the couple) artificially inseminated into her uterus.

Suspended sentence A sentence given after the formal conviction of a crime that the convicted person is not required to serve.

Syllabus A headnote; a short note preceding the text of a reported case that briefly summarizes the rulings of the court on the points decided in the case.

Symbolic speech Nonverbal gestures and actions that are meant to communicate a message.

T

Tenant An individual who occupies or possesses land or premises by way of a grant of an estate of some type, such as in fee, for life, for years, or at will. A person who has the right to temporary use and possession of a particular real property, which has been conveyed to that person by the landlord.

Testator One who makes or has made a will; one who dies leaving a will.

Testify To provide evidence as a witness, subject to an oath or affirmation, in order to establish a particular fact or set of facts.

Testimony Oral evidence offered by a competent witness under oath, which is used to establish some fact or set of facts.

Title In property law, a comprehensive term referring to the legal basis of the ownership of property, encompassing real and personal property and intangible and tangible interests therein; also a document serving as evidence of ownership of property, such as the certificate of title to a motor vehicle.

In regard to legislation, the heading or preliminary part of a particular statute that designates the name by which that act is known.

In the law of trademarks, the name of an item that may be used exclusively by an individual for identification purposes to indicate the quality and origin of the item.

Tortfeasor A wrongdoer; an individual who commits a wrongful act that injures another and for which the law provides a legal right to seek relief; a defendant in a civil tort action.

Tortious Wrongful; conduct of such character as to subject the actor to civil liability under tort law.

Tort law A body of rights, obligations, and remedies that is applied by the courts in civil proceedings to provide relief for persons who have suffered harm from the wrongful acts of others. The person who sustains injury or suffers pecuniary damage as the result of tortious conduct is known as the plaintiff, and the person who is responsible for inflicting the injury and incurs liability for the damage is known as the defendant or tortfeasor.

Trade secret Any valuable commercial information that provides a business with an advantage over competitors who do not have that information.

Trade union An organization of workers in the same skilled occupation or related skilled occupations who act together to secure for all members favorable wages, hours, and other working conditions.

Transfer To remove or convey from one place to another. The removal of a case from one court to another court within the same system where it might have been instituted. An act of the parties, or of the law, by which the title to property is conveyed from one person to another.

Treason The betrayal of one's own country by waging war against it or by consciously or purposely acting to aid its enemies.

Treaty A compact made between two or more independent nations with a view to the public welfare.

Trespass An unlawful intrusion that interferes with one's person or property.

Trial A judicial examination and determination of facts and legal issues arising between parties to a civil or criminal action.

Trial court The court where civil actions or criminal proceedings are first heard.

Truancy The willful and unjustified failure to attend school by one required to do so.

Trust A relationship created at the direction of an individual, in which one or more persons hold the individual's property subject to certain duties to use and protect it for the benefit of others.

Trustee An individual or corporation named by an individual, who sets aside property to be used for the benefit of another person, to manage the property as provided by the terms of the document that created the arrangement.

U

Unenumerated rights Rights that are not expressly mentioned in the written text of a constitution but instead are inferred from the language, history, and structure of the constitution, or cases interpreting it.

Unconstitutional That which is not in agreement with the ideas and regulations of the Constitution.

Uniform commercial code A general and inclusive group of laws adopted, at least partially, by all of the states to further uniformity and fair dealing in business and commercial transactions.

U.S. Constitution *See* Constitution of the United States.

U.S. Court of Appeals *See* Court of appeals.

U.S. Supreme Court *See* Supreme court.

Usury The crime of charging higher interest on a loan than the law permits.

V

Valid Binding; possessing legal force or strength; legally sufficient.

Vandalism The intentional and malicious destruction of or damage to the property of another.

Venue A place, such as the territory, from which residents are selected to serve as jurors.

A proper place, such as the correct court to hear a case because it has authority over events that have occurred within a certain geographical area.

Verdict The formal decision or finding made by a jury concerning the questions submitted to it during a trial. The jury reports the verdict to the court, which generally accepts it.

Veto The refusal of an executive officer to assent to a bill that has been created and approved by the legislature, thereby depriving the bill of any legally binding effect.

Void That which is null and completely without legal force or binding effect.

Voidable That which is not absolutely void, but may be avoided.

Voir dire [*Old French, To speak the truth.*] The preliminary examination of prospective jurors to determine their qualifications and suitability to serve on a jury, in order to ensure the selection of a fair and impartial jury.

Voluntary manslaughter The unlawful killing of a person falling short of malice, premeditation or deliberate intent but too near to these standards to be classified as justifiable homicide.

W

Waive To intentionally or voluntarily relinquish a known right or engage in conduct warranting an inference that a right has been surrendered.

Waiver The voluntary surrender of a known right; conduct supporting an inference that a particular right has been relinquished.

Ward A person, especially an infant or someone judged to be incompetent, placed by the court in the care of a guardian.

Warrant A written order issued by a judicial officer or other authorized person commanding a law enforcement officer to perform some act incident to the administration of justice.

Warranty deed An instrument that transfers real property from one person to another and in which the grantor promises that title is good and clear of any claims.

White collar crime Term for nonviolent crimes that were committed in the course of the offender's occupation, such as commercial fraud or insider trading on the stock market.

Will A document in which a person specifies the method to be applied in the management and distribution of his or her estate after his or her death.

Workers' compensation A system whereby an employer must pay, or provide insurance to pay, the lost wages and medical expenses of an employee who is injured on the job.

Work release program A sentencing alternative designed to permit an inmate to continue regular employment during the daytime but to return to prison at night for lockup.

Writ An order issued by a court requiring that something be done or giving authority to do a specified act.

Writ of assistance A court order issued to enforce an existing judgment.

Writ of certiorari *See* Certiorari.

Writ of habeas corpus *See* Habeas corpus.

Z

Zoning The separation or division of a municipality into districts, the regulation of buildings and structures in such districts in accordance with their construction and the nature and extent of their use, and the dedication of such districts to particular uses designed to serve the general welfare.

ALPHABETICAL LIST OF COURT CASES

Volume I

The following list includes the name of each case covered in this volume of *Great American Court Cases* and the page number on which coverage of the case begins. The case names are arranged in alphabetical order. Names not found here might be located within the cumulative index in the back of this volume.

CHRONOLOGICAL LIST OF COURT CASES

Volume I

The following list includes the name of each case covered in this volume of *Great American Court Cases* and the page number on which coverage of the case begins. The case names are arranged in alphabetical order under the year in which the corresponding case took place. Names not found here might be located within the cumulative index in the back of this volume.

CUMULATIVE INDEX

This index cites cases, people, events, and subjects in all four volumes of Great American Court Cases. Roman numerals refer to volumes.

Department of Defense Authorization Act, **II**: 68

Department of Energy, U.S., **III**: 163

Department of Revenue of Montana v. Kurth Ranch, **II**: 181

Department of Transportation, U.S., **III**: 131

Department of Transportation Act, **III**: 131

deportation, **III**: 88; **IV**: 162-164

desegregation, **III**: 115, 170

Desert Land Act, **IV**: 493

DeShaney v. Winnebago County Department of Social Services, **III**: 278-280 (main)

detention, **IV**: 484-487
  by correctional facilities, **III**: 165-167
  by police officers, **II**: 431-433; **III**: 109
  of juveniles before trial, **III**: 376-379

Developmentally Disabled Assistance and Bill of Rights Act, **III**: 499; **IV**: 220 (box)

Disabilities Education Act, **I**: 162

disabled persons, **I**: 162-164; **III**: 497-506

discharges
  military, **III**: 314-317, 478-480, 490-493

discovery doctrine, **IV**: 477

discovery order, **III**: 220

discrimination
  against African Americans, **I**: 38, 200-201, 212-213, 525-527, 559; **II**: 7-8, 17, 46-47, 188-189, 194-196, 295-298, 507, 516, 539; **III**: 67, 78-80, 83, 108-109, 115-117, 219-222, 580-582; **IV**: 271, 363-367
    by bus companies, **III**: 518-519
    by clubs, **III**: 137-138
    by hotels, **III**: 84-85, 110-112
    by landfill developers, **III**: 205-207, 212-214
    by public schools, **III**: 528-533, 539-542
    by railroads, **III**: 84-85, 511-513
    by restaurants, **III**: 106-107, 113-114
    by schools, **III**: 188-190
    by theaters, **III**: 84-85
    by universities, **III**: 183, 516-517, 523-527, 551-553
    in child custody suits, **III**: 186-187
    in parks, **III**: 534-536
    in prisons, **III**: 537-538
  against aliens, **III**: 133-134, 157-159, 168-169, 356-357
  against Arab Americans, **III**: 197-198
  against Chinese Americans, **I**: 289-291; **III**: 86-89
  against detained suspects, **III**: 165-167
  against Germans, **I**: 511-513

against homeless persons, **III**: 223-225

against homosexuals, **I**: 506; **II**: 65-67; **III**: 471, 475-496

against illegal aliens, **III**: 177-179

against illegitimate children, **II**: 144-145; **III**: 68, 118-120

against Japanese Americans, **III**: 93-101

against Jewish Americans, **III**: 627-629

against Native Americans, **IV**: 470-475, 479-481, 491-492

against non-landowners, **III**: 139-140

against non-party members, **I**: 58-59

against nonresident employees, **III**: 250-252

against nonresidents, **III**: 13-14, 199, 201, 250-252; **IV**: 210-211, 216, 222-223

against pregnant women, **III**: 143-145, 290, 309-311

against Puerto Ricans, **III**: 608

against the disabled, **III**: 498

against the poor, **II**: 70; **III**: 141-142, 428-433, 441-444

against women, **I**: 52-54, 289-291, 559; **III**: 135-136, 215-218, 253-255, 289-311, 314-321, 324-325, 337-338, 343-351; **IV**: 420
  club membership, **III**: 343-344
  employment discrimination, **III**: 559-560
  in labor, **IV**: 293
  in voting, **III**: 74-77, 298-301
  pregnancy, **III**: 309-311
  reproductive rights, **III**: 345-347
  sexual harassment, **III**: 567-569, 575-577
  spousal abuse/cruelty, **III**: 265-267

age, **III**: 148-150, 208-211, 247

by exclusive clubs, **I**: 53 (box); **III**: 343-344

employment, **III**: 13-14, 19-20, 197-198, 247-256, 290-291, 559-560; **IV**: 13-15, 291-293
  affirmative action, **III**: 27-29, 170-173
  against African Americans, **III**: 146-147, 192, 202-204; **IV**: 270
  against nonresidents, **III**: 250-252
  gender-based, **III**: 304-306, 324-325
  job qualification tests, **III**: 146-147
  mandatory leave, **III**: 309-311
  mandatory retirement, **III**: 208-211
  organized labor, **IV**: 144
  racial quotas, **III**: 191-193
  reverse, **III**: 10-12, 15-18, 21-24, 30-32
  sexual harassment, **III**: 567-577

gender-based. *See* discrimination against women; reverse discrimination

genetic, **I**: 558-560

housing, **III**: 68, 123-124, 131-132, 268-270, 520-522
  against African Americans, **III**: 123-124, 131-132, 151-153, 514-515, 520-522

race. *See also* discrimination against specific groups. **II**: 2, 240-242; **III**: 2-3, 174-176, 183-185, 248, 551-553

religious, **I**: 303-305; **III**: 248

reverse, **III**: 2, 4-12, 15-24, 30-37, 170-173, 191-196, 249, 275-277, 312-313, 322-323, 326-336, 339-342, 648

voting
  against African Americans, **III**: 585-590, 593-596, 603-609, 620, 630-631, 634-635, 645-646
  against women, **III**: 74-77, 298-301

disenfranchisement, **III**: 140, 585-587, 589, 624

diversity of citizenship, **II**: 134-135; **IV**: 201-203, 364

divorce, **I**: 385; **III**: 186, 240, 243, 257, 262, 265-267, 275, 318, 468
  a mensa et thoro, **III**: 265
  a vinculo matrimonii, **III**: 265
  reports in school newspapers, **I**: 408

DNA testing, **III**: 234 (box)

Doe v. Bolton, **III**: 200, 418-420 (main), 425, 432, 434, 439

Doe v. General Hospital of the District of Columbia, **III**: 407

Doe v. McMillan, **I**: 541-543 (main)

dogs
  drug-sniffing, **II**: 442-444, 456, 500-501, 536 (box)
  K-9 units, **II**: 536 (box)

Dolan v. City of Tigard, **IV**: 69

domestic partnerships, **III**: 476 (box), 484-489

Donald T. Regan v. Inez Wright, **III**: 188 (main)

Don't Ask-Don't Tell policy, **I**: 506; **III**: 472, 478-480, 490-493; **IV**: 420

Dorr Wars, **IV**: 422

Dothard v. Rawlinson, **III**: 324-325 (main), 347

double jeopardy, **I**: 22 (box); **II**: 9-11, 92-99, 159 (box), 180-183, 290, 348-350; **III**: 56; **IV**: 469

Douglas, William O., **I**: 23, 82, 185, 190, 505; **II**: 174, 383; **III**: 101, 140, 313, 362, 407, 601; **IV**: 12, 78, 331, 389, 431, 545

Dow Chemical Co. v. United States, **II**: 74, 387

Doyle v. Ohio, **II**: 318-319 (main)

juvenile courts, **I:** 396-398; **II:** 219-231, 230 (box); **III:** 370-371, 376-379

Juvenile Justice and Delinquency Prevention Act, **II:** 223 (box)

Juvenile Law and Justice, **III:** 369-371

juvenile law. *See also* children's rights; students' rights. **I:** 532-534; **II:** 2, 219, 222-231, 442-444, 500-501, 510; **III:** 369-386

juveniles. *See also* children

trials as adults, **II:** 35-36, 48-50, 54-55, 219, 222-224; **III:** 377, 384-386

K

K-9 units, **II:** 536 (box)

Kahn v. Shevin, **III:** 312-313 (main)

Kaiser Aetna v. United States , **IV:** 68

Kaiser Aluminum & Chemical Corp. v. Weber et al., **III:** 172

Kansas Sexually Violent Predator Act, **II:** 348-350

Kansas v. Hendricks, **II:** 348-350 (main)

Karcher v. Daggett, **III:** 636-638 (main)

Kass v. Kass, **III:** 92, 261, 468-470 (main)

Kastigar v. United States, **II:** 314-315 (main), 317

Katz v. United States, **I:** 517, 528-529 (main), 530; **II:** 73, 356, 384, 387, 414, 481, 505, 523

Katzenbach v. McClung, **III:** 111, 113-114 (main)

Katzenbach v. Morgan, **III:** 606-609 (main)

Kaufman v. United States, **II:** 401

Keating, Edward, **IV:** 308

Keating-Owen Act, **IV:** 282, 307-310, 384, 533

Kedroff v. St. Nicholas Cathedral, **I:** 146

Keller v. State Bar of California, **I:** 3, 342

Kelley v. Johnson, **I:** 540, 548

Kellie family, **I:** 387

Kemmeter, Anne, **III:** 278

Kendall v. United States, **IV:** 355-357 (main)

Kennedy v. Mendoza-Martinez, **II:** 337 (box); **III:** 167, 361

Kennedy, Anthony M., **I:** 139, 339, 356; **II:** 76; **III:** 482; **IV:** 90

Kennedy, John F., **III:** 170

Kent v. Dulles, **I:** 23-25 (main), 37

Kent v. United States, **II:** 55, 222-224 (main), 226

Kentucky Corrupt Practices Act, **III:** 632-633

Kentucky v. Dennison, **II:** 84-86 (main), 112

Ker v. California, **II:** 395

Ker v. Illinois, **II:** 78

Ker-Frisbie doctrine, **II:** 79

Kevorkian, Jack, **III:** 39, 50 (box)

Keyes v. School District No. 1, **III:** 543-545 (main), 550

Keyishian v. Board of Regents of the University of the State of New York, **I:** 17 (box), 43-44 (main)

Keystone Bituminous Coal Association v. DeBeni, **IV:** 65

kidnapping, **I:** 388 (box); **II:** 28, 36, 40, 48, 78; **IV:** 117

Kilbourn v. Thompson, **IV:** 263-265 (main)

King v. Smith, **III:** 121-122 (main)

King, Martin Luther, Jr., **III:** 509

Kingsley Books v. Brown, **I:** 358

Kingsley International Pictures v. Regents of the State of New York,, **I:** 462

Kingsley v. Kingsley, **III:** 281-283 (main)

Kinsella v. Krueger, **IV:** 152

Kirkpatrick v. Preisler, **III:** 600, 610-612 (main), 636

Knapp Brothers Murder Trial, **II:** 33 (box)

knock and announce requirement, **II:** 356, 527-528, 550-552

Kolender v. Lawson, **II:** 448-450 (main)

Korean War, **IV:** 150-151, 168

Korematsu v. United States, **III:** 68, 97-99 (main), 458

Kovacs v. Cooper, **IV:** 26

KQED-TV, **I:** 392-395

Kramer v. Union Free School District, **III:** 581

Krischer v. McIver, **III:** 40

Ku Klux Klan, **I:** 130, 222, 326, 514; **II:** 43; **III:** 79, 81-83, 508, 583, 585, 588

Ku Klux Klan Act, **III:** 81-83, 108

Kunstler, William M., **I:** 286

L

Labine v. Vincent, **II:** 144

labor law. *See also* corporate law; employment law. **I:** 579-580; **IV:** 45-46, 144, 279-348, 384-385, 504-506, 533-534

labor movement, **II:** 88 (box)

labor unions, **I:** 14-15, 181, 362 (box); **II:** 87; **III:** 88, 172, 250, 304; **IV:** 14, 45-46, 144, 280-288, 291, 294-296, 300-302, 323-324, 343-345, 439

laches, **III:** 175

Ladue v. Gilleo, **I:** 312-313 (main)

LaFollette, Robert, **III:** 163

laissez-faire, **IV:** 144, 279, 534 (box)

Lalli v. Lalli, **II:** 144

Lambert v. Blackwell, **IV:** 224-226 (main)

Lamb's Chapel v. Center Moriches Union Free School District, **I:** 139, 303-305 (main)

Lamont v. Postmaster General of the United States, **I:** 39-40 (main)

landfills, **IV:** 82 (box)

landlord-tenant relationships, **II:** 521; **IV:** 23-25, 50-52

Landmark Communications, Inc. v. Virginia, **I:** 397

landmarks, **I:** 141; **IV:** 212-214

Landmarks Preservation Law, **IV:** 212

language laws, **I:** 511-513

Lanham Act, **IV:** 511

larceny, **I:** 532, 544; **II:** 96, 200, 203

grand, **II:** 98

Larkin v. Grendel's Den, **I:** 136

Lassiter v. Department of Social Services, **II:** 275-276 (main)

Lassiter v. Northampton County Board of Elections, **III:** 601

laundry industry, **IV:** 297-299

lawyers. *See also* right to counsel. **I:** 242-244, 323-325; **II:** 326-328; **III:** 199, 201, 559-560; **IV:** 222-223

residency requirement, **IV:** 222-223

women, **III:** 295-297

layoffs, **III:** 15-17

League of United Latin American Citizens v. Pete Wilson, **III:** 355

Leathers v. Medlock, **I:** 296, 403

Lebron v. National Railroad Passenger Corporation, **I:** 314-316 (main)

Lechmere, Inc. v. NLRB, **IV:** 343-345 (main)

Lee Optical v. Williamson, **III:** 103

Lee v. International Society for Krishna Consciousness, **I:** 302

Lee v. Oregon, **III:** 40

Lee v. Washington, **III:** 537-538 (main)

Lee v. Weisman, **I:** 131-132 (main), 147

Legion of Decency, **I:** 192

legislative branch. *See also* Congress. **IV:** 79-80, 97, 236-238, 349-351, 398-400, 405-408

Lego v. Twomey, **II:** 110

Leisy v. Hardin, **II:** 358-359 (main)

Lemke v. Farmer's Grain Co, **IV:** 455

lemon laws, **IV:** 18

Lemon test, **I:** 83, 98-99, 103, 112, 114, 122, 128, 136, 146, 163 (box), 303

Lemon v. Kurtzman, **I:** 81, 83, 98-99 (main), 103, 112, 114, 119, 122, 128, 131, 135, 146, 155, 160, 163 (box), 303

Lerman v. Chuckleberry Publishing, **I:** 422

Les Amants (The Lovers), **I:** 472

Levy v. Louisiana, **III:** 118-120 (main), 122, 235

liability, **I:** 232-234; **II:** 61; **III:** 56, 64-66, 503-504; **IV:** 92-95, 155 (box)

libel. *See also* defamation. **I:** 166, 250-255, 357, 382, 385-386, 405, 407, 411-412, 418, 421-423, 431-433, 439-460

Libertarian party, **II:** 546-549

Libretti v. United States, **II:** 182

lie detection. *See* polygraph tests

Liebeck v. McDonald's, **III:** 56

Lincoln, Abraham, **I:** 172; **III:** 78, 81; **IV:** 121, 123

Lindbergh, Charles A., **I:** 388 (box)

Lindsley v. Natural Carbonic Gas Co., **III:** 68

Line Item Veto Act, **IV:** 178-185, 351

lineups, **II:** 234

For Reference

Not to be taken from this room